D0065170

9/11

COMMISSION
REPORT

**FULLY UPDATED WITH CONTROVERSIAL
THIRD MONOGRAPH AND NEVER-BEFORE-PUBLISHED
PROGRESS REPORTS FROM THE 9/11 COMMISSIONERS**

**INTRODUCTION BY
THOMAS H. KEAN AND LEE H. HAMILTON**

BARNES & NOBLE

NEW YORK

2006 Barnes & Noble Publishing

ISBN-13: 978-0-7607-8174-6
ISBN-10: 0-7607-8174-5

Printed and bound in the U.S.A. by Maple Vail

1 3 5 7 9 10 8 6 4 2

CONTENTS

LIST OF ILLUSTRATIONS
AND TABLES

COMMISSION MEMBERS

Thomas H. Kean
CHAIR

Lee H. Hamilton
VICE CHAIR

Richard Ben-Veniste

Bob Kerrey

Fred F. Fielding

John F. Lehman

Jamie S. Gorelick

Timothy J. Roemer

Slade Gorton

James R. Thompson

COMMISSION
STAFF

Philip Zelikow, *Executive Director*
Christopher A. Kojm, *Deputy Executive Director*
Daniel Marcus, *General Counsel*

Joanne M. Accolla
Staff Assistant

Alexis Albion
Professional Staff Member

Scott H. Allan, Jr.
Counsel

John A. Azzarello
Counsel

Caroline Barnes
Professional Staff Member

Warren Bass
Professional Staff Member

Ann M. Bennett
Information Control Officer

Mark S. Bittinger
Professional Staff Member

Madeleine Blot
Counsel

Antwion M. Blount
Systems Engineer

Sam Brinkley
Professional Staff Member

Geoffrey Scott Brown
Research Assistant

Daniel Byman
Professional Staff Member

Dianna Campagna
Manager of Operations

Samuel M. W. Caspersen
Counsel

Melissa A. Coffey
Staff Assistant

Lance Cole
Consultant

Marquittia L. Coleman
Staff Assistant

Marco A. Cordero
Professional Staff Member

Rajesh De
Counsel

George W. Delgrosso
Investigator

Gerald L. Dillingham
Professional Staff Member

Thomas E. Dowling
Professional Staff Member

Steven M. Dunne
Deputy General Counsel

Thomas R. Eldridge
Counsel

Alice Falk
Editor

John J. Farmer, Jr.
Senior Counsel & Team Leader

Alvin S. Felzenberg
Deputy for Communications

Lorry M. Fenner
Professional Staff Member

Susan Ginsburg
Senior Counsel & Team Leader

T. Graham Giusti
Security Officer

Nicole Marie Grandrimo
Professional Staff Member

Douglas N. Greenburg
Counsel

Barbara A. Grewe
Senior Counsel, Special Projects

Elinore Flynn Hartz
Family Liaison

Leonard R. Hawley
Professional Staff Member

L. Christine Healey
Senior Counsel & Team Leader

Karen Heitkotter
Executive Secretary

Walter T. Hempel II
Professional Staff Member

C. Michael Hurley
Senior Counsel & Team Leader

Dana J. Hyde
Counsel

John W. Ivicic
Security Officer

Michael N. Jacobson
Counsel

Hunter W. Jamerson
Intern

Bonnie D. Jenkins
Counsel

Reginald F. Johnson
Staff Assistant

R. William Johnstone
Professional Staff Member

Stephanie L. Kaplan
Special Assistant & Managing Editor

Miles L. Kara, Sr.
Professional Staff Member

Janice L. Kephart
Counsel

Hyon Kim
Counsel

Katarzyna Kozaczuk
Financial Assistant

Gordon Nathaniel Lederman
Counsel

Daniel J. Leopold
Staff Assistant

Sarah Webb Linden
Professional Staff Member

Douglas J. MacEachin
Professional Staff Member & Team Leader

Ernest R. May
Senior Adviser

Joseph McBride
Intern

James Miller
Professional Staff Member

Kelly Moore
Professional Staff Member

Charles M. Pereira
Professional Staff Member

John Raidt
Professional Staff Member

John Roth
Senior Counsel & Team Leader

Peter Rundlet
Counsel

Lloyd D. Salvetti
Professional Staff Member

Kevin J. Scheid
Professional Staff Member & Team Leader

Kevin Shaeffer
Professional Staff Member

Tracy J. Shycoff
Deputy for Administration & Finance

Dietrich L. Snell
Senior Counsel & Team Leader

Jonathan DeWees Stull
Communications Assistant

Lisa Marie Sullivan
Staff Assistant

Quinn John Tamm, Jr.
Professional Staff Member

Catharine S. Taylor
Staff Assistant

Yoel Tobin
Counsel

Emily Landis Walker
Professional Staff Member & Family Liaison

Garth Wermter
Senior IT Consultant

Serena B. Wille
Counsel

Peter Yerkes
Public Affairs Assistant

INTRODUCTION TO THIS EDITION

IN JULY 2004, THE 9/11 Commission completed its final report on the terrorist attacks of September 11, 2001—the largest investigation of the U.S. government in history. We found that our government failed in its duty to protect us on that day. We made 41 recommendations to ensure that everything possible was done to prevent another attack. Several of our recommendations were adopted, some suffer from slow implementation, and others are still unaddressed. As a nation, we have not done all that we can and should to protect the American people.

Therefore, we are pleased that Barnes & Noble has decided to reprint the 9/11 Commission's Final Report, the staff monograph on "Four Flights and Civil Aviation Security," and updated report cards of the 9/11 Public Discourse Project. We hope that this new edition will help rekindle citizen interest in our recommendations.

The first part of our mandate was to investigate the "facts and circumstances" of the 9/11 attack. We looked back to provide the most detailed and accurate account we could of a tragic event in our nation's history. We looked back in order to look forward: The second part of our mandate was to provide recommendations to make our country safer and more secure in the future.

After we issued our report and the Commission expired, we and our eight colleagues from the Commission created a private, nonprofit organization for the purpose of public education and advocacy on behalf of the very recommendations we made. The ten of us became the Board of Directors of the 9/11 Public Discourse Project.

In fall 2004, we testified repeatedly before the Congress on behalf of our 41 recommendations. Working closely with the families of 9/11, we fanned out across the country, speaking in every forum that would have us—world affairs councils, chambers of commerce, civic clubs, colleges and high schools, local TV and radio—spreading the message about our work.

We achieved a measure of success. Several of the problems we identified were addressed by the Intelligence Reform and Terrorism Prevention Act, signed into law by the President in December 2004, though implementation of the law is lagging. Other recommendations were sidestepped. This is not acceptable.

So what needs to be done?

First, scarce Homeland Security dollars must be allocated wisely. They must be spent to protect us against the greatest risks. Right now, those funds are spread around more like revenue-sharing projects. For instance, sparsely populated states such as Wyoming still receive more homeland security funding on a per capita basis than do densely populated states such as New York. This pork barrel approach must stop. Three times in 2005 the House passed a good bill that would focus the use of limited resources on areas at greatest risk and with the most vulnerabilities, but it could not reach agreement with the Senate. The Senate needs to work with the House to send a good bill to the President, or scarce dollars will continue to be squandered.

Second, government agencies at the state and local level need to create, regularly update, and practice plans for emergency response. They need to have living, breathing emergency response plans that embrace the Unified Incident Command System. Hurricane Katrina taught us a lesson that we should have learned from 9/11: We cannot wait for a disaster to hit and then look for the plan. All first responders need to know, from the moment they learn of a disaster, who is in charge and what their jobs will be. Louisiana and New Orleans had a paper plan, but because it had not been properly practiced, it wasn't executed.

Third, first responders need a dedicated broadcast frequency so that they can communicate with each other effectively. The Commission recommended that Congress expedite the allocation of a slice of the broadcast spectrum for public safety purposes. These frequencies—ideal for emergency communications because their signals pass through concrete and steel high-rises without difficulty—are now controlled by TV broadcasters. They have been promised for public safety purposes for a decade, and will finally be turned over to first responders in February 2009. But who can say that no disaster will strike before then? Five years after 9/11, it is scandalous that public safety must wait another three years in order to accommodate the politically powerful broadcast industry.

Fourth, greater attention needs to be paid to information sharing. As the Commission's report documented again and again, we missed opportunities to disrupt the 9/11 plot because of our failure to share information. While the federal government is doing a somewhat better job of sharing terrorist threat information within its own structure, overall progress is lagging badly, with huge gaps in information sharing among federal, state, and local authorities. The presidentially appointed Program Manager for Information Sharing did not receive the political support, priority attention, and resources he needed to carry out his task, and has now been replaced. Precious time and momentum have been lost.

Fifth, the FBI must have a greater sense of urgency about the creation of a national security workforce to fight terrorism on American soil. FBI reform has been moving in the right direction, but has been far too slow. Numerous problems impede the Bureau: failure to improve the FBI's inadequate information technology, continuing deficiencies in the FBI's analytic capabilities, shortfalls in information sharing, too much turnover in the workforce and Bureau leadership, and insufficient investment in human capital and training. The Bureau still struggles to make counterterrorism the dominant mission of the agency.

Sixth, the Privacy and Civil Liberties Oversight Board needs to get to work. Sixteen months after its creation by statute, the Board held its first meeting in March 2006. It is the only office within the executive branch that looks across the government to ensure that privacy and civil liberties concerns are appropriately considered when we decide upon and implement new actions to protect ourselves. Now constituted, the Board needs to establish a work plan and move forward expeditiously with its important mission.

Seventh, we need to screen airline passengers against a comprehensive terrorist watchlist before they get on an airplane. Currently, the airlines do the name checking. But because the government wants to protect sensitive information, it does not share all the names on its watchlist with the airlines. The solution recommended by the Commission is a straightforward one: The government should do the name checking of all passengers against its own, comprehensive watchlist. Poor management at the Transportation Security Administration, plus attempts to integrate commercial data into the screening process (setting off a host of civil liberties and privacy issues), has delayed implementing an effective solution indefinitely.

Eighth, Congress needs powerful Intelligence and Homeland Security oversight committees. Because so much information is classified, Congress is the only source of independent oversight of the full breadth of intelligence and homeland security issues before our country. This oversight does not now happen. Therefore, Congress needs oversight committees with more power over the budget and exclusive jurisdiction. Since Congress has given vast authority to the Executive branch in order to protect us against terrorism, it now needs to play its role as a check and balance on the Executive branch, to make sure that agencies are implementing reforms properly. Turf battles have kept the oversight committees weak. To protect our country, as well as our civil liberties, Congress must perform robust oversight of the Executive branch.

Finally, preventing terrorists from gaining access to nuclear weapons must be elevated above all other issues of national security. Nuclear terrorism would have a devastating impact on our people, economy, and way of life. The Commission called for "a maximum effort" against this threat. Given the potential for catastrophic destruction, our level of effort still falls far short. The President should request the personnel and resources, and provide the domestic and international leadership, to secure all weapons-grade nuclear material as soon as possible. Congress and the media also have a continuing responsibility to keep this priority before the public. There is simply no higher priority on the national security agenda.

As we outline in the report cards of the 9/11 Public Discourse Project (which can be found at the end of this volume), there is so much more that needs to be done, and not much time to do it. The terrorists will not wait. If only we can address these recommendations, we will make significant and appreciable progress in providing for the common defense—the first purpose of government. The task is urgent.

The Commission has ended, yet its work must live on. Only through the efforts of an active and engaged citizenry, pressing its elected officials, will necessary reform to prevent another attack take place. We must all remain committed to the implementation of the Commission's recommendations. They are designed to prevent another catastrophic attack on our homeland. There is nothing more important.

Thomas H. Kean
FORMER CHAIR
9/11 Commission

Lee H. Hamilton
FORMER VICE CHAIR
9/11 Commission

April 3, 2006

PREFACE TO
THE 9/11 COMMISSION REPORT

WE PRESENT THE NARRATIVE of this report and the recommendations that flow from it to the President of the United States, the United States Congress, and the American people for their consideration. Ten Commissioners—five Republicans and five Democrats chosen by elected leaders from our nation's capital at a time of great partisan division—have come together to present this report without dissent.

We have come together with a unity of purpose because our nation demands it. September 11, 2001, was a day of unprecedented shock and suffering in the history of the United States. The nation was unprepared. How did this happen, and how can we avoid such tragedy again?

To answer these questions, the Congress and the President created the National Commission on Terrorist Attacks Upon the United States (Public Law 107-306, November 27, 2002).

Our mandate was sweeping. The law directed us to investigate "facts and circumstances relating to the terrorist attacks of September 11, 2001," including those relating to intelligence agencies, law enforcement agencies, diplomacy, immigration issues and border control, the flow of assets to terrorist organizations, commercial aviation, the role of congressional oversight and resource allocation, and other areas determined relevant by the Commission.

In pursuing our mandate, we have reviewed more than 2.5 million pages of documents and interviewed more than 1,200 individuals in ten countries. This included nearly every senior official from the current and previous administrations who had responsibility for topics covered in our mandate.

We have sought to be independent, impartial, thorough, and nonpartisan. From the outset, we have committed to share as much of our investigation as we can with the American people. To that end, we held 19 days of hearings and took public testimony from 160 witnesses.

Our aim has not been to assign individual blame. Our aim has been to provide the fullest possible account of the events surrounding 9/11 and to identify lessons learned.

We learned about an enemy who is sophisticated, patient, disciplined, and lethal. The enemy rallies broad support in the Arab and Muslim world by demanding redress of political grievances, but its hostility toward us and our values is limitless. Its purpose is to rid the world of religious and political pluralism, the plebiscite, and equal rights for women. It makes no distinction between military and civilian targets. *Collateral damage* is not in its lexicon.

We learned that the institutions charged with protecting our borders, civil aviation, and national security did not understand how grave this threat could be, and did not adjust their policies, plans, and practices to deter or defeat it. We learned of fault lines within our government—between foreign and domestic intelligence, and between and within agencies. We learned of the pervasive problems of managing and sharing information across a large and unwieldy government that had been built in a different era to confront different dangers.

At the outset of our work, we said we were looking backward in order to look forward. We hope that the terrible losses chronicled in this report can create something positive—an America that is safer, stronger, and wiser. That September day, we came together as a nation. The test before us is to sustain that unity of purpose and meet the challenges now confronting us.

We need to design a balanced strategy for the long haul, to attack terrorists and prevent their ranks from swelling while at the same time protecting our country against future attacks. We have been forced to think about the way our government is organized. The massive departments and agencies that prevailed in the great struggles of the twentieth century must work together in new ways, so that all the instruments of national power can be combined. Congress needs dramatic changes as well to strengthen oversight and focus accountability.

As we complete our final report, we want to begin by thanking our fellow Commissioners, whose dedication to this task has been profound. We have reasoned together over every page, and the report has benefited from this remarkable dialogue. We want to express our considerable respect for the intellect and judgment of our colleagues, as well as our great affection for them.

We want to thank the Commission staff. The dedicated professional staff, headed by Philip Zelikow, has contributed innumerable hours to the completion of this report, setting aside other important endeavors to take on this all-consuming assignment. They have conducted the exacting investigative work upon which the Commission has built. They have given good advice, and faithfully carried out our guidance. They have been superb.

We thank the Congress and the President. Executive branch agencies have searched records and produced a multitude of documents for us. We thank officials, past and present, who were generous with their time and provided us with insight. The PENTTBOM team at the FBI, the Director's Review Group at the CIA, and Inspectors General at the Department of Justice and the CIA provided great assistance. We owe a huge debt to the investigative labors, painstaking attention to detail, and readiness to share what they have learned.

We have built on the work of several previous Commissions, and we thank the Congressional Joint Inquiry, whose fine work helped us get started. We thank the City of New York for assistance with documents and witnesses, and the Government Printing Office and W.W. Norton & Company for helping to get this report to the broad public.

We conclude this list of thanks by coming full circle: We thank the families of 9/11, whose persistence and dedication helped create the Commission. They have been with us each step of the way, as partners and witnesses. They know better than any of us the importance of the work we have undertaken.

We want to note what we have done, and not done. We have endeavored to provide the most complete account we can of the events of September 11, what happened and why. This final report is only a summary of what we have, citing only a fraction of the sources we have consulted. But in an event of this scale, touching so many issues and organizations, we are conscious of our limits. We have not interviewed every knowledgeable person or found every relevant piece of paper. New information inevitably will come to light. We present this report as a foundation for a better understanding of a landmark in the history of our nation.

We have listened to scores of overwhelming personal tragedies and astounding acts of heroism and bravery. We have examined the staggering impact of the events of 9/11 on the American people and their amazing resilience and courage as they fought back. We have admired their determination to do their best to prevent another tragedy while preparing to respond if it becomes necessary. We emerge from this investigation with enormous sympathy for the victims and their loved ones, and with enhanced respect for the American people. We recognize the formidable challenges that lie ahead.

We also approach the task of recommendations with humility. We have made a limited number of them. We decided consciously to focus on recommendations we believe to be most important, whose implementations can make the greatest difference. We came into this process with strong opinions about what would work. All of us have had to pause, reflect, and sometimes change our minds as we studied these problems and considered the views of others. We hope our report will encourage our fellow citizens to study, reflect—and act.

Thomas H. Kean
CHAIR

Lee H. Hamilton
VICE CHAIR

July 22, 2005

1

"WE HAVE
SOME PLANES"

Tuesday, September 11, 2001, dawned temperate and nearly cloudless in the eastern United States. Millions of men and women readied themselves for work. Some made their way to the Twin Towers, the signature structures of the World Trade Center complex in New York City. Others went to Arlington, Virginia, to the Pentagon. Across the Potomac River, the United States Congress was back in session. At the other end of Pennsylvania Avenue, people began to line up for a White House tour. In Sarasota, Florida, President George W. Bush went for an early morning run.

For those heading to an airport, weather conditions could not have been better for a safe and pleasant journey. Among the travelers were Mohamed Atta and Abdul Aziz al Omari, who arrived at the airport in Portland, Maine.

1.1 INSIDE THE FOUR FLIGHTS

Boarding the Flights

Boston: American 11 and United 175. Atta and Omari boarded a 6:00 A.M. flight from Portland to Boston's Logan International Airport.[1]

When he checked in for his flight to Boston, Atta was selected by a computerized prescreening system known as CAPPS (Computer Assisted Passenger Prescreening System), created to identify passengers who should be subject to special security measures. Under security rules in place at the time, the only consequence of Atta's selection by CAPPS was that his checked bags were held off the plane until it was confirmed that he had boarded the aircraft. This did not hinder Atta's plans.[2]

Atta and Omari arrived in Boston at 6:45. Seven minutes later, Atta apparently took a call from Marwan al Shehhi, a longtime colleague who was at another terminal at Logan Airport. They spoke for three minutes.[3] It would be their final conversation.

Between 6:45 and 7:40, Atta and Omari, along with Satam al Suqami, Wail al Shehri, and Waleed al Shehri, checked in and boarded American Airlines Flight 11, bound for Los Angeles. The flight was scheduled to depart at 7:45.[4]

In another Logan terminal, Shehhi, joined by Fayez Banihammad, Mohand al Shehri, Ahmed al Ghamdi, and Hamza al Ghamdi, checked in for United Airlines Flight 175, also bound for Los Angeles. A couple of Shehhi's colleagues were obviously unused to travel; according to the United ticket agent, they had trouble understanding the standard security questions, and she had to go over them slowly until they gave the routine, reassuring answers.[5] Their flight was scheduled to depart at 8:00.

The security checkpoints through which passengers, including Atta and his colleagues, gained access to the American 11 gate were operated by Globe Security under a contract with American Airlines. In a different terminal, the single checkpoint through which passengers for United 175 passed was controlled by United Airlines, which had contracted with Huntleigh USA to perform the screening.[6]

In passing through these checkpoints, each of the hijackers would have been screened by a walk-through metal detector calibrated to detect items with at least the metal content of a .22-caliber handgun. Anyone who might have set off that detector would have been screened with a hand wand—a procedure requiring the screener to identify the metal item or items that caused the alarm. In addition, an X-ray machine would have screened the hijackers' carry-on belongings. The screening was in place to identify and confiscate weapons and other items prohibited from being carried onto a commercial flight.[7] None of the checkpoint supervisors recalled the hijackers or reported anything suspicious regarding their screening.[8]

While Atta had been selected by CAPPS in Portland, three members of his hijacking team—Suqami, Wail al Shehri, and Waleed al Shehri—were selected in Boston. Their selection affected only the handling of their checked bags, not their screening at the checkpoint. All five men cleared the checkpoint and made their way to the gate for American 11. Atta, Omari, and Suqami took their seats in business class (seats 8D, 8G, and 10B, respectively). The Shehri brothers had adjacent seats in row 2 (Wail in 2A, Waleed in 2B), in the first-class cabin. They boarded American 11 between 7:31 and 7:40. The aircraft pushed back from the gate at 7:40.[9]

Shehhi and his team, none of whom had been selected by CAPPS, boarded United 175 between 7:23 and 7:28 (Banihammad in 2A, Shehri in 2B, Shehhi in 6C, Hamza al Ghamdi in 9C, and Ahmed al Ghamdi in 9D). Their aircraft pushed back from the gate just before 8:00.[10]

Washington Dulles: American 77. Hundreds of miles southwest of Boston, at Dulles International Airport in the Virginia suburbs of Washington, D.C., five more men were preparing to take their early morning flight. At 7:15, a pair of them, Khalid al Mihdhar and Majed Moqed, checked in at the American Airlines ticket counter for Flight 77, bound for Los Angeles. Within the next 20 minutes, they would be followed by Hani Hanjour and two brothers, Nawaf al Hazmi and Salem al Hazmi.[11]

Hani Hanjour, Khalid al Mihdhar, and Majed Moqed were flagged by CAPPS. The Hazmi brothers were also selected for extra scrutiny by the airline's customer service representative at the check-in counter. He did so because one of the brothers did not have photo identification nor could he understand English, and because the agent found both of the passengers to be suspicious. The only consequence of their selection was that their checked bags were held off the plane until it was confirmed that they had boarded the aircraft.[12]

All five hijackers passed through the Main Terminal's west security screening checkpoint; United Airlines, which was the responsible air carrier, had contracted out the work to Argenbright Security.[13] The checkpoint featured closed-circuit television that recorded all passengers, including the hijackers, as they were screened. At 7:18, Mihdhar and Moqed entered the security checkpoint.

Mihdhar and Moqed placed their carry-on bags on the belt of the X-ray machine and proceeded through the first metal detector. Both set off the alarm, and they were directed to a second metal detector. Mihdhar did not trigger the alarm and was permitted through the checkpoint. After Moqed set it off, a screener wanded him. He passed this inspection.[14]

About 20 minutes later, at 7:35, another passenger for Flight 77, Hani Hanjour, placed two carry-on bags on the X-ray belt in the Main Terminal's west checkpoint, and proceeded, without alarm, through the metal detector. A short time later, Nawaf and Salem al Hazmi entered the same checkpoint. Salem al Hazmi cleared the metal detector and was permitted through; Nawaf al Hazmi set off the alarms for both the first and second metal detectors and was then hand-wanded before being passed. In addition, his over-the-shoulder carry-on bag was swiped by an explosive trace detector and then passed. The video footage indicates that he was carrying an unidentified item in his back pocket, clipped to its rim.[15]

When the local civil aviation security office of the Federal Aviation Administration (FAA) later investigated these security screening operations, the screeners recalled nothing out of the ordinary. They could not recall that any of the passengers they screened were CAPPS selectees. We asked a screening expert to review the videotape of the hand-wanding, and he found the quality of the screener's work to have been "marginal at best." The screener should have "resolved" what set off the alarm; and in the case of both Moqed and Hazmi, it was clear that he did not.[16]

At 7:50, Majed Moqed and Khalid al Mihdhar boarded the flight and were seated in 12A and 12B in coach. Hani Hanjour, assigned to seat 1B (first class), soon followed. The Hazmi brothers, sitting in 5E and 5F, joined Hanjour in the first-class cabin.[17]

Newark: United 93. Between 7:03 and 7:39, Saeed al Ghamdi, Ahmed al Nami, Ahmad al Haznawi, and Ziad Jarrah checked in at the United Airlines ticket counter for Flight 93, going to Los Angeles. Two checked bags; two did not. Haznawi was selected by CAPPS. His checked bag was screened for explosives and then loaded on the plane.[18]

The four men passed through the security checkpoint, owned by United Airlines and operated under contract by Argenbright Security. Like the checkpoints in Boston, it lacked closed-circuit television surveillance so there is no documentary evidence to indicate when the hijackers passed through the checkpoint, what alarms may have been triggered, or what security procedures were administered. The FAA interviewed the screeners later; none recalled anything unusual or suspicious.[19]

The four men boarded the plane between 7:39 and 7:48. All four had seats in the first-class cabin; their plane had no business-class section. Jarrah was in seat 1B, closest to the cockpit; Nami was in 3C, Ghamdi in 3D, and Haznawi in 6B.[20]

The 19 men were aboard four transcontinental flights.[21] They were planning to hijack these planes and turn them into large guided missiles, loaded with up to 11,400 gallons of jet fuel. By 8:00 A.M. on the morning of Tuesday, September 11, 2001, they had defeated all the security layers that America's civil aviation security system then had in place to prevent a hijacking.

The Hijacking of American 11

American Airlines Flight 11 provided nonstop service from Boston to Los Angeles. On September 11, Captain John Ogonowski and First Officer Thomas McGuinness piloted the Boeing 767. It carried its full capacity of nine flight attendants. Eighty-one passengers boarded the flight with them (including the five terrorists).[22]

The plane took off at 7:59. Just before 8:14, it had climbed to 26,000 feet, not quite its initial assigned cruising altitude of 29,000 feet. All communications and flight profile data were normal. About this time the "Fasten Seatbelt" sign would usually have been turned off and the flight attendants would have begun preparing for cabin service.[23]

At that same time, American 11 had its last routine communication with the ground when it acknowledged navigational instructions from the FAA's air traffic control (ATC) center in Boston. Sixteen seconds after that transmission, ATC instructed the aircraft's pilots to climb to 35,000 feet. That message and all subsequent attempts to contact the flight were not acknowledged. From this and other evidence, we believe the hijacking began at 8:14 or shortly thereafter.[24]

Reports from two flight attendants in the coach cabin, Betty Ong and Madeline "Amy" Sweeney, tell us most of what we know about how the hijacking happened. As it began, some of the hijackers—most likely Wail al Shehri and Waleed al Shehri, who were seated in row 2 in first class—stabbed the two unarmed flight attendants who would have been preparing for cabin service.[25]

We do not know exactly how the hijackers gained access to the cockpit; FAA rules required that the doors remain closed and locked during flight. Ong speculated that they had "jammed their way" in. Perhaps the terrorists stabbed the flight attendants to get a cockpit key, to force one of them to open the cockpit door, or to lure the captain or first officer out of the cockpit. Or the flight attendants may just have been in their way.[26]

At the same time or shortly thereafter, Atta—the only terrorist on board trained to fly a jet—would have moved to the cockpit from his business-class seat, possibly accompanied by Omari. As this was happening, passenger Daniel Lewin, who was seated in the row just behind Atta and Omari, was stabbed by one of the hijackers—probably Satam al Suqami, who was seated directly behind Lewin. Lewin had served four years as an officer in the Israeli military. He may have made an attempt to stop the hijackers in front of him, not realizing that another was sitting behind him.[27]

The hijackers quickly gained control and sprayed Mace, pepper spray, or some other irritant in the first-class cabin, in order to force the passengers and flight attendants toward the rear of the plane. They claimed they had a bomb.[28]

About five minutes after the hijacking began, Betty Ong contacted the American Airlines Southeastern Reservations Office in Cary, North Carolina, via an AT&T airphone to report an emergency aboard the flight. This was the first of several occasions on 9/11 when flight attendants took action outside the scope of their training, which emphasized that in a hijacking, they were to communicate with the cockpit crew. The emergency call lasted approximately 25 minutes, as Ong calmly and professionally relayed information about events taking place aboard the airplane to authorities on the ground.[29]

At 8:19, Ong reported: "The cockpit is not answering, somebody's stabbed in business class—and I think there's Mace—that we can't breathe—I don't know, I think we're getting hijacked." She then told of the stabbings of the two flight attendants.[30]

At 8:21, one of the American employees receiving Ong's call in North Carolina, Nydia Gonzalez, alerted the American Airlines operations center in Fort Worth, Texas, reaching Craig Marquis, the manager on duty. Marquis soon realized this was an emergency and instructed the airline's dispatcher responsible for the flight to contact the cockpit. At 8:23, the dispatcher tried unsuccessfully to contact the aircraft. Six minutes later, the air traffic control specialist in American's operations center contacted the FAA's Boston Air Traffic Control Center about the flight. The center was already aware of the problem.[31]

Boston Center knew of a problem on the flight in part because just before 8:25 the hijackers had attempted to communicate with the passengers. The microphone was keyed, and immediately one of the hijackers said, "Nobody move. Everything will be okay. If you try to make any moves, you'll endanger yourself and the airplane. Just stay quiet." Air traffic controllers heard the transmission; Ong did not. The hijackers probably did not know how to operate the cockpit radio communication system correctly, and thus inadvertently broadcast their message over the air traffic control channel instead of the cabin public-address channel. Also at 8:25, and again at 8:29, Amy Sweeney got through to the American Flight Services Office in Boston but was cut off after she reported someone was hurt aboard the flight. Three minutes later, Sweeney was reconnected to the office and began relaying updates to the manager, Michael Woodward.[32]

At 8:26, Ong reported that the plane was "flying erratically." A minute later, Flight 11 turned south. American also began getting identifications of the hijackers, as Ong and then Sweeney passed on some of the seat numbers of those who had gained unauthorized access to the cockpit.[33]

Sweeney calmly reported on her line that the plane had been hijacked; a man in first class had his throat slashed; two flight attendants had been stabbed—one was seriously hurt and was on oxygen while the other's wounds seemed minor; a doctor had been requested; the flight attendants were unable to contact the cockpit; and there was a bomb in the cockpit. Sweeney told Woodward that she and Ong were trying to relay as much information as they could to people on the ground.[34]

At 8:38, Ong told Gonzalez that the plane was flying erratically again. Around this time Sweeney told Woodward that the hijackers were Middle Easterners, naming three of their seat numbers. One spoke very little English and one spoke excellent English. The hijackers had gained entry to the cockpit, and she did not know how. The aircraft was in a rapid descent.[35]

At 8:41, Sweeney told Woodward that passengers in coach were under the impression that there was a routine medical emergency in first class. Other flight attendants were busy at duties such as getting medical supplies while Ong and Sweeney were reporting the events.[36]

At 8:41, in American's operations center, a colleague told Marquis that the air traffic controllers declared Flight 11 a hijacking and "think he's [American 11] headed toward Kennedy [airport in New York City]. They're moving everybody out of the way. They seem to have him on a primary radar. They seem to think that he is descending."[37]

At 8:44, Gonzalez reported losing phone contact with Ong. About this same time Sweeney reported to Woodward, "Something is wrong. We are in a rapid descent . . . we are all over the place." Woodward asked Sweeney to look out the window to see if she could determine where they were. Sweeney responded: "We are flying low. We are flying very, very low. We are flying way too low." Seconds later she said, "Oh my God we are way too low." The phone call ended.[38]

At 8:46:40, American 11 crashed into the North Tower of the World Trade Center in New York City.[39] All on board, along with an unknown number of people in the tower, were killed instantly.

The Hijacking of United 175

United Airlines Flight 175 was scheduled to depart for Los Angeles at 8:00. Captain Victor Saracini and First Officer Michael Horrocks piloted the Boeing 767, which had seven flight attendants. Fifty-six passengers boarded the flight.[40]

United 175 pushed back from its gate at 7:58 and departed Logan Airport at 8:14. By 8:33, it had reached its assigned cruising altitude of 31,000 feet. The flight attendants would have begun their cabin service.[41]

The flight had taken off just as American 11 was being hijacked, and at 8:42 the United 175 flight crew completed their report on a "suspicious transmission" overheard from another plane (which turned out to have been Flight 11) just after takeoff. This was United 175's last communication with the ground.[42]

The hijackers attacked sometime between 8:42 and 8:46. They used knives (as reported by two passengers and a flight attendant), Mace (reported by one passenger), and the threat of a bomb (reported by the same passenger). They stabbed members of the flight crew (reported by a flight attendant and one passenger). Both pilots had been killed (reported by one flight attendant). The eyewitness accounts came from calls made from the rear of the plane, from passengers originally seated further forward in the cabin, a sign that passengers and perhaps crew had been moved to the back of the aircraft. Given similarities to American 11 in hijacker seating and in eyewitness reports of tactics and weapons, as well as the contact between the presumed team leaders, Atta and Shehhi, we believe the tactics were similar on both flights.[43]

The first operational evidence that something was abnormal on United 175 came at 8:47, when the aircraft changed beacon codes twice within a minute. At 8:51, the flight deviated from its assigned altitude, and a minute later New York air traffic controllers began repeatedly and unsuccessfully trying to contact it.[44]

At 8:52, in Easton, Connecticut, a man named Lee Hanson received a phone call from his son Peter, a passenger on United 175. His son told him: "I think they've taken over the cockpit—An attendant has been stabbed—and someone else up front may have been killed. The plane is making strange moves. Call United Airlines—Tell them it's Flight 175, Boston to LA." Lee Hanson then called the Easton Police Department and relayed what he had heard.[45]

Also at 8:52, a male flight attendant called a United office in San Francisco, reaching Marc Policastro. The flight attendant reported that the flight had been hijacked, both pilots had been killed, a flight attendant had been stabbed, and the hijackers were probably flying the plane. The call lasted about two minutes, after which Policastro and a colleague tried unsuccessfully to contact the flight.[46]

At 8:58, the flight took a heading toward New York City.[47]

At 8:59, Flight 175 passenger Brian David Sweeney tried to call his wife, Julie. He left a message on their home answering machine that the plane had been hijacked. He then called his mother, Louise Sweeney, told her the flight had been hijacked, and added that the passengers were thinking about storming the cockpit to take control of the plane away from the hijackers.[48]

At 9:00, Lee Hanson received a second call from his son Peter:

> It's getting bad, Dad—A stewardess was stabbed—They seem to have knives and Mace—They said they have a bomb—It's getting very bad on the plane—Passengers are throwing up and getting sick—The plane is making jerky movements—I don't think the pilot is flying the plane—I think we are going down—I think they intend to go to Chicago or someplace and fly into a building—Don't worry, Dad—If it happens, it'll be very fast—My God, my God.[49]

The call ended abruptly. Lee Hanson had heard a woman scream just before it cut off. He turned on a television, and in her home so did Louise Sweeney. Both then saw the second aircraft hit the World Trade Center.[50]

At 9:03:11, United Airlines Flight 175 struck the South Tower of the World Trade Center.[51] All on board, along with an unknown number of people in the tower, were killed instantly.

The Hijacking of American 77

American Airlines Flight 77 was scheduled to depart from Washington Dulles for Los Angeles at 8:10. The aircraft was a Boeing 757 piloted by Captain Charles F. Burlingame and First Officer David Charlebois. There were four flight attendants. On September 11, the flight carried 58 passengers.[52]

American 77 pushed back from its gate at 8:09 and took off at 8:20. At 8:46, the flight reached its assigned cruising altitude of 35,000 feet. Cabin service would have begun. At 8:51, American 77 transmitted its last routine radio communication. The hijacking began between 8:51 and 8:54. As on American 11 and United 175, the hijackers used knives (reported by one passenger) and moved all the passengers (and possibly crew) to the rear of the aircraft (reported by one flight attendant and one passenger). Unlike the earlier flights, the Flight 77 hijackers were reported by a passenger to have box cutters. Finally, a passenger reported that an announcement had been made by the "pilot" that the plane had been hijacked. Neither of the firsthand accounts mentioned any stabbings or the threat or use of either a bomb or Mace, though both witnesses began the flight in the first-class cabin.[53]

At 8:54, the aircraft deviated from its assigned course, turning south. Two minutes later the transponder was turned off and even primary radar contact with the aircraft was lost. The Indianapolis Air Traffic Control Center repeatedly tried and failed to contact the aircraft. American Airlines dispatchers also tried, without success.[54]

At 9:00, American Airlines Executive Vice President Gerard Arpey learned that communications had been lost with American 77. This was now the second American aircraft in trouble. He ordered all American Airlines flights in the Northeast that had not taken off to remain on the ground. Shortly before 9:10, suspecting that American 77 had been hijacked, American headquarters concluded that the second aircraft to hit the World Trade Center might have been Flight 77. After learning that United Airlines was missing a plane, American Airlines headquarters extended the ground stop nationwide.[55]

At 9:12, Renee May called her mother, Nancy May, in Las Vegas. She said her flight was being hijacked by six individuals who had moved them to the rear of the plane. She asked her mother to alert American Airlines. Nancy May and her husband promptly did so.[56]

At some point between 9:16 and 9:26, Barbara Olson called her husband, Ted Olson, the solicitor general of the United States. She reported that the flight had been hijacked, and the hijackers had knives and box cutters. She further indicated that the hijackers were not aware of her phone call, and that they had put all the passengers in the back of the plane. About a minute into the conversation, the call was cut off. Solicitor General Olson tried unsuccessfully to reach Attorney General John Ashcroft.[57]

Shortly after the first call, Barbara Olson reached her husband again. She reported that the pilot had announced that the flight had been hijacked, and she asked her husband what she should tell the captain to do. Ted Olson asked for her location and she replied that the aircraft was then flying over houses. Another passenger told her they were traveling northeast. The Solicitor General then informed his wife of the two previous hijackings and crashes. She did not display signs of panic and did not indicate any awareness of an impending crash. At that point, the second call was cut off.[58]

At 9:29, the autopilot on American 77 was disengaged; the aircraft was at 7,000 feet and approximately 38 miles west of the Pentagon.[59] At 9:32, controllers at the Dulles Terminal Radar Approach Control "observed a primary radar target tracking eastbound at a high rate of speed." This was later determined to have been Flight 77.

At 9:34, Ronald Reagan Washington National Airport advised the Secret Service of an unknown aircraft heading in the direction of the White House. American 77 was then 5 miles west-southwest of the Pentagon and began a 330-degree turn. At the end of the turn, it was descending through 2,200 feet, pointed toward the Pentagon and downtown Washington. The hijacker pilot then advanced the throttles to maximum power and dove toward the Pentagon.[60]

At 9:37:46, American Airlines Flight 77 crashed into the Pentagon, traveling at approximately 530 miles per hour.[61] All on board, as well as many civilian and military personnel in the building, were killed.

The Battle for United 93

At 8:42, United Airlines Flight 93 took off from Newark (New Jersey) Liberty International Airport bound for San Francisco. The aircraft was piloted by Captain Jason Dahl and First Officer Leroy Homer, and there were five flight attendants. Thirty-seven passengers, including the hijackers, boarded the plane. Scheduled to depart the gate at 8:00, the Boeing 757's takeoff was delayed because of the airport's typically heavy morning traffic.[62]

The hijackers had planned to take flights scheduled to depart at 7:45 (American 11), 8:00 (United 175 and United 93), and 8:10 (American 77). Three of the flights had actually taken off within 10 to 15 minutes of their planned departure times. United 93 would ordinarily have taken off about 15 minutes after pulling away from the gate. When it left the ground at 8:42, the flight was running more than 25 minutes late.[63]

As United 93 left Newark, the flight's crew members were unaware of the hijacking of American 11. Around 9:00, the FAA, American, and United were facing the staggering realization of apparent multiple hijackings. At 9:03, they would see another aircraft strike the World Trade Center. Crisis managers at the FAA and the airlines did not yet act to warn other aircraft.[64] At the same time, Boston Center realized that a message transmitted just before 8:25 by the hijacker pilot of American 11 included the phrase, "We have some planes."[65]

No one at the FAA or the airlines that day had ever dealt with multiple hijackings. Such a plot had not been carried out anywhere in the world in more than 30 years, and never in the United States. As news of the hijackings filtered through the FAA and the airlines, it does not seem to have occurred to their leadership that they needed to alert other aircraft in the air that they too might be at risk.[66]

United 175 was hijacked between 8:42 and 8:46, and awareness of that hijacking began to spread after 8:51. American 77 was hijacked between 8:51 and 8:54. By 9:00, FAA and airline officials began to comprehend that attackers were going after multiple aircraft. American Airlines' nationwide ground stop between 9:05 and 9:10 was followed by a United Airlines ground stop. FAA controllers at Boston Center, which had tracked the first two hijackings, requested at 9:07 that Herndon Command Center "get messages to airborne aircraft to increase security for the cockpit." There is no evidence that Herndon took such action. Boston Center immediately began speculating about other aircraft that might be in danger, leading them to worry about a transcontinental flight—Delta 1989—that in fact was not hijacked. At 9:19, the FAA's New England regional office called Herndon and asked that Cleveland Center advise Delta 1989 to use extra cockpit security.[67]

Several FAA air traffic control officials told us it was the air carriers' responsibility to notify their planes of security problems. One senior FAA air traffic control manager said that it was simply not the FAA's place to order the airlines what to tell their pilots.[68] We believe such statements do not reflect an adequate appreciation of the FAA's responsibility for the safety and security of civil aviation.

The airlines bore responsibility, too. They were facing an escalating number of conflicting and, for the most part, erroneous reports about other flights, as well as a continuing lack of vital information from the FAA about the hijacked flights. We found no evidence, however, that American Airlines sent any cockpit warnings to its aircraft on 9/11. United's first decisive action to notify its airborne aircraft to take defensive action did not come until 9:19, when a United flight dispatcher, Ed Ballinger, took the initiative to begin transmitting warnings to his 16 transcontinental flights: "Beware any cockpit intrusion—Two a/c [aircraft] hit World Trade Center." One of the flights that received the warning was United 93. Because Ballinger was still responsible for his other flights as well as Flight 175, his warning message was not transmitted to Flight 93 until 9:23.[69]

By all accounts, the first 46 minutes of Flight 93's cross-country trip proceeded routinely. Radio communications from the plane were normal. Heading, speed, and altitude ran according to plan. At 9:24, Ballinger's warning to United 93 was received in the cockpit. Within two minutes, at 9:26, the pilot, Jason Dahl, responded with a note of puzzlement: "Ed, confirm latest mssg plz—Jason."[70]

The hijackers attacked at 9:28. While traveling 35,000 feet above eastern Ohio, United 93 suddenly dropped 700 feet. Eleven seconds into the descent, the FAA's air traffic control center in Cleveland received the first of two radio transmissions from the aircraft. During the first broadcast, the captain or first officer could be heard declaring "Mayday" amid the sounds of a physical struggle in the cockpit. The second radio transmission, 35 seconds later, indicated that the fight was continuing. The captain or first officer could be heard shouting: "Hey get out of here—get out of here—get out of here."[71]

On the morning of 9/11, there were only 37 passengers on United 93—33 in addition to the 4 hijackers. This was below the norm for Tuesday mornings during the summer of 2001. But there is no evidence that the hijackers manipulated passenger levels or purchased additional seats to facilitate their operation.[72]

The terrorists who hijacked three other commercial flights on 9/11 operated in five-man teams. They initiated their cockpit takeover within 30 minutes of takeoff. On Flight 93, however, the takeover took place 46 minutes after takeoff and there were only four hijackers. The operative likely intended to round out the team for this flight, Mohamed al Kahtani, had been refused entry by a suspicious immigration inspector at Florida's Orlando International Airport in August.[73]

Because several passengers on United 93 described three hijackers on the plane, not four, some have wondered whether one of the hijackers had been able to use the cockpit jump seat from the outset of the flight. FAA rules allow use of this seat by documented and approved individuals, usually air carrier or FAA personnel. We have found no evidence indicating that one of the hijackers, or anyone else, sat there on this flight. All the hijackers had assigned seats in first class, and they seem to have used them. We believe it is more likely that Jarrah, the crucial pilot-trained member of their team, remained seated and inconspicuous until after the cockpit was seized; and once inside, he would not have been visible to the passengers.[74]

At 9:32, a hijacker, probably Jarrah, made or attempted to make the following announcement to the passengers of Flight 93: "Ladies and Gentlemen: Here the captain, please sit down keep remaining sitting. We have a bomb on board. So, sit." The flight data recorder (also recovered) indicates that Jarrah then instructed the plane's autopilot to turn the aircraft around and head east.[75]

The cockpit voice recorder data indicate that a woman, most likely a flight attendant, was being held captive in the cockpit. She struggled with one of the hijackers who killed or otherwise silenced her.[76]

Shortly thereafter, the passengers and flight crew began a series of calls from GTE airphones and cellular phones. These calls between family, friends, and colleagues took place until the end of the flight and provided those on the ground with firsthand accounts. They enabled the passengers to gain critical information, including the news that two aircraft had slammed into the World Trade Center.[77]

At 9:39, the FAA's Cleveland Air Route Traffic Control Center overheard a second announcement indicating that there was a bomb on board, that the plane was returning to the airport, and that they should remain seated.[78] While it apparently was not heard by the passengers, this announcement, like those on Flight 11 and Flight 77, was intended to deceive them. Jarrah, like Atta earlier, may have inadvertently broadcast the message because he did not know how to operate the radio and the intercom. To our knowledge none of them had ever flown an actual airliner before.

At least two callers from the flight reported that the hijackers knew that passengers were making calls but did not seem to care. It is quite possible Jarrah knew of the success of the assault on the World Trade Center. He could have learned of this from messages being sent by United Airlines to the cockpits of its transcontinental flights, including Flight 93, warning of cockpit intrusion and telling of the New York attacks. But even without them, he would certainly have understood that the attacks on the World Trade Center would already have unfolded, given Flight 93's tardy departure from Newark. If Jarrah did know that the passengers were making calls, it might not have occurred to him that they were certain to learn what had happened in New York, thereby defeating his attempts at deception.[79]

At least ten passengers and two crew members shared vital information with family, friends, colleagues, or others on the ground. All understood the plane had been hijacked. They said the hijackers wielded knives and claimed to have a bomb. The hijackers were wearing red bandanas, and they forced the passengers to the back of the aircraft.[80]

Callers reported that a passenger had been stabbed and that two people were lying on the floor of the cabin, injured or dead—possibly the captain and first officer. One caller reported that a flight attendant had been killed.[81]

One of the callers from United 93 also reported that he thought the hijackers might possess a gun. But none of the other callers reported the presence of a firearm. One recipient of a call from the aircraft recounted specifically asking her caller whether the hijackers had guns. The passenger replied that he did not see one. No evidence of firearms or of their identifiable remains was found at the aircraft's crash site, and the cockpit voice recorder gives no indication of a gun being fired or mentioned at any time. We believe that if the hijackers had possessed a gun, they would have used it in the flight's last minutes as the passengers fought back.[82]

Passengers on three flights reported the hijackers' claim of having a bomb. The FBI told us they found no trace of explosives at the crash sites. One of the passengers who mentioned a bomb expressed his belief that it was not real. Lacking any evidence that the hijackers attempted to smuggle such illegal items past the security screening checkpoints, we believe the bombs were probably fake.[83]

During at least five of the passengers' phone calls, information was shared about the attacks that had occurred earlier that morning at the World Trade Center. Five calls described the intent of passengers and surviving crew members to revolt against the hijackers. According to one call, they voted on whether to rush the terrorists in an attempt to retake the plane. They decided, and acted.[84]

At 9:57, the passenger assault began. Several passengers had terminated phone calls with loved ones in order to join the revolt. One of the callers ended her message as follows: "Everyone's running up to first class. I've got to go. Bye."[85]

The cockpit voice recorder captured the sounds of the passenger assault muffled by the intervening cockpit door. Some family members who listened to the recording report that they can hear the voice of a loved one among the din. We cannot identify whose voices can be heard. But the assault was sustained.[86]

In response, Jarrah immediately began to roll the airplane to the left and right, attempting to knock the passengers off balance. At 9:58:57, Jarrah told another hijacker in the cockpit to block the door. Jarrah continued to roll the airplane sharply left and right, but the assault continued. At 9:59:52, Jarrah changed tactics and pitched the nose of the airplane up and down to disrupt the assault. The recorder captured the sounds of loud thumps, crashes, shouts, and breaking glasses and plates. At 10:00:03, Jarrah stabilized the airplane.[87]

Five seconds later, Jarrah asked, "Is that it? Shall we finish it off?" A hijacker responded, "No. Not yet. When they all come, we finish it off." The sounds of fighting continued outside the cockpit. Again, Jarrah pitched the nose of the aircraft up and down. At 10:00:26, a passenger in the background said, "In the cockpit. If we don't we'll die!" Sixteen seconds later, a passenger yelled, "Roll it!" Jarrah stopped the violent maneuvers at about 10:01:00 and said, "Allah is the greatest! Allah is the greatest!" He then asked another hijacker in the cockpit, "Is that it? I mean, shall we put it down?" to which the other replied, "Yes, put it in it, and pull it down."[88]

The passengers continued their assault and at 10:02:23, a hijacker said, "Pull it down! Pull it down!" The hijackers remained at the controls but must have judged that the passengers were only seconds from overcoming them. The airplane headed down; the control wheel was turned hard to the right. The airplane rolled onto its back, and one of the hijackers began shouting "Allah is the greatest. Allah is the greatest." With the sounds of the passenger counterattack continuing, the aircraft plowed into an empty field in Shanksville, Pennsylvania, at 580 miles per hour, about 20 minutes' flying time from Washington, D.C.[89]

Jarrah's objective was to crash his airliner into symbols of the American Republic, the Capitol or the White House. He was defeated by the alerted, unarmed passengers of United 93.

1.2 IMPROVISING A HOMELAND DEFENSE

The FAA and NORAD

On 9/11, the defense of U.S. airspace depended on close interaction between two federal agencies: the FAA and the North American Aerospace Defense Command (NORAD). The most recent hijacking that involved U.S. air traffic controllers, FAA management, and military coordination had occurred in 1993.[90] In order to understand how the two agencies interacted eight years later, we will review their missions, command and control structures, and working relationship on the morning of 9/11.

FAA Mission and Structure. As of September 11, 2001, the FAA was mandated by law to regulate the safety and security of civil aviation. From an air traffic controller's perspective, that meant maintaining a safe distance between airborne aircraft.[91]

Many controllers work at the FAA's 22 Air Route Traffic *Control Centers*. They are grouped under regional offices and coordinate closely with the national Air Traffic Control System *Command Center*, located in Herndon,

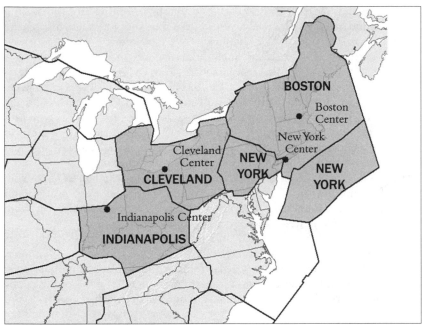

FAA Air Traffic Control Centers

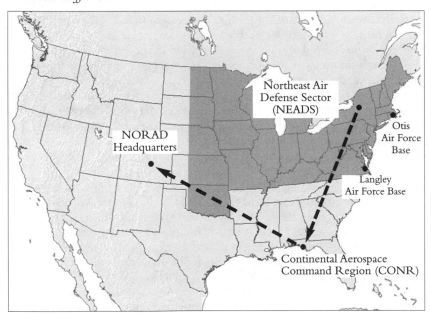

Reporting structure, Northeast Air Defense Sector
Graphics courtesy of ESRI

Virginia, which oversees daily traffic flow within the entire airspace system. FAA headquarters is ultimately responsible for the management of the National Airspace System. The *Operations Center* located at FAA headquarters receives notifications of incidents, including accidents and hijackings.[92]

FAA Control Centers often receive information and make operational decisions independently of one another. On 9/11, the four hijacked aircraft were monitored mainly by the centers in Boston, New York, Cleveland, and Indianapolis. Each center thus had part of the knowledge of what was going on across the system. What Boston knew was not necessarily known by centers in New York, Cleveland, or Indianapolis, or for that matter by the Command Center in Herndon or by FAA headquarters in Washington.

Controllers track airliners such as the four aircraft hijacked on 9/11 primarily by watching the data from a signal emitted by each aircraft's transponder equipment. Those four planes, like all aircraft traveling above 10,000 feet, were required to emit a unique transponder signal while in flight.[93]

On 9/11, the terrorists turned off the transponders on three of the four hijacked aircraft. With its transponder off, it is possible, though more difficult, to track an aircraft by its primary radar returns. But unlike transponder data, primary radar returns do not show the aircraft's identity and altitude. Controllers at centers rely so heavily on transponder signals that they usually do not display primary radar returns on their radar scopes. But they can change the configuration of their scopes so they can see primary radar returns. They did this on 9/11 when the transponder signals for three of the aircraft disappeared.[94]

Before 9/11, it was not unheard of for a commercial aircraft to deviate slightly from its course, or for an FAA controller to lose radio contact with a pilot for a short period of time. A controller could also briefly lose a commercial aircraft's transponder signal, although this happened much less frequently. However, the simultaneous loss of radio and transponder signal would be a rare and alarming occurrence, and would normally indicate a catastrophic system failure or an aircraft crash. In all of these instances, the job of the controller was to reach out to the aircraft, the parent company of the aircraft, and other planes in the vicinity in an attempt to reestablish communications and set the aircraft back on course. Alarm bells would not start ringing until these efforts—which could take five minutes or more—were tried and had failed.[95]

NORAD Mission and Structure. NORAD is a binational command established in 1958 between the United States and Canada. Its mission was, and is, to defend the airspace of North America and protect the continent. That mission does not distinguish between internal and external threats; but because NORAD was created to counter the Soviet threat, it came to define its job as defending against external attacks.[96]

The threat of Soviet bombers diminished significantly as the Cold War ended, and the number of NORAD alert sites was reduced from its Cold War high of 26. Some within the Pentagon argued in the 1990s that the alert sites should be eliminated entirely. In an effort to preserve their mission, members of the air defense community advocated the importance of air sovereignty against emerging "asymmetric threats" to the United States: drug smuggling, "non-state and state-sponsored terrorists," and the proliferation of weapons of mass destruction and ballistic missile technology.[97]

NORAD perceived the dominant threat to be from cruise missiles. Other threats were identified during the late 1990s, including terrorists' use of aircraft as weapons. Exercises were conducted to counter this threat, but they were not based on actual intelligence. In most instances, the main concern was the use of such aircraft to deliver weapons of mass destruction.

Prior to 9/11, it was understood that an order to shoot down a commercial aircraft would have to be issued by the National Command Authority (a phrase used to describe the president and secretary of defense). Exercise planners also assumed that the aircraft would originate from outside the United States, allowing time to identify the target and scramble interceptors. The threat of terrorists hijacking commercial airliners within the United States—and using them as guided missiles—was not recognized by NORAD before 9/11.[98]

Notwithstanding the identification of these emerging threats, by 9/11 there were only seven alert sites left in the United States, each with two fighter aircraft on alert. This led some NORAD commanders to worry that NORAD was not postured adequately to protect the United States.[99]

In the United States, NORAD is divided into three sectors. On 9/11, all the hijacked aircraft were in NORAD's Northeast Air Defense Sector (also known as NEADS), which is based in Rome, New York. That morning NEADS could call on two alert sites, each with one pair of ready fighters: Otis Air National Guard Base in Cape Cod, Massachusetts, and Langley Air Force Base in Hampton, Virginia.[100] Other facilities, not on "alert," would need time to arm the fighters and organize crews.

NEADS reported to the Continental U.S. NORAD Region (CONR) headquarters, in Panama City, Florida, which in turn reported to NORAD headquarters, in Colorado Springs, Colorado.

Interagency Collaboration. The FAA and NORAD had developed protocols for working together in the event of a hijacking. As they existed on 9/11, the protocols for the FAA to obtain military assistance from NORAD required multiple levels of notification and approval at the highest levels of government.[101]

FAA guidance to controllers on hijack procedures assumed that the aircraft pilot would notify the controller via radio or by "squawking" a transponder code of "7500"—the universal code for a hijack in progress. Controllers would notify their supervisors, who in turn would inform management all the way up to FAA headquarters in Washington. Headquarters had a hijack coordinator, who was the director of the FAA Office of Civil Aviation Security or his or her designate.[102]

If a hijack was confirmed, procedures called for the hijack coordinator on duty to contact the Pentagon's National Military Command Center (NMCC) and to ask for a military escort aircraft to follow the flight, report anything unusual, and aid search and rescue in the event of an emergency. The NMCC would then seek approval from the Office of the Secretary of Defense to provide military assistance. If approval was given, the orders would be transmitted down NORAD's chain of command.[103]

The NMCC would keep the FAA hijack coordinator up to date and help the FAA centers coordinate directly with the military. NORAD would receive tracking information for the hijacked aircraft either from joint use radar or from the relevant FAA air traffic control facility. Every attempt would be made to have the hijacked aircraft squawk 7500 to help NORAD track it.[104]

The protocols did not contemplate an intercept. They assumed the fighter escort would be discreet, "vectored to a position five miles directly behind the hijacked aircraft," where it could perform its mission to monitor the aircraft's flight path.[105]

In sum, the protocols in place on 9/11 for the FAA and NORAD to respond to a hijacking presumed that

- the hijacked aircraft would be readily identifiable and would not attempt to disappear;
- there would be time to address the problem through the appropriate FAA and NORAD chains of command; and
- the hijacking would take the traditional form: that is, it would not be a suicide hijacking designed to convert the aircraft into a guided missile.

On the morning of 9/11, the existing protocol was unsuited in every respect for what was about to happen.

American Airlines Flight 11
FAA Awareness. Although the Boston Center air traffic controller realized at an early stage that there was something wrong with American 11, he did not immediately interpret the plane's failure to respond as a sign that it had been hijacked. At 8:14, when the flight failed to heed his instruction to climb to 35,000 feet, the controller repeatedly tried to raise the flight. He reached out to the pilot on the emergency frequency. Though there was no response, he kept trying to contact the aircraft.[106]

At 8:21, American 11 turned off its transponder, immediately degrading the information available about the aircraft. The controller told his supervisor that he thought something was seriously wrong with the plane, although neither suspected a hijacking. The supervisor instructed the controller to follow standard procedures for handling a "no radio" aircraft.[107]

The controller checked to see if American Airlines could establish communication with American 11. He became even more concerned as its route changed, moving into another sector's airspace. Controllers immediately began to move aircraft out of its path, and asked other aircraft in the vicinity to look for American 11.[108]

At 8:24:38, the following transmission came from American 11:

American 11: We have some planes. Just stay quiet, and you'll be okay. We are returning to the airport.

The controller only heard something unintelligible; he did not hear the specific words "we have some planes." The next transmission came seconds later:

American 11: Nobody move. Everything will be okay. If you try to make any moves, you'll endanger yourself and the airplane. Just stay quiet.[109]

The controller told us that he then knew it was a hijacking. He alerted his supervisor, who assigned another controller to assist him. He redoubled his efforts to ascertain the flight's altitude. Because the controller didn't understand the initial transmission, the manager of Boston Center instructed his quality assurance specialist to "pull the tape" of the radio transmission, listen to it closely, and report back.[110]

Between 8:25 and 8:32, in accordance with the FAA protocol, Boston Center managers started notifying their chain of command that American 11 had been hijacked. At 8:28, Boston Center called the Command Center in Herndon to advise that it believed American 11 had been hijacked and was heading toward New York Center's airspace.

By this time, American 11 had taken a dramatic turn to the south. At 8:32, the Command Center passed word of a possible hijacking to the Operations Center at FAA headquarters. The duty officer replied that security personnel at headquarters had just begun discussing the apparent hijack on a conference call with the New England regional office. FAA headquarters began to follow the hijack protocol but did not contact the NMCC to request a fighter escort.[111]

The Herndon Command Center immediately established a teleconference between Boston, New York, and Cleveland Centers so that Boston Center could help the others understand what was happening.[112]

At 8:34, the Boston Center controller received a third transmission from American 11:

American 11: Nobody move please. We are going back to the airport. Don't try to make any stupid moves.[113]

In the succeeding minutes, controllers were attempting to ascertain the altitude of the southbound flight.[114]

Military Notification and Response. Boston Center did not follow the protocol in seeking military assistance through the prescribed chain of command. In addition to notifications within the FAA, Boston Center took the initiative, at 8:34, to contact the military through the FAA's Cape Cod facility. The center also tried to contact a former alert site in Atlantic City, unaware it had been phased out. At 8:37:52, Boston Center reached NEADS. This was the first notification received by the military—at any level—that American 11 had been hijacked:[115]

> **FAA:** Hi. Boston Center TMU [Traffic Management Unit], we have a problem here. We have a hijacked aircraft headed towards New York, and we need you guys to, we need someone to scramble some F-16s or something up there, help us out.
> **NEADS:** Is this real-world or exercise?
> **FAA:** No, this is not an exercise, not a test.[116]

NEADS ordered to battle stations the two F-15 alert aircraft at Otis Air Force Base in Falmouth, Massachusetts, 153 miles away from New York City. The air defense of America began with this call.[117]

At NEADS, the report of the hijacking was relayed immediately to Battle Commander Colonel Robert Marr. After ordering the Otis fighters to battle stations, Colonel Marr phoned Major General Larry Arnold, commanding general of the First Air Force and NORAD's Continental Region. Marr sought authorization to scramble the Otis fighters. General Arnold later recalled instructing Marr to "go ahead and scramble them, and we'll get authorities later." General Arnold then called NORAD headquarters to report.[118]

F-15 fighters were scrambled at 8:46 from Otis Air Force Base. But NEADS did not know where to send the alert fighter aircraft, and the officer directing the fighters pressed for more information: "I don't know where I'm scrambling these guys to. I need a direction, a destination." Because the hijackers had turned off the plane's transponder, NEADS personnel spent the next minutes searching their radar scopes for the primary radar return. American 11 struck the North Tower at 8:46. Shortly after 8:50, while NEADS personnel were still trying to locate the flight, word reached them that a plane had hit the World Trade Center.[119]

Radar data show the Otis fighters were airborne at 8:53. Lacking a target, they were vectored toward military-controlled airspace off the Long Island coast. To avoid New York area air traffic and uncertain about what to do, the fighters were brought down to military airspace to "hold as needed." From 9:09 to 9:13, the Otis fighters stayed in this holding pattern.[120]

In summary, NEADS received notice of the hijacking nine minutes before it struck the North Tower. That nine minutes' notice before impact was the most the military would receive of any of the four hijackings.[121]

United Airlines Flight 175

FAA Awareness. One of the last transmissions from United Airlines Flight 175 is, in retrospect, chilling. By 8:40, controllers at the FAA's New York Center were seeking information on American 11. At approximately 8:42, shortly after entering New York Center's airspace, the pilot of United 175 broke in with the following transmission:

> **UAL 175:** New York UAL 175 heavy.
> **FAA:** UAL 175 go ahead.
> **UAL 175:** Yeah. We figured we'd wait to go to your center. Ah, we heard a suspicious transmission on our departure out of Boston, ah, with someone, ah, it sounded like someone keyed the mikes and said ah everyone ah stay in your seats.
> **FAA:** Oh, okay. I'll pass that along over here.[122]

Minutes later, United 175 turned southwest without clearance from air traffic control. At 8:47, seconds after the impact of American 11, United 175's transponder code changed, and then changed again. These changes were not noticed for several minutes, however, because the same New York Center controller was assigned to both American 11 and United 175. The controller knew American 11 was hijacked; he was focused on searching for it after the aircraft disappeared at 8:46.[123]

At 8:48, while the controller was still trying to locate American 11, a New York Center manager provided the following report on a Command Center teleconference about American 11:

> **Manager, New York Center:** Okay. This is New York Center. We're watching the airplane. I also had conversation with American Airlines, and they've told us that they believe that one of their stewardesses was stabbed and that there are people in the cockpit that have control of the aircraft, and that's all the information they have right now.[124]

The New York Center controller and manager were unaware that American 11 had already crashed.

At 8:51, the controller noticed the transponder change from United 175 and tried to contact the aircraft. There was no response. Beginning at 8:52, the controller made repeated attempts to reach the crew of United 175. Still no response. The controller checked his radio equipment and contacted another controller at 8:53, saying that "we may have a hijack" and that he could not find the aircraft.[125]

Another commercial aircraft in the vicinity then radioed in with "reports over the radio of a commuter plane hitting the World Trade Center." The controller spent the next several minutes handing off the other flights on his scope to other controllers and moving aircraft out of the way of the unidentified aircraft (believed to be United 175) as it moved southwest and then turned northeast toward New York City.[126]

At about 8:55, the controller in charge notified a New York Center manager that she believed United 175 had also been hijacked. The manager tried to notify the regional managers and was told that they were discussing a hijacked aircraft (presumably American 11) and refused to be disturbed. At 8:58, the New York Center controller searching for United 175 told another New York controller "we might have a hijack over here, two of them."[127]

Between 9:01 and 9:02, a manager from New York Center told the Command Center in Herndon:

> **Manager, New York Center:** We have several situations going on here. It's escalating big, big time. We need to get the military involved with us.... We're, we're involved with something else, we have other aircraft that may have a similar situation going on here.[128]

The "other aircraft" referred to by New York Center was United 175. Evidence indicates that this conversation was the only notice received by either FAA headquarters or the Herndon Command Center prior to the second crash that there had been a second hijacking.

While the Command Center was told about this "other aircraft" at 9:01, New York Center contacted New York terminal approach control and asked for help in locating United 175.

> **Terminal:** I got somebody who keeps coasting but it looks like he's going into one of the small airports down there.
> **Center:** Hold on a second. I'm trying to bring him up here and get you—There he is right there. Hold on.
> **Terminal:** Got him just out of 9,500—9,000 now.
> **Center:** Do you know who he is?
> **Terminal:** We're just, we just we don't know who he is. We're just picking him up now.
> **Center (at 9:02):** Alright. Heads up man, it looks like another one coming in.[129]

The controllers observed the plane in a rapid descent; the radar data terminated over Lower Manhattan. At 9:03, United 175 crashed into the South Tower.[130]

Meanwhile, a manager from Boston Center reported that they had deciphered what they had heard in one of the first hijacker transmissions from American 11:

> **Boston Center:** Hey . . . you still there?
> **New England Region:** Yes, I am.
> **Boston Center:** . . . as far as the tape, Bobby seemed to think the guy said that "we have planes." Now, I don't know if it was because it was the accent, or if there's more than one, but I'm gonna, I'm gonna reconfirm that for you, and I'll get back to you real quick. Okay?
> **New England Region:** Appreciate it.
> **Unidentified Female Voice:** They have what?
> **Boston Center:** Planes, as in plural.
> **Boston Center:** It sounds like, we're talking to New York, that there's another one aimed at the World Trade Center.
> **New England Region:** There's another aircraft?
> **Boston Center:** A second one just hit the Trade Center.
> **New England Region:** Okay. Yeah, we gotta get—we gotta alert the military real quick on this.[131]

Boston Center immediately advised the New England Region that it was going to stop all departures at airports under its control. At 9:05, Boston Center confirmed for both the FAA Command Center and the New England Region that the hijackers aboard American 11 said "we have *planes*." At the same time, New York Center declared "ATC zero"—meaning that aircraft were not permitted to depart from, arrive at, or travel through New York Center's airspace until further notice.[132]

Within minutes of the second impact, Boston Center instructed its controllers to inform all aircraft in its airspace of the events in New York and to advise aircraft to heighten cockpit security. Boston Center asked the Herndon Command Center to issue a similar cockpit security alert nationwide. We have found no evidence to suggest that the Command Center acted on this request or issued any type of cockpit security alert.[133]

Military Notification and Response. The first indication that the NORAD air defenders had of the second hijacked aircraft, United 175, came in a phone call from New York Center to NEADS at 9:03. The notice came at about the time the plane was hitting the South Tower.[134]

By 9:08, the mission crew commander at NEADS learned of the second explosion at the World Trade Center and decided against holding the fighters in military airspace away from Manhattan:

> **Mission Crew Commander, NEADS:** This is what I foresee that we probably need to do. We need to talk to FAA. We need to tell 'em if

this stuff is gonna keep on going, we need to take those fighters, put 'em over Manhattan. That's best thing, that's the best play right now. So coordinate with the FAA. Tell 'em if there's more out there, which we don't know, let's get 'em over Manhattan. At least we got some kind of play.[135]

The FAA cleared the airspace. Radar data show that at 9:13, when the Otis fighters were about 115 miles away from the city, the fighters exited their holding pattern and set a course direct for Manhattan. They arrived at 9:25 and established a combat air patrol (CAP) over the city.[136]

Because the Otis fighters had expended a great deal of fuel in flying first to military airspace and then to New York, the battle commanders were concerned about refueling. NEADS considered scrambling alert fighters from Langley Air Force Base in Virginia to New York, to provide backup. The Langley fighters were placed on battle stations at 9:09.[137] NORAD had no indication that any other plane had been hijacked.

American Airlines Flight 77

FAA Awareness. American 77 began deviating from its flight plan at 8:54, with a slight turn toward the south. Two minutes later, it disappeared completely from radar at Indianapolis Center, which was controlling the flight.[138]

The controller tracking American 77 told us he noticed the aircraft turning to the southwest, and then saw the data disappear. The controller looked for primary radar returns. He searched along the plane's projected flight path and the airspace to the southwest where it had started to turn. No primary targets appeared. He tried the radios, first calling the aircraft directly, then the airline. Again there was nothing. At this point, the Indianapolis controller had no knowledge of the situation in New York. He did not know that other aircraft had been hijacked. He believed American 77 had experienced serious electrical or mechanical failure, or both, and was gone.[139]

Shortly after 9:00, Indianapolis Center started notifying other agencies that American 77 was missing and had possibly crashed. At 9:08, Indianapolis Center asked Air Force Search and Rescue at Langley Air Force Base to look for a downed aircraft. The center also contacted the West Virginia State Police and asked whether any reports of a downed aircraft had been received. At 9:09, it reported the loss of contact to the FAA regional center, which passed this information to FAA headquarters at 9:24.[140]

By 9:20, Indianapolis Center learned that there were other hijacked aircraft, and began to doubt its initial assumption that American 77 had crashed. A discussion of this concern between the manager at Indianapolis and the Command Center in Herndon prompted it to notify some FAA field facilities that American 77 was lost. By 9:21, the Command Center, some FAA field facilities, and American Airlines had started to search for American 77. They feared it had been hijacked. At 9:25, the Command Center advised FAA headquarters of the situation.[141]

The failure to find a primary radar return for American 77 led us to investigate this issue further. Radar reconstructions performed after 9/11 reveal that FAA radar equipment tracked the flight from the moment its transponder was turned off at 8:56. But for 8 minutes and 13 seconds, between 8:56 and 9:05, this primary radar information on American 77 was not displayed to controllers at Indianapolis Center.[142] The reasons are technical, arising from the way the software processed radar information, as well as from poor primary radar coverage where American 77 was flying.

According to the radar reconstruction, American 77 reemerged as a primary target on Indianapolis Center radar scopes at 9:05, east of its last known position. The target remained in Indianapolis Center's airspace for another six minutes, then crossed into the western portion of Washington Center's airspace at 9:10. As Indianapolis Center continued searching for the aircraft, two managers and the controller responsible for American 77 looked to the west and southwest along the flight's projected path, not east—where the aircraft was now heading. Managers did not instruct other controllers at Indianapolis Center to turn on their primary radar coverage to join in the search for American 77.[143]

In sum, Indianapolis Center never saw Flight 77 turn around. By the time it reappeared in primary radar coverage, controllers had either stopped looking for the aircraft because they thought it had crashed or were looking toward the west. Although the Command Center learned Flight 77 was missing, neither it nor FAA headquarters issued an all points bulletin to surrounding centers to search for primary radar targets. American 77 traveled undetected for 36 minutes on a course heading due east for Washington, D.C.[144]

By 9:25, FAA's Herndon Command Center and FAA headquarters knew two aircraft had crashed into the World Trade Center. They knew American 77 was lost. At least some FAA officials in Boston Center and the New England Region knew that a hijacker on board American 11 had said "we have some planes." Concerns over the safety of other aircraft began to mount. A manager at the Herndon Command Center asked FAA headquarters if they wanted to order a "nationwide ground stop." While this was being discussed by executives at FAA headquarters, the Command Center ordered one at 9:25.[145]

The Command Center kept looking for American 77. At 9:21, it advised the Dulles terminal control facility, and Dulles urged its controllers to look for primary targets. At 9:32, they found one. Several of the Dulles controllers "observed a primary radar target tracking eastbound at a high rate of speed" and notified Reagan National Airport. FAA personnel at both Reagan National and Dulles airports notified the Secret Service. The aircraft's identity or type was unknown.[146]

Reagan National controllers then vectored an unarmed National Guard C-130H cargo aircraft, which had just taken off en route to Minnesota, to identify and follow the suspicious aircraft. The C-130H pilot spotted it, identified it as a Boeing 757, attempted to follow its path, and at 9:38, seconds after impact, reported to the control tower: "looks like that aircraft crashed into the Pentagon sir."[147]

Military Notification and Response. NORAD heard nothing about the search for American 77. Instead, the NEADS air defenders heard renewed reports about a plane that no longer existed: American 11.

At 9:21, NEADS received a report from the FAA:

FAA: Military, Boston Center. I just had a report that American 11 is still in the air, and it's on its way towards—heading towards Washington.
NEADS: Okay. American 11 is still in the air?
FAA: Yes.
NEADS: On its way towards Washington?
FAA: That was another—it was evidently another aircraft that hit the tower. That's the latest report we have.
NEADS: Okay.
FAA: I'm going to try to confirm an ID for you, but I would assume he's somewhere over, uh, either New Jersey or somewhere further south.
NEADS: Okay. So American 11 isn't the hijack at all then, right?
FAA: No, he is a hijack.
NEADS: He—American 11 is a hijack?
FAA: Yes.
NEADS: And he's heading into Washington?
FAA: Yes. This could be a third aircraft.[148]

The mention of a "third aircraft" was not a reference to American 77. There was confusion at that moment in the FAA. Two planes had struck the World Trade Center, and Boston Center had heard from FAA headquarters in Washington that American 11 was still airborne. We have been unable to identify the source of this mistaken FAA information.

The NEADS technician who took this call from the FAA immediately passed the word to the mission crew commander, who reported to the NEADS battle commander:

Mission Crew Commander, NEADS: Okay, uh, American Airlines is still airborne. Eleven, the first guy, he's heading towards Washington. Okay? I think we need to scramble Langley right now. And I'm gonna take the fighters from Otis, try to chase this guy down if I can find him.[149]

After consulting with NEADS command, the crew commander issued the order at 9:23: "Okay . . . scramble Langley. Head them towards the Washington area. . . . [I]f they're there then we'll run on them. . . . These guys are smart." That order was processed and transmitted to Langley Air Force Base at 9:24. Radar data show the Langley fighters airborne at 9:30. NEADS decided to keep the Otis fighters over New York. The heading of the Langley fighters was adjusted to send them to the Baltimore area. The mission crew commander explained to us that the purpose was to position the Langley fighters between the reported southbound American 11 and the nation's capital.[150]

At the suggestion of the Boston Center's military liaison, NEADS contacted the FAA's Washington Center to ask about American 11. In the course of the conversation, a Washington Center manager informed NEADS: "We're looking—we also lost American 77." The time was 9:34.[151] This was the first notice to the military that American 77 was missing, and it had come by chance. If NEADS had not placed that call, the NEADS air defenders would have received no information whatsoever that the flight was even missing, although the FAA had been searching for it. No one at FAA headquarters ever asked for military assistance with American 77.

At 9:36, the FAA's Boston Center called NEADS and relayed the discovery about an unidentified aircraft closing in on Washington: "Latest report. Aircraft VFR [visual flight rules] six miles southeast of the White House. . . . Six, southwest. Six, southwest of the White House, deviating away." This startling news prompted the mission crew commander at NEADS to take immediate control of the airspace to clear a flight path for the Langley fighters: "Okay, we're going to turn it . . . crank it up. . . . Run them to the White House." He then discovered, to his surprise, that the Langley fighters were not headed north toward the Baltimore area as instructed, but east over the ocean. "I don't care how many windows you break," he said. "Damn it. . . . Okay. Push them back."[152]

The Langley fighters were heading east, not north, for three reasons. First, unlike a normal scramble order, this order did not include a distance to the target or the target's location. Second, a "generic" flight plan—prepared to get the aircraft airborne and out of local airspace quickly—incorrectly led the Langley fighters to believe they were ordered to fly due east (090) for 60 miles. Third, the lead pilot and local FAA controller incorrectly assumed the flight plan instruction to go "090 for 60" superseded the original scramble order.[153]

After the 9:36 call to NEADS about the unidentified aircraft a few miles from the White House, the Langley fighters were ordered to Washington, D.C. Controllers at NEADS located an unknown primary radar track, but "it kind of faded" over Washington. The time was 9:38. The Pentagon had been struck by American 77 at 9:37:46. The Langley fighters were about 150 miles away.[154]

Right after the Pentagon was hit, NEADS learned of another possible hijacked aircraft. It was an aircraft that in fact had not been hijacked at all. After the second World Trade Center crash, Boston Center managers recognized that both aircraft were transcontinental 767 jetliners that had departed Logan Airport. Remembering the "we have some planes" remark, Boston Center guessed that Delta 1989 might also be hijacked. Boston Center called NEADS at 9:41 and identified Delta 1989, a 767 jet that had left Logan Airport for Las Vegas, as a possible hijack. NEADS warned the FAA's Cleveland Center to watch Delta 1989. The Command Center and FAA headquarters watched it too. During the course of the morning, there were multiple erroneous reports of hijacked aircraft. The report of American 11 heading south was the first; Delta 1989 was the second.[155]

NEADS never lost track of Delta 1989, and even ordered fighter aircraft from Ohio and Michigan to intercept it. The flight never turned off its transponder. NEADS soon learned that the aircraft was not hijacked, and tracked Delta 1989 as it reversed course over Toledo, headed east, and landed in Cleveland.[156] But another aircraft was heading toward Washington, an aircraft about which NORAD had heard nothing: United 93.

United Airlines Flight 93

FAA Awareness. At 9:27, after having been in the air for 45 minutes, United 93 acknowledged a transmission from the Cleveland Center controller. This was the last normal contact the FAA had with the flight.[157]

Less than a minute later, the Cleveland controller and the pilots of aircraft in the vicinity heard "a radio transmission of unintelligible sounds of possible screaming or a struggle from an unknown origin."[158]

The controller responded, seconds later: "Somebody call Cleveland?" This was followed by a second radio transmission, with sounds of screaming. The Cleveland Center controllers began to try to identify the possible source of the transmissions, and noticed that United 93 had descended some 700 feet. The controller attempted again to raise United 93 several times, with no response. At 9:30, the controller began to poll the other flights on his frequency to determine if they had heard the screaming; several said they had.[159]

At 9:32, a third radio transmission came over the frequency: "Keep remaining sitting. We have a bomb on board." The controller understood, but chose to respond: "Calling Cleveland Center, you're unreadable. Say again, slowly." He notified his supervisor, who passed the notice up the chain of command. By 9:34, word of the hijacking had reached FAA headquarters.[160]

FAA headquarters had by this time established an open line of communication with the Command Center at Herndon and instructed it to poll all its centers about suspect aircraft. The Command Center executed the request and, a minute later, Cleveland Center reported that "United 93 may have a bomb on board." At 9:34, the Command Center relayed the information concerning United 93 to FAA headquarters. At approximately 9:36, Cleveland advised the Command Center that it was still tracking United 93 and specifically inquired whether someone had requested the military to launch fighter aircraft to intercept the aircraft. Cleveland even told the Command Center it was prepared to contact a nearby military base to make the request. The Command Center told Cleveland that FAA personnel well above them in the chain of command had to make the decision to seek military assistance and were working on the issue.[161]

Between 9:34 and 9:38, the Cleveland controller observed United 93 climbing to 40,700 feet and immediately moved several aircraft out its way. The controller continued to try to contact United 93, and asked whether the pilot could confirm that he had been hijacked.[162] There was no response.

Then, at 9:39, a fourth radio transmission was heard from United 93:

> **Ziad Jarrah:** Uh, this is the captain. Would like you all to remain seated. There is a bomb on board and are going back to the airport, and to have our demands [unintelligible]. Please remain quiet.

The controller responded: "United 93, understand you have a bomb on board. Go ahead." The flight did not respond.[163]

From 9:34 to 10:08, a Command Center facility manager provided frequent updates to Acting Deputy Administrator Monte Belger and other executives at FAA headquarters as United 93 headed toward Washington, D.C. At 9:41, Cleveland Center lost United 93's transponder signal. The controller located it on primary radar, matched its position with visual sightings from other aircraft, and tracked the flight as it turned east, then south.[164]

At 9:42, the Command Center learned from news reports that a plane had struck the Pentagon. The Command Center's national operations manager, Ben Sliney, ordered all FAA facilities to instruct all aircraft to land at the nearest airport. This was an unprecedented order. The air traffic control system handled it with great skill, as about 4,500 commercial and general aviation aircraft soon landed without incident.[165]

At 9:46 the Command Center updated FAA headquarters that United 93 was now "twenty-nine minutes out of Washington, D.C."

At 9:49, 13 minutes after Cleveland Center had asked about getting military help, the Command Center suggested that someone at headquarters should decide whether to request military assistance:

> **FAA Headquarters:** They're pulling Jeff away to go talk about United 93.
> **Command Center:** Uh, do we want to think, uh, about scrambling aircraft?
> **FAA Headquarters:** Oh, God, I don't know.
> **Command Center:** Uh, that's a decision somebody's gonna have to make probably in the next ten minutes.
> **FAA Headquarters:** Uh, ya know everybody just left the room.[166]

At 9:53, FAA headquarters informed the Command Center that the deputy director for air traffic services was talking to Monte Belger about scrambling aircraft. Then the Command Center informed headquarters that controllers had lost track of United 93 over the Pittsburgh area. Within seconds, the Command Center received a visual report from another aircraft, and informed headquarters that the aircraft was 20 miles northwest of Johnstown. United 93 was spotted by another aircraft, and, at 10:01, the Command Center advised FAA headquarters that one of the aircraft had seen United 93 "waving his wings." The aircraft had witnessed the hijackers' efforts to defeat the passengers' counterattack.[167]

United 93 crashed in Pennsylvania at 10:03:11, 125 miles from Washington, D.C. The precise crash time has been the subject of some dispute. The 10:03:11 impact time is supported by previous National Transportation Safety Board analysis and by evidence from the Commission staff's analysis of radar, the flight data recorder, the cockpit voice recorder, infrared satellite data, and air traffic control transmissions.[168]

Five minutes later, the Command Center forwarded this update to headquarters:

> **Command Center:** O.K. Uh, there is now on that United 93.
> **FAA Headquarters:** Yes.
> **Command Center:** There is a report of black smoke in the last position I gave you, fifteen miles south of Johnstown.
> **FAA Headquarters:** From the airplane or from the ground?
> **Command Center:** Uh, they're speculating it's from the aircraft.
> **FAA Headquarters:** Okay.
> **Command Center:** Uh, who, it hit the ground. That's what they're speculating, that's speculation only.[169]

The aircraft that spotted the "black smoke" was the same unarmed Air National Guard cargo plane that had seen American 77 crash into the Pentagon 27 minutes earlier. It had resumed its flight to Minnesota and saw the smoke from the crash of United 93, less than two minutes after the plane went down. At 10:17, the Command Center advised headquarters of its conclusion that United 93 had indeed crashed.[170]

Despite the discussions about military assistance, no one from FAA headquarters requested military assistance regarding United 93. Nor did any manager at FAA headquarters pass any of the information it had about United 93 to the military.

Military Notification and Response. NEADS first received a call about United 93 from the military liaison at Cleveland Center at 10:07. Unaware that the aircraft had already crashed, Cleveland passed to NEADS the aircraft's last known latitude and longitude. NEADS was never able to locate United 93 on radar because it was already in the ground.[171]

At the same time, the NEADS mission crew commander was dealing with the arrival of the Langley fighters over Washington, D.C., sorting out what their orders were with respect to potential targets. Shortly after 10:10, and having no knowledge either that United 93 had been heading toward Washington or that it had crashed, he explicitly instructed the Langley fighters: "negative—negative clearance to shoot" aircraft over the nation's capital.[172]

The news of a reported bomb on board United 93 spread quickly at NEADS. The air defenders searched for United 93's primary radar return and tried to locate other fighters to scramble. NEADS called Washington Center to report:

> **NEADS:** I also want to give you a heads-up, Washington.
> **FAA (DC):** Go ahead.
> **NEADS:** United nine three, have you got information on that yet?
> **FAA:** Yeah, he's down.
> **NEADS:** He's down?
> **FAA:** Yes.
> **NEADS:** When did he land? 'Cause we have got confirmation—
> **FAA:** He did not land.
> **NEADS:** Oh, he's down? Down?
> **FAA:** Yes. Somewhere up northeast of Camp David.
> **NEADS:** Northeast of Camp David.
> **FAA:** That's the last report. They don't know exactly where.[173]

The time of notification of the crash of United 93 was 10:15.[174] The NEADS air defenders never located the flight or followed it on their radar scopes. The flight had already crashed by the time they learned it was hijacked.

Clarifying the Record

The defense of U.S. airspace on 9/11 was not conducted in accord with pre-existing training and protocols. It was improvised by civilians who had never handled a hijacked aircraft that attempted to disappear, and by a military unprepared for the transformation of commercial aircraft into weapons of mass destruction. As it turned out, the NEADS air defenders had nine minutes' notice on the first hijacked plane, no advance notice on the second, no advance notice on the third, and no advance notice on the fourth.

We do not believe that the true picture of that morning reflects discredit on the operational personnel at NEADS or FAA facilities. NEADS commanders and officers actively sought out information, and made the best judgments they could on the basis of what they knew. Individual FAA controllers, facility managers, and Command Center managers thought outside the box in recommending a nationwide alert, in ground-stopping local traffic, and, ultimately, in deciding to land all aircraft and executing that unprecedented order flawlessly.

American Airlines Flight 11 (AA 11)
Boston to Los Angeles

7:59	Takeoff
8:14	Last routine radio communication; likely takeover
8:19	Flight attendant notifies AA of hijacking
8:21	Transponder is turned off
8:23	AA attempts to contact the cockpit
8:25	Boston Center aware of hijacking
8:38	Boston Center notifies NEADS of hijacking
8:46	NEADS scrambles Otis fighter jets in search of AA 11
8:46:40	AA 11 crashes into 1 WTC (North Tower)
8:53	Otis fighter jets airborne
9:16	AA headquarters aware that Flight 11 has crashed into WTC
9:21	Boston Center advises NEADS that AA 11 is airborne heading for Washington
9:24	NEADS scrambles Langley fighter jets in search of AA 11

United Airlines Flight 175 (UA 175)
Boston to Los Angeles

8:14	Takeoff
8:42	Last radio communication
8:42–8:46	Likely takeover
8:47	Transponder code changes
8:52	Flight attendant notifies UA of hijacking
8:54	UA attempts to contact the cockpit
8:55	New York Center suspects hijacking
9:03:11	Flight 175 crashes into 2 WTC (South Tower)
9:15	New York Center advises NEADS that UA 175 was the second aircraft crashed into WTC
9:20	UA headquarters aware that Flight 175 had crashed into WTC

American Airlines Flight 77 (AA 77)
Washington, D.C., to Los Angeles

United Airlines Flight 93 (UA 93)
Newark to San Francisco

8:20	Takeoff
8:51	Last routine radio communication
8:51–8:54	Likely takeover
8:54	Flight 77 makes unauthorized turn to south
8:56	Transponder is turned off
9:05	AA headquarters aware that Flight 77 is hijacked
9:25	Herndon Command Center orders nationwide ground stop
9:32	Dulles tower observes radar of fast-moving aircraft (later identified as AA 77)
9:34	FAA advises NEADS that AA 77 is missing
9:37:46	AA 77 crashes into the Pentagon
10:30	AA headquarters confirms Flight 77 crash into Pentagon

8:42	Takeoff
9:24	Flight 93 receives warning from UA about possible cockpit intrusion
9:27	Last routine radio communication
9:28	Likely takeover
9:34	Herndon Command Center advises FAA headquarters that UA 93 is hijacked
9:36	Flight attendant notifies UA of hijacking; UA attempts to contact the cockpit
9:41	Transponder is turned off
9:57	Passenger revolt begins
10:03:11	Flight 93 crashes in field in Shanksville, PA
10:07	Cleveland Center advises NEADS of UA 93 hijacking
10:15	UA headquarters aware that Flight 93 has crashed in PA; Washington Center advises NEADS that Flight 93 has crashed in PA

More than the actual events, inaccurate government accounts of those events made it appear that the military was notified in time to respond to two of the hijackings, raising questions about the adequacy of the response. Those accounts had the effect of deflecting questions about the military's capacity to obtain timely and accurate information from its own sources. In addition, they overstated the FAA's ability to provide the military with timely and useful information that morning.

In public testimony before this Commission in May 2003, NORAD officials stated that at 9:16, NEADS received hijack notification of United 93 from the FAA.[175] This statement was incorrect. There was no hijack to report at 9:16. United 93 was proceeding normally at that time.

In this same public testimony, NORAD officials stated that at 9:24, NEADS received notification of the hijacking of American 77.[176] This statement was also incorrect. The notice NEADS received at 9:24 was that American 11 had not hit the World Trade Center and was heading for Washington, D.C.[177]

In their testimony and in other public accounts, NORAD officials also stated that the Langley fighters were scrambled to respond to the notifications about American 77,[178] United 93, or both. These statements were incorrect as well. The fighters were scrambled because of the report that American 11 was heading south, as is clear not just from taped conversations at NEADS but also from taped conversations at FAA centers; contemporaneous logs compiled at NEADS, Continental Region headquarters, and NORAD; and other records. Yet this response to a phantom aircraft was not recounted in a single public timeline or statement issued by the FAA or Department of Defense. The inaccurate accounts created the impression that the Langley scramble was a logical response to an actual hijacked aircraft.

In fact, not only was the scramble prompted by the mistaken information about American 11, but NEADS never received notice that American 77 was hijacked. It was notified at 9:34 that American 77 was lost. Then, minutes later, NEADS was told that an unknown plane was 6 miles southwest of the White House. Only then did the already scrambled airplanes start moving directly toward Washington, D.C.

Thus the military did not have 14 minutes to respond to American 77, as testimony to the Commission in May 2003 suggested. It had at most one or two minutes to react to the unidentified plane approaching Washington, and the fighters were in the wrong place to be able to help. They had been responding to a report about an aircraft that did not exist.

Nor did the military have 47 minutes to respond to United 93, as would be implied by the account that it received notice of the flight's hijacking at 9:16. By the time the military learned about the flight, it had crashed.

We now turn to the role of national leadership in the events that morning.

1.3 NATIONAL CRISIS MANAGEMENT

When American 11 struck the World Trade Center at 8:46, no one in the White House or traveling with the President knew that it had been hijacked. While that information circulated within the FAA, we found no evidence that the hijacking was reported to any other agency in Washington before 8:46.[179]

Most federal agencies learned about the crash in New York from CNN.[180] Within the FAA, the administrator, Jane Garvey, and her acting deputy, Monte Belger, had not been told of a confirmed hijacking before they learned from television that a plane had crashed.[181] Others in the agency were aware of it, as we explained earlier in this chapter.

Inside the National Military Command Center, the deputy director of operations and his assistant began notifying senior Pentagon officials of the incident. At about 9:00, the senior NMCC operations officer reached out to the FAA operations center for information. Although the NMCC was advised of the hijacking of American 11, the scrambling of jets was not discussed.[182]

In Sarasota, Florida, the presidential motorcade was arriving at the Emma E. Booker Elementary School, where President Bush was to read to a class and talk about education. White House Chief of Staff Andrew Card told us he was standing with the President outside the classroom when Senior Advisor to the President Karl Rove first informed them that a small, twin-engine plane had crashed into the World Trade Center. The President's reaction was that the incident must have been caused by pilot error.[183]

At 8:55, before entering the classroom, the President spoke to National Security Advisor Condoleezza Rice, who was at the White House. She recalled first telling the President it was a twin-engine aircraft—and then a commercial aircraft—that had struck the World Trade Center, adding "that's all we know right now, Mr. President."[184]

At the White House, Vice President Dick Cheney had just sat down for a meeting when his assistant told him to turn on his television because a plane had struck the North Tower of the World Trade Center. The Vice President was wondering "how the hell could a plane hit the World Trade Center" when he saw the second aircraft strike the South Tower.[185]

Elsewhere in the White House, a series of 9:00 meetings was about to begin. In the absence of information that the crash was anything other than an accident, the White House staff monitored the news as they went ahead with their regular schedules.[186]

The Agencies Confer

When they learned a second plane had struck the World Trade Center, nearly everyone in the White House told us, they immediately knew it was not an accident. The Secret Service initiated a number of security enhancements around the White House complex. The officials who issued these orders did not know that there were additional hijacked aircraft, or that one such aircraft was en route to Washington. These measures were precautionary steps taken because of the strikes in New York.[187]

The FAA and White House Teleconferences. The FAA, the White House, and the Defense Department each initiated a multiagency teleconference before 9:30. Because none of these teleconferences—at least before 10:00—included the right officials from both the FAA and Defense Department, none succeeded in meaningfully coordinating the military and FAA response to the hijackings.

At about 9:20, security personnel at FAA headquarters set up a hijacking teleconference with several agencies, including the Defense Department. The NMCC officer who participated told us that the call was monitored only periodically because the information was sporadic, it was of little value, and there were other important tasks. The FAA manager of the teleconference also remembered that the military participated only briefly before the Pentagon was hit. Both individuals agreed that the teleconference played no role in coordinating a response to the attacks of 9/11. Acting Deputy Administrator Belger was frustrated to learn later in the morning that the military had not been on the call.[188]

At the White House, the video teleconference was conducted from the Situation Room by Richard Clarke, a special assistant to the president long involved in counterterrorism. Logs indicate that it began at 9:25 and included the CIA; the FBI; the departments of State, Justice, and Defense; the FAA; and the White House shelter. The FAA and CIA joined at 9:40. The first topic addressed in the White House video teleconference—at about 9:40—was the physical security of the President, the White House, and federal agencies. Immediately thereafter it was reported that a plane had hit the Pentagon. We found no evidence that video teleconference participants had any prior information that American 77 had been hijacked and was heading directly toward Washington. Indeed, it is not clear to us that the video teleconference was fully under way before 9:37, when the Pentagon was struck.[189]

Garvey, Belger, and other senior officials from FAA headquarters participated in this video teleconference at various times. We do not know who from Defense participated, but we know that in the first hour none of the personnel involved in managing the crisis did. And none of the information conveyed in the White House video teleconference, at least in the first hour, was being passed to the NMCC. As one witness recalled, "[It] was almost like there were parallel decisionmaking processes going on; one was a voice conference orchestrated by the NMCC . . . and then there was the [White House video teleconference]. . . . [I]n my mind they were competing venues for command and control and decisionmaking."[190]

At 10:03, the conference received reports of more missing aircraft, "2 possibly 3 aloft," and learned of a combat air patrol over Washington. There was discussion of the need for rules of engagement. Clarke reported that they were asking the President for authority to shoot down aircraft. Confirmation of that authority came at 10:25, but the commands were already being conveyed in more direct contacts with the Pentagon.[191]

The Pentagon Teleconferences. Inside the National Military Command Center, the deputy director for operations immediately thought the second strike was a terrorist attack. The job of the NMCC in such an emergency is to gather the relevant parties and establish the chain of command between the National Command Authority—the president and the secretary of defense—and those who need to carry out their orders.[192]

On the morning of September 11, Secretary Rumsfeld was having breakfast at the Pentagon with a group of members of Congress. He then returned to his office for his daily intelligence briefing. The Secretary was informed of the second strike in New York during the briefing; he resumed the briefing while awaiting more information. After the Pentagon was struck, Secretary Rumsfeld went to the parking lot to assist with rescue efforts.[193]

Inside the NMCC, the deputy director for operations called for an all-purpose "significant event" conference. It began at 9:29, with a brief recap: two aircraft had struck the World Trade Center, there was a confirmed hijacking of American 11, and Otis fighters had been scrambled. The FAA was asked to provide an update, but the line was silent because the FAA had not been added to the call. A minute later, the deputy director stated that it had just been confirmed that American 11 was still airborne and heading toward D.C. He directed the transition to an air threat conference call. NORAD confirmed that American 11 was airborne and heading toward Washington, relaying the erroneous FAA information already mentioned. The call then ended, at about 9:34.[194]

It resumed at 9:37 as an air threat conference call,* which lasted more than eight hours. The President, Vice President, Secretary of Defense, Vice Chairman of the Joint Chiefs of Staff, and Deputy National Security Advisor Stephen Hadley all participated in this teleconference at various times, as did military personnel from the White House underground shelter and the President's military aide on Air Force One.[195]

Operators worked feverishly to include the FAA, but they had equipment problems and difficulty finding secure phone numbers. NORAD asked three times before 10:03 to confirm the presence of the FAA in the teleconference. The FAA representative who finally joined the call at 10:17 had no familiarity with or responsibility for hijackings, no access to decisionmakers, and none of the information available to senior FAA officials.[196]

---

* All times given for this conference call are estimates, which we and the Department of Defense believe to be accurate within a ± 3 minute margin of error.

We found no evidence that, at this critical time, NORAD's top commanders, in Florida or Cheyenne Mountain, coordinated with their counterparts at FAA headquarters to improve awareness and organize a common response. Lower-level officials improvised—for example, the FAA's Boston Center bypassed the chain of command and directly contacted NEADS after the first hijacking. But the highest-level Defense Department officials relied on the NMCC's air threat conference, in which the FAA did not participate for the first 48 minutes.[197]

At 9:39, the NMCC's deputy director for operations, a military officer, opened the call from the Pentagon, which had just been hit. He began: "An air attack against North America may be in progress. NORAD, what's the situation?" NORAD said it had conflicting reports. Its latest information was "of a possible hijacked aircraft taking off out of JFK en route to Washington D.C." The NMCC reported a crash into the mall side of the Pentagon and requested that the Secretary of Defense be added to the conference.[198]

At 9:44, NORAD briefed the conference on the possible hijacking of Delta 1989. Two minutes later, staff reported that they were still trying to locate Secretary Rumsfeld and Vice Chairman Myers. The Vice Chairman joined the conference shortly before 10:00; the Secretary, shortly before 10:30. The Chairman was out of the country.[199]

At 9:48, a representative from the White House shelter asked if there were any indications of another hijacked aircraft. The deputy director for operations mentioned the Delta flight and concluded that "that would be the fourth possible hijack." At 9:49, the commander of NORAD directed all air sovereignty aircraft to battle stations, fully armed.[200]

At 9:59, an Air Force lieutenant colonel working in the White House Military Office joined the conference and stated he had just talked to Deputy National Security Advisor Stephen Hadley. The White House requested (1) the implementation of continuity of government measures, (2) fighter escorts for Air Force One, and (3) a fighter combat air patrol over Washington, D.C.[201]

By 10:03, when United 93 crashed in Pennsylvania, there had been no mention of its hijacking and the FAA had not yet been added to the teleconference.[202]

The President and the Vice President

The President was seated in a classroom when, at 9:05, Andrew Card whispered to him: "A second plane hit the second tower. America is under attack." The President told us his instinct was to project calm, not to have the country see an excited reaction at a moment of crisis. The press was standing behind the children; he saw their phones and pagers start to ring. The President felt he should project strength and calm until he could better understand what was happening.[203]

The President remained in the classroom for another five to seven minutes, while the children continued reading. He then returned to a holding room shortly before 9:15, where he was briefed by staff and saw television coverage. He next spoke to Vice President Cheney, Dr. Rice, New York Governor George Pataki, and FBI Director Robert Mueller. He decided to make a brief statement from the school before leaving for the airport. The Secret Service told us they were anxious to move the President to a safer location, but did not think it imperative for him to run out the door.[204]

Between 9:15 and 9:30, the staff was busy arranging a return to Washington, while the President consulted his senior advisers about his remarks. No one in the traveling party had any information during this time that other aircraft were hijacked or missing. Staff was in contact with the White House Situation Room, but as far as we could determine, no one with the President was in contact with the Pentagon. The focus was on the President's statement to the nation. The only decision made during this time was to return to Washington.[205]

The President's motorcade departed at 9:35, and arrived at the airport between 9:42 and 9:45. During the ride the President learned about the attack on the Pentagon. He boarded the aircraft, asked the Secret Service about the safety of his family, and called the Vice President. According to notes of the call, at about 9:45 the President told the Vice President: "Sounds like we have a minor war going on here, I heard about the Pentagon. We're at war . . . somebody's going to pay."[206]

About this time, Card, the lead Secret Service agent, the President's military aide, and the pilot were conferring on a possible destination for Air Force One. The Secret Service agent felt strongly that the situation in Washington was too unstable for the President to return there, and Card agreed. The President strongly wanted to return to Washington and only grudgingly agreed to go elsewhere. The issue was still undecided when the President conferred with the Vice President at about the time Air Force One was taking off. The Vice President recalled urging the President not to return to Washington. Air Force One departed at about 9:54 without any fixed destination. The objective was to get up in the air—as fast and as high as possible—and then decide where to go.[207]

At 9:33, the tower supervisor at Reagan National Airport picked up a hotline to the Secret Service and told the Service's operations center that "an aircraft [is] coming at you and not talking with us." This was the first specific report to the Secret Service of a direct threat to the White House. No move was made to evacuate the Vice President at this time. As the officer who took the call explained, "[I was] about to push the alert button when the tower advised that the aircraft was turning south and approaching Reagan National Airport."[208]

American 77 began turning south, away from the White House, at 9:34. It continued heading south for roughly a minute, before turning west and beginning to circle back. This news prompted the Secret Service to order the immediate evacuation of the Vice President just before 9:36. Agents propelled him out of his chair and told him he had to get to the bunker. The Vice President entered the underground tunnel leading to the shelter at 9:37.[209]

Once inside, Vice President Cheney and the agents paused in an area of the tunnel that had a secure phone, a bench, and television. The Vice President asked to speak to the President, but it took time for the call to be connected. He learned in the tunnel that the Pentagon had been hit, and he saw television coverage of smoke coming from the building.[210]

The Secret Service logged Mrs. Cheney's arrival at the White House at 9:52, and she joined her husband in the tunnel. According to contemporaneous notes, at 9:55 the Vice President was still on the phone with the President advising that three planes were missing and one had hit the Pentagon. We believe this is the same call in which the Vice President urged the President not to return to Washington. After the call ended, Mrs. Cheney and the Vice President moved from the tunnel to the shelter conference room.[211]

United 93 and the Shootdown Order

On the morning of 9/11, the President and Vice President stayed in contact not by an open line of communication but through a series of calls. The President told us he was frustrated with the poor communications that morning. He could not reach key officials, including Secretary Rumsfeld, for a period of time. The line to the White House shelter conference room—and the Vice President—kept cutting off.[212]

The Vice President remembered placing a call to the President just after entering the shelter conference room. There is conflicting evidence about when the Vice President arrived in the shelter conference room. We have concluded, from the available evidence, that the Vice President arrived in the room shortly before 10:00, perhaps at 9:58. The Vice President recalled being told, just after his arrival, that the Air Force was trying to establish a combat air patrol over Washington.[213]

The Vice President stated that he called the President to discuss the rules of engagement for the CAP. He recalled feeling that it did no good to establish the CAP unless the pilots had instructions on whether they were authorized to shoot if the plane would not divert. He said the President signed off on that concept. The President said he remembered such a conversation, and that it reminded him of when he had been an interceptor pilot. The President emphasized to us that he had authorized the shootdown of hijacked aircraft.[214]

The Vice President's military aide told us he believed the Vice President spoke to the President just after entering the conference room, but he did not hear what they said. Rice, who entered the room shortly after the Vice President and sat next to him, remembered hearing him inform the President, "Sir, the CAPs are up. Sir, they're going to want to know what to do." Then she recalled hearing him say, "Yes sir." She believed this conversation occurred a few minutes, perhaps five, after they entered the conference room.[215]

We believe this call would have taken place sometime before 10:10 to 10:15.

Among the sources that reflect other important events of that morning, there is no documentary evidence for this call, but the relevant sources are incomplete. Others nearby who were taking notes, such as the Vice President's chief of staff, Scooter Libby, who sat next to him, and Mrs. Cheney, did not note a call between the President and Vice President immediately after the Vice President entered the conference room.[216]

At 10:02, the communicators in the shelter began receiving reports from the Secret Service of an inbound aircraft—presumably hijacked—heading toward Washington. That aircraft was United 93. The Secret Service was getting this information directly from the FAA. The FAA may have been tracking the progress of United 93 on a display that showed its projected path to Washington, not its actual radar return. Thus, the Secret Service was relying on projections and was not aware the plane was already down in Pennsylvania.[217]

At some time between 10:10 and 10:15, a military aide told the Vice President and others that the aircraft was 80 miles out. Vice President Cheney was asked for authority to engage the aircraft.[218] His reaction was described by Scooter Libby as quick and decisive, "in about the time it takes a batter to decide to swing." The Vice President authorized fighter aircraft to engage the inbound plane. He told us he based this authorization on his earlier conversation with the President. The military aide returned a few minutes later, probably between 10:12 and 10:18, and said the aircraft was 60 miles out. He again asked for authorization to engage. The Vice President again said yes.[219]

At the conference room table was White House Deputy Chief of Staff Joshua Bolten. Bolten watched the exchanges and, after what he called "a quiet moment," suggested that the Vice President get in touch with the President and confirm the engage order. Bolten told us he wanted to make sure the President was told that the Vice President had executed the order. He said he had not heard any prior discussion on the subject with the President.[220]

The Vice President was logged calling the President at 10:18 for a two-minute conversation that obtained the confirmation. On Air Force One, the President's press secretary was taking notes; Ari Fleischer recorded that at 10:20, the President told him that he had authorized a shootdown of aircraft if necessary.[221]

Minutes went by and word arrived of an aircraft down in Pennsylvania. Those in the shelter wondered if the aircraft had been shot down pursuant to this authorization.[222]

At approximately 10:30, the shelter started receiving reports of another hijacked plane, this time only 5 to 10 miles out. Believing they had only a minute or two, the Vice President again communicated the authorization to "engage or "take out" the aircraft. At 10:33, Hadley told the air threat conference call: "I need to get word to Dick Myers that our reports are there's an inbound aircraft flying low 5 miles out. The Vice President's guidance was we need to take them out."[223]

Once again, there was no immediate information about the fate of the inbound aircraft. In the apt description of one witness, "It drops below the radar screen and it's just continually hovering in your imagination; you don't know where it is or what happens to it." Eventually, the shelter received word that the alleged hijacker 5 miles away had been a medevac helicopter.[224]

Transmission of the Authorization from the White House to the Pilots

The NMCC learned of United 93's hijacking at about 10:03. At this time the FAA had no contact with the military at the level of national command. The NMCC learned about United 93 from the White House. It, in turn, was informed by the Secret Service's contacts with the FAA.[225]

NORAD had no information either. At 10:07, its representative on the air threat conference call stated that NORAD had "no indication of a hijack heading to DC at this time."[226]

Repeatedly between 10:14 and 10:19, a lieutenant colonel at the White House relayed to the NMCC that the Vice President had confirmed fighters were cleared to engage inbound aircraft if they could verify that the aircraft was hijacked.[227]

The commander of NORAD, General Ralph Eberhart, was en route to the NORAD operations center in Cheyenne Mountain, Colorado, when the shootdown order was communicated on the air threat conference call. He told us that by the time he arrived, the order had already been passed down NORAD's chain of command.[228]

It is not clear how the shootdown order was communicated within NORAD. But we know that at 10:31, General Larry Arnold instructed his staff to broadcast the following over a NORAD instant messaging system: "10:31 Vice president has cleared to us to intercept tracks of interest and shoot them down if they do not respond per [General Arnold]."[229]

In upstate New York, NEADS personnel first learned of the shootdown order from this message:

> **Floor Leadership:** You need to read this. . . . The Region Commander has declared that we can shoot down aircraft that do not respond to our direction. Copy that?
> **Controllers:** Copy that, sir.
> **Floor Leadership:** So if you're trying to divert somebody and he won't divert—
> **Controllers:** DO [Director of Operations] is saying no.
> **Floor Leadership:** No? It came over the chat. . . . You got a conflict on that direction?
> **Controllers:** Right now no, but—
> **Floor Leadership:** Okay? Okay, you read that from the Vice President, right? Vice President has cleared. Vice President has cleared us to

intercept traffic and shoot them down if they do not respond per [General Arnold].[230]

In interviews with us, NEADS personnel expressed considerable confusion over the nature and effect of the order.

The NEADS commander told us he did not pass along the order because he was unaware of its ramifications. Both the mission commander and the senior weapons director indicated they did not pass the order to the fighters circling Washington and New York because they were unsure how the pilots would, or should, proceed with this guidance. In short, while leaders in Washington believed that the fighters above them had been instructed to "take out" hostile aircraft, the only orders actually conveyed to the pilots were to "ID type and tail."[231]

In most cases, the chain of command authorizing the use of force runs from the president to the secretary of defense and from the secretary to the combatant commander. The President apparently spoke to Secretary Rumsfeld for the first time that morning shortly after 10:00. No one can recall the content of this conversation, but it was a brief call in which the subject of shootdown authority was not discussed.[232]

At 10:39, the Vice President updated the Secretary on the air threat conference:

> **Vice President:** There's been at least three instances here where we've had reports of aircraft approaching Washington—a couple were confirmed hijack. And, pursuant to the President's instructions I gave authorization for them to be taken out. Hello?
>
> **SecDef:** Yes, I understand. Who did you give that direction to?
>
> **Vice President:** It was passed from here through the [operations] center at the White House, from the [shelter].
>
> **SecDef:** OK, let me ask the question here. Has that directive been transmitted to the aircraft?
>
> **Vice President:** Yes, it has.
>
> **SecDef:** So we've got a couple of aircraft up there that have those instructions at this present time?
>
> **Vice President:** That is correct. And it's my understanding they've already taken a couple of aircraft out.
>
> **SecDef:** We can't confirm that. We're told that one aircraft is down but we do not have a pilot report that did it.[233]

As this exchange shows, Secretary Rumsfeld was not in the NMCC when the shootdown order was first conveyed. He went from the parking lot to his office (where he spoke to the President), then to the Executive Support Center, where he participated in the White House video teleconference. He moved to the NMCC shortly before 10:30, in order to join Vice Chairman Myers. Secretary Rumsfeld told us he was just gaining situational awareness when he spoke with the Vice President at 10:39. His primary concern was ensuring that the pilots had a clear understanding of their rules of engagement.[234]

The Vice President was mistaken in his belief that shootdown authorization had been passed to the pilots flying at NORAD's direction. By 10:45 there was, however, another set of fighters circling Washington that had entirely different rules of engagement. These fighters, part of the 113th Wing of the District of Columbia Air National Guard, launched out of Andrews Air Force Base in Maryland in response to information passed to them by the Secret Service. The first of the Andrews fighters was airborne at 10:38.[235]

General David Wherley—the commander of the 113th Wing—reached out to the Secret Service after hearing secondhand reports that it wanted fighters airborne. A Secret Service agent had a phone in each ear, one connected to Wherley and the other to a fellow agent at the White House, relaying instructions that the White House agent said he was getting from the Vice President. The guidance for Wherley was to send up the aircraft, with orders to protect the White House and take out any aircraft that threatened the Capitol. General Wherley translated this in military terms to flying "weapons free"—that is, the decision to shoot rests in the cockpit, or in this case in the cockpit of the lead pilot. He passed these instructions to the pilots that launched at 10:42 and afterward.[236]

Thus, while the fighter pilots under NORAD direction who had scrambled out of Langley never received any type of engagement order, the Andrews pilots were operating weapons free—a permissive rule of engagement. The President and the Vice President indicated to us they had not been aware that fighters had been scrambled out of Andrews, at the request of the Secret Service and outside the military chain of command.[237] There is no evidence that NORAD headquarters or military officials in the NMCC knew—during the morning of September 11—that the Andrews planes were airborne and operating under different rules of engagement.

What If?
NORAD officials have maintained consistently that had the passengers not caused United 93 to crash, the military would have prevented it from reaching Washington, D.C. That conclusion is based on a version of events that we now know is incorrect. The Langley fighters were not scrambled in response to United 93; NORAD did not have 47 minutes to intercept the flight; NORAD did not even know the plane was hijacked until after it had crashed. It is appropriate, therefore, to reconsider whether United 93 would have been intercepted.

Had it not crashed in Pennsylvania at 10:03, we estimate that United 93 could not have reached Washington any earlier than 10:13, and probably would have arrived before 10:23. There was only one set of fighters circling Washington during that time frame—the Langley F-16s. They were armed and under NORAD's control. After NEADS learned of the hijacking at 10:07, NORAD would have had from 6 to 16 minutes to locate the flight, receive authorization to shoot it down, and communicate the order to the pilots, who (in the same span) would have had to authenticate the order, intercept the flight, and execute the order.[238]

At that point in time, the Langley pilots did not know the threat they were facing, did not know where United 93 was located, and did not have shoot-down authorization.

First, the Langley pilots were never briefed about the reason they were scrambled. As the lead pilot explained, "I reverted to the Russian threat. . . . I'm thinking cruise missile threat from the sea. You know you look down and see the Pentagon burning and I thought the bastards snuck one by us. . . . [Y]ou couldn't see any airplanes, and no one told us anything." The pilots knew their mission was to divert aircraft, but did not know that the threat came from hijacked airliners.[239]

Second, NEADS did not have accurate information on the location of United 93. Presumably FAA would have provided such information, but we do not know how long that would have taken, nor how long it would have taken NEADS to locate the target.

Third, NEADS needed orders to pass to the pilots. At 10:10, the pilots over Washington were emphatically told, "negative clearance to shoot." Shootdown authority was first communicated to NEADS at 10:31. It is possible that NORAD commanders would have ordered a shootdown in the absence of the authorization communicated by the Vice President, but given the gravity of the decision to shoot down a commercial airliner, and NORAD's caution that a mistake not be made, we view this possibility as unlikely.[240]

NORAD officials have maintained that they would have intercepted and shot down United 93. We are not so sure. We are sure that the nation owes a debt to the passengers of United 93. Their actions saved the lives of countless others, and may have saved either the Capitol or the White House from destruction.

The details of what happened on the morning of September 11 are complex, but they play out a simple theme. NORAD and the FAA were unprepared for the type of attacks launched against the United States on September 11, 2001. They struggled, under difficult circumstances, to improvise a homeland defense against an unprecedented challenge they had never before encountered and had never trained to meet.

At 10:02 that morning, an assistant to the mission crew commander at NORAD's Northeast Air Defense Sector in Rome, New York, was working with his colleagues on the floor of the command center. In a brief moment of reflection, he was recorded remarking that "This is a new type of war."[241]

He was, and is, right. But the conflict did not begin on 9/11. It had been publicly declared years earlier, most notably in a declaration faxed early in 1998 to an Arabic-language newspaper in London. Few Americans had noticed it. The fax had been sent from thousands of miles away by the followers of a Saudi exile gathered in one of the most remote and impoverished countries on earth.

2

THE FOUNDATION OF
THE NEW TERRORISM

2.1 A DECLARATION OF WAR

In February 1998, the 40-year-old Saudi exile Usama Bin Ladin and a fugitive Egyptian physician, Ayman al Zawahiri, arranged from their Afghan headquarters for an Arabic newspaper in London to publish what they termed a fatwa issued in the name of a "World Islamic Front." A fatwa is normally an interpretation of Islamic law by a respected Islamic authority, but neither Bin Ladin, Zawahiri, nor the three others who signed this statement were scholars of Islamic law. Claiming that America had declared war against God and his messenger, they called for the murder of any American, anywhere on earth, as the "individual duty for every Muslim who can do it in any country in which it is possible to do it."[1]

Three months later, when interviewed in Afghanistan by ABC-TV, Bin Ladin enlarged on these themes.[2] He claimed it was more important for Muslims to kill Americans than to kill other infidels. "It is far better for anyone to kill a single American soldier than to squander his efforts on other activities," he said. Asked whether he approved of terrorism and of attacks on civilians, he replied: "We believe that the worst thieves in the world today and the worst terrorists are the Americans. Nothing could stop you except perhaps retaliation in kind. We do not have to differentiate between military or civilian. As far as we are concerned, they are all targets."

Note: Islamic names often do not follow the Western practice of the consistent use of surnames. Given the variety of names we mention, we chose to refer to individuals by the last word in the names by which they are known: Nawaf al Hazmi as Hazmi, for instance, omitting the article "al" that would be part of their name in their own societies. We generally make an exception for the more familiar English usage of "Bin" as part of a last name, as in Bin Ladin. Further, there is no universally accepted way to transliterate Arabic words and names into English. We have relied on a mix of common sense, the sound of the name in Arabic, and common usage in source materials, the press, or government documents. When we quote from a source document, we use its transliteration, e.g., "al Qida" instead of al Qaeda.

Though novel for its open endorsement of indiscriminate killing, Bin Ladin's 1998 declaration was only the latest in the long series of his public and private calls since 1992 that singled out the United States for attack.

In August 1996, Bin Ladin had issued his own self-styled fatwa calling on Muslims to drive American soldiers out of Saudi Arabia. The long, disjointed document condemned the Saudi monarchy for allowing the presence of an army of infidels in a land with the sites most sacred to Islam, and celebrated recent suicide bombings of American military facilities in the Kingdom. It praised the 1983 suicide bombing in Beirut that killed 241 U.S. Marines, the 1992 bombing in Aden, and especially the 1993 firefight in Somalia after which the United States "left the area carrying disappointment, humiliation, defeat and your dead with you."[3]

Bin Ladin said in his ABC interview that he and his followers had been preparing in Somalia for another long struggle, like that against the Soviets in Afghanistan, but "the United States rushed out of Somalia in shame and disgrace." Citing the Soviet army's withdrawal from Afghanistan as proof that a ragged army of dedicated Muslims could overcome a superpower, he told the interviewer: "We are certain that we shall—with the grace of Allah—prevail over the Americans." He went on to warn that "If the present injustice continues . . . , it will inevitably move the battle to American soil."[4]

Plans to attack the United States were developed with unwavering single-mindedness throughout the 1990s. Bin Ladin saw himself as called "to follow in the footsteps of the Messenger and to communicate his message to all nations,"[5] and to serve as the rallying point and organizer of a new kind of war to destroy America and bring the world to Islam.

2.2 BIN LADIN'S APPEAL IN THE ISLAMIC WORLD

It is the story of eccentric and violent ideas sprouting in the fertile ground of political and social turmoil. It is the story of an organization poised to seize its historical moment. How did Bin Ladin—with his call for the indiscriminate killing of Americans—win thousands of followers and some degree of approval from millions more?

The history, culture, and body of beliefs from which Bin Ladin has shaped and spread his message are largely unknown to many Americans. Seizing on symbols of Islam's past greatness, he promises to restore pride to people who consider themselves the victims of successive foreign masters. He uses cultural and religious allusions to the holy Qur'an and some of its interpreters. He appeals to people disoriented by cyclonic change as they confront modernity and globalization. His rhetoric selectively draws from multiple sources—Islam, history, and the region's political and economic malaise. He also stresses grievances against the United States widely shared in the Muslim world. He

Usama Bin Ladin at a news conference in Afghanistan in 1998

inveighed against the presence of U.S. troops in Saudi Arabia, the home of Islam's holiest sites. He spoke of the suffering of the Iraqi people as a result of sanctions imposed after the Gulf War, and he protested U.S. support of Israel.

Islam

Islam (a word that literally means "surrender to the will of God") arose in Arabia with what Muslims believe are a series of revelations to the Prophet Mohammed from the one and only God, the God of Abraham and of Jesus. These revelations, conveyed by the angel Gabriel, are recorded in the Qur'an. Muslims believe that these revelations, given to the greatest and last of a chain of prophets stretching from Abraham through Jesus, complete God's message to humanity. The Hadith, which recount Mohammed's sayings and deeds as recorded by his contemporaries, are another fundamental source. A third key element is the Sharia, the code of law derived from the Qur'an and the Hadith.

Islam is divided into two main branches, Sunni and Shia. Soon after the

Prophet's death, the question of choosing a new leader, or *caliph*, for the Muslim community, or *Ummah*, arose. Initially, his successors could be drawn from the Prophet's contemporaries, but with time, this was no longer possible. Those who became the Shia held that any leader of the Ummah must be a direct descendant of the Prophet; those who became the Sunni argued that lineal descent was not required if the candidate met other standards of faith and knowledge. After bloody struggles, the Sunni became (and remain) the majority sect. (The Shia are dominant in Iran.) The Caliphate—the institutionalized leadership of the Ummah—thus was a Sunni institution that continued until 1924, first under Arab and eventually under Ottoman Turkish control.

Many Muslims look back at the century after the revelations to the Prophet Mohammed as a golden age. Its memory is strongest among the Arabs. What happened then—the spread of Islam from the Arabian Peninsula throughout the Middle East, North Africa, and even into Europe within less than a century—seemed, and seems, miraculous.[6] Nostalgia for Islam's past glory remains a powerful force.

Islam is both a faith and a code of conduct for all aspects of life. For many Muslims, a good government would be one guided by the moral principles of their faith. This does not necessarily translate into a desire for clerical rule and the abolition of a secular state. It does mean that some Muslims tend to be uncomfortable with distinctions between religion and state, though Muslim rulers throughout history have readily separated the two.

To extremists, however, such divisions, as well as the existence of parliaments and legislation, only prove these rulers to be false Muslims usurping God's authority over all aspects of life. Periodically, the Islamic world has seen surges of what, for want of a better term, is often labeled "fundamentalism."[7] Denouncing waywardness among the faithful, some clerics have appealed for a return to observance of the literal teachings of the Qur'an and Hadith. One scholar from the fourteenth century from whom Bin Ladin selectively quotes, Ibn Taimiyyah, condemned both corrupt rulers and the clerics who failed to criticize them. He urged Muslims to read the Qur'an and the Hadith for themselves, not to depend solely on learned interpreters like himself but to hold one another to account for the quality of their observance.[8]

The extreme Islamist version of history blames the decline from Islam's golden age on the rulers and people who turned away from the true path of their religion, thereby leaving Islam vulnerable to encroaching foreign powers eager to steal their land, wealth, and even their souls.

Bin Ladin's Worldview

Despite his claims to universal leadership, Bin Ladin offers an extreme view of Islamic history designed to appeal mainly to Arabs and Sunnis. He draws on fundamentalists who blame the eventual destruction of the Caliphate on leaders who abandoned the pure path of religious devotion.[9] He repeatedly calls on his followers to embrace martyrdom since "the walls of oppression and humiliation cannot be demolished except in a rain of bullets."[10] For those yearning for a lost sense of order in an older, more tranquil world, he offers his "Caliphate" as an imagined alternative to today's uncertainty. For others, he offers simplistic conspiracies to explain their world.

Bin Ladin also relies heavily on the Egyptian writer Sayyid Qutb. A member of the Muslim Brotherhood[11] executed in 1966 on charges of attempting to overthrow the government, Qutb mixed Islamic scholarship with a very superficial acquaintance with Western history and thought. Sent by the Egyptian government to study in the United States in the late 1940s, Qutb returned with an enormous loathing of Western society and history. He dismissed Western achievements as entirely material, arguing that Western society possesses "nothing that will satisfy its own conscience and justify its existence."[12]

Three basic themes emerge from Qutb's writings. First, he claimed that the world was beset with barbarism, licentiousness, and unbelief (a condition he called *jahiliyya*, the religious term for the period of ignorance prior to the revelations given to the Prophet Mohammed). Qutb argued that humans can choose only between Islam and jahiliyya. Second, he warned that more people, including Muslims, were attracted to jahiliyya and its material comforts than to his view of Islam; jahiliyya could therefore triumph over Islam. Third, no middle ground exists in what Qutb conceived as a struggle between God and Satan. All Muslims—as he defined them—therefore must take up arms in this fight. Any Muslim who rejects his ideas is just one more nonbeliever worthy of destruction.[13]

Bin Ladin shares Qutb's stark view, permitting him and his followers to rationalize even unprovoked mass murder as righteous defense of an embattled faith. Many Americans have wondered, "Why do 'they' hate us?" Some also ask, "What can we do to stop these attacks?"

Bin Ladin and al Qaeda have given answers to both these questions. To the first, they say that America had attacked Islam; America is responsible for all conflicts involving Muslims. Thus Americans are blamed when Israelis fight with Palestinians, when Russians fight with Chechens, when Indians fight with Kashmiri Muslims, and when the Philippine government fights ethnic Muslims in its southern islands. America is also held responsible for the governments of Muslim countries, derided by al Qaeda as "your agents." Bin Ladin has stated flatly, "Our fight against these governments is not separate from our fight against you."[14] These charges found a ready audience among millions of Arabs and Muslims angry at the United States because of issues ranging from Iraq to Palestine to America's support for their countries' repressive rulers.

Bin Ladin's grievance with the United States may have started in reaction to specific U.S. policies but it quickly became far deeper. To the second question, what America could do, al Qaeda's answer was that America should abandon the Middle East, convert to Islam, and end the immorality and godlessness of its society and culture: "It is saddening to tell you that you are the worst civilization witnessed by the history of mankind." If the United States did not comply, it would be at war with the Islamic nation, a nation that al Qaeda's leaders said "desires death more than you desire life."[15]

History and Political Context

Few fundamentalist movements in the Islamic world gained lasting political power. In the nineteenth and twentieth centuries, fundamentalists helped articulate anticolonial grievances but played little role in the overwhelmingly secular struggles for independence after World War I. Western-educated lawyers, soldiers, and officials led most independence movements, and clerical influence and traditional culture were seen as obstacles to national progress.

After gaining independence from Western powers following World War II, the Arab Middle East followed an arc from initial pride and optimism to today's mix of indifference, cynicism, and despair. In several countries, a dynastic state already existed or was quickly established under a paramount tribal family. Monarchies in countries such as Saudi Arabia, Morocco, and Jordan still survive today. Those in Egypt, Libya, Iraq, and Yemen were eventually overthrown by secular nationalist revolutionaries.

The secular regimes promised a glowing future, often tied to sweeping ideologies (such as those promoted by Egyptian President Gamal Abdel Nasser's Arab Socialism or the Ba'ath Party of Syria and Iraq) that called for a single, secular Arab state. However, what emerged were almost invariably autocratic regimes that were usually unwilling to tolerate any opposition—even in countries, such as Egypt, that had a parliamentary tradition. Over time, their policies—repression, rewards, emigration, and the displacement of popular anger onto scapegoats (generally foreign)—were shaped by the desire to cling to power.

The bankruptcy of secular, autocratic nationalism was evident across the Muslim world by the late 1970s. At the same time, these regimes had closed off nearly all paths for peaceful opposition, forcing their critics to choose silence, exile, or violent opposition. Iran's 1979 revolution swept a Shia theocracy into power. Its success encouraged Sunni fundamentalists elsewhere.

In the 1980s, awash in sudden oil wealth, Saudi Arabia competed with Shia Iran to promote its Sunni fundamentalist interpretation of Islam, Wahhabism. The Saudi government, always conscious of its duties as the custodian of Islam's holiest places, joined with wealthy Arabs from the Kingdom and other states bordering the Persian Gulf in donating money to build mosques and religious schools that could preach and teach their interpretation of Islamic doctrine.

In this competition for legitimacy, secular regimes had no alternative to offer. Instead, in a number of cases their rulers sought to buy off local Islamist movements by ceding control of many social and educational issues. Emboldened rather than satisfied, the Islamists continued to push for power—a trend especially clear in Egypt. Confronted with a violent Islamist movement that killed President Anwar Sadat in 1981, the Egyptian government combined

harsh repression of Islamic militants with harassment of moderate Islamic scholars and authors, driving many into exile. In Pakistan, a military regime sought
to justify its seizure of power by a pious public stance and an embrace of
unprecedented Islamist influence on education and society.

These experiments in political Islam faltered during the 1990s: the Iranian
revolution lost momentum, prestige, and public support, and Pakistan's rulers
found that most of its population had little enthusiasm for fundamentalist Islam.
Islamist revival movements gained followers across the Muslim world, but failed
to secure political power except in Iran and Sudan. In Algeria, where in 1991
Islamists seemed almost certain to win power through the ballot box, the military preempted their victory, triggering a brutal civil war that continues today.
Opponents of today's rulers have few, if any, ways to participate in the existing
political system. They are thus a ready audience for calls to Muslims to purify
their society, reject unwelcome modernization, and adhere strictly to the Sharia.

Social and Economic Malaise
In the 1970s and early 1980s, an unprecedented flood of wealth led the then
largely unmodernized oil states to attempt to shortcut decades of development.
They funded huge infrastructure projects, vastly expanded education, and created subsidized social welfare programs. These programs established a widespread feeling of entitlement without a corresponding sense of social
obligations. By the late 1980s, diminishing oil revenues, the economic drain
from many unprofitable development projects, and population growth made
these entitlement programs unsustainable. The resulting cutbacks created enormous resentment among recipients who had come to see government largesse
as their right. This resentment was further stoked by public understanding of
how much oil income had gone straight into the pockets of the rulers, their
friends, and their helpers.

Unlike the oil states (or Afghanistan, where real economic development has
barely begun), the other Arab nations and Pakistan once had seemed headed
toward balanced modernization. The established commercial, financial, and
industrial sectors in these states, supported by an entrepreneurial spirit and
widespread understanding of free enterprise, augured well. But unprofitable
heavy industry, state monopolies, and opaque bureaucracies slowly stifled
growth. More importantly, these state-centered regimes placed their highest
priority on preserving the elite's grip on national wealth. Unwilling to foster
dynamic economies that could create jobs attractive to educated young men,
the countries became economically stagnant and reliant on the safety valve of
worker emigration either to the Arab oil states or to the West. Furthermore,
the repression and isolation of women in many Muslim countries have not only
seriously limited individual opportunity but also crippled overall economic
productivity.[16]

By the 1990s, high birthrates and declining rates of infant mortality had produced a common problem throughout the Muslim world: a large, steadily increasing population of young men without any reasonable expectation of suitable or steady employment—a sure prescription for social turbulence. Many of these young men, such as the enormous number trained only in religious schools, lacked the skills needed by their societies. Far more acquired valuable skills but lived in stagnant economies that could not generate satisfying jobs.

Millions, pursuing secular as well as religious studies, were products of educational systems that generally devoted little if any attention to the rest of the world's thought, history, and culture. The secular education reflected a strong cultural preference for technical fields over the humanities and social sciences. Many of these young men, even if able to study abroad, lacked the perspective and skills needed to understand a different culture.

Frustrated in their search for a decent living, unable to benefit from an education often obtained at the cost of great family sacrifice, and blocked from starting families of their own, some of these young men were easy targets for radicalization.

Bin Ladin's Historical Opportunity

Most Muslims prefer a peaceful and inclusive vision of their faith, not the violent sectarianism of Bin Ladin. Among Arabs, Bin Ladin's followers are commonly nicknamed *takfiri*, or "those who define other Muslims as unbelievers," because of their readiness to demonize and murder those with whom they disagree. Beyond the theology lies the simple human fact that most Muslims, like most other human beings, are repelled by mass murder and barbarism whatever their justification.

"All Americans must recognize that the face of terror is not the true face of Islam," President Bush observed. "Islam is a faith that brings comfort to a billion people around the world. It's a faith that has made brothers and sisters of every race. It's a faith based upon love, not hate."[17] Yet as political, social, and economic problems created flammable societies, Bin Ladin used Islam's most extreme, fundamentalist traditions as his match. All these elements—including religion—combined in an explosive compound.

Other extremists had, and have, followings of their own. But in appealing to societies full of discontent, Bin Ladin remained credible as other leaders and symbols faded. He could stand as a symbol of resistance—above all, resistance to the West and to America. He could present himself and his allies as victorious warriors in the one great successful experience for Islamic militancy in the 1980s: the Afghan jihad against the Soviet occupation.

By 1998, Bin Ladin had a distinctive appeal, as he focused on attacking America. He argued that other extremists, who aimed at local rulers or Israel, did not go far enough. They had not taken on what he called "the head of the snake."[18]

Finally, Bin Ladin had another advantage: a substantial, worldwide organization. By the time he issued his February 1998 declaration of war, Bin Ladin had nurtured that organization for nearly ten years. He could attract, train, and use recruits for ever more ambitious attacks, rallying new adherents with each demonstration that his was the movement of the future.

2.3 THE RISE OF BIN LADIN AND AL QAEDA (1988–1992)

A decade of conflict in Afghanistan, from 1979 to 1989, gave Islamist extremists a rallying point and training field. A Communist government in Afghanistan gained power in 1978 but was unable to establish enduring control. At the end of 1979, the Soviet government sent in military units to ensure that the country would remain securely under Moscow's influence. The response was an Afghan national resistance movement that defeated Soviet forces.[19]

Young Muslims from around the world flocked to Afghanistan to join as volunteers in what was seen as a "holy war"—*jihad*—against an invader. The largest numbers came from the Middle East. Some were Saudis, and among them was Usama Bin Ladin.

Twenty-three when he arrived in Afghanistan in 1980, Bin Ladin was the seventeenth of 57 children of a Saudi construction magnate. Six feet five and thin, Bin Ladin appeared to be ungainly but was in fact quite athletic, skilled as a horseman, runner, climber, and soccer player. He had attended Abdul Aziz University in Saudi Arabia. By some accounts, he had been interested there in religious studies, inspired by tape recordings of fiery sermons by Abdullah Azzam, a Palestinian and a disciple of Qutb. Bin Ladin was conspicuous among the volunteers not because he showed evidence of religious learning but because he had access to some of his family's huge fortune. Though he took part in at least one actual battle, he became known chiefly as a person who generously helped fund the anti-Soviet jihad.[20]

Bin Ladin understood better than most of the volunteers the extent to which the continuation and eventual success of the jihad in Afghanistan depended on an increasingly complex, almost worldwide organization. This organization included a financial support network that came to be known as the "Golden Chain," put together mainly by financiers in Saudi Arabia and the Persian Gulf states. Donations flowed through charities or other nongovernmental organizations (NGOs). Bin Ladin and the "Afghan Arabs" drew largely on funds raised by this network, whose agents roamed world markets to buy arms and supplies for the mujahideen, or "holy warriors."[21]

Mosques, schools, and boardinghouses served as recruiting stations in many parts of the world, including the United States. Some were set up by Islamic extremists or their financial backers. Bin Ladin had an important part in this activity. He and the cleric Azzam had joined in creating a "Bureau of Services" (Mektab al Khidmat, or MAK), which channeled recruits into Afghanistan.[22]

The international environment for Bin Ladin's efforts was ideal. Saudi Arabia and the United States supplied billions of dollars worth of secret assistance to rebel groups in Afghanistan fighting the Soviet occupation. This assistance was funneled through Pakistan: the Pakistani military intelligence service (Inter-Services Intelligence Directorate, or ISID), helped train the rebels and distribute the arms. But Bin Ladin and his comrades had their own sources of support and training, and they received little or no assistance from the United States.[23]

April 1988 brought victory for the Afghan jihad. Moscow declared it would pull its military forces out of Afghanistan within the next nine months. As the Soviets began their withdrawal, the jihad's leaders debated what to do next.

Bin Ladin and Azzam agreed that the organization successfully created for Afghanistan should not be allowed to dissolve. They established what they called a base or foundation (al Qaeda) as a potential general headquarters for future jihad.[24] Though Azzam had been considered number one in the MAK, by August 1988 Bin Ladin was clearly the leader (*emir*) of al Qaeda. This organization's structure included as its operating arms an intelligence component, a military committee, a financial committee, a political committee, and a committee in charge of media affairs and propaganda. It also had an Advisory Council (Shura) made up of Bin Ladin's inner circle.[25]

Bin Ladin's assumption of the helm of al Qaeda was evidence of his growing self-confidence and ambition. He soon made clear his desire for unchallenged control and for preparing the mujahideen to fight anywhere in the world. Azzam, by contrast, favored continuing to fight in Afghanistan until it had a true Islamist government. And, as a Palestinian, he saw Israel as the top priority for the next stage.[26]

Whether the dispute was about power, personal differences, or strategy, it ended on November 24, 1989, when a remotely controlled car bomb killed Azzam and both of his sons. The killers were assumed to be rival Egyptians. The outcome left Bin Ladin indisputably in charge of what remained of the MAK and al Qaeda.[27]

Through writers like Qutb, and the presence of Egyptian Islamist teachers in the Saudi educational system, Islamists already had a strong intellectual influence on Bin Ladin and his al Qaeda colleagues. By the late 1980s, the Egyptian Islamist movement—badly battered in the government crackdown following President Sadat's assassination—was centered in two major organizations: the Islamic Group and the Egyptian Islamic Jihad. A spiritual guide for both, but especially the Islamic Group, was the so-called Blind Sheikh, Omar Abdel Rahman. His preaching had inspired the assassination of Sadat. After being in and out of Egyptian prisons during the 1980s, Abdel Rahman found refuge in the United States. From his headquarters in Jersey City, he distributed messages calling for the murder of unbelievers.[28]

The most important Egyptian in Bin Ladin's circle was a surgeon, Ayman al Zawahiri, who led a strong faction of the Egyptian Islamic Jihad. Many of his followers became important members in the new organization, and his own close ties with Bin Ladin led many to think of him as the deputy head of al Qaeda. He would in fact become Bin Ladin's deputy some years later, when they merged their organizations.[29]

Bin Ladin Moves to Sudan

By the fall of 1989, Bin Ladin had sufficient stature among Islamic extremists that a Sudanese political leader, Hassan al Turabi, urged him to transplant his whole organization to Sudan. Turabi headed the National Islamic Front in a coalition that had recently seized power in Khartoum.[30] Bin Ladin agreed to help Turabi in an ongoing war against African Christian separatists in southern Sudan and also to do some road building. Turabi in return would let Bin Ladin use Sudan as a base for worldwide business operations and for preparations for jihad.[31] While agents of Bin Ladin began to buy property in Sudan in 1990,[32] Bin Ladin himself moved from Afghanistan back to Saudi Arabia.

In August 1990, Iraq invaded Kuwait. Bin Ladin, whose efforts in Afghanistan had earned him celebrity and respect, proposed to the Saudi monarchy that he summon mujahideen for a jihad to retake Kuwait. He was rebuffed, and the Saudis joined the U.S.-led coalition. After the Saudis agreed to allow U.S. armed forces to be based in the Kingdom, Bin Ladin and a number of Islamic clerics began to publicly denounce the arrangement. The Saudi government exiled the clerics and undertook to silence Bin Ladin by, among other things, taking away his passport. With help from a dissident member of the royal family, he managed to get out of the country under the pretext of attending an Islamic gathering in Pakistan in April 1991.[33] By 1994, the Saudi government would freeze his financial assets and revoke his citizenship.[34] He no longer had a country he could call his own.

Bin Ladin moved to Sudan in 1991 and set up a large and complex set of intertwined business and terrorist enterprises. In time, the former would encompass numerous companies and a global network of bank accounts and nongovernmental institutions. Fulfilling his bargain with Turabi, Bin Ladin used his construction company to build a new highway from Khartoum to Port Sudan on the Red Sea coast. Meanwhile, al Qaeda finance officers and top operatives used their positions in Bin Ladin's businesses to acquire weapons, explosives, and technical equipment for terrorist purposes. One founding member, Abu Hajer al Iraqi, used his position as head of a Bin Ladin investment company to carry out procurement trips from western Europe to the Far East. Two others, Wadi al Hage and Mubarak Douri, who had become acquainted in Tucson, Arizona, in the late 1980s, went as far afield as China, Malaysia, the Philippines, and the former Soviet states of Ukraine and Belarus.[35]

Bin Ladin's impressive array of offices covertly provided financial and other support for terrorist activities. The network included a major business enterprise in Cyprus; a "services" branch in Zagreb; an office of the Benevolence International Foundation in Sarajevo, which supported the Bosnian Muslims in their conflict with Serbia and Croatia; and an NGO in Baku, Azerbaijan, that was employed as well by Egyptian Islamic Jihad both as a source and conduit for finances and as a support center for the Muslim rebels in Chechnya. He also made use of the already-established Third World Relief Agency (TWRA) headquartered in Vienna, whose branch office locations included Zagreb and Budapest. (Bin Ladin later set up an NGO in Nairobi as a cover for operatives there.)[36]

Bin Ladin now had a vision of himself as head of an international jihad confederation. In Sudan, he established an "Islamic Army Shura" that was to serve as the coordinating body for the consortium of terrorist groups with which he was forging alliances. It was composed of his own al Qaeda Shura together with leaders or representatives of terrorist organizations that were still independent. In building this Islamic army, he enlisted groups from Saudi Arabia, Egypt, Jordan, Lebanon, Iraq, Oman, Algeria, Libya, Tunisia, Morocco, Somalia, and Eritrea. Al Qaeda also established cooperative but less formal relationships with other extremist groups from these same countries; from the African states of Chad, Mali, Niger, Nigeria, and Uganda; and from the Southeast Asian states of Burma, Thailand, Malaysia, and Indonesia. Bin Ladin maintained connections in the Bosnian conflict as well.[37] The groundwork for a true global terrorist network was being laid.

Bin Ladin also provided equipment and training assistance to the Moro Islamic Liberation Front in the Philippines and also to a newly forming Philippine group that called itself the Abu Sayyaf Brigade, after one of the major Afghan jihadist commanders.[38] Al Qaeda helped Jemaah Islamiya (JI), a nascent organization headed by Indonesian Islamists with cells scattered across Malaysia, Singapore, Indonesia, and the Philippines. It also aided a Pakistani group engaged in insurrectionist attacks in Kashmir. In mid-1991, Bin Ladin dispatched a band of supporters to the northern Afghanistan border to assist the Tajikistan Islamists in the ethnic conflicts that had been boiling there even before the Central Asian departments of the Soviet Union became independent states.[39]

This pattern of expansion through building alliances extended to the United States. A Muslim organization called al Khifa had numerous branch offices, the largest of which was in the Farouq mosque in Brooklyn. In the mid-1980s, it had been set up as one of the first outposts of Azzam and Bin Ladin's MAK.[40] Other cities with branches of al Khifa included Atlanta, Boston, Chicago, Pittsburgh, and Tucson.[41] Al Khifa recruited American Muslims to fight in Afghanistan; some of them would participate in terrorist actions in the United States in the early 1990s and in al Qaeda operations elsewhere, including the 1998 attacks on U.S. embassies in East Africa.

2.4 BUILDING AN ORGANIZATION, DECLARING WAR ON THE UNITED STATES (1992–1996)

Bin Ladin began delivering diatribes against the United States before he left Saudi Arabia. He continued to do so after he arrived in Sudan. In early 1992, the al Qaeda leadership issued a fatwa calling for jihad against the Western "occupation" of Islamic lands. Specifically singling out U.S. forces for attack, the language resembled that which would appear in Bin Ladin's public fatwa in August 1996. In ensuing weeks, Bin Ladin delivered an often-repeated lecture on the need to cut off "the head of the snake."[42]

By this time, Bin Ladin was well-known and a senior figure among Islamist extremists, especially those in Egypt, the Arabian Peninsula, and the Afghanistan-Pakistan border region. Still, he was just one among many diverse terrorist barons. Some of Bin Ladin's close comrades were more peers than subordinates. For example, Usama Asmurai, also known as Wali Khan, worked with Bin Ladin in the early 1980s and helped him in the Philippines and in Tajikistan. The Egyptian spiritual guide based in New Jersey, the Blind Sheikh, whom Bin Ladin admired, was also in the network. Among sympathetic peers in Afghanistan were a few of the warlords still fighting for power and Abu Zubaydah, who helped operate a popular terrorist training camp near the border with Pakistan. There were also rootless but experienced operatives, such as Ramzi Yousef and Khalid Sheikh Mohammed, who—though not necessarily formal members of someone else's organization—were traveling around the world and joining in projects that were supported by or linked to Bin Ladin, the Blind Sheikh, or their associates.[43]

In now analyzing the terrorist programs carried out by members of this network, it would be misleading to apply the label "al Qaeda operations" too often in these early years. Yet it would also be misleading to ignore the significance of these connections. And in this network, Bin Ladin's agenda stood out. While his allied Islamist groups were focused on local battles, such as those in Egypt, Algeria, Bosnia, or Chechnya, Bin Ladin concentrated on attacking the "far enemy"—the United States.

Attacks Known and Suspected

After U.S. troops deployed to Somalia in late 1992, al Qaeda leaders formulated a fatwa demanding their eviction. In December, bombs exploded at two hotels in Aden where U.S. troops routinely stopped en route to Somalia, killing two, but no Americans. The perpetrators are reported to have belonged to a group from southern Yemen headed by a Yemeni member of Bin Ladin's Islamic Army Shura; some in the group had trained at an al Qaeda camp in Sudan.[44]

Al Qaeda leaders set up a Nairobi cell and used it to send weapons and trainers to the Somali warlords battling U.S. forces, an operation directly supervised by al Qaeda's military leader.[45] Scores of trainers flowed to Somalia over the ensuing months, including most of the senior members and weapons training experts of al Qaeda's military committee. These trainers were later heard boasting that their assistance led to the October 1993 shootdown of two U.S. Black Hawk helicopters by members of a Somali militia group and to the subsequent withdrawal of U.S. forces in early 1994.[46]

In November 1995, a car bomb exploded outside a Saudi-U.S. joint facility in Riyadh for training the Saudi National Guard. Five Americans and two officials from India were killed. The Saudi government arrested four perpetrators, who admitted being inspired by Bin Ladin. They were promptly executed. Though nothing proves that Bin Ladin ordered this attack, U.S. intelligence subsequently learned that al Qaeda leaders had decided a year earlier to attack a U.S. target in Saudi Arabia, and had shipped explosives to the peninsula for this purpose. Some of Bin Ladin's associates later took credit.[47]

In June 1996, an enormous truck bomb detonated in the Khobar Towers residential complex in Dhahran, Saudi Arabia, that housed U.S. Air Force personnel. Nineteen Americans were killed, and 372 were wounded. The operation was carried out principally, perhaps exclusively, by Saudi Hezbollah, an organization that had received support from the government of Iran. While the evidence of Iranian involvement is strong, there are also signs that al Qaeda played some role, as yet unknown.[48]

In this period, other prominent attacks in which Bin Ladin's involvement is at best cloudy are the 1993 bombing of the World Trade Center, a plot that same year to destroy landmarks in New York, and the 1995 Manila air plot to blow up a dozen U.S. airliners over the Pacific. Details on these plots appear in chapter 3.

Another scheme revealed that Bin Ladin sought the capability to kill on a mass scale. His business aides received word that a Sudanese military officer who had been a member of the previous government cabinet was offering to sell weapons-grade uranium. After a number of contacts were made through intermediaries, the officer set the price at $1.5 million, which did not deter Bin Ladin. Al Qaeda representatives asked to inspect the uranium and were shown a cylinder about 3 feet long, and one thought he could pronounce it genuine. Al Qaeda apparently purchased the cylinder, then discovered it to be bogus.[49] But while the effort failed, it shows what Bin Ladin and his associates hoped to do. One of the al Qaeda representatives explained his mission: "it's easy to kill more people with uranium."[50]

Bin Ladin seemed willing to include in the confederation terrorists from almost every corner of the Muslim world. His vision mirrored that of Sudan's Islamist leader, Turabi, who convened a series of meetings under the label Popular Arab and Islamic Conference around the time of Bin Ladin's arrival in that country. Delegations of violent Islamist extremists came from all the groups represented in Bin Ladin's Islamic Army Shura. Representatives also came from organizations such as the Palestine Liberation Organization, Hamas, and Hezbollah.[51]

Turabi sought to persuade Shiites and Sunnis to put aside their divisions and join against the common enemy. In late 1991 or 1992, discussions in Sudan between al Qaeda and Iranian operatives led to an informal agreement to cooperate in providing support—even if only training—for actions carried out primarily against Israel and the United States. Not long afterward, senior al Qaeda operatives and trainers traveled to Iran to receive training in explosives. In the fall of 1993, another such delegation went to the Bekaa Valley in Lebanon for further training in explosives as well as in intelligence and security. Bin Ladin reportedly showed particular interest in learning how to use truck bombs such as the one that had killed 241 U.S. Marines in Lebanon in 1983. The relationship between al Qaeda and Iran demonstrated that Sunni-Shia divisions did not necessarily pose an insurmountable barrier to cooperation in terrorist operations. As will be described in chapter 7, al Qaeda contacts with Iran continued in ensuing years.[52]

Bin Ladin was also willing to explore possibilities for cooperation with Iraq, even though Iraq's dictator, Saddam Hussein, had never had an Islamist agenda—save for his opportunistic pose as a defender of the faithful against "Crusaders" during the Gulf War of 1991. Moreover, Bin Ladin had in fact been sponsoring anti-Saddam Islamists in Iraqi Kurdistan, and sought to attract them into his Islamic army.[53]

To protect his own ties with Iraq, Turabi reportedly brokered an agreement that Bin Ladin would stop supporting activities against Saddam. Bin Ladin apparently honored this pledge, at least for a time, although he continued to aid a group of Islamist extremists operating in part of Iraq (Kurdistan) outside of Baghdad's control. In the late 1990s, these extremist groups suffered major defeats by Kurdish forces. In 2001, with Bin Ladin's help they re-formed into an organization called Ansar al Islam. There are indications that by then the Iraqi regime tolerated and may even have helped Ansar al Islam against the common Kurdish enemy.[54]

With the Sudanese regime acting as intermediary, Bin Ladin himself met with a senior Iraqi intelligence officer in Khartoum in late 1994 or early 1995. Bin Ladin is said to have asked for space to establish training camps, as well as assistance in procuring weapons, but there is no evidence that Iraq responded to this request.[55] As described below, the ensuing years saw additional efforts to establish connections.

Sudan Becomes a Doubtful Haven

Not until 1998 did al Qaeda undertake a major terrorist operation of its own, in large part because Bin Ladin lost his base in Sudan. Ever since the Islamist regime came to power in Khartoum, the United States and other Western governments had pressed it to stop providing a haven for terrorist organizations. Other governments in the region, such as those of Egypt, Syria, Jordan, and even Libya, which were targets of some of these groups, added their own pressure. At the same time, the Sudanese regime began to change. Though Turabi had been its inspirational leader, General Omar al Bashir, president since 1989, had never been entirely under his thumb. Thus as outside pressures mounted, Bashir's supporters began to displace those of Turabi.

The attempted assassination in Ethiopia of Egyptian President Hosni Mubarak in June 1995 appears to have been a tipping point. The would-be killers, who came from the Egyptian Islamic Group, had been sheltered in Sudan and helped by Bin Ladin.[56] When the Sudanese refused to hand over three individuals identified as involved in the assassination plot, the UN Security Council passed a resolution criticizing their inaction and eventually sanctioned Khartoum in April 1996.[57]

A clear signal to Bin Ladin that his days in Sudan were numbered came when the government advised him that it intended to yield to Libya's demands to stop giving sanctuary to its enemies. Bin Ladin had to tell the Libyans who had been part of his Islamic army that he could no longer protect them and that they had to leave the country. Outraged, several Libyan members of al Qaeda and the Islamic Army Shura renounced all connections with him.[58]

Bin Ladin also began to have serious money problems. International pressure on Sudan, together with strains in the world economy, hurt Sudan's currency. Some of Bin Ladin's companies ran short of funds. As Sudanese authorities became less obliging, normal costs of doing business increased. Saudi pressures on the Bin Ladin family also probably took some toll. In any case, Bin Ladin found it necessary both to cut back his spending and to control his outlays more closely. He appointed a new financial manager, whom his followers saw as miserly.[59]

Money problems proved costly to Bin Ladin in other ways. Jamal Ahmed al Fadl, a Sudanese-born Arab, had spent time in the United States and had been recruited for the Afghan war through the Farouq mosque in Brooklyn. He had joined al Qaeda and taken the oath of fealty to Bin Ladin, serving as one of his business agents. Then Bin Ladin discovered that Fadl had skimmed about $110,000, and he asked for restitution. Fadl resented receiving a salary of only $500 a month while some of the Egyptians in al Qaeda were given $1,200 a month. He defected and became a star informant for the United States. Also testifying about al Qaeda in a U.S. court was L'Houssaine Kherchtou, who told of breaking with Bin Ladin because of Bin Ladin's professed inability to provide him with money when his wife needed a caesarian section.[60]

In February 1996, Sudanese officials began approaching officials from the

United States and other governments, asking what actions of theirs might ease foreign pressure. In secret meetings with Saudi officials, Sudan offered to expel Bin Ladin to Saudi Arabia and asked the Saudis to pardon him. U.S. officials became aware of these secret discussions, certainly by March. Saudi officials apparently wanted Bin Ladin expelled from Sudan. They had already revoked his citizenship, however, and would not tolerate his presence in their country. And Bin Ladin may have no longer felt safe in Sudan, where he had already escaped at least one assassination attempt that he believed to have been the work of the Egyptian or Saudi regimes, or both. In any case, on May 19, 1996, Bin Ladin left Sudan—significantly weakened, despite his ambitions and organizational skills. He returned to Afghanistan.[61]

2.5 AL QAEDA'S RENEWAL IN AFGHANISTAN (1996–1998)

Bin Ladin flew on a leased aircraft from Khartoum to Jalalabad, with a refueling stopover in the United Arab Emirates.[62] He was accompanied by family members and bodyguards, as well as by al Qaeda members who had been close associates since his organization's 1988 founding in Afghanistan. Dozens of additional militants arrived on later flights.[63]

Though Bin Ladin's destination was Afghanistan, Pakistan was the nation that held the key to his ability to use Afghanistan as a base from which to revive his ambitious enterprise for war against the United States.

For the first quarter century of its existence as a nation, Pakistan's identity had derived from Islam, but its politics had been decidedly secular. The army was—and remains—the country's strongest and most respected institution, and the army had been and continues to be preoccupied with its rivalry with India, especially over the disputed territory of Kashmir.

From the 1970s onward, religion had become an increasingly powerful force in Pakistani politics. After a coup in 1977, military leaders turned to Islamist groups for support, and fundamentalists became more prominent. South Asia had an indigenous form of Islamic fundamentalism, which had developed in the nineteenth century at a school in the Indian village of Deoband.[64] The influence of the Wahhabi school of Islam had also grown, nurtured by Saudi-funded institutions. Moreover, the fighting in Afghanistan made Pakistan home to an enormous—and generally unwelcome—population of Afghan refugees; and since the badly strained Pakistani education system could not accommodate the refugees, the government increasingly let privately funded religious schools serve as a cost-free alternative. Over time, these schools produced large numbers of half-educated young men with no marketable skills but with deeply held Islamic views.[65]

Pakistan's rulers found these multitudes of ardent young Afghans a source of potential trouble at home but potentially useful abroad. Those who joined the Taliban movement, espousing a ruthless version of Islamic law, perhaps could bring order in chaotic Afghanistan and make it a cooperative ally. They thus might give Pakistan greater security on one of the several borders where Pakistani military officers hoped for what they called "strategic depth."[66]

It is unlikely that Bin Ladin could have returned to Afghanistan had Pakistan disapproved. The Pakistani military intelligence service probably had advance knowledge of his coming, and its officers may have facilitated his travel. During his entire time in Sudan, he had maintained guesthouses and training camps in Pakistan and Afghanistan. These were part of a larger network used by diverse organizations for recruiting and training fighters for Islamic insurgencies in such places as Tajikistan, Kashmir, and Chechnya. Pakistani intelligence officers reportedly introduced Bin Ladin to Taliban leaders in Kandahar, their main base of power, to aid his reassertion of control over camps near

Khowst, out of an apparent hope that he would now expand the camps and make them available for training Kashmiri militants.[67]

Yet Bin Ladin was in his weakest position since his early days in the war against the Soviet Union. The Sudanese government had canceled the registration of the main business enterprises he had set up there and then put some of them up for public sale. According to a senior al Qaeda detainee, the government of Sudan seized everything Bin Ladin had possessed there.[68]

He also lost the head of his military committee, Abu Ubaidah al Banshiri, one of the most capable and popular leaders of al Qaeda. While most of the group's key figures had accompanied Bin Ladin to Afghanistan, Banshiri had remained in Kenya to oversee the training and weapons shipments of the cell set up some four years earlier. He died in a ferryboat accident on Lake Victoria just a few days after Bin Ladin arrived in Jalalabad, leaving Bin Ladin with a need to replace him not only in the Shura but also as supervisor of the cells and prospective operations in East Africa.[69] He had to make other adjustments as well, for some al Qaeda members viewed Bin Ladin's return to Afghanistan as occasion to go off in their own directions. Some maintained collaborative relationships with al Qaeda, but many disengaged entirely.[70]

For a time, it may not have been clear to Bin Ladin that the Taliban would be his best bet as an ally. When he arrived in Afghanistan, they controlled much of the country, but key centers, including Kabul, were still held by rival warlords. Bin Ladin went initially to Jalalabad, probably because it was in an area controlled by a provincial council of Islamic leaders who were not major contenders for national power. He found lodgings with Younis Khalis, the head of one of the main mujahideen factions. Bin Ladin apparently kept his options open, maintaining contacts with Gulbuddin Hekmatyar, who, though an Islamic extremist, was also one of the Taliban's most militant opponents. But after September 1996, when first Jalalabad and then Kabul fell to the Taliban, Bin Ladin cemented his ties with them.[71]

That process did not always go smoothly. Bin Ladin, no longer constrained by the Sudanese, clearly thought that he had new freedom to publish his appeals for jihad. At about the time when the Taliban were making their final drive toward Jalalabad and Kabul, Bin Ladin issued his August 1996 fatwa, saying that "We . . . have been prevented from addressing the Muslims," but expressing relief that "by the grace of Allah, a safe base here is now available in the high Hindu Kush mountains in Khurasan." But the Taliban, like the Sudanese, would eventually hear warnings, including from the Saudi monarchy.[72]

Though Bin Ladin had promised Taliban leaders that he would be circumspect, he broke this promise almost immediately, giving an inflammatory interview to CNN in March 1997. The Taliban leader Mullah Omar promptly "invited" Bin Ladin to move to Kandahar, ostensibly in the interests of Bin Ladin's own security but more likely to situate him where he might be easier to control.[73]

There is also evidence that around this time Bin Ladin sent out a number of feelers to the Iraqi regime, offering some cooperation. None are reported to have received a significant response. According to one report, Saddam Hussein's efforts at this time to rebuild relations with the Saudis and other Middle Eastern regimes led him to stay clear of Bin Ladin.[74]

In mid-1998, the situation reversed; it was Iraq that reportedly took the initiative. In March 1998, after Bin Ladin's public fatwa against the United States, two al Qaeda members reportedly went to Iraq to meet with Iraqi intelligence. In July, an Iraqi delegation traveled to Afghanistan to meet first with the Taliban and then with Bin Ladin. Sources reported that one, or perhaps both, of these meetings was apparently arranged through Bin Ladin's Egyptian deputy, Zawahiri, who had ties of his own to the Iraqis. In 1998, Iraq was under intensifying U.S. pressure, which culminated in a series of large air attacks in December.[75]

Similar meetings between Iraqi officials and Bin Ladin or his aides may have occurred in 1999 during a period of some reported strains with the Taliban. According to the reporting, Iraqi officials offered Bin Ladin a safe haven in Iraq. Bin Ladin declined, apparently judging that his circumstances in Afghanistan remained more favorable than the Iraqi alternative. The reports describe friendly contacts and indicate some common themes in both sides' hatred of the United States. But to date we have seen no evidence that these or the earlier contacts ever developed into a collaborative operational relationship. Nor have we seen evidence indicating that Iraq cooperated with al Qaeda in developing or carrying out any attacks against the United States.[76]

Bin Ladin eventually enjoyed a strong financial position in Afghanistan, thanks to Saudi and other financiers associated with the Golden Chain. Through his relationship with Mullah Omar—and the monetary and other benefits that it brought the Taliban—Bin Ladin was able to circumvent restrictions; Mullah Omar would stand by him even when other Taliban leaders raised objections. Bin Ladin appeared to have in Afghanistan a freedom of movement that he had lacked in Sudan. Al Qaeda members could travel freely within the country, enter and exit it without visas or any immigration procedures, purchase and import vehicles and weapons, and enjoy the use of official Afghan Ministry of Defense license plates. Al Qaeda also used the Afghan state-owned Ariana Airlines to courier money into the country.[77]

The Taliban seemed to open the doors to all who wanted to come to Afghanistan to train in the camps. The alliance with the Taliban provided al Qaeda a sanctuary in which to train and indoctrinate fighters and terrorists, import weapons, forge ties with other jihad groups and leaders, and plot and staff terrorist schemes. While Bin Ladin maintained his own al Qaeda guesthouses and camps for vetting and training recruits, he also provided support to and benefited from the broad infrastructure of such facilities in Afghanistan made available to the global network of Islamist movements. U.S. intelligence estimates put the total number of fighters who underwent instruction in Bin Ladin–supported camps in Afghanistan from 1996 through 9/11 at 10,000 to 20,000.[78]

In addition to training fighters and special operators, this larger network of guesthouses and camps provided a mechanism by which al Qaeda could screen and vet candidates for induction into its own organization. Thousands flowed through the camps, but no more than a few hundred seem to have become al Qaeda members. From the time of its founding, al Qaeda had employed training and indoctrination to identify "worthy" candidates.[79]

Al Qaeda continued meanwhile to collaborate closely with the many Middle Eastern groups—in Egypt, Algeria, Yemen, Lebanon, Morocco, Tunisia, Somalia, and elsewhere—with which it had been linked when Bin Ladin was in Sudan. It also reinforced its London base and its other offices around Europe, the Balkans, and the Caucasus. Bin Ladin bolstered his links to extremists in South and Southeast Asia, including the Malaysian-Indonesian JI and several Pakistani groups engaged in the Kashmir conflict.[80]

The February 1998 fatwa thus seems to have been a kind of public launch of a renewed and stronger al Qaeda, after a year and a half of work. Having rebuilt his fund-raising network, Bin Ladin had again become the rich man of the jihad movement. He had maintained or restored many of his links with terrorists elsewhere in the world. And he had strengthened the internal ties in his own organization.

The inner core of al Qaeda continued to be a hierarchical top-down group with defined positions, tasks, and salaries. Most but not all in this core swore fealty (or *bayat*) to Bin Ladin. Other operatives were committed to Bin Ladin or to his goals and would take assignments for him, but they did not swear bayat and maintained, or tried to maintain, some autonomy. A looser circle of adherents might give money to al Qaeda or train in its camps but remained essentially independent. Nevertheless, they constituted a potential resource for al Qaeda.[81]

Now effectively merged with Zawahiri's Egyptian Islamic Jihad,[82] al Qaeda promised to become the general headquarters for international terrorism, without the need for the Islamic Army Shura. Bin Ladin was prepared to pick up where he had left off in Sudan. He was ready to strike at "the head of the snake."

Al Qaeda's role in organizing terrorist operations had also changed. Before the move to Afghanistan, it had concentrated on providing funds, training, and weapons for actions carried out by members of allied groups. The attacks on the U.S. embassies in East Africa in the summer of 1998 would take a different form—planned, directed, and executed by al Qaeda, under the direct supervision of Bin Ladin and his chief aides.

The Embassy Bombings

As early as December 1993, a team of al Qaeda operatives had begun casing targets in Nairobi for future attacks. It was led by Ali Mohamed, a former Egyptian army officer who had moved to the United States in the mid-1980s, enlisted in the U.S. Army, and became an instructor at Fort Bragg. He had provided guidance and training to extremists at the Farouq mosque in Brooklyn, including some who were subsequently convicted in the February 1993 attack on the World Trade Center. The casing team also included a computer expert whose write-ups were reviewed by al Qaeda leaders.[83]

The team set up a makeshift laboratory for developing their surveillance photographs in an apartment in Nairobi where the various al Qaeda operatives and leaders based in or traveling to the Kenya cell sometimes met. Banshiri, al Qaeda's military committee chief, continued to be the operational commander of the cell; but because he was constantly on the move, Bin Ladin had dispatched another operative, Khaled al Fawwaz, to serve as the on-site manager. The technical surveillance and communications equipment employed for these casing missions included state-of-the-art video cameras obtained from China and from dealers in Germany. The casing team also reconnoitered targets in Djibouti.[84]

As early as January 1994, Bin Ladin received the surveillance reports, complete with diagrams prepared by the team's computer specialist. He, his top military committee members—Banshiri and his deputy, Abu Hafs al Masri (also known as Mohammed Atef)—and a number of other al Qaeda leaders reviewed the reports. Agreeing that the U.S. embassy in Nairobi was an easy target because a car bomb could be parked close by, they began to form a plan. Al Qaeda had begun developing the tactical expertise for such attacks months earlier, when some of its operatives—top military committee members and several operatives who were involved with the Kenya cell among them—were sent to Hezbollah training camps in Lebanon.[85]

The cell in Kenya experienced a series of disruptions that may in part account for the relatively long delay before the attack was actually carried out. The difficulties Bin Ladin began to encounter in Sudan in 1995, his move to Afghanistan in 1996, and the months spent establishing ties with the Taliban may also have played a role, as did Banshiri's accidental drowning.

In August 1997, the Kenya cell panicked. The London *Daily Telegraph* reported that Madani al Tayyib, formerly head of al Qaeda's finance committee, had turned himself over to the Saudi government. The article said (incorrectly) that the Saudis were sharing Tayyib's information with the U.S. and British authorities.[86] At almost the same time, cell members learned that U.S. and Kenyan agents had searched the Kenya residence of Wadi al Hage, who had become the new on-site manager in Nairobi, and that Hage's telephone was being tapped. Hage was a U.S. citizen who had worked with Bin Ladin in Afghanistan in the 1980s, and in 1992 he went to Sudan to become one of al Qaeda's major financial operatives. When Hage returned to the United States to appear before a grand jury investigating Bin Ladin, the job of cell manager was taken over by Harun Fazul, a Kenyan citizen who had been in Bin Ladin's advance team to Sudan back in 1990. Harun faxed a report on the "security situation" to several sites, warning that "the crew members in East Africa is [sic] in grave danger" in part because "America knows . . . that the followers of [Bin Ladin] . . . carried out the operations to hit Americans in Somalia." The report provided instructions for avoiding further exposure.[87]

On February 23, 1998, Bin Ladin issued his public fatwa. The language had been in negotiation for some time, as part of the merger under way between Bin Ladin's organization and Zawahiri's Egyptian Islamic Jihad. Less than a month after the publication of the fatwa, the teams that were to carry out the embassy attacks were being pulled together in Nairobi and Dar es Salaam. The timing and content of their instructions indicate that the decision to launch the attacks had been made by the time the fatwa was issued.[88]

The next four months were spent setting up the teams in Nairobi and Dar es Salaam. Members of the cells rented residences, and purchased bomb-making materials and transport vehicles. At least one additional explosives expert was brought in to assist in putting the weapons together. In Nairobi, a hotel room was rented to put up some of the operatives. The suicide trucks were purchased shortly before the attack date.[89]

While this was taking place, Bin Ladin continued to push his public message. On May 7, the deputy head of al Qaeda's military committee, Mohammed Atef, faxed to Bin Ladin's London office a new fatwa issued by a group of sheikhs located in Afghanistan. A week later, it appeared in *Al Quds al Arabi*, the same Arabic-language newspaper in London that had first published Bin Ladin's February fatwa, and it conveyed the same message—the duty of Muslims to carry out holy war against the enemies of Islam and to expel the Americans from the Gulf region. Two weeks after that, Bin Ladin gave a video-taped interview to ABC News with the same slogans, adding that "we do not differentiate between those dressed in military uniforms and civilians; they are all targets in this *fatwa*."[90]

By August 1, members of the cells not directly involved in the attacks had mostly departed from East Africa. The remaining operatives prepared and assembled the bombs, and acquired the delivery vehicles. On August 4, they made one last casing run at the embassy in Nairobi. By the evening of August 6, all but the delivery teams and one or two persons assigned to remove the evidence trail had left East Africa. Back in Afghanistan, Bin Ladin and the al Qaeda leadership had left Kandahar for the countryside, expecting U.S. retaliation. Declarations taking credit for the attacks had already been faxed to the joint al Qaeda–Egyptian Islamic Jihad office in Baku, with instructions to stand by for orders to "instantly" transmit them to *Al Quds al Arabi*. One proclaimed "the formation of the Islamic Army for the Liberation of the Holy Places," and two others—one for each embassy—announced that the attack had been carried out by a "company" of a "battalion" of this "Islamic Army."[91]

On the morning of August 7, the bomb-laden trucks drove into the embassies roughly five minutes apart—about 10:35 A.M. in Nairobi and 10:39 A.M. in Dar es Salaam. Shortly afterward, a phone call was placed from Baku to London. The previously prepared messages were then faxed to London.[92]

The attack on the U.S. embassy in Nairobi destroyed the embassy and killed 12 Americans and 201 others, almost all Kenyans. About 5,000 people were injured. The attack on the U.S. embassy in Dar es Salaam killed 11 more people, none of them Americans. Interviewed later about the deaths of the Africans, Bin Ladin answered that "when it becomes apparent that it would be impossible to repel these Americans without assaulting them, even if this involved the killing of Muslims, this is permissible under Islam." Asked if he had indeed masterminded these bombings, Bin Ladin said that the World Islamic Front for jihad against "Jews and Crusaders" had issued a "crystal clear" fatwa. If the instigation for jihad against the Jews and the Americans to liberate the holy places "is considered a crime," he said, "let history be a witness that I am a criminal."[93]

3

COUNTERTERRORISM
EVOLVES

In chapter 2, we described the growth of a new kind of terrorism, and a new terrorist organization—especially from 1988 to 1998, when Usama Bin Ladin declared war and organized the bombing of two U.S. embassies. In this chapter, we trace the parallel evolution of government efforts to counter terrorism by Islamic extremists against the United States.

We mention many personalities in this report. As in any study of the U.S. government, some of the most important characters are institutions. We will introduce various agencies, and how they adapted to a new kind of terrorism.

3.1 FROM THE OLD TERRORISM TO THE NEW:
THE FIRST WORLD TRADE CENTER BOMBING

At 18 minutes after noon on February 26, 1993, a huge bomb went off beneath the two towers of the World Trade Center. This was not a suicide attack. The terrorists parked a truck bomb with a timing device on Level B-2 of the underground garage, then departed. The ensuing explosion opened a hole seven stories up. Six people died. More than a thousand were injured. An FBI agent at the scene described the relatively low number of fatalities as a miracle.[1]

President Bill Clinton ordered his National Security Council to coordinate the response. Government agencies swung into action to find the culprits. The Counterterrorist Center located at the CIA combed its files and queried sources around the world. The National Security Agency (NSA), the huge Defense Department signals collection agency, ramped up its communications intercept network and searched its databases for clues.[2] The New York Field Office of the FBI took control of the local investigation and, in the end, set a pattern for future management of terrorist incidents.

Four features of this episode have significance for the story of 9/11.

First, the bombing signaled a new terrorist challenge, one whose rage and malice had no limit. Ramzi Yousef, the Sunni extremist who planted the bomb, said later that he had hoped to kill 250,000 people.[3]

Second, the FBI and the Justice Department did excellent work investigating the bombing. Within days, the FBI identified a truck remnant as part of a Ryder rental van reported stolen in Jersey City the day before the bombing.[4]

Mohammed Salameh, who had rented the truck and reported it stolen, kept calling the rental office to get back his $400 deposit. The FBI arrested him there on March 4, 1993. In short order, the Bureau had several plotters in custody, including Nidal Ayyad, an engineer who had acquired chemicals for the bomb, and Mahmoud Abouhalima, who had helped mix the chemicals.[5]

The FBI identified another conspirator, Ahmad Ajaj, who had been arrested by immigration authorities at John F. Kennedy International Airport in September 1992 and charged with document fraud. His traveling companion was Ramzi Yousef, who had also entered with fraudulent documents but claimed political asylum and was admitted. It quickly became clear that Yousef had been a central player in the attack. He had fled to Pakistan immediately after the bombing and would remain at large for nearly two years.[6]

The arrests of Salameh, Abouhalima, and Ayyad led the FBI to the Farouq mosque in Brooklyn, where a central figure was Sheikh Omar Abdel Rahman, an extremist Sunni Muslim cleric who had moved to the United States from Egypt in 1990. In speeches and writings, the sightless Rahman, often called the "Blind Sheikh," preached the message of Sayyid Qutb's *Milestones*, characterizing the United States as the oppressor of Muslims worldwide and asserting that it was their religious duty to fight against God's enemies. An FBI informant learned of a plan to bomb major New York landmarks, including the Holland and Lincoln tunnels. Disrupting this "landmarks plot," the FBI in June 1993 arrested Rahman and various confederates.[7]

As a result of the investigations and arrests, the U.S. Attorney for the Southern District of New York prosecuted and convicted multiple individuals, including Ajaj, Salameh, Ayyad, Abouhalima, the Blind Sheikh, and Ramzi Yousef, for crimes related to the World Trade Center bombing and other plots.

An unfortunate consequence of this superb investigative and prosecutorial effort was that it created an impression that the law enforcement system was well-equipped to cope with terrorism. Neither President Clinton, his principal advisers, the Congress, nor the news media felt prompted, until later, to press the question of whether the procedures that put the Blind Sheikh and Ramzi Yousef behind bars would really protect Americans against the new virus of which these individuals were just the first symptoms.[8]

Third, the successful use of the legal system to address the first World Trade Center bombing had the side effect of obscuring the need to examine the character and extent of the new threat facing the United States. The trials did not bring the Bin Ladin network to the attention of the public and policymakers.

The FBI assembled, and the U.S. Attorney's office put forward, some evidence showing that the men in the dock were not the only plotters. Materials taken from Ajaj indicated that the plot or plots were hatched at or near the Khaldan camp, a terrorist training camp on the Afghanistan-Pakistan border. Ajaj had left Texas in April 1992 to go there to learn how to construct bombs. He had met Ramzi Yousef in Pakistan, where they discussed bombing targets in the United States and assembled a "terrorist kit" that included bomb-making manuals, operations guidance, videotapes advocating terrorist action against the United States, and false identification documents.[9]

Yousef was captured in Pakistan following the discovery by police in the Philippines in January 1995 of the Manila air plot, which envisioned placing bombs on board a dozen trans-Pacific airliners and setting them off simultaneously. Khalid Sheikh Mohammed—Yousef's uncle, then located in Qatar—was a fellow plotter of Yousef's in the Manila air plot and had also wired him some money prior to the Trade Center bombing. The U.S. Attorney obtained an indictment against KSM in January 1996, but an official in the government of Qatar probably warned him about it. Khalid Sheikh Mohammed evaded capture (and stayed at large to play a central part in the 9/11 attacks).[10]

The law enforcement process is concerned with proving the guilt of persons apprehended and charged. Investigators and prosecutors could not present all the evidence of possible involvement of individuals other than those charged, although they continued to pursue such investigations, planning or hoping for later prosecutions. The process was meant, by its nature, to mark for the public the events as finished—case solved, justice done. It was not designed to ask if the events might be harbingers of worse to come. Nor did it allow for aggregating and analyzing facts to see if they could provide clues to terrorist tactics more generally—methods of entry and finance, and mode of operation inside the United States.

Fourth, although the bombing heightened awareness of a new terrorist danger, successful prosecutions contributed to widespread underestimation of the threat. The government's attorneys stressed the seriousness of the crimes, and put forward evidence of Yousef's technical ingenuity. Yet the public image that persisted was not of clever Yousef but of stupid Salameh going back again and again to reclaim his $400 truck rental deposit.

3.2 ADAPTATION—AND NONADAPTATION—IN THE LAW ENFORCEMENT COMMUNITY

Legal processes were the primary method for responding to these early manifestations of a new type of terrorism. Our overview of U.S. capabilities for dealing with it thus begins with the nation's vast complex of law enforcement agencies.

The Justice Department and the FBI

At the federal level, much law enforcement activity is concentrated in the Department of Justice. For countering terrorism, the dominant agency under Justice is the Federal Bureau of Investigation. The FBI does not have a general grant of authority but instead works under specific statutory authorizations. Most of its work is done in local offices called field offices. There are 56 of them, each covering a specified geographic area, and each quite separate from all others. Prior to 9/11, the special agent in charge was in general free to set his or her office's priorities and assign personnel accordingly.[11]

The office's priorities were driven by two primary concerns. First, performance in the Bureau was generally measured against statistics such as numbers of arrests, indictments, prosecutions, and convictions. Counterterrorism and counterintelligence work, often involving lengthy intelligence investigations that might never have positive or quantifiable results, was not career-enhancing. Most agents who reached management ranks had little counterterrorism experience. Second, priorities were driven at the local level by the field offices, whose concerns centered on traditional crimes such as white-collar offenses and those pertaining to drugs and gangs. Individual field offices made choices to serve local priorities, not national priorities.[12]

The Bureau also operates under an "office of origin" system. To avoid duplication and possible conflicts, the FBI designates a single office to be in charge of an entire investigation. Because the New York Field Office indicted Bin Ladin prior to the East Africa bombings, it became the office of origin for all Bin Ladin cases, including the East Africa bombings and later the attack on the USS *Cole*. Most of the FBI's institutional knowledge on Bin Ladin and al Qaeda resided there. This office worked closely with the U.S. Attorney for the Southern District of New York to identify, arrest, prosecute, and convict many of the perpetrators of the attacks and plots. Field offices other than the specified office of origin were often reluctant to spend much energy on matters over which they had no control and for which they received no credit.[13]

The FBI's domestic intelligence gathering dates from the 1930s. With World War II looming, President Franklin D. Roosevelt ordered FBI Director J. Edgar Hoover to investigate foreign and foreign-inspired subversion—Communist, Nazi, and Japanese. Hoover added investigation of possible espionage, sabotage, or subversion to the duties of field offices. After the war, foreign intelligence duties were assigned to the newly established Central Intelligence Agency. Hoover jealously guarded the FBI's domestic portfolio against all rivals. Hoover felt he was accountable only to the president, and the FBI's domestic intelligence activities kept growing. In the 1960s, the FBI was receiving significant assistance within the United States from the CIA and from Army Intelligence. The legal basis for some of this assistance was dubious.

Decades of encouragement to perform as a domestic intelligence agency abruptly ended in the 1970s. Two years after Hoover's death in 1972, congressional and news media investigations of the Watergate scandals of the Nixon administration expanded into general investigations of foreign and domestic intelligence by the Church and Pike committees.[14] They disclosed domestic intelligence efforts, which included a covert action program that operated from 1956 to 1971 against domestic organizations and, eventually, domestic dissidents. The FBI had spied on a wide range of political figures, especially individuals whom Hoover wanted to discredit (notably the Reverend Martin Luther King, Jr.), and had authorized unlawful wiretaps and surveillance. The shock registered in public opinion polls, where the percentage of Americans declaring a "highly favorable" view of the FBI dropped from 84 percent to 37 percent. The FBI's Domestic Intelligence Division was dissolved.[15]

In 1976, Attorney General Edward Levi adopted domestic security guidelines to regulate intelligence collection in the United States and to deflect calls for even stronger regulation. In 1983, Attorney General William French Smith revised the Levi guidelines to encourage closer investigation of potential terrorism. He also loosened the rules governing authorization for investigations and their duration. Still, his guidelines, like Levi's, took account of the reality that suspicion of "terrorism," like suspicion of "subversion," could lead to making individuals targets for investigation more because of their beliefs than because of their acts. Smith's guidelines also took account of the reality that potential terrorists were often members of extremist religious organizations and that investigation of terrorism could cross the line separating state and church.[16]

In 1986, Congress authorized the FBI to investigate terrorist attacks against Americans that occur outside the United States. Three years later, it added authority for the FBI to make arrests abroad without consent from the host country. Meanwhile, a task force headed by Vice President George H. W. Bush had endorsed a concept already urged by Director of Central Intelligence William Casey—a Counterterrorist Center, where the FBI, the CIA, and other organizations could work together on international terrorism. While it was distinctly a CIA entity, the FBI detailed officials to work at the Center and obtained leads that helped in the capture of persons wanted for trial in the United States.

The strengths that the FBI brought to counterterrorism were nowhere more brilliantly on display than in the case of Pan American Flight 103, bound from London to New York, which blew up over Lockerbie, Scotland, in December 1988, killing 270 people. Initial evidence pointed to the government of Syria and, later, Iran. The Counterterrorist Center reserved judgment on the perpetrators of the attack. Meanwhile, FBI technicians, working with U.K. security services, gathered and analyzed the widely scattered fragments of the airliner. In 1991, with the help of the Counterterrorist Center, they identified one small fragment as part of a timing device—to the technicians, as distinctive as DNA. It was a Libyan device. Together with other evidence, the FBI put together a case pointing conclusively to the Libyan government. Eventually Libya acknowledged its responsibility.[17] Pan Am 103 became a cautionary tale against rushing to judgment in attributing responsibility for a terrorist act. It also showed again how—given a case to solve—the FBI remained capable of extraordinary investigative success.

FBI Organization and Priorities

In 1993, President Clinton chose Louis Freeh as the Director of the Bureau. Freeh, who would remain Director until June 2001, believed that the FBI's work should be done primarily by the field offices. To emphasize this view he cut headquarters staff and decentralized operations. The special agents in charge gained power, influence, and independence.[18]

Freeh recognized terrorism as a major threat. He increased the number of legal attaché offices abroad, focusing in particular on the Middle East. He also urged agents not to wait for terrorist acts to occur before taking action. In his first budget request to Congress after the 1993 World Trade Center bombing, he stated that "merely solving this type of crime is not enough; it is equally important that the FBI thwart terrorism before such acts can be perpetrated." Within headquarters, he created a Counterterrorism Division that would complement the Counterterrorist Center at the CIA and arranged for exchanges of senior FBI and CIA counterterrorism officials. He pressed for more cooperation between legal attachés and CIA stations abroad.[19]

Freeh's efforts did not, however, translate into a significant shift of resources to counterterrorism. FBI, Justice, and Office of Management and Budget officials said that FBI leadership seemed unwilling to shift resources to terrorism from other areas such as violent crime and drug enforcement; other FBI officials blamed Congress and the OMB for a lack of political will and failure to understand the FBI's counterterrorism resource needs. In addition, Freeh did not impose his views on the field offices. With a few notable exceptions, the field offices did not apply significant resources to terrorism and often reprogrammed funds for other priorities.[20]

In 1998, the FBI issued a five-year strategic plan led by its deputy director, Robert "Bear" Bryant. For the first time, the FBI designated national and economic security, including counterterrorism, as its top priority. Dale Watson, who would later become the head of the new Counterterrorism Division, said that after the East Africa bombings, "the light came on" that cultural change had to occur within the FBI. The plan mandated a stronger intelligence collection effort. It called for a nationwide automated system to facilitate information collection, analysis, and dissemination. It envisioned the creation of a professional intelligence cadre of experienced and trained agents and analysts. If successfully implemented, this would have been a major step toward addressing terrorism systematically, rather than as individual unrelated cases. But the plan did not succeed.[21]

First, the plan did not obtain the necessary human resources. Despite designating "national and economic security" as its top priority in 1998, the FBI did not shift human resources accordingly. Although the FBI's counterterrorism budget tripled during the mid-1990s, FBI counterterrorism spending remained fairly constant between fiscal years 1998 and 2001. In 2000, there were still twice as many agents devoted to drug enforcement as to counterterrorism.[22]

Second, the new division intended to strengthen the FBI's strategic analysis capability faltered. It received insufficient resources and faced resistance from senior managers in the FBI's operational divisions. The new division was supposed to identify trends in terrorist activity, determine what the FBI did not know, and ultimately drive collection efforts. However, the FBI had little appreciation for the role of analysis. Analysts continued to be used primarily in a tactical fashion—providing support for existing cases. Compounding the problem was the FBI's tradition of hiring analysts from within instead of recruiting individuals with the relevant educational background and expertise.[23]

Moreover, analysts had difficulty getting access to the FBI and intelligence community information they were expected to analyze. The poor state of the FBI's information systems meant that such access depended in large part on an analyst's personal relationships with individuals in the operational units or squads where the information resided. For all of these reasons, prior to 9/11 relatively few strategic analytic reports about counterterrorism had been completed. Indeed, the FBI had never completed an assessment of the overall terrorist threat to the U.S. homeland.[24]

Third, the FBI did not have an effective intelligence collection effort. Collection of intelligence from human sources was limited, and agents were inadequately trained. Only three days of a 16-week agents' course were devoted to counterintelligence and counterterrorism, and most subsequent training was received on the job. The FBI did not have an adequate mechanism for validating source reporting, nor did it have a system for adequately tracking and sharing source reporting, either internally or externally. The FBI did not dedicate sufficient resources to the surveillance and translation needs of counterterrorism agents. It lacked sufficient translators proficient in Arabic and other key languages, resulting in a significant backlog of untranslated intercepts.[25]

Finally, the FBI's information systems were woefully inadequate. The FBI lacked the ability to know what it knew: there was no effective mechanism for capturing or sharing its institutional knowledge. FBI agents did create records of interviews and other investigative efforts, but there were no reports officers to condense the information into meaningful intelligence that could be retrieved and disseminated.[26]

In 1999, the FBI created separate Counterterrorism and Counterintelligence divisions. Dale Watson, the first head of the new Counterterrorism Division, recognized the urgent need to increase the FBI's counterterrorism capability. His plan, called MAXCAP 05, was unveiled in 2000: it set the goal of bringing the Bureau to its "maximum feasible capacity" in counterterrorism by 2005. Field executives told Watson that they did not have the analysts, linguists, or technically trained experts to carry out the strategy. In a report provided to Director Robert Mueller in September 2001, one year after Watson presented his plan to field executives, almost every FBI field office was assessed to be operating below "maximum capacity." The report stated that "the goal to 'prevent terrorism' requires a dramatic shift in emphasis from a reactive capability to highly functioning intelligence capability which provides not only leads and operational support, but clear strategic analysis and direction."[27]

Legal Constraints on the FBI and "the Wall"

The FBI had different tools for law enforcement and intelligence.[28] For criminal matters, it could apply for and use traditional criminal warrants. For intelligence matters involving international terrorism, however, the rules were different. For many years the attorney general could authorize surveillance of foreign powers and agents of foreign powers without any court review, but in 1978 Congress passed the Foreign Intelligence Surveillance Act.[29] This law regulated intelligence collection directed at foreign powers and agents of foreign powers in the United States. In addition to requiring court review of proposed surveillance (and later, physical searches), the 1978 act was interpreted by the courts to require that a search be approved only if its "primary purpose" was to obtain foreign intelligence information. In other words, the authorities of the FISA law could not be used to circumvent traditional criminal warrant requirements. The Justice Department interpreted these rulings as saying that criminal prosecutors could be briefed on FISA information but could not direct or control its collection.[30]

Throughout the 1980s and early 1990s, Justice prosecutors had informal arrangements for obtaining information gathered in the FISA process, the understanding being that they would not improperly exploit that process for their criminal cases. Whether the FBI shared with prosecutors information pertinent to possible criminal investigations was left solely to the judgment of the FBI.[31]

But the prosecution of Aldrich Ames for espionage in 1994 revived concerns about the prosecutors' role in intelligence investigations. The Department of Justice's Office of Intelligence Policy and Review (OIPR) is responsible for reviewing and presenting all FISA applications to the FISA Court. It worried that because of the numerous prior consultations between FBI agents and prosecutors, the judge might rule that the FISA warrants had been misused. If that had happened, Ames might have escaped conviction. Richard Scruggs, the acting head of OIPR, complained to Attorney General Janet Reno about the lack of information-sharing controls. On his own, he began imposing information-sharing procedures for FISA material. The Office of Intelligence Policy and Review became the gatekeeper for the flow of FISA information to criminal prosecutors.[32]

In July 1995, Attorney General Reno issued formal procedures aimed at managing information sharing between Justice Department prosecutors and the FBI. They were developed in a working group led by the Justice Department's Executive Office of National Security, overseen by Deputy Attorney General Jamie Gorelick.[33] These procedures—while requiring the sharing of intelligence information with prosecutors—regulated the manner in which such information could be shared from the intelligence side of the house to the criminal side.

These procedures were almost immediately misunderstood and misapplied. As a result, there was far less information sharing and coordination between the FBI and the Criminal Division in practice than was allowed under the department's procedures. Over time the procedures came to be referred to as "the wall." The term "the wall" is misleading, however, because several factors led to a series of barriers to information sharing that developed.[34]

The Office of Intelligence Policy and Review became the sole gatekeeper for passing information to the Criminal Division. Though Attorney General Reno's procedures did not include such a provision, the Office assumed the role anyway, arguing that its position reflected the concerns of Judge Royce Lamberth, then chief judge of the Foreign Intelligence Surveillance Court. The Office threatened that if it could not regulate the flow of information to criminal prosecutors, it would no longer present the FBI's warrant requests to the FISA Court. The information flow withered.[35]

The 1995 procedures dealt only with sharing between agents and criminal prosecutors, not between two kinds of FBI agents, those working on intelligence matters and those working on criminal matters. But pressure from the Office of Intelligence Policy Review, FBI leadership, and the FISA Court built barriers between agents—even agents serving on the same squads. FBI Deputy Director Bryant reinforced the Office's caution by informing agents that too much information sharing could be a career stopper. Agents in the field began to believe—incorrectly—that no FISA information could be shared with agents working on criminal investigations.[36]

This perception evolved into the still more exaggerated belief that the FBI could not share *any* intelligence information with criminal investigators, even if no FISA procedures had been used. Thus, relevant information from the National Security Agency and the CIA often failed to make its way to criminal investigators. Separate reviews in 1999, 2000, and 2001 concluded independently that information sharing was not occurring, and that the intent of the 1995 procedures was ignored routinely.[37] We will describe some of the unfortunate consequences of these accumulated institutional beliefs and practices in chapter 8.

There were other legal limitations. Both prosecutors and FBI agents argued that they were barred by court rules from sharing grand jury information, even though the prohibition applied only to that small fraction that had been presented to a grand jury, and even that prohibition had exceptions. But as interpreted by FBI field offices, this prohibition could conceivably apply to much of the information unearthed in an investigation. There were also restrictions, arising from executive order, on the commingling of domestic information with foreign intelligence. Finally the NSA began putting caveats on its Bin Ladin–related reports that required prior approval before sharing their contents with criminal investigators and prosecutors. These developments further blocked the arteries of information sharing.[38]

Other Law Enforcement Agencies

The Justice Department is much more than the FBI. It also has a U.S. Marshals Service, almost 4,000 strong on 9/11 and especially expert in tracking fugitives, with much local police knowledge. The department's Drug Enforcement Administration had, as of 2001, more than 4,500 agents.[39] There were a number of occasions when DEA agents were able to introduce sources to the FBI or CIA for counterterrorism use.

The Immigration and Naturalization Service (INS), with its 9,000 Border Patrol agents, 4,500 inspectors, and 2,000 immigration special agents, had perhaps the greatest potential to develop an expanded role in counterterrorism. However, the INS was focused on the formidable challenges posed by illegal entry over the southwest border, criminal aliens, and a growing backlog in the applications for naturalizing immigrants. The White House, the Justice Department, and above all the Congress reinforced these concerns. In addition, when Doris Meissner became INS Commissioner in 1993, she found an agency seriously hampered by outdated technology and insufficient human resources. Border Patrol agents were still using manual typewriters; inspectors at ports of entry were using a paper watchlist; the asylum and other benefits systems did not effectively deter fraudulent applicants.[40]

Commissioner Meissner responded in 1993 to the World Trade Center bombing by providing seed money to the State Department's Consular Affairs Bureau to automate its terrorist watchlist, used by consular officers and border inspectors. The INS assigned an individual in a new "lookout" unit to work with the State Department in watchlisting suspected terrorists and with the intelligence community and the FBI in determining how to deal with them when they appeared at ports of entry. By 1998, 97 suspected terrorists had been denied admission at U.S. ports of entry because of the watchlist.[41]

How to conduct deportation cases against aliens who were suspected terrorists caused significant debate. The INS had immigration law expertise and authority to bring the cases, but the FBI possessed the classified information sometimes needed as evidence, and information-sharing conflicts resulted. New laws in 1996 authorized the use of classified evidence in removal hearings, but the INS removed only a handful of the aliens with links to terrorist activity (none identified as associated with al Qaeda) using classified evidence.[42]

Midlevel INS employees proposed comprehensive counterterrorism proposals to management in 1986, 1995, and 1997. No action was taken on them. In 1997, a National Security Unit was set up to handle alerts, track potential terrorist cases for possible immigration enforcement action, and work with the rest of the Justice Department. It focused on the FBI's priorities of Hezbollah and Hamas, and began to examine how immigration laws could be brought to bear on terrorism. For instance, it sought unsuccessfully to require that CIA security checks be completed before naturalization applications were approved.[43] Policy questions, such as whether resident alien status should be revoked upon the person's conviction of a terrorist crime, were not addressed.

Congress, with the support of the Clinton administration, doubled the number of Border Patrol agents required along the border with Mexico to one agent every quarter mile by 1999. It rejected efforts to bring additional resources to bear in the north. The border with Canada had one agent for every 13.25 miles. Despite examples of terrorists entering from Canada, awareness of terrorist activity in Canada and its more lenient immigration laws, and an inspector general's report recommending that the Border Patrol develop a northern border strategy, the only positive step was that the number of Border Patrol agents was not cut any further.[44]

Inspectors at the ports of entry were not asked to focus on terrorists. Inspectors told us they were not even aware that when they checked the names of incoming passengers against the automated watchlist, they were checking in part for terrorists. In general, border inspectors also did not have the information they needed to make fact-based determinations of admissibility. The INS initiated but failed to bring to completion two efforts that would have provided inspectors with information relevant to counterterrorism—a proposed system to track foreign student visa compliance and a program to establish a way of tracking travelers' entry to and exit from the United States.[45]

In 1996, a new law enabled the INS to enter into agreements with state and local law enforcement agencies through which the INS provided training and the local agencies exercised immigration enforcement authority. Terrorist watchlists were not available to them. Mayors in cities with large immigrant populations sometimes imposed limits on city employee cooperation with federal immigration agents. A large population lives outside the legal framework. Fraudulent documents could be easily obtained. Congress kept the number of INS agents static in the face of the overwhelming problem.[46]

The chief vehicle for INS and for state and local participation in law enforcement was the Joint Terrorism Task Force (JTTF), first tried out in New York City in 1980 in response to a spate of incidents involving domestic terrorist organizations. This task force was managed by the New York Field Office of the FBI, and its existence provided an opportunity to exchange information and, as happened after the first World Trade Center bombing, to enlist local officers, as well as other agency representatives, as partners in the FBI investigation. The FBI expanded the number of JTTFs throughout the 1990s, and by

9/11 there were 34. While useful, the JTTFs had limitations. They set priorities in accordance with regional and field office concerns, and most were not fully staffed. Many state and local entities believed they had little to gain from having a full-time representative on a JTTF.[47]

Other federal law enforcement resources, also not seriously enlisted for counterterrorism, were to be found in the Treasury Department.

Treasury housed the Secret Service, the Customs Service, and the Bureau of Alcohol, Tobacco, and Firearms. Given the Secret Service's mission to protect the president and other high officials, its agents did become involved with those of the FBI whenever terrorist assassination plots were rumored.

The Customs Service deployed agents at all points of entry into the United States. Its agents worked alongside INS agents, and the two groups sometimes cooperated. In the winter of 1999–2000, as will be detailed in chapter 6, questioning by an especially alert Customs inspector led to the arrest of an al Qaeda terrorist whose apparent mission was to bomb Los Angeles International Airport.

The Bureau of Alcohol, Tobacco, and Firearms was used on occasion by the FBI as a resource. The ATF's laboratories and analysis were critical to the investigation of the February 1993 bombing of the World Trade Center and the April 1995 bombing of the Alfred P. Murrah Federal Building in Oklahoma City.[48]

Before 9/11, with the exception of one portion of the FBI, very little of the sprawling U.S. law enforcement community was engaged in countering terrorism. Moreover, law enforcement could be effective only after specific individuals were identified, a plot had formed, or an attack had already occurred. Responsible individuals had to be located, apprehended, and transported back to a U.S. court for prosecution. As FBI agents emphasized to us, the FBI and the Justice Department do not have cruise missiles. They declare war by indicting someone. They took on the lead role in addressing terrorism because they were asked to do so.[49]

3.3 ...AND IN THE FEDERAL AVIATION ADMINISTRATION

The Federal Aviation Administration (FAA) within the Department of Transportation had been vested by Congress with the sometimes conflicting mandate of regulating the safety and security of U.S. civil aviation while also promoting the civil aviation industry. The FAA had a security mission to protect the users of commercial air transportation against terrorism and other criminal acts. In the years before 9/11, the FAA perceived sabotage as a greater threat to aviation than hijacking. First, no domestic hijacking had occurred in a decade. Second, the commercial aviation system was perceived as more vulnerable to explosives than to weapons such as firearms. Finally, explosives were perceived as deadlier than hijacking and therefore of greater consequence. In 1996, a presidential commission on aviation safety and security chaired by Vice President Al Gore reinforced the prevailing concern about sabotage and explosives on aircraft. The Gore Commission also flagged, as a new danger, the possibility of attack by surface-to-air missiles. Its 1997 final report did not discuss the possibility of suicide hijackings.[50]

The FAA set and enforced aviation security rules, which airlines and airports were required to implement. The rules were supposed to produce a "layered" system of defense. This meant that the failure of any one layer of security would not be fatal, because additional layers would provide backup security. But each layer relevant to hijackings—intelligence, passenger prescreening, checkpoint screening, and onboard security—was seriously flawed prior to 9/11. Taken together, they did not stop any of the 9/11 hijackers from getting on board four different aircraft at three different airports.[51]

The FAA's policy was to use intelligence to identify both specific plots and general threats to civil aviation security, so that the agency could develop and deploy appropriate countermeasures. The FAA's 40-person intelligence unit was supposed to receive a broad range of intelligence data from the FBI, CIA, and other agencies so that it could make assessments about the threat to aviation. But the large volume of data contained little pertaining to the presence and activities of terrorists in the United States. For example, information on the FBI's effort in 1998 to assess the potential use of flight training by terrorists and the Phoenix electronic communication of 2001 warning of radical Middle Easterners attending flight school were not passed to FAA headquarters. Several top FAA intelligence officials called the domestic threat picture a serious blind spot.[52]

Moreover, the FAA's intelligence unit did not receive much attention from the agency's leadership. Neither Administrator Jane Garvey nor her deputy routinely reviewed daily intelligence, and what they did see was screened for them. She was unaware of a great amount of hijacking threat information from her own intelligence unit, which, in turn, was not deeply involved in the agency's policymaking process. Historically, decisive security action took place only after a disaster had occurred or a specific plot had been discovered.[53]

The next aviation security layer was passenger prescreening. The FAA directed air carriers not to fly individuals known to pose a "direct" threat to civil aviation. But as of 9/11, the FAA's "no-fly" list contained the names of just 12 terrorist suspects (including 9/11 mastermind Khalid Sheikh Mohammed), even though government watchlists contained the names of many thousands of known and suspected terrorists. This astonishing mismatch existed despite the Gore Commission's having called on the FBI and CIA four years earlier to provide terrorist watchlists to improve prescreening. The long-time chief of the FAA's civil aviation security division testified that he was not even aware of the State Department's TIPOFF list of known and suspected terrorists (some 60,000 before 9/11) until he heard it mentioned during the Commission's January 26, 2004, public hearing. The FAA had access to some TIPOFF data, but apparently found it too difficult to use.[54]

The second part of prescreening called on the air carriers to implement an FAA-approved computerized algorithm (known as CAPPS, for Computer Assisted Passenger Prescreening System) designed to identify passengers whose profile suggested they might pose more than a minimal risk to aircraft. Although the algorithm included hijacker profile data, at that time only passengers checking bags were eligible to be selected by CAPPS for additional scrutiny. Selection entailed only having one's checked baggage screened for explosives or held off the airplane until one had boarded. Primarily because of concern regarding potential discrimination and the impact on passenger throughput, "selectees" were no longer required to undergo extraordinary screening of their carry-on baggage as had been the case before the system was computerized in 1997.[55] This policy change also reflected the perception that nonsuicide sabotage was the primary threat to civil aviation.

Checkpoint screening was considered the most important and obvious layer of security. Walk-through metal detectors and X-ray machines operated by trained screeners were employed to stop prohibited items. Numerous government reports indicated that checkpoints performed poorly, often failing to detect even obvious FAA test items. Many deadly and dangerous items did not set off metal detectors, or were hard to distinguish in an X-ray machine from innocent everyday items.[56]

While FAA rules did not expressly prohibit knives with blades under 4 inches long, the airlines' checkpoint operations guide (which was developed in cooperation with the FAA), explicitly permitted them. The FAA's basis for this policy was (1) the agency did not consider such items to be menacing, (2) most local laws did not prohibit individuals from carrying such knives, and (3) such knives would have been difficult to detect unless the sensitivity of metal detectors had been greatly increased. A proposal to ban knives altogether in 1993 had been rejected because small cutting implements were difficult to detect and the number of innocent "alarms" would have increased significantly, exacerbating congestion problems at checkpoints.[57]

Several years prior to 9/11, an FAA requirement for screeners to conduct "continuous" and "random" hand searches of carry-on luggage at checkpoints had been replaced by explosive trace detection or had simply become ignored by the air carriers. Therefore, secondary screening of individuals and their carry-on bags to identify weapons (other than bombs) was nonexistent, except for passengers who triggered the metal detectors. Even when small knives were detected by secondary screening, they were usually returned to the traveler. Reportedly, the 9/11 hijackers were instructed to use items that would be undetectable by airport checkpoints.[58]

In the pre-9/11 security system, the air carriers played a major role. As the

Inspector General of the Department of Transportation told us, there were great pressures from the air carriers to control security costs and to "limit the impact of security requirements on aviation operations, so that the industry could concentrate on its primary mission of moving passengers and aircraft. . . . [T]hose counterpressures in turn manifested themselves as significant weaknesses in security." A longtime FAA security official described the air carriers' approach to security regulation as "decry, deny and delay" and told us that while "the air carriers had seen the enlightened hand of self-interest with respect to safety, they hadn't seen it in the security arena."[59]

The final layer, security on board commercial aircraft, was not designed to counter suicide hijackings. The FAA-approved "Common Strategy" had been elaborated over decades of experience with scores of hijackings, beginning in the 1960s. It taught flight crews that the best way to deal with hijackers was to accommodate their demands, get the plane to land safely, and then let law enforcement or the military handle the situation. According to the FAA, the record had shown that the longer a hijacking persisted, the more likely it was to end peacefully. The strategy operated on the fundamental assumption that hijackers issue negotiable demands (most often for asylum or the release of prisoners) and that, as one FAA official put it, "suicide wasn't in the game plan" of hijackers. FAA training material provided no guidance for flight crews should violence occur.[60]

This prevailing Common Strategy of cooperation and nonconfrontation meant that even a hardened cockpit door would have made little difference in a hijacking. As the chairman of the Security Committee of the Air Line Pilots Association observed when proposals were made in early 2001 to install reinforced cockpit doors in commercial aircraft, "Even if you make a vault out of the door, if they have a noose around my flight attendant's neck, I'm going to open the door." Prior to 9/11, FAA regulations mandated that cockpit doors permit ready access into and out of the cockpit in the event of an emergency. Even so, rules implemented in the 1960s required air crews to keep the cockpit door closed and locked in flight. This requirement was not always observed or vigorously enforced.[61]

As for law enforcement, there were only 33 armed and trained federal air marshals as of 9/11. They were not deployed on U.S. domestic flights, except when in transit to provide security on international departures. This policy reflected the FAA's view that domestic hijacking was in check—a view held confidently as no terrorist had hijacked a U.S. commercial aircraft anywhere in the world since 1986.[62]

In the absence of any recent aviation security incident and without "specific and credible" evidence of a plot directed at civil aviation, the FAA's leadership focused elsewhere, including on operational concerns and the ever-present issue of safety. FAA Administrator Garvey recalled that "every day in 2001 was like the day before Thanksgiving." Heeding calls for improved air service, Congress concentrated its efforts on a "passenger bill of rights," to improve capacity, efficiency, and customer satisfaction in the aviation system. There was no focus on terrorism.[63]

3.4 ... AND IN THE INTELLIGENCE COMMUNITY

The National Security Act of 1947 created the position of Director of Central Intelligence (DCI). Independent from the departments of Defense, State, Justice, and other policy departments, the DCI heads the U.S. intelligence community and provides intelligence to federal entities.

The sole element of the intelligence community independent from a cabinet agency is the CIA. As an independent agency, it collects, analyzes, and disseminates intelligence from all sources. The CIA's number one customer is the president of the United States, who also has the authority to direct it to conduct covert operations.[64] Although covert actions represent a very small fraction of the Agency's entire budget, these operations have at times been controversial and over time have dominated the public's perception of the CIA.

The DCI is confirmed by the Senate but is not technically a member of the president's cabinet. The director's power under federal law over the loose, confederated "intelligence community" is limited.[65] He or she states the community's priorities and coordinates development of intelligence agency budget requests for submission to Congress.

This responsibility gives many the false impression that the DCI has line authority over the heads of these agencies and has the power to shift resources within these budgets as the need arises. Neither is true. In fact, the DCI's real authority has been directly proportional to his personal closeness to the president, which has waxed and waned over the years, and to others in government, especially the secretary of defense.

Intelligence agencies under the Department of Defense account for approximately 80 percent of all U.S. spending for intelligence, including some that supports a national customer base and some that supports specific Defense Department or military service needs.[66] As they are housed in the Defense Department, these agencies are keenly attentive to the military's strategic and tactical requirements.

One of the intelligence agencies in Defense with a national customer base is the National Security Agency, which intercepts and analyzes foreign communications and breaks codes. The NSA also creates codes and ciphers to protect government information. Another is the recently renamed National Geospatial-Intelligence Agency (NGA), which provides and analyzes imagery and produces a wide array of products, including maps, navigation tools, and surveillance intelligence. A third such agency in Defense is the National Reconnaissance Office. It develops, procures, launches, and maintains in orbit information-gathering satellites that serve other government agencies.

The Defense Intelligence Agency supports the secretary of defense, Joint Chiefs of Staff, and military field commanders. It does some collection through human sources as well as some technical intelligence collection. The Army, Navy, Air Force, and Marine Corps have their own intelligence components that collect information, help them decide what weapons to acquire, and serve the tactical intelligence needs of their respective services.

In addition to those from the Department of Defense, other elements in the intelligence community include the national security parts of the FBI; the Bureau of Intelligence and Research in the State Department; the intelligence component of the Treasury Department; the Energy Department's Office of Intelligence and Counterintelligence, the former of which, through leveraging the expertise of the national laboratory system, has special competence in nuclear weapons; the Office of Intelligence of the Coast Guard; and, today, the Directorate of Intelligence Analysis and Infrastructure Protection in the Department of Homeland Security.

The National Security Agency

The National Security Agency's intercepts of terrorist communications often set off alarms elsewhere in the government. Often, too, its intercepts are conclusive elements in the analyst's jigsaw puzzle. NSA engineers build technical systems to break ciphers and to make sense of today's complex signals environment. Its analysts listen to conversations between foreigners not meant for them. They also perform "traffic analysis"—studying technical communications systems and codes as well as foreign organizational structures, including those of terrorist organizations.

Cold War adversaries used very hierarchical, familiar, and predictable military command and control methods. With globalization and the telecommunications revolution, and with loosely affiliated but networked adversaries using commercial devices and encryption, the technical impediments to signals collection grew at a geometric rate. At the same time, the end of the Cold War and the resultant cuts in national security funding forced intelligence agencies to cut systems and seek economies of scale. Modern adversaries are skilled users of communications technologies. The NSA's challenges, and its opportunities, increased exponentially in "volume, variety, and velocity."[67]

The law requires the NSA to not deliberately collect data on U.S. citizens or on persons in the United States without a warrant based on foreign intelligence requirements. Also, the NSA was supposed to let the FBI know of any indication of crime, espionage, or "terrorist enterprise" so that the FBI could obtain the appropriate warrant. Later in this story, we will learn that while the NSA had the technical capability to report on communications with suspected terrorist facilities in the Middle East, the NSA did not seek FISA Court warrants to collect communications between individuals in the United States and foreign countries, because it believed that this was an FBI role. It also did not want to be viewed as targeting persons in the United States and possibly violating laws that governed NSA's collection of foreign intelligence.[68]

An almost obsessive protection of sources and methods by the NSA, and its focus on foreign intelligence, and its avoidance of anything domestic would, as will be seen, be important elements in the story of 9/11.

Technology as an Intelligence Asset and Liability

The application of newly developed scientific technology to the mission of U.S. war fighters and national security decisionmakers is one of the great success stories of the twentieth century. It did not happen by accident. Recent wars have been waged and won decisively by brave men and women using advanced technology that was developed, authorized, and paid for by conscientious and diligent executive and legislative branch leaders many years earlier.

The challenge of technology, however, is a daunting one. It is expensive, sometimes fails, and often can create problems as well as solve them. Some of the advanced technologies that gave us insight into the closed-off territories of the Soviet Union during the Cold War are of limited use in identifying and tracking individual terrorists.

Terrorists, in turn, have benefited from this same rapid development of communication technologies. They simply could buy off the shelf and harvest the products of a $3 trillion a year telecommunications industry. They could acquire without great expense communication devices that were varied, global, instantaneous, complex, and encrypted.

The emergence of the World Wide Web has given terrorists a much easier means of acquiring information and exercising command and control over their operations. The operational leader of the 9/11 conspiracy, Mohamed Atta, went online from Hamburg, Germany, to research U.S. flight schools. Targets of intelligence collection have become more sophisticated. These changes have made surveillance and threat warning more difficult.

Despite the problems that technology creates, Americans' love affair with it leads them to also regard it as the solution. But technology produces its best results when an organization has the doctrine, structure, and incentives to exploit it. For example, even the best information technology will not improve information sharing so long as the intelligence agencies' personnel and security systems reward protecting information rather than disseminating it.

The CIA

The CIA is a descendant of the Office of Strategic Services (OSS), which President Roosevelt created early in World War II after having first thought the FBI might take that role. The father of the OSS was William J. "Wild Bill" Donovan, a Wall Street lawyer. He recruited into the OSS others like himself—well traveled, well connected, well-to-do professional men and women.[69]

An innovation of Donovan's, whose legacy remains part of U.S. intelligence today, was the establishment of a Research and Analysis Branch. There large numbers of scholars from U.S. universities pored over accounts from spies, communications intercepted by the armed forces, transcripts of radio broadcasts, and publications of all types, and prepared reports on economic, political, and social conditions in foreign theaters of operation.

At the end of World War II, to Donovan's disappointment, President Harry Truman dissolved the Office of Strategic Services. Four months later, the President directed that "all Federal foreign intelligence activities be planned, developed and coordinated so as to assure the most effective accomplishment of the intelligence mission related to the national security," under a National Intelligence Authority consisting of the secretaries of State, War, and the Navy, and a personal representative of the president. This body was to be assisted by a Central Intelligence Group, made up of persons detailed from the departments of each of the members and headed by a Director of Central Intelligence.[70]

Subsequently, President Truman agreed to the National Security Act of 1947, which, among other things, established the Central Intelligence Agency, under the Director of Central Intelligence. Lobbying by the FBI, combined with fears of creating a U.S. Gestapo,[71] led to the FBI's being assigned responsibility for internal security functions and counterespionage. The CIA was specifically accorded "no police, subpoena, or law enforcement powers or internal security functions."[72] This structure built in tensions between the CIA and the Defense Department's intelligence agencies, and between the CIA and the FBI.

Clandestine and Covert Action. With this history, the CIA brought to the era of 9/11 many attributes of an elite organization, viewing itself as serving on the nation's front lines to engage America's enemies. Officers in its Clandestine Service, under what became the Directorate of Operations, fanned out into stations abroad. Each chief of station was a very important person in the organization, given the additional title of the DCI's representative in that country. He (occasionally she) was governed by an operating directive that listed operational priorities issued by the relevant regional division of the Directorate, constrained by centrally determined allocations of resources.

Because the conduct of espionage was a high-risk activity, decisions on the clandestine targeting, recruitment, handling, and termination of secret sources and the dissemination of collected information required Washington's approval and action. But in this decentralized system, analogous in some ways to the culture of the FBI field offices in the United States, everyone in the Directorate of Operations presumed that it was the job of headquarters to support the field, rather than manage field activities.

In the 1960s, the CIA suffered exposure of its botched effort to land Cuban exiles at the Bay of Pigs. The Vietnam War brought on more criticism. A prominent feature of the Watergate era was investigations of the CIA by committees headed by Frank Church in the Senate and Otis Pike in the House. They published evidence that the CIA had secretly planned to assassinate Fidel Castro and other foreign leaders. The President had not taken plain responsibility for these judgments. CIA officials had taken most of the blame, saying they had done so in order to preserve the President's "plausible deniability."[73]

After the Watergate era, Congress established oversight committees to ensure that the CIA did not undertake covert action contrary to basic American law. Case officers in the CIA's Clandestine Service interpreted legislation, such as the Hughes-Ryan Amendment requiring that the president approve and report to Congress any covert action, as sending a message to them that covert action often leads to trouble and can severely damage one's career. Controversies surrounding Central American covert action programs in the mid-1980s led to the indictment of several senior officers of the Clandestine Service. During the 1990s, tension sometimes arose, as it did in the effort against al Qaeda, between policymakers who wanted the CIA to undertake more aggressive covert action and wary CIA leaders who counseled prudence and making sure that the legal basis and presidential authorization for their actions were undeniably clear.

The Clandestine Service felt the impact of the post–Cold War peace dividend, with cuts beginning in 1992. As the number of officers declined and overseas facilities were closed, the DCI and his managers responded to developing crises in the Balkans or in Africa by "surging," or taking officers from across the service to use on the immediate problem. In many cases the surge officers had little familiarity with the new issues. Inevitably, some parts of the world and some collection targets were not fully covered, or not covered at all. This strategy also placed great emphasis on close relations with foreign liaison services, whose help was needed to gain information that the United States itself did not have the capacity to collect.

The nadir for the Clandestine Service was in 1995, when only 25 trainees became new officers.[74] In 1998, the DCI was able to persuade the administration and the Congress to endorse a long-range rebuilding program. It takes five to seven years of training, language study, and experience to bring a recruit up to full performance.[75]

Analysis. The CIA's Directorate of Intelligence retained some of its original character of a university gone to war. Its men and women tended to judge one another by the quantity and quality of their publications (in this case, classified publications). Apart from their own peers, they looked for approval and guidance to policymakers. During the 1990s and today, particular value is attached to having a contribution included in one of the classified daily "newspapers"—the Senior Executive Intelligence Brief—or, better still, selected for inclusion in the President's Daily Brief.[76]

The CIA had been created to wage the Cold War. Its steady focus on one or two primary adversaries, decade after decade, had at least one positive effect: it created an environment in which managers and analysts could safely invest time and resources in basic research, detailed and reflective. Payoffs might not be immediate. But when they wrote their estimates, even in brief papers, they could draw on a deep base of knowledge.

When the Cold War ended, those investments could not easily be reallocated to new enemies. The cultural effects ran even deeper. In a more fluid international environment with uncertain, changing goals and interests, intelligence managers no longer felt they could afford such a patient, strategic approach to long-term accumulation of intellectual capital. A university culture with its versions of books and articles was giving way to the culture of the newsroom.

During the 1990s, the rise of round-the-clock news shows and the Internet reinforced pressure on analysts to pass along fresh reports to policymakers at an ever-faster pace, trying to add context or supplement what their customers were receiving from the media. Weaknesses in all-source and strategic analysis were highlighted by a panel, chaired by Admiral David Jeremiah, that critiqued the intelligence community's failure to foresee the nuclear weapons tests by India and Pakistan in 1998, as well as by a 1999 panel, chaired by Donald Rumsfeld, that discussed the community's limited ability to assess the ballistic missile threat to the United States. Both reports called attention to the dispersal of effort on too many priorities, the declining attention to the craft of strategic analysis, and security rules that prevented adequate sharing of information. Another Cold War craft had been an elaborate set of methods for warning against surprise attack, but that too had faded in analyzing new dangers like terrorism.[77]

Security. Another set of experiences that would affect the capacity of the CIA to cope with the new terrorism traced back to the early Cold War, when the Agency developed a concern, bordering on paranoia, about penetration by the Soviet KGB. James Jesus Angleton, who headed counterintelligence in the CIA until the early 1970s, became obsessed with the belief that the Agency harbored one or more Soviet "moles." Although the pendulum swung back after Angleton's forced retirement, it did not go very far. Instances of actual Soviet penetration kept apprehensions high.[78] Then, in the early 1990s, came the Aldrich Ames espionage case, which intensely embarrassed the CIA. Though obviously unreliable, Ames had been protected and promoted by fellow officers while he paid his bills by selling to the Soviet Union the names of U.S. operatives and agents, a number of whom died as a result.

The concern about security vastly complicated information sharing. Information was compartmented in order to protect it against exposure to skilled and technologically sophisticated adversaries. There were therefore numerous restrictions on handling information and a deep suspicion about sending information over newfangled electronic systems, like email, to other agencies of the U.S. government.[79]

Security concerns also increased the difficulty of recruiting officers qualified for counterterrorism. Very few American colleges or universities offered programs in Middle Eastern languages or Islamic studies. The total number of undergraduate degrees granted in Arabic in all U.S. colleges and universities in 2002 was six.[80] Many who had traveled much outside the United States could expect a very long wait for initial clearance. Anyone who was foreign-born or had numerous relatives abroad was well-advised not even to apply. With budgets for the CIA shrinking after the end of the Cold War, it was not surprising that, with some notable exceptions, new hires in the Clandestine Service tended to have qualifications similar to those of serving officers: that is, they were suited for traditional agent recruitment or for exploiting liaison relationships with foreign services but were not equipped to seek or use assets inside the terrorist network.

Early Counterterrorism Efforts

In the 1970s and 1980s, terrorism had been tied to regional conflicts, mainly in the Middle East. The majority of terrorist groups either were sponsored by governments or, like the Palestine Liberation Organization, were militants trying to create governments.

In the mid-1980s, on the basis of a report from a task force headed by Vice President George Bush and after terrorist attacks at airports in Rome and Athens, the DCI created a Counterterrorist Center to unify activities across the Directorate of Operations and the Directorate of Intelligence. The Counterterrorist Center had representation from the FBI and other agencies. In the formal table of organization it reported to the DCI, but in fact most of the Center's chiefs belonged to the Clandestine Service and usually looked for guidance to the head of the Directorate of Operations.[81]

The Center stimulated and coordinated collection of information by CIA stations, compiled the results, and passed selected reports to appropriate stations, the Directorate of Intelligence analysts, other parts of the intelligence community, or to policymakers. The Center protected its bureaucratic turf. The Director of Central Intelligence had once had a national intelligence officer for terrorism to coordinate analysis; that office was abolished in the late 1980s and its duties absorbed in part by the Counterterrorist Center. Though analysts assigned to the Center produced a large number of papers, the focus was support to operations. A CIA inspector general's report in 1994 criticized the Center's capacity to provide warning of terrorist attacks.[82]

Subsequent chapters will raise the issue of whether, despite tremendous talent, energy, and dedication, the intelligence community failed to do enough in coping with the challenge from Bin Ladin and al Qaeda. Confronted with such questions, managers in the intelligence community often responded that they had meager resources with which to work.[83]

Cuts in national security expenditures at the end of the Cold War led to budget cuts in the national foreign intelligence program from fiscal years 1990 to 1996 and essentially flat budgets from fiscal years 1996 to 2000 (except for the so-called Gingrich supplemental to the FY1999 budget and two later, smaller supplementals). These cuts compounded the difficulties of the intelligence agencies. Policymakers were asking them to move into the digitized future to fight against computer-to-computer communications and modern communication systems, while maintaining capability against older systems, such as high-frequency radios and ultra-high- and very-high-frequency (line of sight) systems that work like old-style television antennas. Also, demand for imagery increased dramatically following the success of the 1991 Gulf War. Both these developments, in turn, placed a premium on planning the next generation of satellite systems, the cost of which put great pressure on the rest of the intelligence budget. As a result, intelligence agencies experienced staff reductions, affecting both operators and analysts.[84]

Yet at least for the CIA, part of the burden in tackling terrorism arose from the background we have described: an organization capable of attracting extraordinarily motivated people but institutionally averse to risk, with its capacity for covert action atrophied, predisposed to restrict the distribution of information, having difficulty assimilating new types of personnel, and accustomed to presenting descriptive reportage of the latest intelligence. The CIA, to put it another way, needed significant change in order to get maximum effect in counterterrorism. President Clinton appointed George Tenet as DCI in 1997, and by all accounts terrorism was a priority for him. But Tenet's own assessment, when questioned by the Commission, was that in 2004, the CIA's clandestine service was still at least five years away from being fully ready to play its counterterrorism role.[85] And while Tenet was clearly the leader of the CIA, the intelligence community's confederated structure left open the question of who really was in charge of the entire U.S. intelligence effort.

3.5 ... AND IN THE STATE DEPARTMENT AND THE DEFENSE DEPARTMENT

The State Department

The Commission asked Deputy Secretary of State Richard Armitage in 2004 why the State Department had so long pursued what seemed, and ultimately proved, to be a hopeless effort to persuade the Taliban regime in Afghanistan to deport Bin Ladin. Armitage replied: "We do what the State Department does, we don't go out and fly bombers, we don't do things like that[;] ... we do *our* part in these things."[86]

Fifty years earlier, the person in Armitage's position would not have spoken of the Department of State as having such a limited role. Until the late 1950s, the department dominated the processes of advising the president and Congress on U.S. relations with the rest of the world. The National Security Council was created in 1947 largely as a result of lobbying from the Pentagon for a forum where the military could object if they thought the State Department was setting national objectives that the United States did not have the wherewithal to pursue.

The State Department retained primacy until the 1960s, when the Kennedy and Johnson administrations turned instead to Robert McNamara's Defense Department, where a mini–state department was created to analyze foreign policy issues. President Richard Nixon then concentrated policy planning and policy coordination in a powerful National Security Council staff, overseen by Henry Kissinger.

In later years, individual secretaries of state were important figures, but the department's role continued to erode. State came into the 1990s overmatched by the resources of other departments and with little support for its budget either in the Congress or in the president's Office of Management and Budget.

Like the FBI and the CIA's Directorate of Operations, the State Department had a tradition of emphasizing service in the field over service in Washington. Even ambassadors, however, often found host governments not only making connections with the U.S. government through their own missions in Washington, but working through the CIA station or a Defense attaché. Increasingly, the embassies themselves were overshadowed by powerful regional commanders in chief reporting to the Pentagon.[87]

Counterterrorism

In the 1960s and 1970s, the State Department managed counterterrorism policy. It was the official channel for communication with the governments presumed to be behind the terrorists. Moreover, since terrorist incidents of this period usually ended in negotiations, an ambassador or other embassy official was the logical person to represent U.S. interests.

Keeping U.S. diplomatic efforts against terrorism coherent was a recurring challenge. In 1976, at the direction of Congress, the department elevated its coordinator for combating terrorism to the rank equivalent to an assistant secretary of state. As an "ambassador at large," this official sought to increase the visibility of counterterrorism matters within the department and to help integrate U.S. policy implementation among government agencies. The prolonged crisis of 1979–1981, when 53 Americans were held hostage at the U.S. embassy in Tehran, ended the State Department leadership in counterterrorism. President Carter's assertive national security advisor, Zbigniew Brzezinski, took charge, and the coordination function remained thereafter in the White House.

President Reagan's second secretary of state, George Shultz, advocated active U.S. efforts to combat terrorism, often recommending the use of military force. Secretary of Defense Caspar Weinberger opposed Shultz, who made little headway against Weinberger, or even within his own department. Though Shultz elevated the status and visibility of counterterrorism coordination by appointing as coordinator first L. Paul Bremer and then Robert Oakley, both senior career ambassadors of high standing in the Foreign Service, the department continued to be dominated by regional bureaus for which terrorism was not a first-order concern.

Secretaries of state after Shultz took less personal interest in the problem. Only congressional opposition prevented President Clinton's first secretary of state, Warren Christopher, from merging terrorism into a new bureau that would have also dealt with narcotics and crime. The coordinator under Secretary Madeleine Albright told the Commission that his job was seen as a minor one within the department.[88] Although the description of his status has been disputed, and Secretary Albright strongly supported the August 1998 strikes against Bin Ladin, the role played by the Department of State in counterterrorism was often cautionary before 9/11. This was a reflection of the reality that counterterrorism priorities nested within broader foreign policy aims of the U.S. government.

State Department consular officers around the world, it should not be forgotten, were constantly challenged by the problem of terrorism, for they handled visas for travel to the United States. After it was discovered that Abdel Rahman, the Blind Sheikh, had come and gone almost at will, State initiated significant reforms to its watchlist and visa-processing policies. In 1993, Congress passed legislation allowing State to retain visa-processing fees for border security; those fees were then used by the department to fully automate the terrorist watchlist. By the late 1990s, State had created a worldwide, real-time electronic database of visa, law enforcement, and watchlist information, the core of the post-9/11 border screening systems. Still, as will be seen later, the system had many holes.[89]

The Department of Defense
The Department of Defense is the behemoth among federal agencies. With an annual budget larger than the gross domestic product of Russia, it is an empire. The Defense Department is part civilian, part military. The civilian secretary of defense has ultimate control, under the president. Among the uniformed military, the top official is the chairman of the Joint Chiefs of Staff, who is supported by a Joint Staff divided into standard military staff compartments—J-2 (intelligence), J-3 (operations), and so on.

Because of the necessary and demanding focus on the differing mission of each service, and their long and proud traditions, the Army, Navy, Air Force, and Marine Corps have often fought ferociously over roles and missions in war fighting and over budgets and posts of leadership. Two developments diminished this competition.

The first was the passage by Congress in 1986 of the Goldwater-Nichols

Act, which, among other things, mandated that promotion to high rank required some period of duty with a different service or with a joint (i.e., multiservice) command. This had strong and immediate effects, loosening the loyalties of senior officers to their separate services and causing them to think more broadly about the military establishment as a whole.[90] However, it also may have lessened the diversity of military advice and options presented to the president. The Goldwater-Nichols example is seen by some as having lessons applicable to lessening competition and increasing cooperation in other parts of the federal bureaucracy, particularly the law enforcement and intelligence communities.

The second, related development was a significant transfer of planning and command responsibilities from the service chiefs and their staffs to the joint and unified commands outside of Washington, especially those for Strategic Forces and for four regions: Europe, the Pacific, the Center, and the South. Posts in these commands became prized assignments for ambitious officers, and the voices of their five commanders in chief became as influential as those of the service chiefs.

Counterterrorism

The Pentagon first became concerned about terrorism as a result of hostage taking in the 1970s. In June 1976, Palestinian terrorists seized an Air France plane and landed it at Entebbe in Uganda, holding 105 Israelis and other Jews as hostages. A special Israeli commando force stormed the plane, killed all the terrorists, and rescued all but one of the hostages. In October 1977, a West German special force dealt similarly with a Lufthansa plane sitting on a tarmac in Mogadishu: every terrorist was killed, and every hostage brought back safely. The White House, members of Congress, and the news media asked the Pentagon whether the United States was prepared for similar action. The answer was no. The Army immediately set about creating the Delta Force, one of whose missions was hostage rescue.

The first test for the new force did not go well. It came in April 1980 during the Iranian hostage crisis, when Navy helicopters with Marine pilots flew to a site known as Desert One, some 200 miles southeast of Tehran, to rendezvous with Air Force planes carrying Delta Force commandos and fresh fuel. Mild sandstorms disabled three of the helicopters, and the commander ordered the mission aborted. But foul-ups on the ground resulted in the loss of eight aircraft, five airmen, and three marines. Remembered as "Desert One," this failure remained vivid for members of the armed forces. It also contributed to the later Goldwater-Nichols reforms.

In 1983 came Hezbollah's massacre of the Marines in Beirut. President Reagan quickly withdrew U.S. forces from Lebanon—a reversal later routinely cited by jihadists as evidence of U.S. weakness. A detailed investigation produced a list of new procedures that would become customary for forces deployed abroad. They involved a number of defensive measures, including caution not only about strange cars and trucks but also about unknown aircraft overhead. "Force protection" became a significant claim on the time and resources of the Department of Defense.

A decade later, the military establishment had another experience that evoked both Desert One and the withdrawal from Beirut. The first President Bush had authorized the use of U.S. military forces to ensure humanitarian relief in war-torn Somalia. Tribal factions interfered with the supply missions. By the autumn of 1993, U.S. commanders concluded that the main source of trouble was a warlord, Mohammed Farrah Aidid. An Army special force launched a raid on Mogadishu to capture him. In the course of a long night, two Black Hawk helicopters were shot down, 73 Americans were wounded, 18 were killed, and the world's television screens showed images of an American corpse dragged through the streets by exultant Somalis. Under pressure from Congress, President Clinton soon ordered the withdrawal of U.S. forces. "Black Hawk down" joined "Desert One" as a symbol among Americans in uniform, code phrases used to evoke the risks of daring exploits without maximum preparation, overwhelming force, and a well-defined mission.

In 1995–1996, the Defense Department began to invest effort in planning how to handle the possibility of a domestic terrorist incident involving weapons of mass destruction (WMD). The idea of a domestic command for homeland defense began to be discussed in 1997, and in 1999 the Joint Chiefs developed a concept for the establishment of a domestic Unified Command. Congress killed the idea. Instead, the Department established the Joint Forces Command, located at Norfolk, Virginia, making it responsible for military response to domestic emergencies, both natural and man-made.[91]

Pursuant to the Nunn-Lugar-Domenici Domestic Preparedness Program, the Defense Department began in 1997 to train first responders in 120 of the nation's largest cities. As a key part of its efforts, Defense created National Guard WMD Civil Support Teams to respond in the event of a WMD terrorist incident. A total of 32 such National Guard teams were authorized by fiscal year 2001. Under the command of state governors, they provided support to civilian agencies to assess the nature of the attack, offer medical and technical advice, and coordinate state and local responses.[92]

The Department of Defense, like the Department of State, had a coordinator who represented the department on the interagency committee concerned with counterterrorism. By the end of President Clinton's first term, this official had become the assistant secretary of defense for special operations and low-intensity conflict.[93]

The experience of the 1980s had suggested to the military establishment that if it were to have a role in counterterrorism, it would be a traditional military role—to act against state sponsors of terrorism. And the military had what seemed an excellent example of how to do it. In 1986, a bomb went off at a disco in Berlin, killing two American soldiers. Intelligence clearly linked the bombing to Libya's Colonel Muammar Qadhafi. President Reagan ordered air strikes against Libya. The operation was not cost free: the United States lost two planes. Evidence accumulated later, including the 1988 bombing of Pan Am 103, clearly showed that the operation did not curb Qadhafi's interest in terrorism. However, it was seen at the time as a success. The lesson then taken from Libya was that terrorism could be stopped by the use of U.S. air power that inflicted pain on the authors or sponsors of terrorist acts.

This lesson was applied, using Tomahawk missiles, early in the Clinton administration. George H. W. Bush was scheduled to visit Kuwait to be honored for his rescue of that country in the Gulf War of 1991. Kuwaiti security services warned Washington that Iraqi agents were planning to assassinate the former president. President Clinton not only ordered precautions to protect Bush but asked about options for a reprisal against Iraq. The Pentagon proposed 12 targets for Tomahawk missiles. Debate in the White House and at the CIA about possible collateral damage pared the list down to three, then to one—Iraqi intelligence headquarters in central Baghdad. The attack was made at night, to minimize civilian casualties. Twenty-three missiles were fired. Other than one civilian casualty, the operation seemed completely successful: the intelligence headquarters was demolished. No further intelligence came in about terrorist acts planned by Iraq.[94]

The 1986 attack in Libya and the 1993 attack on Iraq symbolized for the military establishment effective use of military power for counterterrorism—limited retaliation with air power, aimed at deterrence. What remained was the hard question of how deterrence could be effective when the adversary was a loose transnational network.

3.6 ... AND IN THE WHITE HOUSE

Because coping with terrorism was not (and is not) the sole province of any component of the U.S. government, some coordinating mechanism is necessary. When terrorism was not a prominent issue, the State Department could perform this role. When the Iranian hostage crisis developed, this procedure went by the board: National Security Advisor Zbigniew Brzezinski took charge of crisis management.

The Reagan administration continued and formalized the practice of having presidential staff coordinate counterterrorism. After the killing of the marines in Beirut, President Reagan signed National Security Directive 138, calling for a "shift ... from passive to active defense measures" and reprogramming or adding new resources to effect the shift. It directed the State Department "to intensify efforts to achieve cooperation of other governments" and the CIA to "intensify use of liaison and other intelligence capabilities and also to develop plans and capability to preempt groups and individuals planning strikes against U.S. interests."[95]

Speaking to the American Bar Association in July 1985, the President characterized terrorism as "an act of war" and declared: "There can be no place on earth left where it is safe for these monsters to rest, to train, or practice their cruel and deadly skills. We must act together, or unilaterally, if necessary to ensure that terrorists have no sanctuary—anywhere."[96] The air strikes against Libya were one manifestation of this strategy.

Through most of President Reagan's second term, the coordination of counterterrorism was overseen by a high-level interagency committee chaired by the deputy national security adviser. But the Reagan administration closed with a major scandal that cast a cloud over the notion that the White House should guide counterterrorism.

President Reagan was concerned because Hezbollah was taking Americans hostage and periodically killing them. He was also constrained by a bill he signed into law that made it illegal to ship military aid to anticommunist Contra guerrillas in Nicaragua, whom he strongly supported. His national security adviser, Robert McFarlane, and McFarlane's deputy, Admiral John Poindexter, thought the hostage problem might be solved and the U.S. position in the Middle East improved if the United States quietly negotiated with Iran about exchanging hostages for modest quantities of arms. Shultz and Weinberger, united for once, opposed McFarlane and Poindexter.

A staffer for McFarlane and Poindexter, Marine Lieutenant Colonel Oliver North, developed a scheme to trade U.S. arms for hostages and divert the proceeds to the Contras to get around U.S. law. He may have had encouragement from Director of Central Intelligence William Casey.[97]

When the facts were revealed in 1986 and 1987, it appeared to be the 1970s all over again: a massive abuse of covert action. Now, instead of stories about poisoned cigars and Mafia hit men, Americans heard testimony about a secret visit to Tehran by McFarlane, using an assumed name and bearing a chocolate cake decorated with icing depicting a key. An investigation by a special counsel resulted in the indictment of McFarlane, Poindexter, North, and ten others, including several high-ranking officers from the CIA's Clandestine Service. The investigations spotlighted the importance of accountability and official responsibility for faithful execution of laws. For the story of 9/11, the significance of the Iran-Contra affair was that it made parts of the bureaucracy reflexively skeptical about any operating directive from the White House.[98]

As the national security advisor's function expanded, the procedures and structure of the advisor's staff, conventionally called the National Security Council staff, became more formal. The advisor developed recommendations for presidential directives, differently labeled by each president. For President Clinton, they were to be Presidential Decision Directives; for President George W. Bush, National Security Policy Directives. These documents and many others requiring approval by the president worked their way through interagency committees usually composed of departmental representatives at the assistant secretary level or just below it. The NSC staff had senior directors who would sit on these interagency committees, often as chair, to facilitate agreement and to represent the wider interests of the national security advisor.

When President Clinton took office, he decided right away to coordinate counterterrorism from the White House. On January 25, 1993, Mir Amal Kansi, an Islamic extremist from Pakistan, shot and killed two CIA employees at the main highway entrance to CIA headquarters in Virginia. (Kansi drove away and was captured abroad much later.) Only a month afterward came the World Trade Center bombing and, a few weeks after that, the Iraqi plot against former President Bush.

President Clinton's first national security advisor, Anthony Lake, had retained from the Bush administration the staffer who dealt with crime, narcotics, and terrorism (a portfolio often known as "drugs and thugs"), the veteran civil servant Richard Clarke. President Clinton and Lake turned to Clarke to do the staff work for them in coordinating counterterrorism. Before long, he would chair a midlevel interagency committee eventually titled the Counterterrorism Security Group (CSG). We will later tell of Clarke's evolution as adviser on and, in time, manager of the U.S. counterterrorist effort.

When explaining the missile strike against Iraq provoked by the plot to kill President Bush, President Clinton stated: "From the first days of our Revolution, America's security has depended on the clarity of the message: Don't tread on us. A firm and commensurate response was essential to protect our sovereignty, to send a message to those who engage in state-sponsored terrorism, to deter further violence against our people, and to affirm the expectation of civilized behavior among nations."[99]

In his State of the Union message in January 1995, President Clinton promised "comprehensive legislation to strengthen our hand in combating terrorists, whether they strike at home or abroad." In February, he sent Congress proposals to extend federal criminal jurisdiction, to make it easier to deport terrorists, and to act against terrorist fund-raising. In early May, he submitted a bundle of strong amendments. The interval had seen the news from Tokyo in March that a doomsday cult, Aum Shinrikyo, had released sarin nerve gas in a subway, killing 12 and injuring thousands. The sect had extensive properties and laboratories in Japan and offices worldwide, including one in New York. Neither the FBI nor the CIA had ever heard of it. In April had come the bombing of the Murrah federal building in Oklahoma City; immediate suspicions that it had been the work of Islamists turned out to be wrong, and the bombers proved to be American antigovernment extremists named Timothy McVeigh and Terry Nichols. President Clinton proposed to amend his earlier proposals by increasing wiretap and electronic surveillance authority for the FBI, requiring that explosives carry traceable taggants, and providing substantial new money not only for the FBI and CIA but also for local police.[100]

President Clinton issued a classified directive in June 1995, Presidential Decision Directive 39, which said that the United States should "deter, defeat and respond vigorously to all terrorist attacks on our territory and against our citizens." The directive called terrorism both a matter of national security and a crime, and it assigned responsibilities to various agencies. Alarmed by the incident in Tokyo, President Clinton made it the very highest priority for his own staff and for all agencies to prepare to detect and respond to terrorism that involved chemical, biological, or nuclear weapons.[101]

During 1995 and 1996, President Clinton devoted considerable time to seeking cooperation from other nations in denying sanctuary to terrorists. He proposed significantly larger budgets for the FBI, with much of the increase designated for counterterrorism. For the CIA, he essentially stopped cutting allocations and supported requests for supplemental funds for counterterrorism.[102]

When announcing his new national security team after being reelected in 1996, President Clinton mentioned terrorism first in a list of several challenges facing the country.[103] In 1998, after Bin Ladin's fatwa and other alarms, President Clinton accepted a proposal from his national security advisor, Samuel "Sandy" Berger, and gave Clarke a new position as national coordinator for security, infrastructure protection, and counterterrorism. He issued two Presidential Decision Directives, numbers 62 and 63, that built on the assignments to agencies that had been made in Presidential Decision Directive 39; laid out ten program areas for counterterrorism; and enhanced, at least on paper, Clarke's authority to police these assignments. Because of concerns especially on the part of Attorney General Reno, this new authority was defined in precise and limiting language. Clarke was only to "provide advice" regarding budgets and to "coordinate the development of interagency agreed guidelines" for action.[104]

Clarke also was awarded a seat on the cabinet-level Principals Committee when it met on his issues—a highly unusual step for a White House staffer. His interagency body, the CSG, ordinarily reported to the Deputies Committee of subcabinet officials, unless Berger asked them to report directly to the principals. The complementary directive, number 63, defined the elements of the nation's critical infrastructure and considered ways to protect it. Taken together, the two directives basically left the Justice Department and the FBI in charge at home and left terrorism abroad to the CIA, the State Department, and other agencies, under Clarke's and Berger's coordinating hands.

Explaining the new arrangement and his concerns in another commencement speech, this time at the Naval Academy, in May 1998, the President said:

> First, we will use our new integrated approach to intensify the fight against all forms of terrorism: to capture terrorists, no matter where they hide; to work with other nations to eliminate terrorist sanctuaries overseas; to respond rapidly and effectively to protect Americans from terrorism at

home and abroad. Second, we will launch a comprehensive plan to detect, deter, and defend against attacks on our critical infrastructures, our power systems, water supplies, police, fire, and medical services, air traffic control, financial services, telephone systems, and computer networks. . . . Third, we will undertake a concerted effort to prevent the spread and use of biological weapons and to protect our people in the event these terrible weapons are ever unleashed by a rogue state, a terrorist group, or an international criminal organization. . . . Finally, we must do more to protect our civilian population from biological weapons.[105]

Clearly, the President's concern about terrorism had steadily risen. That heightened worry would become even more obvious early in 1999, when he addressed the National Academy of Sciences and presented his most somber account yet of what could happen if the United States were hit, unprepared, by terrorists wielding either weapons of mass destruction or potent cyberweapons.

3.7 . . . AND IN THE CONGRESS

Since the beginning of the Republic, few debates have been as hotly contested as the one over executive versus legislative powers. At the Constitutional Convention, the founders sought to create a strong executive but check its powers. They left those powers sufficiently ambiguous so that room was left for Congress and the president to struggle over the direction of the nation's security and foreign policies.

The most serious question has centered on whether or not the president needs congressional authorization to wage war. The current status of that debate seems to have settled into a recognition that a president can deploy military forces for small and limited operations, but needs at least congressional support if not explicit authorization for large and more open-ended military operations.

This calculus becomes important in this story as both President Clinton and President Bush chose not to seek a declaration of war on Bin Ladin after he had declared and begun to wage war on us, a declaration that they did not acknowledge publicly. Not until after 9/11 was a congressional authorization sought.

The most substantial change in national security oversight in Congress took place following World War II. The Congressional Reorganization Act of 1946 created the modern Armed Services committees that have become so powerful today. One especially noteworthy innovation was the creation of the Joint House-Senate Atomic Energy Committee, which is credited by many with the development of our nuclear deterrent capability and was also criticized for wielding too much power relative to the executive branch.

Ironically, this committee was eliminated in the 1970s as Congress was undertaking the next most important reform of oversight in response to the Church and Pike investigations into abuses of power. In 1977, the House and Senate created select committees to exercise oversight of the executive branch's conduct of intelligence operations.

The Intelligence Committees

The House and Senate select committees on intelligence share some important characteristics. They have limited authorities. They do not have exclusive authority over intelligence agencies. Appropriations are ultimately determined by the Appropriations committees. The Armed Services committees exercise jurisdiction over the intelligence agencies within the Department of Defense (and, in the case of the Senate, over the Central Intelligence Agency). One consequence is that the rise and fall of intelligence budgets are tied directly to trends in defense spending.

The president is required by law to ensure the congressional Intelligence committees are kept fully and currently informed of the intelligence activities of the United States. The committees allow the CIA to some extent to withhold information in order to protect sources, methods, and operations. The CIA must bring presidentially authorized covert action Findings and Memoranda of Notification to the Intelligence committees, and it must detail its failures. The committees conduct their most important work in closed hearings or briefings in which security over classified material can be maintained.

Members of the Intelligence committees serve for a limited time, a restriction imposed by each chamber. Many members believe these limits prevent committee members from developing the necessary expertise to conduct effective oversight.

Secrecy, while necessary, can also harm oversight. The overall budget of the intelligence community is classified, as are most of its activities. Thus, the Intelligence committees cannot take advantage of democracy's best oversight mechanism: public disclosure. This makes them significantly different from other congressional oversight committees, which are often spurred into action by the work of investigative journalists and watchdog organizations.

Adjusting to the Post–Cold War Era

The unexpected and rapid end of the Cold War in 1991 created trauma in the foreign policy and national security community both in and out of government. While some criticized the intelligence community for failing to forecast the collapse of the Soviet Union (and used this argument to propose drastic cuts in intelligence agencies), most recognized that the good news of being relieved of the substantial burden of maintaining a security structure to meet the Soviet challenge was accompanied by the bad news of increased insecurity. In many directions, the community faced threats and intelligence challenges that it was largely unprepared to meet.

So did the intelligence oversight committees. New digitized technologies, and the demand for imagery and continued capability against older systems, meant the need to spend more on satellite systems at the expense of human efforts. In addition, denial and deception became more effective as targets learned from public sources what our intelligence agencies were doing. There were comprehensive reform proposals of the intelligence community, such as those offered by Senators Boren and McCurdy. That said, Congress still took too little action to address institutional weaknesses.[106]

With the Cold War over, and the intelligence community roiled by the Ames spy scandal, a presidential commission chaired first by former secretary of defense Les Aspin and later by former secretary of defense Harold Brown examined the intelligence community's future. After it issued recommendations addressing the DCI's lack of personnel and budget authority over the intelligence community, the Intelligence committees in 1996 introduced implementing legislation to remedy these problems.

The Department of Defense and its congressional authorizing committees rose in opposition to the proposed changes. The President and DCI did not actively support these changes. Relatively small changes made in 1996 gave the DCI consultative authority and created a new deputy for management and assistant DCIs for collection and analysis. These reforms occurred only after the Senate Select Committee on Intelligence took the unprecedented step of threatening to bring down the defense authorization bill. Indeed, rather than increasing the DCI's authorities over national intelligence, the 1990s witnessed movement in the opposite direction through, for example, the transfer of the CIA's imaging analysis capability to the new imagery and mapping agency created within the Department of Defense.

Congress Adjusts

Congress as a whole, like the executive branch, adjusted slowly to the rise of transnational terrorism as a threat to national security. In particular, the growing threat and capabilities of Bin Ladin were not understood in Congress. As the most representative branch of the federal government, Congress closely tracks trends in what public opinion and the electorate identify as key issues. In the years before September 11, terrorism seldom registered as important. To the extent that terrorism did break through and engage the attention of the Congress as a whole, it would briefly command attention after a specific incident, and then return to a lower rung on the public policy agenda.

Several points about Congress are worth noting. First, Congress always has a strong orientation toward domestic affairs. It usually takes on foreign policy and national security issues after threats are identified and articulated by the administration. In the absence of such a detailed—and repeated—articulation, national security tends not to rise very high on the list of congressional priorities. Presidents are selective in their use of political capital for international issues.

In the decade before 9/11, presidential discussion of and congressional and public attention to foreign affairs and national security were dominated by other issues—among them, Haiti, Bosnia, Russia, China, Somalia, Kosovo, NATO enlargement, the Middle East peace process, missile defense, and globalization. Terrorism infrequently took center stage; and when it did, the context was often terrorists' tactics—a chemical, biological, nuclear, or computer threat—not terrorist organizations.[107]

Second, Congress tends to follow the overall lead of the president on budget issues with respect to national security matters. There are often sharp arguments about individual programs and internal priorities, but by and large the overall funding authorized and appropriated by the Congress comes out close to the president's request. This tendency was certainly illustrated by the downward trends in spending on defense, intelligence, and foreign affairs in the first part of the 1990s. The White House, to be sure, read the political signals coming from Capitol Hill, but the Congress largely acceded to the executive branch's funding requests. In the second half of the decade, Congress appropriated some 98 percent of what the administration requested for intelligence programs. Apart from the Gingrich supplemental of $1.5 billion for overall intelligence programs in fiscal year 1999, the key decisions on overall allocation of resources for national security issues in the decade before 9/11—including counterterrorism funding—were made in the president's Office of Management and Budget.[108]

Third, Congress did not reorganize itself after the end of the Cold War to address new threats. Recommendations by the Joint Committee on the Organization of Congress were implemented, in part, in the House of Representatives after the 1994 elections, but there was no reorganization of national security functions. The Senate undertook no appreciable changes. Traditional issues—foreign policy, defense, intelligence—continued to be handled by committees whose structure remained largely unaltered, while issues such as transnational terrorism fell between the cracks. Terrorism came under the jurisdiction of at least 14 different committees in the House alone, and budget and oversight functions in the House and Senate concerning terrorism were also splintered badly among committees. Little effort was made to consider an integrated policy toward terrorism, which might range from identifying the threat to addressing vulnerabilities in critical infrastructure; and the piecemeal approach in the Congress contributed to the problems of the executive branch in formulating such a policy.[109]

Fourth, the oversight function of Congress has diminished over time. In recent years, traditional review of the administration of programs and the implementation of laws has been replaced by "a focus on personal investigations, possible scandals, and issues designed to generate media attention." The unglamorous but essential work of oversight has been neglected, and few members past or present believe it is performed well. DCI Tenet told us: "We ran from threat to threat to threat.... [T]here was not a system in place to say,'You got to go back and do this and this and this.'" Not just the DCI but the entire executive branch needed help from Congress in addressing the questions of counterterrorism strategy and policy, looking past day-to-day concerns. Members of Congress, however, also found their time spent on such everyday matters, or in looking back to investigate mistakes, and often missed the big questions—as did the executive branch. Staff tended as well to focus on parochial considerations, seeking to add or cut funding for individual (often small) programs, instead of emphasizing comprehensive oversight projects.[110]

Fifth, on certain issues, other priorities pointed Congress in a direction that was unhelpful in meeting the threats that were emerging in the months leading up to 9/11. Committees with oversight responsibility for aviation focused overwhelmingly on airport congestion and the economic health of the airlines, not aviation security. Committees with responsibility for the INS focused on the Southwest border, not on terrorists. Justice Department officials told us that committees with responsibility for the FBI tightly restricted appropriations for improvements in information technology, in part because of concerns about the FBI's ability to manage such projects. Committees responsible for South Asia spent the decade of the 1990s imposing sanctions on Pakistan, leaving presidents with little leverage to alter Pakistan's policies before 9/11. Committees with responsibility for the Defense Department paid little heed to developing military responses to terrorism and stymied intelligence reform. All committees found themselves swamped in the minutiae of the budget process, with little time for consideration of longer-term questions, or what many members past and present told us was the proper conduct of oversight.[111]

Each of these trends contributed to what can only be described as Congress's slowness and inadequacy in treating the issue of terrorism in the years before 9/11. The legislative branch adjusted little and did not restructure itself to address changing threats.[112] Its attention to terrorism was episodic and splintered across several committees. Congress gave little guidance to executive branch agencies, did not reform them in any significant way, and did not systematically perform oversight to identify, address, and attempt to resolve the many problems in national security and domestic agencies that became apparent in the aftermath of 9/11.

Although individual representatives and senators took significant steps, the overall level of attention in the Congress to the terrorist threat was low. We examined the number of hearings on terrorism from January 1998 to September 2001. The Senate Armed Services Committee held nine—four related to the attack on the USS *Cole*. The House Armed Services Committee also held nine, six of them by a special oversight panel on terrorism. The Senate Foreign Relations Committee and its House counterpart both held four. The Senate Select Committee on Intelligence, in addition to its annual worldwide threat hearing, held eight; its House counterpart held perhaps two exclusively devoted to counterterrorism, plus the briefings by its terrorist working group. The Senate and House intelligence panels did not raise public and congressional attention on Bin Ladin and al Qaeda prior to the joint inquiry into the attacks of September 11, perhaps in part because of the classified nature of their work. Yet in the context of committees that each hold scores of hearings every year on issues in their jurisdiction, this list is not impressive. Terrorism was a second- or third-order priority within the committees of Congress responsible for national security.[113]

In fact, Congress had a distinct tendency to push questions of emerging national security threats off its own plate, leaving them for others to consider. Congress asked outside commissions to do the work that arguably was at the heart of its own oversight responsibilities.[114] Beginning in 1999, the reports of these commissions made scores of recommendations to address terrorism and homeland security but drew little attention from Congress. Most of their impact came after 9/11.

4

RESPONSES TO AL QAEDA'S INITIAL ASSAULTS

4.1 BEFORE THE BOMBINGS IN KENYA AND TANZANIA

Although the 1995 National Intelligence Estimate had warned of a new type of terrorism, many officials continued to think of terrorists as agents of states (Saudi Hezbollah acting for Iran against Khobar Towers) or as domestic criminals (Timothy McVeigh in Oklahoma City). As we pointed out in chapter 3, the White House is not a natural locus for program management. Hence, government efforts to cope with terrorism were essentially the work of individual agencies.

President Bill Clinton's counterterrorism Presidential Decision Directives in 1995 (no. 39) and May 1998 (no. 62) reiterated that terrorism was a national security problem, not just a law enforcement issue. They reinforced the authority of the National Security Council (NSC) to coordinate domestic as well as foreign counterterrorism efforts, through Richard Clarke and his interagency Counterterrorism Security Group (CSG). Spotlighting new concerns about unconventional attacks, these directives assigned tasks to lead agencies but did not differentiate types of terrorist threats. Thus, while Clarke might prod or push agencies to act, what actually happened was usually decided at the State Department, the Pentagon, the CIA, or the Justice Department. The efforts of these agencies were sometimes energetic and sometimes effective. Terrorist plots were disrupted and individual terrorists were captured. But the United States did not, before 9/11, adopt as a clear strategic objective the elimination of al Qaeda.

Early Efforts against Bin Ladin
Until 1996, hardly anyone in the U.S. government understood that Usama Bin Ladin was an inspirer and organizer of the new terrorism. In 1993, the CIA noted that he had paid for the training of some Egyptian terrorists in Sudan. The State Department detected his money in aid to the Yemeni terrorists who

set a bomb in an attempt to kill U.S. troops in Aden in 1992. State Department sources even saw suspicious links with Omar Abdel Rahman, the "Blind Sheikh" in the New York area, commenting that Bin Ladin seemed "committed to financing 'Jihads' against 'anti Islamic' regimes worldwide." After the department designated Sudan a state sponsor of terrorism in 1993, it put Bin Ladin on its TIPOFF watchlist, a move that might have prevented his getting a visa had he tried to enter the United States. As late as 1997, however, even the CIA's Counterterrorist Center continued to describe him as an "extremist financier."[1]

In 1996, the CIA set up a special unit of a dozen officers to analyze intelligence on and plan operations against Bin Ladin. David Cohen, the head of the CIA's Directorate of Operations, wanted to test the idea of having a "virtual station"—a station based at headquarters but collecting and operating against a subject much as stations in the field focus on a country. Taking his cue from National Security Advisor Anthony Lake, who expressed special interest in terrorist finance, Cohen formed his virtual station as a terrorist financial links unit. He had trouble getting any Directorate of Operations officer to run it; he finally recruited a former analyst who was then running the Islamic Extremist Branch of the Counterterrorist Center. This officer, who was especially knowledgeable about Afghanistan, had noticed a recent stream of reports about Bin Ladin and something called al Qaeda, and suggested to Cohen that the station focus on this one individual. Cohen agreed. Thus was born the Bin Ladin unit.[2]

In May 1996, Bin Ladin left Sudan for Afghanistan. A few months later, as the Bin Ladin unit was gearing up, Jamal Ahmed al Fadl walked into a U.S. embassy in Africa, established his bona fides as a former senior employee of Bin Ladin, and provided a major breakthrough of intelligence on the creation, character, direction, and intentions of al Qaeda. Corroborating evidence came from another walk-in source at a different U.S. embassy. More confirmation was supplied later that year by intelligence and other sources, including material gathered by FBI agents and Kenyan police from an al Qaeda cell in Nairobi.[3]

By 1997, officers in the Bin Ladin unit recognized that Bin Ladin was more than just a financier. They learned that al Qaeda had a military committee that was planning operations against U.S. interests worldwide and was actively trying to obtain nuclear material. Analysts assigned to the station looked at the information it had gathered and "found connections everywhere," including links to the attacks on U.S. troops in Aden and Somalia in 1992 and 1993 and to the Manila air plot in the Philippines in 1994–1995.[4]

The Bin Ladin station was already working on plans for offensive operations against Bin Ladin. These plans were directed at both physical assets and sources of finance. In the end, plans to identify and attack Bin Ladin's money sources did not go forward.[5]

In late 1995, when Bin Ladin was still in Sudan, the State Department and the CIA learned that Sudanese officials were discussing with the Saudi government the possibility of expelling Bin Ladin. U.S. Ambassador Timothy Carney encouraged the Sudanese to pursue this course. The Saudis, however, did not want Bin Ladin, giving as their reason their revocation of his citizenship.[6]

Sudan's minister of defense, Fatih Erwa, has claimed that Sudan offered to hand Bin Ladin over to the United States. The Commission has found no credible evidence that this was so. Ambassador Carney had instructions only to push the Sudanese to expel Bin Ladin. Ambassador Carney had no legal basis to ask for more from the Sudanese since, at the time, there was no indictment outstanding.[7]

The chief of the Bin Ladin station, whom we will call "Mike," saw Bin Ladin's move to Afghanistan as a stroke of luck. Though the CIA had virtually abandoned Afghanistan after the Soviet withdrawal, case officers had reestablished old contacts while tracking down Mir Amal Kansi, the Pakistani gunman who had murdered two CIA employees in January 1993. These contacts contributed to intelligence about Bin Ladin's local movements, business activities, and security and living arrangements, and helped provide evidence that he was spending large amounts of money to help the Taliban. The chief of the Counterterrorist Center, whom we will call "Jeff," told Director George Tenet that the CIA's intelligence assets were "near to providing real-time information about Bin Ladin's activities and travels in Afghanistan." One of the contacts was a group associated with particular tribes among Afghanistan's ethnic Pashtun community.[8]

By the fall of 1997, the Bin Ladin unit had roughed out a plan for these Afghan tribals to capture Bin Ladin and hand him over for trial either in the United States or in an Arab country. In early 1998, the cabinet-level Principals Committee apparently gave the concept its blessing.[9]

On their own separate track, getting information but not direction from the CIA, the FBI's New York Field Office and the U.S. Attorney for the Southern District of New York were preparing to ask a grand jury to indict Bin Ladin. The Counterterrorist Center knew that this was happening.[10] The eventual charge, conspiring to attack U.S. defense installations, was finally issued from the grand jury in June 1998—as a sealed indictment. The indictment was publicly disclosed in November of that year.

When Bin Ladin moved to Afghanistan in May 1996, he became a subject of interest to the State Department's South Asia bureau. At the time, as one diplomat told us, South Asia was seen in the department and the government generally as a low priority. In 1997, as Madeleine Albright was beginning her tenure as secretary of state, an NSC policy review concluded that the United States should pay more attention not just to India but also to Pakistan and Afghanistan.[11] With regard to Afghanistan, another diplomat said, the United States at the time had "no policy."[12]

In the State Department, concerns about India-Pakistan tensions often crowded out attention to Afghanistan or Bin Ladin. Aware of instability and growing Islamic extremism in Pakistan, State Department officials worried most about an arms race and possible war between Pakistan and India. After May 1998, when both countries surprised the United States by testing nuclear weapons, these dangers became daily first-order concerns of the State Department.[13]

In Afghanistan, the State Department tried to end the civil war that had continued since the Soviets' withdrawal. The South Asia bureau believed it might have a carrot for Afghanistan's warring factions in a project by the Union Oil Company of California (UNOCAL) to build a pipeline across the country. While there was probably never much chance of the pipeline actually being built, the Afghan desk hoped that the prospect of shared pipeline profits might lure faction leaders to a conference table. U.S. diplomats did not favor the Taliban over the rival factions. Despite growing concerns, U.S. diplomats were willing at the time, as one official said, to "give the Taliban a chance."[14]

Though Secretary Albright made no secret of thinking the Taliban "despicable," the U.S. ambassador to the United Nations, Bill Richardson, led a delegation to South Asia—including Afghanistan—in April 1998. No U.S. official of such rank had been to Kabul in decades. Ambassador Richardson went primarily to urge negotiations to end the civil war. In view of Bin Ladin's recent public call for all Muslims to kill Americans, Richardson asked the Taliban to expel Bin Ladin. They answered that they did not know his whereabouts. In any case, the Taliban said, Bin Ladin was not a threat to the United States.[15]

In sum, in late 1997 and the spring of 1998, the lead U.S. agencies each pursued their own efforts against Bin Ladin. The CIA's Counterterrorist Center was developing a plan to capture and remove him from Afghanistan. Parts of the Justice Department were moving toward indicting Bin Ladin, making possible a criminal trial in a New York court. Meanwhile, the State Department was focused more on lessening Indo-Pakistani nuclear tensions, ending the Afghan civil war, and ameliorating the Taliban's human rights abuses than on driving out Bin Ladin. Another key actor, Marine General Anthony Zinni, the commander in chief of the U.S. Central Command, shared the State Department's view.[16]

The CIA Develops a Capture Plan

Initially, the DCI's Counterterrorist Center and its Bin Ladin unit considered a plan to ambush Bin Ladin when he traveled between Kandahar, the Taliban capital where he sometimes stayed the night, and his primary residence at the time, Tarnak Farms. After the Afghan tribals reported that they had tried such an ambush and failed, the Center gave up on it, despite suspicions that the tribals' story might be fiction. Thereafter, the capture plan focused on a nighttime raid on Tarnak Farms.[17]

A compound of about 80 concrete or mud-brick buildings surrounded by a 10-foot wall, Tarnak Farms was located in an isolated desert area on the outskirts of the Kandahar airport. CIA officers were able to map the entire site, identifying the houses that belonged to Bin Ladin's wives and the one where

Bin Ladin himself was most likely to sleep. Working with the tribals, they drew up plans for the raid. They ran two complete rehearsals in the United States during the fall of 1997.[18]

By early 1998, planners at the Counterterrorist Center were ready to come back to the White House to seek formal approval. Tenet apparently walked National Security Advisor Sandy Berger through the basic plan on February 13. One group of tribals would subdue the guards, enter Tarnak Farms stealthily, grab Bin Ladin, take him to a desert site outside Kandahar, and turn him over to a second group. This second group of tribals would take him to a desert landing zone already tested in the 1997 Kansi capture. From there, a CIA plane would take him to New York, an Arab capital, or wherever he was to be arraigned. Briefing papers prepared by the Counterterrorist Center acknowledged that hitches might develop. People might be killed, and Bin Ladin's supporters might retaliate, perhaps taking U.S. citizens in Kandahar hostage. But the briefing papers also noted that there was risk in not acting. "Sooner or later," they said, "Bin Ladin will attack U.S. interests, perhaps using WMD [weapons of mass destruction]."[19]

Clarke's Counterterrorism Security Group reviewed the capture plan for Berger. Noting that the plan was in a "very early stage of development," the NSC staff then told the CIA planners to go ahead and, among other things, start drafting any legal documents that might be required to authorize the covert action. The CSG apparently stressed that the raid should target Bin Ladin himself, not the whole compound.[20]

The CIA planners conducted their third complete rehearsal in March, and they again briefed the CSG. Clarke wrote Berger on March 7 that he saw the operation as "somewhat embryonic" and the CIA as "months away from doing anything."[21]

"Mike" thought the capture plan was "the perfect operation." It required minimum infrastructure. The plan had now been modified so that the tribals would keep Bin Ladin in a hiding place for up to a month before turning him over to the United States—thereby increasing the chances of keeping the U.S. hand out of sight. "Mike" trusted the information from the Afghan network; it had been corroborated by other means, he told us. The lead CIA officer in the field, Gary Schroen, also had confidence in the tribals. In a May 6 cable to CIA headquarters, he pronounced their planning "almost as professional and detailed ... as would be done by any U.S. military special operations element." He and the other officers who had worked through the plan with the tribals judged it "about as good as it can be." (By that, Schroen explained, he meant that the chance of capturing or killing Bin Ladin was about 40 percent.) Although the tribals thought they could pull off the raid, if the operation were approved by headquarters and the policymakers, Schroen wrote there was going to be a point when "we step back and keep our fingers crossed that the [tribals] prove as good (and as lucky) as they think they will be."[22]

Military officers reviewed the capture plan and, according to "Mike," "found no showstoppers." The commander of Delta Force felt "uncomfortable" with having the tribals hold Bin Ladin captive for so long, and the commander of Joint Special Operations Forces, Lieutenant General Michael Canavan, was worried about the safety of the tribals inside Tarnak Farms. General Canavan said he had actually thought the operation too complicated for the CIA—"out of their league"—and an effort to get results "on the cheap." But a senior Joint Staff officer described the plan as "generally, not too much different than we might have come up with ourselves." No one in the Pentagon, so far as we know, advised the CIA or the White House not to proceed.[23]

In Washington, Berger expressed doubt about the dependability of the tribals. In his meeting with Tenet, Berger focused most, however, on the question of what was to be done with Bin Ladin if he were actually captured. He worried that the hard evidence against Bin Ladin was still skimpy and that there was a danger of snatching him and bringing him to the United States only to see him acquitted.[24]

On May 18, CIA's managers reviewed a draft Memorandum of Notification (MON), a legal document authorizing the capture operation. A 1986 presidential finding had authorized worldwide covert action against terrorism and probably provided adequate authority. But mindful of the old "rogue elephant" charge, senior CIA managers may have wanted something on paper to show that they were not acting on their own.

Discussion of this memorandum brought to the surface an unease about paramilitary covert action that had become ingrained, at least among some CIA senior managers. James Pavitt, the assistant head of the Directorate of Operations, expressed concern that people might get killed; it appears he thought the operation had at least a slight flavor of a plan for an assassination. Moreover, he calculated that it would cost several million dollars. He was not prepared to take that money "out of hide," and he did not want to go to all the necessary congressional committees to get special money. Despite Pavitt's misgivings, the CIA leadership cleared the draft memorandum and sent it on to the National Security Council.[25]

Counterterrorist Center officers briefed Attorney General Janet Reno and FBI Director Louis Freeh, telling them that the operation had about a 30 percent chance of success. The Center's chief, "Jeff," joined John O'Neill, the head of the FBI's New York Field Office, in briefing Mary Jo White, the U.S. Attorney for the Southern District of New York, and her staff. Though "Jeff" also used the 30 percent success figure, he warned that someone would surely be killed in the operation. White's impression from the New York briefing was that the chances of capturing Bin Ladin alive were nil.[26]

From May 20 to 24, the CIA ran a final, graded rehearsal of the operation, spread over three time zones, even bringing in personnel from the region. The FBI also participated. The rehearsal went well. The Counterterrorist Center planned to brief cabinet-level principals and their deputies the following week, giving June 23 as the date for the raid, with Bin Ladin to be brought out of Afghanistan no later than July 23.[27]

On May 20, Director Tenet discussed the high risk of the operation with Berger and his deputies, warning that people might be killed, including Bin Ladin. Success was to be defined as the exfiltration of Bin Ladin out of Afghanistan.[28] A meeting of principals was scheduled for May 29 to decide whether the operation should go ahead.

The principals did not meet. On May 29, "Jeff" informed "Mike" that he had just met with Tenet, Pavitt, and the chief of the Directorate's Near Eastern Division. The decision was made not to go ahead with the operation. "Mike" cabled the field that he had been directed to "stand down on the operation for the time being." He had been told, he wrote, that cabinet-level officials thought the risk of civilian casualties—"collateral damage"—was too high. They were concerned about the tribals' safety, and had worried that "the purpose and nature of the operation would be subject to unavoidable misinterpretation and misrepresentation—and probably recriminations—in the event that Bin Ladin, despite our best intentions and efforts, did not survive."[29]

Impressions vary as to who actually decided not to proceed with the operation. Clarke told us that the CSG saw the plan as flawed. He was said to have described it to a colleague on the NSC staff as "half-assed" and predicted that the principals would not approve it. "Jeff" thought the decision had been made at the cabinet level. Pavitt thought that it was Berger's doing, though perhaps on Tenet's advice. Tenet told us that given the recommendation of his chief operations officers, he alone had decided to "turn off" the operation. He had simply informed Berger, who had not pushed back. Berger's recollection was similar. He said the plan was never presented to the White House for a decision.[30]

The CIA's senior management clearly did not think the plan would work. Tenet's deputy director of operations wrote to Berger a few weeks later that the CIA assessed the tribals' ability to capture Bin Ladin and deliver him to U.S. officials as low. But working-level CIA officers were disappointed. Before it was canceled, Schroen described it as the "best plan we are going to come up with to capture [Bin Ladin] while he is in Afghanistan and bring him to justice."[31] No capture plan before 9/11 ever again attained the same level of detail and preparation. The tribals' reported readiness to act diminished. And Bin Ladin's security precautions and defenses became more elaborate and formidable.

At this time, 9/11 was more than three years away. It was the duty of Tenet and the CIA leadership to balance the risks of inaction against jeopardizing the lives of their operatives and agents. And they had reason to worry about failure: millions of dollars down the drain; a shoot-out that could be seen as an assassination; and, if there were repercussions in Pakistan, perhaps a coup. The decisions of the U.S. government in May 1998 were made, as Berger has put it, from the vantage point of the driver looking through a muddy windshield moving forward, not through a clean rearview mirror.[32]

Looking for Other Options

The Counterterrorist Center continued to track Bin Ladin and to contemplate covert action. The most hopeful possibility seemed now to lie in diplomacy— but not diplomacy managed by the Department of State, which focused primarily on India–Pakistan nuclear tensions during the summer of 1998. The CIA learned in the spring of 1998 that the Saudi government had quietly disrupted Bin Ladin cells in its country that were planning to attack U.S. forces with shoulder-fired missiles. They had arrested scores of individuals, with no publicity. When thanking the Saudis, Director Tenet took advantage of the opening to ask them to help against Bin Ladin. The response was encouraging enough that President Clinton made Tenet his informal personal representative to work with the Saudis on terrorism, and Tenet visited Riyadh in May and again in early June.[33]

Saudi Crown Prince Abdullah, who had taken charge from the ailing King Fahd, promised Tenet an all-out secret effort to persuade the Taliban to expel Bin Ladin so that he could be sent to the United States or to another country for trial. The Kingdom's emissary would be its intelligence chief, Prince Turki bin Faisal. Vice President Al Gore later added his thanks to those of Tenet, both making clear that they spoke with President Clinton's blessing. Tenet reported that it was imperative to get an indictment against Bin Ladin. The New York grand jury issued its sealed indictment a few days later, on June 10. Tenet also recommended that no action be taken on other U.S. options, such as the covert action plan.[34]

Prince Turki followed up in meetings during the summer with Mullah Omar and other Taliban leaders. Apparently employing a mixture of possible incentives and threats, Turki received a commitment that Bin Ladin would be expelled, but Mullah Omar did not make good on this promise.[35]

On August 5, Clarke chaired a CSG meeting on Bin Ladin. In the discussion of what might be done, the note taker wrote, "there was a dearth of bright ideas around the table, despite a consensus that the [government] ought to pursue every avenue it can to address the problem."[36]

4.2 CRISIS: AUGUST 1998

On August 7, 1998, National Security Advisor Berger woke President Clinton with a phone call at 5:35 A.M. to tell him of the almost simultaneous bombings of the U.S. embassies in Nairobi, Kenya, and Dar es Salaam, Tanzania. Suspicion quickly focused on Bin Ladin. Unusually good intelligence, chiefly from the yearlong monitoring of al Qaeda's cell in Nairobi, soon firmly fixed responsibility on him and his associates.[37]

Debate about what to do settled very soon on one option: Tomahawk cruise missiles. Months earlier, after cancellation of the covert capture operation, Clarke had prodded the Pentagon to explore possibilities for military action. On June 2, General Hugh Shelton, the chairman of the Joint Chiefs of Staff, had directed General Zinni at Central Command to develop a plan, which he had submitted during the first week of July. Zinni's planners surely considered the two previous times the United States had used force to respond to terrorism, the 1986 strike on Libya and the 1993 strike against Iraq. They proposed firing Tomahawks against eight terrorist camps in Afghanistan, including Bin Ladin's compound at Tarnak Farms.[38] After the embassy attacks, the Pentagon offered this plan to the White House.

The day after the embassy bombings, Tenet brought to a principals meeting intelligence that terrorist leaders were expected to gather at a camp near Khowst, Afghanistan, to plan future attacks. According to Berger, Tenet said that several hundred would attend, including Bin Ladin. The CIA described the area as effectively a military cantonment, away from civilian population centers and overwhelmingly populated by jihadists. Clarke remembered sitting next to Tenet in a White House meeting, asking Tenet "You thinking what I'm thinking?" and his nodding "yes."[39] The principals quickly reached a consensus on attacking the gathering. The strike's purpose was to kill Bin Ladin and his chief lieutenants.[40]

Berger put in place a tightly compartmented process designed to keep all planning secret. On August 11, General Zinni received orders to prepare detailed plans for strikes against the sites in Afghanistan. The Pentagon briefed President Clinton about these plans on August 12 and 14. Though the principals hoped that the missiles would hit Bin Ladin, NSC staff recommended the strike whether or not there was firm evidence that the commanders were at the facilities.[41]

Considerable debate went to the question of whether to strike targets outside of Afghanistan, including two facilities in Sudan. One was a tannery believed to belong to Bin Ladin. The other was al Shifa, a Khartoum pharmaceutical plant, which intelligence reports said was manufacturing a precursor ingredient for nerve gas with Bin Ladin's financial support. The argument for hitting the tannery was that it could hurt Bin Ladin financially. The argument for hitting al Shifa was that it would lessen the chance of Bin Ladin's having nerve gas for a later attack.[42]

Ever since March 1995, American officials had had in the backs of their minds Aum Shinrikyo's release of sarin nerve gas in the Tokyo subway. President Clinton himself had expressed great concern about chemical and biological terrorism in the United States. Bin Ladin had reportedly been heard to speak of wanting a "Hiroshima" and at least 10,000 casualties. The CIA reported that a soil sample from the vicinity of the al Shifa plant had tested positive for EMPTA, a precursor chemical for VX, a nerve gas whose lone use was for mass killing. Two days before the embassy bombings, Clarke's staff wrote that Bin Ladin "has invested in and almost certainly has access to VX produced at a plant in Sudan."[43] Senior State Department officials believed that they had received a similar verdict independently, though they and Clarke's staff were probably relying on the same report. Mary McCarthy, the NSC senior director responsible for intelligence programs, initially cautioned Berger that the "bottom line" was that "we will need much better intelligence on this facility before we seriously consider any options." She added that the link between Bin Ladin and al Shifa was "rather uncertain at this point." Berger has told us that he thought about what might happen if the decision went against hitting al Shifa, and nerve gas was used in a New York subway two weeks later.[44]

By the early hours of the morning of August 20, President Clinton and all his principal advisers had agreed to strike Bin Ladin camps in Afghanistan near Khowst, as well as hitting al Shifa. The President took the Sudanese tannery off the target list because he saw little point in killing uninvolved people without doing significant harm to Bin Ladin. The principal with the most qualms regarding al Shifa was Attorney General Reno. She expressed concern about attacking two Muslim countries at the same time. Looking back, she said that she felt the "premise kept shifting."[45]

Later on August 20, Navy vessels in the Arabian Sea fired their cruise missiles. Though most of them hit their intended targets, neither Bin Ladin nor any other terrorist leader was killed. Berger told us that an after-action review by Director Tenet concluded that the strikes had killed 20–30 people in the camps but probably missed Bin Ladin by a few hours. Since the missiles headed for Afghanistan had had to cross Pakistan, the Vice Chairman of the Joint Chiefs was sent to meet with Pakistan's army chief of staff to assure him the missiles were not coming from India. Officials in Washington speculated that one or another Pakistani official might have sent a warning to the Taliban or Bin Ladin.[46]

The air strikes marked the climax of an intense 48-hour period in which Berger notified congressional leaders, the principals called their foreign counterparts, and President Clinton flew back from his vacation on Martha's Vineyard to address the nation from the Oval Office. The President spoke to the congressional leadership from Air Force One, and he called British Prime Minister Tony Blair, Pakistani Prime Minister Nawaz Sharif, and Egyptian President Hosni Mubarak from the White House.[47] House Speaker Newt Gingrich and Senate Majority Leader Trent Lott initially supported the President. The next month, Gingrich's office dismissed the cruise missile attacks as "pinpricks."[48]

At the time, President Clinton was embroiled in the Lewinsky scandal, which continued to consume public attention for the rest of that year and the first months of 1999. As it happened, a popular 1997 movie, *Wag the Dog*, features a president who fakes a war to distract public attention from a domestic scandal. Some Republicans in Congress raised questions about the timing of the strikes. Berger was particularly rankled by an editorial in the *Economist* that said that only the future would tell whether the U.S. missile strikes had "created 10,000 new fanatics where there would have been none."[49]

Much public commentary turned immediately to scalding criticism that the action was too aggressive. The Sudanese denied that al Shifa produced nerve gas, and they allowed journalists to visit what was left of a seemingly harmless facility. President Clinton, Vice President Gore, Berger, Tenet, and Clarke insisted to us that their judgment was right, pointing to the soil sample evidence. No independent evidence has emerged to corroborate the CIA's assessment.[50]

Everyone involved in the decision had, of course, been aware of President Clinton's problems. He told them to ignore them. Berger recalled the President saying to him "that they were going to get crap either way, so they should do the right thing."[51] All his aides testified to us that they based their advice solely on national security considerations. We have found no reason to question their statements.

The failure of the strikes, the "wag the dog" slur, the intense partisanship of the period, and the nature of the al Shifa evidence likely had a cumulative effect on future decisions about the use of force against Bin Ladin. Berger told us that he did not feel any sense of constraint.[52]

The period after the August 1998 embassy bombings was critical in shaping U.S. policy toward Bin Ladin. Although more Americans had been killed in the 1996 Khobar Towers attack, and many more in Beirut in 1983, the overall loss of life rivaled the worst attacks in memory. More ominous, perhaps, was the demonstration of an operational capability to coordinate two nearly simultaneous attacks on U.S. embassies in different countries.

Despite the availability of information that al Qaeda was a global network, in 1998 policymakers knew little about the organization. The reams of new information that the CIA's Bin Ladin unit had been developing since 1996 had not been pulled together and synthesized for the rest of the government. Indeed, analysts in the unit felt that they were viewed as alarmists even within the CIA. A National Intelligence Estimate on terrorism in 1997 had only briefly mentioned Bin Ladin, and no subsequent national estimate would authoritatively evaluate the terrorism danger until after 9/11. Policymakers knew there was a dangerous individual, Usama Bin Ladin, whom they had been trying to capture and bring to trial. Documents at the time referred to Bin Ladin "and his associates" or Bin Ladin and his "network." They did not emphasize the existence of a structured worldwide organization gearing up to train thousands of potential terrorists.[53]

In the critical days and weeks after the August 1998 attacks, senior policymakers in the Clinton administration had to reevaluate the threat posed by Bin

Ladin. Was this just a new and especially venomous version of the ordinary terrorist threat America had lived with for decades, or was it radically new, posing a danger beyond any yet experienced?

Even after the embassy attacks, Bin Ladin had been responsible for the deaths of fewer than 50 Americans, most of them overseas. An NSC staffer working for Richard Clarke told us the threat was seen as one that could cause hundreds of casualties, not thousands.[54] Even officials who acknowledge a vital threat intellectually may not be ready to act on such beliefs at great cost or at high risk.

Therefore, the government experts who believed that Bin Ladin and his network posed such a novel danger needed a way to win broad support for their views, or at least spotlight the areas of dispute. The Presidential Daily Brief and the similar, more widely circulated daily reports for high officials—consisting mainly of brief reports of intelligence "news" without much analysis or context—did not provide such a vehicle. The national intelligence estimate has often played this role, and is sometimes controversial for this very reason. It played no role in judging the threat posed by al Qaeda, either in 1998 or later.

In the late summer and fall of 1998, the U.S. government also was worrying about the deployment of military power in two other ongoing conflicts. After years of war in the Balkans, the United States had finally committed itself to significant military intervention in 1995–1996. Already maintaining a NATO-led peacekeeping force in Bosnia, U.S. officials were beginning to consider major combat operations against Serbia to protect Muslim civilians in Kosovo from ethnic cleansing. Air strikes were threatened in October 1998; a full-scale NATO bombing campaign against Serbia was launched in March 1999.[55]

In addition, the Clinton administration was facing the possibility of major combat operations against Iraq. Since 1996, the UN inspections regime had been increasingly obstructed by Saddam Hussein. The United States was threatening to attack unless unfettered inspections could resume. The Clinton administration eventually launched a large-scale set of air strikes against Iraq, Operation Desert Fox, in December 1998. These military commitments became the context in which the Clinton administration had to consider opening another front of military engagement against a new terrorist threat based in Afghanistan.

A Follow-On Campaign?

Clarke hoped the August 1998 missile strikes would mark the beginning of a sustained campaign against Bin Ladin. Clarke was, as he later admitted, "obsessed" with Bin Ladin, and the embassy bombings gave him new scope for pursuing his obsession. Terrorism had moved high up among the President's concerns, and Clarke's position had elevated accordingly. The CSG, unlike most standing interagency committees, did not have to report through the Deputies Committee. Although such a reporting relationship had been prescribed in the May 1998 presidential directive (after expressions of concern by Attorney General Reno, among others), that directive contained an exception that permitted the CSG to report directly to the principals if Berger so elected. In practice, the CSG often reported not even to the full Principals Committee but instead to the so-called Small Group formed by Berger, consisting only of those principals cleared to know about the most sensitive issues connected with counterterrorism activities concerning Bin Ladin or the Khobar Towers investigation.[56]

For this inner cabinet, Clarke drew up what he called "Political-Military Plan Delenda." The Latin *delenda*, meaning that something "must be destroyed," evoked the famous Roman vow to destroy its rival, Carthage. The overall goal of Clarke's paper was to "immediately eliminate any significant threat to Americans" from the "Bin Ladin network."[57] The paper called for diplomacy to deny Bin Ladin sanctuary; covert action to disrupt terrorist activities, but above all to capture Bin Ladin and his deputies and bring them to trial; efforts to dry up Bin Ladin's money supply; and preparation for follow-on military action. The status of the document was and remained uncertain. It was never formally adopted by the principals, and participants in the Small Group now have little or no recollection of it. It did, however, guide Clarke's efforts.

The military component of Clarke's plan was its most fully articulated element. He envisioned an ongoing campaign of strikes against Bin Ladin's bases in Afghanistan or elsewhere, whenever target information was ripe. Acknowledging that individual targets might not have much value, he cautioned Berger not to expect ever again to have an assembly of terrorist leaders in his sights. But he argued that rolling attacks might persuade the Taliban to hand over Bin Ladin and, in any case, would show that the action in August was not a "one-off" event. It would show that the United States was committed to a relentless effort to take down Bin Ladin's network.[58]

Members of the Small Group found themselves unpersuaded of the merits of rolling attacks. Defense Secretary William Cohen told us Bin Ladin's training camps were primitive, built with "rope ladders"; General Shelton called them "jungle gym" camps. Neither thought them worthwhile targets for very expensive missiles. President Clinton and Berger also worried about the *Economist*'s point—that attacks that missed Bin Ladin could enhance his stature and win him new recruits. After the United States launched air attacks against Iraq at the end of 1998 and against Serbia in 1999, in each case provoking worldwide criticism, Deputy National Security Advisor James Steinberg added the argument that attacks in Afghanistan offered "little benefit, lots of blowback against [a] bomb-happy U.S."[59]

During the last week of August 1998, officials began considering possible follow-on strikes. According to Clarke, President Clinton was inclined to launch further strikes sooner rather than later. On August 27, Under Secretary of Defense for Policy Walter Slocombe advised Secretary Cohen that the available targets were not promising. The experience of the previous week, he wrote, "has only confirmed the importance of defining a clearly articulated rationale for military action" that was effective as well as justified. But Slocombe worried that simply striking some of these available targets did not add up to an effective strategy.[60]

Defense officials at a lower level, in the Office of the Assistant Secretary for Special Operations and Low-Intensity Conflict, tried to meet Slocombe's objections. They developed a plan that, unlike Clarke's, called not for particular strikes but instead for a broad change in national strategy and in the institutional approach of the Department of Defense, implying a possible need for large-scale operations across the whole spectrum of U.S. military capabilities. It urged the department to become a lead agency in driving a national counterterrorism strategy forward, to "champion a national effort to take up the gauntlet that international terrorists have thrown at our feet." The authors expressed concern that "we have not fundamentally altered our philosophy or our approach" even though the terrorist threat had grown. They outlined an eight-part strategy "to be more proactive and aggressive." The future, they warned, might bring "horrific attacks," in which case "we will have no choice nor, unfortunately, will we have a plan." The assistant secretary, Allen Holmes, took the paper to Slocombe's chief deputy, Jan Lodal, but it went no further. Its lead author recalls being told by Holmes that Lodal thought it was too aggressive. Holmes cannot recall what was said, and Lodal cannot remember the episode or the paper at all.[61]

4.3 DIPLOMACY

After the August missile strikes, diplomatic options to press the Taliban seemed no more promising than military options. The United States had issued a formal warning to the Taliban, and also to Sudan, that they would be held directly responsible for any attacks on Americans, wherever they occurred, carried out by the Bin Ladin network as long as they continued to provide sanctuary to it.[62]

For a brief moment, it had seemed as if the August strikes might have shocked the Taliban into thinking of giving up Bin Ladin. On August 22, the reclusive Mullah Omar told a working-level State Department official that the strikes were counterproductive but added that he would be open to a dialogue with the United States on Bin Ladin's presence in Afghanistan.[63] Meeting in Islamabad with William Milam, the U.S. ambassador to Pakistan, Taliban delegates said it was against their culture to expel someone seeking sanctuary but asked what would happen to Bin Ladin should he be sent to Saudi Arabia.[64]

Yet in September 1998, when the Saudi emissary, Prince Turki, asked Mullah Omar whether he would keep his earlier promise to expel Bin Ladin, the

Taliban leader said no. Both sides shouted at each other, with Mullah Omar denouncing the Saudi government. Riyadh then suspended its diplomatic relations with the Taliban regime. (Saudi Arabia, Pakistan, and the United Arab Emirates were the only countries that recognized the Taliban as the legitimate government of Afghanistan.) Crown Prince Abdullah told President Clinton and Vice President Gore about this when he visited Washington in late September. His account confirmed reports that the U.S. government had received independently.[65]

Other efforts with the Saudi government centered on improving intelligence sharing and permitting U.S. agents to interrogate prisoners in Saudi custody. The history of such cooperation in 1997 and 1998 had been strained.[66] Several officials told us, in particular, that the United States could not get direct access to an important al Qaeda financial official, Madani al Tayyib, who had been detained by the Saudi government in 1997.[67] Though U.S. officials repeatedly raised the issue, the Saudis provided limited information. In his September 1998 meeting with Crown Prince Abdullah, Vice President Gore, while thanking the Saudi government for their responsiveness, renewed the request for direct U.S. access to Tayyib.[68] The United States never obtained this access.

An NSC staff–led working group on terrorist finances asked the CIA in November 1998 to push again for access to Tayyib and to see "if it is possible to elaborate further on the ties between Usama bin Ladin and prominent individuals in Saudi Arabia, including especially the Bin Ladin family."[69] One result was two NSC-led interagency trips to Persian Gulf states in 1999 and 2000. During these trips the NSC, Treasury, and intelligence representatives spoke with Saudi officials, and later interviewed members of the Bin Ladin family, about Usama's inheritance. The Saudis and the Bin Ladin family eventually helped in this particular effort and U.S. officials ultimately learned that Bin Ladin was not financing al Qaeda out of a personal inheritance.[70] But Clarke was frustrated about how little the Agency knew, complaining to Berger that four years after "we first asked CIA to track down [Bin Ladin]'s finances" and two years after the creation of the CIA's Bin Ladin unit, the Agency said it could only guess at how much aid Bin Ladin gave to terrorist groups, what were the main sources of his budget, or how he moved his money.[71]

The other diplomatic route to get at Bin Ladin in Afghanistan ran through Islamabad. In the summer before the embassy bombings, the State Department had been heavily focused on rising tensions between India and Pakistan and did not aggressively challenge Pakistan on Afghanistan and Bin Ladin. But State Department counterterrorism officials wanted a stronger position; the department's acting counterterrorism coordinator advised Secretary Albright to designate Pakistan as a state sponsor of terrorism, noting that despite high-level Pakistani assurances, the country's military intelligence service continued "activities in support of international terrorism" by supporting attacks on civilian targets in Kashmir. This recommendation was opposed by the State Department's South Asia bureau, which was concerned that it would damage already sensitive relations with Pakistan in the wake of the May 1998 nuclear tests by both Pakistan and India. Secretary Albright rejected the recommendation on August 5, 1998, just two days before the embassy bombings.[72] She told us that, in general, putting the Pakistanis on the terrorist list would eliminate any influence the United States had over them.[73] In October, an NSC counterterrorism official noted that Pakistan's pro-Taliban military intelligence service had been training Kashmiri jihadists in one of the camps hit by U.S. missiles, leading to the death of Pakistanis.[74]

After flying to Nairobi and bringing home the coffins of the American dead, Secretary Albright increased the department's focus on counterterrorism. According to Ambassador Milam, the bombings were a "wake-up call," and he soon found himself spending 45 to 50 percent of his time working the Taliban–Bin Ladin portfolio.[75] But Pakistan's military intelligence service, known as the ISID (Inter-Services Intelligence Directorate), was the Taliban's primary patron, which made progress difficult.

Additional pressure on the Pakistanis—beyond demands to press the Taliban on Bin Ladin—seemed unattractive to most officials of the State Department. Congressional sanctions punishing Pakistan for possessing nuclear arms prevented the administration from offering incentives to Islamabad.[76] In the words of Deputy Secretary of State Strobe Talbott, Washington's Pakistan policy was "stick-heavy." Talbott felt that the only remaining sticks were additional sanctions that would have bankrupted the Pakistanis, a dangerous move that could have brought "total chaos" to a nuclear-armed country with a significant number of Islamic radicals.[77]

The Saudi government, which had a long and close relationship with Pakistan and provided it oil on generous terms, was already pressing Sharif with regard to the Taliban and Bin Ladin. A senior State Department official concluded that Saudi Crown Prince Abdullah put "a tremendous amount of heat" on the Pakistani prime minister during the prince's October 1998 visit to Pakistan.[78]

The State Department urged President Clinton to engage the Pakistanis. Accepting this advice, President Clinton invited Sharif to Washington, where they talked mostly about India but also discussed Bin Ladin. After Sharif went home, the President called him and raised the Bin Ladin subject again. This effort elicited from Sharif a promise to talk with the Taliban.[79]

Mullah Omar's position showed no sign of softening. One intelligence report passed to Berger by the NSC staff quoted Bin Ladin as saying that Mullah Omar had given him a completely free hand to act in any country, though asking that he not claim responsibility for attacks in Pakistan or Saudi Arabia. Bin Ladin was described as grabbing his beard and saying emotionally, "By Allah, by God, the Americans will still be amazed. The so-called United States will suffer the same fate as the Russians. Their state will collapse, too."[80]

Debate in the State Department intensified after December 1998, when Michael Sheehan became counterterrorism coordinator. A onetime special forces officer, he had worked with Albright when she was ambassador to the United Nations and had served on the NSC staff with Clarke. He shared Clarke's obsession with terrorism, and had little hesitation about locking horns with the regional bureaus. Through every available channel, he repeated the earlier warning to the Taliban of the possible dire consequences—including military strikes—if Bin Ladin remained their guest and conducted additional attacks. Within the department, he argued for designating the Taliban regime a state sponsor of terrorism. This was technically difficult to do, for calling it a state would be tantamount to diplomatic recognition, which the United States had thus far withheld. But Sheehan urged the use of any available weapon against the Taliban. He told us that he thought he was regarded in the department as "a one-note Johnny nutcase."[81]

In early 1999, the State Department's counterterrorism office proposed a comprehensive diplomatic strategy for all states involved in the Afghanistan problem, including Pakistan. It specified both carrots and hard-hitting sticks— among them, certifying Pakistan as uncooperative on terrorism. Albright said the original carrots and sticks listed in a decision paper for principals may not have been used as "described on paper" but added that they were used in other ways or in varying degrees. But the paper's author, Ambassador Sheehan, was frustrated and complained to us that the original plan "had been watered down to the point that nothing was then done with it."[82]

The cautiousness of the South Asia bureau was reinforced when, in May 1999, Pakistani troops were discovered to have infiltrated into an especially mountainous area of Kashmir. A limited war began between India and Pakistan, euphemistically called the "Kargil crisis," as India tried to drive the Pakistani forces out. Patience with Pakistan was wearing thin, inside both the State Department and the NSC. Bruce Riedel, the NSC staff member responsible for Pakistan, wrote Berger that Islamabad was "behaving as a rogue state in two areas—backing Taliban/UBL terror and provoking war with India."[83]

Discussion within the Clinton administration on Afghanistan then concentrated on two main alternatives. The first, championed by Riedel and Assistant Secretary of State Karl Inderfurth, was to undertake a major diplomatic effort to end the Afghan civil war and install a national unity government. The second, favored by Sheehan, Clarke, and the CIA, called for labeling the Taliban a terrorist group and ultimately funneling secret aid to its chief foe, the Northern Alliance. This dispute would go back and forth throughout 1999 and ultimately become entangled with debate about enlisting the Northern Alliance as an ally for covert action.[84]

Another diplomatic option may have been available: nurturing Afghan exile groups as a possible moderate governing alternative to the Taliban. In late 1999, Washington provided some support for talks among the leaders of exile Afghan groups, including the ousted Rome-based King Zahir Shah and Hamid Karzai, about bolstering anti-Taliban forces inside Afghanistan and linking the

Northern Alliance with Pashtun groups. One U.S. diplomat later told us that the exile groups were not ready to move forward and that coordinating fractious groups residing in Bonn, Rome, and Cyprus proved extremely difficult.[85]

Frustrated by the Taliban's resistance, two senior State Department officials suggested asking the Saudis to offer the Taliban $250 million for Bin Ladin. Clarke opposed having the United States facilitate a "huge grant to a regime as heinous as the Taliban" and suggested that the idea might not seem attractive to either Secretary Albright or First Lady Hillary Rodham Clinton—both critics of the Taliban's record on women's rights.[86] The proposal seems to have quietly died.

Within the State Department, some officials delayed Sheehan and Clarke's push either to designate Taliban-controlled Afghanistan as a state sponsor of terrorism or to designate the regime as a foreign terrorist organization (thereby avoiding the issue of whether to recognize the Taliban as Afghanistan's government). Sheehan and Clarke prevailed in July 1999, when President Clinton issued an executive order effectively declaring the Taliban regime a state sponsor of terrorism.[87] In October, a UN Security Council Resolution championed by the United States added economic and travel sanctions.[88]

With UN sanctions set to come into effect in November, Clarke wrote Berger that "the Taliban appear to be up to something."[89] Mullah Omar had shuffled his "cabinet" and hinted at Bin Ladin's possible departure. Clarke's staff thought his most likely destination would be Somalia; Chechnya seemed less appealing with Russia on the offensive. Clarke commented that Iraq and Libya had previously discussed hosting Bin Ladin, though he and his staff had their doubts that Bin Ladin would trust secular Arab dictators such as Saddam Hussein or Muammar Qadhafi. Clarke also raised the "remote possibility" of Yemen, which offered vast uncontrolled spaces. In November, the CSG discussed whether the sanctions had rattled the Taliban, who seemed "to be looking for a face-saving way out of the Bin Ladin issue."[90]

In fact none of the outside pressure had any visible effect on Mullah Omar, who was unconcerned about commerce with the outside world. Omar had virtually no diplomatic contact with the West, since he refused to meet with non-Muslims. The United States learned that at the end of 1999, the Taliban Council of Ministers unanimously reaffirmed that their regime would stick by Bin Ladin. Relations between Bin Ladin and the Taliban leadership were sometimes tense, but the foundation was deep and personal.[91] Indeed, Mullah Omar had executed at least one subordinate who opposed his pro–Bin Ladin policy.[92]

The United States would try tougher sanctions in 2000. Working with Russia (a country involved in an ongoing campaign against Chechen separatists, some of whom received support from Bin Ladin), the United States persuaded the United Nations to adopt Security Council Resolution 1333, which included an embargo on arms shipments to the Taliban, in December 2000.[93] The aim of the resolution was to hit the Taliban where it was most sensitive—

on the battlefield against the Northern Alliance—and criminalize giving them arms and providing military "advisers," which Pakistan had been doing.[94] Yet the passage of the resolution had no visible effect on Omar, nor did it halt the flow of Pakistani military assistance to the Taliban.[95]

U.S. authorities had continued to try to get cooperation from Pakistan in pressing the Taliban to stop sheltering Bin Ladin. President Clinton contacted Sharif again in June 1999, partly to discuss the crisis with India but also to urge Sharif, "in the strongest way I can," to persuade the Taliban to expel Bin Ladin.[96] The President suggested that Pakistan use its control over oil supplies to the Taliban and over Afghan imports through Karachi. Sharif suggested instead that Pakistani forces might try to capture Bin Ladin themselves. Though no one in Washington thought this was likely to happen, President Clinton gave the idea his blessing.[97]

The President met with Sharif in Washington in early July. Though the meeting's main purpose was to seal the Pakistani prime minister's decision to withdraw from the Kargil confrontation in Kashmir, President Clinton complained about Pakistan's failure to take effective action with respect to the Taliban and Bin Ladin. Sharif came back to his earlier proposal and won approval for U.S. assistance in training a Pakistani special forces team for an operation against Bin Ladin. Then, in October 1999, Sharif was deposed by General Pervez Musharraf, and the plan was terminated.[98]

At first, the Clinton administration hoped that Musharraf's coup might create an opening for action on Bin Ladin. A career military officer, Musharraf was thought to have the political strength to confront and influence the Pakistani military intelligence service, which supported the Taliban. Berger speculated that the new government might use Bin Ladin to buy concessions from Washington, but neither side ever developed such an initiative.[99]

By late 1999, more than a year after the embassy bombings, diplomacy with Pakistan, like the efforts with the Taliban, had, according to Under Secretary of State Thomas Pickering, "borne little fruit."[100]

4.4 COVERT ACTION

As part of the response to the embassy bombings, President Clinton signed a Memorandum of Notification authorizing the CIA to let its tribal assets use force to capture Bin Ladin and his associates. CIA officers told the tribals that the plan to capture Bin Ladin, which had been "turned off" three months earlier, was back on. The memorandum also authorized the CIA to attack Bin Ladin in other ways. Also, an executive order froze financial holdings that could be linked to Bin Ladin.[101]

The counterterrorism staff at CIA thought it was gaining a better understanding of Bin Ladin and his network. In preparation for briefing the Senate

Select Committee on Intelligence on September 2, Tenet was told that the intelligence community knew more about Bin Ladin's network "than about any other top tier terrorist organization."[102]

The CIA was using this knowledge to disrupt a number of Bin Ladin–associated cells. Working with Albanian authorities, CIA operatives had raided an al Qaeda forgery operation and another terrorist cell in Tirana. These operations may have disrupted a planned attack on the U.S. embassy in Tirana, and did lead to the rendition of a number of al Qaeda–related terrorist operatives. After the embassy bombings, there were arrests in Azerbaijan, Italy, and Britain. Several terrorists were sent to an Arab country. The CIA described working with FBI operatives to prevent a planned attack on the U.S. embassy in Uganda, and a number of suspects were arrested. On September 16, Abu Hajer, one of Bin Ladin's deputies in Sudan and the head of his computer operations and weapons procurement, was arrested in Germany. He was the most important Bin Ladin lieutenant captured thus far. Clarke commented to Berger with satisfaction that August and September had brought the "greatest number of terrorist arrests in a short period of time that we have ever arranged/facilitated."[103]

Given the President's August Memorandum of Notification, the CIA had already been working on new plans for using the Afghan tribals to capture Bin Ladin. During September and October, the tribals claimed to have tried at least four times to ambush Bin Ladin. Senior CIA officials doubted whether any of these ambush attempts had actually occurred. But the tribals did seem to have success in reporting where Bin Ladin was.[104]

This information was more useful than it had been in the past; since the August missile strikes, Bin Ladin had taken to moving his sleeping place frequently and unpredictably and had added new bodyguards. Worst of all, al Qaeda's senior leadership had stopped using a particular means of communication almost immediately after a leak to the *Washington Times*.[105] This made it much more difficult for the National Security Agency to intercept his conversations. But since the tribals seemed to know where Bin Ladin was or would be, an alternative to capturing Bin Ladin would be to mark his location and call in another round of missile strikes.

On November 3, the Small Group met to discuss these problems, among other topics. Preparing Director Tenet for a Small Group meeting in mid-November, the Counterterrorist Center stressed, "At this point we cannot predict when or if a capture operation will be executed by our assets."[106]

U.S. counterterrorism officials also worried about possible domestic attacks. Several intelligence reports, some of dubious sourcing, mentioned Washington as a possible target. On October 26, Clarke's CSG took the unusual step of holding a meeting dedicated to trying "to evaluate the threat of a terrorist attack in the United States by the Usama bin Ladin network."[107] The CSG members were "urged to be as creative as possible in their thinking" about preventing a Bin Ladin attack on U.S. territory. Participants noted that while the FBI had been given additional resources for such efforts, both it and the CIA were having problems exploiting leads by tracing U.S. telephone numbers and translating documents obtained in cell disruptions abroad. The Justice Department reported that the current guidelines from the Attorney General gave sufficient legal authority for domestic investigation and surveillance.[108]

Though intelligence gave no clear indication of what might be afoot, some intelligence reports mentioned chemical weapons, pointing toward work at a camp in southern Afghanistan called Derunta. On November 4, 1998, the U.S. Attorney's Office for the Southern District of New York unsealed its indictment of Bin Ladin, charging him with conspiracy to attack U.S. defense installations. The indictment also charged that al Qaeda had allied itself with Sudan, Iran, and Hezbollah. The original sealed indictment had added that al Qaeda had "reached an understanding with the government of Iraq that al Qaeda would not work against that government and that on particular projects, specifically including weapons development, al Qaeda would work cooperatively with the Government of Iraq."[109] This passage led Clarke, who for years had read intelligence reports on Iraqi-Sudanese cooperation on chemical weapons, to speculate to Berger that a large Iraqi presence at chemical facilities in Khartoum was "probably a direct result of the Iraq–Al Qida agreement." Clarke added that VX precursor traces found near al Shifa were the "exact formula used by Iraq."[110] This language about al Qaeda's "understanding" with Iraq had been dropped, however, when a superseding indictment was filed in November 1998.[111]

On Friday, December 4, 1998, the CIA included an article in the Presidential Daily Brief describing intelligence, received from a friendly government, about a threatened hijacking in the United States. This article was declassified at our request.

The same day, Clarke convened a meeting of his CSG to discuss both the

---

The following is the text of an item from the Presidential Daily Brief received by President William J. Clinton on December 4, 1998. Redacted material is indicated in brackets.

SUBJECT: Bin Ladin Preparing to Hijack US Aircraft and Other
         Attacks

1. Reporting [—] suggests Bin Ladin and his allies are preparing for attacks in the US, including an aircraft hijacking to obtain the release of Shaykh 'Umar 'Abd al-Rahman, Ramzi Yousef, and Muhammad Sadiq 'Awda. One source quoted a senior member of the Gama'at al-Islamiyya (IG) saying that, as of late October, the IG had completed planning for

an operation in the US on behalf of Bin Ladin, but that the operation was on hold. A senior Bin Ladin operative from Saudi Arabia was to visit IG counterparts in the US soon thereafter to discuss options—perhaps including an aircraft hijacking.

- IG leader Islambuli in late September was planning to hijack a US airliner during the "next couple of weeks" to free 'Abd al-Rahman and the other prisoners, according to what may be a different source.
- The same source late last month said that Bin Ladin might implement plans to hijack US aircraft before the beginning of Ramadan on 20 December and that two members of the operational team had evaded security checks during a recent trial run at an unidentified New York airport. [—]

2. Some members of the Bin Ladin network have received hijack training, according to various sources, but no group directly tied to Bin Ladin's al-Qa'ida organization has ever carried out an aircraft hijacking. Bin Ladin could be weighing other types of operations against US aircraft. According to [—] the IG in October obtained SA-7 missiles and intended to move them from Yemen into Saudi Arabia to shoot down an Egyptian plane or, if unsuccessful, a US military or civilian aircraft.

- A [—] in October told us that unspecified "extremist elements" in Yemen had acquired SA-7s. [—]

3. [—] indicate the Bin Ladin organization or its allies are moving closer to implementing anti-US attacks at unspecified locations, but we do not know whether they are related to attacks on aircraft. A Bin Ladin associate in Sudan late last month told a colleague in Kandahar that he had shipped a group of containers to Afghanistan. Bin Ladin associates also talked about the movement of containers to Afghanistan before the East Africa bombings.

- In other [—] Bin Ladin associates last month discussed picking up a package in Malaysia. One told his colleague in Malaysia that "they" were in the "ninth month [of pregnancy]."
- An alleged Bin Ladin supporter in Yemen late last month remarked to his mother that he planned to work in "commerce" from abroad and said his impending "marriage," which would take place soon, would be a "surprise." "Commerce" and "marriage" often are codewords for terrorist attacks. [—]

hijacking concern and the antiaircraft missile threat. To address the hijacking warning, the group agreed that New York airports should go to maximum security starting that weekend. They agreed to boost security at other East coast airports. The CIA agreed to distribute versions of the report to the FBI and FAA to pass to the New York Police Department and the airlines. The FAA issued a security directive on December 8, with specific requirements for more intensive air carrier screening of passengers and more oversight of the screening process, at all three New York City area airports.[112]

The intelligence community could learn little about the source of the information. Later in December and again in early January 1999, more information arrived from the same source, reporting that the planned hijacking had been stalled because two of the operatives, who were sketchily described, had been arrested near Washington, D.C. or New York. After investigation, the FBI could find no information to support the hijack threat; nor could it verify any arrests like those described in the report. The FAA alert at the New York area airports ended on January 31, 1999.[113]

On December 17, the day after the United States and Britain began their Desert Fox bombing campaign against Iraq, the Small Group convened to discuss intelligence suggesting imminent Bin Ladin attacks on the U.S. embassies in Qatar and Ethiopia. The next day, Director Tenet sent a memo to the President, the cabinet, and senior officials throughout the government describing reports that Bin Ladin planned to attack U.S. targets very soon, possibly over the next few days, before Ramadan celebrations began. Tenet said he was "greatly concerned."[114]

With alarms sounding, members of the Small Group considered ideas about how to respond to or prevent such attacks. Generals Shelton and Zinni came up with military options. Special Operations Forces were later told that they might be ordered to attempt very high-risk in-and-out raids either in Khartoum, to capture a senior Bin Ladin operative known as Abu Hafs the Mauritanian—who appeared to be engineering some of the plots—or in Kandahar, to capture Bin Ladin himself. Shelton told us that such operations are not risk free, invoking the memory of the 1993 "Black Hawk down" fiasco in Mogadishu.[115]

The CIA reported on December 18 that Bin Ladin might be traveling to Kandahar and could be targeted there with cruise missiles. Vessels with Tomahawk cruise missiles were on station in the Arabian Sea, and could fire within a few hours of receiving target data.[116]

On December 20, intelligence indicated Bin Ladin would be spending the night at the Haji Habash house, part of the governor's residence in Kandahar. The chief of the Bin Ladin unit, "Mike," told us that he promptly briefed Tenet and his deputy, John Gordon. From the field, the CIA's Gary Schroen advised: "Hit him tonight—we may not get another chance." An urgent teleconference of principals was arranged.[117]

The principals considered a cruise missile strike to try to kill Bin Ladin. One issue they discussed was the potential collateral damage—the number of innocent bystanders who would be killed or wounded. General Zinni predicted a number well over 200 and was concerned about damage to a nearby mosque. The senior intelligence officer on the Joint Staff apparently made a different calculation, estimating half as much collateral damage and not predicting damage to the mosque. By the end of the meeting, the principals decided against recommending to the President that he order a strike. A few weeks later, in January 1999, Clarke wrote that the principals had thought the intelligence only half reliable and had worried about killing or injuring perhaps 300 people. Tenet said he remembered doubts about the reliability of the source and concern about hitting the nearby mosque. "Mike" remembered Tenet telling him that the military was concerned that a few hours had passed since the last sighting of Bin Ladin and that this persuaded everyone that the chance of failure was too great.[118]

Some lower-level officials were angry. "Mike" reported to Schroen that he had been unable to sleep after this decision. "I'm sure we'll regret not acting last night," he wrote, criticizing the principals for "worrying that some stray shrapnel might hit the Habash mosque and 'offend' Muslims." He commented that they had not shown comparable sensitivity when deciding to bomb Muslims in Iraq. The principals, he said, were "obsessed" with trying to get others—Saudis, Pakistanis, Afghan tribals—to "do what we won't do." Schroen was disappointed too. "We should have done it last night," he wrote. "We may well come to regret the decision not to go ahead."[119] The Joint Staff's deputy director for operations agreed, even though he told us that later intelligence appeared to show that Bin Ladin had left his quarters before the strike would have occurred. Missing Bin Ladin, he said, "would have caused us a hell of a problem, but it was a shot we should have taken, and we would have had to pay the price."[120]

The principals began considering other, more aggressive covert alternatives using the tribals. CIA officers suggested that the tribals would prefer to try a raid rather than a roadside ambush because they would have better control, it would be less dangerous, and it played more to their skills and experience. But everyone knew that if the tribals were to conduct such a raid, guns would be blazing. The current Memorandum of Notification instructed the CIA to capture Bin Ladin and to use lethal force only in self-defense. Work now began on a new memorandum that would give the tribals more latitude. The intention was to say that they could use lethal force if the attempted capture seemed impossible to complete successfully.[121]

Early drafts of this highly sensitive document emphasized that it authorized only a capture operation. The tribals were to be paid only if they captured Bin Ladin, not if they killed him. Officials throughout the government approved this draft. But on December 21, the day after principals decided not to launch the cruise missile strike against Kandahar, the CIA's leaders urged strengthening the language to allow the tribals to be paid whether Bin Ladin was captured *or* killed. Berger and Tenet then worked together to take this line of thought even further.[122]

They finally agreed, as Berger reported to President Clinton, that an extraordinary step was necessary. The new memorandum would allow the killing of Bin Ladin if the CIA and the tribals judged that capture was not feasible (a judgment it already seemed clear they had reached). The Justice Department lawyer who worked on the draft told us that what was envisioned was a group of tribals assaulting a location, leading to a shoot-out. Bin Ladin and others would be captured if possible, but probably would be killed. The administration's position was that under the law of armed conflict, killing a person who posed an imminent threat to the United States would be an act of self-defense, not an assassination. On Christmas Eve 1998, Berger sent a final draft to President Clinton, with an explanatory memo. The President approved the document.[123]

Because the White House considered this operation highly sensitive, only a tiny number of people knew about this Memorandum of Notification. Berger arranged for the NSC's legal adviser to inform Albright, Cohen, Shelton, and Reno. None was allowed to keep a copy. Congressional leaders were briefed, as required by law. Attorney General Reno had sent a letter to the President expressing her concern: she warned of possible retaliation, including the targeting of U.S. officials. She did not pose any legal objection. A copy of the final document, along with the carefully crafted instructions that were to be sent to the tribals, was given to Tenet.[124]

A message from Tenet to CIA field agents directed them to communicate to the tribals the instructions authorized by the President: the United States preferred that Bin Ladin and his lieutenants be captured, but if a successful capture operation was not feasible, the tribals were permitted to kill them. The instructions added that the tribals must avoid killing others unnecessarily and must not kill or abuse Bin Ladin or his lieutenants if they surrendered. Finally, the tribals would not be paid if this set of requirements was not met.[125]

The field officer passed these instructions to the tribals word for word. But he prefaced the directions with a message: "From the American President down to the average man in the street, we want him [Bin Ladin] stopped." If the tribals captured Bin Ladin, the officer assured them that he would receive a fair trial under U.S. law and be treated humanely. The CIA officer reported that the tribals said they "fully understand the contents, implications and the spirit of the message" and that that their response was, "We will try our best to capture Bin Ladin alive and will have no intention of killing or harming him on purpose." The tribals explained that they wanted to prove that their standards of behavior were more civilized than those of Bin Ladin and his band of terrorists. In an additional note addressed to Schroen, the tribals noted that if they were to adopt Bin Ladin's ethics, "we would have finished the job long before," but they had been limited by their abilities and "by our beliefs and laws we have to respect."[126]

Schroen and "Mike" were impressed by the tribals' reaction. Schroen cabled that the tribals were not in it for the money but as an investment in the future of Afghanistan. "Mike" agreed that the tribals' reluctance to kill was not a "showstopper." "From our view," he wrote, "that seems in character and fair enough."[127]

Policymakers in the Clinton administration, including the President and his national security advisor, told us that the President's intent regarding covert action against Bin Ladin was clear: he wanted him dead. This intent was never well communicated or understood within the CIA. Tenet told the Commission that except in one specific case (discussed later), the CIA was authorized to kill Bin Ladin only in the context of a capture operation. CIA senior managers, operators, and lawyers confirmed this understanding. "We always talked about how much easier it would have been to kill him," a former chief of the Bin Ladin unit said.[128]

In February 1999, another draft Memorandum of Notification went to President Clinton. It asked him to allow the CIA to give exactly the same guidance to the Northern Alliance as had just been given to the tribals: they could kill Bin Ladin if a successful capture operation was not feasible. On this occasion, however, President Clinton crossed out key language he had approved in December and inserted more ambiguous language. No one we interviewed could shed light on why the President did this. President Clinton told the Commission that he had no recollection of why he rewrote the language.[129]

Later in 1999, when legal authority was needed for enlisting still other collaborators and for covering a wider set of contingencies, the lawyers returned to the language used in August 1998, which authorized force only in the context of a capture operation. Given the closely held character of the document approved in December 1998, and the subsequent return to the earlier language, it is possible to understand how the former White House officials and the CIA officials might disagree as to whether the CIA was ever authorized by the President to kill Bin Ladin.[130]

The dispute turned out to be somewhat academic, as the limits of available legal authority were not tested. Clarke commented to Berger that "despite 'expanded' authority for CIA's sources to engage in direct action, they have shown no inclination to do so." He added that it was his impression that the CIA thought the tribals unlikely to act against Bin Ladin and hence relying on them was "unrealistic."[131] Events seemed to bear him out, since the tribals did not stage an attack on Bin Ladin or his associates during 1999.

The tribals remained active collectors of intelligence, however, providing good but not predictive information about Bin Ladin's whereabouts. The CIA also tried to improve its intelligence reporting on Bin Ladin by what Tenet's assistant director for collection, the indefatigable Charles Allen, called an "all-out, all-agency, seven-days-a-week" effort.[132] The effort might have had an effect. On January 12, 1999, Clarke wrote Berger that the CIA's confidence in the tribals' reporting had increased. It was now higher than it had been on December 20.[133]

In February 1999, Allen proposed flying a U-2 mission over Afghanistan to build a baseline of intelligence outside the areas where the tribals had coverage. Clarke was nervous about such a mission because he continued to fear that Bin Ladin might leave for someplace less accessible. He wrote Deputy National Security Advisor Donald Kerrick that one reliable source reported Bin Ladin's having met with Iraqi officials, who "may have offered him asylum." Other intelligence sources said that some Taliban leaders, though not Mullah Omar, had urged Bin Ladin to go to Iraq. If Bin Ladin actually moved to Iraq, wrote Clarke, his network would be at Saddam Hussein's service, and it would be "virtually impossible" to find him. Better to get Bin Ladin in Afghanistan, Clarke declared.[134] Berger suggested sending one U-2 flight, but Clarke opposed even this. It would require Pakistani approval, he wrote; and "Pak[istan's] intel[ligence service] is in bed with" Bin Ladin and would warn him that the United States was getting ready for a bombing campaign: "Armed with that knowledge, old wily Usama will likely boogie to Baghdad."[135] Though told also by Bruce Riedel of the NSC staff that Saddam Hussein wanted Bin Ladin in Baghdad, Berger conditionally authorized a single U-2 flight. Allen meanwhile had found other ways of getting the information he wanted. So the U-2 flight never occurred.[136]

4.5 SEARCHING FOR FRESH OPTIONS

"Boots on the Ground?"

Starting on the day the August 1998 strikes were launched, General Shelton had issued a planning order to prepare follow-on strikes and think beyond just using cruise missiles.[137] The initial strikes had been called Operation Infinite Reach. The follow-on plans were given the code name Operation Infinite Resolve.

At the time, any actual military action in Afghanistan would have been carried out by General Zinni's Central Command. This command was therefore the locus for most military planning. Zinni was even less enthusiastic than Cohen and Shelton about follow-on cruise missile strikes. He knew that the Tomahawks did not always hit their targets. After the August 20 strikes, President Clinton had had to call Pakistani Prime Minister Sharif to apologize for a wayward missile that had killed several people in a Pakistani village. Sharif had been understanding, while commenting on American "overkill."[138]

Zinni feared that Bin Ladin would in the future locate himself in cities, where U.S. missiles could kill thousands of Afghans. He worried also lest Pakistani authorities not get adequate warning, think the missiles came from India, and do something that everyone would later regret. Discussing potential repercussions in the region of his military responsibility, Zinni said, "It was easy to take the shot from Washington and walk away from it. We had to live there."[139]

Zinni's distinct preference would have been to build up counterterrorism capabilities in neighboring countries such as Uzbekistan. But he told us that he could not drum up much interest in or money for such a purpose from Washington, partly, he thought, because these countries had dictatorial governments.[140]

After the decision—in which fear of collateral damage was an important factor—not to use cruise missiles against Kandahar in December 1998, Shelton and officers in the Pentagon developed plans for using an AC-130 gunship instead of cruise missile strikes. Designed specifically for the special forces, the version of the AC-130 known as "Spooky" can fly in fast or from high altitude, undetected by radar; guided to its zone by extraordinarily complex electronics, it is capable of rapidly firing precision-guided 25, 40, and 105 mm projectiles. Because this system could target more precisely than a salvo of cruise missiles, it had a much lower risk of causing collateral damage. After giving Clarke a briefing and being encouraged to proceed, Shelton formally directed Zinni and General Peter Schoomaker, who headed the Special Operations Command, to develop plans for an AC-130 mission against Bin Ladin's headquarters and infrastructure in Afghanistan. The Joint Staff prepared a decision paper for deployment of the Special Operations aircraft.[141]

Though Berger and Clarke continued to indicate interest in this option, the AC-130s were never deployed. Clarke wrote at the time that Zinni opposed their use, and John Maher, the Joint Staff's deputy director of operations, agreed that this was Zinni's position. Zinni himself does not recall blocking the option. He told us that he understood the Special Operations Command had never thought the intelligence good enough to justify actually moving AC-130s into position. Schoomaker says, on the contrary, that he thought the AC-130 option feasible.[142]

The most likely explanation for the two generals' differing recollections is that both of them thought serious preparation for any such operations would require a long-term redeployment of Special Operations forces to the Middle East or South Asia. The AC-130s would need bases because the aircraft's unrefueled range was only a little over 2,000 miles. They needed search-and-rescue backup, which would have still less range. Thus an AC-130 deployment had to be embedded in a wider political and military concept involving Pakistan or other neighboring countries to address issues relating to basing and overflight. No one ever put such an initiative on the table. Zinni therefore cautioned about simply ordering up AC-130 deployments for a quick strike; Schoomaker planned for what he saw as a practical strike option; and the underlying issues were not fully engaged. The Joint Staff decision paper was never turned into an interagency policy paper.

The same was true for the option of using ground units from the Special Operations Command. Within the command, some officers—such as Schoomaker—wanted the mission of "putting boots on the ground" to get at Bin Ladin and al Qaeda. At the time, Special Operations was designated as a "supporting command," not a "supported command": that is, it supported a theater commander and did not prepare its own plans for dealing with al Qaeda. Schoomaker proposed to Shelton and Cohen that Special Operations become a supported command, but the proposal was not adopted. Had it been accepted, he says, he would have taken on the al Qaeda mission instead of deferring to Zinni. Lieutenant General William Boykin, the current deputy under secretary of defense for intelligence and a founding member of Delta Force, told us that "opportunities were missed because of an unwillingness to take risks and a lack of vision and understanding."[143]

President Clinton relied on the advice of General Shelton, who informed him that without intelligence on Bin Ladin's location, a commando raid's chance of failure was high. Shelton told President Clinton he would go forward with "boots on the ground" if the President ordered him to do so; however, he had to ensure that the President was completely aware of the large logistical problems inherent in a military operation.[144]

The Special Operations plans were apparently conceived as another quick strike option—an option to insert forces after the United States received actionable intelligence. President Clinton told the Commission that "if we had had really good intelligence about . . . where [Usama Bin Ladin] was, I would have done it." Zinni and Schoomaker did make preparations for possible very high risk in-and-out operations to capture or kill terrorists. Cohen told the Commission that the notion of putting military personnel on the ground without some reasonable certitude that Bin Ladin was in a particular location would have resulted in the mission's failure and the loss of life in a fruitless effort.[145] None of these officials was aware of the ambitious plan developed months earlier by lower-level Defense officials.

In our interviews, some military officers repeatedly invoked the analogy of Desert One and the failed 1980 hostage rescue mission in Iran.[146] They were dubious about a quick strike approach to using Special Operations Forces, which they thought complicated and risky. Such efforts would have required bases in the region, but all the options were unappealing. Pro-Taliban elements of Pakistan's military might warn Bin Ladin or his associates of pending operations. With nearby basing options limited, an alternative was to fly from ships in the Arabian Sea or from land bases in the Persian Gulf, as was done after 9/11. Such operations would then have to be supported from long distances, overflying the airspace of nations that might not have been supportive or aware of U.S. efforts.[147]

However, if these hurdles were addressed, and if the military could then operate regularly in the region for a long period, perhaps clandestinely, it might attempt to gather intelligence and wait for an opportunity. One Special Operations commander said his view of actionable intelligence was that if you "give me the action, I will give you the intelligence."[148] But this course would still be risky, in light both of the difficulties already mentioned and of the danger that U.S. operations might fail disastrously. We have found no evidence that such a long-term political-military approach for using Special Operations Forces in the region was proposed to or analyzed by the Small Group, even though such capability had been honed for at least a decade within the Defense Department.

Therefore the debate looked to some like bold proposals from civilians meeting hypercaution from the military. Clarke saw it this way. Of the military, he said to us, "They were very, very, very reluctant."[149] But from another perspective, poorly informed proposals for bold action were pitted against experienced professional judgment. That was how Secretary of Defense Cohen viewed it. He said to us: "I would have to place my judgment call in terms of, do I believe that the chairman of the Joint Chiefs, former commander of Special Forces command, is in a better position to make a judgment on the feasibility of this than, perhaps, Mr. Clarke?"[150]

Beyond a large-scale political-military commitment to build up a covert or clandestine capability using American personnel on the ground, either military or CIA, there was a still larger option that could have been considered—invading Afghanistan itself. Every official we questioned about the possibility of an invasion of Afghanistan said that it was almost unthinkable, absent a provocation such as 9/11, because of poor prospects for cooperation from Pakistan and other nations and because they believed the public would not support it. Cruise missiles were and would remain the only military option on the table.

The Desert Camp, February 1999
Early in 1999, the CIA received reporting that Bin Ladin was spending much of his time at one of several camps in the Afghan desert south of Kandahar. At the beginning of February, Bin Ladin was reportedly located in the vicinity of the Sheikh Ali camp, a desert hunting camp being used by visitors from a Gulf state. Public sources have stated that these visitors were from the United Arab Emirates.[151]

Reporting from the CIA's assets provided a detailed description of the hunting camp, including its size, location, resources, and security, as well as of Bin Ladin's smaller, adjacent camp.[152] Because this was not in an urban area, missiles launched against it would have less risk of causing collateral damage. On February 8, the military began to ready itself for a possible strike.[153] The next day, national technical intelligence confirmed the location and description of the larger camp and showed the nearby presence of an official aircraft of the United Arab Emirates. But the location of Bin Ladin's quarters could not be pinned down so precisely.[154] The CIA did its best to answer a host of questions about the larger camp and its residents and about Bin Ladin's daily schedule and routines to support military contingency planning. According to reporting from the tribals, Bin Ladin regularly went from his adjacent camp to the larger camp where he visited the Emiratis; the tribals expected him to be at the hunting camp for such a visit at least until midmorning on February 11.[155] Clarke wrote to Berger's deputy on February 10 that the military was then doing targeting work to hit the main camp with cruise missiles and should be in position to strike the following morning.[156] Speaker of the House Dennis Hastert appears to have been briefed on the situation.[157]

No strike was launched. By February 12 Bin Ladin had apparently moved on, and the immediate strike plans became moot.[158] According to CIA and Defense officials, policymakers were concerned about the danger that a strike would kill an Emirati prince or other senior officials who might be with Bin Ladin or close by. Clarke told us the strike was called off after consultations with Director Tenet because the intelligence was dubious, and it seemed to Clarke as if the CIA was presenting an option to attack America's best counterterrorism ally in the Gulf. The lead CIA official in the field, Gary Schroen, felt that the intelligence reporting in this case was very reliable; the Bin Ladin unit chief, "Mike," agreed. Schroen believes today that this was a lost opportunity to kill Bin Ladin before 9/11.[159]

Even after Bin Ladin's departure from the area, CIA officers hoped he might return, seeing the camp as a magnet that could draw him for as long as it was still set up. The military maintained readiness for another strike opportunity.[160] On March 7, 1999, Clarke called a UAE official to express his concerns about possible associations between Emirati officials and Bin Ladin. Clarke later wrote in a memorandum of this conversation that the call had been approved at an interagency meeting and cleared with the CIA.[161] When the former Bin Ladin unit chief found out about Clarke's call, he questioned CIA officials, who denied having given such a clearance.[162] Imagery confirmed that less than a week after Clarke's phone call the camp was hurriedly dismantled, and the site was deserted.[163] CIA officers, including Deputy Director for Operations Pavitt, were irate. "Mike" thought the dismantling of the camp erased a possible site for targeting Bin Ladin.[164]

The United Arab Emirates was becoming both a valued counterterrorism ally of the United States and a persistent counterterrorism problem. From 1999 through early 2001, the United States, and President Clinton personally, pressed the UAE, one of the Taliban's only travel and financial outlets to the outside world, to break off its ties and enforce sanctions, especially those relating to flights to and from Afghanistan.[165] These efforts achieved little before 9/11.

In July 1999, UAE Minister of State for Foreign Affairs Hamdan bin Zayid threatened to break relations with the Taliban over Bin Ladin.[166] The Taliban did not take him seriously, however. Bin Zayid later told an American diplomat that the UAE valued its relations with the Taliban because the Afghan radicals offered a counterbalance to "Iranian dangers" in the region, but he also noted that the UAE did not want to upset the United States.[167]

Looking for New Partners

Although not all CIA officers had lost faith in the tribals' capabilities—many judged them to be good reporters—few believed they would carry out an ambush of Bin Ladin. The chief of the Counterterrorist Center compared relying on the tribals to playing the lottery.[168] He and his associates, supported by Clarke, pressed for developing a partnership with the Northern Alliance, even though doing so might bring the United States squarely behind one side in Afghanistan's long-running civil war.

The Northern Alliance was dominated by Tajiks and drew its strength mainly from the northern and eastern parts of Afghanistan. In contrast, Taliban members came principally from Afghanistan's most numerous ethnic group, the Pashtuns, who are concentrated in the southern part of the country, extending into the North-West Frontier and Baluchistan provinces of Pakistan.[169]

Because of the Taliban's behavior and its association with Pakistan, the Northern Alliance had been able at various times to obtain assistance from Russia, Iran, and India. The alliance's leader was Afghanistan's most renowned military commander, Ahmed Shah Massoud. Reflective and charismatic, he had been one of the true heroes of the war against the Soviets. But his bands had been charged with more than one massacre, and the Northern Alliance was widely thought to finance itself in part through trade in heroin. Nor had Massoud shown much aptitude for governing except as a ruthless warlord. Nevertheless, Tenet told us Massoud seemed the most interesting possible new ally against Bin Ladin.[170]

In February 1999, Tenet sought President Clinton's authorization to enlist Massoud and his forces as partners. In response to this request, the President signed the Memorandum of Notification whose language he personally altered. Tenet says he saw no significance in the President's changes. So far as he was concerned, it was the language of August 1998, expressing a preference for capture but accepting the possibility that Bin Ladin could not be brought out alive. "We were plowing the same ground," Tenet said.[171]

CIA officers described Massoud's reaction when he heard that the United States wanted him to capture and not kill Bin Ladin. One characterized Massoud's body language as "a wince." Schroen recalled Massoud's response as "You guys are crazy—you haven't changed a bit." In Schroen's opinion, the capture proviso inhibited Massoud and his forces from going after Bin Ladin but did not completely stop them.[172] The idea, however, was a long shot. Bin Ladin's usual base of activity was near Kandahar, far from the front lines of Taliban operations against the Northern Alliance.

Kandahar, May 1999

It was in Kandahar that perhaps the last, and most likely the best, opportunity arose for targeting Bin Ladin with cruise missiles before 9/11. In May 1999, CIA assets in Afghanistan reported on Bin Ladin's location in and around Kandahar over the course of five days and nights. The reporting was very detailed and came from several sources. If this intelligence was not "actionable," working-level officials said at the time and today, it was hard for them to imagine how any intelligence on Bin Ladin in Afghanistan would meet the standard. Communications were good, and the cruise missiles were ready. "This was in our strike zone," a senior military officer said. "It was a fat pitch, a home run." He expected the missiles to fly. When the decision came back that they should stand down, not shoot, the officer said, "we all just slumped." He told us he knew of no one at the Pentagon or the CIA who thought it was a bad gamble. Bin Ladin "should have been a dead man" that night, he said.[173]

Working-level CIA officials agreed. While there was a conflicting intelligence report about Bin Ladin's whereabouts, the experts discounted it. At the time, CIA working-level officials were told by their managers that the strikes were not ordered because the military doubted the intelligence and worried about collateral damage. Replying to a frustrated colleague in the field, the Bin Ladin unit chief wrote: "having a chance to get [Bin Ladin] three times in 36 hours and foregoing the chance each time has made me a bit angry. . . . [T]he DCI finds himself alone at the table, with the other princip[als] basically saying 'we'll go along with your decision Mr. Director,' and implicitly saying that the Agency will hang alone if the attack doesn't get Bin Ladin."[174] But the military officer quoted earlier recalled that the Pentagon had been willing to act. He told us that Clarke informed him and others that Tenet assessed the chance of the intelligence being accurate as 50–50. This officer believed that Tenet's assessment was the key to the decision.[175]

Tenet told us he does not remember any details about this episode, except that the intelligence came from a single uncorroborated source and that there was a risk of collateral damage. The story is further complicated by Tenet's absence from the critical principals meeting on this strike (he was apparently out of town); his deputy, John Gordon, was representing the CIA. Gordon recalled having presented the intelligence in a positive light, with appropriate caveats, but stating that this intelligence was about as good as it could get.[176]

Berger remembered only that in all such cases, the call had been Tenet's. Berger felt sure that Tenet was eager to get Bin Ladin. In his view, Tenet did his job responsibly. "George would call and say, 'We just don't have it,'" Berger said.[177]

The decision not to strike in May 1999 may now seem hard to understand. In fairness, we note two points: First, in December 1998, the principals' wariness about ordering a strike appears to have been vindicated: Bin Ladin left his room unexpectedly, and if a strike had been ordered he would not have been hit. Second, the administration, and the CIA in particular, was in the midst of intense scrutiny and criticism in May 1999 because faulty intelligence had just led the United States to mistakenly bomb the Chinese embassy in Belgrade during the NATO war against Serbia. This episode may have made officials more cautious than might otherwise have been the case.[178]

From May 1999 until September 2001, policymakers did not again actively consider a missile strike against Bin Ladin.[179] The principals did give some further consideration in 1999 to more general strikes, reviving Clarke's "Delenda" notion of hitting camps and infrastructure to disrupt al Qaeda's organization. In the first months of 1999, the Joint Staff had developed broader target lists to undertake a "focused campaign" against the infrastructure of Bin Ladin's network and to hit Taliban government sites as well. General Shelton told us that the Taliban targets were "easier" to hit and more substantial.[180]

Part of the context for considering broader strikes in the summer of 1999 was renewed worry about Bin Ladin's ambitions to acquire weapons of mass destruction. In May and June, the U.S. government received a flurry of ominous reports, including more information about chemical weapons training or development at the Derunta camp and possible attempts to amass nuclear material at Herat.[181]

By late June, U.S. and other intelligence services had concluded that al Qaeda was in pre-attack mode, perhaps again involving Abu Hafs the Mauritanian. On June 25, at Clarke's request, Berger convened the Small Group in his office to discuss the alert, Bin Ladin's WMD programs, and his location. "Should we pre-empt by attacking UBL facilities?" Clarke urged Berger to ask his colleagues.[182]

In his handwritten notes on the meeting paper, Berger jotted down the presence of 7 to 11 families in the Tarnak Farms facility, which could mean 60–65 casualties. Berger noted the possible "slight impact" on Bin Ladin and added, "if he responds, we're blamed."[183] The NSC staff raised the option of waiting until after a terrorist attack, and then retaliating, including possible strikes on the Taliban. But Clarke observed that Bin Ladin would probably empty his camps after an attack.[184]

The military route seemed to have reached a dead end. In December 1999, Clarke urged Berger to ask the principals to ask themselves: "Why have there been no real options lately for direct US military action?"[185] There are no notes recording whether the question was discussed or, if it was, how it was answered.

Reports of possible attacks by Bin Ladin kept coming in throughout 1999. They included a threat to blow up the FBI building in Washington, D.C. In September, the CSG reviewed a possible threat to a flight out of Los Angeles or New York.[186] These warnings came amid dozens of others that flooded in.

With military and diplomatic options practically exhausted by the summer of 1999, the U.S. government seemed to be back where it had been in the summer of 1998—relying on the CIA to find some other option. That picture also seemed discouraging. Several disruptions and renditions aimed against the broader al Qaeda network had succeeded.[187] But covert action efforts in Afghanistan had not been fruitful.

In mid-1999, new leaders arrived at the Counterterrorist Center and the Bin Ladin unit. The new director of CTC, replacing "Jeff," was Cofer Black. The new head of the section that included the Bin Ladin unit was "Richard." Black, "Richard," and their colleagues began working on a new operational strategy for attacking al Qaeda; their starting point was to get better intelligence, relying more on the CIA's own sources and less on the tribals.[188]

In July 1999, President Clinton authorized the CIA to work with several governments to capture Bin Ladin, and extended the scope of efforts to Bin Ladin's principal lieutenants. The President reportedly also authorized a covert action under carefully limited circumstances which, if successful, would have resulted in Bin Ladin's death.[189] Attorney General Reno again expressed concerns on policy grounds. She was worried about the danger of retaliation. The CIA also developed the short-lived effort to work with a Pakistani team that we discussed earlier, and an initiative to work with Uzbekistan. The Uzbeks needed basic equipment and training. No action could be expected before March 2000, at the earliest.[190]

In fall 1999, DCI Tenet unveiled the CIA's new Bin Ladin strategy. It was called, simply, "the Plan." The Plan proposed continuing disruption and rendition operations worldwide. It announced a program for hiring and training better officers with counterterrorism skills, recruiting more assets, and trying to penetrate al Qaeda's ranks. The Plan aimed to close gaps in technical intelligence collection (signal and imagery) as well. In addition, the CIA would increase contacts with the Northern Alliance rebels fighting the Taliban.[191]

With a new operational strategy, the CIA evaluated its capture options. None scored high marks. The CIA had no confidence in the Pakistani effort. In the event that Bin Ladin traveled to the Kandahar region in southern Afghanistan, the tribal network there was unlikely to attack a heavily guarded Bin Ladin; the Counterterrorist Center rated the chance of success at less than 10 percent. To the northwest, the Uzbeks might be ready for a cross-border sortie in six months; their chance of success was also rated at less than 10 percent.[192]

In the northeast were Massoud's Northern Alliance forces—perhaps the CIA's best option. In late October, a group of officers from the Counterterrorist Center flew into the Panjshir Valley to meet up with Massoud, a hazardous journey in rickety helicopters that would be repeated several times in the future. Massoud appeared committed to helping the United States collect intelligence on Bin Ladin's activities and whereabouts and agreed to try to capture him if the opportunity arose. The Bin Ladin unit was satisfied that its reporting on Bin Ladin would now have a second source. But it also knew that Massoud would act against Bin Ladin only if his own interests and those of the

United States intersected. By early December, the CIA rated this possibility at less than 15 percent.[193]

Finally, the CIA considered the possibility of putting U.S. personnel on the ground in Afghanistan. The CIA had been discussing this option with Special Operations Command and found enthusiasm on the working level but reluctance at higher levels. CIA saw a 95 percent chance of Special Operations Command forces capturing Bin Ladin if deployed—but less than a 5 percent chance of such a deployment. Sending CIA officers into Afghanistan was to be considered "if the gain clearly outweighs the risk"—but at this time no such gains presented themselves to warrant the risk.[194]

As mentioned earlier, such a protracted deployment of U.S. Special Operations Forces into Afghanistan, perhaps as part of a team joined to a deployment of the CIA's own officers, would have required a major policy initiative (probably combined with efforts to secure the support of at least one or two neighboring countries) to make a long-term commitment, establish a durable presence on the ground, and be prepared to accept the associated risks and costs. Such a military plan was never developed for interagency consideration before 9/11. As 1999 came to a close, the CIA had a new strategic plan in place for capturing Bin Ladin, but no option was rated as having more than a 15 percent chance of achieving that objective.

5

AL QAEDA AIMS AT THE
AMERICAN HOMELAND

5.1 TERRORIST ENTREPRENEURS

By early 1999, al Qaeda was already a potent adversary of the United States. Bin Ladin and his chief of operations, Abu Hafs al Masri, also known as Mohammed Atef, occupied undisputed leadership positions atop al Qaeda's organizational structure. Within this structure, al Qaeda's worldwide terrorist operations relied heavily on the ideas and work of enterprising and strong-willed field commanders who enjoyed considerable autonomy. To understand how the organization actually worked and to introduce the origins of the 9/11 plot, we briefly examine three of these subordinate commanders: Khalid Sheikh Mohammed (KSM), Riduan Isamuddin (better known as Hambali), and Abd al Rahim al Nashiri. We will devote the most attention to Khalid Sheikh Mohammed, the chief manager of the "planes operation."

Khalid Sheikh Mohammed

No one exemplifies the model of the terrorist entrepreneur more clearly than Khalid Sheikh Mohammed, the principal architect of the 9/11 attacks. KSM followed a rather tortuous path to his eventual membership in al Qaeda.[1] Highly educated and equally comfortable in a government office or a terrorist safehouse, KSM applied his imagination, technical aptitude, and managerial skills to hatching and planning an extraordinary array of terrorist schemes. These ideas included conventional car bombing, political assassination, aircraft bombing, hijacking, reservoir poisoning, and, ultimately, the use of aircraft as missiles guided by suicide operatives.

Like his nephew Ramzi Yousef (three years KSM's junior), KSM grew up in Kuwait but traces his ethnic lineage to the Baluchistan region straddling Iran and Pakistan. Raised in a religious family, KSM claims to have joined the Muslim Brotherhood at age 16 and to have become enamored of violent jihad at youth camps in the desert. In 1983, following his graduation from secondary

Detainee Interrogation Reports

Chapters 5 and 7 rely heavily on information obtained from captured al Qaeda members. A number of these "detainees" have firsthand knowledge of the 9/11 plot.

Assessing the truth of statements by these witnesses—sworn enemies of the United States—is challenging. Our access to them has been limited to the review of intelligence reports based on communications received from the locations where the actual interrogations take place. We submitted questions for use in the interrogations, but had no control over whether, when, or how questions of particular interest would be asked. Nor were we allowed to talk to the interrogators so that we could better judge the credibility of the detainees and clarify ambiguities in the reporting. We were told that our requests might disrupt the sensitive interrogation process.

We have nonetheless decided to include information from captured 9/11 conspirators and al Qaeda members in our report. We have evaluated their statements carefully and have attempted to corroborate them with documents and statements of others. In this report, we indicate where such statements provide the foundation for our narrative. We have been authorized to identify by name only ten detainees whose custody has been confirmed officially by the U.S. government.[2]

school, KSM left Kuwait to enroll at Chowan College, a small Baptist school in Murfreesboro, North Carolina. After a semester at Chowan, KSM transferred to North Carolina Agricultural and Technical State University in Greensboro, which he attended with Yousef's brother, another future al Qaeda member. KSM earned a degree in mechanical engineering in December 1986.[3]

Although he apparently did not attract attention for extreme Islamist beliefs or activities while in the United States, KSM plunged into the anti-Soviet Afghan jihad soon after graduating from college. Visiting Pakistan for the first time in early 1987, he traveled to Peshawar, where his brother Zahid introduced him to the famous Afghan *mujahid* Abdul Rasul Sayyaf, head of the Hizbul-Ittihad El-Islami (Islamic Union Party). Sayyaf became KSM's mentor and provided KSM with military training at Sayyaf's Sada camp. KSM claims he then fought the Soviets and remained at the front for three months before being summoned to perform administrative duties for Abdullah Azzam. KSM next took a job working for an electronics firm that catered to the communications needs of Afghan groups, where he learned about drills used to excavate caves in Afghanistan.[4]

Between 1988 and 1992, KSM helped run a nongovernmental organization

(NGO) in Peshawar and Jalalabad; sponsored by Sayyaf, it was designed to aid young Afghan mujahideen. In 1992, KSM spent some time fighting alongside the mujahideen in Bosnia and supporting that effort with financial donations. After returning briefly to Pakistan, he moved his family to Qatar at the suggestion of the former minister of Islamic affairs of Qatar, Sheikh Abdallah bin Khalid bin Hamad al Thani. KSM took a position in Qatar as project engineer with the Qatari Ministry of Electricity and Water. Although he engaged in extensive international travel during his tenure at the ministry—much of it in furtherance of terrorist activity—KSM would hold his position there until early 1996, when he fled to Pakistan to avoid capture by U.S. authorities.[5]

KSM first came to the attention of U.S. law enforcement as a result of his cameo role in the first World Trade Center bombing. According to KSM, he learned of Ramzi Yousef's intention to launch an attack inside the United States in 1991 or 1992, when Yousef was receiving explosives training in Afghanistan. During the fall of 1992, while Yousef was building the bomb he would use in that attack, KSM and Yousef had numerous telephone conversations during which Yousef discussed his progress and sought additional funding. On November 3, 1992, KSM wired $660 from Qatar to the bank account of Yousef's co-conspirator, Mohammed Salameh. KSM does not appear to have contributed any more substantially to this operation.[6]

Yousef's instant notoriety as the mastermind of the 1993 World Trade Center bombing inspired KSM to become involved in planning attacks against the United States. By his own account, KSM's animus toward the United States stemmed not from his experiences there as a student, but rather from his violent disagreement with U.S. foreign policy favoring Israel. In 1994, KSM accompanied Yousef to the Philippines, and the two of them began planning what is now known as the Manila air or "Bojinka" plot—the intended bombing of 12 U.S. commercial jumbo jets over the Pacific during a two-day span. This marked the first time KSM took part in the actual planning of a terrorist operation. While sharing an apartment in Manila during the summer of 1994, he and Yousef acquired chemicals and other materials necessary to construct bombs and timers. They also cased target flights to Hong Kong and Seoul that would have onward legs to the United States. During this same period, KSM and Yousef also developed plans to assassinate President Clinton during his November 1994 trip to Manila, and to bomb U.S.-bound cargo carriers by smuggling jackets containing nitrocellulose on board.[7]

KSM left the Philippines in September 1994 and met up with Yousef in Karachi following their casing flights. There they enlisted Wali Khan Amin Shah, also known as Usama Asmurai, in the Manila air plot. During the fall of 1994, Yousef returned to Manila and successfully tested the digital watch timer he had invented, bombing a movie theater and a Philippine Airlines flight en route to Tokyo. The plot unraveled after the Philippine authorities discovered Yousef's bomb-making operation in Manila; but by that time, KSM was safely

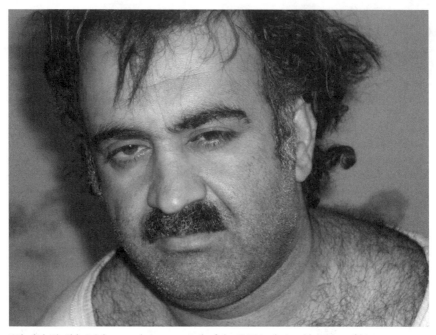

Khalid Sheikh Mohammed, mastermind of the 9/11 plot, at the time of his capture in 2003

back at his government job in Qatar. Yousef attempted to follow through on the cargo carriers plan, but he was arrested in Islamabad by Pakistani authorities on February 7, 1995, after an accomplice turned him in.[8]

KSM continued to travel among the worldwide jihadist community after Yousef's arrest, visiting the Sudan, Yemen, Malaysia, and Brazil in 1995. No clear evidence connects him to terrorist activities in those locations. While in Sudan, he reportedly failed in his attempt to meet with Bin Ladin. But KSM did see Atef, who gave him a contact in Brazil. In January 1996, well aware that U.S. authorities were chasing him, he left Qatar for good and fled to Afghanistan, where he renewed his relationship with Rasul Sayyaf.[9]

Just as KSM was reestablishing himself in Afghanistan in mid-1996, Bin Ladin and his colleagues were also completing their migration from Sudan. Through Atef, KSM arranged a meeting with Bin Ladin in Tora Bora, a mountainous redoubt from the Afghan war days. At the meeting, KSM presented the al Qaeda leader with a menu of ideas for terrorist operations. According to KSM, this meeting was the first time he had seen Bin Ladin since 1989. Although they had fought together in 1987, Bin Ladin and KSM did not yet enjoy an especially close working relationship. Indeed, KSM has acknowledged that Bin Ladin likely agreed to meet with him because of the renown of his nephew, Yousef.[10]

At the meeting, KSM briefed Bin Ladin and Atef on the first World Trade Center bombing, the Manila air plot, the cargo carriers plan, and other activities pursued by KSM and his colleagues in the Philippines. KSM also presented a proposal for an operation that would involve training pilots who would crash planes into buildings in the United States. This proposal eventually would become the 9/11 operation.[11]

KSM knew that the successful staging of such an attack would require personnel, money, and logistical support that only an extensive and well-funded organization like al Qaeda could provide. He thought the operation might appeal to Bin Ladin, who had a long record of denouncing the United States.[12]

From KSM's perspective, Bin Ladin was in the process of consolidating his new position in Afghanistan while hearing out others' ideas, and had not yet settled on an agenda for future anti-U.S. operations. At the meeting, Bin Ladin listened to KSM's ideas without much comment, but did ask KSM formally to join al Qaeda and move his family to Afghanistan.[13]

KSM declined. He preferred to remain independent and retain the option of working with other mujahideen groups still operating in Afghanistan, including the group led by his old mentor, Sayyaf. Sayyaf was close to Ahmed Shah Massoud, the leader of the Northern Alliance. Therefore working with him might be a problem for KSM because Bin Ladin was building ties to the rival Taliban.

After meeting with Bin Ladin, KSM says he journeyed onward to India, Indonesia, and Malaysia, where he met with Jemaah Islamiah's Hambali. Hambali was an Indonesian veteran of the Afghan war looking to expand the jihad into Southeast Asia. In Iran, KSM rejoined his family and arranged to move them to Karachi; he claims to have relocated by January 1997.[14]

After settling his family in Karachi, KSM tried to join the mujahid leader Ibn al Khattab in Chechnya. Unable to travel through Azerbaijan, KSM returned to Karachi and then to Afghanistan to renew contacts with Bin Ladin and his colleagues. Though KSM may not have been a member of al Qaeda at this time, he admits traveling frequently between Pakistan and Afghanistan in 1997 and the first half of 1998, visiting Bin Ladin and cultivating relationships with his lieutenants, Atef and Sayf al Adl, by assisting them with computer and media projects.[15]

According to KSM, the 1998 bombings of the U.S. embassies in Nairobi and Dar es Salaam marked a watershed in the evolution of the 9/11 plot. KSM claims these bombings convinced him that Bin Ladin was truly committed to attacking the United States. He continued to make himself useful, collecting news articles and helping other al Qaeda members with their outdated computer equipment. Bin Ladin, apparently at Atef's urging, finally decided to give KSM the green light for the 9/11 operation sometime in late 1998 or early 1999.[16]

KSM then accepted Bin Ladin's standing invitation to move to Kandahar and work directly with al Qaeda. In addition to supervising the planning and preparations for the 9/11 operation, KSM worked with and eventually led al Qaeda's media committee. But KSM states he refused to swear a formal oath of allegiance to Bin Ladin, thereby retaining a last vestige of his cherished autonomy.[17]

At this point, late 1998 to early 1999, planning for the 9/11 operation began in earnest. Yet while the 9/11 project occupied the bulk of KSM's attention, he continued to consider other possibilities for terrorist attacks. For example, he sent al Qaeda operative Issa al Britani to Kuala Lumpur, Malaysia, to learn about the jihad in Southeast Asia from Hambali. Thereafter, KSM claims, at Bin Ladin's direction in early 2001, he sent Britani to the United States to case potential economic and "Jewish" targets in New York City. Furthermore, during the summer of 2001, KSM approached Bin Ladin with the idea of recruiting a Saudi Arabian air force pilot to commandeer a Saudi fighter jet and attack the Israeli city of Eilat. Bin Ladin reportedly liked this proposal, but he instructed KSM to concentrate on the 9/11 operation first. Similarly, KSM's proposals to Atef around this same time for attacks in Thailand, Singapore, Indonesia, and the Maldives were never executed, although Hambali's Jemaah Islamiah operatives did some casing of possible targets.[18]

KSM appears to have been popular among the al Qaeda rank and file. He was reportedly regarded as an effective leader, especially after the 9/11 attacks. Co-workers describe him as an intelligent, efficient, and even-tempered manager who approached his projects with a single-minded dedication that he expected his colleagues to share. Al Qaeda associate Abu Zubaydah has expressed more qualified admiration for KSM's innate creativity, emphasizing instead his ability to incorporate the improvements suggested by others. Nashiri has been similarly measured, observing that although KSM floated many general ideas for attacks, he rarely conceived a specific operation himself.[19] Perhaps these estimates reflect a touch of jealousy; in any case, KSM was plainly a capable coordinator, having had years to hone his skills and build relationships.

Hambali

Al Qaeda's success in fostering terrorism in Southeast Asia stems largely from its close relationship with Jemaah Islamiah (JI). In that relationship, Hambali became the key coordinator. Born and educated in Indonesia, Hambali moved to Malaysia in the early 1980s to find work. There he claims to have become a follower of the Islamist extremist teachings of various clerics, including one named Abdullah Sungkar. Sungkar first inspired Hambali to share the vision of establishing a radical Islamist regime in Southeast Asia, then furthered Hambali's instruction in jihad by sending him to Afghanistan in 1986. After undergoing training at Rasul Sayyaf's Sada camp (where KSM would later train), Hambali fought against the Soviets; he eventually returned to Malaysia after 18 months in Afghanistan. By 1998, Hambali would assume responsibility for the Malaysia/Singapore region within Sungkar's newly formed terrorist organization, the JI.[20]

Also by 1998, Sungkar and JI spiritual leader Abu Bakar Bashir had accepted Bin Ladin's offer to ally JI with al Qaeda in waging war against Christians and Jews.[21] Hambali met with KSM in Karachi to arrange for JI members to receive training in Afghanistan at al Qaeda's camps. In addition to his close working relationship with KSM, Hambali soon began dealing with Atef as well. Al Qaeda began funding JI's increasingly ambitious terrorist plans, which Atef and KSM sought to expand. Under this arrangement, JI would perform the necessary casing activities and locate bomb-making materials and other supplies. Al Qaeda would underwrite operations, provide bomb-making expertise, and deliver suicide operatives.[22]

The al Qaeda–JI partnership yielded a number of proposals that would marry al Qaeda's financial and technical strengths with JI's access to materials and local operatives. Here, Hambali played the critical role of coordinator, as he distributed al Qaeda funds earmarked for the joint operations. In one especially notable example, Atef turned to Hambali when al Qaeda needed a scientist to take over its biological weapons program. Hambali obliged by introducing a U.S.-educated JI member, Yazid Sufaat, to Ayman al Zawahiri in Kandahar. In 2001, Sufaat would spend several months attempting to cultivate anthrax for al Qaeda in a laboratory he helped set up near the Kandahar airport.[23]

Hambali did not originally orient JI's operations toward attacking the United States, but his involvement with al Qaeda appears to have inspired him to pursue American targets. KSM, in his post-capture interrogations, has taken credit for this shift, claiming to have urged the JI operations chief to concentrate on attacks designed to hurt the U.S. economy.[24] Hambali's newfound interest in striking against the United States manifested itself in a spate of terrorist plans. Fortunately, none came to fruition.

In addition to staging actual terrorist attacks in partnership with al Qaeda, Hambali and JI assisted al Qaeda operatives passing through Kuala Lumpur. One important occasion was in December 1999–January 2000. Hambali accommodated KSM's requests to help several veterans whom KSM had just finished training in Karachi. They included Tawfiq bin Attash, also known as Khallad, who later would help bomb the USS *Cole*, and future 9/11 hijackers Nawaf al Hazmi and Khalid al Mihdhar. Hambali arranged lodging for them and helped them purchase airline tickets for their onward travel. Later that year, Hambali and his crew would provide accommodations and other assistance (including information on flight schools and help in acquiring ammonium nitrate) for Zacarias Moussaoui, an al Qaeda operative sent to Malaysia by Atef and KSM.[25]

Hambali used Bin Ladin's Afghan facilities as a training ground for JI recruits. Though he had a close relationship with Atef and KSM, he maintained JI's institutional independence from al Qaeda. Hambali insists that he did not discuss operations with Bin Ladin or swear allegiance to him, having already given such a pledge of loyalty to Bashir, Sungkar's successor as JI leader. Thus, like any powerful bureaucrat defending his domain, Hambali objected when al Qaeda leadership tried to assign JI members to terrorist projects without notifying him.[26]

Abd al Rahim al Nashiri

KSM and Hambali both decided to join forces with al Qaeda because their terrorist aspirations required the money and manpower that only a robust organization like al Qaeda could supply. On the other hand, Abd al Rahim al Nashiri—the mastermind of the *Cole* bombing and the eventual head of al Qaeda operations in the Arabian Peninsula—appears to have originally been recruited to his career as a terrorist by Bin Ladin himself.

Having already participated in the Afghan jihad, Nashiri accompanied a group of some 30 mujahideen in pursuit of jihad in Tajikistan in 1996. When serious fighting failed to materialize, the group traveled to Jalalabad and encountered Bin Ladin, who had recently returned from Sudan. Bin Ladin addressed them at length, urging the group to join him in a "jihad against the Americans." Although all were urged to swear loyalty to Bin Ladin, many, including Nashiri, found the notion distasteful and refused. After several days of indoctrination that included a barrage of news clippings and television documentaries, Nashiri left Afghanistan, first returning to his native Saudi Arabia and then visiting his home in Yemen. There, he says, the idea for his first terrorist operation took shape as he noticed many U.S. and other foreign ships plying the waters along the southwest coast of Yemen.[27]

Nashiri returned to Afghanistan, probably in 1997, primarily to check on relatives fighting there and also to learn about the Taliban. He again encountered Bin Ladin, still recruiting for "the coming battle with the United States." Nashiri pursued a more conventional military jihad, joining the Taliban forces in their fight against Ahmed Massoud's Northern Alliance and shuttling back and forth between the front and Kandahar, where he would see Bin Ladin and meet with other mujahideen. During this period, Nashiri also led a plot to smuggle four Russian-made antitank missiles into Saudi Arabia from Yemen in early 1998 and helped an embassy bombing operative obtain a Yemeni passport.[28]

At some point, Nashiri joined al Qaeda. His cousin, Jihad Mohammad Ali al Makki, also known as Azzam, was a suicide bomber for the Nairobi attack. Nashiri traveled between Yemen and Afghanistan. In late 1998, Nashiri proposed mounting an attack against a U.S. vessel. Bin Ladin approved. He directed Nashiri to start the planning and send operatives to Yemen, and he later provided money.[29]

Nashiri reported directly to Bin Ladin, the only other person who, according to Nashiri, knew all the details of the operation. When Nashiri had difficulty finding U.S. naval vessels to attack along the western coast of Yemen, Bin

Ladin reportedly instructed him to case the Port of Aden, on the southern coast, instead.[30] The eventual result was an attempted attack on the USS *The Sullivans* in January 2000 and the successful attack, in October 2000, on the USS *Cole*.

Nashiri's success brought him instant status within al Qaeda. He later was recognized as the chief of al Qaeda operations in and around the Arabian Peninsula. While Nashiri continued to consult Bin Ladin on the planning of subsequent terrorist projects, he retained discretion in selecting operatives and devising attacks. In the two years between the *Cole* bombing and Nashiri's capture, he would supervise several more proposed operations for al Qaeda. The October 6, 2002, bombing of the French tanker *Limburg* in the Gulf of Aden also was Nashiri's handiwork. Although Bin Ladin urged Nashiri to continue plotting strikes against U.S. interests in the Persian Gulf, Nashiri maintains that he actually delayed one of these projects because of security concerns.[31] Those concerns, it seems, were well placed, as Nashiri's November 2002 capture in the United Arab Emirates finally ended his career as a terrorist.

5.2 THE "PLANES OPERATION"

According to KSM, he started to think about attacking the United States after Yousef returned to Pakistan following the 1993 World Trade Center bombing. Like Yousef, KSM reasoned he could best influence U.S. policy by targeting the country's economy. KSM and Yousef reportedly brainstormed together about what drove the U.S. economy. New York, which KSM considered the economic capital of the United States, therefore became the primary target. For similar reasons, California also became a target for KSM.[32]

KSM claims that the earlier bombing of the World Trade Center taught him that bombs and explosives could be problematic, and that he needed to graduate to a more novel form of attack. He maintains that he and Yousef began thinking about using aircraft as weapons while working on the Manila air/Bojinka plot, and speculated about striking the World Trade Center and CIA headquarters as early as 1995.[33]

Certainly KSM was not alone in contemplating new kinds of terrorist operations. A study reportedly conducted by Atef, while he and Bin Ladin were still in Sudan, concluded that traditional terrorist hijacking operations did not fit the needs of al Qaeda, because such hijackings were used to negotiate the release of prisoners rather than to inflict mass casualties. The study is said to have considered the feasibility of hijacking planes and blowing them up in flight, paralleling the Bojinka concept. Such a study, if it actually existed, yields significant insight into the thinking of al Qaeda's leaders: (1) they rejected hijackings aimed at gaining the release of imprisoned comrades as too complex, because al Qaeda had no friendly countries in which to land a plane and then negotiate; (2) they considered the bombing of commercial flights in midair—as carried out against Pan Am Flight 103 over Lockerbie, Scotland—a promising means to inflict massive casualties; and (3) they did not yet consider using hijacked aircraft as weapons against other targets.[34]

KSM has insisted to his interrogators that he always contemplated hijacking and crashing large commercial aircraft. Indeed, KSM describes a grandiose original plan: a total of ten aircraft to be hijacked, nine of which would crash into targets on both coasts—they included those eventually hit on September 11 plus CIA and FBI headquarters, nuclear power plants, and the tallest buildings in California and the state of Washington. KSM himself was to land the tenth plane at a U.S. airport and, after killing all adult male passengers on board and alerting the media, deliver a speech excoriating U.S. support for Israel, the Philippines, and repressive governments in the Arab world. Beyond KSM's rationalizations about targeting the U.S. economy, this vision gives a better glimpse of his true ambitions. This is theater, a spectacle of destruction with KSM as the self-cast star—the superterrorist.[35]

KSM concedes that this proposal received a lukewarm response from al Qaeda leaders skeptical of its scale and complexity. Although Bin Ladin listened to KSM's proposal, he was not convinced that it was practical. As mentioned earlier, Bin Ladin was receiving numerous ideas for potential operations—KSM's proposal to attack U.S. targets with commercial airplanes was only one of many.[36]

KSM presents himself as an entrepreneur seeking venture capital and people. He simply wanted al Qaeda to supply the money and operatives needed for the attack while retaining his independence. It is easy to question such a statement. Money is one thing; supplying a cadre of trained operatives willing to die is much more. Thus, although KSM contends he would have been just as likely to consider working with any comparable terrorist organization, he gives no indication of what other groups he thought could supply such exceptional commodities.[37]

KSM acknowledges formally joining al Qaeda, in late 1998 or 1999, and states that soon afterward, Bin Ladin also made the decision to support his proposal to attack the United States using commercial airplanes as weapons. Though KSM speculates about how Bin Ladin came to share his preoccupation with attacking America, Bin Ladin in fact had long been an opponent of the United States. KSM thinks that Atef may have persuaded Bin Ladin to approve this specific proposal. Atef's role in the entire operation is unquestionably very significant but tends to fade into the background, in part because Atef himself is not available to describe it. He was killed in November 2001 by an American air strike in Afghanistan.[38]

Bin Ladin summoned KSM to Kandahar in March or April 1999 to tell him that al Qaeda would support his proposal. The plot was now referred to within al Qaeda as the "planes operation."[39]

The Plan Evolves

Bin Ladin reportedly discussed the planes operation with KSM and Atef in a series of meetings in the spring of 1999 at the al Matar complex near Kandahar. KSM's original concept of using one of the hijacked planes to make a media statement was scrapped, but Bin Ladin considered the basic idea feasible. Bin Ladin, Atef, and KSM developed an initial list of targets. These included the White House, the U.S. Capitol, the Pentagon, and the World Trade Center. According to KSM, Bin Ladin wanted to destroy the White House and the Pentagon, KSM wanted to strike the World Trade Center, and all of them wanted to hit the Capitol. No one else was involved in the initial selection of targets.[40]

Bin Ladin also soon selected four individuals to serve as suicide operatives: Khalid al Mihdhar, Nawaf al Hazmi, Khallad, and Abu Bara al Yemeni. During the al Matar meetings, Bin Ladin told KSM that Mihdhar and Hazmi were so eager to participate in an operation against the United States that they had already obtained U.S. visas. KSM states that they had done so on their own after the suicide of their friend Azzam (Nashiri's cousin) in carrying out the Nairobi bombing. KSM had not met them. His only guidance from Bin Ladin was that the two should eventually go to the United States for pilot training.[41]

Hazmi and Mihdhar were Saudi nationals, born in Mecca. Like the others in this initial group of selectees, they were already experienced mujahideen. They had traveled together to fight in Bosnia in a group that journeyed to the Balkans in 1995. By the time Hazmi and Mihdhar were assigned to the planes operation in early 1999, they had visited Afghanistan on several occasions.[42]

Khallad was another veteran mujahid, like much of his family. His father had been expelled from Yemen because of his extremist views. Khallad had grown up in Saudi Arabia, where his father knew Bin Ladin, Abdullah Azzam, and Omar Abdel Rahman (the "Blind Sheikh"). Khallad departed for Afghanistan in 1994 at the age of 15. Three years later, he lost his lower right leg in a battle with the Northern Alliance, a battle in which one of his brothers died. After this experience, he pledged allegiance to Bin Ladin—whom he had first met as a child in Jeddah—and volunteered to become a suicide operative.[43]

When Khallad applied for a U.S. visa, however, his application was denied. Earlier in 1999, Bin Ladin had sent Khallad to Yemen to help Nashiri obtain explosives for the planned ship-bombing and to obtain a visa to visit the United States, so that he could participate in an operation there. Khallad applied under another name, using the cover story that he would be visiting a medical clinic to obtain a new prosthesis for his leg. Another al Qaeda operative gave Khallad the name of a person living in the United States whom Khallad could use as a point of contact on a visa application. Khallad contacted this individual to help him get an appointment at a U.S. clinic. While Khallad was waiting for the letter from the clinic confirming the appointment, however, he was arrested by Yemeni authorities. The arrest resulted from mistaken identity: Khallad was driving the car of another conspirator in the ship-bombing plot who was wanted by the Yemeni authorities.[44]

Khallad was released sometime during the summer of 1999, after his father and Bin Ladin intervened on his behalf. Khallad learned later that the al Qaeda leader, apparently concerned that Khallad might reveal Nashiri's operation while under interrogation, had contacted a Yemeni official to demand Khallad's release, suggesting that Bin Ladin would not confront the Yemenis if they did not confront him. This account has been corroborated by others. Giving up on acquiring a U.S. visa and concerned that the United States might learn of his ties to al Qaeda, Khallad returned to Afghanistan.[45]

Travel issues thus played a part in al Qaeda's operational planning from the very start. During the spring and summer of 1999, KSM realized that Khallad and Abu Bara, both of whom were Yemenis, would not be able to obtain U.S. visas as easily as Saudi operatives like Mihdhar and Hazmi. Although Khallad had been unable to acquire a U.S. visa, KSM still wanted him and Abu Bara, as well as another Yemeni operative from Bin Ladin's security detail, to participate in the planes operation. Yet because individuals with Saudi passports could travel much more easily than Yemeni, particularly to the United States, there were fewer martyrdom opportunities for Yemenis. To overcome this problem, KSM decided to split the planes operation into two components.[46]

The first part of the planes operation—crashing hijacked aircraft into U.S. targets—would remain as planned, with Mihdhar and Hazmi playing key roles. The second part, however, would now embrace the idea of using suicide operatives to blow up planes, a refinement of KSM's old Manila air plot. The operatives would hijack U.S.-flagged commercial planes flying Pacific routes across East Asia and destroy them in midair, possibly with shoe bombs, instead of flying them into targets. (An alternate scenario apparently involved flying planes into U.S. targets in Japan, Singapore, or Korea.) This part of the operation has been confirmed by Khallad, who said that they contemplated hijacking several planes, probably originating in Thailand, South Korea, Hong Kong, or Malaysia, and using Yemenis who would not need pilot training because they would simply down the planes. All the planes hijacked in the United States and East Asia were to be crashed or exploded at about the same time to maximize the attack's psychological impact.[47]

Training and Deployment to Kuala Lumpur

In the fall of 1999, the four operatives selected by Bin Ladin for the planes operation were chosen to attend an elite training course at al Qaeda's Mes Aynak camp in Afghanistan. Bin Ladin personally selected the veteran fighters who received this training, and several of them were destined for important operations. One example is Ibrahim al Thawar, or Nibras, who would participate in the October 12, 2000, suicide attack on the USS Cole. According to KSM, this training was not given specifically in preparation for the planes operation or any other particular al Qaeda venture. Although KSM claims not to have been involved with the training or to have met with the future 9/11 hijackers at Mes

Aynak, he says he did visit the camp while traveling from Kandahar to Kabul with Bin Ladin and others.[48]

The Mes Aynak training camp was located in an abandoned Russian copper mine near Kabul. The camp opened in 1999, after the United States had destroyed the training camp near Khowst with cruise missiles in August 1998, and before the Taliban granted al Qaeda permission to open the al Faruq camp in Kandahar. Thus, for a brief period in 1999, Mes Aynak was the only al Qaeda camp operating in Afghanistan. It offered a full range of instruction, including an advanced commando course taught by senior al Qaeda member Sayf al Adl. Bin Ladin paid particular attention to the 1999 training session. When Salah al Din, the trainer for the session, complained about the number of trainees and said that no more than 20 could be handled at once, Bin Ladin insisted that everyone he had selected receive the training.[49]

The special training session at Mes Aynak was rigorous and spared no expense. The course focused on physical fitness, firearms, close quarters combat, shooting from a motorcycle, and night operations. Although the subjects taught differed little from those offered at other camps, the course placed extraordinary physical and mental demands on its participants, who received the best food and other amenities to enhance their strength and morale.[50]

Upon completing the advanced training at Mes Aynak, Hazmi, Khallad, and Abu Bara went to Karachi, Pakistan. There KSM instructed them on Western culture and travel. Much of his activity in mid-1999 had revolved around the collection of training and informational materials for the participants in the planes operation. For instance, he collected Western aviation magazines; telephone directories for American cities such as San Diego and Long Beach, California; brochures for schools; and airline timetables, and he conducted Internet searches on U.S. flight schools. He also purchased flight simulator software and a few movies depicting hijackings. To house his students, KSM rented a safehouse in Karachi with money provided by Bin Ladin.[51]

In early December 1999, Khallad and Abu Bara arrived in Karachi. Hazmi joined them there a few days later. On his way to Karachi, Hazmi spent a night in Quetta at a safehouse where, according to KSM, an Egyptian named Mohamed Atta simultaneously stayed on his way to Afghanistan for jihad training.[52]

Mihdhar did not attend the training in Karachi with the others. KSM says that he never met with Mihdhar in 1999 but assumed that Bin Ladin and Atef had briefed Mihdhar on the planes operation and had excused him from the Karachi training.[53]

The course in Karachi apparently lasted about one or two weeks. According to KSM, he taught the three operatives basic English words and phrases. He showed them how to read phone books, interpret airline timetables, use the Internet, use code words in communications, make travel reservations, and rent an apartment. Khallad adds that the training involved using flight simulator computer games, viewing movies that featured hijackings, and reading flight schedules to determine which flights would be in the air at the same time in different parts of the world. They used the game software to increase their familiarity with aircraft models and functions, and to highlight gaps in cabin security. While in Karachi, they also discussed how to case flights in Southeast Asia. KSM told them to watch the cabin doors at takeoff and landing, to observe whether the captain went to the lavatory during the flight, and to note whether the flight attendants brought food into the cockpit. KSM, Khallad, and Hazmi also visited travel agencies to learn the visa requirements for Asian countries.[54]

The four trainees traveled to Kuala Lumpur: Khallad, Abu Bara, and Hazmi came from Karachi; Mihdhar traveled from Yemen. As discussed in chapter 6, U.S. intelligence would analyze communications associated with Mihdhar, whom they identified during this travel, and Hazmi, whom they could have identified but did not.[55]

According to KSM, the four operatives were aware that they had volunteered for a suicide operation, either in the United States or in Asia. With different roles, they had different tasks. Hazmi and Mihdhar were sent to Kuala Lumpur before proceeding to their final destination—the United States. According to KSM, they were to use Yemeni documents to fly to Malaysia, then proceed to the United States using their Saudi passports to conceal their prior travels to and from Pakistan. KSM had doctored Hazmi's Saudi passport so it would appear as if Hazmi had traveled to Kuala Lumpur from Saudi Arabia via Dubai. Khallad and Abu Bara went to Kuala Lumpur to study airport security and conduct casing flights. According to Khallad, he and Abu Bara departed for Malaysia in mid-December 1999. Hazmi joined them about ten days later after briefly returning to Afghanistan to attend to some passport issues.[56]

Khallad had originally scheduled his trip in order to receive a new prosthesis at a Kuala Lumpur clinic called Endolite, and Bin Ladin suggested that he use the opportunity to case flights as well. According to Khallad, Malaysia was an ideal destination because its government did not require citizens of Saudi Arabia or other Gulf states to have a visa. Malaysian security was reputed to be lax when it came to Islamist jihadists. Also, other mujahideen wounded in combat had reportedly received treatment at the Endolite clinic and successfully concealed the origins of their injuries. Khallad said he got the money for the prosthesis from his father, Bin Ladin, and another al Qaeda colleague.[57]

According to Khallad, when he and Abu Bara arrived in Kuala Lumpur they contacted Hambali to let him know where they were staying, since he was to be kept informed of al Qaeda activities in Southeast Asia. Hambali picked up Khallad and Abu Bara and brought them to his home, enlisting the help of a colleague who spoke better Arabic. Hambali then took them to the clinic.[58]

On December 31, Khallad flew from Kuala Lumpur to Bangkok; the next day, he flew to Hong Kong aboard a U.S. airliner. He flew in first class, which he realized was a mistake because this seating assignment on that flight did not afford him a view of the cockpit. He claims to have done what he could to case the flight, testing security by carrying a box cutter in his toiletries kit onto the flight to Hong Kong. Khallad returned to Bangkok the following day. At the airport, the security officials searched his carry-on bag and even opened the toiletries kit, but just glanced at the contents and let him pass. On this flight, Khallad waited until most of the first-class passengers were dozing, then got up and removed the kit from his carry-on. None of the flight attendants took notice.[59]

After completing his casing mission, Khallad returned to Kuala Lumpur. Hazmi arrived in Kuala Lumpur soon thereafter and may even have stayed briefly with Khallad and Abu Bara at Endolite. Mihdhar arrived on January 5, probably one day after Hazmi. All four operatives stayed at the apartment of Yazid Sufaat, the Malaysian JI member who made his home available at Hambali's request. According to Khallad, he and Hazmi spoke about the possibility of hijacking planes and crashing them or holding passengers as hostages, but only speculatively. Khallad admits being aware at the time that Hazmi and Mihdhar were involved in an operation involving planes in the United States but denies knowing details of the plan.[60]

While in Kuala Lumpur, Khallad wanted to go to Singapore to meet Nibras and Fahd al Quso, two of the operatives in Nashiri's ship-bombing operation. An attempt to execute that plan by attacking the USS *The Sullivans* had failed just a few days earlier. Nibras and Quso were bringing Khallad money from Yemen, but were stopped in Bangkok because they lacked visas to continue on to Singapore. Also unable to enter Singapore, Khallad moved the meeting to Bangkok. Hazmi and Mihdhar decided to go there as well, reportedly because they thought it would enhance their cover as tourists to have passport stamps from a popular tourist destination such as Thailand. With Hambali's help, the three obtained tickets for a flight to Bangkok and left Kuala Lumpur together. Abu Bara did not have a visa permitting him to return to Pakistan, so he traveled to Yemen instead.[61]

In Bangkok, Khallad took Hazmi and Mihdhar to one hotel, then went to another hotel for his meeting on the maritime attack plan. Hazmi and Mihdhar soon moved to that same hotel, but Khallad insists that the two sets of operatives never met with each other or anyone else. After conferring with the ship-bombing operatives, Khallad returned to Karachi and then to Kandahar, where he reported on his casing mission to Bin Ladin.[62]

Bin Ladin canceled the East Asia part of the planes operation in the spring of 2000. He evidently decided it would be too difficult to coordinate this attack with the operation in the United States. As for Hazmi and Mihdhar, they had left Bangkok a few days before Khallad and arrived in Los Angeles on January 15, 2000.[63]

Meanwhile, the next group of al Qaeda operatives destined for the planes operation had just surfaced in Afghanistan. As Hazmi and Mihdhar were deploying from Asia to the United States, al Qaeda's leadership was recruiting and training four Western-educated men who had recently arrived in Kandahar. Though they hailed from four different countries—Egypt, the United Arab

Emirates, Lebanon, and Yemen—they had formed a close-knit group as students in Hamburg, Germany. The new recruits had come to Afghanistan aspiring to wage jihad in Chechnya. But al Qaeda quickly recognized their potential and enlisted them in its anti-U.S. jihad.

5.3 THE HAMBURG CONTINGENT

Although Bin Ladin, Atef, and KSM initially contemplated using established al Qaeda members to execute the planes operation, the late 1999 arrival in Kandahar of four aspiring jihadists from Germany suddenly presented a more attractive alternative. The Hamburg group shared the anti-U.S. fervor of the other candidates for the operation, but added the enormous advantages of fluency in English and familiarity with life in the West, based on years that each member of the group had spent living in Germany. Not surprisingly, Mohamed Atta, Ramzi Binalshibh, Marwan al Shehhi, and Ziad Jarrah would all become key players in the 9/11 conspiracy.

Mohamed Atta

Mohamed Atta was born on September 1, 1968, in Kafr el Sheikh, Egypt, to a middle-class family headed by his father, an attorney. After graduating from Cairo University with a degree in architectural engineering in 1990, Atta worked as an urban planner in Cairo for a couple of years. In the fall of 1991, he asked a German family he had met in Cairo to help him continue his education in Germany. They suggested he come to Hamburg and invited him to live with them there, at least initially. After completing a course in German, Atta traveled to Germany for the first time in July 1992. He resided briefly in Stuttgart and then, in the fall of 1992, moved to Hamburg to live with his host family. After enrolling at the University of Hamburg, he promptly transferred into the city engineering and planning course at the Technical University of Hamburg-Harburg, where he would remain registered as a student until the fall of 1999. He appears to have applied himself fairly seriously to his studies (at least in comparison to his jihadist friends) and actually received his degree shortly before traveling to Afghanistan. In school, Atta came across as very intelligent and reasonably pleasant, with an excellent command of the German language.[64]

When Atta arrived in Germany, he appeared religious, but not fanatically so. This would change, especially as his tendency to assert leadership became increasingly pronounced. According to Binalshibh, as early as 1995 Atta sought to organize a Muslim student association in Hamburg. In the fall of 1997, he joined a working group at the Quds mosque in Hamburg, a group designed to bridge the gap between Muslims and Christians. Atta proved a poor bridge, however, because of his abrasive and increasingly dogmatic personality. But among those who shared his beliefs, Atta stood out as a decisionmaker. Atta's friends during this period remember him as charismatic, intelligent, and persuasive, albeit intolerant of dissent.[65]

In his interactions with other students, Atta voiced virulently anti-Semitic and anti-American opinions, ranging from condemnations of what he described as a global Jewish movement centered in New York City that supposedly controlled the financial world and the media, to polemics against governments of the Arab world. To him, Saddam Hussein was an American stooge set up to give Washington an excuse to intervene in the Middle East. Within his circle, Atta advocated violent jihad. He reportedly asked one individual close to the group if he was "ready to fight for [his] belief" and dismissed him as too weak for jihad when the person declined. On a visit home to Egypt in 1998, Atta met one of his college friends. According to this friend, Atta had changed a great deal, had grown a beard, and had "obviously adopted fundamentalism" by that time.[66]

Ramzi Binalshibh

Ramzi Binalshibh was born on May 1, 1972, in Ghayl Bawazir, Yemen. There does not seem to be anything remarkable about his family or early background. A friend who knew Binalshibh in Yemen remembers him as "religious, but not too religious." From 1987 to 1995, Binalshibh worked as a clerk for the International Bank of Yemen. He first attempted to leave Yemen in 1995, when he applied for a U.S. visa. After his application was rejected, he went to Germany and applied for asylum under the name Ramzi Omar, claiming to be a Sudanese citizen seeking asylum. While his asylum petition was pending, Binalshibh lived in Hamburg and associated with individuals from several mosques there. In 1997, after his asylum application was denied, Binalshibh went home to Yemen but returned to Germany shortly thereafter under his true name, this time registering as a student in Hamburg. Binalshibh continually had academic problems, failing tests and cutting classes; he was expelled from one school in September 1998.[67]

According to Binalshibh, he and Atta first met at a mosque in Hamburg in 1995. The two men became close friends and became identified with their shared extremist outlook. Like Atta, by the late 1990s Binalshibh was decrying what he perceived to be a "Jewish world conspiracy." He proclaimed that the highest duty of every Muslim was to pursue jihad, and that the highest honor was to die during the jihad. Despite his rhetoric, however, Binalshibh presented a more amiable figure than the austere Atta, and was known within the community as being sociable, extroverted, polite, and adventuresome.[68]

In 1998, Binalshibh and Atta began sharing an apartment in the Harburg section of Hamburg, together with a young student from the United Arab Emirates named Marwan al Shehhi.[69]

Marwan al Shehhi

Marwan al Shehhi was born on May 9, 1978, in Ras al Khaimah, the United Arab Emirates. His father, who died in 1997, was a prayer leader at the local mosque. After graduating from high school in 1995, Shehhi joined the Emirati military and received half a year of basic training before gaining admission to a military scholarship program that would fund his continued study in Germany.[70]

Shehhi first entered Germany in April 1996. After sharing an apartment in Bonn for two months with three other scholarship students, Shehhi moved in with a German family, with whom he resided for several months before moving into his own apartment. During this period, he came across as very religious, praying five times a day. Friends also remember him as convivial and "a regular guy," wearing Western clothes and occasionally renting cars for trips to Berlin, France, and the Netherlands.[71]

As a student, Shehhi was less than a success. Upon completing a course in German, he enrolled at the University of Bonn in a program for technical, mathematical, and scientific studies. In June 1997, he requested a leave from his studies, citing the need to attend to unspecified "problems" in his home country. Although the university denied his request, Shehhi left anyway, and consequently was compelled to repeat the first semester of his studies. In addition to having academic difficulties at this time, Shehhi appeared to become more extreme in the practice of his faith; for example, he specifically avoided restaurants that cooked with or served alcohol. In late 1997, he applied for permission to complete his course work in Hamburg, a request apparently motivated by his desire to join Atta and Binalshibh. Just how and when the three of them first met remains unclear, although they seemed to know each other already when Shehhi relocated to Hamburg in early 1998. Atta and Binalshibh moved into his apartment in April.[72]

The transfer to Hamburg did not help Shehhi's academic progress; he was directed by the scholarship program administrators at the Emirati embassy to repeat his second semester starting in August 1998, but back in Bonn. Shehhi initially flouted this directive, however, and did not reenroll at the University of Bonn until the following January, barely passing his course there. By the end of July 1999, he had returned to Hamburg, applying to study shipbuilding at the Technical University and, more significantly, residing once again with Atta and Binalshibh, in an apartment at 54 Marienstrasse.[73]

After Shehhi moved in with Atta and Binalshibh, his evolution toward Islamic fundamentalism became more pronounced. A fellow Emirati student who came to Hamburg to visit Shehhi noticed he no longer lived as comfortably as before. Shehhi now occupied an old apartment with a roommate, had no television, and wore inexpensive clothes. When asked why he was living so frugally, Shehhi responded that he was living the way the Prophet had lived.[74] Similarly, when someone asked why he and Atta never laughed, Shehhi retorted, "How can you laugh when people are dying in Palestine?"[75]

Ziad Jarrah

Born on May 11, 1975, in Mazraa, Lebanon, Ziad Jarrah came from an affluent family and attended private, Christian schools. Like Atta, Binalshibh, and
Shehhi, Jarrah aspired to pursue higher education in Germany. In April 1996,
he and a cousin enrolled at a junior college in Greifswald, in northeastern Germany. There Jarrah met and became intimate with Aysel Senguen, the daughter of Turkish immigrants, who was preparing to study dentistry.[76]

Even with the benefit of hindsight, Jarrah hardly seems a likely candidate
for becoming an Islamic extremist. Far from displaying radical beliefs when he
first moved to Germany, he arrived with a reputation for knowing where to
find the best discos and beaches in Beirut, and in Greifswald was known to
enjoy student parties and drinking beer. Although he continued to share an
apartment in Greifswald with his cousin, Jarrah was mostly at Senguen's apartment. Witnesses interviewed by German authorities after 9/11, however, recall
that Jarrah started showing signs of radicalization as early as the end of 1996.
After returning from a trip home to Lebanon, Jarrah started living more strictly
according to the Koran. He read brochures in Arabic about jihad, held forth to
friends on the subject of holy war, and professed disaffection with his previous
life and a desire not to leave the world "in a natural way."[77]

In September 1997, Jarrah abruptly switched his intended course of study
from dentistry to aircraft engineering—at the Technical University of
Hamburg-Harburg. His motivation for this decision remains unclear. The
rationale he expressed to Senguen—that he had been interested in aviation
since playing with toy airplanes as a child—rings somewhat hollow. In any
event, Jarrah appears already to have had Hamburg contacts by this time, some
of whom may have played a role in steering him toward Islamic extremism.[78]

Following his move to Hamburg that fall, he began visiting Senguen in
Greifswald on weekends, until she moved to the German city of Bochum one
year later to enroll in dental school. Around the same time, he began speaking
increasingly about religion, and his visits to Senguen became less and less frequent. He began criticizing her for not being religious enough and for dress-
ing too provocatively. He grew a full beard and started praying regularly. He
refused to introduce her to his Hamburg friends because, he told her, they were
religious Muslims and her refusal to become more observant embarrassed him.
At some point in 1999, Jarrah told Senguen that he was planning to wage a
jihad because there was no greater honor than to die for Allah. Although Jarrah's transformation generated numerous quarrels, their breakups invariably
were followed by reconciliation.[79]

Forming a Cell

In Hamburg, Jarrah had a succession of living accommodations, but he apparently never resided with his future co-conspirators. It is not clear how and
when he became part of Atta's circle. He became particularly friendly with
Binalshibh after meeting him at the Quds mosque in Hamburg, which Jarrah

began attending regularly in late 1997. The worshippers at this mosque featured an outspoken, flamboyant Islamist named Mohammed Haydar Zammar. A well-known figure in the Muslim community (and to German and U.S. intelligence agencies by the late 1990s), Zammar had fought in Afghanistan and relished any opportunity to extol the virtues of violent jihad. Indeed, a witness has reported hearing Zammar press Binalshibh to fulfill his duty to wage jihad. Moreover, after 9/11, Zammar reportedly took credit for influencing not just Binalshibh but the rest of the Hamburg group. In 1998, Zammar encouraged them to participate in jihad and even convinced them to go to Afghanistan.[80]

Owing to Zammar's persuasion or some other source of inspiration, Atta, Binalshibh, Shehhi, and Jarrah eventually prepared themselves to translate their extremist beliefs into action. By late 1999, they were ready to abandon their student lives in Germany in favor of violent jihad. This final stage in their evolution toward embracing Islamist extremism did not entirely escape the notice of the people around them. The foursome became core members of a group of radical Muslims, often hosting sessions at their Marienstrasse apartment that involved extremely anti-American discussions. Meeting three to four times a week, the group became something of a "sect" whose members, according to one participant in the meetings, tended to deal only with each other.[81] Atta's rent checks for the apartment provide evidence of the importance that the apartment assumed as a center for the group, as he would write on them the notation "Dar el Ansar," or "house of the followers."[82]

In addition to Atta, Binalshibh, Shehhi, and Jarrah, the group included other extremists, some of whom also would attend al Qaeda training camps and, in some instances, would help the 9/11 hijackers as they executed the plot:

- Said Bahaji, son of a Moroccan immigrant, was the only German citizen in the group. Educated in Morocco, Bahaji returned to Germany to study electrical engineering at the Technical University of Hamburg-Harburg. He spent five months in the German army before obtaining a medical discharge, and lived with Atta and Binalshibh at 54 Marienstrasse for eight months between November 1998 and July 1999. Described as an insecure follower with no personality and with limited knowledge of Islam, Bahaji nonetheless professed his readiness to engage in violence. Atta and Binalshibh used Bahaji's computer for Internet research, as evidenced by documents and diskettes seized by German authorities after 9/11.[83]
- Zakariya Essabar, a Moroccan citizen, moved to Germany in February 1997 and to Hamburg in 1998, where he studied medical technology. Soon after moving to Hamburg, Essabar met Binalshibh and the others through a Turkish mosque. Essabar turned extremist fairly suddenly, probably in 1999, and reportedly pressured one acquaintance with physical force to become more religious, grow a beard, and

compel his wife to convert to Islam. Essabar's parents were said to have made repeated but unsuccessful efforts to sway him from this lifestyle. Shortly before the 9/11 attacks, he would travel to Afghanistan to communicate the date for the attacks to the al Qaeda leadership.[84]

- Mounir el Motassadeq, another Moroccan, came to Germany in 1993, moving to Hamburg two years later to study electrical engineering at the Technical University. A witness has recalled Motassadeq saying that he would kill his entire family if his religious beliefs demanded it. One of Motassadeq's roommates recalls him referring to Hitler as a "good man" and organizing film sessions that included speeches by Bin Ladin. Motassadeq would help conceal the Hamburg group's trip to Afghanistan in late 1999.[85]

- Abdelghani Mzoudi, also a Moroccan, arrived in Germany in the summer of 1993, after completing university courses in physics and chemistry. Mzoudi studied in Dortmund, Bochum, and Muenster before moving to Hamburg in 1995. Mzoudi described himself as a weak Muslim when he was home in Morocco, but much more devout when he was back in Hamburg. In April 1996, Mzoudi and Motassadeq witnessed the execution of Atta's will.[86]

During the course of 1999, Atta and his group became ever more extreme and secretive, speaking only in Arabic to conceal the content of their conversations.[87] When the four core members of the Hamburg cell left Germany to journey to Afghanistan late that year, it seems unlikely that they already knew about the planes operation; no evidence connects them to al Qaeda before that time. Witnesses have attested, however, that their pronouncements reflected ample predisposition toward taking some action against the United States.[88] In short, they fit the bill for Bin Ladin, Atef, and KSM.

Going to Afghanistan

The available evidence indicates that in 1999, Atta, Binalshibh, Shehhi, and Jarrah decided to fight in Chechnya against the Russians. According to Binalshibh, a chance meeting on a train in Germany caused the group to travel to Afghanistan instead. An individual named Khalid al Masri approached Binalshibh and Shehhi (because they were Arabs with beards, Binalshibh thinks) and struck up a conversation about jihad in Chechnya. When they later called Masri and expressed interest in going to Chechnya, he told them to contact Abu Musab in Duisburg, Germany. Abu Musab turned out to be Mohamedou Ould Slahi, a significant al Qaeda operative who, even then, was well known to U.S. and German intelligence, though neither government apparently knew he was operating in Germany in late 1999. When telephoned by Binalshibh and Shehhi, Slahi reportedly invited these promising recruits to come see him in Duisburg.[89]

Binalshibh, Shehhi, and Jarrah made the trip. When they arrived, Slahi explained that it was difficult to get to Chechnya at that time because many travelers were being detained in Georgia. He recommended they go to Afghanistan instead, where they could train for jihad before traveling onward to Chechnya. Slahi instructed them to obtain Pakistani visas and then return to him for further directions on how to reach Afghanistan. Although Atta did not attend the meeting, he joined in the plan with the other three. After obtaining the necessary visas, they received Slahi's final instructions on how to travel to Karachi and then Quetta, where they were to contact someone named Umar al Masri at the Taliban office.[90]

Following Slahi's advice, Atta and Jarrah left Hamburg during the last week of November 1999, bound for Karachi. Shehhi left for Afghanistan around the same time; Binalshibh, about two weeks later. Binalshibh remembers that when he arrived at the Taliban office in Quetta, there was no one named Umar al Masri. The name, apparently, was simply a code; a group of Afghans from the office promptly escorted him to Kandahar. There Binalshibh rejoined Atta and Jarrah, who said they already had pledged loyalty to Bin Ladin and urged him to do the same. They also informed him that Shehhi had pledged as well and had already left for the United Arab Emirates to prepare for the mission. Binalshibh soon met privately with Bin Ladin, accepted the al Qaeda leader's invitation to work under him, and added his own pledge to those of his Hamburg colleagues. By this time, Binalshibh claims, he assumed he was volunteering for a martyrdom operation.[91]

Atta, Jarrah, and Binalshibh then met with Atef, who told them they were about to undertake a highly secret mission. As Binalshibh tells it, Atef instructed the three to return to Germany and enroll in flight training. Atta—whom Bin Ladin chose to lead the group—met with Bin Ladin several times to receive additional instructions, including a preliminary list of approved targets: the World Trade Center, the Pentagon, and the U.S. Capitol.[92] The new recruits also learned that an individual named Rabia al Makki (Nawaf al Hazmi) would be part of the operation.[93]

In retrospect, the speed with which Atta, Shehhi, Jarrah, and Binalshibh became core members of the 9/11 plot—with Atta designated its operational leader—is remarkable. They had not yet met with KSM when all this occurred. It is clear, then, that Bin Ladin and Atef were very much in charge of the operation. That these candidates were selected so quickly—before comprehensive testing in the training camps or in operations—demonstrates that Bin Ladin and Atef probably already understood the deficiencies of their initial team, Hazmi and Mihdhar. The new recruits from Germany possessed an ideal combination of technical skill and knowledge that the original 9/11 operatives, veteran fighters though they were, lacked. Bin Ladin and Atef wasted no time in assigning the Hamburg group to the most ambitious operation yet planned by al Qaeda.

Bin Ladin and Atef also plainly judged that Atta was best suited to be the tactical commander of the operation. Such a quick and critical judgment invites speculation about whether they had already taken Atta's measure at some earlier meeting. To be sure, some gaps do appear in the record of Atta's known whereabouts during the preceding years. One such gap is February–March 1998, a period for which there is no evidence of his presence in Germany and when he conceivably could have been in Afghanistan.[94] Yet to date, neither KSM, Binalshibh, nor any other al Qaeda figure interrogated about the 9/11 plot has claimed that Atta or any other member of the Hamburg group traveled to Afghanistan before the trip in late 1999.

While the four core Hamburg cell members were in Afghanistan, their associates back in Hamburg handled their affairs so that their trip could be kept secret. Motassadeq appears to have done the most. He terminated Shehhi's apartment lease, telling the landlord that Shehhi had returned to the UAE for family reasons, and used a power of attorney to pay bills from Shehhi's bank account.[95] Motassadeq also assisted Jarrah, offering to look after Aysel Senguen in Jarrah's absence. Said Bahaji attended to similar routine matters for Atta and Binalshibh, thereby helping them remain abroad without drawing attention to their absence.[96]

Preparing for the Operation

In early 2000, Atta, Jarrah, and Binalshibh returned to Hamburg. Jarrah arrived first, on January 31, 2000.[97] According to Binalshibh, he and Atta left Kandahar together and proceeded first to Karachi, where they met KSM and were instructed by him on security and on living in the United States. Shehhi apparently had already met with KSM before returning to the UAE. Atta returned to Hamburg in late February, and Binalshibh arrived shortly thereafter. Shehhi's travels took him to the UAE (where he acquired a new passport and a U.S. visa), Saudi Arabia, Bahrain, and one or more other destinations. Shehhi also returned to Germany, possibly sometime in March.[98]

After leaving Afghanistan, the hijackers made clear efforts to avoid appearing radical. Once back in Hamburg, they distanced themselves from conspicuous extremists like Zammar, whom they knew attracted unwanted attention from the authorities.[99] They also changed their appearance and behavior. Atta wore Western clothing, shaved his beard, and no longer attended extremist mosques. Jarrah also no longer wore a full beard and, according to Senguen, acted much more the way he had when she first met him. And when Shehhi, while still in the UAE in January 2000, held a belated wedding celebration (he actually had been married in 1999), a friend of his was surprised to see that he had shaved off his beard and was acting like his old self again.[100]

But Jarrah's apparent efforts to appear less radical did not completely conceal his transformation from his Lebanese family, which grew increasingly concerned about his fanaticism. Soon after Jarrah returned to Germany, his father asked Jarrah's cousin—a close companion from boyhood—to intercede. The cousin's ensuing effort to persuade Jarrah to depart from "the path he was taking" proved unavailing.[101] Yet Jarrah clearly differed from the other hijackers in that he maintained much closer contact with his family and continued his intimate relationship with Senguen. These ties may well have caused him to harbor some doubts about going through with the plot, even as late as the summer of 2001, as discussed in chapter 7.

After leaving Afghanistan, the four began researching flight schools and aviation training. In early January 2000, Ali Abdul Aziz Ali—a nephew of KSM living in the UAE who would become an important facilitator in the plot—used Shehhi's credit card to order a Boeing 747-400 flight simulator program and a Boeing 767 flight deck video, together with attendant literature; Ali had all these items shipped to his employer's address. Jarrah soon decided that the schools in Germany were not acceptable and that he would have to learn to fly in the United States. Binalshibh also researched flight schools in Europe, and in the Netherlands he met a flight school director who recommended flight schools in the United States because they were less expensive and required shorter training periods.[102]

In March 2000, Atta emailed 31 different U.S. flight schools on behalf of a small group of men from various Arab countries studying in Germany who, while lacking prior training, were interested in learning to fly in the United States. Atta requested information about the cost of the training, potential financing, and accommodations.[103]

Before seeking visas to enter the United States, Atta, Shehhi, and Jarrah obtained new passports, each claiming that his old passport had been lost. Presumably they were concerned that the Pakistani visas in their old passports would raise suspicions about possible travel to Afghanistan. Shehhi obtained his visa on January 18, 2000; Atta, on May 18; and Jarrah, on May 25.[104] Binalshibh's visa request was rejected, however, as were his three subsequent applications.[105] Binalshibh proved unable to obtain a visa, a victim of the generalized suspicion that visa applicants from Yemen—especially young men applying in another country (Binalshibh first applied in Berlin)—might join the ranks of undocumented aliens seeking work in the United States. Before 9/11, security concerns were not a major factor in visa issuance unless the applicant already was on a terrorist watchlist, and none of these four men was. Concerns that Binalshibh intended to immigrate to the United States doomed his chances to participate firsthand in the 9/11 attacks. Although Binalshibh had to remain behind, he would provide critical assistance from abroad to his co-conspirators.

Once again, the need for travel documents dictated al Qaeda's plans.

Travel

It should by now be apparent how significant travel was in the planning undertaken by a terrorist organization as far-flung as al Qaeda. The story of the plot includes references to dozens of international trips. Operations required travel, as did basic communications and the movement of money. Where electronic communications were regarded as insecure, al Qaeda relied even more heavily on couriers.

KSM and Abu Zubaydah each played key roles in facilitating travel for al Qaeda operatives. In addition, al Qaeda had an office of passports and host country issues under its security committee. The office was located at the Kandahar airport and was managed by Atef. The committee altered papers, including passports, visas, and identification cards.[106]

Moreover, certain al Qaeda members were charged with organizing passport collection schemes to keep the pipeline of fraudulent documents flowing. To this end, al Qaeda required jihadists to turn in their passports before going to the front lines in Afghanistan. If they were killed, their passports were recycled for use.[107] The operational mission training course taught operatives how to forge documents. Certain passport alteration methods, which included substituting photos and erasing and adding travel cachets, were also taught. Manuals demonstrating the technique for "cleaning" visas were reportedly circulated among operatives. Mohamed Atta and Zakariya Essabar were reported to have been trained in passport alteration.[108]

The purpose of all this training was twofold: to develop an institutional capacity for document forgery and to enable operatives to make necessary adjustments in the field. It was well-known, for example, that if a Saudi traveled to Afghanistan via Pakistan, then on his return to Saudi Arabia his passport, bearing a Pakistani stamp, would be confiscated. So operatives either erased the Pakistani visas from their passports or traveled through Iran, which did not stamp visas directly into passports.[109]

5.4 A MONEY TRAIL?

Bin Ladin and his aides did not need a very large sum to finance their planned attack on America. The 9/11 plotters eventually spent somewhere between $400,000 and $500,000 to plan and conduct their attack. Consistent with the importance of the project, al Qaeda funded the plotters. KSM provided his operatives with nearly all the money they needed to travel to the United States, train, and live. The plotters' tradecraft was not especially sophisticated, but it was good enough. They moved, stored, and spent their money in ordinary ways, easily defeating the detection mechanisms in place at the time.[110] The origin of the funds remains unknown, although we have a general idea of how al Qaeda financed itself during the period leading up to 9/11.

General Financing

As we explained in chapter 2, Bin Ladin did not fund al Qaeda through a personal fortune and a network of businesses in Sudan. Instead, al Qaeda relied primarily on a fund-raising network developed over time. The CIA now estimates that it cost al Qaeda about $30 million per year to sustain its activities before 9/11 and that this money was raised almost entirely through donations.[111]

For many years, the United States thought Bin Ladin financed al Qaeda's expenses through a vast personal inheritance. Bin Ladin purportedly inherited approximately $300 million when his father died, and was rumored to have had access to these funds to wage jihad while in Sudan and Afghanistan and to secure his leadership position in al Qaeda. In early 2000, the U.S. government discovered a different reality: roughly from 1970 through 1994, Bin Ladin received about $1 million per year—a significant sum, to be sure, but not a $300 million fortune that could be used to fund jihad.[112] Then, as part of a Saudi government crackdown early in the 1990s, the Bin Ladin family was forced to find a buyer for Usama's share of the family company in 1994. The Saudi government subsequently froze the proceeds of the sale. This action had the effect of divesting Bin Ladin of what otherwise might indeed have been a large fortune.[113]

Nor were Bin Ladin's assets in Sudan a source of money for al Qaeda. When Bin Ladin lived in Sudan from 1991 to 1996, he owned a number of businesses and other assets. These could not have provided significant income, as most were small or not economically viable. When Bin Ladin left in 1996, it appears that the Sudanese government expropriated all his assets: he left Sudan with practically nothing. When Bin Ladin arrived in Afghanistan, he relied on the Taliban until he was able to reinvigorate his fund-raising efforts by drawing on ties to wealthy Saudi individuals that he had established during the Afghan war in the 1980s.[114]

Al Qaeda appears to have relied on a core group of financial facilitators who raised money from a variety of donors and other fund-raisers, primarily in the Gulf countries and particularly in Saudi Arabia.[115] Some individual donors surely knew, and others did not, the ultimate destination of their donations. Al Qaeda and its friends took advantage of Islam's strong calls for charitable giving, *zakat*. These financial facilitators also appeared to rely heavily on certain imams at mosques who were willing to divert zakat donations to al Qaeda's cause.[116]

Al Qaeda also collected money from employees of corrupt charities.[117] It took two approaches to using charities for fund-raising. One was to rely on al Qaeda sympathizers in specific foreign branch offices of large, international charities—particularly those with lax external oversight and ineffective internal controls, such as the Saudi-based al Haramain Islamic Foundation.[118] Smaller charities in various parts of the globe were funded by these large Gulf charities and had employees who would siphon the money to al Qaeda.[119]

In addition, entire charities, such as the al Wafa organization, may have wittingly participated in funneling money to al Qaeda. In those cases, al Qaeda operatives controlled the entire organization, including access to bank accounts.[120] Charities were a source of money and also provided significant cover, which enabled operatives to travel undetected under the guise of working for a humanitarian organization.

It does not appear that any government other than the Taliban financially supported al Qaeda before 9/11, although some governments may have contained al Qaeda sympathizers who turned a blind eye to al Qaeda's fundraising activities.[121] Saudi Arabia has long been considered the primary source of al Qaeda funding, but we have found no evidence that the Saudi government as an institution or senior Saudi officials individually funded the organization. (This conclusion does not exclude the likelihood that charities with significant Saudi government sponsorship diverted funds to al Qaeda.)[122]

Still, al Qaeda found fertile fund-raising ground in Saudi Arabia, where extreme religious views are common and charitable giving was both essential to the culture and subject to very limited oversight.[123] Al Qaeda also sought money from wealthy donors in other Gulf states.

Al Qaeda frequently moved the money it raised by *hawala*, an informal and ancient trust-based system for transferring funds.[124] In some ways, al Qaeda had no choice after its move to Afghanistan in 1996: first, the banking system there was antiquated and undependable; and second, formal banking was risky due to the scrutiny that al Qaeda received after the August 1998 East Africa embassy bombings, including UN resolutions against it and the Taliban.[125] Bin Ladin relied on the established hawala networks operating in Pakistan, in Dubai, and throughout the Middle East to transfer funds efficiently. Hawaladars associated with al Qaeda may have used banks to move and store money, as did various al Qaeda fund-raisers and operatives outside of Afghanistan, but there is little evidence that Bin Ladin or core al Qaeda members used banks while in Afghanistan.[126]

Before 9/11, al Qaeda spent funds as quickly as it received them. Actual terrorist operations represented a relatively small part of al Qaeda's estimated $30 million annual operating budget. Al Qaeda funded salaries for jihadists, training camps, airfields, vehicles, arms, and the development of training manuals. Bin Ladin provided approximately $10–$20 million per year to the Taliban in return for safe haven. Bin Ladin also may have used money to create alliances with other terrorist organizations, although it is unlikely that al Qaeda was funding an overall jihad program. Rather, Bin Ladin selectively provided start-up funds to new groups or money for specific terrorist operations.[127]

Al Qaeda has been alleged to have used a variety of illegitimate means, particularly drug trafficking and conflict diamonds, to finance itself. While the drug trade was a source of income for the Taliban, it did not serve the same purpose for al Qaeda, and there is no reliable evidence that Bin Ladin was involved in or made his money through drug trafficking.[128] Similarly, we have seen no persuasive evidence that al Qaeda funded itself by trading in African conflict diamonds.[129] There also have been claims that al Qaeda financed itself through manipulation of the stock market based on its advance knowledge of the 9/11 attacks. Exhaustive investigations by the Securities and Exchange Commission, FBI, and other agencies have uncovered no evidence that anyone with advance knowledge of the attacks profited through securities transactions.[130]

To date, the U.S. government has not been able to determine the origin of the money used for the 9/11 attacks. Ultimately the question is of little practical significance. Al Qaeda had many avenues of funding. If a particular funding source had dried up, al Qaeda could have easily tapped a different source or diverted funds from another project to fund an operation that cost $400,000–$500,000 over nearly two years.

The Funding of the 9/11 Plot

As noted above, the 9/11 plotters spent somewhere between $400,000 and $500,000 to plan and conduct their attack. The available evidence indicates that the 19 operatives were funded by al Qaeda, either through wire transfers or cash provided by KSM, which they carried into the United States or deposited in foreign accounts and accessed from this country. Our investigation has uncovered no credible evidence that any person in the United States gave the hijackers substantial financial assistance. Similarly, we have seen no evidence that any foreign government—or foreign government official—supplied any funding.[131]

We have found no evidence that the Hamburg cell members (Atta, Shehhi, Jarrah, and Binalshibh) received funds from al Qaeda before late 1999. It appears they supported themselves. KSM, Binalshibh, and another plot facilitator, Mustafa al Hawsawi, each received money, in some cases perhaps as much as $10,000, to perform their roles in the plot.[132]

After the Hamburg recruits joined the 9/11 conspiracy, al Qaeda began giving them money. Our knowledge of the funding during this period, before the operatives entered the United States, remains murky. According to KSM, the Hamburg cell members each received $5,000 to pay for their return to Germany from Afghanistan after they had been selected to join the plot, and they received additional funds for travel from Germany to the United States. Financial transactions of the plotters are discussed in more detail in chapter 7.

Requirements for a Successful Attack

As some of the core operatives prepared to leave for the United States, al Qaeda's leaders could have reflected on what they needed to be able to do in order to organize and conduct a complex international terrorist operation to inflict catastrophic harm. We believe such a list of requirements would have included

- leaders able to evaluate, approve, and supervise the planning and direction of the operation;
- communications sufficient to enable planning and direction of the operatives and those who would be helping them;

- a personnel system that could recruit candidates, vet them, indoctrinate them, and give them necessary training;
- an intelligence effort to gather required information and form assessments of enemy strengths and weaknesses;
- the ability to move people; and
- the ability to raise and move the necessary money.

The information we have presented about the development of the planes operation shows how, by the spring and summer of 2000, al Qaeda was able to meet these requirements.

By late May 2000, two operatives assigned to the planes operation were already in the United States. Three of the four Hamburg cell members would soon arrive.

6

FROM THREAT
TO THREAT

IN CHAPTERS 3 AND 4 we described how the U.S. government adjusted its existing agencies and capacities to address the emerging threat from Usama Bin Ladin and his associates. After the August 1998 bombings of the American embassies in Kenya and Tanzania, President Bill Clinton and his chief aides explored ways of getting Bin Ladin expelled from Afghanistan or possibly capturing or even killing him. Although disruption efforts around the world had achieved some successes, the core of Bin Ladin's organization remained intact.

President Clinton was deeply concerned about Bin Ladin. He and his national security advisor, Samuel "Sandy" Berger, ensured they had a special daily pipeline of reports feeding them the latest updates on Bin Ladin's reported location.[1] In public, President Clinton spoke repeatedly about the threat of terrorism, referring to terrorist training camps but saying little about Bin Ladin and nothing about al Qaeda. He explained to us that this was deliberate—intended to avoid enhancing Bin Ladin's stature by giving him unnecessary publicity. His speeches focused especially on the danger of nonstate actors and of chemical and biological weapons.[2]

As the millennium approached, the most publicized worries were not about terrorism but about computer breakdowns—the Y2K scare. Some government officials were concerned that terrorists would take advantage of such breakdowns.[3]

6.1 THE MILLENNIUM CRISIS

"Bodies Will Pile Up in Sacks"
On November 30, 1999, Jordanian intelligence intercepted a telephone call between Abu Zubaydah, a longtime ally of Bin Ladin, and Khadr Abu Hoshar, a Palestinian extremist. Abu Zubaydah said, "The time for training is over." Suspecting that this was a signal for Abu Hoshar to commence a terrorist

operation, Jordanian police arrested Abu Hoshar and 15 others and informed Washington.[4]

One of the 16, Raed Hijazi, had been born in California to Palestinian parents; after spending his childhood in the Middle East, he had returned to northern California, taken refuge in extremist Islamist beliefs, and then made his way to Abu Zubaydah's Khaldan camp in Afghanistan, where he learned the fundamentals of guerrilla warfare. He and his younger brother had been recruited by Abu Hoshar into a loosely knit plot to attack Jewish and American targets in Jordan.[5]

After late 1996, when Abu Hoshar was arrested and jailed, Hijazi moved back to the United States, worked as a cabdriver in Boston, and sent money back to his fellow plotters. After Abu Hoshar's release, Hijazi shuttled between Boston and Jordan gathering money and supplies. With Abu Hoshar, he recruited in Turkey and Syria as well as Jordan; with Abu Zubaydah's assistance, Abu Hoshar sent these recruits to Afghanistan for training.[6]

In late 1998, Hijazi and Abu Hoshar had settled on a plan. They would first attack four targets: the SAS Radisson Hotel in downtown Amman, the border crossings from Jordan into Israel, and two Christian holy sites, at a time when all these locations were likely to be thronged with American and other tourists. Next, they would target a local airport and other religious and cultural sites. Hijazi and Abu Hoshar cased the intended targets and sent reports to Abu Zubaydah, who approved their plan. Finally, back in Amman from Boston, Hijazi gradually accumulated bomb-making materials, including sulfuric acid and 5,200 pounds of nitric acid, which were then stored in an enormous subbasement dug by the plotters over a period of two months underneath a rented house.[7]

In early 1999, Hijazi and Abu Hoshar contacted Khalil Deek, an American citizen and an associate of Abu Zubaydah who lived in Peshawar, Pakistan, and who, with Afghanistan-based extremists, had created an electronic version of a terrorist manual, the *Encyclopedia of Jihad*. They obtained a CD-ROM of this encyclopedia from Deek.[8] In June, with help from Deek, Abu Hoshar arranged with Abu Zubaydah for Hijazi and three others to go to Afghanistan for added training in handling explosives. In late November 1999, Hijazi reportedly swore before Abu Zubaydah the *bayat* to Bin Ladin, committing himself to do anything Bin Ladin ordered. He then departed for Jordan and was at a waypoint in Syria when Abu Zubaydah sent Abu Hoshar the message that prompted Jordanian authorities to roll up the whole cell.[9]

After the arrests of Abu Hoshar and 15 others, the Jordanians tracked Deek to Peshawar, persuaded Pakistan to extradite him, and added him to their catch. Searches in Amman found the rented house and, among other things, 71 drums of acids, several forged Saudi passports, detonators, and Deek's *Encyclopedia*. Six of the accomplices were sentenced to death. In custody, Hijazi's younger brother said that the group's motto had been "The season is coming, and bodies will pile up in sacks."[10]

Diplomacy and Disruption

On December 4, as news came in about the discoveries in Jordan, National Security Council (NSC) Counterterrorism Coordinator Richard Clarke wrote Berger, "If George's [Tenet's] story about a planned series of UBL attacks at the Millennium is true, we will need to make some decisions NOW." He told us he held several conversations with President Clinton during the crisis. He suggested threatening reprisals against the Taliban in Afghanistan in the event of any attacks on U.S. interests, anywhere, by Bin Ladin. He further proposed to Berger that a strike be made during the last week of 1999 against al Qaeda camps in Afghanistan—a proposal not adopted.[11]

Warned by the CIA that the disrupted Jordanian plot was probably part of a larger series of attacks intended for the millennium, some possibly involving chemical weapons, the Principals Committee met on the night of December 8 and decided to task Clarke's Counterterrorism Security Group (CSG) to develop plans to deter and disrupt al Qaeda plots.[12]

Michael Sheehan, the State Department member of the CSG, communicated warnings to the Taliban that they would be held responsible for future al Qaeda attacks. "Mike was not diplomatic," Clarke reported to Berger. With virtually no evidence of a Taliban response, a new approach was made to Pakistan.[13] General Anthony Zinni, the commander of Central Command (CENTCOM), was designated as the President's special envoy and sent to ask General Musharraf to "take whatever action you deem necessary to resolve the Bin Laden problem at the earliest possible time." But Zinni came back empty-handed. As Ambassador William Milam reported from Islamabad, Musharraf was "unwilling to take the political heat at home."[14]

The CIA worked hard with foreign security services to detain or at least keep an eye on suspected Bin Ladin associates. Tenet spoke to 20 of his foreign counterparts. Disruption and arrest operations were mounted against terrorists in eight countries.[15] In mid-December, President Clinton signed a Memorandum of Notification (MON) giving the CIA broader authority to use foreign proxies to detain Bin Ladin lieutenants, without having to transfer them to U.S. custody. The authority was to capture, not kill, though lethal force might be used if necessary.[16] Tenet would later send a message to all CIA personnel overseas, saying, "The threat could not be more real. . . . Do whatever is necessary to disrupt UBL's plans. . . . The American people are counting on you and me to take every appropriate step to protect them during this period." The State Department issued a worldwide threat advisory to its posts overseas.[17]

Then, on December 14, an Algerian jihadist was caught bringing a load of explosives into the United States.

Ressam's Arrest

Ahmed Ressam, 23, had illegally immigrated to Canada in 1994. Using a falsified passport and a bogus story about persecution in Algeria, Ressam entered

Montreal and claimed political asylum. For the next few years he supported himself with petty crime. Recruited by an alumnus of Abu Zubaydah's Khaldan camp, Ressam trained in Afghanistan in 1998, learning, among other things, how to place cyanide near the air intake of a building to achieve maximum lethality at minimum personal risk. Having joined other Algerians in planning a possible attack on a U.S. airport or consulate, Ressam left Afghanistan in early 1999 carrying precursor chemicals for explosives disguised in toiletry bottles, a notebook containing bomb assembly instructions, and $12,000. Back in Canada, he went about procuring weapons, chemicals, and false papers.[18]

In early summer 1999, having learned that not all of his colleagues could get the travel documents to enter Canada, Ressam decided to carry out the plan alone. By the end of the summer he had chosen three Los Angeles–area airports as potential targets, ultimately fixing on Los Angeles International (LAX) as the largest and easiest to operate in surreptitiously. He bought or stole chemicals and equipment for his bomb, obtaining advice from three Algerian friends, all of whom were wanted by authorities in France for their roles in past terrorist attacks there. Ressam also acquired new confederates. He promised to help a New York–based partner, Abdelghani Meskini, get training in Afghanistan if Meskini would help him maneuver in the United States.[19]

In December 1999, Ressam began his final preparations. He called an Afghanistan-based facilitator to inquire into whether Bin Ladin wanted to take credit for the attack, but he did not get a reply. He spent a week in Vancouver preparing the explosive components with a close friend. The chemicals were so caustic that the men kept their windows open, despite the freezing temperatures outside, and sucked on cough drops to soothe their irritated throats.[20] While in Vancouver, Ressam also rented a Chrysler sedan for his travel into the United States, and packed the explosives in the trunk's spare tire well.[21]

On December 14, 1999, Ressam drove his rental car onto the ferry from Victoria, Canada, to Port Angeles, Washington. Ressam planned to drive to Seattle and meet Meskini, with whom he would travel to Los Angeles and case

---

A Case Study in Terrorist Travel
Following a familiar terrorist pattern, Ressam and his associates used fraudulent passports and immigration fraud to travel. In Ressam's case, this involved flying from France to Montreal using a photo-substituted French passport under a false name. Under questioning, Ressam admitted the passport was fraudulent and claimed political asylum. He was released pending a hearing, which he failed to attend. His political asylum claim was denied. He was arrested again, released again, and given another hearing date. Again, he did not show. He was arrested four times

for thievery, usually from tourists, but was neither jailed nor deported. He also supported himself by selling stolen documents to a friend who was a document broker for Islamist terrorists.[22]

Ressam eventually obtained a genuine Canadian passport through a document vendor who stole a blank baptismal certificate from a Catholic church. With this document he was able to obtain a Canadian passport under the name of Benni Antoine Noris. This enabled him to travel to Pakistan, and from there to Afghanistan for his training, and then return to Canada. Impressed, Abu Zubaydah asked Ressam to get more genuine Canadian passports and to send them to him for other terrorists to use.[23]

Another conspirator, Abdelghani Meskini, used a stolen identity to travel to Seattle on December 11, 1999, at the request of Mokhtar Haouari, another conspirator. Haouari provided fraudulent passports and visas to assist Ressam and Meskini's planned getaway from the United States to Algeria, Pakistan, and Afghanistan.[24] One of Meskini's associates, Abdel Hakim Tizegha, also filed a claim for political asylum. He was released pending a hearing, which was adjourned and rescheduled five times. His claim was finally denied two years after his initial filing. His attorney appealed the decision, and Tizegha was allowed to remain in the country pending the appeal. Nine months later, his attorney notified the court that he could not locate his client. A warrant of deportation was issued.[25]

LAX. They planned to detonate the bomb on or around January 1, 2000. At the Immigration and Naturalization Service (INS) preinspection station in Victoria, Ressam presented officials with his genuine but fraudulently obtained Canadian passport, from which he had torn the Afghanistan entry and exit stamps. The INS agent on duty ran the passport through a variety of databases but, since it was not in Ressam's name, he did not pick up the pending Canadian arrest warrants. After a cursory examination of Ressam's car, the INS agents allowed Ressam to board the ferry.[26]

Late in the afternoon of December 14, Ressam arrived in Port Angeles. He waited for all the other cars to depart the ferry, assuming (incorrectly) that the last car off would draw less scrutiny. Customs officers assigned to the port, noticing Ressam's nervousness, referred him to secondary inspection. When asked for additional identification, Ressam handed the Customs agent a Price Costco membership card in the same false name as his passport. As that agent began an initial pat-down, Ressam panicked and tried to run away.[27]

Inspectors examining Ressam's rental car found the explosives concealed in the spare tire well, but at first they assumed the white powder and viscous liquid were drug-related—until an inspector pried apart and identified one of the four timing devices concealed within black boxes. Ressam was placed under arrest. Investigators guessed his target was in Seattle. They did not learn about the Los Angeles airport planning until they reexamined evidence seized in Montreal in 2000; they obtained further details when Ressam began cooperating in May 2001.[28]

Emergency Cooperation

After the disruption of the plot in Amman, it had not escaped notice in Washington that Hijazi had lived in California and driven a cab in Boston and that Deek was a naturalized U.S. citizen who, as Berger reminded President Clinton, had been in touch with extremists in the United States as well as abroad.[29] Before Ressam's arrest, Berger saw no need to raise a public alarm at home—although the FBI put all field offices on alert.[30]

Now, following Ressam's arrest, the FBI asked for an unprecedented number of special wiretaps. Both Berger and Tenet told us that their impression was that more Foreign Intelligence Surveillance Act (FISA) wiretap requests were processed during the millennium alert than ever before.[31]

The next day, writing about Ressam's arrest and links to a cell in Montreal, Berger informed the President that the FBI would advise police in the United States to step up activities but would still try to avoid undue public alarm by stressing that the government had no specific information about planned attacks.[32]

At a December 22 meeting of the Small Group of principals, FBI Director Louis Freeh briefed officials from the NSC staff, CIA, and Justice on wiretaps and investigations inside the United States, including a Brooklyn entity tied to the Ressam arrest, a seemingly unreliable foreign report of possible attacks on seven U.S. cities, two Algerians detained on the Canadian border, and searches in Montreal related to a jihadist cell. The Justice Department released a statement on the alert the same day.[33]

Clarke's staff warned, "*Foreign terrorist sleeper cells are present in the US and attacks in the US are likely.*"[34] Clarke asked Berger to try to make sure that the domestic agencies remained alert. "Is there a threat to civilian aircraft?" he wrote. Clarke also asked the principals in late December to discuss a foreign security service report about a Bin Ladin plan to put bombs on transatlantic flights.[35]

The CSG met daily. Berger said that the principals met constantly.[36] Later, when asked what made her decide to ask Ressam to step out of his vehicle, Diana Dean, a Customs inspector who referred Ressam to secondary inspection, testified that it was her "training and experience."[37] It appears that the heightened sense of alert at the national level played no role in Ressam's detention.

There was a mounting sense of public alarm. The earlier Jordanian arrests had been covered in the press, and Ressam's arrest was featured on network evening news broadcasts throughout the Christmas season.[38]

The FBI was more communicative during the millennium crisis than it had ever been. The senior FBI official for counterterrorism, Dale Watson, was a regular member of the CSG, and Clarke had good relations both with him and with some of the FBI agents handling al Qaeda–related investigations, including John O'Neill in New York. As a rule, however, neither Watson nor these agents brought much information to the group. The FBI simply did not produce the kind of intelligence reports that other agencies routinely wrote and disseminated. As law enforcement officers, Bureau agents tended to write up only witness interviews. Written case analysis usually occurred only in memoranda to supervisors requesting authority to initiate or expand an investigation.[39]

But during the millennium alert, with its direct links into the United States from Hijazi, Deek, and Ressam, FBI officials were briefing in person about ongoing investigations, not relying on the dissemination of written reports. Berger told us that it was hard for FBI officials to hold back information in front of a cabinet-rank group. After the alert, according to Berger and members of the NSC staff, the FBI returned to its normal practice of withholding written reports and saying little about investigations or witness interviews, taking the position that any information related to pending investigations might be presented to a grand jury and hence could not be disclosed under then-prevailing federal law.[40]

The terrorist plots that were broken up at the end of 1999 display the variety of operations that might be attributed, however indirectly, to al Qaeda. The Jordanian cell was a loose affiliate; we now know that it sought approval and training from Afghanistan, and at least one key member swore loyalty to Bin Ladin. But the cell's plans and preparations were autonomous. Ressam's ties to al Qaeda were even looser. Though he had been recruited, trained, and prepared in a network affiliated with the organization and its allies, Ressam's own plans were, nonetheless, essentially independent.

Al Qaeda, and Bin Ladin himself, did have at least one operation of their very own in mind for the millennium period. In chapter 5 we introduced an al Qaeda operative named Nashiri. Working with Bin Ladin, he was developing a plan to attack a ship near Yemen. On January 3, an attempt was made to attack a U.S. warship in Aden, the USS *The Sullivans*. The attempt failed when the small boat, overloaded with explosives, sank. The operatives salvaged their equipment without the attempt becoming known, and they put off their plans for another day.

Al Qaeda's "planes operation" was also coming along. In January 2000, the United States caught a glimpse of its preparations.

A Lost Trail in Southeast Asia

In late 1999, the National Security Agency (NSA) analyzed communications associated with a suspected terrorist facility in the Middle East, indicating that several members of "an operational cadre" were planning to travel to Kuala Lumpur in early January 2000. Initially, only the first names of three were known—"Nawaf," "Salem," and "Khalid." NSA analysts surmised correctly that Salem was Nawaf's younger brother. Seeing links not only with al Qaeda but specifically with the 1998 embassy bombings, a CIA desk officer guessed that "something more nefarious [was] afoot."[41]

In chapter 5, we discussed the dispatch of two operatives to the United States for their part in the planes operation—Nawaf al Hazmi and Khalid al Mihdhar. Two more, Khallad and Abu Bara, went to Southeast Asia to case flights for the part of the operation that was supposed to unfold there.[42] All made their way to Southeast Asia from Afghanistan and Pakistan, except for Mihdhar, who traveled from Yemen.[43]

Though Nawaf's trail was temporarily lost, the CIA soon identified "Khalid" as Khalid al Mihdhar.[44] He was located leaving Yemen and tracked until he arrived in Kuala Lumpur on January 5, 2000.[45] Other Arabs, unidentified at the time, were watched as they gathered with him in the Malaysian capital.[46]

On January 8, the surveillance teams reported that three of the Arabs had suddenly left Kuala Lumpur on a short flight to Bangkok.[47] They identified one as Mihdhar. They later learned that one of his companions was named Alhazmi, although it was not yet known that he was "Nawaf." The only identifier available for the third person was part of a name—Salahsae.[48] In Bangkok, CIA officers received the information too late to track the three men as they came in, and the travelers disappeared into the streets of Bangkok.[49]

The Counterterrorist Center (CTC) had briefed the CIA leadership on the gathering in Kuala Lumpur, and the information had been passed on to Berger and the NSC staff and to Director Freeh and others at the FBI (though the FBI noted that the CIA had the lead and would let the FBI know if a domestic angle arose). The head of the Bin Ladin unit kept providing updates, unaware at first even that the Arabs had left Kuala Lumpur, let alone that their trail had been lost in Bangkok.[50] When this bad news arrived, the names were put on a Thai watchlist so that Thai authorities could inform the United States if any of them departed from Thailand.[51]

Several weeks later, CIA officers in Kuala Lumpur prodded colleagues in Bangkok for additional information regarding the three travelers.[52] In early March 2000, Bangkok reported that Nawaf al Hazmi, now identified for the first time with his full name, had departed on January 15 on a United Airlines flight to Los Angeles. As for Khalid al Mihdhar, there was no report of his departure even though he had accompanied Hazmi on the United flight to Los Angeles.[53] No one outside of the Counterterrorist Center was told any of this. The CIA did not try to register Mihdhar or Hazmi with the State Department's

TIPOFF watchlist—either in January, when word arrived of Mihdhar's visa, or in March, when word came that Hazmi, too, had had a U.S. visa and a ticket to Los Angeles.[54]

None of this information—about Mihdhar's U.S. visa or Hazmi's travel to the United States—went to the FBI, and nothing more was done to track any of the three until January 2001, when the investigation of another bombing, that of the USS *Cole*, reignited interest in Khallad. We will return to that story in chapter 8.

6.2 POST-CRISIS REFLECTION: AGENDA FOR 2000

After the millennium alert, elements of the U.S. government reviewed their performance. The CIA's leadership was told that while a number of plots had been disrupted, the millennium might be only the "kick-off" for a period of extended attacks.[55] Clarke wrote Berger on January 11, 2000, that the CIA, the FBI, Justice, and the NSC staff had come to two main conclusions. First, U.S. disruption efforts thus far had "not put too much of a dent" in Bin Ladin's network. If the United States wanted to "roll back" the threat, disruption would have to proceed at "a markedly different tempo." Second, "sleeper cells" and "a variety of terrorist groups" had turned up at home.[56] As one of Clarke's staff noted, only a "chance discovery" by U.S. Customs had prevented a possible attack.[57] Berger gave his approval for the NSC staff to commence an "after-action review," anticipating new budget requests. He also asked DCI Tenet to review the CIA's counterterrorism strategy and come up with a plan for "where we go from here."[58]

The NSC staff advised Berger that the United States had only been "nibbling at the edges" of Bin Ladin's network and that more terror attacks were a question not of "if" but rather of "when" and "where."[59] The Principals Committee met on March 10, 2000, to review possible new moves. The principals ended up agreeing that the government should take three major steps. First, more money should go to the CIA to accelerate its efforts to "seriously attrit" al Qaeda. Second, there should be a crackdown on foreign terrorist organizations in the United States. Third, immigration law enforcement should be strengthened, and the INS should tighten controls on the Canadian border (including stepping up U.S.-Canada cooperation). The principals endorsed the proposed programs; some, like expanding the number of Joint Terrorism Task Forces, moved forward, and others, like creating a centralized translation unit for domestic intelligence intercepts in Arabic and other languages, did not.[60]

Pressing Pakistan
While this process moved along, diplomacy continued its rounds. Direct pressure on the Taliban had proved unsuccessful. As one NSC staff note put it,

"Under the Taliban, Afghanistan is not so much a state sponsor of terrorism as it is a state sponsored by terrorists."[61] In early 2000, the United States began a high-level effort to persuade Pakistan to use its influence over the Taliban.

In January 2000, Assistant Secretary of State Karl Inderfurth and the State Department's counterterrorism coordinator, Michael Sheehan, met with General Musharraf in Islamabad, dangling before him the possibility of a presidential visit in March as a reward for Pakistani cooperation. Such a visit was coveted by Musharraf, partly as a sign of his government's legitimacy. He told the two envoys that he would meet with Mullah Omar and press him on Bin Ladin. They left, however, reporting to Washington that Pakistan was unlikely in fact to do anything, "given what it sees as the benefits of Taliban control of Afghanistan."[62]

President Clinton was scheduled to travel to India. The State Department felt that he should not visit India without also visiting Pakistan. The Secret Service and the CIA, however, warned in the strongest terms that visiting Pakistan would risk the President's life. Counterterrorism officials also argued that Pakistan had not done enough to merit a presidential visit. But President Clinton insisted on including Pakistan in the itinerary for his trip to South Asia.[63] His one-day stopover on March 25, 2000, was the first time a U.S. president had been there since 1969. At his meeting with Musharraf and others, President Clinton concentrated on tensions between Pakistan and India and the dangers of nuclear proliferation, but also discussed Bin Ladin. President Clinton told us that when he pulled Musharraf aside for a brief, one-on-one meeting, he pleaded with the general for help regarding Bin Ladin. "I offered him the moon when I went to see him, in terms of better relations with the United States, if he'd help us get Bin Ladin and deal with another issue or two."[64]

The U.S. effort continued. Early in May, President Clinton urged Musharraf to carry through on his promise to visit Afghanistan and press Mullah Omar to expel Bin Ladin.[65] At the end of the month, Under Secretary of State Thomas Pickering followed up with a trip to the region.[66] In June, DCI Tenet traveled to Pakistan with the same general message.[67] By September, the United States was becoming openly critical of Pakistan for supporting a Taliban military offensive aimed at completing the conquest of Afghanistan.[68]

In December, taking a step proposed by the State Department some months earlier, the United States led a campaign for new UN sanctions, which resulted in UN Security Council Resolution 1333, again calling for Bin Ladin's expulsion and forbidding any country to provide the Taliban with arms or military assistance.[69] This, too, had little if any effect. The Taliban did not expel Bin Ladin. Pakistani arms continued to flow across the border.

Secretary of State Madeleine Albright told us, "We did not have a strong hand to play with the Pakistanis. Because of the sanctions required by U.S. law, we had few carrots to offer."[70] Congress had blocked most economic and military aid to Pakistan because of that country's nuclear arms program and Musharraf's coup. Sheehan was critical of Musharraf, telling us that the Pakistani leader "blew a chance to remake Pakistan."[71]

Building New Capabilities: The CIA

The after-action review had treated the CIA as the lead agency for any offensive against al Qaeda, and the principals, at their March 10 meeting, had endorsed strengthening the CIA's capability for that role. To the CTC, that meant proceeding with "the Plan," which it had put forward half a year earlier—hiring and training more case officers and building up the capabilities of foreign security services that provided intelligence via liaison. On occasion, as in Jordan in December 1999, these liaison services took direct action against al Qaeda cells.[72]

In the CTC and higher up, the CIA's managers believed that they desperately needed funds just to continue their current counterterrorism effort, for they reckoned that the millennium alert had already used up all of the Center's funds for the current fiscal year; the Bin Ladin unit had spent 140 percent of its allocation. Tenet told us he met with Berger to discuss funding for counterterrorism just two days after the principals' meeting.[73]

While Clarke strongly favored giving the CIA more money for counterterrorism, he differed sharply with the CIA's managers about where it should come from. They insisted that the CIA had been shortchanged ever since the end of the Cold War. Their ability to perform any mission, counterterrorism included, they argued, depended on preserving what they had, restoring what they had lost since the beginning of the 1990s, and building from there—with across-the-board recruitment and training of new case officers, and the reopening of closed stations. To finance the counterterrorism effort, Tenet had gone to congressional leaders after the 1998 embassy bombings and persuaded them to give the CIA a special supplemental appropriation. Now, in the aftermath of the millennium alert, Tenet wanted a boost in overall funds for the CIA *and* another supplemental appropriation specifically for counterterrorism.[74]

To Clarke, this seemed evidence that the CIA's leadership did not give sufficient priority to the battle against Bin Ladin and al Qaeda. He told us that James Pavitt, the head of the CIA's Directorate of Operations, "said if there's going to be money spent on going after Bin Ladin, it should be given to him. . . . My view was that he had had a lot of money to do it and a long time to do it, and I didn't want to put more good money after bad."[75] The CIA had a very different attitude: Pavitt told us that while the CIA's Bin Ladin unit did "extraordinary and commendable work," his chief of station in London "was just as much part of the al Qaeda struggle as an officer sitting in [the Bin Ladin unit]."[76]

The dispute had large managerial implications, for Clarke had found allies in the Office of Management and Budget (OMB). They had supplied him with the figures he used to argue that CIA spending on counterterrorism from its baseline budget had shown almost no increase.[77]

Berger met twice with Tenet in April to try to resolve the dispute. The Deputies Committee met later in the month to review fiscal year 2000 and 2001 budget priorities and offsets for the CIA and other agencies. In the end,

Tenet obtained a modest supplemental appropriation, which funded counter-terrorism without requiring much reprogramming of baseline funds. But the CIA still believed that it remained underfunded for counterterrorism.[78]

Terrorist Financing

The second major point on which the principals had agreed on March 10 was the need to crack down on terrorist organizations and curtail their fund-raising.

The embassy bombings of 1998 had focused attention on al Qaeda's finances. One result had been the creation of an NSC-led interagency committee on terrorist financing. On its recommendation, the President had designated Bin Ladin and al Qaeda as subject to sanctions under the International Emergency Economic Powers Act. This gave the Treasury Department's Office of Foreign Assets Control (OFAC) the ability to search for and freeze any Bin Ladin or al Qaeda assets that reached the U.S. financial system. But since OFAC had little information to go on, few funds were frozen.[79]

In July 1999, the President applied the same designation to the Taliban for harboring Bin Ladin. Here, OFAC had more success. It blocked more than $34 million in Taliban assets held in U.S. banks. Another $215 million in gold and $2 million in demand deposits, all belonging to the Afghan central bank and held by the Federal Reserve Bank of New York, were also frozen.[80] After October 1999, when the State Department formally designated al Qaeda a "foreign terrorist organization," it became the duty of U.S. banks to block its transactions and seize its funds.[81] Neither this designation nor UN sanctions had much additional practical effect; the sanctions were easily circumvented, and there were no multilateral mechanisms to ensure that other countries' financial systems were not used as conduits for terrorist funding.[82]

Attacking the funds of an institution, even the Taliban, was easier than finding and seizing the funds of a clandestine worldwide organization like al Qaeda. Although the CIA's Bin Ladin unit had originally been inspired by the idea of studying terrorist financial links, few personnel assigned to it had any experience in financial investigations. Any terrorist-financing intelligence appeared to have been collected collaterally, as a consequence of gathering other intelligence. This attitude may have stemmed in large part from the chief of this unit, who did not believe that simply following the money from point A to point B revealed much about the terrorists' plans and intentions. As a result, the CIA placed little emphasis on terrorist financing.[83]

Nevertheless, the CIA obtained a general understanding of how al Qaeda raised money. It knew relatively early, for example, about the loose affiliation of financial institutions, businesses, and wealthy individuals who supported extremist Islamic activities.[84] Much of the early reporting on al Qaeda's financial situation and its structure came from Jamal Ahmed al Fadl, whom we have mentioned earlier in the report.[85] After the 1998 embassy bombings, the U.S. government tried to develop a clearer picture of Bin Ladin's finances. A U.S.

interagency group traveled to Saudi Arabia twice, in 1999 and 2000, to get information from the Saudis about their understanding of those finances. The group eventually concluded that the oft-repeated assertion that Bin Ladin was funding al Qaeda from his personal fortune was in fact not true.

The officials developed a new theory: al Qaeda was getting its money elsewhere, and the United States needed to focus on other sources of funding, such as charities, wealthy donors, and financial facilitators. Ultimately, although the intelligence community devoted more resources to the issue and produced somewhat more intelligence,[86] it remained difficult to distinguish al Qaeda's financial transactions among the vast sums moving in the international financial system. The CIA was not able to find or disrupt al Qaeda's money flows.[87]

The NSC staff thought that one possible solution to these weaknesses in the intelligence community was to create an all-source terrorist-financing intelligence analysis center. Clarke pushed for the funding of such a center at Treasury, but neither Treasury nor the CIA was willing to commit the resources.[88]

Within the United States, various FBI field offices gathered intelligence on organizations suspected of raising funds for al Qaeda or other terrorist groups. By 9/11, FBI agents understood that there were extremist organizations operating within the United States supporting a global jihadist movement and with substantial connections to al Qaeda. The FBI operated a web of informants, conducted electronic surveillance, and had opened significant investigations in a number of field offices, including New York, Chicago, Detroit, San Diego, and Minneapolis. On a national level, however, the FBI never used the information to gain a systematic or strategic understanding of the nature and extent of al Qaeda fundraising.[89]

Treasury regulators, as well as U.S. financial institutions, were generally focused on finding and deterring or disrupting the vast flows of U.S. currency generated by drug trafficking and high-level international fraud. Large-scale scandals, such as the use of the Bank of New York by Russian money launderers to move millions of dollars out of Russia, captured the attention of the Department of the Treasury and of Congress.[90] Before 9/11, Treasury did not consider terrorist financing important enough to mention in its national strategy for money laundering.[91]

Border Security
The third point on which the principals had agreed on March 10 was the need for attention to America's porous borders and the weak enforcement of immigration laws. Drawing on ideas from government officials, Clarke's working group developed a menu of proposals to bolster border security. Some reworked or reiterated previous presidential directives.[92] They included

- creating an interagency center to target illegal entry and human traffickers;

- imposing tighter controls on student visas;[93]
- taking legal action to prevent terrorists from coming into the United States and to remove those already here, detaining them while awaiting removal proceedings;[94]
- further increasing the number of immigration agents to FBI Joint Terrorism Task Forces to help investigate immigration charges against individuals suspected of terrorism;[95]
- activating a special court to enable the use of classified evidence in immigration-related national security cases;[96] and
- both implementing new security measures for U.S. passports and working with the United Nations and foreign governments to raise global security standards for travel documents.[97]

Clarke's working group compiled new proposals as well, such as

- undertaking a Joint Perimeter Defense program with Canada to establish cooperative intelligence and law enforcement programs, leading to joint operations based on shared visa and immigration data and joint border patrols;
- staffing land border crossings 24/7 and equipping them with video cameras, physical barriers, and means to detect weapons of mass destruction (WMD); and
- addressing the problem of migrants—possibly including terrorists— who destroy their travel documents so they cannot be returned to their countries of origin.[98]

These proposals were praiseworthy in principle. In practice, however, they required action by weak, chronically underfunded executive agencies and powerful congressional committees, which were more responsive to well-organized interest groups than to executive branch interagency committees. The changes sought by the principals in March 2000 were only beginning to occur before 9/11.

"Afghan Eyes"

In early March 2000, when President Clinton received an update on U.S. covert action efforts against Bin Ladin, he wrote in the memo's margin that the United States could surely do better. Military officers in the Joint Staff told us that they shared this sense of frustration. Clarke used the President's comment to push the CSG to brainstorm new ideas, including aid to the Northern Alliance.[99]

Back in December 1999, Northern Alliance leader Ahmed Shah Massoud had offered to stage a rocket attack against Bin Ladin's Derunta training complex. Officers at the CIA had worried that giving him a green light might cross the line into violation of the assassination ban. Hence, Massoud was told not to take any such action without explicit U.S. authorization.[100] In the spring of 2000, after the CIA had sent out officers to explore possible closer relationships with both the Uzbeks and the Northern Alliance, discussions took place in Washington between U.S. officials and delegates sent by Massoud.[101]

The Americans agreed that Massoud should get some modest technical help so he could work on U.S. priorities—collecting intelligence on and possibly acting against al Qaeda. But Massoud wanted the United States both to become his ally in trying to overthrow the Taliban and to recognize that they were fighting common enemies. Clarke and Cofer Black, the head of the Counterterrorist Center, wanted to take this next step. Proposals to help the Northern Alliance had been debated in the U.S. government since 1999 and, as we mentioned in chapter 4, the U.S. government as a whole had been wary of endorsing them, largely because of the Northern Alliance's checkered history, its limited base of popular support in Afghanistan, and Pakistan's objections.[102]

CIA officials also began pressing proposals to use their ties with the Northern Alliance to get American agents on the ground in Afghanistan for an extended period, setting up their own base for covert intelligence collection and activity in the Panjshir Valley and lessening reliance on foreign proxies. "There's no substitute for face-to-face," one officer told us.[103] But the CIA's institutional capacity for such direct action was weak, especially if it was not working jointly with the U.S. military. The idea was turned down as too risky.[104]

In the meantime, the CIA continued to work with its tribal assets in southern Afghanistan. In early August, the tribals reported an attempt to ambush Bin Ladin's convoy as he traveled on the road between Kabul and Kandahar city—their first such reported interdiction attempt in more than a year and a half. But it was not a success. According to the tribals' own account, when they approached one of the vehicles, they quickly determined that women and children were inside and called off the ambush. Conveying this information to the NSC staff, the CIA noted that they had no independent corroboration for this incident, but that the tribals had acted within the terms of the CIA's authorities in Afghanistan.[105]

In 2000, plans continued to be developed for potential military operations in Afghanistan. Navy vessels that could launch missiles into Afghanistan were still on call in the north Arabian Sea.[106] In the summer, the military refined its list of strikes and Special Operations possibilities to a set of 13 options within the Operation Infinite Resolve plan.[107] Yet planning efforts continued to be limited by the same operational and policy concerns encountered in 1998 and 1999. Although the intelligence community sometimes knew where Bin Ladin was, it had been unable to provide intelligence considered sufficiently reliable to launch a strike. Above all, the United States did not have American eyes on the target. As one military officer put it, we had our hand on the door, but we couldn't open the door and walk in.[108]

At some point during this period, President Clinton expressed his frustration with the lack of military options to take out Bin Ladin and the al Qaeda leadership, remarking to General Hugh Shelton, "You know, it would scare the shit out of al-Qaeda if suddenly a bunch of black ninjas rappelled out of helicopters into the middle of their camp."[109] Although Shelton told the Commission he did not remember the statement, President Clinton recalled this remark as "one of the many things I said." The President added, however, that he realized nothing would be accomplished if he lashed out in anger. Secretary of Defense William Cohen thought that the President might have been making a hypothetical statement. Regardless, he said, the question remained how to get the "ninjas" into and out of the theater of operations.[110] As discussed in chapter 4, plans of this kind were never carried out before 9/11.

In late 1999 or early 2000, the Joint Staff's director of operations, Vice Admiral Scott Fry, directed his chief information operations officer, Brigadier General Scott Gration, to develop innovative ways to get better intelligence on Bin Ladin's whereabouts. Gration and his team worked on a number of different ideas aimed at getting reliable American eyes on Bin Ladin in a way that would reduce the lag time between sighting and striking.[111]

One option was to use a small, unmanned U.S. Air Force drone called the Predator, which could survey the territory below and send back video footage. Another option—eventually dismissed as impractical—was to place a powerful long-range telescope on a mountain within range of one of Bin Ladin's training camps. Both proposals were discussed with General Shelton, the chairman of the Joint Chiefs of Staff, and then briefed to Clarke's office at the White House as the CSG was searching for new ideas. In the spring of 2000, Clarke brought in the CIA's assistant director for collection, Charles Allen, to work together with Fry on a joint CIA-Pentagon effort that Clarke dubbed "Afghan Eyes."[112] After much argument between the CIA and the Defense Department about who should pay for the program, the White House eventually imposed a cost-sharing agreement. The CIA agreed to pay for Predator operations as a 60-day "proof of concept" trial run.[113]

The Small Group backed Afghan Eyes at the end of June 2000. By mid-July, testing was completed and the equipment was ready, but legal issues were still being ironed out.[114] By August 11, the principals had agreed to deploy the Predator.[115] The NSC staff considered how to use the information the drones would be relaying from Afghanistan. Clarke's deputy, Roger Cressey, wrote to Berger that emergency CSG and Principals Committee meetings might be needed to act on video coming in from the Predator if it proved able to lock in Bin Ladin's location. In the memo's margin, Berger wrote that before considering action, "I will want more than verified location: we will need, at least, data on pattern of movements to provide some assurance he will remain in place." President Clinton was kept up to date.[116]

On September 7, the Predator flew for the first time over Afghanistan. When

Clarke saw video taken during the trial flight, he described the imagery to Berger as "truly astonishing," and he argued immediately for more flights seeking to find Bin Ladin and target him for cruise missile or air attack. Even if Bin Ladin were not found, Clarke said, Predator missions might identify additional worthwhile targets, such as other al Qaeda leaders or stocks of chemical or biological weapons.[117]

Clarke was not alone in his enthusiasm. He had backing from Cofer Black and Charles Allen at the CIA. Ten out of 15 trial missions of the Predator over Afghanistan were rated successful. On the first flight, a Predator saw a security detail around a tall man in a white robe at Bin Ladin's Tarnak Farms compound outside Kandahar. After a second sighting of the "man in white" at the compound on September 28, intelligence community analysts determined that he was probably Bin Ladin.[118]

During at least one trial mission, the Taliban spotted the Predator and scrambled MiG fighters to try, without success, to intercept it. Berger worried that a Predator might be shot down, and warned Clarke that a shootdown would be a "bonanza" for Bin Ladin and the Taliban.[119]

Still, Clarke was optimistic about Predator—as well as progress with disruptions of al Qaeda cells elsewhere. Berger was more cautious, praising the NSC staff's performance but observing that this was no time for complacency. "Unfortunately," he wrote, "the light at the end of the tunnel is another tunnel."[120]

6.3 THE ATTACK ON THE USS *COLE*

Early in chapter 5 we introduced, along with Khalid Sheikh Mohammed, two other men who became operational coordinators for al Qaeda: Khallad and Nashiri. As we explained, both were involved during 1998 and 1999 in preparing to attack a ship off the coast of Yemen with a boatload of explosives. They had originally targeted a commercial vessel, specifically an oil tanker, but Bin Ladin urged them to look for a U.S. warship instead. In January 2000, their team had attempted to attack a warship in the port of Aden, but the attempt failed when the suicide boat sank. More than nine months later, on October 12, 2000, al Qaeda operatives in a small boat laden with explosives attacked a U.S. Navy destroyer, the USS *Cole*. The blast ripped a hole in the side of the *Cole*, killing 17 members of the ship's crew and wounding at least 40.[121]

The plot, we now know, was a full-fledged al Qaeda operation, supervised directly by Bin Ladin. He chose the target and location of the attack, selected the suicide operatives, and provided the money needed to purchase explosives and equipment. Nashiri was the field commander and managed the operation in Yemen. Khallad helped in Yemen until he was arrested in a case of mistaken identity and freed with Bin Ladin's help, as we also mentioned earlier. Local al Qaeda coordinators included Jamal al Badawi and Fahd al Quso, who was supposed to film the attack from a nearby apartment. The two suicide operatives chosen were Hassan al Khamri and Ibrahim al Thawar, also known as Nibras. Nibras and Quso delivered money to Khallad in Bangkok during Khallad's January 2000 trip to Kuala Lumpur and Bangkok.[122]

In September 2000, Bin Ladin reportedly told Nashiri that he wanted to replace Khamri and Nibras. Nashiri was angry and disagreed, telling others he would go to Afghanistan and explain to Bin Ladin that the new operatives were already trained and ready to conduct the attack. Prior to departing, Nashiri gave Nibras and Khamri instructions to execute the attack on the next U.S. warship that entered the port of Aden.[123]

While Nashiri was in Afghanistan, Nibras and Khamri saw their chance. They piloted the explosives-laden boat alongside the USS *Cole*, made friendly gestures to crew members, and detonated the bomb. Quso did not arrive at the apartment in time to film the attack.[124]

Back in Afghanistan, Bin Ladin anticipated U.S. military retaliation. He ordered the evacuation of al Qaeda's Kandahar airport compound and fled—first to the desert area near Kabul, then to Khowst and Jalalabad, and eventually back to Kandahar. In Kandahar, he rotated between five to six residences, spending one night at each residence. In addition, he sent his senior advisor, Mohammed Atef, to a different part of Kandahar and his deputy, Ayman al Zawahiri, to Kabul so that all three could not be killed in one attack.[125]

There was no American strike. In February 2001, a source reported that an individual whom he identified as the big instructor (probably a reference to Bin Ladin) complained frequently that the United States had not yet attacked. According to the source, Bin Ladin wanted the United States to attack, and if it did not he would launch something bigger.[126]

The attack on the USS *Cole* galvanized al Qaeda's recruitment efforts. Following the attack, Bin Ladin instructed the media committee, then headed by Khalid Sheikh Mohammed, to produce a propaganda video that included a reenactment of the attack along with images of the al Qaeda training camps and training methods; it also highlighted Muslim suffering in Palestine, Kashmir, Indonesia, and Chechnya. Al Qaeda's image was very important to Bin Ladin, and the video was widely disseminated. Portions were aired on Al Jazeera, CNN, and other television outlets. It was also disseminated among many young men in Saudi Arabia and Yemen, and caused many extremists to travel to Afghanistan for training and jihad. Al Qaeda members considered the video an effective tool in their struggle for preeminence among other Islamist and jihadist movements.[127]

Investigating the Attack

Teams from the FBI, the Naval Criminal Investigative Service, and the CIA were immediately sent to Yemen to investigate the attack. With difficulty, Barbara Bodine, the U.S. ambassador to Yemen, tried to persuade the Yemeni government to accept these visitors and allow them to carry arms, though the Yemenis balked at letting Americans openly carry long guns (rifles, shotguns, automatic weapons). Meanwhile, Bodine and the leader of the FBI team, John O'Neill, clashed repeatedly—to the point that after O'Neill had been rotated out of Yemen but wanted to return, Bodine refused the request. Despite the initial tension, the Yemeni and American investigations proceeded. Within a few weeks, the outline of the story began to emerge.[128]

On the day of the *Cole* attack, a list of suspects was assembled that included al Qaeda's affiliate Egyptian Islamic Jihad. U.S. counterterrorism officials told us they immediately assumed that al Qaeda was responsible. But as Deputy DCI John McLaughlin explained to us, it was not enough for the attack to smell, look, and taste like an al Qaeda operation. To make a case, the CIA needed not just a guess but a link to someone known to be an al Qaeda operative.[129]

Within the first weeks after the attack, the Yemenis found and arrested both Badawi and Quso, but did not let the FBI team participate in the interrogations. The CIA described initial Yemeni support after the *Cole* as "slow and inadequate." President Clinton, Secretary Albright, and DCI Tenet all intervened to help. Because the information was secondhand, the U.S. team could not make its own assessment of its reliability.[130]

On November 11, the Yemenis provided the FBI with new information from the interrogations of Badawi and Quso, including descriptions of individuals from whom the detainees had received operational direction. One of them was Khallad, who was described as having lost his leg. The detainees said that Khallad helped direct the *Cole* operation from Afghanistan or Pakistan. The Yemenis (correctly) judged that the man described as Khallad was Tawfiq bin Attash.[131]

An FBI special agent recognized the name Khallad and connected this news with information from an important al Qaeda source who had been meeting regularly with CIA and FBI officers. The source had called Khallad Bin Ladin's "run boy," and described him as having lost one leg in an explosives accident at a training camp a few years earlier. To confirm the identification, the FBI agent asked the Yemenis for their photo of Khallad. The Yemenis provided the photo on November 22, reaffirming their view that Khallad had been an intermediary between the plotters and Bin Ladin. (In a meeting with U.S. officials a few weeks later, on December 16, the source identified Khallad from the Yemeni photograph.)[132]

U.S. intelligence agencies had already connected Khallad to al Qaeda terrorist operations, including the 1998 embassy bombings. By this time the Yemenis also had identified Nashiri, whose links to al Qaeda and the 1998 embassy bombings were even more well-known.[133]

In other words, the Yemenis provided strong evidence connecting the *Cole* attack to al Qaeda during the second half of November, identifying individual operatives whom the United States knew were part of al Qaeda. During December the United States was able to corroborate this evidence. But the United States did not have evidence about Bin Ladin's personal involvement in the attacks until Nashiri and Khallad were captured in 2002 and 2003.

Considering a Response

The *Cole* attack prompted renewed consideration of what could be done about al Qaeda. According to Clarke, Berger upbraided DCI Tenet so sharply after the *Cole* attack—repeatedly demanding to know why the United States had to put up with such attacks—that Tenet walked out of a meeting of the principals.[134]

The CIA got some additional covert action authorities, adding several other individuals to the coverage of the July 1999 Memorandum of Notification that allowed the United States to develop capture operations against al Qaeda leaders in a variety of places and circumstances. Tenet developed additional options, such as strengthening relationships with the Northern Alliance and the Uzbeks and slowing recent al Qaeda–related activities in Lebanon.[135]

On the diplomatic track, Berger agreed on October 30, 2000, to let the State Department make another approach to Taliban Deputy Foreign Minister Abdul Jalil about expelling Bin Ladin. The national security advisor ordered that the U.S. message "be stern and foreboding." This warning was similar to those issued in 1998 and 1999. Meanwhile, the administration was working with Russia on new UN sanctions against Mullah Omar's regime.[136]

President Clinton told us that before he could launch further attacks on al Qaeda in Afghanistan, or deliver an ultimatum to the Taliban threatening strikes if they did not immediately expel Bin Ladin, the CIA or the FBI had to be sure enough that they would "be willing to stand up in public and say, we believe that he [Bin Ladin] did this." He said he was very frustrated that he could not get a definitive enough answer to do something about the *Cole* attack.[137] Similarly, Berger recalled that to go to war, a president needs to be able to say that his senior intelligence and law enforcement officers have concluded who is responsible. He recalled that the intelligence agencies had strong suspicions, but had reached "no conclusion by the time we left office that it was al Qaeda."[138]

Our only sources for what intelligence officials thought at the time are what they said in informal briefings. Soon after the *Cole* attack and for the remainder of the Clinton administration, analysts stopped distributing written reports about who was responsible. The topic was obviously sensitive, and both Ambassador Bodine in Yemen and CIA analysts in Washington presumed that the government did not want reports circulating around the agencies that might become public, impeding law enforcement actions or backing the President into a corner.[139]

Instead the White House and other principals relied on informal updates as more evidence came in. Though Clarke worried that the CIA might be equivocating in assigning responsibility to al Qaeda, he wrote Berger on November 7 that the analysts had described their case by saying that "it has web feet, flies, and quacks." On November 10, CIA analysts briefed the Small Group of principals on their preliminary findings that the attack was carried out by a cell of Yemeni residents with some ties to the transnational mujahideen network. According to the briefing, these residents likely had some support from al Qaeda. But the information on outside sponsorship, support, and direction of the operation was inconclusive. The next day, Berger and Clarke told President Clinton that while the investigation was continuing, it was becoming increasingly clear that al Qaeda had planned and directed the bombing.[140]

In mid-November, as the evidence of al Qaeda involvement mounted, Berger asked General Shelton to reevaluate military plans to act quickly against Bin Ladin. General Shelton tasked General Tommy Franks, the new commander of CENTCOM, to look again at the options. Shelton wanted to demonstrate that the military was imaginative and knowledgeable enough to move on an array of options, and to show the complexity of the operations. He briefed Berger on the "Infinite Resolve" strike options developed since 1998, which the Joint Staff and CENTCOM had refined during the summer into a list of 13 possibilities or combinations. CENTCOM added a new "phased campaign" concept for wider-ranging strikes, including attacks against the Taliban. For the first time, these strikes envisioned an air campaign against Afghanistan of indefinite duration. Military planners did not include contingency planning for an invasion of Afghanistan. The concept was briefed to Deputy National Security Advisor Donald Kerrick on December 20, and to other officials.[141]

On November 25, Berger and Clarke wrote President Clinton that although the FBI and CIA investigations had not reached a formal conclusion, they believed the investigations would soon conclude that the attack had been carried out by a large cell whose senior members belonged to al Qaeda. Most of those involved had trained in Bin Ladin–operated camps in Afghanistan, Berger continued. So far, Bin Ladin had not been tied personally to the attack and nobody had heard him directly order it, but two intelligence reports suggested that he was involved. When discussing possible responses, though, Berger referred to the premise—al Qaeda responsibility—as an "unproven assumption."[142]

In the same November 25 memo, Berger informed President Clinton about a closely held idea: a last-chance ultimatum for the Taliban. Clarke was developing the idea with specific demands: immediate extradition of Bin Ladin and his lieutenants to a legitimate government for trial, observable closure of all terrorist facilities in Afghanistan, and expulsion of all terrorists from Afghanistan within 90 days. Noncompliance would mean U.S. "force directed at the Taliban itself" and U.S. efforts to ensure that the Taliban would never defeat the Northern Alliance. No such ultimatum was issued.[143]

Nearly a month later, on December 21, the CIA made another presentation to the Small Group of principals on the investigative team's findings. The CIA's briefing slides said that their "preliminary judgment" was that Bin Ladin's al Qaeda group "supported the attack" on the *Cole*, based on strong circumstantial evidence tying key perpetrators of the attack to al Qaeda. The CIA listed the key suspects, including Nashiri. In addition, the CIA detailed the timeline of the operation, from the mid-1999 preparations, to the failed attack on the USS *The Sullivans* on January 3, 2000, through a meeting held by the operatives the day before the attack.[144]

The slides said that so far the CIA had "no definitive answer on [the] crucial question of outside direction of the attack—how and by whom." The CIA noted that the Yemenis claimed that Khallad helped direct the operation from Afghanistan or Pakistan, possibly as Bin Ladin's intermediary, but that it had not seen the Yemeni evidence. However, the CIA knew from both human sources and signals intelligence that Khallad was tied to al Qaeda. The prepared briefing concluded that while some reporting about al Qaeda's role might have merit, those reports offered few specifics. Intelligence gave some ambiguous indicators of al Qaeda direction of the attack.[145]

This, President Clinton and Berger told us, was not the conclusion they needed in order to go to war or deliver an ultimatum to the Taliban threatening war. The election and change of power was not the issue, President Clinton added. There was enough time. If the agencies had given him a definitive answer, he said, he would have sought a UN Security Council ultimatum and given the Taliban one, two, or three days before taking further action against both al Qaeda and the Taliban. But he did not think it would be responsible for a president to launch an invasion of another country just based on a "preliminary judgment."[146]

Other advisers have echoed this concern. Some of Secretary Albright's advisers warned her at the time to be sure the evidence conclusively linked Bin Ladin to the *Cole* before considering any response, especially a military one, because such action might inflame the Islamic world and increase support for the Taliban. Defense Secretary Cohen told us it would not have been prudent to risk killing civilians based only on an assumption that al Qaeda was responsible. General Shelton added that there was an outstanding question as to who was responsible and what the targets were.[147]

Clarke recalled that while the Pentagon and the State Department had reservations about retaliation, the issue never came to a head because the FBI and the CIA never reached a firm conclusion. He thought they were "holding back." He said he did not know why, but his impression was that Tenet and

Reno possibly thought the White House "didn't really want to know," since the principals' discussions by November suggested that there was not much White House interest in conducting further military operations against Afghanistan in the administration's last weeks. He thought that, instead, President Clinton, Berger, and Secretary Albright were concentrating on a last-minute push for a peace agreement between the Palestinians and the Israelis.[148]

Some of Clarke's fellow counterterrorism officials, such as the State Department's Sheehan and the FBI's Watson, shared his disappointment that no military response occurred at the time. Clarke recently recalled that an angry Sheehan asked rhetorically of Defense officials: "Does al Qaeda have to attack the Pentagon to get their attention?"[149]

On the question of evidence, Tenet told us he was surprised to hear that the White House was awaiting a conclusion from him on responsibility for the *Cole* attack before taking action against al Qaeda. He did not recall Berger or anyone else telling him that they were waiting for the magic words from the CIA and the FBI. Nor did he remember having any discussions with Berger or the President about retaliation. Tenet told us he believed that it was up to him to present the case. Then it was up to the principals to decide if the case was good enough to justify using force. He believed he laid out what was knowable relatively early in the investigation, and that this evidence never really changed until after 9/11.[150]

A CIA official told us that the CIA's analysts chose the term "preliminary judgment" because of their notion of how an intelligence standard of proof differed from a legal standard. Because the attack was the subject of a criminal investigation, they told us, the term *preliminary* was used to avoid locking the government in with statements that might later be obtained by defense lawyers in a future court case. At the time, Clarke was aware of the problem of distinguishing between an intelligence case and a law enforcement case. Asking U.S. law enforcement officials to concur with an intelligence-based case before their investigation had been concluded "could give rise to charges that the administration had acted before final culpability had been determined."[151]

There was no interagency consideration of just what military action might have looked like in practice—either the Pentagon's new "phased campaign" concept or a prolonged air campaign in Afghanistan. Defense officials, such as Under Secretary Walter Slocombe and Vice Admiral Fry, told us the military response options were still limited. Bin Ladin continued to be elusive. They felt, just as they had for the past two years, that hitting inexpensive and rudimentary training camps with costly missiles would not do much good and might even help al Qaeda if the strikes failed to kill Bin Ladin.[152]

In late 2000, the CIA and the NSC staff began thinking about the counterterrorism policy agenda they would present to the new administration. The Counterterrorist Center put down its best ideas for the future, assuming it was free of any prior policy or financial constraints. The paper was therefore informally referred to as the "Blue Sky" memo; it was sent to Clarke on December 29. The memo proposed

- A major effort to support the Northern Alliance through intelligence sharing and increased funding so that it could stave off the Taliban army and tie down al Qaeda fighters. This effort was not intended to remove the Taliban from power, a goal that was judged impractical and too expensive for the CIA alone to attain.
- Increased support to the Uzbeks to strengthen their ability to fight terrorism and assist the United States in doing so.
- Assistance to anti-Taliban groups and proxies who might be encouraged to passively resist the Taliban.

The CIA memo noted that there was "no single 'silver bullet' available to deal with the growing problems in Afghanistan." A multifaceted strategy would be needed to produce change.[153]

No action was taken on these ideas in the few remaining weeks of the Clinton administration. Berger did not recall seeing or being briefed on the Blue Sky memo. Nor was the memo discussed during the transition with incoming top Bush administration officials. Tenet and his deputy told us they pressed these ideas as options after the new team took office.[154]

As the Clinton administration drew to a close, Clarke and his staff developed a policy paper of their own, the first such comprehensive effort since the Delenda plan of 1998. The resulting paper, entitled "Strategy for Eliminating the Threat from the Jihadist Networks of al Qida: Status and Prospects," reviewed the threat and the record to date, incorporated the CIA's new ideas from the Blue Sky memo, and posed several near-term policy options.

Clarke and his staff proposed a goal to "roll back" al Qaeda over a period of three to five years. Over time, the policy should try to weaken and eliminate the network's infrastructure in order to reduce it to a "rump group" like other formerly feared but now largely defunct terrorist organizations of the 1980s. "Continued anti-al Qida operations at the current level will prevent some attacks," Clarke's office wrote, "but will not seriously attrit their ability to plan and conduct attacks." The paper backed covert aid to the Northern Alliance, covert aid to Uzbekistan, and renewed Predator flights in March 2001. A sentence called for military action to destroy al Qaeda command-and-control targets and infrastructure and Taliban military and command assets. The paper also expressed concern about the presence of al Qaeda operatives in the United States.[155]

6.4 CHANGE AND CONTINUITY

On November 7, 2000, American voters went to the polls in what turned out to be one of the closest presidential contests in U.S. history—an election campaign during which there was a notable absence of serious discussion of the al Qaeda threat or terrorism. Election night became a 36-day legal fight. Until the Supreme Court's 5–4 ruling on December 12 and Vice President Al Gore's concession, no one knew whether Gore or his Republican opponent, Texas Governor George W. Bush, would become president in 2001.

The dispute over the election and the 36-day delay cut in half the normal transition period. Given that a presidential election in the United States brings wholesale change in personnel, this loss of time hampered the new administration in identifying, recruiting, clearing, and obtaining Senate confirmation of key appointees.

From the Old to the New

The principal figures on Bush's White House staff would be National Security Advisor Condoleezza Rice, who had been a member of the NSC staff in the administration of George H. W. Bush; Rice's deputy, Stephen Hadley, who had been an assistant secretary of defense under the first Bush; and Chief of Staff Andrew Card, who had served that same administration as deputy chief of staff, then secretary of transportation. For secretary of state, Bush chose General Colin Powell, who had been national security advisor for President Ronald Reagan and then chairman of the Joint Chiefs of Staff. For secretary of defense he selected Donald Rumsfeld, a former member of Congress, White House chief of staff, and, under President Gerald Ford, already once secretary of defense. Bush decided fairly soon to keep Tenet as Director of Central Intelligence. Louis Freeh, who had statutory ten-year tenure, would remain director of the FBI until his voluntary retirement in the summer of 2001.

Bush and his principal advisers had all received briefings on terrorism, including Bin Ladin. In early September 2000, Acting Deputy Director of Central Intelligence John McLaughlin led a team to Bush's ranch in Crawford, Texas, and gave him a wide-ranging, four-hour review of sensitive information. Ben Bonk, deputy chief of the CIA's Counterterrorist Center, used one of the four hours to deal with terrorism. To highlight the danger of terrorists obtaining chemical, biological, radiological, or nuclear weapons, Bonk brought along a mock-up suitcase to evoke the way the Aum Shinrikyo doomsday cult had spread deadly sarin nerve agent on the Tokyo subway in 1995. Bonk told Bush that Americans would die from terrorism during the next four years.[156] During the long contest after election day, the CIA set up an office in Crawford to pass intelligence to Bush and some of his key advisers.[157] Tenet, accompanied by his deputy director for operations, James Pavitt, briefed President-elect Bush at Blair House during the transition. President Bush told us he asked Tenet whether the CIA could kill Bin Ladin, and Tenet replied that killing Bin Ladin would have an effect but would not end the threat. President Bush told us Tenet said to him that the CIA had all the authority it needed.[158]

In December, Bush met with Clinton for a two-hour, one-on-one discussion of national security and foreign policy challenges. Clinton recalled saying to Bush, "I think you will find that by far your biggest threat is Bin Ladin and the al Qaeda." Clinton told us that he also said, "One of the great regrets of my presidency is that I didn't get him [Bin Ladin] for you, because I tried to."[159] Bush told the Commission that he felt sure President Clinton had mentioned terrorism, but did not remember much being said about al Qaeda. Bush recalled that Clinton had emphasized other issues such as North Korea and the Israeli-Palestinian peace process.[160]

In early January, Clarke briefed Rice on terrorism. He gave similar presentations—describing al Qaeda as both an adaptable global network of jihadist organizations and a lethal core terrorist organization—to Vice President–elect Cheney, Hadley, and Secretary of State–designate Powell. One line in the briefing slides said that al Qaeda had sleeper cells in more than 40 countries, including the United States.[161] Berger told us that he made a point of dropping in on Clarke's briefing of Rice to emphasize the importance of the issue. Later the same day, Berger met with Rice. He says that he told her the Bush administration would spend more time on terrorism in general and al Qaeda in particular than on anything else. Rice's recollection was that Berger told her she would be surprised at how much more time she was going to spend on terrorism than she expected, but that the bulk of their conversation dealt with the faltering Middle East peace process and North Korea. Clarke said that the new team, having been out of government for eight years, had a steep learning curve to understand al Qaeda and the new transnational terrorist threat.[162]

Organizing a New Administration

During the short transition, Rice and Hadley concentrated on staffing and organizing the NSC.[163] Their policy priorities differed from those of the Clinton administration. Those priorities included China, missile defense, the collapse of the Middle East peace process, and the Persian Gulf.[164] Generally aware that terrorism had changed since the first Bush administration, they paid particular attention to the question of how counterterrorism policy should be coordinated. Rice had asked University of Virginia history professor Philip Zelikow to advise her on the transition.[165] Hadley and Zelikow asked Clarke and his deputy, Roger Cressey, for a special briefing on the terrorist threat and how Clarke's Transnational Threats Directorate and Counterterrorism Security Group functioned.[166]

In the NSC during the first Bush administration, many tough issues were addressed at the level of the Deputies Committee. Issues did not go to the principals unless the deputies had been unable to resolve them. Presidential Decision Directive 62 of the Clinton administration had said specifically that Clarke's Counterterrorism Security Group should report through the Deputies Committee or, at Berger's discretion, directly to the principals. Berger had in practice allowed Clarke's group to function as a parallel deputies committee, reporting directly to those members of the Principals Committee who sat on the special Small Group. There, Clarke himself sat as a de facto principal.

Rice decided to change the special structure that had been built to coordinate counterterrorism policy. It was important to sound policymaking, she felt, that Clarke's interagency committee—like all others—report to the principals through the deputies.[167]

Rice made an initial decision to hold over both Clarke and his entire counterterrorism staff, a decision that she called rare for a new administration. She decided also that Clarke should retain the title of national counterterrorism coordinator, although he would no longer be a de facto member of the Principals Committee on his issues. The decision to keep Clarke, Rice said, was "not uncontroversial," since he was known as someone who "broke china," but she and Hadley wanted an experienced crisis manager. No one else from Berger's staff had Clarke's detailed knowledge of the levers of government. [168]

Clarke was disappointed at what he perceived as a demotion. He also worried that reporting through the Deputies Committee would slow decisionmaking on counterterrorism.[169]

The result, amid all the changes accompanying the transition, was significant continuity in counterterrorism policy. Clarke and his Counterterrorism Security Group would continue to manage coordination. Tenet remained Director of Central Intelligence and kept the same chief subordinates, including Black and his staff at the Counterterrorist Center. Shelton remained chairman of the Joint Chiefs, with the Joint Staff largely the same. At the FBI, Director Freeh and Assistant Director for Counterterrorism Dale Watson remained. Working-level counterterrorism officials at the State Department and the Pentagon stayed on, as is typically the case. The changes were at the cabinet and subcabinet level and in the CSG's reporting arrangements. At the subcabinet level, there were significant delays in the confirmation of key officials, particularly at the Defense Department.

The procedures of the Bush administration were to be at once more formal and less formal than its predecessor's. President Clinton, a voracious reader, received his daily intelligence briefings in writing. He often scrawled questions and comments in the margins, eliciting written responses. The new president, by contrast, reinstated the practice of face-to-face briefings from the DCI. President Bush and Tenet met in the Oval Office at 8:00 A.M., with Vice President Cheney, Rice, and Card usually also present. The President and the DCI both told us that these daily sessions provided a useful opportunity for exchanges on intelligence issues.[170]

The President talked with Rice every day, and she in turn talked by phone at least daily with Powell and Rumsfeld. As a result, the President often felt less need for formal meetings. If, however, he decided that an event or an issue called for action, Rice would typically call on Hadley to have the Deputies Committee develop and review options. The President said that this process often tried his patience but that he understood the necessity for coordination.[171]

Early Decisions

Within the first few days after Bush's inauguration, Clarke approached Rice in an effort to get her—and the new President—to give terrorism very high priority and to act on the agenda that he had pushed during the last few months of the previous administration. After Rice requested that all senior staff identify desirable major policy reviews or initiatives, Clarke submitted an elaborate memorandum on January 25, 2001. He attached to it his 1998 Delenda Plan and the December 2000 strategy paper. "We _urgently_ need ... a Principals level review on the _al Qida_ network," Clarke wrote.[172]

He wanted the Principals Committee to decide whether al Qaeda was "a first order threat" or a more modest worry being overblown by "chicken little" alarmists. Alluding to the transition briefing that he had prepared for Rice, Clarke wrote that al Qaeda "is not some narrow, little terrorist issue that needs to be included in broader regional policy." Two key decisions that had been deferred, he noted, concerned covert aid to keep the Northern Alliance alive when fighting began again in Afghanistan in the spring, and covert aid to the Uzbeks. Clarke also suggested that decisions should be made soon on messages to the Taliban and Pakistan over the al Qaeda sanctuary in Afghanistan, on possible new money for CIA operations, and on "when and how ... to respond to the attack on the USS Cole."[173]

The national security advisor did not respond directly to Clarke's memorandum. No Principals Committee meeting on al Qaeda was held until September 4, 2001 (although the Principals Committee met frequently on other subjects, such as the Middle East peace process, Russia, and the Persian Gulf).[174] But Rice and Hadley began to address the issues Clarke had listed. What to do or say about the _Cole_ had been an obvious question since inauguration day. When the attack occurred, 25 days before the election, candidate Bush had said to CNN, "I hope that we can gather enough intelligence to figure out who did the act and take the necessary action. There must be a consequence."[175] Since the Clinton administration had not responded militarily, what was the Bush administration to do?

On January 25, Tenet briefed the President on the _Cole_ investigation. The written briefing repeated for top officials of the new administration what the CIA had told the Clinton White House in November. This included the "preliminary judgment" that al Qaeda was responsible, with the caveat that no evidence had yet been found that Bin Ladin himself ordered the attack. Tenet told us he had no recollection of a conversation with the President about this briefing.[176]

In his January 25 memo, Clarke had advised Rice that the government should respond to the _Cole_ attack, but "should take advantage of the policy that 'we will respond at a time, place and manner of our own choosing' and not be forced into knee-jerk responses."[177] Before Vice President Cheney visited the CIA in mid-February, Clarke sent him a memo—outside the usual White House document-management system—suggesting that he ask CIA officials "what additional information is needed before CIA can definitively conclude that al-Qida was responsible" for the *Cole*.[178] In March 2001, the CIA's briefing slides for Rice were still describing the CIA's "preliminary judgment" that a "strong circumstantial case" could be made against al Qaeda but noting that the CIA continued to lack "conclusive information on external command and control" of the attack.[179] Clarke and his aides continued to provide Rice and Hadley with evidence reinforcing the case against al Qaeda and urging action.[180]

The President explained to us that he had been concerned lest an ineffectual air strike just serve to give Bin Ladin a propaganda advantage. He said he had not been told about Clinton administration warnings to the Taliban. The President told us that he had concluded that the United States must use ground forces for a job like this.[181]

Rice told us that there was never a formal, recorded decision not to retaliate specifically for the *Cole* attack. Exchanges with the President, between the President and Tenet, and between herself and Powell and Rumsfeld had produced a consensus that "tit-for-tat" responses were likely to be counterproductive. This had been the case, she thought, with the cruise missile strikes of August 1998. The new team at the Pentagon did not push for action. On the contrary, Rumsfeld thought that too much time had passed and his deputy, Paul Wolfowitz, thought that the *Cole* attack was "stale." Hadley said that in the end, the administration's real response to the *Cole* would be a new, more aggressive strategy against al Qaeda.[182]

The administration decided to propose to Congress a substantial increase in counterterrorism funding for national security agencies, including the CIA and the FBI. This included a 27 percent increase in counterterrorism funding for the CIA.[183]

Starting a Review

In early March, the administration postponed action on proposals for increasing aid to the Northern Alliance and the Uzbeks. Rice noted at the time that a more wide-ranging examination of policy toward Afghanistan was needed first. She wanted the review very soon.[184]

Rice and others recalled the President saying, "I'm tired of swatting at flies."[185] The President reportedly also said, "I'm tired of playing defense. I want to play offense. I want to take the fight to the terrorists."[186] President Bush explained to us that he had become impatient. He apparently had heard proposals for rolling back al Qaeda but felt that catching terrorists one by one or even cell by cell was not an approach likely to succeed in the long run. At the same time, he said, he understood that policy had to be developed slowly so that diplomacy and financial and military measures could mesh with one another.[187]

Hadley convened an informal Deputies Committee meeting on March 7, when some of the deputies had not yet been confirmed. For the first time, Clarke's various proposals—for aid to the Northern Alliance and the Uzbeks and for Predator missions—went before the group that, in the Bush NSC, would do most of the policy work. Though they made no decisions on these specific proposals, Hadley apparently concluded that there should be a presidential national security policy directive (NSPD) on terrorism.[188]

Clarke would later express irritation about the deputies' insistence that a strategy for coping with al Qaeda be framed within the context of a regional policy. He doubted that the benefits would compensate for the time lost. The administration had in fact proceeded with Principals Committee meetings on topics including Iraq and Sudan without prior contextual review, and Clarke favored moving ahead similarly with a narrow counterterrorism agenda.[189] But the President's senior advisers saw the al Qaeda problem as part of a puzzle that could not be assembled without filling in the pieces for Afghanistan and Pakistan. Rice deferred a Principals Committee meeting on al Qaeda until the deputies had developed a new policy for their consideration.

The full Deputies Committee discussed al Qaeda on April 30. CIA briefing slides described al Qaeda as the "most dangerous group we face," citing its "leadership, experience, resources, safe haven in Afghanistan, [and] focus on attacking U.S." The slides warned, "There will be more attacks."[190]

At the meeting, the deputies endorsed covert aid to Uzbekistan. Regarding the Northern Alliance, they "agreed to make no major commitment at this time." Washington would first consider options for aiding other anti-Taliban groups.[191] Meanwhile, the administration would "initiate a comprehensive review of U.S. policy on Pakistan" and explore policy options on Afghanistan, "including the option of supporting regime change."[192] Working-level officials were also to consider new steps on terrorist financing and America's perennially troubled public diplomacy efforts in the Muslim world, where NSC staff warned that "we have by and large ceded the court of public opinion" to al Qaeda.

While Clarke remained concerned about the pace of the policy review, he now saw a greater possibility of persuading the deputies to recognize the changed nature of terrorism.[193] The process of fleshing out that strategy was under way.

6.5 THE NEW ADMINISTRATION'S APPROACH

The Bush administration in its first months faced many problems other than terrorism. They included the collapse of the Middle East peace process and, in April, a crisis over a U.S. "spy plane" brought down in Chinese territory. The new administration also focused heavily on Russia, a new nuclear strategy that allowed missile defenses, Europe, Mexico, and the Persian Gulf.

In the spring, reporting on terrorism surged dramatically. In chapter 8, we will explore this reporting and the ways agencies responded. These increasingly alarming reports, briefed to the President and top officials, became part of the context in which the new administration weighed its options for policy on al Qaeda.

Except for a few reports that the CSG considered and apparently judged to be unreliable, none of these pointed specifically to possible al Qaeda action inside the United States—although the CSG continued to be concerned about the domestic threat. The mosaic of threat intelligence came from the Counterterrorist Center, which collected only abroad. Its reports were not supplemented by reports from the FBI. Clarke had expressed concern about an al Qaeda presence in the United States, and he worried about an attack on the White House by "Hizbollah, Hamas, al Qida and other terrorist organizations."[194]

In May, President Bush announced that Vice President Cheney would himself lead an effort looking at preparations for managing a possible attack by weapons of mass destruction and at more general problems of national preparedness. The next few months were mainly spent organizing the effort and bringing an admiral from the Sixth Fleet back to Washington to manage it. The Vice President's task force was just getting under way when the 9/11 attack occurred.[195]

On May 29, at Tenet's request, Rice and Tenet converted their usual weekly meeting into a broader discussion on al Qaeda; participants included Clarke, CTC chief Cofer Black, and "Richard," a group chief with authority over the Bin Ladin unit. Rice asked about "taking the offensive" and whether any approach could be made to influence Bin Ladin or the Taliban. Clarke and Black replied that the CIA's ongoing disruption activities *were* "taking the offensive" and that Bin Ladin could not be deterred. A wide-ranging discussion then ensued about "breaking the back" of Bin Ladin's organization.[196]

Tenet emphasized the ambitious plans for covert action that the CIA had developed in December 2000. In discussing the draft authorities for this program in March, CIA officials had pointed out that the spending level envisioned for these plans was larger than the CIA's entire current budget for counterterrorism covert action. It would be a multiyear program, requiring such levels of spending for about five years.[197]

The CIA official, "Richard," told us that Rice "got it." He said she agreed with his conclusions about what needed to be done, although he complained to us that the policy process did not follow through quickly enough.[198] Clarke and Black were asked to develop a range of options for attacking Bin Ladin's organization, from the least to most ambitious.[199]

Rice and Hadley asked Clarke and his staff to draw up the new presidential directive. On June 7, Hadley circulated the first draft, describing it as "an admittedly ambitious" program for confronting al Qaeda.[200] The draft NSPD's goal was to "eliminate the al Qida network of terrorist groups as a threat to the United States and to friendly governments." It called for a multi-year effort involving diplomacy, covert action, economic measures, law enforcement, public diplomacy, and if necessary military efforts. The State Department was to work with other governments to end all al Qaeda sanctuaries, and also to work with the Treasury Department to disrupt terrorist financing. The CIA was to develop an expanded covert action program including significant additional funding and aid to anti-Taliban groups. The draft also tasked OMB with ensuring that sufficient funds to support this program were found in U.S. budgets from fiscal years 2002 to 2006.[201]

Rice viewed this draft directive as the embodiment of a comprehensive new strategy employing all instruments of national power to eliminate the al Qaeda threat. Clarke, however, regarded the new draft as essentially similar to the proposal he had developed in December 2000 and put forward to the new administration in January 2001.[202] In May or June, Clarke asked to be moved from his counterterrorism portfolio to a new set of responsibilities for cybersecurity. He told us that he was frustrated with his role and with an administration that he considered not "serious about al Qaeda."[203] If Clarke was frustrated, he never expressed it to her, Rice told us.[204]

Diplomacy in Blind Alleys

Afghanistan. The new administration had already begun exploring possible diplomatic options, retracing many of the paths traveled by its predecessors. U.S. envoys again pressed the Taliban to turn Bin Ladin "over to a country where he could face justice" and repeated, yet again, the warning that the Taliban would be held responsible for any al Qaeda attacks on U.S. interests.[205] The Taliban's representatives repeated their old arguments. Deputy Secretary of State Richard Armitage told us that while U.S. diplomats were becoming more active on Afghanistan through the spring and summer of 2001, "it would be wrong for anyone to characterize this as a dramatic shift from the previous administration."[206]

In deputies meetings at the end of June, Tenet was tasked to assess the prospects for Taliban cooperation with the United States on al Qaeda. The NSC staff was tasked to flesh out options for dealing with the Taliban. Revisiting these issues tried the patience of some of the officials who felt they had already been down these roads and who found the NSC's procedures slow. "We weren't going fast enough," Armitage told us. Clarke kept arguing that moves against the Taliban and al Qaeda should not have to wait months for a larger review of U.S. policy in South Asia. "For the government," Hadley said to us, "we moved it along as fast as we could move it along."[207]

As all hope in moving the Taliban faded, debate revived about giving covert assistance to the regime's opponents. Clarke and the CIA's Cofer Black renewed the push to aid the Northern Alliance. Clarke suggested starting with modest aid, just enough to keep the Northern Alliance in the fight and tie down al Qaeda terrorists, without aiming to overthrow the Taliban.[208]

Rice, Hadley, and the NSC staff member for Afghanistan, Zalmay Khalilzad, told us they opposed giving aid to the Northern Alliance alone. They argued that the program needed to have a big part for Pashtun opponents of the Taliban. They also thought the program should be conducted on a larger scale than had been suggested. Clarke concurred with the idea of a larger program, but he warned that delay risked the Northern Alliance's final defeat at the hands of the Taliban.[209]

During the spring, the CIA, at the NSC's request, had developed draft legal authorities—a presidential finding—to undertake a large-scale program of covert assistance to the Taliban's foes. The draft authorities expressly stated that the goal of the assistance was *not* to overthrow the Taliban. But even this program would be very costly. This was the context for earlier conversations, when in March Tenet stressed the need to consider the impact of such a large program on the political situation in the region and in May Tenet talked to Rice about the need for a multiyear financial commitment.[210]

By July, the deputies were moving toward agreement that some last effort should be made to convince the Taliban to shift position and then, if that failed, the administration would move on the significantly enlarged covert action program. As the draft presidential directive was circulated in July, the State Department sent the deputies a lengthy historical review of U.S. efforts to engage the Taliban about Bin Ladin from 1996 on. "These talks have been fruitless," the State Department concluded.[211]

Arguments in the summer brought to the surface the more fundamental issue of whether the U.S. covert action program should seek to overthrow the regime, intervening decisively in the civil war in order to change Afghanistan's government. By the end of a deputies meeting on September 10, officials formally agreed on a three-phase strategy. First an envoy would give the Taliban a last chance. If this failed, continuing diplomatic pressure would be combined with the planned covert action program encouraging anti-Taliban Afghans of all major ethnic groups to stalemate the Taliban in the civil war and attack al Qaeda bases, while the United States developed an international coalition to undermine the regime. In phase three, if the Taliban's policy still did not change, the deputies agreed that the United States would try covert action to topple the Taliban's leadership from within.[212]

The deputies agreed to revise the al Qaeda presidential directive, then being finalized for presidential approval, in order to add this strategy to it. Armitage explained to us that after months of continuing the previous administration's policy, he and Powell were bringing the State Department to a policy of overthrowing the Taliban. From his point of view, once the United States made the commitment to arm the Northern Alliance, even covertly, it was taking action to initiate regime change, and it should give those opponents the strength to achieve complete victory.[213]

Pakistan. The Bush administration immediately encountered the dilemmas that arose from the varied objectives the United States was trying to accomplish in its relationship with Pakistan. In February 2001, President Bush wrote General Musharraf on a number of matters. He emphasized that Bin Ladin and al Qaeda were "a direct threat to the United States and its interests that must be addressed." He urged Musharraf to use his influence with the Taliban on Bin Ladin and al Qaeda.[214] Powell and Armitage reviewed the possibility of acquiring more carrots to dangle in front of Pakistan. Given the generally negative view of Pakistan on Capitol Hill, the idea of lifting sanctions may have seemed far-fetched, but perhaps no more so than the idea of persuading Musharraf to antagonize the Islamists in his own government and nation.[215]

On June 18, Rice met with the visiting Pakistani foreign minister, Abdul Sattar. She "really let him have it" about al Qaeda, she told us.[216] Other evidence corroborates her account. But, as she was upbraiding Sattar, Rice recalled thinking that the Pakistani diplomat seemed to have heard it all before. Sattar urged senior U.S. policymakers to engage the Taliban, arguing that such a course would take time but would produce results. In late June, the deputies agreed to review U.S. objectives. Clarke urged Hadley to split off all other issues in U.S.-Pakistani relations and just focus on demanding that Pakistan move vigorously against terrorism—to push the Pakistanis to do *before* an al Qaeda attack what Washington would demand that they do after. He had made similar requests in the Clinton administration; he had no more success with Rice than he had with Berger.[217]

On August 4, President Bush wrote President Musharraf to request his support in dealing with terrorism and to urge Pakistan to engage actively against al Qaeda. The new administration was again registering its concerns, just as its predecessor had, but it was still searching for new incentives to open up diplomatic possibilities. For its part, Pakistan had done little. Assistant Secretary of State Christina Rocca described the administration's plan to break this logjam as a move from "half engagement" to "enhanced engagement." The administration was not ready to confront Islamabad and threaten to rupture relations. Deputy Secretary Armitage told us that before 9/11, the envisioned new approach to Pakistan had not yet been attempted.[218]

Saudi Arabia. The Bush administration did not develop new diplomatic initiatives on al Qaeda with the Saudi government before 9/11. Vice President Cheney called Crown Prince Abdullah on July 5, 2001, to seek Saudi help in preventing threatened attacks on American facilities in the Kingdom. Secretary of State Powell met with the crown prince twice before 9/11. They discussed topics like Iraq, not al Qaeda. U.S.-Saudi relations in the summer of 2001 were marked by sometimes heated disagreements about ongoing Israeli-Palestinian violence, not about Bin Ladin.[219]

Military Plans
The confirmation of the Pentagon's new leadership was a lengthy process. Deputy Secretary Wolfowitz was confirmed in March 2001 and Under Secre-

tary of Defense for Policy Douglas Feith in July. Though the new officials were briefed about terrorism and some of the earlier planning, including that for Operation Infinite Resolve, they were focused, as Secretary Rumsfeld told us, on creating a twenty-first-century military.[220]

At the Joint Chiefs of Staff, General Shelton did not recall much interest by the new administration in military options against al Qaeda in Afghanistan. He could not recall any specific guidance on the topic from the secretary. Brian Sheridan—the outgoing assistant secretary of defense for special operations and low-intensity conflict (SOLIC), the key counterterrorism policy office in the Pentagon—never briefed Rumsfeld. He departed on January 20; he had not been replaced by 9/11.[221]

Rumsfeld noted to us his own interest in terrorism, which came up often in his regular meetings with Tenet. He thought that the Defense Department, before 9/11, was not organized adequately or prepared to deal with new threats like terrorism. But his time was consumed with getting new officials in place and working on the foundation documents of a new defense policy, the quadrennial defense review, the defense planning guidance, and the existing contingency plans. He did not recall any particular counterterrorism issue that engaged his attention before 9/11, other than the development of the Predator unmanned aircraft system.[222]

The commander of Central Command, General Franks, told us that he did not regard the existing plans as serious. To him a real military plan to address al Qaeda would need to go all the way, following through the details of a full campaign (including the political-military issues of where operations would be based) and securing the rights to fly over neighboring countries.[223]

The draft presidential directive circulated in June 2001 began its discussion of the military by reiterating the Defense Department's lead role in protecting its forces abroad. The draft included a section directing Secretary Rumsfeld to "develop contingency plans" to attack both al Qaeda and Taliban targets in Afghanistan. The new section did not specifically order planning for the use of ground troops, or clarify how this guidance differed from the existing Infinite Resolve plans.[224]

Hadley told us that by circulating this section, a draft Annex B to the directive, the White House was putting the Pentagon on notice that it would need to produce new military plans to address this problem.[225] "The military didn't particularly want this mission," Rice told us.[226]

With this directive still awaiting President Bush's signature, Secretary Rumsfeld did not order his subordinates to begin preparing any new military plans against either al Qaeda or the Taliban before 9/11.

President Bush told us that before 9/11, he had not seen good options for special military operations against Bin Ladin. Suitable bases in neighboring countries were not available and, even if the U.S. forces were sent in, it was not clear where they would go to find Bin Ladin.[227]

President Bush told us that before 9/11 there was an appetite in the government for killing Bin Ladin, not for war. Looking back in 2004, he equated the presidential directive with a readiness to invade Afghanistan. The problem, he said, would have been how to do that if there had not been another attack on America. To many people, he said, it would have seemed like an ultimate act of unilateralism. But he said that he was prepared to take that on.[228]

Domestic Change and Continuity

During the transition, Bush had chosen John Ashcroft, a former senator from Missouri, as his attorney general. On his arrival at the Justice Department, Ashcroft told us, he faced a number of problems spotlighting the need for reform at the FBI.[229]

In February, Clarke briefed Attorney General Ashcroft on his directorate's issues. He reported that at the time, the attorney general acknowledged a "steep learning curve," and asked about the progress of the *Cole* investigation.[230] Neither Ashcroft nor his predecessors received the President's Daily Brief. His office did receive the daily intelligence report for senior officials that, during the spring and summer of 2001, was carrying much of the same threat information.

The FBI was struggling to build up its institutional capabilities to do more against terrorism, relying on a strategy called MAXCAP 05 that had been unveiled in the summer of 2000. The FBI's assistant director for counterterrorism, Dale Watson, told us that he felt the new Justice Department leadership was not supportive of the strategy. Watson had the sense that the Justice Department wanted the FBI to get back to the investigative basics: guns, drugs, and civil rights. The new administration did seek an 8 percent increase in overall FBI funding in its initial budget proposal for fiscal year 2002, including the largest proposed percentage increase in the FBI's counterterrorism program since fiscal year 1997. The additional funds included the FBI's support of the 2002 Winter Olympics in Salt Lake City, Utah (a onetime increase), enhanced security at FBI facilities, and improvements to the FBI's WMD incident response capability.[231]

In May, the Justice Department began shaping plans for building a budget for fiscal year 2003, the process that would usually culminate in an administration proposal at the beginning of 2002. On May 9, the attorney general testified at a congressional hearing concerning federal efforts to combat terrorism. He said that "one of the nation's most fundamental responsibilities is to protect its citizens . . . from terrorist attacks." The budget guidance issued the next day, however, highlighted gun crimes, narcotics trafficking, and civil rights as priorities. Watson told us that he almost fell out of his chair when he saw this memo, because it did not mention counterterrorism. Longtime FBI Director Louis Freeh left in June 2001, after announcing the indictment in the Khobar Towers case that he had worked so long to obtain. Thomas Pickard was the acting director during the summer. Freeh's successor, Robert Mueller, took office just before 9/11.[232]

The Justice Department prepared a draft fiscal year 2003 budget that maintained but did not increase the funding level for counterterrorism in its pending fiscal year 2002 proposal. Pickard appealed for more counterterrorism enhancements, an appeal the attorney general denied on September 10.[233]

Ashcroft had also inherited an ongoing debate on whether and how to modify the 1995 procedures governing intelligence sharing between the FBI and the Justice Department's Criminal Division. But in August 2001, Ashcroft's deputy, Larry Thompson, issued a memorandum reaffirming the 1995 procedures with the clarification that evidence of "any federal felony" was to be immediately reported by the FBI to the Criminal Division. The 1995 procedures remained in effect until after 9/11.[234]

Covert Action and the Predator

In March 2001, Rice asked the CIA to prepare a new series of authorities for covert action in Afghanistan. Rice's recollection was that the idea had come from Clarke and the NSC senior director for intelligence, Mary McCarthy, and had been linked to the proposal for aid to the Northern Alliance and the Uzbeks. Rice described the draft document as providing for "consolidation plus," superseding the various Clinton administration documents. In fact, the CIA drafted two documents. One was a finding that did concern aid to opponents of the Taliban regime; the other was a draft Memorandum of Notification, which included more open-ended language authorizing possible lethal action in a variety of situations. Tenet delivered both to Hadley on March 28. The CIA's notes for Tenet advised him that "in response to the NSC request for drafts that will help the policymakers review their options, each of the documents has been crafted to provide the Agency with the broadest possible discretion permissible under the law." At the meeting, Tenet argued for deciding on a policy before deciding on the legal authorities to implement it. Hadley accepted this argument, and the draft MON was put on hold.[235]

As the policy review moved forward, the planned covert action program for Afghanistan was included in the draft presidential directive, as part of an "Annex A" on intelligence activities to "eliminate the al Qaeda threat."[236] The main debate during the summer of 2001 concentrated on the one new mechanism for a lethal attack on Bin Ladin—an armed version of the Predator drone.

In the first months of the new administration, questions concerning the Predator became more and more a central focus of dispute. Clarke favored resuming Predator flights over Afghanistan as soon as weather permitted, hoping that they still might provide the elusive "actionable intelligence" to target Bin Ladin with cruise missiles. Learning that the Air Force was thinking of equipping Predators with warheads, Clarke became even more enthusiastic about redeployment.[237]

The CTC chief, Cofer Black, argued against deploying the Predator for reconnaissance purposes. He recalled that the Taliban had spotted a Predator in the fall of 2000 and scrambled their MiG fighters. Black wanted to wait until the armed version was ready. "I do not believe the possible recon value outweighs the risk of possible program termination when the stakes are raised by the Taliban parading a charred Predator in front of CNN," he wrote. Military officers in the Joint Staff shared this concern.[238] There is some dispute as to whether or not the Deputies Committee endorsed resuming reconnaissance flights at its April 30, 2001, meeting. In any event, Rice and Hadley ultimately went along with the CIA and the Pentagon, holding off on reconnaissance flights until the armed Predator was ready.[239]

The CIA's senior management saw problems with the armed Predator as well, problems that Clarke and even Black and Allen were inclined to minimize. One (which also applied to reconnaissance flights) was money. A Predator cost about $3 million. If the CIA flew Predators for its own reconnaissance or covert action purposes, it might be able to borrow them from the Air Force, but it was not clear that the Air Force would bear the cost if a vehicle went down. Deputy Secretary of Defense Wolfowitz took the position that the CIA should have to pay for it; the CIA disagreed.[240]

Second, Tenet in particular questioned whether he, as Director of Central Intelligence, should operate an armed Predator. "This was new ground," he told us. Tenet ticked off key questions: What is the chain of command? Who takes the shot? Are America's leaders comfortable with the CIA doing this, going outside of normal military command and control? Charlie Allen told us that when these questions were discussed at the CIA, he and the Agency's executive director, A. B. "Buzzy" Krongard, had said that either one of them would be happy to pull the trigger, but Tenet was appalled, telling them that they had no authority to do it, nor did he.[241]

Third, the Hellfire warhead carried by the Predator needed work. It had been built to hit tanks, not people. It needed to be designed to explode in a different way, and even then had to be targeted with extreme precision. In the configuration planned by the Air Force through mid-2001, the Predator's missile would not be able to hit a moving vehicle.[242]

White House officials had seen the Predator video of the "man in white." On July 11, Hadley tried to hurry along preparation of the armed system. He directed McLaughlin, Wolfowitz, and Joint Chiefs Vice Chairman Richard Myers to deploy Predators capable of being armed no later than September 1. He also directed that they have cost-sharing arrangements in place by August 1. Rice told us that this attempt by Hadley to dictate a solution had failed and that she eventually had to intervene herself.[243]

On August 1, the Deputies Committee met again to discuss the armed

Predator. They concluded that it was legal for the CIA to kill Bin Ladin or one of his deputies with the Predator. Such strikes would be acts of self-defense that would not violate the ban on assassinations in Executive Order 12333. The big issues—who would pay for what, who would authorize strikes, and who would pull the trigger—were left for the principals to settle. The Defense Department representatives did not take positions on these issues.[244]

The CIA's McLaughlin had also been reticent. When Hadley circulated a memorandum attempting to prod the deputies to reach agreement, McLaughlin sent it back with a handwritten comment on the cost-sharing: "we question whether it is advisable to make such an investment before the decision is taken on flying an armed Predator." For Clarke, this came close to being a final straw. He angrily asked Rice to call Tenet. "Either al Qida is a threat worth acting against or it is not," Clarke wrote. "CIA leadership has to decide which it is and cease these bi-polar mood swings."[245]

These debates, though, had little impact in advancing or delaying efforts to make the Predator ready for combat. Those were in the hands of military officers and engineers. General John Jumper had commanded U.S. air forces in Europe and seen Predators used for reconnaissance in the Balkans. He started the program to develop an armed version and, after returning in 2000 to head the Air Combat Command, took direct charge of it.

There were numerous technical problems, especially with the Hellfire missiles. The Air Force tests conducted during the spring were inadequate, so missile testing needed to continue and modifications needed to be made during the summer. Even then, Jumper told us, problems with the equipment persisted. Nevertheless, the Air Force was moving at an extraordinary pace. "In the modern era, since the 1980s," Jumper said to us, "I would be shocked if you found anything that went faster than this."[246]

September 2001

The Principals Committee had its first meeting on al Qaeda on September 4. On the day of the meeting, Clarke sent Rice an impassioned personal note. He criticized U.S. counterterrorism efforts past and present. The "real question" before the principals, he wrote, was "are we serious about dealing with the al Qida threat? . . . Is al Qida a big deal? . . . *Decision makers should imagine themselves on a future day when the CSG has not succeeded in stopping al Qida attacks and hundreds of Americans lay dead in several countries, including the US*," Clarke wrote. "What would those decision makers wish that they had done earlier? That future day could happen at any time."[247]

Clarke then turned to the *Cole*. "*The fact that the USS Cole was attacked during the last Administration does not absolve us of responding for the attack*," he wrote. "Many in al Qida and the Taliban may have drawn the wrong lesson from the Cole: that they can kill Americans without there being a US response, without there being a price. . . . One might have thought that with a $250m hole in a destroyer and 17 dead sailors, the Pentagon might have wanted to respond. Instead, they have often talked about the fact that there is 'nothing worth hitting in Afghanistan' and said 'the cruise missiles cost more than the jungle gyms and mud huts' at terrorist camps." Clarke could not understand "*why we continue to allow the existence of large scale al Qida bases where we know people are being trained to kill Americans.*"[248]

Turning to the CIA, Clarke warned that its bureaucracy, which was "masterful at passive aggressive behavior," would resist funding the new national security presidential directive, leaving it a "hollow shell of words without deeds." The CIA would insist its other priorities were more important. Invoking President Bush's own language, Clarke wrote, "*You are left with a modest effort to swat flies*, to try to prevent specific al Qida attacks by using [intelligence] to detect them and friendly governments' police and intelligence officers to stop them. *You are left waiting for the big attack*, with lots of casualties, after which some major US retaliation will be in order[.]"[249]

Rice told us she took Clarke's memo as a warning not to get dragged down by bureaucratic inertia.[250] While his arguments have force, we also take Clarke's jeremiad as something more. After nine years on the NSC staff and more than three years as the president's national coordinator, he had often failed to persuade these agencies to adopt his views, or to persuade his superiors to set an agenda of the sort he wanted or that the whole government could support.

Meanwhile, another counterterrorism veteran, Cofer Black, was preparing his boss for the principals meeting. He advised Tenet that the draft presidential directive envisioned an ambitious covert action program, but that the authorities for it had not yet been approved and the funding still had not been found. If the CIA was reluctant to use the Predator, Black did not mention it. He wanted "a timely decision from the Principals," adding that the window for missions within 2001 was a short one. The principals would have to decide whether Rice, Tenet, Rumsfeld, or someone else would give the order to fire.[251]

At the September 4 meeting, the principals approved the draft presidential directive with little discussion.[252] Rice told us that she had, at some point, told President Bush that she and his other advisers thought it would take three years or so for their al Qaeda strategy to work.[253] They then discussed the armed Predator.

Hadley portrayed the Predator as a useful tool, although perhaps not for immediate use. Rice, who had been advised by her staff that the armed Predator was not ready for deployment, commented about the potential for using the armed Predator in the spring of 2002.[254]

The State Department supported the armed Predator, although Secretary Powell was not convinced that Bin Ladin was as easy to target as had been suggested. Treasury Secretary Paul O'Neill was skittish, cautioning about the implications of trying to kill an individual.[255]

The Defense Department favored strong action. Deputy Secretary Wolfowitz questioned the United States' ability to deliver Bin Ladin and bring him to justice. He favored going after Bin Ladin as part of a larger air strike, similar to what had been done in the 1986 U.S. strike against Libya. General Myers emphasized the Predator's value for surveillance, perhaps enabling broader air strikes that would go beyond Bin Ladin to attack al Qaeda's training infrastructure.[256]

The principals also discussed which agency—CIA or Defense—should have the authority to fire a missile from the armed Predator.[257]

At the end, Rice summarized the meeting's conclusions. The armed Predator capability was needed but not ready. The Predator would be available for the military to consider along with its other options. The CIA should consider flying reconnaissance-only missions. The principals—including the previously reluctant Tenet—thought that such reconnaissance flights were a good idea, combined with other efforts to get actionable intelligence. Tenet deferred an answer on the additional reconnaissance flights, conferred with his staff after the meeting, and then directed the CIA to press ahead with them.[258]

A few days later, a final version of the draft presidential directive was circulated, incorporating two minor changes made by the principals.[259]

On September 9, dramatic news arrived from Afghanistan. The leader of the Northern Alliance, Ahmed Shah Massoud, had granted an interview in his bungalow near the Tajikistan border with two men whom the Northern Alliance leader had been told were Arab journalists. The supposed reporter and cameraman—actually al Qaeda assassins—then set off a bomb, riddling Massoud's chest with shrapnel. He died minutes later.

On September 10, Hadley gathered the deputies to finalize their three-phase, multiyear plan to pressure and perhaps ultimately topple the Taliban leadership.[260]

That same day, Hadley instructed DCI Tenet to have the CIA prepare new draft legal authorities for the "broad covert action program" envisioned by the draft presidential directive. Hadley also directed Tenet to prepare a separate section "authorizing a broad range of other covert activities, including authority to capture or to use lethal force" against al Qaeda command-and-control elements. This section would supersede the Clinton-era documents. Hadley wanted the authorities to be flexible and broad enough "to cover any additional UBL-related covert actions contemplated."[261]

Funding still needed to be located. The military component remained unclear. Pakistan remained uncooperative. The domestic policy institutions were largely uninvolved. But the pieces were coming together for an integrated policy dealing with al Qaeda, the Taliban, and Pakistan.

7

THE ATTACK LOOMS

7.1 FIRST ARRIVALS IN CALIFORNIA

In chapter 5 we described the Southeast Asia travels of Nawaf al Hazmi, Khalid al Mihdhar, and others in January 2000 on the first part of the "planes operation." In that chapter we also described how Mihdhar was spotted in Kuala Lumpur early in January 2000, along with associates who were not identified, and then was lost to sight when the group passed through Bangkok. On January 15, Hazmi and Mihdhar arrived in Los Angeles. They spent about two weeks there before moving on to San Diego.[1]

Two Weeks in Los Angeles
Why Hazmi and Mihdhar came to California, we do not know for certain. Khalid Sheikh Mohammed (KSM), the organizer of the planes operation, explains that California was a convenient point of entry from Asia and had the added benefit of being far away from the intended target area.[2]

Hazmi and Mihdhar were ill-prepared for a mission in the United States. Their only qualifications for this plot were their devotion to Usama Bin Ladin, their veteran service, and their ability to get valid U.S. visas. Neither had spent any substantial time in the West, and neither spoke much, if any, English.[3]

It would therefore be plausible that they or KSM would have tried to identify, in advance, a friendly contact for them in the United States. In detention, KSM denies that al Qaeda had any agents in Southern California. We do not credit this denial.[4] We believe it is unlikely that Hazmi and Mihdhar—neither of whom, in contrast to the Hamburg group, had any prior exposure to life in the West—would have come to the United States without arranging to receive assistance from one or more individuals informed in advance of their arrival.[5]

KSM says that though he told others involved in the conspiracy to stay away from mosques and to avoid establishing personal contacts, he made an exception in this case and instructed Hazmi and Mihdhar to pose as newly arrived

Saudi students and seek assistance at local mosques. He counted on their breaking off any such relationships once they moved to the East Coast.[6] Our inability to ascertain the activities of Hazmi and Mihdhar during their first two weeks
in the United States may reflect al Qaeda tradecraft designed to protect the
identity of anyone who may have assisted them during that period.

Hazmi and Mihdhar were directed to enroll in English-language classes upon
arriving in Southern California, so that they could begin pilot training as soon
as possible. KSM claims to have steered the two to San Diego on the basis of his
own research, which supposedly included thumbing through a San Diego phone
book acquired at a Karachi flea market. Contradicting himself, he also says that,
as instructed, they attempted to enroll in three language schools in Los Angeles.[7]

After the pair cleared Immigration and Customs at Los Angeles International
Airport, we do not know where they went.[8] They appear to have obtained assis-
tance from the Muslim community, specifically the community surrounding the
King Fahd mosque in Culver City, one of the most prominent mosques in
Southern California.

It is fairly certain that Hazmi and Mihdhar spent time at the King Fahd
mosque and made some acquaintances there. One witness interviewed by the
FBI after the September 11 attacks has said he first met the hijackers at the
mosque in early 2000. Furthermore, one of the people who would befriend
them—a man named Mohdar Abdullah—recalled a trip with Hazmi and
Mihdhar to Los Angeles in June when, on their arrival, the three went to the
King Fahd mosque. There Hazmi and Mihdhar greeted various individuals
whom they appeared to have met previously, including a man named "Khallam." In Abdullah's telling, when Khallam visited the al Qaeda operatives at
their motel that evening, Abdullah was asked to leave the room so that Hazmi,
Mihdhar, and Khallam could meet in private. The identity of Khallam and his
purpose in meeting with Hazmi and Mihdhar remain unknown.[9]

To understand what Hazmi and Mihdhar did in their first weeks in the
United States, evidently staying in Los Angeles, we have investigated whether
anyone associated with the King Fahd mosque assisted them. This subject has
received substantial attention in the media. Some have speculated that Fahad
al Thumairy—an imam at the mosque and an accredited diplomat at the Saudi
Arabian consulate from 1996 until 2003—may have played a role in helping
the hijackers establish themselves on their arrival in Los Angeles. This speculation is based, at least in part, on Thumairy's reported leadership of an extremist faction at the mosque.[10]

A well-known figure at the King Fahd mosque and within the Los Angeles Muslim community, Thumairy was reputed to be an Islamic fundamentalist and a strict adherent to orthodox Wahhabi doctrine. Some Muslims
concerned about his preaching have said he "injected non-Islamic themes into
his guidance/prayers at the [King Fahd] Mosque" and had followers "supportive of the events of September 11, 2001."[11] Thumairy appears to have associ-

ated with a particularly radical faction within the community of local worshippers, and had a network of contacts in other cities in the United States. After 9/11, Thumairy's conduct was a subject of internal debate among some Saudi officials. He apparently lost his position at the King Fahd mosque, possibly because of his immoderate reputation. On May 6, 2003, Thumairy attempted to reenter the United States from Saudi Arabia but was refused entry, based on a determination by the State Department that he might be connected with terrorist activity.[12]

When interviewed by both the FBI and the Commission staff, Thumairy has denied preaching anti-Western sermons, much less promoting violent jihad. More to the point, he claimed not to recognize either Hazmi or Mihdhar. Both denials are somewhat suspect. (He likewise denied knowing Omar al Bayoumi—a man from San Diego we will discuss shortly—even though witnesses and telephone records establish that the two men had contact with each other. Similarly, Thumairy's claim not to know Mohdar Abdullah is belied by Abdullah's contrary assertion.) On the other hand, Thumairy undoubtedly met with and provided religious counseling to countless individuals during his tenure at the King Fahd mosque, so he might not remember two transients like Hazmi and Mihdhar several years later.[13]

The circumstantial evidence makes Thumairy a logical person to consider as a possible contact for Hazmi and Mihdhar. Yet, after exploring the available leads, we have not found evidence that Thumairy provided assistance to the two operatives.[14]

We do not pick up their trail until February 1, 2000, when they encountered Omar al Bayoumi and Caysan Bin Don at a halal food restaurant on Venice Boulevard in Culver City, a few blocks away from the King Fahd mosque. Bayoumi and Bin Don have both told us that they had driven up from San Diego earlier that day so that Bayoumi could address a visa issue and collect some papers from the Saudi consulate. Bayoumi heard Hazmi and Mihdhar speaking in what he recognized to be Gulf Arabic and struck up a conversation. Since Bin Don knew only a little Arabic, he had to rely heavily on Bayoumi to translate for him.[15]

Mihdhar and Hazmi said they were students from Saudi Arabia who had just arrived in the United States to study English. They said they were living in an apartment near the restaurant but did not specify the address. They did not like Los Angeles and were having a hard time, especially because they did not know anyone. Bayoumi told them how pleasant San Diego was and offered to help them settle there. The two pairs then left the restaurant and went their separate ways.[16]

Bayoumi and Bin Don have been interviewed many times about the February 1, 2000, lunch. For the most part, their respective accounts corroborate each other. However, Bayoumi has said that he and Bin Don attempted to visit the King Fahd mosque after lunch but could not find it. Bin Don, on the other hand, recalls visiting the mosque twice that day for prayers, both before and after the meal. Bin Don's recollection is spotty and inconsistent. Bayoumi's version can be challenged as well, since the mosque is close to the restaurant and Bayoumi had visited it, and the surrounding area, on multiple occasions, including twice within six weeks of February 1. We do not know whether the lunch encounter occurred by chance or design. We know about it because Bayoumi told law enforcement that it happened.[17]

Bayoumi, then 42 years old, was in the United States as a business student, supported by a private contractor for the Saudi Civil Aviation Authority, where Bayoumi had worked for over 20 years.[18] The object of considerable media speculation following 9/11, he lives now in Saudi Arabia, well aware of his notoriety. Both we and the FBI have interviewed him and investigated evidence about him.

Bayoumi is a devout Muslim, obliging and gregarious. He spent much of his spare time involved in religious study and helping run a mosque in El Cajon, about 15 miles from San Diego. It is certainly possible that he has dissembled about some aspects of his story, perhaps to counter suspicion. On the other hand, we have seen no credible evidence that he believed in violent extremism or knowingly aided extremist groups.[19] Our investigators who have dealt directly with him and studied his background find him to be an unlikely candidate for clandestine involvement with Islamist extremists.

The Move to San Diego

By February 4, Hazmi and Mihdhar had come to San Diego from Los Angeles, possibly driven by Mohdar Abdullah. Abdullah, a Yemeni university student in his early 20s, is fluent in both Arabic and English, and was perfectly suited to assist the hijackers in pursuing their mission.[20]

After 9/11, Abdullah was interviewed many times by the FBI. He admitted knowing of Hazmi and Mihdhar's extremist leanings and Mihdhar's involvement with the Islamic Army of Aden (a group with ties to al Qaeda) back in Yemen. Abdullah clearly was sympathetic to those extremist views. During a post-9/11 search of his possessions, the FBI found a notebook (belonging to someone else) with references to planes falling from the sky, mass killing, and hijacking. Further, when detained as a material witness following the 9/11 attacks, Abdullah expressed hatred for the U.S. government and "stated that the U.S. brought 'this' on themselves."[21]

When interviewed by the FBI after 9/11, Abdullah denied having advance knowledge of attacks. In May 2004, however, we learned of reports about Abdullah bragging to fellow inmates at a California prison in September–October 2003 that he had known Hazmi and Mihdhar were planning a terrorist attack. The stories attributed to Abdullah are not entirely consistent with each other. Specifically, according to one inmate, Abdullah claimed an unnamed individual had notified him that Hazmi and Mihdhar would be arriving in Los Angeles with plans to carry out an attack. Abdullah allegedly told the same inmate that he had driven the two al Qaeda operatives from Los Angeles to San Diego, but did not say when this occurred. We have been unable to corroborate this account.[22]

Another inmate has recalled Abdullah claiming he first heard about the hijackers' terrorist plans after they arrived in San Diego, when they told him they planned to fly an airplane into a building and invited him to join them on the plane. According to this inmate, Abdullah also claimed to have found out about the 9/11 attacks three weeks in advance, a claim that appears to dovetail with evidence that Abdullah may have received a phone call from Hazmi around that time, that he stopped making calls from his telephone after August 25, 2001, and that, according to his friends, he started acting strangely.[23]

Although boasts among prison inmates often tend to be unreliable, this evidence is obviously important. To date, neither we nor the FBI have been able to verify Abdullah's alleged jailhouse statements, despite investigative efforts.

We thus do not know when or how Hazmi and Mihdhar first came to San Diego. We do know that on February 4, they went to the Islamic Center of San Diego to find Omar al Bayoumi and take him up on his offer of help. Bayoumi obliged by not only locating an apartment but also helping them fill out the lease application, co-signing the lease and, when the real estate agent refused to take cash for a deposit, helping them open a bank account (which they did with a $9,900 deposit); he then provided a certified check from his own account for which the al Qaeda operatives reimbursed him on the spot for the deposit. Neither then nor later did Bayoumi give money to either Hazmi or Mihdhar, who had received money from KSM.[24]

Hazmi and Mihdhar moved in with no furniture and practically no possessions. Soon after the move, Bayoumi used their apartment for a party attended by some 20 male members of the Muslim community. At Bayoumi's request, Bin Don videotaped the gathering with Bayoumi's video camera. Hazmi and Mihdhar did not mingle with the other guests and reportedly spent most of the party by themselves off camera, in a back room.[25]

Hazmi and Mihdhar immediately started looking for a different place to stay. Based on their comment to Bayoumi about the first apartment being expensive, one might infer that they wanted to save money. They may also have been reconsidering the wisdom of living so close to the video camera–wielding Bayoumi, who Hazmi seemed to think was some sort of Saudi spy. Just over a week after moving in, Hazmi and Mihdhar filed a 30-day notice of intention to vacate. Bayoumi apparently loaned them his cell phone to help them check out possibilities for new accommodations.[26]

Their initial effort to move turned out poorly. An acquaintance arranged with his landlord to have Mihdhar take over his apartment. Mihdhar put down a $650 deposit and signed a lease for the apartment effective March 1. Several weeks later, Mihdhar sought a refund of his deposit, claiming he no longer intended to move in because the apartment was too messy. When the landlord refused to refund the deposit, Mihdhar became belligerent. The landlord remembers him "ranting and raving" as if he were "psychotic."[27]

Hazmi and Mihdhar finally found a room to rent in the home of an individual they had met at a mosque in San Diego. According to the homeowner, the future hijackers moved in on May 10, 2000. Mihdhar moved out after only about a month. On June 9, he left San Diego to return to Yemen. Hazmi, on the other hand, stayed at this house for the rest of his time in California, until mid-December; he would then leave for Arizona with a newly arrived 9/11 hijacker-pilot, Hani Hanjour.[28]

While in San Diego, Hazmi and Mihdhar played the part of recently arrived foreign students. They continued to reach out to members of the Muslim community for help. At least initially, they found well-meaning new acquaintances at the Islamic Center of San Diego, which was only a stone's throw from the apartment where they first lived. For example, when they purchased a used car (with cash), they bought it from a man who lived across the street from the Islamic Center and who let them use his address in registering the vehicle, an accommodation "to help a fellow Muslim brother." Similarly, in April, when their cash supply may have been dwindling, Hazmi persuaded the administrator of the Islamic Center to let him use the administrator's bank account to receive a $5,000 wire transfer from someone in Dubai, in the United Arab Emirates (this was KSM's nephew, Ali Abdul Aziz Ali).[29]

Hazmi and Mihdhar visited other mosques as well, mixing comfortably as devout worshippers. During the operatives' critical first weeks in San Diego, Mohdar Abdullah helped them. Translating between English and Arabic, he assisted them in obtaining California driver's licenses and with applying to language and flight schools. Abdullah also introduced them to his circle of friends; he shared an apartment with some of those friends near the Rabat mosque in La Mesa, a few miles from the hijackers' residence.[30]

Abdullah has emerged as a key associate of Hazmi and Mihdhar in San Diego. Detained after 9/11 (first as a material witness, then on immigration charges), he was deported to Yemen on May 21, 2004, after the U.S. Attorney for the Southern District of California declined to prosecute him on charges arising out of his alleged jailhouse admissions concerning the 9/11 operatives. The Department of Justice declined to delay his removal pending further investigation of this new information.[31]

Other friends of Abdullah also translated for Hazmi and Mihdhar and helped them adjust to life in San Diego. Some held extremist beliefs or were well acquainted with known extremists. For example, immediately after 9/11, Osama Awadallah, a Yemeni whose telephone number was found in Hazmi's Toyota at Washington Dulles International Airport, was found to possess photos, videos, and articles relating to Bin Ladin. Awadallah also had lived in a house where copies of Bin Ladin's fatwas and other similar materials were distributed to the residents. Omar Bakarbashat, a Saudi, also met Hazmi and Mihdhar at the Rabat mosque. He admitted helping Hazmi to learn English and taking over the operatives' first apartment in San Diego after they moved out. Bakarbashat apparently had downloaded stridently anti-American Web pages to his computer's hard drive.[32]

Another potentially significant San Diego contact for Hazmi and Mihdhar was Anwar Aulaqi, an imam at the Rabat mosque. Born in New Mexico and thus a U.S. citizen, Aulaqi grew up in Yemen and studied in the United States on a Yemeni government scholarship. We do not know how or when Hazmi and Mihdhar first met Aulaqi. The operatives may even have met or at least talked to him the same day they first moved to San Diego. Hazmi and Mihdhar reportedly respected Aulaqi as a religious figure and developed a close relationship with him.[33]

When interviewed after 9/11, Aulaqi said he did not recognize Hazmi's name but did identify his picture. Although Aulaqi admitted meeting with Hazmi several times, he claimed not to remember any specifics of what they discussed. He described Hazmi as a soft-spoken Saudi student who used to appear at the mosque with a companion but who did not have a large circle of friends.[34]

Aulaqi left San Diego in mid-2000, and by early 2001 had relocated to Virginia. As we will discuss later, Hazmi eventually showed up at Aulaqi's mosque in Virginia, an appearance that may not have been coincidental. We have been unable to learn enough about Aulaqi's relationship with Hazmi and Mihdhar to reach a conclusion.[35]

In sum, although the evidence is thin as to specific motivations, our overall impression is that soon after arriving in California, Hazmi and Mihdhar sought out and found a group of young and ideologically like-minded Muslims with roots in Yemen and Saudi Arabia, individuals mainly associated with Mohdar Abdullah and the Rabat mosque. The al Qaeda operatives lived openly in San Diego under their true names, listing Hazmi in the telephone directory. They managed to avoid attracting much attention.

Flight Training Fails; Mihdhar Bails Out

Hazmi and Mihdhar came to the United States to learn English, take flying lessons, and become pilots as quickly as possible. They turned out, however, to have no aptitude for English. Even with help and tutoring from Mohdar Abdullah and other bilingual friends, Hazmi and Mihdhar's efforts to learn proved futile. This lack of language skills in turn became an insurmountable barrier to learning how to fly.[36]

A pilot they consulted at one school, the Sorbi Flying Club in San Diego, spoke Arabic. He explained to them that their flight instruction would begin with small planes. Hazmi and Mihdhar emphasized their interest in learning to fly jets, Boeing aircraft in particular, and asked where they might enroll to train on jets right away. Convinced that the two were either joking or dreaming, the pilot responded that no such school existed. Other instructors who worked with Hazmi and Mihdhar remember them as poor students who focused on learning to control the aircraft in flight but took no interest in takeoffs or landings. By the end of May 2000, Hazmi and Mihdhar had given up on learning how to fly.[37]

Mihdhar's mind seems to have been with his family back in Yemen, as evidenced by calls he made from the apartment telephone. When news of the birth of his first child arrived, he could stand life in California no longer. In late May and early June of 2000, he closed his bank account, transferred the car registration to Hazmi, and arranged his return to Yemen. According to KSM, Mihdhar was bored in San Diego and foresaw no problem in coming back to the United States since he had not overstayed his visa. Hazmi and Mohdar Abdullah accompanied him to Los Angeles on June 9. After visiting the King Fahd mosque one last time with his friends, Mihdhar left the country the following day.[38]

KSM kept in fairly close touch with his operatives, using a variety of methods. When Bin Ladin called KSM back from Pakistan to Afghanistan in the spring of 2000, KSM asked Khallad (whom we introduced in chapter 5) to maintain email contact with Hazmi in the United States. Mihdhar's decision to strand Hazmi in San Diego enraged KSM, who had not authorized the departure and feared it would compromise the plan. KSM attempted to drop Mihdhar from the planes operation and would have done so, he says, had he not been overruled by Bin Ladin.[39]

Following Mihdhar's departure, Hazmi grew lonely and worried that he would have trouble managing by himself. He prayed with his housemate each morning at 5:00 A.M. and attended services at the Islamic Center. He borrowed his housemate's computer for Internet access, following news coverage of fighting in Chechnya and Bosnia. With his housemate's help, Hazmi also used the Internet to search for a wife (after obtaining KSM's approval to marry). This search did not succeed. Although he developed a close relationship with his housemate, Hazmi preferred not to use the house telephone, continuing the practice he and Mihdhar had adopted of going outside to make phone calls.[40]

After Mihdhar left, other students moved into the house. One of these, Yazeed al Salmi, stands out. In July 2000, Salmi purchased $4,000 in traveler's checks at a bank in Riyadh, Saudi Arabia. On September 5, Hazmi deposited $1,900 of the traveler's checks into his bank account, after withdrawing the same amount in cash. It is possible that Hazmi was simply cashing the traveler's checks for a friend. We do not know; Salmi claims not to remember the transaction. After 9/11, Salmi reportedly confided to Mohdar Abdullah that he had previously known terrorist pilot Hani Hanjour. After living in the same house with Hazmi for about a month, Salmi moved to the La Mesa apartment shared by Abdullah and others.[41]

By the fall of 2000, Hazmi no longer even pretended to study English or take flying lessons. Aware that his co-conspirators in Afghanistan and Pakistan would be sending him a new colleague shortly, he bided his time and worked for a few weeks at a gas station in La Mesa where some of his friends, including Abdullah, were employed. On one occasion, Hazmi told a fellow employee that he was planning to find a better job, and let slip a prediction that he would become famous.[42]

On December 8, 2000, Hani Hanjour arrived in San Diego, having traveled from Dubai via Paris and Cincinnati. Hazmi likely picked up Hanjour at the airport. We do not know where Hanjour stayed; a few days later, both men left San Diego. Before departing, they visited the gas station in La Mesa, where Hazmi reportedly introduced Hanjour as a "long time friend from Saudi Arabia." Hazmi told his housemate that he and his friend "Hani" were headed for San Jose to take flying lessons and told his friends that he would stay in touch. Hazmi promised to return to San Diego soon, and he and Hanjour drove off.[43]

Hazmi did not sever all contact with his friends in San Diego. According to Abdullah, after Hazmi left San Diego in December 2000, he telephoned Abdullah twice: in December 2000 or January 2001, Hazmi said he was in San Francisco and would be attending flight school there; about two weeks later, he said he was attending flight school in Arizona. Some evidence, which we will discuss later, indicates that Hazmi contacted Abdullah again, in August 2001. In addition, during the month following Hazmi's departure from San Diego, he emailed his housemate three times, including a January 2001 email that Hazmi signed "Smer," an apparent attempt to conceal his identity that struck the housemate as strange at the time. Hazmi also telephoned his housemate that he and his friend had decided to take flight lessons in Arizona, and that Mihdhar was now back in Yemen. That was their last contact. When the housemate emailed Hazmi in February and March of 2001 to find out how he was faring, Hazmi did not reply.[44]

The housemate who rented the room to Hazmi and Mihdhar during 2000 is an apparently law-abiding citizen with long-standing, friendly contacts among local police and FBI personnel. He did not see anything unusual enough in the behavior of Hazmi or Mihdhar to prompt him to report to his law enforcement contacts. Nor did those contacts ask him for information about his tenants/housemates.

7.2 THE 9/11 PILOTS IN THE UNITED STATES

The Hamburg Pilots Arrive in the United States
In the early summer of 2000, the Hamburg group arrived in the United States to begin flight training. Marwan al Shehhi came on May 29, arriving in Newark on a flight from Brussels. He went to New York City and waited there for

Mohamed Atta to join him. On June 2, Atta traveled to the Czech Republic by bus from Germany and then flew from Prague to Newark the next day. According to Ramzi Binalshibh, Atta did not meet with anyone in Prague; he simply believed it would contribute to operational security to fly out of Prague rather than Hamburg, the departure point for much of his previous international travel.[45]

Atta and Shehhi had not settled on where they would obtain their flight training. In contrast, Ziad Jarrah had already arranged to attend the Florida Flight Training Center (FFTC) in Venice, Florida. Jarrah arrived in Newark on June 27 and then flew to Venice. He immediately began the private pilot program at FFTC, intending to get a multi-engine license. Jarrah moved in with some of the flight instructors affiliated with his school and bought a car.[46]

While Jarrah quickly settled into training in Florida, Atta and Shehhi kept searching for a flight school. After visiting the Airman Flight School in Norman, Oklahoma (where Zacarias Moussaoui would enroll several months later and where another al Qaeda operative, Ihab Ali, had taken lessons in the mid-1990s), Atta started flight instruction at Huffman Aviation in Venice, Florida, and both Atta and Shehhi subsequently enrolled in the Accelerated Pilot Program at that school. By the end of July, both of them took solo flights, and by mid-August they passed the private pilot airman test. They trained through the summer at Huffman, while Jarrah continued his training at FFTC.[47]

The Hamburg operatives paid for their flight training primarily with funds wired from Dubai by KSM's nephew, Ali Abdul Aziz Ali. Between June 29 and September 17, 2000, Ali sent Shehhi and Atta a total of $114,500 in five transfers ranging from $5,000 to $70,000. Ali relied on the unremarkable nature of his transactions, which were essentially invisible amid the billions of dollars flowing daily across the globe.[48] Ali was not required to provide identification in sending this money and the aliases he used were not questioned.[49]

In mid-September, Atta and Shehhi applied to change their immigration status from tourist to student, stating their intention to study at Huffman until September 1, 2001. In late September, they decided to enroll at Jones Aviation in Sarasota, Florida, about 20 miles north of Venice. According to the instructor at Jones, the two were aggressive, rude, and sometimes even fought with him to take over the controls during their training flights. In early October, they took the Stage I exam for instruments rating at Jones Aviation and failed. Very upset, they said they were in a hurry because jobs awaited them at home. Atta and Shehhi then returned to Huffman.[50]

In the meantime, Jarrah obtained a single-engine private pilot certificate in early August. Having reached that milestone, he departed on the first of five foreign trips he would take after first entering the United States. In October, he flew back to Germany to visit his girlfriend, Aysel Senguen. The two traveled to Paris before Jarrah returned to Florida on October 29. His relationship with her remained close throughout his time in the United States. In addition to his trips, Jarrah made hundreds of phone calls to her and communicated frequently by email.[51]

Jarrah was supposed to be joined at FFTC by Ramzi Binalshibh, who even sent the school a deposit. But Binalshibh could not obtain a U.S. visa. His first applications in May and June 2000 were denied because he lacked established ties in Germany ensuring his return from a trip to the United States. In September, he went home to Yemen to apply for a visa from there, but was denied on grounds that he also lacked sufficient ties to Yemen. In October, he tried one last time, in Berlin, applying for a student visa to attend "aviation language school," but the prior denials were noted and this application was denied as well, as incomplete.[52]

Unable to participate directly in the operation, Binalshibh instead took on the role of coordinating between KSM and the operatives in the United States. Apart from sending a total of about $10,000 in wire transfers to Atta and Shehhi during the summer of 2000, one of Binalshibh's first tasks in his new role as plot coordinator was to assist another possible pilot, Zacarias Moussaoui.[53]

In the fall of 2000, KSM had sent Moussaoui to Malaysia for flight training, but Moussaoui did not find a school he liked. He worked instead on other terrorist schemes, such as buying four tons of ammonium nitrate for bombs to be planted on cargo planes flying to the United States. When KSM found out, he recalled Moussaoui back to Pakistan and directed him to go to the United States for flight training. In early October, Moussaoui went to London. When Binalshibh visited London in December, he stayed at the same 16-room dormitory where Moussaoui was still residing. From London, Moussaoui sent inquiries to the Airman Flight School in Norman, Oklahoma.[54]

Confronting training or travel problems with Hazmi, Mihdhar, Binalshibh, and Moussaoui, al Qaeda was looking for another possible pilot candidate. A new recruit with just the right background conveniently presented himself in Afghanistan.

The Fourth Pilot: Hani Hanjour

Hani Hanjour, from Ta'if, Saudi Arabia, first came to the United States in 1991 to study at the Center for English as a Second Language at the University of Arizona. He seems to have been a rigorously observant Muslim. According to his older brother, Hani Hanjour went to Afghanistan for the first time in the late 1980s, as a teenager, to participate in the jihad and, because the Soviets had already withdrawn, worked for a relief agency there.[55]

In 1996, Hanjour returned to the United States to pursue flight training, after being rejected by a Saudi flight school. He checked out flight schools in Florida, California, and Arizona; and he briefly started at a couple of them before returning to Saudi Arabia. In 1997, he returned to Florida and then, along with two friends, went back to Arizona and began his flight training there in earnest. After about three months, Hanjour was able to obtain his private pilot's license. Several more months of training yielded him a commercial pilot certificate, issued by the Federal Aviation Administration (FAA) in April 1999. He then returned to Saudi Arabia.[56]

Hanjour reportedly applied to the civil aviation school in Jeddah after returning home, but was rejected. He stayed home for a while and then told his family he was going to the United Arab Emirates to work for an airline. Where Hanjour actually traveled during this time period is unknown. It is possible he went to the training camps in Afghanistan.[57]

The fact that Hanjour spent so much time in Arizona may be significant. A number of important al Qaeda figures attended the University of Arizona in Tucson or lived in Tucson in the 1980s and early 1990s.[58] Some of Hanjour's known Arizona associates from the time of his flight training in the late 1990s have also raised suspicion.[59] FBI investigators have speculated that al Qaeda may have directed other extremist Muslims in the Phoenix area to enroll in aviation training. It is clear that when Hanjour lived in Arizona in the 1990s, he associated with several individuals holding extremist beliefs who have been the subject of counterterrorism investigations. Some of them trained with Hanjour to be pilots. Others had apparent connections to al Qaeda, including training in Afghanistan.[60]

By the spring of 2000, Hanjour was back in Afghanistan. According to KSM, Hanjour was sent to him in Karachi for inclusion in the plot after Hanjour was identified in al Qaeda's al Faruq camp as a trained pilot, on the basis of background information he had provided. Hanjour had been at a camp in Afghanistan for a few weeks when Bin Ladin or Atef apparently realized that he was a trained pilot; he was told to report to KSM, who then trained Hanjour for a few days in the use of code words.[61]

On June 20, Hanjour returned home to Saudi Arabia. He obtained a U.S. student visa on September 25 and told his family he was returning to his job in the UAE. Hanjour did go to the UAE, but to meet facilitator Ali Abdul Aziz Ali.[62]

Ali opened a bank account in Dubai for Hanjour and providing the initial funds for his trip. On December 8, Hanjour traveled to San Diego. His supposed destination was an English as a second language program in Oakland, California, which he had scheduled before leaving Saudi Arabia but never attended. Instead, as mentioned earlier, he joined Nawaf al Hazmi in San Diego.[63]

Hazmi and Hanjour left San Diego almost immediately and drove to Arizona. Settling in Mesa, Hanjour began refresher training at his old school, Arizona Aviation. He wanted to train on multi-engine planes, but had difficulties because his English was not good enough. The instructor advised him to discontinue but Hanjour said he could not go home without completing the training. In early 2001, he started training on a Boeing 737 simulator at Pan Am International Flight Academy in Mesa. An instructor there found his work well below standard and discouraged him from continuing. Again, Hanjour persevered; he completed the initial training by the end of March 2001. At that point, Hanjour and Hazmi vacated their apartment and started driving east, anticipating the arrival of the "muscle hijackers"—the operatives who would storm the cockpits and control the passengers. By as early as April 4, Hanjour and Hazmi had arrived in Falls Church, Virginia.[64]

The three pilots in Florida continued with their training. Atta and Shehhi finished up at Huffman and earned their instrument certificates from the FAA in November. In mid-December 2000, they passed their commercial pilot tests and received their licenses. They then began training to fly large jets on a flight simulator. At about the same time, Jarrah began simulator training, also in Florida but at a different center. By the end of 2000, less than six months after their arrival, the three pilots on the East Coast were simulating flights on large jets.[65]

Travels in Early 2001

Jarrah, Atta, and Shehhi, having progressed in their training, all took foreign trips during the holiday period of 2000–2001. Jarrah flew through Germany to get home to Beirut. A few weeks later, he returned to Florida via Germany, with Aysel Senguen. She stayed with him in Florida for ten days, even accompanying him to a flight training session. We do not know whether Atta or al Qaeda leaders knew about Jarrah's trips and Senguen's visit. The other operatives had broken off regular contact with their families. At the end of January 2001, Jarrah again flew to Beirut, to visit his sick father. After staying there for several weeks, Jarrah visited Senguen in Germany for a few days before returning to the United States at the end of February.[66]

While Jarrah took his personal trips, Atta traveled to Germany in early January 2001 for a progress meeting with Ramzi Binalshibh. Binalshibh says Atta told him to report to the al Qaeda leadership in Afghanistan that the three Hamburg pilots had completed their flight training and were awaiting orders. Atta also disclosed that a fourth pilot, Hanjour, had joined Hazmi. Upon returning to Florida, Atta wired Binalshibh travel money. Binalshibh proceeded to Afghanistan, made his report, and spent the next several months there and in Pakistan.[67]

When Atta returned to Florida, Shehhi left for Morocco, traveling to Casablanca in mid-January. Shehhi's family, concerned about not having heard from him, reported him missing to the UAE government. The UAE embassy in turn contacted the Hamburg police and a UAE representative tried to find him in Germany, visiting mosques and Shehhi's last address in Hamburg. After learning that his family was looking for him, Shehhi telephoned them on January 20 and said he was still living and studying in Hamburg. The UAE government then told the Hamburg police they could call off the search.[68]

Atta and Shehhi both encountered some difficulty reentering the United States, on January 10 and January 18, respectively. Because neither presented a

Atta's Alleged Trip to Prague

Mohamed Atta is known to have been in Prague on two occasions: in December 1994, when he stayed one night at a transit hotel, and in June 2000, when he was en route to the United States. On the latter occasion, he arrived by bus from Germany, on June 2, and departed for Newark the following day.[69]

The allegation that Atta met with an Iraqi intelligence officer in Prague in April 2001 originates from the reporting of a single source of the Czech intelligence service. Shortly after 9/11, the source reported having seen Atta meet with Ahmad Khalil Ibrahim Samir al Ani, an Iraqi diplomat, at the Iraqi Embassy in Prague on April 9, 2001, at 11:00 A.M. This information was passed to CIA headquarters.

The U.S. legal attaché ("Legat") in Prague, the representative of the FBI, met with the Czech service's source. After the meeting, the assessment of the Legat and the Czech officers present was that they were 70 percent sure that the source was sincere and believed his own story of the meeting. Subsequently, the Czech intelligence service publicly stated that there was a 70 percent probability that the meeting between Atta and Ani had taken place. The Czech Interior Minister also made several statements to the press about his belief that the meeting had occurred, and the story was widely reported.

The FBI has gathered evidence indicating that Atta was in Virginia Beach on April 4 (as evidenced by a bank surveillance camera photo), and in Coral Springs, Florida on April 11, where he and Shehhi leased an apartment. On April 6, 9, 10, and 11, Atta's cellular telephone was used numerous times to call various lodging establishments in Florida from cell sites within Florida. We cannot confirm that he placed those calls. But there are no U.S. records indicating that Atta departed the country during this period. Czech officials have reviewed their flight and border records as well for any indication that Atta was in the Czech Republic in April 2001, including records of anyone crossing the border who even looked Arab. They have also reviewed pictures from the area near the Iraqi embassy and have not discovered photos of anyone who looked like Atta. No evidence has been found that Atta was in the Czech Republic in April 2001.

According to the Czech government, Ani, the Iraqi officer alleged to have met with Atta, was about 70 miles away from Prague on April 8–9 and did not return until the afternoon of the ninth, while the source was firm that the sighting occurred at 11:00 A.M. When questioned about the reported April 2001 meeting, Ani—now in custody—has denied ever meeting or having any contact with Atta. Ani says that shortly after 9/11, he became concerned that press stories about the alleged meeting might hurt his career. Hoping to clear his name, Ani asked his superiors to approach the Czech government about refuting the allegation. He also denies knowing of any other Iraqi official having contact with Atta.

These findings cannot absolutely rule out the possibility that Atta was in Prague on April 9, 2001. He could have used an alias to travel and a passport under that alias, but this would be an exception to his practice of using his true name while traveling (as he did in January and would in July when he took his next overseas trip). The FBI and CIA have uncovered no evidence that Atta held any fraudulent passports.

KSM and Binalshibh both deny that an Atta-Ani meeting occurred. There was no reason for such a meeting, especially considering the risk it would pose to the operation. By April 2001, all four pilots had completed most of their training, and the muscle hijackers were about to begin entering the United States.

The available evidence does not support the original Czech report of an Atta-Ani meeting.[70]

student visa, both of them had to persuade INS inspectors that they should be admitted so that they could continue their flight training. Neither operative had any problem clearing Customs.[71]

After returning to Florida from their trips, Atta and Shehhi visited Georgia, staying briefly in Norcross and Decatur, and renting a single-engine plane to fly with an instructor in Lawrenceville. By February 19, Atta and Shehhi were in Virginia. They rented a mailbox in Virginia Beach, cashed a check, and then promptly returned to Georgia, staying in Stone Mountain. We have found no explanation for these travels. In mid-March, Jarrah was in Georgia as well, staying in Decatur. There is no evidence that the three pilots met, although Jarrah and Atta apparently spoke on the phone. At the end of the month, Jarrah left the United States again and visited Senguen in Germany for two weeks. In early April, Atta and Shehhi returned to Virginia Beach and closed the mailbox they had opened in February.[72]

By the time Atta and Shehhi returned to Virginia Beach from their travels in Georgia, Hazmi and Hanjour had also arrived in Virginia, in Falls Church. They made their way to a large mosque there, the Dar al Hijra mosque, sometime in early April.[73]

As we mentioned earlier, one of the imams at this mosque was the same Anwar Aulaqi with whom Hazmi had spent time at the Rabat mosque in San Diego. Aulaqi had moved to Virginia in January 2001. He remembers Hazmi from San Diego but has denied having any contact with Hazmi or Hanjour in Virginia.[74]

At the Dar al Hijra mosque, Hazmi and Hanjour met a Jordanian named Eyad al Rababah. Rababah says he had gone to the mosque to speak to the imam, Aulaqi, about finding work. At the conclusion of services, which normally had 400 to 500 attendees, Rababah says he happened to meet Hazmi and Hanjour. They were looking for an apartment; Rababah referred them to a friend who had one to rent. Hazmi and Hanjour moved into the apartment, which was in Alexandria.[75]

Some FBI investigators doubt Rababah's story. Some agents suspect that Aulaqi may have tasked Rababah to help Hazmi and Hanjour. We share that suspicion, given the remarkable coincidence of Aulaqi's prior relationship with Hazmi. As noted above, the Commission was unable to locate and interview Aulaqi. Rababah has been deported to Jordan, having been convicted after 9/11 in a fraudulent driver's license scheme.[76]

Rababah, who had lived in Connecticut, New York, and New Jersey, told investigators that he had recommended Paterson, New Jersey, as a place with an Arabic-speaking community where Hazmi and Hanjour might want to settle. They asked for his help in getting them an apartment in Paterson. Rababah tried without success. He says he then suggested that Hazmi and Hanjour travel with him to Connecticut where they could look for a place to live.[77]

On May 8, Rababah went to Hazmi and Hanjour's apartment to pick them up for the trip to Connecticut. There he says he found them with new roommates—Ahmed al Ghamdi and Majed Moqed. These two men had been sent to America to serve as muscle hijackers and had arrived at Dulles Airport on May 2. Rababah drove Hanjour to Fairfield, Connecticut, followed by Hazmi, who had Moqed and Ghamdi in his car. After a short stay in Connecticut, where they apparently called area flight schools and real estate agents, Rababah drove the four to Paterson to have dinner and show them around. He says that they returned with him to Fairfield that night, and that he never saw them again.[78]

Within a few weeks, Hanjour, Hazmi, and several other operatives moved to Paterson and rented a one-room apartment. When their landlord later paid a visit, he found six men living there—Nawaf al Hazmi, now joined by his younger brother Salem, Hanjour, Moqed, probably Ahmed al Ghamdi, and Abdul Aziz al Omari; Hazmi's old friend Khalid al Mihdhar would soon join them.[79]

Atta and Shehhi had already returned to Florida. On April 11, they moved into an apartment in Coral Springs. Atta stayed in Florida, awaiting the arrival of the first muscle hijackers.[80]

Shehhi, on the other hand, bought a ticket to Cairo and flew there from Miami on April 18. We do not know much more about Shehhi's reason for traveling to Egypt in April than we know about his January trip to Morocco.

Shehhi did meet with Atta's father, who stated in a post-9/11 interview that Shehhi just wanted to pick up Atta's international driver's license and some money. This story is not credible. Atta already had the license with him and presented it during a traffic stop on April 26 while Shehhi was still abroad. Shehhi spent about two weeks in Egypt, obviously more time than would have been needed just to meet with Atta's father. Shehhi could have traveled elsewhere during this time, but no records indicating additional travel have been discovered.[81]

Shehhi returned to Miami on May 2. That day, Atta and Jarrah were together, about 30 miles to the north, visiting a Department of Motor Vehicles office in Lauderdale Lakes, Florida, to get Florida driver's licenses. Back in Virginia, Hazmi and Hanjour were about to leave for Connecticut and New Jersey. As the summer approached, the lead operatives were settled in Florida and New Jersey, waiting for the rest of their contingent to join them.[82]

7.3 ASSEMBLING THE TEAMS

During the summer and early autumn of 2000, Bin Ladin and senior al Qaeda leaders in Afghanistan started selecting the muscle hijackers—the operatives who would storm the cockpits and control the passengers. Despite the phrase widely used to describe them, the so-called muscle hijackers were not at all physically imposing; most were between 5' 5" and 5' 7" in height.[83]

Recruitment and Selection for 9/11
Twelve of the 13 muscle hijackers (excluding Nawaf al Hazmi and Mihdhar) came from Saudi Arabia: Satam al Suqami, Wail al Shehri, Waleed al Shehri, Abdul Aziz al Omari, Ahmed al Ghamdi, Hamza al Ghamdi, Mohand al Shehri, Majed Moqed, Salem al Hazmi, Saeed al Ghamdi, Ahmad al Haznawi, and Ahmed al Nami. The remaining recruit, Fayez Banihammad, came from the UAE. He appears to have played a unique role among the muscle hijackers because of his work with one of the plot's financial facilitators, Mustafa al Hawsawi.[84]

Saudi authorities interviewed the relatives of these men and have briefed us on what they found. The muscle hijackers came from a variety of educational and societal backgrounds. All were between 20 and 28 years old; most were unemployed with no more than a high school education and were unmarried.[85]

Four of them—Ahmed al Ghamdi, Saeed al Ghamdi, Hamza al Ghamdi, and Ahmad al Haznawi—came from a cluster of three towns in the al Bahah region, an isolated and underdeveloped area of Saudi Arabia, and shared the same tribal affiliation. None had a university degree. Their travel patterns and information from family members suggest that the four may have been in contact with each other as early as the fall of 1999.[86]

Five more—Wail al Shehri, Waleed al Shehri, Abdul Aziz al Omari, Mohand al Shehri, and Ahmed al Nami—came from Asir Province, a poor region in southwestern Saudi Arabia that borders Yemen; this weakly policed area is sometimes called "the wild frontier." Wail and Waleed al Shehri were brothers. All five in this group had begun university studies. Omari had graduated with honors from high school, had attained a degree from the Imam Muhammad Ibn Saud Islamic University, was married, and had a daughter.[87]

The three remaining muscle hijackers from Saudi Arabia were Satam al Suqami, Majed Moqed, and Salem al Hazmi. Suqami came from Riyadh. Moqed hailed from a small town called Annakhil, west of Medina. Suqami had very little education, and Moqed had dropped out of university. Neither Suqami nor Moqed appears to have had ties to the other, or to any of the other operatives, before getting involved with extremists, probably by 1999.[88]

Salem al Hazmi, a younger brother of Nawaf, was born in Mecca. Salem's family recalled him as a quarrelsome teenager. His brother Nawaf probably recommended him for recruitment into al Qaeda. One al Qaeda member who knew them says that Nawaf pleaded with Bin Ladin to allow Salem to participate in the 9/11 operation.[89]

Detainees have offered varying reasons for the use of so many Saudi operatives. Binalshibh argues that al Qaeda wanted to send a message to the government of Saudi Arabia about its relationship with the United States. Several other al Qaeda figures, however, have stated that ethnicity generally was not a factor in the selection of operatives unless it was important for security or operational reasons.[90]

KSM, for instance, denies that Saudis were chosen for the 9/11 plot to drive a wedge between the United States and Saudi Arabia, and stresses practical reasons for considering ethnic background when selecting operatives. He says that so many were Saudi because Saudis comprised the largest portion of the pool of recruits in the al Qaeda training camps. KSM estimates that in any given camp, 70 percent of the mujahideen were Saudi, 20 percent were Yemeni, and 10 percent were from elsewhere. Although Saudi and Yemeni trainees were most often willing to volunteer for suicide operations, prior to 9/11 it was easier for Saudi operatives to get into the United States.[91]

Most of the Saudi muscle hijackers developed their ties to extremists two or three years before the attacks. Their families often did not consider these young men religious zealots. Some were perceived as devout, others as lacking in faith. For instance, although Ahmed al Ghamdi, Hamza al Ghamdi, and Saeed al Ghamdi attended prayer services regularly and Omari often served as an imam at his mosque in Saudi Arabia, Suqami and Salem al Hazmi appeared unconcerned with religion and, contrary to Islamic law, were known to drink alcohol.[92]

Like many other al Qaeda operatives, the Saudis who eventually became the muscle hijackers were targeted for recruitment outside Afghanistan— probably in Saudi Arabia itself. Al Qaeda recruiters, certain clerics, and—in a few cases—family members probably all played a role in spotting potential candidates. Several of the muscle hijackers seem to have been recruited through contacts at local universities and mosques.[93]

According to the head of one of the training camps in Afghanistan, some were chosen by unnamed Saudi sheikhs who had contacts with al Qaeda. Omari, for example, is believed to have been a student of a radical Saudi cleric named Sulayman al Alwan. His mosque, which is located in al Qassim Province, is known among more moderate clerics as a "terrorist factory." The province is at the very heart of the strict Wahhabi movement in Saudi Arabia. Saeed al Ghamdi and Mohand al Shehri also spent time in al Qassim, both breaking with their families. According to his father, Mohand al Shehri's frequent visits to this area resulted in his failing exams at his university in Riyadh. Saeed al Ghamdi transferred to a university in al Qassim, but he soon stopped talking to his family and dropped out of school without informing them.[94]

The majority of these Saudi recruits began to break with their families in late 1999 and early 2000. According to relatives, some recruits began to make arrangements for extended absences. Others exhibited marked changes in behavior before disappearing. Salem al Hazmi's father recounted that Salem—who had had problems with alcohol and petty theft—stopped drinking and started attending mosque regularly three months before he disappeared.[95]

Several family members remembered that their relatives had expressed a desire to participate in jihad, particularly in Chechnya. None had mentioned going to Afghanistan. These statements might be true or cover stories. The four recruits from the al Ghamdi tribe, for example, all told their families that they were going to Chechnya. Only two—Ahmed al Ghamdi and Saeed al Ghamdi—had documentation suggesting travel to a Russian republic.[96]

Some aspiring Saudi mujahideen, intending to go to Chechnya, encountered difficulties along the way and diverted to Afghanistan. In 1999, Ibn al Khattab—the primary commander of Arab nationals in Chechnya—reportedly had started turning away most foreign mujahideen because of their inexperience and inability to adjust to the local conditions. KSM states that several of the 9/11 muscle hijackers faced problems traveling to Chechnya and so went to Afghanistan, where they were drawn into al Qaeda.[97]

Khallad has offered a more detailed story of how such diversions occurred. According to him, a number of Saudi mujahideen who tried to go to Chechnya in 1999 to fight the Russians were stopped at the Turkish-Georgian border. Upon arriving in Turkey, they received phone calls at guesthouses in places such as Istanbul and Ankara, informing them that the route to Chechnya via Georgia had been closed. These Saudis then decided to travel to Afghanistan, where they could train and wait to make another attempt to enter Chechnya during the summer of 2000. While training at al Qaeda camps, a dozen of them heard Bin Ladin's speeches, volunteered to become suicide operatives, and eventually were selected as muscle hijackers for the planes operation. Khallad says he met a number of them at the Kandahar airport, where they were helping to provide extra security. He encouraged Bin Ladin to use them. Khallad claims to have been closest with Saeed al Ghamdi, whom he convinced to become a martyr and whom he asked to recruit a friend, Ahmed al Ghamdi, to the same cause. Although Khallad claims not to recall everyone from this group who was later chosen for the 9/11 operation, he says they also included Suqami, Waleed and Wail al Shehri, Omari, Nami, Hamza al Ghamdi, Salem al Hazmi, and Moqed.[98]

According to KSM, operatives volunteered for suicide operations and, for the most part, were not pressured to martyr themselves. Upon arriving in Afghanistan, a recruit would fill out an application with standard questions, such as, What brought you to Afghanistan? How did you travel here? How did you hear about us? What attracted you to the cause? What is your educational background? Where have you worked before? Applications were valuable for determining the potential of new arrivals, for filtering out potential spies from among them, and for identifying recruits with special skills. For instance, as pointed out earlier, Hani Hanjour noted his pilot training. Prospective operatives also were asked whether they were prepared to serve as suicide operatives; those who answered in the affirmative were interviewed by senior al Qaeda lieutenant Muhammad Atef.[99]

KSM claims that the most important quality for any al Qaeda operative was willingness to martyr himself. Khallad agrees, and claims that this criterion had preeminence in selecting the planes operation participants. The second most important criterion was demonstrable patience, Khallad says, because the planning for such attacks could take years.[100]

Khallad claims it did not matter whether the hijackers had fought in jihad previously, since he believes that U.S. authorities were not looking for such operatives before 9/11. But KSM asserts that young mujahideen with clean records were chosen to avoid raising alerts during travel. The al Qaeda training camp head mentioned above adds that operatives with no prior involvement in activities likely to be known to international security agencies were purposefully selected for the 9/11 attacks.[101]

Most of the muscle hijackers first underwent basic training similar to that given other al Qaeda recruits. This included training in firearms, heavy weapons, explosives, and topography. Recruits learned discipline and military life. They were subjected to artificial stresses to measure their psychological fitness and commitment to jihad. At least seven of the Saudi muscle hijackers took this basic training regime at the al Faruq camp near Kandahar. This particular camp appears to have been the preferred location for vetting and training the potential muscle hijackers because of its proximity to Bin Ladin and senior al Qaeda leadership. Two others—Suqami and Moqed—trained at Khaldan, another large basic training facility located near Kabul, where Mihdhar had trained in the mid-1990s.[102]

By the time operatives for the planes operation were picked in mid-2000, some of them had been training in Afghanistan for months, others were just arriving for the first time, and still others may have been returning after prior visits to the camps. According to KSM, Bin Ladin would travel to the camps to deliver lectures and meet the trainees personally. If Bin Ladin believed a trainee held promise for a special operation, that trainee would be invited to the al Qaeda leader's compound at Tarnak Farms for further meetings.[103]

KSM claims that Bin Ladin could assess new trainees very quickly, in about ten minutes, and that many of the 9/11 hijackers were selected in this manner. Bin Ladin, assisted by Atef, personally chose all the future muscle hijackers for the planes operation, primarily between the summer of 2000 and April 2001. Upon choosing a trainee, Bin Ladin would ask him to swear loyalty for a suicide operation. After the selection and oath-swearing, the operative would be sent to KSM for training and the filming of a martyrdom video, a function KSM supervised as head of al Qaeda's media committee.[104]

KSM sent the muscle hijacker recruits on to Saudi Arabia to obtain U.S. visas. He gave them money (about $2,000 each) and instructed them to return to Afghanistan for more training after obtaining the visas. At this early stage, the operatives were not told details about the operation. The majority of the Saudi muscle hijackers obtained U.S. visas in Jeddah or Riyadh between September and November of 2000.[105]

KSM told potential hijackers to acquire new "clean" passports in their home countries before applying for a U.S. visa. This was to avoid raising suspicion about previous travel to countries where al Qaeda operated. Fourteen of the 19 hijackers, including nine Saudi muscle hijackers, obtained new passports. Some of these passports were then likely doctored by the al Qaeda passport division in Kandahar, which would add or erase entry and exit stamps to create "false trails" in the passports.[106]

In addition to the operatives who eventually participated in the 9/11 attacks as muscle hijackers, Bin Ladin apparently selected at least nine other Saudis who, for various reasons, did not end up taking part in the operation: Mohamed Mani Ahmad al Kahtani, Khalid Saeed Ahmad al Zahrani, Ali Abd al Rahman al Faqasi al Ghamdi, Saeed al Baluchi, Qutaybah al Najdi, Zuhair al Thubaiti, Saeed Abdullah Saeed al Ghamdi, Saud al Rashid, and Mushabib al Hamlan. A tenth individual, a Tunisian with Canadian citizenship named Abderraouf Jdey, may have been a candidate to participate in 9/11, or he may have been a candidate for a later attack. These candidate hijackers either backed out, had trouble obtaining needed travel documents, or were removed from the operation by the al Qaeda leadership. Khallad believes KSM wanted between four and six operatives per plane. KSM states that al Qaeda had originally planned to use 25 or 26 hijackers but ended up with only the 19.[107]

Final Training and Deployment to the United States

Having acquired U.S. visas in Saudi Arabia, the muscle hijackers returned to Afghanistan for special training in late 2000 to early 2001. The training reportedly was conducted at the al Matar complex by Abu Turab al Jordani, one of only a handful of al Qaeda operatives who, according to KSM, was aware of the full details of the planned planes operation. Abu Turab taught the operatives how to conduct hijackings, disarm air marshals, and handle explosives. He also trained them in bodybuilding and provided them with a few basic English words and phrases.[108]

According to KSM, Abu Turab even had the trainees butcher a sheep and a camel with a knife to prepare to use knives during the hijackings. The recruits learned to focus on storming the cockpit at the earliest opportunity when the doors first opened, and to worry about seizing control over the rest of the plane later. The operatives were taught about other kinds of attack as well, such as truck bombing, so that they would not be able to disclose the exact nature of their operation if they were caught. According to KSM, the muscle did not learn the full details—including the plan to hijack planes and fly them into buildings—before reaching the United States.[109]

After training in Afghanistan, the operatives went to a safehouse maintained by KSM in Karachi and stayed there temporarily before being deployed to the United States via the UAE. The safehouse was run by al Qaeda operative Abd al Rahim Ghulum Rabbani, also known as Abu Rahmah, a close associate of KSM who assisted him for three years by finding apartments and lending logistical support to operatives KSM would send.

According to an al Qaeda facilitator, operatives were brought to the safehouse by a trusted Pakistani al Qaeda courier named Abdullah Sindhi, who also worked for KSM. The future hijackers usually arrived in groups of two or three, staying at the safe house for as long as two weeks. The facilitator has identified each operative whom he assisted at KSM's direction in the spring of 2001. Before the operatives left Pakistan, each of them received $10,000 from KSM for future expenses.[110]

From Pakistan, the operatives transited through the UAE en route to the United States. In the Emirates they were assisted primarily by al Qaeda operatives Ali Abdul Aziz Ali and Mustafa al Hawsawi. Ali apparently assisted nine future hijackers between April and June 2001 as they came through Dubai. He helped them with plane tickets, traveler's checks, and hotel reservations; he also taught them about everyday aspects of life in the West, such as purchasing clothes and ordering food. Dubai, a modern city with easy access to a major airport, travel agencies, hotels, and Western commercial establishments, was an ideal transit point.[111]

Ali reportedly assumed the operatives he was helping were involved in a big operation in the United States, he did not know the details.[112] When he asked KSM to send him an assistant, KSM dispatched Hawsawi, who had worked on al Qaeda's media committee in Kandahar. Hawsawi helped send the last four operatives (other than Mihdhar) to the United States from the UAE. Hawsawi would consult with Atta about the hijackers' travel schedules to the United States and later check with Atta to confirm that each had arrived. Hawsawi told the muscle hijackers that they would be met by Atta at the airport. Hawsawi also facilitated some of the operation's financing.[113]

The muscle hijackers began arriving in the United States in late April 2001. In most cases, they traveled in pairs on tourist visas and entered the United States in Orlando or Miami, Florida; Washington, D.C.; or New York. Those arriving in Florida were assisted by Atta and Shehhi, while Hazmi and Hanjour took care of the rest. By the end of June, 14 of the 15 muscle hijackers had crossed the Atlantic.[114]

The muscle hijackers supplied an infusion of funds, which they carried as a mixture of cash and traveler's checks purchased in the UAE and Saudi Arabia. Seven muscle hijackers are known to have purchased a total of nearly $50,000 in traveler's checks that were used in the United States. Moreover, substantial deposits into operatives' U.S. bank accounts immediately followed the entry of other muscle hijackers, indicating that those newcomers brought money with them as well. In addition, muscle hijacker Banihammad came to the United States after opening bank accounts in the UAE into which were deposited the equivalent of approximately $30,000 on June 25, 2001. After his June 27 arrival in the United States, Banihammad made Visa and ATM withdrawals from his UAE accounts.[115]

The hijackers made extensive use of banks in the United States, choosing both branches of major international banks and smaller regional banks. All of the hijackers opened accounts in their own name, and used passports and other identification documents that appeared valid on their face. Contrary to numerous published reports, there is no evidence the hijackers ever used false Social Security numbers to open any bank accounts. While the hijackers were not experts on the use of the U.S. financial system, nothing they did would have led the banks to suspect criminal behavior, let alone a terrorist plot to commit mass murder.[116]

The last muscle hijacker to arrive was Khalid al Mihdhar. As mentioned earlier, he had abandoned Hazmi in San Diego in June 2000 and returned to his family in Yemen. Mihdhar reportedly stayed in Yemen for about a month before Khallad persuaded him to return to Afghanistan. Mihdhar complained about life in the United States. He met with KSM, who remained annoyed at his decision to go AWOL. But KSM's desire to drop him from the operation yielded to Bin Ladin's insistence to keep him.[117]

By late 2000, Mihdhar was in Mecca, staying with a cousin until February 2001, when he went home to visit his family before returning to Afghanistan. In June 2001, Mihdhar returned once more to Mecca to stay with his cousin for another month. Mihdhar said that Bin Ladin was planning five attacks on the United States. Before leaving, Mihdhar asked his cousin to watch over his home and family because of a job he had to do.[118]

On July 4, 2001, Mihdhar left Saudi Arabia to return to the United States, arriving at John F. Kennedy International Airport in New York. Mihdhar gave

American Airlines Flight 11

Left to right, *Mohamed Atta*, pilot; *Waleed al Shehri, Wail al Shehri, Satam al Suqami, Abdulaziz al Omari,* hijackers

United Airlines Flight 175

Left to right, *Marwan al Shehhi,* pilot; *Fayez Banihammad, Ahmed al Ghamdi, Hamza al Ghamdi, Mohand al Shehri,* hijackers

American Airlines Flight 77

Left to right, *Hani Hanjour,* pilot; *Nawaf al Hazmi, Khalid al Mihdhar, Majed Moqed, Salem al Hazmi,* hijackers

United Airlines Flight 93

Left to right, *Ziad Jarrah* pilot; *Saeed al Ghamdi, Ahmad al Haznawi, Ahmed al Nami,* hijackers his intended address as the Marriott Hotel, New York City, but instead spent one night at another New York hotel. He then joined the group of hijackers in Paterson, reuniting with Nawaf al Hazmi after more than a year. With two months remaining, all 19 hijackers were in the United States and ready to take the final steps toward carrying out the attacks.[119]

Assistance from Hezbollah and Iran to al Qaeda

As we mentioned in chapter 2, while in Sudan, senior managers in al Qaeda maintained contacts with Iran and the Iranian-supported worldwide terrorist organization Hezbollah, which is based mainly in southern Lebanon and Beirut. Al Qaeda members received advice and training from Hezbollah.

Intelligence indicates the persistence of contacts between Iranian security officials and senior al Qaeda figures after Bin Ladin's return to Afghanistan. Khallad has said that Iran made a concerted effort to strengthen relations with al Qaeda after the October 2000 attack on the USS *Cole*, but was rebuffed because Bin Ladin did not want to alienate his supporters in Saudi Arabia. Khallad and other detainees have described the willingness of Iranian officials to facilitate the travel of al Qaeda members through Iran, on their way to and from Afghanistan. For example, Iranian border inspectors would be told not to place telltale stamps in the passports of these travelers. Such arrangements were particularly beneficial to Saudi members of al Qaeda.[120]

Our knowledge of the international travels of the al Qaeda operatives selected for the 9/11 operation remains fragmentary. But we now have evidence suggesting that 8 to 10 of the 14 Saudi "muscle" operatives traveled into or out of Iran between October 2000 and February 2001.[121]

In October 2000, a senior operative of Hezbollah visited Saudi Arabia to coordinate activities there. He also planned to assist individuals in Saudi Arabia in traveling to Iran during November. A top Hezbollah commander and Saudi Hezbollah contacts were involved.[122]

Also in October 2000, two future muscle hijackers, Mohand al Shehri and Hamza al Ghamdi, flew from Iran to Kuwait. In November, Ahmed al Ghamdi apparently flew to Beirut, traveling—perhaps by coincidence—on the same flight as a senior Hezbollah operative. Also in November, Salem al Hazmi apparently flew from Saudi Arabia to Beirut.[123]

In mid-November, we believe, three of the future muscle hijackers, Wail al Shehri, Waleed al Shehri, and Ahmed al Nami, all of whom had obtained their U.S. visas in late October, traveled in a group from Saudi Arabia to Beirut and then onward to Iran. An associate of a senior Hezbollah operative was on the same flight that took the future hijackers to Iran. Hezbollah officials in Beirut and Iran were expecting the arrival of a group during the same time period. The travel of this group was important enough to merit the attention of senior figures in Hezbollah.[124]

Later in November, two future muscle hijackers, Satam al Suqami and Majed

Moqed, flew into Iran from Bahrain. In February 2001, Khalid al Mihdhar may have taken a flight from Syria to Iran, and then traveled further within Iran to a point near the Afghan border.[125]

KSM and Binalshibh have confirmed that several of the 9/11 hijackers (at least eight, according to Binalshibh) transited Iran on their way to or from Afghanistan, taking advantage of the Iranian practice of not stamping Saudi passports. They deny any other reason for the hijackers' travel to Iran. They also deny any relationship between the hijackers and Hezbollah.[126]

In sum, there is strong evidence that Iran facilitated the transit of al Qaeda members into and out of Afghanistan before 9/11, and that some of these were future 9/11 hijackers. There also is circumstantial evidence that senior Hezbollah operatives were closely tracking the travel of some of these future muscle hijackers into Iran in November 2000. However, we cannot rule out the possibility of a remarkable coincidence—that is, that Hezbollah was actually focusing on some other group of individuals traveling from Saudi Arabia during this same time frame, rather than the future hijackers.[127]

We have found no evidence that Iran or Hezbollah was aware of the planning for what later became the 9/11 attack. At the time of their travel through Iran, the al Qaeda operatives themselves were probably not aware of the specific details of their future operation.

After 9/11, Iran and Hezbollah wished to conceal any past evidence of cooperation with Sunni terrorists associated with al Qaeda. A senior Hezbollah official disclaimed any Hezbollah involvement in 9/11.[128]

We believe this topic requires further investigation by the U.S. government.

7.4 FINAL STRATEGIES AND TACTICS

Final Preparations in the United States

During the early summer of 2001, Atta, assisted by Shehhi, was busy coordinating the arrival of most of the muscle hijackers in southern Florida—picking them up at the airport, finding them places to stay, and helping them settle in the United States.[129]

The majority settled in Florida. Some opened bank accounts, acquired mailboxes, and rented cars. Several also joined local gyms, presumably to stay fit for the operation. Upon first arriving, most stayed in hotels and motels; but by mid-June, they settled in shared apartments relatively close to one another and Atta.[130] Though these muscle hijackers did not travel much after arriving in the United States, two of them, Waleed al Shehri and Satam al Suqami, took unusual trips.

On May 19, Shehri and Suqami flew from Fort Lauderdale to Freeport, the Bahamas, where they had reservations at the Bahamas Princess Resort. The two were turned away by Bahamian officials on arrival, however, because they lacked visas; they returned to Florida that same day. They likely took this trip to renew Suqami's immigration status, as Suqami's legal stay in the United States ended May 21.[131]

On July 30, Shehri traveled alone from Fort Lauderdale to Boston. He flew to San Francisco the next day, where he stayed one night before returning via Las Vegas. While this travel may have been a casing flight—Shehri traveled in first class on the same type of aircraft he would help hijack on September 11 (a Boeing 767) and the trip included a layover in Las Vegas—Shehri was neither a pilot nor a plot leader, as were the other hijackers who took surveillance flights.[132]

The three Hamburg pilots—Atta, Shehhi, and Jarrah—took the first of their cross-country surveillance flights early in the summer. Shehhi flew from New York to Las Vegas via San Francisco in late May. Jarrah flew from Baltimore to Las Vegas via Los Angeles in early June. Atta flew from Boston to Las Vegas via San Francisco at the end of June. Each traveled in first class, on United Airlines. For the east-west transcontinental leg, each operative flew on the same type of aircraft he would pilot on September 11 (Atta and Shehhi, a Boeing 767; Jarrah, a Boeing 757).[133] Hanjour and Hazmi, as noted below, took similar cross-country surveillance flights in August.

Jarrah and Hanjour also received additional training and practice flights in the early summer. A few days before departing on his cross-country test flight, Jarrah flew from Fort Lauderdale to Philadelphia, where he trained at Hortman Aviation and asked to fly the Hudson Corridor, a low-altitude "hallway" along the Hudson River that passes New York landmarks like the World Trade Center. Heavy traffic in the area can make the corridor a dangerous route for an inexperienced pilot. Because Hortman deemed Jarrah unfit to fly solo, he could fly this route only with an instructor.[134]

Hanjour, too, requested to fly the Hudson Corridor about this same time, at Air Fleet Training Systems in Teterboro, New Jersey, where he started receiving ground instruction soon after settling in the area with Hazmi. Hanjour flew the Hudson Corridor, but his instructor declined a second request because of what he considered Hanjour's poor piloting skills. Shortly thereafter, Hanjour switched to Caldwell Flight Academy in Fairfield, New Jersey, where he rented small aircraft on several occasions during June and July. In one such instance on July 20, Hanjour—likely accompanied by Hazmi—rented a plane from Caldwell and took a practice flight from Fairfield to Gaithersburg, Maryland, a route that would have allowed them to fly near Washington, D.C. Other evidence suggests that Hanjour may even have returned to Arizona for flight simulator training earlier in June.[135]

There is no indication that Atta or Shehhi received any additional flight training in June. Both were likely too busy organizing the newly arrived muscle hijackers and taking their cross-country surveillance flights. Atta, moreover, needed to coordinate with his second-in-command, Nawaf al Hazmi.[136]

Although Atta and Hazmi appear to have been in Virginia at about the same time in early April, they probably did not meet then. Analysis of late April communications associated with KSM indicates that they had wanted to get together in April but could not coordinate the meeting.[137] Atta and Hazmi probably first met in the United States only when Hazmi traveled round-trip from Newark to Miami between June 19 and June 25.

After he returned to New Jersey, Hazmi's behavior began to closely parallel that of the other hijackers. He and Hanjour, for instance, soon established new bank accounts, acquired a mailbox, rented cars, and started visiting a gym. So did the four other hijackers who evidently were staying with them in New Jersey. Several also obtained new photo identification, first in New Jersey and then at the Virginia Department of Motor Vehicles, where Hazmi and Hanjour had obtained such documents months earlier, likely with help from their Jordanian friend, Rababah.[138]

Atta probably met again with Hazmi in early July. Returning from his initial cross-country surveillance flight, Atta flew into New York. Rather than return immediately to Florida, he checked into a New Jersey hotel. He picked up tickets to travel to Spain at a travel agency in Paterson on July 4 before departing for Fort Lauderdale. Now that the muscle hijackers had arrived, he was ready to meet with Ramzi Binalshibh for the last time.[139]

The Meeting in Spain

After meeting with Atta in Berlin in January 2001, Binalshibh had spent much of the spring of 2001 in Afghanistan and Pakistan, helping move the muscle hijackers as they passed through Karachi. During the Berlin meeting, the two had agreed to meet later in the year in Kuala Lumpur to discuss the operation in person again. In late May, Binalshibh reported directly to Bin Ladin at an al Qaeda facility known as "Compound Six" near Kandahar.[140]

Bin Ladin told Binalshibh to instruct Atta and the others to focus on their security and that of the operation, and to advise Atta to proceed as planned with the targets discussed before Atta left Afghanistan in early 2000—the World Trade Center, the Pentagon, the White House, and the Capitol. According to Binalshibh, Bin Ladin said he preferred the White House over the Capitol, asking Binalshibh to confirm that Atta understood this preference. Binalshibh says Bin Ladin had given the same message to Waleed al Shehri for conveyance to Atta earlier that spring. Binalshibh also received permission to meet Atta in Malaysia. Atef provided money for the trip, which KSM would help Binalshibh arrange in Karachi.[141]

In early June, Binalshibh traveled by taxi from Kandahar to Quetta, Pakistan, where al Qaeda courier Abu Rahmah took him to KSM. According to Binalshibh, KSM provided a plane ticket to Malaysia and a fraudulent Saudi passport to use for the trip. KSM told him to ask Atta to select a date for the attacks. Binalshibh was to return to Germany and then inform KSM of the date. KSM also gave Binalshibh the email address of Zacarias Moussaoui for future contact. Binalshibh then left for Kuala Lumpur.[142]

Binalshibh contacted Atta upon arriving in Malaysia and found a change in plan. Atta could not travel because he was too busy helping the new arrivals settle in the United States. After remaining in Malaysia for approximately three weeks, Binalshibh went to Bangkok for a few days before returning to Germany. He and Atta agreed to meet later at a location to be determined.[143]

In early July, Atta called Binalshibh to suggest meeting in Madrid, for reasons Binalshibh claims not to know. He says he preferred Berlin, but that he and Atta knew too many people in Germany and feared being spotted together. Unable to buy a ticket to Madrid at the height of the tourist season, Binalshibh booked a seat on a flight to Reus, near Barcelona, the next day. Atta was already en route to Madrid, so Binalshibh phoned Shehhi in the United States to inform him of the change in itinerary.[144]

Atta arrived in Madrid on July 8. He spent the night in a hotel and made three calls from his room, most likely to coordinate with Binalshibh. The next day, Atta rented a car and drove to Reus to pick up Binalshibh; the two then drove to the nearby town of Cambrils. Hotel records show Atta renting rooms in the same area until July 19, when he returned his rental car in Madrid and flew back to Fort Lauderdale. On July 16, Binalshibh returned to Hamburg, using a ticket Atta had purchased for him earlier that day. According to Binalshibh, they did not meet with anyone else while in Spain.[145]

Binalshibh says he told Atta that Bin Ladin wanted the attacks carried out as soon as possible. Bin Ladin, Binalshibh conveyed, was worried about having so many operatives in the United States. Atta replied that he could not yet provide a date because he was too busy organizing the arriving hijackers and still needed to coordinate the timing of the flights so that the crashes would occur simultaneously. Atta said he required about five to six weeks before he could provide an attack date. Binalshibh advised Atta that Bin Ladin had directed that the other operatives not be informed of the date until the last minute. Atta was to provide Binalshibh with advance notice of at least a week or two so that Binalshibh could travel to Afghanistan and report the date personally to Bin Ladin.[146]

As to targets, Atta understood Bin Ladin's interest in striking the White House. Atta said he thought this target too difficult, but had tasked Hazmi and Hanjour to evaluate its feasibility and was awaiting their answer. Atta said that those two operatives had rented small aircraft and flown reconnaissance flights near the Pentagon. Atta explained that Hanjour was assigned to attack the Pentagon, Jarrah the Capitol, and that both Atta and Shehhi would hit the World Trade Center. If any pilot could not reach his intended target, he was to crash the plane. If Atta could not strike the World Trade Center, he planned to crash his aircraft directly into the streets of New York. Atta told Binalshibh that each pilot had volunteered for his assigned target, and that the assignments were subject to change.[147]

During the Spain meeting, Atta also mentioned that he had considered targeting a nuclear facility he had seen during familiarization flights near New York—a target they referred to as "electrical engineering." According to Binalshibh, the other pilots did not like the idea. They thought a nuclear target would be difficult because the airspace around it was restricted, making reconnaissance flights impossible and increasing the likelihood that any plane would be shot down before impact. Moreover, unlike the approved targets, this alternative had not been discussed with senior al Qaeda leaders and therefore did not have the requisite blessing. Nor would a nuclear facility have particular symbolic value. Atta did not ask Binalshibh to pass this idea on to Bin Ladin, Atef, or KSM, and Binalshibh says he did not mention it to them until after September 11.[148]

Binalshibh claims that during their time in Spain, he and Atta also discussed how the hijackings would be executed. Atta said he, Shehhi, and Jarrah had encountered no problems carrying box cutters on cross-country surveillance flights. The best time to storm the cockpit would be about 10–15 minutes after takeoff, when the cockpit doors typically were opened for the first time. Atta did not believe they would need any other weapons. He had no firm contingency plan in case the cockpit door was locked. While he mentioned general ideas such as using a hostage or claiming to have a bomb, he was confident the cockpit doors would be opened and did not consider breaking them down a viable idea. Atta told Binalshibh he wanted to select planes departing on long flights because they would be full of fuel, and that he wanted to hijack Boeing aircraft because he believed them easier to fly than Airbus aircraft, which he understood had an autopilot feature that did not allow them to be crashed into the ground.[149]

Finally, Atta confirmed that the muscle hijackers had arrived in the United States without incident. They would be divided into teams according to their English-speaking ability. That way they could assist each other before the operation and each team would be able to command the passengers in English. According to Binalshibh, Atta complained that some of the hijackers wanted to contact their families to say goodbye, something he had forbidden. Atta, moreover, was nervous about his future communications with Binalshibh, whom he instructed to obtain new telephones upon returning to Germany. Before Binalshibh left Spain, he gave Atta eight necklaces and eight bracelets that Atta had asked him to buy when he was recently in Bangkok, believing that if the hijackers were clean shaven and well dressed, others would think them wealthy Saudis and give them less notice.[150]

As directed, upon returning from Spain, Binalshibh obtained two new phones, one to communicate with Atta and another to communicate with KSM and others, such as Zacarias Moussaoui. Binalshibh soon contacted KSM and, using code words, reported the results of his meeting with Atta. This important exchange occurred in mid-July.[151]

The conversation covered various topics. For example, Jarrah was to send Binalshibh certain personal materials from the hijackers, including copies of their passports, which Binalshibh in turn would pass along to KSM, probably for subsequent use in al Qaeda propaganda.[152]

The most significant part of the mid-July conversation concerned Jarrah's troubled relationship with Atta. KSM and Binalshibh both acknowledge that Jarrah chafed under Atta's authority over him. Binalshibh believes the disagreement arose in part from Jarrah's family visits. Moreover, Jarrah had been on his own for most of his time in the United States because Binalshibh's visa difficulty had prevented the two of them from training together. Jarrah thus felt excluded from the decisionmaking. Binalshibh had to act as a broker between Jarrah and Atta.[153]

Concerned that Jarrah might withdraw from the operation at this late stage, KSM emphasized the importance of Atta and Jarrah's resolving their differences. Binalshibh claims that such concern was unwarranted, and in their mid-July discussion reassured KSM that Atta and Jarrah would reconcile and be ready to move forward in about a month, after Jarrah visited his family. Noting his concern and the potential for delay, KSM at one point instructed Binalshibh to send "the skirts" to "Sally"—a coded instruction to Binalshibh to send funds to Zacarias Moussaoui. While Binalshibh admits KSM did direct him to send Moussaoui money during the mid-July conversation, he denies knowing exactly why he received this instruction—though he thought the money was being provided "within the framework" of the 9/11 operation.[154]

KSM may have instructed Binalshibh to send money to Moussaoui in order to help prepare Moussaoui as a potential substitute pilot for Jarrah. On July 20, 2001, Aysel Senguen, Jarrah's girlfriend, purchased a one-way ticket for Jarrah from Miami to Dusseldorf. On Jarrah's previous four trips from the United States to see Senguen and his family in Lebanon, he had always traveled with a round-trip ticket. When Jarrah departed Miami on July 25, Atta appears to have driven him to the airport, another unique circumstance.[155]

Binalshibh picked up Jarrah at the airport in Dusseldorf on July 25. Jarrah wanted to see Senguen as soon as possible, so he and Binalshibh arranged to meet a few days later. When they did, they had an emotional conversation during which Binalshibh encouraged Jarrah to see the plan through.[156]

While Jarrah was in Germany, Binalshibh and Moussaoui were in contact to arrange for the transfer of funds. Binalshibh received two wire transfers from Hawsawi in the UAE totaling $15,000 and, within days, relayed almost all of this money to Moussaoui in two installments.[157]

Moussaoui had been taking flight lessons at the Airman Flight School in Norman, Oklahoma, since February but stopped in late May. Although at that point he had only about 50 hours of flight time and no solo flights to his credit, Moussaoui began making inquiries about flight materials and simulator training for Boeing 747s. On July 10, he put down a $1,500 deposit for flight simulator training at Pan Am International Flight Academy in Eagan, Minnesota, and by the end of the month, he had received a simulator schedule to train from

August 13 through August 20. Moussaoui also purchased two knives and inquired of two manufacturers of GPS equipment whether their products could be converted for aeronautical use—activities that closely resembled those of the 9/11 hijackers during their final preparations for the attacks.[158]

On August 10, shortly after getting the money from Binalshibh, Moussaoui left Oklahoma with a friend and drove to Minnesota. Three days later, Moussaoui paid the $6,800 balance owed for his flight simulator training at Pan Am in cash and began his training. His conduct, however, raised the suspicions of his flight instructor. It was unusual for a student with so little training to be learning to fly large jets without any intention of obtaining a pilot's license or other goal. On August 16, once the instructor reported his suspicion to the authorities, Moussaoui was arrested by the INS on immigration charges.[159]

KSM denies ever considering Moussaoui for the planes operation. Instead he claims that Moussaoui was slated to participate in a "second wave" of attacks. KSM also states that Moussaoui had no contact with Atta, and we are unaware of evidence contradicting this assertion.[160]

Yet KSM has also stated that by the summer of 2001, he was too busy with the planes operation to continue planning for any second-wave attacks. Moreover, he admits that only three potential pilots were ever recruited for the alleged second wave, Moussaoui plus two others who, by midsummer of 2001, had backed out of the plot.[161] We therefore believe that the effort to push Moussaoui forward in August 2001 lends credence to the suspicion that he was being primed as a possible pilot in the immediate planes operation.

Binalshibh says he assumed Moussaoui was to take his place as another pilot in the 9/11 operation. Recounting a post-9/11 discussion with KSM in Kandahar, Binalshibh claims KSM mentioned Moussaoui as being part of the 9/11 operation. Although KSM never referred to Moussaoui by name, Binalshibh understood he was speaking of the operative to whom Binalshibh had wired money. Binalshibh says KSM did not approve of Moussaoui but believes KSM did not remove him from the operation only because Moussaoui had been selected and assigned by Bin Ladin himself.[162]

KSM did not hear about Moussaoui's arrest until after September 11. According to Binalshibh, had Bin Ladin and KSM learned prior to 9/11 that Moussaoui had been detained, they might have canceled the operation. When Binalshibh discussed Moussaoui's arrest with KSM after September 11, KSM congratulated himself on not having Moussaoui contact the other operatives, which would have compromised the operation. Moussaoui had been in contact with Binalshibh, of course, but this was not discovered until after 9/11.[163]

As it turned out, Moussaoui was not needed to replace Jarrah. By the time Moussaoui was arrested in mid-August, Jarrah had returned to the United States from his final trip to Germany, his disagreement with Atta apparently resolved. The operatives began their final preparations for the attacks.[164]

Readying the Attacks

A week after he returned from meeting Binalshibh in Spain, Atta traveled to Newark, probably to coordinate with Hazmi and give him additional funds. Atta spent a few days in the area before returning to Florida on July 30. The month of August was busy, as revealed by a set of contemporaneous Atta-Binalshibh communications that were recovered after September 11.[165]

On August 3, for example, Atta and Binalshibh discussed several matters, such as the best way for the operatives to purchase plane tickets and the assignment of muscle hijackers to individual teams. Atta and Binalshibh also revisited the question of whether to target the White House. They discussed targets in coded language, pretending to be students discussing various fields of study: "architecture" referred to the World Trade Center, "arts" the Pentagon, "law" the Capitol, and "politics" the White House.[166]

Binalshibh reminded Atta that Bin Ladin wanted to target the White House. Atta again cautioned that this would be difficult. When Binalshibh persisted, Atta agreed to include the White House but suggested they keep the Capitol as an alternate target in case the White House proved too difficult. Atta also suggested that the attacks would not happen until after the first week in September, when Congress reconvened.[167]

Atta and Binalshibh also discussed "the friend who is coming as a tourist"— a cryptic reference to candidate hijacker Mohamed al Kahtani (mentioned above), whom Hawsawi was sending the next day as "the last one" to "complete the group." On August 4, Atta drove to the Orlando airport to meet Kahtani. Upon arrival, however, Kahtani was denied entry by immigration officials because he had a one-way ticket and little money, could not speak English, and could not adequately explain what he intended to do in the United States. He was sent back to Dubai. Hawsawi contacted KSM, who told him to help Kahtani return to Pakistan.[168]

On August 7, Atta flew from Fort Lauderdale to Newark, probably to coordinate with Hazmi. Two days later, Ahmed al Ghamdi and Abdul Aziz al Omari, who had been living in New Jersey with Hazmi and Hanjour, flew to Miami—probably signifying that the four hijacking teams had finally been assigned. While Atta was in New Jersey, he, Hazmi, and Hanjour all purchased tickets for another set of surveillance flights. Like Shehhi, Jarrah, Atta, and Waleed al Shehri before them, Hazmi and Hanjour each flew in first class on the same type of aircraft they would hijack on 9/11 (a Boeing 757), and on transcontinental flights that connected to Las Vegas. This time, however, Atta himself also flew directly to Las Vegas, where all three stayed on August 13–14. Beyond Las Vegas's reputation for welcoming tourists, we have seen no credible evidence explaining why, on this occasion and others, the operatives flew to or met in Las Vegas.[169]

Through August, the hijackers kept busy with their gym training and the pilots took frequent practice flights on small rented aircraft. The operatives also began to make purchases suggesting that the planning was coming to an end. In mid-August, for example, they bought small knives that may actually have been used in the attacks. On August 22, moreover, Jarrah attempted to purchase four GPS units from a pilot shop in Miami. He was able to buy only one unit, which he picked up a few days later when he also purchased three aeronautical charts.[170]

Perhaps most significant, however, was the purchase of plane tickets for September 11. On August 23, Atta again flew to Newark, probably to meet with Hazmi and select flights. All 19 tickets were booked and purchased between August 25 and September 5.[171]

It therefore appears that the attack date was selected by the third week of August. This timing is confirmed by Binalshibh, who claims Atta called him with the date in mid-August. According to Binalshibh, Atta used a riddle to convey the date in code—a message of two branches, a slash, and a lollipop (to non-Americans, 11/9 would be interpreted as September 11). Binalshibh says he called Atta back to confirm the date before passing it to KSM.[172]

KSM apparently received the date from Binalshibh in a message sent through Binalshibh's old Hamburg associate, Zakariya Essabar. Both Binalshibh and KSM claim that Essabar was not privy to the meaning of the message and had no foreknowledge of the attacks. According to Binalshibh, shortly after the date was chosen, he advised Essabar and another Hamburg associate, Said Bahaji, that if they wanted to go to Afghanistan, now was the time because it would soon become more difficult. Essabar made reservations on August 22 and departed Hamburg for Karachi on August 30; Bahaji purchased his tickets on August 20 and departed Hamburg for Karachi on September 3.[173]

Binalshibh also made arrangements to leave for Pakistan during early September, before the attacks, as did Ali and Hawsawi, the plot facilitators in the UAE. During these final days, Binalshibh and Atta kept in contact by phone, email, and instant messaging. Although Atta had forbidden the hijackers to contact their families, he apparently placed one last call to his own father on September 9. Atta also asked Binalshibh to contact the family of one hijacker, pass along goodbyes from others, and give regards to KSM. Jarrah alone appears to have left a written farewell—a sentimental letter to Aysel Senguen.[174]

Hazmi, however, may not have been so discreet. He may have telephoned his former San Diego companion, Mohdar Abdullah, in late August. Several bits of evidence indicate that others in Abdullah's circle may have received word that something big would soon happen. As noted earlier, Abdullah's behavior reportedly changed noticeably. Prior to September 11, both he and Yazeed al Salmi suddenly became intent on proceeding with their planned marriages. One witness quotes Salmi as commenting after the 9/11 attacks, "I knew they were going to do something, that is why I got married." Moreover, as of August 2001, Iyad Kreiwesh and other employees at the Texaco station where Hazmi had worked suddenly were anticipating attention from law enforcement authorities in the near future. Finally, according to an uncorroborated witness account, early on the morning of September 10, Abdullah, Osama Awadallah, Omar Bakarbashat, and others behaved suspiciously at the gas station. According to the witness, after the group met, Awadallah said "it is finally going to happen" as the others celebrated by giving each other high fives.[175]

Dissent within the al Qaeda Leadership

While tactical preparations for the attack were nearing completion, the entire operation was being questioned at the top, as al Qaeda and the Taliban argued over strategy for 2001. Our focus has naturally been on the specifics of the planes operation. But from the perspective of Bin Ladin and Atef, this operation was only one, admittedly key, element of their unfolding plans for the year. Living in Afghanistan, interacting constantly with the Taliban, the al Qaeda leaders would never lose sight of the situation in that country.

Bin Ladin's consistent priority was to launch a major attack directly against the United States. He wanted the planes operation to proceed as soon as possible. Mihdhar reportedly told his cousin during the summer of 2001 that Bin Ladin was reputed to have remarked, "I will make it happen even if I do it by myself."[176]

According to KSM, Bin Ladin had been urging him to advance the date of the attacks. In 2000, for instance, KSM remembers Bin Ladin pushing him to launch the attacks amid the controversy after then-Israeli opposition party leader Ariel Sharon's visit to the Temple Mount in Jerusalem. KSM claims Bin Ladin told him it would be enough for the hijackers simply to down planes rather than crash them into specific targets. KSM says he resisted the pressure.[177]

KSM claims to have faced similar pressure twice more in 2001. According to him, Bin Ladin wanted the operation carried out on May 12, 2001, seven months to the day after the *Cole* bombing. KSM adds that the 9/11 attacks had originally been envisioned for May 2001. The second time he was urged to launch the attacks early was in June or July 2001, supposedly after Bin Ladin learned from the media that Sharon would be visiting the White House. On both occasions KSM resisted, asserting that the hijacking teams were not ready. Bin Ladin pressed particularly strongly for the latter date in two letters stressing the need to attack early. The second letter reportedly was delivered by Bin Ladin's son-in-law, Aws al Madani.[178]

Other evidence corroborates KSM's account. For instance, Mihdhar told his cousin that the attacks were to happen in May, but were postponed twice, first to July, then to September. Moreover, one candidate hijacker remembers a general warning being issued in the al Qaeda camps in July or early August, just like the warnings issued two weeks before the *Cole* bombing and ten days before the eventual 9/11 attacks. During the midsummer alert, al Qaeda members dispersed with their families, security was increased, and Bin Ladin disappeared for about 30 days, until the alert was canceled.[179]

While the details of the operation were strictly compartmented, by the time of the alert, word had begun to spread that an attack against the United States was coming. KSM notes that it was generally well known by the summer of 2001 that he was planning some kind of operation against the United States. Many were even aware that he had been preparing operatives to go to the United States, leading some to conclude that al Qaeda was planning a near-term attack on U.S. soil. Moreover, Bin Ladin had made several remarks that summer hinting at an upcoming attack and generating rumors throughout the worldwide jihadist community. Bin Ladin routinely told important visitors to expect significant attacks against U.S. interests soon and, during a speech at the al Faruq camp, exhorted trainees to pray for the success of an attack involving 20 martyrs. Others have confirmed hearing indications of an impending attack and have verified that such news, albeit without specific details, had spread across al Qaeda.[180]

Although Bin Ladin's top priority apparently was to attack the United States, others had a different view. The Taliban leaders put their main emphasis on the year's military offensive against the Northern Alliance, an offensive that ordinarily would begin in the late spring or summer. They certainly hoped that this year's offensive would finally finish off their old enemies, driving them from Afghanistan. From the Taliban's perspective, an attack against the United States might be counterproductive. It might draw the Americans into the war against them, just when final victory seemed within their grasp.[181]

There is evidence that Mullah Omar initially opposed a major al Qaeda operation directly against the United States in 2001. Furthermore, by July, with word spreading of a coming attack, a schism emerged among the senior leadership of al Qaeda. Several senior members reportedly agreed with Mullah Omar. Those who reportedly sided with Bin Ladin included Atef, Sulayman Abu Ghayth, and KSM. But those said to have opposed him were weighty figures in the organization—including Abu Hafs the Mauritanian, Sheikh Saeed al Masri, and Sayf al Adl. One senior al Qaeda operative claims to recall Bin Ladin arguing that attacks against the United States needed to be carried out immediately to support insurgency in the Israeli-occupied territories and protest the presence of U.S. forces in Saudi Arabia. Beyond these rhetorical appeals, Bin Ladin also reportedly thought an attack against the United States would benefit al Qaeda by attracting more suicide operatives, eliciting greater donations, and increasing the number of sympathizers willing to provide logistical assistance.[182]

Mullah Omar is reported to have opposed this course of action for ideological reasons rather than out of fear of U.S. retaliation. He is said to have preferred for al Qaeda to attack Jews, not necessarily the United States. KSM contends that Omar faced pressure from the Pakistani government to keep al Qaeda from engaging in operations outside Afghanistan. Al Qaeda's chief financial manager, Sheikh Saeed, argued that al Qaeda should defer to the Taliban's wishes. Another source says that Sheikh Saeed opposed the operation, both out of deference to Omar and because he feared the U.S. response to an attack. Abu Hafs the Mauritanian reportedly even wrote Bin Ladin a message basing opposition to the attacks on the Qur'an.[183]

According to KSM, in late August, when the operation was fully planned, Bin Ladin formally notified the al Qaeda Shura Council that a major attack against the United States would take place in the coming weeks. When some council members objected, Bin Ladin countered that Mullah Omar lacked authority to prevent al Qaeda from conducting jihad outside Afghanistan. Though most of the Shura Council reportedly disagreed, Bin Ladin persisted. The attacks went forward.[184]

The story of dissension within al Qaeda regarding the 9/11 attacks is probably incomplete. The information on which the account is based comes from sources who were not privy to the full scope of al Qaeda and Taliban planning. Bin Ladin and Atef, however, probably would have known, at least, that

- The general Taliban offensive against the Northern Alliance would rely on al Qaeda military support.
- Another significant al Qaeda operation was making progress during the summer—a plot to assassinate the Northern Alliance leader, Ahmed Shah Massoud. The operatives, disguised as journalists, were in Massoud's camp and prepared to kill him sometime in August. Their appointment to see him was delayed.[185]

But on September 9, the Massoud assassination took place. The delayed Taliban offensive against the Northern Alliance was apparently coordinated to begin as soon as he was killed, and it got under way on September 10.[186]

As they deliberated earlier in the year, Bin Ladin and Atef would likely have remembered that Mullah Omar was dependent on them for the Massoud assassination and for vital support in the Taliban military operations. KSM remembers Atef telling him that al Qaeda had an agreement with the Taliban to eliminate Massoud, after which the Taliban would begin an offensive to take over Afghanistan. Atef hoped Massoud's death would also appease the Taliban when the 9/11 attacks happened. There are also some scant indications that Omar may have been reconciled to the 9/11 attacks by the time they occurred.[187]

Moving to Departure Positions

In the days just before 9/11, the hijackers returned leftover funds to al Qaeda and assembled in their departure cities. They sent the excess funds by wire transfer to Hawsawi in the UAE, about $26,000 altogether.[188]

The hijackers targeting American Airlines Flight 77, to depart from Dulles, migrated from New Jersey to Laurel, Maryland, about 20 miles from Washington, D.C. They stayed in a motel during the first week in September and spent time working out at a gym. On the final night before the attacks, they lodged at a hotel in Herndon, Virginia, close to the airport.[189]

Further north, the hijackers targeting United Airlines Flight 93, to depart from Newark, gathered in that city from their base in Florida on September 7. Just after midnight on September 8–9, Jarrah received a speeding ticket in Maryland as he headed north on I-95. He joined the rest of his team at their hotel.[190]

Atta was still busy coordinating the teams. On September 7, he flew from Fort Lauderdale to Baltimore, presumably to meet with the Flight 77 team in Laurel. On September 9, he flew from Baltimore to Boston. By then, Shehhi had arrived there, and Atta was seen with him at his hotel. The next day, Atta picked up Omari at another hotel, and the two drove to Portland, Maine, for reasons that remain unknown. In the early morning hours of September 11, they boarded a commuter flight to Boston to connect to American Airlines Flight 11. The two spent their last night pursuing ordinary activities: making ATM withdrawals, eating pizza, and shopping at a convenience store. Their three fellow hijackers for Flight 11 stayed together in a hotel in Newton, Massachusetts, just outside of Boston.[191]

Shehhi and his team targeting United Airlines Flight 175 from Logan Airport spent their last hours at two Boston hotels.[192] The plan that started with a proposal by KSM in 1996 had evolved to overcome numerous obstacles. Now 19 men waited in nondescript hotel rooms to board four flights the next morning.

8

"THE SYSTEM WAS
BLINKING RED"

8.1 THE SUMMER OF THREAT

As 2001 began, counterterrorism officials were receiving frequent but fragmentary reports about threats. Indeed, there appeared to be possible threats almost everywhere the United States had interests—including at home.

To understand how the escalation in threat reporting was handled in the summer of 2001, it is useful to understand how threat information in general is collected and conveyed. Information is collected through several methods, including signals intelligence and interviews of human sources, and gathered into intelligence reports. Depending on the source and nature of the reporting, these reports may be highly classified—and therefore tightly held—or less sensitive and widely disseminated to state and local law enforcement agencies. Threat reporting must be disseminated, either through individual reports or through threat advisories. Such advisories, intended to alert their recipients, may address a specific threat or be a general warning.

Because the amount of reporting is so voluminous, only a select fraction can be chosen for briefing the president and senior officials. During 2001, Director of Central Intelligence George Tenet was briefed regularly regarding threats and other operational information relating to Usama Bin Ladin.[1] He in turn met daily with President Bush, who was briefed by the CIA through what is known as the President's Daily Brief (PDB). Each PDB consists of a series of six to eight relatively short articles or briefs covering a broad array of topics; CIA staff decides which subjects are the most important on any given day. There were more than 40 intelligence articles in the PDBs from January 20 to September 10, 2001, that related to Bin Ladin. The PDB is considered highly sensitive and is distributed to only a handful of high-level officials.[2]

The Senior Executive Intelligence Brief (SEIB), distributed to a broader group of officials, has a similar format and generally covers the same subjects as the PDB. It usually contains less information so as to protect sources and methods. Like their predecessors, the Attorney General, the FBI Director, and Richard Clarke, the National Security Council (NSC) counterterrorism coordinator, all received the SEIB, not the PDB.[3] Clarke and his staff had extensive access to terrorism reporting, but they did not have access to internal, nondisseminated information at the National Security Agency (NSA), CIA, or FBI.

The Drumbeat Begins

In the spring of 2001, the level of reporting on terrorist threats and planned attacks increased dramatically to its highest level since the millennium alert. At the end of March, the intelligence community disseminated a terrorist threat advisory, indicating a heightened threat of Sunni extremist terrorist attacks against U.S. facilities, personnel, and other interests.[4]

On March 23, in connection with discussions about possibly reopening Pennsylvania Avenue in front of the White House, Clarke warned National Security Advisor Condoleezza Rice that domestic or foreign terrorists might use a truck bomb—their "weapon of choice"—on Pennsylvania Avenue. That would result, he said, in the destruction of the West Wing and parts of the residence.[5] He also told her that he thought there were terrorist cells within the United States, including al Qaeda.

The next week, Rice was briefed on the activities of Abu Zubaydah and on CIA efforts to locate him. As pointed out in chapter 6, Abu Zubaydah had been a major figure in the millennium plots. Over the next few weeks, the CIA repeatedly issued warnings—including calls from DCI Tenet to Clarke—that Abu Zubaydah was planning an operation in the near future. One report cited a source indicating that Abu Zubaydah was planning an attack in a country that CIA analysts thought might be Israel, or perhaps Saudi Arabia or India. Clarke relayed these reports to Rice.[6]

In response to these threats, the FBI sent a message to all its field offices on April 13, summarizing reporting to date. It asked the offices to task all resources, including human sources and electronic databases, for any information pertaining to "current operational activities relating to Sunni extremism." It did not suggest that there was a domestic threat.[7]

The interagency Counterterrorism Security Group (CSG) that Clarke chaired discussed the Abu Zubaydah reports on April 19. The next day, a briefing to top officials reported "Bin Ladin planning multiple operations." When the deputies discussed al Qaeda policy on April 30, they began with a briefing on the threat.[8]

In May 2001, the drumbeat of reporting grew louder with reports to top officials that "Bin Ladin public profile may presage attack" and "Bin Ladin network's plans advancing." In early May, a walk-in to the FBI claimed there was a plan to launch attacks on London, Boston, and New York. Attorney General John Ashcroft was briefed by the CIA on May 15 regarding al Qaeda generally and the current threat reporting specifically. The next day brought a report that a phone call to a U.S. embassy had warned that Bin Ladin supporters were planning an attack in the United States using "high explosives." On May 17, based on the previous day's report, the first item on the CSG's agenda was "UBL: Operation Planned in U.S."[9] The anonymous caller's tip could not be corroborated.

Late May brought reports of a possible hostage plot against Americans abroad to force the release of prisoners, including Sheikh Omar Abdel Rahman, the "Blind Sheikh," who was serving a life sentence for his role in the 1993 plot to blow up sites in New York City. The reporting noted that operatives might opt to hijack an aircraft or storm a U.S. embassy. This report led to a Federal Aviation Administration (FAA) information circular to airlines noting the potential for "an airline hijacking to free terrorists incarcerated in the United States." Other reporting mentioned that Abu Zubaydah was planning an attack, possibly against Israel, and expected to carry out several more if things went well. On May 24 alone, counterterrorism officials grappled with reports alleging plots in Yemen and Italy, as well as a report about a cell in Canada that an anonymous caller had claimed might be planning an attack against the United States.[10]

Reports similar to many of these were made available to President Bush in morning intelligence briefings with DCI Tenet, usually attended by Vice President Dick Cheney and National Security Advisor Rice. While these briefings discussed general threats to attack America and American interests, the specific threats mentioned in these briefings were all overseas.

On May 29, Clarke suggested that Rice ask DCI Tenet what more the United States could do to stop Abu Zubaydah from launching "a series of major terrorist attacks," probably on Israeli targets, but possibly on U.S. facilities. Clarke wrote to Rice and her deputy, Stephen Hadley, "When these attacks occur, as they likely will, we will wonder what more we could have done to stop them." In May, CIA Counterterrorist Center (CTC) Chief Cofer Black told Rice that the current threat level was a 7 on a scale of 1 to 10, as compared to an 8 during the millennium.[11]

High Probability of Near-Term "Spectacular" Attacks

Threat reports surged in June and July, reaching an even higher peak of urgency. The summer threats seemed to be focused on Saudi Arabia, Israel, Bahrain, Kuwait, Yemen, and possibly Rome, but the danger could be anywhere—including a possible attack on the G-8 summit in Genoa. A June 12 CIA report passing along biographical background information on several terrorists mentioned, in commenting on Khalid Sheikh Mohammed, that he was recruiting people to travel to the United States to meet with colleagues already there so that they might conduct terrorist attacks on Bin Ladin's behalf. On June 22, the CIA notified all its station chiefs about intelligence suggesting a possible al Qaeda suicide attack on a U.S. target over the next few days. DCI Tenet asked that all U.S. ambassadors be briefed.[12]

That same day, the State Department notified all embassies of the terrorist threat and updated its worldwide public warning. In June, the State Department initiated the Visa Express program in Saudi Arabia as a security measure, in order to keep long lines of foreigners away from vulnerable embassy spaces. The program permitted visa applications to be made through travel agencies, instead of directly at the embassy or consulate.[13]

A terrorist threat advisory distributed in late June indicated a high probability of near-term "spectacular" terrorist attacks resulting in numerous casualties. Other reports' titles warned, "Bin Ladin Attacks May be Imminent" and "Bin Ladin and Associates Making Near-Term Threats." The latter reported multiple attacks planned over the coming days, including a "severe blow" against U.S. and Israeli "interests" during the next two weeks.[14]

On June 21, near the height of the threat reporting, U.S. Central Command raised the force protection condition level for U.S. troops in six countries to the highest possible level, Delta. The U.S. Fifth Fleet moved out of its port in Bahrain, and a U.S. Marine Corps exercise in Jordan was halted. U.S. embassies in the Persian Gulf conducted an emergency security review, and the embassy in Yemen was closed. The CSG had foreign emergency response teams, known as FESTs, ready to move on four hours' notice and kept up the terrorism alert posture on a "rolling 24 hour basis."[15]

On June 25, Clarke warned Rice and Hadley that six separate intelligence reports showed al Qaeda personnel warning of a pending attack. An Arabic television station reported Bin Ladin's pleasure with al Qaeda leaders who were saying that the next weeks "will witness important surprises" and that U.S. and Israeli interests will be targeted. Al Qaeda also released a new recruitment and fund-raising tape. Clarke wrote that this was all too sophisticated to be merely a psychological operation to keep the United States on edge, and the CIA agreed. The intelligence reporting consistently described the upcoming attacks as occurring on a calamitous level, indicating that they would cause the world to be in turmoil and that they would consist of possible multiple—but not necessarily simultaneous—attacks.[16]

On June 28, Clarke wrote Rice that the pattern of al Qaeda activity indicating attack planning over the past six weeks "had reached a crescendo." "A series of new reports continue to convince me and analysts at State, CIA, DIA [Defense Intelligence Agency], and NSA that a major terrorist attack or series of attacks is likely in July," he noted. One al Qaeda intelligence report warned that something "very, very, very, very" big was about to happen, and most of Bin Ladin's network was reportedly anticipating the attack. In late June, the CIA ordered all its station chiefs to share information on al Qaeda with their host governments and to push for immediate disruptions of cells.[17]

The headline of a June 30 briefing to top officials was stark: "Bin Ladin Planning High-Profile Attacks." The report stated that Bin Ladin operatives expected near-term attacks to have dramatic consequences of catastrophic proportions. That same day, Saudi Arabia declared its highest level of terror alert. Despite evidence of delays possibly caused by heightened U.S. security, the planning for attacks was continuing.[18]

On July 2, the FBI Counterterrorism Division sent a message to federal agencies and state and local law enforcement agencies summarizing information regarding threats from Bin Ladin. It warned that there was an increased volume of threat reporting, indicating a potential for attacks against U.S. targets abroad from groups "aligned with or sympathetic to Usama Bin Ladin." Despite the general warnings, the message further stated, "The FBI has no information indicating a credible threat of terrorist attack in the United States." However, it went on to emphasize that the possibility of attack in the United States could not be discounted. It also noted that the July 4 holiday might heighten the threats. The report asked recipients to "exercise extreme vigilance" and "report suspicious activities" to the FBI. It did not suggest specific actions that they should take to prevent attacks.[19]

Disruption operations against al Qaeda–affiliated cells were launched involving 20 countries. Several terrorist operatives were detained by foreign governments, possibly disrupting operations in the Gulf and Italy and perhaps averting attacks against two or three U.S. embassies. Clarke and others told us of a particular concern about possible attacks on the Fourth of July. After it passed uneventfully, the CSG decided to maintain the alert.[20]

To enlist more international help, Vice President Cheney contacted Saudi Crown Prince Abdullah on July 5. Hadley apparently called European counterparts, while Clarke worked with senior officials in the Gulf. In late July, because of threats, Italy closed the airspace over Genoa and mounted antiaircraft batteries at the Genoa airport during the G-8 summit, which President Bush attended.[21]

At home, the CSG arranged for the CIA to brief intelligence and security officials from several domestic agencies. On July 5, representatives from the Immigration and Naturalization Service (INS), the FAA, the Coast Guard, the Secret Service, Customs, the CIA, and the FBI met with Clarke to discuss the current threat. Attendees report that they were told not to disseminate the threat information they received at the meeting. They interpreted this direction to mean that although they could brief their superiors, they could not send out advisories to the field. An NSC official recalls a somewhat different emphasis, saying that attendees were asked to take the information back to their home agencies and "do what you can" with it, subject to classification and distribution restrictions. A representative from the INS asked for a summary of the information that she could share with field offices. She never received one.[22]

That same day, the CIA briefed Attorney General Ashcroft on the al Qaeda threat, warning that a significant terrorist attack was imminent. Ashcroft was told that preparations for multiple attacks were in late stages or already complete and that little additional warning could be expected. The briefing addressed only threats outside the United States.[23]

The next day, the CIA representative told the CSG that al Qaeda members believed the upcoming attack would be "spectacular," qualitatively different from anything they had done to date.[24]

Apparently as a result of the July 5 meeting with Clarke, the interagency committee on federal building security was tasked to examine security measures. This committee met on July 9, when 37 officials from 27 agencies and organizations were briefed on the "current threat level" in the United States. They were told that not only the threat reports from abroad but also the recent convictions in the East Africa bombings trial, the conviction of Ahmed Ressam, and the just-returned Khobar Towers indictments reinforced the need to "exercise extreme vigilance." Attendees were expected to determine whether their respective agencies needed enhanced security measures.[25]

On July 18, 2001, the State Department provided a warning to the public regarding possible terrorist attacks in the Arabian Peninsula.[26]

Acting FBI Director Thomas Pickard told us he had one of his periodic conference calls with all special agents in charge on July 19. He said one of the items he mentioned was the need, in light of increased threat reporting, to have evidence response teams ready to move at a moment's notice, in case of an attack.[27] He did not task field offices to try to determine whether any plots were being considered within the United States or to take any action to disrupt any such plots.

In mid-July, reporting started to indicate that Bin Ladin's plans had been delayed, maybe for as long as two months, but not abandoned. On July 23, the lead item for CSG discussion was still the al Qaeda threat, and it included mention of suspected terrorist travel to the United States.[28]

On July 31, an FAA circular appeared alerting the aviation community to "reports of possible near-term terrorist operations . . . particularly on the Arabian Peninsula and/or Israel." It stated that the FAA had no credible evidence of specific plans to attack U.S. civil aviation, though it noted that some of the "currently active" terrorist groups were known to "plan and train for hijackings" and were able to build and conceal sophisticated explosive devices in luggage and consumer products.[29]

Tenet told us that in his world "the system was blinking red." By late July, Tenet said, it could not "get any worse."[30] Not everyone was convinced. Some asked whether all these threats might just be deception. On June 30, the SEIB contained an article titled "Bin Ladin Threats Are Real." Yet Hadley told Tenet in July that Deputy Secretary of Defense Paul Wolfowitz questioned the reporting. Perhaps Bin Ladin was trying to study U.S. reactions. Tenet replied that he had already addressed the Defense Department's questions on this point; the reporting was convincing. To give a sense of his anxiety at the time, one senior official in the Counterterrorist Center told us that he and a colleague were considering resigning in order to go public with their concerns.[31]

The Calm Before the Storm

On July 27, Clarke informed Rice and Hadley that the spike in intelligence about a near-term al Qaeda attack had stopped. He urged keeping readiness high during the August vacation period, warning that another report suggested an attack had just been postponed for a few months "but will still happen."[32]

On August 1, the FBI issued an advisory that in light of the increased volume of threat reporting and the upcoming anniversary of the East Africa embassy bombings, increased attention should be paid to security planning. It noted that although most of the reporting indicated a potential for attacks on U.S. interests abroad, the possibility of an attack in the United States could not be discounted.[33]

On August 3, the intelligence community issued an advisory concluding that the threat of impending al Qaeda attacks would likely continue indefinitely. Citing threats in the Arabian Peninsula, Jordan, Israel, and Europe, the advisory suggested that al Qaeda was lying in wait and searching for gaps in security before moving forward with the planned attacks.[34]

During the spring and summer of 2001, President Bush had on several occasions asked his briefers whether any of the threats pointed to the United States. Reflecting on these questions, the CIA decided to write a briefing article summarizing its understanding of this danger. Two CIA analysts involved in preparing this briefing article believed it represented an opportunity to communicate their view that the threat of a Bin Ladin attack in the United States remained both current and serious.[35] The result was an article in the August 6 Presidential Daily Brief titled "Bin Ladin Determined to Strike in US." It was the 36th PDB item briefed so far that year that related to Bin Ladin or al Qaeda, and the first devoted to the possibility of an attack in the United States.

The President told us the August 6 report was historical in nature. President Bush said the article told him that al Qaeda was dangerous, which he said he had known since he had become President. The President said Bin Ladin had long been talking about his desire to attack America. He recalled some operational data on the FBI, and remembered thinking it was heartening that 70 investigations were under way. As best he could recollect, Rice had mentioned that the Yemenis' surveillance of a federal building in New York had been looked into in May and June, but there was no actionable intelligence.

He did not recall discussing the August 6 report with the Attorney General or whether Rice had done so. He said that if his advisers had told him there was a cell in the United States, they would have moved to take care of it. That never happened.[36]

Although the following day's SEIB repeated the title of this PDB, it did not contain the reference to hijackings, the alert in New York, the alleged casing

The following is the text of an item from the Presidential Daily Brief received by President George W. Bush on August 6, 2001.[37] Redacted material is indicated by brackets.

Bin Ladin Determined To Strike in US

Clandestine, foreign government, and media reports indicate Bin Ladin since 1997 has wanted to conduct terrorist attacks in the US. Bin Ladin implied in US television interviews in 1997 and 1998 that his followers would follow the example of World Trade Center bomber Ramzi Yousef and "bring the fighting to America."

After US missile strikes on his base in Afghanistan in 1998, Bin Ladin told followers he wanted to retaliate in Washington, according to a [—] service.

An Egyptian Islamic Jihad (EIJ) operative told an [—] service at the same time that Bin Ladin was planning to exploit the operative's access to the US to mount a terrorist strike.

The millennium plotting in Canada in 1999 may have been part of Bin Ladin's first serious attempt to implement a terrorist strike in the US. Convicted plotter Ahmed Ressam has told the FBI that he conceived the idea to attack Los Angeles International Airport himself, but that Bin Ladin lieutenant Abu Zubaydah encouraged him and helped facilitate the operation. Ressam also said that in 1998 Abu Zubaydah was planning his own US attack.

Ressam says Bin Ladin was aware of the Los Angeles operation.

Although Bin Ladin has not succeeded, his attacks against the US Embassies in Kenya and Tanzania in 1998 demonstrate that he prepares operations years in advance and is not deterred by setbacks. Bin Ladin associates surveilled our Embassies in Nairobi and Dar es Salaam as early as 1993, and some members of the Nairobi cell planning the bombings were arrested and deported in 1997.

Al-Qa'ida members—including some who are US citizens—have resided in or traveled to the US for years, and the group apparently maintains a support structure that could aid attacks. Two al-Qua'da members found guilty in the conspiracy to bomb our embassies in East Africa were US citizens, and a senior EIJ member lived in California in the mid-1990s.

A clandestine source said in 1998 that a Bin Ladin cell in New York was recruiting Muslim-American youth for attacks.

We have not been able to corroborate some of the more sensational threat reporting, such as that from a [—] service in 1998 saying that Bin Ladin wanted to hijack a US aircraft to gain the release of "Blind Shaykh" 'Umar 'Abd al-Rahman and other US-held extremists.

Nevertheless, FBI information since that time indicates patterns of suspicious activity in this country consistent with preparations for hijackings or other types of attacks, including recent surveillance of federal buildings in New York.

The FBI is conducting approximately 70 full field investigations throughout the US that it considers Bin Ladin-related. CIA and the FBI are investigating a call to our Embassy in the UAE in May saying that a group of Bin Ladin supporters was in the US planning attacks with explosives.

of buildings in New York, the threat phoned in to the embassy, or the fact that the FBI had approximately 70 ongoing bin Ladin–related investigations.[38] No CSG or other NSC meeting was held to discuss the possible threat of a strike in the United States as a result of this report.

Late in the month, a foreign service reported that Abu Zubaydah was considering mounting terrorist attacks in the United States, after postponing possible operations in Europe. No targets, timing, or method of attack were provided.[39]

We have found no indication of any further discussion before September 11 among the President and his top advisers of the possibility of a threat of an al Qaeda attack in the United States. DCI Tenet visited President Bush in Crawford, Texas, on August 17 and participated in PDB briefings of the President between August 31 (after the President had returned to Washington) and September 10. But Tenet does not recall any discussions with the President of the domestic threat during this period.[40]

Most of the intelligence community recognized in the summer of 2001 that the number and severity of threat reports were unprecedented. Many officials told us that they knew something terrible was planned, and they were desperate to stop it. Despite their large number, the threats received contained few specifics regarding time, place, method, or target. Most suggested that attacks were planned against targets overseas; others indicated threats against unspecified "U.S. interests." We cannot say for certain whether these reports, as dramatic as they were, related to the 9/11 attacks.

Government Response to the Threats

National Security Advisor Rice told us that the CSG was the "nerve center" for running the crisis, although other senior officials were involved over the course of the summer. In addition to his daily meetings with President Bush, and weekly meetings to go over other issues with Rice, Tenet was speaking regularly with Secretary of State Colin Powell and Secretary of Defense Donald Rumsfeld. The foreign policy principals routinely talked on the telephone every day on a variety of topics.[41]

Hadley told us that before 9/11, he and Rice did not feel they had the job of coordinating domestic agencies. They felt that Clarke and the CSG (part of the NSC) were the NSC's bridge between foreign and domestic threats.[42]

There was a clear disparity in the levels of response to foreign versus domestic threats. Numerous actions were taken overseas to disrupt possible attacks—enlisting foreign partners to upset terrorist plans, closing embassies, moving military assets out of the way of possible harm. Far less was done domestically—in part, surely, because to the extent that specifics did exist, they pertained to threats overseas. As noted earlier, a threat against the embassy in Yemen quickly resulted in its closing. Possible domestic threats were more vague. When reports did not specify where the attacks were to take place, officials presumed that they would again be overseas, though they did not rule out a target in the United States. Each of the FBI threat advisories made this point.[43]

Clarke mentioned to National Security Advisor Rice at least twice that al Qaeda sleeper cells were likely in the United States. In January 2001, Clarke forwarded a strategy paper to Rice warning that al Qaeda had a presence in the United States. He noted that two key al Qaeda members in the Jordanian cell involved in the millennium plot were naturalized U.S. citizens and that one jihadist suspected in the East Africa bombings had "informed the FBI that an extensive network of al Qida 'sleeper agents' currently exists in the US." He added that Ressam's abortive December 1999 attack revealed al Qaeda supporters in the United States.[44] His analysis, however, was based not on new threat reporting but on past experience.

The September 11 attacks fell into the void between the foreign and domestic threats. The foreign intelligence agencies were watching overseas, alert to foreign threats to U.S. interests there. The domestic agencies were waiting for evidence of a domestic threat from sleeper cells within the United States. No one was looking for a foreign threat to domestic targets. The threat that was coming was not from sleeper cells. It was foreign—but from foreigners who had infiltrated into the United States.

A second cause of this disparity in response is that domestic agencies did not know what to do, and no one gave them direction. Cressey told us that the CSG did not tell the agencies how to respond to the threats. He noted that the agencies that were operating overseas did not need direction on how to respond; they had experience with such threats and had a "playbook." In contrast, the domestic agencies did not have a game plan. Neither the NSC (including the CSG) nor anyone else instructed them to create one.[45]

This lack of direction was evident in the July 5 meeting with representatives from the domestic agencies. The briefing focused on overseas threats. The domestic agencies were not questioned about how they planned to address the threat and were not told what was expected of them. Indeed, as noted earlier, they were specifically told they could not issue advisories based on the briefing.[46] The domestic agencies' limited response indicates that they did not perceive a call to action.

Clarke reflected a different perspective in an email to Rice on September 15, 2001. He summarized the steps taken by the CSG to alert domestic agencies to the possibility of an attack in the United States. Clarke concluded that domestic agencies, including the FAA, knew that the CSG believed a major al Qaeda attack was coming and could be in the United States.

Although the FAA had authority to issue security directives mandating new security procedures, none of the few that were released during the summer of 2001 increased security at checkpoints or on board aircraft. The information circulars mostly urged air carriers to "exercise prudence" and be alert. Prior to 9/11, the FAA did present a CD-ROM to air carriers and airport authorities describing the increased threat to civil aviation. The presentation mentioned the possibility of suicide hijackings but said that "fortunately, we have no indication that any group is currently thinking in that direction."[47] The FAA conducted 27 special security briefings for specific air carriers between May 1, 2001, and September 11, 2001. Two of these briefings discussed the hijacking threat overseas. None discussed the possibility of suicide hijackings or the use of aircraft as weapons. No new security measures were instituted.[48]

Rice told us she understood that the FBI had tasked its 56 U.S. field offices to increase surveillance of suspected terrorists and to reach out to informants who might have information about terrorist plots. An NSC staff document at the time describes such a tasking as having occurred in late June but does not indicate whether it was generated by the NSC or the FBI. Other than the previously described April 13 communication sent to all FBI field offices, however, the FBI could not find any record of having received such a directive. The April 13 document asking field offices to gather information on Sunni extremism did not mention any possible threat within the United States and did not order surveillance of suspected operatives. The NSC did not specify what the FBI's directives should contain and did not review what had been issued earlier.[49]

Acting FBI Director Pickard told us that in addition to his July 19 conference call, he mentioned the heightened terrorist threat in individual calls with the special agents in charge of field offices during their annual performance review discussions. In speaking with agents around the country, we found little evidence that any such concerns had reached FBI personnel beyond the New York Field Office.[50]

The head of counterterrorism at the FBI, Dale Watson, said he had many discussions about possible attacks with Cofer Black at the CIA. They had expected an attack on July 4. Watson said he felt deeply that something was going to happen. But he told us the threat information was "nebulous." He wished he had known more. He wished he had had "500 analysts looking at Usama Bin Ladin threat information instead of two."[51]

Attorney General Ashcroft was briefed by the CIA in May and by Pickard in early July about the danger. Pickard said he met with Ashcroft once a week in late June, through July, and twice in August. There is a dispute regarding Ashcroft's interest in Pickard's briefings about the terrorist threat situation. Pickard told us that after two such briefings Ashcroft told him that he did not want to hear about the threats anymore. Ashcroft denies Pickard's charge. Pickard says he continued to present terrorism information during further briefings that summer, but nothing further on the "chatter" the U.S. government was receiving.[52]

The Attorney General told us he asked Pickard whether there was intelligence about attacks in the United States and that Pickard said no. Pickard said he replied that he could not assure Ashcroft that there would be no attacks in the United States, although the reports of threats were related to overseas targets. Ashcroft said he therefore assumed the FBI was doing what it needed to do. He acknowledged that in retrospect, this was a dangerous assumption. He did not ask the FBI what it was doing in response to the threats and did not task it to take any specific action. He also did not direct the INS, then still part of the Department of Justice, to take any specific action.[53]

In sum, the domestic agencies never mobilized in response to the threat. They did not have direction, and did not have a plan to institute. The borders were not hardened. Transportation systems were not fortified. Electronic surveillance was not targeted against a domestic threat.[54] State and local law enforcement were not marshaled to augment the FBI's efforts. The public was not warned.

The terrorists exploited deep institutional failings within our government. The question is whether extra vigilance might have turned up an opportunity to disrupt the plot. As seen in chapter 7, al Qaeda's operatives made mistakes. At least two such mistakes created opportunities during 2001, especially in late August.

8.2 LATE LEADS—MIHDHAR, MOUSSAOUI, AND KSM

In chapter 6 we discussed how intelligence agencies successfully detected some of the early travel in the planes operation, picking up the movements of Khalid al Mihdhar and identifying him, and seeing his travel converge with someone they perhaps could have identified but did not—Nawaf al Hazmi—as well as with less easily identifiable people such as Khallad and Abu Bara. These observations occurred in December 1999 and January 2000. The trail had been lost in January 2000 without a clear realization that it had been lost, and without much effort to pick it up again. Nor had the CIA placed Mihdhar on the State Department's watchlist for suspected terrorists, so that either an embassy or a port of entry might take note if Mihdhar showed up again.

On four occasions in 2001, the CIA, the FBI, or both had apparent opportunities to refocus on the significance of Hazmi and Mihdhar and reinvigorate the search for them. After reviewing those episodes we will turn to the handling of the Moussaoui case and some late leads regarding Khalid Sheikh Mohammed.

January 2001: Identification of Khallad

Almost one year after the original trail had been lost in Bangkok, the FBI and the CIA were working on the investigation of the *Cole* bombing. They learned of the link between a captured conspirator and a person called "Khallad." They also learned that Khallad was a senior security official for Bin Ladin who had helped direct the bombing (we introduced Khallad in chapter 5, and returned to his role in the *Cole* bombing in chapter 6).[55]

One of the members of the FBI's investigative team in Yemen realized that he had heard of Khallad before, from a joint FBI/CIA source four months earlier. The FBI agent obtained from a foreign government a photo of the person believed to have directed the *Cole* bombing. It was shown to the source, and he confirmed that the man in that photograph was the same Khallad he had described.[56]

In December 2000, on the basis of some links associated with Khalid al Mihdhar, the CIA's Bin Ladin unit speculated that Khallad and Khalid al Mihdhar might be one and the same.[57]

The CIA asked that a Kuala Lumpur surveillance photo of Mihdhar be shown to the joint source who had identified Khallad. In early January 2001, two photographs from the Kuala Lumpur meeting were shown to the source. One was a known photograph of Mihdhar, the other a photograph of a then unknown subject. The source did not recognize Mihdhar. But he indicated he was 90 percent certain that the other individual was Khallad.[58]

This meant that Khallad and Mihdhar were two different people. It also meant that there was a link between Khallad and Mihdhar, making Mihdhar seem even more suspicious.[59] Yet we found no effort by the CIA to renew the long-abandoned search for Mihdhar or his travel companions.

In addition, we found that the CIA did not notify the FBI of this identification. DCI Tenet and Cofer Black testified before Congress's Joint Inquiry into 9/11 that the FBI had access to this identification from the beginning. But drawing on an extensive record, including documents that were not available to the CIA personnel who drafted that testimony, we conclude this was not the case. The FBI's primary *Cole* investigators had no knowledge that Khallad had been in Kuala Lumpur with Mihdhar and others until after the September 11 attacks. Because the FBI had not been informed in January 2000 about Mihdhar's possession of a U.S. visa, it had not then started looking for him in the United States. Because it did not know of the links between Khallad and Mihdhar, it did not start looking for him in January 2001.[60]

This incident is an example of how day-to-day gaps in information sharing can emerge even when there is mutual goodwill. The information was from a joint FBI/CIA source who spoke essentially no English and whose languages were not understood by the FBI agent on the scene overseas. Issues of travel and security necessarily kept short the amount of time spent with the source. As a result, the CIA officer usually did not translate either questions or answers for his FBI colleague and friend.[61]

For interviews without simultaneous translation, the FBI agent on the scene received copies of the reports that the CIA disseminated to other agencies regarding the interviews. But he was not given access to the CIA's internal operational reports, which contained more detail. It was there—in reporting to which FBI investigators did not have access—that information regarding the January 2001 identification of Khallad appeared. The CIA officer does not recall this particular identification and thus cannot say why it was not shared with his FBI colleague. He might not have understood the possible significance of the new identification.[62]

In June 2000, Mihdhar left California and returned to Yemen. It is possible that if, in January 2001, the CIA had resumed its search for him, placed him on the State Department's TIPOFF watchlist, or provided the FBI with the information, he might have been found—either before or at the time he applied for a new visa in June 2001, or when he returned to the United States on July 4.

Spring 2001: Looking Again at Kuala Lumpur

By mid-May 2001, as the threat reports were surging, a CIA official detailed to the International Terrorism Operations Section at the FBI wondered where the attacks might occur. We will call him "John." Recalling the episode about the Kuala Lumpur travel of Mihdhar and his associates, "John" searched the CIA's databases for information regarding the travel. On May 15, he and an official at the CIA reexamined many of the old cables from early 2000, including the information that Mihdhar had a U.S. visa, and that Hazmi had come to Los Angeles on January 15, 2000.[63]

The CIA official who reviewed the cables took no action regarding them.

"John," however, began a lengthy exchange with a CIA analyst, whom we will call "Dave," to figure out what these cables meant. "John" was aware of how dangerous Khallad was—at one point calling him a "major league killer." He concluded that "something bad was definitely up." Despite the U.S. links evident in this traffic, "John" made no effort to determine whether any of these individuals was in the United States. He did not raise that possibility with his FBI counterpart. He was focused on Malaysia.[64]

"John" described the CIA as an agency that tended to play a "zone defense." He was worrying solely about Southeast Asia, not the United States. In contrast, he told us, the FBI tends to play "man-to-man."[65]

Desk officers at the CIA's Bin Ladin unit did not have "cases" in the same sense as an FBI agent who works an investigation from beginning to end. Thus, when the trail went cold after the Kuala Lumpur meeting in January 2000, the desk officer moved on to different things. By the time the March 2000 cable arrived with information that one of the travelers had flown to Los Angeles, the case officer was no longer responsible for follow-up. While several individuals at the Bin Ladin unit opened the cable when it arrived in March 2000, no action was taken.[66]

The CIA's zone defense concentrated on "where," not "who." Had its information been shared with the FBI, a combination of the CIA's zone defense and the FBI's man-to-man approach might have been productive.

June 2001: The Meeting in New York

"John's" review of the Kuala Lumpur meeting did set off some more sharing of information, getting the attention of an FBI analyst whom we will call "Jane." "Jane" was assigned to the FBI's *Cole* investigation. She knew that another terrorist involved in that operation, Fahd al Quso, had traveled to Bangkok in January 2000 to give money to Khallad.[67]

"Jane" and the CIA analyst, "Dave," had been working together on *Cole*-related issues. Chasing Quso's trail, "Dave" suggested showing some photographs to FBI agents in New York who were working on the *Cole* case and had interviewed Quso.[68]

"John" gave three Kuala Lumpur surveillance pictures to "Jane" to show to the New York agents. She was told that one of the individuals in the photographs was someone named Khalid al Mihdhar. She did not know why the photographs had been taken or why the Kuala Lumpur travel might be significant, and she was not told that someone had identified Khallad in the photographs. When "Jane" did some research in a database for intelligence reports, Intelink, she found the original NSA reports on the planning for the meeting. Because the CIA had not disseminated reports on its tracking of Mihdhar, "Jane" did not pull up any information about Mihdhar's U.S. visa or about travel to the United States by Hazmi or Mihdhar.[69]

"Jane," "Dave," and an FBI analyst who was on detail to the CIA's Bin Ladin unit went to New York on June 11 to meet with the agents about the *Cole* case. "Jane" brought the surveillance pictures. At some point in the meeting she showed the photographs to the agents and asked whether they recognized Quso in any of them. The agents asked questions about the photographs—Why were they taken? Why were these people being followed? Where are the rest of the photographs?[70]

The only information "Jane" had about the meeting—other than the photographs—were the NSA reports that she had found on Intelink. These reports, however, contained caveats that their contents could not be shared with criminal investigators without the permission of the Justice Department's Office of Intelligence Policy and Review (OIPR). Therefore "Jane" concluded that she could not pass on information from those reports to the agents. This decision was potentially significant, because the signals intelligence she did not share linked Mihdhar to a suspected terrorist facility in the Middle East. The agents would have established a link to the suspected facility from their work on the embassy bombings case. This link would have made them very interested in learning more about Mihdhar.[71] The sad irony is that the agents who found the source were being kept from obtaining the fruits of their own work.

"Dave," the CIA analyst, knew more about the Kuala Lumpur meeting. He knew that Mihdhar possessed a U.S. visa, that his visa application indicated that he intended to travel to New York, that Hazmi had traveled to Los Angeles, and that a source had put Mihdhar in the company of Khallad. No one at the meeting asked him what he knew; he did not volunteer anything. He told investigators that as a CIA analyst, he was not authorized to answer FBI questions regarding CIA information. "Jane" said she assumed that if "Dave" knew the answers to questions, he would have volunteered them. The New York agents left the meeting without obtaining information that might have started them looking for Mihdhar.[72]

Mihdhar had been a weak link in al Qaeda's operational planning. He had left the United States in June 2000, a mistake KSM realized could endanger the entire plan—for to continue with the operation, Mihdhar would have to travel to the United States again. And unlike other operatives, Mihdhar was not "clean": he had jihadist connections. It was just such connections that had brought him to the attention of U.S. officials.

Nevertheless, in this case KSM's fears were not realized. Mihdhar received a new U.S. visa two days after the CIA-FBI meeting in New York. He flew to New York City on July 4. No one was looking for him.

August 2001: The Search for Mihdhar and Hazmi Begins and Fails
During the summer of 2001 "John," following a good instinct but not as part of any formal assignment, asked "Mary," an FBI analyst detailed to the CIA's Bin Ladin unit, to review all the Kuala Lumpur materials one more time. She had been at the New York meeting with "Jane" and "Dave" but had not

looked into the issues yet herself. "John" asked her to do the research in her free time.[73]

"Mary" began her work on July 24. That day, she found the cable reporting that Mihdhar had a visa to the United States. A week later, she found the cable reporting that Mihdhar's visa application—what was later discovered to be his first application—listed New York as his destination. On August 21, she located the March 2000 cable that "noted with interest" that Hazmi had flown to Los Angeles in January 2000. She immediately grasped the significance of this information.[74]

"Mary" and "Jane" promptly met with an INS representative at FBI head-quarters. On August 22, the INS told them that Mihdhar had entered the United States on January 15, 2000, and again on July 4, 2001. "Jane" and "Mary" also learned that there was no record that Hazmi had left the country since January 2000, and they assumed he had left with Mihdhar in June 2000. They decided that if Mihdhar was in the United States, he should be found.[75]

They divided up the work. "Mary" asked the Bin Ladin unit to draft a cable requesting that Mihdhar and Hazmi be put on the TIPOFF watchlist. Both Hazmi and Mihdhar were added to this watchlist on August 24.[76]

"Jane" took responsibility for the search effort inside the United States. As the information indicated that Mihdhar had last arrived in New York, she began drafting what is known as a lead for the FBI's New York Field Office. A lead relays information from one part of the FBI to another and requests that a particular action be taken. She called an agent in New York to give him a "heads-up" on the matter, but her draft lead was not sent until August 28. Her email told the New York agent that she wanted him to get started as soon as possible, but she labeled the lead as "Routine"—a designation that informs the receiving office that it has 30 days to respond.[77]

The agent who received the lead forwarded it to his squad supervisor. That same day, the supervisor forwarded the lead to an intelligence agent to open an intelligence case—an agent who thus was behind "the wall" keeping FBI intelligence information from being shared with criminal prosecutors. He also sent it to the *Cole* case agents and an agent who had spent significant time in Malaysia searching for another Khalid: Khalid Sheikh Mohammad.[78]

The suggested goal of the investigation was to locate Mihdhar, determine his contacts and reasons for being in the United States, and possibly conduct an interview. Before sending the lead, "Jane" had discussed it with "John," the CIA official on detail to the FBI. She had also checked with the acting head of the FBI's Bin Ladin unit. The discussion seems to have been limited to whether the search should be classified as an intelligence investigation or as a criminal one. It appears that no one informed higher levels of management in either the FBI or CIA about the case.[79] There is no evidence that the lead, or the search for these terrorist suspects, was substantively discussed at any level above deputy chief of a section within the Counterterrorism Division at FBI headquarters.

One of the *Cole* case agents read the lead with interest, and contacted "Jane" to obtain more information. "Jane" argued, however, that because the agent was designated a "criminal" FBI agent, not an intelligence FBI agent, the wall kept him from participating in any search for Mihdhar. In fact, she felt he had to destroy his copy of the lead because it contained NSA information from reports that included caveats ordering that the information not be shared without OIPR's permission. The agent asked "Jane" to get an opinion from the FBI's National Security Law Unit (NSLU) on whether he could open a criminal case on Mihdhar.[80]

"Jane" sent an email to the *Cole* case agent explaining that according to the NSLU, the case could be opened only as an intelligence matter, and that if Mihdhar was found, only designated intelligence agents could conduct or even be present at any interview. She appears to have misunderstood the complex rules that could apply to this situation.[81]

The FBI agent angrily responded:

Whatever has happened to this—someday someone will die—and wall or not—the public will not understand why we were not more effective and throwing every resource we had at certain "problems."

Let's hope the National Security Law Unit will stand behind their decisions then, especially since the biggest threat to us now, UBL, is getting the most "protection."

"Jane" replied that she was not making up the rules; she claimed that they were in the relevant manual and "ordered by the [FISA] Court and every office of the FBI is required to follow them including FBI NY."[82]

It is now clear that everyone involved was confused about the rules governing the sharing and use of information gathered in intelligence channels. Because Mihdhar was being sought for his possible connection to or knowledge of the *Cole* bombing, he could be investigated or tracked under the existing *Cole* criminal case. No new criminal case was needed for the criminal agent to begin searching for Mihdhar. And as NSA had approved the passage of its information to the criminal agent, he could have conducted a search using all available information. As a result of this confusion, the criminal agents who were knowledgeable about al Qaeda and experienced with criminal investigative techniques, including finding suspects and possible criminal charges, were thus excluded from the search.[83]

The search was assigned to one FBI agent, and it was his very first counterterrorism lead. Because the lead was "routine," he was given 30 days to open an intelligence case and make some unspecified efforts to locate Mihdhar. He started the process a few days later. He checked local New York databases for criminal record and driver's license information and checked the hotel listed on Mihdhar's U.S. entry form. Finally, on September 11, the agent sent a lead to Los Angeles, because Mihdhar had initially arrived in Los Angeles in January 2000.[84]

We believe that if more resources had been applied and a significantly different approach taken, Mihdhar and Hazmi might have been found. They had used their true names in the United States. Still, the investigators would have needed luck as well as skill to find them prior to September 11 even if such searches had begun as early as August 23, when the lead was first drafted.[85]

Many FBI witnesses have suggested that even if Mihdhar had been found, there was nothing the agents could have done except follow him onto the planes. We believe this is incorrect. Both Hazmi and Mihdhar could have been held for immigration violations or as material witnesses in the *Cole* bombing case. Investigation or interrogation of them, and investigation of their travel and financial activities, could have yielded evidence of connections to other participants in the 9/11 plot. The simple fact of their detention could have derailed the plan. In any case, the opportunity did not arise.

Phoenix Memo

The Phoenix memo was investigated thoroughly by the Joint Inquiry and the Department of Justice Inspector General.[86] We will recap it briefly here. In July 2001, an FBI agent in the Phoenix field office sent a memo to FBI headquarters and to two agents on international terrorism squads in the New York Field Office, advising of the "possibility of a coordinated effort by Usama Bin Ladin" to send students to the United States to attend civil aviation schools. The agent based his theory on the "inordinate number of individuals of investigative interest" attending such schools in Arizona.[87]

The agent made four recommendations to FBI headquarters: to compile a list of civil aviation schools, establish liaison with those schools, discuss his theories about Bin Ladin with the intelligence community, and seek authority to obtain visa information on persons applying to flight schools. His recommendations were not acted on. His memo was forwarded to one field office. Managers of the Usama Bin Ladin unit and the Radical Fundamentalist unit at FBI headquarters were addressees, but they did not even see the memo until after September 11. No managers at headquarters saw the memo before September 11, and the New York Field Office took no action.[88]

As its author told investigators, the Phoenix memo was not an alert about suicide pilots. His worry was more about a Pan Am Flight 103 scenario in which explosives were placed on an aircraft. The memo's references to aviation training were broad, including aeronautical engineering.[89] If the memo had been distributed in a timely fashion and its recommendations acted on promptly, we do not believe it would have uncovered the plot. It might well, however, have sensitized the FBI so that it might have taken the Moussaoui matter more seriously the next month.

Zacarias Moussaoui

On August 15, 2001, the Minneapolis FBI Field Office initiated an intelligence investigation on Zacarias Moussaoui. As mentioned in chapter 7, he had entered the United States in February 2001, and had begun flight lessons at Airman Flight School in Norman, Oklahoma. He resumed his training at the Pan Am International Flight Academy in Eagan, Minnesota, starting on August 13. He had none of the usual qualifications for flight training on Pan Am's Boeing 747 flight simulators. He said he did not intend to become a commercial pilot but wanted the training as an "ego boosting thing." Moussaoui stood out because, with little knowledge of flying, he wanted to learn how to "take off and land" a Boeing 747.[90]

The agent in Minneapolis quickly learned that Moussaoui possessed jihadist beliefs. Moreover, Moussaoui had $32,000 in a bank account but did not provide a plausible explanation for this sum of money. He had traveled to Pakistan but became agitated when asked if he had traveled to nearby countries while in Pakistan (Pakistan was the customary route to the training camps in Afghanistan). He planned to receive martial arts training, and intended to purchase a global positioning receiver. The agent also noted that Moussaoui became extremely agitated whenever he was questioned regarding his religious beliefs. The agent concluded that Moussaoui was "an Islamic extremist preparing for some future act in furtherance of radical fundamentalist goals." He also believed Moussaoui's plan was related to his flight training.[91]

Moussaoui can be seen as an al Qaeda mistake and a missed opportunity. An apparently unreliable operative, he had fallen into the hands of the FBI. As discussed in chapter 7, Moussaoui had been in contact with and received money from Ramzi Binalshibh. If Moussaoui had been connected to al Qaeda, questions should instantly have arisen about a possible al Qaeda plot that involved piloting airliners, a possibility that had never been seriously analyzed by the intelligence community.

The FBI agent who handled the case in conjunction with the INS representative on the Minneapolis Joint Terrorism Task Force suspected that Moussaoui might be planning to hijack a plane. Minneapolis and FBI headquarters debated whether Moussaoui should be arrested immediately or surveilled to obtain additional information. Because it was not clear whether Moussaoui could be imprisoned, the FBI case agent decided the most important thing was to prevent Moussaoui from obtaining any further training that he could use to carry out a potential attack.[92]

As a French national who had overstayed his visa, Moussaoui could be detained immediately. The INS arrested Moussaoui on the immigration violation. A deportation order was signed on August 17, 2001.[93]

The agents in Minnesota were concerned that the U.S. Attorney's Office in Minneapolis would find insufficient probable cause of a crime to obtain a criminal warrant to search Moussaoui's laptop computer.[94] Agents at FBI headquarters believed there was insufficient probable cause. Minneapolis therefore sought a special warrant under the Foreign Intelligence Surveillance Act to conduct the search (we introduced FISA in chapter 3).

To do so, however, the FBI needed to demonstrate probable cause that Moussaoui was an agent of a foreign power, a demonstration that was not required to obtain a criminal warrant but was a statutory requirement for a FISA warrant.[95] The case agent did not have sufficient information to connect Moussaoui to a "foreign power," so he reached out for help, in the United States and overseas.

The FBI agent's August 18 message requested assistance from the FBI legal attaché in Paris. Moussaoui had lived in London, so the Minneapolis agent sought assistance from the legal attaché there as well. By August 24, the Minneapolis agent had also contacted an FBI detailee and a CIA desk officer at the Counterterrorist Center about the case.[96]

The FBI legal attaché's office in Paris first contacted the French government on August 16 or 17, shortly after speaking to the Minneapolis case agent on the telephone. On August 22 and 27, the French provided information that made a connection between Moussaoui and a rebel leader in Chechnya, Ibn al Khattab. This set off a spirited debate between the Minneapolis Field Office, FBI headquarters, and the CIA as to whether the Chechen rebels and Khattab were sufficiently associated with a terrorist organization to constitute a "foreign power" for purposes of the FISA statute. FBI headquarters did not believe this was good enough, and its National Security Law Unit declined to submit a FISA application.[97]

After receiving the written request for assistance, the legal attaché in London had promptly forwarded it to his counterparts in the British government, hand-delivering the request on August 21. On August 24, the CIA also sent a cable to London and Paris regarding "subjects involved in suspicious 747 flight training" that described Moussaoui as a possible "suicide hijacker." On August 28, the CIA sent a request for information to a different service of the British government; this communication warned that Moussaoui might be expelled to Britain by the end of August. The FBI office in London raised the matter briefly with British officials as an aside, after a meeting about a more urgent matter on September 3, and sent the British service a written update on September 5. The case was not handled by the British as a priority amid a large number of other terrorist-related inquiries.[98]

On September 4, the FBI sent a teletype to the CIA, the FAA, the Customs Service, the State Department, the INS, and the Secret Service summarizing the known facts regarding Moussaoui. It did not report the case agent's personal assessment that Moussaoui planned to hijack an airplane. It did contain the FAA's comment that it was not unusual for Middle Easterners to attend flight training schools in the United States.[99]

Although the Minneapolis agents wanted to tell the FAA from the beginning about Moussaoui, FBI headquarters instructed Minneapolis that it could not share the more complete report the case agent had prepared for the FAA. The Minneapolis supervisor sent the case agent in person to the local FAA office to fill in what he thought were gaps in the FBI headquarters teletype.[100] No FAA actions seem to have been taken in response.

There was substantial disagreement between Minneapolis agents and FBI headquarters as to what Moussaoui was planning to do. In one conversation between a Minneapolis supervisor and a headquarters agent, the latter complained that Minneapolis's FISA request was couched in a manner intended to get people "spun up." The supervisor replied that was precisely his intent. He said he was "trying to keep someone from taking a plane and crashing into the World Trade Center." The headquarters agent replied that this was not going to happen and that they did not know if Moussaoui was a terrorist.[101]

There is no evidence that either FBI Acting Director Pickard or Assistant Director for Counterterrorism Dale Watson was briefed on the Moussaoui case prior to 9/11. Michael Rolince, the FBI assistant director heading the Bureau's International Terrorism Operations Section (ITOS), recalled being told about Moussaoui in two passing hallway conversations but only in the context that he might be receiving telephone calls from Minneapolis complaining about how headquarters was handling the matter. He never received such a call. Although the acting special agent in charge of Minneapolis called the ITOS supervisors to discuss the Moussaoui case on August 27, he declined to go up the chain of command at FBI headquarters and call Rolince.[102]

On August 23, DCI Tenet was briefed about the Moussaoui case in a briefing titled "Islamic Extremist Learns to Fly."[103] Tenet was also told that Moussaoui wanted to learn to fly a 747, paid for his training in cash, was interested to learn the doors do not open in flight, and wanted to fly a simulated flight from London to New York. He was told that the FBI had arrested Moussaoui because of a visa overstay and that the CIA was working the case with the FBI. Tenet told us that no connection to al Qaeda was apparent to him at the time. Seeing it as an FBI case, he did not discuss the matter with anyone at the White House or the FBI. No connection was made between Moussaoui's presence in the United States and the threat reporting during the summer of 2001.[104]

On September 11, after the attacks, the FBI office in London renewed their appeal for information about Moussaoui. In response to U.S. requests, the British government supplied some basic biographical information about Moussaoui. The British government informed us that it also immediately tasked intelligence collection facilities for information about Moussaoui. On September 13, the British government received new, sensitive intelligence that Moussaoui had attended an al Qaeda training camp in Afghanistan. It passed this intelligence to the United States on the same day. Had this information been available in late August 2001, the Moussaoui case would almost certainly have received intense, high-level attention.[105]

The FBI also learned after 9/11 that the millennium terrorist Ressam, who

by 2001 was cooperating with investigators, recognized Moussaoui as someone who had been in the Afghan camps.[106] As mentioned above, before 9/11
the FBI agents in Minneapolis had failed to persuade supervisors at headquarters that there was enough evidence to seek a FISA warrant to search Moussaoui's computer hard drive and belongings. Either the British information or
the Ressam identification would have broken the logjam.

A maximum U.S. effort to investigate Moussaoui conceivably could have
unearthed his connections to Binalshibh. Those connections might have
brought investigators to the core of the 9/11 plot. The Binalshibh connection
was recognized shortly after 9/11, though it was not an easy trail to find. Dis-
covering it would have required quick and very substantial cooperation from
the German government, which might well have been difficult to obtain.

However, publicity about Moussaoui's arrest and a possible hijacking threat
might have derailed the plot.[107] With time, the search for Mihdhar and Hazmi
and the investigation of Moussaoui might also have led to a breakthrough that
would have disrupted the plot.

Khalid Sheikh Mohammed

Another late opportunity was presented by a confluence of information
regarding Khalid Sheikh Mohammed received by the intelligence community
in the summer of 2001. The possible links between KSM, Moussaoui, and an
individual only later identified as Ramzi Binalshibh would remain undiscov-
ered, however.

Although we readily equate KSM with al Qaeda today, this was not the case
before 9/11. KSM, who had been indicted in January 1996 for his role in the
Manila air plot, was seen primarily as another freelance terrorist, associated
with Ramzi Yousef. Because the links between KSM and Bin Ladin or al
Qaeda were not recognized at the time, responsibility for KSM remained in
the small Islamic Extremist Branch of the Counterterrorist Center, not in the
Bin Ladin unit.

Moreover, because KSM had already been indicted, he became targeted
for arrest. In 1997, the Counterterrorist Center added a Renditions Branch
to help find wanted fugitives. Responsibility for KSM was transferred to this
branch, which gave the CIA a "man-to-man" focus but was not an analytical unit. When subsequent information came, more critical for analysis than
for tracking, no unit had the job of following up on what the information
might mean.[108]

For example, in September 2000, a source had reported that an individual
named Khalid al-Shaykh al-Ballushi was a key lieutenant in al Qaeda. Al-
Ballushi means "from Baluchistan," and KSM is from Baluchistan. Recognizing the possible significance of this information, the Bin Ladin unit sought
more information. When no information was forthcoming, the Bin Ladin unit

dropped the matter.[109] When additional pieces of the puzzle arrived in the spring and summer of 2001, they were not put together.

The first piece of the puzzle concerned some intriguing information associated with a person known as "Mukhtar" that the CIA had begun analyzing in April 2001. The CIA did not know who Mukhtar was at the time—only that he associated with al Qaeda lieutenant Abu Zubaydah and that, based on the nature of the information, he was evidently involved in planning possible terrorist activities.[110]

The second piece of the puzzle was some alarming information regarding KSM. On June 12, 2001, a CIA report said that "Khaled" was actively recruiting people to travel outside Afghanistan, including to the United States where colleagues were reportedly already in the country to meet them, to carry out terrorist-related activities for Bin Ladin. CIA headquarters presumed from the details of the reporting that this person was Khalid Sheikh Mohammed. In July, the same source was shown a series of photographs and identified a photograph of Khalid Sheikh Mohammed as the Khaled he had previously discussed.[111]

The final piece of the puzzle arrived at the CIA's Bin Ladin unit on August 28 in a cable reporting that KSM's nickname was Mukhtar. No one made the connection to the reports about Mukhtar that had been circulated in the spring. This connection might also have underscored concern about the June reporting that KSM was recruiting terrorists to travel, including to the United States. Only after 9/11 would it be discovered that Muhktar/KSM had communicated with a phone that was used by Binalshibh, and that Binalshibh had used the same phone to communicate with Moussaoui, as discussed in chapter 7. As in the Moussaoui situation already described, the links to Binalshibh might not have been an easy trail to find and would have required substantial cooperation from the German government. But time was short, and running out.[112]

Time Runs Out

As Tenet told us, "the system was blinking red" during the summer of 2001. Officials were alerted across the world. Many were doing everything they possibly could to respond to the threats.

Yet no one working on these late leads in the summer of 2001 connected the case in his or her in-box to the threat reports agitating senior officials and being briefed to the President. Thus, these individual cases did not become national priorities. As the CIA supervisor "John" told us, no one looked at the bigger picture; no analytic work foresaw the lightning that could connect the thundercloud to the ground.[113]

We see little evidence that the progress of the plot was disturbed by any government action. The U.S. government was unable to capitalize on mistakes made by al Qaeda. Time ran out.

9

HEROISM AND
HORROR

9.1 PREPAREDNESS AS OF SEPTEMBER 11

Emergency response is a product of preparedness. On the morning of September 11, 2001, the last best hope for the community of people working in or visiting the World Trade Center rested not with national policymakers but with private firms and local public servants, especially the first responders: fire, police, emergency medical service, and building safety professionals.

Building Preparedness
The World Trade Center. The World Trade Center (WTC) complex was built for the Port Authority of New York and New Jersey. Construction began in 1966, and tenants began to occupy its space in 1970. The Twin Towers came to occupy a unique and symbolic place in the culture of New York City and America.

The WTC actually consisted of seven buildings, including one hotel, spread across 16 acres of land. The buildings were connected by an underground mall (the concourse). The Twin Towers (1 WTC, or the North Tower, and 2 WTC, or the South Tower) were the signature structures, containing 10.4 million square feet of office space. Both towers had 110 stories, were about 1,350 feet high, and were square; each wall measured 208 feet in length. On any given workday, up to 50,000 office workers occupied the towers, and 40,000 people passed through the complex.[1]

Each tower contained three central stairwells, which ran essentially from top to bottom, and 99 elevators. Generally, elevators originating in the lobby ran to "sky lobbies" on higher floors, where additional elevators carried passengers to the tops of the buildings.[2]

Stairwells A and C ran from the 110th floor to the raised mezzanine level of the lobby. Stairwell B ran from the 107th floor to level B6, six floors below ground, and was accessible from the West Street lobby level, which was one

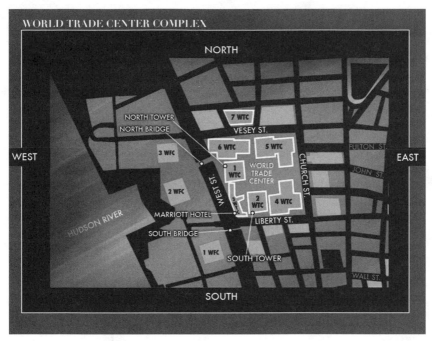

The World Trade Center Complex as of 9/11
Rendering by Marco Crupi

floor below the mezzanine. All three stairwells ran essentially straight up and down, except for two deviations in stairwells A and C where the staircase jutted out toward the perimeter of the building. On the upper and lower boundaries of these deviations were transfer hallways contained within the stairwell proper. Each hallway contained smoke doors to prevent smoke from rising from lower to upper portions of the building; they were kept closed but not locked. Doors leading from tenant space into the stairwells were never kept locked; reentry from the stairwells was generally possible on at least every fourth floor.[3]

Doors leading to the roof were locked. There was no rooftop evacuation plan. The roofs of both the North Tower and the South Tower were sloped and cluttered surfaces with radiation hazards, making them impractical for helicopter landings and as staging areas for civilians. Although the South Tower roof had a helipad, it did not meet 1994 Federal Aviation Administration guidelines.[4]

The 1993 Terrorist Bombing of the WTC and the Port Authority's Response. Unlike most of America, New York City and specifically the World

Trade Center had been the target of terrorist attacks before 9/11. At 12:18 P.M. on February 26, 1993, a 1,500-pound bomb stashed in a rental van was detonated on a parking garage ramp beneath the Twin Towers. The explosion killed six people, injured about 1,000 more, and exposed vulnerabilities in the World Trade Center's and the city's emergency preparedness.[5]

The towers lost power and communications capability. Generators had to be shut down to ensure safety, and elevators stopped. The public-address system and emergency lighting systems failed. The unlit stairwells filled with smoke and were so dark as to be impassable. Rescue efforts by the Fire Department of New York (FDNY) were hampered by the inability of its radios to function in buildings as large as the Twin Towers. The 911 emergency call system was overwhelmed. The general evacuation of the towers' occupants via the stairwells took more than four hours.[6]

Several small groups of people who were physically unable to descend the stairs were evacuated from the roof of the South Tower by New York Police Department (NYPD) helicopters. At least one person was lifted from the North Tower roof by the NYPD in a dangerous helicopter rappel operation— 15 hours after the bombing. General knowledge that these air rescues had occurred appears to have left a number of civilians who worked in the Twin Towers with the false impression that helicopter rescues were part of the WTC evacuation plan and that rescue from the roof was a viable, if not favored, option for those who worked on upper floors. Although they were considered after 1993, helicopter evacuations in fact were not incorporated into the WTC fire safety plan.[7]

To address the problems encountered during the response to the 1993 bombing, the Port Authority spent an initial $100 million to make physical, structural, and technological improvements to the WTC, as well as to enhance its fire safety plan and reorganize and bolster its fire safety and security staffs.[8]

Substantial enhancements were made to power sources and exits. Fluorescent signs and markings were added in and near stairwells. The Port Authority also installed a sophisticated computerized fire alarm system with redundant electronics and control panels, and state-of-the-art fire command stations were placed in the lobby of each tower.[9]

To manage fire emergency preparedness and operations, the Port Authority created the dedicated position of fire safety director. The director supervised a team of deputy fire safety directors, one of whom was on duty at the fire command station in the lobby of each tower at all times. He or she would be responsible for communicating with building occupants during an emergency.[10]

The Port Authority also sought to prepare civilians better for future emergencies. Deputy fire safety directors conducted fire drills at least twice a year, with advance notice to tenants. "Fire safety teams" were selected from among civilian employees on each floor and consisted of a fire warden, deputy fire wardens, and searchers. The standard procedure for fire drills was for fire wardens to lead co-workers in their respective areas to the center of the floor, where they would use the emergency intercom phone to obtain specific information on how to proceed. Some civilians have told us that their evacuation on September 11 was greatly aided by changes and training implemented by the Port Authority in response to the 1993 bombing.[11]

But during these drills, civilians were not directed into the stairwells, or provided with information about their configuration and about the existence of transfer hallways and smoke doors. Neither full nor partial evacuation drills were held. Moreover, participation in drills that were held varied greatly from tenant to tenant. In general, civilians were never told not to evacuate up. The standard fire drill announcement advised participants that in the event of an actual emergency, they would be directed to descend to at least three floors below the fire. Most civilians recall simply being taught to await the instructions that would be provided at the time of an emergency. Civilians were not informed that rooftop evacuations were not part of the evacuation plan, or that doors to the roof were kept locked. The Port Authority acknowledges that it had no protocol for rescuing people trapped above a fire in the towers.[12]

Six weeks before the September 11 attacks, control of the WTC was transferred by net lease to a private developer, Silverstein Properties. Select Port Authority employees were designated to assist with the transition. Others remained on-site but were no longer part of the official chain of command. However, on September 11, most Port Authority World Trade Department employees—including those not on the designated "transition team"— reported to their regular stations to provide assistance throughout the morning. Although Silverstein Properties was in charge of the WTC on September 11, the WTC fire safety plan remained essentially the same.[13]

Preparedness of First Responders
On 9/11, the principal first responders were from the Fire Department of New York, the New York Police Department, the Port Authority Police Department (PAPD), and the Mayor's Office of Emergency Management (OEM).

Port Authority Police Department. On September 11, 2001, the Port Authority of New York and New Jersey Police Department consisted of 1,331 officers, many of whom were trained in fire suppression methods as well as in law enforcement. The PAPD was led by a superintendent. There was a separate PAPD command for each of the Port Authority's nine facilities, including the World Trade Center.[14]

Most Port Authority police commands used ultra-high-frequency radios. Although all the radios were capable of using more than one channel, most PAPD officers used one local channel. The local channels were low-wattage and worked only in the immediate vicinity of that command. The PAPD also had an agencywide channel, but not all commands could access it.[15]

As of September 11, the Port Authority lacked any standard operating procedures to govern how officers from multiple commands would respond to and then be staged and utilized at a major incident at the WTC. In particular, there were no standard operating procedures covering how different commands should communicate via radio during such an incident.

The New York Police Department. The 40,000-officer NYPD was headed by a police commissioner, whose duties were not primarily operational but who retained operational authority. Much of the NYPD's operational activities were run by the chief of department. In the event of a major emergency, a leading role would be played by the Special Operations Division. This division included the Aviation Unit, which provided helicopters for surveys and rescues, and the Emergency Service Unit (ESU), which carried out specialized rescue missions. The NYPD had specific and detailed standard operating procedures for the dispatch of officers to an incident, depending on the incident's magnitude.[16]

The NYPD precincts were divided into 35 different radio zones, with a central radio dispatcher assigned to each. In addition, there were several radio channels for citywide operations. Officers had portable radios with 20 or more available channels, so that the user could respond outside his or her precinct. ESU teams also had these channels but at an operation would use a separate point-to-point channel (which was not monitored by a dispatcher).[17]

The NYPD also supervised the city's 911 emergency call system. Its approximately 1,200 operators, radio dispatchers, and supervisors were civilian employees of the NYPD. They were trained in the rudiments of emergency response. When a 911 call concerned a fire, it was transferred to FDNY dispatch.[18]

The Fire Department of New York. The 11,000-member FDNY was headed by a fire commissioner who, unlike the police commissioner, lacked operational authority. Operations were headed by the chief of department—the sole five-star chief.[19]

The FDNY was organized in nine separate geographic divisions. Each division was further divided into between four to seven battalions. Each battalion contained typically between three and four engine companies and two to four ladder companies. In total, the FDNY had 205 engine companies and 133 ladder companies. On-duty ladder companies consisted of a captain or lieutenant and five firefighters; on-duty engine companies consisted of a captain or lieutenant and normally four firefighters. Ladder companies' primary function was to conduct rescues; engine companies focused on extinguishing fires.[20]

The FDNY's Specialized Operations Command (SOC) contained a limited number of units that were of particular importance in responding to a terrorist attack or other major incident. The department's five rescue companies and seven squad companies performed specialized and highly risky rescue operations.[21]

The logistics of fire operations were directed by Fire Dispatch Operations Division, which had a center in each of the five boroughs. All 911 calls concerning fire emergencies were transferred to FDNY dispatch.[22]

As of September 11, FDNY companies and chiefs responding to a fire used analog, point-to-point radios that had six normal operating channels. Typically, the companies would operate on the same tactical channel, which chiefs on the scene would monitor and use to communicate with the firefighters. Chiefs at a fire operation also would use a separate command channel. Because these point-to-point radios had weak signal strength, communications on them could be heard only by other FDNY personnel in the immediate vicinity. In addition, the FDNY had a dispatch frequency for each of the five boroughs; these were not point-to-point channels and could be monitored from around the city.[23]

The FDNY's radios performed poorly during the 1993 WTC bombing for two reasons. First, the radios signals often did not succeed in penetrating the numerous steel and concrete floors that separated companies attempting to communicate; and second, so many different companies were attempting to use the same point-to-point channel that communications became unintelligible.[24]

The Port Authority installed, at its own expense, a repeater system in 1994 to greatly enhance FDNY radio communications in the difficult high-rise environment of the Twin Towers. The Port Authority recommended leaving the repeater system on at all times. The FDNY requested, however, that the repeater be turned on only when it was actually needed because the channel could cause interference with other FDNY operations in Lower Manhattan. The repeater system was installed at the Port Authority police desk in 5 WTC, to be activated by members of the Port Authority police when the FDNY units responding to the WTC complex so requested. However, in the spring of 2000 the FDNY asked that an activation console for the repeater system be placed instead in the lobby fire safety desk of each of the towers, making FDNY personnel entirely responsible for its activation. The Port Authority complied.[25]

Between 1998 and 2000, fewer people died from fires in New York City than in any three-year period since accurate measurements began in 1946. Firefighter deaths—a total of 22 during the 1990s—compared favorably with the most tranquil periods in the department's history.[26]

Office of Emergency Management and Interagency Preparedness. In 1996, Mayor Rudolph Giuliani created the Mayor's Office of Emergency Management, which had three basic functions. First, OEM's Watch Command was to monitor the city's key communications channels—including radio frequencies of FDNY dispatch and the NYPD—and other data. A second purpose of the OEM was to improve New York City's response to major incidents, including terrorist attacks, by planning and conducting exercises and drills that would involve multiple city agencies, particularly the NYPD and FDNY. Third, the OEM would play a crucial role in managing the city's overall response to an

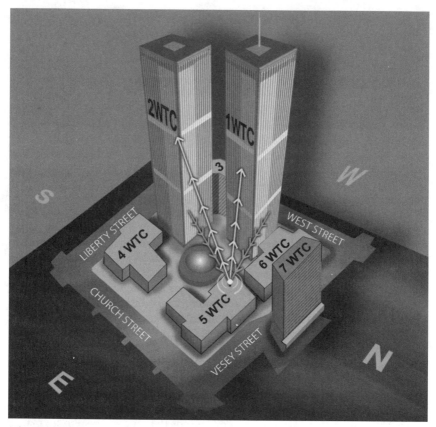

The World Trade Center Radio Repeater System
Rendering by Marco Crupi

incident. After OEM's Emergency Operations Center was activated, designated liaisons from relevant agencies, as well as the mayor and his or her senior staff, would respond there. In addition, an OEM field responder would be sent to the scene to ensure that the response was coordinated.[27]

The OEM's headquarters was located at 7 WTC. Some questioned locating it both so close to a previous terrorist target and on the 23rd floor of a building (difficult to access should elevators become inoperable). There was no backup site.[28]

In July 2001, Mayor Giuliani updated a directive titled "Direction and Control of Emergencies in the City of New York." Its purpose was to eliminate "potential conflict among responding agencies which may have areas

of overlapping expertise and responsibility." The directive sought to accomplish this objective by designating, for different types of emergencies, an
appropriate agency as "Incident Commander." This Incident Commander
would be "responsible for the management of the City's response to the
emergency," while the OEM was "designated the 'On Scene Interagency
Coordinator.'"[29]

Nevertheless, the FDNY and NYPD each considered itself operationally
autonomous. As of September 11, they were not prepared to comprehensively
coordinate their efforts in responding to a major incident. The OEM had not
overcome this problem.

9.2 SEPTEMBER 11, 2001

As we turn to the events of September 11, we are mindful of the unfair perspective afforded by hindsight. Nevertheless, we will try to describe what happened in the following 102 minutes:

- the 17 minutes from the crash of the hijacked American Airlines Flight
  11 into 1 World Trade Center (the North Tower) at 8:46 until the
  South Tower was hit
- the 56 minutes from the crash of the hijacked United Airlines Flight
  175 into 2 World Trade Center (the South Tower) at 9:03 until the
  collapse of the South Tower
- the 29 minutes from the collapse of the South Tower at 9:59 until the
  collapse of the North Tower at 10:28

From 8:46 until 9:03 A.M.
At 8:46:40, the hijacked American Airlines Flight 11 flew into the upper portion of the North Tower, cutting through floors 93 to 99. Evidence suggests
that all three of the building's stairwells became impassable from the 92nd floor
up. Hundreds of civilians were killed instantly by the impact. Hundreds more
remained alive but trapped.[30]

Civilians, Fire Safety Personnel, and 911 Calls
North Tower. A jet fuel fireball erupted upon impact and shot down at least
one bank of elevators. The fireball exploded onto numerous lower floors, including the 77th and 22nd; the West Street lobby level; and the B4 level, four stories
below ground. The burning jet fuel immediately created thick, black smoke that
enveloped the upper floors and roof of the North Tower. The roof of the South
Tower was also engulfed in smoke because of prevailing light winds from the
northwest.[31]

Within minutes, New York City's 911 system was flooded with eyewitness accounts of the event. Most callers correctly identified the target of the attack. Some identified the plane as a commercial airliner.[32]

The first response came from private firms and individuals—the people and companies in the building. Everything that would happen to them during the next few minutes would turn on their circumstances and their preparedness, assisted by building personnel on-site.

Hundreds of civilians trapped on or above the 92nd floor gathered in large and small groups, primarily between the 103rd and 106th floors. A large group was reported on the 92nd floor, technically below the impact but unable to descend. Civilians were also trapped in elevators. Other civilians below the impact zone—mostly on floors in the 70s and 80s, but also on at least the 47th and 22nd floors—were either trapped or waiting for assistance.[33]

It is unclear when the first full building evacuation order was attempted over the public-address system. The deputy fire safety director in the lobby, while immediately aware that a major incident had occurred, did not know for approximately ten minutes that a commercial jet had directly hit the building. Following protocol, he initially gave announcements to those floors that had generated computerized alarms, advising those tenants to descend to points of safety—at least two floors below the smoke or fire—and to wait there for further instructions. The deputy fire safety director has told us that he began instructing a full evacuation within about ten minutes of the explosion. But the first FDNY chiefs to arrive in the lobby were advised by the Port Authority fire safety director—who had reported to the lobby although he was no longer the designated fire safety director—that the full building evacuation announcement had been made within one minute of the building being hit.[34]

Because of damage to building systems caused by the impact of the plane, public-address announcements were not heard in many locations. For the same reason, many civilians may have been unable to use the emergency intercom phones, as they had been advised to do in fire drills. Many called 911.[35]

The 911 system was not equipped to handle the enormous volume of calls it received. Some callers were unable to connect with 911 operators, receiving an "all circuits busy" message. Standard operating procedure was for calls relating to fire emergencies to be transferred from 911 operators to FDNY dispatch operators in the appropriate borough (in this case, Manhattan). Transfers were often plagued by delays and were in some cases unsuccessful. Many calls were also prematurely disconnected.[36]

The 911 operators and FDNY dispatchers had no information about either the location or the magnitude of the impact zone and were therefore unable to provide information as fundamental as whether callers were above or below the fire. Because the operators were not informed of NYPD Aviation's determination of the impossibility of rooftop rescues from the Twin Towers on that day, they could not knowledgeably answer when callers asked whether to go up or down. In most instances, therefore, the operators and the FDNY dispatchers relied on standard operating procedures for high-rise fires—that civilians should stay low, remain where they are, and wait for emergency personnel to reach them. This advice was given to callers from the North Tower for locations both above and below the impact zone. Fire chiefs told us that the evacuation of tens of thousands of people from skyscrapers can create many new problems, especially for individuals who are disabled or in poor health. Many of the injuries after the 1993 bombing occurred during the evacuation.[37]

Although the guidance to stay in place may seem understandable in cases of conventional high-rise fires, FDNY chiefs in the North Tower lobby determined at once that all building occupants should attempt to evacuate immediately. By 8:57, FDNY chiefs had instructed the PAPD and building personnel to evacuate the South Tower as well, because of the magnitude of the damage caused by the first plane's impact.[38]

These critical decisions were not conveyed to 911 operators or to FDNY dispatchers. Departing from protocol, a number of operators told callers that they could break windows, and several operators advised callers to evacuate if they could.[39] Civilians who called the Port Authority police desk located at 5 WTC were advised to leave if they could.[40]

Most civilians who were not obstructed from proceeding began evacuating without waiting for instructions over the intercom system. Some remained to wait for help, as advised by 911 operators. Others simply continued to work or delayed to collect personal items, but in many cases were urged to leave by others. Some Port Authority civilian employees remained on various upper floors to help civilians who were trapped and to assist in the evacuation.[41]

While evacuating, some civilians had trouble reaching the exits because of damage caused by the impact. Some were confused by deviations in the increasingly crowded stairwells, and impeded by doors that appeared to be locked but actually were jammed by debris or shifting that resulted from the impact of the plane. Despite these obstacles, the evacuation was relatively calm and orderly.[42]

Within ten minutes of impact, smoke was beginning to rise to the upper floors in debilitating volumes and isolated fires were reported, although there were some pockets of refuge. Faced with insufferable heat, smoke, and fire, and with no prospect for relief, some jumped or fell from the building.[43]

South Tower. Many civilians in the South Tower were initially unaware of what had happened in the other tower. Some believed an incident had occurred in their building; others were aware that a major explosion had occurred on the upper floors of the North Tower. Many people decided to leave, and some were advised to do so by fire wardens. In addition, Morgan Stanley, which occupied more than 20 floors of the South Tower, evacuated its employees by the decision of company security officials.[44]

Consistent with protocol, at 8:49 the deputy fire safety director in the South Tower told his counterpart in the North Tower that he would wait to hear from "the boss from the Fire Department or somebody" before ordering an evacuation.[45] At about this time, an announcement over the public-address system in

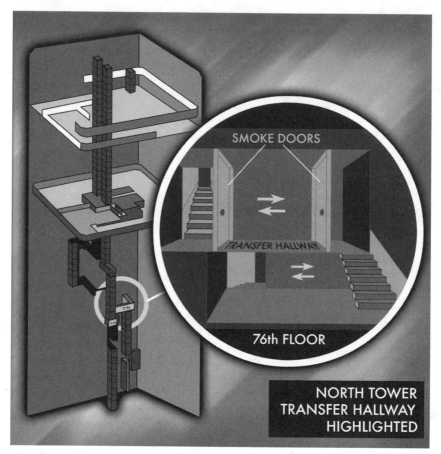

The World Trade Center North Tower Stairwell with Deviation
Rendering by Marco Crupi

the South Tower stated that the incident had occurred in the other building and advised tenants, generally, that their building was safe and that they should remain on or return to their offices or floors. A statement from the deputy fire safety director informing tenants that the incident had occurred in the other building was consistent with protocol; the expanded advice did not correspond to any existing written protocol, and did not reflect any instruction known to have been given to the deputy fire safety director that day. We do not know the reason for the announcement, as both the deputy fire safety director believed to have made it and the director of fire safety for the WTC complex perished in the South Tower's collapse. Clearly, however, the prospect of another plane hitting the second building was beyond the contemplation of anyone giving advice. According to one of the first fire chiefs to arrive, such a scenario was unimaginable, "beyond our consciousness." As a result of the announcement, many civilians remained on their floors. Others reversed their evacuation and went back up.[46]

Similar advice was given in person by security officials in both the ground-floor lobby—where a group of 20 that had descended by the elevators was personally instructed to go back upstairs—and in the upper sky lobby, where many waited for express elevators to take them down. Security officials who gave this advice were not part of the fire safety staff.[47]

Several South Tower occupants called the Port Authority police desk in 5 WTC. Some were advised to stand by for further instructions; others were strongly advised to leave.[48]

It is not known whether the order by the FDNY to evacuate the South Tower was received by the deputy fire safety director making announcements there. However, at approximately 9:02—less than a minute before the building was hit—an instruction over the South Tower's public-address system advised civilians, generally, that they could begin an orderly evacuation if conditions warranted. Like the earlier advice to remain in place, it did not correspond to any prewritten emergency instruction.[49]

FDNY Initial Response
Mobilization. The FDNY response began within five seconds of the crash. By 9:00, many senior FDNY leaders, including 7 of the 11 most highly ranked chiefs in the department, as well as the Commissioner and many of his deputies and assistants, had begun responding from headquarters in Brooklyn. While en route over the Brooklyn Bridge, the Chief of Department and the Chief of Operations had a clear view of the situation on the upper floors of the North Tower. They determined that because of the fire's magnitude and location near the top of the building, their mission would be primarily one of rescue. They called for a fifth alarm, which would bring additional engine and ladder companies, as well as for two more elite rescue units. The Chief of Department arrived at about 9:00; general FDNY Incident Command was transferred to his location on the West Side Highway. In all, 22 of the 32 senior chiefs and commissioners arrived at the WTC before 10:00.[50]

As of 9:00, the units that were dispatched (including senior chiefs responding to headquarters) included approximately 235 firefighters. These units consisted of 21 engine companies, nine ladder companies, four of the department's elite rescue teams, the department's single Hazmat team, two of the city's elite squad companies, and support staff. In addition, at 8:53 nine Brooklyn units were staged on the Brooklyn side of the Brooklyn-Battery Tunnel to await possible dispatch orders.[51]

Operations. A battalion chief and two ladder and two engine companies arrived at the North Tower at approximately 8:52. As they entered the lobby, they encountered badly burned civilians who had been caught in the path of the fireball. Floor-to-ceiling windows in the northwest corner of the West Street level of the lobby had been blown out; some large marble tiles had been dislodged from the walls; one entire elevator bank was destroyed by the fireball. Lights were functioning, however, and the air was clear of smoke.[52]

As the highest-ranking officer on the scene, the battalion chief initially was the FDNY incident commander. Minutes later, the on-duty division chief for Lower Manhattan arrived and took over. Both chiefs immediately began speaking with the former fire safety director and other building personnel to learn whether building systems were working. They were advised that all 99 elevators in the North Tower appeared to be out, and there were no assurances that sprinklers or standpipes were working on upper floors. Chiefs also spoke with Port Authority police personnel and an OEM representative.[53]

After conferring with the chiefs in the lobby, one engine and one ladder company began climbing stairwell C at about 8:57, with the goal of approaching the impact zone as scouting units and reporting back to the chiefs in the lobby. The radio channel they used was tactical 1. Following FDNY high-rise fire protocols, other units did not begin climbing immediately, as the chiefs worked to formulate a plan before sending them up. Units began mobilizing in the lobby, lining up and awaiting their marching orders.[54]

Also by approximately 8:57, FDNY chiefs had asked both building personnel and a Port Authority police officer to evacuate the South Tower, because in their judgment the impact of the plane into the North Tower made the entire complex unsafe—not because of concerns about a possible second plane.[55]

The FDNY chiefs in the increasingly crowded North Tower lobby were confronting critical choices with little to no information. They had ordered units up the stairs to report back on conditions, but did not know what the impact floors were; they did not know if any stairwells into the impact zone were clear; and they did not know whether water for firefighting would be available on the upper floors. They also did not know what the fire and impact zone looked like from the outside.[56]

They did know that the explosion had been large enough to send down a fireball that blew out elevators and windows in the lobby and that conditions were so dire that some civilians on upper floors were jumping or falling from the building. They also knew from building personnel that some civilians were trapped in elevators and on specific floors. According to Division Chief for Lower Manhattan Peter Hayden, "We had a very strong sense we would lose firefighters and that we were in deep trouble, but we had estimates of 25,000 to 50,000 civilians, and we had to try to rescue them."[57]

The chiefs concluded that this would be a rescue operation, not a firefighting operation. One of the chiefs present explained:

We realized that, because of the impact of the plane, that there was some structural damage to the building, and most likely that the fire suppression systems within the building were probably damaged and possibly inoperable....We knew that at the height of the day there were as many as 50,000 people in this building. We had a large volume of fire on the upper floors. Each floor was approximately an acre in size. Several floors of fire would have been beyond the fire-extinguishing capability of the forces that we had on hand. So we determined, very early on, that this was going to be strictly a rescue mission. We were going to vacate the building, get everybody out, and then we were going to get out.[58]

The specifics of the mission were harder to determine, as they had almost no information about the situation 80 or more stories above them. They also received advice from senior FDNY chiefs that while the building might eventually suffer a partial collapse on upper floors, such structural failure was not imminent. No one anticipated the possibility of a total collapse.[59]

Emergency medical services (EMS) personnel were directed to one of four triage areas being set up around the perimeter of the WTC. Some entered the lobby to respond to specific casualty reports. In addition, many ambulance paramedics from private hospitals were rushing to the WTC complex.[60]

NYPD Initial Response
Numerous NYPD officers saw the plane strike the North Tower and immediately reported it to NYPD communications dispatchers.[61]

At 8:58, while en route, the NYPD Chief of Department raised the NYPD's mobilization to level 4, thereby sending to the WTC approximately 22 lieutenants, 100 sergeants, and 800 police officers from all over the city. The Chief of Department arrived at Church and Vesey at 9:00.[62]

At 9:01, the NYPD patrol mobilization point was moved to West and Vesey in order to handle the greater number of patrol officers dispatched in the higher-level mobilization. These officers would be stationed around the perimeter of the complex to direct the evacuation of civilians. Many were diverted on the way to the scene by intervening emergencies related to the attack.[63]

At 8:50, the Aviation Unit of the NYPD dispatched two helicopters to the WTC to report on conditions and assess the feasibility of a rooftop landing or of special rescue operations. En route, the two helicopters communicated with air traffic controllers at the area's three major airports and informed them of the commercial airplane crash at the World Trade Center. The air traffic controllers had been unaware of the incident.[64]

At 8:56, an NYPD ESU team asked to be picked up at the Wall Street heliport to initiate rooftop rescues. At 8:58, however, after assessing the North Tower roof, a helicopter pilot advised the ESU team that they could not land on the roof, because "it is too engulfed in flames and heavy smoke condition."[65]

By 9:00, a third NYPD helicopter was responding to the WTC complex.

NYPD helicopters and ESU officers remained on the scene throughout the morning, prepared to commence rescue operations on the roof if conditions improved. Both FDNY and NYPD protocols called for FDNY personnel to be placed in NYPD helicopters in the event of an attempted rooftop rescue at a high-rise fire. No FDNY personnel were placed in NYPD helicopters on September 11.[66]

The 911 operators and FDNY dispatchers were not advised that rooftop rescues were not being undertaken. They thus were not able to communicate this fact to callers, some of whom spoke of attempting to climb to the roof.[67]

Two on-duty NYPD officers were on the 20th floor of the North Tower at 8:46. They climbed to the 29th floor, urging civilians to evacuate, but did not locate a group of civilians trapped on the 22nd floor.[68]

Just before 9:00, an ESU team began to walk from Church and Vesey to the North Tower lobby, with the goal of climbing toward and setting up a triage center on the upper floors for the severely injured. A second ESU team would follow them to assist in removing those individuals.[69]

Numerous officers responded in order to help injured civilians and to urge those who could walk to vacate the area immediately. Putting themselves in danger of falling debris, several officers entered the plaza and successfully rescued at least one injured, nonambulatory civilian, and attempted to rescue others.[70]

Also by about 9:00, transit officers began shutting down subway stations in the vicinity of the World Trade Center and evacuating civilians from those stations.[71]

Around the city, the NYPD cleared major thoroughfares for emergency vehicles to access the WTC. The NYPD and PAPD coordinated the closing of bridges and tunnels into Manhattan.[72]

PAPD Initial Response
The Port Authority's on-site commanding police officer was standing in the concourse when a fireball erupted out of elevator shafts and exploded onto the mall concourse, causing him to dive for cover. The on-duty sergeant initially instructed the officers in the WTC Command to meet at the police desk in 5 WTC. Soon thereafter, he instructed officers arriving from outside commands to meet him at the fire safety desk in the North Tower lobby. A few of these officers from outside commands were given WTC Command radios.[73]

One Port Authority police officer at the WTC immediately began climbing stairwell C in the North Tower.[74] Other officers began performing rescue and evacuation operations on the ground floors and in the PATH (Port Authority Trans-Hudson) station below the WTC complex.

Within minutes of impact, Port Authority police officers from the PATH, bridges, tunnels, and airport commands began responding to the WTC. The PAPD lacked written standard operating procedures for personnel responding from outside commands to the WTC during a major incident. In addition, officers from some PAPD commands lacked interoperable radio frequencies. As a result, there was no comprehensive coordination of PAPD's overall response.[75]

At 9:00, the PAPD commanding officer of the WTC ordered an evacuation of all civilians in the World Trade Center complex, because of the magnitude of the calamity in the North Tower. This order was given over WTC police radio channel W, which could not be heard by the deputy fire safety director in the South Tower.[76]

Also at 9:00, the PAPD Superintendent and Chief of Department arrived separately and made their way to the North Tower.[77]

OEM Initial Response

By 8:48, officials in OEM headquarters on the 23rd floor of 7 WTC—just to the north of the North Tower—began to activate the Emergency Operations Center by calling such agencies as the FDNY, NYPD, Department of Health, and the Greater Hospital Association and instructing them to send their designated representatives to the OEM. In addition, the Federal Emergency Management Agency (FEMA) was called and asked to send at least five federal Urban Search and Rescue Teams (such teams are located throughout the United States). At approximately 8:50, a senior representative from the OEM arrived in the lobby of the North Tower and began to act as the OEM field responder to the incident. He soon was joined by several other OEM officials, including the OEM Director.[78]

Summary

In the 17-minute period between 8:46 and 9:03 A.M. on September 11, New York City and the Port Authority of New York and New Jersey had mobilized the largest rescue operation in the city's history. Well over a thousand first responders had been deployed, an evacuation had begun, and the critical decision that the fire could not be fought had been made.

Then the second plane hit.

From 9:03 until 9:59 A.M.

At 9:03:11, the hijacked United Airlines Flight 175 hit 2 WTC (the South Tower) from the south, crashing through the 77th to 85th floors. What had been the largest and most complicated rescue operation in city history instantly doubled in magnitude. The plane banked as it hit the building, leaving portions of the building undamaged on impact floors. As a consequence—and in contrast to the situation in the North Tower—one of the stairwells (A) initially remained passable from at least the 91st floor down, and likely from top to bottom.[79]

Civilians, Fire Safety Personnel, and 911 Calls

South Tower. At the lower end of the impact, the 78th-floor sky lobby, hundreds had been waiting to evacuate when the plane hit. Many had attempted but failed to squeeze into packed express elevators. Upon impact, many were killed or severely injured; others were relatively unharmed. We know of at least one civilian who seized the initiative and shouted that anyone who could walk should walk to the stairs, and anyone who could help should help others in need of assistance. As a result, at least two small groups of civilians descended from that floor. Others remained on the floor to help the injured and move victims who were unable to walk to the stairwell to aid their rescue.[80]

Still others remained alive in the impact zone above the 78th floor. Damage was extensive, and conditions were highly precarious. The only survivor known to have escaped from the heart of the impact zone described the 81st floor—where the wing of the plane had sliced through his office—as a "demolition" site in which everything was "broken up" and the smell of jet fuel was so strong that it was almost impossible to breathe. This person escaped by means of an unlikely rescue, aided by a civilian fire warden descending from a higher floor, who, critically, had been provided with a flashlight.[81]

At least four people were able to descend stairwell A from the 81st floor or above. One left the 84th floor immediately after the building was hit. Even at that point, the stairway was dark, smoky, and difficult to navigate; glow strips on the stairs and handrails were a significant help. Several flights down, however, the evacuee became confused when he reached a smoke door that caused him to believe the stairway had ended. He was able to exit that stairwell and switch to another.[82]

Many civilians in and above the impact zone ascended the stairs. One small group reversed its descent down stairwell A after being advised by another civilian that they were approaching a floor "in flames." The only known survivor has told us that their intention was to exit the stairwell in search of clearer air. At the 91st floor, joined by others from intervening floors, they perceived themselves to be trapped in the stairwell and began descending again. By this time, the stairwell was "pretty black," intensifying smoke caused many to pass out, and fire had ignited in the 82nd-floor transfer hallway.[83]

Others ascended to attempt to reach the roof but were thwarted by locked doors. At approximately 9:30 a "lock release" order—which would unlock all areas in the complex controlled by the buildings' computerized security system, including doors leading to the roofs—was transmitted to the Security Command Center located on the 22nd floor of the North Tower. Damage to the software controlling the system, resulting from the impact of the plane, prevented this order from being executed.[84]

Others, attempting to descend, were frustrated by jammed or locked doors in stairwells or confused by the structure of the stairwell deviations. By the lower 70s, however, stairwells A and B were well-lit, and conditions were generally normal.[85]

Some civilians remained on affected floors, and at least one ascended from a lower point into the impact zone, to help evacuate colleagues or assist the injured.[86]

Within 15 minutes after the impact, debilitating smoke had reached at least one location on the 100th floor, and severe smoke conditions were reported throughout floors in the 90s and 100s over the course of the following half hour. By 9:30, a number of civilians who had failed to reach the roof remained on the 105th floor, likely unable to descend because of intensifying smoke in the stairwell. There were reports of tremendous smoke on that floor, but at least one area remained less affected until shortly before the building collapsed. There were several areas between the impact zone and the uppermost floors where conditions were better. At least a hundred people remained alive on the 88th and 89th floors, in some cases calling 911 for direction.[87]

The 911 system remained plagued by the operators' lack of awareness of what was occurring. Just as in the North Tower, callers from below and above the impact zone were advised to remain where they were and wait for help. The operators were not given any information about the inability to conduct rooftop rescues and therefore could not advise callers that they had essentially been ruled out. This lack of information, combined with the general advice to remain where they were, may have caused civilians above the impact not to attempt to descend, although stairwell A may have been passable.[88]

In addition, the 911 system struggled with the volume of calls and rigid standard operating procedures according to which calls conveying crucial information had to wait to be transferred to either EMS or FDNY dispatch.[89] According to one civilian who was evacuating down stairwell A from the heart of the impact zone and who stopped on the 31st floor in order to call 911,

> I told them when they answered the phone, where I was, that I had passed somebody on the 44th floor, injured—they need to get a medic and a stretcher to this floor, and described the situation in brief, and the person then asked for my phone number, or something, and they said—they put me on hold. "You gotta talk to one of my supervisors"—and suddenly I was on hold. And so I waited a considerable amount of time. Somebody else came back on the phone, I repeated the story. And then it happened again. I was on hold a second time, and needed to repeat the story for a third time. But I told the third person that I am only telling you once. I am getting out of the building, here are the details, write it down, and do what you should do.[90]

Very few 911 calls were received from floors below the impact, but at least one person was advised to remain on the 73rd floor despite the caller's protests that oxygen was running out. The last known 911 call from this location came at 9:52.[91]

Evidence suggests that the public-address system did not continue to function after the building was hit. A group of people trapped on the 97th floor, however, made repeated references in calls to 911 to having heard "announcements" to go down the stairs. Evacuation tones were heard in locations both above and below the impact zone.[92]

By 9:35, the West Street lobby level of the South Tower was becoming over-whelmed by injured people who had descended to the lobby but were having difficulty going on. Those who could continue were directed to exit north or east through the concourse and then out of the WTC complex.[93]

By 9:59, at least one person had descended from as high as the 91st floor of that tower, and stairwell A was reported to have been almost empty. Stairwell B was also reported to have contained only a handful of descending civilians at an earlier point in the morning. But just before the tower collapsed, a team of NYPD ESU officers encountered a stream of civilians descending an unidentified stairwell in the 20s. These civilians may have been descending from at or above the impact zone.[94]

North Tower. In the North Tower, civilians continued their evacuation. On the 91st floor, the highest floor with stairway access, all civilians but one were uninjured and able to descend. While some complained of smoke, heat, fumes, and crowding in the stairwells, conditions were otherwise fairly normal on floors below the impact. At least one stairwell was reported to have been "clear and bright" from the upper 80s down.[95]

Those who called 911 from floors below the impact were generally advised to remain in place. One group trapped on the 83rd floor pleaded repeatedly to know whether the fire was above or below them, specifically asking if 911 oper-ators had any information from the outside or from the news. The callers were transferred back and forth several times and advised to stay put. Evidence sug-gests that these callers died.[96]

At 8:59, the Port Authority police desk at Newark Airport told a third party that a group of Port Authority civilian employees on the 64th floor should evacuate. (The third party was not at the WTC, but had been in phone con-tact with the group on the 64th floor.) At 9:10, in response to an inquiry from the employees themselves, the Port Authority police desk in Jersey City con-firmed that employees on the 64th floor should "be careful, stay near the stair-wells, and wait for the police to come up." When the third party inquired again at 9:31, the police desk at Newark Airport advised that they "absolutely" evac-uate. The third party informed the police desk that the employees had previ-ously received contrary advice from the FDNY, which could only have come via 911. These workers were not trapped, yet unlike most occupants on the upper floors, they had chosen not to descend immediately after impact. They eventually began to descend the stairs, but most of them died in the collapse of the North Tower.[97]

All civilians who reached the lobby were directed by NYPD and PAPD offi-cers into the concourse, where other police officers guided them to exit the concourse and complex to the north and east so that they might avoid falling debris and victims.[98]

By 9:55, only a few civilians were descending above the 25th floor in stairwell B; these primarily were injured, handicapped, elderly, or severely over-weight civilians, in some cases being assisted by other civilians.[99]

By 9:59, tenants from the 91st floor had already descended the stairs and exited the concourse. However, a number of civilians remained in at least stair-well C, approaching lower floors. Other evacuees were killed earlier by debris falling on the street.[100]

FDNY Response
Increased Mobilization. Immediately after the second plane hit, the FDNY Chief of Department called a second fifth alarm.[101]

By 9:15, the number of FDNY personnel en route to or present at the scene was far greater than the commanding chiefs at the scene had requested. Five factors account for this disparity. First, while the second fifth alarm had called for 20 engine and 8 ladder companies, in fact 23 engine and 13 ladder com-panies were dispatched. Second, several other units self-dispatched. Third, because the attacks came so close to the 9:00 shift change, many firefighters just going off duty were given permission by company officers to "ride heavy" and became part of those on-duty teams, under the leadership of that unit's officer. Fourth, many off-duty firefighters responded from firehouses separately from the on-duty unit (in some cases when expressly told not to) or from home. The arrival of personnel in excess of that dispatched was particularly pro-nounced in the department's elite units. Fifth, numerous additional FDNY per-sonnel—such as fire marshals and firefighters in administrative positions—who lacked a predetermined operating role also reported to the WTC.[102]

The Repeater System. Almost immediately after the South Tower was hit, senior FDNY chiefs in the North Tower lobby huddled to discuss strategy for the operations in the two towers. Of particular concern to the chiefs—in light of FDNY difficulties in responding to the 1993 bombing—was communica-tions capability. One of the chiefs recommended testing the repeater channel to see if it would work.[103]

Earlier, an FDNY chief had asked building personnel to activate the repeater channel, which would enable greatly-enhanced FDNY portable radio communications in the high-rises. One button on the repeater system activa-tion console in the North Tower was pressed at 8:54, though it is unclear by whom. As a result of this activation, communication became possible between FDNY portable radios on the repeater channel. In addition, the repeater's mas-ter handset at the fire safety desk could hear communications made by FDNY portable radios on the repeater channel. The activation of *transmission* on the master handset required, however, that a second button be pressed. That sec-ond button was never activated on the morning of September 11.[104]

At 9:05, FDNY chiefs tested the WTC complex's repeater system. Because the second button had not been activated, the chief on the master handset could not transmit. He was also apparently unable to hear another chief who was attempting to communicate with him from a portable radio, either because of a technical problem or because the volume was turned down on the console (the normal setting when the system was not in use). Because the repeater channel seemed inoperable—the master handset appeared unable to transmit or receive communications—the chiefs in the North Tower lobby decided not to use it. The repeater system was working at least partially, however, on portable FDNY radios, and firefighters subsequently used repeater channel 7 in the South Tower.[105]

FDNY North Tower Operations. Command and control decisions were affected by the lack of knowledge of what was happening 30, 60, 90, and 100 floors above. According to one of the chiefs in the lobby, "One of the most critical things in a major operation like this is to have information. We didn't have a lot of information coming in. We didn't receive any reports of what was seen from the [NYPD] helicopters. It was impossible to know how much damage was done on the upper floors, whether the stairwells were intact or not."[106] According to another chief present, "People watching on TV certainly had more knowledge of what was happening a hundred floors above us than we did in the lobby. . . . [W]ithout critical information coming in . . . it's very difficult to make informed, critical decisions[.]"[107]

As a result, chiefs in the lobby disagreed over whether anyone at or above the impact zone possibly could be rescued, or whether there should be even limited firefighting for the purpose of cutting exit routes through fire zones.[108]

Many units were simply instructed to ascend toward the impact zone and report back to the lobby via radio. Some units were directed to assist specific groups of individuals trapped in elevators or in offices well below the impact zone. One FDNY company successfully rescued some civilians who were trapped on the 22nd floor as a result of damage caused by the initial fireball.[109]

An attempt was made to track responding units' assignments on a magnetic board, but the number of units and individual firefighters arriving in the lobby made this an overwhelming task. As the fire companies were not advised to the contrary, they followed protocol and kept their radios on tactical channel 1, which would be monitored by the chiefs in the lobby. Those battalion chiefs who would climb would operate on a separate command channel, which also would be monitored by the chiefs in the lobby.[110]

Fire companies began to ascend stairwell B at approximately 9:07, laden with about 100 pounds of heavy protective clothing, self-contained breathing apparatuses, and other equipment (including hoses for engine companies and heavy tools for ladder companies).[111]

Firefighters found the stairways they entered intact, lit, and clear of smoke. Unbeknownst to the lobby command post, one battalion chief in the North Tower found a working elevator, which he took to the 16th floor before beginning to climb.[112]

In ascending stairwell B, firefighters were passing a steady and heavy stream of descending civilians. Firemen were impressed with the composure and total lack of panic shown by almost all civilians. Many civilians were in awe of the firefighters and found their mere presence to be calming.[113]

Firefighters periodically stopped on particular floors and searched to ensure that no civilians were still on it. In a few instances healthy civilians were found on floors, either because they still were collecting personal items or for no apparent reason; they were told to evacuate immediately. Firefighters deputized healthy civilians to be in charge of others who were struggling or injured.[114]

Climbing up the stairs with heavy protective clothing and equipment was hard work even for physically fit firefighters. As firefighters began to suffer varying levels of fatigue, some became separated from others in their unit.[115]

At 9:32, a senior chief radioed all units in the North Tower to return to the lobby, either because of a false report of a third plane approaching or because of his judgment about the deteriorating condition of the building. Once the rumor of the third plane was debunked, other chiefs continued operations, and there is no evidence that any units actually returned to the lobby. At the same time, a chief in the lobby was asked to consider the possibility of a rooftop rescue but was unable to reach FDNY dispatch by radio or phone. Out on West Street, however, the FDNY Chief of Department had already dismissed any rooftop rescue as impossible.[116]

As units climbed higher, their ability to communicate with chiefs on tactical 1 became more limited and sporadic, both because of the limited effectiveness of FDNY radios in high-rises and because so many units on tactical 1 were trying to communicate at once. When attempting to reach a particular unit, chiefs in the lobby often heard nothing in response.[117]

Just prior to 10:00, in the North Tower one engine company had climbed to the 54th floor, at least two other companies of firefighters had reached the sky lobby on the 44th floor, and numerous units were located between the 5th and 37th floors.[118]

FDNY South Tower and Marriott Hotel Operations. Immediately after the repeater test, a senior chief and a battalion chief commenced operations in the South Tower lobby. Almost at once they were joined by an OEM field responder. They were not, however, joined right away by a sizable number of fire companies, as units that had been in or en route to the North Tower lobby at 9:03 were not reallocated to the South Tower.[119]

A battalion chief and a ladder company found a working elevator to the 40th floor and from there proceeded to climb stairwell B. Another ladder company arrived soon thereafter, and began to rescue civilians trapped in an elevator between the first and second floors. The senior chief in the lobby expressed frustration about the lack of units he initially had at his disposal for South Tower operations.[120]

Unlike the commanders in the North Tower, the senior chief in the lobby and the ascending battalion chief kept their radios on repeater channel 7. For the first 15 minutes of the operations, communications among them and the ladder company climbing with the battalion chief worked well. Upon learning from a company security official that the impact zone began at the 78th floor, a ladder company transmitted this information, and the battalion chief directed an engine company staged on the 40th floor to attempt to find an elevator to reach that upper level.[121]

To our knowledge, no FDNY chiefs outside the South Tower realized that the repeater channel was functioning and being used by units in that tower. The senior chief in the South Tower lobby was initially unable to communicate his requests for more units to chiefs either in the North Tower lobby or at the outdoor command post.[122]

From approximately 9:21 on, the ascending battalion chief was unable to reach the South Tower lobby command post because the senior chief in the lobby had ceased to communicate on repeater channel 7. The vast majority of units that entered the South Tower did not communicate on the repeater channel.[123]

The first FDNY fatality of the day occurred at approximately 9:30, when a civilian landed on and killed a fireman near the intersection of West and Liberty streets.[124]

By 9:30, chiefs in charge of the South Tower still were in need of additional companies. Several factors account for the lag in response. First, only two units that had been dispatched to the North Tower prior to 9:03 reported immediately to the South Tower. Second, units were not actually sent until approximately five minutes after the FDNY Chief of Department ordered their dispatch. Third, those units that had been ordered at 8:53 to stage at the Brooklyn-Battery Tunnel—and thus very close to the WTC complex—were not dispatched after the plane hit the South Tower. Fourth, units parked further north on West Street, then proceeded south on foot and stopped at the overall FDNY command post on West Street, where in some cases they were told to wait. Fifth, some units responded directly to the North Tower. (Indeed, radio communications indicated that in certain cases some firemen believed that the South Tower was 1 WTC when in fact it was 2 WTC.) Sixth, some units couldn't find the staging area (at West Street south of Liberty) for the South Tower. Finally, the jumpers and debris that confronted units attempting to enter the South Tower from its main entrance on Liberty Street caused some units to search for indirect ways to enter that tower, most often through the Marriott Hotel, or simply to remain on West Street.[125]

A chief at the overall outdoor command post was under the impression that he was to assist in lobby operations of the South Tower, and in fact his aide already was in that lobby. But because of his lack of familiarity with the WTC complex and confusion over how to get to there, he instead ended up in the Marriott at about 9:35. Here he came across about 14 units, many of which had been trying to find safe access to the South Tower. He directed them to secure the elevators and conduct search-and-rescue operations on the upper floors of the Marriott. Four of these companies searched the spa on the hotel's top floor—the 22nd floor—for civilians, and found none.[126]

Feeling satisfied with the scope of the operation in the Marriott, the chief in the lobby there directed some units to proceed to what he thought was the South Tower. In fact, he pointed them to the North Tower. Three of the FDNY companies who had entered the North Tower from the Marriott found a working elevator in a bank at the south end of the lobby, which they took to the 23rd floor.[127]

In response to the shortage of units in the South Tower, at 9:37 an additional second alarm was requested by the chief at the West and Liberty streets staging area. At this time, the units that earlier had been staged on the Brooklyn side of the Brooklyn-Battery Tunnel were dispatched to the South Tower; some had gone through the tunnel already and had responded to the Marriott, not the South Tower.[128]

Between 9:45 and 9:58, the ascending battalion chief continued to lead FDNY operations on the upper floors of the South Tower. At 9:50, an FDNY ladder company encountered numerous seriously injured civilians on the 70th floor. With the assistance of a security guard, at 9:53 a group of civilians trapped in an elevator on the 78th-floor sky lobby were found by an FDNY company. They were freed from the elevator at 9:58. By that time the battalion chief had reached the 78th floor on stairwell A; he reported that it looked open to the 79th floor, well into the impact zone. He also reported numerous civilian fatalities in the area.[129]

FDNY Command and Control Outside the Towers. The overall command post consisted of senior chiefs, commissioners, the field communications van (Field Comm), numerous units that began to arrive after the South Tower was hit, and EMS chiefs and personnel.[130]

Field Comm's two main functions were to relay information between the overall operations command post and FDNY dispatch and to track all units operating at the scene on a large magnetic board. Both of these missions were severely compromised by the magnitude of the disaster on September 11. First, the means of transmitting information were unreliable. For example, while FDNY dispatch advised Field Comm that 100 people were reported via 911 to be trapped on the 105th floor of the North Tower, and Field Comm then attempted to convey that report to chiefs at the outdoor command post, this information did not reach the North Tower lobby. Second, Field Comm's ability to keep track of which units were operating where was limited, because many units reported directly to the North Tower, the South Tower, or the Marriott. Third, efforts to track units by listening to tactical 1 were severely hampered by the number of units using that channel; as many people tried to speak at once, their transmissions overlapped and often became indecipherable. In the opinion of one of the members of the Field

Comm group, tactical 1 simply was not designed to handle the number of units operating on it that morning.[131]

The primary Field Comm van had access to the NYPD's Special Operations channel (used by NYPD Aviation), but it was in the garage for repairs on September 11. The backup van lacked that capability.[132]

The Chief of Department, along with civilian commissioners and senior EMS chiefs, organized ambulances on West Street to expedite the transport of injured civilians to hospitals.[133]

To our knowledge, none of the chiefs present believed that a total collapse of either tower was possible. One senior chief did articulate his concern that upper floors could begin to collapse in a few hours, and that firefighters thus should not ascend above floors in the 60s. That opinion was not conveyed to chiefs in the North Tower lobby, and there is no evidence that it was conveyed to chiefs in the South Tower lobby either.[134]

Although the Chief of Department had general authority over operations, tactical decisions remained the province of the lobby commanders. The highest-ranking officer in the North Tower was responsible for communicating with the Chief of Department. They had two brief conversations. In the first, the senior lobby chief gave the Chief of Department a status report and confirmed that this was a rescue, not firefighting, operation. In the second conversation, at about 9:45, the Chief of Department suggested that given how the North Tower appeared to him, the senior lobby chief might want to consider evacuating FDNY personnel.[135]

At 9:46, the Chief of Department called an additional fifth alarm, and at 9:54 an additional 20 engine and 6 ladder companies were sent to the WTC. As a result, more than one-third of all FDNY companies now had been dispatched to the WTC. At about 9:57, an EMS paramedic approached the FDNY Chief of Department and advised that an engineer in front of 7 WTC had just remarked that the Twin Towers in fact were in imminent danger of a total collapse.[136]

NYPD Response

Immediately after the second plane hit, the Chief of Department of the NYPD ordered a second Level 4 mobilization, bringing the total number of NYPD officers responding to close to 2,000.[137]

The NYPD Chief of Department called for Operation Omega, which required the protection of sensitive locations around the city. NYPD headquarters were secured and all other government buildings were evacuated.[138]

The ESU command post at Church and Vesey streets coordinated all NYPD ESU rescue teams. After the South Tower was hit, the ESU officer running this command post decided to send one ESU team (each with approximately six police officers) up each of the Twin Towers' stairwells. While he continued to monitor the citywide SOD channel, which NYPD helicopters were using, he also monitored the point-to-point tactical channel that the ESU teams climbing in the towers would use.[139]

The first NYPD ESU team entered the West Street–level lobby of the North Tower and prepared to begin climbing at about 9:15 A.M. They attempted to check in with the FDNY chiefs present, but were rebuffed. OEM personnel did not intervene. The ESU team began to climb the stairs. Shortly thereafter, a second NYPD ESU team entered the South Tower. The OEM field responder present ensured that they check in with the FDNY chief in charge of the lobby, and it was agreed that the ESU team would ascend and support FDNY personnel.[140]

A third ESU team subsequently entered the North Tower at its elevated mezzanine lobby level and made no effort to check in with the FDNY command post. A fourth ESU team entered the South Tower. By 9:59, a fifth ESU team was next to 6 WTC and preparing to enter the North Tower.[141]

By approximately 9:50, the lead ESU team had reached the 31st floor, observing that there appeared to be no more civilians still descending. This ESU team encountered a large group of firefighters and administered oxygen to some of them who were exhausted.[142]

At about 9:56, the officer running the ESU command post on Church and Vesey streets had a final radio communication with one of the ESU teams in the South Tower. The team then stated that it was ascending via stairs, was somewhere in the 20s, and was making slow progress because of the numerous descending civilians crowding the stairwell.[143]

Three plainclothes NYPD officers without radios or protective gear had begun ascending either stairwell A or C of the North Tower. They began checking every other floor above the 12th for civilians. Only occasionally did they find any, and in those few cases they ordered the civilians to evacuate immediately. While checking floors, they used office phones to call their superiors. In one phone call an NYPD chief instructed them to leave the North Tower, but they refused to do so. As they climbed higher, they encountered increasing smoke and heat. Shortly before 10:00 they arrived on the 54th floor.[144]

Throughout this period (9:03 to 9:59), a group of NYPD and Port Authority police officers, as well as two Secret Service agents, continued to assist civilians leaving the North Tower. They were positioned around the mezzanine lobby level of the North Tower, directing civilians leaving stairwells A and C to evacuate down an escalator to the concourse. The officers instructed those civilians who seemed composed to evacuate the complex calmly but rapidly. Other civilians exiting the stairs who were either injured or exhausted collapsed at the foot of these stairs; officers then assisted them out of the building.[145]

When civilians reached the concourse, another NYPD officer stationed at the bottom of the escalator directed them to exit through the concourse to the north and east and then out of the WTC complex. This exit route ensured that civilians would not be endangered by falling debris and people on West Street, on the plaza between the towers, and on Liberty Street.[146]

Some officers positioned themselves at the top of a flight of stairs by 5 WTC that led down into the concourse, going into the concourse when necessary to evacuate injured or disoriented civilians. Numerous other NYPD officers were stationed throughout the concourse, assisting burned, injured, and disoriented civilians, as well as directing all civilians to exit to the north and east. NYPD officers were also in the South Tower lobby to assist in civilian evacuation. NYPD officers stationed on Vesey Street between West Street and Church Street urged civilians not to remain in the area and instead to keep walking north.[147]

At 9:06, the NYPD Chief of Department instructed that no units were to land on the roof of either tower. At about 9:30, one of the helicopters present advised that a rooftop evacuation still would not be possible. One NYPD helicopter pilot believed one portion of the North Tower roof to be free enough of smoke that a hoist could be lowered in order to rescue people, but there was no one on the roof. This pilot's helicopter never attempted to hover directly over the tower. Another helicopter did attempt to do so, and its pilot stated that the severity of the heat from the jet fuel–laden fire in the North Tower would have made it impossible to hover low enough for a rescue, because the high temperature would have destabilized the helicopter.[148]

At 9:51, an aviation unit warned units of large pieces of debris hanging from the building. Prior to 9:59, no NYPD helicopter pilot predicted that either tower would collapse.[149]

Interaction of 911 Calls and NYPD Operations. At 9:37, a civilian on the 106th floor of the South Tower reported to a 911 operator that a lower floor—the "90-something floor"—was collapsing. This information was conveyed inaccurately by the 911 operator to an NYPD dispatcher. The dispatcher further confused the substance of the 911 call by telling NYPD officers at the WTC complex that "the 106th floor is crumbling" at 9:52, 15 minutes after the 911 call was placed. The NYPD dispatcher conveyed this message on the radio frequency used in precincts in the vicinity of the WTC and subsequently on the Special Operations Division channel, but not on City Wide channel 1.[150]

PAPD Response
Initial responders from outside PAPD commands proceeded to the police desk in 5 WTC or to the fire safety desk in the North Tower lobby. Some officers were then assigned to assist in stairwell evacuations; others were assigned to expedite evacuation in the plaza, concourse, and PATH station. As information was received of civilians trapped above ground-level floors of the North Tower, other PAPD officers were instructed to climb to those floors for rescue efforts. Still others began climbing toward the impact zone.[151]

At 9:11, the PAPD Superintendent and an inspector began walking up stairwell B of the North Tower to assess damage near and in the impact zone. The PAPD Chief and several other PAPD officers began ascending a stairwell in order to reach the Windows on the World restaurant on the 106th floor, from which calls had been made to the PAPD police desk reporting at least 100 people trapped.[152]

Many PAPD officers from different commands responded on their own initiative. By 9:30, the PAPD central police desk requested that responding officers meet at West and Vesey and await further instructions. In the absence of a predetermined command structure to deal with an incident of this magnitude, a number of PAPD inspectors, captains, and lieutenants stepped forward at around 9:30 to formulate an on-site response plan. They were hampered by not knowing how many officers were responding to the site and where those officers were operating. Many of the officers who responded to this command post lacked suitable protective equipment to enter the complex.[153]

By 9:58, one PAPD officer had reached the 44th-floor sky lobby of the North Tower. Also in the North Tower, one team of PAPD officers was in the mid-20s and another was in the lower 20s. Numerous PAPD officers were also climbing in the South Tower, including the PAPD ESU team. Many PAPD officers were on the ground floors of the complex—some assisting in evacuation, others manning the PAPD desk in 5 WTC or assisting at lobby command posts.[154]

OEM Response

After the South Tower was hit, OEM senior leadership decided to remain in its "bunker" and continue conducting operations, even though all civilians had been evacuated from 7 WTC. At approximately 9:30, a senior OEM official ordered the evacuation of the facility, after a Secret Service agent in 7 WTC advised him that additional commercial planes were not accounted for. Prior to its evacuation, no outside agency liaisons had reached OEM. OEM field responders were stationed in each tower's lobby, at the FDNY overall command post, and, at least for some period of time, at the NYPD command post at Church and Vesey.[155]

Summary

The emergency response effort escalated with the crash of United 175 into the South Tower. With that escalation, communications as well as command and control became increasingly critical and increasingly difficult. First responders assisted thousands of civilians in evacuating the towers, even as incident commanders from responding agencies lacked knowledge of what other agencies and, in some cases, their own responders were doing.

From 9:59 until 10:28 A.M.

At 9:58:59, the South Tower collapsed in ten seconds, killing all civilians and emergency personnel inside, as well a number of individuals—both first responders and civilians—in the concourse, in the Marriott, and on neighboring streets. The building collapsed into itself, causing a ferocious windstorm and creating a massive debris cloud. The Marriott hotel suffered significant damage as a result of the collapse of the South Tower.[156]

Civilian Response in the North Tower

The 911 calls placed from most locations in the North Tower grew increasingly desperate as time went on. As late as 10:28, people remained alive in some locations, including on the 92nd and 79th floors. Below the impact zone, it is likely that most civilians who were physically and emotionally capable of descending had exited the tower. The civilians who were nearing the bottom of stairwell C were assisted out of the building by NYPD, FDNY, and PAPD personnel. Others, who experienced difficulty evacuating, were being helped by first responders on lower floors.[157]

FDNY Response

Immediate Impact of the Collapse of the South Tower. The FDNY overall command post and posts in the North Tower lobby, the Marriott lobby, and the staging area on West Street south of Liberty all ceased to operate upon the collapse of the South Tower, as did EMS staging areas, because of their proximity to the building.[158]

Those who had been in the North Tower lobby had no way of knowing that the South Tower had suffered a complete collapse. Chiefs who had fled from the overall command post on the west side of West Street took shelter in the underground parking garage at 2 World Financial Center and were not available to influence FDNY operations for the next ten minutes or so.[159]

When the South Tower collapsed, firefighters on upper floors of the North Tower heard a violent roar, and many were knocked off their feet; they saw debris coming up the stairs and observed that the power was lost and emergency lights activated. Nevertheless, those firefighters not standing near windows facing south had no way of knowing that the South Tower had collapsed; many surmised that a bomb had exploded, or that the North Tower had suffered a partial collapse on its upper floors.[160]

We do not know whether the repeater channel continued to function after 9:59.[161]

Initial Evacuation Instructions and Communications. The South Tower's total collapse was immediately communicated on the Manhattan dispatch channel by an FDNY boat on the Hudson River; but to our knowledge, no one at the site received this information, because every FDNY command post had been abandoned—including the overall command post, which included the Field Comm van. Despite his lack of knowledge of what had happened to the South Tower, a chief in the process of evacuating the North Tower lobby sent out an order within a minute of the collapse: "Command to all units in Tower 1, evacuate the building." Another chief from the North Tower lobby soon followed with an additional evacuation order issued on tactical 1.[162]

Evacuation orders did not follow the protocol for giving instructions when a building's collapse may be imminent—a protocol that includes constantly repeating "Mayday, Mayday, Mayday"—during the 29 minutes between the fall of the South Tower and that of the North Tower. In addition, most of the evacuation instructions did not mention that the South Tower had collapsed. However, at least three firefighters heard evacuation instructions which stated that the North Tower was in danger of "imminent collapse."[163]

FDNY Personnel above the Ground Floors of the North Tower. Within minutes, some firefighters began to hear evacuation orders over tactical 1. At least one chief also gave the evacuation instruction on the command channel used only by chiefs in the North Tower, which was much less crowded.[164]

At least two battalion chiefs on upper floors of the North Tower—one on the 23rd floor and one on the 35th floor—heard the evacuation instruction on the command channel and repeated it to everyone they came across. The chief on the 23rd floor apparently aggressively took charge to ensure that all firefighters on the floors in the immediate area were evacuating. The chief on the 35th floor also heard a separate radio communication stating that the South Tower had collapsed (which the chief on the 23rd floor may have heard as well). He subsequently acted with a sense of urgency, and some firefighters heard the evacuation order for the first time when he repeated it on tactical 1. This chief also had a bullhorn and traveled to each of the stairwells and shouted the evacuation order: "All FDNY, get the fuck out!" As a result of his efforts, many firefighters who had not been in the process of evacuating began to do so.[165]

Other firefighters did not receive the evacuation transmissions, for one of four reasons: First, some FDNY radios did not pick up the transmission because of the difficulties of radio communications in high-rises. Second, the numbers trying to use tactical 1 after the South Tower collapsed may have drowned out some evacuation instructions. According to one FDNY lieutenant who was on the 31st floor of the North Tower at the time, "[Tactical] channel 1 just might have been so bogged down that it may have been impossible to get that order through."[166] Third, some firefighters in the North Tower were off-duty and did not have radios. Fourth, some firefighters in the North Tower had been dispatched to the South Tower and likely were on the different tactical channel assigned to that tower.[167]

FDNY personnel in the North Tower who received the evacuation orders did not respond uniformly. Some units—including one whose officer knew that the South Tower had collapsed—either delayed or stopped their evacuation in order to assist nonambulatory civilians. Some units whose members had become separated during the climb attempted to regroup so they could descend together. Some units began to evacuate but, according to eyewitnesses, did not hurry. At least several firefighters who survived believed that they and others would have evacuated more urgently had they known of the South Tower's complete collapse. Other firefighters continued to sit and rest on floors while other companies descended past them and reminded them that they were supposed to evacuate. Some firefighters were determined not to leave the building while other FDNY personnel remained inside and, in one case, convinced others to remain with them. In another case, firefighters had successfully descended to the lobby, where another firefighter then persuaded them to reascend in order to look for specific FDNY personnel.[168]

Other FDNY personnel did not hear the evacuation order on their radio but were advised orally to leave the building by other firefighters and police who were themselves evacuating.[169]

By 10:24, approximately five FDNY companies reached the bottom of stairwell B and entered the North Tower lobby. They stood in the lobby for more than a minute, not certain what to do, as no chiefs were present. Finally, one firefighter—who had earlier seen from a window that the South Tower had collapsed—urged that they all leave, as this tower could fall as well. The units then proceeded to exit onto West Street. While they were doing so, the North Tower began its pancake collapse, killing some of these men.[170]

Other FDNY Personnel. The Marriott Hotel suffered significant damage in the collapse of the South Tower. Those in the lobby were knocked down and enveloped in the darkness of a debris cloud. Some were hurt but could walk. Others were more severely injured, and some were trapped. Several firefighters came across a group of about 50 civilians who had been taking shelter in the restaurant and assisted them in evacuating. Up above, at the time of the South Tower's collapse four companies were descending the stairs single file in a line of approximately 20 men. Four survived.[171]

At the time of the South Tower's collapse, two FDNY companies were either at the eastern side of the North Tower lobby, near the mall concourse, or actually in the mall concourse, trying to reach the South Tower. Many of these men were thrown off their feet by the collapse of the South Tower; they then attempted to regroup in the darkness of the debris cloud and evacuate civilians and themselves, not knowing that the South Tower had collapsed. Several of these firefighters subsequently searched the PATH station below the concourse—unaware that the PAPD had cleared the area of all civilians by 9:19.[172]

At about 10:15, the FDNY Chief of Department and the Chief of Safety, who had returned to West Street from the parking garage, confirmed that the South Tower had collapsed. The Chief of Department issued a radio order for all units to evacuate the North Tower, repeating it about five times. He then directed that the FDNY command post be moved further north on West Street and told FDNY units in the area to proceed north on West Street toward Chambers Street. At approximately 10:25, he radioed for two ladder companies to respond to the Marriott, where he was aware that both FDNY personnel and civilians were trapped.[173]

Many chiefs, including several of those who had been in the North Tower lobby, did not learn that the South Tower had collapsed until 30 minutes or more after the event. According to two eyewitnesses, however, one senior FDNY chief who knew that the South Tower had collapsed strongly expressed the opinion that the North Tower would not collapse, because unlike the South Tower, it had not been hit on a corner.[174]

After the South Tower collapsed, some firefighters on the streets neighboring the North Tower remained where they were or came closer to the North Tower. Some of these firefighters did not know that the South Tower had collapsed, but many chose despite that knowledge to remain in an attempt to save additional lives. According to one such firefighter, a chief who was preparing to mount a search-and-rescue mission in the Marriott, "I would never think of myself as a leader of men if I had headed north on West Street after [the] South Tower collapsed." Just outside the North Tower on West Street one firefighter was directing others exiting the building, telling them when no jumpers were coming down and it was safe to run out. A senior chief had grabbed an NYPD bullhorn and was urging firefighters exiting onto West Street to continue running north, well away from the WTC. Three of the most senior and respected members of the FDNY were involved in attempting to rescue civilians and firefighters from the Marriott.[175]

NYPD Response
A member of the NYPD Aviation Unit radioed that the South Tower had collapsed immediately after it happened, and further advised that all people in the WTC complex and nearby areas should be evacuated. At 10:04, NYPD aviation reported that the top 15 stories of the North Tower "were glowing red" and that they might collapse. At 10:08, a helicopter pilot warned that he did not believe the North Tower would last much longer.[176]

Immediately after the South Tower collapsed, many NYPD radio frequencies became overwhelmed with transmissions relating to injured, trapped, or missing officers. As a result, NYPD radio communications became strained on most channels. Nevertheless, they remained effective enough for the two closest NYPD mobilization points to be moved further from the WTC at 10:06.[177]

Just like most firefighters, the ESU rescue teams in the North Tower had no idea that the South Tower had collapsed. However, by 10:00 the ESU officer running the command post at Church and Vesey ordered the evacuation of all ESU units from the WTC complex. This officer, who had observed the South Tower collapse, reported it to ESU units in the North Tower in his evacuation instruction.[178]

This instruction was clearly heard by the two ESU units already in the North Tower and the other ESU unit preparing to enter the tower. The ESU team on the 31st floor found the full collapse of the South Tower so unfathomable that they radioed back to the ESU officer at the command post and asked him to repeat his communication. He reiterated his urgent message.[179]

The ESU team on the 31st floor conferred with the FDNY personnel there to ensure that they, too, knew that they had to evacuate, then proceeded down stairwell B. During the descent, they reported seeing many firefighters who were resting and did not seem to be in the process of evacuating. They further reported advising these firefighters to evacuate, but said that at times they were not acknowledged. In the opinion of one of the ESU officers, some of these firefighters essentially refused to take orders from cops. At least one firefighter who was in the North Tower has supported that assessment, stating that he was not going to take an evacuation instruction from a cop that morning. However, another firefighter reports that ESU officers ran past him without advising him to evacuate.[180]

The ESU team on the 11th floor began descending stairwell C after receiving the evacuation order. Once near the mezzanine level—where stairwell C ended—this team spread out in chain formation, stretching from several floors down to the mezzanine itself. They used their flashlights to provide a path of beacons through the darkness and debris for civilians climbing down the stairs. Eventually, when no one else appeared to be descending, the ESU team exited the North Tower and ran one at a time to 6 WTC, dodging those who still were jumping from the upper floors of the North Tower by acting as spotters for each other. They remained in the area, conducting additional searches for civilians; all but two of them died.[181]

After surviving the South Tower's collapse, the ESU team that had been preparing to enter the North Tower spread into chain formation and created a path for civilians (who had exited from the North Tower mezzanine) to evacuate the WTC complex by descending the stairs on the north side of 5 and 6 WTC, which led down to Vesey Street. They remained at this post until the North Tower collapsed, yet all survived.[182]

The three plainclothes NYPD officers who had made it up to the 54th floor of the North Tower felt the building shake violently at 9:59 as the South Tower collapsed (though they did not know the cause). Immediately thereafter, they were joined by three firefighters from an FDNY engine company. One of the firefighters apparently heard an evacuation order on his radio, but responded in a return radio communication, "We're not fucking coming out!" However, the firefighters urged the police officers to descend because they lacked the protective gear and equipment needed to handle the increasing smoke and heat. The police officers reluctantly began descending, checking that the lower floors were clear of civilians. They proceeded down stairwell B, poking their heads into every floor and briefly looking for civilians.[183]

Other NYPD officers helping evacuees on the mezzanine level of the North Tower were enveloped in the debris cloud that resulted from the South Tower's collapse. They struggled to regroup in the darkness and to evacuate both themselves and civilians they encountered. At least one of them died in the collapse of the North Tower. At least one NYPD officer from this area managed to evacuate out toward 5 WTC, where he teamed up with a Port Authority police officer and acted as a spotter in advising the civilians who were still exiting when they could safely run from 1 WTC to 5 WTC and avoid being struck by people and debris falling from the upper floors.[184]

At the time of the collapse of the South Tower, there were numerous NYPD officers in the concourse, some of whom are believed to have died there. Those who survived struggled to evacuate themselves in darkness, assisting civilians as they exited the concourse in all directions.[185]

Port Authority Response
The collapse of the South Tower forced the evacuation of the PAPD command post on West and Vesey, compelling PAPD officers to move north. There is no evidence that PAPD officers without WTC Command radios received an evacuation order by radio. Some of these officers in the North Tower decided to evacuate, either on their own or in consultation with other first responders they came across. Some greatly slowed their own descent in order to assist nonambulatory civilians.[186]

After 10:28 A.M.
The North Tower collapsed at 10:28:25 A.M., killing all civilians alive on upper floors, an undetermined number below, and scores of first responders. The FDNY Chief of Department, the Port Authority Police Department Superintendent, and many of their senior staff were killed. Incredibly, twelve firefighters, one PAPD officer, and three civilians who were descending stairwell B of the North Tower survived its collapse.[187]

On September 11, the nation suffered the largest loss of life—2,973—on its soil as a result of hostile attack in its history. The FDNY suffered 343 fatalities— the largest loss of life of any emergency response agency in history. The PAPD suffered 37 fatalities—the largest loss of life of any police force in history. The NYPD suffered 23 fatalities—the second largest loss of life of any police force in history, exceeded only by the number of PAPD officers lost the same day.[188]

Mayor Giuliani, along with the Police and Fire commissioners and the OEM director, moved quickly north and established an emergency operations command post at the Police Academy. Over the coming hours, weeks, and months, thousands of civilians and city, state, and federal employees devoted themselves around the clock to putting New York City back on its feet.[189]

9.3 EMERGENCY RESPONSE AT THE PENTAGON

If it had happened on any other day, the disaster at the Pentagon would be remembered as a singular challenge and an extraordinary national story. Yet the calamity at the World Trade Center that same morning included catastrophic damage 1,000 feet above the ground that instantly imperiled tens of thousands of people. The two experiences are not comparable. Nonetheless, broader les-

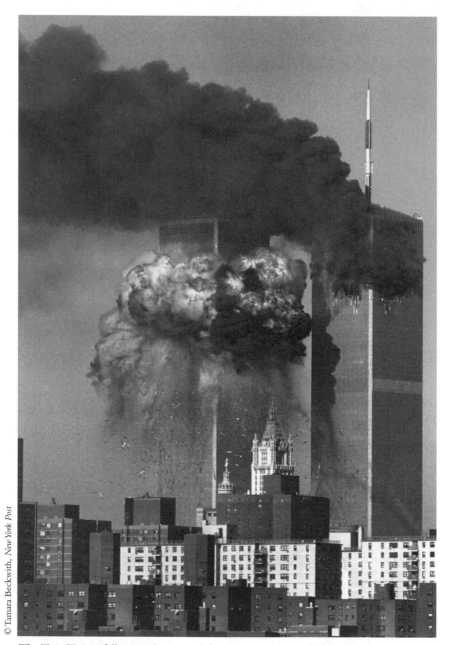

The Twin Towers following the impact of American Airlines Flight 11 and United Airlines Flight 175

The Pentagon, after being struck by American Airlines Flight 77

United Airlines Flight 93 crash site, Shanksville, Pennsylvania

sons in integrating multiagency response efforts are apparent when we analyze the response at the Pentagon.

The emergency response at the Pentagon represented a mix of local, state, and federal jurisdictions and was generally effective. It overcame the inherent complications of a response across jurisdictions because the Incident Command System, a formalized management structure for emergency response, was in place in the National Capital Region on 9/11.[190]

Because of the nature of the event—a plane crash, fire, and partial building collapse—the Arlington County Fire Department served as incident commander. Different agencies had different roles. The incident required a major rescue, fire, and medical response from Arlington County at the U.S. military's headquarters—a facility under the control of the secretary of defense. Since it was a terrorist attack, the Department of Justice was the lead federal agency in charge (with authority delegated to the FBI for operational response). Additionally, the terrorist attack affected the daily operations and emergency management requirements of Arlington County and all bordering and surrounding jurisdictions.[191]

At 9:37, the west wall of the Pentagon was hit by hijacked American Airlines Flight 77, a Boeing 757. The crash caused immediate and catastrophic damage. All 64 people aboard the airliner were killed, as were 125 people inside the Pentagon (70 civilians and 55 military service members). One hundred six people were seriously injured and transported to area hospitals.[192]

While no emergency response is flawless, the response to the 9/11 terrorist attack on the Pentagon was mainly a success for three reasons: first, the strong professional relationships and trust established among emergency responders; second, the adoption of the Incident Command System; and third, the pursuit of a regional approach to response. Many fire and police agencies that responded had extensive prior experience working together on regional events and training exercises. Indeed, at the time preparations were under way at many of these agencies to ensure public safety at the annual meetings of the International Monetary Fund and the World Bank scheduled to be held later that month in Washington, D.C.[193]

Local, regional, state, and federal agencies immediately responded to the Pentagon attack. In addition to county fire, police, and sheriff's departments, the response was assisted by the Metropolitan Washington Airports Authority, Ronald Reagan Washington National Airport Fire Department, Fort Myer Fire Department, the Virginia State Police, the Virginia Department of Emergency Management, the FBI, FEMA, a National Medical Response Team, the Bureau of Alcohol, Tobacco, and Firearms, and numerous military personnel within the Military District of Washington.[194]

Command was established at 9:41. At the same time, the Arlington County Emergency Communications Center contacted the fire departments of Fairfax County, Alexandria, and the District of Columbia to request mutual aid.

The incident command post provided a clear view of and access to the crash site, allowing the incident commander to assess the situation at all times.[195]

At 9:55, the incident commander ordered an evacuation of the Pentagon impact area because a partial collapse was imminent; it occurred at 9:57, and no first responder was injured.[196]

At 10:15, the incident commander ordered a full evacuation of the command post because of the warning of an approaching hijacked aircraft passed along by the FBI. This was the first of three evacuations caused by reports of incoming aircraft, and the evacuation order was well communicated and well coordinated.[197]

Several factors facilitated the response to this incident, and distinguish it from the far more difficult task in New York. There was a single incident, and it was not 1,000 feet above ground. The incident site was relatively easy to secure and contain, and there were no other buildings in the immediate area. There was no collateral damage beyond the Pentagon.[198]

Yet the Pentagon response encountered difficulties that echo those experienced in New York. As the "Arlington County: After-Action Report" notes, there were significant problems with both self-dispatching and communications: "Organizations, response units, and individuals proceeding on their own initiative directly to an incident site, without the knowledge and permission of the host jurisdiction and the Incident Commander, complicate the exercise of command, increase the risks faced by bonafide responders, and exacerbate the challenge of accountability." With respect to communications, the report concludes: "Almost all aspects of communications continue to be problematic, from initial notification to tactical operations. Cellular telephones were of little value. . . . Radio channels were initially oversaturated. . . . Pagers seemed to be the most reliable means of notification when available and used, but most firefighters are not issued pagers."[199]

It is a fair inference, given the differing situations in New York City and Northern Virginia, that the problems in command, control, and communications that occurred at both sites will likely recur in any emergency of similar scale. The task looking forward is to enable first responders to respond in a coordinated manner with the greatest possible awareness of the situation.

9.4 ANALYSIS

Like the national defense effort described in chapter 1, the emergency response to the attacks on 9/11 was necessarily improvised. In New York, the FDNY, NYPD, the Port Authority, WTC employees, and the building occupants themselves did their best to cope with the effects of an unimaginable catastrophe—unfolding furiously over a mere 102 minutes—for which they were unprepared in terms of both training and mindset. As a result of the efforts of first responders, assistance from each other, and their own good instincts and goodwill, the vast majority of civilians below the impact zone were able to evacuate the towers.

The National Institute of Standards and Technology has provided a preliminary estimation that between 16,400 and 18,800 civilians were in the WTC complex as of 8:46 A.M. on September 11. At most 2,152 individuals died at the WTC complex who were not (1) fire or police first responders, (2) security or fire safety personnel of the WTC or individual companies, (3) volunteer civilians who ran to the WTC after the planes' impact to help others, or (4) on the two planes that crashed into the Twin Towers. Out of this total number of fatalities, we can account for the workplace location of 2,052 individuals, or 95.35 percent. Of this number, 1,942 or 94.64 percent either worked or were supposed to attend a meeting at or above the respective impact zones of the Twin Towers; only 110, or 5.36 percent of those who died, worked below the impact zone. While a given person's office location at the WTC does not definitively indicate where that individual died that morning or whether he or she could have evacuated, these data strongly suggest that the evacuation was a success for civilians below the impact zone.[200]

Several factors influenced the evacuation on September 11. It was aided greatly by changes made by the Port Authority in response to the 1993 bombing and by the training of both Port Authority personnel and civilians after that time. Stairwells remained lit near unaffected floors; some tenants relied on procedures learned in fire drills to help them to safety; others were guided down the stairs by fire safety officials based in the lobby. Because of damage caused by the impact of the planes, the capability of the sophisticated building systems may have been impaired. Rudimentary improvements, however, such as the addition of glow strips to the handrails and stairs, were credited by some as the reason for their survival. The general evacuation time for the towers dropped from more than four hours in 1993 to under one hour on September 11 for most civilians who were not trapped or physically incapable of enduring a long descent.

First responders also played a significant role in the success of the evacuation. Some specific rescues are quantifiable, such as an FDNY company's rescue of civilians trapped on the 22d floor of the North Tower, or the success of FDNY, PAPD, and NYPD personnel in carrying nonambulatory civilians out of both the North and South Towers. In other instances, intangibles combined to reduce what could have been a much higher death total. It is impossible to measure how many more civilians who descended to the ground floors would have died but for the NYPD and PAPD personnel directing them—via safe exit routes that avoided jumpers and debris—to leave the complex urgently but calmly. It is impossible to measure how many more civilians would have died but for the determination of many members of the FDNY, PAPD, and NYPD to continue assisting civilians after the South Tower collapsed. It is impossible to measure the calming influence that ascending firefighters had on descending civilians or whether but for the firefighters' presence the poor behavior of a very few civilians could have caused a dangerous and panicked mob flight. But the positive impact of the first responders on the evacuation came at a tremendous cost of first responder lives lost.[201]

Civilian and Private-Sector Challenges

The "first" first responders on 9/11, as in most catastrophes, were private-sector civilians. Because 85 percent of our nation's critical infrastructure is controlled not by government but by the private sector, private-sector civilians are likely to be the first responders in any future catastrophes. For that reason, we have assessed the state of private sector and civilian preparedness in order to formulate recommendations to address this critical need. Our recommendations grow out of the experience of the civilians at the World Trade Center on 9/11.

Lack of Protocol for Rooftop Rescues. Civilians at or above the impact zone in the North Tower had the smallest hope of survival. Once the plane struck, they were prevented from descending because of damage to or impassable conditions in the building's three stairwells. The only hope for those on the upper floors of the North Tower would have been a swift and extensive air rescue. Several factors made this impossible. Doors leading to the roof were kept locked for security reasons, and damage to software in the security command station prevented a lock release order from taking effect. Even if the doors had not been locked, structural and radiation hazards made the rooftops unsuitable staging areas for a large number of civilians; and even if conditions permitted general helicopter evacuations—which was not the case—only several people could be lifted at a time.

The WTC lacked any plan for evacuation of civilians on upper floors of the WTC in the event that all stairwells were impassable below.

Lack of Comprehensive Evacuation of South Tower Immediately after the North Tower Impact. No decision has been criticized more than the decision of building personnel not to evacuate the South Tower immediately after the North Tower was hit. A firm and prompt evacuation order would likely have led many to safety. Even a strictly "advisory" announcement would not have dissuaded those who decided for themselves to evacuate. The advice to stay in place was understandable, however, when considered in its context. At that moment, no one appears to have thought a second plane could hit the South Tower. The evacuation of thousands of people was seen as inherently dangerous. Additionally, conditions were hazardous in some areas outside the towers.[202]

Less understandable, in our view, is the instruction given to some civilians who had reached the lobby to return to their offices. They could have been held in the lobby or perhaps directed through the underground concourse.

Despite the initial advice given over its public-address system, the South Tower was ordered to be evacuated by the FDNY and PAPD within 12 minutes of the North Tower's being hit. If not for a second, unanticipated attack, the evacuation presumably would have proceeded.

Impact of Fire Safety Plan and Fire Drills on Evacuation. Once the South Tower was hit, civilians on upper floors wasted time ascending the stairs instead of searching for a clear path down, when stairwell A was at least initially passable. Although rooftop rescues had not been conclusively ruled out, civilians were not informed in fire drills that roof doors were locked, that rooftop areas were hazardous, and that no helicopter evacuation plan existed.

In both towers, civilians who were able to reach the stairs and descend were also stymied by the deviations in the stairways and by smoke doors. This confusion delayed the evacuation of some and may have obstructed that of others. The Port Authority has acknowledged that in the future, tenants should be made aware of what conditions they will encounter during descent.

Impact of 911 Calls on Evacuation. The NYPD's 911 operators and FDNY dispatch were not adequately integrated into the emergency response. In several ways, the 911 system was not ready to cope with a major disaster. These operators and dispatchers were one of the only sources of information for individuals at and above the impact zone of the towers. The FDNY ordered both towers fully evacuated by 8:57, but this guidance was not conveyed to 911 operators and FDNY dispatchers, who for the next hour often continued to advise civilians not to self-evacuate, regardless of whether they were above or below the impact zones. Nor were 911 operators or FDNY dispatchers advised that rooftop rescues had been ruled out. This failure may have been harmful to civilians on the upper floors of the South Tower who called 911 and were not told that their only evacuation hope was to attempt to descend, not to ascend. In planning for future disasters, it is important to integrate those taking 911 calls into the emergency response team and to involve them in providing up-to-date information and assistance to the public.

Preparedness of Individual Civilians. One clear lesson of September 11 is that individual civilians need to take responsibility for maximizing the probability that they will survive, should disaster strike. Clearly, many building occupants in the World Trade Center did not take preparedness seriously. Individuals should know the exact location of every stairwell in their workplace. In addition, they should have access at all times to flashlights, which were deemed invaluable by some civilians who managed to evacuate the WTC on September 11.

Challenges Experienced by First Responders
The Challenge of Incident Command. As noted above, in July 2001, Mayor Giuliani updated a directive titled "Direction and Control of Emergencies in the City of New York." The directive designated, for different types of emergencies, an appropriate agency as "Incident Commander"; it would be "responsible for the management of the City's response to the emergency." The directive also provided that where incidents are "so multifaceted that no one agency immediately stands out as the Incident Commander, OEM will assign the role of Incident Commander to an agency as the situation demands."[203]

To some degree, the Mayor's directive for incident command was followed on 9/11. It was clear that the lead response agency was the FDNY, and that the other responding local, federal, bistate, and state agencies acted in a supporting role. There was a tacit understanding that FDNY personnel would have primary responsibility for evacuating civilians who were above the ground floors of the Twin Towers, while NYPD and PAPD personnel would be in charge of evacuating civilians from the WTC complex once they reached ground level. The NYPD also greatly assisted responding FDNY units by clearing emergency lanes to the WTC.[204]

In addition, coordination occurred at high levels of command. For example, the Mayor and Police Commissioner consulted with the Chief of the Department of the FDNY at approximately 9:20. There were other instances of coordination at operational levels, and information was shared on an ad hoc basis. For example, an NYPD ESU team passed the news of their evacuation order to firefighters in the North Tower.[205]

It is also clear, however, that the response operations lacked the kind of integrated communications and unified command contemplated in the directive. These problems existed both within and among individual responding agencies.

Command and Control within First Responder Agencies. For a unified incident management system to succeed, each participant must have command and control of its own units and adequate internal communications. This was not always the case at the WTC on 9/11.

Understandably lacking experience in responding to events of the magnitude of the World Trade Center attacks, the FDNY as an institution proved incapable of coordinating the numbers of units dispatched to different points within the 16-acre complex. As a result, numerous units were congregating in the undamaged Marriott Hotel and at the overall command post on West Street by 9:30, while chiefs in charge of the South Tower still were in desperate need of units. With better understanding of the resources already available, additional units might not have been dispatched to the South Tower at 9:37.

The task of accounting for and coordinating the units was rendered difficult, if not impossible, by internal communications breakdowns resulting from the limited capabilities of radios in the high-rise environment of the WTC and from confusion over which personnel were assigned to which frequency. Furthermore, when the South Tower collapsed the overall FDNY command post ceased to operate, which compromised the FDNY's ability to understand the situation; an FDNY marine unit's immediate radio communication to FDNY dispatch that the South Tower had fully collapsed was not conveyed to chiefs at the scene. The FDNY's inability to coordinate and account for the different radio channels that would be used in an emergency of this scale contributed to the early lack of units in the South Tower, whose lobby chief initially could not communicate with anyone outside that tower.[206]

Though almost no one at 9:50 on September 11 was contemplating an imminent total collapse of the Twin Towers, many first responders and civilians were contemplating the possibility of imminent additional terrorist attacks throughout New York City. Had any such attacks occurred, the FDNY's response would have been severely compromised by the concentration of so many of its off-duty personnel, particularly its elite personnel, at the WTC.

The Port Authority's response was hampered by the lack of both standard operating procedures and radios capable of enabling multiple commands to respond in unified fashion to an incident at the WTC. Many officers reporting from the tunnel and airport commands could not hear instructions being issued over the WTC Command frequency. In addition, command and control was complicated by senior Port Authority Police officials becoming directly involved in frontline rescue operations.

The NYPD experienced comparatively fewer internal command and control and communications issues. Because the department has a history of mobilizing thousands of officers for major events requiring crowd control, its technical radio capability and major incident protocols were more easily adapted to an incident of the magnitude of 9/11. In addition, its mission that day lay largely outside the towers themselves. Although there were ESU teams and a few individual police officers climbing in the towers, the vast majority of NYPD personnel were staged outside, assisting with crowd control and evacuation and securing other sites in the city. The NYPD ESU division had firm command and control over its units, in part because there were so few of them (in comparison to the number of FDNY companies) and all reported to the same ESU command post. It is unclear, however, whether non-ESU NYPD officers operating on the ground floors, and in a few cases on upper floors, of the WTC were as well coordinated.

Significant shortcomings within the FDNY's command and control capabilities were painfully exposed on September 11. To its great credit, the department has made a substantial effort in the past three years to address these. While significant problems in the command and control of the PAPD also were exposed on September 11, it is less clear that the Port Authority has adopted new training exercises or major incident protocols to address these shortcomings.[207]

Lack of Coordination among First Responder Agencies. Any attempt to establish a unified command on 9/11 would have been further frustrated by the lack of communication and coordination among responding agencies. Certainly, the FDNY was not "responsible for the management of the City's response to the emergency," as the Mayor's directive would have required. The command posts were in different locations, and OEM headquarters, which could have served as a focal point for information sharing, did not play an integrating role in ensuring that information was shared among agencies on 9/11, even prior to its evacuation. There was a lack of comprehensive coordination between FDNY, NYPD, and PAPD personnel climbing above the ground floors in the Twin Towers.

Information that was critical to informed decisionmaking was not shared among agencies. FDNY chiefs in leadership roles that morning have told us that their decision making capability was hampered by a lack of information from NYPD aviation. At 9:51 A.M., a helicopter pilot cautioned that "large pieces" of the South Tower appeared to be about to fall and could pose a danger to those below. Immediately after the tower's collapse, a helicopter pilot radioed that news. This transmission was followed by communications at 10:08, 10:15, and 10:22 that called into question the condition of the North Tower. The FDNY chiefs would have benefited greatly had they been able to communicate with personnel in a helicopter.

The consequence of the lack of real-time intelligence from NYPD aviation should not be overstated. Contrary to a widely held misperception, no NYPD helicopter predicted the fall of either tower before the South Tower collapsed, and no NYPD personnel began to evacuate the WTC complex prior to that time. Furthermore, the FDNY, as an institution, was in possession of the knowledge that the South Tower had collapsed as early as the NYPD, as its fall had been immediately reported by an FDNY boat on a dispatch channel. Because of internal breakdowns within the department, however, this information was not disseminated to FDNY personnel on the scene.

The FDNY, PAPD, and NYPD did not coordinate their units that were searching the WTC complex for civilians. In many cases, redundant searches of specific floors and areas were conducted. It is unclear whether fewer first responders in the aggregate would have been in the Twin Towers if there had been an integrated response, or what impact, if any, redundant searches had on the total number of first responder fatalities.

Whether the lack of coordination between the FDNY and NYPD on September 11 had a catastrophic effect has been the subject of controversy. We believe that there are too many variables for us to responsibly quantify those consequences. It is clear that the lack of coordination did not affect adversely the evacuation of civilians. It is equally clear, however, that the Incident Command System did not function to integrate awareness among agencies or to facilitate interagency response.[208]

If New York and other major cities are to be prepared for future terrorist attacks, different first responder agencies within each city must be fully coordinated, just as different branches of the U.S. military are. Coordination entails a unified command that comprehensively deploys all dispatched police, fire, and other first responder resources.

In May 2004, New York City adopted an emergency response plan that expressly contemplates two or more agencies jointly being lead agency when responding to a terrorist attack but does not mandate a comprehensive and unified incident command that can deploy and monitor all first responder resources from one overall command post. In our judgment, this falls short of an optimal response plan, which requires clear command and control, common training, and the trust that such training creates. The experience of the military suggests that integrated into such a coordinated response should be a unified field intelligence unit, which should receive and combine information from all first responders—including 911 operators. Such a field intelligence unit could be valuable in large and complex incidents.

Radio Communication Challenges: The Effectiveness and Urgency of Evacuation Instructions. As discussed above, the location of the NYPD ESU command post was crucial in making possible an urgent evacuation order explaining the South Tower's full collapse. Firefighters most certainly would have benefited from that information.

A separate matter is the varied success at conveying evacuation instructions to personnel in the North Tower after the South Tower's collapse. The success of NYPD ESU instruction is attributable to a combination of (1) the strength of the radios, (2) the relatively small numbers of individuals using them, and (3) use of the correct channel by all.

The same three factors worked against successful communication among FDNY personnel. First, the radios' effectiveness was drastically reduced in the high-rise environment. Second, tactical channel 1 was simply overwhelmed by the number of units attempting to communicate on it at 10:00. Third, some firefighters were on the wrong channel or simply lacked radios altogether.

It is impossible to know what difference it made that units in the North Tower were not using the repeater channel after 10:00. While the repeater channel was at least partially operational before the South Tower collapsed, we do not know whether it continued to be operational after 9:59.

Even without the repeater channel, *at least* 24 of the *at most* 32 companies who were dispatched to and actually in the North Tower received the evacuation instruction—either via radio or directly from other first responders. Nevertheless, many of these firefighters died, either because they delayed their evacuation to assist civilians, attempted to regroup their units, lacked urgency, or some combination of these factors. In addition, many other firefighters not dispatched to the North Tower also died in its collapse. Some had their radios on the wrong channel. Others were off-duty and lacked radios. In view of these considerations, we conclude that the technical failure of FDNY radios, while a contributing factor, was not the primary cause of the many firefighter fatalities in the North Tower.[209]

The FDNY has worked hard in the past several years to address its radio deficiencies. To improve radio capability in high-rises, the FDNY has internally developed a "post radio" that is small enough for a battalion chief to carry to the upper floors and that greatly repeats and enhances radio signal strength.[210]

The story with respect to Port Authority police officers in the North Tower is less complicated; most of them lacked access to the radio channel on which the Port Authority police evacuation order was given. Since September 11, the Port Authority has worked hard to integrate the radio systems of their different commands.

. . .

THE LESSON OF 9/11 for civilians and first responders can be stated simply: in the new age of terror, they—we—are the primary targets. The losses America suffered that day demonstrated both the gravity of the terrorist threat and the commensurate need to prepare ourselves to meet it.

The first responders of today live in a world transformed by the attacks on 9/11. Because no one believes that every conceivable form of attack can be prevented, civilians and first responders will again find themselves on the front lines. We must plan for that eventuality. A rededication to preparedness is perhaps the best way to honor the memories of those we lost that day.

10

WARTIME

AFTER THE ATTACKS had occurred, while crisis managers were still sorting out a number of unnerving false alarms, Air Force One flew to Barksdale Air Force Base in Louisiana. One of these alarms was of a reported threat against Air Force One itself, a threat eventually run down to a misunderstood communication in the hectic White House Situation Room that morning.[1]

While the plan at the elementary school had been to return to Washington, by the time Air Force One was airborne at 9:55 A.M. the Secret Service, the President's advisers, and Vice President Cheney were strongly advising against it. President Bush reluctantly acceded to this advice and, at about 10:10, Air Force One changed course and began heading due west. The immediate objective was to find a safe location—not too far away—where the President could land and speak to the American people. The Secret Service was also interested in refueling the aircraft and paring down the size of the traveling party. The President's military aide, an Air Force officer, quickly researched the options and, sometime around 10:20, identified Barksdale Air Force Base as an appropriate interim destination.[2]

When Air Force One landed at Barksdale at about 11:45, personnel from the local Secret Service office were still en route to the airfield. The motorcade consisted of a military police lead vehicle and a van; the proposed briefing theater had no phones or electrical outlets. Staff scrambled to prepare another room for the President's remarks, while the lead Secret Service agent reviewed the security situation with superiors in Washington. The President completed his statement, which for security reasons was taped and not broadcast live, and the traveling party returned to Air Force One. The next destination was discussed: once again the Secret Service recommended against returning to Washington, and the Vice President agreed. Offutt Air Force Base in Nebraska was chosen because of its elaborate command and control facilities, and because it could accommodate overnight lodging for 50 persons. The Secret Service wanted a place where the President could spend several days, if necessary.[3]

Air Force One arrived at Offutt at 2:50 P.M. At about 3:15, President Bush met with his principal advisers through a secure video teleconference.[4] Rice said President Bush began the meeting with the words, "We're at war,"[5] and that Director of Central Intelligence George Tenet said the agency was still assessing who was responsible, but the early signs all pointed to al Qaeda.[6] That evening the Deputies Committee returned to the pending presidential directive they had labored over during the summer.[7]

The secretary of defense directed the nation's armed forces to Defense Condition 3, an increased state of military readiness.[8] For the first time in history, all nonemergency civilian aircraft in the United States were grounded, stranding tens of thousands of passengers across the country. Contingency plans for the continuity of government and the evacuation of leaders had been implemented.[9] The Pentagon had been struck; the White House or the Capitol had narrowly escaped direct attack. Extraordinary security precautions were put in place at the nation's borders and ports.

In the late afternoon, the President overruled his aides' continuing reluctance to have him return to Washington and ordered Air Force One back to Andrews Air Force Base. He was flown by helicopter back to the White House, passing over the still-smoldering Pentagon. At 8:30 that evening, President Bush addressed the nation from the White House. After emphasizing that the first priority was to help the injured and protect against any further attacks, he said: "We will make no distinction between the terrorists who committed these acts and those who harbor them." He quoted Psalm 23—"though I walk through the valley of the shadow of death . . ." No American, he said, "will ever forget this day."[10]

Following his speech, President Bush met again with his National Security Council (NSC), expanded to include Secretary of Transportation Norman Mineta and Joseph Allbaugh, the director of the Federal Emergency Management Agency. Secretary of State Colin Powell, who had returned from Peru after hearing of the attacks, joined the discussion. They reviewed the day's events.[11]

10.1 IMMEDIATE RESPONSES AT HOME

As the urgent domestic issues accumulated, White House Deputy Chief of Staff Joshua Bolten chaired a temporary "domestic consequences" group.[12] The agenda in those first days is worth noting, partly as a checklist for future crisis planners. It began with problems of how to help victims and stanch the flowing losses to the American economy, such as

- Organizing federal emergency assistance. One question was what kind of public health advice to give about the air quality in Lower Manhattan in the vicinity of the fallen buildings.[13]

- Compensating victims. They evaluated legislative options, eventually setting up a federal compensation fund and defining the powers of a special master to run it.
- Determining federal assistance. On September 13, President Bush promised to provide $20 billion for New York City, in addition to the $20 billion his budget director had already guessed might be needed for the country as a whole.[14]
- Restoring civil aviation. On the morning of September 13, the national airspace reopened for use by airports that met newly improvised security standards.
- Reopening the financial markets. After extraordinary emergency efforts involving the White House, the Treasury Department, and the Securities and Exchange Commission, aided by unprecedented cooperation among the usually competitive firms of the financial industry, the markets reopened on Monday, September 17.[15]
- Deciding when and how to return border and port security to more normal operations.
- Evaluating legislative proposals to bail out the airline industry and cap its liability.

The very process of reviewing these issues underscored the absence of an effective government organization dedicated to assessing vulnerabilities and handling problems of protection and preparedness. Though a number of agencies had some part of the task, none had security as its primary mission.

By September 14, Vice President Cheney had decided to recommend, at least as a first step, a new White House entity to coordinate all the relevant agencies rather than tackle the challenge of combining them in a new department. This new White House entity would be a homeland security adviser and Homeland Security Council—paralleling the National Security Council system. Vice President Cheney reviewed the proposal with President Bush and other advisers. President Bush announced the new post and its first occupant—Pennsylvania governor Tom Ridge—in his address to a joint session of Congress on September 20.[16]

Beginning on September 11, Immigration and Naturalization Service agents working in cooperation with the FBI began arresting individuals for immigration violations whom they encountered while following up leads in the FBI's investigation of the 9/11 attacks. Eventually, 768 aliens were arrested as "special interest" detainees. Some (such as Zacarias Moussaoui) were actually in INS custody before 9/11; most were arrested after. Attorney General John Ashcroft told us that he saw his job in directing this effort as "risk minimization," both to find out who had committed the attacks and to prevent a subsequent attack. Ashcroft ordered all special interest immigration hearings closed to the public, family members, and press; directed government attorneys to seek denial of bond until such time as they were "cleared" of terrorist connections by the FBI and other agencies; and ordered the identity of the detainees kept secret. INS attorneys charged with prosecuting the immigration violations had trouble getting information about the detainees and any terrorist connections; in the chaos after the attacks, it was very difficult to reach law enforcement officials, who were following up on other leads. The clearance process approved by the Justice Department was time-consuming, lasting an average of about 80 days.[17]

We have assessed this effort to detain aliens of "special interest." The detainees were lawfully held on immigration charges. Records indicate that 531 were deported, 162 were released on bond, 24 received some kind of immigration benefits, 12 had their proceedings terminated, and 8—one of whom was Moussaoui—were remanded to the custody of the U.S. Marshals Service. The inspector general of the Justice Department found significant problems in the way the 9/11 detainees were treated.[18] In response to a request about the counterterrorism benefits of the 9/11 detainee program, the Justice Department cited six individuals on the special interest detainee list, noting that two (including Moussaoui) were linked directly to a terrorist organization and that it had obtained new leads helpful to the investigation of the 9/11 terrorist attacks.[19] A senior al Qaeda detainee has stated that U.S. government efforts after the 9/11 attacks to monitor the American homeland, including review of Muslims' immigration files and deportation of nonpermanent residents, forced al Qaeda to operate less freely in the United States.[20]

The government's ability to collect intelligence inside the United States, and the sharing of such information between the intelligence and law enforcement communities, was not a priority before 9/11. Guidelines on this subject issued in August 2001 by Deputy Attorney General Larry Thompson essentially recapitulated prior guidance. However, the attacks of 9/11 changed everything. Less than one week after September 11, an early version of what was to become the Patriot Act (officially, the USA PATRIOT Act) began to take shape.[21] A central provision of the proposal was the removal of "the wall" on information sharing between the intelligence and law enforcement communities (discussed in chapter 3). Ashcroft told us he was determined to take every conceivable action, within the limits of the Constitution, to identify potential terrorists and deter additional attacks.[22] The administration developed a proposal that eventually passed both houses of Congress by large majorities and was signed into law on October 26.[23]

Flights of Saudi Nationals Leaving the United States

Three questions have arisen with respect to the departure of Saudi nationals from the United States in the immediate aftermath of 9/11: (1) Did any flights of Saudi nationals take place before national airspace reopened on September 13, 2001? (2) Was there any political intervention to facilitate the departure of Saudi nationals? (3) Did the FBI screen Saudi nationals thoroughly before their departure?

First, we found no evidence that any flights of Saudi nationals, domestic or international, took place before the reopening of national airspace on the morning of September 13, 2001.[24] To the contrary, every flight we have identified occurred after national airspace reopened.[25]

Second, we found no evidence of political intervention. We found no evidence that anyone at the White House above the level of Richard Clarke participated in a decision on the departure of Saudi nationals. The issue came up in one of the many video teleconferences of the interagency group Clarke chaired, and Clarke said he approved of how the FBI was dealing with the matter when it came up for interagency discussion at his level. Clarke told us, "I asked the FBI, Dale Watson . . . to handle that, to check to see if that was all right with them, to see if they wanted access to any of these people, and to get back to me. And if they had no objections, it would be fine with me." Clarke added, "I have no recollection of clearing it with anybody at the White House."[26]

Although White House Chief of Staff Andrew Card remembered someone telling him about the Saudi request shortly after 9/11, he said he had not talked to the Saudis and did not ask anyone to do anything about it. The President and Vice President told us they were not aware of the issue at all until it surfaced much later in the media. None of the officials we interviewed recalled any intervention or direction on this matter from any political appointee.[27]

Third, we believe that the FBI conducted a satisfactory screening of Saudi nationals who left the United States on charter flights.[28] The Saudi government was advised of and agreed to the FBI's requirements that passengers be identified and checked against various databases before the flights departed.[29] The Federal Aviation Administration representative working in the FBI operations center made sure that the

FBI was aware of the flights of Saudi nationals and was able to screen the passengers before they were allowed to depart.[30]

The FBI interviewed all persons of interest on these flights prior to their departures. They concluded that none of the passengers was connected to the 9/11 attacks and have since found no evidence to change that conclusion. Our own independent review of the Saudi nationals involved confirms that no one with known links to terrorism departed on these flights.[31]

10.2 PLANNING FOR WAR

By late in the evening of September 11, the President had addressed the nation on the terrible events of the day. Vice President Cheney described the President's mood as somber.[32] The long day was not yet over. When the larger meeting that included his domestic department heads broke up, President Bush chaired a smaller meeting of top advisers, a group he would later call his "war council."[33] This group usually included Vice President Cheney, Secretary of State Powell, Secretary of Defense Donald Rumsfeld, General Hugh Shelton, Vice Chairman of the Joint Chiefs (later to become chairman) General Myers, DCI Tenet, Attorney General Ashcroft, and FBI Director Robert Mueller. From the White House staff, National Security Advisor Condoleezza Rice and Chief of Staff Card were part of the core group, often joined by their deputies, Stephen Hadley and Joshua Bolten.

In this restricted National Security Council meeting, the President said it was a time for self-defense. The United States would punish not just the perpetrators of the attacks, but also those who harbored them. Secretary Powell said the United States had to make it clear to Pakistan, Afghanistan, and the Arab states that the time to act was now. He said we would need to build a coalition. The President noted that the attacks provided a great opportunity to engage Russia and China. Secretary Rumsfeld urged the President and the principals to think broadly about who might have harbored the attackers, including Iraq, Afghanistan, Libya, Sudan, and Iran. He wondered aloud how much evidence the United States would need in order to deal with these countries, pointing out that major strikes could take up to 60 days to assemble.[34]

President Bush chaired two more meetings of the NSC on September 12. In the first meeting, he stressed that the United States was at war with a new and different kind of enemy. The President tasked principals to go beyond their pre-9/11 work and develop a strategy to eliminate terrorists and punish those who support them. As they worked on defining the goals and objectives of the upcoming campaign, they considered a paper that went beyond al Qaeda to propose the "elimination of terrorism as a threat to our way of life," an aim that would include pursuing other international terrorist organizations in the Middle East.[35]

Rice chaired a Principals Committee meeting on September 13 in the Situation Room to refine how the fight against al Qaeda would be conducted. The principals agreed that the overall message should be that anyone supporting al Qaeda would risk harm. The United States would need to integrate diplomacy, financial measures, intelligence, and military actions into an overarching strategy. The principals also focused on Pakistan and what it could do to turn the Taliban against al Qaeda. They concluded that if Pakistan decided not to help the United States, it too would be at risk.[36]

The same day, Deputy Secretary of State Richard Armitage met with the Pakistani ambassador to the United States, Maleeha Lodhi, and the visiting head of Pakistan's military intelligence service, Mahmud Ahmed. Armitage said that the United States wanted Pakistan to take seven steps:

- to stop al Qaeda operatives at its border and end all logistical support for Bin Ladin;
- to give the United States blanket overflight and landing rights for all necessary military and intelligence operations;
- to provide territorial access to U.S. and allied military intelligence and other personnel to conduct operations against al Qaeda;
- to provide the United States with intelligence information;
- to continue to publicly condemn the terrorist acts;
- to cut off all shipments of fuel to the Taliban and stop recruits from going to Afghanistan; and,
- if the evidence implicated bin Ladin and al Qaeda and the Taliban continued to harbor them, to break relations with the Taliban government.[37]

Pakistan made its decision swiftly. That afternoon, Secretary of State Powell announced at the beginning of an NSC meeting that Pakistani President Musharraf had agreed to every U.S. request for support in the war on terrorism. The next day, the U.S. embassy in Islamabad confirmed that Musharraf and his top military commanders had agreed to all seven demands. "Pakistan will need full US support as it proceeds with us," the embassy noted. "Musharraf said the GOP [government of Pakistan] was making substantial concessions in allowing use of its territory and that he would pay a domestic price. His standing in Pakistan was certain to suffer. To counterbalance that he needed to show that Pakistan was benefiting from his decisions."[38]

At the September 13 NSC meeting, when Secretary Powell described Pakistan's reply, President Bush led a discussion of an appropriate ultimatum to the Taliban. He also ordered Secretary Rumsfeld to develop a military plan against the Taliban. The President wanted the United States to strike the Taliban, step back, wait to see if they got the message, and hit them hard if they did not. He made clear that the military should focus on targets that would influence the Taliban's behavior.[39]

President Bush also tasked the State Department, which on the following day delivered to the White House a paper titled "Game Plan for a Political-Military Strategy for Pakistan and Afghanistan." The paper took it as a given that Bin Ladin would continue to act against the United States even while under Taliban control. It therefore detailed specific U.S. demands for the Taliban: surrender Bin Ladin and his chief lieutenants, including Ayman al Zawahiri; tell the United States what the Taliban knew about al Qaeda and its operations; close all terrorist camps; free all imprisoned foreigners; and comply with all UN Security Council resolutions.[40]

The State Department proposed delivering an ultimatum to the Taliban: produce Bin Ladin and his deputies and shut down al Qaeda camps within 24 to 48 hours, or the United States will use all necessary means to destroy the terrorist infrastructure. The State Department did not expect the Taliban to comply. Therefore, State and Defense would plan to build an international coalition to go into Afghanistan. Both departments would consult with NATO and other allies and request intelligence, basing, and other support from countries, according to their capabilities and resources. Finally, the plan detailed a public U.S. stance: America would use all its resources to eliminate terrorism as a threat, punish those responsible for the 9/11 attacks, hold states and other actors responsible for providing sanctuary to terrorists, work with a coalition to eliminate terrorist groups and networks, and avoid malice toward any people, religion, or culture.[41]

President Bush recalled that he quickly realized that the administration would have to invade Afghanistan with ground troops.[42] But the early briefings to the President and Secretary Rumsfeld on military options were disappointing.[43] Tommy Franks, the commanding general of Central Command (CENTCOM), told us that the President was dissatisfied. The U.S. military, Franks said, did not have an off-the-shelf plan to eliminate the al Qaeda threat in Afghanistan. The existing Infinite Resolve options did not, in his view, amount to such a plan.[44]

All these diplomatic and military plans were reviewed over the weekend of September 15–16, as President Bush convened his war council at Camp David.[45] Present were Vice President Cheney, Rice, Hadley, Powell, Armitage, Rumsfeld, Ashcroft, Mueller, Tenet, Deputy Secretary of Defense Paul Wolfowitz, and Cofer Black, chief of the DCI's Counterterrorist Center.

Tenet described a plan for collecting intelligence and mounting covert operations. He proposed inserting CIA teams into Afghanistan to work with Afghan warlords who would join the fight against al Qaeda.[46] These CIA teams would act jointly with the military's Special Operations units. President Bush later praised this proposal, saying it had been a turning point in his thinking.[47]

General Shelton briefed the principals on the preliminary plan for Afghanistan that the military had put together. It drew on the Infinite Resolve "phased campaign" plan the Pentagon had begun developing in November 2000 as an addition to the strike options it had been refining since 1998. But Shelton added a new element—the possible significant use of ground forces— and that is where President Bush reportedly focused his attention.[48]

After hearing from his senior advisers, President Bush discussed with Rice the contents of the directives he would issue to set all the plans into motion. Rice prepared a paper that President Bush then considered with principals on Monday morning, September 17. "The purpose of this meeting," he recalled saying, "is to assign tasks for the first wave of the war against terrorism. It starts today."[49]

In a written set of instructions slightly refined during the morning meeting, President Bush charged Ashcroft, Mueller, and Tenet to develop a plan for homeland defense. President Bush directed Secretary of State Powell to deliver an ultimatum to the Taliban along the lines that his department had originally proposed. The State Department was also tasked to develop a plan to stabilize Pakistan and to be prepared to notify Russia and countries near Afghanistan when hostilities were imminent.[50]

In addition, Bush and his advisers discussed new legal authorities for covert action in Afghanistan, including the administration's first Memorandum of Notification on Bin Ladin. Shortly thereafter, President Bush authorized broad new authorities for the CIA.[51]

President Bush instructed Rumsfeld and Shelton to develop further the Camp David military plan to attack the Taliban and al Qaeda if the Taliban rejected the ultimatum. The President also tasked Rumsfeld to ensure that robust measures to protect American military forces against terrorist attack were implemented worldwide. Finally, he directed Treasury Secretary Paul O'Neill to craft a plan to target al Qaeda's funding and seize its assets.[52] NSC staff members had begun leading meetings on terrorist fund-raising by September 18.[53]

Also by September 18, Powell had contacted 58 of his foreign counterparts and received offers of general aid, search-and-rescue equipment and personnel, and medical assistance teams.[54] On the same day, Deputy Secretary of State Armitage was called by Mahmud Ahmed regarding a two-day visit to Afghanistan during which the Pakistani intelligence chief had met with Mullah Omar and conveyed the U.S. demands. Omar's response was "not negative on all these points."[55] But the administration knew that the Taliban was unlikely to turn over Bin Ladin.[56]

The pre-9/11 draft presidential directive on al Qaeda evolved into a new directive, National Security Presidential Directive 9, now titled "Defeating the Terrorist Threat to the United States." The directive would now extend to a global war on terrorism, not just on al Qaeda. It also incorporated the President's determination not to distinguish between terrorists and those who harbor them. It included a determination to use military force if necessary to end al Qaeda's sanctuary in Afghanistan. The new directive—formally signed on October 25, after the fighting in Afghanistan had already begun—included new material followed by annexes discussing each targeted terrorist group. The old draft directive on al Qaeda became, in effect, the first annex.[57] The United States would strive to eliminate all terrorist networks, dry up their financial support, and prevent them from acquiring weapons of mass destruction. The goal was the "elimination of terrorism as a threat to our way of life."[58]

10.3 "PHASE TWO" AND THE QUESTION OF IRAQ

President Bush had wondered immediately after the attack whether Saddam Hussein's regime might have had a hand in it. Iraq had been an enemy of the United States for 11 years, and was the only place in the world where the United States was engaged in ongoing combat operations. As a former pilot, the President was struck by the apparent sophistication of the operation and some of the piloting, especially Hanjour's high-speed dive into the Pentagon. He told us he recalled Iraqi support for Palestinian suicide terrorists as well. Speculating about other possible states that could be involved, the President told us he also thought about Iran.[59]

Clarke has written that on the evening of September 12, President Bush told him and some of his staff to explore possible Iraqi links to 9/11. "See if Saddam did this," Clarke recalls the President telling them. "See if he's linked in any way."[60] While he believed the details of Clarke's account to be incorrect, President Bush acknowledged that he might well have spoken to Clarke at some point, asking him about Iraq.[61]

Responding to a presidential tasking, Clarke's office sent a memo to Rice on September 18, titled "Survey of Intelligence Information on Any Iraq Involvement in the September 11 Attacks." Rice's chief staffer on Afghanistan, Zalmay Khalilzad, concurred in its conclusion that only some anecdotal evidence linked Iraq to al Qaeda. The memo found no "compelling case" that Iraq had either planned or perpetrated the attacks. It passed along a few foreign intelligence reports, including the Czech report alleging an April 2001 Prague meeting between Atta and an Iraqi intelligence officer (discussed in chapter 7) and a Polish report that personnel at the headquarters of Iraqi intelligence in Baghdad were told before September 11 to go on the streets to gauge crowd reaction to an unspecified event. Arguing that the case for links between Iraq and al Qaeda was weak, the memo pointed out that Bin Ladin resented the secularism of Saddam Hussein's regime. Finally, the memo said, there was no confirmed reporting on Saddam cooperating with Bin Ladin on unconventional weapons.[62]

On the afternoon of 9/11, according to contemporaneous notes, Secretary Rumsfeld instructed General Myers to obtain quickly as much information as

possible. The notes indicate that he also told Myers that he was not simply interested in striking empty training sites. He thought the U.S. response should consider a wide range of options and possibilities. The secretary said his instinct
was to hit Saddam Hussein at the same time—not only Bin Ladin. Secretary
Rumsfeld later explained that at the time, he had been considering either one
of them, or perhaps someone else, as the responsible party.[63]

According to Rice, the issue of what, if anything, to do about Iraq was really
engaged at Camp David. Briefing papers on Iraq, along with many others, were
in briefing materials for the participants. Rice told us the administration was
concerned that Iraq would take advantage of the 9/11 attacks. She recalled that
in the first Camp David session chaired by the President, Rumsfeld asked what
the administration should do about Iraq. Deputy Secretary Wolfowitz made the
case for striking Iraq during "this round" of the war on terrorism.[64]

A Defense Department paper for the Camp David briefing book on the
strategic concept for the war on terrorism specified three priority targets for
initial action: al Qaeda, the Taliban, and Iraq. It argued that of the three, al Qaeda
and Iraq posed a strategic threat to the United States. Iraq's long-standing
involvement in terrorism was cited, along with its interest in weapons of mass
destruction.[65]

Secretary Powell recalled that Wolfowitz—not Rumsfeld—argued that Iraq
was ultimately the source of the terrorist problem and should therefore be
attacked.[66] Powell said that Wolfowitz was not able to justify his belief that Iraq
was behind 9/11. "Paul was always of the view that Iraq was a problem that
had to be dealt with," Powell told us. "And he saw this as one way of using this
event as a way to deal with the Iraq problem." Powell said that President Bush
did not give Wolfowitz's argument "much weight."[67] Though continuing to
worry about Iraq in the following week, Powell said, President Bush saw
Afghanistan as the priority.[68]

President Bush told Bob Woodward that the decision not to invade Iraq was
made at the morning session on September 15. Iraq was not even on the table
during the September 15 afternoon session, which dealt solely with
Afghanistan.[69] Rice said that when President Bush called her on Sunday, September 16, he said the focus would be on Afghanistan, although he still wanted
plans for Iraq should the country take some action or the administration eventually determine that it had been involved in the 9/11 attacks.[70]

At the September 17 NSC meeting, there was some further discussion of
"phase two" of the war on terrorism.[71] President Bush ordered the Defense
Department to be ready to deal with Iraq if Baghdad acted against U.S. interests, with plans to include possibly occupying Iraqi oil fields.[72]

Within the Pentagon, Deputy Secretary Wolfowitz continued to press the
case for dealing with Iraq. Writing to Rumsfeld on September 17 in a memo
headlined "Preventing More Events," he argued that if there was even a 10 percent chance that Saddam Hussein was behind the 9/11 attack, maximum pri-

ority should be placed on eliminating that threat. Wolfowitz contended that the odds were "far more" than 1 in 10, citing Saddam's praise for the attack, his long record of involvement in terrorism, and theories that Ramzi Yousef was an Iraqi agent and Iraq was behind the 1993 attack on the World Trade Center.[73] The next day, Wolfowitz renewed the argument, writing to Rumsfeld about the interest of Yousef's co-conspirator in the 1995 Manila air plot in crashing an explosives-laden plane into CIA headquarters, and about information from a foreign government regarding Iraqis' involvement in the attempted hijacking of a Gulf Air flight. Given this background, he wondered why so little thought had been devoted to the danger of suicide pilots, seeing a "failure of imagination" and a mind-set that dismissed possibilities.[74]

On September 19, Rumsfeld offered several thoughts for his commanders as they worked on their contingency plans. Though he emphasized the worldwide nature of the conflict, the references to specific enemies or regions named only the Taliban, al Qaeda, and Afghanistan.[75] Shelton told us the administration reviewed all the Pentagon's war plans and challenged certain assumptions underlying them, as any prudent organization or leader should do.[76]

General Tommy Franks, the commanding general of Central Command, recalled receiving Rumsfeld's guidance that each regional commander should assess what these plans meant for his area of responsibility. He knew he would soon be striking the Taliban and al Qaeda in Afghanistan. But, he told us, he now wondered how that action was connected to what might need to be done in Somalia, Yemen, or Iraq.[77]

On September 20, President Bush met with British Prime Minister Tony Blair, and the two leaders discussed the global conflict ahead. When Blair asked about Iraq, the President replied that Iraq was not the immediate problem. Some members of his administration, he commented, had expressed a different view, but he was the one responsible for making the decisions.[78]

Franks told us that he was pushing independently to do more robust planning on military responses in Iraq during the summer before 9/11—a request President Bush denied, arguing that the time was not right. (CENTCOM also began dusting off plans for a full invasion of Iraq during this period, Franks said.) The CENTCOM commander told us he renewed his appeal for further military planning to respond to Iraqi moves shortly after 9/11, both because he personally felt that Iraq and al Qaeda might be engaged in some form of collusion and because he worried that Saddam might take advantage of the attacks to move against his internal enemies in the northern or southern parts of Iraq, where the United States was flying regular missions to enforce Iraqi no-fly zones. Franks said that President Bush again turned down the request.[79]

· · ·

HAVING ISSUED DIRECTIVES to guide his administration's preparations for war, on Thursday, September 20, President Bush addressed the nation before a joint session of Congress. "Tonight," he said, "we are a country awakened to danger."[80] The President blamed al Qaeda for 9/11 and the 1998 embassy bombings and, for the first time, declared that al Qaeda was "responsible for bombing the USS *Cole*."[81] He reiterated the ultimatum that had already been conveyed privately. "The Taliban must act, and act immediately," he said. "They will hand over the terrorists, or they will share in their fate."[82] The President added that America's quarrel was not with Islam: "The enemy of America is not our many Muslim friends; it is not our many Arab friends. Our enemy is a radical network of terrorists, and every government that supports them." Other regimes faced hard choices, he pointed out: "Every nation, in every region, now has a decision to make: Either you are with us, or you are with the terrorists."[83]

President Bush argued that the new war went beyond Bin Ladin. "Our war on terror begins with al Qaeda, but it does not end there," he said. "It will not end until every terrorist group of global reach has been found, stopped, and defeated." The President had a message for the Pentagon: "The hour is coming when America will act, and you will make us proud." He also had a message for those outside the United States. "This is civilization's fight," he said. "We ask every nation to join us."[84]

President Bush approved military plans to attack Afghanistan in meetings with Central Command's General Franks and other advisers on September 21 and October 2. Originally titled "Infinite Justice," the operation's code word was changed—to avoid the sensibilities of Muslims who associate the power of infinite justice with God alone—to the operational name still used for operations in Afghanistan: "Enduring Freedom."[85]

The plan had four phases.

- In *Phase One,* the United States and its allies would move forces into the region and arrange to operate from or over neighboring countries such as Uzbekistan and Pakistan. This occurred in the weeks following 9/11, aided by overwhelming international sympathy for the United States.
- In *Phase Two,* air strikes and Special Operations attacks would hit key al Qaeda and Taliban targets. In an innovative joint effort, CIA and Special Operations forces would be deployed to work together with each major Afghan faction opposed to the Taliban. The Phase Two strikes and raids began on October 7. The basing arrangements contemplated for Phase One were substantially secured—after arduous effort—by the end of that month.
- In *Phase Three,* the United States would carry out "decisive operations" using all elements of national power, including ground troops, to topple the Taliban regime and eliminate al Qaeda's sanctuary in Afghanistan. Mazar-e-Sharif, in northern Afghanistan, fell to a coalition assault by Afghan and U.S. forces on November 9. Four days later the Taliban had fled from Kabul. By early December, all major cities

had fallen to the coalition. On December 22, Hamid Karzai, a Pashtun leader from Kandahar, was installed as the chairman of Afghanistan's interim administration. Afghanistan had been liberated from the rule of the Taliban.

In December 2001, Afghan forces, with limited U.S. support, engaged al Qaeda elements in a cave complex called Tora Bora. In March 2002, the largest engagement of the war was fought, in the mountainous Shah-i-Kot area south of Gardez, against a large force of al Qaeda jihadists. The three-week battle was substantially successful, and almost all remaining al Qaeda forces took refuge in Pakistan's equally mountainous and lightly governed frontier provinces. As of July 2004, Bin Ladin and Zawahiri are still believed to be at large.

- In *Phase Four*, civilian and military operations turned to the indefinite task of what the armed forces call "security and stability operations."

Within about two months of the start of combat operations, several hundred CIA operatives and Special Forces soldiers, backed by the striking power of U.S. aircraft and a much larger infrastructure of intelligence and support efforts, had combined with Afghan militias and a small number of other coalition soldiers to destroy the Taliban regime and disrupt al Qaeda. They had killed or captured about a quarter of the enemy's known leaders. Mohammed Atef, al Qaeda's military commander and a principal figure in the 9/11 plot, had been killed by a U.S. air strike. According to a senior CIA officer who helped devise the overall strategy, the CIA provided intelligence, experience, cash, covert action capabilities, and entrée to tribal allies. In turn, the U.S. military offered combat expertise, firepower, logistics, and communications.[86] With these initial victories won by the middle of 2002, the global conflict against Islamist terrorism became a different kind of struggle.

11
FORESIGHT—AND HINDSIGHT

IN COMPOSING THIS NARRATIVE, we have tried to remember that we write with the benefit and the handicap of hindsight. Hindsight can sometimes see the past clearly—with 20/20 vision. But the path of what happened is so brightly lit that it places everything else more deeply into shadow. Commenting on Pearl Harbor, Roberta Wohlstetter found it "much easier *after* the event to sort the relevant from the irrelevant signals. After the event, of course, a signal is always crystal clear; we can now see what disaster it was signaling since the disaster has occurred. But before the event it is obscure and pregnant with conflicting meanings."[1]

As time passes, more documents become available, and the bare facts of what happened become still clearer. Yet the picture of *how* those things happened becomes harder to reimagine, as that past world, with its preoccupations and uncertainty, recedes and the remaining memories of it become colored by what happened and what was written about it later. With that caution in mind, we asked ourselves, before we judged others, whether the insights that seem apparent now would really have been meaningful at the time, given the limits of what people then could reasonably have known or done.

We believe the 9/11 attacks revealed four kinds of failures: in imagination, policy, capabilities, and management.

11.1 IMAGINATION

Historical Perspective
The 9/11 attack was an event of surpassing disproportion. America had suffered surprise attacks before—Pearl Harbor is one well-known case, the 1950 Chinese attack in Korea another. But these were attacks by major powers.

While by no means as threatening as Japan's act of war, the 9/11 attack was in some ways more devastating. It was carried out by a tiny group of people, not enough to man a full platoon. Measured on a governmental scale, the resources behind it were trivial. The group itself was dispatched by an organization based in one of the poorest, most remote, and least industrialized countries on earth. This organization recruited a mixture of young fanatics and highly educated zealots who could not find suitable places in their home societies or were driven from them.

To understand these events, we attempted to reconstruct some of the context of the 1990s. Americans celebrated the end of the Cold War with a mixture of relief and satisfaction. The people of the United States hoped to enjoy a peace dividend, as U.S. spending on national security was cut following the end of the Soviet military threat.

The United States emerged into the post–Cold War world as the globe's preeminent military power. But the vacuum created by the sudden demise of the Soviet Union created fresh sources of instability and new challenges for the United States. President George H.W. Bush dealt with the first of these in 1990 and 1991 when he led an international coalition to reverse Iraq's invasion of Kuwait. Other examples of U.S. leaders' handling new threats included the removal of nuclear weapons from Ukraine, Belarus, and Kazakhstan; the Nunn-Lugar threat reduction program to help contain new nuclear dangers; and international involvement in the wars in Bosnia and Kosovo.

America stood out as an object for admiration, envy, and blame. This created a kind of cultural asymmetry. To us, Afghanistan seemed very far away. To members of al Qaeda, America seemed very close. In a sense, they were more globalized than we were.

Understanding the Danger

If the government's leaders understood the gravity of the threat they faced and understood at the same time that their policies to eliminate it were not likely to succeed any time soon, then history's judgment will be harsh. Did they understand the gravity of the threat?

The U.S. government responded vigorously when the attack was on our soil. Both Ramzi Yousef, who organized the 1993 bombing of the World Trade Center, and Mir Amal Kansi, who in 1993 killed two CIA employees as they waited to go to work in Langley, Virginia, were the objects of relentless, uncompromising, and successful efforts to bring them back to the United States to stand trial for their crimes.

Before 9/11, al Qaeda and its affiliates had killed fewer than 50 Americans, including the East Africa embassy bombings and the *Cole* attack. The U.S. government took the threat seriously, but not in the sense of mustering anything like the kind of effort that would be gathered to confront an enemy of the first, second, or even third rank. The modest national effort exerted to contain Serbia and its depredations in the Balkans between 1995 and 1999, for example, was orders of magnitude larger than that devoted to al Qaeda.

As best we can determine, neither in 2000 nor in the first eight months of 2001 did any polling organization in the United States think the subject of terrorism sufficiently on the minds of the public to warrant asking a question about it in a major national survey. Bin Ladin, al Qaeda, or even terrorism was not an important topic in the 2000 presidential campaign. Congress and the media called little attention to it.

If a president wanted to rally the American people to a warlike effort, he would need to publicize an assessment of the growing al Qaeda danger. Our government could spark a full public discussion of who Usama Bin Ladin was, what kind of organization he led, what Bin Ladin or al Qaeda intended, what past attacks they had sponsored or encouraged, and what capabilities they were bringing together for future assaults. We believe American and international public opinion might have been different—and so might the range of options for a president—had they been informed of these details. Recent examples of such debates include calls to arms against such threats as Serbian ethnic cleansing, biological attacks, Iraqi weapons of mass destruction, global climate change, and the HIV/AIDS epidemic.

While we now know that al Qaeda was formed in 1988, at the end of the Soviet occupation of Afghanistan, the intelligence community did not describe this organization, at least in documents we have seen, until 1999. A National Intelligence Estimate distributed in July 1995 predicted future terrorist attacks against the United States—and *in* the United States. It warned that this danger would increase over the next several years. It specified as particular points of vulnerability the White House, the Capitol, symbols of capitalism such as Wall Street, critical infrastructure such as power grids, areas where people congregate such as sports arenas, and civil aviation generally. It warned that the 1993 World Trade Center bombing had been intended to kill a lot of people, not to achieve any more traditional political goal.

This 1995 estimate described the greatest danger as "transient groupings of individuals" that lacked "strong organization but rather are loose affiliations." They operate "outside traditional circles but have access to a worldwide network of training facilities and safehavens."[2] This was an excellent summary of the emerging danger, based on what was then known.

In 1996–1997, the intelligence community received new information making clear that Bin Ladin headed his own terrorist group, with its own targeting agenda and operational commanders. Also revealed was the previously unknown involvement of Bin Ladin's organization in the 1992 attack on a Yemeni hotel quartering U.S. military personnel, the 1993 shootdown of U.S. Army Black Hawk helicopters in Somalia, and quite possibly the 1995 Riyadh bombing of the American training mission to the Saudi National Guard.

The 1997 update of the 1995 estimate did not discuss the new intelligence. It did state that the terrorist danger depicted in 1995 would persist. In the update's summary of key points, the only reference to Bin Ladin was this sentence:"Iran and its surrogates, as well as terrorist financier Usama Bin Ladin and his followers, have stepped up their threats and surveillance of US facilities abroad in what also may be a portent of possible additional attacks in the United States."[3] Bin Ladin was mentioned in only two other sentences in the six-page report. The al Qaeda organization was not mentioned. The 1997 update was the last national estimate on the terrorism danger completed before 9/11.[4]

From 1998 to 2001, a number of very good analytical papers were distributed on specific topics. These included Bin Ladin's political philosophy, his command of a global network, analysis of information from terrorists captured in Jordan in December 1999, al Qaeda's operational style, and the evolving goals of the Islamist extremist movement. Many classified articles for morning briefings were prepared for the highest officials in the government with titles such as "Bin Ladin Threatening to Attack US Aircraft [with antiaircraft missiles]" (June 1998), "Strains Surface Between Taliban and Bin Ladin" (January 1999), "Terrorist Threat to US Interests in Caucasus" (June 1999), "Bin Ladin to Exploit Looser Security During Holidays" (December 1999), "Bin Ladin Evading Sanctions" (March 2000), "Bin Ladin's Interest in Biological, Radiological Weapons" (February 2001), "Taliban Holding Firm on Bin Ladin for Now" (March 2001), "Terrorist Groups Said Cooperating on US Hostage Plot" (May 2001), and "Bin Ladin Determined to Strike in the US" (August 2001).[5]

Despite such reports and a 1999 paper on Bin Ladin's command structure for al Qaeda, there were no complete portraits of his strategy or of the extent of his organization's involvement in past terrorist attacks. Nor had the intelligence community provided an authoritative depiction of his organization's relationships with other governments, or the scale of the threat his organization posed to the United States.

Though Deputy DCI John McLaughlin said to us that the cumulative output of the Counterterrorist Center (CTC) "dramatically eclipsed" any analysis that could have appeared in a fresh National Intelligence Estimate, he conceded that most of the work of the Center's 30- to 40-person analytic group dealt with collection issues.[6] In late 2000, DCI George Tenet recognized the deficiency of strategic analysis against al Qaeda. To tackle the problem within the CTC he appointed a senior manager, who briefed him in March 2001 on "creating a strategic assessment capability." The CTC established a new strategic assessments branch during July 2001. The decision to add about ten analysts to this effort was seen as a major bureaucratic victory, but the CTC labored to find them. The new chief of this branch reported for duty on September 10, 2001.[7]

Whatever the weaknesses in the CIA's portraiture, both Presidents Bill Clinton and George Bush and their top advisers told us they got the picture—they understood Bin Ladin was a danger. But given the character and pace of their policy efforts, we do not believe they fully understood just how many people al Qaeda might kill, and how soon it might do it. At some level that is hard to define, we believe the threat had not yet become compelling.

It is hard now to recapture the conventional wisdom before 9/11. For example, a *New York Times* article in April 1999 sought to debunk claims that Bin Ladin was a terrorist leader, with the headline "U.S. Hard Put to Find Proof Bin Laden Directed Attacks."[8] The head of analysis at the CTC until 1999 discounted the alarms about a catastrophic threat as relating only to the danger of chemical, biological, or nuclear attack—and he downplayed even that, writing several months before 9/11: "It would be a mistake to redefine counterterrorism as a task of dealing with 'catastrophic,' 'grand,' or 'super' terrorism, when in fact these labels do not represent most of the terrorism that the United States is likely to face or most of the costs that terrorism imposes on U.S. interests."[9]

Beneath the acknowledgment that Bin Ladin and al Qaeda presented serious dangers, there was uncertainty among senior officials about whether this was just a new and especially venomous version of the ordinary terrorist threat America had lived with for decades, or was radically new, posing a threat beyond any yet experienced. Such differences affect calculations about whether or how to go to war.

Therefore, those government experts who saw Bin Ladin as an unprecedented new danger needed a way to win broad support for their views, or at least spotlight the areas of dispute, and perhaps prompt action across the government. The national estimate has often played this role, and is sometimes controversial for this very reason.[10] Such assessments, which provoke widespread thought and debate, have a major impact on their recipients, often in a wider circle of decisionmakers. The National Intelligence Estimate is noticed in the Congress, for example. But, as we have said, none was produced on terrorism between 1997 and 9/11.

By 2001 the government still needed a decision at the highest level as to whether al Qaeda was or was not "a first order threat," Richard Clarke wrote in his first memo to Condoleezza Rice on January 25, 2001. In his blistering protest about foot-dragging in the Pentagon and at the CIA, sent to Rice just a week before 9/11, he repeated that the "real question" for the principals was "are we serious about dealing with the al Qida threat? . . . Is al Qida a big deal?"

One school of thought, Clarke wrote in this September 4 note, implicitly argued that the terrorist network was a nuisance that killed a score of Americans every 18–24 months. If that view was credited, then current policies might be proportionate. Another school saw al Qaeda as the "point of the spear of radical Islam." But no one forced the argument into the open by calling for a national estimate or a broader discussion of the threat. The issue was never joined as a collective debate by the U.S. government, including the Congress, before 9/11.

We return to the issue of proportion—and imagination. Even Clarke's note challenging Rice to imagine the day after an attack posits a strike that kills "hundreds" of Americans. He did not write "thousands."

Institutionalizing Imagination:
The Case of Aircraft as Weapons

Imagination is not a gift usually associated with bureaucracies. For example, before Pearl Harbor the U.S. government had excellent intelligence that a Japanese attack was coming, especially after peace talks stalemated at the end of November 1941. These were days, one historian notes, of "excruciating uncertainty." The most likely targets were judged to be in Southeast Asia. An attack was coming, "but officials were at a loss to know where the blow would fall or what more might be done to prevent it."[11] In retrospect, available intercepts pointed to Japanese examination of Hawaii as a possible target. But, another historian observes, "in the face of a clear warning, alert measures bowed to routine."[12]

It is therefore crucial to find a way of routinizing, even bureaucratizing, the exercise of imagination. Doing so requires more than finding an expert who can imagine that aircraft could be used as weapons. Indeed, since al Qaeda and other groups had already used suicide vehicles, namely truck bombs, the leap to the use of other vehicles such as boats (the *Cole* attack) or planes is not far-fetched.

Yet these scenarios were slow to work their way into the thinking of aviation security experts. In 1996, as a result of the TWA Flight 800 crash, President Clinton created a commission under Vice President Al Gore to report on shortcomings in aviation security in the United States. The Gore Commission's report, having thoroughly canvassed available expertise in and outside of government, did not mention suicide hijackings or the use of aircraft as weapons. It focused mainly on the danger of placing bombs onto aircraft—the approach of the Manila air plot. The Gore Commission did call attention, however, to lax screening of passengers and what they carried onto planes.

In late 1998, reports came in of a possible al Qaeda plan to hijack a plane. One, a December 4 Presidential Daily Briefing for President Clinton (reprinted in chapter 4), brought the focus back to more traditional hostage taking; it reported Bin Ladin's involvement in planning a hijack operation to free prisoners such as the "Blind Sheikh," Omar Abdel Rahman. Had the contents of this PDB been brought to the attention of a wider group, including key members of Congress, it might have brought much more attention to the need for permanent changes in domestic airport and airline security procedures.[13]

Threat reports also mentioned the possibility of using an aircraft filled with explosives. The most prominent of these mentioned a possible plot to fly an explosives-laden aircraft into a U.S. city. This report, circulated in September 1998, originated from a source who had walked into an American consulate in East Asia. In August of the same year, the intelligence community had received information that a group of Libyans hoped to crash a plane into the

World Trade Center. In neither case could the information be corroborated. In addition, an Algerian group hijacked an airliner in 1994, most likely intending to blow it up over Paris, but possibly to crash it into the Eiffel Tower.[14]

In 1994, a private airplane had crashed onto the south lawn of the White House. In early 1995, Abdul Hakim Murad—Ramzi Yousef's accomplice in the Manila airlines bombing plot—told Philippine authorities that he and Yousef had discussed flying a plane into CIA headquarters.[15]

Clarke had been concerned about the danger posed by aircraft since at least the 1996 Atlanta Olympics. There he had tried to create an air defense plan using assets from the Treasury Department, after the Defense Department declined to contribute resources. The Secret Service continued to work on the problem of airborne threats to the Washington region. In 1998, Clarke chaired an exercise designed to highlight the inadequacy of the solution. This paper exercise involved a scenario in which a group of terrorists commandeered a Learjet on the ground in Atlanta, loaded it with explosives, and flew it toward a target in Washington, D.C. Clarke asked officials from the Pentagon, Federal Aviation Administration (FAA), and Secret Service what they could do about the situation. Officials from the Pentagon said they could scramble aircraft from Langley Air Force Base, but they would need to go to the President for rules of engagement, and there was no mechanism to do so. There was no clear resolution of the problem at the exercise.[16]

In late 1999, a great deal of discussion took place in the media about the crash off the coast of Massachusetts of EgyptAir Flight 990, a Boeing 767. The most plausible explanation that emerged was that one of the pilots had gone berserk, seized the controls, and flown the aircraft into the sea. After the 1999–2000 millennium alerts, when the nation had relaxed, Clarke held a meeting of his Counterterrorism Security Group devoted largely to the possibility of a possible airplane hijacking by al Qaeda.[17]

In his testimony, Clarke commented that he thought that warning about the possibility of a suicide hijacking would have been just one more speculative theory among many, hard to spot since the volume of warnings of "al Qaeda threats and other terrorist threats, was in the tens of thousands—probably hundreds of thousands."[18] Yet the possibility was imaginable, and imagined. In early August 1999, the FAA's Civil Aviation Security intelligence office summarized the Bin Ladin hijacking threat. After a solid recitation of all the information available on this topic, the paper identified a few principal scenarios, one of which was a "suicide hijacking operation." The FAA analysts judged such an operation unlikely, because "it does not offer an opportunity for dialogue to achieve the key goal of obtaining Rahman and other key captive extremists. . . . A suicide hijacking is assessed to be an option of last resort."[19]

Analysts could have shed some light on what kind of "opportunity for dialogue" al Qaeda desired.[20] The CIA did not write any analytical assessments of possible hijacking scenarios.

One prescient pre-9/11 analysis of an aircraft plot was written by a Justice Department trial attorney. The attorney had taken an interest, apparently on his own initiative, in the legal issues that would be involved in shooting down a U.S. aircraft in such a situation.[21]

The North American Aerospace Defense Command imagined the possible use of aircraft as weapons, too, and developed exercises to counter such a threat—from planes coming to the United States from overseas, perhaps carrying a weapon of mass destruction. None of this speculation was based on actual intelligence of such a threat. One idea, intended to test command and control plans and NORAD's readiness, postulated a hijacked airliner coming from overseas and crashing into the Pentagon. The idea was put aside in the early planning of the exercise as too much of a distraction from the main focus (war in Korea), and as too unrealistic. As we pointed out in chapter 1, the military planners assumed that since such aircraft would be coming from overseas; they would have time to identify the target and scramble interceptors.[22]

We can therefore establish that at least some government agencies were concerned about the hijacking danger and had speculated about various scenarios. The challenge was to flesh out and test those scenarios, then figure out a way to turn a scenario into constructive action.

Since the Pearl Harbor attack of 1941, the intelligence community has devoted generations of effort to understanding the problem of forestalling a surprise attack. Rigorous analytic methods were developed, focused in particular on the Soviet Union, and several leading practitioners within the intelligence community discussed them with us. These methods have been articulated in many ways, but almost all seem to have at least four elements in common: (1) think about how surprise attacks might be launched; (2) identify telltale indicators connected to the most dangerous possibilities; (3) where feasible, collect intelligence on these indicators; and (4) adopt defenses to deflect the most dangerous possibilities or at least trigger an earlier warning.

After the end of the Gulf War, concerns about lack of warning led to a major study conducted for DCI Robert Gates in 1992 that proposed several recommendations, among them strengthening the national intelligence officer for warning. We were told that these measures languished under Gates's successors. Responsibility for warning related to a terrorist attack passed from the national intelligence officer for warning to the CTC. An Intelligence Community Counterterrorism Board had the responsibility to issue threat advisories.[23]

With the important exception of analysis of al Qaeda efforts in chemical, biological, radiological, and nuclear weapons, we did not find evidence that the methods to avoid surprise attack that had been so laboriously developed over the years were regularly applied.

Considering what was not done suggests possible ways to institutionalize imagination. To return to the four elements of analysis just mentioned:

1. The CTC did not analyze how an aircraft, hijacked or explosives-laden, might be used as a weapon. It did not perform this kind of analysis from the enemy's perspective ("red team" analysis), even though suicide terrorism had become a principal tactic of Middle Eastern terrorists. If it had done so, we believe such an analysis would soon have spotlighted a critical constraint for the terrorists—finding a suicide operative able to fly large jet aircraft. They had never done so before 9/11.

2. The CTC did not develop a set of telltale indicators for this method of attack. For example, one such indicator might be the discovery of possible terrorists pursuing flight training to fly large jet aircraft, or seeking to buy advanced flight simulators.

3. The CTC did not propose, and the intelligence community collection management process did not set, requirements to monitor such telltale indicators. Therefore the warning system was not looking for information such as the July 2001 FBI report of potential terrorist interest in various kinds of aircraft training in Arizona, or the August 2001 arrest of Zacarias Moussaoui because of his suspicious behavior in a Minnesota flight school. In late August, the Moussaoui arrest was briefed to the DCI and other top CIA officials under the heading "Islamic Extremist Learns to Fly."[24] Because the system was not tuned to comprehend the potential significance of this information, the news had no effect on warning.

4. Neither the intelligence community nor aviation security experts analyzed systemic defenses within an aircraft or against terrorist-controlled aircraft, suicidal or otherwise. The many threat reports mentioning aircraft were passed to the FAA. While that agency continued to react to specific, credible threats, it did not try to perform the broader warning functions we describe here. No one in the government was taking on that role for domestic vulnerabilities.

   Richard Clarke told us that he was concerned about the danger posed by aircraft in the context of protecting the Atlanta Olympics of 1996, the White House complex, and the 2001 G-8 summit in Genoa. But he attributed his awareness more to Tom Clancy novels than to warnings from the intelligence community. He did not, or could not, press the government to work on the systemic issues of how to strengthen the layered security defenses to protect aircraft against hijackings or put the adequacy of air defenses against suicide hijackers on the national policy agenda.

The methods for detecting and then warning of surprise attack that the U.S. government had so painstakingly developed in the decades after Pearl Harbor

did not fail; instead, they were not really tried. They were not employed to analyze the enemy that, as the twentieth century closed, was most likely to launch
a surprise attack directly against the United States.

11.2 POLICY

The road to 9/11 again illustrates how the large, unwieldy U.S. government
tended to underestimate a threat that grew ever greater. The terrorism fostered
by Bin Ladin and al Qaeda was different from anything the government had
faced before. The existing mechanisms for handling terrorist acts had been trial
and punishment for acts committed by individuals; sanction, reprisal, deterrence, or war for acts by hostile governments. The actions of al Qaeda fit neither category. Its crimes were on a scale approaching acts of war, but they were
committed by a loose, far-flung, nebulous conspiracy with no territories or citizens or assets that could be readily threatened, overwhelmed, or destroyed.

Early in 2001, DCI Tenet and Deputy Director for Operations James Pavitt
gave an intelligence briefing to President-elect Bush, Vice President-elect
Cheney, and Rice; it included the topic of al Qaeda. Pavitt recalled conveying
that Bin Ladin was one of the gravest threats to the country.[25]

Bush asked whether killing Bin Ladin would end the problem. Pavitt said
he and the DCI had answered that killing Bin Ladin would have an impact,
but would not stop the threat. The CIA later provided more formal assessments
to the White House reiterating that conclusion. It added that in the long term,
the only way to deal with the threat was to end al Qaeda's ability to use
Afghanistan as a sanctuary for its operations.[26]

Perhaps the most incisive of the advisors on terrorism to the new administration was the holdover Richard Clarke. Yet he admits that his policy advice,
even if it had been accepted immediately and turned into action, would not
have prevented 9/11.[27]

We must then ask when the U.S. government had reasonable opportunities
to mobilize the country for major action against al Qaeda and its Afghan sanctuary. The main opportunities came after the new information the U.S. government received in 1996–1997, after the embassy bombings of August 1998,
after the discoveries of the Jordanian and Ressam plots in late 1999, and after
the attack on the USS *Cole* in October 2000.

The U.S. policy response to al Qaeda before 9/11 was essentially defined
following the embassy bombings of August 1998. We described those decisions
in chapter 4. It is worth noting that they were made by the Clinton administration under extremely difficult domestic political circumstances. Opponents
were seeking the President's impeachment. In addition, in 1998–99 President
Clinton was preparing the government for possible war against Serbia, and he

had authorized major air strikes against Iraq.

The tragedy of the embassy bombings provided an opportunity for a full examination, across the government, of the national security threat that Bin Ladin posed. Such an examination could have made clear to all that issues were at stake that were much larger than the domestic politics of the moment. But the major policy agencies of the government did not meet the threat.

The diplomatic efforts of the Department of State were largely ineffective. Al Qaeda and terrorism was just one more priority added to already-crowded agendas with countries like Pakistan and Saudi Arabia. After 9/11 that changed.

Policymakers turned principally to the CIA and covert action to implement policy. Before 9/11, no agency had more responsibility—or did more—to attack al Qaeda, working day and night, than the CIA. But there were limits to what the CIA was able to achieve in its energetic worldwide efforts to disrupt terrorist activities or use proxies to try to capture or kill Bin Ladin and his lieutenants. As early as mid-1997, one CIA officer wrote to his supervisor: "All we're doing is holding the ring until the cavalry gets here."[28]

Military measures failed or were not applied. Before 9/11 the Department of Defense was not given the mission of ending al Qaeda's sanctuary in Afghanistan.

Officials in both the Clinton and Bush administrations regarded a full U.S. invasion of Afghanistan as practically inconceivable before 9/11. It was never the subject of formal interagency deliberation.

Lesser forms of intervention could also have been considered. One would have been the deployment of U.S. military or intelligence personnel, or special strike forces, to Afghanistan itself or nearby—openly, clandestinely (secretly), or covertly (with their connection to the United States hidden). Then the United States would no longer have been dependent on proxies to gather actionable intelligence. However, it would have needed to secure basing and overflight support from neighboring countries. A significant political, military, and intelligence effort would have been required, extending over months and perhaps years, with associated costs and risks. Given how hard it has proved to locate Bin Ladin even today when there are substantial ground forces in Afghanistan, its odds of sucess are hard to calculate. We have found no indication that President Clinton was offered such an intermediate choice, or that this option was given any more consideration than the idea of invasion.

These policy challenges are linked to the problem of imagination we have already discussed. Since we believe that both President Clinton and President Bush were genuinely concerned about the danger posed by al Qaeda, approaches involving more direct intervention against the sanctuary in Afghanistan apparently must have seemed—if they were considered at all—to be disproportionate to the threat.

Insight for the future is thus not easy to apply in practice. It is hardest to mount a major effort while a problem still seems minor. Once the danger has fully materialized, evident to all, mobilizing action is easier—but it then may be too late.

Another possibility, short of putting U.S. personnel on the ground, was to issue a blunt ultimatum to the Taliban, backed by a readiness to at least launch an indefinite air campaign to disable that regime's limited military capabilities and tip the balance in Afghanistan's ongoing civil war. The United States had warned the Taliban that they would be held accountable for further attacks by Bin Ladin against Afghanistan's U.S. interests. The warning had been given in 1998, again in late 1999, once more in the fall of 2000, and again in the summer of 2001. Delivering it repeatedly did not make it more effective.

As evidence of al Qaeda's responsibility for the *Cole* attack came in during November 2000, National Security Advisor Samuel Berger asked the Pentagon to develop a plan for a sustained air campaign against the Taliban. Clarke developed a paper laying out a formal, specific ultimatum. But Clarke's plan apparently did not advance to formal consideration by the Small Group of principals. We have found no indication that the idea was briefed to the new administration or that Clarke passed his paper to them, although the same team of career officials spanned both administrations.

After 9/11, President Bush announced that al Qaeda was responsible for the attack on the USS *Cole*. Before 9/11, neither president took any action. Bin Ladin's inference may well have been that attacks, at least at the level of the *Cole*, were risk free.[29]

11.3 CAPABILITIES

Earlier chapters describe in detail the actions decided on by the Clinton and Bush administrations. Each president considered or authorized covert actions, a process that consumed considerable time—especially in the Clinton administration—and achieved little success beyond the collection of intelligence. After the August 1998 missile strikes in Afghanistan, naval vessels remained on station in or near the region, prepared to fire cruise missiles. General Hugh Shelton developed as many as 13 different strike options, and did not recommend any of them. The most extended debate on counterterrorism in the Bush administration before 9/11 had to do with missions for the unmanned Predator—whether to use it just to locate Bin Ladin or to wait until it was armed with a missile, so that it could find him and also attack him. Looking back, we are struck with the narrow and unimaginative menu of options for action offered to both President Clinton and President Bush.

Before 9/11, the United States tried to solve the al Qaeda problem with the same government institutions and capabilities it had used in the last stages of the Cold War and its immediate aftermath. These capabilities were insufficient, but little was done to expand or reform them.

For covert action, of course, the White House depended on the Counterterrorist Center and the CIA's Directorate of Operations. Though some officers, particularly in the Bin Ladin unit, were eager for the mission, most were not. The higher management of the directorate was unenthusiastic. The CIA's capacity to conduct paramilitary operations with its own personnel was not large, and the Agency did not seek a large-scale general expansion of these capabilities before 9/11. James Pavitt, the head of this directorate, remembered that covert action, promoted by the White House, had gotten the Clandestine Service into trouble in the past. He had no desire to see this happen again. He thought, not unreasonably, that a truly serious counterterrorism campaign against an enemy of this magnitude would be business primarily for the military, not the Clandestine Service.[30]

As for the Department of Defense, some officers in the Joint Staff were keen to help. Some in the Special Operations Command have told us that they worked on plans for using Special Operations Forces in Afghanistan and that they hoped for action orders. JCS Chairman General Shelton and General Anthony Zinni at Central Command had a different view. Shelton felt that the August 1998 attacks had proved a waste of good ordnance and thereafter consistently opposed firing expensive Tomahawk missiles merely at "jungle gym" terrorist training infrastructure.[31] In this view, he had complete support from Defense Secretary William Cohen. Shelton was prepared to plan other options, but he was also prepared to make perfectly clear his own strong doubts about the wisdom of any military action that risked U.S. lives unless the intelligence was "actionable."[32]

The high price of keeping counterterrorism policy within the restricted circle of the Counterterrorism Security Group and the highest-level principals was nowhere more apparent than in the military establishment. After the August 1998 missile strike, other members of the JCS let the press know their unhappiness that, in conformity with the Goldwater-Nichols reforms, Shelton had been the only member of the JCS to be consulted. Although follow-on military options were briefed more widely, the vice director of operations on the Joint Staff commented to us that intelligence and planning documents relating to al Qaeda arrived in a ziplock red package and that many flag and general officers never had the clearances to see its contents.[33]

At no point before 9/11 was the Department of Defense fully engaged in the mission of countering al Qaeda, though this was perhaps the most dangerous foreign enemy then threatening the United States. The Clinton administration effectively relied on the CIA to take the lead in preparing long-term offensive plans against an enemy sanctuary. The Bush administration adopted this approach, although its emerging new strategy envisioned some yet undefined further role for the military in addressing the problem. Within Defense, both Secretary Cohen and Secretary Donald Rumsfeld gave their principal attention to other challenges.

America's homeland defenders faced outward. NORAD itself was barely able to retain any alert bases. Its planning scenarios occasionally considered the danger of hijacked aircraft being guided to American targets, but only aircraft that were coming from overseas. We recognize that a costly change in NORAD's defense posture to deal with the danger of suicide hijackers, before such a threat had ever actually been realized, would have been a tough sell. But NORAD did not canvass available intelligence and try to make the case.

The most serious weaknesses in agency capabilities were in the domestic arena. In chapter 3 we discussed these institutions—the FBI, the Immigration and Naturalization Service, the FAA, and others. The major pre-9/11 effort to strengthen domestic agency capabilities came in 2000, as part of a millennium after-action review. President Clinton and his principal advisers paid considerable attention then to border security problems, but were not able to bring about significant improvements before leaving office. The NSC-led interagency process did not effectively bring along the leadership of the Justice and Transportation departments in an agenda for institutional change.

The FBI did not have the capability to link the collective knowledge of agents in the field to national priorities. The acting director of the FBI did not learn of his Bureau's hunt for two possible al Qaeda operatives in the United States or about his Bureau's arrest of an Islamic extremist taking flight training until September 11. The director of central intelligence knew about the FBI's Moussaoui investigation weeks before word of it made its way even to the FBI's own assistant director for counterterrorism.

Other agencies deferred to the FBI. In the August 6 PDB reporting to President Bush of 70 full-field investigations related to al Qaeda, news the President said he found heartening, the CIA had simply restated what the FBI had said. No one looked behind the curtain.

The FAA's capabilities to take aggressive, anticipatory security measures were especially weak. Any serious policy examination of a suicide hijacking scenario, critiquing each of the layers of the security system, could have suggested changes to fix glaring vulnerabilities—expanding no-fly lists, searching passengers identified by the CAPPS screening system, deploying Federal Air Marshals domestically, hardening cockpit doors, alerting air crew to a different kind of hijacking than what they had been trained to expect, or adjusting the training of controllers and managers in the FAA and NORAD.

Government agencies also sometimes display a tendency to match capabilities to mission by defining away the hardest part of their job. They are often passive, accepting what are viewed as givens, including that efforts to identify and fix glaring vulnerabilities to dangerous threats would be too costly, too controversial, or too disruptive.

11.4 MANAGEMENT

Operational Management

Earlier in this report we detailed various missed opportunities to thwart the 9/11 plot. Information was not shared, sometimes inadvertently or because of legal misunderstandings. Analysis was not pooled. Effective operations were not launched. Often the handoffs of information were lost across the divide separating the foreign and domestic agencies of the government.

However the specific problems are labeled, we believe they are symptoms of the government's broader inability to adapt how it manages problems to the new challenges of the twenty-first century. The agencies are like a set of specialists in a hospital, each ordering tests, looking for symptoms, and prescribing medications. What is missing is the attending physician who makes sure they work as a team.

One missing element was effective management of transnational operations. Action officers should have drawn on all available knowledge in the government. This management should have ensured that information was shared and duties were clearly assigned across agencies, and across the foreign-domestic divide.

Consider, for example, the case of Mihdhar, Hazmi, and their January 2000 trip to Kuala Lumpur, detailed in chapter 6. In late 1999, the National Security Agency (NSA) analyzed communications associated with a man named Khalid, a man named Nawaf, and a man named Salem. Working-level officials in the intelligence community knew little more than this. But they correctly concluded that "Nawaf" and "Khalid" might be part of "an operational cadre" and that "something nefarious might be afoot."

The NSA did not think its job was to research these identities. It saw itself as an agency to support intelligence consumers, such as CIA. The NSA tried to respond energetically to any request made. But it waited to be asked.

If NSA had been asked to try to identify these people, the agency would have started by checking its own database of earlier information from these same sources. Some of this information had been reported; some had not. But it was all readily accessible in the database. NSA's analysts would promptly have discovered who Nawaf was, that his full name might be Nawaf al Hazmi, and that he was an old friend of Khalid.

With this information and more that was available, managers could have more effectively tracked the movement of these operatives in southeast Asia. With the name "Nawaf al Hazmi," a manager could then have asked the State Department also to check that name. State would promptly have found its own record on Nawaf al Hazmi, showing that he too had been issued a visa to visit the United States. Officials would have learned that the visa had been issued at the same place—Jeddah—and on almost the same day as the one given to Khalid al Mihdhar.

When the travelers left Kuala Lumpur for Bangkok, local officials were able to identify one of the travelers as Khalid al Mihdhar. After the flight left, they learned that one of his companions had the name Alhazmi. But the officials did not know what that name meant.

The information arrived at Bangkok too late to track these travelers as they came in. Had the authorities there already been keeping an eye out for Khalid al Mihdhar as part of a general regional or worldwide alert, they might have tracked him coming in. Had they been alerted to look for a possible companion named Nawaf al Hazmi, they might have noticed him too. Instead, they were notified only after Kuala Lumpur sounded the alarm. By that time, the travelers had already disappeared into the streets of Bangkok.

On January 12, the head of the CIA's al Qaeda unit told his bosses that surveillance in Kuala Lumpur was continuing. He may not have known that in fact Mihdhar and his companions had dispersed and the tracking was falling apart. U.S. officials in Bangkok regretfully reported the bad news on January 13. The names they had were put on a watchlist in Bangkok, so that Thai authorities might notice if the men left the country. On January 14, the head of the CIA's al Qaeda unit again updated his bosses, telling them that officials were continuing to track the suspicious individuals who had now dispersed to various countries.

Unfortunately, there is no evidence of any tracking efforts actually being undertaken by anyone after the Arabs disappeared into Bangkok. No other effort was made to create other opportunities to spot these Arab travelers in case the screen in Bangkok failed. Just from the evidence in Mihdhar's passport, one of the logical possible destinations and interdiction points would have been the United States. Yet no one alerted the INS or the FBI to look for these individuals. They arrived, unnoticed, in Los Angeles on January 15.

In early March 2000, Bangkok reported that Nawaf al Hazmi, now identified for the first time with his full name, had departed on January 15 on a United Airlines flight to Los Angeles. Since the CIA did not appreciate the significance of that name or notice the cable, we have found no evidence that this information was sent to the FBI.

Even if watchlisting had prevented or at least alerted U.S. officials to the entry of Hazmi and Mihdhar, we do not think it is likely that watchlisting, by itself, have prevented the 9/11 attacks. Al Qaeda adapted to the failure of some of its operatives to gain entry into the United States. None of these future hijackers was a pilot. Alternatively, had they been permitted entry and surveilled, some larger results might have been possible had the FBI been patient.

These are difficult what-ifs. The intelligence community might have judged that the risks of conducting such a prolonged intelligence operation were too high—potential terrorists might have been lost track of, for example. The pre-9/11 FBI might not have been judged capable of conducting such an operation. But surely the intelligence community would have preferred to have the chance to make these choices.

From the details of this case, or from the other opportunities we catalogue in the text box, one can see how hard it is for the intelligence community to assemble enough of the puzzle pieces gathered by different agencies to make some sense of them and then develop a fully informed joint plan. Accomplishing all this is especially difficult in a transnational case. We sympathize with the working-level officers, drowning in information and trying to decide what is important or what needs to be done when no particular action has been requested of them.

Who had the job of managing the case to make sure these things were done? One answer is that everyone had the job. The CIA's deputy director for operations, James Pavitt, stressed to us that the responsibility resided with all involved. Above all he emphasized the primacy of the field. The field had the lead in managing operations. The job of headquarters, he stressed, was to support the field, and do so without delay. If the field asked for information or other support, the job of headquarters was to get it—right away.[34]

This is a traditional perspective on operations and, traditionally, it has had great merit. It reminded us of the FBI's pre-9/11 emphasis on the primacy of its field offices. When asked about how this traditional structure would adapt to the challenge of managing a transnational case, one that hopped from place to place as this one did, the deputy director argued that all involved were

---

Operational Opportunities

1. January 2000: the CIA does not watchlist Khalid al Mihdhar or notify the FBI when it learned Mihdhar possessed a valid U.S. visa.

2. January 2000: the CIA does not develop a transnational plan for tracking Mihdhar and his associates so that they could be followed to Bangkok and onward, including the United States.

3. March 2000: the CIA does not watchlist Nawaf al Hazmi or notify the FBI when it learned that he possessed a U.S. visa and had flown to Los Angeles on January 15, 2000.

4. January 2001: the CIA does not inform the FBI that a source had identified Khallad, or Tawfiq bin Attash, a major figure in the October 2000 bombing of the USS *Cole*, as having attended the meeting in Kuala Lumpur with Khalid al Mihdhar.

5. May 2001: a CIA official does not notify the FBI about Mihdhar's U.S. visa, Hazmi's U.S. travel, or Khallad's having attended the Kuala Lumpur meeting (identified when he reviewed all of the relevant traffic because of the high level of threats).

6. June 2001: FBI and CIA officials do not ensure that all relevant information regarding the Kuala Lumpur meeting was shared with the *Cole* investigators at the June 11 meeting.

7. August 2001: the FBI does not recognize the significance of the information regarding Mihdhar and Hazmi's possible arrival in the United States and thus does not take adequate action to share information, assign resources, and give sufficient priority to the search.

8. August 2001: FBI headquarters does not recognize the significance of the information regarding Moussaoui's training and beliefs and thus does not take adequate action to share information, involve higher-level officials across agencies, obtain information regarding Moussaoui's ties to al Qaeda, and give sufficient priority to determining what Moussaoui might be planning.

9. August 2001: the CIA does not focus on information that Khalid Sheikh Mohammed is a key al Qaeda lieutenant or connect information identifying KSM as the "Mukhtar" mentioned in other reports to the analysis that could have linked "Mukhtar" with Ramzi Binalshibh and Moussaoui.

10. August 2001: the CIA and FBI do not connect the presence of Mihdhar, Hazmi, and Moussaoui to the general threat reporting about imminent attacks.

responsible for making it work. Pavitt underscored the responsibility of the particular field location where the suspects were being tracked at any given time. On the other hand, he also said that the Counterterrorist Center was supposed to manage all the moving parts, while what happened on the ground was the responsibility of managers in the field.[35]

Headquarters tended to support and facilitate, trying to make sure everyone was in the loop. From time to time a particular post would push one way, or headquarters would urge someone to do something. But headquarters never really took responsibility for the successful management of this case. Hence the managers at CIA headquarters did not realize that omissions in planning had occurred, and they scarcely knew that the case had fallen apart.

The director of the Counterterrorist Center at the time, Cofer Black, recalled to us that this operation was one among many and that, at the time, it was "considered interesting, but not heavy water yet." He recalled the failure to get the word to Bangkok fast enough, but has no evident recollection of why the case then dissolved, unnoticed.[36]

The next level down, the director of the al Qaeda unit in CIA at the time recalled that he did not think it was his job to direct what should or should not be done. He did not pay attention when the individuals dispersed and things fell apart. There was no conscious decision to stop the operation after the trail was temporarily lost in Bangkok. He acknowledged, however, that perhaps there had been a letdown for his overworked staff after the extreme tension and long hours in the period of the millennium alert.[37]

The details of this case illuminate real management challenges, past and future. The U.S. government must find a way of pooling intelligence and using it to guide the planning of and assignment of responsibilities for *joint operations* involving organizations as disparate as the CIA, the FBI, the State Department, the military, and the agencies involved in homeland security.

Institutional Management

Beyond those day-to-day tasks of bridging the foreign-domestic divide and matching intelligence with plans, the challenges include broader management issues pertaining to how the top leaders of the government set priorities and allocate resources. Once again it is useful to illustrate the problem by examining the CIA, since before 9/11 this agency's role was so central in the government's counterterrorism efforts.

On December 4, 1998, DCI Tenet issued a directive to several CIA officials and his deputy for community management, stating: "We are at war. I want no resources or people spared in this effort, either inside CIA or the Community."[38] The memorandum had little overall effect on mobilizing the CIA or the intelligence community.[39]

The memo was addressed only to CIA officials and the deputy for community management, Joan Dempsey. She faxed the memo to the heads of the major intelligence agencies after removing covert action sections. Only a handful of people received it. The NSA director at the time, Lieutenant General Kenneth Minihan, believed the memo applied only to the CIA and not the NSA, because no one had informed him of any NSA shortcomings. For their part, CIA officials thought the memorandum was intended for the rest of the intelligence community, given that they were already doing all they could and believed that the rest of the community needed to pull its weight.[40]

The episode indicates some of the limitations of the DCI's authority over the direction and priorities of the intelligence community, especially its elements within the Department of Defense. The DCI has to direct agencies without controlling them. He does not receive an appropriation for their activities, and therefore does not control their purse strings. He has little insight into how they spend their resources. Congress attempted to strengthen the DCI's authority in 1996 by creating the positions of deputy DCI for community management and assistant DCIs for collection, analysis and production, and administration. But the authority of these positions is limited, and the vision of central management clearly has not been realized.

The DCI did not develop a management strategy for a war against Islamist terrorism before 9/11. Such a management strategy would define the capabilities the intelligence community must acquire for such a war—from language training to collection systems to analysts. Such a management strategy would necessarily extend beyond the CTC to the components that feed its expertise and support its operations, linked transparently to counterterrorism objectives. It would then detail the proposed expenditures and organizational changes required to acquire and implement these capabilities.

DCI Tenet and his deputy director for operations told us they did have a management strategy for a war on terrorism. It was to rebuild the CIA. They said the CIA as a whole had been badly damaged by prior budget constraints and that capabilities needed to be restored across the board. Indeed, the CTC budget had not been cut while the budgets had been slashed in many other parts of the Agency. By restoring funding across the CIA, a rising tide would lift all boats. They also stressed the synergy between improvements of every part of the Agency and the capabilities that the CTC or stations overseas could draw on in the war on terror.[41]

As some officials pointed out to us, there is a tradeoff in this management approach. In an attempt to rebuild everything at once, the highest priority efforts might not get the maximum support that they need. Furthermore, this approach attempted to channel relatively strong outside support for combating terrorism into backing for across-the-board funding increases. Proponents of the counterterrorism agenda might respond by being less inclined to loosen the purse strings than they would have been if offered a convincing counterterrorism budget strategy. The DCI's management strategy was also focused mainly on the CIA.

Lacking a management strategy for the war on terrorism or ways to see how funds were being spent across the community, DCI Tenet and his aides found it difficult to develop an overall intelligence community budget for a war on terrorism.

Responsibility for domestic intelligence gathering on terrorism was vested solely in the FBI, yet during almost all of the Clinton administration the relationship between the FBI Director and the President was nearly nonexistent. The FBI Director would not communicate directly with the President. His key personnel shared very little information with the National Security Council and the rest of the national security community. As a consequence, one of the critical working relationships in the counterterrorism effort was broken.

The Millennium Exception

Before concluding our narrative, we offer a reminder, and an explanation, of the one period in which the government as a whole seemed to be acting in concert to deal with terrorism—the last weeks of December 1999 preceding the millennium.

In the period between December 1999 and early January 2000, information about terrorism flowed widely and abundantly. The flow from the FBI was particularly remarkable because the FBI at other times shared almost no information. That from the intelligence community was also remarkable, because some of it reached officials—local airport managers and local police departments—who had not seen such information before and would not see it again before 9/11, if then. And the terrorist threat, in the United States even more than abroad, engaged the frequent attention of high officials in the executive branch and leaders in both houses of Congress.

Why was this so? Most obviously, it was because everyone was already on edge with the millennium and possible computer programming glitches ("Y2K") that might obliterate records, shut down power and communication lines, or otherwise disrupt daily life. Then, Jordanian authorities arrested 16 al Qaeda terrorists planning a number of bombings in that country. Those in custody included two U.S. citizens. Soon after, an alert Customs agent caught Ahmed Ressam bringing explosives across the Canadian border with the apparent intention of blowing up Los Angeles airport. He was found to have confederates on both sides of the border.

These were not events whispered about in highly classified intelligence dailies or FBI interview memos. The information was in all major newspapers and highlighted in network television news. Though the Jordanian arrests only made page 13 of the *New York Times*, they were featured on every evening newscast. The arrest of Ressam was on front pages, and the original story and its follow-ups dominated television news for a week. FBI field offices around the country were swamped by calls from concerned citizens. Representatives of the Justice Department, the FAA, local police departments, and major airports had microphones in their faces whenever they showed themselves.[42]

After the millennium alert, the government relaxed. Counterterrorism went back to being a secret preserve for segments of the FBI, the Counterterrorist Center, and the Counterterrorism Security Group. But the experience showed that the government was capable of mobilizing itself for an alert against terrorism. While one factor was the preexistence of widespread concern about Y2K, another, at least equally important, was simply shared information. Everyone knew not only of an abstract threat but of at least one terrorist who had been arrested *in the United States*. Terrorism had a face—that of Ahmed Ressam—and Americans from Vermont to southern California went on the watch for his like.

In the summer of 2001, DCI Tenet, the Counterterrorist Center, and the Counterterrorism Security Group did their utmost to sound a loud alarm, its basis being intelligence indicating that al Qaeda planned something big. But the millennium phenomenon was not repeated. FBI field offices apparently saw no abnormal terrorist activity, and headquarters was not shaking them up.

Between May 2001 and September 11, there was very little in newspapers or on television to heighten anyone's concern about terrorism. Front-page stories touching on the subject dealt with the windup of trials dealing with the East Africa embassy bombings and Ressam. All this reportage looked backward, describing problems satisfactorily resolved. Back-page notices told of tightened security at embassies and military installations abroad and government cautions against travel to the Arabian Peninsula. All the rest was secret.

12

WHAT TO DO?
A GLOBAL STRATEGY

12.1 REFLECTING ON A GENERATIONAL CHALLENGE

THREE YEARS AFTER 9/11, Americans are still thinking and talking about how to protect our nation in this new era. The national debate continues.

Countering terrorism has become, beyond any doubt, the top national security priority for the United States. This shift has occurred with the full support of the Congress, both major political parties, the media, and the American people.

The nation has committed enormous resources to national security and to countering terrorism. Between fiscal year 2001, the last budget adopted before 9/11, and the present fiscal year 2004, total federal spending on defense (including expenditures on both Iraq and Afghanistan), homeland security, and international affairs rose more than 50 percent, from $354 billion to about $547 billion. The United States has not experienced such a rapid surge in national security spending since the Korean War.[1]

This pattern has occurred before in American history. The United States faces a sudden crisis and summons a tremendous exertion of national energy. Then, as that surge transforms the landscape, comes a time for reflection and reevaluation. Some programs and even agencies are discarded; others are invented or redesigned. Private firms and engaged citizens redefine their relationships with government, working through the processes of the American republic.

Now is the time for that reflection and reevaluation. The United States should consider *what to do*—the shape and objectives of a strategy. Americans should also consider *how to do it*—organizing their government in a different way.

Defining the Threat
In the post-9/11 world, threats are defined more by the fault lines within societies than by the territorial boundaries between them. From terrorism to global

disease or environmental degradation, the challenges have become transnational rather than international. That is the defining quality of world politics in the twenty-first century.

National security used to be considered by studying foreign frontiers, weighing opposing groups of states, and measuring industrial might. To be dangerous, an enemy had to muster large armies. Threats emerged slowly, often visibly, as weapons were forged, armies conscripted, and units trained and moved into place. Because large states were more powerful, they also had more to lose. They could be deterred.

Now threats can emerge quickly. An organization like al Qaeda, headquartered in a country on the other side of the earth, in a region so poor that electricity or telephones were scarce, could nonetheless scheme to wield weapons of unprecedented destructive power in the largest cities of the United States.

In this sense, 9/11 has taught us that terrorism against American interests "over there" should be regarded just as we regard terrorism against America "over here." In this same sense, the American homeland is the planet.

But the enemy is not just "terrorism," some generic evil.[2] This vagueness blurs the strategy. The catastrophic threat at this moment in history is more specific. It is the threat posed by *Islamist* terrorism—especially the al Qaeda network, its affiliates, and its ideology.[3]

As we mentioned in chapter 2, Usama Bin Ladin and other Islamist terrorist leaders draw on a long tradition of extreme intolerance within one stream of Islam (a minority tradition), from at least Ibn Taimiyyah, through the founders of Wahhabism, through the Muslim Brotherhood, to Sayyid Qutb. That stream is motivated by religion and does not distinguish politics from religion, thus distorting both. It is further fed by grievances stressed by Bin Ladin and widely felt throughout the Muslim world—against the U.S. military presence in the Middle East, policies perceived as anti-Arab and anti-Muslim, and support of Israel. Bin Ladin and Islamist terrorists mean exactly what they say: to them America is the font of all evil, the "head of the snake," and it must be converted or destroyed.

It is not a position with which Americans can bargain or negotiate. With it there is no common ground—not even respect for life—on which to begin a dialogue. It can only be destroyed or utterly isolated.

Because the Muslim world has fallen behind the West politically, economically, and militarily for the past three centuries, and because few tolerant or secular Muslim democracies provide alternative models for the future, Bin Ladin's message finds receptive ears. It has attracted active support from thousands of disaffected young Muslims and resonates powerfully with a far larger number who do not actively support his methods. The resentment of America and the West is deep, even among leaders of relatively successful Muslim states.[4]

Tolerance, the rule of law, political and economic openness, the extension of greater opportunities to women—these cures must come from within Muslim societies themselves. The United States must support such developments.

But this process is likely to be measured in decades, not years. It is a process that will be violently opposed by Islamist terrorist organizations, both inside Muslim countries and in attacks on the United States and other Western nations. The United States finds itself caught up in a clash *within* a civilization. That clash arises from particular conditions in the Muslim world, conditions that spill over into expatriate Muslim communities in non-Muslim countries.

Our enemy is twofold: al Qaeda, a stateless network of terrorists that struck us on 9/11; and a radical ideological movement in the Islamic world, inspired in part by al Qaeda, which has spawned terrorist groups and violence across the globe. The first enemy is weakened, but continues to pose a grave threat. The second enemy is gathering, and will menace Americans and American interests long after Usama Bin Ladin and his cohorts are killed or captured. Thus our strategy must match our means to two ends: dismantling the al Qaeda network and prevailing in the longer term over the ideology that gives rise to Islamist terrorism.

Islam is not the enemy. It is not synonymous with terror. Nor does Islam teach terror. America and its friends oppose a perversion of Islam, not the great world faith itself. Lives guided by religious faith, including literal beliefs in holy scriptures, are common to every religion, and represent no threat to us.

Other religions have experienced violent internal struggles. With so many diverse adherents, every major religion will spawn violent zealots. Yet understanding and tolerance among people of different faiths can and must prevail.

The present transnational danger is Islamist terrorism. What is needed is a broad political-military strategy that rests on a firm tripod of policies to

- attack terrorists and their organizations;
- prevent the continued growth of Islamist terrorism; and
- protect against and prepare for terrorist attacks.

More Than a War on Terrorism

Terrorism is a tactic used by individuals and organizations to kill and destroy. Our efforts should be directed at those individuals and organizations.

Calling this struggle a war accurately describes the use of American and allied armed forces to find and destroy terrorist groups and their allies in the field, notably in Afghanistan. The language of war also evokes the mobilization for a national effort. Yet the strategy should be balanced.

The first phase of our post-9/11 efforts rightly included military action to topple the Taliban and pursue al Qaeda. This work continues. But long-term success demands the use of all elements of national power: diplomacy, intelligence, covert action, law enforcement, economic policy, foreign aid, public diplomacy, and homeland defense. If we favor one tool while neglecting others, we leave ourselves vulnerable and weaken our national effort.

Certainly the strategy should include offensive operations to counter terrorism. Terrorists should no longer find safe haven where their organizations can grow and flourish. America's strategy should be a coalition strategy, that includes Muslim nations as partners in its development and implementation.

Our effort should be accompanied by a preventive strategy that is as much, or more, political as it is military. The strategy must focus clearly on the Arab and Muslim world, in all its variety.

Our strategy should also include defenses. America can be attacked in many ways and has many vulnerabilities. No defenses are perfect. But risks must be calculated; hard choices must be made about allocating resources. Responsibilities for America's defense should be clearly defined. Planning does make a difference, identifying where a little money might have a large effect. Defenses also complicate the plans of attackers, increasing their risks of discovery and failure. Finally, the nation must prepare to deal with attacks that are not stopped.

Measuring Success

What should Americans expect from their government in the struggle against Islamist terrorism? The goals seem unlimited: Defeat terrorism anywhere in the world. But Americans have also been told to expect the worst: An attack is probably coming; it may be terrible.

With such benchmarks, the justifications for action and spending seem limitless. Goals are good. Yet effective public policies also need concrete objectives. Agencies need to be able to measure success.

These measurements do not need to be quantitative: government cannot measure success in the ways that private firms can. But the targets should be specific enough so that reasonable observers—in the White House, the Congress, the media, or the general public—can judge whether or not the objectives have been attained.

Vague goals match an amorphous picture of the enemy. Al Qaeda and its affiliates are popularly described as being all over the world, adaptable, resilient, needing little higher-level organization, and capable of anything. The American people are thus given the picture of an omnipotent, unslayable hydra of destruction. This image lowers expectations for government effectiveness.

It should not lower them too far. Our report shows a determined and capable group of plotters. Yet the group was fragile, dependent on a few key personalities, and occasionally left vulnerable by the marginal, unstable people often attracted to such causes. The enemy made mistakes—like Khalid al Mihdhar's unauthorized departure from the United States that required him to enter the country again in July 2001, or the selection of Zacarias Moussaoui as a participant and Ramzi Binalshibh's transfer of money to him. The U.S. government was not able to capitalize on those mistakes in time to prevent 9/11.

We do not believe it is possible to defeat all terrorist attacks against Americans, every time and everywhere. A president should tell the American people:

- No president can promise that a catastrophic attack like that of 9/11 will not happen again. History has shown that even the most vigilant and expert agencies cannot always prevent determined, suicidal attackers from reaching a target.

- But the American people are entitled to expect their government to do its very best. They should expect that officials will have realistic objectives, clear guidance, and effective organization. They are entitled to see some standards for performance so they can judge, with the help of their elected representatives, whether the objectives are being met.

12.2 ATTACK TERRORISTS AND THEIR ORGANIZATIONS

The U.S. government, joined by other governments around the world, is working through intelligence, law enforcement, military, financial, and diplomatic channels to identify, disrupt, capture, or kill individual terrorists. This effort was going on before 9/11 and it continues on a vastly enlarged scale. But to catch terrorists, a U.S. or foreign agency needs to be able to find and reach them.

No Sanctuaries
The 9/11 attack was a complex international operation, the product of years of planning. Bombings like those in Bali in 2003 or Madrid in 2004, while able to take hundreds of lives, can be mounted locally. Their requirements are far more modest in size and complexity. They are more difficult to thwart. But the U.S. government must build the capacities to prevent a 9/11-scale plot from succeeding, and those capabilities will help greatly to cope with lesser but still devastating attacks.

A complex international terrorist operation aimed at launching a catastrophic attack cannot be mounted by just anyone in any place. Such operations appear to require

- time, space, and ability to perform competent planning and staff work;
- a command structure able to make necessary decisions and possessing the authority and contacts to assemble needed people, money, and materials;

- opportunity and space to recruit, train, and select operatives with the needed skills and dedication, providing the time and structure required to socialize them into the terrorist cause, judge their trustworthiness, and hone their skills;
- a logistics network able to securely manage the travel of operatives, move money, and transport resources (like explosives) where they need to go;
- access, in the case of certain weapons, to the special materials needed for a nuclear, chemical, radiological, or biological attack;
- reliable communications between coordinators and operatives; and
- opportunity to test the workability of the plan.

Many details in chapters 2, 5, and 7 illustrate the direct and indirect value of the Afghan sanctuary to al Qaeda in preparing the 9/11 attack and other operations. The organization cemented personal ties among veteran jihadists working together there for years. It had the operational space to gather and sift recruits, indoctrinating them in isolated, desert camps. It built up logistical networks, running through Pakistan and the United Arab Emirates.

Al Qaeda also exploited relatively lax internal security environments in Western countries, especially Germany. It considered the environment in the United States so hospitable that the 9/11 operatives used America as their staging area for further training and exercises—traveling into, out of, and around the country and complacently using their real names with little fear of capture.

To find sanctuary, terrorist organizations have fled to some of the least governed, most lawless places in the world. The intelligence community has prepared a world map that highlights possible terrorist havens, using no secret intelligence—just indicating areas that combine rugged terrain, weak governance, room to hide or receive supplies, and low population density with a town or city near enough to allow necessary interaction with the outside world. Large areas scattered around the world meet these criteria.[5]

In talking with American and foreign government officials and military officers on the front lines fighting terrorists today, we asked them: If you were a terrorist leader today, where would you locate your base? Some of the same places come up again and again on their lists:

- western Pakistan and the Pakistan-Afghanistan border region
- southern or western Afghanistan
- the Arabian Peninsula, especially Saudi Arabia and Yemen, and the nearby Horn of Africa, including Somalia and extending southwest into Kenya
- Southeast Asia, from Thailand to the southern Philippines to Indonesia
- West Africa, including Nigeria and Mali
- European cities with expatriate Muslim communities, especially cities

in central and eastern Europe where security forces and border controls are less effective

In the twentieth century, strategists focused on the world's great industrial heartlands. In the twenty-first, the focus is in the opposite direction, toward remote regions and failing states. The United States has had to find ways to extend its reach, straining the limits of its influence.

Every policy decision we make needs to be seen through this lens. If, for example, Iraq becomes a failed state, it will go to the top of the list of places that are breeding grounds for attacks against Americans at home. Similarly, if we are paying insufficient attention to Afghanistan, the rule of the Taliban or warlords and narcotraffickers may reemerge and its countryside could once again offer refuge to al Qaeda, or its successor.

Recommendation: The U.S. government must identify and prioritize actual or potential terrorist sanctuaries. For each, it should have a realistic strategy to keep possible terrorists insecure and on the run, using all elements of national power. We should reach out, listen to, and work with other countries that can help.

We offer three illustrations that are particularly applicable today, in 2004: Pakistan, Afghanistan, and Saudi Arabia.

Pakistan
Pakistan's endemic poverty, widespread corruption, and often ineffective government create opportunities for Islamist recruitment. Poor education is a particular concern. Millions of families, especially those with little money, send their children to religious schools, or madrassahs. Many of these schools are the only opportunity available for an education, but some have been used as incubators for violent extremism. According to Karachi's police commander, there are 859 madrassahs teaching more than 200,000 youngsters in his city alone.[6]

It is hard to overstate the importance of Pakistan in the struggle against Islamist terrorism. Within Pakistan's borders are 150 million Muslims, scores of al Qaeda terrorists, many Taliban fighters, and—perhaps—Usama Bin Ladin. Pakistan possesses nuclear weapons and has come frighteningly close to war with nuclear-armed India over the disputed territory of Kashmir. A political battle among anti-American Islamic fundamentalists, the Pakistani military, and more moderate mainstream political forces has already spilled over into violence, and there have been repeated recent attempts to kill Pakistan's president, Pervez Musharraf.

In recent years, the United States has had three basic problems in its relationship with Pakistan:

- On terrorism, Pakistan helped nurture the Taliban. The Pakistani army and intelligence services, especially below the top ranks, have long been ambivalent about confronting Islamist extremists. Many in the government have sympathized with or provided support to the extremists. Musharraf agreed that Bin Ladin was bad. But before 9/11, preserving good relations with the Taliban took precedence.

- On proliferation, Musharraf has repeatedly said that Pakistan does not barter with its nuclear technology. But proliferation concerns have been long-standing and very serious. Most recently, the Pakistani government has claimed not to have known that one of its nuclear weapons developers, a national figure, was leading the most dangerous nuclear smuggling ring ever disclosed.

- Finally, Pakistan has made little progress toward the return of democratic rule at the national level, although that turbulent process does continue to function at the provincial level and the Pakistani press remains relatively free.

Immediately after 9/11, confronted by the United States with a stark choice, Pakistan made a strategic decision. Its government stood aside and allowed the U.S.-led coalition to destroy the Taliban regime. In other ways, Pakistan actively assisted: its authorities arrested more than 500 al Qaeda operatives and Taliban members, and Pakistani forces played a leading part in tracking down KSM, Abu Zubaydah, and other key al Qaeda figures.[7]

In the following two years, the Pakistani government tried to walk the fence, helping against al Qaeda while seeking to avoid a larger confrontation with Taliban remnants and other Islamic extremists. When al Qaeda and its Pakistani allies repeatedly tried to assassinate Musharraf, almost succeeding, the battle came home.

The country's vast unpoliced regions make Pakistan attractive to extremists seeking refuge and recruits and also provide a base for operations against coalition forces in Afghanistan. Almost all the 9/11 attackers traveled the north-south nexus of Kandahar–Quetta–Karachi. The Baluchistan region of Pakistan (KSM's ethnic home) and the sprawling city of Karachi remain centers of Islamist extremism where the U.S. and Pakistani security and intelligence presence has been weak. The U.S. consulate in Karachi is a makeshift fortress, reflecting the gravity of the surrounding threat.[8]

During the winter of 2003–2004, Musharraf made another strategic decision. He ordered the Pakistani army into the frontier provinces of northwest Pakistan along the Afghan border, where Bin Ladin and Ayman al Zawahiri have reportedly taken refuge. The army is confronting groups of al Qaeda fighters and their local allies in very difficult terrain. On the other side of the frontier, U.S. forces in Afghanistan have found it challenging to organize effective joint operations, given Pakistan's limited capabilities and reluctance to permit U.S. military operations on its soil. Yet in 2004, it is clear that the Pakistani government is trying harder than ever before in the battle against Islamist terrorists.[9]

Acknowledging these problems and Musharraf's own part in the story, we believe that Musharraf's government represents the best hope for stability in Pakistan and Afghanistan.

- In an extraordinary public essay asking how Muslims can "drag ourselves out of the pit we find ourselves in, to raise ourselves up," Musharraf has called for a strategy of "enlightened moderation." The Muslim world, he said, should shun militancy and extremism; the West—and the United States in particular—should seek to resolve disputes with justice and help better the Muslim world.[10]

- Having come close to war in 2002 and 2003, Pakistan and India have recently made significant progress in peacefully discussing their long-standing differences. The United States has been and should remain a key supporter of that process.

- The constant refrain of Pakistanis is that the United States long treated them as allies of convenience. As the United States makes fresh commitments now, it should make promises it is prepared to keep, for years to come.

Recommendation: If Musharraf stands for enlightened moderation in a fight for his life and for the life of his country, the United States should be willing to make hard choices too, and make the difficult long-term commitment to the future of Pakistan. Sustaining the current scale of aid to Pakistan, the United States should support Pakistan's government in its struggle against extremists with a comprehensive effort that extends from military aid to support for better education, so long as Pakistan's leaders remain willing to make difficult choices of their own.

Afghanistan

Afghanistan was the incubator for al Qaeda and for the 9/11 attacks. In the fall of 2001, the U.S.-led international coalition and its Afghan allies toppled the Taliban and ended the regime's protection of al Qaeda. Notable progress has been made. International cooperation has been strong, with a clear UN mandate and a NATO-led peacekeeping force (the International Security Assistance Force, or ISAF). More than 10,000 American soldiers are deployed today in Afghanistan, joined by soldiers from NATO allies and Muslim states. A central government has been established in Kabul, with a democratic constitution, new currency, and a new army. Most Afghans enjoy greater freedom, women and girls are emerging from subjugation, and 3 million children have returned to school. For the first time in many years, Afghans have reason to hope.[11]

But grave challenges remain. Taliban and al Qaeda fighters have regrouped in the south and southeast. Warlords control much of the country beyond Kabul, and the land is awash in weapons. Economic development remains a distant hope. The narcotics trade—long a massive sector of the Afghan economy—is again booming. Even the most hardened aid workers refuse to operate in many regions, and some warn that Afghanistan is near the brink of chaos.[12]

Battered Afghanistan has a chance. Elections are being prepared. It is revealing that in June 2004, Taliban fighters resorted to slaughtering 16 Afghans on a bus, apparently for no reason other than their boldness in carrying an unprecedented Afghan weapon: a voter registration card.

Afghanistan's president, Hamid Karzai, is brave and committed. He is trying to build genuinely national institutions that can overcome the tradition of allocating powers among ethnic communities. Yet even if his efforts are successful and elections bring a democratic government to Afghanistan, the United States faces some difficult choices.

After paying relatively little attention to rebuilding Afghanistan during the military campaign, U.S. policies changed noticeably during 2003. Greater consideration of the political dimension and congressional support for a substantial package of assistance signaled a longer-term commitment to Afghanistan's future. One Afghan regional official plaintively told us the country finally has a good government. He begged the United States to keep its promise and not abandon Afghanistan again, as it had in the 1990s. Another Afghan leader noted that if the United States leaves, "we will lose all that we have gained."[13]

Most difficult is to define the security mission in Afghanistan. There is continuing political controversy about whether military operations in Iraq have had any effect on the scale of America's commitment to the future of Afghanistan. The United States has largely stayed out of the central government's struggles with dissident warlords and it has largely avoided confronting the related problem of narcotrafficking.[14]

Recommendation: The President and the Congress deserve praise for their efforts in Afghanistan so far. Now the United States and the international community should make a long-term commitment to a secure and stable Afghanistan, in order to give the government a reasonable opportunity to improve the life of the Afghan people. Afghanistan must not again become a sanctuary for international crime and terrorism. The United States and the international community should help the Afghan government extend its authority over the country, with a strategy and nation-by-nation commitments to achieve their objectives.

- This is an ambitious recommendation. It would mean a redoubled effort to secure the country, disarm militias, and curtail the age of war-lord rule. But the United States and NATO have already committed themselves to the future of this region—wisely, as the 9/11 story shows—and failed half-measures could be worse than useless.

- NATO in particular has made Afghanistan a test of the Alliance's ability to adapt to current security challenges of the future. NATO must pass this test. Currently, the United States and the international community envision enough support so that the central government can build a truly national army and extend essential infrastructure and minimum public services to major towns and regions. The effort relies in part on foreign civil-military teams, arranged under various national flags. The institutional commitments of NATO and the United Nations to these enterprises are weak. NATO member states are not following through; some of the other states around the world that have pledged assistance to Afghanistan are not fulfilling their pledges.

- The U.S. presence in Afghanistan is overwhelmingly oriented toward military and security work. The State Department presence is woefully understaffed, and the military mission is narrowly focused on al Qaeda and Taliban remnants in the south and southeast. The U.S. government can do its part if the international community decides on a joint effort to restore the rule of law and contain rampant crime and narcotics trafficking in this crossroads of Central Asia.[15]

We heard again and again that the money for assistance is allocated so rigidly that, on the ground, one U.S. agency often cannot improvise or pitch in to help another agency, even in small ways when a few thousand dollars could make a great difference.

The U.S. government should allocate money so that lower-level officials have more flexibility to get the job done across agency lines, adjusting to the circumstances they find in the field. This should include discretionary funds for expenditures by military units that often encounter opportunities to help the local population.

Saudi Arabia

Saudi Arabia has been a problematic ally in combating Islamic extremism. At the level of high policy, Saudi Arabia's leaders cooperated with American diplomatic initiatives aimed at the Taliban or Pakistan before 9/11. At the same time, Saudi Arabia's society was a place where al Qaeda raised money directly from individuals and through charities. It was the society that produced 15 of the 19 hijackers.

The Kingdom is one of the world's most religiously conservative societies, and its identity is closely bound to its religious links, especially its position as the guardian of Islam's two holiest sites. Charitable giving, or *zakat*, is one of the five pillars of Islam. It is broader and more pervasive than Western ideas of charity—functioning also as a form of income tax, educational assistance, foreign aid, and a source of political influence. The Western notion of the separation of civic and religious duty does not exist in Islamic cultures. Funding charitable works is an integral function of the governments in the Islamic world. It is so ingrained in Islamic culture that in Saudi Arabia, for example, a department within the Saudi Ministry of Finance and National Economy collects zakat directly, much as the U.S. Internal Revenue Service collects payroll withholding tax. Closely tied to zakat is the dedication of the government to propagating the Islamic faith, particularly the Wahhabi sect that flourishes in Saudi Arabia.

Traditionally, throughout the Muslim world, there is no formal oversight mechanism for donations. As Saudi wealth increased, the amounts contributed by individuals and the state grew dramatically. Substantial sums went to finance Islamic charities of every kind.

While Saudi domestic charities are regulated by the Ministry of Labor and Social Welfare, charities and international relief agencies, such as the World Assembly of Muslim Youth (WAMY), are currently regulated by the Ministry of Islamic Affairs. This ministry uses zakat and government funds to spread Wahhabi beliefs throughout the world, including in mosques and schools. Often these schools provide the only education available; even in affluent countries, Saudi-funded Wahhabi schools are often the only Islamic schools. Some Wahhabi-funded organizations have been exploited by extremists to further their goal of violent jihad against non-Muslims. One such organization has been the al Haramain Islamic Foundation; the assets of some branch offices have been frozen by the U.S. and Saudi governments.

Until 9/11, few Saudis would have considered government oversight of charitable donations necessary; many would have perceived it as interference in the exercise of their faith. At the same time, the government's ability to finance most state expenditures with energy revenues has delayed the need for a modern income tax system. As a result, there have been strong religious, cultural, and administrative barriers to monitoring charitable spending. That appears to be changing, however, now that the goal of violent jihad also extends to overthrowing Sunni governments (such as the House of Saud) that are not living up to the ideals of the Islamist extremists.[16]

The leaders of the United States and the rulers of Saudi Arabia have long had friendly relations, rooted in fundamentally common interests against the Soviet Union during the Cold War, in American hopes that Saudi oil supplies would stabilize the supply and price of oil in world markets, and in Saudi hopes that America could help protect the Kingdom against foreign threats.

In 1990, the Kingdom hosted U.S. armed forces before the first U.S.-led war against Iraq. American soldiers and airmen have given their lives to help protect Saudi Arabia. The Saudi government has difficulty acknowledging this. American military bases remained there until 2003, as part of an international commitment to contain Iraq.

For many years, leaders on both sides preferred to keep their ties quiet and behind the scenes. As a result, neither the U.S. nor the Saudi people appreciated all the dimensions of the bilateral relationship, including the Saudi role in U.S. strategies to promote the Middle East peace process. In each country, political figures find it difficult to publicly defend good relations with the other.

Today, mutual recriminations flow. Many Americans see Saudi Arabia as an enemy, not as an embattled ally. They perceive an autocratic government that oppresses women, dominated by a wealthy and indolent elite. Saudi contacts with American politicians are frequently invoked as accusations in partisan political arguments. Americans are often appalled by the intolerance, anti-Semitism, and anti-American arguments taught in schools and preached in mosques.

Saudis are angry too. Many educated Saudis who were sympathetic to America now perceive the United States as an unfriendly state. One Saudi reformer noted to us that the demonization of Saudi Arabia in the U.S. media gives ammunition to radicals, who accuse reformers of being U.S. lackeys. Tens of thousands of Saudis who once regularly traveled to (and often had homes in) the United States now go elsewhere.[17]

Among Saudis, the United States is seen as aligned with Israel in its conflict with the Palestinians, with whom Saudis ardently sympathize. Although Saudi Arabia's cooperation against terrorism improved to some extent after the September 11 attacks, significant problems remained. Many in the Kingdom initially reacted with disbelief and denial. In the following months, as the truth became clear, some leading Saudis quietly acknowledged the problem but still did not see their own regime as threatened, and thus often did not respond promptly to U.S. requests for help. Though Saddam Hussein was widely detested, many Saudis are sympathetic to the anti-U.S. insurgents in Iraq, although majorities also condemn jihadist attacks in the Kingdom.[18]

As in Pakistan, Yemen, and other countries, attitudes changed when the terrorism came home. Cooperation had already become significant, but after the bombings in Riyadh on May 12, 2003, it improved much more. The Kingdom openly discussed the problem of radicalism, criticized the terrorists as religiously deviant, reduced official support for religious activity overseas, closed suspect charitable foundations, and publicized arrests—very public moves for a government that has preferred to keep internal problems quiet.

The Kingdom of Saudi Arabia is now locked in mortal combat with al Qaeda. Saudi police are regularly being killed in shootouts with terrorists. In June 2004, the Saudi ambassador to the United States called publicly—in the Saudi press—for his government to wage a jihad of its own against the terrorists. "We must all, as a state and as a people, recognize the truth about these criminals," he declared, "[i]f we do not declare a general mobilization—we will lose this war on terrorism."[19]

Saudi Arabia is a troubled country. Although regarded as very wealthy, in fact per capita income has dropped from $28,000 at its height to the present level of about $8,000. Social and religious traditions complicate adjustment to modern economic activity and limit employment opportunities for young Saudis. Women find their education and employment sharply limited.

President Clinton offered us a perceptive analysis of Saudi Arabia, contending that fundamentally friendly rulers have been constrained by their desire to preserve the status quo. He, like others, made the case for pragmatic reform instead. He hopes the rulers will envision what they want their Kingdom to become in 10 or 20 years, and start a process in which their friends can help them change.[20]

There are signs that Saudi Arabia's royal family is trying to build a consensus for political reform, though uncertain about how fast and how far to go. Crown Prince Abdullah wants the Kingdom to join the World Trade Organization to accelerate economic liberalization. He has embraced the *Arab Human Development Report,* which was highly critical of the Arab world's political, economic, and social failings and called for greater economic and political reform.[21]

Cooperation with Saudi Arabia against Islamist terrorism is very much in the U.S. interest. Such cooperation can exist for a time largely in secret, as it does now, but it cannot grow and thrive there. Nor, on either side, can friendship be unconditional.

Recommendation: The problems in the U.S.-Saudi relationship must be confronted, openly. The United States and Saudi Arabia must determine if they can build a relationship that political leaders on both sides are prepared to publicly defend—a relationship about more than oil. It should include a shared commitment to political and economic reform, as Saudis make common cause with the outside world. It should include a shared interest in greater tolerance and cultural respect, translating into a commitment to fight the violent extremists who foment hatred.

12.3 PREVENT THE CONTINUED GROWTH OF ISLAMIST TERRORISM

In October 2003, reflecting on progress after two years of waging the global war on terrorism, Defense Secretary Donald Rumsfeld asked his advisers: "Are we capturing, killing or deterring and dissuading more terrorists every day than the madrassas and the radical clerics are recruiting, training and deploying against us? Does the US need to fashion a broad, integrated plan to stop the next generation of terrorists? The US is putting relatively little effort into a long-range plan, but we are putting a great deal of effort into trying to stop terrorists. The cost-benefit ratio is against us! Our cost is billions against the terrorists' costs of millions."[22]

These are the right questions. Our answer is that we need short-term action on a long-range strategy, one that invigorates our foreign policy with the attention that the President and Congress have given to the military and intelligence parts of the conflict against Islamist terrorism.

Engage the Struggle of Ideas

The United States is heavily engaged in the Muslim world and will be for many years to come. This American engagement is resented. Polls in 2002 found that among America's friends, like Egypt—the recipient of more U.S. aid for the past 20 years than any other Muslim country—only 15 percent of the population had a favorable opinion of the United States. In Saudi Arabia the number was 12 percent. And two-thirds of those surveyed in 2003 in countries from Indonesia to Turkey (a NATO ally) were very or somewhat fearful that the United States may attack them.[23]

Support for the United States has plummeted. Polls taken in Islamic countries after 9/11 suggested that many or most people thought the United States was doing the right thing in its fight against terrorism; few people saw popular support for al Qaeda; half of those surveyed said that ordinary people had a favorable view of the United States. By 2003, polls showed that "the bottom has fallen out of support for America in most of the Muslim world. Negative views of the U.S. among Muslims, which had been largely limited to countries in the Middle East, have spread. . . . Since last summer, favorable ratings for the U.S. have fallen from 61% to 15% in Indonesia and from 71% to 38% among Muslims in Nigeria."[24]

Many of these views are at best uninformed about the United States and, at worst, informed by cartoonish stereotypes, the coarse expression of a fashionable "Occidentalism" among intellectuals who caricature U.S. values and policies. Local newspapers and the few influential satellite broadcasters—like al Jazeera—often reinforce the jihadist theme that portrays the United States as anti-Muslim.[25]

The small percentage of Muslims who are fully committed to Usama Bin Ladin's version of Islam are impervious to persuasion. It is among the large majority of Arabs and Muslims that we must encourage reform, freedom, democracy, and opportunity, even though our own promotion of these messages is limited in its effectiveness simply because we are its carriers. Muslims themselves will have to reflect upon such basic issues as the concept of jihad, the position of women, and the place of non-Muslim minorities. The United

States can promote moderation, but cannot ensure its ascendancy. Only Muslims can do this.

The setting is difficult. The combined gross domestic product of the 22 countries in the Arab League is less than the GDP of Spain. Forty percent of adult Arabs are illiterate, two-thirds of them women. One-third of the broader Middle East lives on less than two dollars a day. Less than 2 percent of the population has access to the Internet. The majority of older Arab youths have expressed a desire to emigrate to other countries, particularly those in Europe.[26]

In short, the United States has to help defeat an ideology, not just a group of people, and we must do so under difficult circumstances. How can the United States and its friends help moderate Muslims combat the extremist ideas?

Recommendation: The U.S. government must define what the message is, what it stands for. We should offer an example of moral leadership in the world, committed to treat people humanely, abide by the rule of law, and be generous and caring to our neighbors. America and Muslim friends can agree on respect for human dignity and opportunity. To Muslim parents, terrorists like Bin Ladin have nothing to offer their children but visions of violence and death. America and its friends have a crucial advantage—we can offer these parents a vision that might give their children a better future. If we heed the views of thoughtful leaders in the Arab and Muslim world, a moderate consensus can be found.

That vision of the future should stress life over death: individual educational and economic opportunity. This vision includes widespread political participation and contempt for indiscriminate violence. It includes respect for the rule of law, openness in discussing differences, and tolerance for opposing points of view.

Recommendation: Where Muslim governments, even those who are friends, do not respect these principles, the United States must stand for a better future. One of the lessons of the long Cold War was that short-term gains in cooperating with the most repressive and brutal governments were too often outweighed by long-term setbacks for America's stature and interests.

American foreign policy is part of the message. America's policy choices have consequences. Right or wrong, it is simply a fact that American policy regarding the Israeli-Palestinian conflict and American actions in Iraq are dominant staples of popular commentary across the Arab and Muslim world. That does not mean U.S. choices have been wrong. It means those choices must be integrated with America's message of opportunity to the Arab and Muslim world. Neither Israel nor the new Iraq will be safer if worldwide Islamist terrorism grows stronger.

The United States must do more to communicate its message. Reflecting on Bin Ladin's success in reaching Muslim audiences, Richard Holbrooke wondered, "How can a man in a cave outcommunicate the world's leading communications society?" Deputy Secretary of State Richard Armitage worried to us that Americans have been "exporting our fears and our anger," not our vision of opportunity and hope.[27]

Recommendation: Just as we did in the Cold War, we need to defend our ideals abroad vigorously. America does stand up for its values. The United States defended, and still defends, Muslims against tyrants and criminals in Somalia, Bosnia, Kosovo, Afghanistan, and Iraq. If the United States does not act aggressively to define itself in the Islamic world, the extremists will gladly do the job for us.

- **Recognizing that Arab and Muslim audiences rely on satellite television and radio, the government has begun some promising initiatives in television and radio broadcasting to the Arab world, Iran, and Afghanistan. These efforts are beginning to reach large audiences. The Broadcasting Board of Governors has asked for much larger resources. It should get them.**

- **The United States should rebuild the scholarship, exchange, and library programs that reach out to young people and offer them knowledge and hope. Where such assistance is provided, it should be identified as coming from the citizens of the United States.**

An Agenda of Opportunity

The United States and its friends can stress educational and economic opportunity. The United Nations has rightly equated "literacy as freedom."

- The international community is moving toward setting a concrete goal—to cut the Middle East region's illiteracy rate in half by 2010, targeting women and girls and supporting programs for adult literacy.

- Unglamorous help is needed to support the basics, such as textbooks that translate more of the world's knowledge into local languages and libraries to house such materials. Education about the outside world, or other cultures, is weak.

- More vocational education is needed, too, in trades and business skills. The Middle East can also benefit from some of the programs to bridge the digital divide and increase Internet access that have already been developed for other regions of the world.

Education that teaches tolerance, the dignity and value of each individual, and respect for different beliefs is a key element in any global strategy to eliminate Islamist terrorism.

Recommendation: The U.S. government should offer to join with other nations in generously supporting a new International Youth Opportunity Fund. Funds will be spent directly for building and operating primary and secondary schools in those Muslim states that commit to sensibly investing their own money in public education.

Economic openness is essential. Terrorism is not caused by poverty. Indeed, many terrorists come from relatively well-off families. Yet when people lose hope, when societies break down, when countries fragment, the breeding grounds for terrorism are created. Backward economic policies and repressive political regimes slip into societies that are without hope, where ambition and passions have no constructive outlet.

The policies that support economic development and reform also have political implications. Economic and political liberties tend to be linked. Commerce, especially international commerce, requires ongoing cooperation and compromise, the exchange of ideas across cultures, and the peaceful resolution of differences through negotiation or the rule of law. Economic growth expands the middle class, a constituency for further reform. Successful economies rely on vibrant private sectors, which have an interest in curbing indiscriminate government power. Those who develop the practice of controlling their own economic destiny soon desire a voice in their communities and political societies.

The U.S. government has announced the goal of working toward a Middle East Free Trade Area, or MEFTA, by 2013. The United States has been seeking comprehensive free trade agreements (FTAs) with the Middle Eastern nations most firmly on the path to reform. The U.S.-Israeli FTA was enacted in 1985, and Congress implemented an FTA with Jordan in 2001. Both agreements have expanded trade and investment, thereby supporting domestic economic reform. In 2004, new FTAs were signed with Morocco and Bahrain, and are awaiting congressional approval. These models are drawing the interest of their neighbors. Muslim countries can become full participants in the rules-based global trading system, as the United States considers lowering its trade barriers with the poorest Arab nations.

Recommendation: A comprehensive U.S. strategy to counter terrorism should include economic policies that encourage development, more open societies, and opportunities for people to improve the lives of their families and to enhance prospects for their children's future.

Turning a National Strategy into a Coalition Strategy

Practically every aspect of U.S. counterterrorism strategy relies on international cooperation. Since 9/11, these contacts concerning military, law enforcement, intelligence, travel and customs, and financial matters have expanded so dramatically, and often in an ad hoc way, that it is difficult to track these efforts, much less integrate them.

Recommendation: The United States should engage other nations in developing a comprehensive coalition strategy against Islamist terrorism. There are several multilateral institutions in which such issues should be addressed. But the most important policies should be discussed and coordinated in a flexible contact group of leading coalition governments. This is a good place, for example, to develop joint strategies for targeting terrorist travel, or for hammering out a common strategy for the places where terrorists may be finding sanctuary.

Presently the Muslim and Arab states meet with each other, in organizations such as the Islamic Conference and the Arab League. The Western states meet with each other in organizations such as NATO and the Group of Eight summit of leading industrial nations. A recent G-8 summit initiative to begin a dialogue about reform may be a start toward finding a place where leading Muslim states can discuss—and be seen to discuss—critical policy issues with the leading Western powers committed to the future of the Arab and Muslim world.

These new international efforts can create durable habits of visible cooperation, as states willing to step up to their responsibilities join together in constructive efforts to direct assistance and coordinate action.

Coalition warfare also requires coalition policies on what to do with enemy captives. Allegations that the United States abused prisoners in its custody make it harder to build the diplomatic, political, and military alliances the government will need. The United States should work with friends to develop mutually agreed-on principles for the detention and humane treatment of captured international terrorists who are not being held under a particular country's criminal laws. Countries such as Britain, Australia, and Muslim friends, are committed to fighting terrorists. America should be able to reconcile its views on how to balance humanity and security with our nation's commitment to these same goals.

The United States and some of its allies do not accept the application of full Geneva Convention treatment of prisoners of war to captured terrorists. Those

Conventions establish a minimum set of standards for prisoners in internal conflicts. Since the international struggle against Islamist terrorism is not internal, those provisions do not formally apply, but they are commonly accepted as basic standards for humane treatment.

Recommendation: The United States should engage its friends to develop a common coalition approach toward the detention and humane treatment of captured terrorists. New principles might draw upon Article 3 of the Geneva Conventions on the law of armed conflict. That article was specifically designed for those cases in which the usual laws of war did not apply. Its minimum standards are generally accepted throughout the world as customary international law.

Proliferation of Weapons of Mass Destruction

The greatest danger of another catastrophic attack in the United States will materialize if the world's most dangerous terrorists acquire the world's most dangerous weapons. As we note in chapter 2, al Qaeda has tried to acquire or make nuclear weapons for at least ten years. In chapter 4, we mentioned officials worriedly discussing, in 1998, reports that Bin Ladin's associates thought their leader was intent on carrying out a "Hiroshima."

These ambitions continue. In the public portion of his February 2004 worldwide threat assessment to Congress, DCI Tenet noted that Bin Ladin considered the acquisition of weapons of mass destruction to be a "religious obligation." He warned that al Qaeda "continues to pursue its strategic goal of obtaining a nuclear capability." Tenet added that "more than two dozen other terrorist groups are pursuing CBRN [chemical, biological, radiological, and nuclear] materials."[28]

A nuclear bomb can be built with a relatively small amount of nuclear material. A trained nuclear engineer with an amount of highly enriched uranium or plutonium about the size of a grapefruit or an orange, together with commercially available material, could fashion a nuclear device that would fit in a van like the one Ramzi Yousef parked in the garage of the World Trade Center in 1993. Such a bomb would level Lower Manhattan.[29]

The coalition strategies we have discussed to combat Islamist terrorism should therefore be combined with a parallel, vital effort to prevent and counter the proliferation of weapons of mass destruction (WMD). We recommend several initiatives in this area.

Strengthen Counterproliferation Efforts. While efforts to shut down Libya's illegal nuclear program have been generally successful, Pakistan's illicit trade and the nuclear smuggling networks of Pakistani scientist A.Q. Khan have revealed that the spread of nuclear weapons is a problem of global dimensions. Attempts to deal with Iran's nuclear program are still underway. Therefore, the

United States should work with the international community to develop laws and an international legal regime with universal jurisdiction to enable the capture, interdiction, and prosecution of such smugglers by any state in the world where they do not disclose their activities.

Expand the Proliferation Security Initiative. In May 2003, the Bush administration announced the Proliferation Security Initiative (PSI): nations in a willing partnership combining their national capabilities to use military, economic, and diplomatic tools to interdict threatening shipments of WMD and missile-related technology.

The PSI can be more effective if it uses intelligence and planning resources of the NATO alliance. Moreover, PSI membership should be open to non-NATO countries. Russia and China should be encouraged to participate.

Support the Cooperative Threat Reduction Program. Outside experts are deeply worried about the U.S. government's commitment and approach to securing the weapons and highly dangerous materials still scattered in Russia and other countries of the Soviet Union. The government's main instrument in this area, the Cooperative Threat Reduction Program (usually referred to as "Nunn-Lugar," after the senators who sponsored the legislation in 1991), is now in need of expansion, improvement, and resources. The U.S. government has recently redoubled its international commitments to support this program, and we recommend that the United States do all it can, if Russia and other countries will do their part. The government should weigh the value of this investment against the catastrophic cost America would face should such weapons find their way to the terrorists who are so anxious to acquire them.

Recommendation: Our report shows that al Qaeda has tried to acquire or make weapons of mass destruction for at least ten years. There is no doubt the United States would be a prime target. Preventing the proliferation of these weapons warrants a maximum effort—by strengthening counterproliferation efforts, expanding the Proliferation Security Initiative, and supporting the Cooperative Threat Reduction program.

Targeting Terrorist Money

The general public sees attacks on terrorist finance as a way to "starve the terrorists of money." So, initially, did the U.S. government. After 9/11, the United States took aggressive actions to designate terrorist financiers and freeze their money, in the United States and through resolutions of the United Nations. These actions appeared to have little effect and, when confronted by legal challenges, the United States and the United Nations were often forced to unfreeze assets.

The difficulty, understood later, was that even if the intelligence community might "link" someone to a terrorist group through acquaintances or communications, the task of tracing the money from that individual to the terrorist group, or otherwise showing complicity, was far more difficult. It was harder still to do so without disclosing secrets.

These early missteps made other countries unwilling to freeze assets or otherwise act merely on the basis of a U.S. action. Multilateral freezing mechanisms now require waiting periods before being put into effect, eliminating the element of surprise and thus virtually ensuring that little money is actually frozen. Worldwide asset freezes have not been adequately enforced and have been easily circumvented, often within weeks, by simple methods.

But trying to starve the terrorists of money is like trying to catch one kind of fish by draining the ocean. A better strategy has evolved since those early months, as the government learned more about how al Qaeda raises, moves, and spends money.

Recommendation: Vigorous efforts to track terrorist financing must remain front and center in U.S. counterterrorism efforts. The government has recognized that information about terrorist money helps us to understand their networks, search them out, and disrupt their operations. Intelligence and law enforcement have targeted the relatively small number of financial facilitators—individuals al Qaeda relied on for their ability to raise and deliver money—at the core of al Qaeda's revenue stream. These efforts have worked. The death or capture of several important facilitators has decreased the amount of money available to al Qaeda and has increased its costs and difficulty in raising and moving that money. Captures have additionally provided a windfall of intelligence that can be used to continue the cycle of disruption.

The U.S. financial community and some international financial institutions have generally provided law enforcement and intelligence agencies with extraordinary cooperation, particularly in supplying information to support quickly developing investigations. Obvious vulnerabilities in the U.S. financial system have been corrected. The United States has been less successful in persuading other countries to adopt financial regulations that would permit the tracing of financial transactions.

Public designation of terrorist financiers and organizations is still part of the fight, but it is not the primary weapon. Designations are instead a form of diplomacy, as governments join together to identify named individuals and groups as terrorists. They also prevent open fundraising. Some charities that have been identified as likely avenues for terrorist financing have seen their donations diminish and their activities come under more scrutiny, and others have been put out of business, although controlling overseas branches of Gulf-area charities remains a challenge. The Saudi crackdown after the May 2003 terrorist attacks in Riyadh has apparently reduced the funds available to al Qaeda—perhaps drastically—but it is too soon to know if this reduction will last.

Though progress apparently has been made, terrorists have shown considerable creativity in their methods of moving money. If al Qaeda is replaced by smaller, decentralized terrorist groups, the premise behind the government's efforts—that terrorists need a financial support network—may become outdated. Moreover, some terrorist operations do not rely on outside sources of money and may now be self-funding, either through legitimate employment or low-level criminal activity.[30]

12.4 PROTECT AGAINST AND PREPARE FOR TERRORIST ATTACKS

In the nearly three years since 9/11, Americans have become better protected against terrorist attack. Some of the changes are due to government action, such as new precautions to protect aircraft. A portion can be attributed to the sheer scale of spending and effort. Publicity and the vigilance of ordinary Americans also make a difference.

But the President and other officials acknowledge that although Americans may be safer, they are not safe. Our report shows that the terrorists analyze defenses. They plan accordingly.

Defenses cannot achieve perfect safety. They make targets harder to attack successfully, and they deter attacks by making capture more likely. Just increasing the attacker's odds of failure may make the difference between a plan attempted, or a plan discarded. The enemy also may have to develop more elaborate plans, thereby increasing the danger of exposure or defeat.

Protective measures also prepare for the attacks that may get through, containing the damage and saving lives.

Terrorist Travel

More than 500 million people annually cross U.S. borders at legal entry points, about 330 million of them noncitizens. Another 500,000 or more enter illegally without inspection across America's thousands of miles of land borders or remain in the country past the expiration of their permitted stay. The challenge for national security in an age of terrorism is to prevent the very few people who may pose overwhelming risks from entering or remaining in the United States undetected.[31]

In the decade before September 11, 2001, border security—encompassing travel, entry, and immigration—was not seen as a national security matter. Public figures voiced concern about the "war on drugs," the right level and kind of immigration, problems along the southwest border, migration crises originating in the Caribbean and elsewhere, or the growing criminal traffic in humans. The immigration system as a whole was widely viewed as increasingly dysfunctional and badly in need of reform. In national security circles, however, only smuggling of weapons of mass destruction carried weight, not the entry of terrorists who might use such weapons or the presence of associated foreign-born terrorists.

For terrorists, travel documents are as important as weapons. Terrorists must travel clandestinely to meet, train, plan, case targets, and gain access to attack. To them, international travel presents great danger, because they must surface to pass through regulated channels, present themselves to border security officials, or attempt to circumvent inspection points.

In their travels, terrorists use evasive methods, such as altered and counterfeit passports and visas, specific travel methods and routes, liaisons with corrupt government officials, human smuggling networks, supportive travel agencies, and immigration and identity fraud. These can sometimes be detected.

Before 9/11, no agency of the U.S. government systematically analyzed terrorists' travel strategies. Had they done so, they could have discovered the ways in which the terrorist predecessors to al Qaeda had been systematically but detectably exploiting weaknesses in our border security since the early 1990s.

We found that as many as 15 of the 19 hijackers were potentially vulnerable to interception by border authorities. Analyzing their characteristic travel documents and travel patterns could have allowed authorities to intercept 4 to 15 hijackers and more effective use of information available in U.S. government databases could have identified up to 3 hijackers.[32]

Looking back, we can also see that the routine operations of our immigration laws—that is, aspects of those laws not specifically aimed at protecting against terrorism—inevitably shaped al Qaeda's planning and opportunities. Because they were deemed not to be bona fide tourists or students as they claimed, five conspirators that we know of tried to get visas and failed, and one was denied entry by an inspector. We also found that had the immigration system set a higher bar for determining whether individuals are who or what they claim to be—and ensuring routine consequences for violations—it could potentially have excluded, removed, or come into further contact with several hijackers who did not appear to meet the terms for admitting short-term visitors.[33]

Our investigation showed that two systemic weaknesses came together in our border system's inability to contribute to an effective defense against the 9/11 attacks: a lack of well-developed counterterrorism measures as a part of border security and an immigration system not able to deliver on its basic commitments, much less support counterterrorism. These weaknesses have been reduced but are far from being overcome.

Recommendation: Targeting travel is at least as powerful a weapon against terrorists as targeting their money. The United States should combine terrorist travel intelligence, operations, and law enforcement in a strategy to intercept terrorists, find terrorist travel facilitators, and constrain terrorist mobility.

Since 9/11, significant improvements have been made to create an integrated watchlist that makes terrorist name information available to border and law enforcement authorities. However, in the already difficult process of merging border agencies in the new Department of Homeland Security—"changing the engine while flying" as one official put it[34]—new insights into terrorist travel have not yet been integrated into the front lines of border security.

The small terrorist travel intelligence collection and analysis program currently in place has produced disproportionately useful results. It should be expanded. Since officials at the borders encounter travelers and their documents first and investigate travel facilitators, they must work closely with intelligence officials.

Internationally and in the United States, constraining terrorist travel should become a vital part of counterterrorism strategy. Better technology and training to detect terrorist travel documents are the most important immediate steps to reduce America's vulnerability to clandestine entry. Every stage of our border and immigration system should have as a part of its operations the detection of terrorist indicators on travel documents. Information systems able to authenticate travel documents and detect potential terrorist indicators should be used at consulates, at primary border inspection lines, in immigration services offices, and in intelligence and enforcement units. All frontline personnel should receive some training. Dedicated specialists and ongoing linkages with the intelligence community are also required. The Homeland Security Department's Directorate of Information Analysis and Infrastructure Protection should receive more resources to accomplish its mission as the bridge between the frontline border agencies and the rest of the government counterterrorism community.

A Biometric Screening System

When people travel internationally, they usually move through defined channels, or portals. They may seek to acquire a passport. They may apply for a visa. They stop at ticket counters, gates, and exit controls at airports and seaports. Upon arrival, they pass through inspection points. They may transit to another gate to get on an airplane. Once inside the country, they may seek another form of identification and try to enter a government or private facility. They may seek to change immigration status in order to remain.

Each of these checkpoints or portals is a screening—a chance to establish that people are who they say they are and are seeking access for their stated purpose, to intercept identifiable suspects, and to take effective action.

The job of protection is shared among these many defined checkpoints. By taking advantage of them all, we need not depend on any one point in the system to do the whole job. The challenge is to see the common problem across agencies and functions and develop a conceptual framework—an architecture—for an effective screening system.[35]

Throughout government, and indeed in private enterprise, agencies and firms at these portals confront recurring judgments that balance security, efficiency, and civil liberties. These problems should be addressed systemically, not in an ad hoc, fragmented way. For example:

What information is an individual required to present and in what form? A fundamental problem, now beginning to be addressed, is the lack of standardized information in "feeder" documents used in identifying individuals. Biometric identifiers that measure unique physical characteristics, such as facial features, fingerprints, or iris scans, and reduce them to digitized, numerical statements called algorithms, are just beginning to be used. Travel history, however, is still recorded in passports with entry-exit stamps called cachets, which al Qaeda has trained its operatives to forge and use to conceal their terrorist activities.

How will the individual and the information be checked? There are many databases just in the United States—for terrorist, criminal, and immigration history, as well as financial information, for instance. Each is set up for different purposes and stores different kinds of data, under varying rules of access. Nor is access always guaranteed. Acquiring information held by foreign governments may require painstaking negotiations, and records that are not yet digitized are difficult to search or analyze. The development of terrorist indicators has hardly begun, and behavioral cues remain important.

Who will screen individuals, and what will they be trained to do? A wide range of border, immigration, and law enforcement officials encounter visitors and immigrants and they are given little training in terrorist travel intelligence. Fraudulent travel documents, for instance, are usually returned to travelers who are denied entry without further examination for terrorist trademarks, investigation as to their source, or legal process.

What are the consequences of finding a suspicious indicator, and who will take action? One risk is that responses may be ineffective or produce no further information. Four of the 9/11 attackers were pulled into secondary border inspection, but then admitted. More than half of the 19 hijackers were flagged by the Federal Aviation Administration's profiling system when they arrived for their flights, but the consequence was that bags, not people, were checked. Competing risks include "false positives," or the danger that rules may be applied with insufficient training or judgment. Overreactions can impose high costs too—on individuals, our economy, and our beliefs about justice.

- A special note on the importance of trusting subjective judgment: One potential hijacker was turned back by an immigration inspector as he tried to enter the United States. The inspector relied on intuitive experience to ask questions more than he relied on any objective factor that could be detected by "scores" or a machine. Good people who have worked in such jobs for a long time understand this phenomenon well. Other evidence we obtained confirmed the importance of letting experienced gate agents or security screeners ask questions and use their judgment. This is not an invitation to arbitrary exclusions. But any effective system has to grant some scope, perhaps in a little extra inspection or one more check, to the instincts and discretion of well trained human beings.

Recommendation: The U.S. border security system should be integrated into a larger network of screening points that includes our transportation system and access to vital facilities, such as nuclear reactors. The President should direct the Department of Homeland Security to lead the effort to design a comprehensive screening system, addressing common problems and setting common standards with systemwide goals in mind. Extending those standards among other governments could dramatically strengthen America and the world's collective ability to intercept individuals who pose catastrophic threats.

We advocate a system for screening, not categorical profiling. A screening system looks for particular, identifiable suspects or indicators of risk. It does not involve guesswork about who might be dangerous. It requires frontline border officials who have the tools and resources to establish that people are who they say they are, intercept identifiable suspects, and disrupt terrorist operations.

The U.S. Border Screening System

The border and immigration system of the United States must remain a visible manifestation of our belief in freedom, democracy, global economic growth, and the rule of law, yet serve equally well as a vital element of counterterrorism. Integrating terrorist travel information in the ways we have described is the most immediate need. But the underlying system must also be sound.

Since September 11, the United States has built the first phase of a biometric screening program, called US VISIT (the United States Visitor and Immigrant Status Indicator Technology program). It takes two biometric identifiers—digital photographs and prints of two index fingers—from travel-ers. False identities are used by terrorists to avoid being detected on a watch-list. These biometric identifiers make such evasions far more difficult.

So far, however, only visitors who acquire visas to travel to the United States are covered. While visitors from "visa waiver" countries will be added to the program, beginning this year, covered travelers will still constitute only about 12 percent of all noncitizens crossing U.S. borders. Moreover, exit data are not uniformly collected and entry data are not fully automated. It is not clear the system can be installed before 2010, but even this timetable may be too slow, given the possible security dangers.[36]

- Americans should not be exempt from carrying biometric passports or otherwise enabling their identities to be securely verified when they enter the United States; nor should Canadians or Mexicans. Cur-rently U.S. persons are exempt from carrying passports when return-ing from Canada, Mexico, and the Caribbean. The current system enables non-U.S. citizens to gain entry by showing minimal identifi-cation. The 9/11 experience shows that terrorists study and exploit America's vulnerabilities.

- To balance this measure, programs to speed known travelers should be a higher priority, permitting inspectors to focus on greater risks. The daily commuter should not be subject to the same measures as first-time travelers. An individual should be able to preenroll, with his or her identity verified in passage. Updates of database information and other checks can ensure ongoing reliability. The solution, requir-ing more research and development, is likely to combine radio fre-quency technology with biometric identifiers.[37]

- The current patchwork of border screening systems, including several frequent traveler programs, should be consolidated with the USVISIT system to enable the development of an integrated system, which in turn can become part of the wider screening plan we suggest.

- The program allowing individuals to travel from foreign countries through the United States to a third country, without having to obtain a U.S. visa, has been suspended. Because "transit without visa" can be exploited by terrorists to enter the United States, the program should not be reinstated unless and until transit passage areas can be fully secured to prevent passengers from illegally exiting the airport.

Inspectors adjudicating entries of the 9/11 hijackers lacked adequate infor-mation and knowledge of the rules. All points in the border system—from con-sular offices to immigration services offices—will need appropriate electronic access to an individual's file. Scattered units at Homeland Security and the State

Department perform screening and data mining: instead, a government-wide team of border and transportation officials should be working together. A modern border and immigration system should combine a biometric entry-exit system with accessible files on visitors and immigrants, along with intelligence on indicators of terrorist travel.

Our border screening system should check people efficiently and welcome friends. Admitting large numbers of students, scholars, businesspeople, and tourists fuels our economy, cultural vitality, and political reach. There is evidence that the present system is disrupting travel to the United States. Overall, visa applications in 2003 were down over 32 percent since 2001. In the Middle East, they declined about 46 percent. Training and the design of security measures should be continuously adjusted.[38]

Recommendation: The Department of Homeland Security, properly supported by the Congress, should complete, as quickly as possible, a biometric entry-exit screening system, including a single system for speeding qualified travelers. It should be integrated with the system that provides benefits to foreigners seeking to stay in the United States. Linking biometric passports to good data systems and decisionmaking is a fundamental goal. No one can hide his or her debt by acquiring a credit card with a slightly different name. Yet today, a terrorist can defeat the link to electronic records by tossing away an old passport and slightly altering the name in the new one.

Completion of the entry-exit system is a major and expensive challenge. Biometrics have been introduced into an antiquated computer environment. Replacement of these systems and improved biometric systems will be required. Nonetheless, funding and completing a biometrics-based entry-exit system is an essential investment in our national security.

Exchanging terrorist information with other countries, consistent with privacy requirements, along with listings of lost and stolen passports, will have immediate security benefits. We should move toward real-time verification of passports with issuing authorities. The further away from our borders that screening occurs, the more security benefits we gain. At least some screening should occur before a passenger departs on a flight destined for the United States. We should also work with other countries to ensure effective inspection regimes at all airports.[39]

The international community arrives at international standards for the design of passports through the International Civil Aviation Organization (ICAO). The global standard for identification is a digital photograph; fingerprints are optional. We must work with others to improve passport standards and provide foreign assistance to countries that need help in making the transition.[40]

Recommendation: The U.S. government cannot meet its own obligations to the American people to prevent the entry of terrorists without a major effort to collaborate with other governments. We should do more to exchange terrorist information with trusted allies, and raise U.S. and global border security standards for travel and border crossing over the medium and long term through extensive international cooperation.

Immigration Law and Enforcement

Our borders and immigration system, including law enforcement, ought to send a message of welcome, tolerance, and justice to members of immigrant communities in the United States and in their countries of origin. We should reach out to immigrant communities. Good immigration services are one way of doing so that is valuable in every way—including intelligence.

It is elemental to border security to know who is coming into the country. Today more than 9 million people are in the United States outside the legal immigration system. We must also be able to monitor and respond to entrances between our ports of entry, working with Canada and Mexico as much as possible.

There is a growing role for state and local law enforcement agencies. They need more training and work with federal agencies so that they can cooperate more effectively with those federal authorities in identifying terrorist suspects.

All but one of the 9/11 hijackers acquired some form of U.S. identification document, some by fraud. Acquisition of these forms of identification would have assisted them in boarding commercial flights, renting cars, and other necessary activities.

Recommendation: Secure identification should begin in the United States. The federal government should set standards for the issuance of birth certificates and sources of identification, such as drivers licenses. Fraud in identification documents is no longer just a problem of theft. At many entry points to vulnerable facilities, including gates for boarding aircraft, sources of identification are the last opportunity to ensure that people are who they say they are and to check whether they are terrorists.[41]

Strategies for Aviation and Transportation Security

The U.S. transportation system is vast and, in an open society, impossible to secure completely against terrorist attacks. There are hundreds of commercial airports, thousands of planes, and tens of thousands of daily flights carrying more than half a billion passengers a year. Millions of containers are imported annually through more than 300 sea and river ports served by more than 3,700 cargo and passenger terminals. About 6,000 agencies provide transit services through buses, subways, ferries, and light-rail service to about 14 million Americans each weekday.[42]

In November 2001, Congress passed and the President signed the Aviation and Transportation Security Act. This act created the Transportation Security Administration (TSA), which is now part of the Homeland Security Department. In November 2002, both the Homeland Security Act and the Maritime Transportation Security Act followed. These laws required the development of strategic plans to describe how the new department and TSA would provide security for critical parts of the U.S. transportation sector.

Over 90 percent of the nation's $5.3 billion annual investment in the TSA goes to aviation—to fight the last war. The money has been spent mainly to meet congressional mandates to federalize the security checkpoint screeners and to deploy existing security methods and technologies at airports. The current efforts do not yet reflect a forward-looking strategic plan systematically analyzing assets, risks, costs, and benefits. Lacking such a plan, we are not convinced that our transportation security resources are being allocated to the greatest risks in a cost-effective way.

- Major vulnerabilities still exist in cargo and general aviation security. These, together with inadequate screening and access controls, continue to present aviation security challenges.
- While commercial aviation remains a possible target, terrorists may turn their attention to other modes. Opportunities to do harm are as great, or greater, in maritime or surface transportation. Initiatives to secure shipping containers have just begun. Surface transportation systems such as railroads and mass transit remain hard to protect because they are so accessible and extensive.

Despite congressional deadlines, the TSA has developed neither an integrated strategic plan for the transportation sector nor specific plans for the various modes—air, sea, and ground.

Recommendation: Hard choices must be made in allocating limited resources. The U.S. government should identify and evaluate the transportation assets that need to be protected, set risk-based priorities for defending them, select the most practical and cost-effective ways of doing so, and then develop a plan, budget, and funding to implement the effort. The plan should assign roles and missions to the relevant authorities (federal, state, regional, and local) and to private stakeholders. In measuring effectiveness, perfection is unattainable. But terrorists should perceive that potential targets are defended. They may be deterred by a significant chance of failure.

Congress should set a specific date for the completion of these plans and hold the Department of Homeland Security and TSA accountable for achieving them.

The most powerful investments may be for improvements in technologies with applications across the transportation modes, such as scanning technologies designed to screen containers that can be transported by plane, ship, truck, or rail. Though such technologies are becoming available now, widespread deployment is still years away.

In the meantime, the best protective measures may be to combine improved methods of identifying and tracking the high-risk containers, operators, and facilities that require added scrutiny with further efforts to integrate intelligence analysis, effective procedures for transmitting threat information to transportation authorities, and vigilance by transportation authorities and the public.

A Layered Security System

No single security measure is foolproof. Accordingly, the TSA must have multiple layers of security in place to defeat the more plausible and dangerous forms of attack against public transportation.

- The plan must take into consideration the full array of possible enemy tactics, such as use of insiders, suicide terrorism, or standoff attack. Each layer must be effective in its own right. Each must be supported by other layers that are redundant and coordinated.
- The TSA should be able to identify for Congress the array of potential terrorist attacks, the layers of security in place, and the reliability provided by each layer. TSA must develop a plan as described above to improve weak individual layers and the effectiveness of the layered systems it deploys.

On 9/11, the 19 hijackers were screened by a computer-assisted screening system called CAPPS. More than half were identified for further inspection, which applied only to their checked luggage.

Under current practices, air carriers enforce government orders to stop certain known and suspected terrorists from boarding commercial flights and to apply secondary screening procedures to others. The "no-fly" and "automatic selectee" lists include only those individuals who the U.S. government believes pose a direct threat of attacking aviation.

Because air carriers implement the program, concerns about sharing intelligence information with private firms and foreign countries keep the U.S. government from listing all terrorist and terrorist suspects who should be included. The TSA has planned to take over this function when it deploys a new screening system to take the place of CAPPS. The deployment of this system has been delayed because of claims it may violate civil liberties.

Recommendation: Improved use of "no-fly" and "automatic selectee" lists should not be delayed while the argument about a successor to CAPPS continues. This screening function should be performed by the TSA, and it should utilize the larger set of watchlists maintained by the federal government. Air carriers should be required to supply the information needed to test and implement this new system.

CAPPS is still part of the screening process, still profiling passengers, with the consequences of selection now including personal searches of the individual and carry-on bags. The TSA is dealing with the kind of screening issues that are being encountered by other agencies. As we mentioned earlier, these screening issues need to be elevated for high-level attention and addressed promptly by the government. Working through these problems can help clear the way for the TSA's screening improvements and would help many other agencies too.

The next layer is the screening checkpoint itself. As the screening system tries to stop dangerous people, the checkpoint needs to be able to find dangerous items. Two reforms are needed soon: (1) screening people for explosives, not just their carry-on bags, and (2) improving screener performance.

Recommendation: The TSA and the Congress must give priority attention to improving the ability of screening checkpoints to detect explosives on passengers. As a start, each individual selected for special screening should be screened for explosives. Further, the TSA should conduct a human factors study, a method often used in the private sector, to understand problems in screener performance and set attainable objectives for individual screeners and for the checkpoints where screening takes place.

Concerns also remain regarding the screening and transport of checked bags and cargo. More attention and resources should be directed to reducing or mitigating the threat posed by explosives in vessels' cargo holds. The TSA should expedite the installation of advanced (in-line) baggage-screening equipment. Because the aviation industry will derive substantial benefits from this deployment, it should pay a fair share of the costs. The TSA should require that every passenger aircraft carrying cargo must deploy at least one hardened container to carry any suspect cargo. TSA also needs to intensify its efforts to identify, track, and appropriately screen potentially dangerous cargo in both the aviation and maritime sectors.

The Protection of Civil Liberties

Many of our recommendations call for the government to increase its presence in our lives—for example, by creating standards for the issuance of forms of identification, by better securing our borders, by sharing information gathered by many different agencies. We also recommend the consolidation of authority over the now far-flung entities constituting the intelligence community. The Patriot Act vests substantial powers in our federal government. We have seen the government use the immigration laws as a tool in its counterterrorism effort. Even without the changes we recommend, the American public has vested enormous authority in the U.S. government.

At our first public hearing on March 31, 2003, we noted the need for balance as our government responds to the real and ongoing threat of terrorist attacks. The terrorists have used our open society against us. In wartime, government calls for greater powers, and then the need for those powers recedes after the war ends. This struggle will go on. Therefore, while protecting our homeland, Americans should be mindful of threats to vital personal and civil liberties. This balancing is no easy task, but we must constantly strive to keep it right.

This shift of power and authority to the government calls for an enhanced system of checks and balances to protect the precious liberties that are vital to our way of life. We therefore make three recommendations.

First, as we will discuss in chapter 13, to open up the sharing of information across so many agencies and with the private sector, the President should take responsibility for determining what information can be shared by which agencies and under what conditions. Protection of privacy rights should be one key element of this determination.

Recommendation: As the President determines the guidelines for information sharing among government agencies and by those agencies with the private sector, he should safeguard the privacy of individuals about whom information is shared.

Second, Congress responded, in the immediate aftermath of 9/11, with the Patriot Act, which vested substantial new powers in the investigative agencies of the government. Some of the most controversial provisions of the Patriot Act are to "sunset" at the end of 2005. Many of the act's provisions are relatively noncontroversial, updating America's surveillance laws to reflect technological developments in a digital age. Some executive actions that have been criticized are unrelated to the Patriot Act. The provisions in the act that facilitate the sharing of information among intelligence agencies and between law enforcement and intelligence appear, on balance, to be beneficial. Because of concerns regarding the shifting balance of power to the government, we think that a full and informed debate on the Patriot Act would be healthy.

Recommendation: The burden of proof for retaining a particular governmental power should be on the executive, to explain (a) that the power actually materially enhances security and (b) that there is ade-

quate supervision of the executive's use of the powers to ensure protection of civil liberties. If the power is granted, there must be adequate guidelines and oversight to properly confine its use.

Third, during the course of our inquiry, we were told that there is no office within the government whose job it is to look across the government at the actions we are taking to protect ourselves to ensure that liberty concerns are appropriately considered. If, as we recommend, there is substantial change in the way we collect and share intelligence, there should be a voice within the executive branch for those concerns. Many agencies have privacy offices, albeit of limited scope. The Intelligence Oversight Board of the President's Foreign Intelligence Advisory Board has, in the past, had the job of overseeing certain activities of the intelligence community.

Recommendation: At this time of increased and consolidated government authority, there should be a board within the executive branch to oversee adherence to the guidelines we recommend and the commitment the government makes to defend our civil liberties.

We must find ways of reconciling security with liberty, since the success of one helps protect the other. The choice between security and liberty is a false choice, as nothing is more likely to endanger America's liberties than the success of a terrorist attack at home. Our history has shown us that insecurity threatens liberty. Yet, if our liberties are curtailed, we lose the values that we are struggling to defend.

Setting Priorities for National Preparedness

Before 9/11, no executive department had, as its first priority, the job of defending America from domestic attack. That changed with the 2002 creation of the Department of Homeland Security. This department now has the lead responsibility for problems that feature so prominently in the 9/11 story, such as protecting borders, securing transportation and other parts of our critical infrastructure, organizing emergency assistance, and working with the private sector to assess vulnerabilities.

Throughout the government, nothing has been harder for officials—executive or legislative—than to set priorities, making hard choices in allocating limited resources. These difficulties have certainly afflicted the Department of Homeland Security, hamstrung by its many congressional overseers. In delivering assistance to state and local governments, we heard—especially in New York—about imbalances in the allocation of money. The argument concentrates on two questions.

First, how much money should be set aside for criteria not directly related to risk? Currently a major portion of the billions of dollars appropriated for state and local assistance is allocated so that each state gets a certain amount, or an allocation based on its population—wherever they live.

Recommendation: Homeland security assistance should be based strictly on an assessment of risks and vulnerabilities. Now, in 2004, Washington, D.C., and New York City are certainly at the top of any such list. We understand the contention that every state and city needs to have some minimum infrastructure for emergency response. But federal homeland security assistance should not remain a program for general revenue sharing. It should supplement state and local resources based on the risks or vulnerabilities that merit additional support. Congress should not use this money as a pork barrel.

The second question is, Can useful criteria to measure risk and vulnerability be developed that assess all the many variables? The allocation of funds should be based on an assessment of threats and vulnerabilities. That assessment should consider such factors as population, population density, vulnerability, and the presence of critical infrastructure within each state. In addition, the federal government should require each state receiving federal emergency preparedness funds to provide an analysis based on the same criteria to justify the distribution of funds in that state.

In a free-for-all over money, it is understandable that representatives will work to protect the interests of their home states or districts. But this issue is too important for politics as usual to prevail. Resources must be allocated according to vulnerabilities. We recommend that a panel of security experts be convened to develop written benchmarks for evaluating community needs. We further recommend that federal homeland security funds be allocated in accordance with those benchmarks, and that states be required to abide by those benchmarks in disbursing the federal funds. The benchmarks will be imperfect and subjective; they will continually evolve. But hard choices must be made. Those who would allocate money on a different basis should then defend their view of the national interest.

Command, Control, and Communications

The attacks on 9/11 demonstrated that even the most robust emergency response capabilities can be overwhelmed if an attack is large enough. Teamwork, collaboration, and cooperation at an incident site are critical to a successful response. Key decisionmakers who are represented at the incident command level help to ensure an effective response, the efficient use of resources, and responder safety. Regular joint training at all levels is, moreover, essential to ensuring close coordination during an actual incident.

Recommendation: Emergency response agencies nationwide should adopt the Incident Command System (ICS). When multiple agencies or multiple jurisdictions are involved, they should adopt a unified command. Both are proven frameworks for emergency response. We strongly support the decision that federal homeland security funding will be contingent, as of October 1, 2004, upon the adoption and regular use of ICS and unified command procedures. In the future, the Department of Homeland Security should consider making funding contingent on aggressive and realistic training in accordance with ICS and unified command procedures.

The attacks of September 11, 2001 overwhelmed the response capacity of most of the local jurisdictions where the hijacked airliners crashed. While many jurisdictions have established mutual aid compacts, a serious obstacle to multi-jurisdictional response has been the lack of indemnification for mutual-aid responders in areas such as the National Capital Region.

Public safety organizations, chief administrative officers, state emergency management agencies, and the Department of Homeland Security should develop a regional focus within the emergency responder community and promote multi-jurisdictional mutual assistance compacts. Where such compacts already exist, training in accordance with their terms should be required. Congress should pass legislation to remedy the long-standing indemnification and liability impediments to the provision of public safety mutual aid in the National Capital Region and where applicable throughout the nation.

The inability to communicate was a critical element at the World Trade Center, Pentagon, and Somerset County, Pennsylvania, crash sites, where multiple agencies and multiple jurisdictions responded. The occurrence of this problem at three very different sites is strong evidence that compatible and adequate communications among public safety organizations at the local, state, and federal levels remains an important problem.

Recommendation: Congress should support pending legislation which provides for the expedited and increased assignment of radio spectrum for public safety purposes. Furthermore, high-risk urban areas such as New York City and Washington, D.C., should establish signal corps units to ensure communications connectivity between and among civilian authorities, local first responders, and the National Guard. Federal funding of such units should be given high priority by Congress.

Private-Sector Preparedness

The mandate of the Department of Homeland Security does not end with government; the department is also responsible for working with the private sector to ensure preparedness. This is entirely appropriate, for the private sector controls 85 percent of the critical infrastructure in the nation. Indeed, unless a terrorist's target is a military or other secure government facility, the "first" first responders will almost certainly be civilians. Homeland security and national preparedness therefore often begins with the private sector.

Preparedness in the private sector and public sector for rescue, restart, and recovery of operations should include (1) a plan for evacuation, (2) adequate communications capabilities, and (3) a plan for continuity of operations. As we examined the emergency response to 9/11, witness after witness told us that despite 9/11, the private sector remains largely unprepared for a terrorist attack. We were also advised that the lack of a widely embraced private-sector preparedness standard was a principal contributing factor to this lack of preparedness.

We responded by asking the American National Standards Institute (ANSI) to develop a consensus on a "National Standard for Preparedness" for the private sector. ANSI convened safety, security, and business continuity experts from a wide range of industries and associations, as well as from federal, state, and local government stakeholders, to consider the need for standards for private sector emergency preparedness and business continuity.

The result of these sessions was ANSI's recommendation that the Commission endorse a voluntary National Preparedness Standard. Based on the existing American National Standard on Disaster/Emergency Management and Business Continuity Programs (NFPA 1600), the proposed National Preparedness Standard establishes a common set of criteria and terminology for preparedness, disaster management, emergency management, and business continuity programs. The experience of the private sector in the World Trade Center emergency demonstrated the need for these standards.

Recommendation: We endorse the American National Standards Institute's recommended standard for private preparedness. We were encouraged by Secretary Tom Ridge's praise of the standard, and urge the Department of Homeland Security to promote its adoption. We also encourage the insurance and credit-rating industries to look closely at a company's compliance with the ANSI standard in assessing its insurability and creditworthiness. We believe that compliance with the standard should define the standard of care owed by a company to its employees and the public for legal purposes. Private-sector preparedness is not a luxury; it is a cost of doing business in the post-9/11 world. It is ignored at a tremendous potential cost in lives, money, and national security.

13

HOW TO DO IT? A DIFFERENT WAY OF ORGANIZING THE GOVERNMENT

As presently configured, the national security institutions of the U.S. government are still the institutions constructed to win the Cold War. The United States confronts a very different world today. Instead of facing a few very dangerous adversaries, the United States confronts a number of less visible challenges that surpass the boundaries of traditional nation-states and call for quick, imaginative, and agile responses.

The men and women of the World War II generation rose to the challenges of the 1940s and 1950s. They restructured the government so that it could protect the country. That is now the job of the generation that experienced 9/11. Those attacks showed, emphatically, that ways of doing business rooted in a different era are just not good enough. Americans should not settle for incremental, ad hoc adjustments to a system designed generations ago for a world that no longer exists.

We recommend significant changes in the organization of the government. We know that the quality of the people is more important than the quality of the wiring diagrams. Some of the saddest aspects of the 9/11 story are the outstanding efforts of so many individual officials straining, often without success, against the boundaries of the possible. Good people can overcome bad structures. They should not have to.

The United States has the resources and the people. The government should combine them more effectively, achieving unity of effort. We offer five major recommendations to do that:

- unifying strategic intelligence and operational planning against Islamist terrorists across the foreign-domestic divide with a National Counterterrorism Center;
- unifying the intelligence community with a new National Intelligence Director;

- unifying the many participants in the counterterrorism effort and their knowledge in a network-based information-sharing system that transcends traditional governmental boundaries;
- unifying and strengthening congressional oversight to improve quality and accountability; and
- strengthening the FBI and homeland defenders.

13.1 UNITY OF EFFORT ACROSS THE FOREIGN-DOMESTIC DIVIDE

Joint Action

Much of the public commentary about the 9/11 attacks has dealt with "lost opportunities," some of which we reviewed in chapter 11. These are often characterized as problems of "watchlisting," of "information sharing," or of "connecting the dots." In chapter 11 we explained that these labels are too narrow. They describe the symptoms, not the disease.

In each of our examples, no one was firmly in charge of managing the case and able to draw relevant intelligence from anywhere in the government, assign responsibilities across the agencies (foreign or domestic), track progress, and quickly bring obstacles up to the level where they could be resolved. Responsibility and accountability were diffuse.

The agencies cooperated, some of the time. But even such cooperation as there was is not the same thing as joint action. When agencies cooperate, one defines the problem and seeks help with it. When they act jointly, the problem and options for action are defined differently from the start. Individuals from different backgrounds come together in analyzing a case and planning how to manage it.

In our hearings we regularly asked witnesses: Who is the quarterback? The other players are in their positions, doing their jobs. But who is calling the play that assigns roles to help them execute as a team?

Since 9/11, those issues have not been resolved. In some ways joint work has gotten better, and in some ways worse. The effort of fighting terrorism has flooded over many of the usual agency boundaries because of its sheer quantity and energy. Attitudes have changed. Officials are keenly conscious of trying to avoid the mistakes of 9/11. They try to share information. They circulate—even to the President—practically every reported threat, however dubious.

Partly because of all this effort, the challenge of coordinating it has multiplied. Before 9/11, the CIA was plainly the lead agency confronting al Qaeda. The FBI played a very secondary role. The engagement of the departments of Defense and State was more episodic.

- Today the CIA is still central. But the FBI is much more active, along with other parts of the Justice Department.
- The Defense Department effort is now enormous. Three of its unified commands, each headed by a four-star general, have counterterrorism as a primary mission: Special Operations Command, Central Command (both headquartered in Florida), and Northern Command (headquartered in Colorado).
- A new Department of Homeland Security combines formidable resources in border and transportation security, along with analysis of domestic vulnerability and other tasks.
- The State Department has the lead on many of the foreign policy tasks we described in chapter 12.
- At the White House, the National Security Council (NSC) now is joined by a parallel presidential advisory structure, the Homeland Security Council.

So far we have mentioned two reasons for joint action—the virtue of joint planning and the advantage of having someone in charge to ensure a unified effort. There is a third: the simple shortage of experts with sufficient skills. The limited pool of critical experts—for example, skilled counterterrorism analysts and linguists—is being depleted. Expanding these capabilities will require not just money, but time.

Primary responsibility for terrorism analysis has been assigned to the Terrorist Threat Integration Center (TTIC), created in 2003, based at the CIA headquarters but staffed with representatives of many agencies, reporting directly to the Director of Central Intelligence. Yet the CIA houses another intelligence "fusion" center: the Counterterrorist Center that played such a key role before 9/11. A third major analytic unit is at Defense, in the Defense Intelligence Agency. A fourth, concentrating more on homeland vulnerabilities, is at the Department of Homeland Security. The FBI is in the process of building the analytic capability it has long lacked, and it also has the Terrorist Screening Center.[1]

The U.S. government cannot afford so much duplication of effort. There are not enough experienced experts to go around. The duplication also places extra demands on already hard-pressed single-source national technical intelligence collectors like the National Security Agency.

Combining Joint Intelligence and Joint Action

A "smart" government would *integrate* all sources of information to see the enemy as a whole. Integrated all-source analysis should also inform and shape strategies to collect more intelligence. Yet the Terrorist Threat Integration Center, while it has primary responsibility for terrorism analysis, is formally proscribed from having any oversight or operational authority and is not part of any operational entity, other than reporting to the director of central intelligence.[2]

The government now tries to handle the problem of joint management, informed by analysis of intelligence from all sources, in two ways.

- First, agencies with lead responsibility for certain problems have constructed their own interagency entities and task forces in order to get cooperation. The Counterterrorist Center at CIA, for example, recruits liaison officers from throughout the intelligence community. The military's Central Command has its own interagency center, recruiting liaison officers from all the agencies from which it might need help. The FBI has Joint Terrorism Task Forces in 84 locations to coordinate the activities of other agencies when action may be required.

- Second, the problem of joint operational planning is often passed to the White House, where the NSC staff tries to play this role. The national security staff at the White House (both NSC and new Homeland Security Council staff) has already become 50 percent larger since 9/11. But our impression, after talking to serving officials, is that even this enlarged staff is consumed by meetings on day-to-day issues, sifting each day's threat information and trying to coordinate everyday operations.

Even as it crowds into every square inch of available office space, the NSC staff is still not sized or funded to be an executive agency. In chapter 3 we described some of the problems that arose in the 1980s when a White House staff, constitutionally insulated from the usual mechanisms of oversight, became involved in direct operations. During the 1990s Richard Clarke occasionally tried to exercise such authority, sometimes successfully, but often causing friction.

Yet a subtler and more serious danger is that as the NSC staff is consumed by these day-to-day tasks, it has less capacity to find the time and detachment needed to advise a president on larger policy issues. That means less time to work on major new initiatives, help with legislative management to steer needed bills through Congress, and track the design and implementation of the strategic plans for regions, countries, and issues that we discuss in chapter 12.

Much of the job of operational coordination remains with the agencies, especially the CIA. There DCI Tenet and his chief aides ran interagency meetings nearly every day to coordinate much of the government's day-to-day work. The DCI insisted he did not make policy and only oversaw its implementation. In the struggle against terrorism these distinctions seem increasingly artificial. Also, as the DCI becomes a lead coordinator of the government's operations, it becomes harder to play all the position's other roles, including that of analyst in chief.

The problem is nearly intractable because of the way the government is currently structured. Lines of operational authority run to the expanding executive departments, and they are guarded for understandable reasons: the DCI commands the CIA's personnel overseas; the secretary of defense will not yield to others in conveying commands to military forces; the Justice Department will not give up the responsibility of deciding whether to seek arrest warrants. But the result is that each agency or department needs its own intelligence apparatus to support the performance of its duties. It is hard to "break down stovepipes" when there are so many stoves that are legally and politically entitled to have cast-iron pipes of their own.

Recalling the Goldwater-Nichols legislation of 1986, Secretary Rumsfeld reminded us that to achieve better joint capability, each of the armed services had to "give up some of their turf and authorities and prerogatives." Today, he said, the executive branch is "stove-piped much like the four services were nearly 20 years ago." He wondered if it might be appropriate to ask agencies to "give up some of their existing turf and authority in exchange for a stronger, faster, more efficient government wide joint effort."[3] Privately, other key officials have made the same point to us.

We therefore propose a new institution: a civilian-led unified joint command for counterterrorism. It should combine strategic intelligence and joint operational planning.

In the Pentagon's Joint Staff, which serves the chairman of the Joint Chiefs of Staff, intelligence is handled by the J-2 directorate, operational planning by J-3, and overall policy by J-5. Our concept combines the J-2 and J-3 functions (intelligence and operational planning) in one agency, keeping overall policy coordination where it belongs, in the National Security Council.

Recommendation: We recommend the establishment of a National Counterterrorism Center (NCTC), built on the foundation of the existing Terrorist Threat Integration Center (TTIC). Breaking the older mold of national government organization, this NCTC should be a center for joint operational planning *and* joint intelligence, staffed by personnel from the various agencies. The head of the NCTC should have authority to evaluate the performance of the people assigned to the Center.

- Such a joint center should be developed in the same spirit that guided the military's creation of unified joint commands, or the shaping of earlier national agencies like the National Reconnaissance Office, which was formed to organize the work of the CIA and several defense agencies in space.

NCTC—Intelligence. The NCTC should lead strategic analysis, pooling all-source intelligence, foreign and domestic, about transnational terrorist organizations with global reach. It should develop *net* assessments (comparing enemy capabilities and intentions against U.S. defenses and countermeasures). It should also provide warning. It should do this work by drawing on the efforts of the CIA, FBI, Homeland Security, and other departments and agencies. It should task collection requirements both inside and outside the United States.

- The intelligence function (J-2) should build on the existing TTIC structure and remain distinct, as a national intelligence center, within the NCTC. As the government's principal knowledge bank on Islamist terrorism, with the main responsibility for strategic analysis and net assessment, it should absorb a significant portion of the analytical talent now residing in the CIA's Counterterrorist Center and the DIA's Joint Intelligence Task Force—Combatting Terrorism (JITF-CT).

NCTC—Operations. The NCTC should perform joint planning. The plans would assign operational responsibilities to lead agencies, such as State, the CIA, the FBI, Defense and its combatant commands, Homeland Security, and other agencies. The NCTC should *not* direct the actual execution of these operations, leaving that job to the agencies. The NCTC would then track implementation; it would look across the foreign-domestic divide and across agency boundaries, updating plans to follow through on cases.[4]

- The joint operational planning function (J-3) will be new to the TTIC structure. The NCTC can draw on analogous work now being done in the CIA and every other involved department of the government, as well as reaching out to knowledgeable officials in state and local agencies throughout the United States.

- The NCTC should *not* be a policymaking body. Its operations and planning should follow the policy direction of the president and the National Security Council.

Consider this hypothetical case. The NSA discovers that a suspected terrorist is traveling to Bangkok and Kuala Lumpur. The NCTC should draw on joint intelligence resources, including its own NSA counterterrorism experts, to analyze the identities and possible destinations of these individuals. Informed by this analysis, the NCTC would then organize and plan the management of the case, drawing on the talents and differing kinds of experience among the several agency representatives assigned to it—assigning tasks to the CIA overseas, to Homeland Security watching entry points into the United States, and to the FBI. If military assistance might be needed, the Special Operations Command could be asked to develop an appropriate concept for such an operation. The NCTC would be accountable for tracking the progress of the case, ensuring that the plan evolved with it, and integrating the information into a warning. The NCTC would be responsible for being sure that intelligence gathered from the activities in the field became part of the government's institutional memory about Islamist terrorist personalities, organizations, and possible means of attack.

In each case the involved agency would make its own senior managers aware of what it was being asked to do. If those agency heads objected, and the issue could not easily be resolved, then the disagreement about roles and missions could be brought before the National Security Council and the president.

NCTC—Authorities. The head of the NCTC should be appointed by the president, and should be equivalent in rank to a deputy head of a cabinet department. The head of the NCTC would report to the national intelligence director, an office whose creation we recommend below, placed in the Executive Office of the President. The head of the NCTC would thus also report indirectly to the president. This official's nomination should be confirmed by the Senate and he or she should testify to the Congress, as is the case now with other statutory presidential offices, like the U.S. trade representative.

- To avoid the fate of other entities with great nominal authority and little real power, the head of the NCTC must have the right to concur in the choices of personnel to lead the operating entities of the departments and agencies focused on counterterrorism, specifically including the head of the Counterterrorist Center, the head of the FBI's Counterterrorism Division, the commanders of the Defense Department's Special Operations Command and Northern Command, and the State Department's coordinator for counterterrorism.[5] The head of the NCTC should also work with the director of the Office of Management and Budget in developing the president's counterterrorism budget.

- There are precedents for surrendering authority for joint planning while preserving an agency's operational control. In the international context, NATO commanders may get line authority over forces assigned by other nations. In U.S. unified commands, commanders plan operations that may involve units belonging to one of the services. In each case, procedures are worked out, formal and informal, to define the limits of the joint commander's authority.

The most serious disadvantage of the NCTC is the reverse of its greatest virtue. The struggle against Islamist terrorism is so important that any clear-cut centralization of authority to manage and be accountable for it may concentrate too much power in one place. The proposed NCTC would be given the authority of planning the activities of other agencies. Law or executive order must define the scope of such line authority.

The NCTC would not eliminate interagency policy disputes. These would still go to the National Security Council. To improve coordination at the White House, we believe the existing Homeland Security Council should soon be merged into a single National Security Council. The creation of the NCTC should help the NSC staff concentrate on its core duties of assisting the president and supporting interdepartmental policymaking.

We recognize that this is a new and difficult idea precisely because the authorities we recommend for the NCTC really would, as Secretary Rumsfeld foresaw, ask strong agencies to "give up some of their turf and authority in exchange for a stronger, faster, more efficient government wide joint effort." Countering transnational Islamist terrorism will test whether the U.S. government can fashion more flexible models of management needed to deal with the twenty-first-century world.

An argument against change is that the nation is at war, and cannot afford to reorganize in midstream. But some of the main innovations of the 1940s and 1950s, including the creation of the Joint Chiefs of Staff and even the construction of the Pentagon itself, were undertaken in the midst of war. Surely the country cannot wait until the struggle against Islamist terrorism is over.

"Surprise, when it happens to a government, is likely to be a complicated, diffuse, bureaucratic thing. It includes neglect of responsibility, but also responsibility so poorly defined or so ambiguously delegated that action gets lost."[6] That comment was made more than 40 years ago, about Pearl Harbor. We hope another commission, writing in the future about another attack, does not again find this quotation to be so apt.

13.2 UNITY OF EFFORT IN THE INTELLIGENCE COMMUNITY

In our first section, we concentrated on counterterrorism, discussing how to combine the analysis of information from all sources of intelligence with the joint planning of operations that draw on that analysis. In this section, we step back from looking just at the counterterrorism problem. We reflect on whether the government is organized adequately to direct resources and build the intelligence capabilities it will need not just for countering terrorism, but for the broader range of national security challenges in the decades ahead.

The Need for a Change

During the Cold War, intelligence agencies did not depend on seamless integration to track and count the thousands of military targets—such as tanks and missiles—fielded by the Soviet Union and other adversary states. Each agency concentrated on its specialized mission, acquiring its own information and then sharing it via formal, finished reports. The Department of Defense had given birth to and dominated the main agencies for technical collection of intelligence. Resources were shifted at an incremental pace, coping with challenges that arose over years, even decades.

We summarized the resulting organization of the intelligence community in chapter 3. It is outlined below.

Members of the U.S. Intelligence Community

Office of the Director of Central Intelligence, which includes the Office of the Deputy Director of Central Intelligence for Community Management, the Community Management Staff, the Terrorism Threat Integration Center, the National Intelligence Council, and other community offices

The Central Intelligence Agency (CIA), which performs human source collection, all-source analysis, and advanced science and technology

National intelligence agencies:
- National Security Agency (NSA), which performs signals collection and analysis
- National Geospatial-Intelligence Agency (NGA), which performs imagery collection and analysis

---

- National Reconnaissance Office (NRO), which develops, acquires, and launches space systems for intelligence collection
- Other national reconnaissance programs

Departmental intelligence agencies:
- Defense Intelligence Agency (DIA) of the Department of Defense
- Intelligence entities of the Army, Navy, Air Force, and Marines
- Bureau of Intelligence and Research (INR) of the Department of State
- Office of Terrorism and Finance Intelligence of the Department of Treasury
- Office of Intelligence and the Counterterrorism and Counterintelligence Divisions of the Federal Bureau of Investigation of the Department of Justice
- Office of Intelligence of the Department of Energy
- Directorate of Information Analysis and Infrastructure Protection (IAIP) and Directorate of Coast Guard Intelligence of the Department of Homeland Security

The need to restructure the intelligence community grows out of six problems that have become apparent before and after 9/11:

- *Structural barriers to performing joint intelligence work.* National intelligence is still organized around the collection disciplines of the home agencies, not the joint mission. The importance of integrated, all-source analysis cannot be overstated. Without it, it is not possible to "connect the dots." No one component holds all the relevant information.

  By contrast, in organizing national defense, the Goldwater-Nichols legislation of 1986 created joint commands for operations in the field, the Unified Command Plan. The services—the Army, Navy, Air Force, and Marine Corps—organize, train, and equip their people and units to perform their missions. Then they assign personnel and units to the joint combatant commander, like the commanding general of the Central Command (CENTCOM). The Goldwater-Nichols Act required officers to serve tours outside their service in order to win promotion. The culture of the Defense Department was transformed, its collective mind-set moved from service-specific to "joint," and its operations became more integrated.[7]

- *Lack of common standards and practices across the foreign-domestic divide.* The leadership of the intelligence community should be able to pool information gathered overseas with information gathered in the United States, holding the work—wherever it is done—to a common standard of quality in how it is collected, processed (e.g., translated), reported, shared, and analyzed. A common set of personnel standards for intelligence can create a group of professionals better able to operate in joint activities, transcending their own service-specific mind-sets.

- *Divided management of national intelligence capabilities.* While the CIA was once "central" to our national intelligence capabilities, following the end of the Cold War it has been less able to influence the use of the nation's imagery and signals intelligence capabilities in three national agencies housed within the Department of Defense: the National Security Agency, the National Geospatial-Intelligence Agency, and the National Reconnaissance Office. One of the lessons learned from the 1991 Gulf War was the value of national intelligence systems (satellites in particular) in precision warfare. Since that war, the department has appropriately drawn these agencies into its transformation of the military. Helping to orchestrate this transformation is the under secretary of defense for intelligence, a position established by Congress after 9/11. An unintended consequence of these developments has been the far greater demand made by Defense on technical systems, leaving the DCI less able to influence how these technical resources are allocated and used.

- *Weak capacity to set priorities and move resources.* The agencies are mainly organized around what they collect or the way they collect it. But the priorities for collection are national. As the DCI makes hard choices about moving resources, he or she must have the power to reach across agencies and reallocate effort.

- *Too many jobs.* The DCI now has at least three jobs. He is expected to run a particular agency, the CIA. He is expected to manage the loose confederation of agencies that is the intelligence community. He is expected to be the analyst in chief for the government, sifting evidence and directly briefing the President as his principal intelligence adviser. No recent DCI has been able to do all three effectively. Usually what loses out is management of the intelligence community, a difficult task even in the best case because the DCI's current authorities are weak. With so much to do, the DCI often has not used even the authority he has.

- *Too complex and secret.* Over the decades, the agencies and the rules surrounding the intelligence community have accumulated to a depth that practically defies public comprehension. There are now 15 agencies or parts of agencies in the intelligence community. The community and the DCI's authorities have become arcane matters, understood only by initiates after long study. Even the most basic information about how much money is actually allocated to or within the intelligence community and most of its key components is shrouded from public view.

The current DCI is responsible for community performance but lacks the three authorities critical for any agency head or chief executive officer: (1) control over purse strings, (2) the ability to hire or fire senior managers, and (3) the ability to set standards for the information infrastructure and personnel.[8]

The only budget power of the DCI over agencies other than the CIA lies in coordinating the budget requests of the various intelligence agencies into a single program for submission to Congress. The overall funding request of the 15 intelligence entities in this program is then presented to the president and Congress in 15 separate volumes.

When Congress passes an appropriations bill to allocate money to intelligence agencies, most of their funding is hidden in the Defense Department in order to keep intelligence spending secret. Therefore, although the House and Senate Intelligence committees are the authorizing committees for funding of the intelligence community, the final budget review is handled in the Defense Subcommittee of the Appropriations committees. Those committees have no subcommittees just for intelligence, and only a few members and staff review the requests.

The appropriations for the CIA and the national intelligence agencies—NSA, NGA, and NRO—are then given to the secretary of defense. The secretary transfers the CIA's money to the DCI but disburses the national agencies' money directly. Money for the FBI's national security components falls within the appropriations for Commerce, Justice, and State and goes to the attorney general.[9]

In addition, the DCI lacks hire-and-fire authority over most of the intelligence community's senior managers. For the national intelligence agencies housed in the Defense Department, the secretary of defense must seek the DCI's concurrence regarding the nomination of these directors, who are presidentially appointed. But the secretary may submit recommendations to the president without receiving this concurrence. The DCI cannot fire these officials. The DCI has even less influence over the head of the FBI's national security component, who is appointed by the attorney general in consultation with the DCI.[10]

Combining Joint Work with Stronger Management

We have received recommendations on the topic of intelligence reform from many sources. Other commissions have been over this same ground. Thoughtful bills have been introduced, most recently a bill by the chairman of the House Intelligence Committee Porter Goss (R-Fla.), and another by the ranking minority member, Jane Harman (D-Calif.). In the Senate, Senators Bob Graham (D-Fla.) and Dianne Feinstein (D-Calif.) have introduced reform proposals as well. Past efforts have foundered, because the president did not support them; because the DCI, the secretary of defense, or both opposed them; and because some proposals lacked merit. We have tried to take stock of these experiences, and borrow from strong elements in many of the ideas that have already been developed by others.

Recommendation: The current position of Director of Central Intelligence should be replaced by a National Intelligence Director with two main areas of responsibility: (1) to oversee national intelligence centers on specific subjects of interest across the U.S. government and (2) to manage the national intelligence program and oversee the agencies that contribute to it.

First, the National Intelligence Director should oversee *national intelligence centers* to provide all-source analysis and plan intelligence operations for the whole government on major problems.

- One such problem is counterterrorism. In this case, we believe that the center should be the intelligence entity (formerly TTIC) inside the National Counterterrorism Center we have proposed. It would sit there alongside the operations management unit we described earlier, with both making up the NCTC, in the Executive Office of the President. Other national intelligence centers—for instance, on counterproliferation, crime and narcotics, and China—would be housed in whatever department or agency is best suited for them.

- The National Intelligence Director would retain the present DCI's role as the principal intelligence adviser to the president. We hope the president will come to look directly to the directors of the national intelligence centers to provide all-source analysis in their areas of responsibility, balancing the advice of these intelligence chiefs against the contrasting viewpoints that may be offered by department heads at State, Defense, Homeland Security, Justice, and other agencies.

Second, the National Intelligence Director should manage the national intelligence program and oversee the component agencies of the intelligence community. (See diagram.)[11]

- The National Intelligence Director would submit a unified budget for national intelligence that reflects priorities chosen by the National Security Council, an appropriate balance among the varieties of technical and human intelligence collection, and analysis. He or she would receive an appropriation for national intelligence and apportion the funds to the appropriate agencies, in line with that budget, and with authority to reprogram funds among the national intelligence agencies to meet any new priority (as counterterrorism was in the 1990s). The National Intelligence Director should approve and submit nominations to the president of the individuals who would lead the CIA, DIA, FBI Intelligence Office, NSA, NGA, NRO, Information Analysis and Infrastructure Protection Directorate of the Department of Homeland Security, and other national intelligence capabilities.[12]

- The National Intelligence Director would manage this national effort with the help of three deputies, each of whom would also hold a key position in one of the component agencies.[13]
  - foreign intelligence (the head of the CIA)
  - defense intelligence (the under secretary of defense for intelligence)[14]
  - homeland intelligence (the FBI's executive assistant director for intelligence or the under secretary of homeland security for information analysis and infrastructure protection)

  Other agencies in the intelligence community would coordinate their work within each of these three areas, largely staying housed in the same departments or agencies that support them now.

  Returning to the analogy of the Defense Department's organization, these three deputies—like the leaders of the Army, Navy, Air Force, or Marines—would have the job of acquiring the systems, training the people, and executing the operations planned by the national intelligence centers.

  And, just as the combatant commanders also report to the secretary of defense, the directors of the national intelligence centers—e.g., for counterproliferation, crime and narcotics, and the rest—also would report to the National Intelligence Director.

- The Defense Department's military intelligence programs—the joint military intelligence program (JMIP) and the tactical intelligence and related activities program (TIARA)—would remain part of that department's responsibility.

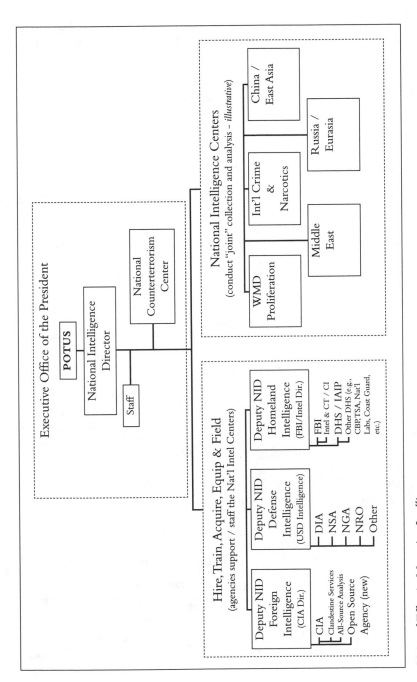

Executive Office of the President

POTUS

National Intelligence Director

Staff

National Counterterrorism Center

National Intelligence Centers
(conduct "joint" collection and analysis – *illustrative*)

WMD Proliferation

Int'l Crime & Narcotics

Middle East

Russia / Eurasia

China / East Asia

Hire, Train, Acquire, Equip & Field
(agencies support / staff the Nat'l Intel Centers)

Deputy NID Foreign Intelligence (CIA Dir.)

CIA
— Clandestine Services
— All-Source Analysis
— Open Source Agency (new)

Deputy NID Defense Intelligence (USD Intelligence)

— DIA
— NSA
— NGA
— NRO
— Other

Deputy NID Homeland Intelligence (FBI/Intel Dir.)

— FBI Intel & CT / CI
— DHS / IAIP
— Other DHS (e.g., CBP,TSA, Nat'l Labs, Coast Guard, etc.)

Unity of Effort in Managing Intelligence

- The National Intelligence Director would set personnel policies to establish standards for education and training and facilitate assignments at the national intelligence centers and across agency lines. The National Intelligence Director also would set information sharing and information technology policies to maximize data sharing, as well as policies to protect the security of information.

- Too many agencies now have an opportunity to say no to change. The National Intelligence Director should participate in an NSC executive committee that can resolve differences in priorities among the agencies and bring the major disputes to the president for decision.

The National Intelligence Director should be located in the Executive Office of the President. This official, who would be confirmed by the Senate and would testify before Congress, would have a relatively small staff of several hundred people, taking the place of the existing community management offices housed at the CIA.

In managing the whole community, the National Intelligence Director is still providing a service function. With the partial exception of his or her responsibilities for overseeing the NCTC, the National Intelligence Director should support the consumers of national intelligence—the president and policymaking advisers such as the secretaries of state, defense, and homeland security and the attorney general.

We are wary of too easily equating government management problems with those of the private sector. But we have noticed that some very large private firms rely on a powerful CEO who has significant control over how money is spent and can hire or fire leaders of the major divisions, assisted by a relatively modest staff, while leaving responsibility for execution in the operating divisions.

There are disadvantages to separating the position of National Intelligence Director from the job of heading the CIA. For example, the National Intelligence Director will not head a major agency of his or her own and may have a weaker base of support. But we believe that these disadvantages are outweighed by several other considerations:

- The National Intelligence Director must be able to directly oversee intelligence collection inside the United States. Yet law and custom has counseled against giving such a plain domestic role to the head of the CIA.

- The CIA will be one among several claimants for funds in setting national priorities. The National Intelligence Director should not be both one of the advocates and the judge of them all.

- Covert operations tend to be highly tactical, requiring close attention. The National Intelligence Director should rely on the relevant joint mission center to oversee these details, helping to coordinate closely with the White House. The CIA will be able to concentrate on building the capabilities to carry out such operations and on providing the personnel who will be directing and executing such operations in the field.

- Rebuilding the analytic and human intelligence collection capabilities of the CIA should be a full-time effort, and the director of the CIA should focus on extending its comparative advantages.

Recommendation: The CIA Director should emphasize (a) rebuilding the CIA's analytic capabilities; (b) transforming the clandestine service by building its human intelligence capabilities; (c) developing a stronger language program, with high standards and sufficient financial incentives; (d) renewing emphasis on recruiting diversity among operations officers so they can blend more easily in foreign cities; (e) ensuring a seamless relationship between human source collection and signals collection at the operational level; and (f) stressing a better balance between unilateral and liaison operations.

The CIA should retain responsibility for the direction and execution of clandestine and covert operations, as assigned by the relevant national intelligence center and authorized by the National Intelligence Director and the president. This would include propaganda, renditions, and nonmilitary disruption. We believe, however, that one important area of responsibility should change.

Recommendation: Lead responsibility for directing and executing paramilitary operations, whether clandestine or covert, should shift to the Defense Department. There it should be consolidated with the capabilities for training, direction, and execution of such operations already being developed in the Special Operations Command.

- Before 9/11, the CIA did not invest in developing a robust capability to conduct paramilitary operations with U.S. personnel. It relied on proxies instead, organized by CIA operatives without the requisite military training. The results were unsatisfactory.

- Whether the price is measured in either money or people, the United States cannot afford to build two separate capabilities for carrying out secret military operations, secretly operating standoff missiles, and secretly training foreign military or paramilitary forces. The United States should concentrate responsibility and necessary legal authorities in one entity.

- The post-9/11 Afghanistan precedent of using joint CIA-military teams for covert and clandestine operations was a good one. We believe this proposal to be consistent with it. Each agency would concentrate on its comparative advantages in building capabilities for joint missions. The operation itself would be planned in common.

- The CIA has a reputation for agility in operations. The military has a reputation for being methodical and cumbersome. We do not know if these stereotypes match current reality; they may also be one more symptom of the civil-military misunderstandings we described in chapter 4. It is a problem to be resolved in policy guidance and agency management, not in the creation of redundant, overlapping capabilities and authorities in such sensitive work. The CIA's experts should be integrated into the military's training, exercises, and planning. To quote a CIA official now serving in the field: "One fight, one team."

Recommendation: Finally, to combat the secrecy and complexity we have described, the overall amounts of money being appropriated for national intelligence and to its component agencies should no longer be kept secret. Congress should pass a separate appropriations act for intelligence, defending the broad allocation of how these tens of billions of dollars have been assigned among the varieties of intelligence work.

The specifics of the intelligence appropriation would remain classified, as they are today. Opponents of declassification argue that America's enemies could learn about intelligence capabilities by tracking the top-line appropriations figure. Yet the top-line figure by itself provides little insight into U.S. intelligence sources and methods. The U.S. government readily provides copious information about spending on its military forces, including military intelligence. The intelligence community should not be subject to that much disclosure. But when even aggregate categorical numbers remain hidden, it is hard to judge priorities and foster accountability.

13.3 UNITY OF EFFORT IN SHARING INFORMATION

Information Sharing

We have already stressed the importance of intelligence analysis that can draw on all relevant sources of information. The biggest impediment to all-source analysis—to a greater likelihood of connecting the dots—is the human or systemic resistance to sharing information.

The U.S. government has access to a vast amount of information. When databases not usually thought of as "intelligence," such as customs or immigration information, are included, the storehouse is immense. But the U.S. government has a weak system for processing and using what it has. In interviews around the government, official after official urged us to call attention to frustrations with the unglamorous "back office" side of government operations.

In the 9/11 story, for example, we sometimes see examples of information that could be accessed—like the undistributed NSA information that would have helped identify Nawaf al Hazmi in January 2000. But someone had to ask for it. In that case, no one did. Or, as in the episodes we describe in chapter 8, the information is distributed, but in a compartmented channel. Or the information is available, and someone does ask, but it cannot be shared.

What all these stories have in common is a system that requires a demonstrated "need to know" before sharing. This approach assumes it is possible to know, in advance, who will need to use the information. Such a system implicitly assumes that the risk of inadvertent disclosure outweighs the benefits of wider sharing. Those Cold War assumptions are no longer appropriate. The culture of agencies feeling they own the information they gathered at taxpayer expense must be replaced by a culture in which the agencies instead feel they have a duty to the information—to repay the taxpayers' investment by making that information available.

Each intelligence agency has its own security practices, outgrowths of the Cold War. We certainly understand the reason for these practices. Counterintelligence concerns are still real, even if the old Soviet enemy has been replaced by other spies.

But the security concerns need to be weighed against the costs. Current security requirements nurture overclassification and excessive compartmentation of information among agencies. Each agency's incentive structure opposes sharing, with risks (criminal, civil, and internal administrative sanctions) but few rewards for sharing information. No one has to pay the long-term costs of overclassifying information, though these costs—even in literal financial terms—are substantial. There are no punishments for *not* sharing information. Agencies uphold a "need-to-know" culture of information protection rather than promoting a "need-to-share" culture of integration.[15]

Recommendation: Information procedures should provide incentives for sharing, to restore a better balance between security and shared knowledge.

Intelligence gathered about transnational terrorism should be processed, turned into reports, and distributed according to the same quality standards, whether it is collected in Pakistan or in Texas.

The logical objection is that sources and methods may vary greatly in different locations. We therefore propose that when a report is first created, its data be separated from the sources and methods by which they are obtained. The

report should begin with the information in its most shareable, but still meaningful, form. Therefore the maximum number of recipients can access some
form of that information. If knowledge of further details becomes important,
any user can query further, with access granted or denied according to the rules
set for the network—and with queries leaving an audit trail in order to determine who accessed the information. But the questions may not come at all
unless experts at the "edge" of the network can readily discover the clues that
prompt to them.[16]

We propose that information be shared horizontally, across new networks
that transcend individual agencies.

- The current system is structured on an old mainframe, or hub-and-
spoke, concept. In this older approach, each agency has its own database. Agency users send information to the database and then can
retrieve it from the database.

- A decentralized network model, the concept behind much of the
information revolution, shares data horizontally too. Agencies would
still have their own databases, but those databases would be searchable
across agency lines. In this system, secrets are protected through the
design of the network and an "information rights management"
approach that controls access to the data, not access to the whole network. An outstanding conceptual framework for this kind of "trusted
information network" has been developed by a task force of leading
professionals in national security, information technology, and law
assembled by the Markle Foundation. Its report has been widely discussed throughout the U.S. government, but has not yet been converted into action.[17]

**Recommendation: The president should lead the government-wide
effort to bring the major national security institutions into the information revolution. He should coordinate the resolution of the legal,
policy, and technical issues across agencies to create a "trusted information network."**

- No one agency can do it alone. Well-meaning agency officials are
under tremendous pressure to update their systems. Alone, they may
only be able to modernize the stovepipes, not replace them.

- Only presidential leadership can develop government-wide concepts
and standards. Currently, no one is doing this job. Backed by the Office
of Management and Budget, a new National Intelligence Director
empowered to set common standards for information use throughout
the community, and a secretary of homeland security who helps

extend the system to public agencies and relevant private-sector data-bases, a government-wide initiative can succeed.

- White House leadership is also needed because the policy and legal issues are harder than the technical ones. The necessary technology already exists. What does not are the rules for acquiring, accessing, sharing, and using the vast stores of public and private data that may be available. When information sharing works, it is a powerful tool. Therefore the sharing and uses of information must be guided by a set of practical policy guidelines that simultaneously empower and constrain officials, telling them clearly what is and is not permitted.

"This is government acting in new ways, to face new threats," the most recent Markle report explains. "And while such change is necessary, it must be accomplished while engendering the people's trust that privacy and other civil liberties are being protected, that businesses are not being unduly burdened with requests for extraneous or useless information, that taxpayer money is being well spent, and that, ultimately, the network will be effective in protect-ing our security." The authors add: "Leadership is emerging from all levels of government and from many places in the private sector. What is needed now is a plan to accelerate these efforts, and public debate and consensus on the goals."[18]

13.4 UNITY OF EFFORT IN THE CONGRESS

Strengthen Congressional Oversight of Intelligence and Homeland Security

Of all our recommendations, strengthening congressional oversight may be among the most difficult and important. So long as oversight is governed by current congressional rules and resolutions, we believe the American people will not get the security they want and need. The United States needs a strong, stable, and capable congressional committee structure to give America's national intelligence agencies oversight, support, and leadership.

Few things are more difficult to change in Washington than congressional committee jurisdiction and prerogatives. To a member, these assignments are almost as important as the map of his or her congressional district. The Amer-ican people may have to insist that these changes occur, or they may well not happen. Having interviewed numerous members of Congress from both par-ties, as well as congressional staff members, we found that dissatisfaction with congressional oversight remains widespread.

The future challenges of America's intelligence agencies are daunting. They include the need to develop leading-edge technologies that give our policymakers and warfighters a decisive edge in any conflict where the interests of the United States are vital. Not only does good intelligence win wars, but the best intelligence enables us to prevent them from happening altogether.

Under the terms of existing rules and resolutions the House and Senate intelligence committees lack the power, influence, and sustained capability to meet this challenge. While few members of Congress have the broad knowledge of intelligence activities or the know-how about the technologies employed, all members need to feel assured that good oversight is happening. When their unfamiliarity with the subject is combined with the need to preserve security, a mandate emerges for substantial change.

Tinkering with the existing structure is not sufficient. Either Congress should create a joint committee for intelligence, using the Joint Atomic Energy Committee as its model, or it should create House and Senate committees with combined authorizing and appropriations powers.

Whichever of these two forms are chosen, the goal should be a structure—codified by resolution with powers expressly granted and carefully limited—allowing a relatively small group of members of Congress, given time and reason to master the subject and the agencies, to conduct oversight of the intelligence establishment and be clearly accountable for their work. The staff of this committee should be nonpartisan and work for the entire committee and not for individual members.

The other reforms we have suggested—for a National Counterterrorism Center and a National Intelligence Director—will not work if congressional oversight does not change too. Unity of effort in executive management can be lost if it is fractured by divided congressional oversight.

Recommendation: Congressional oversight for intelligence—and counterterrorism—is now dysfunctional. Congress should address this problem. We have considered various alternatives: A joint committee on the old model of the Joint Committee on Atomic Energy is one. A single committee in each house of Congress, combining authorizing and appropriating authorities, is another.

- The new committee or committees should conduct continuing studies of the activities of the intelligence agencies and report problems relating to the development and use of intelligence to all members of the House and Senate.

- We have already recommended that the total level of funding for intelligence be made public, and that the national intelligence program be appropriated to the National Intelligence Director, not to the secretary of defense.[19]

- We also recommend that the intelligence committee should have a subcommittee specifically dedicated to oversight, freed from the consuming responsibility of working on the budget.

- The resolution creating the new intelligence committee structure should grant subpoena authority to the committee or committees. The majority party's representation on this committee should never exceed the minority's representation by more than one.

- Four of the members appointed to this committee or committees should be a member who also serves on each of the following additional committees: Armed Services, Judiciary, Foreign Affairs, and the Defense Appropriations subcommittee. In this way the other major congressional interests can be brought together in the new committee's work.

- Members should serve indefinitely on the intelligence committees, without set terms, thereby letting them accumulate expertise.

- The committees should be smaller—perhaps seven or nine members in each house—so that each member feels a greater sense of responsibility, and accountability, for the quality of the committee's work.

The leaders of the Department of Homeland Security now appear before 88 committees and subcommittees of Congress. One expert witness (not a member of the administration) told us that this is perhaps the single largest obstacle impeding the department's successful development. The one attempt to consolidate such committee authority, the House Select Committee on Homeland Security, may be eliminated. The Senate does not have even this.

Congress needs to establish for the Department of Homeland Security the kind of clear authority and responsibility that exist to enable the Justice Department to deal with crime and the Defense Department to deal with threats to national security. Through not more than one authorizing committee and one appropriating subcommittee in each house, Congress should be able to ask the secretary of homeland security whether he or she has the resources to provide reasonable security against major terrorist acts within the United States and to hold the secretary accountable for the department's performance.

Recommendation: Congress should create a single, principal point of oversight and review for homeland security. Congressional leaders are best able to judge what committee should have jurisdiction over this department and its duties. But we believe that Congress does have the obligation to choose one in the House and one in the Senate, and that this committee should be a permanent standing committee with a nonpartisan staff.

Improve the Transitions between Administrations
In chapter 6, we described the transition of 2000–2001. Beyond the policy issues we described, the new administration did not have its deputy cabinet officers in place until the spring of 2001, and the critical subcabinet officials were not confirmed until the summer—if then. In other words, the new administration—like others before it—did not have its team on the job until at least six months after it took office.

Recommendation: Since a catastrophic attack could occur with little or no notice, we should minimize as much as possible the disruption of national security policymaking during the change of administrations by accelerating the process for national security appointments. We think the process could be improved significantly so transitions can work more effectively and allow new officials to assume their new responsibilities as quickly as possible.

- Before the election, candidates should submit the names of selected members of their prospective transition teams to the FBI so that, if necessary, those team members can obtain security clearances immediately after the election is over.

- A president-elect should submit lists of possible candidates for national security positions to begin obtaining security clearances immediately after the election, so that their background investigations can be complete before January 20.

- A single federal agency should be responsible for providing and maintaining security clearances, ensuring uniform standards–including uniform security questionnaires and financial report requirements, and maintaining a single database. This agency can also be responsible for administering polygraph tests on behalf of organizations that require them.

- A president-elect should submit the nominations of the entire new national security team, through the level of under secretary of cabinet departments, not later than January 20. The Senate, in return, should adopt special rules requiring hearings and votes to confirm or reject national security nominees within 30 days of their submission. The Senate should not require confirmation of such executive appointees below Executive Level 3.

- The outgoing administration should provide the president-elect, as soon as possible after election day, with a classified, compartmented list that catalogues specific, operational threats to national security; major military or covert operations; and pending decisions on the possible use of force. Such a document could provide both notice and a checklist, inviting a president-elect to inquire and learn more.

13.5 ORGANIZING AMERICA'S DEFENSES IN THE UNITED STATES

The Future Role of the FBI

We have considered proposals for a new agency dedicated to intelligence collection in the United States. Some call this a proposal for an "American MI-5," although the analogy is weak—the actual British Security Service is a relatively small worldwide agency that combines duties assigned in the U.S. government to the Terrorist Threat Integration Center, the CIA, the FBI, and the Department of Homeland Security.

The concern about the FBI is that it has long favored its criminal justice mission over its national security mission. Part of the reason for this is the demand around the country for FBI help on criminal matters. The FBI was criticized, rightly, for the overzealous domestic intelligence investigations disclosed during the 1970s. The pendulum swung away from those types of investigations during the 1980s and 1990s, though the FBI maintained an active counterintelligence function and was the lead agency for the investigation of foreign terrorist groups operating inside the United States.

We do not recommend the creation of a new domestic intelligence agency. It is not needed if our other recommendations are adopted—to establish a strong national intelligence center, part of the NCTC, that will oversee counterterrorism intelligence work, foreign and domestic, and to create a National Intelligence Director who can set and enforce standards for the collection, processing, and reporting of information.

Under the structures we recommend, the FBI's role is focused, but still vital. The FBI does need to be able to direct its thousands of agents and other employees to collect intelligence in America's cities and towns—interviewing informants, conducting surveillance and searches, tracking individuals, working collaboratively with local authorities, and doing so with meticulous attention to detail and compliance with the law. The FBI's job in the streets of the United States would thus be a domestic equivalent, operating under the U.S. Constitution and quite different laws and rules, to the job of the CIA's operations officers abroad.

Creating a new domestic intelligence agency has other drawbacks.

- The FBI is accustomed to carrying out sensitive intelligence collection operations in compliance with the law. If a new domestic intelligence agency were outside of the Department of Justice, the process of legal oversight—never easy—could become even more difficult.

Abuses of civil liberties could create a backlash that would impair the collection of needed intelligence.

- Creating a new domestic intelligence agency would divert attention of the officials most responsible for current counterterrorism efforts while the threat remains high. Putting a new player into the mix of federal agencies with counterterrorism responsibilities would exacerbate existing information-sharing problems.

- A new domestic intelligence agency would need to acquire assets and personnel. The FBI already has 28,000 employees; 56 field offices, 400 satellite offices, and 47 legal attaché offices; a laboratory, operations center, and training facility; an existing network of informants, cooperating defendants, and other sources; and relationships with state and local law enforcement, the CIA, and foreign intelligence and law enforcement agencies.

- Counterterrorism investigations in the United States very quickly become matters that involve violations of criminal law and possible law enforcement action. Because the FBI can have agents working criminal matters and agents working intelligence investigations concerning the same international terrorism target, the full range of investigative tools against a suspected terrorist can be considered within one agency. The removal of "the wall" that existed before 9/11 between intelligence and law enforcement has opened up new opportunities for cooperative action within the FBI.

- Counterterrorism investigations often overlap or are cued by other criminal investigations, such as money laundering or the smuggling of contraband. In the field, the close connection to criminal work has many benefits.

Our recommendation to leave counterterrorism intelligence collection in the United States with the FBI still depends on an assessment that the FBI—if it makes an all-out effort to institutionalize change—can do the job. As we mentioned in chapter 3, we have been impressed by the determination that agents display in tracking down details, patiently going the extra mile and working the extra month, to put facts in the place of speculation. In our report we have shown how agents in Phoenix, Minneapolis, and New York displayed initiative in pressing their investigations.

FBI agents and analysts in the field need to have sustained support and dedicated resources to become stronger intelligence officers. They need to be rewarded for acquiring informants and for gathering and disseminating information differently and more broadly than usual in a traditional criminal investigation. FBI employees need to report and analyze what they have learned in ways the Bureau has never done before.

Under Director Robert Mueller, the Bureau has made significant progress in improving its intelligence capabilities. It now has an Office of Intelligence, overseen by the top tier of FBI management. Field intelligence groups have been created in all field offices to put FBI priorities and the emphasis on intelligence into practice. Advances have been made in improving the Bureau's information technology systems and in increasing connectivity and information sharing with intelligence community agencies.

Director Mueller has also recognized that the FBI's reforms are far from complete. He has outlined a number of areas where added measures may be necessary. Specifically, he has recognized that the FBI needs to recruit from a broader pool of candidates, that agents and analysts working on national security matters require specialized training, and that agents should specialize within programs after obtaining a generalist foundation. The FBI is developing career tracks for agents to specialize in counterterrorism/counterintelligence, cyber crimes, criminal investigations, or intelligence. It is establishing a program for certifying agents as intelligence officers, a certification that will be a prerequisite for promotion to the senior ranks of the Bureau. New training programs have been instituted for intelligence-related subjects.

The Director of the FBI has proposed creating an Intelligence Directorate as a further refinement of the FBI intelligence program. This directorate would include units for intelligence planning and policy and for the direction of analysts and linguists.

We want to ensure that the Bureau's shift to a preventive counterterrorism posture is more fully institutionalized so that it survives beyond Director Mueller's tenure. We have found that in the past the Bureau has announced its willingness to reform and restructure itself to address transnational security threats, but has fallen short—failing to effect the necessary institutional and cultural changes organization-wide. We want to ensure that this does not happen again. Despite having found acceptance of the Director's clear message that counterterrorism is now the FBI's top priority, two years after 9/11 we also found gaps between some of the announced reforms and the reality in the field. We are concerned that management in the field offices still can allocate people and resources to local concerns that diverge from the national security mission. This system could revert to a focus on lower-priority criminal justice cases over national security requirements.

Recommendation: A specialized and integrated national security workforce should be established at the FBI consisting of agents, analysts, linguists, and surveillance specialists who are recruited, trained, rewarded, and retained to ensure the development of an institutional

culture imbued with a deep expertise in intelligence and national security.

- The president, by executive order or directive, should direct the FBI to develop this intelligence cadre.

- Recognizing that cross-fertilization between the criminal justice and national security disciplines is vital to the success of both missions, all new agents should receive basic training in both areas. Furthermore, new agents should begin their careers with meaningful assignments in both areas.

- Agents and analysts should then specialize in one of these disciplines and have the option to work such matters for their entire career with the Bureau. Certain advanced training courses and assignments to other intelligence agencies should be required to advance within the national security discipline.

- In the interest of cross-fertilization, all senior FBI managers, including those working on law enforcement matters, should be certified intelligence officers.

- The FBI should fully implement a recruiting, hiring, and selection process for agents and analysts that enhances its ability to target and attract individuals with educational and professional backgrounds in intelligence, international relations, language, technology, and other relevant skills.

- The FBI should institute the integration of analysts, agents, linguists, and surveillance personnel in the field so that a dedicated team approach is brought to bear on national security intelligence operations.

- Each field office should have an official at the field office's deputy level for national security matters. This individual would have management oversight and ensure that the national priorities are carried out in the field.

- The FBI should align its budget structure according to its four main programs—intelligence, counterterrorism and counterintelligence, criminal, and criminal justice services—to ensure better transparency on program costs, management of resources, and protection of the intelligence program.[20]

- The FBI should report regularly to Congress in its semiannual program reviews designed to identify whether each field office is appropriately addressing FBI and national program priorities.

- The FBI should report regularly to Congress in detail on the qualifications, status, and roles of analysts in the field and at headquarters. Congress should ensure that analysts are afforded training and career opportunities on a par with those offered analysts in other intelligence community agencies.

- The Congress should make sure funding is available to accelerate the expansion of secure facilities in FBI field offices so as to increase their ability to use secure email systems and classified intelligence product exchanges. The Congress should monitor whether the FBI's information-sharing principles are implemented in practice.

The FBI is just a small fraction of the national law enforcement community in the United States, a community comprised mainly of state and local agencies. The network designed for sharing information, and the work of the FBI through local Joint Terrorism Task Forces, should build a reciprocal relationship, in which state and local agents understand what information they are looking for and, in return, receive some of the information being developed about what is happening, or may happen, in their communities. In this relationship, the Department of Homeland Security also will play an important part.

The Homeland Security Act of 2002 gave the under secretary for information analysis and infrastructure protection broad responsibilities. In practice, this directorate has the job to map "terrorist threats to the homeland against our assessed vulnerabilities in order to drive our efforts to protect against terrorist threats."[21] These capabilities are still embryonic. The directorate has not yet developed the capacity to perform one of its assigned jobs, which is to assimilate and analyze information from Homeland Security's own component agencies, such as the Coast Guard, Secret Service, Transportation Security Administration, Immigration and Customs Enforcement, and Customs and Border Protection. The secretary of homeland security must ensure that these components work with the Information Analysis and Infrastructure Protection Directorate so that this office can perform its mission.[22]

Homeland Defense

At several points in our inquiry, we asked, "Who is responsible for defending us at home?" Our national defense at home is the responsibility, first, of the Department of Defense and, second, of the Department of Homeland Security. They must have clear delineations of responsibility and authority.

We found that NORAD, which had been given the responsibility for defending U.S. airspace, had construed that mission to focus on threats coming from outside America's borders. It did not adjust its focus even though the intelligence community had gathered intelligence on the possibility that terrorists might turn to hijacking and even use of planes as missiles. We have been assured that NORAD has now embraced the full mission. Northern Command has been established to assume responsibility for the defense of the domestic United States.

Recommendation: The Department of Defense and its oversight committees should regularly assess the adequacy of Northern Command's strategies and planning to defend the United States against military threats to the homeland.

The Department of Homeland Security was established to consolidate all of the domestic agencies responsible for securing America's borders and national infrastructure, most of which is in private hands. It should identify those elements of our transportation, energy, communications, financial, and other institutions that need to be protected, develop plans to protect that infrastructure, and exercise the mechanisms to enhance preparedness. This means going well beyond the preexisting jobs of the agencies that have been brought together inside the department.

Recommendation: The Department of Homeland Security and its oversight committees should regularly assess the types of threats the country faces to determine (a) the adequacy of the government's plans—and the progress against those plans—to protect America's critical infrastructure and (b) the readiness of the government to respond to the threats that the United States might face.

.   .   .

We look forward to a national debate on the merits of what we have recommended, and we will participate vigorously in that debate.

APPENDIX A

COMMON ABBREVIATIONS

CAP	combat air patrol
CAPPS	Computer Assisted Passenger Prescreening System
CENTCOM	Central Command
CIA	Central Intelligence Agency
CONR	Continental U.S. NORAD Region
CSG	Counterterrorism Security Group
CTC	Counterterrorist Center
DIA	Defense Intelligence Agency
DCI	Director of Central Intelligence
ESU	Emergency Service Unit (NYPD)
FAA	Federal Aviation Administration
FBI	Federal Bureau of Investigation
FDNY	Fire Department of New York
FFTC	Florida Flight Training Center
FISA	Foreign Intelligence Surveillance Act
FISC	Foreign Intelligence Surveillance Court
INS	Immigration and Naturalization Service
ISID	Inter-Services Intelligence Directorate (Pakistan)
JCS	Joint Chiefs of Staff
JI	Jemaah Islamiah
JTTF	Joint Terrorism Task Force
KSM	Khalid Sheikh Mohammed
Legat	legal attaché
MAK	Mektab al Khidmat
MON	memorandum of notification
NEADS	Northeast Air Defense Sector
NCTC	National Counterterrorism Center
NGO	nongovernmental organization
NMCC	National Military Command Center

NORAD	North American Aerospace Defense Command
NTSB	National Transportation Safety Board
NSA	National Security Agency
NSC	National Security Council
NSPD	national security policy directive
NYPD	New York Police Department
OEM	Office of Emergency Management (New York City)
OFAC	Office of Foreign Assets Control
OIPR	Office of Intelligence Policy and Review
OMB	Office of Management and Budget
PAPD	Port Authority Police Department
PDD	presidential decision directive
PEOC	Presidential Emergency Operations Center
SEC	Securities and Exchange Commission
TSA	Transportation Security Administration
TTIC	Terrorist Threat Integration Center
UBL	Usama Bin Ladin
WMD	weapons of mass destruction
WTC	World Trade Center
WTO	World Trade Organization

APPENDIX B

TABLE OF NAMES

U.S. OFFICIALS

Madeleine Albright — Secretary of State, 1997–2001

Charles Allen — Assistant Director of Central Intelligence for Collection, 1998–

Richard Armitage — Deputy Secretary of State, 2001–

Larry Arnold — Commander, First Air Force and Commander of the Continental U.S. North American Aerospace Defense Command (NORAD) Region, 1997–2002

John Ashcroft — Attorney General, 2001–

Monte Belger — Acting Deputy Administrator, Federal Aviation Administration 1997–2002

Samuel "Sandy" Berger — National Security Advisor, 1997–2001; Deputy National Security Advisor 1993–1997

J. Cofer Black — Director, DCI Counterterrorist Center, 1999–2002

Joshua Bolten — White House Deputy Chief of Staff, 2001–2003

Robert "Bear" Bryant — Deputy Director, Federal Bureau of Investigation, 1997–1999

George H. W. Bush — 41st President of the United States, 1989–1993; Vice President, 1981–1989

George W. Bush — 43rd President of the United States, 2001–

Andrew Card, Jr. — White House Chief of Staff, 2001–

Richard B. Cheney — Vice President of the United States, 2001–

Richard Clarke — National Counterterrorism Coordinator, NSC, 1997–2001

William J. Clinton — 42nd President of the United States, 1993–2001

William Cohen — Secretary of Defense, 1997–2001

Roger Cressey   NSC counterterrorism official, 1999–2001
Ralph Eberhart   Commander in Chief, NORAD and U.S. Space
                         Command, 2000–
Tommy Franks   Commander, U.S. Central Command (CENT-
                         COM), 2001–2003
Louis Freeh   Director, Federal Bureau of Investigation, 1993–2001
Scott Fry   Director of Operations for the Joint Chiefs of
                         Staff, 1998–2000
Jane Garvey   Administrator, Federal Aviation Administration,
                         1997–2002
Newt Gingrich   Speaker of the House, 1995–1999
Rudolph Giuliani   Mayor, City of New York, 1994–2001
John Gordon   Deputy Director of Central Intelligence, 1997–2000
Al Gore, Jr.   Vice President of the United States, 1993–2001
Scott Gration   Fry's Chief Information Operations Officer,
                         2000–2001
Stephen Hadley   Deputy National Security Advisor, 2001–
Dennis Hastert   Speaker of the House, 1999–
Karl Inderfurth   Assistant Secretary of State for South Asia,
                         1997–2001
Donald Kerrick   Deputy National Security Advisor, 2000–2001
Zalmay Khalilzad   NSC Senior Director for Near East and South
                         Asia and Special Envoy to Afghanistan,
                         2001–2003
Anthony Lake   National Security Advisor, 1993–1997
Trent Lott   Senate Majority Leader, 1996–2001
Mary McCarthy   NSC senior director for intelligence, 1998–2001
John McLaughlin   Deputy Director of Central Intelligence,
                         2000–2004
William Milam   U.S. Ambassador to Pakistan, 1998–2001
Norman Mineta   Secretary of Transportation, 2001–
Robert Mueller   Director, Federal Bureau of Investigation, 2001–
Richard Myers   Chairman of the Joint Chiefs, September 2001–;
                         Joint Chiefs Vice Chairman, 2000–2001
John O'Neill   FBI Special Agent in Charge for National Secu-
                         rity, New York Field Office, 1997–2001; Chief
                         of Security of the World Trade Center, killed
                         on 9/11
Paul O'Neill   Secretary of the Treasury, 2001–2002
James Pavitt   Deputy Director of Operations, CIA,
                         1999–2004
Thomas Pickard   Acting Director, Federal Bureau of Investigation,
                         June 25, 2001–September 4, 2001

Thomas Pickering	Under Secretary of State, 1997–2000
Colin Powell	Secretary of State, 2001–
Ronald Reagan	40th President of the United States, 1981–1989
Janet Reno	Attorney General, 1993–2001
Condoleezza Rice	National Security Advisor, 2001–
Bill Richardson	Ambassador to the United Nations, 1997–1998
Thomas Ridge	First Secretary of Homeland Security, 2003–; Homeland Security Advisor, 2001–2003
Bruce Riedel	Senior Director for Near East and South Asia, NSC, 1997–2001
Christina Rocca	Assistant Secretary of State for South Asia, 2001–
Michael Rolince	FBI Section Chief, International Terrorism Operations Section, 1998–2002
Donald Rumsfeld	Secretary of Defense, 2001–
Peter Schoomaker	Commander, Special Operations Command, 1997–2000
Gary Schroen	CIA Station Chief, Islamabad, 1996–1999
Michael Sheehan	Counterterrorism Coordinator, U.S. Department of State, 1998–2000
Hugh Shelton	Chairman of the Joint Chiefs of Staff, 1997–2001
Walter Slocombe	Under Secretary of Defense for Policy, 1994–2001
James Steinberg	Deputy National Security Advisor, 1996–2000
Strobe Talbott	Deputy Secretary of State, 1994–2001
George Tenet	Director of Central Intelligence, 1997–2004
Larry Thompson	Deputy Attorney General, 2001–2003
Dale Watson	Executive Assistant Director for Counterterrorism and Counterintelligence, FBI, 2001–2002
Paul Wolfowitz	Deputy Secretary of Defense, 2001–
Anthony Zinni	Commander, U.S. Central Command (CENTCOM), 1997–2000

OTHERS

Abdullah bin Abdul Aziz	Crown Prince and de facto regent of Saudi Arabia, 1995–
Mohdar Abdullah	Yemeni; student in San Diego who assisted two 9/11 hijackers
Sayf al Adl	Egyptian; high-ranking member of al Qaeda military committee
Mahmud Ahmed	Director General of Pakistan's Inter-Services Intelligence Directorate, 1999–2001
Mohammed Farrah Aidid	Somali warlord who challenged U.S. presence in Somalia in the early 1990s (deceased)

Ali Abdul Aziz Ali	(a.k.a. Ammar al Baluchi) Pakistani; KSM's nephew; financial and travel facilitator for 9/11 plot
Ahmad Khalil Ibrahim Samir al Ani	Iraqi intelligence officer who allegedly met with Atta in Prague, Czech Republic; currently in U.S. custody
Mohamed Atta	Egyptian; tactical leader of 9/11 plot; pilot/hijacker (AA 11) (deceased)
Mohammed Atef	(a.k.a. Abu Hafs al Masri) Egyptian; al Qaeda military commander (deceased)
Tawfiq bin Attash	(a.k.a. Khallad, Waleed bin Attash) Yemeni; senior al Qaeda operative connected to the U.S. embassy bombings, the USS *Cole* attack, and the 9/11 attacks; currently in U.S. custody
Anwar Aulaqi	U.S. citizen; Imam at Rabat mosque (San Diego, CA) and later at Dar al Hijra mosque (Falls Church, VA), who associated with two 9/11 hijackers
Abdullah Azzam	Palestinian; founder of the Maktab al Khidmat, which provided logistical support to mujahideen in Afghanistan (deceased)
Jamal al Badawi	Yemeni; co-conspirator arrested in Yemen for the USS *Cole* attack
Said Bahaji	German son of Moroccan immigrant; Hamburg cell associate
Saeed al Baluchi	Saudi; candidate 9/11 hijacker
Fayez Banihammad	Emirati; 9/11 hijacker (UA 175) (deceased)
Abu Ubaidah al Banshiri	Egyptian; al Qaeda military commander until 1996 (deceased)
Abu Bara al Yemeni	(a.k.a. Abu al Bara al Ta'izi, Suhail Shurabi, and Barakat) Yemeni; potential suicide bomber in original 9/11 plot
Ramzi Binalshibh	Yemeni; Hamburg cell member; coordinator for 9/11 plot; currently in U.S. custody
Omar Hassan Ahmed al Bashir	President of Sudan, 1989–
Abu Bakar Bashir	Indonesian; spiritual leader and founder of Jemaah Islamiya, al Qaeda–affiliated terrorist group in Southeast Asia
Omar al Bayoumi	Saudi; assisted two 9/11 hijackers in San Diego, CA
Khalil Deek	U.S. citizen; created electronic version of *Encyclopedia of Jihad*; believed to be involved in millen-

nium plot to destroy tourist landmarks in Jordan

Caysan Bin Don	(a.k.a Isamu Dyson, a.k.a Clayton Morgan) U.S. citizen; met two 9/11 hijackers in Los Angeles and San Diego, CA
Zakariya Essabar	Moroccan; Hamburg cell associate
Jamal Ahmed Mohamed al Fadl	Sudanese; al Qaeda member who defected to the United States in 1996
Ahmed al Ghamdi	Saudi; 9/11 hijacker (UA 175) (deceased)
Ali Abd al Rahman al Faqasi al Ghamdi	(a.k.a. Abu Bakr al Azdi) Saudi; candidate 9/11 hijacker; currently in U.S. custody
Hamza al Ghamdi	Saudi; 9/11 hijacker (UA 175) (deceased)
Saeed al Ghamdi	Saudi; 9/11 hijacker (UA 93) (deceased)
Saeed ("Jihad") al Ghamdi	Saudi; candidate 9/11 hijacker
Hassan Ghul	Pakistani; al Qaeda facilitator; currently in U.S. custody
Abu Hafs al Masri	see Mohammed Atef
Abu Hafs al Mauritani	Mauritanian; senior al Qaeda theologian
Wadi al Hage	U.S. citizen; al Qaeda operative; Bin Ladin's personal assistant; convicted in embassy bombings trial
Mushabib al Hamlan	Saudi; candidate 9/11 hijacker
Hani Hanjour	Saudi; 9/11 pilot/hijacker (AA 77) (deceased)
Mustafa al Hawsawi	Saudi; al Qaeda media committee member; financial and travel facilitator for 9/11 plot
Nawaf al Hazmi	Saudi; 9/11 hijacker (AA 77) (deceased)
Salem al Hazmi	Saudi; 9/11 hijacker (AA 77) (deceased)
Ahmad al Haznawi	Saudi; 9/11 hijacker (UA 93) (deceased)
Gulbuddin Hekmatyar	Afghani; founder and leader of the Hizb-e-Islami, a Taliban opposition group; Prime Minister of Afghanistan, 1993–1994; 1996
Saddam Hussein	President of Iraq, 1979-2003
Zein al Abideen Mohamed Hussein	(a.k.a. Abu Zubaydah) Palestinian; al Qaeda associate; currently in U.S. custody
Abu Hajer al Iraqi	see Mamdouh Mahmud Salim
Riduan Isamuddin	(a.k.a. Hambali) Indonesian; operational leader of Jemaah Islamiya; currently in U.S. custody
Ziad Jarrah	Lebanese; 9/11 pilot/hijacker (UA 93) (deceased)
Abderraouf Jdey	(a.k.a. Faruq al Tunisi) Tunisian/Canadian; candidate 9/11 hijacker

Mohamed al Kahtani	Saudi; candidate 9/11 hijacker; currently in U.S. custody
Mir Amal Kansi	Pakistani; extremist who killed two CIA employees at CIA headquarters in Virginia in 1993 (executed)
Hamid Karzai	Interim Leader and later President of Afghanistan, Dec. 2001–
Younis Khalis	Afghani; leader of Hizb-e-Islami; hosted UBL upon his return to Afghanistan in 1996
Khallad	*see* Tawfiq bin Attash
Wali Khan Amin Shah	(a.k.a. Osama Asmurai) Turkmen; early associate of Usama Bin Ladin; convicted in Manila air (Bojinka) plot
Ibn al Khattab	Saudi; mujahid leader in Chechnya
L'Houssaine Kherchtou	(a.k.a. Joe the Moroccan, Abu Talal) Moroccan; former al Qaeda member who broke with Bin Ladin and became a U.S. government informant
Usama Bin Ladin	(UBL) Saudi; head of al Qaeda
Ibn al Shaykh al Libi	Libyan; head of jihadist training camp in Afghanistan
Ahmed al Nami	Saudi; 9/11 hijacker (UA 93) (deceased)
Sheikh Saeed al Masri	Egyptian; head of al Qaeda finance committee
Ahmed Shah Massoud	Leader of Afghanistan's Northern Alliance, a Taliban opposition group (assassinated Sept. 9, 2001)
Khalid al Mihdhar	Saudi; 9/11 hijacker (AA 77) (deceased)
Khalid Sheikh Mohammed	(KSM) (a.k.a. Mukhtar) Pakistani; mastermind of 9/11 attacks; currently in U.S. custody
Majed Moqed	Saudi; 9/11 hijacker (AA 77) (deceased)
Mounir el Motassadeq	Moroccan; Hamburg cell associate
Zacarias Moussaoui	French; arrested in the U.S. in connection with the 9/11 attacks
Hosni Mubarak	President of Egypt, 1981–
Pervez Musharraf	Leader of Pakistan, 1999–
Abdelghani Mzoudi	Moroccan; Hamburg cell associate
Qutaybah al Najdi	Saudi; candidate 9/11 hijacker
Abd al Rahim al Nashiri	(a.k.a. Mullah Bilal) Saudi; mastermind of USS *Cole* attack; currently in U.S. custody
Mullah Mohammed Omar	Leader of Afghanistan's Taliban, which ruled most of the country from 1996 to 2001
Abdul Aziz al Omari	Saudi; 9/11 hijacker (AA 11) (deceased)
Muammar Qadhafi	Leader of Libya, 1970–

Fahd al Quso	Yemeni; al Qaeda co-conspirator arrested in Yemen for the USS *Cole* attack
Sayyid Qutb	Egyptian writer; member of Muslim Brotherhood (deceased)
Eyad al Rababah	Jordanian; Virginia resident who helped Hazmi and Hanjour
Abd al Rahim Ghulum Rabbani	(a.k.a. Abu Rahmah) Saudi; al Qaeda member who worked closely with KSM in Karachi and assisted many of the 9/11 hijackers
Sheikh Omar Abdel Rahman	(a.k.a. the Blind Sheikh) Egyptian cleric; convicted for crimes related to 1993 World Trade Center bombing and 1995 plots against other NY landmarks
Saud al Rashid	Saudi; candidate 9/11 hijacker
Ahmed Ressam	(a.k.a. Benni Antoine Noris) Algerian; convicted in millennium plot to bomb Los Angeles International Airport
Mamdouh Mahmud Salim	(a.k.a. Abu Hajer al Iraqi) Iraqi; chief procurement officer for al Qaeda in Sudan; arrested in connection with 1998 embassy bombings
Yazeed al Salmi	Saudi; briefly a housemate of a 9/11 hijacker in San Diego
Abdul Rasul Sayyaf	Afghani; head of the Hizbul-Ittihad El-Islami, and KSM's mentor
Aysel Senguen	German; fiancée of 9/11 hijacker Jarrah
Nawaz Sharif	Pakistani Prime Minister, 1990–1993, 1997–1999
Marwan al Shehhi	Emirati; 9/11 pilot/hijacker (UA 175) (deceased)
Mohand al Shehri	Saudi; 9/11 hijacker (UA 175) (deceased)
Wail al Shehri	Saudi; 9/11 hijacker (AA 11) (deceased)
Waleed al Shehri	Saudi; 9/11 hijacker (AA 11) (deceased)
Mohamedou Ould Slahi	(a.k.a. Abu Musab) Mauritanian; recruited 9/11 hijackers in Germany
Yazid Sufaat	Malaysian; member of Jemaah Islamiya
Satam al Suqami	Saudi; 9/11 hijacker (AA 11) (deceased)
Madani al Tayyib	Saudi; former head of al Qaeda finance committee
Zuhair al Thubaiti	Saudi; candidate 9/11 hijacker
Fahad al Thumairy	Saudi; Imam of King Fahd mosque in Los Angeles; accredited diplomat at Saudi Consulate in Los Angeles
Hassan al Turabi	Sudan's longtime hard-line ideological leader and Speaker of the country's National Assembly

	during the 1990s
Prince Turki bin Faisal	Saudi intelligence chief prior to 9/11
Ramzi Yousef	(a.k.a. Abdul Basit) Pakistani; convicted master-mind of and co-conspirator in 1993 WTC bombing and Manila air (Bojinka) plots
Khalid Saeed Ahmad al Zahrani	Saudi; candidate 9/11 hijacker
Mohammed Haydar Zammar	German citizen from Syria; jihadist; possible recruiter of Hamburg cell members
Ayman al Zawahiri	Egyptian; UBL's deputy and leader of Egyptian Islamic Jihad terrorist group
Hamdan Bin Zayid	Emirati; Minister of State for Foreign Affairs of the United Arab Emirates
Abu Zubaydah	*see* Zein al Abideen Mohamed Hussein

APPENDIX C

COMMISSION HEARINGS

The Commission held 12 public hearings during the course of its investigation, convening for a total of 19 days and receiving testimony from 160 witnesses. The following is a list of hearings and witnesses in order of their appearance. All witnesses appearing during the 2004 calendar year testified under oath.

FIRST PUBLIC HEARING
Alexander Hamilton Customs House, New York, N.Y.
March 31–April 1, 2003

The Honorable George Pataki, Governor, State of New York
The Honorable Michael R. Bloomberg, Mayor, City of New York

The Experience of the Attack
Harry Waizer, survivor, Cantor Fitzgerald, LP
David Lim, Police Department, Port Authority of New York and New Jersey
Lee Ielpi, Fire Department of New York (retired)
Lieutenant Colonel Brian Birdwell, United States Army
Craig Sincock, United States Army (retired)

Representatives of the Victims
Stephen Push, Families of September 11
Mary Fetchet, Voices of September 11
Mindy Kleinberg, September 11 Advocates
Allison Vadhan, Families of Flight 93

The Attackers, Intelligence, and Counterterrorism Policy
Daniel Byman, Georgetown University
Abraham D. Sofaer, Hoover Institution
Brian Jenkins, RAND Corporation
Magnus Ranstorp, University of St. Andrews

Borders, Money, and Transportation Security
Glenn Fine, Inspector General, U.S. Department of Justice
Lee Wolosky, Boies, Schiller & Flexner LLP
Gerald Dillingham, Director, Civil Aviation Issues, General Accounting Office

Law Enforcement, Domestic Intelligence, and Homeland Security
Michael Wermuth, RAND Corporation
Steven Brill, Author, *After: How America Confronted the September 12 Era*
Zoë Baird, Markle Foundation
Randy Larsen, ANSER Institute for Homeland Security

Immediate Response to the Attacks
Shawn Kelley, Assistant Chief, Arlington County Fire Department
William Baker, American Society of Civil Engineers
Ken Holden, Commissioner, New York City Department of Design and Construction

SECOND PUBLIC HEARING
Congress and Civil Aviation Security
Hart Senate Office Building, Washington, D.C.
May 22–23, 2003

Congressional Oversight
Representative Nancy Pelosi (D-Calif.)
Senator John McCain (R-Az.)
Senator Joseph Lieberman (D-Conn.)

Intelligence Oversight and the Joint Inquiry
Senator Bob Graham (D-Fla.)
Senator Richard Shelby (R-Ala.)
Representative Porter Goss (R-Fla.)
Representative Jane Harman (D-Calif.)

Affected Constituencies
Senator Charles Schumer (D-N.Y.)
Senator Hillary Rodham Clinton (D-N.Y.)
Senator Jon Corzine (D-N.J.)
Senator Frank Lautenberg (D-N.J.)
Representative Jerrold Nadler (D-N.Y.)
Representative Christopher Shays (R-Conn.)

State of the System: Civil Aviation Security on September 11
Jane Garvey, former Administrator, Federal Aviation Administration
Kenneth Mead, Inspector General, Department of Transportation
James May, Air Transport Association of America

Bogdan Dzakovic, Civil Aviation Security Inspector,
   Transportation Security Agency

September 11, 2001: The Attacks and the Response
The Honorable Norman Mineta, Secretary of Transportation
Major General Craig McKinley, Commander, 1st Air Force and the
   Continental United States NORAD Region (CONR)
Lieutenant General Mike Canavan (retired), former Associate Administrator for
   Civil Aviation Security, Federal Aviation Administrator

Reforming Civil Aviation Security: Next Steps
Stephen McHale, Deputy Administrator, Transportation Security Agency
Major General O.K. Steele (retired), former Associate Administrator for
   Civil Aviation Security, Federal Aviation Administration
Mary Schiavo, former Inspector General, Department of Transportation

THIRD PUBLIC HEARING
Terrorism, al Qaeda, and the Muslim World
Russell Senate Office Building, Washington, D.C.
July 9, 2003

Al Qaeda
Rohan Gunaratna, Institute for Defence and Strategic Studies
Mamoun Fandy, United States Institute of Peace
Marc Sageman, University of Pennsylvania

States and Terrorism
Laurie Mylroie, American Enterprise Institute
Judith Yaphe, National Defense University
Murhaf Jouejati, Middle East Institute and George Washington University
Mark Gasiorowski, Louisiana State University

The Challenge within the Muslim World
Rachel Bronson, Council on Foreign Relations
Steven Emerson, The Investigative Project
Gilles Kepel, Institute of Political Studies, Paris
Dennis Ross, Washington Institute for Near East Policy

FOURTH PUBLIC HEARING
Intelligence and the War on Terrorism
Russell Senate Office Building, Washington, D.C.
October 14, 2003

Leadership of U.S. Intelligence
James R. Schlesinger, former Director of Central Intelligence and
   Secretary of Defense

John M. Deutch, former Director of Central Intelligence and
Deputy Secretary of Defense

Intelligence and National Security Policy
James B. Steinberg, The Brookings Institution and former Deputy
National Security Advisor

Warning of Transnational Threats
Richard Kerr, former Deputy Director of Central Intelligence
Mary O. McCarthy, former National Intelligence Officer for Warning,
Central Intelligence Agency
John Gannon, Staff Director, House Select Committee on Homeland Security

FIFTH PUBLIC HEARING
Private/Public Sector Partnerships for Emergency Preparedness
Drew University, Madison, N.J.
November 19, 2003

Highlights of New Jersey's Public/Private Sector Partnerships
The Honorable James E. McGreevey, Governor, State of New Jersey

The Challenge of Private Sector Preparedness
John Degnan, The Chubb Corporation

Skyscraper Safety Issues from 9/11 Family Members
Monica Gabrielle, Skyscraper Safety Campaign
Sally Regenhard, Skyscraper Safety Campaign

Public/Private Initiatives Since 9/11
Michael F. Byrne, Director, Office of National Capital Region Coordination,
Department of Homeland Security
Dennis J. Reimer, Oklahoma National Memorial Institute for
Prevention of Terrorism
Richard A. Andrews, National Center for Crisis and Continuity Coordination

Private Sector Experience on 9/11
William Y. Yun, Fiduciary Trust Company International

**Standards for Emergency Management and
Business Continuity**
Glenn Corbett, John Jay College of Criminal Justice
Randall Yim, Director, National Preparedness Team, General Accounting Office

Future Strategies for Private Sector Preparedness
William G. Raisch, Greater New York Safety Council
Peter R. Orszag, The Brookings Institution
James Haviaris, Rockefeller Group Development Corporation
Thomas Susman, Ropes & Gray

SIXTH PUBLIC HEARING
Security and Liberty
Russell Senate Office Building, Washington, D.C.
December 8, 2003

Intelligence Collection within the United States
Larry D. Thompson, former Deputy Attorney General of the United States
Philip B. Heymann, former Deputy Attorney General of the United States
Stephen J. Schulhofer, New York University, School of Law

Protecting Privacy, Preventing Terrorism
Judith A. Miller, former General Counsel, Department of Defense
Stewart A. Baker, former General Counsel, National Security Agency
Marc Rotenberg, Electronic Privacy Information Center

Preventive Detention: Use of Immigration Laws and Enemy Combatant Designations to Combat Terrorism
Jan Ting, Temple University
Khaled Medhat Abou El Fadl, UCLA School of Law
David Martin, University of Virginia School of Law and former General
    Counsel, Immigration and Naturalization Service, Department of Justice

Government Organization and Domestic Intelligence
The Honorable William P. Barr, former Attorney General of the United States
John J. Hamre, former Deputy Secretary of Defense
John MacGaffin, former Associate Deputy Director for Operations,
    Central Intelligence Agency

SEVENTH PUBLIC HEARING
Borders, Transportation, and Managing Risk
Hart Senate Office Building, Washington, D.C.
January 26–27, 2004

The Border Security System Prior to September 11
Mary A. Ryan, former Assistant Secretary for Consular Affairs,
    Department of State
Doris Meissner, former Commissioner, Immigration and Naturalization Service,
    Department of Justice

An Incident in Florida
Jose E. Melendez-Perez, Inspector, Customs and Border Protection,
    Department of Homeland Security

Visas and Watchlisting Today
Maura Harty, Assistant Secretary for Consular Affairs, Department of State
Russell E. Travers, Deputy Director, Information Sharing and Knowledge

Management Department, Terrorist Threat Integration Center, Central Intelligence Agency

Donna A. Bucella, Director, Terrorist Screening Center, Federal Bureau of Investigation

The Response to September 11 on the Borders

James Ziglar, former Commissioner, Immigration and Naturalization Service, Department of Justice

Robert C. Bonner, Commissioner, Customs and Border Protection, Department of Homeland Security

Peter F. Verga, Principal Deputy Assistant Secretary for Homeland Defense, Department of Defense

Aviation Security on 9/11: The Regulators

Jane F. Garvey, former Administrator, Federal Aviation Administration

Cathal L. "Irish" Flynn, former Associate Administrator of Civil Aviation Security, Federal Aviation Administration

Claudio Manno, Assistant Administrator for Intelligence, Transportation Security Administration

Aviation Security on 9/11: The Airlines

Edmond L. Soliday, former Vice President of Safety, Quality Assurance, and Security, United Airlines

Andrew P. Studdert, former Chief Operating Officer, United Airlines

Gerard J. Arpey, Chief Executive Officer, American Airlines

Timothy J. Ahern, Vice President–DFW Hub, and former Vice President of Safety, Security, and Environmental, American Airlines

Acts of Courage in the Sky

Nydia Gonzalez, Manager, Southeast Reservations Center, American Airlines

Risk Management after September 11

James M. Loy, Deputy Secretary, Department of Homeland Security

EIGHTH PUBLIC HEARING

Counterterrorism Policy
Hart Senate Office Building, Washington, D.C.
March 23–24, 2004

Diplomacy

The Honorable Madeleine K. Albright, former Secretary of State

The Honorable Colin L. Powell, Secretary of State

The Military

The Honorable William S. Cohen, former Secretary of Defense

The Honorable Donald H. Rumsfeld, Secretary of Defense

Intelligence Policy

The Honorable George J. Tenet, Director of Central Intelligence

National Policy Coordination

The Honorable Samuel R. Berger, former Assistant to the President for
    National Security Affairs
Richard A. Clarke, former National Coordinator for Counterterrorism,
    National Security Council
Richard L. Armitage, Deputy Secretary of State

NINTH PUBLIC HEARING
Hart Senate Office Building, Washington, D.C.
April 8, 2004

The Honorable Condoleezza Rice, Assistant to the President for
    National Security Affairs

TENTH PUBLIC HEARING
Law Enforcement and Intelligence
Hart Senate Office Building, Washington, D.C.
April 13–14, 2004

**Law Enforcement, Counterterrorism, and Intelligence Collection in
    the United States Prior to 9/11**

The Honorable Louis J. Freeh, former Director, Federal Bureau of Investigation
The Honorable Janet Reno, former Attorney General of the United States

Threats and Responses in 2001

Thomas J. Pickard, former Acting Director, Federal Bureau of Investigation
Ambassador J. Cofer Black, former Director, Counterterrorism Center,
    Central Intelligence Agency
The Honorable John Ashcroft, Attorney General of the United States

The Performance of the Intelligence Community

The Honorable George J. Tenet, Director of Central Intelligence

Preventing Future Attacks Inside the United States

John O. Brennan, Director, Terrorist Threat Integration Center,
    Central Intelligence Agency
Lieutenant General Patrick M. Hughes, Assistant Secretary for Information
    Analysis, Department of Homeland Security
John S. Pistole, Executive Assistant Director for Counterterrorism and
    Counterintelligence, Federal Bureau of Investigation
James L. Pavitt, Deputy Director of Operations, Central Intelligence Agency

FBI Leadership and Initiatives Post-9/11

The Honorable Robert S. Mueller III, Director, Federal Bureau of Investigation
Maureen Baginski, Executive Assistant Director for Intelligence,
    Federal Bureau of Investigation

ELEVENTH PUBLIC HEARING
Emergency Response
New School University, New York, N.Y.
May 18–19, 2004

Alan Reiss, former Director, World Trade Center, Port Authority of
New York and New Jersey
Joseph Morris, former Chief, Port Authority of New York and
New Jersey Police Department
Bernard B. Kerik, former Commissioner, New York Police Department
Thomas Von Essen, former Commissioner, Fire Department of New York
Richard Sheirer, former Director, New York City Office of
Emergency Management
Raymond W. Kelly, Commissioner, New York Police Department
Nicholas Scoppetta, Commissioner, Fire Department of New York
Joseph F. Bruno, Director, New York City Office of Emergency Management
The Honorable Rudolph W. Giuliani, former Mayor, City of New York
Dennis Smith, Author, *Report from Ground Zero*
Jerome M. Hauer, former Commissioner, New York City Office of
Emergency Management
Edward P. Plaugher, Chief, Arlington County Fire Department
The Honorable Michael R. Bloomberg, Mayor, City of New York
The Honorable Thomas J. Ridge, Secretary of Homeland Security

TWELFTH PUBLIC HEARING
The 9/11 Plot and National Crisis Management
National Transportation Safety Board Conference Center,
Washington, D.C.
June 16–17, 2004

Al Qaeda
Mary Deborah Doran, Special Agent, Federal Bureau of Investigation
Patrick J. Fitzgerald, U.S. Attorney for the Northern District of Illinois
CIA Officials

Outline of the 9/11 Plot
Jacqueline Maguire, Special Agent, Federal Bureau of Investigation
James N. Fitzgerald, Special Agent, Federal Bureau of Investigation
Adam B. Drucker, Supervisory Special Agent, Federal Bureau of Investigation
CIA Officials

Military Response on 9/11
General Richard B. Myers, United States Air Force, Chairman,
Joint Chiefs of Staff

Admiral (select) Charles Joseph Leidig, United States Navy,
  Deputy Director for Operations, National Military Command Center
General Ralph E. Eberhart, United States Air Force, Commander,
  North American Aerospace Defense Command (NORAD) and
  United States Northern Command
Major General Larry Arnold, United States Air Force (retired),
  former Commander, Continental United States NORAD Region (CONR)

FAA Response on 9/11

Monte R. Belger, former Acting Deputy Administrator, Federal Aviation
  Administration
Jeff Griffith, former Deputy Director, Air Traffic Control,
  Federal Aviation Administration
John S. White, former Facility Manager, Air Traffic Control Systems
  Command Center, Federal Aviation Administration
Benedict Sliney, Operations Manager, New York Terminal Radar Approach
  Control, Federal Aviation Administration

NOTES

For simplicity, we have adopted the following citation conventions in these endnotes.

Dozens of government agencies and other entities provided the Commission with more than 2.5 million pages of documents and other materials, including more than 1,000 hours of audiotapes. In general, we cite documents and other materials by providing the agency or entity of origin, the type of document (e.g., memo, email, report, or record), the author and recipient, the title (in quotes) or a description of the subject, and the date. We use the following abbreviations for the agencies and entities that produced the bulk of these documents: AAL—American Airlines; CIA—Central Intelligence Agency; DCI—Director of Central Intelligence; DHS—Department of Homeland Security; DOD—Department of Defense; DOJ—Department of Justice; DOS—Department of State; DOT—Department of Transportation; EPA—Environmental Protection Agency; FAA—Federal Aviation Administration; FBI—Federal Bureau of Investigation; FDNY—Fire Department of New York; GAO—General Accounting Office; INS—Immigration and Naturalization Service; NEADS—Northeast Air Defense Sector; NSA—National Security Agency; NSC—National Security Council; NTSB—National Transportation Safety Board; NYPD—New York Police Department; OEM—Office of Emergency Management, City of New York; PANYNJ or Port Authority—Port Authority of New York and New Jersey; PAPD—Port Authority Police Department; SEC—Securities and Exchange Commission; Treasury—Department of Treasury; TSA—Transportation Security Administration; UAL—United Air Lines; USSS—United States Secret Service.

Interviews, meetings, briefings, and site visits conducted by Commissioners or by members of the Commission staff are cited, for example, as "George Tenet interview (Jan. 22, 2004)." Testimony by witnesses at one of the Commission's 12 public hearings is cited as "Condoleezza Rice testimony, Apr. 8, 2004."Written statements for the record provided by witnesses at one of our public hearings are cited as "Thomas Ridge prepared statement, May 19, 2004."

At the request of intelligence community agencies (including the FBI), we use the first name and last initial, only the first name, or in a few instances an alias or title when referring to working-level employees in those agencies. At the request of several intelligence agencies, we cite most reports from the CIA and other intelligence agencies generically as "Intelligence report," followed by a description of the subject and date. In a few instances in which we were given access to highly sensitive documents or information, we cite generically to documents or information provided to the Commission.

Our investigation built on the work of many others, including the Joint Inquiry of the Senate Select Committee on Intelligence and the House Permanent Select Committee on Intelligence into Intelligence Community Activities Before and After the Terrorist Attacks of September 11, 2001, which we refer to as the "Joint Inquiry." We cite as "Joint Inquiry report, Dec. 2002" the Report of the U.S. Senate Select Committee on Intelligence and U.S. House Permanent Select Committee on Intelligence, S. Rep. No. 107-351, H.R. Rep. No. 107-792, 107th Cong., 2d sess. (2002), indicating "classified version" where appropriate. Testimony presented during hearings conducted by the Joint Inquiry is cited as "Joint Inquiry testimony of George Tenet, Oct. 17, 2002," indicating "closed hearing" where appropriate. We cite interviews conducted by the Joint Inquiry staff as "Joint Inquiry interview of Cofer Black," with the date of the interview.

Another major source for our investigation were the thousands of interviews conducted by the Federal Bureau of Investigation during its investigation of the 9/11 attacks, which it refers to as "Penttbom." FBI agents write up their interviews on forms called 302s, which we cite as "FBI report of investigation, interview of John Smith, Oct. 4, 2001," using the date of the interview. We cite interviews conducted by other agencies by agency name and date of the interview; for example, an interview conducted by the Department of Justice Office of Inspector General is cited as "DOJ Inspector General interview of Mary Jones, July 9, 2002."

1 "We Have Some Planes"

1. No physical, documentary, or analytical evidence provides a convincing explanation of why Atta and Omari drove to Portland, Maine, from Boston on the morning of September 10, only to return to Logan on Flight 5930 on the morning of September 11. However, Atta reacted negatively when informed in Portland that he would have to check in again in Boston. Michael Touhey interview (May 27, 2004). Whatever their reason, the Portland Jetport was the nearest airport to Boston with a 9/11 flight that would have arrived at Logan in time for the passengers to transfer to American Airlines Flight 11, which had a scheduled departure time of 7:45 A.M. See Tom Kinton interview (Nov. 6, 2003); Portland International Jetport site visit (Aug. 18, 2003).

Like the other two airports used by the 9/11 hijackers (Newark Liberty International Airport and Washington Dulles International Airport), Boston's Logan International Airport was a "Category X" airport: i.e., among the largest facilities liable to highest threat, and generally subject to greater security requirements. See FAA report, "Civil Aviation Security Reference Handbook," May 1999, pp. 117–118. Though Logan was selected for two of the hijackings (as were both American and United Airlines), we found no evidence that the terrorists targeted particular airports or airlines. Nothing stands out about any of them with respect to the only security layer that was relevant to the actual hijackings: checkpoint screening. See FAA briefing materials, "Assessment and Testing Data for BOS, EWR, and IAD," Oct. 24, 2001. Despite security problems at Logan (see, e.g., two local Fox 25 television investigative reports in February and April 2001, and an email in August 2001 from a former FAA special agent to the agency's leadership regarding his concerns about lax security at the airport), no evidence suggests that such issues entered into the terrorists' targeting: they simply booked heavily fueled east-to-west transcontinental flights of the large Boeing aircraft they trained to fly that were scheduled to take off at nearly the same time. See Matt Carroll, "Fighting Terror Sense of Alarm; Airlines Foiled Police Logan Probe," *Boston Globe,* Oct. 17, 2001, p. B1.

2. CAPPS was an FAA-approved automated system run by the airlines that scored each passenger's profile to identify those who might pose a threat to civil aviation. The system also chose passengers at random to receive additional security scrutiny. Ten out of the 19 hijackers (including 9 out of 10 on the two American Airlines flights) were identified via the CAPPS system. According to the procedures in place on 9/11, in addition to those flagged by the CAPPS algorithm, American's ticket agents were to mark as "selectees" those passengers who did not provide correct responses to the required security questions, failed to show proper identification, or met other criteria. See FAA report, "Air Carrier Standard Security Program," May 2001, pp. 75–76; FAA record of interview, Donna Thompson, Sept. 23, 2001; Chuck Severance interview (Apr. 15, 2004); Jim Dillon interview (Apr. 15, 2004); Diane Graney interview (Apr. 16, 2004). It appears that Atta was selected at random. See Al Hickson briefing (June 8, 2004).

3. The call was placed from a pay phone in Terminal C (between the screening checkpoint and United 175's boarding gate). We presume Shehhi made the call, but we cannot be sure. Logan International Airport site visit (Aug. 15, 2003); see also FBI response to Commission briefing request no. 6, undated (topic 11).

4. Flight 11 pushed back from Gate 32 in Terminal B at 7:40. See AAL response to the Commission's February 3, 2004, requests, Mar. 15, 2004.

5. See UAL letter, "Flight 175—11Sep01 Passenger ACI Check-in History," July 11, 2002. Customer service representative Gail Jawahir recalled that her encounter with the Ghamdis occurred at "shortly before 7 A.M.," and when shown photos of the hijackers, she indicated that Mohand al Shehri resembled one of the two she checked in (suggesting they were Banihammad and Shehri). However, she also recalled that the men had the same last name and had assigned seats on row 9 (i.e., the Ghamdis), and that account has been adopted here. In either case, she almost certainly was dealing with one set of the Flight 175 hijackers. See FBI reports of investigation, interviews of Gail Jawahir, Sept. 21, 2001; Sept. 28, 2001. Even had the hijackers been unable to understand and answer the two standard security questions, the only consequence would have been the screening of their carry-on and checked bags for explosives. See FAA report, "Air Carrier Standard Security Program," May 2001, p. 76.

6. For Flight 11, two checkpoints provided access to the gate. The second was opened at 7:15 A.M. The FAA conducted many screener evaluations between September 11, 1999, and September 11, 2001. At the primary checkpoints, in aggregate, screeners met or exceeded the average for overall, physical search, and X-ray detection, while falling below the norm for metal detection. No FAA Special Assessments (by "red teams") were done at Logan security checkpoints during the two years prior to September 11, 2001. See FAA briefing materials, "Assessment and Testing Data for BOS, EWR, and IAD," Oct. 24, 2001.

7. See Air Transport Association/Regional Airlines Association (ATA/RAA) report, "Air Carriers Checkpoint Operations Guide," Aug. 1999; FAA report, "Air Carrier Standard Security Program," May 2001, appendix VI.

8. Mary Carol Turano interview (Mar. 11, 2004); FBI reports of investigation, interview of Nilda Cora, Oct. 4, 2001; interview of William Thomas, Sept. 14, 2001; interview of Jennifer Gore, Sept. 12, 2001; interview of Claudia Richey, Sept. 15, 2001; interview of Rosarito Rivera, Sept. 25, 2001.

9. See TSA report, "Selectee Status of September 11th Hijackers," undated. For boarding and seating information, see AAL record, SABRE information on Flight 11, Sept. 11, 2001. These boarding times from the American system are approximate only; for Flight 11, they indicated that some passengers "boarded" after the aircraft had pushed back from the gate. See AAL response to the Commission's February 3, 2004, requests, Mar. 15, 2004.

10. See TSA report, "Selectee Status of September 11th Hijackers," undated; see also UAL letter, "Flight 175—11 Sep01 Passenger ACI Check-in History," July 11, 2002.

11. The Hazmis checked in at 7:29; the airline has not yet been able to confirm the time of Hanjour's check-in. However, it had to have taken place by 7:35, when he appears on the checkpoint videotape. See AAL record, SABRE information for Flight 77, Sept. 11, 2001; AAL response to the Commission's February 3, 2004, requests, Mar. 15, 2004; Metropolitan Washington Airports Authority videotape, Dulles main terminal checkpoints, Sept. 11, 2001.

12. See TSA report, "Selectee Status of September 11th Hijackers," undated; see also FAA report, "Selectee List AALA #77," undated; FBI report of investigation, interview of Vaughn Allex, Sept. 12, 2001; Vaughn Allex interview (July 13, 2004).

13. The FAA conducted many screener evaluations at Dulles between September 11, 1999, and September 11, 2001. While the test results for physical search exceeded the national average, both the metal detector and X-ray results were below average. See FAA briefing materials, "Assessment and Testing Data for BOS, EWR, and IAD," Oct. 24, 2001.

14. Metropolitan Washington Airports Authority videotape, Dulles main terminal checkpoints, Sept. 11, 2001; see also Tim Jackson interview (Apr. 12, 2004).

15. Metropolitan Washington Airports Authority videotape, Dulles main terminal checkpoints, Sept. 11, 2001; see also Tim Jackson interview (Apr. 12, 2004).

16. For investigation findings, see FAA report, "American Airlines Flight #77: Hijacking and Crash into the Pentagon, Sept. 11, 2001," undated. For screener evaluations, see Tim Jackson interview (Apr. 12, 2004).

17. See AAL record, SABRE information for Flight 77, Sept. 11, 2001; AAL response to the Commission's February 3, 2004, requests, Mar. 15, 2004.

18. UAL record, Flight 93 EWR bag loading status, Sept. 11, 2001; UAL record, Flight 93 EWR ACI passenger history, Sept. 11, 2001; UAL record, Flight 93 EWR full bag history, Sept. 11, 2001; TSA report, "Selectee Status of September 11th Hijackers," undated; FBI report, "The Final 24 Hours," Dec. 8, 2003.

19. The FAA conducted many screener evaluations at Newark between September 11, 1999, and September 11, 2001. Detection rates for metal detection, physical searches, and X-rays all met or exceeded the national averages. See FAA briefing materials, "Assessment and Testing Data for BOS, EWR, and IAD," Oct. 24, 2001; see also FAA report, "United Airlines Flight 93, September 11, 2001, Executive Report," Jan. 30, 2002.

20. UAL record, Flight 93 EWR ACI passenger history, Sept. 11, 2001; see also FBI report, "The Final 24 Hours," Dec. 8, 2003.

21. While Flights 11 and 77 were at or slightly above the average number of passengers for the respective flights that summer, Flights 175 and 93 were well below their averages. We found no evidence to indicate that the hijackers manipulated the passenger loads on the aircraft they hijacked. Financial records did not reveal the purchase of any tickets beyond those the hijackers used for themselves. See FBI response to Commission briefing request no. 6, undated (topic 8); AAL report, "Average Load Factor by Day-of-Week," undated (for Flights 11 and 77 from June 11, 2001, to Sept. 9, 2001); AAL response to the Commission's supplemental document requests, Jan. 20, 2004; UAL report, Flight 175 BOS-LAX Load Factors, undated (from June 1, 2001, to Sept. 11, 2001); UAL report, "Explanation of Load Factors," undated.

22. See AAL response to the Commission's February 3, 2004, requests, Mar. 15, 2004; AAL record, Dispatch Environmental Control/Weekly Flight Summary for Flight 11, Sept. 11, 2001; AAL report, "Flight Attendant Jump Seat Locations During Takeoff And Flight Attendant Typical Cabin Positions During Start of Cabin Service," undated; AAL report, "Passenger Name List, Flight 11/September 11," undated.

23. Commission analysis of NTSB and FAA air traffic control and radar data. See AAL record, Dispatch Environmental Control/Weekly Flight Summary for Flight 11, Sept. 11, 2001; NTSB report, "Flight Path Study—American Airlines Flight 11," Feb. 19, 2002; Bill Halleck and Peggy Houck interview (Jan. 8, 2004). The initial service assignments for flight attendants on American 11 would have placed Karen Martin and Bobbi Arestegui in first class; Sara Low and Jean Roger in business class; Dianne Snyder in the midcabin galley; Betty Ong and Amy Sweeney in coach; and Karen Nicosia in the aft galley. Jeffrey Collman would have been assigned to work in coach, but to assist in first class if needed. See AAL report, "Flight Attendant Jump Seat Locations During Takeoff And Flight Attendant Typical Cabin Positions During Start of Cabin Service," undated; Bob Jordan briefing (Nov. 20, 2003).

24. NTSB report, Air Traffic Control Recording—American Airlines Flight 11, Dec. 21, 2001; NTSB report, Air Traffic Control Recording—United Airlines Flight 175, Dec. 21, 2001. Given that the cockpit crew of American 11 had been acknowledging all previous instructions from air traffic control that morning within a matter of seconds, and that when the first reporting of the hijacking was received a short time later (the 8:19 call from Betty Ong) a number of actions had already been taken by the hijackers, it is most likely that the hijacking occurred at 8:14 A.M.

25. An early draft of an executive summary prepared by FAA security staff for the agency's leadership referred to an alleged report of a shooting aboard Flight 11. We believe this report was erroneous for a number of reasons—there is no evidence that the hijackers purchased firearms, use of a gun would be inconsistent with the otherwise

common tactics employed by the hijackers, the alleged shooting victim was seated where witness accounts place the stabbing victim (9B), and, most important, neither Betty Ong nor Amy Sweeney, the only two people who communicated to the ground from aboard the aircraft, reported the presence of a gun or a shooting. Both reported knives and stabbings. AAL transcript, telephone call from Betty Ong to Nydia Gonzalez, Sept. 11, 2001; AAL transcript, telephone call from Nydia Gonzalez to Craig Marquis, Sept. 11, 2001; AAL transcript, telephone call from Nancy Wyatt to Ray Howland, Sept. 11, 2001; Michael Woodward interview (Jan. 25, 2004). The General Accounting Office looked into the gun story and was unable to corroborate it. GAO report, summary of briefing re investigation, Aug. 30, 2002.

26. Craig Marquis interview (Nov. 19, 2003); Michael Woodward interview (Jan. 25, 2004); Jim Dillon interview (Apr. 15, 2004). See also AAL transcript, telephone call from Betty Ong to Nydia Gonzalez, Sept. 11, 2001. At the time of the hijacking, American Airlines flight attendants all carried cockpit keys on their person. See Craig Marquis, Craig Parfitt, Joe Bertapelle, and Mike Mulcahy interview (Nov. 19, 2003).

27. AAL transcript, telephone call from Nydia Gonzalez to Craig Marquis, Sept. 11, 2001; Obituary, "Daniel Lewin," *Washington Post*, Sept. 22, 2001, p. B7.

28. AAL transcript, telephone call from Betty Ong to Nydia Gonzalez, Sept. 11, 2001; AAL transcript, telephone call from Nydia Gonzalez to Craig Marquis, Sept. 11, 2001. Regarding the claim of a bomb, see Michael Woodward interview (Jan. 25, 2004).

29. Calls to American's reservations office are routed to the first open line at one of several facilities, among them the center in Cary, N.C. See Nydia Gonzalez interview (Nov. 19, 2003). On standard emergency training, see FAA report, "Air Carrier Standard Security Program," May 2001, pp. 139j–139o; Don Dillman briefing (Nov. 18, 2003); Bob Jordan briefing (Nov. 20, 2003). The call from Ong was received initially by Vanessa Minter and then taken over by Winston Sadler; realizing the urgency of the situation, he pushed an emergency button that simultaneously initiated a tape recording of the call and sent an alarm notifying Nydia Gonzalez, a supervisor, to pick up on the line. Gonzalez was paged to respond to the alarm and joined the call a short time later. Only the first four minutes of the phone call between Ong and the reservations center (Minter, Sadler, and Gonzalez) was recorded because of the time limit on the recently installed system. See Nydia Gonzalez interview (Nov. 19, 2003); Nydia Gonzalez testimony, Jan. 27, 2004.

30. AAL transcript, telephone call from Betty Ong to Nydia Gonzalez, Sept. 11, 2001.

31. See Nydia Gonzalez interview (Nov. 19, 2003); Craig Marquis interviews (Nov. 19, 2003; Apr. 26, 2004); AAL record, Dispatch Environmental Control/Weekly Flight Summary for Flight 11, Sept. 11, 2001; AAL transcript, telephone call from Bill Halleck to BOS ATC, Sept. 11, 2001. The Air Carrier Standard Security Program required airlines to immediately notify the FAA and FBI upon receiving information that an act or suspected act of airplane piracy was being committed.

32. See FAA recording, Boston Air Route Traffic Control Center, position 46R, at 8:25 A.M.; Air Traffic Control Recording—American Airlines Flight 11, Dec. 21, 2001. Starting at 8:22, Amy Sweeney attempted by airphone to contact the American Airlines flight services office at Logan, which managed the scheduling and operation of flight attendants. Sweeney's first attempt failed, as did a second at 8:24. When she got through to Nunez, the latter thought she had reported her flight number as 12. Michael Woodward, supervisor at the Boston office, hearing that a problem had been reported aboard an American airplane, went to American's gate area at Logan with his colleague Beth Williams. Woodward noted that the morning bank of flights had all departed Boston and the gate area was quiet. He further realized that Flight 12 had not even departed yet, so he and Williams returned to the office to try to clarify the situation. See FBI report, "American Airlines Airphone Usage," Sept. 20, 2001; Michael Woodward interview (Jan. 25, 2004). The phone call between Sweeney and Woodward lasted about 12 minutes (8:32–8:44) and was not taped. See AAL email, Woodward to Schmidt, "Flight 11 Account of events," Sept. 19, 2001; AAL notes, Michael Woodward handwritten notes, Sept. 11, 2001; FBI report of investigation, interview of Michael Woodward, Sept. 13, 2001; AAL report, interview of Michael Woodward, Sept. 11, 2001; AAL transcript, telephone call from Nancy Wyatt to Ray Howland, Sept. 11, 2001.

33. See AAL transcript, telephone call from Nydia Gonzalez to Craig Marquis, Sept. 11, 2001; NTSB report, "Flight Path Study—American Airlines Flight 11," Feb. 19, 2002. AAL transcript, telephone call from Nydia Gonzalez to Craig Marquis, Sept. 11, 2001; AAL transcript, telephone call from Nancy Wyatt to Ray Howland, Sept. 11, 2001.

34. Michael Woodward interview (Jan. 25, 2004).

35. AAL transcript, telephone call from Nydia Gonzalez to Craig Marquis, Sept. 11, 2001; Michael Woodward interview (Jan. 25, 2004); AAL, Michael Woodward notes, Sept. 11, 2001. Also at this time American Airlines completed its "lockout" procedure for Flight 11, which restricted access to information about a hijacked flight in accordance with the Air Carrier Standard Security program. See FAA report, "Air Carrier Standard Security Program," May 2001, p. 110.

36. AAL transcript, telephone call from Nancy Wyatt to Ray Howland, Sept. 11, 2001; Michael Woodward interview (Jan. 25, 2004).

37. AAL transcript, telephone call from Nydia Gonzalez to Craig Marquis, Sept. 11, 2001.

38. Ibid.; Michael Woodward interview (Jan. 25, 2004).

39. NTSB report, "Flight Path Study—American Airlines Flight 11," Feb. 19, 2002.

40. The 56 passengers represented a load factor of 33.33 percent of the airplane's seating capacity of 168, below the 49.22 percent for Flight 175 on Tuesdays in the three-month period prior to September 11, 2001. See UAL report, Flight 175 BOS-LAX Load Factors, undated (from June 1, 2001, to Sept. 11, 2001). Nine passengers holding reservations for Flight 175 did not show for the flight. They were interviewed and cleared by the FBI. FAA report, "Executive Summary," Sept. 12, 2001; FAA report, "Executive Summary, Chronology of a Multiple Hijacking Crisis, September 11, 2001," Sept. 17, 2001; UAL record, Flight 175 ACARS report, Sept. 11, 2001; UAL record, Flight 175 Flight Data Recap, Sept. 11, 2001.

41. FAA report, "Executive Summary," Sept. 12, 2001; FAA report, "Executive Summary, Chronology of a Multiple Hijacking Crisis, September 11, 2001," Sept. 17, 2001; NTSB report, "Flight Path Study—United Airlines 175," Feb. 19, 2002; NTSB report, Air Traffic Control Recording—United Airlines Flight 175, Dec. 21, 2001. At or around this time, flight attendants Kathryn Laborie and Alfred Marchand would have begun cabin service in first class; with Amy King and Robert Fangman in business class; and with Michael Tarrou, Amy Jarret, and Alicia Titus in economy class. See UAL report, "Flight 175 Flight Attendant Positions/Jumpseats," undated. United flight attendants, unlike those at American, did not carry cockpit keys. Instead, such keys were stowed in the cabin—on Flight 175, in the overhead bin above seats 1A and 1B in first class. See Don Dillman briefing (Nov. 18, 2003); Bob Jordan briefing (Nov. 20, 2003).

42. Asked by air traffic controllers at 8:37 to look for an American Airlines 767 (Flight 11), United 175 reported spotting the aircraft at 8:38. At 8:41, the flight crew reported having "heard a suspicious transmission" from another aircraft shortly after takeoff, "like someone keyed the mike and said everyone stay in your seats." See NTSB report, Air Traffic Control Recording—United Airlines Flight 175, Dec. 21, 2001.

43. See Marc Policastro interview (Nov. 21, 2003); FBI reports of investigation, interview of Lee Hanson, Sept. 11, 2001; interview of Marc Policastro, Sept. 11, 2001; interview of Louise Sweeney, Sept. 28, 2001; interview of Ronald May, Sept. 11, 2001. On both American 11 and United 175, Boeing 767 double-aisled aircraft, the hijackers arrayed themselves similarly: two seated in first class close to the cockpit door, the pilot hijacker seated close behind them, and at least one other hijacker seated close behind the pilot hijacker. Hijackers were seated next to both the left and right aisles. On American 77 and United 93, Boeing 757 single-aisle aircraft, the pilot hijacker sat in the first row, closest to the cockpit door. See FBI report, "Summary of Penttbom Investigation," Feb. 29, 2004, pp. 67-69; AAL schematics for Flight 11 and Flight 77; UAL schematics for Flight 175 and Flight 93.

44. NTSB report, "Flight Path Study—United Airlines 175," Feb. 19, 2002; NTSB report, Air Traffic Control Recording—United Airlines Flight 175, Dec. 21, 2001.

45. See FBI report of investigation, interview of Lee Hanson, Sept. 11, 2001.

46. Flight crew on board UAL aircraft could contact the United office in San Francisco (SAMC) simply by dialing *349 on an airphone. See FBI report of investigation, interview of David Price, Jan. 24, 2002. At some point before 9:00, SAMC notified United's headquarters of the emergency call from the flight attendant. See Marc Policastro interview (Nov. 21, 2003); FBI report of investigation, interview of Marc Policastro, Sept. 11, 2001; Rich Miles interiew (Nov. 21, 2003).

47. NTSB report, "Flight Path Study—United Airlines 175," Feb. 19, 2002.

48. See FBI reports of investigation, interview of Julie Sweeney, Oct. 2, 2001; interview of Louise Sweeney, Sept. 28, 2001.

49. See FBI report of investigation, interview of Lee Hanson, Sept. 11, 2001.

50. See ibid.; interview of Louise Sweeney, Sept. 28, 2001.

51. NTSB report, "Flight Path Study—United Airlines 175," Feb. 19, 2002.

52. AAL report, "Flight Attendant Jump Seat Locations During Takeoff And Flight Attendant Typical Cabin Positions During Start of Cabin Service," undated; AAL email, Young to Clark, "Flight Crews," Sept. 12, 2001; AAL record, Dispatch Environmental Control/Weekly Flight Summary for Flight 11, Sept. 11, 2001.

53. AAL record, System Operations Command Center (SOCC) log, Sept. 11, 2001, p. 2; NTSB report, "Flight Path Study—American Airlines Flight 77," Feb. 19, 2002. Flight attendant Renee May would likely have started working in the first-class galley; Michele Heidenberger would have been in the aft galley; Jennifer Lewis would have been in first class; and Kenneth Lewis would have been in the main cabin. On cabin service, see AAL report, "Flight Attendant Jump Seat Locations During Takeoff And Flight Attendant Typical Cabin Positions During Start of Cabin Service," undated. For cruising altitude, see NTSB report, "Flight Path Study—American Airlines Flight 77," Feb. 19, 2002. On events in the cabin, see FAA recording, Indianapolis Air Traffic Control Center, position HNN R, Sept. 11, 2001; FBI report of investigation, interview of Theodore Olson, Sept. 11, 2001; FBI report of investigation, interview of Ronald and Nancy May, Sept. 12, 2001; AAL record, Dispatch Environmental Control/Weekly Flight Summary for Flight 11, Sept. 11, 2001.

54. Air traffic control notified American's headquarters of the problem, and the airline began attempts to contact the flight by 8:59 via ACARS. See NTSB report, "Flight Path Study—American Airlines Flight 77," Feb. 19, 2002. On American 11, the transponder signal was turned off at 8:21; on United 175, the code was changed at 8:47; on American 77, the signal was turned off at 8:56; and on United 93, the signal was turned off at 9:41. See FAA report, "Summary of Air Traffic Hijack Events: September 11, 2001," Sept. 17, 2001; Richard Byard interview (Sept.

24, 2003); Linda Povinelli interview (Sept. 24, 2003); see also NTSB report, Air Traffic Control Recording—American Airlines Flight 77, Dec. 21, 2001; AAL record, Dispatch Environmental Control/Weekly Flight Summary for Flight 11, Sept. 11, 2001.

55. Gerard Arpey interview (Jan. 8, 2004); Larry Wansley interview (Jan. 8, 2004); AAL record, System Operations Command Center (SOCC) log, Sept. 11, 2001.

56. FBI report, "American Airlines Airphone Usage," Sept. 20, 2001; FBI report of investigation, interview of Ronald and Nancy May, Sept. 12, 2001.

57. The records available for the phone calls from American 77 do not allow for a determination of which of four "connected calls to unknown numbers" represent the two between Barbara and Ted Olson, although the FBI and DOJ believe that all four represent communications between Barbara Olson and her husband's office (all family members of the Flight 77 passengers and crew were canvassed to see if they had received any phone calls from the hijacked flight, and only Renee May's parents and Ted Olson indicated that they had received such calls). The four calls were at 9:15:34 for 1 minute, 42 seconds; 9:20:15 for 4 minutes, 34 seconds; 9:25:48 for 2 minutes, 34 seconds; and 9:30:56 for 4 minutes, 20 seconds. FBI report, "American Airlines Airphone Usage," Sept. 20, 2001; FBI report of investigation, interview of Theodore Olson, Sept. 11, 2001; FBI report of investigation, interview of Helen Voss, Sept. 14, 2001; AAL response to the Commission's supplemental document request, Jan. 20, 2004.

58. FBI report, "American Airlines Airphone Usage," Sept. 20, 2001; FBI report of investigation, interview of Theodore Olson, Sept. 11, 2001.

59. See FAA report, "Report of Aircraft Accident," Nov. 13, 2001; John Hendershot interview (Dec. 22, 2003); FAA report, "Summary of Air Traffic Hijack Events: September 11, 2001," Sept. 17, 2001; NTSB report, "Flight Path Study—American Airlines Flight 77," Feb. 19, 2002; Commission analysis of radar data.

60. See FAA report, "Summary of Air Traffic Hijack Events: September 11, 2001," Sept. 17, 2001; NTSB report, "Flight Path Study—American Airlines Flight 77," Feb. 19, 2002; FAA report, "Report of Aircraft Accident," Nov. 13, 2001.

61. See NTSB report, "Flight Path Study—American Airlines Flight 77," Feb. 19, 2002; TSA report, "Criminal Acts Against Civil Aviation for 2001," Aug. 20, 2002, p. 41.

62. The flight attendant assignments and seating included Chief Flight Attendant Deborah Welsh (first class, seat J1 at takeoff); Sandra Bradshaw (coach, seat J5); Wanda Green (first class, seat J4); Lorraine Bay (coach, seat J3); and CeeCee Lyles (coach, seat J6). See UAL response to Commission questions for the record, Apr. 5, 2004; FAA report, "Chronology of the September 11 Attacks and Subsequent Events Through October 24, 2001," undated; UAL records, copies of electronic boarding passes for Flight 93, Sept. 11, 2001; Bob Varcadipane interview (May 4, 2004); Newark Tower briefing (May 4, 2004).

63. Although the flight schedule indicates an 8:00 A.M. "departure," this was the time the plane left the gate area. Taxiing from the gate to the runway normally took about 15 minutes. Bob Varcadipane interview (May 4, 2004); Newark Tower briefing (May 4, 2004).

64. Commission analysis of FAA air traffic control data. On the FAA's awareness of multiple hijackings, see AAL transcript, telephone call from Nydia Gonzalez to Craig Marquis, Sept. 11, 2001; Craig Marquis interview (Nov. 19, 2003); AAL record, System Operations Command Center (SOCC) log, Sept. 11, 2001; UAL System Operations Control briefing (Nov. 20, 2003); Rich Miles interview (Nov. 21, 2003); UAL report, "Timeline: Dispatch/SMFDO Activities—Terrorist Crisis," undated.

65. FAA audio file, Boston Center, position 46R, 8:24:38 and 8:24:56; Peter Zalewski interview (Sept. 23, 2003).

66. On September 6, 1970, members of the Popular Front for the Liberation of Palestine hijacked a Pan American Boeing 747, a TWA Boeing 707, and a Swissair DC-8. On September 9, a British airliner was hijacked as well. An attempt to hijack an Israeli airliner was thwarted. The Pan American plane landed in Cairo and was blown up after its passengers were released. The other three aircraft were flown to Dawson Field, near Amman, Jordan; the passengers were held captive, and the planes were destroyed. The international hijacking crisis turned into a civil war, as the Jordanian government used force to restore its control of the country. See FAA report, Civil Aviation Reference Handbook, May 1999, appendix D.

The FAA knew or strongly suspected that Flight 11 was a hijacking 11 minutes after it was taken over; Flight 175, 9 minutes after it was taken over. There is no evidence to indicate that the FAA recognized Flight 77 as a hijacking until it crashed into the Pentagon.

67. FAA audio file, Herndon Command Center, line 5114, 9:07:13; FAA audio file, Herndon Command Center, position 15, 9:19. At 9:07, Boston Air Traffic Control Center recommended to the FAA Command Center that a cockpit warning be sent to the pilots of all commercial aircraft to secure their cockpits. While Boston Center sent out such warnings to the commercial flights in its sector, we could find no evidence that a nationwide warning was issued by the ATC system.

68. Ellen King interview (Apr. 5, 2004). FAA air traffic control tapes indicate that at 9:19 the FAA Air Traffic Control System Command Center in Herndon ordered controllers to send a cockpit warning to Delta 1989 because, like American 11 and United 175, it was a transcontinental flight departing Boston's Logan Airport.

69. For American Airlines' response, see AAL briefing (Apr. 26, 2004). For Ballinger's warnings, see Ed Ballinger interview (Apr. 14, 2004). A companywide order for dispatchers to warn cockpits was not issued until 9:21. See UAL report, "Timeline: Dispatch/SMFDO Activities—Terrorist Crisis," undated. While one of Ballinger's col-

leagues assisted him, Ballinger remained responsible for multiple flights. See Ed Ballinger interview (Apr. 14, 2004). American Airlines' policy called for the flight dispatcher to manage only the hijacked flight, relieving him of responsibilities for all other flights. On American Airlines' policy, see Craig Marquis, Craig Parfitt, Joe Bertapelle, and Mike Mulcahy interview (Nov. 19, 2003). United Airlines had no such "isolation" policy. UAL System Operations Control briefing (Nov. 20, 2003).

70. On FDR, see NTSB report, "Specialist's Factual Report of Investigation—Digital Flight Data Recorder" for United Airlines Flight 93, Feb. 15, 2002; on CVR, see FBI report, "CVR from UA Flight #93," Dec. 4, 2003; Commission review of Aircraft Communication and Reporting System (ACARS) messages sent to and from Flight 93 (which indicate time of message transmission and receipt); see UAL record, Ed Ballinger ACARS log, Sept. 11, 2001. At 9:22, after learning of the events at the World Trade Center, Melody Homer, the wife of co-pilot Leroy Homer, had an ACARS message sent to her husband in the cockpit asking if he was okay. See UAL record, ACARS message, Sept. 11, 2001.

71. On FDR, see NTSB report, "Specialist's Factual Report of Investigation—Digital Flight Data Recorder" for United Airlines Flight 93, Feb. 15, 2002; on CVR, see FBI report, "CVR from UA Flight #93," Dec. 4, 2003; FAA report, "Summary of Air Traffic Hijack Events: September 11, 2001," Sept. 17, 2001; NTSB report, Air Traffic Control Recording—United Airlines Flight 93, Dec. 21, 2001.

72. The 37 passengers represented a load factor of 20.33 percent of the plane's seating capacity of 182, considerably below the 52.09 percent for Flight 93 on Tuesdays in the three-month period prior to September 11 (June 11–September 4, 2001). See UAL report, Flight 93 EWR–SFO load factors, undated. Five passengers holding reservations for Flight 93 did not show for the flight. All five were interviewed and cleared by the FBI. FBI report, "Flight #93 'No Show' Passengers from 9/11/01," Sept. 18, 2001.

73. INS record, Withdrawal of Application for Admission for Mohamed al Kahtani, Aug. 4, 2001.

74. See FAA regulations, Admission to flight deck, 14 C.F.R. § 121.547 (2001); UAL records, copies of boarding passes for United 93, Sept. 11, 2001. One passenger reported that ten first-class passengers were aboard the flight. If that number is accurate, it would include the four hijackers. FBI report of investigation, interview of Lisa Jefferson, Sept. 11, 2001; UAL record, Flight 93 passenger manifest, Sept. 11, 2001. All but one of the six passengers seated in the first-class cabin communicated with the ground during the flight, and none mentioned anyone from their cabin having gone into the cockpit before the hijacking. Moreover, it is unlikely that the highly regarded and experienced pilot and co-pilot of Flight 93 would have allowed an observer into the cockpit before or after takeoff who had not obtained the proper permission. See UAL records, personnel files of Flight 93 pilots. For jumpseat information, see UAL record, Weight and Balance Information for Flight 93 and Flight 175, Sept. 11, 2001; AAL records, Dispatch Environmental Control/Weekly Flight Summary for Flight 11 and Flight 77, Sept. 11, 2001.

75. Like Atta on Flight 11, Jarrah apparently did not know how to operate the communication radios; thus his attempts to communicate with the passengers were broadcast on the ATC channel. See FBI report, "CVR from UA Flight #93," Dec. 4, 2003. Also, by 9:32 FAA notified United's headquarters that the flight was not responding to radio calls. According to United, the flight's nonresponse and its turn to the east led the airline to believe by 9:36 that the plane was hijacked. See Rich Miles interview (Nov. 21, 2003); UAL report, "United dispatch SMFDO activities—terrorist crisis," Sept. 11, 2001.

76. In accordance with FAA regulations, United 93's cockpit voice recorder recorded the last 31 minutes of sounds from the cockpit via microphones in the pilots' headsets, as well as in the overhead panel of the flight deck. This is the only recorder from the four hijacked airplanes to survive the impact and ensuing fire. The CVRs and FDRs from American 11 and United 175 were not found, and the CVR from American Flight 77 was badly burned and not recoverable. See FBI report, "CVR from UA Flight #93," Dec. 4, 2003; see also FAA regulations, 14 C.F.R. §§ 25.1457, 91.609, 91.1045, 121.359; Flight 93 CVR data. A transcript of the CVR recording was prepared by the NTSB and the FBI.

77. All calls placed on airphones were from the rear of the aircraft. There was one airphone installed in each row of seats on both sides of the aisle. The airphone system was capable of transmitting only eight calls at any one time. See FBI report of investigation, airphone records for flights UAL 93 and UAL 175 on Sept. 11, 2001, Sept. 18, 2001.

78. FAA audio file, Cleveland Center, position Lorain Radar; Flight 93 CVR data; FBI report, "CVR from UA Flight #93," Dec. 4, 2003.

79. FBI reports of investigation, interviews of recipients of calls from Todd Beamer, Sept. 11, 2001, through June 11, 2002; FBI reports of investigation, interviews of recipients of calls from Sandy Bradshaw, Sept. 11, 2001, through Oct. 4, 2001. Text messages warning the cockpit of Flight 93 were sent to the aircraft by Ed Ballinger at 9:24. See UAL record, Ed Ballinger's ACARS log, Sept. 11, 2001.

80. We have relied mainly on the record of FBI interviews with the people who received calls. The FBI interviews were conducted while memories were still fresh and were less likely to have been affected by reading the accounts of others or hearing stories in the media. In some cases we have conducted our own interviews to supplement or verify the record. See FBI reports of investigation, interviews of recipients of calls from Todd Beamer, Mark Bingham, Sandy Bradshaw, Marion Britton, Thomas Burnett, Joseph DeLuca, Edward Felt, Jeremy Glick, Lauren Grandcolas, Linda Gronlund, CeeCee Lyles, Honor Wainio.

81. FBI reports of investigation, interviews of recipients of calls from Thomas Burnett, Sept. 11, 2001; FBI reports of investigation, interviews of recipients of calls from Marion Britton, Sept. 14, 2001, through Nov. 8, 2001; Lisa Jefferson interview (May 11, 2004); FBI report of investigation, interview of Lisa Jefferson, Sept. 11, 2001; Richard Belme interview (Nov. 21, 2003).

82. See Jere Longman, *Among the Heroes—United Flight 93 and the Passengers and Crew Who Fought Back* (Harper-Collins, 2002), p. 107; Deena Burnett interview (Apr. 26, 2004); FBI reports of investigation, interviews of recipients of calls from Jeremy Glick, Sept. 11, 2001, through Sept. 12, 2001; Lyzbeth Glick interview (Apr. 22, 2004). Experts told us that a gunshot would definitely be audible on the CVR. The FBI found no evidence of a firearm at the crash site of Flight 93. See FBI response to Commission briefing request no. 6, undated (topic 11). The FBI collected 14 knives or portions of knives at the Flight 93 crash site. FBI report, "Knives Found at the UA Flight 93 Crash Site," undated.

83. FBI response to Commission briefing request no. 6, undated (topic 11); FBI reports of investigation, interviews of recipients of calls from Jeremy Glick, Sept. 11, 2001, through Sept. 12, 2001.

84. See FBI reports of investigation, interviews of recipients of calls from United 93.

85. FBI reports of investigation, interviews of recipients of calls from United 93. For quote, see FBI report of investigation, interview of Philip Bradshaw, Sept. 11, 2001; Philip Bradshaw interview (June 15, 2004); Flight 93 FDR and CVR data. At 9:55:11 Jarrah dialed in the VHF Omni-directional Range (VOR) frequency for the VOR navigational aid at Washington Reagan National Airport, further indicating that the attack was planned for the nation's capital.

86. Flight 93 FDR and CVR data.

87. Ibid.

88. Ibid.

89. Ibid. The CVR clearly captured the words of the hijackers, including words in Arabic from the microphone in the pilot headset up to the end of the flight. The hijackers' statements, the clarity of the recording, the position of the microphone in the pilot headset, and the corresponding manipulations of flight controls provide the evidence. The quotes are taken from our listening to the CVR, aided by an Arabic speaker.

90. In 1993, a Lufthansa aircraft was hijacked from its Frankfurt to Cairo route and diverted to JFK Airport in New York. The event lasted for 11 hours and was resolved without incident. Tamara Jones and John J. Goldman, "11-Hour Hijack Ends Without Injury in N.Y.," *Los Angeles Times*, Feb. 12, 1993, p. A1.

91. The second half of the twentieth century witnessed a tremendous growth of the air transport industry, and the FAA's corresponding responsibilities grew enormously from the 1960s through 2001. Throughout that time, the FAA focused on setting and maintaining safety and efficiency standards. Since no plane had been hijacked inside the United States since 1991, sabotage was perceived as the most significant threat to civil aviation. For a broader discussion of the perception of the threat, see section 3.3.

92. FAA report, "Administrator's Fact Book," July 2001; Benedict Sliney interview (May 21, 2004); John McCartney interview (Dec. 17, 2003).

93. FAA regulations, Air Traffic Control transponder and altitude reporting equipment and use, 14 CFR § 91.215 (2001).

94. DOD radar files, 84th Radar Evaluation Squadron, "9/11 Autoplay," undated; Charles Thomas interview (May 4, 2004); John Thomas interview (May 4, 2004); Joseph Cooper interview (Sept. 22, 2003); Tim Spence interview (Sept. 30, 2003). For general information on approaching terminals, see FAA report, "Aeronautical Information Manual," Feb. 19, 2004. Times assigned to audio transmissions were derived by the Commission from files provided by the FAA and the Northeast Air Defense Sector (NEADS) based on audio time stamps contained within the files provided by the sender. FAA tapes are certified accurate to Universal Coordinated Time by quality assurance specialists at FAA air traffic facilities. NEADS files are time-stamped as accurate to the Naval Observatory clock. We also compared audio times to certified transcripts when available.

95. FAA Boston Center site visit (Sept. 22–24, 2003).

96. NORAD's mission is set forth in a series of renewable agreements between the United States and Canada. According to the agreement in effect on 9/11, the "primary missions" of NORAD were "aerospace warning" and "aerospace control" for North America. *Aerospace warning* was defined as "the monitoring of man-made objects in space and the detection, validation, and warning of attack against North America whether by aircraft, missiles, or space vehicles." *Aerospace control* was defined as "providing surveillance and control of the airspace of Canada and the United States." See DOS memo, Exchange of Notes Between Canada and the United States Regarding Extension of the NORAD Agreement, Mar. 28, 1996; see also DOS press release, "Extension of NORAD Agreement," June 16, 2000 (regarding the extension of the 1996 Agreement unchanged). For NORAD's defining its job as defending against external attacks, see Ralph Eberhart interview (Mar. 1, 2004).

97. DOD report, "NORAD Strategy Review: Final Report," July 1992, p. 55.

98. For assumptions of exercise planners, see Paul Goddard and Ken Merchant interview (Mar. 4, 2004). For the authority to shoot down a commercial aircraft prior to 9/11, granted to NORAD but not used against Payne Stewart's plane in 1999 after the pilot and passengers lost consciousness, see Richard Myers interview (Feb. 17, 2004). A 1998 White House tabletop exercise chaired by Richard Clarke included a scenario in which a terrorist

group loaded a Learjet with explosives and took off for a suicide mission to Washington. Military officials said they could scramble fighter jets from Langley Air Force Base to chase the aircraft, but they would need "executive" orders to shoot it down. Chuck Green interview (Apr. 21, 2004). For no recognition of this threat, see Ralph Eberhart interview (Mar. 1, 2004).

99. Richard Myers interview (Feb. 17, 2004).

100. Donald Quenneville interview (Jan. 7, 2004); Langley Air Force Base 119th Fighter Wing briefing (Oct. 6–7, 2003).

101. Collin Scoggins interviews (Sept. 22, 2003; Jan. 8, 2004); FAA report, "Crisis Management Handbook for Significant Events," Feb. 15, 2000; DOD memo, CJCS instruction, "Aircraft Piracy (Hijacking) and Destruction of Derelict Airborne Objects," June 1, 2001.

102. See FAA regulations, Hijacked Aircraft, Order 7110.65M, para.10-2-6 (2001); David Bottiglia interview (Oct. 1, 2003); FAA report, "Crisis Management Handbook for Significant Events," Feb. 15, 2000. From interviews of controllers at various FAA centers, we learned that an air traffic controller's first response to an aircraft incident is to notify a supervisor, who then notifies the traffic management unit and the operations manager in charge. The FAA center next notifies the appropriate regional operations center (ROC), which in turn contacts FAA headquarters. Biggio stated that for American 11, the combination of three factors—loss of radio contact, loss of transponder signal, and course deviation—was serious enough for him to contact the ROC in Burlington, Mass. However, without hearing the threatening communication from the cockpit, he doubts Boston Center would have recognized or labeled American 11 "a hijack." Terry Biggio interview (Sept. 22, 2003); see also Shirley Miller interview (Mar. 30, 2004); Monte Belger interview (Apr. 20, 2004).

103. FAA regulations, Special Military Operations, Requests for Service, Order 7610.4J, paras. 7-1-1, 7-1-2 (2001); DOD memo, CJCS instruction, "Aircraft Piracy (Hijacking) and Destruction of Derelict Airborne Objects," June 1, 2001.

104. Ralph Eberhart interview (Mar. 1, 2004); Alan Scott interview (Feb. 4, 2004); Robert Marr interview (Jan. 23, 2004); FAA regulations, Position Reports within NORAD Radar Coverage, Order 7610.4J, para. 7-4-2 (2001); DOD memo, CJCS instruction, "Aircraft Piracy (Hijacking) and Destruction of Derelict Airborne Objects," June 1, 2001.

105. FAA regulations, Air/Ground Communications Security, Order 7610.4J, para. 7-1-6 (2001); FAA regulations, Vectors, Order 7610.4J, para. 7-2-3 (2001).

106. Peter Zalewski interview (Sept. 22, 2003); Terry Biggio interviews (Sept. 22, 2003; Jan. 8, 2004); Collin Scoggins interview (Sept. 22, 2003); Daniel Bueno interview (Sept. 22, 2003). For evidence of the numerous attempts by air traffic control to raise American 11, see FAA memo, "Full Transcript; Aircraft Accident; AAL11; New York, NY; September 11, 2001," Feb. 15, 2002, p. 7.

107. DOD radar files, 84th Radar Evaluation Squadron, "9/11 Autoplay," undated; Peter Zalewski interview (Sept. 22, 2003); John Schippani interview (Sept. 22, 2003).

108. Peter Zalewski interview (Sept. 22, 2003); John Schippani interview (Sept. 22, 2003).

109. FAA memo, "Full Transcript; Aircraft Accident; AAL11; New York, NY; September 11, 2001," Feb. 15, 2002, p. 11; Peter Zalewski interview (Sept. 23, 2003).

110. Peter Zalewski interview (Sept. 23, 2003); John Schippani interview (Sept. 22, 2003); Terry Biggio interviews (Sept. 22, 2003; Jan. 8, 2004); Robert Jones interview (Sept. 22, 2003).

111. FAA memo, "Full Transcript; Aircraft Accident; AAL11; New York, NY; September 11, 2001," Apr. 19, 2002, p. 2; FAA record, Boston Center daily record of facility operation, Sept. 11, 2001; Terry Biggio interviews (Sept. 22, 2003; Jan. 8, 2004); Daniel Bueno interview (Sept. 22, 2004). See also FAA memo, "Transcription of 9/11 Tapes," Oct. 2, 2003, p. 2; FAA audio file, Herndon Command Center, line 4525, 8:32–8:33.

112. See FAA memo, "Transcription of 9/11 Tapes," Oct. 2, 2003, pp. 2–3; FAA record, New England Region Daily Log, Sept. 11, 2001; Daniel Bueno interview (Sept. 22, 2003); Terry Biggio interviews (Sept. 22, 2003; Jan. 8, 2004).

113. FAA memo, "Full Transcript; Aircraft Accident; AAL11; New York, NY; September 11, 2001," Feb. 15, 2002, p. 12.

114. FAA memo, "Full Transcript; Aircraft Accident; AAL11; New York, NY; September 11, 2001," Jan. 28, 2002, p. 5.

115. FAA memo, "Full Transcript; Aircraft Accident; AAL11; New York, NY; September 11, 2001," Apr. 19, 2002, p. 5; Terry Biggio interview (Sept. 22, 2003); Collin Scoggins interviews (Sept. 22, 2003; Jan. 8, 2004); Daniel Bueno interview (Sept. 22, 2003).

116. On 9/11, NORAD was scheduled to conduct a military exercise, Vigilant Guardian, which postulated a bomber attack from the former Soviet Union. We investigated whether military preparations for the large-scale exercise compromised the military's response to the real-world terrorist attack on 9/11. According to General Eberhart, "it took about 30 seconds" to make the adjustment to the real-world situation. Ralph Eberhart testimony, June 17, 2004. We found that the response was, if anything, expedited by the increased number of staff at the sectors and at NORAD because of the scheduled exercise. See Robert Marr interview (Jan. 23, 2004).

117. For the distance between Otis Air Force Base and New York City, see William Scott testimony, May 23, 2003. For the order from NEADS to Otis to place F-15s at battle stations, see NEADS audio file, Weapons Director Technician position, channel 14, 8:37:15. See also interviews with Otis and NEADS personnel: Jeremy Powell interview (Oct. 27, 2003); Michael Kelly interview (Oct. 14, 2003); Donald Quenneville interview (Jan. 7, 2004), and interviews with Otis fighter pilots: Daniel Nash interview (Oct. 14, 2003); Timothy Duffy interview (Jan. 7, 2004). According to Joseph Cooper from Boston Center, "I coordinated with Huntress ["Huntress" is the call sign for NEADS]. I advised Huntress we had a hijacked aircraft. I requested some assistance. Huntress requested and I supplied pertinent information. I was advised aircraft might be sent from Otis." FAA record, Personnel Statement of Joseph Cooper, Oct. 30, 2001.

118. Robert Marr interview (Jan. 23, 2004); Leslie Filson, *Air War Over America* (First Air Force, 2003), p. 56; Larry Arnold interview (Feb. 3, 2004).

119. NEADS audio file, Weapons Director Technician position, channel 14; 8:45:54; Daniel Nash interview (Oct. 14, 2003); Michael Kelly interview (Oct. 14, 2003); Donald Quenneville interview (Jan. 7, 2004); Timothy Duffy interview (Jan. 7, 2004); NEADS audio file, Mission Crew Commander position, channel 2, 8:44:58; NEADS audio file, Identification Technician position, channel 5, 8:51:13.

120. FAA audio file, Boston Center, position 31R; NEADS audio file, Mission Crew Commander position, channel 2, 8:58:00; NEADS audio file, Mission Crew Commander position, channel 2, 8:54:55. Because of a technical issue, there are no NEADS recordings available of the NEADS senior weapons director and weapons director technician position responsible for controlling the Otis scramble. We found a single communication from the weapons director or his technician on the Guard frequency at approximately 9:11, cautioning the Otis fighters: "remain at current position [holding pattern] until FAA requests assistance." See NEADS audio file, channel 24. That corresponds to the time after the Otis fighters entered the holding pattern and before they headed for New York. NEADS controllers were simultaneously working with a tanker to relocate close to the Otis fighters. At 9:10, the senior director on the NEADS floor told the weapons director, "I want those fighters closer in." NEADS audio file, Identification Technician position, channel 5. At 9:10:22, the Otis fighters were told by Boston Center that the second tower had been struck. At 9:12:54, the Otis fighters told their Boston Center controller that they needed to establish a combat air patrol over New York, and they immediately headed for New York City. See FAA audio files, Boston Center, position 31R. This series of communications explains why the Otis fighters briefly entered and then soon departed the holding pattern, as the radar reconstruction of their flight shows. DOD radar files, 84th Radar Evaluation Squadron, "9/11 Autoplay," undated.

121. In response to allegations that NORAD responded more quickly to the October 25, 1999, plane crash that killed Payne Stewart than it did to the hijacking of American 11, we compared NORAD's response time for each incident. The last normal transmission from the Stewart flight was at 9:27:10 A.M. Eastern Daylight Time. The Southeast Air Defense Sector was notified of the event at 9:55, 28 minutes later. In the case of American 11, the last normal communication from the plane was at 8:13 A.M. EDT. NEADS was notified at 8:38, 25 minutes later. We have concluded there is no significant difference in NORAD's reaction to the two incidents. See NTSB memo, Aircraft Accident Brief for Payne Stewart incident, Oct. 25, 1999; FAA email, Gahris to Myers, "ZJX Timeline for N47BA accident," Feb. 17, 2004.

122. FAA memo, "Full Transcript; Aircraft Accident; UAL175; New York, NY; September 11, 2001," May 8, 2002, pp. 5–6.

123. FAA audio file, New York Center, position R42, 8:42–8:45; FAA memo, "Full Transcript; Aircraft Accident; UAL175; New York, NY; September 11, 2001," May 8, 2002, pp. 6–8; DOD radar files, 84th Radar Evaluation Squadron, "9/11 Autoplay," undated. The FAA-produced timeline notes, "Based on coordination received from [Boston Center] indicating a possible hijack, most of the controller's attention is focused on AAL 11." See FAA report, "Summary of Air Traffic Hijack Events September 11, 2001," Sept. 17, 2001; see also David Bottiglia interview (Oct. 1, 2003); FAA memo, "Full Transcript; Aircraft Accident; UAL175; New York, NY; September 11, 2001," May 8, 2002, p. 9.

124. FAA audio file, Herndon Command Center, New York Center position, line 5114, 8:48.

125. FAA memo, "Full Transcript; Aircraft Accident; UAL175; New York, NY; September 11, 2001," May 8, 2002, pp. 12, 14.

126. Ibid., p. 15. At 8:57, the following exchange between controllers occurred: "I got some handoffs for you. We got some incidents going over here. Is Delta 2433 going to be okay at thirty-three? I had to climb him for traffic. I let you United 175 just took off out of think we might have a hijack over here. Two of them." See FAA memo, "Full Transcript; Aircraft Accident; UAL175; New York, NY; September 11, 2001," May 8, 2002.

127. See FAA report, "Summary of Air Traffic Hijack Events September 11, 2001," Sept. 17, 2001; Evanna Dowis interview (Sept. 30, 2004); Michael McCormick interview (Dec. 15, 2003); FAA record, Personnel Statement of Michael McCormick, Oct. 17, 2001. See also FAA memo, "Full Transcript; Aircraft Accident; UAL175; New York, NY; September 11, 2001," May 8, 2002, p. 17.

128. FAA memo, "Full Transcript; Command Center; NOM Operational Position; September 11, 2001," Oct. 14, 2003, pp. 15–17.

129. FAA memo, "Full Transcript; Aircraft Accident; UAL175; New York, NY; September 11, 2001," Jan. 17, 2002, p. 3.

130. "N90 [New York Terminal Radar Approach] controller stated 'at approximately 9:00 a.m., I observed an unknown aircraft south of the Newark, New Jersey Airport, northeast bound and descending out of twelve thousand nine hundred feet in a rapid rate of descent, the radar target terminated at the World Trade Center.'" FAA report, "Summary of Air Traffic Hijack Events September 11, 2001," Sept. 17, 2001. Former NORAD official Alan Scott testified that the time of impact of United 175 was 9:02. William Scott testimony, May 23, 2003. We have determined that the impact time was 9:03:11 based on our analysis of FAA radar data and air traffic control software logic.

131. FAA audio file, Herndon Command Center, New York Center position, line 5114, 9:02:34.

132. Ibid., 9:03; FAA audio file, Herndon Command Center, Cleveland/Boston position, line 5115, 9:05; Michael McCormick interview (Oct. 1, 2003); David LaCates interview (Oct. 2, 2003).

133. FAA Audio File, Herndon Command Center, Boston Center position, line 5115, 9:05–9:07.

134. Joseph McCain interview (Oct. 28, 2003); Robert Marr (Jan. 23, 2004); James Fox interview (Oct. 29, 2003); Dawne Deskins interview (Oct. 30, 2003).

135. NEADS audio file, Mission Crew Commander position, channel 2, 9:07:32.

136. Daniel Nash interview (Oct. 14, 2003); Timothy Duffy interview (Jan. 7, 2004).

137. Because the Otis fighters had expended a great deal of fuel in flying first to military airspace and then to New York, the battle commanders were concerned about refueling. As NEADS personnel looked for refueling tankers in the vicinity of New York, the mission crew commander considered scrambling the Langley fighters to New York to provide backup for the Otis fighters until the NEADS Battle Cab (the command area that overlooks the operations floor) ordered "battle stations only at Langley." The alert fighters at Langley Air Force Base were ordered to battle stations at 9:09. Colonel Marr, the battle commander at NEADS, and General Arnold, the CONR commander, both recall that the planes were held on battle stations, as opposed to scrambling, because they might be called on to relieve the Otis fighters over New York City if a refueling tanker was not located, and also because of the general uncertainty of the situation in the sky. According to William Scott at the Commission's May 23, 2003, hearing, "At 9:09, Langley F-16s are directed to battle stations, just based on the general situation and the breaking news, and the general developing feeling about what's going on." See NEADS audio file, Mission Crew Commander, channel 2, 9:08:36; Robert Marr interview (Oct. 27, 2003); Larry Arnold interview (Feb. 3, 2004). See also Colonel Marr's statement that "[t]he plan was to protect New York City." Filson, *Air War Over America*, p. 60.

138. Commission analysis of FAA radar data and air traffic control transmissions.

139. The Indianapolis Center controller advised other Indianapolis Center personnel of the developing situation. They agreed to "sterilize" the airspace along the flight's westerly route so the safety of other planes would not be affected. John Thomas interview (May 4, 2004).

140. John Thomas interview (Sept. 24, 2003). According to the FAA-produced timeline, at 9:09 Indianapolis Center "notified Great Lakes Regional Operations Center a possible aircraft accident of AMERICAN 77 due to the simultaneous loss of radio communications and radar identification." FAA report, "Summary of Air Traffic Hijack Events September 11, 2001," Sept. 17, 2001.

141. FAA audio file, Herndon Command Center, National Operations Manager position, line 4525; FAA audio file, Herndon Command Center, National Traffic Management Officer east position, line 4530; FAA memo, "Full Transcription; Air Traffic Control System Command Center, National Traffic Management Officer, East Position; September 11, 2001," Oct. 21, 2003, p. 13.

142. Primary radar contact for Flight 77 was lost because the "preferred" radar in this geographic area had no primary radar system, the "supplemental" radar had poor primary coverage, and the FAA ATC software did not allow the display of primary radar data from the "tertiary" and "quadrary" radars.

143. David Boone interview (May 4, 2004); Charles Thomas interview (May 4, 2004); John Thomas interview (May 4, 2004); Commission analysis of FAA radar data and air traffic control software logic.

144. John Thomas interview (May 4, 2004); Charles Thomas interview (May 4, 2004). We have reviewed all FAA documents, transcripts, and tape recordings related to American 77 and have found no evidence that FAA headquarters issued a directive to surrounding centers to search for primary radar targets. Review of the same materials also indicates that no one within FAA located American 77 until the aircraft was identified by Dulles controllers at 9:32. For much of that time, American 77 was traveling through Washington Center's airspace. The Washington Center's controllers were looking for the flight, but they were not told to look for primary radar returns.

145. John White interview (May 7, 2004); Ellen King interview (Apr. 5, 2004); Linda Schuessler interview (Apr. 6, 2004); Benedict Sliney interview (May 21, 2004); FAA memo, "Full Transcription; Air Traffic Control System Command Center, National Traffic Management Officer, East Position; September 11, 2001," Oct. 21, 2003, pp. 14, 27.

146. John Hendershot interview (Dec. 22, 2003).

147. FAA memo, "Partial Transcript; Aircraft Accident; AAL77; Washington, DC; September 11, 2001," Sept. 20, 2001, p. 7.

148. NEADS audio file, Identification Technician position, channel 7, 9:21:10.

149. NEADS audio file, Mission Crew Commander, channel 2, 9:21:50; Kevin Nasypany interview (Jan. 22–23, 2004).

150. NEADS audio file, Mission Crew Commander, Channel 2, 9:22:34. The mission commander thought to put the Langley scramble over Baltimore and place a "barrier cap" between the hijack and Washington, D.C. Kevin Nasypany interview (Jan. 22–23, 2004).

151. NEADS audio file, Identification Technician position, channel 5, 9:32:10; ibid., 9:33:58.

152. For first quote, see NEADS audio file, Identification Technician position, channel 5, 9:35:50. For second quote, see NEADS audio file, Identification Technician position, channel 7, 9:36:34; Kevin Nasypany interview (Jan. 22–23, 2004). For the third quote, see NEADS audio file, Mission Crew Commander, channel 2, 9:39; 9:39:37; Kevin Nasypany interview (Jan. 22–23, 2004).

153. Dean Eckmann interview (Dec. 1, 2003); FAA memo, "Partial Transcript; Scramble Aircraft; QUIT25; September 11, 2001," Sept. 4, 2003, pp. 2–4 (Peninsular Radar position); FAA memo, "Partial Transcript; Scramble Aircraft; QUIT25; September 11, 2001," Sept. 4, 2003, pp. 2–5 (East Feeder Radar position).

154. NEADS audio file, Mission Crew Commander, channel 2, 9:38:02; Dawne Deskins interview (Oct. 30, 2003). The estimated time of impact of Flight 77 into the Pentagon is based on Commission analysis of FDR, air traffic control, radar, and Pentagon elevation and impact site data.

155. Joseph Cooper interview (Sept. 22, 2003); NEADS audio file, Identification Technician position, recorder 1, channel 7, 9:41.

156. NEADS audio file, Mission Crew Commander position, channel 2, 9:42:08.

157. FAA memo, "Full Transcript; Aircraft Accident; N591UA (UAL93); Somerset, PA; September 11, 2001," May 10, 2002, p. 10.

158. The United 93 timeline in FAA report, "Summary of Air Traffic Hijack Events September 11, 2001," Sept. 17, 2001, states that at 9:28:17 "a radio transmission of unintelligible sounds of possible screaming or a struggle from an unknown origin was heard over the ZOB [Cleveland Center] radio." See FAA memo, "Full Transcript; Aircraft Accident; N591UA (UAL93); Somerset, PA; September 11, 2001," May 10, 2002, p. 11.

159. The United 93 timeline in FAA report, "Summary of Air Traffic Hijack Events September 11, 2001," Sept. 17, 2001, states that at 9:28:54 a "second radio transmission, mostly unintelligible, again with sounds of possible screaming or a struggle and a statement, 'get out of here, get out of here' from an unknown origin was heard over the ZOB [Cleveland Center] radio." FAA audio file, Cleveland Center, Lorain Radar position; FAA memo, "Full Transcript; Aircraft Accident; N591UA (UAL93); Somerset, PA; September 11, 2001," May 10, 2002, p. 11. At 9:31:48, ExecJet 56 also called in, reporting that "we're just answering your call. We did hear that, uh, yelling too." The FAA responded at 9:31:51, "Okay, thanks. We're just trying to figure out what's going on." FAA memo, "Full Transcript; Aircraft Accident; N591UA (UAL93); Somerset, PA; September 11, 2001," May 10, 2002, p. 15.

160. FAA memo, "Full Transcript; Aircraft Accident; N591UA (UAL93); Somerset, PA; September 11, 2001," May 10, 2002, p. 15.

161. FAA memo, "Full Transcription; Air Traffic Control System Command Center, National Traffic Management Officer, East Position; September 11, 2001," Oct. 21, 2003, pp. 10, 13; FAA audio file, Herndon Command Center, New York Center position, line 5154.

162. FAA memo, "Full Transcript; Aircraft Accident; N591UA (UAL93); Somerset, PA; September 11, 2001," May 10, 2002, p. 19.

163. Ibid., p. 23.

164. FAA memo, "Full Transcription; Air Traffic Control System Command Center, National Traffic Management Officer, East Position; September 11, 2001," Oct. 21, 2003, pp. 16–17; FAA audio file, Cleveland Center, Lorain Radar position; FAA memo, "Full Transcript; Aircraft Accident; N591UA (UAL93); Somerset, PA; September 11, 2001," May 10, 2002, pp. 26–32.

165. FAA memo, "Full Transcription; Air Traffic Control System Command Center, National Traffic Management Officer, East Position; September 11, 2001," Oct. 21, 2003, pp. 17–19.

166. For 9:46 quotation, see ibid., pp. 19–20. For 9:49 discussion about military assistance, see ibid., p. 21.

167. For 9:53 discussion about scrambling aircraft, see ibid., p. 23. Neither Monte Belger nor the deputy director for air traffic services could recall this discussion in their interviews with us. Monte Belger interview (Apr. 20, 2004); Peter Challan interview (Mar. 26, 2004). Subsequently Belger told us he does not believe the conversation occurred. Monte Belger, email to the Commission, July 12, 2004. However, tapes from the morning reveal that at 9:53 a staff person from headquarters told the Command Center "Peter's talking to Monte now about scrambling." FAA memo, "Full Transcription; Air Traffic Control System Command Center, National Traffic Management Officer, East Position; September 11, 2001," Oct. 21, 2003, p. 23. For discussions about the status of United 93, see ibid., pp. 24–27.

168. Ibid., pp. 23–27. We also reviewed a report regarding seismic observations on September 11, 2001, whose authors conclude that the impact time of United 93 was "10:06:05±5 (EDT)." Won-Young Kim and G. R. Baum, "Seismic Observations during September 11, 2001, Terrorist Attack," spring 2002 (report to the Maryland Depart-

ment of Natural Resources). But the seismic data on which they based this estimate are far too weak in signal-to-noise ratio and far too speculative in terms of signal source to be used as a means of contradicting the impact time established by the very accurate combination of FDR, CVR, ATC, radar, and impact site data sets. These data sets constrain United 93's impact time to within 1 second, are airplane- and crash-site specific, and are based on time codes automatically recorded in the ATC audiotapes for the FAA centers and correlated with each data set in a process internationally accepted within the aviation accident investigation community. Furthermore, one of the study's principal authors now concedes that "seismic data is not definitive for the impact of UA 93." Email from Won-Young Kim to the Commission, "Re: UA Flight 93," July 7, 2004; see also Won-Young Kim, "Seismic Observations for UA Flight 93 Crash near Shanksville, Pennsylvania during September 11, 2001," July 5, 2004.

169. FAA memo, "Full Transcription; Air Traffic Control System Command Center, National Traffic Management Officer, East Position; September 11, 2001," Oct. 21, 2003, p. 31.

170. For 10:17 discussion, see ibid., p. 34. For communication regarding "black smoke," see FAA memo, "Full Transcript; Aircraft Accident; N591UA (UAL93) Somerset, PA; September 11, 2001," May 10, 2002, pp. 16–18 (Cleveland Center, Imperial Radar position). This report from the C-130H was recorded on ATC audio about 1 minute and 37 seconds after the impact time of United 93 as established by NTSB and Commission analysis of FDR, CVR, radar, and impact data sets—more than a minute before the earliest impact time originally posited by the authors of the seismic data report.

171. NEADS audio file, Identification Technician, channel 5, 10:07.

172. NEADS audio file, Mission Crew Commander, channel 2, 10:10.

173. NEADS audio file, Identification Technician, channel 4, 10:14.

174. DOD record, NEADS MCC/T Log Book, Sept. 11, 2001.

175. William Scott testimony, May 23, 2003.

176. Larry Arnold testimony, May 23, 2003.

177. See DOD record, NEADS MCC/T Log Book, Sept. 11, 2001. The entry in this NEADS log records the tail number not of American 77 but of American 11: "American Airlines #N334AA hijacked." See also DOD record, Surveillance Log Book, Sept. 11, 2001.

178. William Scott testimony, May 23, 2003; DOD briefing materials, "Noble Eagle; 9-11 Timeline," undated.

179. For lack of knowledge about the hijacking, see, e.g., White House transcript, Card interview with Ron Fournier of the Associated Press, Aug. 7, 2002. For information on the hijacking within the FAA, see the discussion of American 11 in section 1.2.

180. See White House record, Situation Room Log, Sept. 11, 2001; White House record, Presidential Emergency Operations Center (PEOC) Watch Log, Sept. 11, 2001; DOD record, Senior Operations Officer log, Sept. 11, 2001.

181. Jane Garvey interview (Jun. 30, 2004); Monte Belger interview (Apr. 20, 2004).

182. For notifications, see DOD record, Assistant Deputy Director Operations Passdown Log, Sept. 11, 2001. For the call to the FAA, see DOD record, Senior Operations Officer log, Sept. 11, 2001 ("9:00 NMCC called FAA, briefed of explosion at WTC possibly from aircraft crash. Also, hijacking of American Flight 11 from Boston to LA, now enroute to Kennedy"). For the scrambling of jets not being discussed, see Ryan Gonsalves interview (May 14, 2004).

183. Secret Service records show the motorcade arriving between 8:50 and 8:55. USSS record, shift log, Sept. 11, 2001 (8:55); USSS record, Command Post Protectee Log, Sept. 11, 2001 (8:50). For Andrew Card's recollection, see Andrew Card meeting (Mar. 31, 2004). For the President's reaction, see Andrew Card meeting (Mar. 31, 2004); White House transcript, President Bush interview with Bob Schieffer of CBS News, Apr. 17, 2002.

184. White House transcript, Rice interview with Evan Thomas of *Newsweek*, Nov. 1, 2001, p. 2; see also White House record, President's Daily Diary, Sept. 11, 2001.

185. White House transcript, Vice President Cheney interview with *Newsweek*, Nov. 19, 2001, p. 1.

186. For Rice's meeting, see White House transcript, Rice interview with Bob Woodward of the *Washington Post*, Oct. 24, 2001, pp. 360–361. For White House staff monitoring the news, see, e.g., White House transcript, Rice interview with Evan Thomas, Nov. 11, 2001, p. 388.

187. On White House staff reaction, see White House transcript, Rice interview with Bob Woodward, Oct. 24, 2001, p. 361; Andrew Card meeting (Mar. 31, 2004). On security enhancements, see USSS memo, interview with Carl Truscott, Oct. 1, 2001, p. 1. On security measures being precautionary, see Carl Truscott interview (Apr. 15, 2004).

188. For the time of the teleconference, see FAA record, Chronology ADA-30, Sept. 11, 2001. For recollections of the NMCC officer, see Charles Chambers interview (Apr. 23, 2004). For recollections of the FAA manager, see Michael Weikert interview (May 7, 2004). For Belger's reaction, see Monte Belger testimony, June 17, 2004.

189. For the times of the video teleconference, see White House record, Situation Room Communications Log, Sept. 11, 2001 (9:25 start); CIA notes, Cofer Black timeline, Sept. 11, 2001 (CIA representatives joining at 9:40); FAA record, Chronology ADA-30, Sept. 11, 2001 (FAA representatives joining at 9:40).

190. Patrick Gardner interview (May 12, 2004). For participants, see Jane Garvey interview (Oct. 21, 2003); Monte Belger interview (Apr. 20, 2004); Jeff Griffith interview (Mar. 31, 2004). On the absence of Defense officials, see John Brunderman interview (May 17, 2004). The White House video teleconference was not connected into the area of the NMCC where the crisis was being managed. Thus the director of the operations team—who was on the phone with NORAD—did not have the benefit of information being shared on the video teleconference. See, e.g., Charles Leidig interview (Apr. 29, 2004); Montague Winfield interview (Apr. 26, 2004); Patrick Gardner interview (May 12, 2004). Moreover, when the Secretary and Vice Chairman later participated in the White House video teleconference, they were necessarily absent from the NMCC and unable to provide guidance to the operations team. See DOD report, OT-2 Analysis of NMCC Response to Terrorist Attack on 11 SEP 01, Oct. 4, 2001; John Brunderman interview (May 17, 2004).

191. NSC notes, Paul Kurtz notes, Sept. 11, 2001; Paul Kurtz meeting (Dec. 22, 2003). For shootdown authority having already been conveyed, see DOD transcript, Air Threat Conference Call, Sept. 11, 2001.

192. Charles Leidig interview (Apr. 29, 2004). For the job of the NMCC in an emergency, see NMCC briefing (July 21, 2003).

193. For the Secretary's activities, see DOD memo, interview of Donald Rumsfeld, Dec. 23, 2002; Stephen Cambone interview (July 8, 2004).

194. Charles Leidig interview (Apr. 29, 2004). Secure teleconferences are the NMCC's primary means of coordinating emergencies, and they fall into two categories: "event" and "threat." Event conferences seek to gather information. If the situation escalates, a threat conference may be convened. On 9/11, there was no preset teleconference for a domestic terrorist attack. NMCC and National Military Joint Intelligence Center (NMJIC) briefing (July 21, 2003). For the content of the conferences on 9/11, see DOD transcript, Air Threat Conference Call, Sept. 11, 2001.

195. See DOD transcript, Air Threat Conference Call, Sept. 11, 2001; see also White House notes, Thomas Gould notes, Sept. 11, 2001.

196. On difficulties in including the FAA, see NMCC and NMJIC briefing (July 21, 2003); John Brunderman interview (May 17, 2004). On NORAD and the time of the FAA's joining, see DOD transcript, Air Threat Conference Call, Sept. 11, 2001. For the FAA representative, see Rayford Brooks interview (Apr. 15, 2004).

197. Richard Myers interview (Feb. 17, 2004); Charles Leidig interview (Apr. 29, 2004).

198. DOD transcript, Air Threat Conference Call, Sept. 11, 2001.

199. On the briefing, see ibid. The Vice Chairman was on Capitol Hill when the Pentagon was struck, and he saw smoke as his car made its way back to the building. Richard Myers interview (Feb. 17, 2004). For the Chairman being out of the country, see DOD record, Deputy Director for Operations Passdown Log, Sept. 11, 2001.

200. DOD transcript, Air Threat Conference Call, Sept. 11, 2001.

201. Ibid.

202. Ibid.

203. For the President being informed at 9:05, see White House record, President's Daily Diary, Sept. 11, 2001. For Card's statement, see White House transcript, Card interview with Ron Fournier, Aug. 7, 2002. For the President's reaction, see President Bush and Vice President Cheney meeting (Apr. 29, 2004).

204. For the President's activities, see Education Channel videotape, "Raw Footage of President Bush at Emma E. Booker Elementary School," Sept. 11, 2001 (remaining in classroom); Deborah Loewer meeting (Feb. 6, 2004) (in the holding room). For his calls, see White House record, President's Daily Diary, Sept. 11, 2001 (9:15 call to Vice President); Deborah Loewer meeting (Feb. 6, 2004) (call to Rice); President Bush and Vice President Cheney meeting (Apr. 29, 2004) (call to Pataki); White House record, Secure Switchboard Log, Sept. 11, 2001 (call to Mueller). For the decision to make a statement, see Ari Fleischer interview (Apr. 22, 2004). For the Secret Service's perspective, see Edward Marinzel interview (Apr. 21, 2004).

205. On the return to Washington, see Deborah Loewer meeting (Feb. 6, 2004); Andrew Card meeting (Mar. 31, 2004). On consulting with senior advisers, see Ari Fleischer interview (Apr. 22, 2004). On information about additional aircraft, see, e.g., Andrew Card meeting (Mar. 31, 2004). On decisions and the focus on the President's speech, see President Bush and Vice President Cheney meeting (Apr. 29, 2004); Ari Fleischer interview (Apr. 22, 2004); Andrew Card meeting (Mar. 31, 2004).

206. On the motorcade, see USSS record, shift log, Sept. 11, 2001 (departing 9:35, arriving 9:45); USSS record, Command Post Protectee Log, Sept. 11, 2001 (departing 9:36, arriving 9:42). Fleischer deduced from his notes that the President learned about the Pentagon while in the motorcade. Ari Fleischer interview (Apr. 22, 2004). For the President's actions and statements to the Vice President, see Ari Fleischer interview (Apr. 22, 2004); White House notes, Ari Fleischer notes, Sept. 11, 2001.

207. On not returning to Washington, see Edward Marinzel interview (Apr. 21, 2004); USSS memo, interview of Edward Marinzel, Oct. 3, 2001; Andrew Card meeting (Mar. 31, 2004). For additional sources on the President's desire to return, see White House transcript, Vice President Cheney interview with Newsweek, Nov. 19, 2001, p. 5. For the Vice President's recollection, see President Bush and Vice President Cheney meeting (Apr. 29, 2004). For time of departure, see USSS record, Command Post Protectee Log, Sept. 11, 2001. On Air Force One's objectives on takeoff, see Edward Marinzel interview (Apr. 21, 2004).

208. USSS memo, interview of Gregory LaDow, Oct. 1, 2001, p. 1. Shortly after the second attack in New York, a senior Secret Service agent charged with coordinating the President's movements established an open line with his counterpart at the FAA, who soon told him that there were more planes unaccounted for—possibly hijacked—in addition to the two that had already crashed. Though the senior agent told someone to convey this information to the Secret Service's operations center, it either was not passed on or was passed on but not disseminated; it failed to reach agents assigned to the Vice President, and the Vice President was not evacuated at that time. See Nelson Garabito interview (Mar. 11, 2004); USSS memo, interview of Nelson Garabito, Oct. 1, 2001; see also Terry Van Steenbergen interview (Mar. 30, 2004).

209. American 77's route has been determined through Commission analysis of FAA and military radar data. For the evacuation of the Vice President, see White House transcript, Vice President Cheney interview with *Newsweek*, Nov. 19, 2001, p. 2; USSS memo, interview of Rocco Delmonico, Oct. 1, 2001 (evacuation of the White House); see also White House notes, Mary Matalin notes, Sept. 11, 2001. On the time of entering the tunnel, see USSS report, "Executive Summary: U.S. Secret Service Timeline of Events, September 11–October 3, 2001," Oct. 3, 2001, p. 2. Secret Service personnel told us that the 9:37 entry time in their timeline was based on alarm data, which is no longer retrievable. USSS briefing (Jan. 29, 2004).

210. White House transcript, Vice President Cheney interview with *Newsweek*, Nov. 19, 2001, p. 4; President Bush and Vice President Cheney meeting (Apr. 29, 2004).

211. On Mrs. Cheney, see USSS report, "Executive Summary: U.S. Secret Service Timeline of Events, September 11–October 3, 2001," Oct. 3, 2001, p. 2 (time of arrival); White House transcript, Lynne Cheney interview with *Newsweek*, Nov. 9, 2001, p. 2 (joining the Vice President). For the contemporaneous notes, see White House notes, Lynne Cheney notes, Sept. 11, 2001. On the content of the Vice President's call, see White House transcript, Vice President Cheney interview with *Newsweek*, Nov. 19, 2001, p. 5. According to the Vice President, there was "one phone call from the tunnel. And basically I called to let him know that we were a target and I strongly urged him not to return to Washington right away, that he delay his return until we could find out what the hell was going on." For their subsequent movements, see White House transcript, Vice President Cheney interview with *Newsweek*, Nov. 19, 2001, p. 5; White House transcript, Lynne Cheney interview with *Newsweek*, Nov. 9, 2001, p. 2.

212. On communications problems, see, e.g., President Bush and Vice President Cheney meeting (Apr. 29, 2004). On lack of an open line, see, e.g., Deborah Loewer meeting (Feb. 6, 2004).

213. On the Vice President's call, see President Bush and Vice President Cheney meeting (Apr. 29, 2004). For the Vice President's time of arrival in the shelter conference room, see White House record, PEOC Shelter Log, Sept. 11, 2001 (9:58); USSS memo, OVP 9/11 Timeline, Nov. 17, 2001 (9:52; Mrs. Cheney arrived White House and joined him in tunnel); White House notes, Lynne Cheney notes, Sept. 11, 2001 (9:55; he is on phone with President); White House transcript, Lynne Cheney interview with *Newsweek*, Nov. 9, 2001, p. 2 ("And when I got there, he was on the phone with the President . . . But from that first place where I ran into him, I moved with him into what they call the PEOC"); White House transcript, Vice President Cheney interview with *Newsweek*, Nov. 19, 2001, p. 4 (9:35 or 9:36 arrival; he estimated a 15-minute stay); Carl Truscott interview (Apr. 15, 2004) (arrived with Rice and the Vice President in conference room; called headquarters immediately; call logged at 10:00); President Bush and Vice President Cheney meeting, Apr. 29, 2004 (Vice President viewed television footage of Pentagon ablaze in tunnel); White House transcript, Rice interview with Evan Thomas, Nov. 1, 2001, p. 388 (Rice viewed television footage of Pentagon ablaze in Situation Room). For the Vice President's recollection about the combat air patrol, see President Bush and Vice President Cheney meeting (Apr. 29, 2004); White House transcript, President Bush interview with Bob Woodward and Dan Balz, Dec. 17, 2001, p. 16.

214. President Bush and Vice President Cheney meeting (Apr. 29, 2004); see also White House transcript, Vice President Cheney interview with *Newsweek*, Nov. 19, 2001, pp. 7–8.

215. Douglas Cochrane meeting (Apr. 16, 2004); Condeleeza Rice meeting (Feb. 7, 2004). For Rice entering after the Vice President, see USSS report, "Executive Summary: U.S. Secret Service Timeline of Events, September 11–October 3, 2001," Oct. 3, 2001, p. 2; Carl Truscott interview (Apr. 15, 2004).

216. In reconstructing events that occurred in the PEOC on the morning of 9/11, we relied on (1) phone logs of the White House switchboard; (2) notes of Lewis Libby, Mrs. Cheney, and Ari Fleischer; (3) the tape (and then transcript) of the air threat conference call; and (4) Secret Service and White House Situation Room logs, as well as four separate White House Military Office logs (the PEOC Watch Log, the PEOC Shelter Log, the Communications Log, and the 9/11 Log).

217. DOD transcript, Air Threat Conference Call, Sept. 11, 2001. For one open line between the Secret Service and the FAA, see note 208. At Secret Service headquarters, personnel from the intelligence division were also on a phone conference with FAA headquarters. Chuck Green interview (Mar. 10, 2004). For notification of an inbound aircraft at 10:02, see USSS record, Intelligence Division timeline, Sept. 11, 2001; USSS record, Crisis Center Incident Monitor, Sept. 11, 2001. For the FAA's projection, see Tim Grovack interview (Apr. 8, 2004). For Secret Service updates, see DOD transcript, Air Threat Conference Call, Sept. 11, 2001.

218. White House notes, Lynne Cheney notes, Sept. 11, 2001; White House notes, Lewis Libby notes, Sept. 11, 2001.

219. For Libby's characterization, see White House transcript, Scooter Libby interview with *Newsweek*, Nov. 2001. For the Vice President's statement, see President Bush and Vice President Cheney meeting (Apr. 29, 2004). For the second authorization, see White House notes, Lynne Cheney notes, Sept. 11, 2001; White House notes, Lewis Libby notes, Sept. 11, 2001.

220. Joshua Bolten meeting (Mar. 18, 2004); see also White House notes, Lewis Libby notes, Sept. 11, 2001 ("10:15–18: Aircraft 60 miles out, confirmed as hijack—engage? VP: Yes. JB [Joshua Bolten]: Get President and confirm engage order").

221. For the Vice President's call, see White House record, Secure Switchboard Log, Sept. 11, 2001; White House record, President's Daily Diary, Sept. 11, 2001; White House notes, Lewis Libby notes, Sept. 11, 2001. Fleischer's 10:20 note is the first mention of shootdown authority. See White House notes, Ari Fleischer notes, Sept. 11, 2001; see also Ari Fleischer interview (Apr. 22, 2004).

222. DOD transcript, Air Threat Conference Call, Sept. 11, 2001.

223. On reports of another plane, see White House notes, Lynne Cheney notes, Sept. 11, 2001; White House notes, Lewis Libby notes, Sept. 11, 2001. On the Vice President's authorization, see ibid.; DOD transcript, Air Threat Conference Call, Sept. 11, 2001. For Hadley's statement, see DOD transcript, Air Threat Conference Call, Sept. 11, 2001.

224. For the quotation, see White House transcript, Libby interview with *Newsweek*, Nov. 2001. On the aircraft's identity, see White House record, White House Military Office Log, Sept. 11, 2001.

225. On the NMCC, see DOD transcript, Air Threat Conference Call, Sept. 11, 2001. On the Secret Service's contacts with the FAA, see notes 208, 217. On the Secret Service conveying information to the White House, see DOD transcript, Air Threat Conference Call, Sept. 11, 2001; Nelson Garabito interview (Mar. 11, 2004).

226. DOD transcript, Air Threat Conference Call, Sept. 11, 2001.

227. Ibid.

228. Ralph Eberhart interview (Mar. 1, 2004). On the morning of 9/11, General Eberhart was in his office at headquarters—roughly 30 minutes away from Cheyenne Mountain, where the operations center is located.

229. DOD record, Continental Region chat log, Sept. 11, 2001.

230. NEADS audio file, Mission Crew Commander position, channel 2, 10:32:12. For the text of the chat log message, see DOD record, Continental Region chat log, Sept. 11, 2001.

231. For the statements of NEADS personnel, see Robert Marr interview (Jan. 23, 2004) (NEADS commander); Kevin Nasypany interview (Jan. 22, 2004) (mission commander); James Fox interview (Oct. 29, 2004) (senior weapons director). On the understanding of leaders in Washington, see DOD transcript, Air Threat Conference Call, Sept. 11, 2001. For the orders to Langley pilots, see NEADS audio file, Weapons Director position, recorder 1, channel 2, 10:10–11.

232. For evidence of the President speaking to Rumsfeld, see White House notes, Ari Fleischer notes, Sept. 11, 2001. On inability to recall this conversation, see Donald Rumsfeld interview (Jan. 30, 2004).

233. DOD note, transcript of Air Threat Conference Call, Sept. 11, 2001.

234. Donald Rumsfeld interview (Jan. 30, 2004). At 11:15, Secretary Rumsfeld spoke to the President and told him DOD was working on refining the rules of engagement so pilots would have a better understanding of the circumstances under which an aircraft could be shot down. See, e.g., DOD notes, Stephen Cambone notes, Sept. 11, 2001. DOD did not circulate written rules of engagement until sometime after 1:00 P.M. See DOD memo, rules of engagement, Sept. 11, 2001 (faxed to Andrews Air Force Base at 1:45 P.M.).

235. David Wherley interview (Feb. 27, 2004).

236. The 113th Wing first learned from the FAA tower at Andrews that the Secret Service wanted fighters airborne. The FAA tower had been contacted by personnel at FAA headquarters, who were on an open line with senior agents from the President's detail. See Nelson Garabito interview (Mar. 11, 2004); Terry Van Steenbergen interview (Mar. 30, 2004). On the Secret Service agent relaying instructions, see USSS memo, Beauchamp to AD-Inspection, September 11 experience, Feb. 23, 2004. On the order to fly weapons free, see David Wherley interview (Feb. 27, 2004); DOD memo, interview of David Wherley, Oct. 3, 2001, p. 12.

237. President Bush and Vice President Cheney meeting (Apr. 29, 2004).

238. These estimates are based on analysis of Boeing 757 maximum operating speed data, FAA and military radar data, and assumptions regarding how the airplane would be operated en route to the Washington, D.C., area. The shortest time frame assumes maximum speed without regard to overspeed warnings, a straight-line path, and no time allowed for maneuvering or slowing to aim and crash the airplane into its target. The probable time frame allows for speeds consistent with the observed operation of the airplane prior to its final maneuvers and crash, as well as for maneuvers and slowing in the D.C. area to take aim. According to radar data, the fighters from Langley Air Force Base arrived over Washington at about 10:00 A.M. Two of the three Langley fighters were fully armed (i.e., with missiles and guns); the third fighter carried only guns. Craig Borgstrom interview (Dec. 1, 2003).

239. For the pilots' awareness, see Dean Eckmann interview (Dec. 1, 2003); Bradley Derrig interview (Dec. 1, 2003); Craig Borgstrom interview (Dec. 1, 2003). For the quotation, see Dean Eckmann interview (Dec. 1, 2003).

240. For no authority at 10:10, see NEADS audio file, Mission Crew Commander, channel 2. For shootdown

authority at 10:31, see DOD record, Continental Region chat log, Sept. 11, 2001. For possibility of ordering a shoot-down, see Larry Arnold interview (Feb. 2, 2004).

241. NEADS audio file, Identification Technician position, recorder 1, channel 4, 10:02:22.

2 The Foundation of the New Terrorism

1. "Text of World Islamic Front's Statement Urging Jihad Against Jews and Crusaders," *Al Quds al Arabi*, Feb. 23, 1998 (trans. Foreign Broadcast Information Service), which was published for a large Arab world audience and signed by Usama Bin Ladin, Ayman al Zawahiri (emir of the Egyptian Islamic Jihad), Abu Yasir Rifa'i Ahmad Taha (leader of the Egyptian Islamic Group), Mir Hamzah (secretary of the Jamiat ul Ulema e Pakistan), and Fazlul Rahman (head of the Jihad Movement in Bangladesh).

2. "Hunting Bin Ladin," PBS *Frontline* broadcast, May 1998 (online at www.pbs.org/wgbh/pages/frontline/shows/binladen/who/interview.html).

3. Usama Bin Ladin, "Declaration of War Against the Americans Occupying the Land of the Two Holy Places," Aug. 23, 1996 (trans., online at www.terrorismfiles.org/individuals/declaration_of_jihad1.html).

4. "Hunting Bin Ladin," PBS *Frontline* broadcast, May 1998.

5. Ibid.

6. For a classic passage conveying the nostalgic view of Islam's spread, see Henri Pirenne, *A History of Europe*, trans. Bernard Miall (University Books, 1956), pp. 25–26.

7. See Martin Marty and R. Scott Appleby, eds., *Fundamentalism Observed*, vol. 1 (Univ. of Chicago Press, 1994).

8. See Emmanuel Sivan, *Radical Islam: Medieval Theology and Modern Politics*, enlarged ed. (Yale Univ. Press, 1990).

9. From the perspective of Islamic, not Arab, history, the Baghdad Caliphate's destruction by the Mongols in 1292 marks the end not of Islamic greatness but of Arab dominance of the Muslim world. Moghul India, Safavid Persia, and, above all, the Ottoman Empire were great Islamic powers that arose long after the Baghdad Caliphate fell.

10. Bin Ladin, "Declaration of War," Aug. 23, 1996.

11. The Muslim Brotherhood, which arose in Egypt in 1928 as a Sunni religious/nationalist opposition to the British-backed Egyptian monarchy, spread throughout the Arab world in the mid–twentieth century. In some countries, its oppositional role is nonviolent; in others, especially Egypt, it has alternated between violent and nonviolent struggle with the regime.

12. Sayyid Qutb, *Milestones* (American Trust Publications, 1990). Qutb found sin everywhere, even in rural midwestern churches. Qutb's views were best set out in Sayyid Qutb, "The America I Have Seen" (1949), reprinted in Kamal Abdel-Malek, ed., *America in an Arab Mirror: Images of America in Arabic Travel Literature: An Anthology* (Palgrave, 2000).

13. For a good introduction to Qutb, see National Public Radio broadcast, "Sayyid Qutb's America," May 6, 2003 (online at www.npr.org/display_pages/features/feature_1253796.html).

14. "Bin Laden's 'Letter to America,'" *Observer Worldview*, Nov. 24, 2002 (trans., online at http://observer.guardian.co.uk/worldview/story/0,11581,845725,00.html). The al Qaeda letter was released in conjunction with the release of an audio message from Bin Ladin himself.

15. Ibid.

16. See *Arab Human Development Report 2003* (United Nations, 2003), a report prepared by Arabs that examines not only standard statistical data but also more sensitive social indicators recently identified by the Nobel Prize–winning economist Amartya Sen. It says little, however, about the political dimensions of economic and social trends. See Mark LeVine, "The UN Arab Human Development Report: A Critique," *Middle East Report*, July 26, 2002 (online at www.merip.org/mero/mer0072602.html).

17. President Bush, remarks at roundtable with Arab- and Muslim-American leaders, Sept. 10, 2002 (online at www.whitehouse.gov/news/releases/2002/09/20020910-7.html).

18. See, e.g., Intelligence report, interrogation of Zubaydah, Oct. 29, 2002; CIA analytic report, "Bin Ladin's Terrorist Operations: Meticulous and Adaptable," CTC 00-40017CSH, Nov. 2, 2000.

19. "Open resistance flared so quickly that only two months after the invasion . . . almost the entire population of Kabul climbed on their rooftops and chanted with one voice, 'God is great.' This open defiance of the Russian generals who could physically destroy their city was matched throughout the countryside." General (Ret.) Mohammed Yahya Nawwroz and Lester W. Grau, "The Soviet War in Afghanistan; History and Harbinger of Future War?" *Military Review* (Fort Leavenworth Foreign Military Studies Office), Sept./Oct. 1995, p. 2.

20. Rohan Gunaratna, *Inside Al Qaeda: Global Network of Terror* (Columbia Univ. Press, 2002), pp. 16–23. Regarding UBL's access to his family's fortune, see Rick Newcomb interview (Feb. 4, 2004); William Wechsler interview (Jan. 7, 2004).

21. Government's Evidentiary Proffer Supporting the Admissibility of Co-Conspirator Statements, *United States v. Enaam Arnaout*, No. 02-CR-892 (N.D. Ill. filed Jan. 6, 2003).

22. Intelligence report, Terrorism: Usama Bin Ladin's Historical Links to 'Abdallah Azzam, Apr. 18, 1997. By

most accounts, Bin Ladin initially viewed Azzam as a mentor, and became in effect his partner by providing financial backing for the MAK.

23. In his memoir, Ayman al Zawahiri contemptuously rejects the claim that the Arab mujahideen were financed (even "one penny") or trained by the United States. See Zawahiri, "Knights Under the Prophet's Banner," *Al Sharq al Awsat*, Dec. 2, 2001. CIA officials involved in aiding the Afghan resistance regard Bin Ladin and his "Arab Afghans" as having been militarily insignificant in the war and recall having little to do with him. Gary Schroen interview (Mar. 3, 2003).

24. See Abdullah Azzam, "Al Qaeda al Sulbah" (The solid foundation), *Al Jihad*, Apr. 1988, p. 46.

25. A wealth of information on al Qaeda's evolution and history has been obtained from materials seized in recent years, including files labeled "Tareekh Usama" (Usama's history) and "Tareekh al Musadat" (History of the Services Bureau). For descriptions of and substantial excerpts from these files, see Government's Evidentiary Proffer Supporting the Admissibility of Co-Conspirator Statements, *United States v. Arnaout*, Jan. 6, 2003. See also Intelligence report, Terrorism: Historical Background of the Islamic Army and bin Ladin's Move from Afghanistan to Sudan, Nov. 26, 1996; DOD document, "Al-Qaeda," AFGP-2002-000080 (translated). For a particularly useful insight into the evolution of al Qaeda—written by an early Bin Ladin associate, Adel Batterjee, under a pseudonym—see Basil Muhammad, *Al Ansar al Arab fi Afghanistan* (The Arab volunteers in Afghanistan) (Benevolence International Foundation (BIF) and World Association of Muslim Youth, 1991).

26. Government's Evidentiary Proffer Supporting the Admissibility of Co-Conspirator Statements, *United States v. Arnaout*, Jan. 6, 2003.

27. See FBI report of investigation, interview of Jamal al Fadl, Nov. 10, 1996; Gunaratna, *Inside Al Qaeda*, p. 23.

28. Daniel Benjamin and Steven Simon, *The Age of Sacred Terror* (Random House, 2002), pp. 6–7, 57–63, 83–85; *United States v. Rahman*, 189 F.3d 88, 104–105, 123–124 (2d Cir. Aug. 16, 1996).

29. Gunaratna, *Inside Al Qaeda*, pp. 25–27; DOD document, "Union Agreement between Jama'at Qaedat Ansar Allah (The Base Group of Allah Supporters) and Jama'at Al-Jihad (Jihad Group)," AFGP-2002-000081, undated; Benjamin and Simon, *Age of Sacred Terror*, p. 103.

30. Trial testimony of Jamal al Fadl, *United States v. Usama bin Laden*, No. S(7) 98 Cr. 1023 (S.D. N.Y.), Feb. 6, 2001 (transcript pp. 218–219, 233); Feb. 13, 2001 (transcript pp. 514–516); Feb. 20, 2001 (transcript p. 890). Fadl says this invitation was delivered by a Sudanese delegation that visited Bin Ladin in Afghanistan. See also CIA analytic report, "Al-Qa'ida in Sudan, 1992–1996: Old School Ties Lead Down Dangerous Paths," CTC 2003-40028CHX, Mar. 10, 2003.

31. See Intelligence report, Terrorism: Historical Background of the Islamic Army and bin Ladin's Move from Afghanistan to Sudan, Nov. 26, 1996.

32. Trial testimony of Fadl, *United States v. bin Laden*, Feb. 6, 2001 (transcript pp. 220–224).

33. For Bin Ladin's confrontation with the Saudi regime, see, e.g., Peter L. Bergen, *Holy War Inc.: Inside the Secret World of Osama bin Ladin* (Touchstone, 2001), pp. 80–82. On aid provided by a dissident member of the royal family, see Intelligence report, interrogation of KSM, Sept. 27, 2003; Intelligence report, interrogation of Khallad, Sept. 26, 2003. See also FBI report of investigation, interview of Fadl, Nov. 10, 1996.

34. Gunaratna, *Inside Al Qaeda*, p. 34.

35. Intelligence report, Bin Ladin's business activities in 1992, Mar. 31, 1994; Intelligence report, Terrorism: Historical Background of the Islamic Army and bin Ladin's Move from Afghanistan to Sudan, Nov. 26, 1996; CIA analytic report, "Old School Ties," Mar. 10, 2003.

36. Trial testimony of Fadl, *United States v. bin Laden*, Feb. 6, 2001 (transcript pp. 301–302, 305–306, 315–317, 367–368); Intelligence report, Terrorism: Historical Background of the Islamic Army and bin Ladin's Move from Afghanistan to Sudan, Nov. 26, 1996; CIA analytic report, "Old School Ties," Mar. 10, 2003.

37. See Intelligence report, Bin Ladin's business activities in 1992, Mar. 31, 1994; Intelligence report, Shipment of Arms and Boats to Yemen for Use by an Islamic Extremist, Aug. 9, 1996; Intelligence report, Terrorism: Responsibilities and Background of Islamic Army Shura Council, Dec. 19, 1996; CIA analytic report, "Old School Ties," Mar. 10, 2003; FBI reports of investigation, interviews of Fadl, Nov. 10, 1996; Nov. 12, 1996; CIA analytic report, "Usama Bin Ladin: Al-Qa'ida's Business and Financial Links in Southeast Asia," CTC 2002-40066CH, June 6, 2002. For Bin Ladin's involvement in the Bosnian conflicts, see Evan F. Kohlmann, *Al-Qaida's Jihad in Europe: The Afghan-Bosnian Network* (Berg, 2004).

38. Trial testimony of Fadl, *United States v. bin Laden*, Feb. 7, 2001 (transcript p. 354); FBI reports of investigation, interviews of Fadl, Nov. 10, 1996; Dec. 21, 1998; "RP Cops Aware of Long-Term Rightwing Muslim Connection," *Manila Times*, Apr. 26, 2002.

39. Trial testimony of Fadl, *United States v. bin Laden*, Feb. 7, 2001 (transcript pp. 354–355); FBI report of investigation, interview of Fadl, Feb. 4, 1998. See also Republic of Singapore, Ministry of Home Affairs, Report to Parliament, "The Jemaah Islamiyah Arrests and the Threat of Terrorism," Jan. 7, 2003.

40. Benjamin and Simon, *Age of Sacred Terror*, pp. 100, 235.

41. See CIA analytic report, "Arizona: Long-Term Nexus For Islamic Extremists," CTC 2002-30037H, May 15, 2002; Steven Emerson, *American Jihad* (Free Press, 2002), pp. 129–137.

42. Intelligence report, Fatwa to attack U.S. interests in Saudi Arabia and movement of explosives to Saudi Arabia, Jan. 8 1997; trial testimony of Fadl, *United States v. bin Laden*, Feb. 6, 2001 (transcript pp. 265–266); trial testimony of L'Houssaine Kherchtou, *United States v. bin Laden*, Feb. 21, 2001 (transcript p. 1163); FBI reports of investigation, interviews of Fadl, Nov. 10, 1996; Nov. 12, 1996; FBI report of investigation, interview of confidential source, Sept. 16, 1999.

43. On Wali Khan's relationship with Bin Ladin, see Intelligence report, Usama Bin Ladin's Historical Links to 'Abdallah Azzam, Apr. 18, 1997; FBI report of investigation, interview of Fadl, Nov. 10, 1996; Muhammad, *Al Ansar al Arab fi Afghanistan*. On the Blind Sheikh, Bin Ladin eventually spoke publicly of his admiration. See ABC News interview, "To Terror's Source," May 28, 1998. In late 1992, Abu Zubaydah confided to his diary that he was getting ready to go to one of al Qaeda's military camps: "Perhaps later I will tell you about the Qa'ida and Bin Ladin group." Intelligence report, translation of Abu Zubaydah's diary, June 9, 2002. Ramzi Yousef and Khalid Sheikh Mohammed masterminded the 1995 Manila air plot, and KSM helped fund Yousef's attempt to blow up the World Trade Center in 1993. Intelligence report, interrogation of KSM, Jan. 9, 2004. The Blind Sheikh was linked to Yousef and the 1993 World Trade Center attack, while Wali Khan was convicted together with Yousef for the Manila air conspiracy.

44. Intelligence report, Usama Bin Ladin Links to a Southern Yemeni Group, Mar. 5, 1997; FBI report of investigation, interview of Fadl, Nov. 10, 1996; CIA analytic report, "Old School Ties," Mar. 10, 2003, p. 4.

45. U.S. intelligence did not learn of al Qaeda's role in Somalia until 1996. Intelligence report, Bin Ladin's Activities in Somalia and Sudanese NIF Support, Apr. 30, 1997.

46. Intelligence report, Bin Ladin's Activities in Eritrea, Mar. 10, 1997; FBI report of investigation, interview of confidential source, Sept. 16, 1999; FBI report of investigation, interview of Essam Mohamed al Ridi, Dec. 7, 1999; trial testimony of Essam Mohamed al Ridi, *United States v. bin Laden*, Feb. 14, 2001 (transcript pp. 578–593); trial testimony of Fadl, *United States v. bin Laden*, Feb. 6, 2001 (transcript pp. 279–285). In June 1998, Bin Ladin was indicted on charges arising out of the Somalia attack in the U.S. District Court for the Southern District of New York.

47. For background about the attack on the training facility, see, e.g., Benjamin and Simon, *Age of Sacred Terror*, pp. 132, 242. On the proposed attack in Saudi Arabia, see Intelligence report, Fatwa to attack U.S. interests in Saudi Arabia and movement of explosives to Saudi Arabia, Jan. 8, 1997; FBI reports of investigation, interviews of Fadl, Nov. 12, 1996; Feb. 13, 1998. On associates taking credit, see Intelligence report made available to the Commission.

48. CIA analytic report, "Khobar Bombing: Saudi Shia, Iran, and Usama Bin Ladin All Suspects," CTC 96-30015, July 5, 1996; DIA analytic report, Defense Intelligence Threat Review 96-007, July 1996; Intelligence report made available to the Commission. See also Benjamin and Simon, *Age of Sacred Terror*, pp. 224–225, 300–302.

49. Intelligence report, Usama Bin Ladin's Attempts to Acquire Uranium, Mar. 18, 1997; CIA analytic report, "Usama Bin Ladin Trying to Develop WMD Capability?" CTC 97-30002, Jan. 6, 1997; trial testimony of Fadl, *United States v. bin Laden*, Feb. 7, 2001 (transcript pp. 357–366); Feb. 13, 2001 (transcript pp. 528–529); Feb. 20, 2001 (transcript pp. 982–985).

50. Trial testimony of Fadl, *United States v. bin Laden*, Feb. 13, 2001 (transcript p. 528).

51. CIA analytic report, "Old School Ties," Mar. 10, 2003.

52. Intelligence report, Establishment of a Tripartite Agreement Among Usama Bin Ladin, Iran, and the NIF, Jan. 31, 1997; Intelligence report, Cooperation Among Usama Bin Ladin's Islamic Army, Iran, and the NIF, Jan. 31 1997; FBI report of investigation, interview of Fadl, Nov. 10, 1996; trial testimony of Fadl, *United States v. bin Laden*, Feb. 6, 2001 (transcript pp. 290–293); FBI report of investigation, interview of confidential source, Sept. 16, 1999.

53. CIA analytic report, "Ansar al-Islam: Al Qa'ida's Ally in Northeastern Iraq," CTC 2003-40011CX, Feb. 1, 2003.

54. Ibid.; Intelligence report, al Qaeda and Iraq, Aug. 1, 1997.

55. Intelligence reports, interrogations of detainee, May 22, 2003; May 24, 2003. At least one of these reports dates the meeting to 1994, but other evidence indicates the meeting may have occurred in February 1995. Greg interview (June 25, 2004).

Two CIA memoranda of information from a foreign government report that the chief of Iraq's intelligence service and a military expert in bomb making met with Bin Ladin at his farm outside Khartoum on July 30, 1996. The source claimed that Bin Ladin asked for and received assistance from the bomb-making expert, who remained there giving training until September 1996, which is when the information was passed to the United States. See Intelligence reports made available to the Commission. The information is puzzling, since Bin Ladin left Sudan for Afghanistan in May 1996, and there is no evidence he ventured back there (or anywhere else) for a visit. In examining the source material, the reports note that the information was received "third hand," passed from the foreign government service that "does not meet directly with the ultimate source of the information, but obtains the information from him through two unidentified intermediaries, one of whom merely delivers the information to the Service." The same source claims that the bomb-making expert had been seen in the area of Bin Ladin's Sudan farm in December 1995.

56. Intelligence report, Possible Islamic Army Foreknowledge of an "Egyptian Operation" and Logistical and

Security Assistance Provided for the Attackers, Feb. 13, 1997; FBI report of investigation, interview of Fadl, Nov. 4, 1997.

57. Tim Carney interview (Dec. 4, 2003).

58. Trial testimony of L'Houssaine Kherchtou, *United States v. bin Laden*, Feb. 21, 2001 (transcript pp. 1280–1282).

59. On the Sudanese economy, see, e.g., Benjamin and Simon, *Age of Sacred Terror*, pp. 114–115, 132–133. For details about Saudi pressure on the Bin Ladin family, see, e.g., Frank G. interview (Mar. 2, 2004). Regarding management of Bin Ladin's finances, see CIA analytic report, "Usama Bin Ladin: Al-Qa'ida's Financial Facilitators," OTI IA 2001-134-HXC, Oct. 18, 2001; CIA analytic report, "Shaykh Sa'id: Al-Qa'ida's Loyal Senior Accountant," CTC 2003-30072H, July 2, 2003; Intelligence reports, interrogations of detainee, Sept. 17, 1998; Aug. 4, 1999. On the financial crisis in al Qaeda at this time, see trial testimony of L'Houssaine Kherchtou, *United States v. bin Laden*, Feb. 21, 2001 (transcript pp. 1282–1284).

60. Trial testimony of Fadl, *United States v. bin Laden*, Feb. 6, 2001 (transcript pp. 165–174, 190–205, 255–258); Feb. 7, 2001 (transcript pp. 382–391); trial testimony of L'Houssaine Kherchtou, *United States v. bin Laden*, Feb. 21, 2001 (transcript pp. 1282–1284).

61. Because the U.S. embassy in Khartoum had been closed in response to terrorist threats, the U.S. Ambassador to Sudan was working out of the embassy in Nairobi. The Sudanese regime notified him there by fax. See Tim Carney interview (Dec. 4, 2003); Donald Petterson interview (Sept. 30, 2003); DOS cable, Nairobi 7020, "Sudan: Foreign Minister on Developments re Terrorism and Peace," May 21, 1996. On the attempted assassination of Bin Ladin, see FBI report of investigation, interview of L'Houssaine Kherchtou, Oct. 15, 2000; FBI report of investigation, interview of confidential source, Sept. 16, 1999.

62. Intelligence report, interrogation of KSM, July 23, 2003.

63. Ahmed Rashid, *Taliban: Militant Islam, Oil and Fundamentalism in Central Asia* (Yale Univ. Press, 2000), p. 133; Steve Coll, *Ghost Wars: The Secret History of the CIA, Afghanistan, and bin Laden, from the Soviet Invasion to September 10, 2001* (Penguin, 2004), p. 9; Intelligence reports, interrogations of KSM, July 12, 2003; Sept. 27, 2003; Intelligence report, interrogation of Khallad, Sept. 27, 2003. The current Afghan Foreign Minister told us that one of Bin Ladin's planes landed in Islamabad for refueling. See Abdullah Abdullah interview (Oct. 23, 2003).

64. Rashid, *Taliban*, pp. 88–90.

65. See Owen Bennet Jones, *Pakistan: Eye of the Storm* (Yale Univ. Press, 2002); Raffat Pasha interview (Oct. 25, 2003); Rashid, *Taliban*; Waleed Ziad, "How the Holy Warriors Learned to Hate," *New York Times*, June 18, 2004, p. A31.

66. See, e.g., Marvin Weinbaum interview (Aug. 12, 2003); William Milam interview (Dec. 29, 2003). Milam described "strategic depth" as Pakistan's need for a friendly, pliable neighbor on the west due to its hostile relationship with India on the east.

67. On Pakistan's consent, see Ahmed Rashid interview (Oct. 27, 2003); see also Rashid, *Taliban*, p. 139; Intelligence report, Terrorism: Activities of Bin Ladin's in Pakistan, Afghanistan, and India, July 14, 1997; FBI investigation, interview of former al Qaeda associate, Mar. 19, 2001, p. 26. On the Afghanistan-Pakistan-centered network of guesthouses and training camps, see CIA analytic report, "Sketch of a South Asia–Based Terrorist Training and Logistic Network," DI TR 95-12, Dec. 1995; CIA analytic report, "The Rise of UBL and Al-Qa'ida and the Intelligence Community Response," Mar. 19, 2004 (draft), p. 11.

68. On Bin Ladin's money problems, see trial testimony of L'Houssaine Kherchtou, *United States v. bin Laden*, Feb. 21, 2003 (transcript pp. 1282–1286); Frank G. and Mary S. briefing (July 15, 2003); DOS cable, Nairobi 11468, "Sudan: Major Usama Bin Ladin Asset Deregistered," Aug. 6, 1996; Intelligence report, interrogation of KSM, July 30, 2003. See also Robert Block, "In War on Terrorism, Sudan Struck a Blow by Fleecing Bin Laden," *Wall Street Journal*, Dec. 3, 2001, p. A1.

69. FBI report of investigation, interview of confidential source, Sept. 16, 1999; trial testimony of Ashif Juma, *United States v. bin Laden*, Feb. 15, 2001 (transcript pp. 626–627); trial testimony of L'Houssaine Kherchtou, *United States v. bin Laden*, Feb. 22, 2001 (transcript pp. 1264–1267); FBI report of investigation, interview of L'Houssaine Kherchtou, Aug. 28, 2000. See also Intelligence report, interrogation of Khallad, Sept. 27, 2003.

70. See trial testimony of L'Houssaine Kherchtou, *United States v. bin Laden*, Feb. 22, 2001 (transcript pp. 1282–1286).

71. Intelligence report, interrogation of KSM, July 12, 2003; Gunaratna, *Inside Al Qaeda*, p. 41; Rashid, *Taliban*, pp. 19–21, 133.

72. For Bin Ladin's 1996 fatwa, see Bin Ladin, "Declaration of War," Aug. 23, 1996. On constraints from the Sudanese, see Intelligence report, interrogation of KSM, Feb. 20, 2004. On warnings from the Saudi monarchy, see Intelligence report, Timeline of events from 1993 bombing of World Trade Center through 9/11 (citing cables from Apr. 1997).

73. On Bin Ladin's promise to Taliban leaders, see government exhibit no. 1559-T, *United States v. bin Laden*. For the Bin Ladin interview, see CNN broadcast, interview of Bin Ladin by Peter Arnett on Mar. 20, 1997, May 9, 1997 (available online at http://news.findlaw.com/cnn/docs/binladen/binladenintvw-cnn.pdf). According to

KSM, Bin Ladin moved to Kandahar "by order of Emir Al-Mouminin," that is, Mullah Omar. See Intelligence report, interrogation of KSM, July 12, 2003. On the Taliban's invitation to UBL, see Mike briefing (Dec. 12, 2003); Rashid, *Taliban*, p. 129. Rashid has also described the move as part of Bin Ladin's plan to solidify his relationship with, and eventually gain control over, the Taliban. Ahmed Rashid interview (Oct. 27, 2003).

74. Intelligence report, unsuccessful Bin Ladin probes for contact with Iraq, July 24, 1998; Intelligence report, Saddam Hussein's efforts to repair relations with Saudi government, 2001.

75. Intelligence report, Iraq approach to Bin Ladin, Mar. 16, 1999.

76. CIA analytic report, "Ansar al-Islam: Al Qa'ida's Ally in Northeastern Iraq," CTC 2003-40011CX, Feb. 1, 2003. See also DIA analytic report, "Special Analysis: Iraq's Inconclusive Ties to Al-Qaida," July 31, 2002; CIA analytic report, "Old School Ties," Mar. 10, 2003. We have seen other intelligence reports at the CIA about 1999 contacts. They are consistent with the conclusions we provide in the text, and their reliability is uncertain. Although there have been suggestions of contacts between Iraq and al Qaeda regarding chemical weapons and explosives training, the most detailed information alleging such ties came from an al Qaeda operative who recanted much of his original information. Intelligence report, interrogation of al Qaeda operative, Feb. 14, 2004. Two senior Bin Ladin associates have adamantly denied that any such ties existed between al Qaeda and Iraq. Intelligence reports, interrogations of KSM and Zubaydah, 2003 (cited in CIA letter, response to Douglas Feith memorandum, "Requested Modifications to 'Summary of Body of Intelligence Reporting on Iraq–al Qaida Contacts (1990–2003),'" Dec. 10, 2003, p. 5).

77. On Gulf-based donors to Bin Ladin, see Frank G. and Mary S. briefing (July 15, 2003); CIA analytic report, "Saudi-Based Financial Support for Terrorist Organizations," CTC 2002-40117CH, Nov. 14, 2002. On the relationship between Bin Ladin and Omar, see Intelligence report, interrogation of detainee, Feb. 20, 2002. On relations between the Arabs in Afghanistan and the Taliban, see ibid. On financial relations, see CIA analytic report, "Ariana Afghan Airlines: Assets and Activities," OTI IR 1999-170CX, July 29, 1999; CIA, NID, "Near East: UAE: Imposition of Sanctions Could Disrupt Bin Ladin's Finances," June 9, 1999.

78. CIA analytic report, "Afghanistan: An Incubator for International Terrorism," CTC 01-40004, Mar. 27, 2001; CIA analytic report, "Al-Qa'ida Still Well Positioned to Recruit Terrorists," July 1, 2002, p. 1.

79. The number of actual al Qaeda members seems to have been relatively small during the period before 9/11, although estimates vary considerably, from the low hundreds to as many as 5,000. For the low hundreds, see Intelligence report, interrogation of KSM, Dec. 3, 2003. For 5,000, see Intelligence report, interrogation of Khallad, Nov. 26, 2003. Khallad added that because pledging *bayat* was secret, the number of al Qaeda members can only be speculative. On al Qaeda's training and indoctrination, see minutes from the August 1988 meeting leading to the official formation of al Qaeda, cited in Government's Evidentiary Proffer Supporting the Admissibility of Co-conspirator Statements, *United States v. Arnaout*, Jan. 6, 2003, p. 36.

80. By 1996, al Qaeda apparently had established cooperative relationships with at least 20 Sunni Islamic extremist groups in the Middle East, South Asia, Africa, and East Asia, as well as with elements of the Saudi opposition. See CIA analytic report, "Old School Ties," Mar. 10, 2003, p. 3. On ties with Southeast Asia and the Malaysian-Indonesian JI, see, e.g., Intelligence report, interrogation of Hambali, Sept. 5, 2003. On Pakistani militant ties to Bin Ladin, see CIA analytic report, "Terrorism: Extremists Planning Attacks Against US Interests in Pakistan," Nov. 29, 2001, p. 1 and appendix B; see also Gunaratna, *Inside Al Qaeda*, pp. 169–171, 199; Benjamin and Simon, *Age of Sacred Terror*, pp. 286–287. On Europe, see, e.g., trial testimony of Fadl, *United States v. bin Laden*, Feb. 6, 2001 (transcript pp. 301, 315–316), Feb. 7, 2001 (transcript p. 368). On London, see, e.g., Intelligence report, interrogation of detainee, Sept. 17, 1997. On Balkans, see Government's Evidentiary Proffer Supporting the Admissibility of Co-Conspirator Statements, *United States v. Arnaout*, Jan. 6, 2003; Kohlmann, *Al-Qaida's Jihad in Europe*.

81. See, e.g., "Tareekh Usama" and "Tareekh al Musadat" (described in note 25). See also FBI report of investigation, interviews of Mohammad Rashed Daoud al 'Owhali, Aug. 22–25, 1998; FBI report of investigation, interview of Nasser Ahmad Nasser al Bahri, Oct. 3, 2001, p. 8.

82. The merger was de facto complete by February 1998, although the formal "contract" would not be signed until June 2001. See Intelligence report, Incorporation of Zawahiri's Organization into Bin Ladin's Al-Qa'ida, and Recent [1998] Activities of Egyptian Associates of Al-Qa'ida, Sept. 22, 1998; see also Intelligence report, interrogation of detainee, Feb. 8, 2002.

83. FBI report of investigation, interview of confidential source, Sept. 16, 1999; FBI report of investigation, interview of L'Houssaine Kherchtou, Aug. 28, 2000; Benjamin and Simon, *Age of Sacred Terror*, pp. 123–124.

84. On the group's surveillance and photography activities, see trial testimony of L'Houssaine Kherchtou, *United States v. bin Laden*, Feb. 21, 2001 (transcript pp. 1499–1500); FBI reports of investigation, interviews of L'Houssaine Kherchtou, Aug. 18, 2000; Oct. 18, 2000; see also FBI report of investigation, interview of confidential source, Sept. 16, 1999. On Bin Ladin's use of technical equipment to promote his intelligence/security capabilities, see Intelligence report, Terrorism: Usama Bin Ladin's Intelligence Capabilities and Techniques, Dec. 5, 1996.

85. On the surveillance reports and the Hezbollah training camps, see FBI report of investigation, interview of confidential source, Sept. 16, 1999; see also Intelligence report, Al Qaeda Targeting Study of U.S. Embassy Nairobi, prepared 23 December 1993, Apr. 5, 1999; Intelligence report, Establishment of a Tripartite Agreement Among

Usama Bin Ladin, Iran, and the NIF, Jan. 31, 1997; Intelligence report, Cooperation Among Usama Bin Ladin's Islamic Army, Iran, and the NIF, Jan. 31 1997; FBI report of investigation, interview of Fadl, Nov. 10, 1996. Bin Ladin told his operatives he wanted them to study Hezbollah's 1983 truck bombing of U.S. marines in Lebanon that killed 241 and led to the American pullout from Lebanon. See, e.g., statement of Ali Mohamed in support of change of plea, *United States v. Ali Mohamed*, No. S(7) 98 Cr. 1023 (S.D. N.Y.), Oct. 20, 2000 (transcript p. 30); trial testimony of Fadl, *United States v. bin Laden*, Feb. 6, 2001 (transcript pp. 292–293); FBI report of investigation, interview of Fadl, Mar. 10, 1997; FBI report of investigation, interview of confidential source, Sept. 16, 1999.

86. Hugh Davies, "Saudis Detain Member of Anti-American Terror Group," *Daily Telegraph* (London), Aug. 2, 1997.

87. For general information on Hage, see Oriana Gill, "Hunting Bin Laden: A Portrait of Wadih El Hage, Accused Terrorist," PBS *Frontline* broadcast, Sept. 12, 2001. On returning to the United States, Hage was met at the airport by FBI agents, interrogated, and called the next day before the federal grand jury then investigating Bin Ladin. Because he lied to the grand jury about his association with Bin Ladin and al Qaeda, he was arrested immediately after the embassy bombings a year later. Testimony of Patrick Fitzgerald before the Senate Judiciary Committee, Oct. 21, 2003, pp. 3–4. On Hage's phone taps, see introduction of stipulation (government exhibit no. 36), *United States v. bin Laden*, Feb. 27, 2001 (transcript pp. 1575–1576). For Harun's fax, see government exhibit no. 300A-T, *United States v. bin Laden*.

88. "World Islamic Front's Statement Urging Jihad," *Al Quds al Arabi*, Feb. 23, 1998; closing statement by Asst. U.S. Attorney Ken Karas, *United States v. bin Laden*, May 1, 2001 (transcript pp. 5369, 5376–5377). On related activities in Kenya and Tanzania, see FBI report of investigation, interviews of Mohamed Sadeeq Odeh, Aug. 15–28, 1998.

89. FBI report of investigation, interviews of Mohamed Sadeeq Odeh, Aug. 15–28, 1998; closing statement by Asst. U.S. Attorney Ken Karas, *United States v. bin Laden*, May 1, 2001 (transcript pp. 5239, 5408, 5417).

90. For the Atef fax, see government exhibit no. 1636-T, *United States v. bin Laden*. For the fatwa, see government exhibit no. 1602-T, *United States v. bin Laden* (translation of "Clergymen in Afghanistan Issue a Fatwa calling for the Removal of American Forces from the Gulf," *Al Quds al Arabi*, May 14, 1998). For the interview, see ABC News interview, "To Terror's Source," May 28, 1998.

91. See closing statement by Asst. U.S. Attorney Ken Karas, *United States v. bin Laden*, May 2, 2001 (transcript pp. 5426–5439); see also FBI report of investigation, interviews of Mohammad Rashed Daoud al 'Owhali, Aug. 22–25, 1998, p. 9. Copies of the declarations issued by "The Islamic Army for the Liberation of the Holy Places" taking credit for the operation were recovered from a raid in Baku, Azerbaijan, after the bombings in September 1998. See also government exhibit no. 1557C-T, *United States v. bin Laden* ("The formation of the Islamic Army for the Liberation of the Holy Places"); government exhibit no. 1557D-T, *United States v. bin Laden* ("Al-Aqsa Mosque operation"); government exhibit no. 1557E-T, *United States v. bin Laden* ("The Holy Ka'ba operation").

92. Closing statement by Asst. U.S. Attorney Ken Karas, *United States v. bin Laden*, May 2, 2001 (transcript p. 5445).

93. ABC News interview, "Terror Suspect: An Interview with Osama Bin Laden," Dec. 22, 1998 (conducted in Afghanistan by ABC News producer Rahimullah Yousafsai).

3 Counterterrorism Evolves

1. Brief of the United States, *United States v. Ramzi Ahmed Yousef*, Lead No. 98-1041 (2d Cir. filed Aug. 25, 2000), pp. 42–43; John Miller and Michael Stone, with Chris Mitchell, *The Cell: Inside the 9/11 Plot, and Why the FBI and CIA Failed to Stop It* (Hyperion, 2002), pp. 95, 99.

2. On President Clinton's tasking the NSC, see Richard Clarke interview (Dec. 18, 2003). On the role of different U.S. government agencies, see Steve Coll, *Ghost War: The Secret History of the CIA, Afghanistan, and bin Laden, from the Soviet Invasion to September 10, 2001* (Penguin, 2004), p. 251.

3. Trial testimony of Brian Parr, *United States v. Yousef*, No. S12 93 CR 180 (KTD) (S.D. N.Y.), Oct. 22, 1997 (transcript p. 4694).

4. On the process of identification, see Joseph Malone interview (May 25, 2004).

5. *United States v. Salameh*, 152 F.3d 88, 107–108 (2d Cir. 1998); Miller and Stone, *The Cell*, pp. 104–105, 107, 109. Abouhalima had fled to the Middle East after the bombing, and was picked up by Egyptian authorities and returned to the United States in late March 1993. Brief of the United States, *United States v. Mohammed A. Salameh*, Lead No. 94-1312 (2d Cir. filed Jan. 17, 1997), p. 64 and n. ***.

6. *United States v. Salameh*, 152 F.3d at 107–108, n. 2; *United States v. Yousef*, 327 F.3d 56, 78–79 (2d Cir. 2003); Miller and Stone, *The Cell*, p. 119; Daniel Benjamin and Steven Simon, *The Age of Sacred Terror* (Random House, 2002), p. 12.

7. On Rahman's ties to the Farouq mosque, see Miller and Stone, *The Cell*, pp. 54–55. On Rahman's message, see *United States v. Rahman*, 189 F.3d 88, 104 (2d Cir. 1999); Brief for the United States, *United States v. Siddig Ibrahim Siddig Ali*, Lead No. 96-1044 (2d Cir. filed July 3, 1997), pp. 10, 15. See also DOS Inspector General report, "Review

of the Visa-Issuance Process Phase I: Circumstances Surrounding the Issuance of Visas to Sheikh Omar Ali Ahmed Abdel Rahman," Mar. 1994, pp. 6, 8, 36. On the informant's reports, see *United States v. Rahman*, 189 F.3d at 106–107. On the landmarks plot, see *United States v. Rahman*, 189 F.3d at 108–111, 123–127; Miller and Stone, *The Cell*, p. 116.

8. These prosecutions also had the unintended consequence of alerting some al Qaeda members to the U.S. government's interest in them. In February 1995, the government filed a confidential court document listing Usama Bin Ladin and scores of other people as possible co-conspirators in the New York City landmarks plot. Ali Mohamed, who was on the list, obtained a copy and faxed it to a close Bin Ladin aide for distribution. Statement of Ali Mohamed in support of change of plea, *United States v. Ali Mohamed*, No. S(7) 98 Cr. 1023 (S.D. N.Y.), Oct. 20, 2000 (transcript p. 29); Statements of Prosecutor and Judge, *United States v. Bin Laden*, No. S(7) 98 Cr. 1023 (S.D. N.Y.), Mar. 26, 2001 (transcript pp. 3338–3339); Patrick Fitzgerald interview (Jan. 28, 2004).

9. On Ajaj's travels to Khaldan and interactions with KSM, see *United States v. Salameh*, 152 F.3d at 107–108. Ajaj had entered the United States on a B-2 tourist visa at New York City on September 9, 1991. INS alien file, No. A72215823, Sept. 9, 1991.

10. On Yousef's capture and the Manila air plot, see *United States v. Yousef*, 327 F.3d at 79–82. On KSM, see Joint Inquiry report (classified version), pp. 324–328; CIA analytical report, "WTC 1993: The Solid Case for al-Qa'ida Involvement," CTC 2002-40084H, July 11, 2002; Intelligence report, interrogation of KSM, May 27, 2003; James Risen and David Johnston, "Threats and Responses: Counterterrorism; Qaeda Aide Slipped Away Long Before Sept. 11 Attack," *New York Times*, Mar. 8, 2003, p. A12.

11. For a general history of the FBI, supporting the subsequent text (unless otherwise noted), see Athan G. Theoharis, et al., *The FBI: A Comprehensive Reference Guide* (Onyx Press, 1999); the FBI's authorized history, FBI report, "History of the FBI" (online at www.fbi.gov/libref/historic/history/historymain.htm); the FBI's history as told by the Federation of American Scientists, "History of the FBI," updated June 18, 2003 (online at www.fas.org/irp/agency/doj/fbi/fbi_hist.htm). For discussion of field office autonomy, see FBI letter, Kalish to Wolf, responses to questions posed by the Subcommittee on Commerce, Justice, State, and Judiciary of the House Appropriations Committee, May 24, 2004, pp. 47–48.

12. See, e.g., Dan C. interview (Aug. 27, 2003); Ruben Garcia interview (Apr. 29, 2004); DOJ Inspector General interview of William Gore, Oct. 24, 2002.

13. The Washington Field Office was originally assigned the East Africa bombings case because it generally has responsibility for investigating crimes overseas. When the attack was determined to be al Qaeda–related, responsibility shifted to the New York Field Office. See generally Kevin C. interview (Aug. 25, 2003). This created significant friction between agents in the respective offices. Edward Curran and Sidney Caspersen interview (Jan. 20, 2004). On the concept of the office of origin, see FBI memo, Kalish to Wolf, responses to questions from the Subcommittee on Commerce, Justice, State, and Judiciary of the House Appropriations Committee, pp. 47–48; testimony of Robert S. Mueller III before the Subcommittee on the Departments of Commerce, Justice, and State, the Judiciary and Related Agencies of the House Appropriations Committee, June 18, 2003; FBI report, "Counterterrorism Program Since September 2001," Apr. 14, 2004, p. 20.

14. On the impact of Watergate, see generally Kathryn Olmsted, *Challenging the Secret Government: The Post-Watergate Investigations of the CIA and FBI* (Univ. of North Carolina Press, 1996).

15. David M. Alpern with Anthony Marro and Stephan Lesher, "This Is Your New FBI," *Newsweek*, Jan. 5, 1976, p. 14.

16. On the Levi guidelines and the Smith modifications, see John T. Elliff, "Symposium: National Security and Civil Liberties: The Attorney General's Guidelines for FBI Investigations," *Cornell Law Review*, vol. 69 (Apr. 1984), p. 785. On the line between church and state, see Floyd Abrams, "The First Amendment and the War against Terrorism," *University of Pennsylvania Journal of Constitutional Law*, vol. 5 (Oct. 2002).

17. On Pan Am bombing investigation, see Commission analysis of U.S. counterterrorism strategy from 1968 to 1993; FBI report, "History of the FBI."

18. Louis Freeh interview (Jan. 6, 2004); Federation of American Scientists, "History of the FBI;" DOJ Inspector General report, "Federal Bureau of Investigation Casework and Human Resource Allocation," Sept. 2003, pp. iv, vi, viii, x, xiii.

19. For quote, see FBI report, "Congressional Budget Justification Book Fiscal Year 1995," undated, p. 6. On Freeh's efforts, see Howard M. Shapiro, "The FBI in the 21st Century," *Cornell International Law Journal*, vol. 28 (1995), pp. 219–228; Louis Freeh interview (Jan. 6, 2004). On Freeh's budget request, see FBI report, "Congressional Budget Justification Book Fiscal Year 1995," undated.

20. Janet Reno interview (Dec. 16, 2003); Dale Watson interview (Feb. 5, 2004); Stephen Colgate interview (May 19, 2004); OMB budget examiner interview (Apr. 27, 2004).

21. On the plan, see FBI report, "Strategic Plan: 1998–2003, 'Keeping Tomorrow Safe,'" May 8, 1998. For Watson's recollections, see Dale Watson interview (Jan. 6, 2004).

22. For the mid-1990s numbers, see FBI memo, Freeh to Reno, "Reorganization of FBI Headquarters—Establishment of Counterterrorism Division and Investigative Services Division," Apr. 22, 1999. For the 1998–2001 num-

bers, see DOJ Inspector General report, "Review of the Federal Bureau of Investigation's Counterterrorism Program: Threat Assessment, Strategic Planning, and Resource Management," Sept. 2002, p. 67. For the failure to shift resources, see DOJ Inspector General report, "FBI Casework and Human Resource Allocation," Sept. 2003, pp. iv, vi, viii, x, xiii. For the comparison to drug agents, see testimony of Dick Thornburgh before the Subcommittee on Commerce, State, Justice, the Judiciary, and Related Agencies of the House Appropriations Committee, June 18, 2003, p. 20.

23. Dale Watson interview (Feb. 5, 2004); Virginia Bollinger interview (Feb. 2, 2004); Robert Bryant interview (Dec. 18, 2003).

24. On the state of information technology at FBI, see Virginia Bollinger interview (Jan. 28, 2004); Mark Miller interview (Dec. 23, 2003). On the lack of an overall assessment, see DOJ Inspector General report, "Review of the FBI's Counterterrorism Program," Sept. 2002, pp. ii–iii.

25. For training statistics, see DOJ Inspector General report, "Review of the FBI's Counterterrorism Program," Sept. 2002, p. 74. For translation resources, see FBI report, "FY 2002 Counterterrorism Division Program Plan Summary," undated, p. 4. Since 9/11, the FBI has recruited and processed more than 30,000 translator applicants. This has resulted in the addition of nearly 700 new translators. FBI report, "The FBI's Counterterrorism Program Since September 2001," Apr. 14, 2004. The FBI's hiring process includes language testing, a personnel security interview, polygraph, and a full background investigation. The FBI must maintain rigorous security and proficiency standards with respect to its permanent and contract employees. Even as the FBI has increased its language services cadre, the demand for translation services has also greatly increased. Thus, the FBI must not only continue to bring on board more linguists, it must also continue to take advantage of technology and best practices to prioritize its workflow, enhance its capabilities, and ensure compliance with its quality control program. FBI linguists interviews (July 31, 2003–May 10, 2004); Margaret Gulotta interview (May 10, 2004). See DOJ Inspector General report, "A Review of the FBI's Actions in Connection with Allegations Raised by Contract Linguist Sibel Edmonds," July 1, 2004; Sibel Edmonds interview (Feb. 11, 2004).

26. Wilson Lowery interview (Jan. 28, 2004); Janet Reno testimony, Apr. 13, 2004; Helen S. interview (Dec. 29, 2003); Stephen Colgate interview (May 19, 2004); Robert Dies interview (Feb. 4, 2004).

27. FBI report, "Director's Report on Counterterrorism," Sept. 1, 2001, pp. I-1–I-14. On FBI reorganization, see FBI memo, Freeh to Reno, "Reorganization of FBI Headquarters—Establishment of Counterterrorism Division and Investigative Services Division," Apr. 22, 1999. On Watson's observation, see Dale Watson interview (Feb. 4, 2004). On MAXCAP 05, see FBI memo, description of MAXCAP 05, undated (draft likely prepared after Aug. 31, 2001, for incoming Director Mueller). On field executives' views, see FBI report, Counterterrorism Division, International Terrorism Program, "Strategic Program Plan, FY 2001–06," undated, p. 30.

28. International terrorism intelligence cases were designated as 199 matters; international terrorism criminal cases were designated as 265 matters. In 2003, these designations were eliminated; all international terrorism matters now receive the same designation, 315.

29. For historical information on FISA, see Americo R. Cinquegrana, "The Walls (and Wires) have Ears: The Background and First Ten Years of the Foreign Intelligence Surveillance Act of 1978," *University of Pennsylvania Law Review,* vol. 137 (1989), pp. 793, 802–805. For the statute, see 50 U.S.C. §§ 1801 et seq. As enacted in 1978, FISA permitted orders authorizing electronic surveillance. It did not refer to physical searches. In 1994, the statute was amended to permit orders authorizing physical searches. See Pub. L. No. 103-359, 108 Stat. 3423, 3443 (Oct. 14, 1994); 50 U.S.C. §§ 1821–1829. See generally, William C. Banks and M. E. Bowman, "Executive Authority for National Security Surveillance," *American University Law Review,* vol. 50 (2000), pp. 1–130.

30. On the history of courts applying the primary purpose standard, see *In re Sealed Case,* 310 F.3d 717, 725–726 (FISC Ct. Rev. 2002), in which the FISC Court of Review concluded that these courts had ruled in error. See also DOJ report, "Final Report of the Attorney General's Review Team on the Handling of the Los Alamos National Laboratory Investigation" (hereinafter "Bellows Report"), May 2000, appendix D. On DOJ interpretation of FISA, see DOJ memo, Dellinger to Vatis, "Standards for Searchers Under Foreign Intelligence Act," Feb. 14, 1995; Royce Lamberth interview (Mar. 26, 2004); Bellows Report, pp. 711–712; DOJ Inspector General interview of Marion Bowman, May 28, 2003.

31. Bellows Report, pp. 711–712; DOJ Inspector General interview of Marion Bowman, May 28, 2003.

32. Bellows Report, pp. 712–714, n. 947, appendix D tabs 2, 3; Richard Scruggs interview (May 26, 2004); Larry Parkinson interview (Feb. 24, 2004). Because OIPR had ultimate authority to decide what was presented to the FISA Court, it wielded extraordinary power in the FISA process.

33. The group included representatives from the FBI, OIPR, and the Criminal Division. In addition, the U.S. Attorney for the Southern District of New York was given an opportunity to comment on the procedures. The procedures that were eventually issued were agreed to by all involved in the drafting process. As a member of the Commission, Gorelick has recused herself from participation in this aspect of our work.

34. On Reno's July 1995 memo, see DOJ Inspector General report, "A Review of the FBI's Handling of Intelligence Information Related to the September 11 Attacks," July 2004, pp. 27–34; Bellows Report, p. 709, appen-

dix D tab 23. Some barriers were proposed by OIPR in the FISA applications and subsequently adopted by the FISC; others, less formally recorded, were believed by the FBI to be equally applicable.

35. On the misapplication of the procedures and the role of OIPR, see Bellows Report, pp. 721–722; Marion Bowman interview (Mar. 6, 2004); Fran Fragos Townsend meeting (Feb. 13, 2004). On the OIPR as gatekeeper, see MichaelVatis interview (Jan. 21, 2004); Larry Parkinson interview (Feb. 24, 2004). On OIPR's stated defense, see David Kris interview (May 19, 2004); Richard Scruggs interview (May 26, 2004). On OIPR's threat, see Larry Parkinson interview (Feb. 24, 2004); Thomas A. interview (Mar. 16, 2004). On the lack of information flow, see Bellows Report, pp. 722, 724–725, 729–731.

36. For Bryant's comment, see David Kris interview (Jan. 15, 2004); Bellows Report, p. 714. On barriers between agents on same squads, see Larry Parkinson interview (Feb. 24, 2004); MichaelVatis interview (Jan. 21, 2004); DOJ Inspector General interview of Thomas A., May 28, 2003. On incorrect interpretation by field agents, see Joint Inquiry report, pp. 363, 367–368; Larry Parkinson interview (Feb. 24, 2004); MichaelVatis interview (Jan. 21, 2004); DOJ Inspector General interview of Thomas A., May 28, 2003; DOJ Inspector General interview of Jane, Nov. 4, 2002.

37. For an example of the barriers between agents, see DOJ emails, Jane to Steve B., interpreting the wall to apply to non-FISA information, Aug. 29, 2001; David Kris interview (Jan. 15, 2004). On the NSA barriers, see DOJ Inspector General interview of Jane, Nov. 4, 2002. These barriers were reinforced by caveats NSA began placing on all of its Bin Ladin–related reports and later on all of its counterterrorism-related reports—whether or not the information was subject to the attorney general's order—which required approval before the report's contents could be shared with criminal investigators. Ibid. On the several reviews of the process, see Bellows Report, pp. 709, 722; DOJ Inspector General report, "The Handling of FBI Intelligence Information Related to the Justice Department's Campaign Finance Investigation," July 1999, pp. 15–16, 255, 256, 328–330, 340, 344; GAO report, "FBI Intelligence Investigations: Coordination Within Justice on Counterintelligence Criminal Matters Is Limited," July 2001, pp. 3–5.

38. In December 1999, NSA began placing caveats on all of its Bin Ladin reports that precluded sharing of any of the reports' contents with criminal prosecutors or FBI agents investigating criminal matters without first obtaining OIPR's permission. These caveats were initially created at the direction of Attorney General Reno and applied solely to reports of information gathered from three specific surveillances she had authorized. Because NSA decided it was administratively too difficult to determine whether particular reports derived from the specific surveillances authorized by the attorney general, NSA decided to place this caveat on all its terrorism-related reports. In November 2000, in response to direction from the FISA Court, NSA modified these caveats to require that consent for sharing the information with prosecutors or criminal agents be obtained from NSA's Customer Needs and Delivery Services group. See DOJ memo, Reno to Freeh, E.O. 12333 authorized surveillance of a suspected al Qaeda operative, Dec. 24, 1999; NSA email, William L. to Brian C., "dissemination of terrorism reporting," Dec. 29, 1999; NSA memo, Ann D. to others, "Reporting Guidance," Dec. 30. 1999; Intelligence report, Nov. 6, 2000. See also discussion of the history of the NSA caveats in the notes to Chapter 8.

39. See DEA report, "DEA Staffing & Budget" (figures for 1972 to 2003) (online at www.usdoj.gov/dea/agency/staffing.htm). For USMS staffing, see DOJ information provided to the Commission.

40. On the number of agents, see INS newsletter, "INS Commissioner Meissner Announces Departure," Jan. 2001; INS news release, "INS to Hire More than 800 Immigration Inspectors Nationwide," Jan. 12, 2001; Gregory Bednarz prepared statement, Oct. 9, 2003, p. 5. On the INS's main challenges, see, e.g., Eric Holder interview (Jan. 28, 2004); Jamie Gorelick interview (Jan. 13, 2004); Doris Meissner interview (Nov. 25, 2003). On the White House views, see, e.g., White House press release, "Fact Sheet on Immigration Enforcement Act," May 3, 1995. On DOJ's concerns, see INS newsletter, Remarks of Attorney General Reno on Oct. 24, 2000, Jan. 2001, pp. 16, 26. To assess congressional views, we reviewed all conference and committee reports relating to congressional action on INS budget requests for fiscal years 1995 through 2001 and all Senate and House immigration hearings from 1993 to 2001. On outdated technology, see Gus de la Vina interview (Nov. 19, 2003); Doris Meissner interview (Nov. 25, 2003).

41. On Meissner's response, see Doris Meissner interview (Nov. 25, 2003). On the lookout unit, see Tim G. interview (Oct. 1, 2002). On the number of denials of entry, see Majority Staff Report, Hearing on "Foreign Terrorists in America: Five Years after the World Trade Center" before the Subcommittee on Technology, Terrorism, and Government Information of the Senate Judiciary Committee, Feb. 24, 1998, p. 145.

42. Majority Staff Report, Hearing on "Foreign Terrorists in America: Five Years after the World Trade Center," Feb. 24, 1998, p. 152; 8 U.S.C. § 1534(e)(1)(A). On the low level of removals, see Daniel Cadman interview (Oct. 9, 2003); Rocky Concepcion interview (June 15, 2004).

43. On the 1986 plan, see INS report, Investigations Division, "Alien Terrorists and Undesirables: A Contingency Plan," May 1986; Daniel Cadman interview (Oct. 17, 2003). On the 1995 plan, see INS memo, Bramhall to Bednarz and Hurst, "Draft Counter-Terrorism Strategy Outline," Aug. 11, 1995. On the 1997 plan, see INS email, Cadman to others, "EAC briefing document," Dec. 5, 1997 (attachment titled "Counterterrorism/National Secu-

rity Strategy and Casework Oversight"). On the work of the National Security Unit and the Intelligence Unit, see Daniel Cadman interview (Oct. 17, 2003); Cliff Landesman interview (Oct. 27, 2003).

44. For number of agents on Canadian border, the Canadian situation generally, and the inspector general's recommendations, see INS report, "Northern Border Strategy," Jan. 9, 2001; DOJ Inspector General report, "Follow-up Review of the Border Patrol Efforts Along the Northern Border," Apr. 2000 (inspection plan). On terrorists entering the United States via Canada, see, e.g., INS record, Record of Deportable Alien, Abu Mezer, June 24, 1996. Mezer was able to stay in the United States despite apprehensions for his illegal entries along the northern border.

45. The inspectors' views are drawn from our interviews with 26 border inspectors who had contact with the 9/11 hijackers. On the incomplete INS projects, see Illegal Immigration Reform and Immigrant Responsibility Act, Pub. L. No. 104-208, 110 Stat. 3009 (1996), §§ 110, 641.

46. For the 1996 law, see 8 U.S.C. § 1357 (1996). On unauthorized immigration, see Migration Policy Institute report, "Immigration Facts: Unauthorized Immigration to the United States," Oct. 2003 (online at www.migrationpolicy.org/pubs/two_unauthorized_immigration_us.pdf). On the initiation of city noncooperation, see New York Mayor Ed Koch's 1987 order prohibiting city line workers, but not police or the Department of Corrections, from transmitting information respecting any alien to federal immigration authorities. On backlogs, see testimony of Dr. Demetrios G. Papademetriou before the Subcommittee on Immigration, Border Security and Claims of the House Judiciary Committee, Mar. 11, 2004. On the overwhelmed INS, see James Ziglar testimony, Jan. 26, 2004.

47. On the relationship between the FBI and state and local police forces, see William Bratton et al. interview (Nov. 20, 2003); David Cohen interview (Feb. 4, 2004). On the New York JTTF, see Mary Jo White, "Prosecuting Terrorism in New York," *Middle East Quarterly*, spring 2001 (online at www.meforum.org/article/25). On the pre-9/11 number of JTTFs, see Louis Freeh prepared statement for the Joint Inquiry, Oct. 8, 2002, p. 18. On the effectiveness of JTTFs, see Washington Field Office agent interview (Aug. 4, 2003); Phoenix JTTF member interview (Oct. 20, 2003); Phoenix Field Office agent interview (Oct. 21, 2003); Art C. interview (Dec. 4, 2003).

48. Treasury report, "1995 Highlights of The Bureau of Alcohol, Tobacco and Firearms," undated (online at www.atf.gov/pub/gen_pub/annualrpt/1995/index.htm); ATF report, "ATF Snapshot," Jan. 30, 1998 (online at www.atf.gov/about/snap1998.htm).

49. Dale Watson interview (Feb. 4, 2004); Frank P. interview (Aug. 26, 2003); Dan C. interview (Aug. 27, 2003); Louis Freeh interview (Jan. 8. 2004).

50. See Federal Aviation Reauthorization Act, Pub. L. No. 104-264, 110 Stat. 3213 (1996), codified at 49 U.S.C. § 40101; Federal Aviation Authorization Act, H.R. Rep. No. 104-848, 104th Cong., 2d sess. (1996) (notes on conference substitute for § 401). On responsibility for protection, see 49 U.S.C. § 44903(b). On sabotage, see FAA report, Aviation Security Advisory Committee, "Domestic Security Baseline Final Report," Dec. 12, 1996; FAA report, "Civil Aviation Security: Objectives and Priorities," Mar. 18, 1999 (staff working paper). See also Jane Garvey prepared statement, May 22, 2003; *Report of the President's Commission on Aviation Security and Terrorism* (Pan Am/Lockerbie Commission), May 15, 1990, pp. 113–114; *Final Report of the White House Commission on Aviation Safety and Security* (Gore Commission), Feb. 12, 1997. While the sabotage of commercial aircraft, including Pan Am 103 in 1998, had claimed many lives, hijackings had also been deadly, including the 1985 hijacking of an Egypt Air flight in which 60 people were killed and 35 injured; the 1986 hijacking of Pan Am 73 in which 22 people were killed and 125 injured; and the 1996 hijacking of an Ethiopian Airlines flight in which 123 people were killed. See FAA report, "Civil Aviation Security Reference Handbook," May 1999. Commissioners Ben-Veniste, Gorelick, and Thompson have recused themselves from our work on aviation security matters.

51. See GAO report, "Aviation Security: Additional Actions Needed to Meet Domestic and International Challenges," Jan. 27, 1994; GAO report, "Aviation Security: Urgent Issues Need to Be Addressed," Sept. 11, 1996; GAO report, "Aviation Security: Slow Progress in Addressing Long-Standing Screener Performance Problems," Mar. 16, 2000; GAO report, "Aviation Security: Long-Standing Problems Impair Airport Screeners' Performance," June 28, 2000; testimony of Kenneth M. Mead, DOT Inspector General, Joint Hearing on Actions Needed to Improve Aviation Security before the Subcommittee on Oversight of Government Management, Restructuring and the District of Columbia of the Senate Governmental Affairs Committee, Sept. 25, 2001. On rules regulating access to security sensitive areas of commercial airports, see FAA regulations, "Airport Security," 14 C.F.R. § 107; FAA report, "Air Carrier Standard Security Program," May 2001.

52. The FAA maintained formal agreements with the CIA, FBI, Department of State, Department of Defense, and NSA to receive data of interest as outlined in the agreement. In addition, the FAA posted liaisons with the CIA, FBI, and Department of State to facilitate the flow of intelligence and threat information. See Claudio Manno interview (Oct. 1, 2003); Matt K. interview (Feb. 13, 2004). FAA civil aviation security officials reported that the agency's intelligence watch received about 200 pieces of intelligence per day. See Claudio Manno interview (Oct. 1, 2003). The analysis regarding the passage of FBI information was based on a review of the FAA's Intelligence Case Files. The FBI analyst who worked on the 1998 tasking indicated that the information was shared with the FAA liaison to the Bureau, but the liaison did not recall having seen it. Cathal Flynn interview (Sept. 9, 2003); Matt K. interview (Feb. 13, 2004).

53. Regarding intelligence reports, the Daily Intelligence Summary (DIS) prepared by the FAA's Office of Civil Aviation Intelligence was reviewed first by an assistant to Acting Deputy Administrator Belger, who would inform him of any information that she felt merited his attention. Belger in turn would determine whether the information needed to be raised with Administrator Garvey. Garvey told us that she maintained an open door policy and counted on her security staff to keep her informed on any pressing issues. Jane Garvey interview (Oct. 21, 2003); Monte Belger interview (Nov. 24, 2003); Cathal Flynn interview (Sept. 9, 2003); Shirley Miller interview (Mar. 30, 2004); Claudio Manno interview (Oct. 1, 2003). Regarding the intelligence unit, see Nicholas Grant interview (May 26, 2004); Claudio Manno interview (Oct. 1, 2003); Mike Canavan interview (Nov. 4, 2003); Alexander T. Wells, *Commercial Aviation Safety* (McGraw-Hill, 2001), p. 308.

54. On the threat to civil aviation, see Lee Longmire interview (Oct. 28, 2003). On CAPPS, also known as CAPS (Computer Assisted Profiling System), see FAA security directive, "Threat to Air Carriers," SD 97-01, Oct. 27, 1997. The profile was derived from information on the Passenger Name Record and did not include factors such as race, creed, color, or national origin. In addition to those chosen by the algorithm, a number of other passengers were selected at random, both to address concerns about discrimination and to deter terrorists from figuring out the algorithm and gaming the system. On no-fly lists, see FAA security directive, "Threat to U.S. Air Carriers," SD 95, Apr. 24, 2000. Some of the individuals on the no-fly list were in U.S. custody as of 9/11. See Kevin G. Hall, Alfonso Chardy, and Juan O. Tamayo, "Mix-Up Almost Permitted Deportation of Men Suspected of Terrorist Activities," *Miami Herald*, Sept. 19, 2001; FAA security directive, "Threat to U.S. Aircraft Operators," SD 108-1, Aug. 28, 2001. On the Gore Commission, see *Final Report of the White House Commission on Aviation Safety and Security*, Feb. 12, 1997, p. 28. On the TIPOFF database (used to screen visa applicants and persons seeking permission to enter the United States against the names of known or suspected terrorists), see DOS cable, State 182167, "Fighting Terrorism: Visas Viper Procedures," Oct. 19, 2001. Finally, on the watchlist, officials told us that large lists were difficult to implement, particularly when they weren't accompanied by numeric data such as date of birth that would enable an air carrier to distinguish the terrorist from others around the world who had his or her name. In addition, the U.S. intelligence community was required to approve the "no-fly" listing of an individual in order to protect sources and methods. Matt Kormann interview (Feb. 13, 2004).

55. On selectees, see James Padgett interview (Oct. 7, 2003). Their bags were either screened for explosives or held off their flight until they were confirmed to be aboard. See FAA security directive, "Threat to Air Carriers," SD 97-01 Oct. 27, 1997. Under the previous noncomputerized profiling system, selectees were subject to secondary screening of their carry-on belongings, and checked baggage. See FAA security directive, "Threat to Air Carriers," SD 96-05, Aug. 19, 1996.

56. FAA report, "Air Carrier Standard Security Program," May 2001; FAA regulations, "Screening of Passengers and Property," 14 C.F.R. § 108.9 (1999); Leo Boivin interview (Sept. 17, 2003).

57. "Knives with blades under 4 inches, such as Swiss Army Knives, scout knives, pocket utility knives, etc. may be allowed to enter the sterile area. However, some knives with blades under 4 inches could be considered by a reasonable person to be a 'menacing knife' and/or may be illegal under local law and should not be allowed to enter the sterile area." See FAA regulations, Air Carriers Checkpoint Operations Guide, Aug. 1999; see also Air Transport Association Regional Airlines Association report, "Checkpoint Operations Guide," Aug. 1999; Cathal Flynn interview (Sept. 9, 2003); Lee Longmire interview (Oct. 28, 2003); Leo Boivin interview (Sept. 17, 2003). A 1994 FAA assessment of the threat to civil aviation in the United States stated that "system vulnerabilities also exist with respect to hijackings . . . aircraft can be hijacked with either fake weapons or hoax explosive devices. Cabin crew or passengers can also be threatened with objects such as short blade knives, which are allowable on board aircraft." See FAA report, "The Threat to U.S. Civil Aviation in the United States," Sept. 1994.

58. On random and continuous screening, see Janet Riffe interview (Feb. 26, 2004); FAA report, "Air Carrier Standard Security Program," May 2001. On the 9/11 hijackers, see Intelligence report, interrogation of Ramzi Binalshibh, Oct. 1, 2002; FAA records, Intelligence Case File 98–96.

59. Courtney Tucker interview (June 3, 2004); Kenneth Mead prepared statement, May 22, 2003. Some air carrier officials, however, enjoyed a strong reputation for leadership in aviation security, including United Airlines' Ed Soliday. Bruce Butterworth interview (Sept. 29, 2003); Cathal Flynn interview (Sept. 9, 2003); Steven Jenkins interview (Feb. 24, 2004).

60. Mike Morse interview (Sept. 15, 2003). Regarding training, see FAA report, "Air Carrier Standard Security Program," May 2001.

61. On a hardened cockpit door making little difference, see Tim Ahern interview (Oct. 8, 2004). For regulations governing the doors, see FAA regulations, "Miscellaneous Equipment" (emergency exit), 14 C.F.R. § 121.313 (2001); FAA regulations, "Closing and locking of flight crew compartment door," 14 C.F.R. § 121.587 (2001). Also compromising cockpit security was the use of common locks (one key fit the cockpits of all Boeing aircraft) and the absence of procedures to properly manage and safeguard cockpit keys. Michael Woodward interview (Jan. 25, 2004). For the quote on reinforced cockpit doors, see Byron Okada, "Air Rage Prompts Call for Safety Measures: The FAA Is Expected to Release a Report Today," *Fort Worth Star-Telegram*, Jan. 10, 2001, p. 1.

62. James Underwood interview (Sept. 17, 2004); Mike Canavan interview (Nov. 4, 2003).

63. Jane Garvey interview (Oct. 21, 2003).

64. As defined by statute, *covert action* "means an activity or activities of the United States Government to influence political, economic, or military conditions abroad, where it is intended that the role of the United States Government will not be apparent or acknowledged publicly, but does not include—(1) activities the primary purpose of which is to acquire intelligence[.]" 50 U.S.C. § 413b(e). Executive Order 12333, titled "United States Intelligence Activities," terms covert action "special activities," defined as "activities conducted in support of national foreign policy objectives abroad which are planned and executed so that the role of the United States Government is not apparent or acknowledged publicly, and functions in support of such activities[.]" E.O. 12333 § 3.4(h). Pursuant to that order, the CIA has primary responsibility for covert action; another nonmilitary agency may conduct covert action only if the president determines that it "is more likely to achieve a particular objective." Ibid. § 1.8(e).

65. See 50 U.S.C. § 401a(4).

66. DCI report, "National Foreign Intelligence Program Historical Data FY 1985 to FY 2003," Feb. 11, 2004.

67. For quote, see Joint Inquiry testimony of Michael Hayden, June 18, 2002; see also Michael Hayden interview (Dec. 10, 2003).

68. Michael Hayden interview (Dec. 10, 2003).

69. For the CIA's early years, see John Ranelagh, *The Agency: The Rise and Decline of the CIA* (Simon & Schuster, 1986). For the Agency's more recent history, see Robert M. Gates, *From the Shadows: The Ultimate Insider's Story of Five Presidents and How They Won the Cold War* (Simon & Schuster, 1996).

70. Regarding the dissolution of the OSS and creation of the CIG, see Michael Warner, *Central Intelligence: Origin and Evolution* (Center for the Study of Intelligence, 2001); Executive Order 9621, "Termination of the Office of Strategic Services and Disposition of its Functions," Sept. 20, 1945; "Presidential Directive on Coordination of Foreign Intelligence Activities," Jan. 22, 1946 (11 Fed. Reg. 1337, 1339).

71. Regarding fears of creating a U.S. Gestapo, see Amy Zegart, *Flawed by Design: The Evolution of the CIA, JCS and NSC* (Stanford Univ. Press, 1999), p. 268, n. 6.

72. National Security Act of 1947, Pub. L. No. 80-253, § 102(d)(3), codified at 50 U.S.C. § 403-3(d)(1).

73. On plausible deniability, see, e.g., Ranelagh, *The Agency*, pp. 341–345; Evan Thomas, *The Very Best Men: Four Who Dared: The Early Years of the CIA* (Simon & Schuster, 1995), pp. 230–235.

74. James Pavitt interview (Jan. 8, 2004).

75. Steve Kappes interview (May 7, 2004); James Pavitt interview (Jan. 8, 2004).

76. Jami Miscik interview (Aug. 29, 2003).

77. Mary McCarthy, Fritz Ermarth, and Charles Allen briefing (Aug. 14, 2003).

78. See Tom Mangold, *Cold Warrior: James Jesus Angleton, the CIA's Master Spy Hunter* (Simon & Schuster, 1991).

79. Ruth David interview (June 10, 2003).

80. "According to the 2002 Integrated Postsecondary Education Data System statistics, American colleges granted only six degrees in Arabic in the survey year." Joint Inquiry report (unclassified version), p. 344.

81. Leo Hazelwood interview (Aug. 25, 2003); Duane Clarridge interview (Sept. 16, 2003).

82. Charles Allen interview (Sept. 22, 2003); Duane Clarridge interview (Sept. 16, 2003); David Carey interview (Oct. 31, 2003); Leo Hazelwood interview (Aug. 25, 2003); John Helgerson interview (Sept. 5, 2003); Robert Vickers interview (Sept. 17, 2003); CIA Inspector General report, "The Agency's Counterterrorism Effort," Oct. 1994.

83. Cofer Black testimony, Apr. 13, 2004.

84. James Pavitt interview (Jan. 8, 2004).

85. George Tenet testimony, Mar. 24, 2004; George Tenet testimony, Apr. 14, 2004.

86. Richard Armitage interview (Jan. 12, 2004).

87. See Dana Priest, *The Mission: Waging War and Keeping Peace with America's Military* (W.W. Norton, 2003).

88. Michael Sheehan interview (Dec. 16, 2003).

89. See DOS report, Bureau of Consular Affairs, "1990 Report of the Visa Office," Oct. 1991; DOS Inspector General report, "Review of the Visa-Issuing Process; Phase I: Circumstances Surrounding the Issuance of Visas to Sheik Omar Ahmed Ali Abdel Rahman," Mar. 1994; Mary Ryan interviews (Sept. 29, 2003; Oct. 9, 2003); DOS briefing materials, presentation on consular systems delivered to the Information Resources Management Program Board, Apr. 26, 1995; DOS report, "History of the Department of State During the Clinton Presidency (1993–2001)," undated (online at www.state.gov/r/pa/ho/pubs/c6059.htm); Foreign Relations Authorization Act, Pub. L. No. 103-236 (1994), § 140(a).

90. See Gordon N. Lederman, *Reorganizing the Joint Chiefs of Staff: The Goldwater-Nichols Act of 1986* (Greenwood, 1999).

91. William Cohen interview (Feb. 5, 2004); John Hamre interview (Dec. 9, 2003); Hugh Shelton interview (Dec. 5, 2004); Cohen Group meeting (Dec. 12, 2003).

92. See Monterey Institute of International Studies report, "Nunn-Lugar-Domenici Domestic Preparedness and WMD Civil Support Teams," Oct. 2001 (online at http://cns.miis.edu/research/cbw/120city.htm); National Defense Authorization Act for Fiscal Year 1997, Pub. L. No. 104-201, 110 Stat. 2422 (1996); DOD report, "Domes-

tic Preparedness Program in the Defense Against Weapons of Mass Destruction," May 1, 1997 (online at www.defenselink.mil/pubs/domestic/toc.html).

93. John Hamre interview (Dec. 9, 2003); Henry Allen Holmes interview (Nov. 10, 2003); Brian Sheridan interview (Feb. 25, 2004).

94. Charles Allen interview (Jan. 27, 2004).

95. Commission analysis of U.S. counterterrorism strategy from 1968 to 1993.

96. President Reagan, "Remarks at the Annual Convention of the American Bar Association," July 8, 1985 (online at www.reagan.utexas.edu/resource/speeches/1985/70885a.htm).

97. See *Report of the President's Special Review Board* (Tower Commission) (GPO, 1987); Theodore Draper, *A Very Thin Line: The Iran-Contra Affairs* (Simon & Schuster, 1991).

98. James Pavitt interview (Jan. 8, 2004).

99. President Clinton, "Address to the Nation on the Strike on Iraqi Intelligence Headquarters," June 26, 1993.

100. President Clinton, "Address Before a Joint Session of the Congress on the State of the Union," Jan. 24, 1995; President Clinton, "Message to the Congress Transmitting Proposed Legislation To Combat Terrorism," Feb. 9, 1995; President Clinton, "Message to the Congress Transmitting Proposed Legislation To Combat Terrorism," May 3, 1995.

101. Presidential Decision Directive/NSC-39, "U.S. Policy on Counterterrorism," June 21, 1995.

102. President Clinton, "Remarks by the President in a Congressional Meeting," July 29, 1996.

103. President Clinton, "Remarks Announcing the Second Term National Security Team and an Exchange With Reporters," Dec. 5, 1996.

104. Presidential Decision Directive/NSC-62, "Protection Against Unconventional Threats to the Homeland and Americans Overseas," May 22, 1998; Presidential Decision Directive/NSC-63, "Critical Infrastructure Protection," May 22, 1998.

105. President Clinton, "Commencement Address at the United States Naval Academy in Annapolis, Maryland," May 22, 1998.

106. See Ernest R. May, "Intelligence: Backing into the Future," *Foreign Affairs*, Summer 1992.

107. For Congress's domestic orientation, see Lee H. Hamilton, *How Congress Works and Why You Should Care* (Indiana Univ. Press, 2004), pp.18–19. For presidential focus prior to 9/11, see President Clinton, "Commencement Address at the United States Naval Academy in Annapolis, Maryland," May 22, 1998; President Clinton, "Keeping America Secure for the 21st Century," Jan. 22, 1999.

108. Hamilton, *How Congress Works*, p. 17. Our review of the classified schedules of authorization from 1995 to 2001 found that Congress generally supported the top line requests made by the administration for intelligence, never reducing it by more than 2 or 3 percent; however, the congressional oversight committees did reallocate the administration's requests significantly, sometimes increasing programs like counterterrorism that they believed were being underfunded. On the intelligence budget, see George Tenet prepared statement, Mar. 24, 2004, pp. 23–26. The DCI added that frustrations with getting additional funding requests arose mainly from the administration. See ibid.

109. Joint Committee on the Organization of Congress, Final Report, Dec. 1993; "Contract with America," 1994; Statement of Rep. Saxby Chambliss, Hearing on Intelligence Gaps in Counterterrorism before the Special Oversight Panel on Terrorism of the House Armed Services Committee, Sept. 5, 2002.

110. Hamilton, *How Congress Works*, p. 106; Richard Durbin interview (Apr. 27, 2004); Dianne Feinstein interview (June 1, 2004); Peter Hoekstra interview (June 2, 2004); Chris Shays interview (June 2, 2004); Dana Priest, "Congressional Oversight of Intelligence Criticized," *Washington Post,* Apr. 27, 2004, p. A1. For Tenet quote, see George Tenet testimony, Mar. 24, 2004.

111. For neglect of airline security, see Commission analysis of the *Congressional Daily Digest* and the *Congressional Record* using the search term "aviation security." See also FAA briefing materials, "FAA Hearing/Briefing Activity Prior to September 11, 2001," undated. For the focus on the Southwest border, see Commission analysis of the hearing records of the subcommittees on immigration of the House and Senate Judiciary committees from 1993 through 2001. On restricting the FBI's appropriations, see Robert Dies interview (Feb. 4, 2004); Stephen Colgate interview (May 19, 2004). On sanctions on Pakistan, see Strobe Talbott interview (Jan. 15, 2004); Karl Inderfurth interview (Feb. 18, 2004); Christina Rocca interview (Jan. 29, 2004). On the lack of time for oversight, see Hamilton, *How Congress Works*, p. 112; see also Center for Strategic and International Studies meeting (July 23, 2003); Jay Rockefeller meeting (Oct. 16, 2003). On the Senate Appropriations Committee, the long-serving Chair (Ted Stevens) and Ranking Minority Member (Daniel Inouye) of the Defense Appropriations Subcommittee conduct at least weekly oversight sessions of the intelligence community, always behind closed doors, the effectiveness of which we cannot judge.

112. Although some members of the House sought the creation of a Select Committee on Terrorism in the beginning of 2001, the Speaker asked the intelligence ccommittee to set up a terrorism working group instead. Under Rep. Saxby Chambliss and Rep. Jane Harman, it held several briefings before 9/11 and became a subcommittee of the Intelligence Committee immediately afterward.

113. Rep. Christopher Shays of Connecticut, chairman of the National Security Subcommittee of the Government Reform Committee, held 12 wide-ranging hearings on terrorism between 1999 and July 2001, with special attention on domestic preparedness and response to terrorist attack. Though the intelligence oversight panels' work was largely secret, the intelligence community's annual worldwide threat testimony before the Senate Select Committee on Intelligence was public testimony (typically followed by a closed session). From 1997 through 2001, the threat of terrorism rose on the priority list from third (1997–1998) to second (1999–2000) to first in 2001. See Commission analysis of congressional hearings on terrorism.

114. Congress created three commissions in 1998. One, chaired jointly by former senators Gary Hart and Warren Rudman, examined national security challenges for the twenty-first century. This commission included stark warnings about possible domestic terrorist attacks and recommended a new institution devoted to identifying and defending vulnerabilities in homeland security. See Phase III Report of the U.S. Commission on National Security/21st Century, "Road Map for National Security: Imperative for Change," Feb. 15, 2001. A second, chaired by former governor James G. Gilmore of Virginia, studied domestic preparedness to cope with attacks using weapons of mass destruction and presented five reports. See, e.g., Fifth Annual Report to the President and the Congress of the Advisory Panel to Assess Domestic Response Capabilities for Terrorism Involving Weapons of Mass Destruction, "Forging America's New Normalcy: Securing our Homeland, Preserving our Liberty," Dec. 15, 2003. The third, chaired by L. Paul Bremer, the former State Department counterterrorism coordinator, with vice chair Maurice Sonnenberg, a member of the President's Foreign Intelligence Advisory Board, focused specifically on terrorist threats and what could be done to prepare for them. See Report of the National Commission on Terrorism, "Countering the Threat of International Terrorism," June 2000.

4 Responses to Al Qaeda's Initial Assaults

1. On financing of Egyptian terrorists, see Intelligence report, Sudanese links to Egypt's Gama'at al-Islamiya and training of Egyptians, July 14, 1993; Intelligence report, funding by Bin Ladin of Gama'at al-Islamiya by Bin Ladin and composition of its Sudanese wing, July 22, 1993. On aid to Yemeni terrorists, see DOS memo, attached to Bin Ladin "Viper" file, Aug. 28, 1993. CTC documents describing Bin Ladin as an "extremist financier" include Intelligence report, Bin Ladin links to materials related to WMD, Mar. 20, 1997; Intelligence report, Bin Ladin's financial support to Egyptian, Algerian, and Libyan extremists, June 17, 1997.

2. Richard Clarke interview (Dec. 18. 2003). Of the 200 people at the Center, the new Bin Ladin unit had about 12. Mike interview (Dec. 11, 2003). Staffing of the UBL unit had risen to 40–50 employees by Sept. 11, 2001, out of about 390 CTC employees. Richard interview (Dec. 11, 2003); CIA response to Commission questions for the record, Jan. 21, 2004.

3. On Fadl, see, e.g., Intelligence reports on historical background of Bin Ladin's army (Nov. 26, 1996; Apr. 18, 1997); on the structure of al Qaeda and leadership composition (Dec. 18, 1996; Dec. 19, 1996; Dec. 19, 1996); on roles and responsibilities of the organizational component (Dec. 19, 1996); on objectives and direction (Jan. 8, 1997; Jan. 27, 1997); on the financial infrastructure and networks (Dec. 30, 1996; Jan. 3, 1997); on connections and collaboration with other terrorist groups and supporters (Jan 8, 1997; Jan. 31, 1997; Jan 31, 1997; Feb. 7, 1997); on activities in Somalia (Apr. 30, 1997); on Bin Ladin's efforts to acquire WMD materials (Mar. 18, 1997). On the other walk-in source, see CIA cable, Jan. 3, 1997. Material from the Nairobi cell was introduced into evidence during the testimony of FBI Special Agent Daniel Coleman, *United States v. Usama Bin Laden*, No. S(7) 98 Cr. 1023 (S.D. N.Y.), Feb. 21, 2001 (transcript pp. 1078–1088, 1096–1102).

4. Mike interview (Dec. 11, 2003).

5. Daniel Benjamin and Steven Simon, *The Age of Sacred Terror* (Random House, 2002), pp. 269–270; Mike interview (Dec. 11, 2003); Richard Clarke interview (Dec. 18, 2003); George Tenet interview (Jan. 22, 2004).

6. On Sudanese discussions with Saudi officials, see Frank interview (Mar. 18, 2004); Ron interview (Mar. 18, 2004). Timothy Carney believed the Saudis told Sudan that they did not want Bin Ladin. Timothy Carney interview (Dec. 4, 2003).

7. The CIA official who held one-on-one discussions with Erwa said that Erwa never offered to expel Bin Ladin to the United States or render him to another country. Mark interview (May 12, 2004). For Carney's instructions and the lack of a U.S. indictment, see Timothy Carney interview (Dec. 4, 2003). On the indictment issue and the supposed Sudanese offer to give up Bin Ladin, see Samuel Berger interview (Jan. 14, 2004).

In early May 1996, the CIA received intelligence that Bin Ladin might be leaving Sudan. Though this reporting was described as "very spotty," it would have been passed along to the DCI's office because of high concern about Bin Ladin at the time. But it did not lead to plans for a U.S. operation to snatch Bin Ladin, because there was no indictment against him. Ron interview (Mar. 18, 2004); Frank interview (Mar. 18, 2004). It appears, however, that if another country had been willing to imprison Bin Ladin, the CIA might have tried to work out a scenario for apprehending him. CIA cable, May 8, 1996. The Sudanese government did not notify the United States that Bin Ladin had left the country until about two days after his departure. DOS cable, Nairobi 07020, "Sudan: Foreign Minister on Developments," May 21, 1996.

President Clinton, in a February 2002 speech to the Long Island Association, said that the United States did not accept a Sudanese offer and take Bin Ladin because there was no indictment. President Clinton speech to the Long Island Association, Feb. 15, 2002 (videotape of speech). But the President told us that he had "misspoken" and was, wrongly, recounting a number of press stories he had read. After reviewing this matter in preparation for his Commission meeting, President Clinton told us that Sudan never offered to turn Bin Ladin over to the United States. President Clinton meeting (Apr. 8, 2004). Berger told us that he saw no chance that Sudan would have handed Bin Ladin over and also noted that in 1996, the U.S. government still did not know of any al Qaeda attacks on U.S. citizens. Samuel Berger interview (Jan. 14, 2004).

Alleged Sudanese offers to cooperate on counterterrorism have been the subject of much recent controversy. After repeatedly demanding that Sudan stop supporting terrorist groups, in 1993 the U.S. government designated the country a state sponsor of terrorism. Diplomatic discussions continued but had little impact on Sudanese support for terrorism or on other issues, such as human rights. In the fall of 1995, the United States conducted a Sudan policy review and, supported by a vocal segment of Congress, the White House sought to pressure and isolate the Sudanese. Susan Rice interview (Jan. 9, 2004).

After Bin Ladin left Sudan in May 1996, some State Department officials, including Ambassador Carney, criticized the NSC's hard-line policy, which he felt provided no "carrots" for Sudanese moderates to cooperate on counterterrorism. He also faulted the NSC for not reopening the U.S. embassy in Khartoum (closed in early 1996) when security concerns there were reevaluated. State's Sudan desk officer agreed, noting that the embassy was an excellent vehicle for gathering information on terrorists. According to one State official, NSC policymakers' views were too firmly set to engage and test the Sudanese on counterterrorism. Timothy Carney interview (Dec. 4, 2003); David Shinn interview (Aug. 29, 2003); Stephen Schwartz interview (Dec. 30, 2003).

But supporters of the tough line, such as the NSC's Susan Rice, argued that any conciliatory statements from Khartoum belied its unhelpful actions. For example, she noted, though Sudan did eventually expel Bin Ladin, his al Qaeda network retained a presence in the country. Susan Rice interview (Jan. 9, 2004). In addition, the CIA's Africa Division, whose operatives had engaged the Sudanese on counterterrorism in early 1996, would conclude that "there is no indication that Sudanese involvement with terrorism has decreased in the past year." They saw the Sudanese gestures toward cooperating as "tactical retreats" aimed at deceiving Washington in hopes of having sanctions removed. CIA memo, Walter to Acting DCI, "Africa Division's Recommendations Regarding Sudan," Dec. 17, 1996. The CIA official who ran the Sudanese portfolio and met with the Sudanese on numerous occasions told us the Sudanese were not going to deliver, and the perceived moderates "were just flat-out lying." Mark interview (May 12, 2004).

In February 1997, the Sudanese sent letters to President Clinton and Secretary of State Albright, extending an invitation for a U.S. counterterrorism inspection mission to visit Sudan. The Sudanese also used private U.S. citizens to pass along offers to cooperate. Mansoor Ijaz interview (May 7, 2004); Janet McElligot interview (Oct. 20, 2003). But these offers were dismissed because the NSC viewed Sudan as all talk and little action. U.S. officials also feared that the Sudanese would exploit any positive American responses, including trips to the region by U.S. officials, for their own political purposes. See Joint Inquiry interview of David Williams, June 26, 2002. Today, Sudan is still listed as a state sponsor of terrorism.

8. Mike interview (Dec. 11, 2003). On local contacts, see Gary Schroen interview (Mar. 3, 2004). On "Jeff's" views, see CIA memo, "DCI Talking Points Regarding Operations Against Usama Bin Ladin," Aug. 25, 1997.

9. See Joint Inquiry briefing by Mike, Sept. 12, 2002. For briefings to the NSC, see NSC email, Clarke to Berger, "Threat Warning: Usama bin Ladin," Mar. 7, 1998; Mary McCarthy interview (Dec. 8, 2003); CIA memos, summary of weekly Berger/Tenet meeting, May 1, 1998.

10. CIA memos, summary of weekly Berger/Tenet meeting, May 1, 1998.

11. Karl Inderfurth interview (Feb. 18, 2004).

12. Peter Tomsen interview (Oct. 8, 2003).

13. For State Department officials' views, see Strobe Talbott interview (Jan. 15, 2004); Karl Inderfurth interview (Feb. 18, 2004).

14. On the civil war and UNOCAL, see Karl Inderfurth interview (Feb. 18, 2004); Robin Raphel interview (Dec. 8, 2003). The former UNOCAL chief for the pipeline project, Marty Miller, denied working exclusively with the Taliban and told us that his company sought to work with all Afghan factions to bring about the necessary stability to proceed with the project. Marty Miller interview (Nov. 7, 2003). UNOCAL hired, among others, Robert Oakley, the former ambassador to Pakistan. Oakley told us that he counseled the company about the internal dynamics of Afghanistan and Pakistan but never lobbied the State Department on UNOCAL's behalf. Robert Oakley interview (Sept. 7, 2003); see also "Advisory Consulting Agreement" between UNOCAL and Oakley, Oct. 1996. On giving the Taliban a chance, see Marvin Weinbaum interview (Aug. 12, 2003).

15. See Madeleine Albright, speech at Nashir Bagh refugee camp in western Pakistan, Nov. 18, 1997. For a description of the Richardson mission, see Bill Richardson interview (Dec. 15, 2003); Karl Inderfurth interview (Feb. 18, 2004).

16. Marvin Weinbaum interview (Aug. 12, 2003). See also Strobe Talbott interview (Jan. 15, 2004). For Zinni's

view, see Anthony Zinni interview (Jan. 29, 2004).

17. Gary Schroen interview (Mar. 3, 2004). For more details, see Steve Coll, *Ghost Wars: The Secret History of the CIA, Afghanistan, and bin Laden, from the Soviet Invasion to September 10, 2001* (Penguin, 2004), p. 379.

18. Coll, *Ghost Wars*, pp. 343, 391; Gary Schroen interview (Mar. 3, 2004); Joint Inquiry briefing by Mike, Sept. 12, 2002.

19. For a description of the plan, the content of briefing papers, and the Berger-Tenet meeting, see CIA memo, Jeff to Tenet, "Information Paper on Usama Bin Ladin," Feb. 12, 1998 (with attached paper for Tenet's meeting with Berger on Feb. 13, 1998, "Next Steps Against Usama Bin Ladin"). The paper also briefly noted other options the CIA could be pursuing against Bin Ladin: paramilitary or sabotage attacks—possibly lethal—against Bin Ladin's facilities in Kandahar and Sudan, or even intelligence support for U.S. military strikes. On the Kansi operation, see Coll, *Ghost Wars*, p. 373.

20. NSC note, Simon to Berger, update on Feb. 24 meeting, Feb. 27, 1998.

21. Joint Inquiry briefing by Mike, Sept. 12, 2002; NSC email, Clarke to Berger, "Threat Warning: Usama Bin Ladin," Mar. 7, 1998.

22. Mike interview (Jan. 6, 2004); CIA email, Schroen to Mike, "Capture Op," May 5, 1998; CIA cable, "Comments on [Tribals'] Planning for UBL Rendition," May 6, 1998. For the modification of the plan, see CIA memo, "Tentative Timeline for the Bin Ladin Capture Operation," May 19, 1998. For details on some CIA officers' concerns, see Coll, *Ghost Wars*, pp. 393–394.

23. CIA cable, "19 May 98 Briefing for JSOC," May 27, 1998; CIA cable, "Developments in the [Tribals'] Operation at the HQs End," May 26, 1998; Joint Inquiry interview of Michael Canavan, Sept. 3, 2002.

24. CIA memos, summary of weekly Berger/Tenet meeting, May 1, 1998.

25. CIA memo, summary of Covert Action Planning Group meeting, May 18, 1998; CIA memo, "Tentative Timeline for the Bin Ladin Capture Operation," May 19, 1998. The summary of the meeting notes that the initiative was not an assassination, despite the inaccurate comments of some in the NSC.

26. Mike interviews (Dec. 11, 2003; Jan. 6, 2004); Jeff interview (Dec. 17, 2003); Mary Jo White interview (May 17, 2004).

27. CIA cable, "20–24 May 98 Full Mission Profile of the U.S. Side of the Bin Ladin Capture Operation," May 27, 1998; CIA cable, "Developments in the [Tribals'] Operation at the HQs End," May 26, 1998.

28. CIA memo, summary of weekly Berger/Tenet meeting, May 20, 1998. It is unclear if a decision had been made at this point on where to bring Bin Ladin.

29. Mike interview (Dec. 11, 2003); CIA cable, "The [Tribals'] Operations," May 29, 1998.

30. Richard Clarke interview (Dec. 18, 2003), in which he also noted that Tenet did not approve of the plan. For Clarke's comments to the NSC, see CIA cable, "Info from State on Status of Political Approvals for [Tribals']," May 29, 1998. See Jeff interview (Dec. 17, 2003); James Pavitt interview (Jan. 8, 2004); George Tenet interview (Jan. 22, 2004), in which he also said he did not tell the Principals Committee his reasons for canceling the operation because there was no reason for the principals to hear details of an unsound plan. See also Samuel Berger interview (Jan. 14, 2004).

31. CIA memo, DDO to Berger, "Timing of the UBL Rendition Operation," June 15, 1998; for Schroen, see CIA cable, "Comments on [Tribals'] Planning for UBL Rendition," May 6, 1998.

32. See, e.g., Samuel Berger interview (Jan. 14, 2004).

33. On Saudi disruptions generally, see CIA report, "Additional Background on the Saudi discovery of an UBL Network in Saudi Arabia," undated (appears to be May 1998). On the DCI's visits to Saudi Arabia, see Intelligence reports made available to the Commission.

34. See Intelligence reports made available to the Commission.

35. Coll, *Ghost Wars*, pp. 400–402.

36. CIA note, Pillar to Wentworth/Ramanujam, summary of Aug. 5, 1998, CSG meeting on Bin Ladin, Aug. 6, 1998.

37. See, e.g., CIA briefing materials, "Bombings in Nairobi and Dar es Salaam—An Update," Aug. 14, 1998.

38. DOD memo, "Chronology of Planning," Dec. 14, 1998.

39. Richard Clarke interview (Dec. 18, 2003).

40. NSC email, Clarke to Berger, Aug. 8, 1998; Samuel Berger interview (Jan. 14, 2004); CIA memo, "Khowst and the Meeting of Islamic Extremist Leaders on 20 Aug.," Aug. 17, 1998.

41. NSC notes, checklist re military strikes, Aug. 14, 1998 (author appears to be Clarke). On the military plans, see DOD memo, "Chronology of Planning," Dec. 14, 1998.

42. President Clinton meeting (Apr. 8, 2004); Samuel Berger interview (Jan. 14, 2004).

43. NSC emails, Simon to Kerrick, Aug. 5, 1998. For the report of Bin Ladin's comment, see, e.g., NSC email, Clarke to Berger, July 15, 1998. EMPTA stands for O-ethyl methylphosphonothioic acid.

44. NSC memo, McCarthy to Berger, re Shifa, Aug. 11, 1998; Samuel Berger interview (Jan. 14, 2004).

45. For a timeline of the decisionmaking events, see NSC memo to Steinberg et al., Aug. 17, 1999. The list of concurrences is drawn from talking points prepared for Berger's use with the main four leaders of the House and

Senate; the list explicitly mentions the Attorney General. NSC email, Clarke to Berger, Aug. 19, 1998. Reno told us she did not mention her concerns to the President but discussed them with Berger, Tenet, White House Counsel Charles Ruff, and DOJ staff. Janet Reno interview (Dec. 16, 2003).

46. NSC email, Clarke to Kerrick, "Timeline," Aug. 19, 1998; Samuel Berger interview (Jan. 14, 2004). We did not find documentation on the after-action review mentioned by Berger. On Vice Chairman Joseph Ralston's mission in Pakistan, see William Cohen interview (Feb. 5, 2004). For speculation on tipping off the Taliban, see, e.g., Richard Clarke interview (Dec. 18, 2003).

47. NSC email, Clarke to Kerrick, "Timeline," Aug. 19, 1998.

48. For initial support by Gingrich and Lott, see, e.g., Steven Thomma and Richard Parker, "U.S. Strikes Afghan, Sudan Sites, Retaliating for Embassy Attacks," *Philadelphia Inquirer,* Aug. 21, 1998, p. A1. For a reaction to the later criticism by Gingrich's office, see NSC email, Simon to Berger, Sept. 10, 1998.

49. Editorial, "Punish and Be Damned," *Economist,* Aug. 29, 1998, p. 16. For a summary of skeptical public reaction, see Benjamin and Simon, *Age of Sacred Terror,* pp. 354–363.

50. See NSC memo, McCarthy and Clarke to Berger, Apr. 17, 2000, reporting that on balance, they think the CIA claim was valid. See also President Clinton meeting (Apr. 8, 2004); Vice President Gore meeting (Apr. 9, 2004); Samuel Berger interview (Jan. 14, 2004); George Tenet interview (Jan. 22, 2004); Richard Clarke interview (Dec. 19, 2003).

51. Samuel Berger interview (Jan. 22, 2004). President Clinton told us that he had directed his national security team to focus exclusively on responding to the embassy bombings. President Clinton meeting (Apr. 8, 2004). See also William Cohen testimony, Mar. 23, 2004. When "wag the dog" allegations were again raised during the December 1998 Desert Fox campaign over Iraq, Defense Secretary Cohen, formerly a Republican senator, told members of Congress that he would have resigned if he believed the President was using the military for any purpose other than national security. William Cohen interview (Feb. 5, 2004).

52. Samuel Berger interview (Jan. 22, 2004).

53. CIA analytic report, "Foreign Terrorist Threat in the U.S.: Revisiting our 1995 Estimate," Apr. 1997.

54. Daniel Benjamin interview (Dec. 4, 2003).

55. On the Balkan crises, see Tim Judah, *The Serbs: History, Myth and the Destruction of Yugoslavia* (Yale Univ. Press, 2000).

56. On Clarke's obsession with terrorism and Bin Ladin, see Richard Clarke interview (Feb. 3, 2004); Richard A. Clarke, *Against All Enemies: Inside America's War on Terror* (Free Press, 2004), p. 234. On the CSG and the Small Group, see Samuel Berger interview (Jan. 11, 2004).

57. NSC memo, "Political Military Plan DELENDA," Sept. 1998 (attached to NSC memo, Clarke to Rice, Jan. 25, 2001).

58. Ibid. See also NSC memo, Clarke to Berger, Sept. 7, 1998.

59. Handwritten note from Steinberg on NSC memo, Clarke to Berger, Apr. 14, 2000. For the views of Small Group members, see William Cohen interview (Feb. 5, 2004); Hugh Shelton interview (Feb. 5, 2004); President Clinton meeting (Apr. 8, 2004); Samuel Berger interview (Jan. 14, 2004); Madeleine Albright interview (Jan. 7, 2004); James Steinberg interview (Dec. 5, 2003).

60. Richard Clarke interview (Jan. 12, 2004); DOD memo, Slocombe to Cohen, Aug. 27, 1998.

61. DOD memo, "Towards a More Aggressive Counterterrorism Posture," undated, pp. 1, 7. The principal author of this paper was Thomas Kuster, a career civil servant and former special forces officer. He told us that this paper was drafted in September 1998. On this episode, see Thomas Kuster interviews (Dec. 9, 2003; Mar. 5, 2004); Allen Holmes interview (Mar. 10, 2004); Jan Lodal interview (Mar. 5, 2004).

62. DOS cable, Islamabad 06863, "Afghanistan: Demarche to Taliban on New Bin Ladin Threat," Sept. 14, 1998. See also NSC memo, Clarke to principals, "Possible New Attacks on US by UBL Network," Sept. 12, 1998, which suggested language for the demarche, including a warning that future attacks would bring "severe consequences." NSC email, Clarke to Berger, Sept. 19, 1998, indicates that the State Department used both its embassy in Islamabad and a direct call to Mullah Omar's office to deliver the warning.

63. DOS memo, "Mullah Omar's 8/22 Contact with State Department," Aug. 22, 1998.

64. DOS cable, Islamabad 007665, "High-Level Taliban Official Gives the Standard Line on Bin Ladin with a Couple of Nuances," Oct. 12, 1998.

65. NSC memo, Sept. 24, 1998; Coll, *Ghost Wars,* p. 414.

66. The CIA in particular pressed the Saudis hard on intelligence sharing. DCI Tenet met with Crown Prince Abdullah, Ambassador Bandar, the minister of defense and aviation, and other senior officials repeatedly and pressed them on counterterrorism. See, e.g., CIA memo, Tenet to Berger, Tenet's meeting with Crown Prince Abdullah in Jeddah, June 7, 1998. As late as July 3, 2001, the DCI was pressing Bandar, conveying the urgent need for information. CIA cable, DCI meeting with Bandar, July 3, 2001.

67. See, e.g., Mike interview (Dec. 11, 2003). The Saudis, however, were reluctant to provide details of incomplete investigations and highly sensitive to any information related to Saudi nationals, particularly those in the Kingdom. See CIA memo, Saudi CT Cooperation, June 18, 1998.

68. CIA talking points, Vice President's meeting with Crown Prince Abdullah, Sept. 24, 1998; NSC memo,

Simon to Berger, "Talking Points for Lott-Gingrich Meeting," Sept. 24, 1998.

69. NSC memo, Wechsler, summary of conclusions of Nov. 16, 1998, meeting of Working Group on UBL's Finances.

70. Rick Newcomb interview (Feb. 4, 2004); Treasury memo, Office of Foreign Asset Control to DOS, "Draft Cable on Meeting with Two of UBL's Brothers," May 19, 2000; DOS cable, State 035243, "January 2000 Meeting Regarding UBL Finances," Feb. 27, 2000; Frank G. interview (Mar. 2, 2004). The U.S. government team learned that the Bin Ladin family sold UBL's share of the inheritance and, at the direction of the Saudi government, placed the money into a specified account then frozen by the Saudi government in 1994.

71. NSC memo, Clarke to Berger, Roadmap, Nov. 3, 1998. According to Clarke, Tenet's deputy, John Gordon, agreed that there was no senior CIA manager to answer these questions and promised to fix that.

72. DOS memo, McKune to Albright, "State Sponsorship of Terrorism: Pakistan," Feb. 1998. For the rejection of the proposed designation, see handwritten notes on the McKune memo.

73. Madeleine Albright interview (Jan. 7, 2004).

74. NSC memo, Simon to NSC officials, Oct. 6, 1998. Links between Pakistan's military intelligence service and Harakat ul Ansar trainees at Bin Ladin camps near Khowst were also discussed in DOS memo, Inderfurth to Talbott, "Pakistani Links to Kashmiri Militants," Aug. 23, 1998.

75. William Milam interview (Dec. 29, 2003).

76. By the fall of 1999, the Glenn, Pressler, and Symington amendments prohibited most economic and military assistance to Pakistan. Clinton administration officials told us that these sanctions made it impossible to offer "carrots" to Pakistan, and that before 9/11, waiving sanctions was not feasible because of the Musharraf coup, non-proliferation concerns, and Congress's pro-India orientation. Karl Inderfurth interview (Feb. 18, 2004); Strobe Talbott interview (Feb. 8, 2004).

77. Strobe Talbott interview (Feb. 8, 2004). Berger agreed with Talbott that using other sticks, such as blocking loans from international financial institutions, would have risked a collapse of the Pakistani government and the rise of Islamists to power in a nuclear-armed country. Samuel Berger interview (Jan. 14, 2004).

78. DOS memo, Pickering to Albright, "Berger meeting on UBL," Nov. 3, 1998.

79. White House reports made available to the Commission. President Clinton met with Prime Minister Sharif on December 2, 1999, and called him on December 18, 1999.

80. NSC email, Clarke to Berger, Dec. 9, 1998. The event described in the intelligence report was said to have occurred on November 17, 1998. Intelligence officials now tell us that there are some doubts about the accuracy of the report.

81. Michael Sheehan interview (Dec. 16, 2003). For Sheehan's background, see Madeleine Albright, with Bill Woodward, *Madam Secretary* (Miramax, 2003), pp. 369–370. For one of Sheehan's warnings, see DOS cable, Abu Dhabi 002212, "Messages for the Taliban," Apr. 9, 1999.

82. Michael Sheehan interviews (Dec. 16, 2003; March 2004). For Albright's views, see Madeleine Albright interview (Jan. 7, 2004). NSC memo, Principals' Decision Paper, Mar. 8, 1999. In May 1999, Albright approved a State Department diplomatic strategy calling for increased high-level pressure on the Taliban and the three countries that recognized it—and for unilateral sanctions if this failed. DOS memo, Inderfurth, Indyk, and Sheehan to Albright, "A New Bin Ladin Strategy," May 15, 1999.

83. NSC email, Riedel to Berger and Clarke, June 8, 1999.

84. See Karl Inderfurth interview (Feb. 18, 2004); DOS memo, Inderfurth to Albright, May 6, 1999; Michael Sheehan interview (Dec. 16, 2003). Although Sheehan told us he was initially skeptical about supporting the Northern Alliance, he eventually came around in the fall of 2000.

85. For aid to the exile groups, see Karl Inderfurth interview (Feb. 18, 2004); Peter Tomsen interview (July 14, 2004). The aid was later cut because of alleged accounting deficiencies. For the diplomat's views, see Christina Rocca interview (Jan. 29, 2004). But Peter Tomsen, the State Department's special envoy to the Afghan resistance in the late 1980s, believed that neither administration did enough to assemble an anti-Taliban ruling coalition inside and outside Afghanistan. Peter Tomsen interview (Oct. 8, 2003); see also letter from Peter Tomsen to the Commission, June 30, 2004.

86. NSC memo, Clarke to Berger, Roadmap, May 18, 1999.

87. DOS memo, Inderfurth to Albright, May 6, 1999; DOS memo, Oakley to Pickering, "Designating the Taliban a FTO," Apr. 22, 1999; Executive Order 13129, July 4, 1999. Since 1979, the secretary of state has had the authority to name "state sponsors of terrorism," subjecting such countries to significant economic sanctions. Being designated a "foreign terrorist organization" also brings sanctions and stigmatizes a regime. While the U.S. government did not use either designation against the Taliban, the sanctions under this executive order mimicked the sanctions that would have been implemented under them.

88. UN Security Council Resolution (UNSCR) 1267, Oct. 15, 1999. UNSCR 1267 demanded that the Taliban render Bin Ladin to justice within 30 days; upon noncompliance, UN member states were called on to restrict takeoff and landing rights of Taliban-owned aircraft. The sanctions also required member states to freeze Taliban funds and financial resources. But Taliban "charter flights" continued to fly between Afghanistan and the UAE. Judy Pasternak and Stephen Braun, "Emirates Looked Other Way While Al Qaeda Funds Flowed," *Los Angeles*

Times, Jan. 20, 2002, p. A1. Enforcing the financial restrictions also proved a challenge—especially in the Middle East. Anthony Wayne interview (Jan. 14, 2004); Frank G. interview (Mar. 2, 2004); DOS report, "Usama Bin Ladin Intelligence Update," Nov. 19, 1999.

89. NSC email, Clarke to Berger, Oct. 30, 1999.

90. Ibid.; NSC memo, Benjamin to CSG, Nov. 12, 1999. Earlier, Clarke had worried that the expulsion of Bin Ladin might mean he would move to Somalia or Libya, where he might be even harder to target. NSC email, Clarke to Berger, Oct. 8, 1998.

91. See Intelligence report, relations between al Qaeda and the Taliban, Feb. 20, 2002.

92. Intelligence report, March 2000.

93. UNSCR 1333, Dec. 19, 2000.

94. Edmund Hull interview (Oct. 18, 2003).

95. Ambassador Milam characterized UNSCR 1267 and UNSCR 1333 as "punchless." DOS cable, Islamabad 000656, "Options for dealing with Afghan terrorism problem," Feb. 6, 2001. But Ambassador Sheehan indicated that even if UNSCR 1333 failed to stop the arms flow from Pakistan to the Taliban, it had enormous symbolic importance. He also noted that UNSCR 1333 must have stigmatized the Taliban because they "went ballistic over the sanctions." Sheehan added that UNSCR 1333 made Saudi Arabia and the UAE "very nervous" about their relationships with the Taliban. Michael Sheehan interview (Dec. 16, 2003).

96. White House cable to U.S. Embassy, Islamabad, message to Prime Minister Sharif, June 16, 1999; Madeleine Albright prepared statement, Mar. 24, 2004.

97. White House cable to U.S. Embassy, Islamabad, message to Prime Minister Sharif, June 16, 1999; Samuel Berger interview (Jan. 14, 2004); President Clinton meeting (Apr. 8, 2004); NSC memo, Clarke and McCarthy to Berger, Aug. 2, 1999.

98. President Clinton meeting (Apr. 8, 2004); DOS memo, Sheehan to Albright, "S/CT Update on Critical Issues," July 9, 1999.

99. Samuel Berger interview (Jan. 14, 2004); President Clinton meeting (Apr. 8, 2004).

100. Thomas Pickering interview (Dec. 22, 2003).

101. See Executive Order 13099, Aug. 20, 1998.

102. CIA talking points, information on Bin Ladin for the DCI's Sept. 2, 1998, briefing to the Senate Select Committee on Intelligence, Sept. 2, 1998.

103. For the Tirana raid and resulting operations, see Benjamin and Simon, *Age of Sacred Terror*, pp. 261, 264; Clarke, *Against All Enemies*, p. 183; CIA talking points, "CIA Operation Results in Capture of Two Bin Ladin Operatives," July 7, 1998; CIA memo, Jeff to Tenet, "Biweekly Developments in CT Policy," July 15, 1998. For other operations, see NSC memo, Benjamin to Berger, Oct. 9, 1998. For the arrest of Abu Hajer, see CIA report, "Apprehension of Senior UBL Lieutenant in Germany," Sept. 22, 1998; NSC memo, Benjamin to Berger, Oct. 9, 1998; NSC email, Clarke to Berger, Sept. 17, 1998. For an overview of the CIA's efforts to disrupt al Qaeda, see Joint Inquiry testimony of George Tenet, Oct. 17, 2002. For Clarke's comment to Berger, see NSC email, Clarke to Berger, Sept. 25, 1998.

104. For ambush attempts, see Joint Inquiry report (classified version), pp. 312–313; CIA memo, "Status of the Bin Ladin Capture Operation," Sept. 30, 1998 (part of materials for Small Group meeting). For CIA officials' doubts, see James Pavitt interview (Jan. 8, 2004); Jeff interview (Dec. 17, 2003). On the quality of the tribals' reporting, see Charles Allen interview (Jan. 27, 2004). The tribals' extensive reporting on Bin Ladin's location is reflected in near daily UBL Situation Reports prepared for the DCI from December 1998 to January 2001.

105. See Martin Sieff, "Terrorist Is Driven by Hatred for U.S., Israel," *Washington Times*, Aug. 21, 1998, p. 1. Regarding the leak, see Mary C. interview (Oct. 25, 2003); Richard Taylor interview (Dec. 10, 2003); Don Kerr interview (Sept. 9, 2003).

106. NSC memo, Clarke to Berger, Roadmap, Nov. 3, 1998; NSC talking points, Nov. 3, 1998. The quoted sentence is in boldface.

107. NSC memo, summary of conclusions of Oct. 26, 1998, CSG Meeting, Oct. 28, 1998; NSC notes, CSG Agenda: "Bin Ladin Penetration of the United States," Oct. 26, 1998. For the threat against Washington, see NSC memo, Clarke to Berger, Weekly Report, July 3, 1998; NSC email, Clarke to various NSC staff, Sept. 7, 1998; NSC memo, Clarke to Berger, Roadmap, Nov. 3, 1998.

108. NSC memo, summary of conclusions of Oct. 26, 1998, CSG meeting, Oct. 28, 1998.

109. Indictment, *United States v. Usama Bin Laden*, No. 98 Cr. (S.D. N.Y. unsealed Nov. 4, 1998), p. 3. For the reports concerning Derunta, see NSC memo, Clarke to Berger, Roadmap, Nov. 3, 1998.

110. NSC email, Clarke to Berger, Nov. 4, 1998. Evidence on Iraqi ties to al Qaeda is summarized in chapter 2.

111. Patrick Fitzgerald testimony, June 16, 2004.

112. The PDB was a summary of Intelligence report, planning by UBL to hijack U.S. airplane, Dec. 4, 1998. For the immediate responses, see NSC memo, summary of conclusions of Dec. 4, 1998, CSG meeting; FAA security directive, "Threat to Air Carriers," SD 108-98, Dec. 8, 1998. We requested declassification of this document; the declassified document was delivered on July 13, 2004.

113. On further information, see Intelligence report, possible arrest of persons involved in hijacking plan, Dec. 18, 1998; Intelligence report, timeframe for completion of hijacking operation, Dec. 24, 1998; Intelligence report, claim that Bin Ladin postponed hijacking, Jan. 8, 1999; CIA analytic report, "Reporting on Al-Qaida plans to Use Aircraft as Terrorist Weapons," Aug. 26, 2002. After 9/11, the U.S. government checked again with the foreign government to determine if there could be any connection between the attacks and these 1998–1999 reports. The foreign government had no intelligence of such links, but judged that the 1998 plan could have influenced planning for the 9/11 operation. Ibid.

On the FBI followup in 1998–1999, see FBI memo, Jack S. to FAA ACI, "FBI Investigative Efforts," Jan. 27, 1999; FAA records, information in FAA Intelligence Case File 98-0199B. A Saudi who had just completed pilot training, boarding a flight to return to Saudi Arabia, had been arrested at JFK Airport in late November 1998. He had been carrying an inert hand grenade, which was detected by a checkpoint screener. The terminal was evacuated, and police found miscellaneous gun parts, pistol ammunition, and military paraphernalia in the man's checked bags. FAA record, "Security Summary NY-99-007," undated. The man was released after a few days in jail and, assisted by the local Saudi consulate, had returned to Saudi Arabia. The new threat information caused the FBI and the CIA to look again at this case. FBI agents found that the man's statements about his flight training were true and that his firearms were legally registered. The Saudi investigators reported that the Saudi had enjoyed shooting at a gun club in Texas, where he had completed his flight training for a commercial pilot's license. The Saudis further indicated that the man had no apparent political motive, and the results of a security investigation in the Kingdom were negative. FAA memo, Matthew K. to Jack S. and Tom K., Saudi national, Jan. 17, 1999; FBI memo, Jack S. to FAA ACI, "FBI Investigative Efforts," Jan. 27, 1999; Intelligence report (to FAA), Saudi information, Apr. 13, 1999. For the expiration of the FAA security directive, see FAA security directive, SD 108-95; FAA record, "SD/EA Status: 108 Security Directives," May 20, 2002.

114. NSC notes, Clarke briefing notes for Berger for Small Group, Dec. 17, 1998; CIA memo, "Bin Ladin Ready to Attack," Dec. 18, 1998.

115. NSC notes, Clarke briefing notes for Berger for Small Group, Dec. 17, 1998; NSC memo, Benjamin to Berger, Dec. 18, 1998; DOD memo, "UBL Campaign: Talking Points for Qandahar Attack," Jan. 11, 1999; Hugh Shelton interview (Feb. 5, 2004).

116. NSC memo, Benjamin to Berger, Dec. 18, 1998; DOD order, Execute Order (EXORD), Dec. 18, 1998.

117. NSC memo, Benjamin to Berger, Dec. 18, 1998; Mike interview (Jan. 6, 2004); CIA emails, Mike to Schroen, "Urgent re UBL," and Schroen's response, Dec. 20, 1998.

118. John Maher III interview (Apr. 4, 2004). Maher said he found General Zinni's figures to be "shockingly high." On the principals' decision against recommending an attack, see NSC memo, Clarke to Berger, Jan. 12, 1999. See also George Tenet interview (Jan. 22, 2004); Mike interview (Feb. 6, 2004).

119. CIA email, Mike to Schroen, "Your Note," Dec. 21, 1998; CIA email, Schroen to Mike, "Re Urgent re UBL," Dec. 20, 1998.

120. John Maher III interview (Apr. 22, 2004).

121. CIA report, "Further Options Available Against UBL," Nov. 18, 1998; CIA talking points, "Options for Attacking the Usama Bin Ladin Problem," Nov. 24, 1998. On the MON, see Randy Moss interview (Feb. 6, 2004); James Baker interview (Feb. 4, 2004).

122. NSC note, Dec. 20, 1998. There is no indication as to who wrote this note or to whom it was directed. It was cleared with Berger, Reno, Assistant Attorney General Randy Moss, and CTC's "Jeff," and briefed in substance to Leon Fuerth, national security adviser to Vice President Gore, and to Deputy DCI Gordon. See also attached CIA memo, Gordon to Berger, Dec. 21, 1998; NSC memo, Berger to President Clinton, Dec. 24, 1998.

123. NSC memo, Berger to President Clinton, Dec. 24, 1998; Randy Moss interview (Feb. 6, 2004); James Baker interview (Feb. 4, 2004). Both Moss and Baker told us they concluded that killing Bin Ladin did not violate the assassination ban contained in Executive Order 12333.

124. NSC memo, Berger to President Clinton, Dec. 24, 1998; Janet Reno interview (Dec. 16, 2003). See also Randy Moss interview (Feb. 6, 2004). Tenent told us he does not recall this episode.

125. CIA cable, message from the DCI, Dec. 26, 1998.

126. CIA cable, instructions passed to tribals and response, Dec. 27, 1998.

127. CIA cable, comments on tribals' response, Dec. 27, 1998. "Mike" noted that the tribals' reaction had "attracted a good deal of attention" back at CIA headquarters. CIA cable, comments from Schroen, Dec. 28, 1998. Schroen commented that the tribals' response was an effort to appear statesmanlike and take the moral high ground.

128. See President Clinton meeting (Apr. 8, 2004); Samuel Berger interview (Jan. 1, 2004); Richard Clarke interview (Jan. 12, 2004). For a CIA senior intelligence manager, operator, and lawyer's view, see George Tenet interview (Jan. 22, 2004); Gary Schroen interview (Jan. 6, 2004); Doug B. interview (Nov. 17, 2003); Mike interview (Jan. 6, 2004).

129. James Baker interview (Feb. 4, 2004); President Clinton meeting (Apr. 8, 2004).

130. NSC memo, McCarthy to CIA, Dec. 1999.

131. NSC memo, Clarke to Berger, Jan. 12, 1999.

132. NSC email, Ward to Clarke and others, Jan. 5, 1999.

133. NSC memo, Clarke to Berger, Jan. 12, 1999.

134. NSC email, Clarke to Kerrick, Feb. 10, 1999; Charles Allen interview (Jan. 27, 2004).

135. NSC email, Clarke to Berger, Feb. 11, 1999. The email in fact misspells "boogie" as "boggie."

136. NSC email, Riedel to NSC front office, Feb. 16, 1999. The email does not provide Riedel's source. For Berger's authorization, see NSC notes, TNT note, Feb. 12, 1999.

137. DOD memo, "Chronology of Planning," Dec. 14, 1998.

138. DOS cable, Washington 157093, "Aug. 21 telephone conversation between POTUS and Prime Minister Sharif," Aug. 26, 1998. Sharif was cordial but disagreed with the U.S. decision to strike.

139. Anthony Zinni interview (Jan. 29, 2004).

140. Ibid.

141. DOD memo, Headquarters SOC, "Planning Directive for Infinite Resolve," Dec. 23, 1998. On basing options, see DOD memo, "Summary of Conclusions: AC-130 Deployment Decision Paper," Jan. 12, 1999.

142. NSC memo, Clarke to Berger and Steinberg, Roadmap for Feb. 2, 1999, Small Group meeting, undated; John Maher III interview (Apr. 22, 2004); Anthony Zinni interview (Jan. 29, 2004); Peter Schoomaker interview (Feb. 19, 2004).

143. Peter Schoomaker interview (Feb. 19, 2004); William Boykin interview (Nov. 7, 2003).

144. Hugh Shelton interview (Feb. 5, 2004).

145. President Clinton meeting (Apr. 8, 2004); William Cohen interview (Feb. 5, 2004).

146. Hugh Shelton interview (Feb. 5, 2004); William Boykin interview (Nov. 7, 2003).

147. General Zinni reminded us that in addition to severing military-to-military relations with Pakistan after the 1998 nuclear test, the United States had not shipped to Pakistan the F-16s Pakistan had bought prior to the test. Instead, the United States kept the money Pakistan paid for the F-16s to fund storage of the aircraft. Meanwhile, Pakistani pilots were crashing and dying. "Guess how they [felt] about the United States of America," Zinni said. Nevertheless, Zinni told us that Musharraf was someone who would actually work with the United States if he was given the chance to do so. Anthony Zinni interview (Jan. 29, 2004).

148. William Boykin interview (Nov. 7, 2003).

149. Richard Clarke interview (Jan. 12, 2004).

150. William Cohen testimony (Mar. 23, 2004).

151. CIA report, "UBL Situation Report," Feb. 2, 1999. Public sources include Coll, Ghost Wars, pp. 447–449; Benjamin and Simon, Age of Sacred Terror, p. 281.

152. CIA cable, "Update on Location of an Activity at Sheikh Ali's Camps," Feb. 7, 1999.

153. DOD order, MOD 001 to CJCS warning order, Feb. 8, 1999.

154. CIA reports, "UBL Situation Report," Feb. 6–10, 1999.

155. CIA cable, "Support for Military Contingency Planning," Feb. 10, 1999.

156. NSC email, Clarke to Kerrick, Feb. 10, 1999.

157. CIA talking points, "CIA Operations Against UBL," Feb. 10, 1999.

158. CIA reports, "UBL Situation Reports," Feb. 11–12, 1999.

159. John Maher III interview (Apr. 22, 2004); Richard Clarke interview (Jan. 12, 2004); Gary Schroen interview (Mar. 3, 2004); Mike interview (Jan. 6, 2004).

160. Mike briefing (Mar. 11, 2004); John Maher III interview (Apr. 22, 2004).

161. NSC memo, Clarke, secure teleconference between UAE Chief of Staff Muhammad bin Zayid and Clarke, Mar. 7, 1999.

162. Mike interview (Jan. 6, 2004). Maher told us he thinks it "almost impossible" that the CIA cleared Clarke's call. John Maher III interview (Apr. 22, 2004).

163. Days before overhead imagery confirmed the location of the hunting camp, Clarke had returned from a visit to the UAE, where he had been working on counterterrorism cooperation and following up on a May 1998 UAE agreement to buy F-16 aircraft from the United States. His visit included one-on-one meetings with Army Chief of Staff bin Zayid, as well as talks with Sheikh Muhammad bin Rashid, the ruler of Dubai. Both agreed to try to work with the United States in their efforts against Bin Ladin. NSC memo, Clarke to Berger, Trip Report, Feb. 8, 1999; Theodore Kattouf interview (Apr. 21, 2004). On February 10, as the United States considered striking the camp, Clarke reported that during his visit bin Zayid had vehemently denied rumors that high-level UAE officials were in Afghanistan. NSC email, Clarke to Kerrick, UBL update, Feb. 10, 1999. Subsequent reporting, however, suggested that high-level UAE officials had indeed been at the desert camp. CIA memo, "Recent High Level UAE Visits to Afghanistan," Feb. 19, 1999. General Shelton also told us that his UAE counterpart said he had been hunting at a desert camp in Afghanistan at about this time. Hugh Shelton interview (Feb. 5, 2004).

164. Mike briefing (Mar. 3, 2004). Talking points for the DCI to use at a late March Small Group meeting note that concurrently with the UAE being "tipped off" to the CIA's knowledge of the camp, one of the tribal network's major subsources (within Bin Ladin's Taliban security detail) was dispatched to the north, further handicapping reporting efforts. CIA talking points, "Locating Bin Ladin," Mar. 29, 1999.

165. Theodore Kattouf interview (Apr. 21, 2004). Kattouf was the U.S. ambassador to the UAE from 1999 to 2001. He indicated that high-level UAE officials would agree to restrict Afghan flights but told him that the government had a difficult time enforcing this. For communications with the UAE, see White House letter, President Clinton to bin Zayid, July 23, 1999; DOS memo, Sheehan to Albright, "Signs of Progress on our UBL strategy," Sept. 12, 1999.

166. DOS memo, Indyk and Sheehan to Albright, "UAE Gives Ultimatum to Taliban on Bin Laden," July 16, 1999, and attached transcript of conversation between Hamdan bin Zayid and Mullah Mutawakkil, "Informal Translation of UAE Note," July 14, 1999; DOS cable, Abu Dhabi 04644, "Taliban Refuse to Expel Bin Ladin Despite UAEG Ultimatum: Need to Stiffen UAE Resolve to Take the Necessary Next Steps," July 19, 1999.

167. DOS memo, Indyk and Sheehan to Albright, "UAE Gives Ultimatum to Taliban on Bin Laden," July 16, 1999.

168. Jeff interview (Dec. 17, 2003). Schroen, however, told us that the tribals' reporting was 50–60 percent accurate. Gary Schroen interview (Mar. 3, 2004).

169. For discussion of the Taliban generally, see Ahmed Rashid, *Taliban: Militant Islam, Oil and Fundamentalism in Central Asia* (Yale Univ. Press, 2000).

170. Ibid.; Benjamin and Simon, *Age of Sacred Terror*, pp. 338–399; George Tenet interview (Jan. 22, 2004).

171. George Tenet interview (Jan. 22, 2004).

172. Richard interview (Dec. 12, 2003); Gary Schroen interview (Mar. 3, 2004).

173. John Maher III interview (Apr. 22, 2004). For an account of the reporting from this period written by Mike, see CIA memo, Jeff to Tenet, "Tracking Usama Bin Ladin, 14–20 May 1999," May 21, 1999. Mike's account was also used to prepare the DCI for a May 25, 1999, Principals Committee meeting. CIA briefing materials, "Background Information: Evaluating the Quality of Intelligence on Bin Ladin (UBL) in Qandahar, 13–20 May, 1999," undated (probably May 25, 1999).

174. CIA email, Mike to Schroen, "Re: Your Note," May 17, 1999.

175. John Maher III interview (Apr. 22, 2004).

176. George Tenet interview (Jan. 22, 2004); John Gordon interview (May 13, 2004).

177. Samuel Berger interview (Jan. 14, 2004).

178. The May 1999 intelligence on Bin Ladin's location in Kandahar came as criticism of the CIA over the recent bombing of the Chinese embassy in Belgrade was at its peak. The DCI later testified that this bombing was the result of a CIA mistake. Testimony of George Tenet before the House Permanent Select Committee on Intelligence, July 22, 1999. On Bin Ladin's whereabouts during the December 1998 episode, see John Maher III interview (Apr. 22, 2004).

179. Cruise missiles were readied for another possible strike in early July 1999. But none of the officials we have interviewed recalled that an opportunity arose at that time justifying the consideration of a strike. See, e.g., John Maher III interview (Apr. 22, 2004).

180. Hugh Shelton interview (Feb. 5, 2004); DOD briefing materials, UBL JCS Focused Campaign, undated.

181. NSC memo, Benjamin to Berger and Steinberg, Apr. 29, 1999; NSC email, Clarke to Berger, May 26, 1999.

182. NSC memo, Clarke to Berger, June 24, 1999. For Clarke's request to Berger to convene the Small Group, see NSC memo, Clarke to Berger, Analysis/Options re UBL, Jun. 13, 1999. See also NSC email, Storey to Berger and Clarke, June 24, 1999.

183. Berger notes on NSC memo, Clarke to Berger, June 24, 1999.

184. NSC memo, Clarke to Berger, June 24, 1999.

185. NSC memo, Clarke to Berger, UBL review for Dec. 3, 1999, Small Group meeting, Dec. 2, 1999.

186. NSC memo, CSG agenda, Sept. 24, 1999.

187. According to CTC talking points for the CSG in June 1999, more than 40 members of al Qaeda had been imprisoned over the past year. CIA talking points, C/CTC TPs/Backgrounder for CSG, June 7, 1999. Figures cited in the DCI's letter to President Clinton in October, however, are slightly different: CTC had helped render 32 terrorists to justice since July 1998, more than half of whom were al Qaeda. CIA letter, Tenet to President Clinton, "CIA's Counterterrorism Efforts," Oct. 16, 1999.

188. See CIA cable, "Usama Bin Ladin: The Way Ahead," Aug. 25, 1999, soliciting comments from various stations on "possible new approaches to capturing UBL and disrupting operations." The evolution of some of this thinking can be seen throughout the summer of 1999. See, e.g., CIA briefing materials, CTC UBL Update: "Must Do Some Fundamental Rethinking," July 20, 1999 (Afghan assets are not capable of mounting a UBL capture operation or ambush); CIA briefing materials, CTC UBL Update: "Problems with Capturing UBL," Aug. 3, 1999 (tribals are good reporters but are unlikely to capture Bin Ladin because of the risks involved, so there is a need to identify a new group to undertake a capture operation).

189. July 1999 Memorandum of Notification.

190. See James Baker interview (Feb. 4, 2004); Janet Reno interview (Dec. 16, 2003); Randy Moss interview (Jan. 22, 2004); George Tenet interview (Jan. 22, 2004). On the Pakistani and Uzbek capture teams, see CIA memo,

"Outline of Program to Build Pakistan Team to Seek the Capture and Rendition of Usama Bin Ladin and his Lieu-tenants," July 27, 1999; CIA memo, CIA Outline of Program to Build Uzbek and other teams to Seek the Cap-ture and Rendition of Usama Bin Ladin and his Lieutenants, July 27, 1999; CIA briefing materials, talking points for the DCI for the Aug. 3 Small Group meeting, Aug. 3, 1999 (Other Pakistani Involvement in Efforts to Capture UBL; Uzbek and other programs). On the Uzbeks' readiness, see CIA briefing materials, "Executive Summary for UBL Conference," Sept. 16, 1999.

191. CIA briefing materials, "Executive Summary for UBL Conference," Sept. 16, 1999. For its preface, the Plan quoted a memo Tenet had sent to the CIA's senior management in December 1998: "We are at war with Usama bin Ladin."

192. Ibid. See also the following briefings of the Plan: CIA briefing materials, CTC/NSC Briefing on the Plan, Sept. 29, 1999; CIA briefing materials, Executive Summary: UBL Conference, prepared for Berger, Nov. 30, 1999; CIA briefing materials, CTC briefing for the NSC Small Group, Dec. 2/3, 1999.

193. This figure increased through the fall of 1999, from less than 5 percent on September 16 to less than 10 percent by November 30, and finally to less than 15 percent by early December. CIA briefing materials, "Execu-tive Summary for UBL Conference," Sept. 16, 1999; CIA briefing materials, Executive Summary: UBL Confer-ence, prepared for Berger, Nov. 30, 1999; CIA briefing materials, CTC briefing for the NSC Small Group, Dec. 2/3, 1999. On Massoud, see also CIA briefing materials, "DDCI UBL Update," Oct. 29, 1999; CIA briefing mate-rials, "DCI UBL Update," Nov. 12, 1999.

194. CIA briefing materials, "Executive Summary for UBL Conference," Sept. 16, 1999. For the JSOC esti-mate, see CIA briefing materials, Executive Summary: UBL Conference, prepared for Berger, Nov. 30, 1999.

5 Al Qaeda Aims at the American Homeland

1. Though KSM and Bin Ladin knew each other from the anti-Soviet campaign of the 1980s, KSM apparently did not begin working with al Qaeda until after the 1998 East Africa embassy bombings. Intelligence reports, inter-rogations of KSM, Nov. 21, 2003; Jan. 9, 2004; Feb. 19, 2004.

2. Those detainees are Khalid Sheikh Mohammed, Abu Zubaydah, Riduan Isamuddin (also known as Ham-bali), Abd al Rahim al Nashiri, Tawfiq bin Attash (also known as Khallad), Ramzi Binalshibh, Mohamed al Kah-tani, Ahmad Khalil Ibrahim Samir al Ani, Ali Abd al Rahman al Faqasi al Ghamdi (also known as Abu Bakr al Azdi), and Hassan Ghul.

3. On KSM's relationship to Yousef and his ethnicity, see CIA analytic report, Khalid Sheik Muhammad's Nephews, CTC 2003-300013, Jan. 31, 2003. On KSM's biography, see Intelligence report, interrogation of KSM, July 12, 2003; FBI electronic communication, requests for information on KSM colleges/universities, June 10, 2002.

4. In an uncorroborated post-capture claim that may be mere bravado, KSM has stated that he considered assas-sinating Rabbi Meir Kahane when Kahane lectured in Greensboro at some point between 1984 and 1986. Intel-ligence report, interrogation of KSM, July 12, 2003. On KSM's connection to Sayyaf, see Intelligence reports, interrogations of KSM, July 3, 2003; July 12, 2003; FBI electronic communication, "Summary of Information . . . with regard to . . . KSM," July 8, 1999. On KSM's battle experience and his electronics work, see Intelligence reports, interrogations of KSM, July 3, 2003; July 12, 2003. On KSM's anti-Soviet activities, see Intelligence report, inter-rogation of KSM, Feb. 17, 2004 (in which KSM says he apparently met Bin Ladin for the first time when the Sayyaf group and Bin Ladin's Arab mujahideen group were next to each other along the front line).

5. Intelligence report, interrogation of KSM, July 12, 2003 (in which KSM also notes that his group contin-ued fighting in the Jalalabad area, and his brother Abid was killed there). KSM claims that Ramzi Yousef visited the NGO's establishment in Jalalabad while Yousef was undergoing training. KSM adds that between 1993 and 1996, he traveled to China, the Philippines, Pakistan, Bosnia (a second time), Brazil, Sudan, and Malaysia. Most, if not all, of this travel appears to have been related to his abiding interest in carrying out terrorist operations. Although KSM claims that Sheikh Abdallah was not a member, financier, or supporter of al Qaeda, he admits that Abdallah under-wrote a 1995 trip KSM took to join the Bosnia jihad. Intelligence report, interrogation of KSM, July 23, 2003.

6. On KSM's learning of Yousef's plans, see Intelligence report, interrogation of KSM, Jan. 9, 2004 (in which KSM also contends that Yousef never divulged to him the intended target of the attack). On KSM/Yousef phone conversations, see Intelligence report, interrogation of KSM, Feb. 17, 2004 (in which KSM also says that most of his phone conversations with Yousef were social in nature, but that Yousef did discuss mixing explosives ingredients once or twice and that on one occasion, Yousef asked him to send the passport Yousef had in his true name, Abdul Basit). On KSM's money transfer, see FBI report, Tradebom investigation, Mar. 20, 1993.

7. Evidence gathered at the time of Yousef's February 1995 arrest included dolls wearing clothes containing nitrocellulose. FBI evidence, Manila air investigation. On KSM's rationale for attacking the United States, see Intel-ligence report, interrogation of KSM, Sept. 5, 2003 (in this regard, KSM's statements echo those of Yousef, who delivered an extensive polemic against U.S. foreign policy at his January 1998 sentencing). On the Manila air plot, see Intelligence reports, interrogations of KSM, Apr. 17, 2003; July 12, 2003 (in which KSM also says *bojinka* is not Serbo-Croatian for "big bang," as has been widely reported, but rather a nonsense word he adopted after hearing

it on the front lines in Afghanistan). According to KSM, the plot was to receive financing from a variety of sources, including associates of co-conspirator Wali Khan and KSM's own funds. Intelligence reports, interrogations of KSM, Nov. 26, 2003; Jan. 9, 2004; Feb. 19, 2004. On activities during the summer of 1994, see Intelligence reports, interrogations of KSM, May 3, 2003; July 12, 2003; Nov. 10, 2003; Feb. 21, 2004; Feb. 24, 2004.

8. On recruiting Wali Khan in Karachi, see FBI report of investigation, interview of Abdul Hakim Murad, Apr. 13, 1995; Intelligence report, interrogation of KSM, July 12, 2003 (in which KSM recounts how he knew Wali Khan from Afghanistan). On the testing of the timer, see Brief for the United States of America, *United States v. Ramzi Ahmed Yousef,* No. 98-1041(L) (2d Cir. filed Aug. 25, 2000), pp. 85–86, 88–91. The latter explosion caused the death of a passenger and extensive damage to the aircraft, which was forced to make an emergency landing in Okinawa. In 1996, Yousef was convicted on charges arising out of the Bojinka plot, including the bombing of the Philippine Airlines flight. See ibid., p. 8. On KSM's travels, see generally Intelligence report, interrogation of KSM, July 12, 2003. Yousef managed to escape to Pakistan, but his accomplice, Murad—whom KSM claims to have sent to Yousef with $3,000 to help fund the operation—was arrested and disclosed details of the plot while under interrogation. Contrary to Murad's confession, in which he described his intended role as one of the five operatives who would plant bombs on board the targeted aircraft, KSM has said that Murad's role was limited to carrying the $3,000 from Dubai to Manila. Intelligence reports, interrogations of KSM, Feb. 19, 2004; (two reports); Feb. 24, 2004; Apr. 2, 2004. This aspect of KSM's account is not credible, as it conflicts not just with Murad's confession but also with physical evidence tying Murad to the very core of the plot, and with KSM's own statements elsewhere that Murad was involved in planning and executing the operation. Intelligence reports, interrogations of KSM, Aug. 18, 2003; Jan. 9, 2004; Feb. 24, 2004 (in which KSM also claims that while he was in Qatar in February 1995, he and Yousef consulted by telephone regarding the cargo carrier plan, and Yousef proceeded with the operation despite KSM's advice that he hide instead). We have uncovered no evidence that KSM was present at the guesthouse in Islamabad where Yousef's arrest took place, as has been suggested in the press.

9. Intelligence report, interrogation of KSM, July 12, 2003. KSM's presence in Bosnia coincided with a police station bombing in Zagreb where the timing device of the bomb (a modified Casio watch) resembled those manufactured by KSM and Yousef in the Philippines for the Manila air operation. FBI report, Manila air investigation, May 23, 1999. On the Sudanese trip and Afghanistan, see Intelligence report, interrogation of SM, July 12, 2003 (in which KSM also claims to have encountered Sayf al Adl while in Yemen; apparently KSM has not divulged the substance of this meeting).

10. Intelligence report, interrogation of KSM, Jan. 9, 2004. In another interrogation report, however, KSM downplays the significance of his relationship to Yousef in enabling him to meet with Bin Ladin. Specifically, KSM notes that Yousef was not a member of al Qaeda and that Yousef never met Bin Ladin. Intelligence report, interrogation of KSM, Feb. 19, 2004.

11. Intelligence reports, interrogations of KSM, July 12, 2003; Jan. 9, 2004; Feb. 19, 2004. With respect to KSM's additional proposal to bomb cargo planes by shipping jackets containing nitrocellulose, KSM states that Bin Ladin expressed interest in changing the operation so that it would involve a suicide operative. Intelligence report, interrogation of KSM, Nov. 10, 2003.

12. Intelligence report, interrogation of KSM, Feb. 19, 2004.

13. Probably inflating his own role, KSM says he and a small group of colleagues, including Yousef and Wali Khan, were among the earliest advocates of attacking the United States. KSM asserts that Bin Ladin and some of the other jihadist leaders concentrated on overthrowing Arab regimes and argued for limiting confrontation with the United States to places like Somalia. On KSM's description of Bin Ladin's agenda, see Intelligence report, interrogation of KSM, Nov. 13, 2003. As discussed in chapter 2, we do not agree with this assessment. On Bin Ladin's reactions to KSM's proposal, see Intelligence reports, interrogations of KSM, July 12, 2003; Jan. 9, 2004; Feb. 19, 2004. On KSM's intent to target the United States and Bin Ladin's interest in Somalia, see Intelligence report, interrogation of KSM, Nov. 13, 2003.

14. On KSM's independence, see Intelligence report, interrogation of KSM, Jan. 9, 2004. Even after he began working with Bin Ladin and al Qaeda, KSM concealed from them his ongoing relationship with Sayyaf. Intelligence report, interrogation of KSM, July 30, 2003. Although KSM says he would have accepted the support of another organization to stage a 9/11-type operation, there is no evidence he ever peddled this idea to any other group. Intelligence report, interrogation of KSM, Feb. 19, 2004. On his travels after meeting Bin Ladin, see Intelligence report, interrogation of KSM, July 12, 2003. Hambali also was one of the founders of Konsojaya, a Malaysian company run by a close associate of Wali Khan. FBI report, Manila air investigation, May 23, 1999. Hambali claims he was asked to serve on the company's board of directors as a formality and insists that he did not recognize the "Arabs" who were to run the company or play any role in its operations. Intelligence report, interrogation of Hambali, Nov. 19, 2003.

15. Intelligence reports, interrogations of KSM, July 12, 2003; Feb. 19, 2004 (two reports). KSM maintains that he provided similar services for other mujahideen groups at this time, including the Libyan Islamic Fighting Group and a group headed by Abu Zubaydah. Intelligence report, interrogation of KSM, Feb. 19, 2004.

16. On KSM's understanding of Bin Ladin's commitment, see Intelligence report, interrogation of KSM, Feb.

19, 2004. On KSM's assistance to al Qaeda, see Intelligence reports, interrogations of KSM, July 12, 2003 (two reports). On Bin Ladin's decision to approve 9/11 operation, see Intelligence report, interrogation of KSM, Jan. 9, 2004. KSM has observed that the East Africa bombings and the subsequent bombing of the USS *Cole* yielded a recruiting bonanza for al Qaeda, as increasing numbers of Arab youth became enamored of the idea of waging jihad against the United States. Intelligence report, interrogation of KSM, Sept. 5, 2003.

17. On KSM's decision to move to Kandahar, see Intelligence report, interrogation of KSM, Jan. 9, 2004. On the media committee, see Intelligence report, interrogation of KSM, July 12, 2003 (in which KSM also says that as head of the media committee, he would take charge of producing the propaganda video al Qaeda issued following the bombing of the USS *Cole*). On the oath, see Intelligence report, interrogation of KSM, Nov. 13, 2003 (in which KSM also claims his reluctance stemmed from a concern that he would lose the ability to persevere with the 9/11 operation should Bin Ladin subsequently decide to cancel it).

18. On a possible Southeast Asian operation, see Intelligence report, interrogation of Hambali, Sept. 4, 2003. On a possible U.S. operation, see Intelligence reports, interrogations of KSM, June 27, 2003; July 14, 2003. On a possible Israeli operation, see Intelligence report, interrogation of KSM, June 30, 2003. On other possible targets discussed with Atef, see Intelligence report, interrogation of Hambali, Sept. 4, 2003 (Thailand); Intelligence report, interrogation of KSM, Apr. 4, 2004 (Singapore, Indonesia, Maldives).

19. For an example of KSM's popularity, see Intelligence report, interrogation of al Qaeda facilitator, Oct. 11, 2002. See also Intelligence report, interrogation of Abu Zubaydah, Nov. 7, 2002; Intelligence report, interrogation of Nashiri, Feb. 10, 2003.

20. Intelligence reports, interrogations of Hambali, Jan. 14, 2003; Mar. 5, 2004.

21. Rohan Gunaratna, *Inside Al Qaeda: Global Network of Terror* (Columbia Univ. Press, 2002), pp. 187, 199.

22. On the trip to Karachi, see Intelligence report, interrogation of Hambali, Sept. 12, 2003. On Hambali's relationship with Atef and receipt of al Qaeda funds, see Intelligence report, interrogation of Hambali, Mar. 5, 2004. Al Qaeda began providing funds to JI for terrorist operations as early as 1999. Intelligence report, interrogation of detainee, Mar. 3, 2004.

23. On Hambali's role as coordinator, see Intelligence report, interrogation of detainee, Mar. 4, 2004. On Sufaat, see Intelligence report, interrogation of KSM, Apr. 12, 2003; Intelligence report, interrogation of detainee, Apr. 30, 2003. In 1987, Sufaat received a bachelor's degree in biological sciences, with a minor in chemistry, from California State University, Sacramento. Sufaat did not start on the al Qaeda biological weapons program until after JI's December 2000 church bombings in Indonesia, in which he was involved. Intelligence report, interrogation of Hambali, Sept. 8, 2003. On Sufaat's schooling, see Intelligence report, interrogation of detainee, Dec. 14, 2001.

24. Intelligence report, interrogation of KSM, June 9, 2003. KSM also maintains that he persuaded Hambali to focus on "soft" targets in Singapore, such as oil tankers, the U.S. and Israeli embassies, and Western airlines. Intelligence report, interrogation of KSM, June 24, 2003.

25. As discussed in greater detail in section 5.2, Khallad was sent by Bin Ladin to Kuala Lumpur to case U.S. airline flights in the Far East for possible future attacks there, whereas Hazmi and Mihdhar were on the first leg of their travel from Karachi to Los Angeles, where they would arrive on January 15, 2000. Intelligence report, interrogation of KSM, July 31, 2003. On Hambali's assistance at KSM's request, see Intelligence report, interrogation of KSM, July 31, 2003; Intelligence report, interrogation of Khallad, Aug. 8, 2003. On assistance to Moussaoui, see Intelligence report, interrogation of KSM, Mar. 24, 2003; Intelligence report, interrogation of detainee, Apr. 9, 2002. According to statements attributed to Hambali and Sufaat, in each of these instances the al Qaeda guests were lodged at Sufaat's condominium, an apartment on the outskirts of Kuala Lumpur. Intelligence report, interrogation of detainee, Jan. 22, 2002; Intelligence reports, interrogations of Hambali, Sept. 8, 2003; Sept. 12, 2003.

26. On Hambali's relationship with Bin Ladin, see Intelligence reports, interrogations of Hambali, Aug. 29, 2003; Sept. 5, 2003 (in which Hambali also explains his relationship with al Qaeda as follows: he received his marching orders from JI, but al Qaeda would lead any joint operation involving members of both organizations). On Hambali's objections, see Intelligence report, interrogation of KSM, July 8, 2003. On KSM's coordination with Hambali, see Intelligence report, interrogation of KSM, Apr. 17, 2003. On KSM's recognition of Hambali's domain, see Intelligence report, interrogation of KSM, Aug. 18, 2003. According to KSM, his close relationship with Hambali prompted criticism from Bashir, the JI leader, who thought Hambali should focus more directly on Indonesia and Malaysia instead of involving himself in al Qaeda's broader terrorist program. Indeed, KSM describes Hambali as an al Qaeda member working in Malaysia. Intelligence report, interrogation of KSM, Aug. 18, 2003. Nashiri observes that al Qaeda's standard security practice dictated that no senior member could manage terrorist activities in a location where another senior member was operating. Intelligence report, interrogation of Nashiri, Jan. 14, 2003. Yet al Qaeda's deference to Hambali's turf apparently had limits. Khallad says he and Hambali never discussed the intended Southeast Asia portion of the original 9/11 plan. Intelligence report, interrogation of Khallad, Apr. 27, 2004.

27. On Nashiri's recruitment, see FBI report of investigation, interview of Nasser Ahmad Naser al Bahri, a.k.a. Abu Jandal, Sept. 17–Oct. 2, 2001. On Nashiri's refusal to swear allegiance, see Intelligence report, interrogation of

KSM, Nov. 21, 2003. On Nashiri's idea for his first terrorist operation and his travels, see Intelligence reports, interrogations of Nashiri, Nov. 21, 2002; Dec. 26, 2002.

28. Intelligence report, interrogation of Nashiri, Dec. 26, 2002. Although Nashiri's account of this episode dates his return to Afghanistan in 1996, the 1997 date is likely more accurate. On Nashiri's involvement in the missile-smuggling and embassy-bombing plots, see Intelligence report, seizure of antitank missiles in Saudi Arabia, June 14, 1998; FBI report of investigation, interview of Mohammad Rashed Daoud al Owahli, Sept. 9, 1998, p. 6.

29. For Nashiri's version, which may not be true, see Intelligence report, interrogation of Nashiri, Dec. 26, 2002. On communication between Nashiri and Bin Ladin about attacking U.S. vessels, see Intelligence report, interrogation of Nashiri, Nov. 21, 2002. The reporting of Nashiri's statements on this subject is somewhat inconsistent, especially as to the exact timing of the original proposal. Some corroboration does exist, however, for Nashiri's claim that the original proposal was his. A detainee says that 9/11 hijacker Khalid al Mihdhar told him about the maritime operation sometime in late 1999 and credited Nashiri as its originator. Intelligence report, interrogation of detainee, Dec. 2, 2001.

30. Intelligence report, interrogation of Nashiri, Jan. 27, 2003. Nashiri claims not to have had any telephone or email contact with Bin Ladin while planning the *Cole* operation; rather, whenever Bin Ladin wanted to meet, he would have an al Qaeda member travel to Pakistan to summon Nashiri by telephone. Ibid.

31. As an example of Nashiri's status, see FBI report of investigation, interview of Abu Jandal, Sept. 17–Oct. 2, 2001 (in which Nashiri is described as widely known to be one of al Qaeda's most committed terrorists and, according to one of his mujahideen colleagues, so extreme in his ferocity in waging jihad that he "would commit a terrorist act 'in Mecca inside the Ka'aba itself' [the holiest site in Islam] if he believed there was a need to do so"). On Nashiri's role on the Arabian Peninsula, see Intelligence report, interrogation of Khallad, Jan. 14, 2004. Nashiri also enjoyed a reputation as a productive recruiter for al Qaeda. See Intelligence report, interrogation of Abu Zubaydah, Aug. 29, 2002. On Nashiri's discretion, see, e.g., Intelligence report, interrogation of Nashiri, Nov. 20, 2002. On Nashiri seeking Bin Ladin's approval, see Intelligence report, interrogation of KSM, Jan. 14, 2004. On the *Limburg* operation, see Intelligence report, interrogation of Nashiri, May 21, 2003. On Nashiri's security concerns, see Intelligence report, interrogation of Nashiri, Feb. 20, 2003.

32. See Intelligence reports, interrogations of KSM, July 1, 2003; Sept. 5, 2003.

33. For KSM's learning from the first World Trade Center bombing and his interest in a more novel form of attack, see Intelligence report, interrogation of KSM, July 1, 2003. For KSM's interest in aircraft as weapons and speculation about striking the World Trade Center and CIA, see Intelligence report, interrogation of KSM, Feb. 19, 2004. KSM has stated that he and Yousef at this time never advanced the notion of using aircraft as weapons past the idea stage. Intelligence report, interrogation of KSM, Apr. 2, 2004.

After 9/11, some Philippine government officials claimed that while in Philippine custody in February 1995, KSM's Manila air plot co-conspirator Abdul Hakim Murad had confessed having discussed with Yousef the idea of attacking targets, including the World Trade Center, with hijacked commercial airliners flown by U.S.-trained Middle Eastern pilots. See Peter Lance, *1000 Years for Revenge: International Terrorism and the FBI—the Untold Story* (HarperCollins, 2003), pp. 278–280. In Murad's initial taped confession, he referred to an idea of crashing a plane into CIA headquarters. Lance gave us his copy of an apparent 1995 Philippine National Police document on an interrogation of Murad. That document reports Murad describing his idea of crashing a plane into CIA headquarters, but in this report Murad claims he was thinking of hijacking a commercial aircraft to do it, saying the idea had come up in a casual conversation with Yousef with no specific plan for its execution. We have seen no pre-9/11 evidence that Murad referred in interrogations to the training of other pilots, or referred in this casual conversation to targets other than the CIA. According to Lance, the Philippine police officer, who after 9/11 offered the much more elaborate account of Murad's statements reported in Lance's book, claims to have passed this added information to U.S. officials. But Lance states the Philippine officer declined to identify these officials. Peter Lance interview (Mar. 15, 2004). If such information was provided to a U.S. official, we have seen no indication that it was written down or disseminated within the U.S. government. Incidentally, KSM says he never discussed his idea for the planes operation with Murad, a person KSM regarded as a minor figure. Intelligence report, interrogation of KSM, Apr. 2, 2004.

34. Intelligence report, 1996 Atef study on airplane hijacking operations, Sept. 26, 2001.

35. Intelligence reports, interrogations of KSM, July 12, 2003; Nov. 6, 2003. Abu Zubaydah, who worked closely with the al Qaeda leadership, has stated that KSM originally presented Bin Ladin with a scaled-down version of the 9/11 plan, and that Bin Ladin urged KSM to expand the operation with the comment, "Why do you use an axe when you can use a bulldozer?" Intelligence report, interrogation of Abu Zubaydah, May 16, 2003. The only possible corroboration we have found for Abu Zubaydah's statement is Khallad's suggestion that Bin Ladin may have expanded KSM's original idea for an attack using planes. Intelligence report, interrogation of Khallad, Apr. 22, 2004. Neither Abu Zubaydah nor Khallad claims to have been present when KSM says he first pitched his proposal to Bin Ladin in 1996.

36. For the scheme's lukewarm reception, see Intelligence report, interrogation of KSM, Nov. 6, 2003. For Bin Ladin's response, see Intelligence reports, interrogations of KSM, Aug. 18, 2003; Feb. 19, 2004.

37. Intelligence report, interrogation of KSM, Feb. 19, 2004.

38. For KSM's joining al Qaeda, see Intelligence report, interrogation of KSM, Nov. 13, 2003. KSM has provided inconsistent information about whether Bin Ladin first approved his proposal for what became the 9/11 attacks in late 1998 or in early 1999. Compare Intelligence reports, interrogations of KSM, Aug. 18, 2003; Jan. 9, 2004; Feb. 19, 2004; Apr. 3, 2004. For KSM's antipathy to the United States, see Intelligence report, interrogation of KSM, Feb. 19, 2004. For Atef's role, see Intelligence report, interrogation of KSM, Jan. 9, 2004. For Atef's death, see DOS report, "Comprehensive List of Terrorists and Groups Identified Under Executive Order 13224," Dec. 31, 2001.

39. Intelligence report, interrogation of KSM, Aug. 18, 2003.

40. Intelligence reports, interrogations of KSM, Aug. 18, 2003; Feb. 20, 2004; Apr. 30, 2004. An earlier KSM interrogation report, however, states that Bin Ladin preferred the Capitol over the White House as a target. Intelligence report, interrogation of KSM, Apr. 17, 2003. KSM has admitted that his statement in a post-9/11 interview with Al Jazeera reporter Yosri Fouda—that an al Qaeda "reconnaissance committee" had identified 30 potential targets in the United States during the late 1990s—was a lie designed to inflate the perceived scale of the 9/11 operation. Intelligence report, interrogation of KSM, Feb. 23, 2004. For the specific targets, see Intelligence report, selection of 9/11 targets, Aug. 13, 2003 (citing KSM interrogation).

41. For the four individuals, see Intelligence report, interrogation of KSM, Aug. 18, 2003. Abu Bara al Yemeni is also known by the names Abu al Bara al Taizi, Suhail Shurabi, and Barakat. Ibid. KSM has also stated that he did not learn of the selection of Hazmi and Mihdhar for the planes operation until November 1999. Intelligence report, interrogation of KSM, Apr. 2, 2004. For Mihdhar's and Hazmi's eagerness, see Intelligence reports, interrogations of KSM, Jan. 9, 2004; Feb. 20, 2004 . For Bin Ladin's instruction, see Intelligence report, interrogation of KSM, Feb. 20, 2004. Hazmi obtained a B-1/B-2 multiple-entry visa issued at Jiddah, Saudi Arabia, on April 3, 1999; Mihdhar obtained the same type of visa at the same location on April 7, 1999. DOS records, NIV applicant details for Hazmi and Mihdhar, Nov. 8, 2001. Hazmi and Mihdhar both obtained new passports shortly before they applied for visas. FBI report, "Summary of Penttbom Investigation," Jan. 31, 2003, p. 9.

42. For Hazmi and Mihdhar's city of birth, see CIA analytic report, "11 September: The Plot and the Plotters," CTC 2003-40044HC, June 1, 2003, pp. 49–50. For their travel to Bosnia, see Intelligence report, interrogation of Saudi al Qaeda member, Oct. 3, 2001. For their visits to Afghanistan, see Intelligence reports, interrogations of detainee, Feb. 5, 2002; Feb. 11, 2002; Intelligence reports, interrogations of Saudi al Qaeda member, Oct. 2, 2001; Oct. 18, 2001.

43. Intelligence reports, interrogations of Khallad, June 25, 2003; Sept. 5, 2003.

44. For Khallad's visa application under a false name and its rejection, see DOS record, visa application of Salah Saeed Mohammed bin Yousaf (alias for Khallad), Apr. 3, 1999; Intelligence report, interrogation of Khallad, Aug. 20, 2003. Khallad's visa denial was based not on terrorism concerns but apparently on his failure to submit sufficient documentation in support of his application. See DOS record, NIV applicant detail, Mar. 31, 2004. For Khallad's 1999 mission to Yemen, see Intelligence report, interrogation of Khallad, Aug. 20, 2003. For the U.S. point of contact, see Intelligence report, interrogation of Khallad, Aug. 22, 2003. Khallad claims he cannot remember his U.S. contact's full name but says it sounded like "Barzan." According to the CIA, "Barzan" is possibly identifiable with Sarbarz Mohammed, the person who resided at the address in Bothell, Washington, that Khallad listed on his visa application as his final destination. Ibid. For his contacts with "Barzan" and his arrest, see ibid.; Intelligence report, interrogation of Khallad, Aug. 20, 2003. Nashiri has confirmed that Khallad had been assigned to help procure explosives for the ship-bombing plot, and that his arrest caused work on the operation to stop temporarily. Intelligence report, interrogation of Nashiri, Feb. 21, 2004.

45. For the interventions, see Intelligence report, interrogation of Khallad, Aug. 20, 2003. Khallad has provided inconsistent information as to his release date. Ibid. (June 1999); Intelligence report, interrogation of Khallad, Jan. 6, 2004 (August 1999). Khallad's brother reportedly has confirmed that Khallad was released from custody only after negotiations with the Yemeni director for political security in which a deal was struck prohibiting Khallad and his associates from conducting operations in Yemen. Intelligence report, interrogation of detainee, Oct. 1, 2002. For his giving up on a visa and his return to Afghanistan, see Intelligence reports, interrogations of Khallad, July 31, 2003; Aug. 22, 2003.

46. For KSM's realization of visa complications, see Intelligence report, interrogation of KSM, Aug. 18, 2003. According to both KSM and Khallad, Abu Bara never applied for a U.S. visa. Intelligence report, interrogation of KSM, Feb. 20, 2004; Intelligence report, interrogation of Khallad, Feb. 17, 2004. KSM has noted that Ramzi Binalshibh, another Yemeni slated early on to participate in the 9/11 attacks, likewise would prove unable to acquire a U.S. visa the following year. Intelligence report, interrogation of KSM, Jan. 7, 2004. For KSM's desire to keep Khallad and Abu Bara involved, see Intelligence report, interrogation of KSM, Aug. 18, 2003. For Saudis being chosen for the planes operation, see Intelligence reports, interrogations of KSM, Jan. 7, 2004; Jan. 23, 2004. For KSM's splitting the operation into two parts, see Intelligence report, interrogation of KSM, Aug. 18, 2003; Intelligence report, interrogation of Khallad, Apr. 27, 2004.

47. For the second part of the operation, see Intelligence report, interrogation of KSM, Aug. 18. 2003. For the

alternate scenario, see Intelligence report, interrogation of KSM, Apr. 30, 2004; Intelligence report, interrogation of Khallad, Apr. 21, 2004. Khallad has provided contradictory statements about the number of planes to be destroyed in East Asia. Intelligence reports, interrogations of Khallad, Aug. 13, 2003; Apr. 5, 2004. According to Khallad, Thailand, South Korea, Hong Kong, and Malaysia were likely origins of the flights because Yemenis did not need visas to enter them. Intelligence report, interrogation of Khallad, Aug. 13, 2003. For the importance of simultaneity, see Intelligence report, interrogation of KSM, Aug. 18, 2003.

48. For the four operatives' training, see Intelligence report, interrogation of KSM, Aug. 18, 2003. For the elite nature of the course and Nibras's participation, see Intelligence reports, interrogations of Khallad, Sept. 8, 2003; Sept. 11, 2003; Intelligence report, interrogation of KSM, July 15, 2003. For KSM's view, see ibid.; Intelligence report, interrogation of KSM, Aug. 18, 2003. For KSM's visit, see Intelligence report, interrogation of KSM, Feb. 20, 2004.

49. For a description of the camp and the commando course, see Intelligence report, interrogation of KSM, July 15, 2003. For Bin Ladin's interest and the decision on the number of trainees, see Intelligence report, interrogation of Khallad, Sept. 8, 2003.

50. For the nature of the commando course, see Intelligence report, interrogation of Khallad, Sept. 8, 2003. KSM claims that the course proved so rigorous that Mihdhar quit after a week and returned to his family in Yemen. Intelligence report, interrogation of KSM, Aug. 18, 2003. However, two of Mihdhar's al Qaeda colleagues who were present during the training have provided different accounts. Khallad apparently has stated both that Bin Ladin pulled Mihdhar and Nawaf al Hazmi out of the course early and that Mihdhar actually completed the course. See Intelligence reports, interrogations of Khallad, Sept. 1, 2003; May 21, 2004. See also FBI report of investigation, interview of Abu Jandal, Oct. 2, 2001 (indicating that Mihdhar completed the course).

51. For instruction on Western culture and travel, see Intelligence reports, interrogations of KSM, Mar. 24, 2003; June 15, 2004; Intelligence report, interrogation of Khallad, Aug. 21, 2003. For KSM's mid-1999 activity and Bin Ladin's payment, see Intelligence report, interrogation of KSM, Feb. 20, 2004. According to KSM, he received a total of $10,000 from Bin Ladin for 9/11-related expenses. Intelligence report, interrogation of KSM, Apr. 5, 2004.

52. For Khallad, Abu Bara, and Hazmi's travels, see Intelligence report, interrogation of KSM, May 30, 2003. Khallad has provided a second version, namely that all three traveled together to Karachi. Intelligence report, interrogation of Khallad, July 31, 2003. For Hazmi and Atta's simultaneous presence in Quetta, see Intelligence reports, interrogations of KSM, Feb. 20, 2004; Mar. 31, 2004. KSM maintains it was a coincidence. Ibid.

53. Intelligence report, interrogation of KSM, Mar. 31, 2004. In his initial post-capture statements, KSM claimed that Mihdhar did not have to attend the training because he had previously received similar training from KSM. Intelligence report, interrogation of KSM, Mar. 24, 2003. KSM subsequently expressed uncertainty about why Bin Ladin and Atef excused Mihdhar from the training. Intelligence report, interrogation of KSM, Feb. 20, 2004.

54. For the varying accounts of the course's length, see Intelligence reports, interrogations of KSM, Aug. 18, 2003; Feb. 20, 2004; Intelligence reports, interrogations of Khallad, Nov. 6, 2003; July 31, 2003. For KSM's description, see Intelligence reports, interrogations of KSM, Mar. 24, 2003; Aug. 18, 2003; Feb. 20, 2004. For Khallad's description, see Intelligence report, interrogation of Khallad, Apr. 5, 2004. KSM says that he permitted the trainees to view Hollywood films about hijackings only after he edited the films to cover the female characters. Intelligence report, interrogation of KSM, Nov. 10, 2003. For the use of game software and discussions of casing flights, see Intelligence report, interrogation of Khallad, Nov. 6, 2003. For KSM's instructions regarding casing, see Intelligence report, interrogation of Khallad, July 31, 2003. For visits to travel agencies, see Intelligence report, interrogation of Khallad, Aug. 13, 2003.

55. For the travels of Khallad, Abu Bara, and Hazmi via Karachi, see Intelligence report, interrogation of KSM, Aug. 18, 2003. For Mihdhar's travel from Yemen, see FBI report, "Hijackers Timeline," Nov. 14, 2003 (citing 265A-NY-280350, serial 24808).

56. For the operatives' knowledge, see Intelligence report, interrogation of KSM, Aug. 18, 2003. For Hazmi and Mihdhar being sent to Malaysia, see Intelligence report, interrogation of KSM, July 29, 2003. For passport doctoring, see Intelligence report, interrogation of KSM, Aug. 18, 2003. For casing, see Intelligence report, interrogation of KSM, July 29, 2003. For Khallad and Abu Bara's departure, as well as Hazmi's travel, see Intelligence report, interrogation of KSM, July 31, 2003. Khallad maintains that Abu Bara did not participate in the casing operation and simply traveled to Kuala Lumpur as Khallad's companion. Intelligence report, interrogation of Khallad, May 30, 2003.

57. For the trip's original purpose and Bin Ladin's suggestion, see Intelligence report, interrogation of Khallad, July 31, 2003. On Malaysia, Endolite, and the financing of Khallad's trip, see Intelligence report, interrogation of Khallad, Aug. 22, 2003.

58. On informing Hambali, see Intelligence report, interrogation of KSM, Aug. 18, 2003. For Hambali's assistance, see Intelligence report, interrogation of Khallad, July 31, 2003; Intelligence report, interrogation of Hambali, Sept. 4, 2003. For the colleague who spoke Arabic, see Intelligence report, interrogation of Khallad, May 30, 2003.

59. For the dates of Khallad's travel, his mistake in seating, and his other efforts to case flights, see Intelligence reports, interrogations of Khallad, July 31, 2003; Aug. 21, 2003. Khallad says he put the box cutter alongside tubes

of toothpaste and shaving cream with metallic exteriors, so that if the metal detector at the airport was triggered, the inspector would attribute the alarm to the other items. He also carried art supplies, which he hoped would explain the presence of a box cutter if anyone asked. Ibid.

60. For Khallad's return to Kuala Lumpur, see Intelligence report, interrogation of Khallad, May 30, 2003. For Hazmi's arrival and stay at the clinic, see Intelligence report, interrogation of Khallad, July 31, 2003. For Mihdhar's arrival, see FBI report, "Hijackers Timeline," Nov. 14, 2003 (citing 265A-NY-280350, serial 24808). For their stay at Sufaat's apartment, see CIA analytic report, "The Plot and the Plotters," June 1, 2003, p. 11; Intelligence report, interrogation of Khallad, Aug. 22, 2003. For Khallad's discussions with Hazmi and Khallad's knowledge of the operation, see Intelligence report, interrogation of Khallad, July 31, 2003.

61. For the Bangkok meeting, see CIA analytic report, "The Plot and the Plotters," June 1, 2003, pp. 49–50. For relocation of the meeting to Bangkok, see Intelligence reports, interrogations of Khallad, Aug. 18, 2003; Jan. 7, 2004. Fahd al Quso, a close friend of Khallad's, accompanied Nibras on the trip to Bangkok to take money to Khallad. Quso claims that the amount was $36,000. FBI report of investigation, interview of Quso, Jan. 31, 2001. Khallad claims that it was only $10,000 to $12,000. Intelligence reports, interrogations of Khallad, May 30, 2003; Aug. 18, 2003. Khallad has identified contradictory purposes for the money: a donation to charities benefiting amputees, see Intelligence report, interrogation of Khallad, Aug. 8, 2003; and to advance the ship-bombing operation, see Intelligence report, interrogation of Khallad, Jan. 7, 2004. Khallad has explicitly denied giving any of the money he received from Nibras and Quso to Hazmi and Mihdhar. Intelligence reports, interrogations of Khallad, Aug. 8, 2003; Jan. 7, 2004. Given the separate reporting from KSM that he gave Hazmi and Mihdhar $8,000 each before they traveled to the United States, we have insufficient evidence to conclude that the Nibras/Quso money helped finance the planes operation. Intelligence report, interrogation of KSM, June 15, 2004. For Hazmi and Mihdhar's interest in traveling to Bangkok, see Intelligence report, interrogation of Khallad, Jan. 7, 2004. For Hambali's assistance, see Intelligence report, interrogation of Khallad, Aug. 8, 2003. For Abu Bara's return to Yemen, see Intelligence report, interrogation of Khallad, May 30, 2003.

62. For the hotel arrangements, see Intelligence report, interrogation of Khallad, Jan. 7, 2004. For the two groups not meeting with each other, see Intelligence report, interrogation of Khallad, Aug. 18, 2003. For Khallad's subsequent actions, see Intelligence report, interrogation of Khallad, July 31, 2003.

63. For Bin Ladin's cancellation of the East Asian operation, see Intelligence report, interrogation of KSM, Aug. 18, 2003. For Hazmi and Mihdhar's departure, see Intelligence report, interrogation of Khallad, Aug. 8, 2003. For their arrival in Los Angeles, see FBI report, "Hijackers Timeline," Nov. 14, 2003 (citing 265A-NY-280350-CG, serial 4062; 265A-NY-280350-302, serial 7134).

64. On Atta's family background, see FBI report, "Hijackers Timeline," Nov. 14, 2003 (citing FBI electronic communication from Cairo dated Sept. 13, 2001); CIA analytic report, "The Plot and the Plotters," June 1, 2003, p. 23. For details on his study in Germany, see German Bundeskriminalamt (BKA) report, investigative summary re Atta, June 24, 2002; Federal Prosecutor General (Germany), response to Commission letter, June 25, 2004, pp. 3–4. Atta's host family in Hamburg soon asked him to move out. Between 1993 and 1998, Atta shared a one-bedroom apartment in Hamburg with a fellow student, who moved out after having problems with Atta and was succeeded by another roommate. See German BKA report, investigative summary re Atta, June 24, 2002. On Atta's character, see German BKA investigation of Said Bahaji, summary of interrogation of Shahid Nickels on Oct. 30, 2001.

65. On the Muslim student association in Hamburg, see Intelligence report, interrogation of Ramzi Binalshibh, Oct. 2, 2002. On the Muslim-Christian working group and Atta, see German BKA investigation of Bahaji, summary of interrogation of Michael Krause on Oct. 11, 2001; German BKA investigation of Bahaji, summary of interrogation of Nickels on Oct. 30, 2001. Much of the information about Atta and his friends in Hamburg comes from Nickels, a German national who converted to Islam while in high school and spent considerable time with Atta's circle between 1997 and 1999. Nickels testified at the trials in Germany of Mounir el Motassadeq and Abdelghani Mzoudi on 9/11-related charges.

66. German BKA investigation of Bahaji, summary of interrogation of Nickels on Oct. 30, 2001, pp. 8, 15; federal prosecutor's closing argument, Motassadeq trial, Feb. 5, 2003. On Atta's fundamentalism, see FBI electronic communication, "Khaled A. Shoukry," June 17, 2002.

67. German BKA report, investigative summary re Binalshibh, July 4, 2002; Federal Prosecutor General (Germany), response to Commission letter, June 25, 2004, pp. 3–4; FBI report of investigation, interview of Fuad Omar Bazarah, Apr. 9, 2004; Intelligence report, interrogation of Binalshibh, Sept. 24, 2002. Binalshibh used various names, such as Ramzi Omar and Ramzi al Sheiba. In May 1998, months before he was expelled from school, German authorities had issued a warrant to arrest and deport "Ramzi Omar." German BKA report, investigative summary re Binalshibh, July 4, 2002. But Binalshibh was no longer using this alias, so the German authorities did not discover that he and Ramzi Omar were the same person until after the attacks of September 11. Ibid.

68. Intelligence report, interrogation of Binalshibh, Oct. 2, 2002; German BKA investigation of Bahaji, summary of interrogation of Nickels on Oct. 30, 2001; German BKA report, investigative summary re Binalshibh, July 4, 2002.

69. German BKA report, investigative summary re Binalshibh, July 4, 2002.

70. CIA analytic report, "The Plot and the Plotters," June 1, 2003, p. 23; German BKA report, investigative summary re Shehhi, July 9, 2002.

71. German BKA report, investigative summary re Shehhi, July 9, 2002; Federal Prosecutor General (Germany), response to Commission letter, June 25, 2004, pp. 3–4; FBI electronic communication, summary of testimony of Mohamed Abdulla Mohamed Awady on Oct. 24, 2003, at the Mzoudi trial, Dec. 5, 2003.

72. German BKA report, investigative summary re Shehhi, July 9, 2002.

73. Ibid.

74. FBI electronic communication, summary of testimony of Mohamed Abdulla Mohamed Awady on Oct. 24, 2003, at the Mzoudi trial, Dec. 5, 2003.

75. Federal prosecutor's closing argument, Motassadeq trial, Feb. 5, 2003.

76. German BKA report, investigative summary re Jarrah, July 18, 2002; Federal Prosecutor General (Germany), response to Commission letter, June 25, 2004, pp. 3–4. In 1999, Jarrah and Senguen allegedly married in an Islamic ceremony not recognized under German law. Senguen has only acknowledged that she and Jarrah were engaged. German BKA report, investigative summary re Jarrah, July 18, 2002.

77. German BKA report, investigative summary re Jarrah, July 18, 2002.

78. Ibid.

79. Ibid.

80. On Jarrah's accommodations in Hamburg and his meeting with Binalshibh, see ibid. On Jarrah and Zammar, see German BKA investigation of Bahaji, summary of interrogation of Nickels on Oct. 30, 2001; see generally Intelligence report, interrogation of Binalshibh, Nov. 6, 2003; Intelligence report, "Terrorism: Background Information on Usama Bin Ladin Associate Muhammad Haydar Zammar," Jan. 14, 2002. For Zammar encouraging jihad, see Intelligence report, interrogation of detainee, Jan. 14, 2002.

81. Intelligence report, interrogation of Binalshibh, Nov. 6, 2003; German BKA investigation of Bahaji, summary of interrogation of Nickels on Oct. 30, 2001. On one occasion, German authorities intercepted a call in which such a gathering was mentioned. An individual phoning Zammar's house on February 17, 1999, was told that he was away on a trip to a distant, "bad" region, but that "people" at 54 Marienstrasse knew where he was. The same conversation revealed that these "people" included "Said, Mohamed Amir, [and] Omar," likely a reference to the apartment's original occupants, Said Bahaji, Atta, and Binalshibh. Federal Prosecutor General (Germany), response to Commission letter, June 25, 2004, p. 9. Shehhi also appears to have lived there briefly, in November 1998 and again in the summer of 1999. German BKA report, investigative summary re Shehhi, July 9, 2002. The Marienstrasse apartment remained an important location for the group even after Binalshibh, Atta, and Shehhi all moved out, as some of their closest associates, including Zakariya Essabar and Abdelghani Mzoudi, moved in. See German BKA report, investigative summary re Binalshibh, July 4, 2002.

82. German BKA report, investigative summary re Bahaji, Mar. 6, 2002. A document containing a biography of Bin Ladin—seized from the residence of Said Bahaji, a member of Atta's circle—also contains the phrase "Dar el Ansar," which refers to the name of a guesthouse Bin Ladin established in Afghanistan for mujahideen recruits. Ibid.

83. German BKA investigation of Bahaji, summary of interrogation of Nickels on Nov. 7, 2001; German BKA report, investigative summary re Bahaji, Mar. 6, 2002; federal prosecutor's closing argument, Motassadeq trial, Feb. 5, 2003. The diskettes seized from Bahaji's residence also contained bomb-making instructions. Federal Prosecutor General (Germany), response to Commission letter, June 25, 2004, p. 10. A videotape of Bahaji's October 9, 1999, wedding at the Quds mosque, recovered by German authorities after the September 11 attacks, depicts Binalshibh giving a speech denouncing Jews as a problem for all Muslims. On the videotape, Binalshibh also reads a Palestinian war poem, and Shehhi and Mzoudi sing a jihad song. Also shown attending the wedding are Jarrah and Zammar. FBI report, "Hijackers Timeline," Nov. 14, 2003 (citing 265A-NY-280350-BN-415).

84. German BKA report, investigative summary re Essabar; CIA report, interrogation of Binalshibh, May 27, 2003; federal prosecutor's closing argument, Motassadeq trial, Feb. 5, 2003. After arriving in Afghanistan in 2001, he became a member of al Qaeda's media committee. Intelligence report, interrogations of KSM and Binalshibh, May 27, 2003.

85. German BKA report, investigative summary re Motassadeq, Oct. 22, 2001.

86. German BKA report, investigative summary re Mzoudi, Jan. 13, 2003; German BKA report, investigative summary re Motassadeq, Oct. 22, 2001. Mzoudi and Motassadeq were both tried in Germany on charges related to the 9/11 attacks. Mzoudi was acquitted in February 2004, in part because Binalshibh was not produced as a witness. Motassadeq was convicted in 2003 for being an accessory to the attacks and received a 15-year prison sentence, but his conviction was reversed. See Richard Bernstein, "Germans Free Moroccan Convicted of a 9/11 Role," New York Times, Apr. 8, 2004, p. A18.

87. Summary of Judgment and Sentencing Order by Hanseatic Regional High Court, Motassadeq trial, Feb. 19, 2003; German BKA investigation of Bahaji, summary of interrogation of Nickels on Oct. 30, 2001. According to Nickels, who was distancing himself from the group by this time, "Atta was just too strange." Ibid.

88. Shehhi and other members of the group used to frequent a library in Hamburg to use the Internet. According to one of the librarians, in 1999 Shehhi, unprompted, inveighed against America, and boasted that "something was going to happen" and that "there would be thousands of dead people." FBI electronic communication, summary of testimony of Angela Duile on Aug. 28, 2003, at Mzoudi trial, Oct. 27, 2003. Another witness who lived in the same dormitory as Motassadeq testified that in late 1998 or early 1999, he overheard a conversation in which Motassadeq told someone that "we will do something bad again" and that "we will dance on their graves." The conversation also contained a reference to the "burning of people." FBI electronic communication, summary of testimony of Holger Liszkowski on Sept. 9, 2003, at Mzoudi trial, Nov. 17, 2003. On another occasion, according to the same witness, Motassadeq apparently identified Atta as "our pilot." Another witness recalled Atta ominously observing in 1999 that the United States was not omnipotent and that "something can be done." German BKA investigation of Bahaji, summary of interrogation of Nickels on Nov. 20, 2001.

89. Intelligence reports, interrogations of Binalshibh, Oct. 7, 2002; May 20, 2003.

90. Intelligence report, interrogation of Binalshibh, May 20, 2003. A detainee has confirmed Binalshibh's account about being advised to go to Afghanistan rather than trying to travel directly to Chechnya. The detainee dates the Slahi meeting to October 1999. Intelligence report, interrogation of detainee, Oct. 17, 2003. The detainee, however, also suggests that Slahi and Binalshibh may have met earlier in 1999 in Frankfurt, through a mutual acquaintance. Intelligence report, interrogation of detainee, Oct. 27, 2003. The acquaintance apparently tells a different story, claiming that Slahi introduced him to Binalshibh and Jarrah at Slahi's home in 1997 or 1998, and that he later lived with them in Hamburg. Intelligence report, interrogation of detainee, July 2, 2003.

91. FBI report, "Summary of Penttbom Investigation," Feb. 29, 2004, p. 8; Intelligence reports, interrogations of Binalshibh, Sept. 24, 2002; Mar. 4, 2003; May 20, 2003.

92. On meetings with Atef and Bin Ladin, see Intelligence reports, interrogations of Binalshibh, Dec. 10, 2002; Mar. 4, 2003; Mar. 31, 2003; Intelligence report, interrogation of KSM, Feb. 20, 2004. Atta reportedly had between two and five meetings with Bin Ladin before leaving Kandahar and was the only 9/11 hijacker who knew the entire scope of the operation from the outset. Intelligence report, comments of Binalshibh on Atta, Apr. 21, 2003.

93. Intelligence report, interrogation of Binalshibh, Dec. 10, 2002. According to KSM, Bin Ladin designated Hazmi to be Atta's second in command. Intelligence report, interrogation of KSM, Feb. 20, 2004.

94. In addition, Atta obtained a new passport in June 1998, even though his current one was still valid for nearly a year, a sign that he may have been following the al Qaeda practice of concealing travel to Pakistan. Federal Prosecutor General (Germany), response to Commission letter, June 25, 2004, p. 11.

95. German BKA report, investigative summary re Motassadeq, Oct. 22, 2001; Summary of Judgment and Sentencing Order by Hanseatic Regional High Court, Motassadeq trial, Feb. 19, 2003. Motassadeq continued to handle some of Shehhi's affairs even after Shehhi returned to Hamburg. Most importantly, in March 2000, Motassadeq paid Shehhi's semester fees at the university, to ensure Shehhi's continued receipt of scholarship payments from the UAE. Ibid.

96. German BKA report, investigative summary re Motassadeq, Oct. 22, 2001. After 9/11, Motassadeq admitted to German authorities that Shehhi had asked him to handle matters in a way that would conceal Shehhi's absence. Motassadeq also would claim later that he did not know why his friends had gone to Afghanistan, saying he thought they were planning to go fight in Chechnya. For assistance provided by both Motassadeq and Bahaji, see Federal Prosecutor General (Germany), response to Commission letter, June 25, 2004, pp. 13–14.

97. Jarrah encountered a minor problem during his return trip to Hamburg. On January 30, 2000, while transiting Dubai on his way from Karachi to Germany, Jarrah drew questioning from UAE authorities about an overlay of the Qu'ran that appeared on one page of his passport. The officials also noticed the religious tapes and books Jarrah had in his possession, but released him after he pointed out that he had lived in Hamburg for a number of years and was studying aircraft construction there. FBI report, "Summary of Penttbom Investigation," Feb. 29, 2004, p. 13.

98. Intelligence report, interrogation of Binalshibh, Sep. 24, 2002; FBI report, "Summary of Penttbom Investigation," Feb. 29, 2004, pp. 11, 13. According to a KSM interrogation report, Shehhi may have been present for at least some of the training that Atta and Binalshibh received in Karachi. Intelligence report, interrogation of KSM, Mar. 31, 2004.

99. Intelligence report, interrogation of Binalshibh, Nov. 6, 2003. Binalshibh and the others kept their distance from Zammar even before visiting Afghanistan and getting their instructions from Bin Ladin and Atef. Ibid.

100. On Atta, see FBI analytic report, "The 11 September Hijacker Cell Model," Feb. 2003, p. 28. On Jarrah, see German BKA report, investigative summary re Jarrah, July 18, 2002. Note that although Jarrah's attitude was now much more congenial, he told Senguen nothing about being in Afghanistan. On Shehhi's wedding celebration, see German BKA report, investigative summary re Shehhi, July 9, 2002; on his changed appearance and behavior, see FBI electronic communication, summary of testimony of Mohamed Abdulla Mohamed Awady on Oct. 24, 2003, at the Mzoudi trial, Dec. 5, 2003.

101. German BKA report, investigative summary re Jarrah, July 18, 2002.

102. On Ali Abdul Aziz Ali, also known as Ammar al Baluchi, see FBI report, "Summary of Penttbom Investi-

gation," Feb. 29, 2004, p. 78. Ali, in turn, would ship these materials to his uncle, KSM, in Karachi. Intelligence report, interrogation of Ali Abdul Aziz Ali, Feb. 11, 2004. On Jarrah, see German BKA report, investigative summary re Jarrah, July 18, 2002. Following his sudden decision to study aircraft engineering in Hamburg, Jarrah had expressed interest in becoming a pilot around the end of 1998, well before he traveled to Afghanistan. According to Senguen, Jarrah told her about friends of his who had interrupted their studies to join the Germany army so that they could become pilots. Jarrah's pre-Afghanistan interest in aviation also is confirmed by a January 22, 1999, email recovered after the September 11, 2001, attacks, in which Jarrah told a friend from Beirut that he might "come next year and . . . have something to tell about airplanes." Ibid. On Binalshibh, see Intelligence report, interrogation of Binalshibh, Sept. 24, 2002.

103. Summary of Judgment and Sentencing Order by Hanseatic Regional High Court, Motassadeq trial, Feb. 19, 2003, pp. 10–11. Zacarias Moussaoui later would benefit from the results of all this research. Following his August 2001 arrest, the FBI discovered among his possessions a fax copy of an advertisement for U.S. flight schools. According to Binalshibh, notes in the margin of the advertisement were written by Atta. Intelligence report, interrogation of Binalshibh, Dec. 19, 2002.

104. DOS record, NIV applicant detail, Marwan al Shehhi, Mohamed Atta, Ziad Jarrah, Nov. 8, 2001. The visa applications were destroyed by the State Department according to routine document handling practices before their significance was known.

105. DOS records, visa applications of Ramzi Binalshibh, May 17, 2000; June 15, 2000; Oct. 25 2000. CIA analytic report, "The Plot and the Plotters," June 1, 2003, pp. 9–10; German BKA report, investigative summary re Binalshibh, July 4, 2002. Atta had twice explored the possibility of obtaining a U.S. green card shortly before his November 1999 trip to Afghanistan. FBI report, "Summary of Penttbom Investigation," Feb. 29, 2004, p. 8. Both Binalshibh and Jarrah listed the same person as a point of contact in the United States, an Indonesian national who had previously lived in Hamburg. Although this individual knew some members of the Hamburg cell, including Mohamed Atta and Razmi Binalshibh, there is no indication that any of the hijackers actually contacted him while they were in the United States. See German BKA report, investigative summary re Jarrah, July 18, 2002. Binalshibh had applied for a visa years earlier along with Fuad Bazarah, a co-worker in Yemen whose father contacted the U.S. embassy on Binalshibh's behalf. Bazarah obtained a visa application and moved to Los Angeles, but Binalshibh's application was denied. Bazarah would later live in Los Angeles with Ramez Noaman, an individual who knew Nawaf al Hazmi in San Diego. FBI electronic communication, "Penttbom," Oct. 23, 2001.

106. Intelligence report, interrogation of KSM, Sept. 9, 2003; CIA analytic report, Al Qaeda travel issues, Jan. 2004, p. 1. On the role of KSM, see, e.g., Intelligence report, interrogation of Binalshibh, Oct. 11, 2002. On the role of Abu Zubaydah, see, e.g., Intelligence report, biographical information on Abu Zubayda, Feb. 25, 2002. Al Qaeda also relied on outside travel facilitators, including fraudulent document vendors, corrupt officials, travel agencies, and smugglers, to help move operatives around the world by obtaining fraudulent documents, arranging visas (real or fake), making airline reservations, etc. See CIA analytic report, "Clandestine Travel Facilitators: Key Enablers of Terrorism," Dec. 31, 2002; CIA analytic report, Al Qaeda travel issues, Jan. 2004.

107. On passport collection schemes, see Intelligence report, interrogation of KSM, Sept. 9, 2003. On recycled passports, see Intelligence report, Collection of passports June 7, 2002.

108. See Intelligence reports, interrogations of KSM, Nov. 12, 2003; May 25, 2004; CIA analytic report, Al Qaeda travel issues, Jan. 2004, pp. 1, 3, 19. A detainee has admitted attending several security and specialized courses, including ones in counterfeiting and seal removal. Intelligence report, interrogation of al Qaeda associates, Apr. 11, 2002. Atta reportedly learned alteration techniques in Afghanistan, cleaning Ramzi Binalshibh's passport of its Pakistani visa and travel cachets. CIA analytic report, Al Qaeda travel issues, Jan. 2004, p. 1.

109. Intelligence report, Information on Mujahideen Travel, Mar. 13, 2002.

110. Intelligence report, interrogation of KSM, July 25, 2003. A small amount of the plot's backing came from Shehhi's own funds. He received a salary from the UAE military, which was sponsoring his studies in Germany, through December 23, 2000. Binalshibh apparently used some of this money to wire just over $10,000 to Shehhi in the United States and pay some of his own plot-related expenses. Adam Drucker interview (Jan. 12, 2004); FBI Report, "Summary of Penttbom Investigation," Feb. 29, 2004, pp. 20–22.

111. CIA analytic report, "Terrorism: Amount of Money It Takes to Keep al-Qa'ida Functioning," Aug. 7, 2002; CIA analytic report, "Terrorism: Al-Qa'ida Operating on a Shoestring," undated (post-9/11); Frank G. interview (Mar. 2, 2004).

112. In the wake of the East Africa embassy bombings, the NSC led trips to Saudi Arabia in 1999 and 2000 to meet with Saudi officials on terrorist financing. These meetings, and subsequent interviews of Bin Ladin family members in the United States, helped the U.S. government revise its understanding of Bin Ladin's wealth. Rick Newcomb interview (Feb. 4, 2004); William Wechsler interview (Jan. 7, 2004).

113. See William Wechsler interview (Jan. 7, 2004); Rick Newcomb interview (Feb. 4, 2004); Frank G. interview (Mar. 2, 2004); Frank G. and Mary S. briefing (July 15, 2003). See also DOS cable, State 035243, "January 2000 Meeting Regarding UBL Finances," Feb. 27, 2000; DOS cable, Riyadh 000475, "The Saudi Binladin Group: Builders to the King," Feb. 16, 1999; Treasury memo, Office of Foreign Asset Control to DOS, Draft Cable on Meet-

ing with Two of UBL's Brothers, May 19, 2000; Youssef M. Ibrahim, "Saudis Strip Citizenship from Backers of Militants," *New York Times*, Apr. 10, 1994, p. 15; "Saudi Family Disassociates Itself from 'Terrorist' Member," Associated Press, Feb. 19, 1994.

114. Frank G. and Mary S. briefing (July 15, 2003); Frank G. interview (Mar. 2, 2004); Intelligence report, interrogation of KSM, July 30, 2003; Robert Block, "In War on Terrorism, Sudan Struck a Blow by Fleecing Bin Laden," *Wall Street Journal*, Dec. 3, 2001, p. A1. Despite substantial evidence to the contrary and his own assertion that Bin Ladin arrived in Afghanistan with no money, KSM has told his interrogators that he believes the bulk of the money (85–95 percent) for the planes operation came from Bin Ladin's personal fortune. Intelligence reports, interrogations of KSM, July 30, 2003; Apr. 5, 2004; June 15, 2004.

115. Frank G. interview (Mar. 2, 2004); CIA analytic report, Financial Support for Terrorist Organizations, CTC 2002-40117CH, Nov. 14, 2002. The United States was not a primary source of al Qaeda funding, although some funds raised in the United States may have made their way to al Qaeda or its affiliated groups. Frank G. and Mary S. briefing (July 15, 2003).

116. Frank G. interview (Mar. 2, 2004); CIA analytic report, "Identifying al-Qa'ida's Donors and Fundraisers: A Status Report," CTC 2002-40029CH, Feb. 27, 2002.

117. CIA analytic report, "Identifying al-Qa'ida's Donors and Fundraisers: A Status Report," Feb. 27, 2002; CIA analytic report, spectrum of al Qaeda donors, CTC 2003-30199HC, Oct. 30, 2003; Frank G. interview (Mar. 2, 2004).

118. CIA analytic report, "How Bin Ladin Commands a Global Terrorist Network," CTC 99-40003, Jan. 27, 1999; CIA analytic report, "Gauging the War against al-Qa'ida's Finances," CTC 2002-30078CH, Aug. 8, 2002; CIA analytic report, paper on Al-Haramain, CTC 2002-30014C, Mar. 22, 2002.

119. CIA analytic report, "Al Qa'ida's Financial Ties to Islamic Youth Programs," CTC 2002-40132HCX, Jan. 17, 2003; CIA analytic report, Al Qaeda Financial Network, CTC 2002-40094H, Aug. 7, 2002.

120. Frank G. interview (Mar. 2, 2004); CIA analytic report, Financial Links of Al Qaeda Operative, CTC 2002-30060CH, June 27, 2002.

121. Frank G. and Mary S. briefing (July 15, 2003). The Taliban's support was limited to the period immediately following Bin Ladin's arrival in Afghanistan, before he reinvigorated fund-raising efforts. By 9/11, al Qaeda was returning the favor, providing substantial financial support to the Taliban.

122. David Aufhauser interview (Feb. 12, 2004). We have found no evidence that Saudi Princess Haifa al Faisal provided any funds to the conspiracy, either directly or indirectly. See Adam Drucker interview (May 19, 2004).

123. On limited Saudi oversight, see Bob Jordan interview (Jan. 14, 2004). In Saudi Arabia, *zakat* is broader and more pervasive than Western ideas of charity, in that it functions not only as charity but also as social welfare, educational assistance, foreign aid, a form of income tax, and a source of political influence.

124. A *hawala*, at least in the "pure" form, transfers value without the use of a negotiable instrument or other commonly recognized method for the exchange of money. For example, a U.S. resident who wanted to send money to a person in another country, such as Pakistan, would give her money, in dollars, to a U.S.-based hawaladar. The U.S. hawaladar would then contact his counterpart in Pakistan, giving the Pakistani hawaladar the particulars of the transaction, such as the amount of money, the code, and perhaps the identity of the recipient. The ultimate recipient in Pakistan would then go to the Pakistani hawaladar and receive his money, in rupees, from whatever money the Pakistani hawaladar has on hand. As far as the sender and ultimate recipient are concerned, the transaction is then complete. The two hawaladars would have a variety of mechanisms to settle their debt, either through offsetting transactions (e.g., someone in Pakistan sending money to the United States using the same two hawaladars), a periodic settling wire transfer from the U.S. hawaladar's bank to the Pakistani hawaladar's bank, or a commercial transaction, such as the U.S. hawaladar paying a debt or an invoice, in dollars, that the Pakistani hawaladar owes in the United States. Hawalas typically do not have a large central control office for settling transactions, maintaining instead a loose association with other hawaladars to transfer value, generally without any formal or legally binding agreements. See Treasury report, "A Report to Congress in Accordance with Section 359 of the [USA PATRIOT Act]" Nov. 2002; Treasury report, "Hawala: The Hawala Alternate Remittance System and its Role in Money Laundering," undated (prepared by the Financial Crimes Enforcement Network in cooperation with INTERPOL, probably in 1996).

125. Frank G. and Mary S. briefing (July 15, 2003); CIA analytic report Al-Qa'ida Financiers, CTC 2002-30138H, Jan. 3, 2003. Moreover, because al Qaeda initially was living hand to mouth, there was no need to store funds.

126. CIA analytic report, "Pursuing the Bin Ladin Financial Target," CTC 01-40003HCS, Apr. 12, 2001; CIA analytic report, "Couriers, Hawaladars Key to Moving Al-Qa'ida Money," CTC 2003-40063CH, May 16, 2003.

127. For al Qaeda spending, see Frank G. and Mary S. briefing (July 15, 2003). The 1998 U.S. embassy bombings in East Africa cost approximately $10,000. CIA analytic report, "Gauging the War on Terrorism: Most 11 September Practices Still Viable," Jan. 30, 2002; Intelligence report, interrogation of KSM, June 3, 2003. Although there is evidence that al Qaeda experienced funding shortfalls as part of the cyclical fund-raising process (with more money coming during the holy month of Ramadan), we are not aware of any intelligence indicating that terror-

ist acts were interrupted as a result. For al Qaeda expenditures, see, e.g., CIA analytic report, "Usama Bin Ladin's Finances: Some Estimates of Wealth, Income, and Expenditures," CTC IR 98-40006, Nov. 17, 1998. For payments to the Taliban, see Frank G. and Mary S. briefing (July 15, 2003); CIA analytic report, "Terrorism: Amount of Money It Takes to Keep al-Qa'ida Functioning," PWR080702-05, Aug. 7, 2002. On start-up funds, see Frank G. interview (Mar. 2, 2004).

128. Doug Wankel interview (Mar. 15, 2004); Frank G. and Mary S. briefing (July 15, 2003). Although some reporting alleges that Bin Ladin may have been an investor, or even had an operational role, in drug trafficking before 9/11, this intelligence cannot be substantiated. Ibid. Frank G. interview (Mar. 2, 2004). No evidence indicates any such involvement in drug trafficking, and none of the detained al Qaeda operatives has indicated that this was a method of fund-raising.

129. "Conflict diamonds" refers to rough diamonds that finance armed conflict in Africa. The international community has tried to restrict trade in such gems. FBI report, "Allegations of Al Qaeda Trafficking in Conflict Diamonds," July 18, 2003; CIA analytic report, "Terrorism: Assessing al-Qa'ida and Hizballah Ties to Conflict Diamonds," CTC 2002-40121CH, Jan. 13, 2003; CIA analytic report, "Couriers, Hawaladars Key to Moving Al-Qa'ida Money," CTC 2003-40063CH, May 16, 2003; DOS cable, Brussels 05994, "WP Reporter Claims More Witnesses to 2001 Al-Qaida/Conflict Diamonds Link," Dec. 12, 2002; DOS cable, Brussels 001054, terrorism and conflict diamonds, Mar. 1, 2002. Greg R. interviews (Oct. 3, 2003; July 6, 2004); Alan White interview (June 23, 2004); FBI situation reports and supporting documents from the Sierra Leone trip, Feb. 2004.

130. Highly publicized allegations of insider trading in advance of 9/11 generally rest on reports of unusual pre-9/11 trading activity in companies whose stock plummeted after the attacks. Some unusual trading did in fact occur, but each such trade proved to have an innocuous explanation. For example, the volume of put options—investments that pay off only when a stock drops in price—surged in the parent companies of United Airlines on September 6 and American Airlines on September 10—highly suspicious trading on its face. Yet, further investigation has revealed that the trading had no connection with 9/11. A single U.S.-based institutional investor with no conceivable ties to al Qaeda purchased 95 percent of the UAL puts on September 6 as part of a trading strategy that also included *buying* 115,000 shares of American on September 10. Similarly, much of the seemingly suspicious trading in American on September 10 was traced to a specific U.S.-based options trading newsletter, faxed to its subscribers on Sunday, September 9, which recommended these trades. These examples typify the evidence examined by the investigation. The SEC and the FBI, aided by other agencies and the securities industry, devoted enormous resources to investigating this issue, including securing the cooperation of many foreign governments. These investigators have found that the apparently suspicious consistently proved innocuous. Joseph Cella interview (Sept. 16, 2003; May 7, 2004; May 10–11, 2004); FBI briefing (Aug. 15, 2003); SEC memo, Division of Enforcement to SEC Chair and Commissioners, "Pre-September 11, 2001 Trading Review," May 15, 2002; Ken Breen interview (Apr. 23, 2004); Ed G. interview (Feb. 3, 2004).

131. The hijackers spent more than $270,000 in the United States, and the costs associated with Moussaoui were at least $50,000. The additional expenses included travel to obtain passports and visas, travel to the United States, expenses incurred by the plot leaders and facilitators, and the expenses incurred by the people selected to be hijackers who ultimately did not participate. For many of these expenses, we have only fragmentary evidence and/or unconfirmed detainee reports, and can make only a rough estimate of costs. The $400,000 to $500,000 estimate does not include the cost of running training camps in Afghanistan, where the hijackers were recruited and trained, or the marginal cost of the training itself. Finally, the architect of the plot, KSM, put the total cost at approximately $400,000, apparently excluding Moussaoui's expenses. Intelligence reports, interrogations of KSM, June 3, 2003; Apr. 5, 2004. Our investigation has uncovered no evidence that the 9/11 conspirators employed hawala as a means to move the money that funded the operation. Indeed, the surviving plot participants have either not mentioned hawala or have explicitly denied using it to send money to the United States. Adam Drucker interview (Jan. 12, 2004; Intelligence report, interrogation of KSM, Apr. 5, 2004; Intelligence report, interrogation of detainee, Apr. 2, 2004; Intelligence report, interrogation of Ramzi Binalshibh, Apr. 7, 2004. On domestic U.S. and foreign government funding, see, e.g., Adam Drucker interviews (Jan. 12, 2004; May 19, 2004); Dennis Lormel interview (Jan. 16, 2004); FBI response to Commission question for the record, July 13, 2004. As discussed in chapter 7, we have examined three transactions involving individuals in San Diego. Based on all of the evidence, we have concluded that none of these transactions involved a net transfer of funds to the hijackers.

132. Shehhi received a salary from the UAE military, which was sponsoring his studies in Germany. Adam Drucker interview (Jan. 12, 2004). For funds received by facilitators, see Intelligence report, interrogation of KSM, Apr. 5, 2004; Intelligence report, interrogation of Binalshibh, Apr. 9, 2004. Notwithstanding persistent press reports to the contrary, there is no convincing evidence that the Spanish al Qaeda cell, led by Imad Barkat Yarkas and al Qaeda European financier Mohammed Galeb Kalaje Zouaydi, provided any funding to support the 9/11 attacks or the Hamburg participants. Zouaydi may have provided funds to Hamburg associate Mamoun Darkazanli—see, e.g., FBI letterhead memorandum, Yarkas and Spanish Cell investigation, Jan. 8, 2003—but there is no evidence that Zouaydi provided money to the plot participants or that any of his funds were used to support the plot. Adam Drucker interview (Jan. 12, 2004); Ed G. interview (Feb. 3, 2004).

6 From Threat to Threat

1. President Clinton was a voracious reader of intelligence. He received the President's Daily Brief (PDB), Senior Executive Intelligence Brief (SEIB), and the State Department's intelligence updates daily, as well as other products episodically. Berger, Clarke, and Chief of Staff John Podesta received daily Bin Ladin "Situation Reports" from the CIA detailing Bin Ladin's reported location and movements. Berger told us he would tell President Clinton if there was anything in these reports that he needed to know. Samuel Berger interview (Jan. 14, 2004). Information on distribution of Bin Ladin Situation Reports provided to the Commission by CIA.

2. President Clinton spoke of terrorism in numerous public statements. In his August 5, 1996, remarks at George Washington University, he called terrorism "the enemy of our generation." He usually spoke of terrorism in two related contexts: new technologies and the greater openness engendered by post–Cold War globalization; and weapons of mass destruction (WMD), especially—and increasingly over time—the threat from biological and chemical weapons. President Clinton repeatedly linked terrorist groups and WMD as transnational threats for the new global era. See, e.g., President Clinton remarks, "On Keeping America Secure for the 21st Century," Jan. 22, 1999 (at the National Academy of Sciences, Washington, D.C.), in which he spoke directly to these topics.

3. President Clinton spoke of the Y2K computer problem in his January 19, 1999, State of the Union address. On Y2K concerns, see John Podesta interview (Jan. 15, 2004). On concerns about extremist groups exploiting millennial opportunities, see, e.g., CIA briefing materials, CTC for the DCI, "Millennium Threat," Dec. 16, 1999.

4. Judith Miller, "Holy Warriors: Dissecting a Terror Plot from Boston to Amman," *New York Times*, Jan. 15, 2001, p. A1; CIA analytic report, "Bin Ladin's Terrorist Operations: Meticulous and Adaptable," CTC 00-400117, Nov. 2, 2000 (appendix B: "Bin Ladin's Role in the Anti-U.S. 'Millennial' Plots").

5. Ibid. On Hoshar and Hijazi, see Jason Burke, *Al Qaeda: Casting a Shadow of Terror* (I. B. Tauris, 2003), p. 188. Khaldan and Derunta were terrorist training camps in Afghanistan controlled by Abu Zubaydah. While the camps were not al Qaeda facilities, Abu Zubaydah had an agreement with Bin Ladin to conduct reciprocal recruiting efforts whereby promising trainees at the camps could be invited to join al Qaeda. See Intelligence report, interrogation of Abu Zubaydah, July 10, 2002.

6. Miller, "Holy Warriors," Jan. 15, 2001; CIA analytic report, "Bin Ladin's Terrorist Operations," Nov. 2, 2000 (appendix B).

7. CIA analytic report, "Bin Ladin's Terrorist Operations," Nov. 2, 2000 (appendix B).

8. FBI electronic communication, "Ahmed Ressam; Usama bin Ladin; Sbih Benyamin; Lucia Garofalo; Bouabide Chamchi," Dec. 29, 1999; Miller, "Holy Warriors," Jan. 15, 2001. The *Encyclopedia* is a multivolume instruction manual containing lessons on weapons handling, tactics, covert operations, bomb making, and other topics. The manual was originally created in the late 1980s by Afghanistan-based extremists, who considered it essential for waging terrorist operations and guerrilla warfare in the jihad against the Soviets. For more on the origins of the *Encyclopedia*, see Intelligence report, interrogation of Abu Zubaydah, June 24, 2003. Although Deek's precise role within the extremist community is unknown, his name appears variously as a staff member, instructor, and technical guru for the Khaldan and Derunta terrorist training camps in Afghanistan. Intelligence has revealed no extant links to the al Qaeda inner circle. For more on Deek, see FBI electronic communication, "Usama Bin Laden; Penttbomb; Taliban," May 25, 2002.

9. Testimony of Dale Watson before the Senate Select Committee on Intelligence, Feb. 9, 2000, p. 4; Miller, "Holy Warriors," Jan. 15, 2001.

10. Testimony of Dale Watson before the Senate Select Committee on Intelligence, Feb. 9, 2000, pp. 3–4; FBI electronic communication, "Ahmed Ressam; Usama bin Ladin; Sbih Benyamin; Lucia Garofalo; Bouabide Ghamchi," Dec. 29, 1999; Miller, "Holy Warriors," Jan. 15, 2001. On the fate of Hoshar and Hijazi's accomplices, see DOS cable, Amman 05158, "Security Court Convicts UBL Suspects of Plotting," Sept. 18, 2000.

11. NSC note, Clarke to Berger, Dec. 4, 1999; Richard Clarke interview (Jan. 12, 2004). In the margin next to Clarke's suggestion to attack al Qaeda facilities in the week before January 1, 2000, Berger wrote "no."

12. NSC memo, Berger to President Clinton, Dec. 9, 1999.

13. NSC email, Clarke to Berger, Dec. 14, 1999. The State Department, through the U.S. embassy in Riyadh, also asked the Saudis to relay the same threat to the Taliban. The diplomat said the United States was delivering "a strong and unmistakable message to the Taliban that should such attacks occur, they and Bin Ladin will be subject to swift and serious response." See DOS cable, Riyadh 003900, "Saudis on USG Warning to Taliban Concerning UBL Threats," Dec. 14, 1999. Berger wrote President Clinton that the State Department's warning seemed to barely register with the Taliban. See NSC memo, Berger to President Clinton, terrorist threat at the millennium, Dec. 18, 1999.

14. See NSC memo, talking points for Zinni, Dec. 20, 1999; Anthony Zinni interview (Jan. 19, 2004); NSC email, Clarke to Berger, Dec. 22, 1999 (in which Clarke writes that "the Milam mission has largely failed"); NSC memo, Riedel re Milam call (attached to the Clarke email).

15. George Tenet interview (Jan. 22, 2004); George Tenet prepared statement, Mar. 24, 2004, p. 22.

16. Randy Moss interview (Feb. 6, 2004). In sending the draft MON to the CIA, the NSC's senior director for intelligence programs, Mary McCarthy, cited only the August 1998 and July 1999 MONs as relevant prece-

dents—indicating that these new authorities were limited to using the capture and rendition approach. There was no indication that this MON authorized kill authority, although lethal force could be used in self-defense. See NSC memo, McCarthy to CIA, Dec. 1999.

17. CIA cable, "DCI message and update on Millennium threat," Dec. 20, 1999; NSC email, Cressey to Berger's office and others, Dec. 23, 1999.

18. Trial testimony of Ahmed Ressam, *United States v. Mokhtar Haouari*, No. S4 00 Cr. 15 (S.D. N.Y.), July 3, 2001 (transcript pp. 536–569); July 5, 2001 (transcript p. 624); FBI report of investigation, interviews of Ahmed Ressam, May 10, 2001; May 24, 2001. Ressam's recruitment by Abderraouf Hannachi (a Khaldan alumnus) is noted in Deposition of Ahmed Ressam, *In re: Letters Rogatory, August 1, 2001* (S.D. N.Y.), Jan. 23, 2002 (transcript pp. 32–33). See also PBS *Frontline* broadcast, "Trail of a Terrorist," Oct. 25, 2001 (online at www.pbs.org/wgbh/pages/frontline/shows/trail).

19. Trial testimony of Ressam, *United States v. Haouari*, July 3, 2001 (transcript pp. 570–584); FBI report of investigation, interview of Ressam, Aug. 7, 2001.

20. FBI report of investigation, interview of Ressam, May 10, 2001; Hal Bernton, Mike Carter, David Heath, and James Neff, "The Terrorist Within: The Story Behind One Man's Holy War Against America," *Seattle Times*, June 23–July 7, 2002 (part 11, "The Ticking Bomb").

21. Trial testimony of Ressam, *United States v. Haouari*, July 5, 2001 (transcript p. 605); Deposition of Ressam, *In re: Letters Rogatory* (S.D. N.Y.), Jan. 23, 2002 (transcript p. 23).

22. Trial testimony of Ressam, *United States v. Haouari,* July 3, 2001; Bernton, Carter, Heath, and Neff, "The Terrorist Within," June 23–July 7, 2002 (part 6, "It Takes a Thief"). A friend of Ressam's, Fateh Kamel, would pay Ressam for stolen passports, credit cards and other identity documents. Kamel is now serving eight years in prison in France for activities related to association with terrorist enterprises. Bruce Crumley, "Fighting Terrorism: Lessons from France," *Time*, Sept. 24, 2001 (online at www.time.com/time/nation/article/0,8599,176139,00.html). Ressam testified that he also sold stolen documents to Mohktar Haouari. See trial testimony of Ressam, *United States v. Haouari*, July 5, 2001 (transcript pp. 631–632).

23. PBS *Frontline* broadcast, "Trail of a Terrorist." Leo Nkounga was the document broker and an illegal alien in Canada from Cameroon who failed to surrender himself for deportation in 1993. Canadian deportation order, Adjudication file no. AOT93-0077, Sept. 15, 1993. He said he obtained two genuine Canadian passports for Ressam by submitting fake baptismal certificates to Canadian authorities. CBC News broadcast, *Disclosure*, "Target Terrorism," Mar. 26, 2002 (online at www.cbc.ca/disclosure/archives/020326_leo/resources.html). Ressam told border officials that he did not have a visa for Pakistan because he was only transiting on his way to India. FBI report of investigation, interview of Ressam, May 15, 2001, p. 7.

24. FBI case profile (part of materials provided to Dale Watson), "Abdelghani Meskini," Feb. 8, 2000. Meskini, who spoke English, was to drive Ressam and to give him money, but Ressam never showed since he was arrested at the border. Meskini was arrested on Dec. 30, 1999, and charged with material support and interstate fraud. See Testimony of Dale Watson before the Senate Select Committee on Intelligence, Feb. 9, 2000, pp. 11–12. On passports and visas provided by Haouari, see *United States v. Haouari*, 319 F. 3d 88, 91 (2d Cir. 2002).

25. INS alien file, No. A73603119, Abdel Hakim Tizegha. There is no record of Tizegha's entry into the United States.

26. Trial testimony of Ressam, *United States v. Haouari*, July 5, 2001 (transcript pp. 605–607, 613); FBI report of investigation, interview of Ressam, May 10, 2001; Opening Statement, *United States v. Ahmed Ressam*, No. CR99-666C JCC (W.D. Wash.), Mar. 13, 2001 (transcript p. 33).

27. Trial testimony of Diana Dean and Mark Johnson, *United States v. Ressam*, Mar. 13, 2001 (transcript pp. 116, 165). On the unraveling of the Ressam case, see Bernton, Carter, Heath and Neff, "The Terrorist Within," June 23–July 7, 2002 (part 15, "Puzzle Pieces").

28. Trial testimony of Mark Johnson, *United States v. Ressam*, Mar. 13, 2001 (transcript p. 124).

29. NSC memo, Berger to President Clinton, terrorism threat at the millennium, Dec. 9, 1999.

30. NSC email, Clarke to Berger, Dec. 11, 1999.

31. Samuel Berger interview (Jan. 14, 2004); George Tenet interview (Jan. 22, 2004).

32. NSC memo, Berger to President Clinton, terrorist threat at the millennium, Dec. 18, 1999.

33. NSC email, Clarke to Berger, roadmap for Small Group, Dec. 22, 1999; NSC email, Cressey to Berger and others, Dec. 23, 1999.

34. NSC memo, "The Millennium Terrorist Alert—Next Steps," undated (attached to NSC draft memo, "Review of Terrorism Alert and Lessons Learned," Jan. 3, 2000). In the original document, the quotation is underlined, not italicized. See also NSC memo, "Principals Meeting: Millennium Terrorism," undated (likely Dec. 1999); NSC email, Clarke to Berger, roadmap for Small Group, Dec. 22, 1999.

35. NSC email, Clarke to Berger, roadmap for Small Group, Dec. 22, 1999.

36. Samuel Berger interview (Jan. 14, 2004). See also Richard Clarke interview (Jan. 12, 2004); Roger Cressey interview (Dec. 15, 2003).

37. Trial testimony of Diana Dean, *United States v. Ressam,* Mar. 13, 2001 (transcript p. 124).

38. Vanderbilt University, Television News Archive, Dec. 22, 1999–Jan. 4, 2000.

39. On the FBI's standard operating procedure, see Samuel Berger interview (Jan. 14, 2004); John Podesta interview (Jan. 15, 2004); James Steinberg interview (Dec. 4, 2003); Richard Clarke interviews (Dec. 18, 2004; Jan. 12, 2004); Paul Kurtz interview (Dec. 16, 2003).

40. See James Steinberg interview (Dec. 4, 2003). According to Steinberg, the millennium crisis was the only time that the FBI effectively shared information with the NSC. Before that, White House officials complained, they got nothing from the FBI—and were told that they were being deliberately kept out of the loop on grounds of propriety. See also Samuel Berger interview (Jan. 14, 2004); Richard Clarke interview (Jan. 12, 2004); Roger Cressey interview (Dec. 15, 2003). In fact, it was completely appropriate for the NSC to be briefed by the FBI on its national security investigations. Moreover, the legal bar to sharing information was often exaggerated. Only information actually presented to the grand jury could not be disclosed. See Rule 6(e) of the Federal Rules of Criminal Procedure, which establishes rules for grand jury secrecy.

41. Intelligence report, Activities of Bin Ladin associates, Dec. 29, 1999; Intelligence report, review of 9/11 hijackers' activities, Sept. 23, 2002; CIA cable, "Activities of Bin Ladin Associate Khalid Revealed," Jan. 4, 2000.

42. Intelligence report, meetings between Khallad and perpetrators of the 9/11 attacks, May 30, 2003.

43. Intelligence report, Activities of Bin Ladin associates, Jan. 2, 2000; CIA cable, "Activities of Bin Ladin Associate Khalid Revealed," Jan. 4, 2000; CIA email, CTC to NSA, Another UBL related report, Jan. 3, 2000.

44. CIA cable, "Activities of Bin Ladin Associate Khalid Revealed," Jan. 4, 2000. His Saudi passport—which contained a visa for travel to the United States—was photocopied and forwarded to CIA headquarters. This information was not shared with FBI headquarters until August 2001. An FBI agent detailed to the Bin Ladin unit at CIA attempted to share this information with colleagues at FBI headquarters. A CIA desk officer instructed him not to send the cable with this information. Several hours later, this same desk officer drafted a cable distributed solely within CIA alleging that the visa documents had been shared with the FBI. She admitted she did not personally share the information and cannot identify who told her they had been shared. We were unable to locate anyone who claimed to have shared the information. Contemporaneous documents contradict the claim that they were shared. DOJ Inspector General interview of Doug M., Feb. 12, 2004; DOJ Inspector General interview of Michael, Oct. 31, 2002; CIA cable, Jan. 5, 2000; DOJ Inspector General report, "A Review of the FBI's Handling of Intelligence Information Related to the 9/11 Attacks," July 2, 2004, p. 282.

45. CIA cables, "Identification of UBL Associate Khalid Transiting Dubai," Jan. 4, 2000; "UBL Associate Travel to Malaysia—Khalid Bin Muhammad bin 'Abdallah al-Mihdhar," Jan. 5, 2000; "Arrival of UBL Associate Khalid Bin Muhammad bin 'Abdallah al-Mihdhar," Jan. 6, 2000.

46. CIA cable, "UBL Associates Travel to Malaysia and Beyond—Khalid Bin Muhammad bin 'Abdallah al-Midhar," Jan. 6, 2000.

47. CIA cable, "UBL Associates Depart Malaysia," Jan. 8, 2000.

48. CIA cable, "UBL Associates: Flight Manifest," Jan. 9, 2000. None of the CIA personnel at CIA headquarters or in the field had checked NSA databases or asked NSA to do so. If this had been done, on the basis of other unreported intelligence associated with the same sources, analysts would have been able to quickly learn "Nawaf" was likely Nawaf al Hazmi. Such analysis was not conducted until after 9/11. After 9/11 it also was determined that Salahsae was part of a name being used by Tawfiq bin Attash, also known as Khallad. One reason he was traveling around East Asia at this time is that he was helping to plan possible hijackings on aircraft in connection with an early idea for what would become the 9/11 plot.

49. CIA cable, "Efforts to Locate al-Midhar," Jan. 13, 2000. We now know that two other al Qaeda operatives flew to Bangkok to meet Khallad to pass him money. See chapter 8. That was not known at the time. Mihdhar was met at the Kuala Lumpur airport by Ahmad Hikmat Shakir, an Iraqi national. Reports that he was a lieutenant colonel in the Iraqi Fedayeen have turned out to be incorrect. They were based on a confusion of Shakir's identity with that of an Iraqi Fedayeen colonel with a similar name, who was later (in September 2001) in Iraq at the same time Shakir was in police custody in Qatar. See CIA briefing by CTC specialists (June 22, 2004); Walter Pincus and Dan Eggen, "Al Qaeda Link to Iraq May Be Confusion over Names," Washington Post, June 22, 2004, p. A13.

50. Richard interview (Dec. 11, 2003); CIA briefing materials, UBL unit briefing slides, Jan. 3–Jan. 14, 2000; Intelligence reports, "UBL Situation Report," Jan. 5, 10, 12, 2000; CIA email, Rob to John and others, "Malaysia—for the record," Jan. 6, 2000.

51. CIA cable, "Efforts to Locate al-Midhar," Jan. 13, 2000.

52. CIA cable, "UBL Associates: Identification of Possible UBL Associates," Feb. 11, 2000.

53. CIA cable, "UBL Associates: Identification of Possible UBL Associates," Mar. 5, 2000. Presumably the departure information was obtained back in January, on the days that these individuals made their departures. Because these names were watchlisted with the Thai authorities, we cannot yet explain the delay in reporting the news. But since nothing was done with this information even in March, we do not attribute much significance to this failure alone.

54. See, e.g., Joint Inquiry testimony of George Tenet, Oct. 17, 2002, pp. 110–112; DOJ Inspector General interview of John, Nov. 1, 2002.

55. CIA briefing, CTC Update, "Islamic Extremist Terrorist Threat," Jan. 5, 7, 2000; George Tenet interview (Jan. 22, 2004). Tenet described the millennium alert as probably the most difficult operational environment the CIA had ever faced.

56. NSC memo, Clarke to Berger, "Post-Millennium Soul Searching," Jan. 11, 2000.

57. NSC memo, "Review of Terrorism Alert and Lessons Learned," Jan. 3, 2000 (draft). This paper is part of a packet Clarke sent to Deputy Attorney General Thompson, copying White House officials, on Sept. 17, 2001.

58. NSC memo, McCarthy to Berger, need for new strategy, Jan. 5, 2000.

59. NSC memo, Kurtz to Berger, roadmap for March 10 PC meeting, Mar. 8, 2000.

60. NSC memo, Cressey to Berger, Summary of Conclusions for March 10, 2000, PC on Millennium After- Action Review, Apr. 3, 2000; Samuel Berger letter to the Commission, "Comments on Staff Statements 5–8," May 13, 2004, p. 9.

61. NSC memo, "The Millennium Terrorist Alert—Next Steps," undated.

62. DOS memo, Sheehan and Inderfurth to Albright, "Pakistan Trip Report—A Counterterrorism Perspective," Jan. 26, 2000; DOS cable, Islamabad 00396, "Inderfurth Delegation Meeting with General Musharraf," Jan. 24, 2000.

63. In February 2000, the CIA began receiving information about a possible Bin Ladin–associated plot to attack Air Force One with Stinger missiles if President Clinton visited Pakistan; this information was deemed credible by early March. The CIA also reviewed reported threats to the President in Bangladesh and India. CIA briefing, "Reported Plan To Attack U.S. Presidential Plane If He Visits Pakistan," Feb. 18, 2000; NSC email, Clarke to Berger, terrorism update, Feb. 29, 2000; CIA briefing, chief of CTC for the President, "Threats to the President's Visit to Asia," Mar. 2, 2000; NSC memo, Kurtz, "Summary of Conclusions of March 14, 2000 Meeting on Clinton Trip to South Asia;" NSC email, Kurtz to Berger, two new threats to assassinate the President in Bangladesh, Mar. 16, 2000. Berger told us that the Secret Service was vehemently opposed to a presidential visit to Islamabad; it took the extraordinary step of meeting twice with the President and offering very serious warnings. Samuel Berger interview (Jan. 14, 2004).

64. President Clinton meeting (Apr. 8, 2004). President Clinton told us he offered Musharraf aid and help in improving U.S.-Pakistani relations. A conversation that day between the two leaders in the presence of several close advisers is described in DOS cable, State 073803, "Memorandum of the President's Conversation with Pervez Musharraf on March 25, 2000," Apr. 19, 2000. A third meeting was apparently held in front of additional aides. Berger told that President Clinton did not want to press the Bin Ladin issue too heavily at the main meeting because ISID (Inter-Services Intelligence Directorate) members were present. Samuel Berger interview (Jan. 14, 2004).

65. NSC email, Camp for Berger, "Musharraf's Proposed Afghanistan Trip," May 8, 2000. Clarke wrote Berger that Musharraf seemed to have "said the right things to Omar." NSC email, Clarke to Berger, May 11, 2000.

66. DOS cable, Islamabad 002902, "Summary of May 26, 2000 Meeting Between Pickering and Musharraf," May 29, 2000.

67. DOS cable, Islamabad 79983, "DCI Meets with Chief Executive General Musharraf," June 21, 2000. Musharraf agreed to create a counterterrorism working group to coordinate efforts between Pakistani agencies and the CIA. Tenet noted that he was not asking the Pakistanis to deliver Bin Ladin next Tuesday; the DCI said he was "ambitious, but not crazy."

68. DOS cable, State 185645, "Concern that Pakistan is Stepping up Support to Taliban's Military Campaign in Afghanistan," Sept. 26, 2000.

69. UN Security Council Resolution (UNSCR) 1333, Dec. 19, 2000. UNSCR 1333 also called for countries to withdraw their officials and agents from the Taliban-held part of Afghanistan. Sheehan said that the new UN sanctions were aimed at the Taliban's primary supporters: Pakistan, Saudi Arabia, and the United Arab Emirates. Michael Sheehan interview (Dec. 16, 2003).

70. Madeleine Albright prepared statement, Mar. 23, 2004, p. 11; Madeleine Albright interview (Jan. 7, 2004).

71. Michael Sheehan interview (Dec. 16, 2003).

72. The CIA appears to have briefed President Clinton on its "Next Steps and New Initiatives" in February 2000, noting the need to hire and train the right officers with the necessary skills and deploy them to the right places, as well as to work with foreign liaison. The CIA noted in its briefing that the President should press foreign leaders to maintain pressure on terrorists. See CIA briefing materials, "Targeting the Terrorists: Next Steps and New Initiatives," Feb. 1, 2000 (for the President); NSC email, Cressey to Berger, "CT Briefing for Clinton," Feb. 8, 2000.

73. For the CTC's perspective, see CIA briefing materials, "Talking Points for the DCI for the Principals Committee meeting on Terrorism: The Millennium Alert—After Action Review," Mar. 9, 2000. Deputy Chief of CTC Ben Bonk noted in the talking points that the CTC had obligated 50 percent of its fiscal year 2000 budget by Jan. 31, 2000, spending about 15 percent of its budget directly on the millennium surge. He stated that without a supplemental, it would be impossible for the CTC to continue at its current pace, let alone increase the operational tempo. On Tenet meeting with Berger, see George Tenet interview (Jan. 28, 2004).

74. Joan Dempsey interview (Nov. 12, 2003); George Tenet interview (Jan. 22, 2004). Tenet called the supple-

mental appropriation "a lifesaver." See, for example, the request for supplemental appropriations in CIA briefing materials, "Targeting the Terrorists: Next Steps and New Initiatives," Feb. 1, 2000 (for the President).

75. Richard Clarke interview (Feb. 3, 2004).

76. James Pavitt interview (Jan. 8, 2004).

77. Richard Clarke interviews (Dec. 18, 2003; Feb. 3, 2004).

78. CIA memos, summary of weekly Berger/Tenet meeting, Apr. 5, 12, 2000; NSC memo, "April 19, 2000 Agenda for Deputies Committee Meeting on CT: The Millennium Threat FY00 and FY01 Budget Review;" NSC memo, "Summary of Conclusions of April 18, 2000 CSG Meeting," Apr. 26, 2000. On May 2, 2000, Berger was updated on budget issues relating to the CIA and other agencies; there was agreement on the most critical items to be funded, but not on the source of that funding. In CIA's case, it had already reprogrammed over $90 million, but Tenet wanted to use most of this money on non-counterterrorism programs. NSC memo, Kurtz to Berger, "Budget Issues," May 2, 2000. On June 29, 2000, the President authorized raising the CIA's covert action funding ceiling. NSC memo, McCarthy to CSG, "DCI Wants to Raise Funding Ceiling," May 8, 2000; NSC memo, McCarthy to others July 7, 2000 (appendix on authorities). But funding issues in other agencies remained unresolved. Clarke complained that neither Treasury nor Justice would identify offsets. Clarke encouraged OMB to tell both departments that if they would not identify offsets then OMB would. NSC email, Clarke to Rudman and Mitchell, May 9, 2000. On August 1, 2000, Clarke wrote Berger that one of five goals by the end of the Clinton administration was to secure appropriations for cybersecurity and millennium after-action review projects. NSC memo, Clarke to Berger, "Goals and Wildcards," Aug. 1, 2000. As late as September 2000, Clarke was advising Berger that unfunded counterterrorism requests continued to be his number one priority. NSC note, Clarke to Berger, Sept. 9, 2000.

79. Executive Order 13099 (Aug. 20, 1998); Rick Newcomb interview (Feb. 4, 2004); Robert McBride interview (Nov. 19–20, 2003); NSC memo, Kurtz to Berger, June 28, 2000. OFAC did freeze accounts belonging to Salah Idris, the owner of the al Shifa facility bombed in response to the East Africa embassy bombings. Idris filed suit against his bank and OFAC. OFAC subsequently authorized the unfreezing of those accounts. James Risen, "To Bomb Sudan Plant, or Not: A Year Later, Debates Rankle," *New York Times*, Oct. 27, 1999, p. A1. The inability to freeze funds is attributed in part to a lack of intelligence on the location of Bin Ladin's money, OFAC's reluctance or inability to rely on what classified information there may have been, and Bin Ladin's transfer of assets into the hands of trusted third parties or out of the formal financial system by 1998. Even if OFAC had received better intelligence from the intelligence community, it would have been powerless to stop the bulk of the problem. Al Qaeda money flows depended on an informal network of hawalas and Islamic institutions moving money from Gulf supporters to Afghanistan. These funds would not therefore have touched the U.S. formal financial system. OFAC's authorities are only against U.S. persons, financial institutions, and businesses. Frank G. and Mary S. briefing (July 15, 2003); Rick Newcomb interview (Feb. 4, 2003).

80. Executive Order 13129; Treasury memo, Newcomb to Johnson, "Blocking of Taliban-Controlled Assets," undated (probably Oct. 18, 1999).

81. DOS cable, State 184471, Sept. 30, 1999; 18 U.S.C. § 2339B.

82. The Financial Action Task Force, a multilateral government organization dedicated to standard setting, focused on money laundering, particularly as it related to crimes such as drug trafficking and large-scale fraud that involved vast amounts of illegally procured money. Although the UN General Assembly adopted the International Convention for the Suppression of Financing Terrorism in December 1999, the convention did not enter into force until April 2002.

83. Doug M. interview (Dec. 16, 2003); Frank G. interview (Mar. 2, 2004). See also Mike interview (Dec. 11, 2003), setting forth the goals of the UBL station; none relate specifically to terrorist financing. Another witness recalled that the UBL station made some effort to gather intelligence on al Qaeda financing, but it proved to be too hard a target, the CIA had too few sources and, as a result, little quality intelligence was produced. Ed G. interview (Feb. 3, 2004). Some attributed the problem to the CIA's separation of terrorist-financing analysis from other counterterrorism activities. Within the Directorate of Intelligence, a group was devoted to the analysis of all financial issues, including terrorist financing. Called the Office of Transnational Issues (OTI), Illicit Transaction Groups (ITG), it dealt with an array of issues besides terrorist financing, including drug trafficking, drug money laundering, alien smuggling, sanctions, and corruption. ITG was not part of the CTC, although it rotated a single analyst to CTC. Moreover, OTI analysts were separated from the operational side of terrorist financing at CTC, which planned operations against banks and financial facilitators. William Wechsler interview (Jan. 7, 2004); Frank G. and Mary S. briefing (July 15, 2003).

84. CIA analytic report, "Funding Islamic Extremist Movements: The Role of Islamic Financial Institutions," OTI 97-10035CX, Dec. 1997.

85. Mike interview (Dec. 11, 2003).

86. CIA analytic reports, "Usama Bin Ladin: Some Saudi Financial Ties Probably Intact," OTI IR 99-005CX, Jan. 11, 1999; "How Bin Ladin Commands a Global Terrorist Network," CTC 99-40003, Jan. 27, 1999; "Islamic Terrorists: Using Nongovernmental Organizations Extensively," CTC 99-40007, Apr. 9, 1999.

87. See NSC memo, Kurtz to Berger, June 28, 2000; NSC document, TNT to Berger, Nov. 3, 1998, roadmap for Small Group, undated. The problem continued until 9/11. Intelligence reporting was so limited that one CIA intelligence analyst told us that, unassisted, he could read and digest the universe of intelligence reporting on al Qaeda financial issues in the three years prior to the 9/11 attacks. Frank G. and Mary S. briefing (July 15, 2003).

88. Richard Clarke interview (Feb. 3, 2004); see, e.g., NSC memo, Clarke to CSG, "Concept of Operations for Task Force Test of the Foreign Terrorist Asset Tracking Center," Nov. 1, 2000; Treasury memo, Romey to Sloan, "FTAT SCIF," May 17, 2001; Treasury memo, Newcomb to Sloan, "Response to Romey Memo," May 23, 2001. Despite post-9/11 declarations to the contrary, on the eve of 9/11 FTAT had funds appropriated, but no people hired, no security clearances, and no space to work. Treasury memo, Newcomb to Dam, "Establishing the Foreign Asset Tracking Center," Aug. 3, 2001. One Treasury official described CIA's posture as "benign neglect" toward the Foreign Terrorist Asset Tracking Center (FTATC), and characterized the CIA as believing that financial tracking had limited utility. Treasury memo, Mat Burrows to O'Neill, "Your PC on Counterterrorism on 4 September," Sept. 4, 2001. National Security Advisor Rice told us she and her staff had determined by spring 2001 that terrorist financing proposals were a good option, so Treasury continued to plan to establish an office for 24 financing analysts. Condoleezza Rice meeting (Feb. 7, 2004). In fact, as noted above, Treasury failed to follow through on the establishment of the FTATC until after 9/11.

89. This assessment is based on an extensive review of FBI files and interviews with agents and supervisors at FBI Headquarters and various field offices.

90. Although there was an increased focus on money laundering, several significant legislative and regulatory initiatives designed to close vulnerabilities in the U.S. financial system failed to gain traction. Some of these, such as a move to control foreign banks with accounts in the United States, died as a result of banking industry pressure. Others, such as the regulation of money remitters within the United States, were mired in bureaucratic inertia and a general antiregulatory environment. In any event, it is an open question whether such legislative or regulatory initiatives would have significantly harmed al Qaeda, which generally made little use of the U.S. financial system to move or store its money.

91. Treasury report, "The 2001 National Money Laundering Strategy," Sept. 2001.

92. NSC email, Berger's office to executive secretaries, "Millennium Alert After Action Review," Mar. 9, 2000.

93. PDD-62, "Protection Against Unconventional Threats to the Homeland and Americans Overseas," May 22, 1998, pp. 8–9; NSC email, Berger's office to executive secretaries, "Millennium Alert After Action Review," Mar. 9, 2000.

94. PDD-62, May 22, 1998; PDD-39, "U.S. Policy on Counterterrorism," June 21, 1995, p. 2.

95. NSC email, Berger's office to executive secretaries, "Millennium Alert After Action Review," Mar. 9, 2000.

96. PDD-62, May 22, 1998, p. 9. Congress had authorized the Alien Terrorist Removal Court at the request of the Justice Department in 1996, and it was established in 1997. Clarke noted the court had not been "highly useful." NSC email, Berger's office to executive secretaries, "Millennium Alert After Action Review," Mar. 9, 2000. Indeed, it had not been used at all.

97. PDD-62, May 22, 1998, p. 8; NSC memo, Clarke, "Summary of Conclusions for March 31, 2000 Millennium Alert Immigration Review Meeting," Apr. 13, 2000. One provision from PDD-62 *not* updated and reiterated in 2000 was a directive to CIA to ensure that names (and aliases) of terrorists were collected and disseminated to State, INS, and the FBI in a timely way, so that the border agencies could place them on a watchlist and the FBI could identify them in the United States.

98. NSC email, Berger's office to executive secretaries, "Millennium Alert After Action Review," Mar. 9, 2000.

99. Richard Clarke interview (Feb. 3, 2004); Samuel Berger interview (Jan. 14, 2004); Scott Fry interview (Dec. 29, 2003); Scott Gration interview (March 3, 2004); NSC email, Clarke to Berger, Mar. 2, 2000. Clarke apparently took the comment as a presidential instruction to take another look at what additional actions could be taken against Bin Ladin. Given diplomatic failures to directly pressure the Taliban through Pakistan, the NSC staff saw increased support to the Northern Alliance and Uzbeks as alternative options. NSC memo, "The Millennium Terrorist Alert— Next Steps," undated.

100. A good account of the episode is found in Steve Coll, *Ghost Wars: The Secret History of the CIA, Afghanistan, and bin Laden, from the Soviet Invasion to September 10, 2001* (Penguin, 2004), pp. 487–491; see also ibid., pp. 495–496, 502–503, 517–519; Richard interview (Dec. 11, 2003). "Richard" told us the attack had already occurred when CIA headquarters heard about it; "within this building, they were breathless," he remarked. The CIA concern was apparently over possible casualties and whether, by sharing intelligence with Massoud on Bin Ladin's possible location, the CIA might have violated the assassination ban. Tenet did not recall the incident, saying it was no doubt just "a blip" on his screen within the context of the millennium alerts. George Tenet interview (Jan. 22, 2004). The incident was, however, noticed by the NSC counterterrorism staff, which pointedly asked to be kept in the loop in the future. NSC memo, "Review of Terrorism Alert and Lessons Learned," Jan. 3, 2000 (draft).

101. See, e.g., CIA officers' visits to Tashkent noted in CIA briefing materials, DCI Update, "Islamic Extremist Terrorist Threat," Feb. 18, 2000; CIA briefing materials, EXDIR Update, Visit to Tashkent, Apr. 5, 2000. CTC teams were deployed to Afghanistan to meet with Massoud on March 13–21, 2000, and possibly on April 24–28,

2000. CIA briefing materials, EXDIR Update, "Islamic Extremist Terrorist Threat," Mar. 6, 2000; CIA briefing materials, "CTC PowerPoint," Apr. 3, 2000. Massoud's representatives also met with Clarke, the State Department's Michael Sheehan, and CIA senior managers in Washington. CIA briefing materials, "DDO Update," May 22, 2000.

102. On Black and Clarke's positions, see Cofer Black interview (Dec. 9, 2003); Roger Cressey interview (Dec. 15, 2003). On reasons for caution, see, e.g., Strobe Talbott interview (Jan. 15, 2004).

103. See, e.g., CIA briefing materials, CTC Update for the DDCI, July 7, 2000 ("Direct engagement with Massoud will enhance our ability to report on UBL and increase retaliation options if . . . we are attacked by UBL").

104. The deputy chief for operations of CTC, "Henry," told us that going into the Afghanistan sanctuary was essential. He and Black proposed direct engagement with Massoud to the CIA's senior management, but the idea was rejected because of what "Henry" called "a question of resources"—the CIA did not have effective means to get personnel in or out of Afghanistan. When he proposed sending a CIA team into northern Afghanistan to meet with Massoud in August 2000, the idea was turned down; local helicopters were not deemed airworthy, and land access was too risky. Henry interview (Nov. 18, 2003); Henry briefing (Apr. 22, 2004).

105. The alleged attempt was reported on August 10, 2000; see CIA memo, Bonk to McCarthy and Clarke, "Attempted Interdiction of Suspect Bin Ladin's Convoy," Aug. 11, 2000. For doubts as to whether the tribals made this attempt, see Cofer Black interview (Dec. 9, 2003); Richard interview (Dec. 11, 2003).

106. The Joint Chiefs of Staff Warning Order of July 6, 1999, was still in effect. See DOD memo, "Military Response Options," Oct. 23, 2000.

107. The 13 options included B-2 bombers, missiles, AC-130 gunships, the armed UAV, and raids to capture and destroy al Qaeda leaders and targets. DOD briefing materials, Joint Chiefs of Staff, "Operation Infinite Resolve Brief," June 2000.

108. Scott Gration interview (Mar. 3, 2004). See also Scott Fry interview (Dec. 29, 2003).

109. This quotation is taken from Daniel Benjamin and Steven Simon, *The Age of Sacred Terror* (Random House, 2002), p. 318. President Clinton confirmed that he made this statement. President Clinton meeting (Apr. 8, 2004).

110. President Clinton meeting (Apr. 8, 2004); Hugh Shelton interview (Feb. 5, 2004); William Cohen interview (Feb. 5, 2004).

111. Scott Gration interview (Mar. 3, 2004); Scott Fry interview (Dec. 29, 2003).

112. NSC memo, Clarke to CSG members, "Follow-Up to bin Ladin Review," Apr. 25, 2000. See also CIA briefing materials, "DDCI Update," Apr. 21, 2000 (J-39 "has decided to do everything possible to support CIA's UBL efforts"). This reportedly included J-39's belief that it would be able to pay for all costs—though, as it turned out, that would not be the case. CIA managers were reluctant to go ahead with either the telescope or the Predator options. Executive Director David Carey told us they saw the projects as a "distraction" that would pull personnel and resources away from other, high-priority activities, such as worldwide disruptions. The telescope program, for instance, was considered too challenging and risky for the CIA's Afghan assets; development continued through the summer, but the idea was eventually dropped. David Carey interview (Oct. 31, 2003); Scott Fry interview (Dec. 29, 2003); Scott Gration interview (Mar. 3, 2004).

113. According to Charles Allen, the CIA's senior management, especially within the Directorate of Operations, was originally averse to the Predator program mostly because of the expense—approximately $3 million, which the directorate claimed it did not have. Charles Allen interview (Jan. 27, 2004). The argument between CIA and DOD over who would pay for proposed operations continued for months. On the CIA side see, for example, CIA briefing materials, "DDO Update," May 22, 26, 2000 (at which the DCI was told that unless funding was identified within the next 10 days, the military advised that the Predator could not be deployed that fiscal year; the military was waiting for an NSC request that it fund the projects). See also NSC memo, Clarke to Tenet, June 25, 2000 ("The other CSG agencies are unanimous that the Predator project is our highest near-term priority and that funding should be shifted to it"). Clarke noted that the CSG plan was to use DOD money to jump-start the program. On the cost-sharing agreement, see NSC memo, Kurtz to Berger, June 28, 2000; NSC memo, "Small Group agenda," June 29, 2000. Eventually, "after some pushing," the CIA found $2 million from its funds to pay for two months of trial flights. DOD agreed to fund $2.4 million. NSC memo, Kurtz to Berger, June 28, 2000.

114. NSC memo, Kurtz to Berger, June 28, 2000. On UAV tests, see CIA briefing materials, "DCI Update," July 14, 2000. On modifications, see NSC memo, Clarke to Berger, update, July 18, 2000.

115. NSC memo, Clarke to Berger, "Predator," Aug. 11, 2000.

116. NSC memo, Cressey to Berger, Aug. 18, 2000 (underlining in the original); NSC memo, Cressey to Berger, Aug. 21, 2000 (attaching informational memo to President Clinton).

117. NSC note, Clarke to Berger, Sept. 9, 2000.

118. John Maher III interview (Apr. 22, 2004). The CIA's Ben Bonk told us he could not guarantee from analysis of the video feed that the man in the white robe was in fact Bin Ladin, but he thinks Bin Ladin is the "highest probability person." (Bin Ladin is unusually tall.) Ben Bonk briefing (Mar. 11, 2004). Intelligence analysts seem to have determined this might have been Bin Ladin very soon after the September 28 sighting; two days later, Clarke wrote to Berger that there was a "very high probability" Bin Ladin had been located. NSC note, Clarke to Berger, "Procedures for Protecting Predator," Sept. 30, 2000.

119. NSC note, Clarke to Berger, "Procedures for Protecting Predator," Sept. 30, 2000. Clarke pointed to a silver lining: "The fact that its existence has become at least partially known, may for a while change the al Qida movement patterns," he wrote, but "it may also serve as a healthy reminder to al Qida and the Taliban that they are not out of our thoughts or sight." Ibid.

120. Clarke wrote to Berger that "it might be a little gloomy sitting around the fire with the al Qida leadership these days." NSC note, Clarke to Berger, Sept. 9, 2000.

121. For the number of dead and wounded, see Indictment, *United States v. Jamal Ahmed Mohammed Ali al-Badawi*, No. S12 98 Cr. 1023 (KTD) (S.D. N.Y. filed May 15, 2003), p. 16.

122. See Intelligence report, interrogation of Abd al Rahim al Nashiri, Feb. 21, 2004. For Khallad, see Intelligence report, interrogation of Khallad, Aug. 20, 2003. For Khamri and Nibras's full names, Quso's responsibility to film the attack, and Nibras and Quso delivering money, see Indictment, *United States v. al-Badawi*, May 15, 2003, pp. 13–14. Badawi was supposed to film the attack but had to travel, so he instructed Quso to do it instead. FBI notes, notes of Nov. 11 and 13 executive conference call, Nov. 13, 2000, p. 2. For Quso's admission of delivering money, see Al S. interviews (Aug. 26, 2003; Sept. 15, 2003).

123. For Bin Ladin's decision, Nashiri's trip to protest, and Nashiri's instructions, see Intelligence report, interrogation of Nashiri, Feb. 21, 2004. For a report that Nashiri did not instruct the operatives to attack, see Intelligence report, interrogation of Nashiri, Nov. 21, 2002.

124. For the attack, see Indictment, *United States v. al-Badawi*, May 15, 2003, p. 16. For Quso not filming the attack, see FBI report of investigation, interview of Fahd Mohammed Ahmad al-Quso, Feb. 3, 2001, p. 8. Quso apparently fell asleep and missed the attack. See FBI notes, notes of Nov. 11 and 13 executive conference call, Nov. 13, 2000, p. 2.

125. For Bin Ladin's order to evacuate and subsequent actions, see Intelligence report, interrogation of Abu Zubaydah, Dec. 13, 2003. For Bin Ladin's, Atef's, and Zawahiri's movements, see Intelligence report, interrogation of Khallad, Sept. 27, 2003.

126. Intelligence report, Terrorism Activities, Oct. 1, 2001.

127. For the media committee, the video, and its effect, see Intelligence report, autobiography of KSM, July 12, 2003; Intelligence report, interrogation of KSM, Apr. 4, 2003. On the bombing of the *Cole* sparking jihadist recruitment, see Intelligence report, interrogation of Khallad, Sept. 5, 2003.

128. See Barbara Bodine interview (Oct. 21, 2003); Al S. interviews (Aug. 26, 2003; Sept. 15, 2003). On the problems with having Americans bring firearms into the country, see also NSC email, Clarke to Berger, USS *Cole*—situation report for PC meeting, Oct. 13, 2000. U.S. officials cannot travel to a country without the clearance of the U.S. ambassador to that country.

129. For suspicion of Egyptian Islamic Jihad, see NSC memo, Berger to President Clinton, update on *Cole* attack, Oct. 12, 2000. For McLaughlin's statement, see John McLaughlin interview (Jan. 21, 2004). In this vein, the State Department advised the investigation not to rush to judgment that al Qaeda was responsible. Barbara Bodine interview (Oct. 21, 2003).

130. For Yemen barring the FBI, see Al S. interviews (Aug. 26, 2003; Sept. 15, 2003). For the CIA's characterization, see CIA report, threat to U.S. personnel in Yemen, Oct. 18, 2000. For the high-level interventions, see Samuel Berger interview (Jan. 14, 2004); Kenneth Pollack interview (Sept. 24, 2003); CIA cable, CIA talking points for Tenet's call to chief of Yemen intelligence, Oct. 26, 2000. On secondhand information, see John McLaughlin interview (Jan. 21, 2004).

131. FBI notes, notes of Nov. 11 and 13 executive conference call, Nov. 13, 2000; FBI electronic communication, "Summary of information from Yemen intelligence," Jan. 10, 2001.

132. For the FBI agent's role, see Al S. interviews (Aug. 26, 2003; Sept. 15, 2003). For Yemen providing the photograph, see FBI electronic communication, "Summary of information from Yemen intelligence," Jan. 10, 2001. For the source identifying the photograph, see FBI electronic communication, "Source reporting on al Qaeda," Jan. 16, 2001.

133. For Khallad's involvement in the embassy bombings, see FBI report of investigation, interview of Mohammad Rashed Daoud al Owhali, Sept. 9, 1998. For Yemen identifying Nashiri, see FBI electronic communication, "Information provided by Yemen intelligence," Dec. 17, 2000.

134. Richard Clarke interview (Feb. 3, 2004). Richard Miniter offers an account of the Clinton administration's deliberations about the *Cole* in Richard Miniter, *Losing Bin Laden: How Bill Clinton's Failures Unleashed Global Terror* (Regnery, 2003), pp. 222–227. Berger told us the account is "a crock." Samuel Berger interview (Jan. 14, 2004). Clarke was less critical. Richard Clarke interview (Feb. 3, 2004).

135. For the additional covert action authorities, see NSC memo, McCarthy to Berger, new covert action authorities, Oct. 31, 2000. For Tenet developing options, see NSC memo, Berger to President Clinton, update on *Cole* investigation, Nov. 25, 2000.

136. For Berger's authorization, see NSC memo, TNT to Berger, responding to Taliban's September overture, Oct. 20, 2000. For Berger's statement, see NSC memo, Berger to TNT, reply to Oct. 20, 2000, memo. For the admin-

istration working with Russia, see NSC memo, Berger to President Clinton, update on *Cole* investigation, Nov. 25, 2000.

137. President Clinton meeting (Apr. 8, 2004).

138. Samuel Berger interview (Jan. 14, 2004).

139. In the first ten days after the bombing, between October 13 and 23, at least three high-level briefing items discussed responsibility for the attack. The next such briefing item we can find summarized the evidence for the new Bush administration on January 25, 2001. On the guidance, and the presumed reasons for it, see Barbara Bodine interview (Oct. 21, 2003); Pattie Kindsvater interview (Mar. 29, 2004); Ben Bonk statement during John McLaughlin interview (Jan. 21, 2004); see also John McLaughlin interview (Jan. 21, 2004); Richard interview (Dec. 11, 2003).

140. For Clarke's statement, see NSC email, Clarke to Berger, Nov. 7, 2000. For the November 10 briefing, see CIA briefing materials, preliminary findings regarding the *Cole* attack for the Nov. 10, 2000, Small Group meeting, undated (appears to be Nov. 10, 2000). For Berger and Clarke's communication with the President, see NSC memo, Berger to President Clinton, USS *Cole* investigation update, Nov. 25, 2000.

141. See Gregory Newbold interview (Sept. 29, 2003); William Cohen interview (Feb. 5, 2004). For Shelton tasking Franks, see DOD memo, Joint Chiefs of Staff tasking, Mod 005 to Joint Planning Directive to U.S. Central Command, Nov. 30, 2000. For Shelton briefing Berger, see NSC memo, Berger to President Clinton, USS *Cole* investigation update, Nov. 25, 2000. For the 13 options, see also DOD briefing materials, Operation Infinite Resolve Contingency Plan Brief, undated. For the briefing to Kerrick, see DOD briefing materials, briefing to Lt. Gen. Kerrick, Dec. 20, 2000. For the briefing of other DOD officials, see DOD briefing materials, "Evolution of Infinite Resolve Planning, Summary of TLAM Availability (1998–2001), Evolution of the Armed Predator Program," Mar. 19, 2004, p. 5.

142. NSC memo, Berger to President Clinton, USS *Cole* investigation update, Nov. 25, 2000.

143. Ibid. For Clarke's ideas, see NSC memo, Clarke to Sheehan and Hull, "Ultimatum Strategy with the Taliban," Nov. 25, 2000.

144. CIA briefing materials, "Intelligence Assessment: The Attack on the USS Cole," Dec. 21, 2000.

145. Ibid.

146. President Clinton meeting (Apr. 8, 2004); Samuel Berger interview (Jan. 14, 2004).

147. For Albright's advisers, see DOS memo, Inderfurth to Albright, Dec. 19, 2000; DOS memo, Hull and Eastham to Albright, preparation for Principals Committee meeting, Dec. 21, 2000. See also DOS briefing materials, talking points for Principals Committee meeting, Dec. 21, 2000; William Cohen interview (Feb. 5, 2004); Hugh Shelton interview (Feb. 5, 2004).

148. Richard Clarke interview (Feb. 3, 2004)

149. Richard Clarke, *Against All Enemies: Inside America's War on Terror* (Free Press, 2004), p. 224. Sheehan has not disavowed Clarke's quote.

150. George Tenet interview (Jan. 28, 2004).

151. Pattie Kindsvater interview (Mar. 29, 2004). For Clarke's awareness, see NSC email, Clarke to Cressey, "Considerations," Oct. 25, 2000.

152. For the lack of meaningful targets, see Scott Fry interview (Dec. 29, 2003); Walter Slocombe interview (Dec. 19, 2003).

153. CIA memo, Black to Clarke, "NSC Requests on Approaches for Dealing with Problems in Afghanistan," Dec. 29, 2000.

154. See Samuel Berger letter to the Commission, "Comments on Staff Statements 5–8," May 13, 2004. For the Blue Sky memorandum's proposals being rolled into proposals considered by the new administration, see George Tenet interview (Jan. 28, 2004); John McLaughlin interview (Jan. 21, 2004). On the internal CIA draft of the Blue Sky memorandum, Deputy Director for Operations James Pavitt added a handwritten note that he posed no objection if the memorandum was for transition discussion purposes, but "I do not believe a proposal of this magnitude should be on the table for implementation" so late in the Clinton administration. He also questioned the proposal for support to Massoud. CIA memo, "Options to Undermine Usama Bin Ladin and al-Qa'ida," Dec. 18, 2000.

155. NSC memo, "Strategy for Eliminating the Threat from the Jihadist Networks of al Qida: Status and Prospects," undated (appears to be Dec. 29, 2001), attached to NSC memo, Clarke to Rice, Jan. 25, 2001.

156. Ben Bonk interview (Jan. 21, 2004); John McLaughlin interview (Jan. 21, 2004).

157. Robert McNamara, Jr., interview (Apr. 19, 2004).

158. President Bush and Vice President Cheney meeting (Apr. 29, 2004); Condoleezza Rice meeting (Feb. 7, 2004); James Pavitt interview (Jan. 8, 2004). Pavitt also recalls telling the President-elect that killing Bin Ladin would not end the threat. Vice President–elect Cheney, Rice, Hadley, and White House Chief of Staff–designate Andrew Card also attended the briefing, which took place about a week before the inauguration. The President noted that Tenet did not say he did not have authority to kill Bin Ladin. Tenet told us he recalled the meeting with Bush but not what he said to the President-elect. George Tenet interview (Jan. 28, 2004). He told us, however, that if circumstances changed and he needed more authority, he would have come back to either President Clinton or Pres-

ident Bush and asked for the additional authority. See George Tenet testimony, Mar. 24, 2004. The Blair House CIA briefing is recounted in some detail in Bob Woodward, *Bush at War* (Simon & Schuster, 2002), pp. 34–35.

159. President Clinton meeting (Apr. 8, 2004).

160. President Bush and Vice President Cheney meeting (Apr. 29, 2004).

161. NSC briefing materials, "CT Briefing for Bush-Cheney Transition Team, APNSA-Designate Rice, "Policy, Organization, Priorities," undated. Powell was briefed by the full CSG, at his request.

162. Richard Clarke interview (Feb. 3, 2004); Samuel Berger interview (Jan. 14, 2004); Condoleezza Rice meeting (Feb. 7, 2004); Roger Cressey interview (Dec. 15, 2003); Paul Kurtz interviews (Dec. 16, 2003; Dec. 22, 2003).

163. Condoleezza Rice meeting (Feb. 7, 2004); Stephen Hadley meeting (Jan. 31, 2004). Hadley told us that he was able to do less policy development than in a normal two-month transition.

164. Public references by candidate and then President Bush about terrorism before 9/11 tended to reflect these priorities, focusing on state-sponsored terrorism and WMD as a reason to mount a missile defense. See, e.g., President Bush remarks, Warsaw University, June 15, 2001.

165. Rice and Zelikow had been colleagues on the NSC staff during the first Bush administration and were coauthors of a book concerning German unification. See Philip Zelikow and Condoleezza Rice, *Germany Unified and Europe Transformed: A Study in Statecraft* (Harvard Univ. Press, 1995). As the Executive Director of the Commission, Zelikow has recused himself from our work on the Clinton-Bush transition at the National Security Council.

166. Philip Zelikow interview (Oct. 8, 2003).

167. Condoleezza Rice meeting (Feb. 7, 2004).

168. Ibid.

169. Richard Clarke interviews (Dec. 18, 2003; Feb. 3, 2004); Roger Cressey interview (Dec. 15, 2003). As Clarke put it, "There goes our ability to get quick decisions." Richard Clarke interview (Feb. 3, 2004). However, Paul Kurtz told the Commission that even though Clarke complained about losing his seat on the Principals Committee on terrorism issues, Kurtz saw no functional change in Clarke's status. Paul Kurtz interviews (Dec. 16, 2003; Dec. 22, 2003).

170. President Bush and Vice President Cheney meeting (Apr. 29, 2004); George Tenet interview (Jan. 28, 2004).

171. President Bush and Vice President Cheney meeting (Apr. 29, 2004).

172. NSC memo, Clarke to Rice, al Qaeda review, Jan. 25, 2001 (italics and underlining of the word *urgently* in original). Clarke's staff called on other occasions for early Principals Committee decisions, including in a "100 Day Plan" that called for cabinet-level decisions on the Northern Alliance, Uzbekistan, Predator, and the *Cole*. See NSC memo, Fenzel to Rice, Feb. 16, 2001. Other requests for early PCs are found in NSC email, Fenzel to Hadley, "Early PC Meeting Priorities," Feb. 2, 2001; NSC email, Cressey to NSC Front Office, "TNT Meeting Priorities," Feb. 7, 2001; NSC email, Cressey to Moran, "Aid to NA," Feb. 12, 2001; NSC memo, Cressey to Rice, Mar. 2, 2001.

173. NSC memo, Clarke to Rice, al Qaeda review, Jan. 25, 2001.

174. The Bush administration held 32 Principals Committee meetings on subjects other than al Qaeda before 9/11. Condoleezza Rice testimony, Apr. 8, 2004; White House information provided to the Commission. Rice told us the Administration did not need a principals meeting on al Qaeda because it knew that al Qaeda was a major threat. Condoleezza Rice meeting (Feb. 7, 2004) Condoleezza Rice testimony, Apr. 8, 2004.

175. CNN broadcast, "CNN Ahead of the Curve," Oct. 13, 2000. Vice presidential candidate Dick Cheney also urged swift retaliation against those responsible for bombing the destroyer, saying: "Any would-be terrorist out there needs to know that if you're going to attack, you'll be hit very hard and very quick. It's not time for diplomacy and debate. It's time for action." Associated Press, "Cheney: Swift Retaliation Needed," Oct. 13, 2000.

176. George Tenet interview (Jan. 28, 2004).

177. NSC memo, Clarke to Rice, al Qaeda review, Jan. 25, 2001.

178. NSC memo, Clarke to Vice President Cheney, Feb. 15, 2001.

179. CIA briefing materials, "UBL Strategic Overview and USS COLE Attack Update," Mar. 27, 2001. These briefing slides appear to have been recycled from slides prepared on Jan. 10, 2001.

180. In early March, Cressey wrote Rice and Hadley that at a belated wedding reception at Tarnak Farms for one of Bin Ladin's sons, the al Qaeda leader had read a new poem gloating about the attack on the *Cole*. NSC email, Cressey to Rice and Hadley, "BIN LADIN on the USS COLE," Mar. 2, 2001. A few weeks later, Cressey wrote Hadley that while the law enforcement investigation went on, "we know all we need to about who did the attack to make a policy decision." NSC email, Cressey to Hadley, "Need for Terrorism DC Next Week," Mar. 22, 2001. Around this time, Clarke wrote Rice and Hadley that the Yemeni prime minister had told State Department counterterrorism chief Hull that while Yemen was not saying so publicly, Yemen was 99 percent certain that Bin Ladin was responsible for the *Cole*. NSC email, Clarke to NSC Front Office, "Yemen's View on the USS Cole," Mar. 24, 2001. In June, Clarke wrote Rice and Hadley that a new al Qaeda video claimed responsibility for the *Cole*. NSC email, Clarke to Rice and Hadley, "Al Qida Video Claims Responsibility for Cole Attack," June 21, 2001. Later that month, two Saudi jihadists arrested by Bahraini authorities during the threat spike told their captors that their al Qaeda training camps in Afghanistan had held celebratory parties over the *Cole* attack. NSC email,

Clarke to NSC Front Office and others, "Captured Al Qida Terrorist Met UBL Then Were to Attack US in Saudi Arabia," June 29, 2001.

181. President Bush and Vice President Cheney meeting (Apr. 29, 2004).

182. Condoleezza Rice meeting (Feb. 7, 2004); Donald Rumsfeld meeting (Jan. 30, 2004); Paul Wolfowitz interview (Jan. 20, 2004); Stephen Hadley meeting (Jan. 31, 2004).

183. See CIA memo, "History of Funding for CIA Counterterrorism," Aug. 12, 2002. One of Clarke's concerns had been the level of funding for counterterrorism in the new administration's first budget. See, e.g., NSC memo, Clarke to Vice President Cheney, Feb. 15, 2001.

184. NSC note to Hadley, undated (attached to NSC memo, Cressey to Rice, aid to Northern Alliance and Uzbekistan, Mar. 2, 2001).

185. Condoleezza Rice meeting (Feb. 7, 2004). Rice remembered President Bush using this phrase in May 2001, when warnings of terrorist threats began to multiply. However, speaking on background to the press in August 2002, Richard Clarke described a directive from the President in March 2001 to "stop swatting at flies" and "just solve this problem." A reporter then said to Clarke that he understood Bush to have given that direction in May, and Clarke said: "No, it was March." Fox News transcript, "Clarke Praises Bush Team in '02," Mar. 24, 2004 (online at www.foxnews.com/printer_friendly_story/0,3566,115085,00.html).

186. Barton Gellman, "A Strategy's Cautious Evolution: Before Sept. 11, the Bush Anti-Terror Effort Was Mostly Ambition," *Washington Post*, Jan. 20, 2001, p. A1.

187. President Bush and Vice President Cheney meeting (Apr. 29, 2004).

188. NSC notes, John Bellinger notes from March 7, 2001, meeting; NSC email, Cressey to Rice and Hadley, "BIN LADIN on the USS COLE," Mar. 2, 2001; CIA briefing materials, Deputies Committee Briefing, "Countering the Threat from al-Qa'ida," Mar. 7, 2001.

189. Condoleezza Rice meeting (Feb. 7, 2004). On the Iraq PC, see Bob Woodward, *Plan of Attack* (Simon & Schuster, 2004), p. 13. On the Sudan PC, see NSC memo, "Summary of Conclusions for March 27, 2001 Principals Committee Meeting on Sudan," Apr. 10, 2001; CIA notes, Houdek's notes on March 27, 2001, Principals Committee meeting. On others, see NSC document, list of meetings, Jan. 20 to Sept. 11, 2001, undated.

190. CIA briefing materials, "U.S. Policy Against Al Qa'ida" (for the Apr. 30, 2001, Deputies Committee meeting). On the DC meeting, see also NSC email, Clarke to NSC Front Office, "Request for DC on al Qida Terrorism," Apr. 16, 2001. DCI Tenet had already talked with Rice and Hadley about Bin Ladin and al Qaeda, the Taliban, and the Predator program. See, e.g., CIA memos, summary of weekly Rice/Tenet meeting, Jan. 24, 2001; Feb. 7, 2001; Mar. 8, 2001 (when Rice received CIA assessments on the possible impact of Taliban actions against al Qaeda and on the likely regional impact of increased aid to anti-Taliban groups in Afghanistan). Both Secretary Powell and Secretary Rumsfeld appear to have already been briefed on these topics by the DCI as well. See, e.g., CIA briefing materials, talking points on the Predator for DCI meeting with Rumsfeld, Feb. 9, 2001; CIA briefing materials, talking points on Bin Ladin, the Taliban and Afghanistan for DCI meetings with Powell, Feb. 13, 2001; Mar. 13, 2001.

191. NSC memo, Summary of Conclusions for Apr. 30, 2001, Deputies Committee meeting.

192. Ibid.

193. NSC memo, Policy Coordinating Committee (PCC) Chairman's Summary Paper, "Key Issues for Al-Qida Deputies Meeting," Apr. 19, 2001.

194. For threats considered by the CSG, see NSC memo, agenda for March 19 CSG videoconference, Mar. 19, 2001 (agenda item about UBL interest in targeting a passenger plane at Chicago airport); NSC memo, agenda for CSG threat videoconference, May 17, 2001 (agenda item, "UBL: Operation Planned in US"). For Clarke's concern about an al Qaeda presence in the United States, see NSC briefing materials, TNT to Rice, counterterrorism briefing for Bush/Cheney transition team, undated, which noted that al Qaeda had "sleeper cells" in more than 40 countries, including the United States; NSC memo, "Strategy for Eliminating the Threat from the Jihadist Networks of al Qida: Status and Prospects," undated (appears to be Dec. 29, 2000), attached to NSC memo, Clarke to Rice, Jan. 25, 2001, discussing al Qaeda's presence in the United States. For Clarke's concerns about an attack on the White House, see NSC email, Clarke to Rice, briefing on Pennsylvania Ave, Mar. 23, 2001.

195. For the President's announcement, see White House press release, "Statement by the President, Domestic Preparedness Against Weapons of Mass Destruction," May 8, 2001 (online at www.whitehouse.gov/news/releases/2001/05/print/02010508.html).

196. CIA memo, summary of weekly Rice/Tenet meeting, May 29, 2001.

197. Ibid.

198. Richard interview (Dec. 11, 2003).

199. CIA memo, summary of weekly Rice/Tenet meeting, May 29, 2001.

200. NSC memo, Hadley to Armitage, Wolfowitz, McLaughlin, and O'Keefe, "Next Steps on al-Qida," June 7, 2001.

201. NSC memo, draft National Security Presidential Directive, undated; Condoleezza Rice testimony, Apr. 8, 2004.

202. See, e.g., Condoleezza Rice testimony, Apr. 8, 2004; Richard Clarke interview (Feb. 3, 2004).

203. Richard Clarke interview (Jan. 12, 2004).

204. Condoleezza Rice meeting (Feb. 7, 2004).

205. DOS cable, State 111711, "Demarche on Threat by Afghan-based Terrorists," June 27, 2001. Under Secretary of State for Political Affairs Marc Grossman knew of Sheehan's severe demands and instructed Ambassador Milam to reiterate them to the Taliban. Marc Grossman interview (Jan. 20, 2004).

206. In early July 2001, shortly before retiring, Ambassador Milam met one last time with Taliban Deputy Foreign Minister Jalil in Islamabad. Milam tried to dispel any confusion about where Bin Ladin fit into U.S.-Taliban relations—the Saudi terrorist was the issue, and he had to be expelled. DOS cable, Islamabad 3628, "Taliban's Mullah Jalil's July 2 Meeting With The Ambassador," July 3, 2001. The State Department's South Asia bureau called for a less confrontational stance toward the Taliban. It opposed a policy to overthrow the Taliban and was cautious about aiding the Northern Alliance. DOS memo, Rocca to Grossman, "Your Participation in Deputies Committee Meeting, Friday, June 29, 2001," June 28, 2001; see DOS memo, "Pakistan/Afghanistan DC-Covert Action Issue," undated (appears to be mid-June 2001); Richard Armitage interview (Jan. 12, 2004).

207. For the Deputies Committee meeting, see NSC memo, Summary of Conclusions of June 29, 2001, Deputies Committee meeting, undated (attached to NSC memo, Biegun to executive secretaries, July 6, 2001). For officials who were impatient with the pace of the Deputies' Committee review, see, e.g., Richard Armitage interview (Jan. 12, 2004); John McLaughlin interview (Jan. 21, 2004). For Clarke's arguments, see NSC memo, PCC Chairman's Summary Paper, "Key Issues for Al-Qida Deputies Meeting," Apr. 19, 2001. See also Richard Armitage testimony, Mar. 24, 2004; Stephen Hadley meeting (Jan. 31, 2004).

208. For Clarke and Black renewing their push, see, e.g., Cofer Black interview (Dec. 9, 2003). For Clarke's suggestion, see NSC email, Cressey to Moran, various matters concerning al Qaeda, Feb. 12, 2001.

209. Condoleezza Rice meeting (Feb. 7, 2004); Stephen Hadley meeting (Jan. 31, 2004); Zalmay Khalilzad interview (Nov. 21, 2003). For Clarke's view, see NSC memo, Clarke to Rice, al Qaeda review, Jan. 25, 2001.

210. For the draft authorities, see CIA briefing materials, talking points for DCI meeting with Rice on the draft Afghanistan counterterrorism finding and the draft UBL Memorandum of Notification, Mar. 28, 2001. For the draft explicitly stating that the goal was not to overthrow the Taliban, see Jonathan F. interview (Jan. 19, 2004).

211. See NSC email, Clarke to Khalilzad, Crawford, and Cressey, "Option for integrated al Qida-Afghan-Pakistan paper," June 30, 2001. For State's view, see DOS memo, "U.S. Engagement with the Taliban on Usama Bin Laden," undated (attached to NSC memo, Biegun to executive secretaries, July 16, 2001).

212. For an outline of the policy, see NSC memo, "Afghanistan: A Comprehensive Strategy," undated (attached to NSC memo, Biegun memo to executive secretaries, Sept. 7, 2001). For the September 10 meeting, see NSC memo, Biegun to executive secretaries, Summary of Conclusions for Sept. 10, 2001, Deputies Committee meeting on Afghanistan, India, and Pakistan, Sept. 26, 2001.

213. For the September 10 meeting, see NSC memo, Biegun to executive secretaries, Summary of Conclusions for Sept. 10, 2001, Deputies Committee meeting on Afghanistan, India and Pakistan, Sept. 26, 2001. For Armitage's view, see Richard Armitage interview (Jan. 12, 2004).

214. Colin Powell prepared statement, Mar. 23, 2004, p. 5.

215. For reviewing the possibility of more carrots, see DOS memo, Hull and Usrey to Grossman, "Deputies Committee Meeting on Terrorism and al Qaida," Apr. 20, 2001. For the possibility of lifting sanctions, see Colin Powell interview (Jan. 21, 2004); Richard Armitage interview (Jan. 12, 2004); DOS memo, "Engagement with Pakistan: From Negative to Positive," undated (appears to be May 29, 2001).

216. Condoleezza Rice meeting (Feb. 7, 2004).

217. For Rice's view on Sattar, see Condoleezza Rice meeting (Feb. 7, 2004). For Sattar urging the United States to engage the Taliban, see DOS cable, State 109130, "The Secretary's Lunch With Pakistani Foreign Minister Abdul Sattar," June 22, 2001. For the deputies agreeing to review objectives, see NSC memo, Summary of Conclusions of June 29, 2001, Deputies Committee meeting, undated (attached to NSC memo, Biegun to executive secretaries, July 6, 2001). For Clarke urging Hadley, see NSC memo, Clarke to Hadley, "DC on Pakistan," June 27, 2001.

218. See White House letter, President Bush to Musharraf, Aug. 4, 2001. For Rocca's view, see DOS memo, "Engagement with Pakistan: From Negative to Positive," undated (possibly May 29, 2001); Christina Rocca interview (Jan. 29, 2004). For Armitage's comment, see Richard Armitage interview (Jan. 12, 2004).

219. For the Vice President's call, see CIA briefing materials, "Efforts to Counter the Bin Ladin Threat," Sept. 12, 2001. For Powell's meetings, see DOS cable, State 041824, "Secretary's 26 February Meeting With Saudi Crown Prince Abdullah," Mar. 8, 2001; DOS cable, State 117132, "The Secretary's June 29 Meeting With Saudi Crown Prince Abdullah," July 5, 2001.

220. Paul Wolfowitz interview (Jan. 20, 2004); Donald Rumsfeld interview (Jan. 30, 2004).

221. For Shelton's recollection, see Hugh Shelton interview (Feb. 5, 2004). For Sheridan's departure, see Austin Yamada interview (Dec. 23, 2003); Brian Sheridan interview (Feb. 24, 2004).

222. Donald Rumsfeld interview (Jan. 30, 2004). Rumsfeld had been a member of the Bremer-Sonnenberg Commission on Terrorism, created by Congress in 1998.

223. Tommy Franks interview (Apr. 9, 2004).

224. For Annex B, see NSC memo, draft National Security Presidential Directive, undated (attached to NSC email, Biegun to executive secretaries, July 13, 2001). The annex said that Pentagon planning was also to include options to eliminate weapons of mass destruction that the al Qaeda network might acquire or make.

225. Stephen Hadley meeting (Jan. 31, 2004).

226. Condoleezza Rice meeting (Feb. 7, 2004).

227. President Bush and Vice President Cheney meeting (Apr. 29, 2004).

228. Ibid.

229. John Ashcroft interview (Dec. 17, 2003).

230. NSC email, Clarke to Rice and Hadley, "Courtesy call on AG," Feb. 22, 2001.

231. On the FBI strategy, see FBI report, Counterterrorism Division, International Terrorism Program, "Strategic Program Plan FY 2001–2006," undated (appears to be from summer 2000). On Watson's recollections, see Dale Watson interview (Jan. 6, 2004). On the FBI budget proposal, see statement of Attorney General John Ashcroft, Hearing on U.S. Federal Efforts to Combat Terrorism before the Subcommittee on Commerce, Justice, and State, the Judiciary, and Related Agencies of the Senate Appropriations Committee, May 9, 2001. See DOJ memo, Comments on Staff Statement 12, Apr. 7, 2004.

232. Testimony of John Ashcroft, Hearing on U.S. Federal Efforts to Combat Terrorism before the Subcommittee on Commerce, Justice, and State, the Judiciary, and Related Agencies of the Senate Appropriations Committee, May 9, 2001. On DOJ's priorities, see DOJ memo, Ashcroft to Heads of Department Components, "Guidance for Preparing FY 2003 Budgets," May 10, 2001. On Watson's reaction, see Dale Watson interview (Jan. 6, 2004).

233. DOJ letter, Ashcroft to Daniels, transmitting the Department of Justice FY 2003 budget request, Sept. 10, 2001; Thomas Pickard interview (Jan. 21, 2004). Pickard told us that he approached Ashcroft and asked him to reconsider DOJ's denial of the FBI's original counterterrorism budget request in light of the continuing threat. It was not uncommon for FBI budget requests to be reduced by the attorney general or by OMB before being submitted to Congress; this had occurred during the previous administration.

234. In chapter 3, we discuss how this problem arose. By 2001, it had become worse. During 2000, the FBI had erred in preparing some of its applications for FISA surveillance, misstating how much information had been shared with criminal prosecutors and the nature of the walls between the intelligence and law enforcement functions within the FBI. In March 2001, Judge Royce Lamberth, chief judge of the FISA Court, chastised the FBI, sending a letter to Ashcroft announcing he was banning an offending supervisory agent from appearing before the court. Judge Lamberth also met personally with Ashcroft and his acting deputy, Robert Mueller, to complain about the performance of the FBI and the Office of Intelligence Policy and Review (OIPR). Judge Lamberth letter to Ashcroft, Mar. 9, 2001; John Ashcroft interview (Dec. 17, 2003). In May 2001, Ashcroft altered the FISA application process to ensure greater accuracy. See DOJ memo, Ashcroft to Freeh, "The Foreign Intelligence Surveillance Act (FISA) Process," May 18, 2001.

In July 2001, the General Accounting Office criticized the way the 1995 procedures were being applied and criticized OIPR and FBI for not complying with the information-sharing requirements of the 1995 procedures. This was the third report in as many years by a government agency indicating that the procedures were not working as planned. In October 2000, December 2000, and March 2001, proposals for reform to the 1995 procedures were put forth by senior DOJ officials. None resulted in reform. One impediment was that the respective DOJ components could not agree on all the proposed reforms. A second impediment was a concern that such reforms would require a challenge to the FISA Court's position on the matter. This was considered risky because the FISA Court of Review had never convened, and one of the judges had previously voiced skepticism regarding the constitutionality of the FISA statute. Deputy Attorney General Larry Thompson did ask the court to accept the modifications described in the text, which were distributed as part of his August 2001 memorandum reaffirming the 1995 procedures. See DOJ memo, Thompson to the Criminal Division, the Office of Intelligence Policy and Review, and the FBI, "Intelligence Sharing," Aug. 6, 2001.

235. This tasking may have occurred before Rice's March 15, 2001, meeting with Tenet. See CIA memo, "Talking Points for DCI Meeting with Rice," Mar. 15, 2001. For Rice's recollections, see Condoleezza Rice meeting (Feb. 7, 2004). Attorney General John Ashcroft told us he told Rice on March 7, 2001, that his lawyers had determined that the existing legal authorities for covert action against Bin Ladin were unclear and insufficient, and that he suggested new, explicit kill authorities be developed. John Ashcroft testimony, Apr. 13, 2004. On the CIA draft documents, see CIA memo, "Talking Points for the DCI on the Draft Afghanistan Counterterrorism Finding and the Draft UBL MON," Mar. 27, 2001. For the description of the meeting, see CIA memo, Moseman to Tenet, Mar. 28, 2001.

236. NSC memo, Sturtevant to Griffin, Levin, Krongard, Watson, and others, July 12, 2001.

237. See, e.g., NSC note, Clarke to Berger, Sept. 23, 2000; Richard Clarke interview (Feb. 3, 2004).

238. CIA memo, Black to Clarke, Jan. 25, 2001. For a Joint Staff view, see, e.g., Scott Gration interview (Mar. 3, 2004). The mission commander for the Predator flights, Air Force Major Mark A. Cooter, had registered his opposition to redeploying the aircraft back in December 2000: "given the cost/benefit from these continued missions it seems senseless." DOD letter, Cooter to Alec B., "Continued Flight Operations," Nov. 14, 2000 (attached to CIA memo, Black to DCI and others, Predator Operation, Nov. 17, 2000).

239. See NSC memo, Summary of Conclusions of Deputies Committee meeting, Apr. 30, 2001. This document noted a consensus in favor of reconnaissance missions commencing in July. But DDCI McLaughlin told us that he and Black believed that no such decision had been made at the meeting. Hadley told us he believed that a decision had been made at the meeting to fly such missions. See John McLaughlin interview (Jan. 2, 2004). See also CIA briefing materials, "Summary of April 30, 2001 Deputies Committee meeting," May 3, 2001; Stephen Hadley meeting (Jan. 31, 2004). For Rice's perspective, see Condoleezza Rice meeting (Feb. 7, 2004).

240. Allen described the "quibbling" over financing the Predator program as "ridiculous." Charles Allen interview (Jan. 27, 2004). For a CIA senior management perspective, see, e.g., John McLaughlin interview (Jan. 21, 2004). The Defense Department's view is suggested in CIA briefing materials, "Summary of April 30, 2001 Deputies Committee meeting," May 3, 2001.

241. George Tenet interview (Jan. 28, 2004); Charles Allen interview (Jan. 27, 2004).

242. John Maher III interview (Apr. 22, 2004); Scott Gration interview (Mar. 3, 2004); John Jumper interview (Mar. 3, 2004).

243. On Hadley's efforts and directions, see NSC memo, Hadley to McLaughlin, Wolfowitz, and Myers, "Re: Predator," July 11, 2001. On Rice's intervention, see NSC memo, Biegun to executive secretaries, July 31, 2001; CIA memo, Campbell to McLaughlin, Pavitt, and others, Aug. 2, 2001. The White House told us that it cannot find a formal Summary of Conclusions for this meeting.

244. On the Deputies Committee meeting, see NSC memo, Biegun to executive secretaries, July 31, 2001; CIA memo, Campbell to McLaughlin, Pavitt, and others, Aug. 2, 2001. The White House told us that it cannot find a formal Summary of Conclusions for this meeting.

245. NSC memo, Hadley to Armitage, Wolfowitz, Myers, and McLaughlin, resolving Predator issues, Aug. 3, 2001 (including McLaughlin's handwritten comment); NSC email, Clarke to Rice and Hadley, "Need to place a call to Tenet," Aug. 8, 2001.

246. John Maher III interview (Apr. 22, 2004); John Jumper interview (Mar. 3, 2004); see also Scott Gration interview (Mar. 3, 2004).

247. NSC memo, Clarke to Rice, "Observations at the Principals Meeting on Al Qida," Sept. 4, 2001 (text italicized here is underlined in the original).

248. Ibid.

249. Ibid.

250. Condoleezza Rice testimony, Apr. 8, 2004.

251. CIA memo, Black to Tenet, Sept. 4, 2001.

252. Various interviews with participants, as well as the Maher memo (see note 255 below), make it clear that the meeting focused on Predator, not the presidential directive.

253. Condoleezza Rice meeting (Feb. 7, 2004).

254. Ibid.; NSC memo, Cressey to Rice, September 4 PC on counterterrorism, Sept. 3, 2001.

255. CIA memo, Maher to limited group, "Principals Committee meeting, Sept. 4, 2001," Sept. 4, 2001. We have not found a formal summary of conclusions, which would usually be prepared after a Principals Committee meeting.

256. Ibid.

257. Ibid.

258. Ibid.

259. NSC memo, Clarke to CSG members, Sept. 7, 2001.

260. On Massoud's assassination, see Coll, *Ghost Wars*, pp. 574–575. On the Sept. 10 meeting, see NSC memo, Biegun to executive secretaries, "Summary of Conclusions for Sept. 10, 2001 Deputies Committee meeting on Afghanistan, India and Pakistan," Sept. 26, 2001. Note that the agenda for this meeting, distributed on September 7, 2001, listed its topics as "Pakistan, India, and Afghanistan"; the Summary of Conclusions, written after 9/11, flipped the order of the topics.

261. NSC memo, Hadley to Tenet, Sept. 10, 2001.

7 The Attack Looms

1. FBI report, "Summary of Penttbom Investigation," Feb. 29, 2004 (classified version), p. 16.

2. Intelligence report, interrogation of KSM, May 19, 2003. Although KSM's stated reasons for sending Hazmi and Mihdhar to California do not seem especially compelling, we have uncovered no evidence tending to establish any more plausible explanation for the California destination. The possibility that the two hijackers were pursuing another al Qaeda mission on the West Coast, while certainly conceivable—see, e.g., CIA analytic report,

"Alternate View: Two 11 September Hijackers Possibly Involved in Previous US Plot," CTC 2002-30064, July 5, 2002—conflicts with the organization's preference for having its 9/11 operatives concentrate on that mission exclusively.

3. Intelligence reports, interrogations of KSM, May 19, 2003; Aug. 14, 2003.

4. Intelligence report, interrogation of KSM, Aug. 18, 2003. According to Hambali, in late 1999 or early 2000 KSM sent an al Qaeda operative named Issa al Britani to visit Hambali in Malaysia. At the end of the visit, Issa provided Hambali with two addresses—one in the United States ("possibly in California") and one in South Africa—and told Hambali he could contact "people in those locations" if he "needed help." Hambali claims he never contacted anyone at either address or passed either address to anyone else, and claims not to remember the addresses. Intelligence report, interrogation of Hambali, Sept. 12, 2003. In an assessment of KSM's reporting, the CIA concluded that protecting operatives in the United States appeared to be a "major part" of KSM's resistance efforts. For example, in response to questions about U.S. zip codes found in his notebooks, KSM provided the less than satisfactory explanation that he was planning to use the zip codes to open new email accounts. CIA report, Intelligence Community Terrorist Threat Assessment, "Khalid Shaykh Muhammed's Threat Reporting—Precious Truths, Surrounded by a Bodyguard of Lies," Apr. 3, 2003, pp. 4–5.

5. Notably, as discussed in chapter 5, precisely such arrangements—in the form of lodging and travel assistance provided by Hambali's minions—were in place when the first contingent of operatives (including Hazmi and Mihdhar) journeyed to Kuala Lumpur in late 1999 and early 2000.

6. Intelligence report, interrogation of KSM, May 19, 2003.

7. Intelligence reports, interrogations of KSM, May 19, 2003; Aug. 14, 2003. KSM also has stated that in addition to providing Hazmi and Mihdhar with a San Diego telephone book, he gave them another directory "possibly covering Long Beach, California." Intelligence report, interrogation of KSM, June 15, 2004.

8. Although Hazmi and Mihdhar told immigration authorities on January 15, 2000, that they would be staying at the Sheraton Hotel in Los Angeles, their names do not appear in the hotel's registration records for the second half of January. FBI searches of the records of other hotels near the airport and smaller establishments in Culver City failed to locate the hijackers, as did our own investigation. See FBI report, "Hijackers Timeline," Nov. 14, 2003 (Apr. 3, 1999, entry, citing 265A-NY-280350-CG, serial 4062; 265A-NY-280350-302, serial 7134); Commission investigation in Culver City; Vicki G. interview (Sept. 30, 2003).

9. For the FBI source's claims, see FBI letterhead memorandum, Penttbom investigation, Oct. 8, 2002. For Abdullah's recollections, see FBI report of investigation, interview of Mohdar Abdullah, Jan. 15, 2002. Other reporting indicates that Hazmi and Mihdhar spent time at the King Fahd mosque. A scholar lecturing at the mosque was reportedly approached by either Hazmi or Mihdhar about performing a wedding ceremony. Khalil A. Khalil interview (Feb. 24, 2004). On "Khallam," see FBI electronic communication, "Fahad Althumairy," Sept. 4, 2002; FBI electronic communication, "Ziyat Kharfan," Jan. 8, 2002 (giving description of visitor with whom Hazmi and Mihdhar met at mosque). The Khallam story has never been corroborated. The FBI considered the possibility that Khallam might be Khallad, the al Qaeda member whose role in the 9/11 plot and the *Cole* attack we discussed in chapter 5. This speculation was based on reporting that Khallad was in the United States in June 2000 and was seen in the company of Fahad al Thumairy, an imam at the mosque. FBI electronic communication, investigation of *Cole* bombing, interview of witness, Mar. 19, 2003; CIA cable, source reporting, Mar. 18, 2003. Neither we nor the FBI have found any travel documentation establishing Khallad's presence in the United States at any time. We doubt that the person allegedly seen with Thumairy actually was Khallad.

10. Patrick J. McDonnell, "Saudi Envoy in L.A. Is Deported," *Los Angeles Times*, May 10, 2003, p. B1; Michael Isikoff and Daniel Klaidman, with Jamie Reno, "Failure to Communicate," *Newsweek*, Aug. 4, 2003, p. 34. As of January 2000, Thumairy was employed by the Saudi Arabian Ministry of Islamic Affairs, Religious Endowments and Religious Guidance, to act as the consulate's liaison to the mosque. FBI electronic communication, "Fahad Al Thumairy," Sept. 4, 2002. Before 9/11, Saudi imams employed by the ministry often were dispatched to help serve Muslim communities around the world, sometimes—as in Thumairy's case—with diplomatic status in the host country. On Thumairy's leadership, see FBI letterhead memorandum, investigation of Mohammed bin Suleiman al Muhanna, July 9, 2003; FBI letterhead memorandum, investigation of Mohamed Ibrahim Aliter, Dec. 2, 2002.

11. FBI electronic communication, "Abdulaziz Alroomi," Apr. 2, 2003.

12. FBI letterhead memorandum, investigation of Khaled Charif, Dec. 4, 2002. After 9/11, arguments arose within the Saudi government over whether to allow reputedly radical imams, including Thumairy, to work for the Saudi government in the United States. FBI letterhead memorandum, investigation of Mohammed bin Suleiman al Muhanna, July 9, 2003. In May 2003, the U.S. government settled the matter, at least in Thumairy's case, by refusing to let him back into the country. DOS memo, Karl Hoffman to the Commission, June 8, 2004, and the attached materials.

13. On Thumairy's religious views, see FBI letterhead memorandum, investigation of Mohamed Aliter, Dec. 2, 2002; Fahad al Thumairy interviews (Feb. 23–25, 2004). However, two witnesses we interviewed who knew Thumairy and used to hear him preach at the King Fahd mosque deny that he promoted extremism. Sami A. Mekhemar interview (Apr. 21, 2004); Interview (Apr. 23, 2004). Despite the disparate views as to whether Thumairy

qualified as an extremist while he was in Los Angeles, it does appear that both the Saudi Arabian government and the leadership of the mosque attempted to discipline him in the summer of 2002 and early 2003 for espousing extremist views. Thumairy denies incurring any such disciplinary measures. Fahad al Thumairy interviews (Feb. 23–25, 2004); FBI letterhead memorandum, investigation of Mohammed bin Suleiman al Muhanna, July 9, 2003. On Bayoumi, see Khalil A. Khalil interview (Feb. 24, 2004). Bayoumi and Thumairy had numerous telephonic contacts between December 1998 and December 2000. Specifically, Bayoumi called Thumairy's home telephone 10 times during this period, and Thumairy called Bayoumi's cellular and home phones 11 times between December 3 and December 20, 2000. FBI electronic communication, "Fahad Al-Thumairy," Nov. 20, 2002. Bayoumi recalls consulting with Thumairy, solely on religious matters, both by telephone and in person at the mosque. Omar al Bayoumi interview (Oct. 16–17, 2003). As to Thumairy's contact with Mohdar Abdullah, see FBI electronic communication, "Fahad Althumairy," Oct. 25, 2002; FBI report of investigation, interview of Mohdar Abdullah, July 23, 2002. According to one individual, Abdullah visited the mosque frequently and was "very close" to radical followers of Thumairy. FBI electronic communication, "Fahad Althumairy," Oct. 25, 2002.

14. We have checked, for example, the records for apartments where Thumairy is known to have placed Saudi visitors during 2001. The most intriguing lead concerns an Arabic-speaking taxicab driver, Qualid Benomrane, who was arrested on immigration charges in early 2002. When asked to look at a series of photographs that included the 19 hijackers involved in the 9/11 attacks, Benomrane responded ambiguously, seeming first to pick out the photographs of Hazmi and Mihdhar but then denying that he recognized them. Later in the interview, Benomrane told the FBI about driving "two Saudis" around Los Angeles and to San Diego's Sea World after being introduced to them by Thumairy at the King Fahd mosque before 9/11. According to Benomrane, someone at the consulate had asked Thumairy to assist the two Saudis, who had recently arrived in Los Angeles and had moved to an apartment near the mosque. FBI electronic communication, "Fahad Althumairy," Sept. 4, 2002; Ashour E. interview (May 20, 2004); FBI reports of investigation, interviews of Qualid Moncef Benomrane, Mar. 7, 2002; Mar. 13, 2002; May 23, 2002. Working with agencies of the U.S. government, we have attempted to locate and interview Benomrane overseas, since he was deported in 2002. After checking many possible avenues of corroboration for this story, our investigation has not substantiated the hypothesis that Benomrane's "two Saudis" were Hazmi and Mihdhar. In fact, we have established that Benomrane did not obtain a taxi license, or even a driver's license, until months after he could be supposed to have chauffeured Hazmi and Mihdhar. Moreover, before his deportation, Benomrane described the two Saudis as sons of a sick father who was seeking medical treatment in Los Angeles. Ibid. We have found evidence corroborating this account.

15. FBI document made available to the Commission; Caysan Bin Don interview (Apr. 20, 2004); Omar al Bayoumi interview (Oct. 16–17, 2003); Interview (Apr. 23, 2004). In Bin Don's presence, Bayoumi met with a still-unidentified consular employee whom Bayoumi already knew and whom Bin Don says he saw in Anaheim as recently as November 2003. The employee provided Bayoumi with Qur'ans and other religious materials during the February 1, 2000, meeting. Omar al Bayoumi interview (Oct. 16–17, 2003). At the time of the February 1, 2000, restaurant encounter, Bin Don, a U.S. citizen, went by the name Isamu Dyson.

16. Caysan Bin Don interview (Apr. 20, 2004); FBI report of investigation, interview of Isamu Dyson, Oct. 8, 2001.

17. See Caysan Bin Don interview (Apr. 20, 2004); FBI report of investigation, interview of Isamu Dyson, Oct. 8, 2001. Bin Don himself has been inconsistent about visiting the mosque. In his initial interviews, he recalled praying with Bayoumi at the consulate before lunch and visiting the mosque only once, after the meal; when we interviewed him recently, however, he stated that both prayer sessions took place at the mosque. For Bayoumi's visits to Los Angeles, see FBI report of investigation, recovery of hotel records, Jan. 15, 2002. Although Bayoumi might deny visiting the mosque on February 1 to conceal some contact he may have made there that day, we have seen no evidence of such contact.

18. Saudi Civil Aviation Authority employment records for Bayoumi, Mar. 2000–Jan. 2002 (provided by the FBI); FBI report of investigation, "Connections of San Diego PENTTBOMB Subjects to the Government of Saudi Arabia," undated; FBI letterhead memorandum, investigation of Bayoumi, Apr. 15, 2002. While in San Diego, Bayoumi was officially employed by Ercan, a subsidiary of a contractor for the Saudi Civil Aviation Administration, although a fellow employee described Bayoumi as a "ghost employee," noting that he was one of many Saudis on the payroll who was not required to work. In April 2000, Bayoumi received a promotion and his status was also adjusted from "single" to "married" (despite the fact that he was already married). As a result, his salary was raised and his "other allowances" stipend increased significantly, from approximately $465 to $3,925 a month, remaining at that level until December 2000. In January 2001, the stipend was reduced to $3,427. It stayed constant until August 2001, when Bayoumi left the United States. Saudi Civil Aviation Authority employment records for Bayoumi, Mar. 2000–Jan. 2002 (provided by the FBI); Richard L. Lambert prepared statement, June 26, 2003, pp. 7–9; FBI reports of investigation, interviews of Samuel George Coombs, Apr. 8, 2002; July 24, 2002; Aug. 26, 2002.

19. On Bayoumi's activities, see FBI electronic communication, interview of Bayoumi, Sept. 17, 2003. Although Bayoumi admits knowing Thumairy, no telephone records document any contact between the two just before Bayoumi's lunch with Hazmi and Mihdhar in Los Angeles. Nor do individuals who regard Thumairy as an extremist

place Bayoumi in Thumairy's circle of associates. KSM has denied knowing Bayoumi. Intelligence report, interrogation of KSM, Aug. 18, 2003.

Bayoumi was once the subject of an FBI counterterrorism investigation, prompted by allegations about him that appear to have been groundless. On the closing of the investigation, see FBI electronic communication, "Omar Ahmed Al Bayoumi," June 7, 1999. Another possible source of suspicion is his passport, which contains a cachet that intelligence investigators associate with possible adherence to al Qaeda. It is a marking that can be obtained by especially devout Muslims. Although we believe the marking suggests the need for further inquiry, it is not the kind of fraudulent manipulation that would conclusively link the document with a terrorist organization. INS records, copy of Bayoumi passport; CIA analytic report, Al-Qa'ida Travel Issues, CTC 2004-40002H, Nov. 14, 2003, pp. ii, 18.

20. On Abdullah's assistance to the hijackers, see FBI electronic communication, Abdullah investigation, May 19, 2004. In a post-9/11 interview with law enforcement, Abdullah claimed that Bayoumi specifically asked him "to be the individual to acclimate the hijackers to the United States, particularly San Diego, California." FBI report of investigation, interview of Mohdar Abdullah, July 23, 2002. Bayoumi, however, denies even introducing Hazmi and Mihdhar to Abdullah, much less asking him to assist them. Omar al Bayoumi interview (Oct. 16–17, 2003).

21. FBI report of investigation, interview of Mohdar Abdullah, July 23, 2002; FBI electronic communication, "Osama Bassnan," Oct. 17, 2001; FBI report of investigation, interview of Mohdar Abdullah, Sept. 22, 2001; FBI electronic communication, "Shareef Abdulmuttaleb el Arbi," Feb. 4, 2003. For the possibility of the notebook belonging to someone else, see FBI report, Behavioral Analysis Activity, Oct. 4, 2001.

22. FBI electronic communication, interview of Charles Sabah Toma, May 18, 2004.

23. On Abdullah's claims of advance knowledge, see FBI electronic communication, interview, May 17, 2004. On Abdullah's telephone use after August 25, 2001, and acting strangely, see FBI report of investigation, interview, Sept. 24, 2001; FBI report of investigation, interview of Mohdar Abdullah, July 23, 2002; Danny G. interviews (Nov. 18, 2003; May 24, 2004).

24. The hijackers' mode of transportation and the exact date of their arrival in San Diego are not known. On their locating Bayoumi on February 4 and his assistance, see Richard L. Lambert prepared statement, June 26, 2003, pp. 6–7; Omar al Bayoumi interview (Oct. 16–17, 2003); FBI report of investigation, interview of Omar al Bayoumi, Aug. 4–5, 2003. The rental application states that Hazmi and Mihdhar resided in Bayoumi's apartment from January 15 to February 2, 2000, but Bayoumi denies it, and we have found no reason to dispute his denial. According to Bayoumi, he was in such a hurry to complete the rental transaction that he signed the application form without reading it. Bayoumi also denies receiving any money from Hazmi or Mihdhar for helping them with the apartment. Omar al Bayoumi interview (Oct. 16–17, 2003). On opening an account, see FBI report, "Summary of Penttbom Investigation," Feb. 29, 2004, p. 12.

Contrary to highly publicized allegations, we have found no evidence that Hazmi or Mihdhar received money from another Saudi citizen, Osama Bassnan.

25. Omar al Bayoumi interview (Oct. 16–17, 2003). According to Bayoumi, he originally intended to hold the party at his own apartment, but moved it to the hijackers' apartment when one of the guests created an awkward social circumstance by bringing his wife; Bayoumi solved the problem by having the friend's wife stay with his own wife in Bayoumi's apartment and moving the party to the hijackers' residence. Bayoumi maintains that a visiting sheikh was the party's principal honoree. Ibid. Although Bin Don has recalled that the party was intended to welcome Hazmi and Mihdhar to the community, this is belied by the hijackers' apparent decision to sequester themselves in the back room, and by the account of another party attendee. Caysan Bin Don interview (Apr. 20, 2004); Khalid Abdulrab al Yafai interview (Feb. 24, 2004). Of the two operatives, only Mihdhar appears briefly on the video shot by Bin Don. Bayoumi videotape of party (provided by the FBI).

26. On the hijackers' efforts to relocate, see Omar al Bayoumi interview (Oct. 16–17, 2003); Interview (Apr. 23, 2004); FBI report, "San Diego Brief to 9/11 Commission," June 26, 2003, p. 17. Telephone records indicate that on February 9 and February 14, 2000, Bayoumi's cell phone was used to call the landlord of the operatives' acquaintance, Hashim al Attas, who had decided to vacate his apartment. On February 15, 2000, when the landlord returned a page from Bayoumi's cell phone, Hazmi answered the phone. Steve O. interview (Nov. 17, 2003); FBI report of investigation, interview of George Harb, Oct. 30, 2001. Hazmi and Mihdhar appear to have used Bayoumi's cell phone until telephone service (subscribed in Hazmi's name) was installed in their apartment.

27. FBI report of investigation, interview of George Harb, Sept. 16, 2001. The hijackers may actually have lived in Attas's apartment for a short while. Bayoumi has stated that he recalls hearing that Hazmi and Mihdhar moved into the apartment for two weeks but then returned to their original apartment while Bayoumi was in Washington, D.C. FBI report of investigation, interview of Omar al Bayoumi, Aug. 4–6, 2003. This account is confirmed by Attas's girlfriend, who recalls that Attas met Mihdhar and Hazmi either through friends or at the mosque, and that the pair moved into Attas's apartment for approximately two weeks before moving out and taking Attas's furnishings with them. FBI report, "San Diego Brief to 9/11 Commission," June 26, 2003, p. 18.

28. Interview (Apr. 23, 2004). Hazmi and Mihdhar did not officially vacate their first apartment until May 31, 2000. FBI report, "Hijackers Timeline," Nov. 14, 2003 (citing 265A-NY-280350-SD, serial 1445). The exact details

of the hijackers' move to their final San Diego address are not altogether clear, as their landlord—who has been interviewed many times by the FBI and once by us—has provided various accounts of how he first met them. See also FBI electronic communication, Penttbom investigation, Oct. 3, 2001. On Mihdhar's travels, see Interview (Apr. 23, 2004); FBI report, "Summary of Penttbom Investigation," Feb. 29, 2004 (classified version), p. 46. On Hazmi's departure, see FBI report, "San Diego Brief to 9/11 Commission," June 26, 2003, p. 18.

29. On the purchase of the car, see FBI report, "Hijackers Timeline," Nov. 14, 2003 (citing Bank of America records). Law enforcement officials recovered the blue 1988 Toyota from the parking lot at Dulles International Airport on September 11. On the wire transfer, see FBI report of investigation, interview, Sept. 17, 2001. After 9/11, the mosque administrator came forward because he feared he had unwittingly aided the hijackers. He recalled Hazmi and Mihdhar arriving at the mosque on their own and describing themselves as clerks employed by the Saudi Arabian government. The two said they needed help finding a school where they could study English, which neither spoke well enough, in the administrator's opinion, to permit them to become pilots. The administrator also suspected that Mihdhar might have been an intelligence agent of the Saudi government. After first declining Hazmi's request for a loan, the administrator agreed to permit him to use the administrator's bank account to receive the $5,000 wire transfer. Claiming to have been suspicious of the entire transaction, the administrator distanced himself from Hazmi and Mihdhar, but not before they had received the assistance they needed. Ibid. We have no evidence contradicting the administrator's account.

30. On visits to other mosques, see FBI letterhead memorandum, investigation of Ali Ahmad Mesdaq, Jan. 28, 2002; FBI reports of investigation, interviews of Samir Abdoun, Oct. 28, 2001; May 15, 2002. On Bayoumi's assistance, see Richard L. Lambert prepared statement, June 26, 2003, p. 7; FBI electronic communication, "Jay Steven Barlow," Sept. 24, 2002. On April 12, 2000, Hazmi registered for a one-month class in conversational English. FBI report, "Hijackers Timeline," Nov. 14, 2003 (Apr. 12, 2000, entry, citing Bank of America records).

31. Even before learning of Abdullah's alleged jailhouse conversations, we attempted to interview him in November 2003, while he was incarcerated and awaiting deportation. Through counsel, Abdullah refused to be interviewed unless he was released from custody. The U.S. Department of Justice declined to obtain an order of use immunity so that Abdullah's testimony could be compelled. See Commission letter to Daniel Levin, DOJ, Dec. 31, 2003; DOJ letter, Daniel Levin to the Commission, Jan. 5, 2004. On Abdullah's deportation, see FBI electronic communication, Abdullah investigation, July 1, 2004. Abdullah appears to be at liberty in Yemen, although he claims Yemeni authorities are watching him. H. G. Reza, "Deported Friend of Terrorists in Report," Los Angeles Times, June 17, 2004, p. A31.

32. On Awadallah, see FBI electronic communication, interview of Osama Awadallah, June 6, 2002; FBI electronic communication, interview of Osama Awadallah, Feb. 4, 2003. On Bakarbashat, see FBI report of investigation, interview of Omar Bakarbashat, Sept. 17, 2001; FBI electronic communication, Penttbom investigation, Apr. 11, 2002. Another associate of Hazmi and Mihdhar referred to them after the September 11 attacks as "more than heroes." FBI letterhead memorandum, "Diah Thabet," Oct. 25, 2002.

33. On Anwar Aulaqi, see Wade A. interview (Oct. 16, 2003). The FBI investigated Aulaqi in 1999 and 2000 after learning that he may have been contacted by a possible procurement agent for Bin Ladin. During this investigation, the FBI learned that Aulaqi knew individuals from the Holy Land Foundation and others involved in raising money for the Palestinian terrorist group Hamas. Sources alleged that Aulaqi had other extremist connections. FBI electronic communication, background searches, Feb. 3, 2000; FBI report of investigation, interview, Sept. 24, 2001; FBI electronic communication, interview, Oct. 8, 2002. None of this information was considered strong enough to support a criminal prosecution. For evidence of possible early contacts between Hazmi/Mihdhar and Aulaqi, see Steve O. interview (Nov. 17, 2003), noting that four calls took place between Aulaqi's phone and Bayoumi's phone on February 4, 2000, the day Bayoumi helped Hazmi and Mihdhar find an apartment and perhaps lent them his phone.

One witness remembered meeting Hazmi through Aulaqi and Mohdar Abdullah, and later meeting Mihdhar at Aulaqi's mosque. This same witness recalled seeing Hazmi and Mihdhar in the guest room on the second floor of the mosque and, on one occasion, leaving the room just after Aulaqi, at the conclusion of a meeting. FBI reports of investigation, interviews of Samir Abdoun, Oct. 28, 2001; May 15, 2002; FBI report of investigation, interview of Anwar Aulaqi, Sept. 25, 2001; FBI electronic communication, Penttbom investigation, Sept. 15, 2002.

34. FBI reports of investigation, interviews of Anwar Aulaqi, Sept. 17, 2001; Sept. 19, 2001.

35. Aulaqi took a position at the Dar al Hijra mosque in early 2001. By the time we sought to interview him in 2003, he had left the United States, reportedly returning to Yemen. We attempted to locate and interview him in Yemen, working with U.S. agencies and the Yemeni government, as well as other governments that might have knowledge of his whereabouts. Those attempts were unsuccessful.

36. Whereas Hazmi managed to speak broken English, Mihdhar did not even have this much command of the language, which he appeared uninterested in learning. Interview (Apr. 23, 2004); FBI report of investigation, interview of Omar Bakarbashat, Sept. 17, 2001; FBI report of investigation, interview of Ramez Noaman, Oct. 1, 2001. On April 4, 2000, Hazmi took his first flying lesson, a one-hour introductory session at the National Air College in San Diego. Exactly one month later, Hazmi and Mihdhar purchased flight equipment from an instructor at the

Sorbi Flying Club in San Diego. On May 5, both of them took a lesson at Sorbi, followed by a second lesson at the same school five days later. FBI report, "Summary of Penttbom Investigation," Feb. 29, 2004, p. 18.

37. On the Sorbi Flying Club, see FBI report of investigation, interview of Khaled al Kayed, Sept. 15, 2001. For other instructors' views, see FBI electronic communication, Penttbomb investigation, Apr. 11, 2002.

38. On Mihdhar's phone calls, see, e.g., FBI report, "Hijackers Timeline," Nov. 14, 2003 (Mar. 20, 2000, entry, citing 265A-NY-280350-19426). On Mihdhar's travels, see FBI report, "Summary of Penttbom Investigation," Feb. 29, 2004 (classified version), p. 17. On KSM's views, see Intelligence report, interrogation of KSM, May 19, 2003. On Mihdhar's status, see INS record, NIIS record of Mihdhar, June 10, 2000.

39. On KSM's communication methods, see Intelligence report, interrogation of KSM, Oct. 15, 2003. Even here, the West Coast operatives' language limitation posed a problem, as KSM had to send emails in Arabic using the English alphabet. Ibid. In addition to having his nephew Ali Abdul Aziz Ali transmit funds to the operatives in the United States, KSM used Ali as an intermediary for telephone messages. Intelligence report, interrogation of detainee, Jan. 7, 2004. On Khallad's role, see Intelligence reports, interrogations of KSM, Oct. 15, 2003; Aug. 18, 2003; Intelligence report, interrogation of Khallad, Feb. 17, 2004. On KSM's annoyance with and views on Mihdhar, see Intelligence reports, interrogations of KSM, June 15, 2004; May 19, 2003.

40. Intelligence report, interrogation of Khallad, Feb. 17, 2004; FBI report of investigation, interview, Sept. 24, 2001; FBI electronic communication, Penttbom investigation, Sept. 15, 2001; FBI electronic communication, interview, July 26, 2002; Interview (Apr. 23, 2004); FBI electronic communication, Penttbom investigation, Sept. 15, 2001. Both KSM and Khallad were aware of Hazmi's interest in finding a bride, and KSM reportedly went so far as to promise Hazmi a monthly stipend of $700 in the event he succeeded in marrying. Intelligence reports, interrogations of KSM, Aug. 6, 2003; Jan. 9, 2004. Although Hazmi did not use his housemate's telephone to make calls, he apparently received calls on it, including calls from an individual named Ashraf Suboh, who called the house 16 times between July 20 and November 18, 2000. Suboh's name and address appear in a printed email recovered during searches at an al Qaeda site in Pakistan in May 2002. The document was dated Jan. 9, 2001, and included his name and a mailing address. FBI letterhead memorandum, San Diego investigation, July 2, 2002.

41. Salmi arrived in San Diego on August 7, 2000, and three days later moved into the house where Hazmi resided. Omar al Bayoumi—who reported (at least nominally) to Salmi's uncle at the Saudi Civil Aviation ministry—found this accommodation for Salmi, although Salmi claims not to have known Bayoumi before coming to San Diego. FBI report of investigation, interview of Yazeed al Salmi, Oct. 8, 2001. On Salmi's move to Abdullah's house in La Mesa, see FBI report of investigation, interview of Salmi, Sept. 21, 2001. On possible financial links, see FBI report, "Hijackers Timeline," Nov. 14, 2003 (citing 265A-NY-280350-302, serial 59279); FBI electronic communication, Information and questions re Salmi interview, June 9, 2004; FBI report of investigation, interview of Salmi, June 17, 2004. For Salmi's possible link to Hanjour, see FBI report of investigation, interview of Abdullah, July 23, 2002. We made efforts with the assistance of the FBI to interview Salmi, but without success. The FBI interviewed Salmi on its own in June 2004 but failed to ask about his reported childhood ties to Hanjour. FBI report of investigation interview of Yazeed al Salmi, June 14, 2004.

42. At KSM's direction, Khallad notified Hazmi that another operative, who turned out to be Hanjour, would be joining Hazmi soon. Intelligence report, interrogation of Khallad, Feb. 17, 2004. On Hazmi's work at the gas station and his statement about becoming famous, see FBI report of investigation, interview, May 21, 2002. The owner of the gas station, Osama Mustafa, and the manager of the station, Iyad Kreiwesh, have both been the subject of FBI counterterrorism investigations. The investigations did not yield evidence of criminal conduct. Thumairy, the Saudi imam in Los Angeles, allegedly presided over Kreiwesh's wedding at the King Fahd mosque, witnessed by Abdullah and Benomrane, likely around September 2000. FBI report of investigation, interview of Mohdar Abdullah, July 23, 2002; 4377 Parks Avenue, San Diego record, "Application to Rent and Rental Deposit," Sept. 21, 2000.

43. On Hanjour's travel to San Diego, see INS record, NIIS record of Hanjour, Dec. 8, 2000. Hazmi's housemate remembers him taking an unexplained trip to the San Diego airport around this time. FBI report of investigation, interview, Sept. 24, 2001. On Hanjour and Hazmi leaving San Diego and the visit to the gas station, see FBI report of investigation, interview of Mohdar Abdullah, Sept. 19, 2001. On Hazmi's comment to his housemate, see Interview (Apr. 23, 2004). Although Hazmi's housemate claims that the "Hani" whom Hazmi introduced him to is not the same person pictured in Hanjour's photograph, we have little doubt that the housemate did in fact see Hanjour on the day he and Hazmi left San Diego. Ibid.; FBI electronic communication, Penttbom investigation, Sept. 15, 2001.

44. On Hazmi's contact with Abdullah, see FBI report of investigation, interview of Mohdar Abdullah, Sept. 19, 2001; FBI report of investigation, interview of Ramez Noaman, Oct. 1, 2001. On Hazmi's contact with his housemate, see FBI reports of investigation, interviews, Sept. 24, 2001; July 26, 2002. On Hazmi's contact to acquaintances in San Diego, see Danny G. interviews (Nov. 18, 2003; May 24, 2004).

45. For Shehhi's arrival, see INS record, NIIS record of Shehhi, May 29, 2000; Customs record, secondary inspection record of Shehhi, May 29, 2000. For Shehhi going to New York City, see FBI report, "Hijackers Timeline," Dec. 5, 2003 (May 30, 2000, entry citing Dresdner bank records). For Atta's travel to the Czech Republic,

see ibid. (June 2, 2000, entry citing Teletype, Sept. 21, 2001, 280350-PR, serial 111). Upon entry, Atta received the customary authorization to stay six months as a tourist. For Atta's arrival in Newark on June 3, 2000, see INS record, non-NIIS record of Atta, June 3, 2000. For Atta's apparent motivation, see CIA analytic report, "11 September: The Plot and the Plotters," CTC 2003-40044HC, June 1, 2003, p. 13; Intelligence reports, interrogations of Binalshibh, Oct. 2, 2002; Mar. 3, 2004.

46. Demonstrating Atta and Shehhi's uncertainty regarding flight schools, Atta emailed a New Hampshire school on June 5, 2000, see FBI report, "Hijackers Timeline," Dec. 5, 2003 (citing 265A-NY-280350-302, serial 3975); and inquired with a New Jersey school on June 22, 2000, see ibid. (citing 265A-NY-280350-NK, serial 15965). As they looked at flight schools on the East Coast, Atta and Shehhi stayed in a series of short-term rentals in New York City. Ibid. (June 19, 2000, entry citing 265A-NY-280350-302, serials 80926, 86069; June 25, 2000, entry citing 265A-NY-280350-302, serial 74902). For Jarrah's travel and training, see INS record, NIIS record of Jarrah, June 27, 2000; FBI letterhead memorandum, profile of Jarrah, Mar. 20, 2002. For Jarrah living with instructors, see ibid. For Jarrah purchasing a vehicle, see FBI briefing materials, Penttbom, Dec. 10–11, 2003, p. 150 (citing 265A-NY-280350-302, serials 21113, 66098).

47. For Atta and Shehhi visiting the Oklahoma school, see FBI report, "Hijackers Timeline," Dec. 5, 2003 (July 2, 2000, entry citing FBI electronic communication, Sept. 13, 2001). For Moussaoui's enrollment, see Superseding Indictment, *United States v. Moussaoui*, Crim. No. 01-455-A (E.D. Va. filed July 16, 2002), para. 44. For Atta's initial training in Florida, see FBI report, "Hijackers Timeline," Dec. 5, 2003 (July 7, 2000, entry citing 265A-NY-280350-TP-5382). Atta and Shehhi did not take their return flight to New York, and there are no travel records indicating how they traveled from Oklahoma to Florida. Ibid. (July 7, 2000, entry citing FBI electronic communication, Sept. 19, 2001). For Atta and Shehhi's enrollment in the advanced course, see ibid. (July 17, 2000, entry citing 265A-NY-280350, serial 4234; 265A-NY-280350-CE, serial 632). The two also soon rented an apartment and opened a joint bank account. Ibid. (July 13, 2000, entry citing 265A-NY-280350-TP-5679; July 7, 2000, entry citing 265A-NY-280350-302-16752). Atta bought a car. FBI briefing materials, Penttbom, Dec. 10–11, 2003, p. 150. For their solo flights, see FBI report, "Hijackers Timeline," Dec. 5, 2003 (July 30, 2000, entry citing 265A-NY-280350-CE-624, 632). For passing the test, see ibid. (Aug. 14, 2000, entry citing 265A-NY-280350-302, serials 9715, 26590). For Atta and Shehhi continuing training, see ibid. (Sept. 1, 2000, entry citing 265A-NY-280350-2435). For Jarrah's training, see ibid. (June 27, 2000, entry citing 265A-NY-280350-TP (FD-302), serial 1442).

48. Ali reportedly received the money sent to the United States from KSM in Pakistan and via courier. Intelligence reports, interrogations of detainee, Feb. 11, 2004 (two reports). Ramzi Binalshibh wired some funds withdrawn from Shehhi's bank account in Germany, a total of more than $10,000 in four transfers between June 13 and September 27, 2000. FBI report, "Summary of Penttbom Investigation," Feb. 29, 2004, pp. 16–17; German BKA (Bundeskriminalamt) report, investigative summary re Binalshibh, July 4, 2002, pp. 39–41.

49. Adam Drucker interview (Jan. 12, 2004); wire transfer documents (provided by the FBI), pp. 6–37. Ali did provide identification for his initial wire transfer to Hazmi in April that, along with some contact information he provided when he made subsequent transfers, helped the FBI unravel his aliases after 9/11. Intelligence reports, interrogations of detainee, Feb. 11, 2004 (two reports).

50. The applications of Atta and Shehhi for student status include the same supporting financial documentation. See INS record, Atta application to change status, Sept. 19, 2000; INS record, Shehhi application to change status, Sept. 15, 2000. For Atta and Shehhi's enrolling at Jones Aviation, see FBI report, "Hijackers Timeline," Dec. 5, 2003 (Sept. 23, 2000, entry citing SunTrust Financial Records). For Atta and Shehhi's behavior, see FBI report of investigation, interview of Ivan Chirivella, Sept. 15, 2001. For their failure, haste, and return to Huffman, see FBI report, "Hijackers Timeline," Dec. 5, 2003 (Oct. 4, 2000, entry citing 265A-NY-280350-TP, serial 1474; 265A-NY-280350-302, serial 1361).

51. For Jarrah's certificate, see FBI letterhead memorandum, profile of Jarrah, Mar. 20, 2002. For Jarrah's leaving the United States, see FBI report, "Hijackers Timeline," Dec. 5, 2003 (Oct. 7, 2000, entry citing 265A-NY-280350-302-7134). For Jarrah and Senguen's travel to Paris, see FBI letterhead memorandum, profile of Jarrah, Mar. 20, 2002. For Jarrah's return to the United States, see FBI report, "Hijackers Timeline," Dec. 5, 2003 (Oct. 29, 2000, entry citing INS NIIS Report; 265A-NY-280350-302, serial 7134). For their telephone contact, see FBI letterhead memorandum, profile of Jarrah, Mar. 20, 2002. For their email contact, see FBI electronic communication, Penttbom investigation, Sept. 18, 2001, p. 5.

52. For Binalshibh's deposit, see FBI report, "Hijackers Timeline," Dec. 5, 2003 (June 27, 2000, entry citing 265A-NY-280350-TP (FD-302), serial 1442; 265A-NY-280350-TP, serial 9500). For his May and June visa applications, see DOS records, Binalshibh visa applications, May 31, 2000; July 18, 2000; FBI briefing materials, Penttbom, Dec. 10–11, 2003, pp. 136–137; CIA analytic report, "The Plot and the Plotters," June 1, 2003, pp. 10, 12. For his September application in Yemen, see DOS record, Binalshibh visa application, Sept. 16, 2000. For his October application in Berlin, see DOS record, Binalshibh visa application, Nov. 1, 2000. Even after the last application was rejected, Binalshibh sought ways to get a visa, such as by marrying a U.S. citizen. He corresponded by email with a woman in California, but Atta told him to discontinue this effort. Intelligence report, interrogation of Binalshibh, Sept. 24, 2002.

Essabar may have been intended to replace Binalshibh. Like Atta, Shehhi, and Jarrah, Essabar obtained a new passport even though his old one was nearly a year from expiration, evidently to conceal his prior travel to Afghanistan during the first half of 2000. On December 12, 2000, and January 28, 2001—after Binalshibh's four U.S. visa applications had been denied—Essabar made two unsuccessful U.S. visa applications, stating that he wished to visit the United States during the week of February 15, 2001. DOS records, Essabar visa applications, Dec. 12, 2000; Jan. 8, 2001. See Federal Prosecutor General (Germany), response to Commission letter, June 25, 2004, p. 14. Neither Binalshibh nor Essabar were denied visas based on terrorism concerns.

53. FBI report, "Summary of Penttbom Investigation," Feb. 29, 2004 (classified version), p. 82.

54. For KSM sending Moussaoui to Malaysia, see Intelligence Report, interrogation of KSM, Mar. 24, 2003. For Moussaoui not finding a flight school, see Intelligence report, interrogation of detainee, Jan. 22, 2002. For the ammonium nitrate purchase, see Intelligence report, interrogation of detainee, Apr. 9, 2002; Intelligence report, interrogation of detainee, Apr. 12, 2004. For the cargo planes operation, see Intelligence report, interrogation of detainee, Apr. 12, 2004. For KSM's reaction, see Intelligence Report, interrogation of KSM, Mar. 24, 2003. For Moussaoui's and Binalshibh's trips and Moussaoui's emails, see FBI report, "Summary of Penttbom Investigation," Feb. 29, 2004 (classified version), p. 85. There are no witnesses who report that Moussaoui and Binalshibh actually met in London, but Moussaoui's subsequent travel to Afghanistan implies that he received instructions from Binalshibh. See ibid., p. 86. Somewhere in his travels, Moussaoui obtained the funds he would bring to the United States. He declared $35,000 upon arrival on February 23, 2001, and he deposited $32,000 into a Norman, Oklahoma, bank account on February 26. FBI report, "Summary of Penttbom Investigation," Feb. 29, 2004, p. 78.

55. For Hanjour's entry, see INS record, NIIS record of Hanjour, Oct. 3, 1991. For his university studies, see FBI report, "Hijackers Timeline," Dec. 5, 2003 (Oct. 14, 1991, entry citing 265A-NY-280350-PX, serial 3792). For Hanjour being religious, see FBI letterhead memorandum, Penttbom investigation, Jan. 4, 2004, p. 10. One witness interviewed by the FBI after 9/11 remembers Hanjour and Nawaf al Hazmi becoming so entranced during a prayer that both men began to cry. FBI report of investigation, interview of Mourad Jdaini, Sept. 22, 2001. For Hanjour's trip to Afghanistan, his initial studies in the United States, his rejection by the Saudi flight school, and his desire for flight training in the United States, see Intelligence report, interviews of Saudi hijackers' families, Dec. 22, 2001; FBI report of investigation, interview of Adnan Khalil, Sept. 29, 2001.

56. For Hanjour's 1996 trip to the United States, see, e.g., FBI report, "Hijackers Timeline," Dec. 5, 2003 (Apr. 1, 1996, entry citing 265A-NT-280350, serial 2746; 265A-NT-280350-302, serial 9130). For his interest in flight training in Florida and his training in California, see FBI report of investigation, interview of Adnan Khalil, Sep. 14, 2001; FBI report, "Hijackers Timeline," Dec. 5, 2003 (Sept. 3, 1996, entry citing 265A-NY-280350-SF, serial 1847). For his 1996 flight instruction in Arizona and return to Saudi Arabia, see ibid. (Sept. 29, 1996, entry citing 265A-NY-280350-IN, serial 953; Nov. 26, 1996, entry citing INS: 265A-NY-280350-NK). For his return to Florida, see FBI letterhead memorandum, investigation of Bandar al Hazmi, Jan. 15, 2002. For his 1998 flight training in Arizona, see FBI report, "Hijackers Timeline," Dec. 5, 2003 (Feb. 2, 1998, entry citing 265A-NY-280350-IN, serial 4468). For his flight training in Arizona with his two friends, see ibid. (Feb. 24, 2000, entry citing 265A-NY-280530-IN, serial 4468). Hanjour initially was nervous if not fearful in flight training. FBI letterhead memorandum, investigation of Lotfi Raissi, Jan. 4, 2004, p. 11. His instructor described him as a terrible pilot. FBI letterhead memorandum, interview of James McRae, Sept. 17, 2001.

We have seen no evidence of a familial relationship between Bandar al Hazmi and hijackers Nawaf al Hazmi and Salem al Hazmi. Tim T. interview (Jan. 5, 2004); Ken Williams interview (May 11, 2004). Bandar al Hazmi claims he met Hanjour in Florida, as they were both studying at the same English-language institute. FBI letterhead memorandum, investigation of Bandar al Hazmi, Jan. 15, 2002. Rayed Abdullah, who knew Bandar al Hazmi from high school, says he moved to Florida to become a commercial pilot after speaking with Bandar al Hazmi, and claims he met Hanjour upon arriving in Florida. FBI report of investigation, interview of Rayed Abdullah, Sept. 15, 2001; FBI letterhead memorandum, investigation of Abdullah Rayed Abdullah, Nov. 16, 2001, p. 8. This account is not credible, because Abdullah arrived in the United States on November 15, 1997, the day *before* Hanjour arrived. Ken Williams interview (May 11, 2004); FBI report, "Hijackers Timeline," Dec. 5, 2003 (citing 265A-NY-280350-NK, serial 1379). The three of them did attend language school together but not until after all three had arrived in the United States. FBI report of investigation, interview of Rayed Abdullah, Sept. 15, 2001. The Phoenix FBI office remains suspicious of Abdullah and Hazmi and their association with Hanjour. Ken Williams interview (May 11, 2004). (Williams is the FBI agent who authored what is referred to as the "Phoenix memo," discussed in chapter 8.)

For Hanjour obtaining his pilot's license in three months, see FBI report of investigation, interview of Amro Hassan, Sept. 17, 2001, p. 2. For Hanjour receiving his commercial pilot's license, see FBI report, "Hijackers Timeline," Dec. 5, 2003 (Apr. 15, 1999, entry citing 265A-NY-280350-PX, serial 334). For Hanjour's apparent return to Saudi Arabia, see ibid. (Apr. 28, 1999, entry citing INS I-94, 265A-NY-280350-NK, serial 1379). Bandar al Hazmi continued his training at Arizona Aviation with intermittent trips home to Saudi Arabia, before departing the United States for the last time in January 2000. Tim T. interview (Jan. 5, 2004); FBI report of investigation, interview of Amro Hassan, Sept. 19, 2001. Rayed Abdullah trained at Arizona Aviation and obtained a private pilot's license in December 1998. FBI letterhead memorandum, investigation of Rayed Abdullah, May 5, 2001, p. 9. Abdullah then worked as a computer programmer in Arizona before resuming flight training during the summer of 2001. FBI report of investigation, interview of Rayed Abdullah, Sept. 16, 2001, p. 5.

57. Intelligence report, interviews of Saudi hijackers' families, Dec. 22, 2001.

58. Al Qaeda figures at the university or in Tucson included Mubarak al Duri, reportedly Bin Ladin's principal procurement agent for weapons of mass destruction; Muhammad Bayazid, an al Qaeda arms procurer and trainer; Wadi al Hage, an operative convicted for the East Africa bombings; and Wail Julaidan, a Saudi extremist with ties to al Qaeda. CIA and FBI joint analytic report, "Arizona: Long Term Nexus for Islamic Extremists," May 15, 2002, p. 3.

59. Rayed Abdullah, who lived and trained with Hanjour, was a leader at the Islamic Cultural Center in Phoenix and reportedly gave extremist speeches at the mosque. Ken Williams interview (Jan. 7, 2004); FBI electronic communication, Rayed Abdullah, Sept. 22, 2003. Another Hanjour associate, Faisal al Salmi, took flight training with Rayed Abdullah but wanted to keep his training secret. FBI letterhead memorandum, investigation of Rayed Abdullah, May 5, 2001; FBI report of investigation, interview of Malek Seif, Oct. 25, 2001. When polygraphed on whether he had taken flight training at the behest of an organization, al Salmi's negative response was deemed deceptive. FBI electronic communication, investigation of Zakaria Soubra, June 5, 2002, p. 8.

60. For al Qaeda activity in Arizona, see Ken Williams interview (Jan. 7, 2004). On al Qaeda directing individuals in the Phoenix area to enroll in flight training without telling them why, see FBI electronic communication, investigation of Rayed Abdullah, Sept. 22, 2003. Ghassan al Sharbi, who was captured in March 2002 in Pakistan along with Abu Zubaydah, studied at Embry-Riddle Aeronautical University in Prescott, Arizona. Greg Krikorian, "Detainee Facing Deportation Summoned to Probe," Los Angeles Times, Jan. 24, 2003; Ken Williams interview (Jan. 7, 2004). Although Sharbi has not been tied to the 9/11 attacks, he reportedly attended the training camps in Afghanistan and swore bayat to Bin Ladin during the summer of 2001. FBI memorandum, investigation of Hamed al Sulami, Aug. 1, 2002, p. 6.

After he left the camps, Sharbi looked for his friend Hamdan al Shalawi, another student in Arizona, for a secret project. Shalawi reportedly trained in the camps in November 2000, learning how to conduct "Khobar Towers"–type attacks that he and a colleague planned to execute in Saudi Arabia. FBI electronic communication, investigation of Hamdan al Shalawi, Oct. 16, 2003, p. 2; Intelligence report, trace request on Shalawi, Nov. 27, 2000. Shalawi, however, denies this, claiming to have been studying in Arizona at the time, which neither the FBI nor we have been able to confirm. Shalawi was involved in a widely publicized incident in November 1999, when he and his friend Muhammed al Qudhaieen were detained because the crew of a cross-country America West flight reported that Qudhaieen had attempted to open the cockpit door on two occasions. FBI letterhead memorandum, Hamed al Sulami, July 25, 2002, p. 7. After the 9/11 attacks, FBI agents in Phoenix considered whether the incident was a "dry run" for the attacks. See, e.g., FBI letterhead memorandum, investigation of Fahad al Wahedi, Nov. 8, 2002, p. 4. In our interviews of Shalawi and Qudhaieen, they both claimed that Qudhaieen was only looking for the lavatory on the plane. Mohammad al Qudhaieen interview (Oct. 25, 2003); Hamdan al Shalawi interview (Oct. 22, 2003). Shalawi admits having gone to Afghanistan, but only once in the late 1980s after the war with the Soviet Union. Shalawi interview (Oct. 22, 2003).

Finally, another admitted associate of Hani Hanjour in Arizona, Hamed al Sulami, has had telephone contact with Sulayman al Alwan, a radical Saudi cleric from Qassim Province who was reported to be Abu Zubaydah's spiritual advisor and, as discussed later in this chapter, may have had a role in recruiting one or more of the muscle hijackers. FBI memorandum, investigation of Hamed al Sulami, Aug. 1, 2002, p. 2; FBI memorandum, investigation of Fahad al Wahedi, Nov. 8, 2002, p. 4; CIA analytic report, "The Plot and the Plotters," June 1, 2003, p. 27.

61. For Hanjour's meeting KSM, experience in the camp, and incorporation into the 9/11 operation, see Intelligence report, interrogation of KSM, Feb. 20, 2004. It is unknown how Hanjour got to the camps or who may have directed him to go there. For new arrivals' procedures, see Intelligence report, interrogation of KSM, May 15, 2003.

62. For Hanjour returning home and obtaining a visa, see DOS records, visa applications for Hanjour, Sept. 10, 2000; Sept. 25, 2000. For Hanjour's statement to his family, see Intelligence report, interviews of Saudi hijackers' families, Dec. 22, 2001. For the meeting, see Intelligence report, interrogation of detainee, Jan. 7, 2004.

63. Ali initially gave Hanjour $3,000 to open the account and later deposited another $5,000 into the account. See FBI report, financial timeline of 9/11 hijackers, Dec. 9, 2004, p. 36 (Dec. 5, 2000, and Jan. 28, 2001, entries). Intelligence report, interrogation of detainee, Feb. 11, 2004. Hanjour also maintained another account, into which more than $9,600 was deposited. While in the United States, he accessed both accounts via ATM. FBI Report, "Summary of Penttbom Investigation," Feb. 29, 2004, pp. 9, 11, 13, 17–18, 19. For Hanjour's travel and supposed destination, see INS record, NIIS record of Hanjour, Dec. 8, 2000; DOS record, Hanjour visa application, Sept. 25, 2000. For his enrollment but failure to attend, see FBI report, "Hijackers Timeline," Dec. 5, 2003 (Nov. 6, 2000, entry citing 265A-NY-280350-302, serial 11165; 265A-NY-280350-SF, serial 160).

64. For Hanjour's refresher training, see FBI report, "Hijackers Timeline," Dec. 5, 2003 (Dec. 13, 2000, entry citing 265A-NY-280350-IN, serial 29652). For his desire to train on multi-engine planes, his language difficulties, the instructor's advice, and his reaction, see FBI report of investigation, interview of Rodney McAlear, Apr. 10,

2002. For his training at Pan Am International Flight Academy and completion by March 2001, see FBI report, "Hijackers Timeline," Dec. 5, 2003 (Feb. 8, 2001, entries citing 265A-NY-280350, serial 2870; 265A-NY-280350-PX, serials 334, 1033). For the Academy's instructor's reaction, see FBI report of investigation, interview of James Milton, Apr. 12, 2002; FBI electronic communication, Penttbom investigation, Sept. 16, 2001, pp. 2–3. For his perseverance, see ibid., p. 3. For vacating their apartment, see FBI report, "Hijackers Timeline," Dec. 5, 2003 (Mar. 31, 2001, entry citing 265A-NY-280350-PX, serial 762). During the cross-country drive, Hazmi received a speeding ticket in Oklahoma on April 1, 2001. Ibid. (citing 265A-NY-280350-W, serial 693, items k2453, k2454; 265A-NY-280350-OC, serial 1541; 265A-NY-280350-302, serials 58753, 58757). For arrival in Virginia, see ibid. (citing 265A-NY-280350-NH, serial 1859).

65. For Atta's training at Huffman, see, e.g., FBI report, "Hijackers Timeline," Dec. 5, 2003 (Nov. 19, 2000, entry citing 265A-280350-TP-5382). For Atta's certificate, see ibid. (Nov. 20, 2000, entry citing FAA records). For Shehhi's training at Huffman, see FBI report of investigation, interview of Erik Seiberlich, Sept. 12, 2001. For Shehhi's certificate, see FBI report, "Summary of Penttbom Investigation," Feb. 29, 2004, p. 20. For Atta and Shehhi taking the commercial pilot test, see FBI report, "Hijackers Timeline," Dec. 5, 2003 (Dec. 19, 2000, entry citing 265A-NY-280350-302-9715, serial 26590). For Atta and Shehhi's commercial pilot licenses, see ibid. (Dec. 21, 2000, entries citing FAA records; 265A-NY-280350-302-2340). For Atta and Shehhi's simulator training, see ibid. (Dec. 30, 2000, entry citing 265A-NY-280350-302, serial 1177). For Jarrah's training, see ibid. (Dec. 15, 2000, entries citing 265D-NY-280350-1399, serial 8048).

66. For Jarrah's trip to Beirut and return trip with Senguen, see FBI letterhead memorandum, profile of Jarrah, Mar. 20, 2002. For Senguen accompanying Jarrah to flight training, see German BKA report, investigative summary re Jarrah, July 18, 2002, p. 60. According to Binalshibh, Senguen visited Jarrah in order to verify that he actually was studying to become a pilot. Intelligence report, interrogation of Binalshibh, June 9, 2004. For Jarrah's second trip to Beirut and visiting Senguen, see FBI letterhead memorandum, profile of Jarrah, Mar. 20, 2002; FBI electronic communication, Penttbom investigation, Sept. 18, 2001, p. 5.

67. For Atta's trip to Germany and meeting with Binalshibh, see Intelligence reports, interrogations of Binalshibh, Sept. 24, 2002; Dec. 10, 2002; FBI Penttbom timeline briefing (Dec. 10–11, 2003). For Atta giving money to Binalshibh, see ibid. For Atta returning to Florida, see FBI report, "Hijackers Timeline," Dec. 5, 2003 (Jan. 10, 2001, entry citing INS NIIS report; 265A-NY-280350-302, serial 7134). For Binalshibh's trip to Afghanistan, see FBI Penttbom timeline briefing (Dec. 10–11, 2003).

68. For Shehhi's trip, see FBI report, "Hijackers Timeline," Dec. 5, 2003 (Jan. 11 and 12, 2001, entries citing 265A-NY-280350-TP, serials 11182, 11183; 265A-NY-280350-OUT, serials 2248, 2256, Intelligence report). We do not have information on what Shehhi did in Morocco. Atta's cell phone was used on January 2 to call the Moroccan embassy in Washington, D.C. before Shehhi left. FBI report, "Hijackers Timeline," Dec. 5, 2003 (citing cellular telephone records). Shehhi's trip occurred at a time when Abdelghani Mzoudi, one of the Hamburg cell associates, was also in Morocco. Mzoudi claims he went home to Morocco to get married but could not because he was injured in a car accident there. German BKA report, investigative summary re Mzoudi, Jan. 13, 2003, p. 43. He denies having met with Shehhi, and neither German nor U.S. investigators have uncovered evidence of a meeting. See Federal Prosecutor General (Germany), response to Commission letter, June 25, 2004. For Shehhi's family contacting the UAE embassy, which contacted Hamburg police, and the UAE official's search, see German BKA report, investigative summary re Shehhi, July 9, 2002, p. 23. For Shehhi's call home, see FBI report, "Hijackers Timeline," Dec. 5, 2003 (citing 265A-NY-280350-BN-98). For the search being called off, see German BKA report, investigative summary re Shehhi, July 9, 2002, p. 24.

69. Reports that Atta was in the Prague airport on May 30–31, 2000, and that he was turned back because he lacked a visa appear to be a case of mistaken identity: a Pakistani traveler with a name similar to Atta's attempted to enter the Czech Republic from Saudi Arabia via Germany but was forced to return to Germany because he lacked a valid Czech visa. CIA cable, report re traveler to Prague, Dec. 8, 2001.

70. For Czech source reporting and credibility assessment, see CIA briefing (Jan. 28, 2004); Eliska T. interview (May 20, 2004). For the information being reported to CIA, see CIA briefing (Jan. 28, 2004). For the leak and the ministers' statements, see CIA briefing (Jan. 28, 2004); Shirley interview (Apr. 29, 2004). On April 4, 2001, Atta cashed an $8,000 check at a bank in Virginia Beach; he appears on a bank surveillance tape. For FBI evidence of Atta being in Virginia Beach, see FBI report, "Hijackers Timeline," Dec. 5, 2003 (Apr. 4, 2001, entry citing 265A-NY-280350-302-615, 688, 896, 898). For FBI evidence of Atta being in Coral Springs, see ibid. (Apr. 11, 2001, entries citing 265A-NY-280350-302, serial 381; 265A-NY-280350-MM, serials 3817, 5214). For Czech government finding no evidence of Atta's presence and having evidence that Ani was not in Prague, see CIA briefing (Jan. 28, 2004). Aside from scrutinizing various official records, the Czech government also reviewed surveillance photos taken outside the Iraqi embassy. CIA briefing (Jan. 28, 2004); Shirley interview (Apr. 29, 2004). None of the people photographed that day resembled Atta, although the surveillance only operated from 8:00 A.M. to 3:00 P.M. CIA cable, review of surveillance photos, Feb. 27, 2002. For Ani's denials of any meetings and request to superiors, see CIA briefing (Jan. 28, 2004); Intelligence report, interrogation of Ahmad Khalil Ibrahim Samir al Ani, Oct. 1, 2003. For KSM's denial of the meeting, see Shirley interview (Apr. 29, 2004). Binalshibh has stated that Atta and

he were so close that Atta probably would have told him of a meeting with an Iraqi official. Intelligence report, interrogation of Binalshibh, Oct. 2, 2002. Binalshibh also stated that Bin Ladin was upset with Iraqi leader Saddam Hussein for committing atrocities against Iraqi Muslims, and that Bin Ladin would never have approved such a meeting. Intelligence report, interrogation of Binalshibh, Oct. 4, 2002. For Atta not using an alias during his July 2001 trip, see FBI memo, Penttbom investigation, Jan. 14, 2002.

71. Atta was admitted as a tourist for an eight-month stay, even though the legal limit for tourists is six months. Shehhi was admitted for a four-month "business" stay. The Atta and Shehhi applications to change status were ultimately adjudicated on July 17 and August 9, 2001. Each received until October 1, 2001, to complete his studies. For Atta's INS inspection, see INS records, NIIS record of Atta, Jan. 10, 2001; copy of Atta's Egyptian passport; Atta's inspection results; student/school form presented by Atta; primary and secondary inspectors interviews (Mar. 25, 2004). For Shehhi's INS inspection, see INS records, NIIS record of Shehhi, Jan. 18, 2001; Shehhi's inspection results; primary inspector interview (Mar. 26, 2004); secondary inspector interview (Mar. 22, 2004).

72. For Atta and Shehhi staying in Norcross and Decatur, see FBI report, "Hijackers Timeline," Dec. 5, 2003 (Jan. 25, 2001, entry citing 265A-NY-280350-3631; 265A-NY-280350-AT-141). For the plane rental in Lawrenceville, see ibid. (Jan. 31, 2001, entry citing 265A-NY-280350, serial 13850). These locations are all near Atlanta. For return to Virginia, see ibid. (Feb. 20, 2001, entry citing 265A-NY-280350-NF-48, 51). For mailbox rental, see ibid. (Feb. 20, 2001, entry citing 265A-NY-280350-NF-48). For check cashing, see FBI report, "Summary of Penttbom Investigation," Feb. 29, 2004, p. 26. For return to Georgia, see FBI report, "Hijackers Timeline," Dec. 5, 2003 (Feb. 21, 2001, entry citing 65A-NY-280350-302, serial 49563). For Jarrah staying in Decatur, see FBI report, "Hijackers Timeline," Dec. 5, 2003 (Mar. 15, 2001, entry citing 265A-NY-280350, serial 15661). For Atta-Jarrah call, see FBI letterhead memorandum, profile of Jarrah, Mar. 20, 2002. For Jarrah's apparent visit with Senguen, see INS records, NIIS record for Jarrah, Feb. 25, 2001 (with departure date of Mar. 30, 2001); NIIS record for Jarrah, Apr. 13, 2001. For Atta and Shehhi returning to Virginia Beach, see FBI report, "Hijackers Timeline," Dec. 5, 2003 (Apr. 3, 2001, entry citing FBI electronic communication, Sept. 17, 2001). For Atta closing the mailbox, see ibid. (Apr. 4, 2001, entry citing FBI electronic communication, Sept. 18, 2001).

73. For Atta and Shehhi arriving in Virginia, see FBI report, "Hijackers Timeline," Dec. 5, 2003 (Apr. 3, 2001, entry citing 265A-NY-280350-302-615, 688, 896, 898). For Hazmi and Hanjour arriving in Virginia, see ibid. (Apr. 4, 2001, entry citing 265A-NY-280350-NH, serial 1859). For their attendance at the Dar al Hijra mosque, see FBI electronic communication, request for interviews, Aug. 6, 2002.

74. For Aulaqi moving to Virginia, see FBI electronic communication, analysis related to Penttbom investigation, Oct. 23, 2001. For his denial of contacts with Hazmi and Hanjour, see FBI report of investigation, interview of Anwar Aulaqi, Sept. 17, 2001.

75. The apartment was already occupied by two other individuals. The al Qaeda operatives spent little time with their roommates, but did mention at one point that they had considered going to Afghanistan for jihad. FBI report of investigation, interview of Ahmad Ahmad, Oct. 4, 2002. For Hazmi and Hanjour meeting Rababah, see FBI electronic communication, request for interviews of certain individuals, Aug. 6, 2002. For Rababah seeking work at the mosque, his meeting them, and his assistance in finding them an apartment, see FBI report of investigation, interview of Eyad al Rababah, June 10, 2002. For Hazmi and Hanjour renting the apartment, see FBI report of investigation, interview of Derar Mohammed Saleh, Jan. 16, 2003.

76. For FBI agents' suspicions, see Jim B. interview (Nov. 6, 2003). Rababah was reluctant to admit meeting the hijackers at the mosque and initially told a story about meeting them for the first time at a store. Rababah attributed his initial prevarication to wanting to protect the mosque from anti-Arab sentiment following September 11. FBI report of investigation, interview of Eyad al Rababah, June 10, 2002; Robert B. interview (Nov. 6, 2003). For Rababah's deportation, see Peter A. interview (Oct. 10, 2003).

77. FBI report of investigation, interview of Eyad al Rababah, June 10, 2002.

78. For Rababah going to the apartment and finding new roommates, see FBI report of investigation, interview of Eyad al Rababah, June 10, 2002. For the trips to Connecticut and New Jersey, see FBI report, "Hijackers Timeline," Dec. 5, 2003 (May 8, 2001, entries citing 265A-NY-280350-NH, serial 1859); FBI electronic communication, summary of Penttbom investigation, June 3, 2002. For the telephone calls, see FBI report, "Hijackers Timeline," Dec. 5, 2003 (May 8, 2001, entry citing 265A-NY-280350-NH, serial 1859). For return to Connecticut and Rababah not seeing the hijackers again, see ibid. (May 10, 2001, entry citing 265A-NY-280350-NH, serial 1859); FBI report of investigation, interview of Eyad al Rababah, June 10, 2002.

79. For the apartment rental in New Jersey, see FBI report of investigation, interview of Eyad al Rababah, June 10, 2002; FBI report, "Hijackers Timeline," Dec. 5, 2003 (May 21, 2001, entry citing 265A-NY-280350-302, serials 25453, 25445). For the landlord finding six people, see FBI report of investigation, interview of Jimi Nouri, Sept. 19, 2001. Although no specific evidence places Omari in the apartment, the muscle hijackers based in New Jersey likely lived together, as they apparently conducted other activities jointly, such as obtaining identification cards. See, e.g., FBI report, "Hijackers Timeline," Dec. 5, 2003 (July 1, 2001, entries citing 265A-NY-280350-FD-302, serials 4718, 11815, 20900, 21529).

80. For Atta's renting the apartment, see FBI report, "Hijackers Timeline," Dec. 5, 2003 (citing 265A-NY-

280350-302, serial 381; 265A-NY-280350-MM, serial 3817). For Shehhi's presence in Florida, see, e.g., ibid. (Apr. 13, 2001, entry citing 265A-NY-280350-302, serial 17575).

81. For Shehhi's ticket purchase, see FBI report, "Hijackers Timeline," Dec. 5, 2003 (Apr. 13, 2001, entry citing 265A-NY-280350-302, serial 17575; Apr. 18, 2001 entry citing 265A-NY-280350-CG, serial 1928; 265A-NY-280350-302, serial 16379; Apr. 19, 2001, entry citing CIA report; 265A-NY-280350-302, serial 17575). For Shehhi's visit with Atta's father, see ibid. (Apr. 20, 2001, entry citing CIA report). For Atta having license during April 26, 2001, traffic stop and Shehhi spending two weeks abroad, see ibid. (citing 265A-NY-280350-MM, serial 2746; May 2, 2001, entry citing 265A-NY-280350-302, serial 16379; 265A-NY-280350-CG, serial 1928); FBI Penttbom timeline briefing (Dec. 10-11, 2003).

82. For Shehhi's return, see INS record, NIIS record of Shehhi, May 2, 2001. For Atta and Jarrah obtaining driver's licenses, see FBI report, "Hijackers Timeline," Dec. 5, 2003 (May 2, 2001, entry citing 265A-NY-280350-MM, serial 59). Also on May 2, Atta and two unidentified companions appeared at the Miami District Immigration Office, where an inspector reduced Atta's authorized length of stay by two months, correcting the mistake made back in January. Interview of inspector (Mar. 25, 2004).

83. For a description of the muscle hijackers, see CIA analytic report, "The Plot and the Plotters," June 1, 2003, pp. 34–52.

84. On Banihammad, see CIA analytic report, "Facilitating Disaster: An Overview of 11 September Finance," CTC 2002-40093H, Aug. 22, 2002, p. 4

85. Intelligence reports, interviews of Saudi hijackers' families, Dec. 22, 2001; July 17, 2002; Saudi Arabian Mabahith briefing (Oct. 17, 2003) (disclosing that two of the muscle hijackers had married shortly before joining the plot and only one, Wail al Shehri, was employed, as a physical education teacher).

86. CIA analytic report, "The Plot and the Plotters," June 1, 2003, p. 25.

87. Ibid.

88. Ibid., p. 26.

89. Ibid., p. 25. On Nawaf's efforts on behalf of his brother, see CIA analytic report, "Afghanistan Camps Central to 11 September Plot: Can al-Qa'ida Train on the Run?" CTC 2003-40071CH, June 20, 2003, p. 1; Intelligence report, interrogation of detainee, Oct. 18, 2001.

90. Intelligence report, interrogation of Binalshibh, Feb. 18, 2004; Intelligence report, interrogations of KSM and another detainee, Feb. 18, 2004; Intelligence report, interrogation of Abu Zubaydah, Feb. 19, 2004; Intelligence report, interrogation of Nashiri, Feb. 2004; Intelligence report, interrogation of detainee, Feb. 18, 2004.

91. Intelligence report, interrogation of KSM, Jan 7, 2004. Khallad agrees about the recruit pool, but also argues that operatives' ethnicity was important for symbolic reasons, citing the Nairobi and Dar es Salaam embassy bombings and the planes operation as examples. In the planes operation, Khallad notes, Bin Ladin selected operatives from Mecca (Mihdhar and the Hazmi brothers) and would have used more had they been available. Moreover, with respect to the remaining Saudi muscle hijackers, Khallad claims Bin Ladin chose them because he wanted the 9/11 attacks to resound across Saudi Arabia, especially among the southern tribes and those of the hijackers themselves. According to Khallad, Bin Ladin wanted operatives from strong tribal areas of Saudi Arabia and chose two Saudi brothers from the al Shehri tribe, of which their father was a leader. Intelligence report, interrogation of Khallad, Feb. 18, 2004.

92. CIA analytic report, "The Plot and the Plotters," June 1, 2003, pp. 24, 26. According to Saudi authorities, none of the hijackers had any record of extremist activity, but Satam al Suqami and Salem al Hazmi both had minor criminal offense records. Saudi Arabian Mabahith briefing (Oct. 17, 2003).

93. CIA analytic report, "Afghanistan Camps Central to 11 September Plot," June 20, 2003, pp. 1–2.

94. For trainer's comments, see Intelligence report, interrogation of detainee, Feb. 8, 2002. For Omari's, Ghamdi's, and Shehri's backgrounds, see CIA analytic report, "The Plot and the Plotters," June 1, 2003, p. 27; Intelligence reports, interviews of Saudi hijackers' families, Dec. 22, 2001; July 17, 2002.

95. CIA analytic report, "The Plot and the Plotters," June 1, 2003, p. 26; Intelligence reports, interviews of Saudi hijackers' families, Dec. 22, 2001; July 17, 2002. According to Saudi authorities, a substantial number of the hijackers isolated themselves and became religious only within a few months of leaving the Kingdom. All but Ahmad al Haznawi, who called his aunt to inquire about his sick mother, ceased contact with their families about six months before the attacks. Saudi Arabian Mabahith briefing (Oct. 17, 2003).

96. CIA analytic report, "The Plot and the Plotters," June 1, 2003, p. 26; Intelligence reports, interviews of Saudi hijackers' families, Dec. 22, 2001; July, 17, 2002.

97. On Khattab, see CIA analytic report, "The Plot and the Plotters," June 1, 2003, p. 26, n. 2. For KSM's claim, see Intelligence report, interrogation of KSM, May 15, 2003. For difficulties traveling to Chechnya, see also Saudi Arabian Mabahith briefing (Oct. 17, 2003).

98. Intelligence reports, interrogations of Khallad, Sept. 5, 2003; Mar. 26, 2004; Jan. 8, 2004; Jan. 7, 2004. Khallad claims he also encouraged Salem al Hazmi to participate in a suicide operation. Intelligence report, interrogation of Khallad, Apr. 13, 2004.

99. Intelligence reports, interrogations of KSM, May 15, 2003; Jan. 9, 2004; Oct. 21, 2003. KSM does acknowl-

edge that the commander of al Faruq training camp was known to urge trainees to swear bayat. Moreover, peer pressure certainly appears to have been a factor in swaying recruits to choose "martyrdom." Intelligence report, interrogation of KSM, Apr. 30, 2004.

100. Intelligence report, interrogation of KSM, Feb. 18, 2004; Intelligence report, interrogation of Khallad, Jan. 8, 2004.

101. Intelligence report, interrogation of Khallad, Feb. 18, 2004; Intelligence report, interrogation of KSM, Jan. 7, 2004; Intelligence report, interrogation of detainee, Feb. 8, 2003.

102. CIA analytic report, "Afghanistan Camps Central to 11 September Plot," June 20, 2003, pp. 2–3.

103. Ibid., p. 8; Intelligence report, interrogation of KSM, May 15, 2003.

104. Intelligence reports, interrogations of KSM, May 15, 2003; Jan. 9, 2004; Apr. 2, 2004; Intelligence report, interrogation of Khallad, Apr. 13, 2004; Intelligence report, interrogation of detainee, Apr. 14, 2004. For description of martyrdom video filming, see Intelligence report, interrogation of KSM, May 21, 2004.

105. Intelligence report, interrogation of Khallad, Apr. 13, 2004; Intelligence reports, interrogations of KSM, Aug. 20, 2003; Apr. 13, 2004; Apr. 5, 2004; Apr. 3, 2004.

Dates of U.S. visas obtained in 2000: Ahmed al Ghamdi (September 3), Saeed al Ghamdi (September 4), Hamza al Ghamdi (October 17), Mohand al Shehri (October 23), Wail and Waleed al Shehri (October 24), Ahmed al Nami (October 28), Ahmad al Haznawi (November 12), Majed Moqed (November 20), and Satam al Suqami (November 21). Five Saudi muscle hijackers obtained visas in 2001: Ahmed al Nami (April 23), Saeed al Ghamdi (June 12), Khalid al Mihdhar (June 13), Abdul Aziz Omari (June 18) and Salem al Hazmi (June 20). For Nami, Ghamdi, and Mihdhar, this was their second visa, and each applied using a new passport. Banihammad, the only non-Saudi muscle hijacker, also obtained his visa much later than most of the Saudi muscle hijackers, on June 18, 2001. See Commission analysis of DOS records; CIA analytic report, "The Plot and the Plotters," June 1, 2003, p. 55. According to KSM, the three hijackers who obtained their first visas much later than the others were not replacements for unsuccessful candidates. KSM simply wanted to get as many hijackers into the United States as possible to enhance the odds for success, even if each flight ended up with as many as six or seven. Intelligence report, interrogation of KSM, Feb. 20, 2004.

106. Only the passports of Satam al Suqami and Abdul Aziz al Omari were recovered after 9/11. Both had been doctored. According to KSM, two hijacker passports were damaged in the doctoring process. These may have belonged to Saeed al Ghamdi and Ahmed al Nami, as both acquired new passports and new U.S. visas, although the old visas were still valid. Of the hijacker visa applications we were able to review, all were incomplete. Tourist visas were granted anyway. On obtaining "clean" passports and the two damaged passports, see Intelligence reports, interrogations of KSM, July 3, 2003; Sept. 9, 2003. Wail and Waleed al Shehri had a family member in the Saudi passport office who provided them with new passports for their trip to the United States. See CIA analytic report, Al Qaeda Travel Issues, CTC 2004-40002H, Jan. 2004, p. 12.

107. Intelligence report, interrogation of Khallad, Apr. 5, 2004; Intelligence report, interrogation of KSM, Mar. 20, 2004. The candidate operatives were

1. **Muhammad Mani Ahmad al Kahtani.** Currently in custody, he is the last known Saudi muscle candidate to be sent to the United States, in early August 2001, to round out the number of hijackers. As discussed later in this chapter, he was refused entry. Secretary of Defense interview with David Frost (BBC), June 27, 2004, available at www.defenselink.mil. CIA analytic report, "Threat Threads: Recent Advances in Understanding 11 September," CTC 2002-30086CH, Sept. 16, 2002, p. 4; Intelligence report, interrogation of KSM, July 3, 2003; Intelligence report, interrogation of detainee, Apr. 3, 2003.

2. **Khalid Saeed Ahmad al Zahrani.** He traveled to Afghanistan illegally after being prohibited by Saudi authorities from leaving Saudi Arabia. After being assigned to a mission in the U.S., he secretly reentered the Kingdom but failed in an attempt to have his name removed from the list of prohibited travelers so that he could obtain a U.S. visa. See Intelligence reports, interrogations of detainee, Apr. 20, 2002; Oct. 4, 2002; Apr. 3, 2003.

3. **Ali Abd al Rahman al Faqasi al Ghamdi.** (aka Abu Bakr al Azdi) He reportedly was to have been part of the planes operation but was held in reserve by Bin Ladin for a later, even larger operation. Like other muscle hijackers, he reportedly set out for Chechnya but diverted to Afghanistan. See Intelligence reports, interrogations of Abu Bakr al Azdi, July 23, 2003; Sept. 25, 2003; Intelligence report, interrogation of Khallad, Nov. 6, 2003.

4 and 5. **Saeed al Baluchi** and **Qutaybah al Najdi.** Both were sent to Saudi Arabia via Bahrain, where Najdi was stopped and briefly questioned by airport security officials. Both were so frightened by the experience that they withdrew from the operation. KSM urged Baluchi to obtain a U.S. visa, but Baluchi refused, fearing that he might be watchlisted at the U.S. embassy. See Intelligence report, interrogation of Khallad, July 9, 2003; Intelligence reports, interrogations of KSM, Mar. 27, 2003; July 3, 2003; Feb. 20, 2004.

6. **Zuhair al Thubaiti:** He has reportedly admitted membership in al Qaeda, stating "proudly" that

he was among a select number of operatives who had the personal endorsement of Bin Ladin. He was not ultimately selected for the 9/11 attacks because the al Qaeda leadership considered him too high-strung and lacking the necessary temperament. CIA analytic report, "Threat Threads," Sept. 16, 2002, p. 3; Intelligence reports, interrogations of detainee, May 21, 2002; June 17, 2002; June 20, 2002; Intelligence reports, interrogations of KSM, Feb. 20, 2004 (two reports).

7. **Saeed Abdullah Saeed ("Jihad") al Ghamdi.** He arranged to travel to Afghanistan in March 2000, swore allegiance to Bin Ladin (agreeing to serve as a suicide operative), and was sent to Saudi Arabia by KSM with 9/11 hijacker Ahmad al Haznawi to obtain a U.S. visa, but his visa application was denied because he appeared to be intending to immigrate. DOS record, Ghamdi visa application, Nov. 13, 2000. CIA analytic report, "Threat Threads," Sept. 16, 2002, p. 4; Intelligence reports, interrogations of detainee, Apr. 11, 2002; Sept. 11, 2002; Intelligence report, interrogation of KSM, Feb. 20, 2004.

8. **Saud al Rashid.** Describing him as headstrong and immature, KSM says he disappeared after being sent to Saudi Arabia for a U.S. visa, either because he had second thoughts or because his family interceded and confiscated his passport. Passport photos of Rashid and three 9/11 hijackers—Nawaf al Hazmi, Mihdhar, and Omari—were found together during a May 2002 raid in Karachi. After discovery of the photos in 2002, Rashid turned himself in to the Saudi authorities, but he has since been released from custody. In a Commission interview, he has admitted training in Afghanistan but denies hearing of al Qaeda before returning from Afghanistan or meeting Bin Ladin, KSM, or any 9/11 hijacker other than Ahmad al Haznawi, whom he claims seeing only once or twice at a guesthouse. He has no credible explanation why photos of him were found with those of three other hijackers, or why others identified him as a candidate hijacker. See Intelligence report, interrogation of KSM, Mar. 27, 2003; June 11, 2003; July 3, 2003; Feb. 20, 2004; Intelligence report, interrogation of Khallad, July 9, 2003; Saud al Rashid interview (Feb. 24, 2004).

9. **Mushabib al Hamlan.** Sent to Saudi Arabia to acquire a U.S. visa, he and his travel companion, 9/11 hijacker Ahmed al Nami, both applied for and received visas on October 28, 2000. Hamlan never returned to Afghanistan, probably dropping out either because he changed his mind or because his family intervened.

In December 1999, while still in high school in Saudi Arabia, Hamlan became involved with a group that gathered periodically to watch jihad propaganda tapes, and was encouraged by a mentor named Bandar Marui to pursue jihad, especially as practiced in the Bosnia-Herzegovina and Russian-Afghan wars and a book titled *Gladiator of Passion.* As instructed, Hamlan acquired a passport, on February 15, 2000, and agreed to go to Afghanistan after the hajj in mid-March 2000. He and two travel companions obtained Pakistani visas in Sharjah, UAE, and traveled to Islamabad, where al Qaeda facilitator Hassan Ghul took them to a guesthouse managed by Abu Zubaydah. Days later, two men helped Hamlan cross the Pakistan-Afghanistan border.

At the Khaldan camp, Hamlan received military training courses. Upon hearing that the camp was to be closed, he and others traveled to al Faruq camp near Kandahar, where they received more training. He also met and proclaimed allegiance to Bin Ladin at this time. Injured during a further training session, Hamlan was assigned to guard the airport, where he met future hijacker Ahmed al Nami (whose recent laser eye surgery had interrupted his training). An individual named Abu Basir al Yemeni indoctrinated the two in Bin Ladin's anti-U.S. position and extolled the virtues of martyrdom. Hamlan and Nami eventually agreed to approach Abu Hafs al Mauritani about participating in a suicide operation. The day after visiting Abu Hafs, Hamlan and Nami heard from Abu Basir that Bin Ladin was planning an attack against the United States. After taking their passports, Abu Basir arranged for Hamlan and Nami to meet Bin Ladin and instructed them to use the following phrase to express their desire to become martyrs: "I want to be one of this religion's bricks and glorify this religion." The al Qaeda leader accepted both applicants.

In October 2000, Abu Basir took Hamlan and Nami to meet KSM, who impressed on them the high expectations for martyrs and instructed them on using coded telephone numbers. He returned their passports, which had been altered and now contained forged tourism stamps for Singapore, Malaysia, Turkey, and Egypt. KSM told them to meet with Atef before returning to Saudi Arabia, where they should contact hijacker future 9/11 hijacker Waleed al Shehri for additional documentation.

After meeting with Atef, Hamlan and Nami traveled by car and by air to an address KSM had given them in Tehran, where arrangements were made for them to fly to Qatar. From Qatar they traveled onward to the UAE and then to Mecca. Nami contacted KSM and received coded instructions to go to Jeddah, call Waleed al Shehri, and obtain visas at the U.S. consulate. In Jeddah, they briefly shared an apartment with Shehri, who provided them with directions to the consulate and showed them how to fill out the visa application. After acquiring visas, Hamlan and Nami presented their passports to Shehri for inspection and returned to Mecca. Nami called KSM, who told them to return to Afghanistan the next day.

Despite instructions to the contrary, Hamlan insisted on calling his family before leaving Saudi Arabia because he had begun to have second thoughts after acquiring the visa. Told by his brother that their mother had fallen ill. Hamlan decided not to return to Afghanistan even after Nami reminded him of his allegiance to Bin Ladin and commitment to complete the suicide mission. In Riyadh, he told his brothers that he had been on jihad in Chechnya. Fearing that they might ask for his passport, he removed the U.S. visa—as later confirmed by forensic analysis performed by Saudi authorities. Hamlan returned to college and resumed living with his parents, who confiscated his passport.

Thereafter, Hamlan received a visit at the college from a former associate at al Faruq camp, Khalid al Zahrani, who asked why he had not returned to Afghanistan. Zahrani admitted having been sent by KSM to convince Hamlan to return to Afghanistan. Hamlan never did. Intelligence report, interrogation of detainee, Mar. 16, 2003.

10. **Abderraouf Jdey, a.k.a. Faruq al Tunisi.** A Canadian passport holder, he may have trained in Afghanistan with Khalid al Mihdhar and Nawaf al Hazmi and received instruction from KSM with Atta and Binalshibh. A letter recovered from a safehouse in Pakistan, apparently written by Sayf al Adl, also suggests that Jdey was initially part of the 9/11 operation at the same time as the Hamburg group. A videotape of Jdey's martyrdom statement was found in the rubble of Atef's house near Kabul following a November 2001 airstrike, together with a martyrdom video of Binalshibh. While both Binalshibh and Khallad confirm Jdey's status as an al Qaeda recruit, KSM says Jdey was slated for a "second wave" of attacks but had dropped out by the summer of 2001 while in Canada. FBI briefing (June 24, 2004); Intelligence report, interrogation of Binalshibh, Sept. 11, 2003; Intelligence report, interrogation of Khallad, May 21, 2004; Intelligence report, interrogation of KSM, July 1, 2003.

108. On the few operatives fully aware of the plot and Abu Turab's training, see Intelligence report, interrogation of KSM, Feb. 23, 2004. Abu Turab was the son-in-law of Ayman al Zawahiri. Intelligence report, interrogation of Zubaydah, Feb. 18, 2004. KSM also taught the muscle hijackers English and provided lessons about airplanes. Intelligence report, interrogation of KSM, Apr. 2, 2004. Binalshibh also has discussed this training in post-capture statements, describing it as hand-to-hand combat training. Intelligence report, interrogation of Binalshibh, Jan. 8, 2004. According to Binalshibh, after returning to Afghanistan, muscle hijacker recruits fought on the front lines alongside the Taliban and participated in the March 2001 destruction of the giant Buddha statues in Bamian Province, Afghanistan. Intelligence report, interrogation of Binalshibh, Mar. 31, 2004.

109. Intelligence report, interrogation of KSM, Feb. 23, 2004. According to KSM, the muscle hijackers learned about the specific targets and the Atta's completed operational plan only in late August. Intelligence report, interrogation of KSM, Apr. 2, 2004.

110. On the facilitator's comments, see Intelligence reports, interrogations of detainee, Sept. 14, 2002; Oct. 3, 2002; May 5, 2003 (two reports), in which he claims also to have assisted the Hamburg pilots and Binalshibh. On KSM's funding of the hijackers, see Intelligence reports, interrogations of KSM, June 15, 2004; July 25, 2003.

111. On Ali's role and the transit of the hijackers, see Intelligence report, interrogation of detainee, Feb. 12, 2004. According to the detainee, the operatives arrived with their own money to buy plane tickets and anything else they needed. Ali referred them to places where they could obtain travelers checks. He also helped Ahmed al Ghamdi, one of the earliest operatives to transit Dubai, acquire a mobile phone account so that the operatives could use that number as a travel agency point of contact. Ibid.

112. In May 2001, however, Ali asked KSM to participate in a suicide mission and offered to travel to the United States and assist the operatives there. As discussed in a set of Atta-Binalshibh exchanges in August 2001, Ali (referred to by the nickname "Losh") appears to have contacted Atta and expressed the desire to join the operation. Ali actually applied for a U.S. visa on August 27, 2001, listing his intended arrival date as September 4 for a one-week stay. His application was denied because he appeared to be an economic immigrant. DOS record, visa application of Ali Abdul Aziz Ali, Aug. 27, 2001. Intelligence report, interrogation of detainee, Nov. 17, 2003; Intelligence report, documents captured with KSM, Sept. 24, 2003; CIA notes, "DRG Research Notes," Jan. 17, 2004; FBI report, "Summary of Penttbom Investigation," Feb. 29, 2004, p. 72.

113. Intelligence reports, interrogations of detainee, May 6, 2003; Jan. 8, 2004. See also Intelligence report, interrogation of Binalshibh, Sept. 11, 2003. Hawsawi's role as financial facilitator appears to have begun when he and hijacker Banihammad opened bank accounts at the same UAE bank while Banihammad was his way to the United States. Banihammad, who was from the UAE, was familiar with the country's procedures and helped Hawsawi complete his account application. Banihammad gave Hawsawi roughly $3,000 and granted him power of attorney over his account so that Hawsawi could forward the bank card to him in the United States. After Banihammad arrived in the United States, Hawsawi deposited $4,900 into the account. FBI report, "Summary of Penttbom Investigation," Feb. 29, 2004, p. 29.

114. All but 2 of the 15 muscle hijackers were admitted as tourists, affording a six-month stay in the United States (except in the case of Mihdhar, who received four months). The first pair to arrive were Waleed al Shehri (Flight 11) and Satam al Suqami (Flight 11), who flew from the UAE to London and arrived in Orlando on April 23, 2001, where Atta most likely met them. Suqami was admitted as a business visitor, allowing him only a one-month stay and thus making him an illegal overstay by May 21, 2001. INS records, NIIS records of Waleed al Shehri and Satam al Suqami, Apr. 23, 2001. Suqami was the only hijacker not to obtain a U.S. identification document.

Shehri and another individual (presumably Suqami) settled in Hollywood, Florida, moving into a motel on April 30. FBI report, "Hijackers Timeline," Dec. 5, 2003 (citing London EC, serial 2236; 315N-NY-280350-302, serial 7134; 315N-NY-280350, serial 8082).

The next set, Ahmed al Ghamdi (Flight 175) and Moqed (Flight 77), arrived at Dulles Airport on May 2, 2001, on a flight from London originating in Dubai. INS records, NIIS records of Ghamdi and Moqed, May 2, 2001. Although Customs declarations of the two indicate that Moqed claimed to be carrying more than $10,000, the Customs Service generated no report of this event. Both Ghamdi and Moqed gave the Hyatt Hotel in Washington as their intended destination, but instead moved into the apartment in Alexandria, Virginia, that Nawaf al Hazmi and Hani Hanjour had rented. FBI report, "Hijackers Timeline," Dec. 5, 2003 (citing flight manifest and Customs records, referenced in 265A-NY-280350, serial 2746; 265A-NY-280359-RY, serial 5; 265A-NY-280350-302, New Hampshire ECs dated Sept. 28, 2001, Sept. 29, 2001; 265A-NY-280350, serial 9776; 265A-NY-280350-IN, serial 5151; 265A-NY-280350-302).

Hamza al Ghamdi (Flight 175), Mohand al Shehri (Flight 175), and Ahmed al Nami (Flight 93) arrived in Miami on May 28, 2001. INS records, NIIS records of Hamza al Ghamdi, Mohand al Shehri, and Ahmed al Nami, May 28, 2001. The three had taken a flight from London after starting out in Dubai. Atta probably picked up the group at the airport, having rented a Ford Explorer for the day. Shehri and Nami gave the Sheraton in Miami as their intended destination, but do not appear to have stayed there. Marwan al Shehhi helped them settle in Florida. Within a few days, Shehhi found the group an apartment in Delray Beach, Florida. FBI report, "Hijackers Timeline," Dec. 5, 2003 (citing 265A-NY-280350-NK, serial 2851; 265A-NY-280350-CG, serial 1928; 265A-NY-280350-NK, serial 2851; 265A-NY-280350-DL, serial 1778; 265A-NY-280350-DL, 838; 265D-NY-280350-A, serial 16; 265A-NY-280350-NK, serial 2851; 265A-NY-280350-MM-302, serial 11703).

Haznawi (Flight 93) and Wail al Shehri (Flight 11) arrived in Miami from London on June 8, 2001 using the same route as the previous three. INS records, NIIS records of Haznawi and Wail al Shehri (June 8, 2001). FBI report, "Hijackers Timeline," Dec. 5, 2003 (citing 265A-NY-280350-RY, serial 5).

Saeed al Ghamdi (Flight 93) and Banihammad (Flight 175) arrived in Orlando from London on June 27, 2001. INS records, NIIS records of Saeed al Ghamdi and Banihammad, June 27, 2001. Saeed al Ghamdi was questioned by immigration authorities as a possible intending immigrant, as he spoke little English, had no return ticket, and listed no address on his arrival record. INS record, inspection results for Ghamdi, June 27, 2001; primary inspector interview (Mar. 17, 2004); secondary inspector interview (Apr. 19, 2004). Ghamdi and Banihammad presumably stayed with the hijackers who preceded them or with Atta and Shehhi in the Hollywood, Florida, apartment. Post-9/11 investigation revealed that during this time period Atta and Shehhi also checked into hotels or rented apartments with unidentified males, probably the newly arrived muscle hijackers. FBI report, "Hijackers Timeline," Dec. 5, 2003 (citing 265A-NY-280350-302-19615; 265A-NY-280350-MM, serial 3255; 265A-NY-280350-MM-302, serial 34927; 265A-NY-280350-MM-Sub, serial 3255; 265A-NY-280350-RY, serial 5; 265A-NY-280350-MM-302, serial 34927; 265A-NY-280350-MM, serials 48418, 2374, 4449, 4696; 265A-NY-280350, serials 925, 449, 18695).

The remaining hijackers entered the United States through New York. Salem al Hazmi (Flight 77) and Omari (Flight 11) arrived at JFK on June 29, 2001, from Dubai with a connection in Zurich. INS records, arrival records of Salem al Hazmi and Omari, June 29, 2001. They likely were picked up by Salem's older brother Nawaf—who was then living in Paterson, New Jersey, with Hani Hanjour—the following day, for on June 30, Nawaf had a minor car accident traveling eastbound on the George Washington Bridge, toward JFK. FBI report, "Hijackers Timeline," Dec. 5, 2003 (citing Bern EC Sept. 15, 2001; INS NIIS report; 265A-NY-280350-302, serial 7134; 265A-NY-280350-HQ, serial 11297; Bern EC (Omari PNR, Swiss Air); 265A-NY-280350-302, serial 60839). On Salem al Hazmi in the Paterson apartment, see FBI report of investigation, interview of Jimi Nouri, Oct. 6, 2001, p. 5.

115. FBI report, "Summary of Penttbom Investigation," Feb. 29, 2004, pp. 29–41; Adam Drucker interview (Jan. 12, 2004).

116. In some cases, bank employees completed the Social Security number fields on the new account application with a hijacker's date of birth or visa control number, but did so on their own to complete the form. Adam Drucker interview (Jan. 12, 2004). Contrary to persistent media reports, no financial institution filed a Suspicious Activity Report (SAR)—which U.S. law requires banks to file within 30 days of a suspicious transaction—with respect to any transaction of any of 19 hijackers before 9/11. A number of banks did file SARs after 9/11, when the hijackers' names became public. Adam Drucker interview (Jan. 12, 2004); James Sloan interview (Nov. 14, 2003). Nor should SARs have been filed. The hijackers' transactions themselves were not extraordinary or remarkable. See Commission analysis of financial transactions; Adam Drucker interview (Jan. 12, 2004); Dennis Lormel interview (Jan. 16, 2004).

117. Intelligence report, interrogation of Khallad, Mar. 26, 2004; Intelligence report, interrogation of KSM, May 19, 2003.

118. Intelligence reports, interrogations of detainee, Nov. 27, 2001; Feb. 5, 2002.

119. FBI report, "Hijackers Timeline," Dec. 5, 2003 (citing 315N-NY-280350-DL, serial 2812; 315N-NY-280350-302, serial 21529; 315N-NY-280350-NK, serials 21529, 11815, 4718).

120. Intelligence reports, interrogations of detainee, Oct. 18, 2001; Mar. 13, 2002; Intelligence report, interrogation of detainee, Mar. 7, 2002; Intelligence reports, interrogations of KSM, Aug. 20, 2003; Sept. 12, 2003, July 16, 2004; Intelligence report, interrogation of Khallad, Sept. 12, 2003; Intelligence report, interrogation of detainee, Sept. 30, 2003; CIA analytic report, "Iran and al-Qa'ida: Ties Forged in Islamic Extremism," CTC 2004-40009HCX, March 2004, pp. i, 6-12.

121. Intelligence report, analysis of Hezbollah, Iran, and 9/11, Dec. 20, 2001; Intelligence report, interrogation of Binalshibh, July 16, 2004.

122. Ibid.; Intelligence report, Hezbollah activities, Oct. 11, 2001; Intelligence report, operative's travel to Saudi Arabia, Aug. 9, 2002.

123. Intelligence reports, hijacker activities, Oct. 11, 2001; Oct. 29, 2001; Nov. 14, 2001; Intelligence report, operative's claimed identification of photos of two Sept. 11 hijackers, Aug. 9, 2002.

124. Intelligence reports, hijacker activities, Nov. 14, 2001; Oct. 2, 2001; Oct. 31, 2001.

125. Intelligence reports, hijacker activities, Oct. 19, 2001; Dec. 7, 2001.

126. Intelligence report, interrogation of KSM, July 16, 2004; Intelligence report; interrogation of Binalshibh, July 16, 2004.

127. Intelligence report, analysis of Hezbollah, Iran, and 9/11, Dec. 20, 2001.

128. Intelligence report, Hezbollah and Sunni terrorist activities, Sept. 21, 2001; Intelligence report, Hezbollah denies involvement in 9/11, Sept. 22, 2001.

129. For Atta and Shehhi's efforts, see FBI report, "Summary of Penttbom Investigation," Feb. 29, 2004, pp. 25–37.

130. Ibid., pp. 29–41.

131. FBI report, "Hijackers Timeline," Dec. 5, 2003 (citing 315N-NY-280350-302, serials 12436, 7134); see Intelligence report, interrogation of KSM, June 15, 2004; Intelligence report, interrogation of Binalshibh, June 9, 2004. Another example of unusual travel was a trip by Suqami on July 10 from Fort Lauderdale to Orlando; he stayed at a hotel in Lake Buena Vista with an unidentified male through July 12. FBI report, "Summary of Penttbom Investigation," Feb. 29, 2004, p. 31.

132. FBI report, "Hijackers Timeline," Dec. 5, 2003 (citing 315N-NY-280350-302, serial 27063; 315N-NY-280350-DL, serial 2245); Commission investigation in Las Vegas.

133. FBI report, "Summary of Penttbom Investigation," Feb. 29, 2001, pp. 41–44.

134. FBI letterhead memorandum, profile of Jarrah, Mar. 20, 2002.

135. FBI report, "Hijackers Timeline," Dec. 5, 2003 (citing 315N-NY-280350-302, serial 7228; 315N-NY-280350-F, serial 99; 315N-NY-280350-NK, serial 263). Documents from Sawyer Aviation in Phoenix, Arizona, show Hanjour joining the flight simulator club on June 23, 2001, with Faisal al Salmi, Rayed Abdullah, and Lotfi Raissi. FBI report of investigation, interview of Jennifer Stangel, Sept. 14, 2001. But the documents are inconclusive, as there are no invoices or payment records for Hanjour, while such documents do exist for the other three. FBI memo, Penttbom investigation, Oct. 7, 2001; FBI memo, Penttbom investigation, summary of dispatch sheets, Oct. 12, 2001; Don W. and Steve B. interview (Jan. 6, 2004). One Sawyer employee identified Hanjour as being there during the time period, though she was less than 100 percent sure. FBI report of investigation, interview of Tina Arnold, Oct. 17, 2001. Another witness identified Hanjour as being with Salmi in the Phoenix area during the summer of 2001. FBI letterhead memorandum, investigation of Lotfi Raissi, Jan. 4, 2004, p. 18. Documentary evidence for Hanjour, however, shows that he was in New Jersey for most of June, and no travel records have been recovered showing that he returned to Arizona after leaving with Hazmi in March. Nevertheless, the FBI's Phoenix office believes it plausible that Hanjour returned to Arizona for additional training. FBI electronic communication, Penttbom investigation, Feb. 19, 2002.

136. Intelligence report, interrogation of Binalshibh, Oct. 1, 2002.

137. CIA cable, communications analysis, Sept. 11, 2003.

138. On Hazmi, see FBI report, "Summary of Penttbom Investigation," Feb. 29, 2004, p. 46. On obtaining photo identification, see ibid.; FBI report, "Hijackers Timeline," Dec. 5, 2003 (citing 315N-NY-280350-NK, serial 1243; 315N-NY-280350-BS, serial 352; 315N-NY-280350-302, serials 33059, 64343).

139. FBI report, "Summary of Penttbom Investigation," Feb. 29, 2004, p. 47.

140. For Binalshibh moving the muscle hijackers, see Intelligence report, interrogation of Binalshibh, June 9, 2004. According to Binalshibh, he took each of the muscle hijackers shopping for clothes and set them up with email accounts during their time in Karachi. Ibid. For meeting with Atta and Bin Ladin, see Intelligence reports, interrogations of Binalshibh, Sept. 24, 2002; Feb. 18, 2004. Binalshibh has provided inconsistent information about who else was present during his meeting with Bin Ladin. In one interview, Binalshibh claimed he attended two different meetings, one of which was attended by Bin Ladin, Atef, KSM, and Abu Turab al Jordani, and the second of which was attended just by Bin Ladin, Atef, and KSM. More recently, however, Binalshibh has mentioned only one meeting and has claimed he alone met with Bin Ladin because Atef and KSM were busy with other matters. Compare Intelligence report, interrogation of Binalshibh, Dec. 11, 2002, with Intelligence report, interrogation of Binalshibh, Feb. 18, 2004.

141. On Binalshibh's meeting with Bin Ladin, Intelligence reports, interrogations of Binalshibh, Dec. 11, 2002; Sept. 24, 2002; Feb. 18, 2004; Apr. 7, 2004. KSM claims that the White House and the Capitol were both acceptable targets and had been on the list since the spring of 1999. Intelligence report, interrogation of KSM, Apr. 2, 2004. On Binalshibh's receipt of money, Intelligence reports, interrogations of Binalshibh, Oct. 23, 2002; Dec. 11, 2002. In one report, Binalshibh says that Atef provided him with $3,000; in another he claims it was $5,000.

142. Intelligence reports, interrogations of Binalshibh, Sept. 24, 2002; Oct. 23, 2002; Dec. 11, 2002.

143. Intelligence reports, interrogations of Binalshibh, Sept. 24, 2002; Dec. 11, 2002.

144. Intelligence reports, interrogations of Binalshibh, Oct. 1, 2002; Mar. 7, 2003; Apr. 8, 2004.

145. FBI report, "Summary of Penttbom Investigation," Feb. 29, 2004, p. 48. Intelligence reports, interrogations of Binalshibh, Oct. 1, 2002; Mar. 7, 2003; Dec. 21, 2002. Atta had a stopover in Zurich, where he bought two Swiss Army knives and withdrew 1,700 Swiss francs from his SunTrust bank account. He may have intended to use the knives during the attacks. It is unknown why he withdrew the money. FBI report, "Summary of Penttbom Investigation," Feb. 29, 2004, p. 47.

Although U.S. authorities have not uncovered evidence that anyone met with Atta or Binalshibh in Spain in July 2001, Spanish investigators contend that members of the Spanish al Qaeda cell were involved in the July meeting and were connected to the 9/11 attacks. In an indictment of the Spanish cell members dated September 17, 2003, the Spanish government relies on three main points. First is a 1997 trip to the United States by Ghasoub al Abrash Ghalyoun, a Syrian living in Spain. During the trip, Ghalyoun videotaped a number of U.S. landmarks, including the World Trade Center. The Spanish indictment alleges that an al Qaeda courier was in Ghalyoun's town in Spain shortly after the trip and that the courier probably delivered the tape to al Qaeda leaders in Afghanistan. Second, the Spanish government contends that during the relevant time period, an individual named Muhammed Belfatmi was near the town where the Atta-Binalshibh meeting took place. and that Belfatmi traveled to Karachi shortly before September 11 on the same flight as Said Bahaji, one of Atta's Hamburg associates, and even stayed at the same hotel. Finally, Spanish authorities rely on an intercepted telephone conversation between cell leader Imad Eddin Barakat Yarkas and an individual named "Shakur" in August 2001, in which "Shakur" describes himself as entering "the field of aviation" and "slitting the throat of the bird." "Shakur" has been identified by Spanish authorities as Farid Hilali. Although we cannot rule out the possibility that other facts will come to light as the Spanish case progresses to trial, we have not found evidence that individuals in Spain participated in the July meeting or in the 9/11 plot. See Baltasar Garzon interview (Feb. 13, 2004); Indictment, Central Investigating Court No. 5, Madrid, Sept. 17, 2003, pp. 151–200, 315–366; Superseding Indictment, Central Investigating Court No. 5, Madrid, April 28, 2004.

146. Intelligence reports, interrogations of Binalshibh, Oct. 1, 2002; Mar. 7, 2003; Apr. 17, 2003.

147. Intelligence reports, interrogations of Binalshibh, Oct. 1, 2002; Mar. 7, 2003; Sept. 11, 2003; Oct. 11, 2003; Feb. 18, 2004; Apr. 7, 2004. KSM claims to have assigned the Pentagon specifically to Hanjour, the operation's most experienced pilot. Intelligence report, interrogation of KSM, Feb. 20, 2004.

148. Intelligence reports, interrogations of Binalshibh, Mar. 7, 2003; Oct. 11, 2003. Binalshibh since has denied that the term *electrical engineering* was used to refer to a potential nuclear target despite having said so earlier. Intelligence report, interrogation of Binalshibh, Sept. 11, 2003. KSM has admitted that he considered targeting a nuclear power plant as part of his initial proposal for the planes operation. See chapter 5.2. He has also stated that Atta included a nuclear plant in his preliminary target list, but that Bin Ladin decided to drop that idea. Intelligence report, interrogation of KSM, Mar. 12, 2002.

149. Intelligence reports, interrogations of Binalshibh, Oct. 1, 2002; Mar. 7, 2003; Feb. 18, 2004.

150. Intelligence reports, interrogations of Binalshibh, Sept. 24, 2002; Oct. 1, 2002; Mar. 7, 2003; Apr. 17, 2003.

151. On Binalshibh's new phones, see Intelligence report, interrogation of Binalshibh, Dec. 21, 2002. On Binalshibh's call to KSM, see Intelligence reports, interrogations of Binalshibh, Oct. 1, 2002; Mar. 31, 2003. CIA cable, Sept. 10, 2003; CIA report, Director's Review Group, Oct. 2003.

152. Intelligence report, interrogation of KSM, Oct. 31, 2003; Intelligence report, interrogation of Binalshibh, Nov. 1, 2003. KSM may also have intended to include these documents as part of the historical file he maintained about the 9/11 operation. He says the file included letters and email communications among those involved with the attacks, but was lost in Afghanistan when he fled after September 11. Intelligence report, interrogation of KSM, Oct. 15, 2003.

153. Intelligence reports, interrogations of Binalshibh, Nov. 1, 2003; Oct. 11, 2003; Intelligence report, interrogation of KSM, Oct. 31, 2002.

154. Intelligence reports, interrogations of Binalshibh, Oct. 31, 2002; Dec. 19, 2002; Apr. 17, 2003; Oct. 11, 2003; Nov. 1, 2003; Intelligence report interrogation of KSM, Sept. 11, 2003.

155. FBI letterhead memorandum, Penttbom investigation, Mar. 20, 2002, p. 60; FBI report, "Hijackers Timeline," Dec. 5, 2003 (citing 315N-NY-280350-302, serial 20874); Jarrah travel documents (provided by the FBI).

156. Intelligence reports, interrogations of Binalshibh, Dec. 11, 2002; Apr. 8, 2004.

157. According to Binalshibh, Jarrah was not aware of Moussaoui or the wire transfers. Intelligence reports,

interrogations of Binalshibh, Dec. 11, 2002; Apr. 17, 2003. FBI report, "Summary of Penttbom Investigation," Feb. 29, 2004 (classified version), pp. 89–90.

158. FBI report, Moussaoui, Zacarias, a.k.a. Shaqil, Aug. 18, 2001, pp. 7, 11; FBI briefing materials, Penttbom, Dec. 10–11, 2003, p. 148 (citing 315N-NY-280350-302, serial 98252).

159. FBI report, "Summary of Penttbom Investigation," Feb. 29, 2004 (classified version), p. 90; DOJ Inspector General interview of John Weess, Oct. 22, 2002; FBI letterhead memorandum, "Moussaoui, Zacarias," Aug. 31, 2001.

160. Intelligence report, interrogation of KSM, July 2, 2003; Intelligence report, interrogation of KSM, Sept. 11, 2003.

161. Intelligence reports, interrogations of KSM, July 1, 2003; July 8, 2003. In addition to Moussaoui, the two al Qaeda operatives identified by KSM as candidates for the second wave of attacks were Abderraouf Jdey, a.k.a. Faruq al Tunisi (a Canadian passport holder, discussed earlier as a candidate hijacker) and Zaini Zakaria, a.k.a. Mussa (a Jemaah Islamiah member who worked in Hambali's Malaysia stronghold and was directed by Atef to enroll in flight training sometime in 2000, according to KSM). Intelligence report, interrogation of KSM, July 8, 2003; Intelligence report, interrogation of Hambali, Mar. 4, 2004.

162. Intelligence report, interrogation of Binalshibh, Apr. 17, 2003. According to Binalshibh, KSM said that the operative had been raised and educated in Europe and that his arrest resulted, at least in part, from his having been insufficiently discreet. KSM identified this operative as an exception in Bin Ladin's overall record of selecting the right people for the 9/11 attacks. Intelligence report, interrogation of Binalshibh, Dec. 18, 2002. Subsequently, however, Binalshibh has sought, somewhat incredibly, to exculpate a host of individuals, including Moussaoui, from complicity in the 9/11 plot. Intelligence report, interrogation of Binalshibh, Apr. 2, 2004.

163. For Binalshibh's claims, see Intelligence reports, interrogations of Binalshibh, Nov. 7, 2002; Feb. 13, 2003; Feb. 27, 2003. On KSM, see intelligence report, interrogation of KSM, July 2, 2003.

164. Jarrah returned to the United States on August 5, 2001. INS record, arrival record of Jarrah, Aug. 5, 2001.

165. FBI report, "Hijackers Timeline," Dec. 5, 2003 (citing 315N-NY-280350-302, serial 14139; Boston electronic communication). The communications were recovered from materials seized during the March 2003 capture of KSM. For background, see Intelligence reports, interrogations of KSM, Aug. 13, 2002 (two cables); Intelligence report, documents captured with KSM, Sept. 24, 2003.

166. Intelligence reports, interrogation of KSM, Aug. 12, 2003. Binalshibh, however, has denied that *law* and *politics* referred to two separate targets; he claims that both terms referred to the U.S. Capitol, even though in the context of the exchange it seems clear that two different targets were contemplated. Intelligence report, interrogations of Binalshibh, Sept. 11, 2003 (two reports).

167. CIA notes, "DRG Research Notes," Jan. 17, 2004. In another exchange between Atta and Binalshibh on September 9—two days before the attacks—it still appears as though the White House would be the primary target for the fourth plane and the U.S. Capitol the alternate. See CIA report, Documents captured with KSM, Sept. 24, 2003.

168. On the Atta-Binalshibh communication, see Intelligence report, interrogation of Binalshibh, Sept. 11, 2003. On Kahtani's attempt to enter the U.S., see INS record, withdrawal of application for admission of Kahtani, Aug. 4, 2001. For Hawsawi, see Intelligence report, interrogation of detainee, Apr. 3, 2003.

169. On Atta's trip to Newark, see FBI report, "Summary of Penttbom Investigation," Feb. 29, 2004, p. 50. On arrivals in Florida, see FBI report, "Hijackers Timeline," Dec. 5, 2004 (citing 315N-NY-280350, serials 388, 5860; 315N-NY-280350-BS, serial 294; 315N-NY-280350-302, serial 66933). On travel to Las Vegas, see ibid. (citing 315N-NY-280350-LV, serial 53299; 315N-NY-280350-302, serial 110). Atta's flight from Washington, D.C., arrived in Las Vegas within an hour of Hazmi and Hanjour's arrival. Ibid. The three hijackers stayed in Las Vegas only one night, departing on August 14. Ibid. (citing 315N-NY-280350-DL, serial 829; 315N-NY-280350-SD, serial 569; 315N-NY-280350-302, serial 165970). Detainee interviews have not explained the Las Vegas meeting site. See, e.g., Intelligence report, interrogation of Binalshibh, Nov. 5, 2003.

170. FBI report, "Summary of Penttbom Investigation," Feb. 29, 2004, pp. 52–57. Hanjour successfully conducted a challenging certification flight supervised by an instructor at Congressional Air Charters of Gaithersburg, Maryland, landing at a small airport with a difficult approach. The instructor thought Hanjour may have had training from a military pilot because he used a terrain recognition system for navigation. Eddie Shalev interview (Apr. 9, 2004).

171. FBI report, "Summary of Penttbom Investigation," Feb. 29, 2004, pp. 57–60. According to Binalshibh, Atta deliberately selected morning flights because he anticipated that the most people would be at work then. Intelligence report, interrogation of Binalshibh, June 3, 2004.

172. Intelligence reports, interrogations of Binalshibh, Oct. 1, 2002; Dec. 17, 2002; Dec. 21, 2002.

173. On KSM's receipt of date of attacks, see Intelligence report, interrogations of KSM and Binalshibh, May 27, 2003. Although Binalshibh also has claimed that he called KSM with the date after receiving the information from Atta, KSM insists that he learned of the date in a letter delivered by Essabar, and that it would have been a serious breach of communications security to communicate the date over the phone. Intelligence reports, interrogations of Binalshibh, Oct. 1, 2002; Dec. 17, 2002. Intelligence report, interrogation of KSM, Feb. 20, 2004. Most

recently, Binalshibh has claimed that he neither called nor sent a letter to KSM, but rather passed a verbal message via Essabar. Intelligence report, interrogation of Binalshibh, Apr. 8, 2004. On Binalshibh's communication to Essabar, see Intelligence reports, interrogations of Binalshibh, Dec. 17, 2002; Nov. 6, 2003; Apr. 8, 2004.

174. On Binalshibh's travel, see FBI report, "Summary of Penttbom Investigation," Feb. 29, 2004 (classified version), p. 84. On Binalshibh's communication with Atta, see Intelligence report, Documents captured with KSM, Sept. 24, 2003; Intelligence report, interrogation of Binalshibh, Sept. 11, 2003. On Atta's call to his father, see Intelligence report, re Atta, Sept. 13, 2001. On Jarrah's letter, see German BKA report, investigative summary re Jarrah, July 18, 2002, p. 67.

175. Shortly after 9/11, Abdullah told at least one witness that the FBI was asking questions about his having received a phone a call from Hazmi in August. FBI report of investigation, interview, Sept. 24, 2001. In a July 2002 FBI interview, Abdullah asked whether the FBI had taped the call. FBI report of investigation, interview of Mohdar Abdullah, July 23, 2002. Also on possibility of Hazmi-Abdullah contact shortly before 9/11, see Danny G. interviews (Nov. 18, 2003; May 24, 2004). On the change in Abdullah's mood, see FBI report of investigation, interview of Mohdar Abdullah, July 23, 2001. On the sudden interest of Abdullah and Salmi in proceeding with marriage plans, see FBI report of investigation, interview, Sept. 24, 2001; FBI report of investigation, interview of Samir Abdoun, Oct. 21, 2001. On anticipated law enforcement interest in gas station employees and September 10, 2001, meeting, see FBI report of investigation, interview, May 21, 2002.

176. Intelligence report, interrogation of detainee, Feb. 5, 2002.

177. Intelligence reports, interrogations of KSM, Aug. 14, 2003; Feb. 20, 2004.

178. Intelligence reports, interrogations of KSM, June 3, 2003; Feb. 20, 2004; Apr. 3, 2004.

179. Intelligence reports, interrogations of detainee, Nov. 27, 2001; Feb. 5, 2002. Intelligence report, interrogation of detainee, May 30, 2002.

180. Intelligence report, interrogation of KSM, Jan. 9, 2004; Intelligence report, interrogation of detainee, June 27, 2003; Intelligence report, interrogation of detainee, Feb. 5, 2002. KSM also says that he and Atef were so concerned about this lack of discretion that they urged Bin Ladin not to make any additional remarks about the plot. According to KSM, only Bin Ladin, Atef, Abu Turab al Jordani, Binalshibh, and a few of the senior hijackers knew the specific targets, timing, operatives, and methods of attack. Intelligence reports, interrogations of KSM, Oct. 27, 2003; Feb. 23, 2004. Indeed, it was not until midsummer that Egyptian Islamic Jihad leader Ayman al Zawahiri learned of the operation, and only after his group had cemented its alliance with al Qaeda and Zawahiri had become Bin Ladin's deputy. Intelligence report, interrogation of KSM, Jan. 9, 2004.

181. See Intelligence report, interrogation of KSM, July 24, 2003.

182. On Omar's opposition, see, e.g., Intelligence report, interrogation of detainee, May 30, 2002, in which the detainee says that when Bin Ladin returned after the general alert during July, he spoke to his confidants about Omar's unwillingness to allow an attack against the United States to originate from Afghanistan. See also Intelligence report, interrogation of KSM, Oct. 27, 2003. There is some discrepancy about the position of Zawahiri. According to KSM, Zawahiri believed in following the injunction of Mullah Omar not to attack the United States; other detainees, however, have said that Zawahiri was squarely behind Bin Ladin. Intelligence report, interrogation of detainee, June 20, 2002; Intelligence report, interrogation of detainee, June 27, 2003; Intelligence report, interrogation of KSM, Sept. 26, 2003.

183. Intelligence report, interrogation of KSM, Jan. 9, 2004; Intelligence reports, interrogations of detainee, June 27, 2003; Dec. 26, 2003. On Abu Hafs's views, see Intelligence report, interrogation of detainee, Oct. 7, 2003.

184. Intelligence reports, interrogations of KSM, Oct. 27, 2003; Sept. 27, 2003, in which Bin Ladin had sworn bayat to Omar upon first moving to Afghanistan, following the Shura Council's advice. KSM claims he would have disobeyed even had the council ordered Bin Ladin to cancel the operation. Intelligence report, interrogation of KSM, Jan. 9, 2004.

185. See Intelligence report, interrogation of KSM, July 24, 2003.

186. Abdul Faheem Khan interview (Oct. 23, 2003); see also Arif Sarwari interview (Oct. 23, 2003).

187. Intelligence reports, interrogations of KSM, May 8, 2003; July 24, 2003.

188. FBI report, "Hijackers Timeline," Dec. 5, 2003 (citing 315N-NY-280350, serial 3112; Western Union records; 315N-NY-280350-302, serials 28398, 37864). In addition, Nawaf al Hazmi attempted to send Hawsawi the debit card for Mihdhar's bank account, which still contained approximately $10,000. The package containing the card was intercepted after the FBI found the Express Mail receipt for it in Hazmi's car at Dulles Airport on 9/11. FBI report, "Summary of Penttbom Investigation," Feb. 29, 2004, p. 61.

189. FBI report, "Hijackers Timeline," Dec. 5, 2003 (citing 315N-NY-280350-WF, serial 64; 315N-NY-280350-BA, serials 273, 931, 628; 315N-NY-280350-302, serials 10092, 17495).

190. FBI report, "Hijackers Timeline," Dec. 5, 2003 (citing 315N-NY-280350, serials 6307, 9739). In the early morning hours of September 11, Jarrah made one final call to Senguen from his hotel. FBI report, "Hijackers Timeline," Dec. 5, 2003. The conversation was brief and, according to Senguen, not unusual. FBI electronic communication, Penttbom investigation, Sept. 18, 2001, pp. 5–6.

191. FBI report, "Hijackers Timeline," Dec. 5, 2003 (citing 315N-NY-280350-FD-302; 315N-NY-280350-

SD, serial 1522; 315N-NY-280350-302, serials 16597, 5029, 6072, 11098, 11114, 11133, 4119; 315N-NY-280350-BS, serials 349, 19106, 16624; 315N-NY-280350-CD, serial 373; 315N-NY-280350, serials 7441, 21340; 315N-NY-280350-AT, serial 135). There have been many speculations about why Atta scheduled the Portland flight. Although he may have believed that security was more relaxed at the smaller airport, he and Omari had to pass through security again at Logan. Ibid. (citing 315N-NY-280350-BS, serial 2909). Interrogation of detainees has produced no solid explanation for the trip. See, e.g., Intelligence report, interrogation of Binalshibh, Mar. 3, 2004.

192. FBI report, "Hijackers Timeline," Dec. 5, 2003 (citing 315N-NY-280350, serial 2268; 315N-NY-280350-302, serials 32036, 9873; 315N-NY-280350-LO, serial 2).

8 "The System Was Blinking Red"

1. Beginning in December 1999, these briefings were conducted based on slides created by the CIA's Bin Ladin unit. See Richard interview (Dec. 11, 2003). We were able to review the slides to identify the subjects of the respective briefings.

2. The exact number of persons who receive the PDB varies by administration. In the Clinton administration, up to 25 people received the PDB. In the Bush administration, distribution in the pre-9/11 time period was limited to six people. The Commission received access to about four years of articles from the PDB related to Bin Ladin, al Qaeda, the Taliban, and key countries such as Afghanistan, Pakistan, and Saudi Arabia, including all the Commission requested. The White House declined to permit all commissioners to review these sensitive documents. The Commission selected four representatives—the Chair, the Vice Chair, Commissioner Gorelick, and the Executive Director—as its review team. All four reviewed all of the more than 300 relevant articles. Commissioner Gorelick and the Executive Director prepared a detailed summary, reviewed by the White House for constitutional and especially sensitive classification concerns, that was then made available to all Commissioners and designated staff. Except for the August 6, 2001, PDB article, the summary could not include verbatim quotations, for example the titles of the articles, but could paraphrase the substance. Two of the articles—the December 4, 1998, hijacking article (in chapter 4) and the August 6, 2001, article discussing Bin Ladin's plans to attack in the United States (in this chapter)—were eventually declassified.

3. The CIA produced to the Commission all SEIB articles relating to al Qaeda, Bin Ladin, and other subjects identified by the Commission as being relevant to its mission from January 1998 through September 20, 2001.

4. See CIA, SEIB, "Sunni Terrorist Threat Growing," Feb. 6, 2001; CIA cable, "Intelligence Community Terrorist Threat Advisory," Mar. 30, 2001.

5. See NSC email, Clarke to Rice, Briefing on Pennsylvania Avenue, Mar. 23, 2001.

6. See NSC email, Clarke to Rice and Hadley, Terrorism Update, Mar. 30, 2001; NSC email, Clarke to Rice, Terrorist Threat Warning, Apr. 10, 2001.

7. See FBI electronic communication, heightened threat advisory, Apr. 13, 2001.

8. See NSC email, Cressey to Rice and Hadley, Threat Update, Apr. 19, 2001; CIA, SEIB, "Bin Ladin Planning Multiple Operations," Apr. 20, 2001; NSC memo, Clarke for Hadley, "Briefing Notes for al Qida Meeting," undated (appears to be from April 2001).

9. For threats, see CIA, SEIB, "Bin Ladin Public Profile May Presage Attack," May 3, 2001; CIA, SEIB, "Bin Ladin Network's Plans Advancing," May 26, 2001; FBI report, Daily UBL/Radical Fundamentalist Threat Update, ITOS Threat Update Webpage, May 7, 2001 (the walk-in's claim was later discredited). For Attorney General briefing, see CIA briefing materials, "Briefing for the Attorney General, 15 May 2001, Al-Qa'ida," undated. For more threats and CSG discussion, see Intelligence report, Threat Report, May 16, 2001; NSC memo, CSG agenda, May 17, 2001.

10. See CIA, SEIB, "Terrorist Groups Said Cooperating on US Hostage Plot," May 23, 2001; FAA information circular, "Possible Terrorist Threat Against American Citizens," IC-2001-08, June 22, 2001 (this IC expired on August 22, 2001); CIA, SEIB, "Bin Ladin Network's Plans Advancing," May 26, 2001; NSC email, Clarke to Rice and Hadley, "A day in the life of Terrorism intelligence," May 24, 2001.

11. See NSC email, Clarke to Rice and Hadley, Stopping Abu Zubaydah's attacks, May 29, 2001. For threat level, see White House document, "Selected Summer 2001 Threat Response Activities," undated, pp. 1–2 (provided to the Commission by President Bush on Apr. 29, 2004).

12. The information regarding KSM was not captioned as a threat. It was part of a longer cable whose subject line was "Terrorism: Biographical Information on Bin Ladin Associates in Afghanistan." The cable reported further that KSM himself was regularly traveling to the United States. See Intelligence report, June 12, 2001. This was doubted by the CIA's Renditions Branch, which had been looking for KSM since 1997. It noted, however, that if the source was talking about the "real" KSM, the CIA had both "a significant threat and opportunity to pick him up." See CIA cable, request additional information on KSM, June 26, 2001. A month later, a report from the source indicated that the information regarding KSM's travel to the United States was current as of the summer of 1998. It noted further, however, that KSM continued his old activities but not specifically the travel to the United States. Significantly, it confirmed that the source was talking about the "real" KSM. See CIA cable, follow-up source on

KSM, July 11, 2001. As noted in chapter 7, KSM has said that it was generally well known by the summer of 2001 that he was planning an operation in the United States. Roger Cressey told us he did not recall seeing this reporting, although he would have had access to it. Roger Cressey interview (June 23, 2004).

For the summer threat reporting and actions taken in response, see NSC memo, Clarke/Cressey agenda for June 22 CSG meeting, June 20, 2001; CIA, SEIB, "Bin Ladin and Associates Making Near-Term Threats," June 25, 2001; CIA, SEIB, "Bin Ladin Planning High-Profile Attacks," June 30, 2001; CIA cable, "Threat UBL Attack Against US Interests Next 24–48 Hours," June 22, 2001; FBI report, Daily UBL/Radical Fundamentalist Threat Update, ITOS Threat Update Webpage, June 22, 2001.

13. DOS cable, Riyadh 02326, "U.S. Visa Express Program Transforms NIV Scene in Saudi Arabia," Aug. 19, 2001; NSC memo, Current US Terrorism Alert, July 3, 2001.

14. See CIA cable, "Possible Threat of Imminent Attack from Sunni Extremists," June 23, 2001; CIA, SEIB, "Bin Ladin Attacks May be Imminent," June 23, 2001; CIA, SEIB, "Bin Ladin and Associates Making Near-Term Threats," June 25, 2001.

15. See NSC memo, Clarke to CSG regarding that day's CSG meeting, June 22, 2001; NSC memo, Current U.S. Terrorism Alert, July 3, 2001. For the readiness of FESTs, see NSC email, Clarke to Rice and Hadley, Terrorism Threat Update, June 25, 2001.

16. See NSC email, Clarke to Rice and Hadley, Possibility of an al Qaeda Attack, June 25, 2001; CIA report, Foreign Broadcast Information Service, "MBC TV Carries Video Report on Bin Ladin, Followers in Training," June 24, 2001; CIA, SEIB, "Bin Ladin Threats Are Real," June 30, 2001; John McLaughlin interview (Jan. 21, 2004); CIA cable, "Continued Threat/Potential Attack by UBL," June 29, 2001.

17. See NSC email, Clarke to Rice and Hadley, Possibility of an al Qaeda Attack, June 28, 2001; NSC email, Clarke for Rice and others, Terrorist Alert, June 30, 2001.

18. See NSC email, Clarke to Rice and others, Terrorist Alert, June 30, 2001; CIA, SEIB, "Bin Ladin Planning High-Profile Attacks," June 30, 2001; CIA, SEIB, "Planning for Bin Ladin Attacks Continues, Despite Delays," July 2, 2001.

19. FBI report, National Law Enforcement Telecommunications System (NLETS) message, "National Threat Warning System—Potential Anti-U.S. Terrorist Attacks," July 2, 2001.

20. By July 3, DCI Tenet had asked about 20 of his counterparts in friendly foreign intelligence services to detain specific al Qaeda members and to generally harass al Qaeda–affiliated cells. NSC memo, Current U.S. Terrorism Alert, July 3, 2001. For specific disruption activities and maintaining alert, see NSC email, Clarke to Rice and Hadley, Threat Updates, July 6, 2001; Richard Clarke interview (Jan. 12, 2004).

21. For the Cheney call see President Bush and Vice President Cheney meeting (Apr. 29, 2004). For the Hadley call see NSC email, Clarke to Rice and Edelman, Terrorism Alert, July 2, 2001. For the G-8 summit see Associated Press Online, "Bush Faced Threat at G-8 Summit," Sept. 26, 2001.

22. Veronica C. interview (May 25, 2004); INS memo, Veronica C. to Cadman, "Briefing at the NSC," July 9, 2001; Roger Cressey interview (June 23, 2004). The Customs representative, Ricardo C., did send out a general advisory that was based solely on historical facts, such as the Ressam case, to suggest there was a threat. Ricardo C. interview (June 12, 2004).

23. See CIA memo, "CTC Briefing for the Attorney General on the Usama Bin Ladin Terrorist Threat," July 5, 2001, and the accompanying CIA briefing materials, "DCI Update Terrorist Threat Review," July 3, 2001.

24. See NSC email, Clarke to Rice and Hadley, Threat Updates, July 6, 2001.

25. Ibid.; see also FBI memo, Kevin G. to Watson, "Protective Services Working Group (PSWG) Meeting Held at FBIHQ 7/9/01," July 16, 2001, and accompanying attendance sheets.

26. FBI report, Daily UBL/Radical Fundamentalist Threat Update, ITOS Threat Update Webpage, July 20, 2001.

27. Thomas Pickard interview (Apr. 8, 2004).

28. See CIA, SEIB, "Bin Ladin Plans Delayed but Not Abandoned," July 13, 2001; CIA, SEIB, "One Bin Ladin Operation Delayed, Others Ongoing," July 25, 2001; NSC memo, Cressey to CSG, Threat SVTS, July 23, 2001.

29. FAA information circular, "Continued Middle Eastern Threats to Civil Aviation," IC-2001-04A, July 31, 2001.

30. George Tenet interview (Jan. 28, 2004).

31. See CIA, SEIB, "Bin Ladin Threats Are Real," June 30, 2001. For Tenet's response to DOD's concerns about possible deception, see CIA memo, weekly meeting between Rice and Tenet, July 17, 2001; John McLaughlin interview (Jan. 21, 2004); Richard interview (Dec. 11, 2003).

32. NSC email, Clarke to Rice and Hadley, Threats Update, July 27, 2001.

33. FBI report, NLETS message, "Third Anniversary of the 1998 U.S. Embassy Bombings in East Africa Approaches; Threats to U.S. Interests Continue," Aug. 1, 2001.

34. CIA cable, "Threat of Impending al Qaeda Attack to Continue Indefinitely," Aug. 3, 2001.

35. CIA letter, Tenet to the Commission, Mar. 26, 2004; Barbara S. interview (July 13, 2004); Dwayne D. interview (July 13, 2004).

36. President Bush and Vice President Cheney meeting (Apr. 29, 2004). For Rice's reaction to the August 6 PDB article, see Condoleezza Rice testimony, Apr. 8, 2004.

37. The CTC analyst who drafted the briefing drew on reports over the previous four years. She also spoke with an FBI analyst to obtain additional information. The FBI material was written up by the CIA analyst and included in the PDB. A draft of the report was sent to the FBI analyst to review. The FBI analyst did not, however, see the final version, which added the reference to the 70 investigations. Barbara S. interviews (Apr. 12, 2004); Joint Inquiry interview of Jen M., Nov. 20, 2002. Because of the attention that has been given to the PDB, we have investigated each of the assertions mentioned in it.

The only information that actually referred to a hijacking in this period was a walk-in at an FBI office in the United States who mentioned hijackings among other possible attacks. The source was judged to be a fabricator. FBI report, Daily UBL/Radical Fundamentalist Threat Update, ITOS Threat Update Webpage, Aug. 1, 2001.

The FBI conducted an extensive investigation of the two individuals who were stopped after being observed taking photographs of two adjacent buildings that contained FBI offices. The person taking the photographs told the FBI that he was taking them for a co-worker in Indiana who had never been to New York and wanted to see what it looked like. The picture taker was in New York to obtain further information regarding his pending citizenship application. He had an appointment at 26 Federal Plaza, where the relevant INS offices were located. This same building houses portions of the FBI's New York Field Office. Before going into the building the individual pulled out the camera and took four photographs. When the FBI attempted to contact the co-worker (and roommate) who had requested some photographs, it was determined that he had fled without receiving his last paycheck after learning that the FBI had asked his employer some questions about him. Further investigation determined that he was an illegal alien using forged identity documents. Despite two years of investigation, the FBI was unable to find the co-worker or determine his true identity. The FBI closed the investigation on June 9, 2003, when it concluded that it was unable to connect the men's activities to terrorism. Matthew interview (June 18, 2004); FBI case file, no. 266A-NY-279198.

The 70 full-field investigations number was a generous calculation that included fund-raising investigations. It also counted each individual connected to an investigation as a separate full-field investigation. Many of these investigations should not have been included, such as the one that related to a dead person, four that concerned people who had been in long-term custody, and eight that had been closed well before August 6, 2001. Joint Inquiry interview of Elizabeth and Laura, Nov. 20, 2002; FBI report, "70 UBL Cases," undated (produced to the Joint Inquiry on Aug. 12, 2002).

The call to the UAE was originally reported by the CIA on May 16. It came from an anonymous caller. Neither the CIA nor the FBI was able to corroborate the information in the call. FBI report, Daily UBL/Radical Fundamentalist Threat Update, ITOS Threat Update Webpage, May 16, 2001.

38. See CIA, SEIB, "Bin Ladin Determined to Strike in US," Aug. 7, 2001; see also Roger Cressey interview (June 23, 2004). The Deputy Director of Central Intelligence testified that the FBI information in the PDB was omitted from the SEIB because of concerns about protecting ongoing investigations, because the information had been received from the FBI only orally, and because there were no clear, established ground rules regarding SEIB contents. John McLaughlin testimony, Apr. 14, 2004.

39. Intelligence report, Consideration by Abu Zubaydah to Attack Targets in the United States, Aug. 24, 2001.

40. George Tenet interview (July 2, 2004).

41. Condoleezza Rice testimony, Apr. 8, 2004; Condoleezza Rice meeting (Feb. 7, 2004).

42. Stephen Hadley meeting (Jan. 31, 2004).

43. It is also notable that virtually all the information regarding possible domestic threats came from human sources. The information on overseas threats came mainly from signals intelligence. Officials believed that signals intelligence was more reliable than human intelligence. Roger Cressey interview (June 23, 2004).

44. NSC memo, Clarke to Rice, al Qaeda review, Jan. 25, 2001 (attaching NSC memo, "Strategy for Eliminating the Threat from the Jihadists Networks of al Qida: Status and Prospects," Dec. 2000). Clarke had also mentioned domestic terrorist cells in connection with the possibility of reopening Pennsylvania Avenue. See NSC email, Clarke to Rice, Briefing on Pennsylvania Avenue, Mar. 23, 2001.

45. Roger Cressey interview (June 23, 2004).

46. This approach was consistent with how this same issue was addressed almost exactly a year earlier, despite the fact that by 2001 the threat level was higher than it had ever been previously. On June 30, 2000, NSC counterterrorism staffers met with INS, Customs, and FBI officials to review border and port security measures. The NSC staff's Paul Kurtz wrote to then national security adviser Samuel Berger, "We noted while there was no information regarding potential attacks in the U.S. they should inform their officers to remain vigilant." NSC email, Kurtz to Berger, Steinberg, and Rudman, warning re: UBL threat reporting, June 30, 2000.

47. FAA briefing materials, Office of Civil Aviation Security, "The Transnational Threat to Civil Aviation," undated (slide 24). The presentation did indicate, however, that if a hijacker was intending to commit suicide in a spectacular explosion, the terrorist would be likely to prefer a domestic hijacking. Between July 27 and September 11, 2001, the FAA did issue five new Security Directives to air carriers requiring them to take some specific secu-

rity measures. Two continued certain measures that had been in place for at least a year. Others related only to carrying specific passengers. See FAA security directives, SD 108-98, July 27, 2001; SD 108-00, July 27, 2001; SD 108-00, July 27, 2001; SD 108-01, Aug. 21, 2001; SD 108-01, Aug. 31, 2001. In order to issue more general warnings without directing carriers to take specific action, the FAA issued Information Circulars. Of the eight such circulars issued between July 2 and September 11, 2001, five highlighted possible threats overseas. See FAA information circulars, "Possible Terrorist Threat—Arabian Peninsula," IC-2001-11, July 18, 2001; "Recent Terrorist Activity in the Middle East," IC-2001-03B, July 26, 2001; "Continued Middle Eastern Threats to Civil Aviation," IC-2001-04A, July 31, 2001; "Violence Increases in Israel," IC-2001-07A, Aug. 28, 2001; "ETA Bombs Airports in Spain," IC-2001-13, Aug. 29, 2001. One, issued on August 16, warned about the potential use of disguised weapons. FAA information circular, "Disguised Weapons," IC-2001-12, Aug. 16, 2001.

48. FAA report, "Record of Air Carrier Briefings—4/18/01 to 9/10/01," undated.

49. See Condoleezza Rice testimony, Apr. 8, 2004; NSC memo, U.S. Terrorism Alert, July 3, 2001; FBI electronic communication, Heightened Threat Advisory, Apr. 13, 2001. For the lack of NSC direction, see Roger Cressey interview (June 23, 2004).

50. Thomas Pickard interview (Apr. 8, 2004). For example, an international terrorism squad supervisor in the Washington Field Office told us he was not aware of an increased threat in the summer of 2001, and his squad did not take any special actions to respond to it. The special agent in charge of the Miami Field Office told us he did not learn of the high level of threat until after September 11. See Washington Field Office agent interview (Apr. 1, 2004); Hector Pesquera interview (Oct. 3, 2003).

51. Dale Watson interview (Jan. 6, 2004).

52. See Thomas Pickard interviews (Jan. 21, 2004; Apr. 8, 2004); Thomas Pickard testimony, Apr. 13, 2004; Thomas Pickard letter to the Commission, June 24, 2004; John Ashcroft testimony, Apr. 13, 2004. We cannot resolve this dispute. Pickard recalls the alleged statement being made at a briefing on July 12. The Department of Justice has informed us that the only people present at that briefing were Pickard, Ashcroft, Deputy Attorney General Larry Thompson, and Ashcroft's chief of staff, David Ayres. There are no records of the discussions at these briefings. Thompson and Ayres deny Ashcroft made any such statement. Dale Watson, who did not attend any of the briefings, told us that Pickard complained after one of the briefings that Ashcroft did not want to be briefed on the threats because "nothing ever happened." Ruben Garcia, head of the FBI's Criminal Division, who attended some of Pickard's briefings of the Attorney General but not the one at which Pickard alleges Ashcroft made the statement, recalls that Ashcroft was "not enthusiastic" about the classified portions of the briefings that related to counterterrorism. We have been told that Pickard and Ashcroft did not have a good relationship. This may have influenced their views on the facts surrounding their meetings. Larry Thompson interview (Jan. 29, 2004); Dale Watson interview (June 3, 2004); Ruben Garcia interview (Apr. 29, 2004); Thompson and Ayres letter to the Commission, July 12, 2004.

53. See Thomas Pickard interviews (Jan. 21, 2004; Apr. 8, 2004); John Ashcroft meeting (Dec. 17, 2003); John Ashcroft testimony, Apr. 13, 2004.

54. Indeed, the number of FISA warrants in effect in the summer of 2001 may well have been less than it was at the beginning of the year. Because of problems with inaccuracies in the applications, FISAs were allowed to lapse rather than be renewed with continuing inaccuracies. Michael Rolince interview (Apr. 12, 2004); Marion Bowman interview (Mar. 6, 2004).

55. See CIA cable, Base/FBI comments on draft cable, Nov. 27, 2000; FBI electronic communication, USS Cole investigation, Nov. 21, 2000; FBI electronic communication, USS Cole investigation, Jan. 10, 2001 (draft).

56. For the recollection of the FBI agent, see Al S. interviews (Aug. 26, 2003; Sept. 15, 2003). See also FBI report of investigation, interview of source, July 18, 2000; attachment to FBI electronic communication, USS Cole investigation, Jan. 10, 2001 (draft); FBI electronic communication, UBL investigation, Jan. 16, 2001.

57. For speculation regarding identities, see CIA cable, "Photo of UBL Associate," Dec. 27, 2000. Retrospective analysis of available information would have answered that question, but that analysis was not done until after 9/11. For analysis, see Intelligence report, Retrospective review of 11 September 2001 hijackers' activities, Sept. 23, 2002.

58. CIA cable, "Request for January 2000 Malaysian Surveillance Photos," Dec. 12, 2000; CIA cable, "Photo of UBL Associate," Dec. 27, 2000; CIA cable, "Review of Malaysia 'Khaled' Photos," Jan. 5, 2001.

59. The CIA knew that Mihdhar and Khallad had both been to Bangkok in January 2000. They had not yet discovered that Khallad, traveling under an alias, had actually flown to Bangkok with Mihdhar. Still, as Director Tenet conceded in his testimony before the Joint Inquiry, the Kuala Lumpur meeting took on additional significance once Khallad was identified as having attended the meeting. See Joint Inquiry report, p. 149.

60. For Tenet and Black testimony, see Joint Inquiry testimony of George Tenet, Oct. 17, 2002; Joint Inquiry testimony of Cofer Black, Sept. 26, 2002. For documents not available to CIA personnel who drafted the testimony, see, e.g., FBI electronic communication, UBL investigation, Jan. 16, 2001; FBI emails between Al S. and Michael D., re: source, Jan. 9-11, 2001; FBI electronic communication, USS Cole investigation, Jan. 4, 2001; DOJ Inspector General interview of Jennifer M., Dec. 9, 2002. For the views of the FBI investigators, see DOJ Inspec-

tor General interviews of Steve B., Sept. 16, 2002; Nov. 14, 2002; Al S. interviews (Aug. 26, 2003; Sept. 15, 2003). The DOJ Inspector General came to the same conclusion. See DOJ Inspector General report, "A Review of the FBI's Handling of Intelligence Information Related to the September 11 Attacks" (hereinafter "DOJ IG 9/11 Report"), July 2, 2004, pp. 308–310.

61. DOJ Inspector General interview of Michael D., Nov. 6, 2002; Michael D. interview (May 4, 2004); DOJ Inspector General interview of Chris, Nov. 27, 2002.

62. For the internal CIA reports to which the FBI did not have access, see CIA cable, "UBL Operative Khallad," Jan. 3, 2001; CIA cable, source debriefing, Jan. 5, 2001. The FBI agent informed us that he was unaware how such internal CIA communications worked, or that the operational cables even existed, and so did not know to ask for them. Such messages are routinely not shared in order to protect intelligence sources and methods. In this case, application of the routine procedure did not serve that purpose because the FBI agent was aware of the source's identity as well as the methods used to obtain the information. Moreover, the FBI agent also may have been absent from the room when the identification was made. The source had brought a sheaf of documents with him that the FBI agent left the room to copy while the interview of the witness continued. Because of the circumstances of the interview site, the agent would have been absent for a significant period of time. In addition, the case officer was frequently given photographs from a broad range of CIA stations to show to this particular witness. He did not focus on the purpose of showing the photographs; he was only concerned with whether the source recognized the individuals. DOJ Inspector General interview of Michael D., Nov. 6, 2002; Michael D. interview (May 4, 2004); DOJ Inspector General interview of Chris, Nov. 27, 2002.

63. John interview (Apr. 2, 2004). See also CIA email, Dave to John, "Re: Liaison Response," May 18, 2001. The old reporting from early 2000 that was reexamined included CIA cable, "Transit of UBL Associate Khalid Through Dubai," Jan. 4, 2000; CIA cable, "Recent Influx of Suspected UBL Associates to Malaysia," Jan. 5, 2000; CIA cable, "UBL Associates: Flight Manifest for MH072," Jan. 9, 2000; CIA cable, "UBL Associates: Identification of Possible UBL Associates," Mar. 5, 2000. For cable information, see CIA records, audit of cable databases.

64. For a record of the exchange between John and Dave, see CIA emails, Dave to John, May 17, 18, 24, 2001; CIA email, Richard to Alan, identification of Khallad, July 13, 2001. For the account of John's FBI counterpart, see Michael Rolince interview (Apr. 12, 2004). For John's focus on Malaysia, see DOJ Inspector General interview of John, Nov. 1, 2002.

65. DOJ Inspector General interview of John, Nov. 1, 2002.

66. For the account of the desk officer, see DOJ Inspector General interview of Michael D., Oct. 31, 2002. For cable information, see CIA records, audit of cable databases.

67. DOJ Inspector General interviews of Jane, Nov. 4, 2002; July 16, 2003.

68. DOJ Inspector General interview of Jane, Nov. 4, 2002; DOJ Inspector General interview of Dave, Oct. 31, 2002.

69. DOJ Inspector General interviews of Jane, Nov. 4, 2002; July 16, 2003.

70. DOJ Inspector General interview of Jane, Nov. 4, 2002; DOJ Inspector General interview of Dave, Oct. 31, 2002; DOJ Inspector General interview of Russ F., Sept. 17, 2002; DOJ Inspector General interview of Steve B., Sept. 16, 2002.

71. "Jane" did not seek OIPR's permission to share this information at the meeting. "Jane" also apparently did not realize that one of the agents in attendance was a designated intelligence agent, so she could have shared all of the information with that agent regardless of the caveats. No one who was at the meeting suggested that option, however. DOJ Inspector General interview of Steve B., Sept. 16, 2002; DOJ Inspector General interview of Jane, July 16, 2003. These caveats were different from the legal limits we discussed in section 3.2. The Attorney General's July 1995 procedures concerned FISA information developed in an FBI intelligence investigation. This, however, was NSA information. These particular caveats were the result of the Justice Department's and NSA's overabundance of caution in December 1999. During the millennium crisis, Attorney General Reno authorized electronic surveillance of three U.S. persons overseas. Because the searches were not within the United States, no FISA warrant was needed. Reno approved the surveillances pursuant to section 2.5 of Executive Order 12333 with the proviso that the results of these particular surveillances not be shared with criminal investigators or prosecutors without the approval of the Office of Intelligence Policy and Review. Because of the complexity of determining whether particular reporting was the fruit of particular surveillances, NSA decided to place these caveats on all its Bin Ladin–related reporting, not just reporting on the surveillances authorized by Reno. As a result, these caveats were placed on the reports relating to Mihdhar even though they were not covered by Reno's December 1999 order. See DOJ memo, Reno to Freeh, FISA surveillance of a suspected al Qaeda operative, Dec. 24, 1999; NSA email, William L. to Karen C., "distribution restrictions," Dec. 10, 1999; NSA email, William L. to Anthony L., "doj restrictions," Dec. 20, 1999; NSA email, William L. to Brian C., "dissemination of terrorism reporting," Dec. 29, 1999. See also NSA memo, Ann D. to others, "Reporting Guidance," Dec. 30, 1999.

In May 2000, it was brought to the Attorney General's attention that these caveats prevented certain attorneys in the Terrorism and Violent Crime Section (TVCS) from reading the reporting. After discussions with NSA, the caveats were changed to specifically permit dissemination of these reports to designated attorneys in the TVCS and two attorneys in the U.S. Attorney's Office for the Southern District of New York. See NSA memo, Joan R. to Townsend and Reynolds, "Resumed Delivery of Classified Intelligence to TVCS," June 9, 2000; NSA memo, Hayden to Asst. Attorney General, "Proposal to Provide UBL-related Product to U.S. Attorney's Office/Southern District of New York," Aug. 30, 2000.

72. For the facts known by Dave at this time, see CIA records, audit of cable databases; see also CIA email, Dave to John, timeline entries, May 15, 2001. For CIA analyst's role, see DOJ Inspector General interview of Dave, Oct. 31, 2002. For Jane's account, see DOJ Inspector General interview of Jane, July 16, 2003.

73. DOJ Inspector General interview of Mary, Oct. 29, 2002.

74. For Mary's account, see DOJ Inspector General interview of Mary, Oct. 29, 2002. For the reporting regarding Mihdhar and Hazmi, see CIA cable, Khalid's passport, Jan. 4, 2000; CIA cable, Mihdhar's visa application, Jan. 5, 2000; CIA cable, Hazmi entered U.S., Mar. 6, 2000. For Mary's cable access information, see CIA records, audit of cable databases.

75. DOJ Inspector General interview of Mary, Oct. 29, 2002; DOJ Inspector General interview of Jane, Nov. 4, 2002.

76. DOJ Inspector General interview of Mary, Oct. 29, 2002; Intelligence report, Watchlisting of Bin Ladin–related individuals, Aug. 23, 2001; Joint Inquiry testimony of Christopher Kojm, Sept. 19, 2002. The watchlist request included Mihdhar, Nawaf al Hazmi, Salah Saeed Mohammed Bin Yousaf (they did not yet realize this was an alias for Tawfiq bin Attash, a.k.a. Khallad), and Ahmad Hikmat Shakir (who assisted Mihdhar in Kuala Lumpur).

77. Jane told investigators that she viewed this matter as just another lead and so assigned no particular urgency to the matter. DOJ Inspector General interviews of Jane, July 16, 2003; Nov. 4, 2002. For the draft lead, see attachment to FBI email, Jane to Craig D., "Re: FFI Request," Aug. 28, 2001. For the final version, see FBI electronic communication, "Request to Open a Full Field Investigation," Aug. 28, 2001.

78. FBI email, Craig D. to John L., "Fwd: Re: FFI Request," Aug. 28, 2001; FBI email, John L. to Steve and others, "Fwd: Re: FFI Request," Aug. 28, 2001. For an introduction to these legal limits and "the wall," see section 3.2. In December 2000, pursuant to concerns of the FISA Court, the New York Field Office began designating certain agents as either intelligence or criminal agents. Intelligence agents could see FISA materials and any other information that bore cautions about sharing without obtaining the FISA Court's permission or permission from the Justice Department's OIPR. FBI electronic communication, "Instructions re FBI FISA Policy," Dec. 7, 2000.

79. While one witness recalls a discussion with a senior FBI official, that official denies that such a discussion took place. The other alleged participant does not recall such a meeting. John interview (Apr. 2, 2004); Michael Rolince interview (Apr. 12, 2004); Jane interview (July 13, 2004); DOJ Inspector General interview of Rodney M., Nov. 5, 2002. For investigation's goal, see FBI electronic communication, "Request to Open a Full Field Investigation," Aug. 28, 2001.

80. DOJ Inspector General interviews of Jane, July 16, 2003; Nov. 4, 2002; DOJ Inspector General interviews of Steve B., Sept. 16, 2002; Nov. 14, 2002; Jane interview (July 13, 2004). FBI email, Jane to John L., "Fwd: Re: FFI Request," Aug. 29, 2001.

The analyst's email, however, reflects that she was confusing a broad array of caveats and legal barriers to information sharing and rules governing criminal agents' use of information gathered through intelligence channels. There was no broad prohibition against sharing information gathered through intelligence channels with criminal agents. This type of sharing occurred on a regular basis in the field. The court's procedures did not apply to all intelligence gathered regardless of collection method or source. Moreover, once information was properly shared, the criminal agent could use it for further investigation.

81. FBI email, Jane to Steve, NSLU Response, Aug. 29, 2001. "Jane" says she only asked whether there was sufficient probable cause to open the matter as a criminal case and whether the criminal agent could attend any interview if Mihdhar was found. She said the answer she received to both questions was no. She did not ask whether the underlying information could have been shared. Jane interview (July 13, 2004). The NSLU attorney denies advising that the agent could not participate in an interview and notes that she would not have given such inaccurate advice. The attorney told investigators that the NSA caveats would not have precluded criminal agents from joining in any search for Mihdhar or from participating in any interview. Moreover, she said that she could have gone to the NSA and obtained a waiver of any such caveat because there was no FISA information involved in this case. There are no records of the conversation between "Jane" and the attorney. "Jane" did not copy the attorney on her email to the agent, so the attorney did not have an opportunity to confirm or reject the advice "Jane" was giving to the agent. DOJ Inspector General interview of Sherry S., Nov. 7, 2002.

"Jane" asked the New York agent assigned to the Mihdhar search to sign a FISA acknowledgment form indicating the agent understood how he had to treat FISA information. Because no FISA information was involved, she should not have required him to sign such a form. To the extent she believed, incorrectly, that the Attorney General's 1995 procedures applied to this situation, there was in fact an exception in place for New York. DOJ Inspector General interview of Sherry S., Nov. 7, 2002. More fundamentally, "Jane" apparently understood the welter of restrictions to mean, in workday shorthand, that any information gathered by intelligence agencies should not be shared with criminal agents. This was incorrect. DOJ Inspector General interviews of Jane, July 16, 2003; Nov. 4, 2002.

82. FBI emails between Steve B. and Jane, re: NSLU Response, Aug. 29, 2001. While the agent expressed his frustration with the situation to "Jane," he made no effort to press the matter further by discussing his concerns with either his supervisor or the chief division counsel in New York.

83. Attorney General Ashcroft testified to us that this and similar information-sharing issues arose from Attorney General Reno's 1995 guidelines, discussed in chapter 3, and specifically from a March 1995 memorandum of then Deputy Attorney General Jamie Gorelick. John Ashcroft testimony, Apr. 13, 2004; DOJ memo, Gorelick to White, "Instructions on Separation of Certain Foreign Counterintelligence and Criminal Investigations," Mar. 4, 1995.

We believe the Attorney General's testimony does not fairly or accurately reflect the significance of the 1995 documents and their relevance to the 2001 discussions. Whatever the merits of the March 1995 Gorelick memorandum and the subsequent July 1995 Attorney General procedures on information sharing, they did not apply to the information the analyst decided she could not share with the criminal agent. As discussed earlier, the reason "Jane" decided she could not share information was because the initial information on Mihdhar had been analyzed by the NSA. This reason was unrelated to either of the 1995 documents. The Gorelick memorandum applied to two particular criminal cases, neither of which was involved in the summer 2001 information-sharing discussions. As the FBI agent observed in his email, Part A of the 1995 procedures applied only to information obtained pursuant to a FISA warrant. None of the Mihdhar material was FISA information. There was an exemption for the Southern District of New York from Part B of the 1995 procedures, so they did not apply. Also, the 1995 procedures did not govern whether information could be shared between intelligence and criminal agents within the FBI, a separation that the Bureau did not begin making formally until long after the procedures were in place. The 1995 procedures governed only the sharing of information with criminal prosecutors. Even in that situation, the restriction obliged running the information through the OIPR screen.

What had happened, as we discussed in chapter 3, was a growing battle within the Justice Department during the 1990s, and between parts of Justice and the FISA Court, over the scope of OIPR's screening function and the propriety of using FISA-derived information in criminal matters. The FISA Court's concern with FBI sloppiness in its FISA applications also began to take a toll: the court began designating itself as the gatekeeper for the sharing of intelligence information; the FBI was required to separately designate criminal and intelligence agents; and the court banned one supervisory FBI agent from appearing before it. By late 2000, these factors had culminated in a set of complex rules and a widening set of beliefs—a bureaucratic culture—that discouraged FBI agents from even seeking to share intelligence information. Neither Attorney General acted to resolve the conflicting views within the Justice Department. Nor did they challenge the strict interpretation of the FISA statute set forth by the FISA Court and OIPR. Indeed, this strict interpretation remained in effect until the USA PATRIOT Act was passed after 9/11.

Simply put, there was no legal reason why the information the analyst possessed could not have been shared with the criminal agent. On August 27, "Jane" requested the NSA's permission to share the information with the criminal agents, but she intended for the information only to help the criminal agents in their ongoing *Cole* investigation. She still did not believe they could be involved in the intelligence investigation even if the NSA permitted the information to be shared. DOJ IG 9/11 Report, July 2, 2004, p. 339. The next day the NSA notified its representative at FBI headquarters that it had approved the passage of the information to the criminal agents. NSC email, Carlene C. to Richard K., "Response to FBI Sanitization Request," Aug. 28, 2001. Thus, "Jane" had permission to share the information with the criminal agent prior to their August 29 emails.

84. DOJ Inspector General interview of Robert F., Dec. 18, 2002; FBI electronic communication, Los Angeles lead, Sept. 10, 2001.

85. Hazmi and Mihdhar used their true names to obtain California driver's licenses and open New Jersey bank accounts. Hazmi also had a car registered and had been listed in the San Diego telephone book. Searches of readily available databases could have unearthed the driver's licenses, the car registration, and the telephone listing. A search on the car registration would have unearthed a license check by the South Hackensack Police Department that would have led to information placing Hazmi in the area and placing Mihdhar at a local hotel for a week in early July 2001. The hijackers actively used the New Jersey bank accounts, through ATM, debit card, and cash transactions, until September 10. Among other things, they used their debit cards to pay for hotel rooms; and Hazmi used his card on August 27 to purchase tickets on Flight 77 for himself and his brother (and fellow hijacker), Salem al Hazmi. These transactions could have helped locate them if the FBI had obtained the bank records in time. There would have been no easy means, however, to determine the existence of these accounts, and obtaining bank cooperation pre-9/11 might have been problematic. The most likely means of successfully finding the men in the short time available was one not often used pre-9/11 for suspected terrorists: an FBI BOLO (be on the lookout) combined with a media campaign. This alone might have delayed or disrupted the plot, even if the men had not been physically located before September 11. But this would have been considered only if the FBI believed that they were about to carry out an imminent attack. No one at the FBI—or any other agency—believed that at the time.

See FBI report, financial spreadsheet re: 9/11 hijackers, undated; South Hackensack, N.J., Police Department report, Detective Bureau Report, Oct. 17, 2001 (case no. 20018437). According to Ramzi Binalshibh, had KSM known that Moussaoui had been arrested, he would have canceled the 9/11 attacks. Intelligence report, interrogation of Ramzi Binalshibh, Feb. 14, 2003. The publicity regarding Mihdhar and Hazmi might have had a similar effect because they could have been identified by the airlines and might have jeopardized the operation.

86. Joint Inquiry report, pp. xiii, 325–335; DOJ IG 9/11 Report, July 2, 2004, pp. 59–106.

87. FBI electronic communication, Phoenix memo, July 10, 2001.

88. Ibid.; Joint Inquiry report, pp. 325–335; DOJ IG 9/11 Report, July 2, 2004, pp. 59–106.

89. DOJ Inspector General interview of Kenneth Williams, July 22, 2003.

90. Unlike Moussaoui, the typical student at Pan Am Flight Academy holds an FAA Airline Transport Pilot rating or the foreign equivalent, is employed by an airline, and has several thousand flight hours. Moussaoui also stood out for several other reasons. He had paid nearly $9,000 in cash for the training, yet had no explanation for the source of these funds; he had asked to fly a simulated flight from London's Heathrow Airport to New York's John F. Kennedy Airport; and he was also particularly interested in the operation of the aircraft doors. FBI electronic communication, Request OIPR permission to contact U.S. Attorney's Office regarding Zacarias Moussaoui, Aug. 18, 2001. For a detailed, step-by-step chronology of activities taken regarding Moussaoui prior to September 11, see DOJ IG 9/11 Report, July 2, 2004, pp. 109–197.

91. FBI electronic communication, Request OIPR permission to contact U.S. Attorney's Office regarding Zacarias Moussaoui, Aug. 18, 2001.

92. DOJ Inspector General interview of Harry S., June 6, 2002; DOJ Inspector General interview of Greg J., July 9, 2002; FBI letterhead memorandum, Zacarias Moussaoui, Aug. 19, 2001.

93. DOJ IG 9/11 Report, July 2, 2004, p. 128.

94. Criminal search warrants must be approved by Department of Justice attorneys before submission to the court. Therefore, approval from the Minneapolis U.S. Attorney's Office was required before a criminal search warrant could be obtained. DOJ Inspector General interview of Coleen Rowley, July 16, 2002. Another agent, however, said that he spoke to an Assistant U.S. Attorney in the Minneapolis office and received advice that the facts were almost sufficient to obtain a criminal warrant. DOJ Inspector General interview of Greg J., July 9, 2002. The Assistant United States Attorney said that if the FBI had asked for a criminal warrant that first night, he would have sought it. He believed that there was sufficient probable cause for a criminal warrant at that time. DOJ Inspector General interview of William K., May 29, 2003. Mary Jo White, the former U.S. Attorney for the Southern District of New York, told us that based on her review of the evidence known pre-9/11, she would have approved a criminal search warrant. Mary Jo White interview (May 17, 2004). Because the agents never presented the information to the Minneapolis U.S. Attorney's Office before 9/11, we cannot know for sure what its judgment would have been or whether a judge would have signed the warrant. In any event, the Minneapolis agents were concerned that if they tried to first obtain a criminal warrant but the U.S. Attorney's Office or the judge refused, the FISA Court might reject an application for a FISA warrant on the grounds that the agents were attempting to make an end run around the criminal process. Therefore, it was judged too risky to seek a criminal warrant unless it was certain that it would be approved. DOJ Inspector General interview of Greg J., July 9, 2002. In addition, FBI headquarters specifically instructed Minneapolis that it could not open a criminal investigation. DOJ IG 9/11 Report, July 2, 2004, p. 138. Finally, the Minneapolis Field Office mistakenly believed that the 1995 Attorney General procedures required OIPR's approval before it could contact the U.S. Attorney's Office about obtaining a criminal warrant.

95. The FISA definition of "foreign power" includes "a group engaged in international terrorism or activities in preparation therefor."

96. FBI electronic communication, Request to contact U.S. Attorney's Office regarding Zacarias Moussaoui, Aug. 18, 2001. For CTC contact, see FBI email, Harry S. to Chuck F., "Please Pass To [desk officer]," Aug. 24, 2001; FBI email, Harry S. to Chuck F., "Re: Fwd: 199M-MP-60130 (Zacarias Moussaoui)," Aug. 24, 2001.

97. DOJ Inspector General interview of Greg J., July 9, 2002; FBI electronic communication, Moussaoui investigation, Aug. 22, 2002; FBI electronic communication, Moussaoui investigation, Aug. 30, 2002.

98. FBI letterhead memorandum, Zacarias Moussaoui, Aug. 21, 2001; CIA cable, subjects involved in suspicious 747 flight training, Aug. 24, 2001; CIA cable, "Zacarias Moussaoui and Husayn 'Ali Hasan Ali-Attas," Aug. 28, 2001; Joseph H., interview (May 4, 2004); FBI letterhead memorandum, Zacarias Moussaoui, Sept. 5, 2001.

99. FBI teletype, "Zacarias Moussaoui—International Terrorism," Sept. 4, 2001.

100. DOJ Inspector General interview of Greg J., July 9, 2002.

101. Minneapolis may have been more concerned about Moussaoui's intentions because the case agent and the supervisory agent were both pilots. They were, therefore, more highly sensitized to the odd nature of Moussaoui's actions and comments regarding flying. DOJ Inspector General interview of Greg J., July 9, 2002; DOJ Inspector General interview of Harry S., June 20, 2002.

102. DOJ Inspector General interview of Michael Rolince, May 5, 2004; Michael Rolince interview (Apr. 12, 2004); DOJ IG 9/11 Report, July 2, 2004, pp. 168–170, 188.

103. CIA briefing materials, DCI Update, "Islamic Extremist Learns to Fly," Aug. 23, 2001. Deputy Director of Central Intelligence John McLaughlin testified that he was told about Moussaoui several days before Tenet was briefed, although he did not recall the specific date of the briefing. John McLaughlin testimony, Apr. 14, 2004.

104. George Tenet interviews (Jan. 28, 2004; July 2, 2004).

105. For the renewed request, see FBI letterhead memorandum, Zacarias Moussaoui, Sept. 11, 2001. For the initial British response, see British Security Service memo, re: Zacarias Moussaoui, Sept. 12, 2001; information provided to the Commission by the British government; British liaison telex, "Zacarias Moussaoui—Background Information," Sept. 13, 2001. See also Joseph H. interview (May 4, 2004).

106. Joint Inquiry report (classified version), pp. 340–341. Notably, the FBI analyst "Mary" who was looking at the Mihdhar information suggested that the U.S. government talk to Ressam to see if he knew anything about Mihdhar. See CIA email, Mary to John, seeking identification by Ressam, Aug. 21, 2001. There is no evidence that Ressam was asked about Moussaoui or Mihdhar prior to 9/11.

107. According to Ramzi Binalshibh, had KSM known that Moussaoui had been arrested, he would have cancelled the 9/11 attacks. Intelligence report, interrogation of Ramzi Binalshibh, Feb. 14, 2003.

108. Joint Inquiry report (classified version), pp. 329–331; Joint Inquiry interview of Mike, Alice, Larry, John, Terry, Aug. 12, 2002.

109. CIA cable, Key UBL personalities, Sept. 25, 2000.

110. CIA cable, Mukhtar information, May 23, 2002.

111. CIA cable, Biographical Information on Key UBL Associates in Afghanistan, June 11, 2001; Intelligence report, biographical information on Bin Ladin associates in Afghanistan, June 12, 2001. For the subsequent identification, see CIA cable, follow-up source on KSM, July 11, 2001.

112. For the reporting identifying Mukhtar as KSM, see CIA cable, source information re: KSM, Aug. 28, 2001.

113. John interview (Apr. 2, 2004).

9 Heroism and Horror

1. For the WTC's layout, see Port Authority diagrams, "World Trade Center Concourse Level," "Concourse Level," and "Plaza Level," undated. For the number of square feet of office space, see Federal Emergency Management Agency (FEMA) report, "World Trade Center Building Performance Study," undated. For the number of workers and passersby, see Port Authority briefing (May 13, 2004).

For the dimensions, see FEMA report, "World Trade Center Building Performance Study," undated. In addition, the outside of each tower was covered by a frame of 14-inch-wide steel columns; the centers of the steel columns were 40 inches apart. These exterior walls bore most of the weight of the building. The interior core of the buildings was a hollow steel shaft, in which elevators and stairwells were grouped. Ibid. For stairwells and elevators, see Port Authority response to Commission interrogatory, May 2004.

2. See Port Authority response to Commission interrogatory, May 2004.

3. Ibid. These deviations were necessary because of the placement of heavy elevators and machine rooms, and were located between the 42nd and 48th floors and the 76th and 82nd floors in both towers. For the doors being closed but unlocked, see Port Authority briefing (May 13, 2004).

4. For rooftop access and evacuations, see Port Authority response to Commission interrogatory, May 2004. For the helipad not conforming, see PANYNJ interview 14 (July 8, 2004). In the interests of promoting candor and protecting privacy, we agreed not to identify most individuals we interviewed. Individuals are identified by a code, and individuals' ranks or units are disclosed only in a broad manner.

5. For the 1993 attack's effect, see Alan Reiss testimony, May 18, 2004. For the attack's testing the city's response capability, see FDNY report, "Report from the Chief of Department, Anthony L. Fusco," in William Manning, ed., *The World Trade Center Bombing: Report and Analysis* (FEMA, undated), p. 11.

6. For the towers' loss of power and the other effects, see New York City report, "Report of the World Trade Center Review Committee," 1995, p. 4. For generators' shutting down, see Port Authority briefing (May 13, 2004). For the rescue efforts, see FDNY report, "Report from the Chief of Department, Anthony L. Fusco," in Manning, ed., *The World Trade Center Bombing*, p. 11. For the evacuation time, see PANYNJ interview 5 (May 15, 2004).

7. For information on rooftop evacuations, see Port Authority response to Commission interrogatory, May 2004; NYPD interview 25, Aviation (June 21, 2004). For the rappel rescue, see Port Authority response to Commission interrogatory, May 2004. For figure of 15 hours, see "World Trade Center Bombing," *NY Cop Online Magazine*, Dec. 12, 2000 (online at www.nycop.com). For the general false impression, see Civilian interview 3 (May 4, 2004); Commission analysis of letters written to the Occupational Safety and Health Administration (OSHA) concerning the September 11 attacks. For the WTC fire safety plan, see Port Authority response to Commission interrogatory, May 2004.

8. For the upgrades, see Port Authority memorandum to the Commission for Nov. 3, 2003, meeting; Port Authority briefing (May 13, 2004).

9. For the upgrades, see Port Authority memorandum to the Commission for Nov. 3, 2003, meeting; Port

Authority response to Commission interrogatory, May 2004. For the fire alarm, see PANYNJ interview 10 (June 16, 2004); PANYNJ interview 7 (June 2, 2004).

10. Port Authority memorandum to Commission for Nov. 3, 2003 meeting; WTC interview 6 (May 25, 2004).

11. For fire safety teams, see PANYNJ Interview 7 (Jun. 2, 2004). For fire drill procedures, see Civilian interview 1 (Mar. 2, 2004); Civilian interview 10 (Mar. 24, 2004). For aids to the September 11 evacuation, see, e.g., Civilian interview 14 (Apr. 7, 2004); Civilian interview 20 (May 4, 2004); Civilian interview 21 (May 4, 2004); Civilian Interview 13 (Mar. 25, 2004).

12. For instructions to civilians, see, e.g., Civilian interview 20 (May 4, 2004); Civilian interview 21 (May 4, 2004); Civilian interview 12 (May 4, 2004); Stanley Praimnath testimony, May 18, 2004 (videotaped). For civilians' participation, see Civilian interview 10 (Mar. 24, 2004); Civilian interview 15 (Apr. 21, 2004); Commission analysis of letters written to OSHA concerning the September 11 attacks. For civilians not being instructed not to evacuate up, see Port Authority briefing (May 13, 2004). For the standard fire drill announcement, see Port Authority response to Commission interrogatory, May 2004. For civilians' recollection, see Civilian interview 1 (Mar. 2, 2004); Civilian interview 13 (Mar. 25, 2004); Civilian interview 10 (Mar. 24, 2004). For Port Authority acknowledgment of lack of a protocol, see PANYNJ interview 2 (Apr. 14, 2004).

13. For SPI transition, see PANYNJ Interview 11 (Jun. 23, 2004); Alan Reiss prepared statement, May 18, 2004, p. 8. For fire safety plan, see PANYNJ Interview 8 (June 6, 2004).

14. See Port Authority Police Department (PAPD) report, "Port Authority of New York and New Jersey," undated (online at www.panynj.gov).

15. PANYNJ interview 4 (May 10, 2004).

16. For 40,000 officers, see NYPD information provided to the Commission, July 9, 2004. For standard operating procedures, see NYPD regulations, "Patrol Guide: Rapid Mobilization," and "Patrol Guide: Mobilization Readiness Levels," Jan. 1, 2000.

17. For the 35 radio zones, see NYPD report, "Radio Zones," undated. For other citywide radio channels, see, e.g., NYPD report, "Transit Patrol VHF," undated; NYPD interview 18, ESU (Feb. 24, 2004).

18. For the NYPD supervising the emergency call system and employing more than 1,200 people, see NYPD report, "Communications Section," undated (online at www.nyc.gov/html/nypd/html/otsd/ commsec.html). For fire emergencies being transferred to the FDNY dispatch, see FDNY interview 28, Dispatch (Jan. 29, 2004).

19. See FDNY email to the Commission, July 9, 2004; Thomas Von Essen interview (Apr. 7, 2004). For operations being headed by the sole five-star chief, see FDNY regulations, "Regulations" chapter of "Operational Procedures and Policies," July 1999.

20. For department organization, see FDNY report, "Unit Location Chart," Sept. 11, 2001; FDNY regulations, "Firefighting Procedures," "Engine Company," and "Ladder Company Operations" chapters of "Operational Procedures and Policies," July 1999.

21. FDNY interview 48, SOC (Mar. 11, 2004).

22. FDNY interview 28, Dispatch (Jan. 29, 2004). Each center was staffed at all times with a supervisor and seven dispatchers who worked in 12-hour tours. Positions included a decision dispatcher, responsible for directing the appropriate fire apparatus to the scene; a voice alarm or notification dispatcher, responsible for intra- and interagency communications; a radio in and radio out dispatcher who tracked the movement of fire apparatuses; and three alarm dispatchers, responsible for sending the appropriate number of units to a fire scene to correspond with the designated alarm level. Ibid.

23. FDNY regulations, "Communications" chapter of "Operational Procedures and Policies," July 1999; FDNY interview 60, HQ (May 11, 2004); FDNY interview 64, HQ (June 30, 2004).

24. FDNY report, "Report from the Chief of Department, Anthony L. Fusco," in Manning, ed., The World Trade Center Bombing, p. 11.

25. PANYNJ interview 1 (Nov. 6, 2003); PANYNJ interview 4 (May 10, 2004). In early 2001, New York provided its firefighters with new digital radios. The procurement process for these radios remains controversial, and they proved unpopular with the rank and file, who believed that adequate training in their use had not been provided. The new radios were withdrawn shortly after they had been introduced into the field. While the new radios briefly were in service, the WTC repeater channel could be left on at all times, because the new radios operated on entirely different frequencies and thus were not vulnerable to interference from the repeater system. Thomas Von Essen interview (Apr. 7, 2004). For the new radios permitting the repeater to stay on, see PANYNJ interview 1 (Nov. 6, 2003); PANYNJ interview 4 (May 10, 2004).

26. For civilian fatalities, see New York City press release, Office of the Mayor Press Release No. 042-01, Feb. 8, 2001. For firefighter fatalities, see Terry Golway, So Others Might Live (Basic Books, 2002), p. 304.

27. For the creation of the Office of Emergency Management (OEM), see Rudolph Giuliani interview (Apr. 20, 2004). For OEM's purposes, see Richard Sheirer interview (Apr. 7, 2004). For OEM's sending field responder, see ibid.; OEM interview 1 (Feb. 12, 2004). Other data monitored by OEM's Watch Command included Emergency Medical Service data regarding patterns of illness (to spot a potential epidemic in its early stages), live video feeds from New York Harbor and city streets, and television news channels. Richard Sheirer interview (Apr. 7, 2004);

OEM interview 3 (Mar. 16, 2004). The Watch Command's monitoring of EMS data proved instrumental in an extremely early identification and then highly effective containment of the 1999 West Nile outbreak, which likely would have resulted in many more fatalities but for OEM. Richard Sheirer interview (Apr. 7, 2004).

28. Richard Sheirer testimony (May 18, 2004); OEM interview 3 (Mar. 16, 2004).

29. New York City memo, "Direction and Control of Emergencies in the City of New York," July 2001 (signed by Mayor Giuliani).

30. For the exact time of impact, see FAA analysis of American 11 radar returns and Commission analysis of FAA radar data and air traffic control software logic. For the zone of impact, see National Institute of Standards and Technology (NIST) report, "Interim Report on the Federal Building Fire Safety Investigation of the World Trade Center," June 28, 2004. On people alive on the 92nd floor and above after the impact, see Commission analysis of conditions on tower floors and advice received by civilians in the towers based on (1) calls to NYPD 911 from or concerning people in the towers on September 11, 2001, and (2) transcripts of recorded calls to the Port Authority police desk from people in the towers on September 11, 2001 (hereafter "Commission analysis of 911/PAPD calls"). Everyone alive on the 91st floor was able to evacuate. Civilian interview 7 (Mar. 22, 2004); Civilian interview 6 (Mar. 22, 2004). For civilians being alive but trapped, see Commission analysis of 911/PAPD calls; Civilian interview 17 (May 11, 2004); Civilian interview 2 (Mar. 19, 2004).

31. For fire in the 77th floor elevator and damage to the 22nd floor, see Commission analysis of 911/PAPD calls; Port Authority transcripts of recorded Port Authority calls and radio channels, Sept. 11, 2001, vol. II, channel 8, p. 4 (22nd floor). For a fireball in the lobby, see PAPD interview 1, WTC Command (Oct. 14, 2003); Civilian interview 14 (Apr. 7, 2004). Burning jet fuel descended at least one elevator bank. FDNY interview 4, Chief (Jan. 8, 2004). For the roofs being engulfed and the winds, see, e.g., NYPD interview 16, Aviation (Apr. 1, 2004).

32. Commission analysis of 911/PAPD calls.

33. Ibid.

34. For the on-duty fire safety director's perspective, see WTC interview 6 (May 25, 2004). For the chiefs being told by the Port Authority fire safety director that the evacuation order was given earlier, see PANYNJ interview 13 (Nov. 20, 2003). For him no longer being the designated fire safety director, see PANYNJ interview 11 (June 23, 2004).

35. For public announcements not being heard, see, e.g., Civilian interview 6 (Mar. 22, 2004); Civilian interview 7 (Mar. 22, 2004); Civilian interview 9 (Mar. 23, 2004); Civilian interview 14 (Apr. 7, 2004); Commission analysis of 911/PAPD calls. The evacuation tone was heard in some locations below the impact. Civilian interview 7 (Mar. 22, 2004); Commission analysis of 911/PAPD calls. For some emergency intercoms being unusable, see WTC interview 9 (June 8, 2004); Port Authority transcripts of recorded Port Authority calls and radio channels, Sept. 11, 2001. For evidence that some were usable, see WTC interview 6 (May 25, 2004).

36. For callers being disconnected, see Commission analysis of 911/PAPD calls. For the standard operating procedure and only a few people being available, causing calls to be transferred, see FDNY interview 28, Dispatch (Jan. 29, 2004). For delays and terminations, see Commission analysis of 911/PAPD calls.

37. For operators' and dispatchers' situational awareness and instructions to callers, see Commission analysis of 911/PAPD calls. For standard operating procedures for a high-rise fire, see FDNY interview 28, Dispatch (Jan. 29, 2004). For the fire chiefs' view, see FDNY interview 61, Chief (May 12, 2004); FDNY interview 62, Chief (May 12, 2004). For many injuries occurring during the evacuation, see Zachary Goldfarb and Steven Kuhr, "EMS Response to the Explosion," in Manning, ed., *The World Trade Center Bombing*, p. 94.

38. FDNY interview 15, Chief (Jan. 14, 2004): FDNY interview 4, Chief (Jan. 8, 2004).

39. For operators' and dispatchers' lack of knowledge, see Commission analysis of 911/PAPD calls. For operators departing from protocol, see ibid.

40. Commission analysis of 911/PAPD calls; Port Authority transcripts of recorded Port Authority calls and radio channels, Sept. 11, 2001, vol. II, channel 9, pp. 1–2, 23–24; channel 10, pp. 2, 6, 23.

41. See Civilian interview 6 (Mar. 22, 2004); Civilian interview 7 (Mar. 22, 2004); Civilian interview 14 (Apr. 7, 2004); Civilian interview 9 (Mar. 23, 2004). For Port Authority employees remaining, see Civilian interview 6 (Mar. 22, 2004); Civilian interview 7 (Mar. 22, 2004), Port Authority report, *September 11 Special Awards Ceremony*, vol. 1, undated (recognitions 2, 3, 4, and 5).

42. For trouble reaching exits, see, e.g., Civilian interview 9 (Mar. 23, 2004). For "locked" doors, see, e.g., Civilian interview 6 (Mar. 22, 2004); Civilian Interview 14 (Apr. 7, 2004); WTC interview 9 (June 8, 2004); Civilian interview 7 (Mar. 22, 2004).

43. For smoke rising and its effect, see Commission analysis of 911/PAPD calls. For people jumping, see Civilian interview 13 (Mar. 25, 2004); Commission analysis of 911/PAPD calls; Port Authority transcripts of recorded Port Authority calls and radio channels, vol. II, WTC channel 26 (channel W), Sept. 11, 2001, pp. 4–6.

44. There is no evidence of a dispute between Morgan Stanley and the Port Authority over the Port Authority's "defend in place" evacuation policy before September 11. For occupants who were unaware of what happened, see, e.g., Civilian interview 1 (Mar. 2, 2004). For civilians concluding that the incident had occurred in the other building, see Civilian interview 13 (Mar. 25, 2004); Civilian interview 1 (Mar. 2, 2004). For others being aware that

a major incident had occurred, see, e.g., Civilian interview 13 (Mar. 25, 2004); Civilian interview 10 (Mar. 24, 2004). Some of them could actually feel the heat from the explosion in the North Tower. See, e.g., Civilian interview 10 (Mar. 24, 2004); Civilian interview 15 (Apr. 21, 2004). For people deciding to leave or being advised to do so by fire wardens, see, e.g., Civilian interview 1 (Mar. 2, 2004); Civilian interview 8 (Mar. 23, 2004); Civilian statement 1, undated. For Morgan Stanley occupying 20 floors and ordering its employees to leave, see Civilian interview 19 (June 6, 2004).

45. Port Authority, transcripts of recorded Port Authority calls and radio channels, Sept. 11, 2001, vol. II, channel 17, p. 1; PANYNJ interview 7 (June 2, 2004). Fire command stations were equipped with manuals containing prescripted announcements corresponding to a number of specified emergencies. Once the FDNY arrived on the scene, however, all decisions relating to evacuation or other emergency procedures were left to its discretion.

46. When a notable event occurred, it was standard procedure for the on-duty deputy fire safety director to make an "advisory" announcement to tenants who were affected by or might be aware of the incident, in order to acknowledge the incident and to direct tenants to stand by for further instructions. The purpose of advisory announcements, as opposed to "emergency" announcements (such as to evacuate), was to reduce panic. PANYNJ interview 7 (June 2, 2004); Port Authority response to Commission interrogatory, May 2004. For the content of the announcement, see, e.g., Brian Clark testimony, May 18, 2004 (videotaped); Civilian interview 3 (May 4, 2004); Civilian interview 13 (Mar. 25, 2004); Civilian statement 1, undated. For the protocol and prescripted announcements and the death of the director of fire safety and the deputy fire safety director, see PANYNJ interview 7 (June 2, 2004); PANYNJ interview 12 (July 7, 2004). For people not thinking a second plane would hit, see, e.g., PANYNJ interview 7 (June 2, 2004). For the quotation, see FDNY interview 63, Chief (May 16, 2004). For civilians remaining, see Civilian interview 1 (Mar. 2, 2004); Civilian interview 13 (Mar. 25, 2004); Civilian interview 8 (Mar. 23, 2004); Civilian interview 16 (Apr. 27, 2004); Commission analysis of letters written to OSHA concerning the September 11 attacks. For civilians returning after evacuating, see Civilian interview 1 (Mar. 2, 2004); Civilian interview 11 (Mar. 25, 2004); Civilian interview 4 (Mar. 16, 2004); Commission analysis of letters written to OSHA concerning the September 11 attacks.

47. For advice on the ground floor, see Civilian interview 4 (Mar. 16, 2004). Nineteen of them returned upstairs, where 18 died; the 20th was told by her supervisor, who was in the group, to leave rather than return upstairs. The supervisor also survived. Civilian interview 4 (Mar. 16, 2004). For advice in the sky lobbies, see, e.g., Civilian interview 15 (Apr. 21, 2004). For security officials not being part of the fire safety staff, see PANYNJ interview 7 (June 2, 2004).

48. For people told to stand by, see Port Authority transcripts of recorded Port Authority calls and radio channels, Sept. 11, 2001, vol. II, channel 8, pp. 7–8. For people advised to leave, see ibid., vol. II, channel 9, pp. 2, 4, 9.

49. It is also not known if the deputy fire safety director received the order by the PAPD to evacuate the complex; however, the Port Authority has told us that deputy fire safety directors did not generally take direct orders from the PAPD under the regular chain of command. PANYNJ interview 7 (June 2, 2004). For the announcement, see Civilian interview 16 (Apr. 27, 2004); Civilian interview 13 (Mar. 25, 2004). For the announcement's deviating from protocol, see PANYNJ interview 7 (June 2, 2004).

50. For senior leaders' response by 9:00 A.M., see FDNY interview 18, Chief (Jan. 22, 2004); FDNY interview 54, Chief (Apr. 15, 2004); FDNY interview 5, Chief (Dec. 16, 2003); FDNY interview 52, Chief (Apr. 5, 2004); FDNY interview 27, HQ (Jan. 28, 2004). For the Chief of Department's and Chief of Operation's actions, see FDNY interview 18, Chief (Jan. 22, 2004). For senior leaders' response by 9:59, see FDNY report, McKinsey & Company, "FDNY Report," Aug. 19, 2002, p. 32.

51. FDNY interview 60, HQ (May 11, 2004); see FDNY record, computer-aided dispatch report, Sept. 11, 2001, 08:47:20–9:00:00.

52. For the chief's and companies' arrival, see Jules Naudet and Gedeon Naudet, video footage, Sept. 11, 2001; FDNY interview 4, Chief (Jan. 8, 2004). For burned civilians, see FDNY interview 29, Battalion 1 (Jan. 29, 2004). For the building's physical conditions, see FDNY interview 16, Battalion 1 (Jan. 20, 2004). For conditions in the lobby, see Jules Naudet and Gedeon Naudet, video footage, Sept. 11, 2001.

53. For the initial incident commander and command post location, see Jules Naudet and Gedeon Naudet, video footage, Sept. 11, 2001; FDNY interview 4, Chief (Jan. 8, 2004). For the transfer of incident command, see FDNY interview 15, Chief (Jan. 14, 2004). For ascertaining building systems' status from building personnel, see FDNY interview 4, Chief (Jan. 8, 2004); PANYNJ interview 13 (Nov. 20, 2003); FDNY interview 15, Chief (Jan. 14, 2004). For speaking with OEM and PAPD officials, see FDNY interview 15, Chief (Jan. 14, 2004); Jules Naudet and Gedeon Naudet, video footage, Sept. 11, 2001.

54. For the ladder and engine companies' climb, see FDNY interview 59, Battalion 2 (Apr. 22, 2004); Jules Naudet and Gedeon Naudet, video footage, Sept. 11, 2001. For tactical 1, see FDNY interview 59, Battalion 2 (Apr. 22, 2004). For other units lining up in the lobby, see Jules Naudet and Gedeon Naudet, video footage, Sept. 11, 2001.

55. For FDNY instructing building personnel and PAPD to evacuate the South Tower, see FDNY interview

4, Chief (Jan. 8, 2004); FDNY interview 15, Chief (Jan. 14, 2004); PANYNJ interview 13 (Nov. 20, 2003). For lack of concern about a second plane, see FDNY interview 63, Chief (May 16, 2004).

56. FDNY interview 4, Chief (Jan. 8, 2004); FDNY interview 15, Chief (Jan. 14, 2004).

57. For their situational awareness, see FDNY interview 4, Chief (Jan. 8, 2004); FDNY interview 15, Chief (Jan. 14, 2004) (quotation).

58. Peter Hayden testimony, May 18, 2004 (videotaped).

59. On the lack of information, see FDNY interview 4, Chief (Jan. 8, 2004); FDNY interview 15, Chief (Jan. 14, 2004).

60. On the staging areas, see FDNY interview 47, Chief (Mar. 11, 2004); FDNY interview 44, Chief (Mar. 8, 2004); FDNY interview 33, EMS (Feb. 9, 2004). For EMS's response, see Jules Naudet and Gedeon Naudet, video footage, Sept. 11, 2001. For private ambulances responding, see FDNY interview 35, EMS (Feb. 10, 2004).

61. NYPD recordings, City Wide 1, Special Operations Division, and Divisions 1, 2, and 3 radio channels, Sept. 11, 2001.

62. For the Chief of Department's actions, see NYPD interview 8, HQ (Feb. 24, 2004). For the number of officers, see NYPD regulations, "Patrol Guide: Rapid Mobilization," Jan. 1, 2000; NYPD recordings, City Wide 1 and Divisions 1, 2, and 3 radio channels, Sept. 11, 2001.

63. For shifting the mobilization point, see NYPD interview 17, 1st Precinct (Apr. 1, 2004). For stationing officers around the perimeter, see NYPD recordings, City Wide 1, Special Operations Division, and Divisions 1, 2, and 3 radio channels, Sept. 11, 2001. For officers being diverted, see, e.g., NYPD interview 21, 6th Precinct (May 4, 2004).

64. For the helicopters' dispatch, see NYPD records, "Aviation Unit Flight Data Sheets," Sept. 11, 2001. For communications with air traffic controllers and their situational awareness, see NYPD interview 12, Aviation (Mar. 10, 2004); NYPD interview 14, Aviation (Mar. 11, 2004); NYPD interview 13, Aviation (Mar. 10, 2004); NYPD interview 16, Aviation (Apr. 1, 2004).

65. NYPD recording, Special Operations Division radio channel, Sept. 11, 2001.

66. For the third helicopter, see NYPD records, "Aviation Unit Flight Data Sheets," Sept. 11, 2001. For the helicopters' subsequent actions and protocol, see NYPD interview 12, Aviation (Mar. 10, 2004); NYPD interview 14, Aviation (Mar. 11, 2004); NYPD interview 13, Aviation (Mar. 10, 2004); NYPD interview 16, Aviation (Apr. 1, 2004); NYPD interview 15, ESU (Mar. 11, 2004).

67. Commission analysis of 911/PAPD calls; NYPD recordings, City Wide 1, Special Operations, and Division 1, 2, and 3 radio channels, Sept. 11, 2001.

68. NYPD memo, requests for departmental recognition 4 and 6, Jun. 26, 2002. For those on the 22nd floor apparently not being located, see PANYNJ recognition 1, undated.

69. NYPD interview 15, ESU (Mar. 11, 2004); NYPD interview 18, ESU (Feb. 24, 2004).

70. For other officers' positioning, see NYPD interview 20, Manhattan South Task Force (May 4, 2004); NYPD interview 21, 6th Precinct (May 4, 2004); NYPD interview 19, 13th Precinct (May 4, 2004); NYPD interview 4, Housing (Feb. 17, 2004); PAPD interview 4, Port Authority Bus Terminal Command (Nov. 20, 2003). For officers assisting in the North Tower evacuation, see NYPD memo, request for departmental recognition 1 and 2, June 26, 2002.

71. NYPD recording, Transit Division 1 radio channel, Sept. 11, 2001.

72. NYPD recordings, City Wide 1, Special Operations Division, and Divisions 1, 2, and 3 radio channels, Sept. 11, 2001.

73. For the on-site commanding officer's actions, see PAPD interview 1, WTC command (Oct. 14, 2003). For the on-duty sergeant's initial instructions, see PAPD statement 3, WTC Command (Nov. 12, 2001). For his instructions to meet at the desk, see PAPD statement 3, WTC Command (Nov. 12, 2001); PAPD statement 12, WTC Command (Mar. 28, 2002). On the scarcity of radios, see PAPD statement 9, PATH Command (Jan. 28, 2002); PAPD statement 8, WTC Command (Jan. 12, 2002).

74. PAPD interview 7, WTC Command (Nov. 25, 2003).

75. For the response, see PAPD statement 2, WTC Command (Nov. 10, 2001). For the lack of such written standard operating procedures, see PAPD interview 3, LaGuardia Airport Command (Nov. 20, 2003); PAPD regulations, "Manual of Police Division Instructions," undated (in existence before 9/11). Instead, the PAPD relied on tradition to dictate its response procedures. On the lack of interoperable frequencies, see PANYNJ interview 4 (May 10, 2004); PAPD statement 9, PATH Command (Jan. 28, 2002).

76. For the evacuation order, see PAPD statement 3, WTC Command (Nov. 12, 2001); PAPD interview 1, WTC Command (Oct. 14, 2003). For its transmission, see Port Authority transcripts of recorded Port Authority calls and radio channels, Sept. 11, 2001, vol. II, channel W, p. 7.

77. PAPD statement 1, Administrative Command, Nov. 2, 2001; PAPD statement 4, Administrative Command, Nov. 24, 2001.

78. For the Emergency Operations Center's activation, see OEM interview 3 (Mar. 16, 2004); OEM interview 2 (Mar. 4, 2004). For the request for search teams, see OEM interview 5 (Mar. 19, 2004). For the senior OEM offi-

cial's arrival, see OEM interview 4 (Mar. 18, 2004). For other OEM officials' arrival, see Richard Sheirer interview (Apr. 7, 2004); OEM interview 6 (Mar. 24, 2004).

79. For the time of impact, see FAA analysis of United Airlines Flight 175 radar returns and Commission analysis of FAA radar data and air traffic control software logic. For the impact zone, see NIST report, "Interim Report on the Federal Building and Fire Safety Investigation of the World Trade Center," June 18, 2004, appendix H–41. For portions undamaged, see Civilian interview 10 (Mar. 24, 2004). For stairwell A remaining passable, see Civilian interview 8 (Mar. 23, 2004); Civilian interview 1 (Mar. 2, 2004); Civilian interview 13 (Mar. 25, 2004); Civilian interview 4 (Mar. 16, 2004).

80. For the sky lobby, see Civilian interview 10 (Mar. 24, 2004). For the condition of people on the impact floors, see Civilian interview 10 (Mar. 24, 2004); Civilian interview 4 (Mar. 16, 2004); Commission analysis of 911/PAPD calls. For events in the sky lobby after impact, see Civilian interview 10 (Mar. 24, 2004).

81. For conditions in the impact zone above the 78th floor, see Civilian interview 4 (Mar. 16, 2004); Civilian interview 3 (May 4, 2004); Commission analysis of 911/PAPD calls. For conditions on the 81st floor, see Civilian interview 4 (Mar. 16, 2004); Civilian interview 3 (May 4, 2004).

82. For the four people, see Civilian interview 1 (Mar. 2, 2004); Civilian interview 13 (Mar. 25, 2004); Civilian interview 4 (Mar. 16, 2004); Civilian interview 8 (Mar. 23, 2004). For the first person to descend stairwell A, see Civilian interview 13 (Mar. 25, 2004).

83. For civilians ascending the stairs, see Civilian interview 8 (Mar. 23, 2004); Civilian interview 16 (Apr. 27, 2004); Civilian interview 1 (Mar. 2, 2004); Commission analysis of letters written to OSHA concerning the September 11 attacks. For the intention of the group ascending the stairwell and the conditions, see Civilian interview 8 (Mar. 23, 2004).

84. On civilians finding locked doors, see, e.g., Civilian interview 16 (Apr. 27, 2004); Commission analysis of letters written to OSHA concerning the September 11 attacks. On the lock release order, see Port Authority transcripts of recorded Port Authority calls and radio channels, Sept. 11, 2001, vol. II, channel X, pp. 25–31; Port Authority response to Commission interrogatory, May 2004. The Security Command Center did not control access areas in the Observation Deck and other private tenant spaces. It is unknown whether there were any prior or subsequent orders or attempts to release the building's locks.

85. For trouble descending, see Brian Clark testimony, May 18, 2004 (videotaped); Richard Fern testimony, May 18, 2004 (videotaped); Commission analysis of letters written to OSHA concerning the September 11 attacks. The conditions of stairwell C are unknown. For conditions in stairwells, see, e.g., Civilian Interview 1 (Mar. 2, 2004); Civilian Interview 13 (Mar. 25, 2004).

86. For some civilians remaining, see Civilian interview 10 (Mar. 24, 2004). For some civilians ascending, see, e.g., Civilian interview 1 (Mar. 2, 2004); Civilian interview 11 (Mar. 25, 2004).

87. For conditions in the 90s and 100s, see Commission analysis of 911/PAPD calls. For the 105th floor and the condition of the less affected area, see Civilian interview 16 (Apr. 27, 2004). For the other areas of the 105th, 88th, and 89th floors, see Commission analysis of 911/PAPD calls.

88. For the callers, see Commission analysis of 911/PAPD calls. There are many variables to consider in determining whether, and to what extent, stairwell A was actually a viable exit. Knowing that the stairway was initially passable from at least the 91st floor down, we can conclude that it was likely open from top to bottom, on floors farther removed from the impact. However, in areas near the impact zone some doors leading to the stairwell may have jammed. We know that access to stairway A was possible from at least the 81st and 84th floors, and from several other floors between the 84th and 91st floor. It is likely that access was possible from floors higher up as well. It is not known, however, whether 911 callers had a clear path to the stairwell entrance from their locations. Damage caused by the impact of the plane, and the resulting smoke and heat, may have prevented some from being able to reach the entrance to the staircase; but the stated locations of at least some callers indicate that they were near stairwell A on their floor. Based on conditions described by civilians who descended stairwell A from at or above the impact zone, we conclude that stairwell A may have become effectively impassable as the morning progressed.

89. Commission analysis of 911/PAPD calls.

90. Brian Clark testimony, May 18, 2004 (videotaped); Civilian interview 1 (Mar. 2, 2004); Commission analysis of 911/PAPD calls.

91. Commission analysis of 911/PAPD calls.

92. Civilian interview 1 (Mar. 2, 2004); Civilian interview 8 (Mar. 23, 2004); Civilian interview 13 (Mar. 25, 2004); Civilian interview 4 (Mar. 16, 2004); Commission analysis of 911/PAPD calls.

93. OEM interview 1 (Feb. 12, 2004); PANYNJ interview 7 (June 2, 2004); Civilian interview 13 (Mar. 25, 2004); Civilian interview 1 (Mar. 2, 2004); Civilian interview 8 (Mar. 23, 2004).

94. Civilian interview 8 (Mar. 23, 2004); Civilian interview 1 (Mar. 2, 2004); Civilian interview 4 (Mar. 16, 2004); Civilian interview 13 (Mar. 25, 2004); NYPD interview 15, ESU (Mar. 11, 2004).

95. Civilian interview 6 (Mar. 22, 2004); Civilian interview 7 (Mar. 22, 2004) (quotation); Civilian interview 9 (Mar. 3, 2004); Civilian interview 14 (Apr. 7, 2004).

96. Commission analysis of 911/PAPD calls. It is not clear whether callers from below the impact were trapped

in offices or otherwise obstructed from proceeding, or were simply calling to seek advice. In any case, the 911 operators and FDNY dispatchers who advised them did not appear to be basing their advice on these or other factual considerations.

97. Port Authority transcripts of recorded Port Authority calls and radio channels, Sept. 11, 2001.

98. For the evacuation route for civilians, see Civilian interview 6 (Mar. 22, 2004); Civilian interview 7 (Mar. 22, 2004); Civilian interview 14 (Apr. 7, 2004); Civilian interview 9 (Mar. 23, 2004); PANYNJ interview 7 (Jun. 2, 2004).

99. FDNY interview 40, Battalion 4 (Feb. 12, 2004); FDNY interview 16, Battalion 1 (Jan. 20, 2004); FDNY interview 24, Battalion 6 (Jan. 23, 2004); FDNY interview 29, Battalion 1 (Jan. 29, 2004); NYPD interview 6, ESU (Feb. 19, 2004); NYPD interview 10, ESU (Mar. 1, 2004); FDNY interview, transcript 10, Battalion 2, Dec. 6, 2001.

100. Civilian interview 7 (Mar. 22, 2004); Civilian interview 6 (Mar. 22, 2004); PAPD interview 4, Port Authority Bus Terminal Command (Nov. 20, 2003); NYPD interview 10, ESU (Mar. 1, 2004). For people killed by debris, see, e.g., WTC interview 9 (June 8, 2004).

101. FDNY records, computer-aided dispatch report, alarm box 8087, Sept. 11, 2001, 09:10:02; FDNY interview 45, HQ (Mar. 8, 2004).

102. For the 23 engines and 13 ladders dispatched, see FDNY records, computer-aided dispatch report, Sept. 11, 2001, 09:08:28–09:15:00. For units that self-dispatched, see FDNY interview 60, HQ (May 11, 2004); FDNY report, McKinsey & Company, "FDNY Report," Aug. 19, 2002, p. 35. For units riding heavy, see ibid., p. 131; FDNY interview 25, Battalion 1 (Jan. 23, 2004); FDNY interview 21, Battalion 1 (Jan. 22, 2004); FDNY interview 7, Battalion 4 (Jan. 9, 2004); FDNY interview 9, Battalion 8 (Jan. 9, 2004); FDNY interview 50, Battalion 11 (Mar. 17, 2004); FDNY interview 31, Battalion 1 (Jan. 30, 2004); FDNY interview 34, Battalion 1 (Feb. 9, 2004). For extra personnel being a particular issue for SOC companies, see FDNY report, 9/11 fatalities list. For firefighters responding when told not to, see FDNY interview 46, Battalion 10 (Mar. 9, 2004). For firefighters responding from firehouses separately from the on-duty unit, see FDNY interview 46, Battalion 10 (Mar. 9, 2004); FDNY interview, transcript 26, Battalion 2, Jan. 16, 2002; FDNY interview, transcript 14, Battalion 32, Dec. 12, 2001; FDNY interview, transcript 19, Battalion 2, Jan. 8, 2002. For firefighters responding from home, see FDNY interview 14, Battalion 1 (Jan. 13, 2004); FDNY interview 17, Battalion 6 (Jan. 22, 2004); FDNY interview 19, Battalion 4 (Jan. 22, 2004); FDNY interview, transcript 6, Battalion 6 (Oct. 12, 2001); FDNY interview 11, Battalion 1 (Jan. 13, 2004); FDNY interview, transcript 2, Battalion 2, Oct. 9, 2001. For numerous additional FDNY personnel reporting, see FDNY interview 3, Chief (Jan. 7, 2004); FDNY interview 8, Fire Marshall (Jan. 9, 2004).

103. FDNY interview 15, Chief (Jan. 14, 2004); Jules Naudet and Gedeon Naudet, video footage, Sept. 11, 2001.

104. For FDNY personnel requesting the repeater's activation, see FDNY interview 4, Chief (Jan. 8, 2004). For one button on the repeater channel being activated, see PANYNJ interview 1 (Nov. 6, 2003); PANYNJ interview 4 (May 10, 2004); Port Authority records, measurements of repeater activation tones on Sept. 11, 2001, undated. For it being unclear who triggered activation, see WTC interview 6 (May 25, 2004). For the mechanics of activating the repeater, see PANYNJ interview 1 (Nov. 6, 2003); PANYNJ interview 4 (May 10, 2004).

105. For the testing of the repeater system, see Port Authority recording, WTC channel 30 (repeater channel), Sept. 11, 2001. For the master handset not being able to transmit, see PANYNJ interview 1 (Nov. 6, 2003); PANYNJ interview 4 (May 10, 2004); Port Authority records, measurements of repeater activation tones on Sept. 11, 2001, undated. For the chief on the handset not being able to hear, see Port Authority recording, WTC channel 30 (repeater channel), Sept. 11, 2001. On why he could not hear, see PANYNJ interview 1 (Nov. 6, 2003); PANYNJ interview 4 (May 10, 2004). For the repeater channel being in use in the South Tower, see Port Authority recording, WTC channel 30 (repeater channel), Sept. 11, 2001.

106. FDNY interview 15, Chief (Jan. 14, 2004); FDNY interview 4, Chief (Jan. 8, 2004); FDNY interview 5, Chief (Dec. 16, 2003). For the quotation, see Joseph Pfeifer testimony, May 18, 2004 (videotaped).

107. Peter Hayden testimony, May 18, 2004 (videotaped).

108. FDNY interview 15, Chief (Jan. 14, 2004); FDNY interview 4, Chief (Jan. 8, 2004); FDNY interview 5, Chief (Dec. 16, 2003).

109. On units ascending to the impact zone, see, e.g., FDNY interview 16, Battalion 1 (Jan. 20, 2004); FDNY interview 40, Battalion 4 (Feb. 12, 2004). On tasks below the impact zone, see FDNY interview 9, Battalion 8 (Jan. 9, 2004); FDNY interview, transcript 16, Battalion 31, Dec. 20, 2001. For rescuing civilians on the 22nd floor, see PANYNJ recognition 1, undated.

110. See FDNY interview 58, Division 3 (Apr. 22, 2004). For units using tactical 1, see FDNY interview 15, Chief (Jan. 14, 2004); FDNY interview 40, Battalion 4 (Feb. 12, 2004); FDNY interview 23, Chief (Jan. 23, 2004).

111. See FDNY interview 29, Battalion 1 (Jan. 29, 2004); FDNY interview 16, Battalion 1 (Jan. 20, 2004); Jules Naudet and Gedeon Naudet, video footage, Sept. 11, 2001. For equipment being carried, see ibid.

112. FDNY interview 38 , Battalion 4 (Feb. 11, 2004). For the working elevator, see FDNY interview 23, Chief (Jan. 23, 2004).

113. FDNY interview 38, Battalion 4 (Feb. 11, 2004); FDNY interview 25, Battalion 1 (Jan. 23, 2004); FDNY

interview 40, Battalion 4 (Feb. 12, 2004); FDNY interview 24, Battalion 6 (Jan. 23, 2004); FDNY interview 10, Battalion 1 (Jan. 12, 2004); FDNY interview 20, Battalion 6 (Jan. 22, 2004).

114. FDNY interview 23, Chief (Jan. 23, 2004); FDNY interview 30, Battalion 4 (Jan. 30, 2004); FDNY interview 13, Battalion 1 (Jan. 13, 2004); FDNY interview 29, Battalion 1 (Jan. 29, 2004); FDNY interview 26, Battalion 8 (Jan. 28, 2004).

115. FDNY interview 40, Battalion 4 (Feb. 12, 2004); FDNY interview 20, Battalion 6 (Jan. 22, 2004); FDNY interview 16, Battalion 1 (Jan. 20, 2004); FDNY interview 29, Battalion 1 (Jan. 29, 2004); FDNY interview 13, Battalion 1 (Jan. 13, 2004); NYPD interview 6, ESU (Feb. 19, 2004); FDNY interview 23, Chief (Jan. 23, 2004); FDNY interview 25, Battalion 1 (Jan. 23, 2004).

116. For the instruction to return to the lobby, see FDNY interview 5, Chief (Dec. 16, 2003); Jules Naudet and Gedeon Naudet video footage, Sept. 11, 2001. For the rumor being debunked, the other chief continuing operations, and no evidence of units returning, see Jules Naudet and Gedeon Naudet, video footage, Sept. 11, 2001; FDNY interview 15, Chief (Jan. 14, 2004). For the chief in lobby asked about helicopters, see FDNY interview, transcript 7, Chief, Oct. 23, 2001. For the rejection of helicopters, see Rudolph Giuliani interview (Apr. 20, 2004).

117. For the diminished communications, see FDNY interview 29, Battalion 1 (Jan. 29, 2004); FDNY interview, transcript 5, Battalion 6 (Oct. 12, 2001); FDNY interview 42, Field Comm (Feb. 13, 2004); Jules Naudet and Gedeon Naudet, video footage, Sept. 11, 2001; FDNY interview 15, Chief (Jan. 14, 2004); FDNY interview 5, Chief (Dec. 16, 2003). For lobby chiefs hearing nothing in response, see FDNY interview 15, Chief (Jan. 14, 2004); FDNY interview 5, Chief (Dec. 16, 2003).

118. For firefighters on the 54th floor, see NYPD interview 23, Intelligence (June 10, 2004). For firefighters on the 44th floor, see PAPD interview 7, WTC Command (Nov. 25, 2004). For firefighters between the 5th and 37th floors, see, e.g., FDNY interview 29, Battalion 1 (Jan. 29, 2004); FDNY interview 40, Battalion 4 (Feb. 12, 2004).

119. For their commencing operations, see Port Authority recording, WTC channel 30 (repeater channel), Sept. 11, 2001. For OEM field responder joining, see OEM interview 1 (Feb. 12, 2004). For units not rerouting to South Tower, see OEM interview 1 (Feb. 12, 2004); Port Authority recording, WTC channel 30 (repeater channel), Sept. 11, 2001; FDNY interview, transcript 4, Battalion 4, Oct. 9, 2001; FDNY interview, transcript 20, Battalion 10 (Jan. 10, 2001).

120. For the ladder company in stairwell B, see Port Authority recording, WTC channel 30 (repeater channel), Sept. 11, 2001. For the other ladder company, see OEM interview 1 (Feb. 12, 2004). For the senior chief's perspective, see Port Authority recording, WTC channel 30 (repeater channel), Sept. 11, 2001.

121. Port Authority recording, WTC channel 30 (repeater channel), Sept. 11, 2001.

122. For the chiefs' situational awareness, see Port Authority recording, WTC channel 30 (repeater channel), Sept. 11, 2001; FDNY interview 4, Chief (Jan. 8, 2004); FDNY 15, Chief (Jan. 14, 2004); FDNY interview 43, Chief (Mar. 3, 2004). For the senior chief's perspective, see Port Authority recording, WTC channel 30 (repeater channel), Sept. 11, 2001.

123. Port Authority recording, WTC channel 30 (repeater channel), Sept. 11, 2001. It is unknown whether the lobby chief ceased to communicate on the repeater channel because of technical problems or because he simply switched channels in order to be able to communicate with chiefs outside the South Tower. The FDNY strongly maintains that there must have been a technical problem resulting from the impact of one of the planes, because they do not believe this chief would have switched channels without first so advising on the repeater channel. FDNY letter to the Commission, July, 2, 2004. However, the repeater channel subsequently worked very well for FDNY personnel on the 78th floor and in an elevator on the 40th floor. Port Authority recording, WTC channel 30 (repeater channel), Sept. 11, 2001.

124. FDNY interview 37, Battalion 35 (Feb. 10, 2004); FDNY interview 2, Battalion 48 (Dec. 15, 2003); FDNY interview, transcript 11, Battalion 32, Dec. 12, 2001.

125. On the need for more companies, see FDNY interview 6, HQ (Jan. 8, 2004). For only two units being dispatched, see OEM interview 1 (Feb. 12, 2004); Port Authority recording, WTC channel 30 (repeater channel), Sept. 11, 2001; FDNY interview, transcript 4, Battalion 4, Oct. 9, 2001; FDNY interview, transcript 20, Battalion 10, Jan. 10, 2001. For the delayed dispatch, see FDNY records, computer-aided dispatch report, alarm box 8087, Sept. 11, 2001, 09:03:00–09:10:02. For units staged at the Brooklyn-Battery tunnel, see ibid., alarm box 1377, Sept. 11, 2001, 08:52:59–09:47:05. On units who parked and walked, see FDNY interview 46, Battalion 10 (Mar. 9, 2004); FDNY interview, transcript 24, Battalion 35, Jan. 25, 2002; FDNY interview, transcript 22, Battalion 7, Jan. 16, 2002. For confusion about the towers, see FDNY interview, transcript 8, Chief, Oct. 23, 2001; Port Authority recording, WTC channel 30 (repeater channel), Sept. 11, 2001. On the inability to find the staging area, see FDNY interview 2, Battalion 48 (Dec. 15, 2003); FDNY interview, transcript 17, Battalion 12, Dec. 20, 2001. On jumpers and debris, see FDNY interview 2, Battalion 48 (Dec. 15, 2003); FDNY interview 22, Battalion 28 (Jan. 22, 2004); FDNY interview 39, Battalion 35 (Feb. 11, 2004); FDNY interview, transcript 11, Battalion 32, Dec. 12, 2001; FDNY interview, transcript 15, Battalion 48, Dec. 13, 2001; FDNY interview, transcript 17, Battalion 12, Dec. 20, 2001.

126. For the chief's perspective, see FDNY interview 43, Chief (Mar. 3, 2004). For the four companies, see FDNY interview, transcript 13, Battalion 11, Dec. 12, 2001.

127. FDNY interview 43, Chief (Mar. 3, 2004). For finding working elevator in North Tower, see FDNY interview 53, Battalion 11 (Apr. 14, 2004).

128. For the second alarm, see FDNY interview 6, HQ (Jan. 8, 2004). For the other units, see FDNY records, computer-aided dispatch report, alarm box 1377, Sept. 11, 2001, 09:42:45–09:47:05. For some having gone through the tunnel and responded to the Marriott, see FDNY interview, transcript 3, Battalion 48, Dec. 13, 2001.

129. Port Authority recording, WTC channel 30 (repeater channel), Sept. 11, 2001.

130. FDNY interview 42, Field Comm (Feb. 13, 2004); FDNY interview 45, HQ (Mar. 8, 2004); FDNY interview 46, Battalion 10 (Mar. 9, 2004); FDNY interview 18, Chief (Jan. 22, 2004); FDNY interview 27, HQ (Jan. 28, 2004); FDNY interview 47, Chief (Mar. 11, 2004); OEM interview 6 (Mar. 24, 2004).

131. FDNY interview 42, Field Comm (Feb. 13, 2004).

132. Ibid.

133. FDNY interview 27, HQ (Jan. 28, 2004).

134. For no chief fearing a total collapse, see FDNY interview 45, HQ (Mar. 8, 2004); Thomas Von Essen interview (Apr. 7, 2004); FDNY interview 52, Chief (Apr. 5, 2004); FDNY interview 4, Chief (Jan. 8, 2004); FDNY interview 15, Chief (Jan. 14, 2004); FDNY interview 5, Chief (Dec. 16, 2003). For one chief's perspective, see FDNY interview 52, Chief (Apr. 5, 2004). For the opinion not being conveyed, see FDNY interview 4, Chief (Jan. 8, 2004); FDNY interview 15, Chief (Jan. 14, 2004); FDNY interview 5, Chief (Dec. 16, 2003).

135. FDNY interview 5, Chief (Dec. 16, 2003).

136. For the fifth alarm, see FDNY records, computer-aided dispatch report, alarm box 2033, Sept. 11, 2001, 09:54:29. On numbers dispatched, see ibid., Sept. 11, 2001, 08:47:20–09:54:29. For the paramedic, see FDNY interview 32, Chief (Feb. 9, 2004).

137. NYPD interview 8, HQ (Feb. 24, 2004). Each Level 4 mobilization fields about 1,000 officers.

138. NYPD interview 8, HQ (Feb. 24, 2004).

139. NYPD interview 15, ESU (Mar. 11, 2004); NYPD interview 18, ESU (Feb. 24, 2004).

140. For the ESU team's arrival in the North Tower and attempt to talk with the FDNY chiefs without OEM intervention, see Jules Naudet and Gedeon Naudet, video footage, Sept. 11, 2001; NYPD interview 5, ESU (Feb. 19, 2004); NYPD interview 6, ESU (Feb. 19, 2004). For the decision to have the ESU team ascend, see NYPD interview 15, ESU (Mar. 11, 2004); NYPD interview 18, ESU (Feb. 24, 2004). For the first ESU team in the South Tower checking in with the FDNY command post there, see OEM interview 1 (Feb. 12, 2004).

141. For the ESU teams' preparations and one team entering the South Tower, see NYPD interview 15, ESU (Mar. 11, 2004); NYPD interview 18, ESU (Feb. 24, 2004). For the fifth team's status at 9:59, see NYPD interview 15, ESU (Mar. 11, 2004); NYPD interview 18, ESU (Feb. 24, 2004); NYPD interview 7, ESU (Feb. 20, 2004). For the team at the North Tower, see NYPD interview 11, ESU (Mar. 9, 2004); NYPD interview 10, ESU (Mar. 1, 2004).

142. NYPD interview 6, ESU (Feb. 19, 2004).

143. New York City Police Museum interview of Kenneth Winkler, Apr. 17, 2003 (videotaped); NYPD interview 15, ESU (Mar. 11, 2004).

144. NYPD interview 22, Intelligence (June 10, 2004); NYPD interview 23, Intelligence (June 10, 2004); NYPD interview 24, Intelligence (June 15, 2004).

145. NYPD interview 20, Manhattan South Task Force (May 4, 2004); NYPD interview 21, 6th Precinct (May 4, 2004); NYPD interview 19, 13th Precinct (May 4, 2004); NYPD interview 4, Housing (Feb. 17, 2004); PAPD interview 4, Port Authority Bus Terminal Command (Nov. 20, 2003).

146. NYPD interview 19, 13th Precinct (May 4, 2004); NYPD interview 2, Transit (Jan. 2, 2004).

147. For the instructions to civilians, see NYPD interview 3, HQ (Jan. 15, 2004). For the officers at 5 WTC and the concourse, see NYPD memo, requests for departmental recognition 3 and 5, June 26, 2002; NYPD memo, request for departmental recognition 3, June 26, 2002. For officers in the South Tower, see NYPD memo, request for departmental recognition 6, June 26, 2002; NYPD memo, request for departmental recognition 4, June 26, 2002.

148. For the Chief of Department's instructions, see NYPD interview 8, HQ (Feb. 24, 2004). For the helicopter's perspective, see NYPD recordings, City Wide 1 and Special Operations Division radio channels, Sept. 11, 2001. For pilot's belief and the helicopter not hovering, see NYPD interview 12, Aviation (Mar. 10, 2004). For the other helicopter, see NYPD interview 16, Aviation (Apr. 1, 2004); NYPD interview 1, Aviation (Sept. 26, 2003).

149. For the warning, see NYPD recording, Special Operations Division radio channel, Sept. 11, 2001. For no pilot predicting a collapse, see, e.g., NYPD interview 12, Aviation (Mar. 10, 2004); NYPD interview 14, Aviation (Mar. 11, 2004).

150. For the 911 call, see Commission analysis of 911/PAPD calls. For the inaccurate conveyance, see NYPD report, McKinsey & Company, "NYPD Call-routing and Message Dispatch: Draft Summary Report," July 23, 2002.

151. For the initial responders and the assignments, see PAPD statement 3, WTC Command, Nov. 12, 2001; PAPD statement 12, WTC Command, Mar. 28, 2002. For officers assigned to rescue, see Port Authority transcripts

of recorded Port Authority calls and radio channels, Sept. 11, 2001, vol. II, channel W, p. 26. For others climbing toward the impact zone, see PAPD statement 4, Administration Command, Nov. 24, 2001.

152. For the PAPD Superintendent and inspector's ascent, see PAPD statement 3, WTC Command, Nov. 12, 2001. For the PAPD Chief's and officers' ascent, see PANYNJ statement 1, Feb. 1, 2002. For the calls to the PAPD desk, see Port Authority transcripts of recorded Port Authority calls and radio channels, Sept. 11, 2001, vol. II, channel 10, pp. 16–17.

153. For officers responding on their own initiative, see PAPD interview 8, JFK Command (Mar. 31, 2004); PAPD statement 11, WTC Command, Mar. 28, 2002. For the desk's instructions, see PAPD statement 10, Port Authority Bus Terminal Command, Mar. 20, 2002; PAPD interview 3, LaGuardia Command (Nov. 20, 2003). For formulating an ad hoc plan, see PAPD interview 3, LaGuardia Command (Nov. 20, 2003); PAPD statement 6, Port Authority Bus Terminal Command, Jan. 4, 2002. For poor situational awareness, see PAPD statement 7, Administrative Command, Jan. 6, 2002; PAPD interview 8, JFK Command (Mar. 31, 2004). For the lack of equipment, see PAPD interview 9, LaGuardia Command (Apr. 1, 2004); PAPD statement 13, Port Newark Command, Mar. 5, 2002.

154. On the PAPD officer reaching the 44th floor, see PAPD interview 7, WTC Command (Nov. 25, 2003). For the PAPD teams, see PAPD statement 4, Administrative Command, Nov. 24, 2001; PAPD interview 1, WTC Command (Oct. 14, 2003). For the officers climbing, see PAPD statement 3, WTC Command, Nov. 12, 2001. For officers on the ground floors, see PAPD interview 4, Port Authority Bus Terminal Command (Nov. 20, 2003); PAPD interview 2, Holland Tunnel Command (Oct. 27, 2003); PAPD statement 2, WTC Command, Nov. 10, 2001.

155. On remaining in the bunker, see OEM interview 3 (Mar. 16, 2004). For the evacuation order, see OEM interview 4 (Mar. 18, 2004). On liaisons and OEM, see OEM interview 3 (Mar. 16, 2004). For field responders' placement, see OEM interview 6 (Mar. 24, 2004); OEM interview 1 (Feb. 12, 2004); Richard Sheirer interview (Apr. 7, 2004); OEM interview 7 (Mar. 31, 2004); FDNY interview, transcript 25, OEM, Oct. 17, 2001.

156. NIST report, "Progress Report on the Federal Building and Fire Safety Investigation of the WTC," June 18, 2004, appendix H, p. 40.

157. For information about 911 calls, see Commission analysis of 911/PAPD calls. For people alive on the 92nd and 79th floors, see ibid.; Civilian interview 5 (May 26, 2004). For civilians being assisted, see PAPD interview 4, Port Authority Bus Terminal Command (Nov. 6, 2004); NYPD interview 10, ESU (Mar. 1, 2004); FDNY interview, transcript 10, Battalion 2, Dec. 6, 2001. For injured civilians being assisted, see FDNY interview, transcript 10, Battalion 2, Dec. 6, 2001; FDNY interview 40, Battalion 4 (Feb. 12, 2004); PAPD interview 6, Lincoln Tunnel Command (Nov. 24, 2003).

158. For the overall command post, see FDNY interview 52, Chief (Apr. 5, 2004). For the North Tower lobby, see FDNY interview 4, Chief (Jan. 8, 2004). For South Tower staging, see FDNY interview 6, HQ (Jan. 8, 2004). For EMS staging areas, see FDNY interview 32, Chief (Feb. 9, 2004); FDNY interview 35, EMS (Feb. 10, 2004).

159. For situational awareness in North Tower lobby, see FDNY interview 15, Chief (Jan. 14, 2004). For overall command post, see FDNY interview 52, Chief (Apr. 5, 2004).

160. For the collapse's effect on the firefighters, see FDNY interview 29, Battalion 1 (Jan. 29, 2004); FDNY interview 40, Battalion 4 (Feb. 12, 2004); FDNY interview 25, Battalion 1 (Jan. 23, 2004); FDNY interview 24, Battalion 6 (Jan. 23, 2004); FDNY interview 23, Chief (Jan. 23, 2004); FDNY interview 16, Battalion 1 (Jan. 20, 2004). For the reaction of firefighters not facing the south, see FDNY interview 7, Battalion 4 (Jan. 9, 2004); FDNY interview 10, Battalion 1 (Jan. 12, 2004); FDNY interview 12, Battalion 4 (Jan. 13, 2004); FDNY interview 26, Battalion 8 (Jan. 28, 2004); FDNY interview 29, Battalion 1 (Jan. 29, 2004); FDNY interview 16, Battalion 1 (Jan. 20, 2004).

161. It is possible that the repeater channel satellite on the roof of 5 WTC was damaged or destroyed when the South Tower collapsed. That the repeater channel stopped recording transmissions at 9:59 does not mean transmissions no longer could be made on it.

162. For the FDNY boat radioing of the collapse, see FDNY recording, FDNY Manhattan Dispatch Channel, Sept. 11, 2001. For the van being abandoned, see FDNY interview 42, Field Comm (Feb. 13, 2004). For the order one minute after the collapse, see FDNY interview 4, Chief (Jan. 8, 2004); Jules Naudet and Gedeon Naudet, video footage, Sept. 11, 2001. For the subsequent order, see FDNY interview 40, Battalion 4 (Feb. 12, 2004).

163. For evacuation instructions, our analysis is based on more than 100 interviews we conducted and our review of 500 internal FDNY interview transcripts. For three firefighters hearing "imminent collapse," see FDNY interview, transcript 20, Battalion 10, Jan. 10, 2002; FDNY interview, transcript 23, Battalion 7, Jan. 21, 2002; FDNY interview, transcript 21, Battalion 8, Jan. 9, 2002.

164. For firefighters hearing orders over tactical 1, see, e.g., FDNY interview 40, Battalion 4 (Feb. 12, 2004); FDNY interview 29, Battalion 1 (Jan. 29, 2004). For one chief giving the instruction, see FDNY interview 23, Chief (Jan. 23, 2004).

165. For the chief on the 35th floor and the first instruction, see FDNY interview 23, Chief (Jan. 23, 2004). For the chief on the 23rd floor, see FDNY interview 29, Battalion 1 (Jan. 29, 2004); FDNY interview 16, Battalion 1 (Jan. 20, 2004). For the chief on the 35th floor hearing of the South Tower collapse and taking subsequent

action, see FDNY interview 23, Chief (Jan. 23, 2004). For firefighters beginning to evacuate because of these chiefs, see, e.g., FDNY interview 16, Battalion 1 (Jan. 20, 2004); FDNY interview, transcript 9, Battalion 6, Dec. 5, 2001.

166. For radios not working in high-rise environments, see FDNY interview 9, Battalion 8 (Jan. 9, 2004); FDNY interview 13, Battalion 1 (Jan. 13, 2004). For tactical 1 being overburdened, see FDNY interview 16, Battalion 1 (Jan. 20, 2004). For the quotation, see FDNY interview, transcript 9, Battalion 6, Dec. 5, 2001.

167. For off-duty firefighters in the North Tower, see NYPD interview 6, ESU (Feb. 19, 2004); FDNY interview 24, Battalion 6 (Jan. 23, 2004). For firefighters dispatched to the South Tower, see FDNY interview 53, Battalion 11 (Apr. 14, 2004); FDNY interview, transcript 20, Battalion 10, Jan. 10, 2001.

168. For units stopping or delaying evacuation to help, see FDNY interview 40, Battalion 4 (Feb. 12, 2004); FDNY interview 59, Battalion 2 (Apr. 22, 2004); FDNY interview, transcript 3, Battalion 2, Oct. 9, 2001; FDNY interview, transcript 5, Battalion 6, Oct. 12, 2001. For companies first trying to regroup, see FDNY interview, transcript 3, Battalion 2, Oct. 9, 2001; FDNY interview, transcript 4, Battalion 4, Oct. 9, 2001. For the lack of urgency, see FDNY interview 57, SOC (Apr. 15, 2004); FDNY interview 25, Battalion 1 (Jan. 23, 2004); FDNY interview 16, Battalion 1 (Jan. 20, 2004); FDNY interview, transcript 9, Battalion 6, Dec. 5, 2001; FDNY interview, transcript 4, Battalion 4, Oct. 9, 2001; FDNY interview, transcript 3, Battalion 2, Oct. 9, 2001. For the belief that urgency would have increased on learning of the South Tower's collapse, see FDNY interview, transcript 9, Battalion 6, Dec. 5, 2001; FDNY interview, transcript 5, Battalion 6, Oct. 12, 2001. For firefighters sitting and not evacuating, see FDNY interview 16, Battalion 1 (Jan. 20, 2004); NY State Court interview 1 (June 22, 2004). For firefighters not leaving while others remained and convincing others to stay with them, see FDNY interview, transcript 4, Battalion 4, Oct. 9, 2001; FDNY interview 57, SOC (Apr. 15, 2004).

169. FDNY interview 57, SOC (Apr. 15, 2004); FDNY interview 55, Battalion 8 (Apr. 15, 2004); FDNY interview, transcript 9, Battalion 6, Dec. 5, 2001; FDNY interview 59, Battalion 2 (Apr. 22, 2004); FDNY interview 10, Battalion 1 (Jan. 12, 2004); FDNY interview 7, Battalion 4 (Jan. 9, 2004); FDNY interview 13, Battalion 1 (Jan. 13, 2004); FDNY interview 23, Chief (Jan. 23, 2004); FDNY interview 26, Battalion 8 (Jan. 28, 2004); FDNY interview 12, Battalion 4 (Jan. 13, 2004).

170. FDNY interview 59, Battalion 2 (Apr. 22, 2004).

171. For hotel's damage, see Jules Naudet and Gedeon Naudet, video footage, Sept. 11, 2001. For individuals in the lobby, see FDNY interview 43, Chief (Mar. 3, 2004); FDNY interview 36, Chief (Feb. 10, 2004); FDNY interview 1, Chief (Mar. 26, 2004). On assisting the civilians, see FDNY interview 43, Chief (Mar. 3, 2004). For the line of 20 men and the 4 survivors, see FDNY interview, transcript 13, Battalion 11, Dec. 12, 2001.

172. For the two companies and their actions, see FDNY interview 22, Battalion 28 (Jan. 22, 2004); FDNY interview 37, Battalion 35 (Feb. 10, 2004); FDNY interview 39, Battalion 35 (Feb. 11, 2004); FDNY interview 41, Battalion 35 (Feb. 12, 2004); FDNY interview, transcript 12, Battalion 35, Dec. 12, 2001. For the PAPD having cleared the area, see PAPD statement 3, WTC command, Nov. 12, 2001. For FDNY personnel checking the area afterward, see FDNY interview, transcript 12, Battalion 35, Dec. 12, 2001.

173. For the senior leaders confirming the collapse, and the Chief of Department issuing a radio order, see FDNY interview 52, Chief (Apr. 5, 2004). For his ordering the post's relocation and two companies to respond, see FDNY interview 45, HQ (Mar. 8, 2004).

174. For the chiefs' delay in learning of the collapse, see FDNY interview 4, Chief (Jan. 8, 2004); FDNY interview 56, Chief (Apr. 23, 2004). On one chief's view of the North Tower, see FDNY interview 51 (Apr. 2, 2004); FDNY interview 36, Chief (Feb. 10, 2004).

175. For firefighters' actions after the collapse, see FDNY interview 49, Chief (Mar. 17, 2004); FDNY interview 52, Chief (Apr. 5, 2004); FDNY interview 36, Chief (Feb. 10, 2004); FDNY interview 45, HQ (Mar. 8, 2004); FDNY interview 51 (Apr. 2, 2004); FDNY interview 22, Battalion 28 (Jan. 22, 2004); FDNY interview 1, Chief (Mar. 26, 2004); FDNY interview, transcript 1, Battalion 7, Jan. 28, 2001; FDNY interview, transcript 12, Battalion 35, Dec. 12, 2001. For some not knowing about the collapse but others knowing and remaining to help, see FDNY interview 49, Chief (Mar. 17, 2004); FDNY interview 52, Chief (Apr. 5, 2004); FDNY interview 36, Chief (Feb. 10, 2004); FDNY interview 45, HQ (Mar. 8, 2004). For the quotation, see FDNY interview 49, Chief (Mar. 17, 2004). For the firefighter directing those exiting, see FDNY interview 29, Battalion 1 (Jan. 29, 2004); FDNY interview 24, Battalion 6 (Jan. 23, 2004). For the using a bullhorn, see FDNY interview 52, Chief (Apr. 5, 2004). For the three senior members' actions, see FDNY interview 51 (Apr. 2, 2004).

176. NYPD recordings, City Wide 1 and Special Operations Division radio channels, Sept. 11, 2001; see also NYPD interview 12, Aviation (Mar. 10, 2004); NYPD interview 14, Aviation (Mar. 11, 2004); NYPD interview 13, Aviation (Mar. 10, 2004); NYPD interview 16, Aviation (Apr. 1, 2004).

177. NYPD recordings, City Wide 1, Special Operations Division, and Divisions 1, 2, and 3 radio channels, Sept. 11, 2001; NPYD interview 15, ESU (Mar. 11, 2004); NYPD interview 18, ESU (Feb. 24, 2004).

178. For the ESU teams' situational awareness, see, e.g., NYPD interview 5, ESU (Feb. 19, 2004); NYPD interview 6, ESU (Feb. 19, 2004). For the evacuation order, see NYPD interview 15, ESU (Mar. 11, 2004); NYPD interview 18, ESU (Feb. 24, 2004).

179. For the message being clearly heard, see, e.g., NYPD interview 5, ESU (Feb. 19, 2004); NYPD interview

6, ESU (Feb. 19, 2004). For the subsequent exchange, see NYPD interview 6, ESU (Feb. 19, 2004); NYPD interview 5, ESU (Feb. 19, 2004); NYPD interview 15, ESU (Mar. 11, 2004); NYPD interview 18, ESU (Feb. 24, 2004).

180. For the ESU team's perspective, see NYPD interview 5, ESU (Feb. 19, 2004); NYPD interview 6, ESU (Feb. 19, 2004). For a firefighter stating he would not take instructions from the NYPD, see FDNY interview 38, Battalion 4 (Feb. 11, 2004). For a firefighter alleging that ESU officers passed him without sharing evacuation instruction, see FDNY interview 57, SOC (Apr. 15, 2004). A member of the only ESU team that this firefighter could have encountered above the 11th floor states that his team did share its evacuation instruction with firefighters it encountered. NYPD interview 6, ESU (Feb. 19, 2004).

181. NYPD interview 11, ESU (Mar. 9, 2004); NYPD interview 10, ESU (Mar. 1, 2004).

182. NYPD interview 7, ESU (Feb. 20, 2004); NYPD interview 15, ESU (Mar. 11, 2004); NYPD interview 18, ESU (Feb. 24, 2004).

183. NYPD interview 22, Intelligence (June 10, 2004); NYPD interview 23, Intelligence (June 10, 2004); NYPD interview 24, Intelligence (June 15, 2004).

184. NYPD interview 20, Manhattan South Task Force (May 4, 2004); NYPD interview 21, 6th Precinct (May 4, 2004); NYPD interview 4, Housing (Feb. 17, 2004); PAPD interview 4, Port Authority Bus Terminal Command (Nov. 20, 2003).

185. For officers being in the concourse, see NYPD recordings, City Wide 1, Special Operations Division, and Divisions 1, 2, and 3 radio channels, Sept. 11, 2001. For the survivors' actions, see NYPD memo, requests for departmental recognition 3, 4, 5 and 6, June 26, 2002; NYPD interview 19, 13th Precinct (May 4, 2004); NYPD interview 2, Transit (Jan. 2, 2004).

186. For the collapse's effect, see PAPD interview 3, LaGuardia Command (Nov. 20, 2003). For officers not receiving the evacuation order, see PAPD interview 7, WTC Command (Nov. 25, 2003); PAPD interview 5, Lincoln Tunnel Command (Nov. 24, 2003). For officers deciding to evacuate, see PAPD interview 10, GW Bridge Command (Sept. 25, 2003); PAPD statement 5, Lincoln Tunnel Command (Dec. 10, 2001). For officers slowing their descent, see PAPD interview 10, GW Bridge Command (Sept. 25, 2003).

187. For the North Tower collapsing at 10:28:25, see NIST report, "Progress Report on the Federal Building and Fire Safety Investigation of the WTC," June 18, 2004, appendix H, p. 40. For those in stairwell B who survived the North Tower's collapse, see FDNY report, Division 3 report on operations on Sept. 11, 2001, undated; Dennis Cauchon and Martha Moore, "Miracles Emerge from Debris," *USA Today*, Sept. 6, 2002, p. A1.

188. According to the number of death certificates issued by the New York City Medical Examiner's Office, the WTC attacks killed 2,749 nonterrorists, including nonterrorist occupants of the hijacked aircraft. New York City Office of the Chief Medical Examiner report, "WTC Victim List," undated (as of July 9, 2004). The Pentagon attack killed 184 nonterrorists, including the occupants of the hijacked aircraft. FBI report, list of Pentagon victims, undated (as of July 9, 2004). Forty nonterrorists died in the crash of United Airlines Flight 93 in Pennsylvania. FBI report, list of Flight 93 victims, undated (as of July 9, 2004). Our conclusion that these first responder death totals were the largest in U.S. history is based on our inability to find contrary evidence. For FDNY fatalities, see FDNY report, September 11 tribute, undated (online at www.ci.nyc.ny.us/html/fdny/media/tribute/tribute.html). For PAPD fatalities, see PAPD report, "In Memoriam," undated (online at www.panynj.gov/AboutthePortAuthority/PortAuthorityPolice/InMemoriam/). For NYPD fatalities, see NYPD report, "NYPD Memorial: 2001 Heroes," undated (online at www.ci.nyc.ny.us/html/nypd/html/memorial_01.html).

189. Rudolph Giuliani interview (Apr. 20, 2004); OEM interview 3 (Mar. 16, 2004); Richard Sheirer interview (Apr. 7, 2004); Thomas Von Essen interview (Apr. 7, 2004); Bernard Kerik interview (Apr. 6, 2004).

190. The Incident Command System (ICS) is a formalized management structure for command, control, and coordination during an emergency response. ICS provides a means to coordinate the efforts of individual agencies as they work toward the three main priorities of most emergencies—life safety, incident stability, and property/environment conservation. Within ICS, incident command is organized into five major components: the command function, the planning section, the operations section, the logistics section, and the finance/administration section. When multiple agencies or jurisdictions are involved in a response, ICS provides for and can evolve into a unified command, with a decisionmaker from each key agency represented at the incident command level. For the system being used on 9/11, see, e.g., Arlington County, Virginia, report, Titan Systems Corp., "Arlington County: After-Action Report on the Response to the September 11 Terrorist Attack on the Pentagon," 2002, pp. 11, A-20–A-21.

191. Grant C. Peterson, "Introduction: Arlington County and the After-Action Report," July 28, 2003 (presented at conference in Arlington, Va., "Local Response to Terrorism: Lessons Learned from the 9/11 Attack on the Pentagon").

192. For the death toll, see FBI report, list of Pentagon victims, undated. For patient care and victim disposition, see Arlington County, "After-Action Report," pp. B-1, B-12–B-15.

193. For reasons the response was mainly a success, see Arlington County, "After-Action Report," pp. 11–12; Edward Plaugher interview (Oct. 16, 2003). For preparations for the International Monetary Fund and the World

Bank meetings, see "Washington Is Seeking Support to Handle Protests at 2 Meetings," *New York Times*, Aug. 18, 2001, p. A8; Arlington County, "After-Action Report," pp. 12, A-4, C-26.

194. For a list of the response agencies, see James Schwartz and Christopher Combs, "Incident Command, Joint Operations Center and Incident Communications," July 28, 2003 (presented at conference in Arlington, Va., "Local Response to Terrorism: Lessons Learned from the 9/11 Attack on the Pentagon"). When the Bureau of Alcohol, Tobacco, and Firearms moved from the Department of the Treasury to the Department of Justice after 9/11 in connection with the creation of DHS, it was renamed the Bureau of Alcohol, Tobacco, Firearms and Explosives (still abbreviated ATF); see ATF press release, "ATF Moves to the Department of Justice," Jan. 24, 2003.

195. For the establishment of incident command on September 11, see Arlington County, "After-Action Report," appendix 1, p. 1-1; Schwartz and Combs, "Incident Command."

196. Arlington County, "After-Action Report," appendix 1, p. 1-1. Other sources put the time of the partial collapse as late as 10:14. See Edward P. Plaugher, "Fire & EMS," July 28, 2003 (presented at conference in Arlington, Va., "Local Response to Terrorism: Lessons Learned from the 9/11 Attack on the Pentagon").

197. Ibid., pp. A-30–A-31.

198. Edward A. Flynn, "Law Enforcement," July 28, 2003 (presented at conference in Arlington, Va., on "Local Response to Terrorism: Lessons Learned from the 9/11 Attack on the Pentagon").

199. Arlington County, "After-Action Report," pp. 12–13.

200. For the estimate, see NIST report, "WTC Investigation Progress," June 22–23, 2004. For the updated death certificate information, see New York City report, "WTC Victim List," June 21, 2004. The analysis in this paragraph is based upon the following sources: CNN, "September 11: A Memorial," updated 2004 (online at www.cnn.com/SPECIALS/2001/memorial/index.html); company contacts, June 29, 2004 (online at http://worldtradeaftermath.com/wta/contacts/companies_list.asp?letter=a); CNN, WTC tenants, 2001 (online at www.cnn.com/SPECIALS/2001/trade.center/tenants1.html); September 11 personal tributes, June 19, 2004 (online at www.legacy.com/LegacyTribute/Sept11.asp); September 11 personal profiles, Oct. 11, 2003 (online at www.september11victims.com/september11Victims); *New York Times, Portraits: 9/11/01: The Collected "Portraits of Grief"* (Times Books, 2002). It is possible that a person who worked above the impact zone had not yet reached his or her office and was killed below the impact zone, either by falling debris, by the fireballs that exploded into the lobby, or by being trapped in an elevator. Individuals below the impact zone may have been killed for the same reasons. Individuals may also have been killed while in the process of evacuating.

201. Ironically, had the towers remained up longer, scores more first responders would have died. Twenty-six additional FDNY companies—more than 150 firefighters—were en route at the time of the South Tower's collapse, and scores more PAPD officers on Church and Vesey were preparing to enter the towers.

202. The "advisory" announcement directed by protocol (without the expanded instruction for occupants to return to their floors) would have given greater leeway to those who judged, based on a firsthand awareness of conditions on their floors (e.g., some could feel heat from North Tower explosion), that evacuation was warranted. In retrospect, occupants would only have had to reach a point below the 77th floor to be safe.

203. Appended to the directive was a list of different types of emergencies with designated Incident Commanders. Terrorist incidents were subdivided according to the types of attack. Conventional weapons and bomb threats were assigned to the NYPD, while chemical, biological, and nuclear attacks designated "NYPD or FDNY" as the Incident Commander. The directive noted: "The handling of a threat of a chemical or biological release or the use of conventional weapons falls to the NYPD. Dealing with the consequences of the explosion or release is the responsibility of the FDNY. The investigation that follows, once the consequences of the event have been mitigated, is the responsibility of the NYPD. Any conflicts regarding the issue of Command at these incidents will be resolved by OEM." New York City memo, Office of the Mayor, "Direction and Control of Emergencies in the City of New York," July 2001.

204. For the NYPD clearing lanes, see, e.g., FDNY interview 43, Chief (Mar. 3, 2004).

205. For the Mayor and Police Commissioner's consultation with the FDNY Chief of Department, see Rudolph Giuliani interview (Apr. 20, 2004).

206. The FDNY's lack of command and control had some unintended positive consequences. One battalion chief was dispatched to the South Tower but instead responded to the North Tower, where he was instrumental in saving many lives after the South Tower collapsed. Some FDNY units dispatched to the South Tower—where they would have perished—instead were mistakenly sent to the North Tower and in many cases survived.

207. For the FDNY addressing these issues, see generally FDNY report, McKinsey & Company, "FDNY Report," Aug. 19, 2002; Peter Hayden interview (Jan. 14, 2004). For the PAPD not changing standard operating procedures or training, see PAPD regulations, "Manual of Police Division Instructions," undated (in existence before and after 9/11); Barry Pickard interview (Nov. 24, 2003).

208. One instance in which the FDNY/NYPD rivalry may have had an impact on the total fatalities was the alleged failure of ESU officers descending past at least two firefighters after 9:59 in the North Tower to share their evacuation instructions. It should be noted, however, that at least one firefighter has conceded that he, too, descended past other stationary firefighters without telling them to evacuate. In addition, according to one of the ESU offi-

cers and one of the firefighters in the North Tower, at least some FDNY personnel were unwilling to take evacuation orders from police that morning.

209. Based on more than 100 interviews we conducted and our review of 500 internal FDNY interview transcripts, we conclude that out of these 32 companies, all on-duty members of 19 companies are likely to have known to evacuate (Engine Companies 1, 4, 7, 9, 15, 16, 21, 24, 28, 33, 39, and 65; Ladder Companies 1, 5, 6, 8, 9, 110; and Rescue 1). We also conclude that at least some members of each of five companies knew to evacuate (two firefighters from Ladder Company 10; the officer of Ladder Company 20; all but the officer of Engine Company 10; at least two firefighters from Squad 18; and at least three firefighters from Engine 6). We do not know whether members of the eight other companies knew to evacuate (Engine Companies 55, 207, and 226; Rescue 2, 3, and 4; Hazmat 1; and Squad 1) because they all died, and we have come across no on-point eyewitness accounts related to their operations. It is very possible that at least some of these firefighters did hear the evacuation order but nevertheless failed to evacuate in the only 29-minute period between the collapse of the two towers. In addition, it is possible that several of the eight companies for which we have no record of their receiving evacuation instructions were in the South Tower and thus died in its earlier collapse.

210. Eric Lipton, "A New Weapon for Firefighters," *New York Times*, May 30, 2004, p. 27.

10 Wartime

1. All times are Eastern Daylight Time. Sometime around 10:30, after the decision had already been made not to return to Washington, a reported threat to "Angel"—the code word for Air Force One—was widely disseminated in the Presidential Emergency Operations Center (PEOC) and aboard Air Force One. Notes from the morning indicate that Vice President Cheney informed President Bush in a phone conversation shortly after 10:30 that an anonymous threat had been phoned into the White House that was viewed as credible. At about the same time, news of the threat was conveyed on the air threat conference call.

The Secret Service's Intelligence Division tracked down the origin of this threat and, during the day, determined that it had originated in a misunderstanding by a watch officer in the White House Situation Room. The director of the White House Situation Room that day disputes this account. But the Intelligence Division had the primary job of running down the story, and we found their witnesses on this point to be credible. During the afternoon of September 11 the leadership of the Secret Service was satisfied that the reported threat to "Angel" was unfounded.

At the White House press briefing on September 12, spokesperson Ari Fleischer described the threat to Air Force One as "real and credible." White House transcript, Press Briefing by Ari Fleischer, Sept. 12, 2001 (online at www.whitehouse.gov/news/releases/2001/09/print/20010912-8.html). Fleischer told us he cited the information in good faith. Indeed, Fleischer had conferred with Vice President Cheney and Karen Hughes before the briefing, and they had decided to let people know about the threat, all of them believing it was true. According to Fleischer, only weeks later did he learn—from press reports—that the threat was unfounded. We have not found any evidence that contradicts his account. Ari Fleischer interview (Apr. 22, 2004); Chuck Green interview (Mar. 10, 2004); Deborah Loewer meeting (Feb. 6, 2004); Ralph Sigler meeting (May 10, 2004); Andrew Card meeting (Mar. 31, 2004); Edward Marinzel interview (Apr. 21, 2004); Secret Service briefing (Jan. 29, 2004).

2. Edward Marinzel interview (Apr. 21, 2004); USSS memo, interview with Edward Marinzel, Oct. 3, 2001; President Bush and Vice President Cheney meeting (Apr. 29, 2004); Ari Fleischer interview (Apr. 22, 2004); Deborah Loewer meeting (Feb. 6, 2004); White House record, PEOC Watch Log, Sept. 11, 2001.

3. Commission analysis of Air Force One radar data; Edward Marinzel interview (Apr. 21, 2004); USSS memo, interview with Edward Marinzel, Oct. 3, 2001; Deborah Loewer meeting (Feb. 6, 2004).

4. White House record, Situation Room Communications Log, Sept. 11, 2001.

5. White House transcript, Rice interview with Bob Woodward of the *Washington Post*, Oct. 24, 2001, p. 367. In the interview, Rice also said the President characterized the war as "global in nature." Ibid.

6. See White House transcript, Rice interview with Scott Pelley of CBS, Aug. 2, 2002, p. 408; but see Rice's statement to Bob Woodward: "In the first video conference, the assumption that everybody kind of shared was that it was global terrorists. . . . I don't believe anybody said this is likely al Qaeda. I don't think so." White House transcript, Rice interview with Bob Woodward, Oct. 24, 2001, p. 367.

7. NSC memo, Summary of Conclusions of Deputies Committee Meeting (held by secure teleconference), Sept. 11, 2001.

8. The Secretary's decision was broadcast on the air threat conference call at 10:43. A minute later, Secretary Rumsfeld spoke to the Vice President, and he asked Rumsfeld to run the issue by the President. At 10:45 conferees were told to "hold off" on Defcon 3, but a minute later the order was reinstated. Rumsfeld believed the matter was urgent and, having consulted DOD directives, concluded he had the authority to issue the order and would brief the President. Rumsfeld briefed the President on the decision at 11:15. See DOD transcript, Air Threat Conference Call, Sept. 11, 2001; Stephen Cambone interviews (July 8, 2004; July 12, 2004); DOD notes, Stephen Cambone notes, Sept. 11, 2001.

9. The 9/11 crisis tested the U.S. government's plans and capabilities to ensure the continuity of constitutional government and the continuity of government operations. We did not investigate this topic, except as needed in order to understand the activities and communications of key officials on 9/11. The Chair, Vice Chair, and senior staff were briefed on the general nature and implementation of these continuity plans.

10. White House transcript, Statement by the President in His Address to the Nation, Sept. 11, 2001 (online at www.whitehouse.gov/news/releases/2001/09/20010911-16.html).

11. White House transcript, Rice interview with Bob Woodward, Oct. 24, 2001, p. 371.

12. Joshua Bolten meeting (Mar. 18, 2004); see also Steven Brill, *After: How America Confronted the September 12 Era* (Simon & Schuster, 2003), pp. 50–51.

13. The collapse of the World Trade Center towers on the morning of September 11 coated Lower Manhattan with a thick layer of dust from the debris and fire. For days a plume of smoke rose from the site. Between September 11 and September 21, 2001, EPA issued five press releases regarding air quality in Lower Manhattan. A release on September 16 quoted the claim of the assistant secretary for labor at OSHA that tests show "it is safe for New Yorkers to go back to work in New York's financial district." (OSHA's responsibility extends only to indoor air quality for workers, however.) The most controversial press release, on September 18, quoted EPA Administrator Christine Whitman as saying that the air was "safe" to breathe. This statement was issued the day after the financial markets reopened. The EPA Office of Inspector General investigated the issuance of these press releases and concluded that the agency did not have enough data about the range of possible pollutants other than asbestos to make a judgment, lacked public health benchmarks for appropriate levels of asbestos and other pollutants, and had imprecise methods for sampling asbestos in the air; it also noted that more than 25 percent of the bulk dust samples collected before September 18 showed the presence of asbestos above the agency's 1 percent benchmark. EPA Inspector General report, "EPA's Response to the World Trade Center Collapse: Challenges, Successes, and Areas for Improvement," Aug. 21, 2003.

We do not have the expertise to examine the scientific accuracy of the pronouncements in the press releases. The issue is the subject of pending civil litigation.

We did examine whether the White House improperly influenced the content of the press releases so that they would intentionally mislead the public. The EPA press releases were coordinated with Samuel Thernstrom, associate director for communications at the White House Council on Environmental Quality. Oral reports, interviews with EPA officials, and materials on the EPA's Web site were not coordinated through the White House. Although the White House review process resulted in some editorial changes to the press releases, these changes were consistent with what the EPA had already been saying without White House clearance. See, e.g., David France and Erika Check, "Asbestos Alert; How much of the chemical does the World Trade Center wreckage contain?" *Newsweek Web Exclusive*, Sept. 14, 2001 (quoting EPA Administrator Whitman as saying the air quality is not a health problem); Andrew C. Revkin, "After the Attacks: The Chemicals; Monitors Say Health Risk From Smoke Is Very Small," *New York Times*, Sept. 14, 2001, p. A6 (EPA says levels of airborne asbestos below threshold of concern); Hugo Kugiya, "Terrorist Attacks; Asbestos Targeted in Cleanup Effort; EPA's Whitman: 'No reason for concern,'" *Newsday*, Sept. 16, 2001, p. W31 (Whitman says there is no reason for concern given EPA tests for asbestos). There were disputes between the EPA's communications person and the White House coordinator regarding the press releases. The EPA communications person said she felt extreme pressure from the White House coordinator, and felt that they were no longer her press releases. EPA Inspector General interview of Tina Kreisher, Aug. 28, 2002. The White House coordinator, however, told us that these disputes were solely concerned with process, not the actual substance of the releases. Samuel Thernstrom interview (Mar. 31, 2004). Former EPA administrator Christine Whitman agreed with the White House coordinator. Christine Whitman interview (June 28, 2004) The documentary evidence supports this claim. Although Whitman told us she spoke with White House senior economic adviser Lawrence Lindsey regarding the need to get the financial markets open quickly, she denied he pressured her to declare the air was safe due to economic expediency. We found no evidence of pressure on EPA to say the air was safe in order to permit the markets to reopen. Moreover, the most controversial release that specifically declared the air safe to breathe was released after the markets had already reopened.

The EPA did not have the health-based benchmarks needed to assess the extraordinary air quality conditions in Lower Manhattan after 9/11. The EPA and the White House therefore improvised and applied standards developed for other circumstances in order to make pronouncements regarding air safety, advising workers at Ground Zero to use protective gear and advising the general population that the air was safe. Whether those improvisations were appropriate is still a subject for medical and scientific debate. See EPA Inspector General report, "EPA's Response to the World Trade Center Collapse," Aug. 21, 2003, pp. 9–19.

14. Brill, *After*, pp. 47–50.

15. We studied this episode and interviewed many of the participants. The NYSE, Amex, and Nasdaq have developed plans for coordination and cooperation in the event of a disaster affecting one or all of them, but these plans do not include other exchanges or international components. The White House efforts during the crisis were coordinated by the President's Working Group on Financial Markets, a group created in the 1980s.

16. Brill, *After*, pp. 53–55, 89–91. Following interim reports in 1999 and 2000, a congressional commission

chaired by former senators Gary Hart and Warren Rudman, and directed by retired general Charles Boyd, had, in January 2001, recommended the creation of a cabinet department dedicated to "homeland security." In May 2001, President Bush named Vice President Cheney to head a task force on problems of national preparedness. His recently hired coordinator, Admiral Steven Abbot, had started work just before the 9/11 attack.

17. Ashcroft told us that he established a "hold until cleared" policy because of the high rate of flight from deportation proceedings. John Ashcroft testimony, Apr. 13, 2004. For closure of hearings and secrecy of the detainee names, see DOJ email, Chief Immigration Judge Michael Creppy to all immigration judges, "Cases requiring special procedures," Sept. 21, 2001. This policy has been challenged in two U.S. courts of appeals. The Sixth Circuit held that there is a constitutional right of public access to these hearings; the Third Circuit reached the opposite result. The Supreme Court has not yet decided to resolve this "circuit split." See *Detroit Free Press v. Ashcroft*, 303 F.3d 681 (6th Cir. 2002); *North Jersey Media Group, Inc. v. Ashcroft*, 308 F.3d 198 (3d Cir. 2002), *cert. denied*, 123 S.Ct. 2215 (2003). For the length of the clearance process, see DOJ Inspector General report, "The September 11 Detainees: A Review of the Treatment of Aliens Held on Immigration Charges in Connection with the Investigation of the September 11 Attacks," Apr. 2003, p. 51.

18. DOJ Inspector General report, "The September 11 Detainees," Apr. 2003, pp. 142–150, 195–197.

19. John Ashcroft testimony, Apr. 13, 2004; DOJ record, "Special Interest Cases," Sept. 16, 2003. These numbers do not add up to 768 because we have not included all categories. Some of those remanded to the Marshals Service were held as material witnesses, and individuals were released "on bond" only after they were "cleared" by the FBI of any connection to 9/11. For the response to our questions about the 9/11 detainee program, see DOJ emails, Daniel Levin to the Commission, July 9, 2004; July 13, 2004. There is one exception to the statement in the text that the detainees were lawfully held on immigration charges; one detainee was held for a short time "despite the fact that there was no valid immigration charge." DOJ Inspector General report, "The September 11 Detainees," Apr. 2003, p. 15, n. 22. See also Khaled Medhat Abou El Fadl testimony, Dec. 8, 2003.

20. Intelligence report, interrogation of KSM, May 10, 2003.

21. The complete title of the Act is Uniting and Strengthening America by Providing Appropriate Tools Required to Intercept and Obstruct Terrorism (USA PATRIOT ACT) Act of 2001, Pub. L. No. 107-56, 115 Stat. 273 (signed into law Oct. 26, 2001).

22. John Ashcroft interview (Dec. 17, 2003).

23. On the early development of the Patriot Act, see, e.g., Brill, *After*, pp. 73–76, 120–125.

24. During the morning of September 11, the FAA suspended all nonemergency air activity in the national airspace. While the national airspace was closed, decisions to allow aircraft to fly were made by the FAA working with the Department of Defense, Department of State, U.S. Secret Service, and the FBI. The Department of Transportation reopened the national airspace to U.S. carriers effective 11:00 A.M. on September 13, 2001, for flights out of or into airports that had implemented the FAA's new security requirements. See FAA response to Commission questions for the record, June 8, 2004.

25. After the airspace reopened, nine chartered flights with 160 people, mostly Saudi nationals, departed from the United States between September 14 and 24. In addition, one Saudi government flight, containing the Saudi deputy defense minister and other members of an official Saudi delegation, departed Newark Airport on September 14. Every airport involved in these Saudi flights was open when the flight departed, and no inappropriate actions were taken to allow those flights to depart. See City of St. Louis Airport Authority, Lambert–St. Louis International Airport response to Commission questions for the record, May 27, 2004; Los Angeles International Airport response to Commission questions for the record, June 2, 2004; Greater Orlando Aviation Authority, Orlando International Airport response to Commission questions for the record, June 8, 2004; Metropolitan Washington Airports Authority, Washington Dulles International Airport response to Commission questions for the record, June 8, 2004; Port Authority of New York and New Jersey, JFK Airport response to Commission questions for the record, June 4, 2004; Massachusetts Port Authority, Logan International Airport, and Hanscom Airfield response to Commission questions for the record, June 17, 2004; Las Vegas–McCarran International Airport response to Commission questions for the record, June 22, 2004; Port Authority of New York and New Jersey, Newark Airport response to supplemental question for the record, July 9, 2004.

Another particular allegation is that a flight carrying Saudi nationals from Tampa, Florida, to Lexington, Kentucky, was allowed to fly while airspace was closed, with special approval by senior U.S. government officials. On September 13, Tampa police brought three young Saudis they were protecting on an off-duty security detail to the airport so they could get on a plane to Lexington. Tampa police arranged for two private investigators to provide security on the flight. They boarded a chartered Learjet. Dan Grossi interview (May 24, 2004); Manuel Perez interview (May 27, 2004); John Solomon interview (June 4, 2004); Michael Fendle interview (June 4, 2004). The plane took off at 4:37 P.M., after national airspace was open, more than five hours after the Tampa airport had reopened, and after other flights had arrived at and departed from that airport. Hillsborough County Aviation Authority, Tampa International Airport response to Commission questions for the record, June 7, 2004. The plane's pilot told us there was "nothing unusual whatsoever" about the flight other than there were few airplanes in the sky. The company's owner and director of operations agreed, saying that "it was just a routine little trip for us" and that he would have heard if there had been anything unusual about it. The pilot said he followed standard procedures and filed his flight plan with the FAA prior to the flight, adding, "I was never questioned about it." Christopher Steele interview (June 14, 2004); Barry Ellis interview (June 14, 2004). FAA records confirm this account. FAA supplemental response to Commission questions for the record, June 8, 2004. When the plane arrived at Lexington Blue Grass Airport, that airport had also been open for more than five hours. Lexington-Fayette Urban County Airport Board, Blue Grass Airport response to Commission questions for the record, June 8, 2004. The three Saudi nationals debarked from the plane and were met by local police. Their private security guards were paid, and the police then escorted the three Saudi passengers to a hotel where they joined relatives already in Lexington. Mark Barnard interview (June 7, 2004). The FBI is alleged to have had no record of the flight and denied that it occurred, hence contributing to the story of a "phantom flight." This is another misunderstanding. The FBI was initially misinformed about how the Saudis got to Lexington by a local police officer in Lexington who did not have firsthand knowledge of the matter. The Bureau subsequently learned about the flight. James M. interview (June 18, 2004).

26. Richard Clarke interview (Jan. 12, 2004).

27. Andrew Card meeting (Mar. 31, 2004); President Bush and Vice President Cheney meeting (Apr. 29, 2004); Condoleezza Rice meeting (Feb. 7, 2004); Prince Bandar interview (May 5, 2004); Richard Clarke interview (Jan. 12, 2004); Richard Clarke testimony, Mar. 24, 2004 ("I would love to be able to tell you who did it, who brought this proposal to me, but I don't know"). Instead, the matter was handled as follows. Within days of September 11, fearing reprisals against Saudi nationals, Rihab Massoud, the deputy chief of mission at the Saudi embassy in Washington, D.C., called Dale Watson, the FBI's assistant director for counterterrorism, and asked for help in getting some of its citizens out of the country. Rihab Massoud interview (May 11, 2004). At about the same time, Michael Rolince, chief of the FBI's international terrorism operations section, also heard from an FBI official in Newark about a proposed flight of Saudis out of the country. Michael Rolince interview (June 9, 2004). We believe this was the Saudi deputy defense minister's flight. Rolince says he told the Newark official that the Saudis should not be allowed to leave without having the names on their passports matched to their faces, and their names run through FBI case records to see whether they had surfaced before. Rolince and Watson briefed Robert Mueller, the director of the FBI, about the issue and how they were handling it. The State Department played a role as well in flights involving government officials or members of the royal family. State coordinated with the FBI and FAA to allow screening by the FBI of flights with Saudi nationals on board. There is no evidence that State tried to limit the screening. DOS record, Log of USA 9-11 Terrorist Attack Task Force, Sept. 13, 2001; Jack S. interview (June 14, 2004). The FBI effectively approved the Saudi flights at the level of a section chief. Having an opportunity to check the Saudis was useful to the FBI. This was because the U.S. government did not, and does not, routinely run checks on foreigners who are *leaving* the United States. This procedure was convenient to the FBI, as the Saudis who wished to leave in this way would gather and present themselves for record checks and interviews, an opportunity that would not be available if they simply left on regularly scheduled commercial flights.

28. These flights were screened by law enforcement officials, primarily the FBI. For example, one flight, the so-called Bin Ladin flight, departed the United States on September 20 with 26 passengers, most of them relatives of Usama Bin Ladin. Screening of this flight was directed by an FBI agent in the Baltimore Field Office who was also a pilot. This agent, coordinating with FBI headquarters, sent an electronic communication to each of the field offices through which the Bin Ladin flight was scheduled to pass, including the proposed flight manifest and directing what screening should occur. He also monitored the flight as it moved around the country—from St. Louis to Los Angeles to Orlando to Washington Dulles, and to Boston Logan—correcting for any changes in itinerary to make sure there was no lapse in FBI screening at these locations. Again, each of the airports through which the Bin Ladin flight passed was open, and no special restrictions were lifted to accommodate its passage. James C. interview (June 3, 2004).

The Bin Ladin flight and other flights we examined were screened in accordance with policies set by FBI headquarters and coordinated through working-level interagency processes. Michael Rolince interview (June 9, 2004). Although most of the passengers were not interviewed, 22 of the 26 people on the Bin Ladin flight were interviewed by the FBI. Many were asked detailed questions. None of the passengers stated that they had any recent contact with Usama Bin Ladin or knew anything about terrorist activity. See, e.g., FBI report of investigation, interview of Mohammed Saleh Bin Laden, Sept. 21, 2001. As Richard Clarke noted, long before 9/11 the FBI was following members of the Bin Ladin family in the United States closely. Richard Clarke testimony, Mar. 24, 2004. Two of the passengers on this flight had been the subjects of preliminary investigations by the FBI, but both their cases had been closed, in 1999 and March 2001, respectively, because the FBI had uncovered no derogatory information on either person linking them to terrorist activity. Their cases remained closed as of 9/11, were not reopened before they departed the country on this flight, and have not been reopened since. FBI electronic communication, Summary of Information Regarding Flights taken by Saudi Citizens Out of the U.S. Shortly After September 11, 2001, Oct. 29, 2003, pp. 9–10.

29. Michael Rolince interview (June 9, 2004). Massoud corroborates this account. He said the FBI required the names and personal information of all departing passengers sponsored for departure by the Saudi Embassy. Rihab Massoud interview (May 11, 2004).

30. Jack S. interview (June 14, 2004).

31. The FBI checked a variety of databases for information on the Bin Ladin flight passengers and searched the aircraft. Because it was not clear to us whether the TIPOFF terrorist watchlist was checked by the FBI, the Terrorist Screening Center checked the names of individuals on the flight manifests of six Saudi flights against the current TIPOFF watchlist at our request prior to our hearing in April 2004. There were no matches. At our request, based on additional information, the Terrorist Screening Center in June and July 2004 rechecked the names of individuals believed to be on these six flights, the names of individuals on three more charter flights, the names of individuals on the flight containing the Saudi Deputy Defense Minister, and the names of Saudi nationals on commercial flights that journalists have alleged are suspect. There were no matches. Tim D. interviews (Apr. 12, 2004; June 30, 2004; July 9, 2004); FBI memo, Terrorist Screening Center to Director's Office, "Request by 9/11 Commission Task Force to screen the airline passenger lists through the TDSB and TIPOFF databases," Mar. 30, 2004.

32. White House transcript, Vice President Cheney interview with Charlie Gibson of ABC, Sept. 4, 2002, p. 11.

33. "The only ... true advice I receive is from our war council." White House transcript, President Bush interview with Bob Woodward and Dan Balz of the *Washington Post*, Dec. 20, 2001.

34. On Secretary Rumsfeld's remarks, see White House transcript, President Bush interview with Bob Woodward and Dan Balz, Dec. 20, 2001. The President's adviser, Karen Hughes, who was in the interview, listed the points Rumsfeld made at the smaller NSC meeting. Ibid.

35. On the President's tasking in the earlier meeting held that day, see NSC memo, Summary of Conclusions for NSC Meeting Held on September 12, 2001, Dec. 17, 2001. On the paper that went beyond al Qaeda, see NSC memo, Deputies Draft Paper (attached to Agenda for NSC Meeting Scheduled for Sept. 12, 2001). The Summary of Conclusions for the afternoon meeting indicates that the paper was discussed.

On giving priority to preventing terrorists from acquiring weapons of mass destruction, see White House transcript, Hadley interview with Dan Balz and Bob Woodward, Jan. 11, 2002, p. 535.

36. NSC memo, Summary of Conclusions for Principals Committee Meeting Held on September 13, 2001. In addition to the usual members of President Bush's war cabinet, Secretary of Transportation Mineta and FAA security chief Canavan also attended.

37. DOS cable, State 158711, "Deputy Secretary Armitage's Meeting with General Mahmud: Actions and Support Expected of Pakistan in Fight Against Terrorism," Sept. 14, 2001. On September 14, 2001, the U.S. Embassy in Islamabad sent Musharraf's answer to the State Department by cable.

38. DOS cable, Islamabad 5123, "Musharraf Accepts the Seven Points," Sept. 14, 2001.

39. NSC memo, Summary of Conclusions of NSC Meeting Held on September 13, 2001. According to the Summary of Conclusions, this meeting of the President and his advisers took place in the White House Situation Room; however, the agenda alerting agencies to the meeting specified that it would be conducted via the secure video teleconference system (SVTS). Thus, it is unclear whether the attendees met face-to-face at the White House or held their meeting remotely via SVTS.

40. State Department memo, "Gameplan for Polmil Strategy for Pakistan and Afghanistan," Sept. 14, 2001 (tasked by President Bush). The paper was sent to the White House on September 14, 2001. The demand to free all imprisoned foreigners reflected the U.S. government's concern about the welfare of several foreign aid workers in Afghanistan who had been imprisoned by the Taliban in August 2001. Two young American women, Heather Mercer and Dayna Curry of the organization "Shelter Now International," were among those arrested and charged with promoting Christianity. The Taliban and other Islamists found their activities an affront to Islam and in violation of Afghanistan's laws and the regime's tenets. Wendy Chamberlin interview (Oct. 28, 2003). Powell stated that the President wanted to get the hostages out but that desire would not restrain American action. White House transcript, President Bush interview with Bob Woodward and Dan Balz, Dec. 20, 2001.

41. State Department memo, "Gameplan for Polmil Strategy for Pakistan and Afghanistan," Sept. 14, 2001.

42. White House transcript, President Bush interview with Bob Woodward and Dan Balz, Dec. 20, 2001.

43. Stephen Hadley meeting (Jan. 31, 2004). Hadley told us that the White House was not satisfied with the Defense Department's plans to use force in Afghanistan after 9/11. Ibid.; see also White House transcript, Rice interview with John King of CNN, Aug. 2, 2002, p. 421.

44. Tommy Franks interview (Apr. 9, 2004).

45. NSC memo, Hadley to recipients, "Discussion Paper for NSC meeting at Camp David on 14 September," Sept. 14, 2001.

46. CIA memo, "Going to War," Sept. 15, 2001.

47. White House transcript, President Bush interview with Bob Woodward and Dan Balz, Dec. 20, 2001.

48. DOD briefing materials, "Evolution of Infinite Resolve Planning (AQ, UBL)," undated (provided to the Commission on Mar. 19, 2004). According to Deputy National Security Advisor Stephen Hadley, the President responded to Shelton by saying that the boots-on-the-ground option was an interesting idea. He wanted to know what the CIA would do when ground forces were in Afghanistan. White House transcript, Hadley interview with Dan Balz and Bob Woodward, Jan. 11, 2002, p. 545.

49. NSC memo, "Conclusions of National Security Council Meeting," Sept. 17, 2001; White House transcript, President Bush interview with Bob Woodward and Dan Balz, Dec. 20, 2001.

50. NSC memo, "Conclusions of National Security Council Meeting," Sept. 17, 2001.

51. See NSC memo, Rice to Cheney, Powell, O'Neill, Rumsfeld, Ashcroft, Gonzales, Card, Tenet, and Shelton, Sept. 16, 2001.

52. NSC memo, "Conclusions of National Security Council Meeting," Sept. 17, 2001.

53. NSC memo, Summary of Conclusions of Terrorist Fund-raising Meeting Held on September 18, 2001.

54. DOS briefing materials, "Fact Sheet on Response to Terrorist Attacks in US," Sept. 17, 2001.

55. DOS cable, State 161279, "Deputy Secretary Armitage–Mamoud Phone Call," Sept. 18, 2001.

56. White House transcript, Vice President Cheney interview with Dan Balz and Bob Woodward, Jan. 18, 2002, pp. 7–8.

57. Stephen Hadley meeting (Jan. 31, 2004).

58. See National Security Presidential Directive 9, Oct. 25, 2001.

59. President Bush and Vice President Cheney meeting (Apr. 29, 2004). On Iran, see Condoleezza Rice testimony, Apr. 8, 2004.

60. Richard A. Clarke, *Against All Enemies: Inside America's War on Terror* (Free Press, 2004), p. 32. According to Clarke, he responded that "al Qaeda did this." When the President pressed Clarke to check if Saddam was involved and said that he wanted to learn of any shred of evidence, Clarke promised to look at the question again, but added that the NSC and the intelligence community had looked in the past for linkages between al Qaeda and Iraq and never found any real linkages. Ibid.

61. President Bush told us that Clarke had mischaracterized this exchange. On the evening of September 12, the President was at the Pentagon and then went to the White House residence. He dismissed the idea that he had been wandering around the Situation Room alone, saying, "I don't do that." He said that he did not think that any president would roam around looking for something to do. While Clarke said he had found the President's tone "very intimidating," ("Clarke's Take on Terror," CBSnews.com, Mar. 21, 2004, online at www.cbsnews.com/stories /2004/03/19/60minutes/printable607356.shtml), President Bush doubted that anyone would have found his manner intimidating. President Bush and Vice President Cheney meeting (Apr. 29, 2004). Roger Cressey, Clarke's deputy, recalls this exchange with the President and Clarke concerning Iraq shortly after 9/11, but did not believe the President's manner was intimidating. Roger Cressey interview (June 23, 2004).

62. NSC memo, Kurtz to Rice, Survey of Intelligence Information on any Iraq Involvement in the September 11 Attacks, Sept. 18, 2001. On *60 Minutes* (CBS, Mar. 21, 2004), Clarke said that the first draft of this memo was returned by the NSC Front Office because it did not find a tie between Iraq and al Qaeda; Rice and Hadley deny that they asked to have the memo redone for this reason.

63. See DOD notes, Victoria Clarke notes, Sept. 11, 2001; DOD notes, Stephen Cambone notes, Sept. 11, 2001. Cambone's notes indicate this exchange took place at 2:40 P.M. on September 11, 2001. Steven Cambone interview (July 15, 2004).

64. Condoleezza Rice meeting (Feb. 7, 2004). For an account of Rumsfeld's and Wolfowitz's position on Iraq, see Bob Woodward, *Bush at War* (Simon & Schuster, 2002), pp. 83–84. Rice told us that the *Bush at War* account of the Camp David discussions on Iraq accorded with her memory.

65. DOD memo, Office of the Under Secretary of Defense for Policy, "War on Terrorism: Strategic Concept," Sept. 14, 2001.

66. Colin Powell interview (Jan. 21, 2004). Rumsfeld told Bob Woodward that he had no recollection of Wolfowitz's remarks at Camp David. DOD transcript, "Secretary Rumsfeld Interview with the Washington Post," Jan. 9, 2002 (online at www.defenselink.mil/transcripts/2002/t02052002_t0109wp.html).

67. Colin Powell interview (Jan. 21, 2004). Powell raised concerns that a focus on Iraq might negate progress made with the international coalition the administration was putting together for Afghanistan. Taking on Iraq at this time could destroy the international coalition. Ibid.

68. Colin Powell interview (Jan. 21, 2004).

69. White House transcript, President Bush interview with Bob Woodward and Dan Balz, Dec. 20, 2001.

70. Condoleezza Rice meeting (Feb. 7, 2004).

71. NSC memo, "Conclusions of National Security Council Meeting," Sept. 17, 2001.

72. Condoleezza Rice testimony, Apr. 8, 2004; see also Bob Woodward, *Plan of Attack* (Simon & Schuster, 2004), p. 22.

73. DOD memo, Wolfowitz to Rumsfeld, "Preventing More Events," Sept. 17, 2001. We review contacts between Iraq and al Qaeda in chapter 2. We have found no credible evidence to support theories of Iraqi government involvement in the 1993 WTC bombing. Wolfowitz added in his memo that he had attempted in June to get the CIA to explore these theories.

74. DOD memo, Wolfowitz to Rumsfeld, "Were We Asleep?" Sept. 18, 2001.

75. DOD memo, Rumsfeld to Shelton, "Some Thoughts for CINCs as They Prepare Plans," Sept. 19, 2001. In a memo that appears to be from Under Secretary of Defense Douglas Feith to Rumsfeld, dated September 20, the author expressed disappointment at the limited options immediately available in Afghanistan and the lack of ground options. The author suggested instead hitting terrorists outside the Middle East in the initial offensive, perhaps delib-

erately selecting a non–al Qaeda target like Iraq. Since U.S. attacks were expected in Afghanistan, an American attack in South America or Southeast Asia might be a surprise to the terrorists. The memo may have been a draft never sent to Rumsfeld, or may be a draft of points being suggested for Rumsfeld to deliver in a briefing to the President. DOD memo, Feith to Rumsfeld, "Briefing Draft," Sept. 20, 2001.

76. Hugh Shelton interview (Feb. 5, 2004).

77. Tommy Franks interview (Apr. 9, 2004).

78. NSC memo, memorandum of conversation from meeting of President Bush with Prime Minister Blair, Sept. 20, 2001.

79. Tommy Franks interview (Apr. 9, 2004).

80. White House transcript, President Bush's Address to a Joint Session of Congress and the American People, Sept. 20, 2001. British Prime Minister Tony Blair attended the session.

81. Ibid. Several NSC officials, including Clarke and Cressey, told us that the mention of the *Cole* in the speech to Congress marked the first public U.S. declaration that al Qaeda had been behind the October 2000 attack. Clarke said he added the language on this point to the speech. Richard Clarke interview (Feb. 3, 2004); Roger Cressey interview (Dec. 15, 2003).

82. White House transcript, President Bush's Address to a Joint Session of Congress and the American People, Sept. 20, 2001. President Bush told the *Washington Post* that he considered having Powell deliver the ultimatum to the Taliban, but determined it would have more impact coming directly from the president. White House transcript, President Bush interview with Bob Woodward and Dan Balz, Dec. 20, 2001.

83. White House transcript, President Bush's Address to a Joint Session of Congress and the American People, Sept. 20, 2001.

84. Ibid.

85. Tommy Franks interview (Apr. 9, 2004). Vice Chairman of the Joint Chiefs of Staff Richard Myers and Major General Del Dailey, commander of Joint Special Operations Command, also attended the September 21 meeting. The meeting was in direct response to the President's September 17 instruction to Rumsfeld to develop a military campaign plan for Afghanistan. The original "Infinite Justice" name was a continuation of a series of names begun in August 1998 with Operation Infinite Reach, the air strikes against Bin Ladin's facilities in Afghanistan and Sudan after the embassy bombings. The series also included Operation Infinite Resolve, a variety of proposed follow-on strikes on al Qaeda targets in Afghanistan.

86. DOD Special Operations Command and Central Command briefings (Sept. 15–16, 2003; Apr. 8–9, 2004; Apr. 28, 2004); Tommy Franks interview (Apr. 9, 2004). On death of Atef, see Daniel Benjamin and Steven Simon, *Age of Sacred Terror*, p. 349; Henry, "The CIA in Afghanistan, 2001–2002," *Studies in Intelligence* (classified version), vol. 47, no. 2 (2003), pp. 1, 11. See Donald Rumsfeld testimony, Mar. 23, 2004 (nearly two-thirds of the known leaders of al Qaeda had been killed or captured).

11 Foresight—and Hindsight

1. Roberta Wohlstetter, *Pearl Harbor: Warning and Decision* (Stanford Univ. Press, 1962), p. 387.

2. Intelligence Community analytic report, "The Foreign Terrorist Threat in the United States," NIE 95-13, July 1995, pp. v, vii–viii, 10–11, 13, 18.

3. Intelligence Community analytic report, "The Foreign Terrorist Threat in the US: Revisiting Our 1995 Estimate," ICB 97-8, Apr. 1997, p. 1.

4. For Bin Ladin being mentioned in only two other sentences, see ibid.

5. Titles are drawn from articles in the National Intelligence Daily and the Senior Executive Intelligence Brief.

6. John McLaughlin interview (Jan. 21, 2004).

7. Ibid.; Pattie Kindsvater interview (Sept. 12, 2003).

8. Tim Weiner, "U.S. Hard Put to Find Proof Bin Laden Directed Attacks," *New York Times*, Apr. 13, 1999, p. A1.

9. Paul R. Pillar, *Terrorism and U.S. Foreign Policy* (Brookings Institution Press, 2001), p. 23; see also ibid., pp. 5, 21–22.

10. For a concise statement of the role of the national estimate process, see Task force sponsored by the Council on Foreign Relations, *Making Intelligence Smarter: The Future of U.S. Intelligence* (Council on Foreign Relations, 1996), pp. 34–35 (additional views of Richard Betts).

11. Waldo Heinrichs, *Threshold of War: Franklin D. Roosevelt and American Entry into World War II* (Oxford Univ. Press, 1988), p. 215.

12. For the response being routine, see Gordon Prange, *At Dawn We Slept: The Untold Story of Pearl Harbor* (McGraw-Hill, 1981), pp. 732–733. For a brief summary of these routines and the reasons why the intercepts were not properly digested, see Graham Allison and Philip Zelikow, *Essence of Decision*, 2d ed. (Longman, 1999), p. 194, n. 72.

13. PDBs were not routinely briefed to congressional leaders, though this item could have been in some other intelligence briefing. It was not circulated in the NID or SEIB. For the September 1998 report, see Intelligence report, "Terrorism: Possible Attack on a U.S. City," Sept. 8, 1998.

14. For the August report, see Intelligence report, "Terrorism: Alleged Threat by Arab Terrorists to Attack the World Trade Center in New York," Aug. 12, 1998. An FAA civil aviation security official believed the plan was improbable because Libyan planes were required to operate within airspace limitations and the Libyans did not possess aircraft with the necessary range to make good on the threat. Jack S. interview (June 13, 2004). On September 30, 1999, the FAA closed the file on the August report after investigation could not corroborate the report, and the source's credibility was deemed suspect. FAA report, Transportation Security Intelligence ICF Report 980162, undated; but see FAA/TSA rebuttal to the Joint Inquiry's Sept. 18, 2002, staff statement, undated, p. 1 (stating that the FAA did not formally analyze this threat). The Algerian hijackers had placed explosives in key areas of the cabin. However, there was some speculation in the media based on reports from a passenger aboard the plane that the hijackers had discussed crashing it into the Eiffel Tower. FAA report, FAA Intelligence Case File 94-305, undated.

15. For Murad's idea, see chapter 5, note 33.

16. For Clarke's involvement in the 1996 Olympics, see Richard Clarke interview (Dec. 18, 2003). For the 1998 exercise, see Chuck Green interview (Apr. 21, 2004); NSC briefing paper, Nov. 10, 1998.

17. For the report of the National Transportation Safety Board, see NTSB report, "Aircraft Accident Brief," Mar. 13, 2002 (online at www.ntsb.gov/Publictn/2002/aab0201.htm). For the early 2000 CSG discussion, see NSC note, CSG SVTS agenda, Jan. 31, 2000.

18. Richard Clarke testimony, Mar. 24, 2004.

19. FAA memo, Office of Civil Aviation Security Intelligence, "Usama Bin Ladin/World Islamic Front Hijacking Threat," Intelligence Note 99-06, Aug. 4, 1999, pp. 5–6.

20. Ibid.

21. As part of his 34-page analysis, the attorney explained why he thought that a fueled Boeing 747, used as a weapon, "must be considered capable of destroying virtually any building located anywhere in the world." DOJ memo, Robert D. to Cathleen C., "Aerial Intercepts and Shoot-downs: Ambiguities of Law and Practical Considerations," Mar. 30, 2000, p. 10. Also, in February 1974, a man named Samuel Byck attempted to commandeer a plane at Baltimore Washington International Airport with the intention of forcing the pilots to fly into Washington and crash into the White House to kill the president. The man was shot by police and then killed himself on the aircraft while it was still on the ground at the airport.

22. For NORAD's hypothesis of aircraft as weapons, see, e.g., Ralph Eberhardt interview (Mar. 1, 2004). For the 2001 Positive Force 01 exercise, see DOD briefing (Apr. 29, 2004); Tom Cecil and Mark Postgate interview (June 7, 2004).

23. For the Gates report's recommendations, see DCI task force report, "Improving Intelligence Warning," May 29, 1992. For strengthening of the warning official, see DCI memo, "Warning," July 17, 1992. For the recommendations languishing, see Charles Allen interview (Sept. 22, 2003). For CTC having responsibility for warning, see Robert Vickers interview (Sept. 17, 2003). For the Board's warnings, see, e.g., Community Counterterrorism Board report, "Intelligence Community Terrorist Threat Advisory: Bin Ladin Orchestrating Possible Anti-US Attacks," June 30, 2000.

24. CIA briefing materials, "DCI Update," Aug. 23, 2001.

25. James Pavitt interview (Jan. 8, 2004). For more on this meeting, see Condoleezza Rice meeting (Feb. 7, 2004); George Tenet interview (Jan. 28, 2004).

26. For the briefing to the President-elect, see James Pavitt interview (Jan. 8, 2004). The CIA's formal analysis of what would happen if Bin Ladin alone was removed as compared with the importance of shutting down the sanctuary was offered in several places. See, e.g., CIA analytic report, "Likely Impact of Taliban Actions Against Al Qaeda," Feb. 21, 2001 (provided as background for Tenet meetings with Rice on Feb. 23 and Mar. 7, 2001).

27. Richard Clarke testimony, Mar. 24, 2004.

28. Mike interview (Dec. 11, 2003) (reading from CIA email, Mike to Winston Wiley, Aug. 27, 1997).

29. For President Bush's statement of al Qaeda's responsibility for the *Cole* attack, see White House transcript, "Address to a Joint Session of Congress and the American People," Sept. 20, 2001 (online at www.whitehouse.gov/news/releases/2001/09/20010920-8.html).

30. For Pavitt's view, see James Pavitt interview (Jan. 8, 2004).

31. Hugh Shelton interview (Feb. 5, 2004). Zinni was concerned about excessive collateral damage caused by Tomahawk strikes. See Anthony Zinni interview (Jan. 29, 2004).

32. For Shelton's view, see Hugh Shelton interview (Feb. 5, 2004). For Cohen's view, see William Cohen interview (Feb. 5, 2004).

33. Russell Honore interview (Oct. 29, 2003).

34. James Pavitt interview (Jan. 8, 2004).

35. Ibid.

36. Cofer Black interview (Dec. 9, 2003).

37. Rich interview (Dec. 11, 2003).

38. CIA memo, Tenet to Gordon and others, "Usama Bin Ladin," Dec. 4, 1998, p. 2.

39. See, e.g., Joan Dempsey interview (Nov. 12, 2003); Jeff B. interview (Dec. 11, 2003); Louis Andre interview

(Nov. 10, 2003); Mary C. interview (Oct. 25, 2003); Maureen Baginski interview (Nov. 15, 2003); Thomas Wilson interview (Dec. 4, 2003). Assistant DCI Charles Allen did redouble his efforts to coordinate and improve collection at the tactical level, but this was not a plan to address larger weaknesses in the fundamental capabilities of the intelligence community. See Charles Allen interview (Sept. 22, 2003).

40. For Dempsey's action, see Joan Dempsey interview (Nov. 12, 2003). For Minihan's view, see Joint Inquiry interview of Kenneth Minihan, Sept. 12, 2002. For the CIA viewing the memorandum as intended for non-CIA intelligence agencies, see Dave Carey interview (Oct. 31, 2003).

41. George Tenet interview (Jan. 22, 2004); James Pavitt interview (Jan. 8, 2004).

42. For the *New York Times* article about the Jordanian arrests, see Reuters, "Jordan Seizes 13 and Links Them to Afghan Explosives Training," *New York Times*, Dec. 16, 1999, p. A13. For the Ressam story being on the front page, see, e.g., Sam Howe Verhovek with Tim Weiner, "Man Seized with Bomb Parts at Border Spurs U.S. Inquiry," *New York Times*, Dec. 18, 1999, p. A1. For television coverage, see Vanderbilt University Television News Archive, Dec. 13, 22–31, 1999.

12 What to Do? A Global Strategy

1. For spending totals, see David Baumann, "Accounting for the Deficit," *National Journal*, June 12, 2004, p. 1852 (combining categories for defense discretionary, homeland security, and international affairs).

2. White House press release, "National Strategy for Combating Terrorism," Feb. 2003 (online at www.whitehouse.gov/news/releases/2003/02/20030214-7.html).

3. "Islamist terrorism is an immediate derivative of *Islamism*. This term distinguishes itself from *Islamic* by the fact that the latter refers to a religion and culture in existence over a millennium, whereas the first is a political/religious phenomenon linked to the great events of the 20th century. Furthermore Islamists define themselves as 'Islamiyyoun/Islamists' precisely to differentiate themselves from 'Muslimun/Muslims.' . . . Islamism is defined as 'an Islamic militant, anti-democratic movement, bearing a holistic vision of Islam whose final aim is the restoration of the caliphate.'" Mehdi Mozaffari, "Bin Laden and Islamist Terrorism," *Militaert Tidsskrift*, vol. 131 (Mar. 2002), p. 1 (online at www.mirkflem.pup.blueyonder.co.uk/pdf/islamistterrorism.pdf). The Islamist movement, born about 1940, is a product of the modern world, influenced by Marxist-Leninist concepts about revolutionary organization. "Islamists consider Islam to be as much a religion as an 'ideology,' a neologism which they introduced and which remains anathema to the ulamas (the clerical scholars)." Olivier Roy, *The Failure of Political Islam*, trans. Carol Volk (Harvard Univ. Press, 1994), p. 3. Facing political limits by the end of the 1990s, the extremist wing of the Islamist movement "rejected the democratic references invoked by the moderates; and as a result, raw terrorism in its most spectacular and destructive form became its main option for reviving armed struggle in the new millennium." Gilles Kepel, *Jihad: The Trail of Political Islam*, trans. Anthony Roberts (Harvard Univ. Press, 2002), p. 14.

4. Opening the Islamic Conference of Muslim leaders from around the world on October 16, 2003, then Malaysian prime minister Mahathir Mohamad said: "Today we, the whole Muslim *ummah* [community of believers] are treated with contempt and dishonour. Our religion is denigrated. Our holy places desecrated. Our countries are occupied. Our people are starved and killed. None of our countries are truly independent. We are under pressure to conform to our oppressors' wishes about how we should behave, how we should govern our lands, how we should think even." He added: "There is a feeling of hopelessness among the Muslim countries and their people. They feel that they can do nothing right. They believe that things can only get worse. The Muslims will forever be oppressed and dominated by the Europeans and Jews." The prime minister's argument was that the Muslims should gather their assets, not striking back blindly, but instead planning a thoughtful, long-term strategy to defeat their worldwide enemies, which he argued were controlled by the Jews. "But today the Jews rule the world by proxy. They get others to fight and die for them." Speech at the Opening of the Tenth Session of the Islamic Summit Conference, Oct. 16, 2003 (online at www.oicsummit2003.0rg.my/speech_03.php).

5. CIA map, "Possible Remote Havens for Terrorist and Other Illicit Activity," May 2003.

6. For the numbers, see Tariq interview (Oct. 20, 2003).

7. For Pakistan playing a key role in apprehending 500 terrorists, see Richard Armitage testimony, Mar. 23, 2004.

8. For Pakistan's unpoliced areas, see Tasneem Noorani interview (Oct. 27, 2003).

9. Pakistanis and Afghanis interviews (Oct. 2003); DOD Special Operations Command and Central Command briefings (Sept. 15–16, 2004); U.S. intelligence official interview (July 9, 2004).

10. Pervez Musharraf, "A Plea for Enlightened Moderation: Muslims Must Raise Themselves Up Through Individual Achievement and Socioeconomic Emancipation," *Washington Post*, June 1, 2004, p. A23.

11. For a review of ISAF's role, see NATO report, "NATO in Afghanistan," updated July 9, 2004 (online at www.nato.int/issues/afghanistan).

12. United States Institute of Peace report, "Establishing the Rule of Law in Afghanistan," Mar. 2004, pp. 1–3 (online at www.usip.org/pubs/specialreports/sr117.html).

13. For the change, see Lakhdar Brahimi interview (Oct. 24, 2003); U.S. officials in Afghanistan interview (Oct.

2003). For the request that the United States remain, see Kandahar province local leaders interview (Oct. 21, 2003). For the effect of the United States leaving, see Karim Khalili interview (Oct. 23, 2003).

14. Some have criticized the Bush administration for neglecting Afghanistan because of Iraq. Others, including General Franks, say that the size of the U.S. military commitment in Afghanistan has not been compromised by the commitments in Iraq. We have not investigated the issue and cannot offer a judgment on it.

15. Even if the U.S. forces, stretched thin, are reluctant to take on this role, "a limited, but extremely useful, change in the military mandate would involve intelligence sharing with civilian law enforcement and a willingness to take action against drug warehouses and heroin laboratories." United States Institute of Peace report, "Establishing the Rule of Law in Afghanistan," Mar. 2004, p. 17.

16. For barriers to Saudi monitoring of charities, see, e.g., Robert Jordan interview (Jan. 14, 2004); David Aufhauser interview (Feb. 12, 2004).

17. For the Saudi reformer's view, see Members of *majles al-shura* interview (Oct. 14, 2003).

18. Neil MacFarquhar, "Saudis Support a Jihad in Iraq, Not Back Home," *New York Times,* Apr. 23, 2004, p. A1.

19. Prince Bandar Bin Sultan, "A Diplomat's Call for War," *Washington Post,* June 6, 2004, p. B4 (translation of original in *Al-Watan,* June 2, 2004).

20. President Clinton meeting (Apr. 8, 2004).

21. For Jordan's initiatives, see testimony of William Burns before the Subcommittee on the Middle East and Central Asia of the House International Relations Committee, Mar. 19, 2003 (online at www.house.gov /international_relations/108/burn0319.htm). For the report, see United Nations Development Programme report, *Arab Human Development Report 2003: Building a Knowledge Society* (United Nations, 2003) (online at www.miftah.org/Doc/Reports/Englishcomplete2003.pdf).

22. DOD memo, Rumsfeld to Myers, Wolfowitz, Pace, and Feith, "Global War on Terrorism," Oct. 16, 2003 (online at www.usatoday.com/news/washington/executive/rumsfeld-memo.htm).

23. For the statistics, see James Zogby, *What Arabs Think: Values, Beliefs, and Concerns* (Zogby International, 2002). For fear of a U.S. attack, see Pew Global Attitudes Project report, *Views of a Changing World: June 2003* (Pew Research Center for the People and the Press, 2003), p. 2. In our interviews, current and former U.S. officials dealing with the Middle East corroborated these findings.

24. For polling soon after 9/11, see Pew Research Center for the People and the Press report, "America Admired, Yet Its New Vulnerability Seen as Good Thing, Say Opinion Leaders; Little Support for Expanding War on Terrorism" (online at http://people-press.org/reports/print.php3?ReportID=145). For the quotation, see Pew Global Attitudes Project report, "War With Iraq Further Divides Global Publics But World Embraces Democratic Values and Free Markets," June 3, 2003 (online at www.pewtrusts.com/ideas/ideas_item.cfm?content_ item_id=1645&content_type_id=7).

25. For the Occidentalist "creed of Islamist revolutionaries," see, e.g., Avishai Margalit and Ian Buruma, *Occidentalism: The West in the Eyes of Its Enemies* (Penguin Press, 2004).

26. We draw these statistics, significantly, from the U.S. government's working paper circulated in April 2004 to G-8 "sherpas" in preparation for the 2004 G-8 summit. The paper was leaked and published in *Al-Hayat.* "U.S. Working Paper for G-8 Sherpas," *Al-Hayat,* Feb. 13, 2004 (online at http://english.daralhayat.com/Spec/02-2004/Article-20040213-ac40bdaf-c0a8-01ed-004e-5e7ac897d678/story.html).

27. Richard Holbrooke, "Get the Message Out," *Washington Post,* Oct. 28, 2001, p. B7; Richard Armitage interview (Jan. 12, 2004).

28. Testimony of George Tenet, "The Worldwide Threat 2004: Challenges in a Changing Global Context," before the Senate Select Committee on Intelligence, Feb. 24, 2004.

29. U.S. Department of Energy Advisory Board report, "A Report Card on the Department of Energy's Nonproliferation Programs with Russia," Jan. 10, 2001, p. vi.

30. For terrorists being self-funding, see United Nations report, "Second Report of the [UN] Monitoring Group, Pursuant to Security Council Resolution 1390," Sept. 19, 2002, p. 13.

31. For legal entry, see White House report, Office of Homeland Security, "The National Strategy for Homeland Security," July 2002, p. 20 (online at www.whitehouse.gov/homeland/book/index.html). For illegal entry, see Chicago Council on Foreign Relations task force report, *Keeping the Promise: Immigration Proposals from the Heartland* (Chicago Council on Foreign Relations, 2004), p. 28.

32. The names of at least three of the hijackers (Nawaf al Hazmi, Salem al Hazmi, and Khalid al Mihdhar) were in information systems of the intelligence community and thus potentially could have been watchlisted. Had they been watchlisted, the connections to terrorism could have been exposed at the time they applied for a visa or at the port of entry. The names of at least three of the hijackers (Nawaf al Hazmi, Salem al Hazmi, and Khalid al Mihdhar), were in information systems of the intelligence community and thus potentially could have been watchlisted. Had they been watchlisted, their terrorist affiliations could have been exposed either at the time they applied for a visa or at the port of entry. Two of the hijackers (Satam al Suqami and Abdul Aziz al Omari) presented passports manipulated in a fraudulent manner that has subsequently been associated with al Qaeda. Based on our review of their visa and travel histories, we believe it possible that as many as eleven additional hijackers (Wail al Shehri,

Waleed al Shehri, Mohand al Shehri, Hani Hanjour, Majed Moqed, Nawaf al Hazmi, Hamza al Ghamdi, Ahmed al Ghamdi, Saeed al Ghamdi, Ahmed al Nami, and Ahmad al Haznawi) held passports containing these same fraudulent features, but their passports have not been found so we cannot be sure. Khalid al Mihdhar and Salem al Hazmi presented passports with a suspicious indicator of Islamic extremism. There is reason to believe that the passports of three other hijackers (Nawaf al Hazmi, Ahmed al Nami, and Ahmad al Haznawi) issued in the same Saudi passport office may have contained this same indicator; however, their passports have not been found, so we cannot be sure.

33. Khallad Bin Attash, Ramzi Binalshibh, Zakariya Essabar, Ali Abdul Aziz Ali, and Saeed al Ghamdi (not the individual by the same name who became a hijacker) tried to get visas and failed. Kahtani was unable to prove his admissibility and withdrew his application for admission after an immigration inspector remained unpersuaded that he was a tourist. All the hijackers whose visa applications we reviewed arguably could have been denied visas because their applications were not filled out completely. Had State visa officials routinely had a practice of acquiring more information in such cases, they likely would have found more grounds for denial. For example, three hijackers made statements on their visa applications that could have been proved false by U.S. government records (Hani Hanjour, Saeed al Ghamdi, and Khalid al Mihdhar), and many lied about their employment or educational status. Two hijackers could have been denied admission at the port of entry based on violations of immigration rules governing terms of admission—Mohamed Atta overstayed his tourist visa and then failed to present a proper vocational school visa when he entered in January 2001; Ziad Jarrah attended school in June 2000 without properly adjusting his immigration status, an action that violated his immigration status and rendered him inadmissible on each of his six subsequent reentries into the United States between June 2000 and August 5, 2001. There were possible grounds to deny entry to a third hijacker (Marwan al Shehhi). One hijacker violated his immigration status by failing to enroll as a student after entry (Hani Hanjour); two hijackers overstayed their terms of admission by four and eight months respectively (Satam al Suqami and Nawaf al Hazmi). Atta and Shehhi attended a flight school (Huffman Aviation) that the Justice Department's Inspector General concluded should not have been certified to accept foreign students, see DOJ Inspector General's report, "The INS' Contacts with Two September 11 Terrorists: A Review of the INS's Admissions of Atta and Shehhi, its Processing of their Change of Status Applications, and its Efforts to Track Foreign Students in the United States," May 20, 2002.

34. John Gordon interview (May 13, 2004).

35. For a description of a layering approach, see Stephen Flynn, *America the Vulnerable: How the U.S. Has Failed to Secure the Homeland and Protect Its People from Terrorism* (HarperCollins, 2004), p. 69.

36. The logical and timely rollout of such a program is hampered by an astonishingly long list of congressional mandates. The system originated in the Illegal Immigration Reform and Immigrant Responsibility Act of 1996 and applied to all non-U.S. citizens who enter or exit the United States at any port of entry. Pub. L. No. 104-208, 110 Stat. 3009 (1996), § 110. The Data Management Improvement Act of 2000 altered this mandate by incorporating a requirement for a searchable centralized database, limiting the government's ability to require new data from certain travelers and setting a series of implementation deadlines. Pub. L. No. 106-215, 114 Stat. 337 (2000), § 2(a). The USA PATRIOT Act mandated that the Attorney General and Secretary of State "particularly focus" on having the entry-exit system include biometrics and tamper-resistant travel documents readable at all ports of entry. Pub. L. No. 107-56, 115 Stat. 272 (2001), § 1008(a). In the Enhanced Border Security and Visa Entry Reform Act, Congress directed that, not later than October 26, 2004, the attorney general and the secretary of state issue to all non-U.S. citizens only machine-readable, tamper-resistant visas and other travel and entry documents that use biometric identifiers and install equipment at all U.S. ports of entry to allow biometric authentication of such documents. Pub. L. No. 107-173, 116 Stat. 543 (2002), § 303(b). The Act also required that increased security still facilitate the free flow of commerce and travel. Ibid. § 102(a)(1)(C). The administration has requested a delay of two years for the requirement of tamper-proof passports. Testimony of Thomas Ridge before the House Judiciary Committee, Apr. 21, 2004 (online at www.dhs.gov/dhspublic/display?theme=45&content=3498&print=true). Program planners have set a goal of collecting information, confirming identity, providing information about foreign nationals throughout the entire immigration system, and ultimately enabling each point in the system to assess the lawfulness of travel and any security risks.

37. There are at least three registered traveler programs underway, at different points in the system, designed and run by two different agencies in the Department of Homeland Security (outside the U.S. VISIT system), which must ultimately be the basis for access to the United States.

38. For the statistics, see DOS report, "Workload Statistics by Post Regions for All Visa Classes" June 18, 2004. One post-9/11 screening process, known as Condor, has conducted over 130,000 extra name-checks. DOS letter, Karl Hofmann to the Commission, Apr. 5, 2004. The checks have caused significant delays in some cases but have never resulted in visas being denied on terrorism grounds. For a discussion of visa delays, see General Accounting Office report, "Border Security: Improvements Needed to Reduce Time Taken to Adjudicate Visas for Science Students and Scholars," Feb. 2004. We do not know all the reasons why visa applications have dropped so significantly. Several factors beyond the visa process itself include the National Security Entry-Exit Registration System, which requires additional screening processes for certain groups from Arab and Muslim countries; the Iraq war; and per-

haps cyclical economic factors. For the cost to the United States of visa backlogs, see National Foreign Trade Council report, "Visa Backlog Costs U.S. Exporters More Than $30 Billion Since 2002, New Study Finds," June 2, 2004 (online at www.nftc.org/newsflash/newsflash.asp?Mode=View&articleid=1686&Category=All).

39. These issues are on the G-8 agenda. White House press release, "G-8 Secure and Facilitated Travel Initiative (SAFTI)," June 9, 2004 (online at www.whitehouse.gov/news/releases/2004/06/20040609-51.html). Lax passport issuance standards are among the vulnerabilities exploited by terrorists, possibly including two of the 9/11 hijackers. Three models exist for strengthened prescreening: (1) better screening by airlines, such as the use of improved document authentication technology; (2) posting of border agents or inspectors in foreign airports to work cooperatively with foreign counterparts; and (3) establishing a full preinspection regime, such as now exists for travel to the United States from Canada and Ireland. All three models should be pursued, in addition to electronic prescreening .

40. Among the more important problems to address is that of varying transliterations of the same name. For example, the current lack of a single convention for transliterating Arabic names enabled the 19 hijackers to vary the spelling of their names to defeat name-based watchlist systems and confuse any potential efforts to locate them. While the gradual introduction of biometric identifiers will help, that process will take years, and a name match will always be useful. The ICAO should discuss the adoption of a standard requiring a digital code for all names that need to be translated into the Roman alphabet, ensuring one common spelling for all countries.

41. On achieving more reliable identification, see Markle Foundation task force report, *Creating a Trusted Information Network for Homeland Security* (Markle Foundation, 2003), p. 72 (online at www.markle.org).

42. General Accounting Office report, *Mass Transit: Federal Action Could Help Transit Agencies Address Security Challenges*, GAO-03-263, Dec. 2002 (online at www.gao.gov/new.items/d03263.pdf).

13 How to Do It? A Different Way of Organizing the Government

1. The Bush administration clarified the respective missions of the different intelligence analysis centers in a letter sent by Secretary Ridge, DCI Tenet, FBI Director Mueller, and TTIC Director Brennan to Senators Susan Collins and Carl Levin on April 13, 2004. The letter did not mention any element of the Department of Defense. It stated that the DCI would define what analytical resources he would transfer from the CTC to TTIC no later than June 1, 2004. DCI Tenet subsequently told us that he decided that TTIC would have primary responsibility for terrorism analysis but that the CIA and the Defense Intelligence Agency would grow their own analysts. TTIC will have tasking authority over terrorism analysts in other intelligence agencies, although there will need to be a board to supervise deconfliction. George Tenet interview (July 2, 2004). We have not received any details regarding this plan.

2. "TTIC has no operational authority. However, TTIC has the authority to task collection and analysis from Intelligence Community agencies, the FBI, and DHS through tasking mechanisms we will create. The analytic work conducted at TTIC creates products that inform each of TTIC's partner elements, as well as other Federal departments and agencies as appropriate." Letter from Ridge and others to Collins and Levin, Apr. 13, 2004.

3. Donald Rumsfeld prepared statement, Mar. 23, 2004, p. 20.

4. In this conception, the NCTC should plan actions, assigning responsibilities for operational direction and execution to other agencies. It would be built on TTIC and would be supported by the intelligence community as TTIC is now. Whichever route is chosen, the scarce analytical resources now dispersed among TTIC, the Defense Intelligence Agency's Joint Interagency Task Force—Combatting Terrorism (JITF-CT), and the DCI's Counterterrorist Center (CTC) should be concentrated more effectively than they are now.

- The DCI's Counterterrorist Center would become a CIA unit, to handle the direction and execution of tasks assigned to the CIA. It could have detailees from other agencies, as it does now, to perform this operational mission. It would yield much of the broader, strategic analytic duties and personnel to the NCTC. The CTC would rely on the restructured CIA (discussed in section 13.2) to organize, train, and equip its personnel.
- Similarly, the FBI's Counterterrorism Division would remain, as now, the operational arm of the Bureau to combat terrorism. As it does now, it would work with other agencies in carrying out these missions, retaining the JTTF structure now in place. The Counterterrorism Division would rely on the FBI's Office of Intelligence to train and equip its personnel, helping to process and report the information gathered in the field.
- The Defense Department's unified commands—SOCOM, NORTHCOM, and CENTCOM—would be the joint operational centers taking on DOD tasks. Much of the excellent analytical talent that has been assembled in the Defense Intelligence Agency's JITF-CT should merge into the planned NCTC.
- The Department of Homeland Security's Directorate for Information Analysis and Infrastructure Protection should retain its core duties, but the NCTC should have the ultimate responsibility for producing *net* assessments that utilize Homeland Security's analysis of domestic vulnerabilities and integrate all-source analysis of foreign intelligence about the terrorist enemy.
- The State Department's counterterrorism office would be a critical participant in the NCTC's work, taking the lead in directing the execution of the counterterrorism foreign policy mission.

The proposed National Counterterrorism Center should offer one-stop shopping to agencies with counterterrorism and homeland security responsibilities. That is, it should be an authoritative reference base on the transnational terrorist organizations: their people, goals, strategies, capabilities, networks of contacts and support, the context in which they operate, and their characteristic habits across the life cycle of operations—recruitment, reconnaissance, target selection, logistics, and travel. For example, this Center would offer an integrated depiction of groups like al Qaeda or Hezbollah worldwide, overseas, and in the United States.

The NCTC will not eliminate the need for the executive departments to have their own analytic units. But it would enable agency-based analytic units to become smaller and more efficient. In particular, it would make it possible for these agency-based analytic units to concentrate on analysis that is tailored to their agency's specific responsibilities.

A useful analogy is in military intelligence. There, the Defense Intelligence Agency and the service production agencies (like the Army's National Ground Intelligence Center) are the institutional memory and reference source for enemy order of battle, enemy organization, and enemy equipment. Yet the Joint Staff and all the theater commands still have their own J-2s. They draw on the information they need, tailoring and applying it to their operational needs. As they learn more from their tactical operations, they pass intelligence of enduring value back up to the Defense Intelligence Agency and the services so it can be evaluated, form part of the institutional memory, and help guide future collection.

In our proposal, that reservoir of institutional memory about terrorist organizations would function for the government as a whole, and would be in the NCTC.

5. The head of the NCTC would thus help coordinate the operational side of these agencies, like the FBI's Counterterrorism Division. The intelligence side of these agencies, such as the FBI's Office of Intelligence, would be overseen by the National Intelligence Director we recommend later in this chapter.

6. The quotation goes on: "It includes gaps in intelligence, but also intelligence that, like a string of pearls too precious to wear, is too sensitive to give to those who need it. It includes the alarm that fails to work, but also the alarm that has gone off so often it has been disconnected. It includes the unalert watchman, but also the one who knows he'll be chewed out by his superior if he gets higher authority out of bed. It includes the contingencies that occur to no one, but also those that everyone assumes somebody else is taking care of. It includes straightforward procrastination, but also decisions protracted by internal disagreement. It includes, in addition, the inability of individual human beings to rise to the occasion until they are sure it is the occasion—which is usually too late. . . . Finally, as at Pearl Harbor, surprise may include some measure of genuine novelty introduced by the enemy, and some sheer bad luck." Thomas Schelling, foreword to Roberta Wohlstetter, *Pearl Harbor: Warning and Decision* (Stanford Univ. Press, 1962), p. viii.

7. For the Goldwater-Nichols Act, see Pub. L. No. 99-433, 100 Stat. 992 (1986). For a general discussion of the act, see Gordon Lederman, *Reorganizing the Joint Chiefs of Staff: The Goldwater-Nichols Act of 1986* (Greenwood, 1999); James Locher, *Victory on the Potomac: The Goldwater-Nichols Act Unifies the Pentagon* (Texas A&M Univ. Press, 2003).

8. For a history of the DCI's authority over the intelligence community, see CIA report, Michael Warner ed., *Central Intelligence; Origin and Evolution* (CIA Center for the Study of Intelligence, 2001). For the Director's view of his community authorities, see DCI directive, "Director of Central Intelligence Directive 1/1: The Authorities and Responsibilities of the Director of Central Intelligence as Head of the U.S. Intelligence Community," Nov. 19, 1998.

9. As Norman Augustine, former chairman of Lockheed Martin Corporation, writes regarding power in the government, "As in business, cash is king. If you are not in charge of your budget, you are not king." Norman Augustine, *Managing to Survive in Washington: A Beginner's Guide to High-Level Management in Government* (Center for Strategic and International Studies, 2000), p. 20.

10. For the DCI and the secretary of defense, see 50 U.S.C. § 403-6(a). If the director does not concur with the secretary's choice, then the secretary is required to notify the president of the director's nonconcurrence. Ibid. For the DCI and the attorney general, see 50 U.S.C. § 403-6(b)(3).

11. The new program would replace the existing National Foreign Intelligence Program.

12. Some smaller parts of the current intelligence community, such as the State Department's intelligence bureau and the Energy Department's intelligence entity, should not be funded out of the national intelligence program and should be the responsibility of their home departments.

13. The head of the NCTC should have the rank of a deputy national intelligence director, e.g., Executive Level II, but would have a different title.

14. If the organization of defense intelligence remains as it is now, the appropriate official would be the under secretary of defense for intelligence. If defense intelligence is reorganized to elevate the responsibilities of the director of the DIA, then that person might be the appropriate official.

15. For the information technology architecture, see Ruth David interview (June 10, 2003). For the necessity of moving from need-to-know to need-to-share, see James Steinberg testimony, Oct. 14, 2003. The Director still has no strategy for removing information-sharing barriers and—more than two years since 9/11—has only appointed a working group on the subject. George Tenet prepared statement, Mar. 24, 2004, p. 37.

16. The intelligence community currently makes information shareable by creating "tearline" reports, with the nonshareable information at the top and then, below the "tearline," the portion that recipients are told they can share. This proposal reverses that concept. All reports are created as tearline data, with the shareable information at the top and with added details accessible on a system that requires permissions or authentication.

17. See Markle Foundation Task Force report, *Creating a Trusted Information Network for Homeland Security* (Markle Foundation, 2003); Markle Foundation Task Force report, *Protecting America's Freedom in the Information Age* (Markle Foundation, 2002) (both online at www.markle.org).

18. Markle Foundation Task Force report, *Creating a Trusted Information Network*, p. 12. The pressing need for such guidelines was also spotlighted by the Technology and Privacy Advisory Committee appointed by Secretary Rumsfeld to advise the Department of Defense on the privacy implications of its Terrorism Information Awareness Program. Technology and Privacy Advisory Committee report, *Safeguarding Privacy in the Fight Against Terrorism* (2004) (online at www.sainc.com/tapac/TAPAC_Report_Final_5-10-04.pdf). We take no position on the particular recommendations offered in that report, but it raises issues that pertain to the government as a whole—not just to the Department of Defense.

19. This change should eliminate the need in the Senate for the current procedure of sequential referral of the annual authorization bill for the national foreign intelligence program. In that process, the Senate Armed Services Committee reviews the bill passed by the Senate Select Committee on Intelligence before the bill is brought before the full Senate for consideration.

20. This recommendation, and measures to assist the Bureau in developing its intelligence cadre, are included in the report accompanying the Commerce, Justice and State Appropriations Act for Fiscal Year 2005, passed by the House of Representatives on July 7, 2004. H.R. Rep. No. 108-576, 108th Cong., 2d sess. (2004), p. 22.

21. Letter from Ridge and others to Collins and Levin, Apr. 13, 2004.

22. For the directorate's current capability, see Patrick Hughes interview (Apr. 2, 2004).

INTERIM REPORTS

THE 9/11 COMMISSION released two interim reports during the approximately twenty-month-long investigation into the events surrounding the September 11, 2001, terrorist attacks against the United States. Each of these documents outlined the progress the Commission had made to that point and laid out plans for the next phase of the investigation. The second report is the more detailed of the two, and shows how much the focus of the Commission's efforts had sharpened by late summer 2003, when it was released. Moreover, the reports reveal the cooperative and bipartisan spirit that guided the Commission's members as they approached the daunting tasks of rallying the support of numerous civilian and governmental sources and examining millions of pages of documentary evidence.

**First Interim Report of the
National Commission on Terrorist Attacks Upon the United States**

Thomas H. Kean, Chair, and Lee H. Hamilton, Vice Chair

July 8, 2003

BACKGROUND

The 9/11 Commission will report on the facts and circumstances surrounding the attacks of September 11, 2001. It will review, identify, and evaluate lessons learned and make recommendations for the future. While we analyze the terrorist danger around the world, we are also addressing sensitive policy and intelligence issues across the federal government and beyond. In the last six months, the Commission has launched the most wide-ranging outside investigation of American national security in the history of the United States. We make this point so that the public will understand that the issues we are addressing have few, if any, precedents.

With a staff of more than 60 in three offices, two in Washington, DC and one in New York City, the Commission has received thousands of documents and is meeting with officials in every area of its work. The Commission is fully funded. Its professional staff has deep expertise. The staff now has the necessary security clearances. We are also able to build on work that has already been done inside the government.

STATUS REPORT

This is a critical time for the Commission. We have worked hard to stay on schedule to complete our work by the end of May 2004, as required by our statute, but the coming weeks will determine whether we will be able to do our job within the time allotted. The task in front of us is monumental. Time is slipping by. Every day lost complicates our work. Extensive and prompt cooperation from the U.S. government, the Congress, state and local agencies, and private firms is essential. This report offers an initial evaluation of this cooperation.

When he signed the bill that created the Commission, President Bush pledged his cooperation. He and his subordinates have made significant efforts to keep that promise. Security clearances for commissioners and staff were expedited. The President designated a senior official at the Justice Department to facilitate Executive Branch cooperation with the Commission.

Yet it is also clear that the Administration underestimated the scale of the Commission's work and the full breadth of support required. The facilitation job previously assigned to

www.9-11commission.gov

an already busy top official at Justice has now been transferred to another senior Justice official working full-time to support the Commission along with four deputies.

Every bit of that help will be needed in expediting responses to the 26 briefing requests and 44 *sets* of document requests, many with dozens of categorical areas of inquiry, that have already been filed with 16 different agencies. While thousands of documents are flowing in—some in boxes and some digitized—most of the documents we need are still to come. These documents are critical in their own right and to help our staff prepare for their hundreds of interviews with individual officials.

We now detail the status with respect to many agencies:

- The document requests already filed with the Executive Office of the President cover every major part of the EOP, including the NSC. We will not go into detail on the substance of these or other requests. We can say that we have received and are in the process of receiving access to a wide range of sensitive documents and that, to date, no requested access has been denied. Many more documents are being requested. Conditions have been imposed, in some cases, with respect to our access to and usage of these materials. Our discussions continue.

- The Central Intelligence Agency has been arranging needed briefings and providing intelligence products, including essential information that has been developed since 9/11. DCI Tenet composed a strong review group and team of analysts to look back at the pre-9/11 record. Their work has been invaluable. The CIA has been slower in producing the internal documents that we have requested on management and resource choices in the pre-9/11 war on terrorism.

- The Federal Bureau of Investigation got off to a slow start in responding to the Commission's requests. When Director Mueller became aware of the Commission's concerns, he assigned additional agents and staff to assist us. He and his staff have provided us with detailed briefings on the PENTTBOM investigation and the counterterrorism reforms undertaken by the FBI since 9/11. The FBI is now moving constructively to help us utilize the records compiled in the largest criminal inquiry ever conducted by the Bureau. Especially helpful, the Bureau has helped us access documents in a searchable electronic form.

- The Department of Justice has assisted the White House in resolving issues that have arisen in agency responses to our requests. But records requested from DOJ are overdue, and the Department has not yet been able to resolve important issues related to the Moussaoui case. We also disagree with the Administration's general insistence on having agency representatives present during interviews of serving officials, and this matter is still under discussion.

- The problems that have arisen so far with the Department of Defense are becoming particularly serious. We have not received responses to requests relating to NORAD and other DOD components, including the JCS and the

Department's historical office. Delays are lengthening and agency points of contact have so far been unable to resolve them. In the last few days, we have been assured that the Department's leaders will address these concerns. We look forward to seeing the results.

- The Department of State has responded helpfully to all requests made so far. The Department of the Treasury has also been responsive, as have officials at the Securities and Exchange Commission.

- The Department of Transportation and the Federal Aviation Administration have gradually been responsive to the Commission. But we still have some important additional information to obtain from them.

- The record of support from the Department of Homeland Security so far is mixed. Elements of the former Immigration and Naturalization Service have been slow in providing briefings, although there are recent signs of improvement. The Transportation Security Administration has provided a substantial volume of material to us. The Secret Service has also been helpful.

- Relevant congressional committees have displayed good will, but we have encountered problems in obtaining adequate access to the materials compiled by the Joint Inquiry. Through cooperation, almost all of those problems have been resolved. More tests will be coming as the Commission extends its scrutiny of congressional resource allocation and oversight.

- It is still too soon to assess cooperation by local agencies such as New York City, the Port Authority, or Arlington County, or private sector entities such as the relevant airlines.

We believe the President when he says he is committed to assisting the Commission. The White House has demonstrated that commitment in some vital ways, but the next few weeks will be crucial. We will need strong support from the White House to insure that we are able to receive the materials we require in sufficient time to meet the statutory deadline.

We acknowledge the challenge faced in responding to these requests by officials already busy with other tasks. But we must look backward in order to look forward. The contemporary history of the country passed a watershed on 9/11. We must do the job we are required to do by law so that we may understand how we came to this turning point in the way we think about our security and to understand the choices that lie ahead.

We will provide another interim report on our progress in September.

Second Interim Report of the
National Commission on Terrorist Attacks Upon the United States

Thomas H. Kean, Chair, and Lee H. Hamilton, Vice Chair

September 23, 2003

The National Commission on Terrorist Attacks Upon the United States—the 9-11 Commission—continues to work, and we intend to report to the nation no later than our statutory deadline of May 27, 2004. We will speak this afternoon about our access to documents, what we have done, and what we plan to do. We will outline some of the investigative and policy questions before us.

ACCESS

We turn first to the issue we left open at the time of our July 8 report. Are we getting the help we need so that we can complete our job in the time allotted to us by law?

- Since our July report, Executive Branch agencies have significantly improved their performance in responding to our document requests. There are still pending requests, and many documents have yet to be produced. Key agencies have assigned additional people to produce documents. Agencies initially slow in responding, including the Department of Defense, have worked hard to assist the Commission.

- While there have been some unnecessary delays, we now have over 10,000 documents in hand, and have access to documents from the Executive Branch numbering more than two million pages. This is already more than four times what was provided to the Congressional Joint Inquiry. The flow of documents to us continues.

- Production appears to be nearing completion in the critical area of high-level agency records on policy deliberations if all current commitments are met. The Executive Branch agencies have agreed to produce these records. Some have been slow. We have received many of these documents only recently. We have been assured that the remainder will be made available in the next two weeks. If they are not, we will not hesitate to inform the public.

- The Commission has obtained access to many of the key White House and National Security Council documents we have sought from this administration and its predecessor. The access we already have is on a unique breadth and scale.

www.9-11commission.gov

Pending requests seek additional sensitive documents. We have been conducting extensive negotiations so that the Commission gets the additional information it needs. Although we have received certain assurances, we are still negotiating with the White House. We will inform the public promptly if the Commission does not receive the access it needs.

- The CIA and the Departments of State, Defense, Justice, and Homeland Security have generally been responsive to the Commission's requests. In many cases this has required some extraordinary efforts, which we appreciate. In the case of some particular requests, agencies have been unable to locate any responsive documents, or only a few where we would have expected there to have been more. In all cases, we will obtain certifications by senior responsible officials as to the completeness of their production.

- The FBI has provided the largest amount of material to the Commission. It also has the largest number of documents relevant to our work. We have needed to create very unusual working arrangements to facilitate the Commission's access to the remaining FBI information we need to receive. The Bureau has agreed to these procedures and, from the top, has expressed a firm commitment to make them work.

- There are many more agencies we could mention in the public sector, including at the regional and local level. We have also been obtaining documents from some private firms. Again, in general, these agencies and firms have been responsive to our requests.

WHAT WE HAVE DONE

We have just passed the second anniversary of the attacks. No one has waited for answers longer than the families of the victims. We thank them for their patience and support. We are working to earn their patience. Let's talk about what we have been doing.

- We and our staff of 65, in two offices in Washington and one in New York City, have been evaluating the mountain of documents in our possession.

- We have received 87 briefings from agency officials.

- We have conducted more than 200 interviews of individual witnesses.

- We have heard from 58 policy and fact witnesses in our public hearings.

Our interviews are not just in Washington. We are going to FBI Field Offices, military bases, airports, air traffic control facilities, and immigration checkpoints, and interviewing first responders from across the country.

WHAT WE PLAN TO DO

- Our public hearings will continue, although we will defer the factual hearings in order to permit the staff work necessary for those hearings to be fruitful. Instead, we will focus the remainder of our hearings in this calendar year on important policy issues.

- In October we will explore questions of organization and leadership. Should we restructure the intelligence community and create a Director of National Intelligence? Should we change the way we prepare and issue warnings of terrorist attacks?

- In November we will hear testimony on best practices for emergency preparedness.

- In December we will examine reforms by the FBI and whether we need a new agency to gather intelligence in the United States, what some have called an American version of Britain's MI-5. We will look at whether our nation is striking the right balance of security and liberty.

Based on what we learn in our document review and classified interviews, we will begin a series of public hearings on factual issues in January with the principal figures of the Bush and Clinton administrations. We will hear testimony, including from Cabinet-level officials, on how they did their jobs in the run-up to the 9-11 attacks and—in the case of current officials—how they see their jobs today.

- We will hold a hearing in January on the immediate response to the hijackings by those responsible for our air security system and by our nation's leaders.

- We will hold a two-day hearing at the end of January on border and transportation security issues. We will look at watchlists, visas and foreign visitors, immigration law enforcement, and aviation security.

- We will hold a three-day hearing in February on law enforcement and intelligence collection inside the United States. We will hear from the Justice Department, the FBI, Homeland Security, and state and local officials.

- Later in February, we will hold two more days of hearings, on terrorist safe havens and permissive environments, then and now, and we will look at broader issues of international cooperation.

- In March, we will hold four days of hearings. We will hear from senior officials, then and now, at Defense, CIA, the State Department, Treasury, and the National Security Council staff.

- In April, we will hold hearings telling the story—as authoritatively as we can—of the 9-11 plot and what happened on that day. We will look at emergency response, at the local and national level.

Taken together, our plan is for 14 days of hearings between January and April. We will hear from some 55 senior officials, past and present.

At the end of May we will release a report to the nation. We will want it to be as widely available as possible. That public report will be backed by a number of volumes of detailed monographs.

QUESTIONS

As we get access to so much information, many are anxious to hear what we have learned. We understand their impatience. Yet we are engaged in what may be the largest investigation of U.S. government actions and policy in American history. Waiting for the right answers is better than rushing to judgment with the wrong ones.

The questions we must answer begin with the past.

- We are developing a full depiction of the conspiracy to attack this country; how the plotters analyzed our weaknesses, the strategies they developed, the actions they took, and those who helped them.

- We must understand the enemy that chose war against America.

- We are seeking to understand militant forces within the Islamic world, and the religious, governmental, and financial institutions—and ideologies—that support them.

- We are evaluating the events and policies that may have contributed to the development of this threat.

- We are considering how we collected and analyzed foreign intelligence. The CIA was created in part to avoid another Pearl Harbor. Generations of experts worked on better ways to warn against surprise attacks. We are exploring how, or whether, those methods were employed to warn against this one. We are also exploring the way intelligence efforts were conducted within the United States, and how well our foreign and domestic agencies combined their efforts against a transnational enemy.

- We are analyzing the policies our leaders crafted to combat terrorism and prevent such a devastating attack. What actions were chosen, or readied, with the tools of diplomacy, military power, or more secret means—whether against terrorist sanctuaries or terrorist finance?

- We are assessing how America's other defenses performed as well, looking at how terrorists penetrated our borders and how they boarded and seized four commercial airliners.

- We are reconstructing the events of September 11, minute by minute, so that we can see the strengths and weaknesses in the way the air traffic control system, our air defenses, the national command authorities, and local emergency responders understood and responded to the attack.

In addition to describing the facts and circumstances surrounding the attack, our report will emphasize the most important policy recommendations. We want recommendations that can be implemented, work in the real world, and make a difference. And we will not go away the day after we release our report. We will work hard to explain our recommendations and win support for them.

We do not bring our recommendations before you today. That work remains to be done. However, we are clear about some of the central policy questions we will need to address:

- Is the Intelligence Community organized properly to carry out the war on terrorism? Does the Director of Central Intelligence need greater authority over agencies and resources?

- Is our military properly organized to defend us at home as well as defeat our enemies abroad?

- Do we have a government-wide, unified strategy for counterterrorism with the best balance of diplomacy, law enforcement, financial measures, military action, covert action, and public diplomacy? Are we meeting the challenge today and are we postured well for the future?

- What are the best methods of identifying, tracking, and disrupting terrorist funding, and how effective have we been in getting cooperation from key foreign governments?

- Which reforms in our immigration and border system since September 11 have made Americans more secure, and which hold the most promise for the future?

- Has the FBI carried out enough reform and the right reforms? Or do we need a new domestic intelligence agency?

- Do we have the proper policies, resource levels and risk management priorities to protect our aviation and other transportation systems?

- What measures have been taken to improve agency cooperation across federal, state, and local levels, how effective are they, and what more needs to be done to respond to future attacks?

We certainly will take up additional questions as our work progresses, but we know that these key policy questions are before us.

LOOKING BACK—AND FORWARD

The Commission is not choosing between examining the past or the future. We are doing both. We are looking backward in order to look forward.

We will try to learn how and why America was attacked so that we can suggest ways to keep such a tragedy from happening again. You have our dedication to that effort.

Thank you for your time and attention, and we would be pleased to respond to your questions.

THIRD MONOGRAPH:
THE FOUR FLIGHTS AND
CIVIL AVIATION SECURITY

ON SEPTEMBER 12, 2005, the National Archives and Records administration re-released the third monograph of the 9/11 Commission Report: "The Four Flights and Civil Aviation Security."

Unlike the commission's previous two monographs, which were released shortly after the full 9/11 Commission Report and contained the full records of information that were used in preparing the final report, this third monograph contains material that further explains the chronology of the events taking place aboard the four flights on September 11, 2001, as well as the Commission's findings regarding civil aviation security.

A version of this monograph was first released on January 28, 2005, with much of its text redacted by the executive branch. This updated version, made public on September 12, 2005, although still partly "blacked out," declassifies dozens of passages, in response to criticism from former Commission members that this third monograph contains information that is vital to the public's understanding of what went wrong.

In a joint statement through the 9/11 Public Discourse Project, Thomas H. Kean and Lee H. Hamilton, former Chair and Vice Chair of the 9/11 Commission said, "While we still believe that the entire document could be made available to the public without damaging national security, we welcome this step forward. The additional detail provided in this version of the monograph will make a further contribution to the public record of the facts and circumstances of the 9/11 attacks established by the final report of the 9/11 Commission."

SUBJECT TO CLASSIFICATION REVIEW

Staff Report, August 26, 2004

Table of Contents

Preface

Part 1. "We Have Some Planes": The Four Flights—a Chronology

Part 2. Civil Aviation Security and the 9/11 Attacks

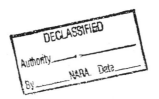

PART I: THE FOUR FLIGHTS

American Airlines Flight 11
United Air Lines Flight 175
American Airlines Flight 77
United Air Lines Flight 93

(Note to reader: All times indicated are Eastern Daylight Time unless otherwise specified).

1.1 AMERICAN AIRLINES FLIGHT 11

Colgan Air Flight 5930
The Flight 11 story begins on the morning of September 11, 2001, in Portland, Maine, aboard Colgan Air Flight 5930 headed for Logan International Airport.[1] Two of the Flight 11 hijackers, Mohamed Atta and Abdul Aziz al Omari, were aboard the flight on their way to Boston.

Hijacker Arrival at the Airport and Check-in. At *5:40 A.M.* on September 11, 2001, a car rented by Mohamed Atta in Boston on September 9 entered the Portland International Jetport parking facility.[2]

5:43 A.M. Atta and Omari checked in at the US Airways counter at the Portland Jetport. Atta checked two bags, Omari none.[3] The agent who checked in the two hijackers recalled that when he handed Atta his boarding pass, Atta asked why he was not given a boarding pass for his connecting flight on American Airlines from Boston to Los Angeles. The agent explained to Atta that he would have to check in with American Airlines in Boston to obtain the boarding pass for the second leg of his itinerary. The agent remembered that Atta clenched his jaw and looked as though he was about to get angry. Atta stated that he was assured he would have "one-step check-in." The agent told them that they had better get going if they were to make their flight. He said that Atta looked as if he were about to say something in anger but turned to leave. Both Atta and Omari departed for the security checkpoint.[4]

Hijacker Prescreening Selectee Status. When he checked in at the Portland airport, Atta was randomly selected for additional security scrutiny by the Computer Assisted Passenger Prescreening System (CAPPS). The Federal Aviation Administration (FAA), required air carriers to apply the system to their passengers to identify those who might be a security risk.[5] FAA rules required that the checked bags of CAPPS selectees be screened for explosives, or their bags held off the airplane until the passenger boarded.[6] Because US Airways at Portland Jetport did not have explosives detection screening equipment for checked bags at that time, Atta's luggage was subject to the matching procedure.[7] The application of this procedure was designed to stop a nonsuicide bomber—one who might place a bomb in a bag and then leave the airport. At this time, the FAA believed that such bombers were among the greatest threats to civil aviation security.

Checkpoint Security Screening. At *5:45 A.M.*, Atta and Omari arrived at the sole security checkpoint at the Portland International Jetport.[8] This checkpoint was under the custodial responsibility of Delta Airlines, which contracted for security screening services with Globe Aviation Services. The checkpoint had two lanes, each outfitted with a walk-through metal detector and X-ray equipment to help detect weapons.[9]

The checkpoint videotape was seized as evidence by the FBI and reviewed by the Commission.[10] The videotape showed that Atta and Omari entered the walk through metal detector at *5:45:03 A.M.* A screener was stationed at the device to monitor the screening. Though not conclusive, the video suggests that neither of the subjects set off the metal detector. Both Atta and Omari proceeded from the magnetometer immediately to the X-ray belt. Atta picked up a black shoulder bag. Omari claimed a similar bag, and also a smaller black case that he held in both hands. The item cannot be identified but resembled a camera or camcorder case. Neither of the bags was physically examined by a screener, a step that is required if the X-ray monitor displays a suspicious item. Both of the subjects passed out of view of the video camera at *5:45:15 A.M.*

Hijacker Boarding. Seating aboard the Colgan flight was open rather than assigned.[11] Eight passengers boarded the flight, including Atta and Omari.[12] The flight crew included a pilot and a first officer who also served as the flight attendant. Atta and Omari were the last to board the aircraft and sat in the last row of the plane—row 9.[13]

The Flight. Colgan Air Flight 5930 was a Beechcraft 1900—a 19-seat regional airliner. It departed from Gate 11 on time at *6:00 A.M.*, arriving at Gate B9 (A) at Boston Logan International Airport at approximately *6:45 A.M.*, one hour before the scheduled departure of Flight 11.[14]

Purpose of the Flight. No physical, documentary, or analytical evidence found either by the Commission or by law enforcement agencies provides a clear reason why Atta and Omari drove to Portland from Boston on the morning of September 10 only to return to Logan International Airport on Flight 5930 on the morning of September 11.[15]

The most plausible theory is that the hijackers chose to fly into Boston to avoid suspicion that might have been aroused if they had arrived at Logan at approximately the same time as eight other young Middle Eastern males to check in for Flight 11 and Flight 175. Such an intent might also explain why Atta appeared to be so upset that he had to check in again in Boston to get a boarding pass for Flight 11.

It is also possible that they traveled to Portland to preserve operational security. If the hijackers' plot had been discovered by U.S. intelligence or law enforcement, or by the U.S. aviation security system, the two terrorists would be apprehended during their check-in at the Portland airport. That outcome would have been preferable to being stopped at Logan Airport, where other members of Atta's hijack team were also checking in, and where conspirators intending to hijack Flight 175 were assembling at the same time.[16]

Telephone records show that a phone call was placed from a pay phone in the gate area from which Flight 175 departed to Atta's cell phone at *6:52 A.M.*[17] This call strongly suggests that the two hijacking teams engaged in tactical communications, such as situational reporting and possible "go" or "no go" determinations, at the last moment.

The Massport Aviation Director told the Commission that Portland was the nearest airport to Boston with a flight that would have arrived at Logan in time for the passengers to transfer to Flight 11.[18]

We also considered the possibility that Atta, the leader of the 9/11 hijackers, might have believed that he and Omari were more likely to successfully pass through checkpoint screening at a smaller airport, carrying items such as Mace or pepper spray, than they were at Logan Airport.

However, two considerations would have made this a faulty assumption. First, public sources would not have supported the notion that smaller airports had more porous checkpoints. For instance, in the winter and spring of 2001, a Fox news special investigation publicly described serious shortcomings in the detection capabilities at Logan Airport's security screening checkpoints, including the ease with which knives could be carried through checkpoints.[19] Second, Atta and Omari were required to go through another security checkpoint when they arrived at Logan in order to enter the terminal from which Flight 11 departed.

We believe that Atta's apparent anger about not receiving his boarding pass for Flight 11 when he checked in for Flight 5930 is a strong indication that he hoped to enter the system and obtain his final boarding pass along with Omari at Portland, separately from the other hijackers The hijackers checked-in and went through the checkpoints (at least in the case of the Flight 77 hijackers who were videotaped), in pairs or by themselves. This provides additional evidence that the hijackers did not want to make themselves conspicuous by congregating.

American Airlines Flight 11
Hijackers. Mohamed Atta (pilot); Abdul Aziz al Omari; Waleed al Shehri; Wail al Shehri; Satam al Suqami.

Hijacker Weapon Purchases. Atta purchased two Victorinox Swiss Army knives at the Zurich Airport on July 8, 2001, and a Leatherman multi-tool in Boynton Beach, Florida, on August 30, 2001.[20]

Hijacker Arrival at Airport and Check-in. At *6:45 A.M.*, Atta and Omari arrived at Boston Logan airport, Terminal B, Gate B9A. Atta and Omari still had their carry-on shoulder bags. Atta's two checked bags were unloaded from the Colgan Air flight. The luggage tags indicated that they should be transferred to American Airlines Flight 11 from Boston to Los Angeles International Airport. FAA security rules did not require additional screening or special security handling of Atta's luggage.

After exiting the aircraft, Atta and Omari crossed a parking lot that separated their arrival and departure terminals. They were observed asking for directions.[21]

Also at *6:45 A.M.*, Wail al Shehri, Waleed al Shehri, and Satam al Suqami arrived at Logan Airport and parked their rental car at the airport's central parking facility.[22]

Hijacker Prescreening. According to ticket records, Wail al Shehri, Waleed al Shehri, and Satam al Suqami were selected by CAPPS.[23] Waleed al Shehri did not check a bag. The others checked in one each.[24] Their checked luggage was screened by an explosives detection system and loaded aboard the aircraft.[25] Under FAA security rules in effect at the time, the hijackers' designation as "selectees" did not require that they undergo any screening of their person or carry-on bags beyond what was required of passengers not selected by CAPPS.[26]

Checkpoint Security Screening. Because the airport's security checkpoints and gate area were not monitored by video surveillance equipment at that time, no conclusive evidence exists regarding when and how the Flight 11 hijackers passed through checkpoint screening. To reach their departure gate after checking in, all five hijackers would have been required to pass through one of two checkpoints, both of which were operated by Globe Aviation Services under a contract with American Airlines.[27] The smaller checkpoint opened at 7:15 A.M. and was used mainly for overflow traffic from the other. We believe it most likely that the hijackers would have chosen to pass through the busier checkpoint in the hopes of being less conspicuous.

At the checkpoint, each of the individual's carry-on belongings would have been screened by an X-ray machine. The purpose of this screening was to identify and confiscate weapons and other items prohibited from being carried onto a commercial flight.[28] Also, the passenger would pass through a walk-through metal detector calibrated at that time to detect items with at least the metal content of a small-caliber handgun. If any one of the hijackers triggered the walk-through magnetometer, he would have been screened with a handheld metal detector—a procedure requiring the screener to identify the item or items that caused the alarm. Any items found that were prohibited or restricted under the checkpoint operating rules and guidelines would not be allowed past the checkpoint. The checkpoint supervisors did not recall the hijackers or report anything suspicious regarding their screening.[29]

6:52 A.M. Atta received a phone call from a pay phone in Terminal C at Logan International Airport—the terminal from which Flight 175 was due to depart.[30]

Hijacker Boarding. At approximately *7:31 A.M.*, Wail al Shehri and Waleed al Shehri boarded. Atta and Omari followed at approximately *7:39 A.M.* Suqami boarded a minute later.[31]

Flight Profile. Flight 11 provided daily, nonstop service from Boston's Logan International Airport (BOS) to Los Angeles International Airport (LAX). On September 11, it was scheduled for a 7:45 A.M. departure.[32] The aircraft was a Boeing 767, tail number N334AA.[33]

Captain John Ogonowski and First Officer Thomas McGuinness piloted the plane. It carried its full capacity of nine flight attendants:

- Karen Martin (Position 1), assigned to the forward left jumpseat (1L), located between the first-class cabin and the cockpit entrance;
- Kathleen Nicosia (Position 2), assigned to the left aft jumpseat (3L) at the back of the aircraft;
- Betty Ong (Position 3), assigned to the right aft jumpseat (3R) at the back of the aircraft behind the coach section;
- Dianne Snyder (Position 4), assigned to the mid-galley jumpseat (2R);
- Barbara "Bobbi" Arestegui (Position 5), assigned to the forward right jumpseat (1R Center), which was in the forward galley between the cockpit and the first-class cabin;
- Jeffrey Collman (Position 6), assigned to the middle left jumpseat (2L) located in the middle galley within the main cabin;
- Sara Low (Position 7), assigned to the middle right jumpseat (2R) in the middle galley within the main cabin;
- Jean Roger (Position 8), assigned to the forward left jumpseat (1L Center) in the forward galley; and
- Madeline "Amy" Sweeney (Position 9), assigned to the left aft jumpseat (3L) at the back of the aircraft behind the coach section.[34]

The aircraft had a capacity of 158 passengers: 9 seats in first class, 30 in business class, and 119 in coach.[35] On September 11, the flight carried 81 passengers (including the 5 terrorists) with 2 pilots and 9 flight attendants, for a total of 92 people on board.

All 9 of the first-class seats were occupied, 2 of them by hijackers Waleed al Shehri (2B) and Wail al Shehri (2A). Nineteen of the 30 seats in business class were occupied (49 percent), 3 by hijackers Atta (8D), Omari (8G), and Suqami (10B).[36] Fifty-three of the 119 coach seats were occupied (44 percent), none of them by hijackers.

The percentage of seats occupied on the aircraft—also known as the "load factor"—on September 11, 2001, was 51 percent, compared to an average load factor for Flight 11 of almost 39 percent on Tuesdays over the three months preceding 9/11.[37] Thus, the load factor on this flight was somewhat above the norm. The Commission found no ticketing, passenger occupancy, or financial evidence to indicate that the hijackers purchased additional seats beyond the ones they actually used in order to limit the number of passengers they would need to control during the operation.[38]

As noted above, all of the hijackers were accounted for in checking in and boarding the flight. American's records do not reflect the use of a cockpit jump seat by anyone other than the Flight 11 pilot and first officer.[39]

Under American Airline's policy in effect on 9/11, every crew member, including each of the flight attendants, had a key to the cockpit. The airline's Flight Standards Manual instructed the crews to guard their keys carefully.[40] Rules implemented in the 1960s required that air crews keep the cockpit door closed and locked during flight,[41] though the requirement was not always observed by flight crews or enforced by the FAA.

The American Airlines dispatcher in charge of Flight 11 said that all aspects of preflight preparation were routine. She reported having no preflight communications with the pilot or aircraft because no problems or issues in need of resolution arose.[42]

Flight 11 was loaded with 76,400 pounds of fuel, above the average fuel load of 70,000 pounds.[43]

The Flight. At *7:40 A.M.*, Flight 11 pushed back from Gate 32 and taxied to its departure runway. It took off at *7:59 A.M.*[44]

Shortly before *8:14 A.M.*, Flight 11 reached an altitude of 26,000 feet, just shy of its initial cruising altitude of 29,000 feet. Up to this point, all communications and the flight's appearance to air traffic controllers were normal.[45] While cabin service generally did not start until after the cruising altitude was reached, some pilots under the proper circumstances would turn off the "Fasten Seatbelt" signs earlier, thereby permitting the flight attendants to begin cabin service. It is not known if such a head start was allowed on this flight, but it is very likely that flight attendants would at least have begun preparations for service.[46]

FAA air traffic controller Peter Zalewski, stationed at the Boston Air Route Traffic Control Center (Boston Center) radioed directional instructions: "American 11 turn twenty degrees right." Flight 11 replied: "twenty right American 11." This was the last routine communication received from the flight. Seconds later, air traffic control radioed Flight 11 again, this time instructing the aircraft to climb to 35,000 feet. The flight did not respond. Over the next ten minutes, air traffic control tried nine times to contact the flight. All attempts were unsuccessful.[47]

According to the flight attendant's assigned seats, Karen Martin was in the first-class cabin and Bobbi Arestegui in the first-class galley, or kitchen. Sara Low and Jean Roger would have been serving business-class passengers, with Dianne Snyder in the mid-galley. Betty Ong and Amy Sweeney would have been working in coach, with Karen Nicosia in the rear galley. Jeffrey Collman would have been assigned to work in coach, or to assist in first class if needed.[48]

The Hijacking. At *around 8:14 A.M. or shortly thereafter,*[49] the hijackers began their takeover of the aircraft. Information supplied by eyewitness accounts indicates that the hijackers initiated and sustained their command of the aircraft using knives (as reported by two flight attendants); violence, including stabbing and slashing (as reported by two flight attendants); the threat of violence (as indicated by a hijacker in radio transmissions received by air traffic control); Mace (reported by one flight attendant); the threat of a bomb, either fake or real (reported by one flight attendant); and deception about their intentions (as indicated by a hijacker in a radio transmission received by air traffic control).

8:19 A.M.[50] Flight attendant Betty Ong contacted the American Airlines Southeastern Reservations Office in Cary, North Carolina, via AT&T air phone to report an emergency aboard the flight. Flight attendants know the reservations 800 number because they call it frequently to help passengers with reservations questions. Calls to the number are routed to the first open line at one of several facilities, including the one in Cary.[51]

The emergency call from Betty Ong lasted approximately 25 minutes (*8:19 A.M.–8:44 A.M.*). Ong relayed vital information about events taking place aboard the airplane to authorities on the ground. Her call was received initially at the reservations office by an American Airlines employee. The call was transferred to another employee who, realizing the urgency of the situation, pushed an emergency button that simultaneously initiated a tape recording of the call and sent an alarm notifying Nydia Gonzalez, the reservations office supervisor, to pick up on the line. Gonzalez was paged to respond to the alarm and joined the call a short time later. Only the first four minutes of the phone call between Ong and the reservations center was tape-recorded because the recently installed recording system at that time contained a default time limit.[52]

8:19 A.M. Ong reported, "The cockpit is not answering, somebody's stabbed in business class—and I think there's mace—that we can't breathe—I don't know, I think we're getting hijacked."[53]

While the reported "stabbing" in business class may have been an attack on the flight attendants, or on an unnamed victim, this may quite possibly have been the initial report of the attack (recounted with more specificity later) on a passenger in business class, seated in 9B—directly behind Atta and Omari, and in front of Suqami. The passenger was a 31-year-old man who had served four years as an officer in the Israeli military.[54]

8:20 A.M. Ong reported that two flight attendants had been stabbed.[55]

As noted above, American Airlines flight attendants all carried cockpit keys on their person. Although no information was provided from the flight about exactly how the hijackers gained access to the cockpit, it is possible the stabbings of the flight attendants could have been for the purpose of acquiring a key, of forcing one of them to open the cockpit door, or of luring the captain or first officer out of the cockpit.

Also at *8:20 A.M.*, the American Airlines dispatcher at the airline's operations center in Texas who was responsible for transatlantic flights received a communication from an American Airlines flight traveling from Seattle to Boston that air traffic control had asked the aircraft to try to contact Flight 11. This was the first indication she had of any problem on the flight.[56]

8:21 A.M. The transponder on Flight 11 was switched off, making it more difficult for FAA air traffic control centers to identify the flight and monitor its flight path.[57]

Also at *8:21 A.M.*, Gonzalez joined the call from Ong. Realizing the seriousness of the situation, she used another phone line to contact Craig Marquis, manager on duty, at the American Airlines System Operations Control (SOC) in Fort Worth, Texas, and informed the airline's headquarters that there was a problem aboard Flight 11. Gonzalez's emergency call to the SOC was recorded at the airline's headquarters. Gonzalez notified Marquis that Flight 11 was reporting an emergency, that stabbings had taken place, and that the flight attendants could not reach the cockpit.

After confirming Gonzalez's identity and position, at *8:22 A.M.* Marquis acknowledged the emergency and indicated to Gonzalez that he would "get ATC [air traffic control] on here." At this same time, while Marquis was relating this information to Gonzalez, Ong reported to Gonzalez's colleague: "I think the guys [hijackers] are up there. They might have gone there, jammed their way up there, or something. Nobody can call the cockpit. We can't even get inside." Thirty seconds after contacting American Airlines' headquarters, Gonzalez rejoined the call from Ong.[58]

Also at *8:22 A.M.*, flight attendant Madeline "Amy" Sweeney tried to contact the American Airlines flight services office at Logan International Airport by air phone. The office she was attempting to call managed the scheduling and operation of flight attendants, and its phone number was well known to the American flight attendants operating out of Boston.[59] Sweeney's initial attempt to get through to the office failed.[60]

8:23 A.M. The American Airlines flight dispatcher sent an Aircraft Communications and Reporting System (ACARS) text message to Flight 11: "Good Morning. . .ATC looking for you on [radio frequency] 135.32."[61] ACARS is an email system that enables those in the cockpit of an in-flight aircraft and company personnel on the ground to rapidly communicate with one another. The dispatcher received no response to his message.

Also at *8:23 A.M.*, the tape recording of the call between Ong and the reservations center ceased because of the default time limit on the system. However, Gonzalez remained on the line with Ong for the next 21 minutes. Gonzalez continued to report the information she received from the flight attendant to the American Airlines SOC. The call between American's reservations facility and the SOC continued to be taped by the SOC until its conclusion.[62]

8:24 A.M. Ong told Gonzalez that the hijackers were in the cockpit.[63] Sweeney attempted another call to the flight services office. It also failed.[64]

Shortly before *8:25 A.M.*, air traffic controller Zalewski heard two clicks over the frequency assigned to the flight, and radioed in response, "Is that American eleven trying to call?" Five seconds later, a voice with a foreign accent addressed the passengers. "We have some planes. Just stay quiet and you'll be okay. We're returning to the airport." [65] Because the wrong button was pushed, this message was heard not by the passengers but by air traffic control. The controller did not comprehend the first sentence ("planes"); it was understood 30 minutes later after a facility manager was able to locate and replay the tape. (See *9:03 A.M.* entry below.)

Seconds later, Boston Center heard the following transmission from the same foreign voice: "Nobody move. Everything will be okay. If you try to make any moves, you'll endanger yourself and the airplane. Just stay quiet."[66] According to Ong's simultaneous reporting, no announcements had been made from the cockpit to the passengers. This suggests that the hijackers' announcements were not heard in the cabin, and that they did not know how to operate the radio properly.

8:25 A.M. After hearing the second transmission from the aircraft, controllers at Boston Center believed that Flight 11 had been hijacked.[67]

Also at *8:25 A.M.*, an American Airlines air traffic control (ATC) specialist at the SOC sent another ACARS message to Flight 11: "Plz contact Boston Center ASAP...They have lost radio contact and your transponder signal." Again, the aircraft did not respond to this or subsequent ACARS messages attempting to reestablish contact with the cockpit.[68]

At the same time, Sweeney's third call to the American Airlines Flight Services Office at Boston finally was connected to an American Airlines' employee. Sweeney told her that someone was hurt aboard Flight 12, and then the phone call was cut off. The recipient of the call passed the information to Michael Woodward, the flight service manager. Woodward went to American's gate area at Logan with a colleague. The supervisor noted that the morning flights had all departed Boston and the gate area was quiet. He further realized that Flight 12 was a flight to Boston from the West Coast that had not even left yet, so he and his colleague returned to the office to try to clarify the nature of the emergency call.[69]

Between *8:25 A.M.* and *8:32 A.M.*, in accordance with the FAA protocol, Boston Center managers started notifying their chain of command that Flight 11 had been hijacked.[70]

8:26 A.M. Ong reported to Gonzalez that the plane was "flying erratically." Gonzalez passed this information to the SOC.[71]

8:28 A.M., Boston Center called the FAA Air Traffic Control System Command Center in Herndon, Virginia (Herndon Command Center) to advise management that it believed Flight 11 had been hijacked and was heading toward New York Center's airspace. By this point in time, Flight 11 had taken a dramatic turn to the south. Command Center immediately established a teleconference between Boston, New York and Cleveland Centers to allow Boston Center to provide situational awareness to the centers that adjoined Boston in the event the rogue aircraft entered their airspace.[72]

8:29 A.M. An air traffic control specialist at the American Airlines' SOC contacted Boston Center to ask about the status of Flight 11.

8:31 A.M. A controller at Boston Center told the American Airlines air traffic control specialist that the last known altitude of the aircraft was below 29,000 feet and that "He [Flight 11] was heading west. But right now he's pointed southwest of Albany." The controller also said the transponder had been lost and that "the controller heard a threat in the background, but that's unconfirmed and we're trying to pull the tape at this time."[73]

8:32 A.M. The Herndon Command Center notified the Operations Center at FAA headquarters in Washington, D.C., of the possible hijacking of Flight 11, and was told that FAA security personnel at headquarters had just begun discussing the hijacking on a conference call with the agency's New England regional office.[74]

Also at *8:32 A.M.*,[75] the American Airlines flight service manager at Logan, Michael Woodward, returned to his office and discovered that Sweeney had called again and was speaking with an employee in the office. Woodward, who was a friend of Sweeney's, took over the call. Sweeney said that she was sitting in the back of the plane next to Ong, who was still on the phone with Gonzalez.

The phone call between Sweeney and Woodward lasted approximately 12 minutes. It was not taped. According to Woodward, Sweeney was calm and collected. She provided the following information: she was sitting in the back of the aircraft next to Betty Ong; the plane had been hijacked; a man in first class had had his throat slashed; two flight attendants had been stabbed—one flight attendant had been stabbed seriously and was on oxygen while another flight attendant's wounds were not as serious and seemed to be okay; a doctor had been paged; the flight attendants were unable to contact the cockpit; and there was a bomb in the cockpit.[76]

Sweeney told Woodward that she and Ong were trying to relay as much information as they could to people on the ground.[77]

Sometime *after 8:30 A.M. but before 8:45 A.M.*, American Airlines Executive Vice President Gerard Arpey made a routine call to the airline's SOC and was informed that personnel there were on the phone with a flight attendant who was reporting violence and a cockpit intrusion on one of the company's flights. He tried unsuccessfully to contact American Airlines' Chairman Don Carty to apprise him of the situation. He immediately went to the SOC and learned that colleagues were setting up the company's System Operations Command Center (SOCC) in order to manage the emergency.[78]

8:33 A.M. The SOC manager on duty, Craig Marquis, received a report from the SOC air traffic control specialist about the specialist's just-completed call to Boston Center. The specialist told him that the aircraft was at "29,000 feet. They've lost Comm [communications] with 'em. Turned off his transponder. Tracking his primary only. Was westbound. Turned southbound. Said the controller heard on the frequency the pilot apparently adjust his mike—lot of loud voices—that sounded threatening—something about return or I'll kill ya or something to that effect—or threatening dialogue."[79] American headquarters now suspected that Flight 11 had been hijacked.[80]

Also at *8:33 A.M.*, Gonzalez received a report from Ong providing the first indication of a fatality on board. Gonzalez passed the information on to Marquis at *8:34 A.M.* as follows: "They think they might have a fatality on the flight. One of our passengers, possibly on 9B, Levin or Lewis, might have been fatally stabbed."[81]

8:34 A.M., While FAA headquarters received its initial notification that Flight 11 had been hijacked, the Boston controller received a third transmission from Flight 11: "Nobody move please. We are going back to the airport. Don't try to make any stupid moves."[82]

Also at *8:34 A.M.*, in an attempt to get fighter aircraft airborne to track Flight 11, Boston Center's managers decided not to wait for the request for military assistance to be passed up the FAA chain of command, and took the initiative by calling a manager at the FAA Cape Cod facility. They asked the Cape Cod manager to contact Otis Air Force Base in Cape Cod, Massachusetts to get fighters airborne to "tail" the hijacked aircraft.[83]

8:35 A.M. Gonzalez confirmed the details of a report by Ong regarding the identity of one of the hijackers: "He's the one that's in the—he's in the cockpit. Okay you said Tom Sukani? Okay—Okay and he was in 10B. Okay, okay, so he's one of the persons that are in the cockpit. And as far as weapons, all they have are just knives?"[84]

8:36 A.M. Marquis received Gonzalez's report about the hijacker she referred to as "Tom al Sukani" (i.e., Satam al Suqami), who had been seated in 10B.[85] He then initiated action to "lockout" American Airlines Flight 11. This procedure is standard for airlines in safety and security incidents. It acknowledges an emergency on the flight and isolates information so that the case can be managed by top leadership at the airlines in a way that protects information from being altered or released, and also protects the identities of the passengers and crew.

8:37 A.M.- 8:38 A.M., Gonzalez reported to Marquis that the passengers had been moved out of first class and back to coach and that the plane was flying erratically again. American completed its lockout of Flight 11.[86] Also at 8:38 A.M., Gonzalez reported that the plane was in a rapid descent. Marquis asked a fellow employee in the SOC if Flight 11 was descending. The employee replied, "We don't know. The transponder is off so we have no active read on him."[87]

8:37:52 A.M. Boston Center called the North American Aerospace Defense Command's (NORAD) Northeast Air Defense Sector (NEADS) and notified NEADS about the suspected hijacking of Flight11.[88] The United States' military defense of its homeland on 9/11 began with this call. Indeed, this was the first notification received by the military – at any level – that Flight 11 had been hijacked.

First notification to NORAD that AA11 was hijacked.

Graphic courtesy of ESRI

The report of the hijack was relayed immediately to Battle Commander Colonel Robert Marr at NEADS, who was stationed in the Battle Cab in preparation for a scheduled NORAD exercise. Col. Marr confirmed that the hijacking was "real-world" then ordered fighter pilots at Otis Air Force Base in Massachusetts to battle-stations.[89]

Col. Marr then phoned Maj. General Larry Arnold, commanding General of the First Air Force and the Continental U.S. NORAD Region (CONR) commander. Col. Marr advised him of the situation, and sought authorization to scramble the Otis fighters in response to the reported hijacking. General Arnold instructed Col. Marr "to go ahead and scramble the airplanes and we'd get permission later. And the reason for that is that the procedure…if you follow the book, is they [law enforcement officials] go to the duty officer of the national military center, who in turn makes an inquiry to NORAD for the availability of fighters, who then gets permission from someone representing the Secretary of Defense. Once that is approved then we scramble an aircraft. We didn't wait for that."[90] General Arnold then picked up the phone and talked to the operations deputy at NORAD, who told him `Yeah, we'll work with the National Military Command Center (NMCC). Go ahead and scramble the aircraft.'"[91]

At *8:40 A.M.*, NEADS placed two F-15 alert aircraft at Otis Air Force Base in Massachusetts, located about 153 miles away from New York City, on battle stations.[92]

Also at *8:40 A.M.*, information about Flight 11 started to be conveyed within the Air Traffic Control system. Boston Center, through the Herndon Command Center, provided a report to New York TRACON on Flight 11.

Also at *8:40 A.M.*, an American Airlines employee in Boston who was standing next to Michael Woodward as he talked to Sweeney contacted an employee in American Airlines' SOC. She reported the content of the ongoing call between Woodward and Sweeney, including that Sweeney said the hijackers were Middle Eastern men seated in 10B, 9D, and 9G; one spoke very little English and one spoke excellent English; she did not know how they had gained entry to the cockpit; and the aircraft was in a rapid descent.[93]

8:41 A.M. Sweeney told Woodward that passengers in coach were under the impression that there was a routine medical emergency in first class. She said that the other flight attendants were attending to duties, including getting medical supplies, while she and Ong reported the events.[94]

Also at *8:41 A.M.*, Marquis instructed an unidentified colleague in the SOC: "Tell ATC to handle this as an emergency." The colleague replied, "They have in there it's been hijacked." The manager responded: "It is. Okay."[95]

The colleague then informed Marquis, "They think he's [Flight 11] headed toward Kennedy. They're moving everybody out of the way. They seem to have him on a primary radar. They seem to think that he is descending."[96]

8:43 A.M. A Herndon Command Center air traffic specialist warned Washington en route center that Flight 11 was a "possible hijack" and would be headed towards Washington Center's airspace if it continued on a southbound track.

8:44 A.M., Gonzalez reported to Marquis that phone contact with Ong had been terminated: "We, I think we might have lost her."[97] About this same time, Sweeney reported to Woodward in Boston, "Something is wrong. We are in a rapid descent . . . we are all over the place." Woodward asked Sweeney to look out the window to see if she could determine where they were. Sweeney told him, "We are flying low. We are flying very, very low. We are flying way too low." Seconds later she said, "Oh my God we are way too low" and then the phone call ended.[98]

8:45 A.M. The American Airlines employee listening to the call between Woodward and Sweeney reported to the SOC: , "She [Sweeney] started screaming and saying something's wrong and now he's [Woodward] having trouble—now he thinks he might be disconnected. Okay, we just lost connection."[99]

Also at *8:45 A.M.*, the American Airlines director of security learned of the hijacking. He contacted the special agent in charge of the FBI's Dallas Field Office to tell him that a hijacking was taking place.[100]

8:46 A.M. The order to scramble the Otis fighters was passed from the NEADS Battle Commander (BC) to his Mission Crew Commander (MCC), who passed it to the Weapons Director (WD).[101] Almost immediately, however, a problem arose. The Weapons Director asked: "MCC. I don't know where I'm scrambling these guys to. I need a direction, a destination."[102] Because the hijackers had turned off the plane's transponder, the plane appeared only as a primary track on radar. The fighters were vectored to military air space near Long Island while NEADS personnel searched frantically for the missing flight. [103]

8:46:40 A.M. American Airlines Flight 11 crashed into the North Tower of the World Trade Center in New York City.[104] All on board and an unknown number in the building were killed on impact.

By *8:50 A.M.,* American Airlines headquarters learned that an aircraft had struck the World Trade Center via a telephone call from an American employee at LaGuardia Airport. The airline did not know the plane was Flight 11.[105]

8:53 A.M. Although the Otis fighters were airborne, neither the fighter pilots nor the NEADS officers were aware that Flight 11 had crashed into the World Trade Center's North Tower. When NEADS learned of the crash, the fighters were placed in a holding pattern in military airspace to await further instruction. NEADS had no knowledge that a second hijacked aircraft, United 175, was bearing down on the South Tower. The Otis fighters remained in a holding pattern until word reached NEADS that the second aircraft had crashed into the World Trade Center.

At about *9:03 A.M.,* Boston Center reported to the FAA's New England regional office that the hijackers stated, "We have some planes" during the 8:25 A.M. transmission from Flight 11 [106]

9:16 A.M. The American Airlines SOC air traffic control specialist called an official at the FAA's Herndon Command Center and informed her that American "thought" Flight 11 had been the first aircraft to crash into the World Trade Center.[107]

9:21 A.M. NEADS received a report from Boston Center that "it was evidently another aircraft that hit the tower" and that Flight 11 was still airborne and "heading towards Washington."[108] NEADS personnel immediately began an active search for the aircraft.

9:23 A.M. After consulting with the NEADS Battle Commander, the NEADS Mission Crew Commander issued an order to scramble alert fighters from Langley Air Force Base in Virginia in response to the report that Flight 11 was headed towards Washington DC.[109] The initial strategy of NEADS personnel was to use the alert fighters scrambled from Otis Air Force Base at 8:46 A.M. to chase down Flight 11 if they could find the aircraft, and to vector the Langley fighters on a northerly heading to an area between the (reported) southbound Flight 11 and the nation's capital.[110]

9:24 A.M. The order to scramble the Langley fighters was processed and transmitted by NEADS to Langley Air Force Base. [111]

Shortly after *9:24 A.M.*, out of concern over leaving New York's airspace unprotected, NEADS commanders decided to cancel the plan to pursue Flight 11 with the Otis fighters.[112]

9:27 A.M. The military's situational awareness was summarized on the NEADS watch floor as follows: "Three planes unaccounted for. American Airlines 11 may still be airborne but the flight that – United 175 to the World Trade Center. We're not sure who the other one is."[113]

9:30 A.M. Radar data showed the Langley fighters airborne. On the floor at NEADS, the ID Technicians continued to attempt to locate American 11 after the Langley fighters were airborne.[114]

By *9:30 A.M.*, American Airlines confirmed that Flight 11 had crashed into the World Trade Center.[115]

Alleged Gun Use on Flight 11. The Commission investigated an allegation that a gun was used aboard American Airlines Flight 11. The allegation arose from a notation in an initial executive summary produced on September 11, 2001, by FAA staff indicating that FAA headquarters had received a report of a shooting on the plane from an American Airlines employee at the company's operations center.[116] The report did not mention a stabbing. In interviews with the Commission, the individual alleged to have made the report to the FAA denied having done so.[117]

Regardless of what reports were received in the chaotic environment of the various operations centers at the FAA, the airports, and the airlines, authoritative information about whether a shooting occurred on Flight 11 could have come only from individuals on the aircraft who were reporting events to contacts on the ground.

As noted above, two flight attendants aboard American Airlines Flight 11 placed calls to ground contacts to report what was happening on the aircraft. Neither in the tape recordings of the calls nor in the accounts of the witnesses to the calls is the presence of a gun or the occurrence of a shooting reported.[118] These witnesses' accounts of the phone calls are consistent and are quite specific about the presence of knives and the stabbing or slashing of two crew members and a passenger.

In order to accept the accuracy of the initial FAA executive summary concerning a shooting (disregarding the evidence by eyewitnesses to the contrary), one would have to believe that the American Airlines operations center relayed to the FAA the account of a shooting that no witness recalls while neglecting to include the account of a stabbing that was widely reported, including to personnel in the operations center. This seems highly implausible.

In fact, the victim of the alleged shooting that was noted in the FAA executive summary was seated in 9B. That seat, according to several of the witness accounts from the aircraft, was assigned to the passenger who was stabbed.[119]

Both the FBI and the General Accounting Office investigated the story of a gun aboard Flight 11 and could find nothing to substantiate the version in the executive summary. In addition, while investigators have uncovered evidence of numerous knife purchases by the 19 hijackers leading up to September 11, 2001, there was no evidence that they purchased or possessed firearms.[120]

Furthermore, the tactics of all four hijacking teams involved in the plot were similar. No evidence has been uncovered to suggest that the hijackers on any of the other flights used firearms. Evidence shows that common tactics were used among the flights including the use of knives, the threat of a bomb (either real or simulated) reported on three flights, and the presence of Mace reported on two flights. It seems unlikely that one of the teams would depart from the tactical discipline of the plotters' mutual strategy.

Evidently, the account of the attack on the business-class passenger—the only attack on a passenger reported by eyewitnesses—became garbled as it was relayed between airline and FAA authorities in the confusion of the rapidly unfolding events of the day.

1.2 UNITED AIR LINES FLIGHT 175

Hijackers. Marwan al Shehhi (pilot); Mohand al Shehri; Hamza al Ghamdi; Fayez Banihammad; Ahmed al Ghamdi.

Hijacker Weapon Purchase. On August 13, 2001, Marwan al Shehhi purchased two short-bladed knives, a Cliphanger Viper and an Imperial Tradesman Dual Edge. On the same day and in the same city, Fayez Banihammad bought a Stanley two-piece snap knife set (a type of multi-tool), and Hamza al Ghamdi purchased a Leatherman Wave multi-tool.[121]

Hijacker Arrival at Airport and Check-in. At *6:20 A.M.*,[122] Ahmed al Ghamdi and Hamza al Ghamdi checked in at the United Air Lines (UAL) ticket counter at Logan International Airport in Boston.[123] They approached a United Air Lines customer service representative, who immediately referred them to another agent because one of the men presented a "certificate" that the first agent was unfamiliar with.[124]

This second customer service representative said that one of the two men told her that he needed a ticket. She examined his documents and found that he already had a UAL envelope with an itinerary and ticket in his hand. She told him that he did not need a ticket but could check-in. The United agent recalled that the men checked two bags. She thought each had one carry-on bag resembling a briefcase. She recalled that each man had "problems" answering the standard security questions, and that she had to repeat them "very slowly." After the questioning, the men departed the counter area for the security checkpoint.[125]

6:20 A.M. Ahmed al Ghamdi checked two bags that were loaded on the aircraft at *6:31 A.M.*[126]

6:45 A.M. Marwan al Shehhi checked a single bag. It was loaded on the plane at *6:51 A.M.*[127]

6:52 A.M. A call was placed to Mohamed Atta's cell phone from a pay phone in Terminal C located between the screening checkpoint and the departure gate.[128] The call lasted three minutes and was most likely a last-minute check between Atta, who had just arrived in Boston, and Marwan al Shehhi.[129]

6:53 A.M. Fayez Banihammad (listed in the airline passenger record as Fayez Ahmed) and Mohand al Shehri (listed as Mohald) checked in. Banihammad checked two bags, which were loaded at *6:57 A.M.*[130]

Hijacker Prescreening. None of the Flight 175 hijackers was selected for additional security scrutiny by the CAPPS system.[131]

Checkpoint Security Screening. Because Logan Airport did not use video cameras to monitor activities at security checkpoints, we could not establish with certainty when the five hijackers passed through security screening or how they were processed. Judging from when they checked in for the flight, we estimated they were screened within the time frames as follow:

To reach their departure gate, after checking in, the hijackers had to pass through a checkpoint in Terminal C before boarding.[132] The checkpoint was under the custodial responsibility of United Air Lines. It had contracted the screening duties to Huntleigh USA Corporation. None of the checkpoint supervisors recalled the hijackers or reported anything suspicious regarding their screening.[133]

Hijacker Boarding. Fayez Banihammad boarded the flight at *7:23 A.M.* He was seated in 2A (first class). Mohand al Shehri boarded at the same time and sat next to him in 2B. *Four minutes later*, both Marwan al Shehhi, seated in 6C (business class), and Ahmed al Ghamdi, seated in 9D (business class), embarked. At *7:28 A.M.*, Hamza al Ghamdi was the last hijacker to board the flight; he sat in 9C (business class).[134]

Flight Profile. The flight was scheduled to depart Logan at 8:00 A.M. for Los Angeles International Airport. The aircraft was a Boeing 767, with tail number N612UA.[135]

Captain Victor Saracini and First Officer Michael Horrocks piloted the plane. The flight attendants were

- Robert Fangman, assigned to the middle center jump seat between the middle galley and coach;

- Amy Jarret, assigned to the right jump seat, located in the back of the plane between coach and the rear galley;
- Amy King, assigned to the forward center jump seat, located between the forward galley and the first-class cabin;
- Kathryn Laborie, assigned to the forward left jump seat next to the cockpit entrance;
- Alfred Marchand, assigned the forward center jump seat, located between the forward galley and the first-class cabin;
- Michael Tarrou, assigned to the rear left jump seat, located in the back of the plane between coach and the rear galley; and
- Alicia Titus, assigned to the middle center jump seat between the middle galley and coach.[136]

The aircraft had a capacity of 168 passengers: 10 in first class, 33 in business class, and 125 in coach. The flight carried 56 passengers (including 5 hijackers) with 2 pilots and 7 flight attendants, for a total of 65 people on board.

Nine of the 10 first-class seats were occupied, including 2 by hijackers Banihammad and Mohand al Shehri. Eleven of the 33 business-class seats were occupied, 3 by hijackers Shehhi, Hamza al Ghamdi, and Ahmed al Ghamdi; and 36 of the 125 coach seats were occupied, none by hijackers.[137]

The 56 passengers represented a load factor of one-third of the plane's passenger capacity. This figure is considerably below the 49 percent average load factor for Flight 175 for Tuesdays in the three-month period prior to September 11. It represented the third-lowest load factor among the scheduled flights during that period,[138] when Tuesdays were the least traveled day for Flight 175.[139]

There is no evidence that the Flight 175 hijackers purchased additional tickets for the flight beyond the ones they actually used.[140]

All the hijackers were accounted for on the flight, and according to United's records, no paperwork was filed to indicate that any cockpit jumpseat was occupied by anyone other than flight crew.[141]

Under United Air Lines policy at the time, a key to the cockpit door was stowed in a designated place near the cockpit door.[142]

Flight 175 was loaded with 76,000 pounds of fuel,[143] a normal amount for the cross-country flight.[144]

The Flight. At *7:58 A.M.*, Flight 175 pushed back from Gate 19 in Terminal C, and it departed Logan Airport at *8:14 A.M.*[145]

At *8:19 A.M.*, Flight 175 made radio contact with a Boston Center air traffic controller.[146]

8:33 A.M. Flight 175 reached its assigned cruising altitude of 31,000 feet.[147] At or around this time, flight attendants Laborie and Marchand would have begun cabin service in first class, while flight attendants King and Fangman would have done the same in business class, and Tarrou, Jarret, and Titus would have served coach class.[148]

8:37 A.M. FAA air traffic controllers asked the flight crew of Flight 175 to look for American Airlines Flight 11.[149]

8:38 A.M. The crew of Flight 175 radioed air traffic control that they had spotted the aircraft at 28,000 or 29,000 feet. FAA air traffic control told them to turn their aircraft to avoid Flight 11.[150]

8:40 A.M. Control of Flight 175 was passed from Boston Center to the New York Air Traffic Control Center at Ronkonkoma, New York (New York Center).[151]

8:41 A.M. The flight crew of Flight 175 reported to air traffic controllers that "we heard a suspicious transmission [from another aircraft] on our departure out of Boston—like someone keyed the mike and said everyone stay in your seats."[152]

United's system operations control manager in Chicago reported that though he normally received relevant information about United flights from FAA air traffic control, on September 11, 2001, he did not recall receiving information about any air traffic control communications with or from Flight 175, including the *8:41 A.M.* report.[153] The other senior United Air Lines officials working in the operations center on 9/11 confirmed that they were never told of this communication, though they stated that air traffic controllers would "first and foremost" communicate directly with pilots. Furthermore, these officials reported that they never received any communication on the morning of September 11, 2001, from the FAA or the air traffic control system advising United to contact its aircraft about the hijackings.[154]

At *8:42 A.M.*, the flight crew of Flight 175 completed their report on the "suspicious transmission" they had received from another plane. This represented the flight's last communication with the ground.[155]

The Hijacking. Between *8:42 A.M.* and *8:46 A.M.*, the hijackers began their takeover of the flight. The hijackers initiated and sustained their command of the aircraft using knives (as reported by two passengers and a flight attendant), Mace (reported by one passenger), and the threat of a bomb (reported by the same passenger). They stabbed flight crew members (as reported by a flight attendant and one passenger) and killed both pilots, (as reported by a flight attendant).

All of these eyewitness accounts were provided via phone calls (as described below) from the back of the plane, even though the passengers calling had each been assigned a seat in the front or middle of the cabin.[156]

Given the similarities to Flight 11 in hijacker seating and in the eyewitness reports of tactics and weapons, as well as the close contact between presumed team leaders Atta and Shehhi, it is likely the hijacking unfolded in much the same manner as on Flight 11.

8:47 A.M. Flight 175's transponder code changed twice within a one-minute period.[157] David Bottiglia, the New York Center air traffic controller responsible for Flight 175 was also handling Flight 11, which he was told had been hijacked. At this point he was trying to locate Flight 11 and did not notice the transponder code changes on Flight 175 until *8:51 A.M.*[158]

8:50 A.M. Delta Airlines Flight 1489 radioed in and advised David Bottiglia there was "a lot of smoke in lower Manhattan" and the World Trade Center looked like it was on fire.[159] The controller acknowledged the message at 8:51 A.M., and agreed to pass on any news, then noticed a change in the transponder reading from Flight 175. The controller asked Flight 175 to recycle its transponder to the proper code.[160] There was no response.

Also at *8:51 A.M.*, Flight 175 deviated from its assigned altitude.[161]

8:52 A.M. David Bottiglia made the first of five unsuccessful attempts over a three-minute period to contact the flight.[162] While continuing his attempts to contact Flight 175, David Bottiglia spent the next several minutes handing off the other flights on his scope to other controllers and moving aircraft out of the way of the unidentified aircraft (believed to be Flight 175) as it moved southwest and then turned northeast toward New York City.[163]

Also at *8:52 A.M.*, Lee Hanson received a phone call from his son, passenger Peter Burton Hanson,[164] who told him that the flight was being hijacked. "I think they've taken over the cockpit—An attendant has been stabbed—and someone else up front may have been killed. The plane is making strange moves. Call United Air Lines—Tell them it's Flight 175, Boston to LA." Lee Hanson then called the Easton, Connecticut, Police Department, relayed the information from his son to a police captain, and asked for his help.[165]

Also at *8:52 A.M.*,[166] Marc Policastro, an employee at the United Air Lines maintenance office in San Francisco (SAMC), received a phone call from a male flight attendant[167] on Flight 175 who reported that the aircraft had been hijacked, both pilots had been killed, a flight attendant had been stabbed, and he believed the hijackers were flying the plane. The call lasted about two minutes. Policastro tried unsuccessfully to contact the flight via ACARS.[168] Another employee at the maintenance office also tried to contact Flight 175 with an ACARS message around this time, with a message requesting the flight crew to confirm reports of an incident onboard.[169] None of these or any subsequent attempts to contact Flight 175 were acknowledged from the aircraft.

Beginning at 8:52 A.M. and continuing until 8:59 A.M., a passenger unsuccessfully tried a total of four times to reach his wife on both her business and home phone lines.[170]

Meanwhile, at United's (UAL) headquarters in Chicago, the air traffic control coordinator called an official at the FAA Herndon Command Center to confirm that the plane that had just crashed into the World Trade Center was not a United plane. He was informed that the aircraft was a hijacked American Airlines 757.[171] Shortly thereafter, the UAL coordinator briefed the director of United's systems operations center, and the shift manager of United's flight dispatch, about the call. The dispatch manager attempted to notify top corporate officials but was unable to do so because the UAL pager system was not working.[172]

At *approximately 8:55 A.M.* a New York Center supervisor notified the center's operations manager of her belief that Flight 175 had been hijacked.[173]

8:57 A.M. Flight 175 turned to the northeast and leveled off at 28,500 feet. *One minute later*, it headed toward New York City.[174]

8:58 A.M. David Bottiglia, the New York Center controller searching for Flight 175, told another New York controller "we might have a hijack over here, two of them."[175]

8:59 A.M. Passenger Brian David Sweeney[176] attempted to call his wife, Julie. He left a message on their home answering machine telling her that the plane had been hijacked.[177]

Also at *8:59 A.M.*, an employee at United's maintenance office in San Francisco sent three ACARS messages to Flight 175. Each read, "I heard of a reported incident aboard your acft [aircraft]. Plz verify all is normal."[178]

Shortly before 9:00 A.M., one of this employee's supervisors in the San Francisco office called United's station operations control manager in Chicago to tell him of the reported hijacking of Flight 175.[179] The operations center manager initially thought the report referred to the American Airlines hijacking, but the supervisor in San Francisco reiterated that it was about Flight 175.[180] The Chicago manager notified his boss, United's operations center director, who in turn contacted United's chief operating officer, Andy Studdert, and the company's CEO, James Goodwin.[181] The employee supervisor also called the airline's security chief. The SOC director and the supervisor began the process of activating the crisis center at United's headquarters, which took about 30 minutes to complete.[182]

At *approximately 9:00 A.M.*, the FAA's New York Center informed the UAL air traffic control coordinator that Flight 175 was missing from radar.[183]

9:00 A.M.[184] Passenger Brian David Sweeney called his mother and told her that his flight had been hijacked. He said that the passengers were thinking about storming the cockpit to wrest control of the plane away from the hijackers. He thought they were flying somewhere over Ohio. Immediately after the call from her son, Mrs. Sweeney turned on the television and saw the second aircraft crash into the South Tower of the World Trade Center.[185]

Also at *9:00 A.M.*,[186] Lee Hanson received a second call from his son who told him: It's getting bad, Dad—A stewardess was stabbed—They seem to have knives and Mace—They said they have a bomb—It's getting very bad on the plane—Passengers are throwing up and getting sick—The plane is making jerky movements—I don't think the pilot is flying the plane—I think we are going down—I think they intend to go to Chicago or someplace and fly into a building.[187]

The call ended abruptly. Hanson did not know whether his son had hung up or the phone had malfunctioned. After the call, Hanson turned on his television. He watched as the second plane slammed into the South Tower.[188]

9:01 or 9:02 A.M. A United flight dispatch manager went to the desk of Ed Ballinger, the dispatcher responsible for the airline's East to West Coast flights. He told the dispatcher of the information just received by the operations center manager from the San Francisco maintenance office that had led them to suspect Flight 175 had been hijacked.[189]

Between *9:01 A.M. and 9:02 A.M.*, a manager from New York Center told the FAA Command Center: "We have several situations going on here. It's escalating big, big time. We need to get the military involved with us. . . . We're, we're involved with something else, we have other aircraft that may have a similar situation going on here."[190] The "other aircraft" referred to by New York Center was Flight 175. The evidence suggests this conversation was the only notice received by either FAA headquarters or the Herndon Command Center prior to the second crash that there had been a second hijacking. While the Herndon Command Center was told about this "other aircraft" at *9:01 A.M.*, New York Center contacted New York terminal approach control and asked for assistance in locating Flight 175. At *9:02 A.M.*, as New York terminal approach controllers located Flight 175 rapidly descending into lower Manhattan, a New York Center manager stated, "[a]lright. Heads up man, it looks like another one coming in."[191]

At **9:03 a.m.**, Terry Biggio, a manager from FAA's Boston Center, reported to an FAA New England region representative that they had deciphered what the hijackers on board American 11 said during the first radio transmission (at 8:25 A.M.). Biggio reported that the hijackers said "we have planes." He then emphasized that they said "planes as in plural." As the air traffic controllers in Boston came to the tragic realization that the hijackers may have hijacked multiple commercial aircraft, Flight 175 was about to strike the South Tower of the World Trade Center.[192]

9:03 A.M. Ballinger sent an ACARS message to the aircraft: "How is the ride. Anything dispatch can do for you." Another ACARS was sent at the same time by the UAL air traffic control coordinator: "NY approach lookin for ya on [frequency] 127.4."

9:03 A.M. NEADS air defenders received their first notice of a second hijacked aircraft when New York Center told a NEADS Identification Technician that Flight 175 was a "second possible hijack."[193]

9:03:11 A.M.[194] United Air Lines Flight 175 crashed into the South Tower of the World Trade Center. The aircraft was traveling at over 587 miles per hour at impact.[195] All on board and an unknown number in the building were killed instantly.

9:03:22 A.M. Seconds after Flight 175 crashed into the South Tower, Terry Biggio, Boston Center's manager, advised the New England Region that New York confirmed that a second plane had struck the World Trade Center.[196]

Shortly after, unaware that Flight 175 had flown into the World Trade Center, Ballinger again attempted to communicate with the aircraft. He sent the same ACARS message: "How is the ride. Anything dispatch can do for you."[197] Meanwhile, the airline's air traffic control coordinator re-sent his ACARS message, "NY approach lookin for ya on 127.4."[198]

9:04 A.M. Terry Biggio immediately advised New England Region that Boston Center was going to stop all departures at airports under its control and suggested they "do the same elsewhere."[199]

Between *9:04 A.M. and 9:07 A.M.*, the NEADS Identification Technicians were on the phone with FAA Boston Center seeking further information on Flight 175 when Boston Center confirmed a second crash at the World Trade Center.[200]

9:05 A.M. On an open line monitored by Herndon Command Center, Terry Biggio contacted the New England Region and confirmed that the hijackers on board American 11 said "we have planes."[201]

9:05 A.M. New York Center declared "ATC zero"—meaning that aircraft were not permitted to depart from, arrive at, or travel through New York Center's airspace until further notice.[202]

9:07 A.M. Fearing there may be additional attacks after the second WTC crash, Terry Biggio asked a New England Region manager if warnings to increase cockpit security could be sent to airborne aircraft via "ACARS or something." Biggio was particularly concerned about warning airborne international flights scheduled to arrive at JFK International Airport. While Boston Center did not want to alarm any airborne aircraft, they were considering using the radio frequencies to alert international flight crews to heighten their cockpit security. On the advice of a New England Region representative, Boston Center decided to contact Air Transport Association ("ATA") representatives through Herndon Command Center and ask the ATA representatives to formally request that airline companies warn their aircraft to heighten cockpit security. Not content to rely on the airlines to warn their aircraft, Terry Biggio decided that Boston Center would issue a Notice to Airmen ("NOTAM") to heighten cockpit security in light of the attacks on New York.[203]

By *9:08 A.M.,* the mission crew commander at NEADS learned of the second explosion at the World Trade Center and decided against holding the fighters in military airspace away from Manhattan. Anticipating additional attacks on New York, the mission crew commander told his crew:

> This is what I foresee that we probably need to do. We need to talk to FAA. We need to tell 'em if this stuff is gonna keep on going, we need to take those fighters, put 'em over Manhattan. That's best thing, that's the best play right now. So coordinate with the FAA. Tell 'em if there's more out there, which we don't know, let's get 'em over Manhattan. At least we got some kind of play.[204]

9:09 A.M. After learning about the second crash at the World Trade Center, NEADS ordered alert fighters at Langley Air Force Base to battle stations. Colonel Marr, the battle commander at NEADS, and General Arnold, the CONR Commander, both recall that the planes were held on battle stations, as opposed to scrambling, because they might be called upon to relieve the Otis fighters over New York City if a refueling tanker was not located, and also because of the general uncertainty of the situation in the sky.[205] After initially considering scrambling the Langley fighters to New York to provide backup for the Otis fighters, they decided to leave the Langley jets on "battle stations only."[206]   NORAD had no indication that any other plane had been hijacked.

9:09 A.M. to 9:10 A.M. Terry Biggio instructed all air traffic controllers in Boston Center to use their radio frequencies to inform all aircraft within Boston Center's airspace of the events unfolding in New York and to advise the aircraft to heighten cockpit security in light of those events. Boston air traffic controllers immediately executed Biggio's order.[207]

9:10 A.M. A UAL dispatch operations shift manager's timeline log entry noted, "At that point a second aircraft had hit the WTC, but we didn't know it was our United flight."[208]

Between 9:10 A.M. and 9:20 A.M., The United dispatch operations manager spoke with the American Airlines dispatch operations manager about the two crashes into the World Trade Center. The American official believed both aircraft were his; the United official was increasingly "confident" that the second plane was Flight 175. In slow motion and enlarged images of the second impact on CNN, he could see that the airplane did not have the shiny metallic color of American jets.[209]

9:12 A.M. A staff analyst in United headquarters alerted United dispatch, flight safety, and flight operations personnel about the American Airlines crash and the missing UAL Flight 175.[210]

9:13 A.M. Radar data show the Otis fighters were approximately 115 miles away from New York City when they exited their holding pattern and set a course direct for Manhattan.[211]

At approximately **9:15 A.M.**, Daniel Bueno, another Boston Center manager, asked the Herndon Command Center to contact all FAA centers in the country and instruct them to issue a similar cockpit security alert to all airborne aircraft. Commission staff has found no evidence to suggest that the Command Center acted on Bueno's request or issued any type of nationwide cockpit security alert.[212] One Command Center manager told Commission staff that the FAA culture and mindset on 9/11 was such that they would never have relayed this message directly to all pilots. She said the FAA would pass situational awareness to the airline company representatives who, in turn, would determine if such action was necessary.[213]

9:19 A.M. Ballinger sent the following ACARS message to his airborne flights: "Beware any cockpit intrusion…Two aircraft in NY hit trade center builds."[214]

9:20 A.M. The UAL dispatch operations manager now believed that the second aircraft to crash into the World Trade Center was Flight 175. Its identity was still unconfirmed.[215]

9:22 A.M. The UAL system operations control manager issued an advisory, under the name of UAL Chief Operating Officer Andy Studdert, to all UAL facilities—including the flight dispatchers—stating that Flight 175 had been involved in an accident in New York City and that the crisis center had been activated.[216] Just prior to the Studdert advisory, United headquarters began the lockout procedure to restrict access to passenger and crew information about the flight.[217]

9:23 A.M. Ballinger sent out his "cockpit intrusion" message to Flight 175.[218] At this time, while the dispatcher was aware that two large aircraft (including one United airliner) had crashed into the World Trade Center and that Flight 175 had been hijacked, he was not aware that Flight 175 had crashed.[219]

9:25 A.M. The Otis fighters arrived over Manhattan and established a combat air patrol (CAP) over the city.[220]

1.3 AMERICAN AIRLINES FLIGHT 77

Hijackers: Hani Hanjour (pilot); Khalid al Mihdhar; Nawaf al Hazmi; Salem al Hazmi; Majed Moqed.

Hijacker Weapon Purchases. On August 27, Nawaf al Hazmi purchased Leatherman multi-tool knives.[221]

Hijacker Check-in and Checkpoint Security Screening. At approximately *7:15 A.M.,* Majed Moqed and Khalid al Mihdhar checked in at the American Airlines ticket counter at Dulles and proceeded to checkpoint screening.[222]

Security screening for Flight 77 was conducted at the east and west checkpoints in the Main Terminal. United Air Lines had custodial responsibility for the screening and contracted out the work to Argenbright Security. All five of the hijackers passed through the same checkpoint. Closed-circuit television recorded all passengers, including the hijackers, as they were screened.[223]

7:18 A.M. Moqed and Mihdhar entered the security screening checkpoint. They placed their carry-on bags on the X-ray machine belt and proceeded through the first walk-through metal detector. Both set off the alarm and were directed to a second metal detector. While Mihdhar did not trigger the second metal detector and was permitted through the checkpoint, Moqed failed once again. A security officer screened him with a hand-held metal detection wand. He passed this cursory inspection.[224]

At approximately *7:29 A.M.,* Nawaf al Hazmi and Salem al Hazmi checked in at the American ticket counter.[225]

7:35 A.M. Hani Hanjour placed two carry-on bags on the X-ray belt and passed through the metal detector. He picked up his carry-on bags and proceeded through the checkpoint.

7:36 A.M., Nawaf and Salem al Hazmi entered the same checkpoint. Salem, with one carry-on bag, successfully cleared the magnetometer and was permitted through the checkpoint. Nawaf set off the alarms for both the first and second magnetometers. He was hand-wanded and his shoulder bag was swiped by an explosive trace detector before he was allowed to proceed. The video footage showed that he was carrying an unidentified item clipped to the rim of his back pants pocket.[226]

Hijacker Prescreening Selectee Status. CAPPS selected all five of the Flight 77 hijackers for added security scrutiny. Hanjour, Mihdhar, and Moqed were chosen by the computer algorithm. Nawaf al Hazmi and Salem al Hazmi were both made CAPPS selectees at the discretion of the airline's customer service representative who checked them in.[227] The agent told us that one of the hijackers (Salem, we believe) presented identification without a picture and did not seem to be able to understand English. He said that he thought both were suspicious and made sure he made both of them selectees.

The only consequence of selection, however, was that their bags were held off the plane until it was confirmed that they had boarded the aircraft.[228]

Thus, Hanjour, Nawaf al Hazmi, and Mihdhar, who did not check any bags on September 11, suffered no consequences from their selection by the system. For Salem al Hazmi, who checked two bags, and Moqed, who checked one bag, the sole consequence was that their baggage was not loaded onto Flight 77 until after their boarding was confirmed.[229]

Hijacker Boarding. At approximately *7:50 A.M.*, Moqed and Mihdhar boarded Flight 77 and were seated in seats 12A and 12B of coach, respectively. Hanjour, assigned to seat 1B, in first class, boarded at approximately *7:52 A.M.* Finally, Nawaf al Hazmi and Salem al Hazmi, occupying seats 5E and 5F in first class, boarded at approximately *7:55 A.M.*[230]

Flight Profile. Flight 77 provided nonstop service between Washington Dulles International Airport and Los Angeles International Airport. It was scheduled to depart at 8:10 A.M. The aircraft was a Boeing 757, tail number N644AA.[231]

Captain Charles F. Burlingame and First Officer David Charlebois piloted the plane. The flight attendants on Flight 77 were

- Michele Heidenberger, assigned to the rear left jump seat in the very back of the plane at takeoff;
- Jennifer G. Lewis, assigned to the right middle jump seat between first class and coach (and therefore between the hijackers in 5E and 5F and those in 12A and 12B);
- Kenneth E. Lewis, assigned to the right rear jump seat; and
- Renee May, assigned to the forward left jump seat next to the entry area and between the first row of first class and the cockpit.[232]

The aircraft had a capacity of 176 passengers, 22 in first class and 154 in coach. On September 11, 2001, the flight carried 58 passengers (including 5 hijackers) with 2 pilots and 4 flight attendants for a total of 64 people on board. Fifteen of the 22 first-class seats were occupied, 3 by hijackers. Forty-three of the 154 economy seats aboard were occupied, 2 by hijackers.

The 58 passengers represented a load factor of 33.0 percent of the plane's passenger capacity of 176. This figure is almost identical to the 32.8 percent average load factor for Flight 77 for Tuesdays in the three-month period prior to September 11. During that time, Tuesdays were the least traveled day for Flight 77.[233]

The Commission has found no ticketing, passenger occupancy, or financial evidence to indicate that the hijackers purchased additional seats (beyond the ones they actually used) in order to limit the number of passengers they would need to control during the operation.[234]

All the hijackers were assigned seats as they checked in and boarded the flight. According to American's records, "no documentation for a jump seat passenger was filed for Flight 77."[235] There is no evidence to suggest that any hijacker was admitted into the cockpit and permitted to sit in a jump seat prior to the takeover.

As on Flight 11, under American Airline policy in effect on 9/11, every crew member, including each of the flight attendants, had a key to the cockpit.[236]

Flight 77 was loaded with 49,900 pounds of fuel. The amount of fuel was below the average (59,400 pounds) for the flight during 2001.[237]

The Flight. Flight 77 pushed back from Dulles Gate D-26 at *8:09 A.M.*[238]

8:20 A.M. Flight 77 took off from Dulles.[239]

8:40 A.M. After proceeding normally through air space controlled by the Washington Air Traffic Control Center (Washington Center), Flight 77 was handed off to the Indianapolis Air Traffic Control Center (Indianapolis Center), with which it made routine radio contact.[240]

8:46 A.M. Flight 77 reached its assigned cruising altitude of 35,000 feet.[241] Cabin service would have begun, with Renee May likely working in the first-class galley between the cockpit and first class, Michele Heidenberger in the galley at the rear of the plane, Jennifer Lewis circulating in first-class, and Kenneth Lewis in the main cabin.[242]

8:51 A.M. Flight 77 transmitted its last routine radio communication, an acknowledgment from the cockpit crew to air traffic control's navigational instructions.[243]

The Hijacking. *Between 8:51 A.M. and 8:54 A.M.*, the hijackers began their takeover of the aircraft. They initiated and sustained their command of the aircraft using knives and box cutters (reported by one passenger) and moved all of the passengers (and possibly crew) to the rear of the aircraft (reported by one flight attendant and one passenger).

Neither of the firsthand accounts to come from Flight 77, from a flight attendant and from a passenger, mentioned any actual use of violence (e.g., stabbings) or the threat or use of either a bomb or Mace. Both of these witnesses began the flight in the first-class cabin.

8:54 A.M. The aircraft deviated from its assigned course by making a slight turn to the south.[244]

8:56 A.M. The transponder was switched off, and the aircraft was lost on primary radar.[245] The controller tracking Flight 77 continued to look for it. He searched along its projected flight path and the airspace to the southwest where it had started to turn. No primary targets appeared. He tried the radios, first calling the aircraft directly, then the airline. Again there was nothing. At this point, the Indianapolis Center controller had no knowledge of the situation in New York. He did not know that other aircraft had been hijacked. He believed Flight 77 had experienced serious electrical and/or mechanical failure, and was gone. At the same time, the Indianapolis Center made the first of ten unsuccessful attempts over the next six and a half minutes to contact the aircraft via radio.[246]

Shortly after *8:56 A.M.*, the Indianapolis Center controller reached out to controllers in other sectors at Indianapolis Center to advise them of the situation.[247] The controllers agreed to "sterilize the air space" along the flight's projected westerly route so that other planes would not be affected by Flight 77.[248] Two Indianapolis Center managers joined the controller responsible for Flight 77 in searching for the flight. The managers did not instruct other controllers at Indianapolis Center to turn on their primary radar coverage to join in the search for Flight 77.

By *8:58 A.M.*, FAA air traffic control contacted American to advise the airline that contact had been lost with Flight 77. Shortly thereafter, American Airlines dispatchers made the first of several unsuccessful attempts over three minutes to contact Flight 77, using the ACARS email system to advise the flight crew to contact the Indianapolis Air Traffic Control Center.[249]

9:00 A.M. American Airlines Executive Vice President Gerard Arpey learned that communication had been lost with Flight 77. He ordered all American Airlines flights in the Northeast that had not taken off to remain on the ground.[250]

Also at *9:00 A.M.*, Flight 77 headed east and shortly thereafter began to descend.[251]

9:02 A.M. The FAA's air traffic controllers told American Airlines that they did not know the location of Flight 77 and were unable to contact it.[252] *Three minutes later*, American began lockout procedures to protect information about the flight.[253]

9:05 A.M. Flight 77 re-emerged as a primary target on Indianapolis Center radar scopes, well east of its last known position.[254] However, the aircraft was not detected by air traffic controllers because they were searching along its projected flight path to the west and southwest.

At *approximately 9:07 A.M.*, Flight 77 leveled off at 25,000 feet and made a slight course change to the east-northeast.[255]

By *9:08 A.M.*, officials in American Airlines' SOC had concluded that the second aircraft to hit the World Trade Center might have been Flight 77.[256]

9:08 A.M. The FAA's Indianapolis Center contacted Air Force Search and Rescue in Langley, Virginia, to request that they be on the lookout for an accident involving Flight 77 because of the simultaneous loss of radio communications and all radar contact.[257]

9:09 A.M. Indianapolis Center called the FAA Great Lakes Regional Office to notify it of a possible accident involving American 77.[258]

At some time *between 9:00 A.M. and 9:10 A.M.*, an American Airlines air traffic control specialist at SOC who was in communication with the Herndon Command Center notified SOC air traffic control manager that he had learned United was "missing a plane." American headquarters extended its ground stop nationwide.[259]

9:11 A.M. Renee May, a flight attendant, attempted to call her parents but the call did not connect. A second call to the same number at *9:12 A.M.* did go through.[260] In the conversation, May told her mother that her flight was being hijacked by six individuals who had moved them—the mother was not sure whether her daughter meant all the passengers or just the crew—to the rear of the plane. May asked her mother to call American Airlines and make sure that they knew about the hijacking, giving her three phone numbers in Northern Virginia to call.

At some point *between 9:12 A.M. and the crash of Flight 77 into the Pentagon (9:37:46 A.M.)*, Renee May's parents reached an American Airlines employee at Reagan National Airport in Washington, D.C., giving her the information provided by their daughter, including her phone number on board and the flight number.[261] Initially, the American employee thought the Mays were talking about the aircraft that had crashed into the World Trade Center. May's mother reiterated that she was speaking of Flight 77, still in the air. At some point after completing the call, the American employee was told to evacuate the building. On her way out, she heard explosions from the direction of the Pentagon, though she was not sure that it was the crash of an aircraft. She informed a flight services manager at the airport about her conversation with May's parents.[262]

Around 9:15 A.M., after confirming that two airliners had struck the World Trade Center American ordered all of its airborne flights to land.[263]

9:16 A.M. An American Airlines air traffic control specialist phoned an official at the Herndon Command Center to inquire about the status of New York City air traffic. Over the course of this conversation, which lasted two and a half minutes, the specialist said that American "thought" Flight 11 had crashed into the World Trade Center. Flight 77, he said, was "missing." As he made his report, he received an update from American's SOC indicating that Flight 77 also might have crashed into the towers. He updated the ATC official but wondered how Flight 77 could have gotten to New York City. The ATC official replied that the second crash might not have been Flight 77 because "we [ATC] have another call sign" for that incident. At that point, though, the Herndon Command Center was not sure of the identity of either of the two crashed aircraft and provided no further information.[264]

At some point *between 9:16 A.M. and 9:26 A.M.*,[265] Barbara Olson, a Flight 77 passenger, called her husband, Ted Olson, the solicitor general of the United States. Olson spoke to his wife for about one minute before the call was cut off.[266] She reported that the flight had been hijacked and the hijackers were wielding knives and box cutters. She did not mention stabbing or slashing of the crew or passengers. The hijackers, she said, were not aware of her phone call. All of the passengers were in the back of the plane. Barbara Olson had been seated in first class.[267]

After this call, Ted Olson tried unsuccessfully to reach Attorney General John Ashcroft. He contacted the Department of Justice Command Center and requested that they send someone to his office.[268] He also told the Department of Justice Command Center that his wife's flight had been hijacked and gave them the flight number.

By no later than *9:18 A.M.*, FAA centers in Indianapolis, Cleveland, and Washington were aware that Flight 77 was missing and that two aircraft had struck the World Trade Center.[269]

By *9:20 A.M.*, Indianapolis Center learned that there were other hijacked aircraft in the system, and began to doubt its initial assumption that Flight 77 had crashed.[270] A discussion of this concern between the manager at Indianapolis and the Herndon Command Center prompted the Command Center to notify some FAA field facilities that Flight 77 was lost.

Between 9:20 A.M. and 9:31 A.M.,[271] Barbara Olson again called her husband. During their second conversation, she reported that the pilot had announced that the flight had been hijacked and she asked her husband what she should tell the captain to do. Ted Olson asked for her location. She said that the aircraft was flying over houses. Another passenger told her they were traveling northeast. Ted Olson informed his wife of the two previous hijackings and crashes, but she did not display signs of panic or indicate any awareness of an impending crash. The call abruptly ended.[272]

By *9:21 A.M.*, the Herndon Command Center, some FAA field facilities, and American Airlines had started to search for Flight 77. They feared it had been hijacked.[273]

9:21 A.M. Herndon Command Center advised a supervisor at the Dulles Terminal Radar Approach Control (TRACON) facility that the FAA had lost contact with Flight 77 and was trying to find the aircraft. Controllers at Dulles TRACON were advised that a commercial aircraft was missing and instructed to look for primary targets.[274]

9:24 A.M. The FAA's Great Lakes Regional Office notified the agency's headquarters in Washington, D.C., that Flight 77 might have been involved in an accident.[275]

9:25 A.M. Herndon Command Center advised FAA headquarters that Flight 77 was lost in Indianapolis Center's airspace. It could not be located on radar.[276]

Also at *9:25 A.M.* Ben Sliney, the Herndon Command Center National Operations Manager, ordered a "nationwide ground stop," which prevented any aircraft from taking off in the United States.[277]

9:29 A.M. Flight 77 was now flying at 7,000 feet and was approximately 38 miles west of the Pentagon.[278]

At or shortly after *9:32 A.M.*, controllers at the Dulles TRACON "observed a primary radar target tracking eastbound at a high rate of speed," and notified Reagan National Airport of the approaching aircraft. This was later determined to have been Flight 77.[279]

9:34 A.M. Flight 77 was 5 miles west-southwest of the Pentagon. It began a 330-degree right turn. At the end of the turn, the plane descended through 2,200 feet pointed toward the Pentagon and downtown Washington D.C.[280]

Also at *9:34 A.M.* NEADS Identification Technicians who, at 9:21 A.M., had been told by Boston Center that Flight 11 was still airborne and heading south, contacted the Operations Manager at Washington Center to provide an update on the evolving situation. In the course of the conversation, the Operations Manager informed NEADS that Flight 77 was lost.[281] He did not inform NEADS that it was hijacked because he did not know. This discussion was the first notice to the military that Flight 77 was missing, and it had come by chance.[282] If NEADS had not placed that call to Washington Center, the NEADS air defenders would have received no information whatsoever that Flight 77 was even missing.

Also at *9:34 A.M.*, an update by the American Airlines SOC indicated that Flights 11 and 77 had been the aircraft that crashed into the World Trade Center.[283]

At approximately *9:36 A.M.*, Reagan Airport controllers then vectored an unarmed National Guard C-130H cargo aircraft, which had just taken off en route to Minnesota, to identify and follow the primary target identified by Dulles TRACON. The C-130H pilot spotted it, identified it as a Boeing 757, and attempted to follow its path.[284]

9:36 A.M. The FAA's Boston Center – which had learned of the unidentified primary radar target tracking eastbound via an FAA conference call line – called NEADS and relayed the report of the aircraft closing in on Washington. The aircraft that still had not been linked with the missing Flight 77. Boston Center told NEADS: "Latest report. Aircraft VFR [Visual Flight Rules] six miles southeast of the White House…Six, southwest. Six, southwest of the White House, deviating away."[285] This startling news prompted the Mission Crew Commander at NEADS to order "AFIO" (Authorization for Interceptor Operations), which entailed taking immediate control of the Langley fighters from the FAA. He then ordered the fighters to proceed directly towards Washington DC: "Okay, we're going to turn it … crank it up…Run them to the White House."[286]

Shortly after *9:36 A.M.*, the Mission Crew Commander at NEADS discovered, to his surprise, that the Langley fighters were not headed north as the scramble order had instructed, but east over the ocean. His response was emotional, "I don't care how many windows you break," he said, "Damn it...Okay. Push them back."[287]

9:37:46 A.M., American Airlines Flight 77 crashed into the Pentagon. The aircraft was traveling at approximately 530 miles per hour on impact.[288] All on board were killed, along with 125 civilian and military personnel in the Pentagon.[289] The Langley fighters were approximately 150 miles away.

At approximately *9:38 A.M.*, the C-130H aircraft reported to Reagan Airport controllers that the aircraft it was attempting to follow crashed into the Pentagon.[290]

9:42 A.M. American's director of safety programs,[291] who happened to be in Washington, DC at the time, confirmed for American Airlines officials that "something has hit the Pentagon."[292]

Also at *9:42 A.M.,* the Herndon Command Center learned from news reports that a plane had struck the Pentagon. The Command Center's national operations manager, Ben Sliney, ordered all FAA facilities to instruct all aircraft to land at the nearest airport. This was an unprecedented order. The air traffic control system handled it with great skill, as about 4,500 commercial and general aviation aircraft soon landed without incident.[293]

9:45 A.M. An official at American headquarters called United headquarters to inform them that an aircraft had hit the Pentagon and that American believed it was a U.S. Airways turbojet.[294]

At approximately *10:00 A.M.*, the Langley fighters established a Combat Air Patrol (CAP) over Washington, DC.

By no later than 10:30 A.M., American confirmed that Flight 77 had crashed into the Pentagon.[295]

1.4 UNITED AIR LINES FLIGHT 93

Hijackers: Ziad Samir Jarrah (pilot); Saeed al Ghamdi; Ahmed al Nami; Ahmad al Haznawi.

Hijacker Weapon Purchases. Personal financial records do not reflect weapons purchases by any of the hijackers. However, the FBI recovered 14 knives or portions of knives, including a box cutter, at the Flight 93 crash site.

Hijacker Arrival at Airport and Check-in. At *7:03 A.M.*, Saeed al Ghamdi checked in at the United Air Lines ticket counter at Newark airport but checked no baggage. Ahmed al Nami checked two bags. At *7:24 A.M.*, Ahmad al Haznawi checked a single bag. Finally, at *7:39 A.M.*, Ziad Jarrah checked in at the UAL ticket counter; he did not have any luggage.[296]

Hijacker Prescreening. Only Ahmad al Haznawi was selected by CAPPS. His checked bag was screened for explosives and then loaded on the plane after confirmation that Haznawi was on board.[297]

Checkpoint Security Screening. Because Newark Airport, like Logan in Boston, did not use video cameras to monitor activities at security checkpoints, we could not establish with certainty how the five hijackers were processed when they passed through security screening.

To reach their departure gate, after checking in, the hijackers had to pass through a single checkpoint that serviced United Air Lines flights from the concourse from which Flight 93 departed. The checkpoint was the custodial responsibility of United Air Lines and operated under contract by Argenbright Security. The FAA interviewed each of the screeners on duty at the checkpoint, and none of them reported anything unusual or suspicious.[298]

Hijacker Boarding. At *7:39 A.M.*, Haznawi and Ghamdi boarded the aircraft. Haznawi sat in 6B (first class) and Ghamdi in 3D (first class). At *7:40 A.M.*, Nami boarded and sat in 3C (first class). At *7:48 A.M.*, Jarrah boarded and sat in 1B (first class).[299]

Flight Profile. In September 2001 and during certain other periods earlier in the year, United Air Lines Flight 93 provided daily, nonstop service from Newark (Liberty) International Airport in New Jersey to San Francisco International Airport.[300] On September 11, it was scheduled for an 8:00 A.M. departure.[301] The aircraft was a Boeing 757. Tail number N591UA.

The plane was piloted by Captain Jason Dahl and First Officer Lee Roy Homer. Five flight attendants provided cabin services:
- Chief flight attendant Deborah Welsh, assigned to seat seat J1 in first class;
- Sandra Bradshaw, assigned to seat J5 in coach;
- Wanda Green, assigned to seat J4 in first class;

- Lorraine Bay, assigned to seat J3 in coach; and
- CeeCee Lyles, assigned to seat J6 in coach.[302]

On September 11, 2001, the flight carried 37 passengers (including 4 hijackers) with two pilot and 5 flight attendants for a total of 44 people on board.

Ten passengers were seated in first class, including all four of the hijackers; the other 27 were in coach. There was no business class on Flight 93.[303]

The 37 passengers (including the four hijackers) represented a load factor of 20 percent of the plane's passenger capacity of 182. This figure is considerably below the 52 percent average load factor for Flight 93 for Tuesdays in the three-month period prior to September 11; indeed, it represents the lowest load factor among these flights during that time span.[304] In this three-month period, Tuesdays were the least traveled day for Flight 93.[305]

There is no evidence that Flight 93 hijackers purchased additional tickets for the flight beyond the ones they used.[306] As on the other three flights, all the hijackers were accounted for in checking in and boarding the flight, and according to United's records, no paperwork was filed to indicate that any cockpit jump seat was occupied by anyone other than flight crew.[307] Thus, there is no evidence to suggest that any hijacker was admitted into the cockpit and permitted to sit in a jump seat prior to the takeover.

On Flight 93, the cockpit key was kept in a storage compartment in the front of the airplane. It was United Air Lines' policy at the time not to provide individual flight attendants with a key to the cockpit door.[308]

Flight 93 was loaded with 48,700 pounds of fuel, which was a normal amount for the flight.[309]

The Flight. At *8:00 A.M.*, Flight 93 pushed back from gate 17A at Newark Airport and taxied to its departure area. Because of typical local air traffic congestion, the flight was delayed 42 minutes.[310] It remained in a holding status until *8:42 A.M.*, when it departed.[311]

9:02 A.M. The flight reached its cruising altitude of 35,000 feet.[312] Under normal circumstances, the pilot would turn off the seatbelt sign once the aircraft reached cruising altitude, usually about 20 minutes into the flight.[313]

Upon commencement of cabin service, it is likely that flight attendants Deborah Welsh and Wanda Green would have worked in first class, while Lorraine Bay, CeeCee Lyles, and Sandra Bradshaw would have been in coach.[314]

Beginning at *9:03 A.M.*, several dispatchers sent ACARS messages to several United flights indicating that aircraft had crashed into the World Trade Center. These messages provided no details or warnings, however.

9:08 A.M. Ballinger, the United flight dispatcher, began to send out ACARS messages notifying United's transcontinental flights that had not yet taken off that a ground stop had been ordered for commercial aircraft in the New York area.[315]

At *9:19 A.M.*, shortly after he became aware of the second crash into the World Trade Center, Ballinger began sending cockpit warnings via text messages to the 16 transcontinental flights under his jurisdiction, including Flight 93. The messages were sent out in groups; Flight 93 received its message several minutes later.[316] This represented the first occasion on 9/11 when either American or United sent out such a warning to their airborne aircraft.

9:21 A.M. Ballinger received a routine ACARS message from the aircraft: "Good mornin' . . . Nice clb [climb] outta EWR [Newark airport] after a nice tour of the apt [apartment] courts y [and] grnd cntrl. 20 N EWC At 350 occl [occasional] lt [light] chop. Wind 290/50 ain't helping. J." The last notation was presumably the signature for Captain Jason Dahl, who was personally acquainted with the dispatcher.[317]

Also at *9:21 A.M.*, the UAL air traffic control coordinator sent out a message to UAL dispatchers: "There may be Addnl hijackings in progress. You may want to advise your flts to stay on alert and shut down all cockpit access Inflt. [inflight] Sandy per Mgmt."[318]

9:22 A.M. An ACARS text message was sent to First Officer LeRoy Homer at the request of his wife, who was concerned about her husband after hearing about the attacks on the World Trade Center.[319]

9:23 A.M. Ballinger sent an ACARS message to Flight 93's flight deck: "Beware any cockpit intrusion—Two a/c [aircraft] hit World Trade Center." This was the same message the dispatcher had begun transmitting to the airline's transcontinental flights at 9:19 A.M. in response to information United headquarters had received about the hijacking of Flight 175 and the events at the World Trade Center.[320]

After reporting experiencing some "light chop" at 35,000 feet, Flight 93 was handed off to Cleveland Air Traffic Control Center (Cleveland Center).[321] Several seconds later, Flight 93 established radio contact with Cleveland Center: "Morning Cleveland, United Ninety-three with you at, three-five-oh (35,000 feet), intermittent light chop."[322] The controller did not respond to this initial transmission as he had sixteen flights under his control, and was issuing new routes to several aircraft based upon the decisions in New York and Boston to ground-stop all aircraft.[323]

9:25 A.M. Flight 93 again radioed Cleveland Center, checking in at 35,000 feet. The controller replied, "United ninety-three, Cleveland, roger."[324]

At approximately *9:25 A.M.*, FAA headquarters requested the Herndon Command Center to "get an awareness up to all the traffic management coordinators or the traffic management units to report any unusual circumstances direct to the Command Center of loss of identification, or any radio, uh, any unusual radio transmissions."[325]

9:26 A.M. The Cleveland controller handling Flight 93 engaged in conversations with several aircraft about the evolving "serious" situation in New York City and the prospects for flights to be allowed to land in Philadelphia.[326]

Also at *9:26 A.M.*, Flight 93 asked for confirmation of the ACARS message sent at *9:23 A.M.* and received in the cockpit at *9:24 A.M.* "Ed cofirm latest mssg plz—Jason."[327]

9:27 A.M. The Flight 93 flight crew responded to routine radio contact from the FAA air traffic control center in Cleveland. This was the last communication from the flight's cockpit crew.[328]

The Hijacking. At *9:28 A.M.*, the hijackers began their takeover of the aircraft. They wielded knives (reported by at least five callers); engaged in violence, including stabbing (reported by at least four callers and indicated by the sounds of the cockpit struggle transmitted over the radio); relocated the passengers to the back of the plane (reported by at least two callers); threatened use of a bomb, either real or fake (reported by at least three callers); and engaged in deception about their intentions (as indicated by the hijacker's radio transmission received by FAA air traffic control).

9:28 A.M. The aircraft was traveling 35,000 feet above eastern Ohio. It suddenly began to descend, dropping 685 feet over the next half minute. Eleven seconds into the descent, Cleveland Center overheard the first of two radio transmissions from the Flight 93 cockpit. The captain or first officer declared "Mayday" amid sounds of a physical struggle in the cockpit. [329] While the controller did not understand what was said, he began to try to identify the possible source of the transmissions and noticed Flight 93's rapid descent. The Cleveland controller replied over the radio: "Somebody call Cleveland?"[330] There was no reply.

The second radio transmission, 35 seconds later, indicated that the clash was still in progress. The captain or first officer shouted: "Hey get out of here—get out of here—get out of here."[331] The screaming in this second radio transmission was heard by the Cleveland controller responsible for Flight 93. [332]

While this appears to show the exact time that the hijackers invaded the cockpit, we have found no conclusive evidence to indicate precisely when the terrorists took over the main cabin or moved passengers seated in the first-class cabin back to coach—a tactic reported by several passengers during phone calls to parties on the ground. We believe that it is most likely that the four hijackers breached the cockpit at the same time that they took over the front of the plane and pushed passengers back into the coach cabin. Taking over the cabin first would likely have alerted the flight deck to a problem, and waiting to control or move passengers once the cockpit was secured would have increased the risk of passenger intervention, particularly if the passengers had witnessed the hijackers displacing the crew from the controls.

The terrorists who hijacked the three other commercial flights on 9/11 operated in five-man teams. They initiated their cockpit takeover operations within 30 minutes of takeoff, most likely after the seatbelt sign had been turned off and the flight attendants were beginning cabin service. On Flight 93, however, there were only four hijackers. They waited approximately 46 minutes after takeoff to begin their assault. We were unable to determine why they waited so long.

At approximately *9:30 A.M.*, air traffic control informed United headquarters that Flight 93 was not responding to attempted radio contacts.[333]

9:30 A.M. The Cleveland controller began to poll the other flights on his frequency to determine if they heard the screaming; several said they had.[334]

At approximately *9:31 A.M.*, the National Traffic Management Officer on duty at the Herndon Command Center relayed to air traffic control facilities (including Cleveland Center) the request from FAA Headquarters to report any unusual circumstances to the Command Center.

9:31 A.M. United dispatchers were advised by United headquarters officials that there was a potential problem with Flight 93. The airline's air traffic control coordinator and another employee each sent an ACARS message to the flight asking it to establish radio contact with air traffic control. There was no response to these or any subsequent ACARS messages.[335]

9:32 A.M.[336] The Cleveland controller overheard a transmission of threatening language from Flight 93: "Ladies and Gentlemen: Here the captain, please sit down keep remaining sitting. We have a bomb on board. So, sit." The cockpit voice recording also indicates that a woman, most likely a flight attendant, was being held captive in the cockpit. Moments after hearing the threatening transmission from Flight 93, Cleveland Center reported to the Herndon Command Center that the flight may have a bomb on board. [337]

Also at *9:32 A.M.*, Ballinger began sending a new ACARS message ("High security alert. Secure cockpit.") to his flights. This communication was transmitted to Flight 93 at *9:33 A.M.*[338]

9:34 A.M. Herndon Command Center relayed the reports it had received on Flight 93 to FAA headquarters.

Between *9:34 A.M.* and *9:38 A.M.*, the Cleveland controller observed Flight 93 climbing to 40,700 feet and immediately moved several aircraft out of its way. The controller continued to try to contact Flight 93, and asked whether the pilot could confirm that he had been hijacked.[339] There was no response. As the flight continued to climb, the controller moved decisively to clear the other flights in his sector from Flight 93's path.

Additionally, between *9:34 A.M.* and *10:08 A.M.*, a Herndon Command Center facility manager provided several updates to the FAA Deputy Administrator and other executives at the agency's headquarters as Flight 93 approached the Washington, DC area.

At approximately *9:36 A.M.*, Cleveland Center advised the Herndon Command Center that they were still tracking Flight 93 and inquired specifically whether someone had requested the military to launch fighter aircraft to intercept the flight. They added that they were prepared to contact a nearby military base to request fighter aircraft assistance. The Command Center told Cleveland Center that FAA personnel above them in the chain of command had to make the decision to request military assistance.[340]

9:36 A.M.[341] A flight attendant contacted the United Air Lines maintenance facility in San Francisco. (The same facility that the flight attendant aboard United 175 had called to report the hijacking of that flight). The San Francisco phone number is one that flight crews know to call in order to report mechanical and systems problems, obtain advice on troubleshooting, and request maintenance while in flight. Her call was first answered by a United maintenance employee and was subsequently taken over by a manager at the facility. The manager described the flight attendant as "shockingly calm." The flight attendant, reporting from the back of the plane, told the maintenance employees that hijackers were in the cabin behind the first-class curtain and in the cockpit. They had announced they had a bomb on the plane. The hijackers had pulled a knife. They had killed a flight attendant. The manager reported the emergency to his supervisor, who passed the information to the United Air Lines crisis center. The manager then instructed the air phone operator to try and reestablish contact with the plane, but the effort was unsuccessful.[342]

This began a series of calls from the flight that provided vital information both to the ground and to the passengers. At least two callers from the flight reported that the hijackers knew that passengers were making calls but did not seem to care. The cockpit voice recorder does not provide evidence of whether Jarrah, the pilot, was aware of these calls or indicate why the hijackers allowed them to take place.

At least ten passengers and two crew members shared vital information with family, friends, colleagues, or others on the ground, including:[343] the plane had been hijacked; the hijackers wielded knives; the hijackers had entered the cockpit; the hijackers had a bomb; hijackers wore red bandanas; passengers were forced to the back of the aircraft; a passenger had been stabbed (reported by at least two callers), and the victim had died (reported by one); two individuals were lying on the floor of the aircraft injured or dead, possibly the captain and first officer; and a flight attendant had been killed.

The calls provided information very similar to that received from the other hijacked aircraft, including the hijackers' use of knives, violence, the threat of a bomb, relocation of passengers to the back of the aircraft and cockpit intrusion. There is, of course, no means of ascertaining the location of callers who were using cellular phones inside the aircraft. However, calls were made from air phones installed in the last nine rows of the aircraft. The air phone system aboard the flight limited to eight the number of calls that could be made at one time.[344]

9:36 A.M. Flight 93 reversed course and headed east. The hijackers struggled to control a defiant hostage, most likely a flight attendant in the cockpit, eventually killing or otherwise silencing her.[345]

Also at *9:36 A.M.*, the United manager of flight dispatch operations advised Ballinger that Flight 93 was "off track, heading for D.C."[346] By this point, United headquarters believed the aircraft had been hijacked.[347] Another UAL dispatcher, assisting Ballinger, sent an ACARS message to Flight 93, asking, "How's the wx.(?) Can dispatch be of any assistance?"[348]

9:37 A.M. A passenger called his mother. He told her that he was on United Air Lines Flight 93 and it was being hijacked; that the plane had been taken over by three guys, and that they said they have a bomb.[349]

One of the key mysteries associated with Flight 93 is that at least five passengers described the presence of three hijackers on the plane, rather than the four who were actually aboard.[350] Some have wondered whether such reporting might suggest that one of the hijackers was positioned in the cockpit from the outset of the flight and remained unseen by the passengers. FAA rules allowed commercial air carriers to permit properly credentialed and approved individuals, usually air carrier personnel such as pilots or operational personnel, to ride in the cockpit jump seat (located directly behind the pilot and first officer).[351]

We cannot know with certainty whether a hijacker had gained access to the cockpit prior to the violent takeover of the aircraft, but we believe it unlikely that a hijacker occupied the jump seat prior to the takeover. All four of Flight 93's hijackers were issued tickets for seats in the first-class cabin and used their tickets to enter the aircraft. None of the paperwork required by United Air Lines to authorize a jump seat occupant for Flight 93 had been filed.[352]

One of the passengers who contacted a party on the ground reported that ten first-class passengers were on the flight. This figure is consistent with the four terrorists and the six nonhijackers who boarded the aircraft holding tickets for first-class seats.[353]

Five of the six nonhijacker passengers in first-class seats contacted the ground by phone to share information about the hijacking.[354] These individuals would have been best positioned to observe whether a passenger among them had gotten up during the flight and entered the cockpit before the violent takeover of the aircraft. None of the callers reported the occurrence of such an event. Moreover, the pilot and co-pilot of Flight 93 were experienced, well-regarded professionals, unlikely to allow any observer into the cockpit, pre- or post-takeoff, who had not obtained the permission needed for such privileges.[355]

Finally, the pilot hijacker was the critical link in the terrorist operation. It is reasonable to expect that the hijackers would take all precautions necessary to protect the one among them required to fly the plane. Given their unwillingness to risk his death or injury during the takeover of the aircraft, it made operational sense for the pilot hijacker to remain seated and inconspicuous until he was needed, most likely after the cockpit had been seized.

9:37 A.M. A passenger made the first of several calls to his wife. During these calls, he reported that: the plane had been hijacked; the hijackers claimed to have a bomb; and a passenger had been knifed. He thought one of them had a gun. He didn't think they had a bomb because he couldn't see it. The passenger asked his wife if she had heard about any other planes. His wife informed him about the World Trade Center. The passenger asked if the planes that crashed into the towers were commercial.

In one of the later calls to his wife, the passenger reported that the passenger that had been knifed had died; that "they" were in the cockpit; and that a group of passengers were getting ready to do something.[356]

Between *9:37 A.M. and 9:57 A.M.*, a passenger was in contact his wife and his mother-in-law, who immediately called 911 on her cell phone. The passenger told his family that Flight 93 had been hijacked by three "Iranian-looking" males, with dark skin and bandanas; one of the males stated that he was in possession of a bomb in a red box and one was armed with a knife; the captain had not made any announcements; the hijackers had herded the passengers into the rear of the plane; the three hijackers had entered the cockpit. He and other passengers were contemplating "rushing" the hijackers; he did not observe any guns in the possession of the hijackers; the passengers were voting on whether to storm the cockpit and retake control of the airplane.[357]

9:39 A.M. The Cleveland Center controller overheard the following radio transmission from Flight 93: "Uh, is the captain. Would like you all to remain seated. There is a bomb on board and are going back to the airport, and to have our demands [unintelligible]. Please remain quiet."[358]

It is quite possible Jarrah knew that the attacks on the World Trade Center had succeeded. Text messages sent by United Air Lines to the cockpits of its transcontinental flights, including Flight 93, warned of possible cockpit intrusion and told of the attacks in New York.[359] But even if Jarrah had not read these messages, he must have understood, given Flight 93's tardy departure from Newark, that the attacks on the World Trade Center would already have unfolded. If he knew that the passengers were making calls, he must have failed to understand that they were sure to learn of the New York attacks and would immediately see through his ruse that the aircraft was simply "returning to the airport."

9:39 A.M. A passenger called her husband and left a message that the flight had been hijacked.[360]

9:40 A.M. The United air traffic control coordinator for West Coast flights notified the Herndon Command Center that Flight 93 was not responding to the airline's attempts to contact it. It was also off course.[361]

9:40 A.M. As he continued to update his 9:32 A.M. "secure cockpit" message to his flights, Ballinger sent the following ACARS transmission to Flight 93: "High security alert. Secure cockpit. Two airliner hit NY Trade Center. And 1 aircraft in IAD missing. And one in EWR missing . . . too. UAL 175/93 missing." At *9:41 A.M.,* the dispatcher sent the same message to Flight 93, with the following addition at the end: "UAL 175/93 found."[362]

9:41 A.M. The transponder on the plane was turned off.[363] The Cleveland controller located the aircraft on primary radar, and matched his reading with visual sightings from other aircraft to follow the Flight 93 as it turned east and, ultimately, south.[364]

9:41 A.M. The Herndon Command Center notified headquarters that Flight 93 had reversed course from its intended flight path and was descending and heading eastbound.[365]

9:42 A.M. While Command Center employees informed FAA field facilities of the order to land all aircraft, one of the Command Center managers continued to give FAA headquarters several updates on the progress and location of Flight 93.

9:43 A.M. A passenger contacted his father to inform him that his flight had been hijacked.[366]

9:44 A.M. A passenger contacted GTE air phone operators. His connection lasted for the remainder of the flight. He noted the following: The flight had been hijacked, and the captain and first officer were lying on the floor of the first-class cabin and were injured or possibly dead. One of the hijackers had a red belt with a bomb strapped to his waist. Two of the hijackers, who had knives, entered the cockpit and closed the door behind them. At some point the hijackers closed the curtain between first class and coach so that passengers could not see into first class; those in the rear of the plane were not being monitored by the hijackers. The plane was going up and down and had turned or changed direction. He and some other passengers were planning something and he was going to put the phone down.

At some point *between 9:45 A.M. and 9:50 A.M.*, the United station operations control manager received a report from the San Francisco maintenance office about the call from the Flight 93 flight attendant advising that the aircraft had been hijacked. He immediately passed this information on to Ballinger and the crisis center. He also attempted to initiate a lockout of Flight 93. The United computer system, however, was not set up at that time to deal with two such procedures simultaneously[367]—and United had already effected a lockout of Flight 175.

9:46 A.M. A United employee at the maintenance facility in San Francisco sent the following ACARS message to Flight 93: "Heard report of incident. Plz confirm all is normal."

Also at *9:46 A.M.*, a passenger contacted her sister and left a voice mail message: her flight had been hijacked by terrorists and they said they had a bomb; she knew that terrorists had already flown a couple of planes into the World Trade Center; it looked like they were going to take this one down as well.[368]

Also at *9:46 A.M.* the Herndon Command Center updated FAA headquarters that Flight 93 was tracking towards Washington, DC and was 29 minutes away from the city.[369]

9:48 A.M. A flight attendant called her husband, using an air phone, and left a message: the aircraft had been hijacked; there were three hijackers; the plane had turned around; and she'd heard that planes had flown into the World Trade Center.[370]

9:49 A.M. A passenger called her boyfriend: her plane was hijacked; the hijackers had cut two passengers' throats; she knew that two planes had crashed into the WTC.[371]

9:49 A.M. Thirteen minutes after initially questioned by Cleveland Center about getting military help, Herndon Command Center suggested to FAA headquarters that someone should decide whether to request military assistance.[372]

9:50 A.M. Ballinger continued to send ACARS messages to the airline's transcontinental flights, including Flight 93, advising them to "land ASP at nearest UAL airport—ORD terrorist. No one in to cockpit—Land asp." He sent a second message advising the aircraft to land anywhere as soon as possible. He sent the same message again one minute later.[373]

9:50 A.M. A flight attendant called her husband to report the emergency. The call lasted approximately eight minutes. She seemed to be aware of the other hijackings that morning. Her husband told her he was watching the television and confirmed to her that two planes had crashed into the World Trade Center. The flight attendant told her husband that the plane had been hijacked by three men. She said the hijackers were carrying knives and had put on red headbands as they were hijacking the plane. She said that the passengers had been moved to the rear of the plane and that the hijackers were up front. She said that she thought the plane may have been over the Mississippi because they were passing over a large river. She said that the passengers were discussing how to overpower the hijackers, including preparing hot water to throw on the hijackers and then to rush them.

9:53 A.M., FAA headquarters informed Herndon Command Center that the Deputy Director for Air Traffic Services was talking to Deputy Administrator Monte Belger about scrambling aircraft.[374]

9:54 A.M. A passenger phoned her stepmother and told her that the plane had been hijacked. The call lasted approximately four and a half minutes. Before hanging up, the passenger said she had to go because they were trying to break into the cockpit.[375]

9:55 A.M. The pilot hijacker, presumably Jarrah, dialed into the flight computer the navigational code for Reagan National Airport, in order to fly the aircraft toward Washington, D.C.[376]

An air phone operator, who had been on the line with a passenger since 9:44 A.M, heard someone say: "Are you guys ready? Okay! Let's roll!" Shortly thereafter she heard screaming followed by silence.[377]

9:56 A.M. Herndon Command Center informed FAA headquarters they lost track of Flight 93 over the Pittsburgh area.[378] Within seconds, the Command Center relocated Flight 93 and informed headquarters.

The Flight attendant who had called her husband at **9:50 A.M.** ended her phone call. She said, "Everyone is running up to first class. I've got to go. Bye." She hung up the phone.[379]

9:57 A.M. The passengers began their revolt. The sounds of the passenger uprising captured by the cockpit voice recorder suggest that a great struggle began at the back of the airplane and progressed toward the front. The evidence from the CVR indicates that the struggle continued for the duration of the flight.[380]

9:58 A.M. A passenger called 911 in Westmoreland County, Pennsylvania, from his cell phone to report a hijacking in progress.[381]

Also at **9:58 A.M.**, a flight attendant contacted her husband by cell phone. She told him again that the plane had been hijacked and they were forcing their way into the cockpit.[382]

In response to the passenger revolt, Jarrah immediately began to roll the airplane to the left and right, attempting to knock the passengers off balance. At **9:58:57**, Jarrah told another hijacker in the cockpit to block the door. Jarrah continued to roll the airplane sharply left and right, but the assault continued.

At **9:59:52**, Jarrah changed tactics and pitched the nose of the airplane up and down to disrupt the assault. The recorder captured the sounds of loud thumps, crashes, shouts, and breaking glasses and plates. At **10:00:03**, Jarrah stabilized the airplane.[383]

Five seconds later, Jarrah asked, "Is that it? Shall we finish it off?" A hijacker responded, "No. Not yet. When they all come, we finish it off." The sounds of fighting continued outside the cockpit. Again, Jarrah pitched the nose of the aircraft up and down. At **10:00:26**, a passenger in the background said, "In the cockpit. If we don't we'll die!" Sixteen seconds later, a passenger yelled "Roll it!"

At this same time, Herndon Command Center advised FAA headquarters that "United ninety three was spotted by a VFR at eight thousand feet, eleven, eleven miles south of Indianhead, just north of Cumberland, Maryland.[384]

At about *10:01 A.M.*, Jarrah stopped his violent maneuvers and said, "Allah is the greatest! Allah is the greatest!" He then asked another hijacker in the cockpit, "Is that it? I mean, shall we put it down?" to which the other replied, "Yes, put it in it, and pull it down."[385]

At *10:01 A.M.*, two minutes before Flight 93 crashed, Command Center updated FAA headquarters that the flight was "rocking its wings."[386]

The passengers continued their assault and at *10:02:23*, a hijacker said, "Pull it down! Pull it down!" The hijackers remained at the controls but must have judged that the passengers were only seconds from overcoming them. The airplane headed down; the control wheel was turned hard to the right. The airplane rolled onto its back, and one of the hijackers began shouting "Allah is the greatest. Allah is the greatest."[387]

10:03:11 A.M. With the sounds of the passenger counterattack continuing, Flight 93 crashed into an empty field in Shanksville, Pennsylvania, at 580 miles per hour, about 20 minutes' flying time from Washington, D.C.[388]

10:07 A.M. Unaware that the aircraft had already crashed, Cleveland Center notified NEADS that Flight 93 had a bomb onboard and passed them the aircraft's last known latitude and longitude. NEADS was never able to locate Flight 93 on radar because it had already crashed. The call was the first notification the military – at any level – received about Flight 93.[389] No one from FAA headquarters, which was informed of the hijacking at 9:34 A.M., requested military assistance

regarding Flight 93. In fact, the executive level managers at FAA headquarters did not forward to the military any of the information they received from Herndon Command Center regarding Flight 93.[390]

10:10 A.M. Ballinger sent an ACARS message to Flight 93: "Don't divert to DC. Not an option." He sent the same message again one minute later.

Also at *10:10 A.M.*, when the information that Flight 93 had turned off its transponder and had a potential bomb on board reached the mission crew commander, he was dealing with the arrival of the Langley fighters over Washington DC and what their orders were with respect to potential targets. While NEADS searched for the radar track on Flight 93, the Mission Crew Commander instructed his Weapons Director on the current rules of engagement (ROE) for the fighters, stating that they did not have clearance (permission) to shoot down targets and that their tasking was to identify aircraft by type and tail number.[391]

At approximately *10:11 A.M.*, as the news of a bomb on board Flight 93 spread throughout the floor, the Mission Crew Commander tried to locate fighter assets to scramble toward the plane. He established contact with an Air National Guard Unit in Syracuse, New York to expedite launching aircraft to respond to Flight 93. The Syracuse unit reported that it would be able to launch fighters with loaded guns (no missiles) in "approximately 15 minutes."[392]

10:13 A.M. The Herndon Command Center advised FAA headquarters of its conclusion that Flight 93 had crashed.[393]

10:15 A.M. NEADS contacted Washington Center to provide them with an update on the situation with Flight 93, only to be informed by the center that Flight 93 had crashed.[394] By this same time, United headquarters had confirmed that an aircraft had crashed near Johnstown, Pennsylvania, and believed that this was Flight 93.[395]

10:17 A.M. An operational alert message was sent out to United Air Lines personnel from Andy Studdert: "UAL 93-11 EWR-SFO has been involved in an accident. Crisis Center has been activated."[396]

10:27 A.M. United Air Lines advised American Airlines of the crash of Flight 93.[397]

10:31 A.M. NEADS received its first official ROE for their fighters (via a NORAD instant messaging system) stating that the Vice President had authorized the military to shoot down tracks that did not respond to their direction.[398] The NEADS air defenders expressed considerable confusion over the nature and effect of this specific ROE in interviews with Commission staff.[399] Indeed, Colonel Marr indicated to staff that he actually believes he withheld the ROE from the NEADS floor for several minutes because he was unsure of its ramifications,[400] while both the Mission Crew Commander and the Weapons Director indicated that they withheld the order from the pilots flying Combat Air Patrol over Washington, DC and New York City because they were unsure how the pilots would or should proceed with such guidance.[401]

1.5 HIJACKER TACTICS

Flight Selection. The hijackers strategically planned the flights they chose—early morning departures from East Coast airports aboard large Boeing 757 and 767 for which they had trained. The planes carried large amounts of fuel for their transcontinental flights, maximizing the destructive power of the crash.

Ticket Purchase and seating. Each of the hijackers purchased a ticket between mid- and late August. There is no evidence to suggest that the hijackers or their associates purchased unused tickets for the hijacked flights. The seats selected by each hijacker team appear to have been determined by aircraft type. The Boeing 757 was a single-aisle plane; the Boeing 767 had two aisles. Thus for Flights 77 and 93 (both 757s), the probable hijacker pilot was seated in the very front of the plane, a position that gave him ready access to the cockpit. The other hijackers were seated close behind in first class (or, in the case of two hijackers on Flight 77, in the forward part of coach), covering both sides of the aisle. For the twin-aisled Flights 11 and 175, a layout that offered more operational maneuverability, the hijacker pilot sat in business class with accomplices both in front in first class and just behind, covering both aisles. The seating arrangements chosen by the hijackers facilitated the isolation of the front of the aircraft and the hijacker pilot's entry into the cockpit. [402]

Cockpit Access. Exactly how the hijackers gained access to the cockpit is not known. The strength of the cockpit doors in use on 9/11 would not have precluded forced entry.[403] However, cockpit keys were available aboard the aircraft.[404] On September 11, 2001, a single key fit the cockpit doors of all Boeing 757 and 767 aircraft. While the hijacking response doctrine, known as the commercial aviation community's "Common Strategy," taught the flight crew to try to keep hijackers out of the cockpit, it above all urged nonconfrontation and cooperation.[405] There is no way to know whether the terrorists had access to a key; but if not, access to the cockpit could be gained by luring the pilots out of the cockpit, threatening violence, or forcing the door open. There was no evidence to suggest any of the hijackers sat in a jump seat in the cockpit. Each of the hijackers had an assigned seat and appears to have used it.[406]

Weapons and Tactics. The hijackers likely gained control of the forward section of the cabin after the aircraft's seatbelt sign was turned off, the flight attendants had begun cabin service, and passengers were allowed to begin to move around the cabin.[407] The hijackers took over the aircraft by force or threat of force, as reported on all four flights.

Records of purchases by the hijackers, as well as evidence discovered at the crash sites (primarily the site of Flight 93), indicate that the primary weapons of choice were knives with a blade less than 4 inches long.[408] The use of knives was cited on all four flights by flight crew and passengers. Box cutters were specifically indicated only in one report from Flight 77. A box cutter–type implement, along with a variety of short-bladed knives, was found at the crash site of Flight 93.

The hijackers gained access to the cockpit and sealed off the front of the aircraft from the passengers and cabin crew, moving them to the back of the aircraft. This was reported, with slight variation, on all four flights. Reports from two of the hijacked aircraft (Flights 11 and 175) indicated the presence of Mace in the cabin. Both Mace and other irritants such as pepper spray were items specifically prohibited under FAA rules.

We believe the terrorists created a "sterile" area around the cockpit by isolating the passengers and attempting to keep them away from the forward cabin. The hijackers used the threat of bombs to frighten and control the passengers. This was reported on all flights except Flight 77. The hijackers also used announcements on Flight 11 and Flight 93 that the aircraft was returning to the airport to make passengers believe they were in no immediate danger if they cooperated.

Initially, these tactics, techniques, and communications resembled those of a traditional hijacking for the purpose of taking hostages or transportation. This was the scenario that the "Common Strategy" was designed to address.

As the hijackings progressed, however, there was evidence of growing awareness on board the aircraft that something beyond a traditional hijacking was under way. Callers from both Flights 11 and 175 noted early in the process very erratic flying patterns and talked about the possibility that the hijackers were piloting the aircraft. One Flight 175 passenger predicted the hijackers intended to fly the aircraft into a building. Another said the passengers were considering storming the cockpit.

Later, well into the hijacking of Flight 77, at least one passenger was told that two planes had crashed into the World Trade Center. In the case of Flight 93, the growing awareness among the passengers and crew of what had already occurred on other flights spurred a revolt.

Pilot Training. To successfully carry out the 9/11 attacks, at least one member of the team had to be able to pilot the plane, navigate it to the desired location, and direct it into the intended target. These tasks required adequate training and preparation.

FAA and FBI records show that 4 of the 19 hijackers, one aboard each flight, received flight training, possessed FAA certificates as qualified pilots and honed their skills at flight simulator facilities.[409] FAA certification required that a candidate complete a certain amount of flight training and pass both a written exam and a practical skills test.[410] Each of the four pilots received flight training in the United States, which is recognized as having one of the world's most advanced pilot training education and certification systems in the world; thus many pilots from many nations train here.[411]

Of the five hijackers on Flight 11, only Mohamed Atta held a certificate from the FAA as a qualified private and commercial pilot, including a rating in operating multi-engine aircraft. Atta received his commercial pilot certificate in December 2000.[412] He also received Boeing flight simulator training.

According to experts consulted by Commission staff, the simulator familiarized a pilot with the cockpit controls and the proper operation of the Boeing 757 and 767. It gave the pilot the operational proficiency, "feel," and confidence necessary to fly the aircraft. It was essential training for the hijacker pilots.[413]

Knowledge of the aircraft, including its flight management system computer and autopilot function, could be gained through simulator training, the operational manual (which was widely available), and flight simulator software sold by many public outlets.[414] Flight manuals and instruction videotapes were found among the belongings left behind by the hijackers.

Of the five hijackers aboard Flight 175, only Marwan al Shehhi held an FAA pilot certification. Shehhi earned his commercial pilot certificate in December 2000, on the same day and at the same school as Atta. He also received Boeing flight simulator training.[415]

Of the five hijackers aboard Flight 77, Hani Hanjour alone had completed flight training. He received his commercial multi-engine pilot certificate from the FAA in April 1999. He had extensive flight training in the United States, and was perhaps the most experienced and highly trained pilot among the 9/11 hijackers.[416] The Pentagon, his target, was particularly difficult to hit because of its low profile.

Ziad Jarrah was the only one of the four hijackers aboard Flight 93 with flight training and FAA pilot certification. Jarrah was awarded his private pilot certificate from the FAA in November 2000. He also received Boeing flight simulator training. Jarrah had logged only 100 flight hours, and did not possess a commercial pilot certificate or multi-engine rating.[417]

Flying the Aircraft. Their training enabled the pilots to hit their intended targets. The onboard Flight Management System in use could be programmed in such a way that it would navigate the aircraft automatically to a location as precise as a building, at a speed and altitude of the hijacker's choosing, provided the hijackers possessed the precise positioning data necessary.[418] The "black box" flight data recorders recovered from Flight 93 and Flight 77 indicate that the hijacker pilots used navigational codes for the Washington, D.C., area. Financial records indicate that Jarrah, the hijacker pilot of Flight 93, had purchased a global positioning satellite system.[419] He had attempted to buy four GPS units, but only one was available.

Whether the hijackers flew the aircraft manually, engaged the Flight Management System to take them to a programmed destination, or employed some combination of both methods, experts consulted by the Commission staff believe their training and experience adequately prepared them to complete the mission.[420]

SUMMARY TABLES

Table 1: Hijack Times and FAA Awareness of Hijack

Flight	Time of Impact	Hijack Time*	Time of FAA Awareness of Hijack	Time Between Hijacking and FAA Awareness
AA11	8:46:40	8:14–8:20	8:25	5–11 min
UA175	9:03:11	8:42–8:46	8:55	9–13 min
AA77	9:37:46	8:51–8:54	9:24**	30–33 min
UA93	10:03:11	9:28	9:28	0 min

*Estimated

**Between 8:56 and 9:09, the relevant FAA center believed AA77
had crashed. Between 9:09 and 9:21, based on the events in
New York, information from American Airlines, and the inability
to confirm the crash on the ground, the FAA began to believe
that AA77 might also be hijacked. By 9:24, this belief was communicated to FAA headquarters.

Table 2: FAA Awareness of Hijack and FAA Warning to the Military

Flight	Time of Impact	Time of FAA Awareness of Hijack	Time of FAA Warning to Military	Time Between FAA Awareness and Warning to Military
AA11	8:46:40	8:25	8:38	13 min
UA175	9:03:11	8:55	9:03	8 min
AA77	9:37:46	9:24**	no warning**	N/A**
UA93	10:03:11	9:28	10:07	39 min

**Between 8:56 and 9:09, the relevant FAA center believed AA77 had crashed. Between 9:09 and 9:21, based on the events in New York, information from American Airlines, and the inability to confirm the crash on the ground, the FAA began to believe that AA77 might also be hijacked. By 9:24, this belief was communicated to FAA headquarters.

Table 3: FAA Warning to the Military

Flight	Time of Impact	Notification as Established by Commission Staff		Notification Presented by Military to Commission, May 2003	
		Time	Warning	Time	Warning
AA11	8:46:40	8:38	9 min	8:40	7 min
UA175	9:03:11	9:03	0 min	9:05	0 min
AA77	9:37:46	None*	0 min	9:24	14 min
UA93	10:03:11	10:07	0 min	9:16	47 min

*There was no notification received by NEADS that American 77 was hijacked. Washington Center informed NEADS at 9:34 that American 77 was lost in Indianapolis Center's airspace and could not be found. This notification was separate from and preceded the information NEADS received at 9:36 from Boston Center that there was an "aircraft VFR six miles southeast of the White House...six southwest." NEADS did not know that aircraft, which struck the Pentagon a minute later, was American 77.

PART II: CIVIL AVIATION SECURITY AND THE 9/11 ATTACKS

2.1 THE THREAT

Pre-9/11. A great challenge in conducting an analysis of a catastrophic and transformational event is trying to recapture the reality of that time as experienced by the people who lived it, including those in policymaking positions. Hindsight confers an enhanced understanding of the rush of past events, but the perspective it provides can be distorted. To answer fully the question of why the civil aviation system failed to stop the attacks that day, we must recall the world before September 11.

Former FAA administrator Jane Garvey testified:

> On September 10, we were not a nation at war. On September 10, we were a nation bedeviled by delays, concerned about congestion, and impatient to keep moving. . .And on September 10, based on intelligence reporting, we saw explosive devices on aircraft as the most dangerous threat. We were also concerned about what we now think of as traditional hijacking, in which the hijacker seizes control of the aircraft for transportation, or in which passengers are held as hostages to further some political agenda.[421]

The Commission staff found no evidence that the FAA knew, or possessed intelligence indicating, that Bin Ladin, al Qaeda, al Qaeda affiliates, or any other group was plotting to hijack commercial planes in the United States and use them as weapons.[422] Administrator Garvey and Claudio Manno, Director of FAA's Office of Civil Aviation Intelligence on 9/11, testified to that effect before the Commission.[423]

Nevertheless, the FAA had indeed considered the possibility that terrorists would hijack a plane and use it as a weapon. In the spring of 2001, FAA intelligence distributed an unclassified CD-ROM presentation to air carriers and airports, including Logan, Newark, and Dulles. The presentation cited the possibility that terrorist might conduct suicide hijacking but stated: "fortunately, we have no indication that any group is currently thinking in that direction."[424]

In 1998 and 1999, the FAA intelligence unit produced reports about the hijacking threat posed by Bin Ladin and al Qaeda, including the possibility that the terrorist group might try to hijack a commercial jet and slam it into a U.S. landmark. It viewed this possibility as "unlikely" and a "last resort." FAA perceived as far more likely that al Qaeda would hijack a flight overseas, where the terrorists had access to safe havens. They believe that from these safe havens, Bin Ladin could use passengers to bargain for the release of Islamic extremists imprisoned in the United States.[425]

Many officials pointed out to us that despite numerous reports and assessments regarding the growing terrorist threat, the U.S. civil aviation system had been enjoying a period of relative peace. By 2001, it had been over a decade since a U.S. air carrier had been hijacked or bombed.[426]

Even terrorist experts perceived positive trends. Writing in 1999, aviation security expert and former Gore Commission member Brian Jenkins observed that the battle between terrorism and security has "continued for the past 30 years with security gradually gaining. In the early 1970s, more than 30 percent of international terrorist attacks were targeted against commercial aviation; it is less than 10 percent today."[427]

The absence of attacks instilled a confidence that U.S. counterterrorism, at least domestically, was working, allowing the FAA to focus on other serious policy challenges facing civil aviation, including capacity problems, the industry's economic woes, the demand for better customer service, and the ever present issue of safety. To the extent there was a threat, numerous FAA and air carrier officials told us the threat was predominantly overseas.

The fact that the civil aviation system seems to have been lulled into a false sense of security is striking not only because of what happened on 9/11 but also in light of the intelligence assessments, including those conducted by the FAA's own security branch, that raised alarms about the growing terrorist threat to civil aviation throughout the 1990s and into the new century. This heightened threat was attributed in large part to Usama Bin Ladin who, in 1998, had declared war on the United States and also threatened to attack aviation, including the hijacking of U.S. aircraft.[428]

Indeed, since 1996, the domestic aviation system had operated at a security level that was, in effect, a permanent code orange. Specifically, it was the level required when "information indicates that a terrorist group or other hostile entity with a known capability of attacking civil aviation is likely to carry out attacks against U.S. targets; or civil disturbances with a direct impact on civil aviation have begun or are imminent."[429] (See appendix 2.)

This was preceeded by the 1995 National Intelligence Estimate on terrorism that highlighted the growing domestic threat of terrorist attack, including a risk to civil aviation:

> Should terrorists launch new attacks, we believe their preferred targets will be U.S. Government facilities and national symbols, financial and transportation infrastructure nodes, or public gathering places. Civil aviation remains a particularly attractive target in light of the fear and publicity that the downing of an airline would evoke and the revelations last summer of the US air transport sector's vulnerabilities.

Numerous documents, reports and assessments produced by the FAA's intelligence division through the late 1990s and up to 9/11 reported on the growing threat posed by terrorists. For example, between March 14 and May 15, 2001, the FAA's Office of Civil Aviation Intelligence conducted a series of classified briefings for security officials at 19 of the nation's largest airports, including Newark, Boston's Logan and Washington Dulles. The briefing highlighted the threat posed by terrorists in general and Bin Ladin in particular, including his threats against aviation. The renewed interest in hijacking by terrorist groups was also covered.[430]

Perceived Aviation Security Threat. While hostage taking was the dominant concern in regard to hijacking, sabotage was the threat that concerned civil aviation security officials most. After 9/11, FAA Administrator Garvey told a Senate Committee that prior to that day, "all our Security Directives, all of our security recommendations have been geared toward explosives. This [9/11] was a whole new world for us."[431] She later told the Commission that "based on intelligence reporting, we saw explosive devices as the most dangerous threat."[432]

An act of sabotage or a traditional hijacking to obtain hostages was the threat to aviation foremost in the mind of FAA security officials during the summer of 2001, as they were apprised of the increased "chatter" being picked up by U.S. intelligence agencies indicating an imminent terrorist attack.

The concern grew in the Spring of 2001 when al Qaeda operative Ahmed Ressam (who planned to bomb Los Angeles International Airport at the millenium) and the al Qaeda conspirators who blew up two U.S. embassies in Africa in 1998 were convicted in U.S. courts.[433]

One of the FAA's liaisons to the intelligence community told the Commission that the intelligence community sensed, particularly in June and July 2001, that "something was going to happen" that summer. Most of the community, he said, was looking for the event to occur abroad.[434]

Much of this threat information was contained in the daily intelligence summaries produced by FAA's security branch for the agency's leaders. The summaries were based on reporting it received from the U.S. intelligence community and other sources. Among the 105 summaries issued between April 1, 2001, and September 10, 2001, almost half mentioned Bin Ladin, al Qaeda, or both, mostly in regard to overseas threats.[435]

Of the 52 summaries mentioning Bin Ladin or al Qaeda, 5 mentioned hijacking as a capability al Qaeda was training for or possessed. Two mentioned suicide operations, but not connected to a threat to aviation.[436] One of the summaries, which will be discussed later, mentioned air defense measures being undertaken in Genoa, Italy, for the G-8 summit to protect the event from possible air attack by terrorists (including their use of an explosives-laden aircraft as a weapon).[437]

The National Security Council's Counterterrorism Security Group (CSG) responded to the threat reporting that summer by inviting the FAA to attend a meeting in early July 2001 at the White House to discuss with domestic agency officials heightened security concerns[438] General Michael Canavan, the FAA's top security official, attended the meeting.

He recalled that the White House counterterrorism officials emphasized that an attack would likely take place overseas.[439] Other FAA officials questioned by the Commission, including Administrator Garvey, told us that leading up to 9/11 they too understood the threat to be primarily abroad.[440]

Canavan testified to the Commission, "We really had no credible or actionable intelligence that told us this was really going to happen. In other words, this is a real threat. ███████████████████████████ None of it was ever talked about being in the United States."[441]

In the course of our investigation FAA intelligence officials stated that such specific intelligence is rare in the counterterrorism environment. Nevertheless, because the intelligence that summer did not provided details about a specific plot, the security directives issued by the FAA that summer required no significant upgrade of security at domestic checkpoints, such as prohibiting knives or requiring Computer Assisted Passenger Prescreening System (CAPPS) selectees to undergo additional screening of their person or carry-on bags. Nor did the FAA implement any additional measures, such as increasing the presence of air marshals or imposing the other high-security measures it took in the aftermath of the 9/11 attacks.[442]

The first security directives that went out after the early July CSG meeting were issued on July 27, 2001. One concerned special security procedures involving charter flights to or from Cuba, another extended measures in place for clearing law enforcement officers' identification before they would be allowed to access sterile areas in airports,[443] and a third added an Egyptian thought to be insane to the no-fly list. Before 9/11, two other security directives went out, one in late August adding a few more names to the no-fly list, and another regarding heightened security for flights carrying the author Salman Rushdie (against whom a fatwa had been issued). None of these affected general security procedures at checkpoints or aboard aircraft.[444]

In 2001, the FAA issued 16 information circulars. These publications were designed to warn airports and air carriers about security issues but did not specify or require any security measures they should take.

The first circular sent out after the July CSG meeting appeared on July 12. It updated a 1994 advisory about the threat posed by surface-to-air missiles. Six more circulars were distributed before 9/11, five of them highlighting overseas concerns. Among them was a circular issued on July 31 that mentioned hijacking. It alerted the aviation community to "reports of possible near-term terrorist operations . . . particularly on the Arabian Peninsula and/or Israel" and contained the following language:

The FAA does not have any credible information regarding specific plans by terrorist groups to attack U.S. civil aviation interests. Nevertheless, some of the currently active groups are known to plan and train for hijacking and have the capability to construct sophisticated IEDs. . . . The FAA encourages all U.S. carriers to exercise prudence and demonstrate a high degree of alertness.[445]

Administrator Garvey told the Commission that she was aware of the heightened threat during the summer of 2001. However, both FAA Deputy Administrator Monte Belger and his assistant told us in separate interviews that they were basically unaware of the threat posed by Usama Bin Ladin and al Qaeda prior to September 11, 2001.[446]

While the airlines had been instructed by the FAA to "demonstrate a high degree of alertness," neither of the senior operations executives of the airlines whose planes were hijacked on 9/11 were aware of the heightened threat environment that summer.[447]

The Commission was contacted by veteran commercial pilots who said that they were never made aware of the threat conditions that summer, and that they believe they should have been.

Sabotage. As stated by Administrator Garvey, prior to 9/11 the FAA viewed sabotage as the preeminent threat to civil aviation, particularly on the domestic front. The 1980s had seen a tremendous growth in the number of casualties from aircraft sabotage, including the 1985 bombing of an Air India flight that killed 329 people, the 1987 bombing of a Korean Air flight that killed 115 people, and the 1988 bombing of Pan Am 103 that killed 270 people.[448]

Throughout the 1990s, terrorist activities and other factors reinforced the FAA's view, including the foiled 1995 plot to blow up 12 U.S. jetliners over the Pacific, devised by Ramzi Yousef, mastermind of the 1993 attack on the World Trade Center; the TWA 800 disaster in 1996 (which was at first thought to be an act of sabotage but was later judged by federal investigators to be a fuel tank explosion caused by an electrical short circuit); and terrorist innovations in building improvised explosive devices (IEDs).[449]

In reaction to the TWA 800 disaster, President Clinton created the White House Commission on Aviation Safety and Security, chaired by Vice President Al Gore and commonly referred to as the Gore Commission. Its most significant security recommendations, issued in February 1997, dealt with the bomb threat to aircraft including the deployment of explosive detection systems at the nation's airports.[450]

FAA planning documents in effect on 9/11 listed the array of threats to civil aviation perceived by the agency and the measures to counter them. They also reflected the FAA's concern about sabotage. ███████████████████████████ The documents did not list suicide hijacking as a threat.

Civil aviation security officials focused on bombing in part because they believed measures to counter it were not nearly as pervasive or advanced as those in place to foil hijackings, which included checkpoint screening with metal detectors and X-ray machines. For this reason, the effort to deploy explosives detection technology to screen checked baggage became a priority for the FAA following the Pan Am 103 disaster in 1988.

Moreover, the absence of hijackings was cited by a number of FAA and air carrier security officials as evidence that checkpoint screening was working effectively to stop hijacking and that sabotage was the greater threat.[452] One former high-ranking Department of Transportation security official told us that in his view, the lack of incidents suggested that the nation had won the battle against hijacking.[453] The security director for a major air carrier told us that the approach to checkpoint security was "if it ain't broke, don't fix it."[454]

Because sabotage was considered deadlier than hijacking it was viewed as the greater menace—particularly considering that traditional hijackers wanted either transportation—such as the hijackings to Cuba in the late 1960s and early 1970s—or political concessions.

Hijacking. Despite the system's view of the relative threat posed by hijacking and sabotage, statistics showed that hijacking had always been the most prevalent means of attacking civil aviation. According to the Rand–St. Andrews University chronology of terrorist attacks, between 1972 and 1996 hijacking represented 87 percent of attacks against civil aviation.[455] Between 1996 and 2000 there were 64 hijackings worldwide but only 3 incidents of sabotage. Between 1996 and 2001, 15 hijackings took place. No cases of sabotage occurred. As of 2000, the incidence of hijacking was on the increase worldwide.[456]

And while sabotage had been the deadlier form of attack, hijackings had also often proved fatal. The 1985 hijacking of an Egypt Air flight killed 60 people and injured 35; the 1986 hijacking of Pan Am 73 killed 22 people and injured 125; and the 1996 hijacking of an Ethiopian Airlines flight killed 123 people.[457]

As noted previously, the FAA intelligence unit did perceive that the hijacking threat was on the rise prior to 9/11, but primarily as an overseas concern. Nevertheless, in a July 17, 2001, proposed rulemaking, the FAA expressly cited the presence of terrorist cells in the United States and their interest in targeting the transportation sector.[458]

We asked the top security official at the Department of Transportation on 9/11 why policymakers continued to view the risk of hijacking to be overseas, when the FAA's own public documents cited an urgent and growing domestic threat. He said that in hindsight he had asked himself that same question many times.[459]

A synopsis of the FAA's view of the hijacking threat was set forth in an advisory issued to air carriers and airports on April 27, 2000, four months after five Islamist extremists hijacked Indian Airlines Flight 814 to Kandahar, Afghanistan, to win the release of incarcerated fellow extremists. The circular stated:

> Most international hijackings in the 1990's were attributed to individuals motivated by personal factors like escaping social, political or economic conditions in their homeland. They were largely unprofessional and rarely involved violence against passengers or crew. Conditions for a terrorist seizure of an airliner were not as favorable as in the previous two decades. Arrests of key group members, disruption of cells, struggles within the groups, restraints placed by terrorist state sponsors and the lack of terrorist safe haven airports may all have contributed to making this option less desirable. . . . We believe that the situation has changed. We assess that the prospect for terrorist hijacking has increased and that U.S. airliners could be targeted in an attempt to obtain the release of indicted or convicted terrorists imprisoned in the United States. . . . We assess that the terrorist hijacking of a U.S. airliner is more probable outside the United States due to access to safe havens. Although a hijacking within the U.S. would likely result in a larger number of American hostages, it would be operationally more difficult to accomplish. We do not rule it out, but at least two logistical factors would make it more difficult. First, the terrorist support structure in the U.S. is less developed than overseas, and second, if an aircraft were hijacked with the objective of flying it to a safe haven, it would need to be refueled.[460]

The expiration date on the advisory was "indefinite," and it had not been replaced as of September 11, 2001.

However, the FAA's security briefings to airports in the spring of 2001 contained an important caveat. It stated that from the hijackers' perspective, "A domestic hijacking would likely result in a greater number of American hostages but would be operationally more difficult. We don't rule it out. . . . If, however, the intent of the hijacker is not to exchange hostages for prisoners, but to commit suicide in a spectacular explosion, a domestic hijacking would probably be preferable."[461]

2.2 THE CIVIL AVIATION SECURITY LAYERS

Purpose of the Aviation Security System. Federal law required the FAA to protect U.S. civil aviation from piracy and sabotage. An FAA report produced in June 2001 stated the agency's mission more specifically: "The objective of the civil aviation security system is to prevent terrorist acts against civil aviation. The security system necessary to protect the traveling public must be capable of detecting, assessing, and ensuring that threat objects such as explosives, weapons, or chemical or biological agents are not allowed on aircraft."[462]

Policy Setting and Implementation. As the United States responded to attacks on commercial aviation, particularly the rash of hijackings in the 1970s, and high-profile disasters such as Pan Am 103, the roles and responsibilities for planning, implementing, and enforcing the nation's aviation security system took shape, and were vested in five primary institutions:

1. The Federal Aviation Administration was responsible for setting and enforcing regulations "to protect passengers and property on an aircraft in air transportation . . . against an act of criminal violence or aircraft piracy."[463]
2. Air carriers were responsible for screening passengers and baggage for weapons and prohibited items (explosives and incendiary devices), controlling access to aircraft, and training air crews in emergency response.[464]
3. Airport authorities were responsible for controlling access to sensitive airport facilities, including the Air Operation Area (AOA), and providing law enforcement services to airport facilities.
4. U.S. intelligence agencies were responsible for collecting and sharing with the FAA intelligence information bearing on threats to aviation, and, together with law enforcement, for stopping such plots from being carried out.
5. Congress was responsible for enacting aviation security statutes, performing oversight of the national civil aviation system, and funding the FAA.

Together, the institutions of civil aviation security were responsible for protecting 1.8 million passengers daily as they traveled aboard more than 25,000 flights, leaving from and arriving at more than 563 domestic airports.[465]

Layered System. The basic approach to achieving civil aviation security before 9/11 was described by the President's Commission on Aviation Security and Terrorism in its May 1990 report. This document summarized the FAA's security approach as a system of redundant, interrelated security measures based on the theory that if one measure fails, another will back it up.[466] Civil aviation security authorities repeatedly emphasized the importance of a layered system of protection for airline passengers, aircraft, and facilities. Such a system afforded protection that no single layer of security could have provided independently.[467]

FAA security inspections, Department of Transportation Inspector General audits, and General Accounting Office investigations found persistent deficiencies in all areas of aviation security. This was powerful evidence that no single layer of security could be relied on to sufficiently protect passengers and aircraft from piracy and sabotage.

On the morning of September 11, 2001, national civil aviation security consisted of six major layers of defense. They were

- intelligence
- airport access control
- passenger prescreening
- passenger checkpoint screening

- checked baggage/cargo/mail screening for explosives
- aircraft and onboard security

Only those layers relevant to the 9/11 plot—intelligence, passenger prescreening, passenger checkpoint screening, and onboard security—are addressed in the following staff analysis.

Intelligence

Intelligence was considered to be the first layer of security— the linchpin of the U.S. civil aviation security system. The FAA relied on intelligence to identify specific plots against civil aviation so that the U.S. intelligence community or law enforcement could foil them before the terrorists got to the airport.

Intelligence and other information helped shape the agency's view of the terrorist threat to civil aviation, and was to inform the policies, practices and procedures necessary to protect passengers and commercial flights from hijacking and sabotage.

Without strong intelligence function that was well connected to policymakers, the task of designing and operating a rational and effective security system would be difficult.

Although it did not collect raw intelligence, the FAA maintained an intelligence unit that operated a 24-hour watch where data was assessed by trained analysts. The FAA was the agency primarily responsible for assessing intelligence for its relevance specifically to U.S. commercial aviation.[468] The unit received nearly 200 pieces of threat related information daily from U.S. intelligence agencies, particularly the FBI, CIA, and State Department, [469] as well as other sources of information bearing on civil aviation security, including academia and the media.[470]

Between 1993 and September 11, 2001, the FAA opened more than 1,200 intelligence case files to track, study, and report on many different threats to U.S. commercial aviation.[471] While the intelligence unit had no investigative powers, if certain information required particular investigative follow-up, FAA analysts would request the FBI or CIA to conduct further inquiry.

Important intelligence information derived from these cases would be included in daily intelligence summaries and other finished intelligence products and assessments bearing on civil aviation security.[472] The distribution of the daily intelligence summary to the FAA's top policymakers was one of the primary means the intelligence unit endeavored to keep leadership properly informed.[473]

If the information provided specific information about a threat to a particular flight or airport, the FAA's intelligence unit would notify the affected air carrier or airport directly.[474] If, however, the threat required the implementation of some extraordinary security measure, FAA's top security official—the associate administrator of civil aviation security— was empowered to order action through the issuance of a security directive.[475] The directive would specify what measure was required, who was required to implement it, when it was to be implemented and over what time period.[476]

To ensure that security measures were properly calibrated to the threat, the FAA relied, in part, on its "Security Directive Working Group." This panel was made up of representatives from the three main divisions of FAA Civil Aviation Security—intelligence, operations, and policy. The group would convene to assess the adequacy of operations in regard to a particular threat and was authorized to make recommendations to the FAA associate administrator about whether to order the enhancement of security measures. The Commission requested documentation regarding any working group meetings held in 2001 regarding the high threat period that summer, but TSA was unable to find such documentation.

In addition to issuing security directives FAA could invoke various alert levels as part of its "Aviation Security Contingency Plan.". The plan outlined specific threat levels and the accompanying required countermeasures "to ensure that the FAA, airport operators, and air carriers are able to respond on short notice to all civil aviation threats." The various alert levels represented the level of threat perceived by the FAA in light of incidents and intelligence estimates.[477]

Although the FAA's Office of Intelligence had a highly capable staff, it was not well connected to the agency's top policymakers. Intelligence that indicated a real and growing threat leading up to 9/11 did not stimulate significant increases in security procedures. FAA policymakers required either a security incident or "specific and credible" evidence of an "actionable" threat before they would take urgent action to strengthen security.[478] This was despite the fact that such intelligence was recognized as being rare in the counterterrorism environment.

Since 9/11 public commentators and some Commission witnesses and interviewees cited the intelligence community's failure to connect the dots regarding the 9/11 attacks. We examined what the FAA knew about the following:

- the domestic presence and activities of international terrorists groups;
- the interest of Usama Bin Ladin and al Qaeda in hijacking;
- terrorists training as pilots for terrorist purposes; and
- the interest of terrorist groups in the use of aircraft as weapons.

Domestic Presence of International Terrorist Groups. FAA records indicate that the agency did understand that terrorists were present in the United States and posed a threat to commercial aviation.[479] In 1998, the FAA issued a security directive that read in part:

> The threat posed by foreign terrorists in the United States has increased, and the FAA believes that the threat will continue for the foreseeable future. . . . Of specific concern are individuals, groups and states hostile to the United States which continue to threaten violence against America and

American citizens in retaliation for U.S. policies. . . . A terrorist attack in the United States could occur with little or no warning.[480]

Another security directive issued in 1998 cited the 1993 attack on the World Trade Center and stated: "This attack dramatically demonstrated the capabilities and intent of International terrorists to operate in the United States." It went on to mention Bin Ladin and radical Islamic terrorist groups in general and stated: "Civil aviation has been a prominent target of these and other transnational terrorists. In the past several years, information has been received that individuals in the United States associated with loosely affiliated extremists have discussed targeting commercial aircraft and civil aviation facilities. Loosely, affiliated extremists have also shown a particular interest in media reporting regarding airline and airport security."[481]

In addition, a July 17, 2001, *Federal Register* notice from the FAA stated:

> Terrorism can occur anytime, anywhere in the United States. Members of foreign terrorist groups, representatives from State sponsors of terrorism and radical fundamentalist elements from many nations are present in the United States. . .Thus an increasing threat to civil aviation from both foreign and potentially domestic ones exists and needs to be prevented and countered.

This language was in support of a proposed rule to improve passenger screening and other security measures that Congress ordered in 1996. According to FAA officials, it had been held up by the Office of Management and Budget because of concerns over costs, and was still not in effect as of 9/11.[482]

FAA officials told us that what information they did receive about the presence and activities of foreign terrorist groups in the United States was general and anecdotal. They said they received little from the intelligence community regarding specific plots or the activities and capabilities of these groups.[483] One senior FAA official told us that FAA was being told that those terrorists who were present in the United States were engaged in "fund-raising rather than actual terrorist people plotting."[484]

In addition, FAA intelligence officials told us that they had perceived weaknesses in domestic reporting. There were several reasons for these flaws. First, although the FBI was the lead government agency on counterterrorism issues, its primary focus was on collecting evidence for criminal cases, not on the collection and dissemination of intelligence. The CIA, meanwhile, was focused on the terrorist threat overseas. And although the State Department maintained the government's terrorist watchlist, that watchlist was not fully shared with the FAA (for reasons that we discuss later).

Second, there were indications of strain between some members of the intelligence community. One top FAA security official informed us that his refrain to the intelligence community prior to 9/11 was "You guys can tell us what's happening on a street in Kabul, but you can't tell us what's going on in Atlanta."[488] The former head of the FAA's Civil Aviation Security branch told us that he when asked counterparts in the intelligence community if the FAA could receive higher levels of information, his requests were not greeted warmly by some. In his interview with us, he characterized their attitude toward the FAA as "condescending."[489]

Third, FAA officials stated that even when useful information on domestic activities was developed by the intelligence community it was not always shared with them. As an example, these officials cited the failure to apprise the FAA of the "Phoenix EC" memo written in the summer of 2001 by an FBI special agent regarding his concerns about flight training being undertaken by Middle Eastern men at U.S. flight schools.[490] One high-ranking official at the FAA testified that had this memo been received by the FAA, an intelligence case file would have been opened specifically on pilot training, and appropriate investigative and collection follow-up would have been requested.[491]

Moreover, this intelligence might have put the information the FAA later received about the arrest of Zacarias Moussaoui into sharper focus. Moussaoui was arrested by the Immigration and Naturalization Service in August 2001 following reports of suspicious behavior in flight school.

But FAA intelligence officials were not the only ones who did not know about the Phoenix EC memo. The FBI's civil aviation program manager and the FAA's liaison to the FBI were also kept in the dark.[492] Nor were they aware that in 1998 the FBI tasked its field offices to examine whether Islamist extremists in their area were taking flying lessons.[493]

There are several explanations for this apparent breakdown in communications. The Civil Aviation Security program at FBI headquarters was handled by a single FBI employee who, until 1998, served in this capacity on a part-time basis.[494] We found no formal process for ensuring that the manager received all information pertinent to aviation security threats. Her access depended on her personal relationships with field agents responsible for the airports. A former head of the Air Transport Association told the Commission that the air carriers had long advocated the establishment of a civil aviation security unit within FBI headquarters. The absence of one, he said, was "the single greatest failure prior to 9/11."[495]

The FAA employee who was assigned to the FBI reported that, in fact, he served as a "detailee" to the FBI, not as a "liaison."[496] As a detailee he spent nearly 40 percent of his time working on FBI assignments, including the investigation of the 1998 bombings of two U.S. embassies in Africa. In theory, his assignment to the Radical Fundamentalist Unit at FBI placed him in a unit where he could receive timely and important terrorist information that could benefit the FAA. However, he was responsible for many tasks, and the dual responsibilities imposed on him by two masters made it impossible for him to devote his full attention to civil aviation security issues.

One FAA official told us that in 2000, the Defense Intelligence Agency hosted a conference at which analysts, including representatives from the FAA, discussed cases in which hijackers possessed advanced knowledge of aircraft and piloting skills.

We found no documentation to indicate that the FAA was aware that FBI headquarters had tasked field offices to review whether Islamist extremists were training in aviation schools in the late 1990s. We also found no evidence that the FAA asked the FBI to canvass flight-training facilities for terrorists.[511]

Also in 1994, a private plane piloted by a suicidal youth crashed into the south lawn of the White House.[514]

As discussed earlier, in 2000 and 2001, FAA's intelligence branch produced a presentation for airports and air carriers throughout the country that mentioned the possibility of a domestic suicide hijacking but reassuringly added that no group currently seemed to be making such plans.[528] The intelligence unit had begun to think about suicide tactics because the Algerian terrorist group known as GIA, the Armed Islamic Group, and al Qaeda had all begun to use suicide attacks in the late 1990s. The FAA's head of civil aviation security on 9/11 told us that he always knew it was a possibility, but said he never saw specific threat information.[529]

In addition, both FAA and airline officials told us that their view of the suicide threat to aviation was influenced by a presentation at an aviation security conference in 1997 by a leading expert in suicide terrorism from the Middle East. He did not believe that these tactics would be used in aviation.[530]

Even though the FAA was working on efforts to deploy additional explosives detection technology at airports throughout the country, before 2001 the primary measure to combat sabotage was still the practice of positive passenger bag match (PPBM). PPBM required that the air carrier confirm a passenger had boarded the plane before loading his or her checked luggage. The assumption behind the practice was that the attacker was not suicidal, reflecting the FAA's view that suicide terrorism was not a priority threat. If it had been, PPBM would have been a very poor countermeasure.[531]

In summary, although suicide hijacking would be a consequential event, FAA considered it unlikely because it was unprecedented, there was no specific and credible evidence to suggest it would happen, and at least one top suicide terrorism expert dismissed it as a tactic terrorists would employ in the aviation arena.

If intelligence failed to detect a terrorist plot, passenger prescreening was the next layer of protection.

Passenger Prescreening

Passenger prescreening before 9/11 had two main components designed to help keep dangerous people and their weapons off commercial aircraft.

The first was the FAA list of individuals known to pose a threat to commercial aviation, referred to as the no-fly list. On the basis of information it received from the intelligence community, the FAA was authorized to issue directives requiring air carriers to prohibit listed individuals from boarding aircraft or, in designated cases, to ensure that the passenger received enhanced screening before boarding.[532]

To be listed in a security directive, an individual had to pose a "direct" threat to aviation. In other words, ███████████████████████████████████████
██
██

Only a very few individuals among the thousands listed as known or suspected terrorists by the U.S. government were placed on the FAA no-fly list or ordered to undergo extraordinary security procedures. As of September 11, the list of individuals whom FAA sought to prohibit from flying comprised 12 people; it included subjects wanted in connection with the 1995 Manila air plot to blow up a dozen U.S. aircraft in the Pacific, among them Khalid Sheikh Mohammed, the mastermind behind the attacks of September 11, 2001. Another list contained the names of three individuals who were required to receive enhanced screening, including a physical search, before being allowed to board a commercial aircraft.[534]

We did not find any evidence of a concerted effort by the FAA to obtain the names of all suspected terrorists and to list them in order to prevent them from flying. Nor did we find evidence that the FAA was directed to make such an effort by the Department of Transportation or the White House, or that the State Department, which managed the TIPOFF terrorist list, was ordered to share the list with the FAA.

The former head of FAA Civil Aviation Security, Cathal "Irish" Flynn, testified that he did not know about the government's TIPOFF list of known and suspected terrorists until the Commission's hearings on the topic in January 2004.[535] Another FAA intelligence official indicated that FAA had access to a system called TIPOFF "light," which was an older database of names that the FAA considered to be outdated and unusable because most names were not accompanied by biographic data, such as a date of birth, that would have enabled the aviation system to positively identify individuals that should be prohbited from flying distinct from innocent people who share the same name. [536]

The FAA's intelligence chief told us that often the basis for the listing of an individual as a threat was classified and thus the name was not shared with uncleared people or organizations. Because of classification concerns, he stated, it was very difficult to get clearance from the intelligence community to release the information, absent a direct threat to aviation. Thus, if the FAA wanted to use all 60,000 names in TIPOFF, each would have to be individually cleared.[537]

Interviewees also told us that the intelligence community was reluctant to share names of known and suspected terrorists with air carriers, particularly foreign carriers that fly to the United States, out of fear the information could be shared with host governments or even with the terrorists themselves. [538]

Two of the 9/11 hijackers, Nawaf al Hazmi and Khalid al Mihdhar, had been placed on the TIPOFF terrorist watchlist in late August. Their names were not shared with the FAA and therefore were not included in the no-fly list on September 11, 2001.[539]

Such limited use of terrorist watchlists seems to have contravened the recommendations of the White House Commission on Aviation Safety and Security. In 1997, the Gore Commission recommended: "The FBI and CIA should develop a system that would allow important intelligence information on known or suspected terrorists to be used in passenger profiling without compromising the integrity of the intelligence."[540]

While the civil aviation security system did not use lists of known or suspected terrorists to keep suspect individuals from boarding commercial aircraft, the FAA did require the air carriers to systematically prescreen passengers to predict who might be a security risk. This was the second element of prescreening—a program to identify those passengers on each flight who, because they matched profile criteria developed by the FAA (not including race, creed, color, or national origin), might pose more than a "minimal threat" to aviation. Those who met the criteria, the "selectees," were subject to additional security measures.[541]

In August 1996, the FAA began requiring air carriers to use a manual prescreening process to identify potential security threats. Under this program, the airline representative at the check-in counter assessed the passenger according to criteria established by the FAA. The criteria focused on certain data contained in the passenger's ticket record, including ███████ on the passenger's response to a set of security questions, and on the passenger's presentation of proper identification, such as a driver's license or passport. After considering these factors, the air carrier would determine whether the passenger should be selected to receive additional security measures.[542]

If a passenger was selected, his or her checked baggage tags and boarding pass were specially marked. The bags would be screened for explosives, or held off the plane until it was confirmed that the passenger had boarded. The passenger's carry-on items would be subject to a hand search or opened and assessed using FAA-approved explosives detection equipment. Using this method, screeners were better able to detect dangerous and deadly items ██████████████.[543]

In October 1997, the FAA issued a security directive requiring air carriers to replace the manual passenger prescreening system with an automated one known as the Computer Assisted Passenger Prescreening System (CAPPS), which would automatically score each passenger's security risk according to an algorithm of "factors" and "weights."[544] FAA officials believed that automating the system would make the process fairer and more reliable than the manual system that depended on airline personnel.[545] One air carrier security official said that some customer service personnel would deliberately fail to "select" a passenger who met the criteria in order to avoid the hassle of imposing additional security measures.[546]

CAPPS, like the manual system that preceded it, assessed factors ███████████ and weighted them according to a computerized formula. The system also assigned selectee status to a random sampling of passengers on each flight in order to address concerns about discrimination and to keep terrorists from gaming the system by learning how to avoid selection. In addition, FAA rules required that air carriers apply selectee security measures to individuals who could not provide appropriate government identification, those who could not correctly answer two security questions ███████████.[547]

Under CAPPS, the air carrier was responsible for examining each selectee's checked baggage for explosives using an FAA-approved method, including screening with explosive detection equipment, screening with a trace detection system designed to identify the residue of explosives on the outside of the bag, examination by a bomb-sniffing dog, and physical search. Selectees were no longer required to undergo any additional screening of their person or carry-on baggage at the checkpoint.[548] Up to 7 percent of all passengers were designated as selectees by the CAPPS system in place on September 11, 2001.[549]

Automated profiling was an inexact science. It identified many individuals who posed no particular threat to aviation and operated without empirical evidence that it captured all of those who were. While the system relied, in part, on hijacker profiles for its design, it targeted only those who checked bags.[550] The limited consequences of "selection" reflected the FAA's view that nonsuicide bombing was the most substantial risk to domestic aircraft.

One architect of CAPPS told us that the reason selection did not entail additional scrutiny at the checkpoint was policymakers' fear that checkpoint screeners would devote too much attention to CAPPS selectees and would fail to thoroughly screen other passengers.[551]

According to the former head of the airlines' trade association, the decision not to screen a selected person's carry-on bags was questionable given the "abysmally" poor performance of screening and given the wide range of dangerous items that were undetectable by the screening equipment in use at the time.[552] And an FAA security official told us that many of her colleagues believed that abandoning carry-on hand searches had led to a decrease in security.[553]

As originally conceived, passenger prescreening was supposed to be far more robust. In a 1996 report, an FAA security advisory group recommended CAPPS and called on airlines to apply an "FAA-approved passive profile to all passengers enplaning at U.S. airports to identify selectees, whose persons and property (checked baggage and carry-on bags/items) will receive additional security scrutiny."[554]

In fact, under Aviation Security Alert Level III which was an effect on 9/11, screeners were supposed to physically search or screen, with an approved device, the carry-on property of CAPPS selectees, and "hand wand or pat down that person."[555] This practice was not required by the security directive implementing CAPPS and was not in evidence at either the Portland Jetport or Dulles Airport where surveillance video recorded the checkpoint screening of the hijackers.[556]

We believe that a number of factors were influential in scaling back the consequences of CAPPS selection, among them the desire to limit the purchase of expensive explosives detection technology,[557] concerns about customer dissatisfaction with delays and "hassle,"[558] the need to avoid operational delays,[559] and the fear of potential discrimination or the appearance of it.[560] Issues of discrimination were central to the debate over passenger prescreening from its inception.[561] Applying secondary screening to the selectees' person and carry-on belongings was particularly controversial. One senior FAA security official said that the "procedure of escorting selectees and dumping out their carry-on at the gate" generated opposition from the American Civil Liberties Union and the Department of Justice.[562]

Even with the consequences of selection restricted to explosives screening or matching checked bags, the air carriers were under pressure from the FAA that threatened to undercut CAPPS' effectiveness. In a January 11, 1998, letter to United Air Lines, the FAA conditionally approved the air carrier's plan to implement the CAPPS system provided that the carrier ensured that

> There will be no lines forming at your EDS [explosives detection system] machines and that in the rare cases where lines might form, the persons in those lines will be from sufficiently diverse racial, ethnic and national origin groups so as to minimize any possibility of problematic stigmatization. Once UA implements the CAPPS program, we plan to monitor UA's security operations, and any consumer complaints filed with DOT, to ensure that your assurances regarding the absence or passenger make-up of lines at EDS equipment are correct.[563]

One airline official told us that his company was informed that if at least three out of five people in a line of selectees awaiting screening were of the same ethnicity, its program would be deemed discriminatory.[564]

For a terrorist traveling lightly, or who had intentions other than to sabotage the flight using checked baggage, prescreening did not represent a layer of security that needed to be overcome.

On 9/11 10 of the 19 hijackers were selected for additional baggage screening: nine flew on Colgan or American Airlines and one on United. Two of them, Hani Hanjour and Mohamed Atta, were pilots. The Commission asked the Transportation Security Administration to independently score the hijackers using the CAPPS algorithm in effect on 9/11 to determine if the air carriers had properly prescreened the hijackers. The agency found that the algorithm had been applied correctly and the selection designations were appropriate.[565]

In any case, the selection process was not the primary problem with CAPPS. Those hijackers identified by the system as risks to the aircraft carried their weapons—knives, box cutters, Mace or pepper spray, and fake bombs—on their person or in their carry-on bags.[566] Had CAPPS required selectees to be subject to a secondary search of their person, carry-on bags, or both, perhaps screeners could have found and confiscated the prohibited items; perhaps an alert screener would have identified the component parts of a fake bomb; perhaps the additional screening would have exposed a rattled hijacker; or perhaps any knives found by the screeners would have been confiscated as they used the "common sense" urged of them by FAA rules and the discretion provided them by the airline's checkpoint operations guide to prohibit menacing items.

Checkpoint Screening for Weapons

The most obvious and vital element of aviation security was checkpoint screening for weapons. Federal rules required air carriers "to conduct screening . . . to prevent or deter the carriage aboard airplanes of any explosive, incendiary, or a deadly or dangerous weapon on or about each individual's person or accessible property, and the carriage of any explosive or incendiary in checked baggage."[567] The former associate administrator for civil aviation security, Irish Flynn, testified before the Commission that "checkpoint screening was the primary measure to prevent hijackings of aircraft."[568] More than half a billion passengers per year were screened by government-certified equipment operated and maintained according to FAA specifications.

In most instances, air carriers entered into contracts with private security companies to conduct screening operations.[569] The staffing levels, training requirements, testing, and supervision of checkpoint screening personnel were set out in FAA regulations and enforced by the agency's security operation unit. Requirements for screeners included 40 hours of instruction and on-the-job training, with recurrent training and assessments.

Screeners relied on metal detectors, X-ray machines, physical searches, and bomb detection technology. Metal detectors were calibrated to detect guns and large knives to prevent passengers from carrying such items beyond the checkpoint.[570] Prohibited items such as guns would be confiscated. Restricted items such as box cutters were not allowed in the cabin, but the passenger would be given the option of placing the article in his or her checked baggage for transport.

All firearms were prohibited from being carried past a checkpoint, except those in the possession of authorized law enforcement officers. Knives with blades 4 inches long or longer also were expressly barred.[571]

Neither FAA regulations nor the Air Carrier Standard Security Program specifically identified a three-and-one-half-inch knife that locks into place, such as those purchased by the 9/11 hijackers and like knives found at the crash site of Flight 93 in Pennsylvania, as "deadly or dangerous." However, federal rules advised screeners to use "common sense" in determining what would be allowed past a checkpoint.[572] The airlines' checkpoint operations guide—which the airlines developed in cooperation with the FAA to implement the agency's rules—explicitly permitted knives with blades less than 4 inches long.[573]

> Knives with blades under 4 inches, such as Swiss Army Knives, scout knives, pocket utility knives, etc. may be allowed to enter the sterile areas. However some knives with blades under 4 inches could be considered by a reasonable person to

be a "menacing knife" and/or may be illegal under local law and should not be allowed to enter the sterile area.[574]

When asked whether screeners were truly expected to exercise discretion and common sense in making determinations about what that was not expressly prohibited could pass the checkpoint, one interviewee who oversaw checkpoint screening for an air carrier said, "It didn't work that way."[575]

However, under the air carrier's operations guide in place on September 11, 2001, "box cutters" were classified as restricted items, which "are not permitted in the passenger cabin of an aircraft. The [checkpoint] supervisor must be notified if an item in this category is encountered. Passengers may be given the option of having these items transported as checked baggage."[576] The COG provided no guidance on how to distinguish between permissible "pocket knives" and restricted "box cutter."[577]

The president of the Air Transport Association, testified before the Commission that while box-cutting devices were considered a restricted item posing a potential danger and could be kept off the aircraft, "the pre-9/11 screening system was not designed to detect or prohibit these types of small items."[578]

Indeed, prior to 9/11, checkpoints were not tested for their ability to detect knives, because short knives were not FAA-approved "test items."[579] This omission ignored the use of knives in deadly hijackings elsewhere around the world, as well as a 1994 FAA assessment of the threat to U.S. civil aviation that listed among "system vulnerabilities" to hijackers: "cabin crew or passengers can also be threatened with objects such as short-blade knives, which are allowable on board aircraft."[580]

The FAA based its policy on short-bladed knives on a number of factors: (1) the agency did not consider such items to be menacing;[581] (2) most local laws did not prohibit individuals from carrying such knives; and (3) the knives would have been difficult to detect unless the sensitivity of metal detectors had been greatly increased. A 1993 proposal to ban knives altogether had been rejected because small cutting implements were difficult to detect and the number of innocent "alarms" would have increased significantly, exacerbating congestion problems at checkpoints.[582]

Even if the system had detected such a knife carried by a hijacker on 9/11, the knife most likely would have been returned and carried onto the plane. Mace and pepper spray, in contrast, were categorized as "hazardous materials," which passengers were prohibited from carrying without the express permission of the airline.

By 2001, any confidence that checkpoint screening was functioning effectively was belied by numerous public studies by the General Accounting Office[583] and the Department of Transportation's Office of Inspector General.[584] Over the previous 20 years, government auditors and FAA enforcement inspectors had documented serious and chronic weaknesses in the systems deployed to screen passengers and baggage for carry-on weapons or bombs.[585] The trend in performance leading up to 9/11 was not encouraging. A 2001 report produced on behalf of the FAA found that "both carry-on and metal detection screening performance has declined significantly from 1999-2000."[586] The April 2000 GAO assessment of passenger and baggage screening was representative of independent evaluations of that system's effectiveness through September 11, 2001:

> FAA and the airline industry have made little progress in improving the effectiveness of airport checkpoint screeners. Screeners are not adequately detecting dangerous objects and long-standing problems affecting screeners' performance remain, such as the rapid screener turnover and the inattention to screener training. FAA's efforts to address these problems are behind schedule.[587]

Among the problems that plagued checkpoints was the high turnover among screeners, who earned only minimum wage. This workforce was paid by the financially troubled and cost-conscious aviation industry, which—according to many FAA interviewees— viewed mimimizing the cost of security as more important than maximizing its effectiveness.[588]

Technology also played a role. Metal detectors and X-ray equipment were the tools of effective screening, but both had substantial limitations.[589] These technological limitations and the tendency of screeners to perform poorly when tested on finding even the most easily detectable items were well known to aviation security policymakers. The FAA also fully understood that terrorists were unlikely to stow a weapon in a carry-on bag in a such a way that it would be easily recognized by an X-ray machine operator.

In its proposed rulemaking action of July 17, 2001, which aimed at updating basic security requirements (including checkpoint screening), the FAA itself noted that "publicity about problems with U.S. domestic civil aviation security measures increases the potential for attack here."[590] Given this knowledge, the FAA's decision not to require more thorough searching of CAPPS selectees seems questionable. The proposed rule that accompanied the FAA's caution sought to require federal certification of screening companies and to increase the training of their employees. Though Congress had ordered the drafting of regulations to implement these reforms in 1996, they still had not been completed as of September 11, 2001, mainly because of concerns about their cost.

Moreover, in the late 1990s the FAA's requirement that checkpoint screeners conduct "continuous" and "random" hand searches of carry-on luggage for deadly and dangerous items had been largely replaced with a requirement to swipe them for explosives. FAA security officials told us that the "continuous" and "random" secondary screening of carry-on bags was often ignored by the airlines.[591] Screeners no longer were regularly opening the stream of carry-on luggage; instead, they were relying on devices that scanned for traces of explosives. Without randomly hand searching carry-on items, however, they had little chance of detecting a prohibited item that would not trigger the metal detector or that was well hidden in carry-on luggage.

Screeners also had ill-defined objectives and performance goals. Although the FAA tested checkpoints on their ability to detect prohibited items in order to prevent violence aboard an aircraft,[592] federal regulations governing security checkpoints required that carriers conduct screening to "prevent or deter" the carrying of a deadly or dangerous weapon onto an aircraft.

Requiring that checkpoints be able to detect weapons was a more rigorous standard than deterrence, which could be accomplished simply by an appearance of effective screening. The president of the Air Transportation Association testified before the Commission that "This [checkpoint] system was specifically designed as a . . . prevent-or-deter system, and was not a more intrusive prevent-and-detect system."[593] In fact, the air carriers had successfully fought off the FAA's efforts to change the standard to "prevent and detect."

The regulations' requirement to prevent *or* deter, moreover, seemed to provide a choice. Regulators and those who believed a higher standard of checkpoint performance should be imposed could point to the "prevention" language as the relevant standard, while those whose interests might be served by a less rigor could point to "deterrence" language. Indeed, air carrier security officials interviewed by the Commission staff spoke of their responsibility to "deter" the carrying of a weapon past a checkpoint and suggested that the absence of hijackings indicated success.

This disagreement was not merely semantic: it had real consequences. As a senior civil aviation security official told us, screening just for deterrence was unlikely to deter in the long run.[594] Deterrence is measured by the absence of incidents rather than the ability to stop them. But in the age of terrorism, when an unprecedented and devastating blow can occur anytime and anywhere, the fact that an incident has not yet occurred cannot be relied on as the sole indicator that security is sufficient and working well.

Despite the documented shortcomings of the screening system, the long stretch of time more than a decade—without a domestic hijacking or bombing was perceived by many within the system as confirmation that it was working.[595] This view explains, in part, why a transportation security official told us that the agency thought it had won the battle against hijacking.[596] In fact, one of the primary reasons that the secondary screening of passengers selected by the prescreening program was restricted to checked bags was officials' belief that checkpoint screening was working sufficiently well. As events proved, their confidence was misplaced.

One former FAA Red Team member who testified before the Commission aptly observed, "From a security point of view, there is no difference between defending against a hijacker that wants to do a September 11 thing or a hijacker who wants to go to Miami. The key word is you're defending against a hijacking, and you worry about his motivation later."[597] In 1990, the President's Commission on Aviation Security and Terrorism noted that the airline industry referred to checkpoint screening "as the first line of defense. It may, in fact, be the last line of defense. If someone is able to defeat this security measure, that person can gain access to passengers, crew and aircraft with relative ease."[598]

We turn now to how prescreening worked on September 11 with respect to the four hijacked flights.

9/11 CHECKPOINTS

United was the custodial air carrier for three of the checkpoints used to screen the passengers of the hijacked flights, and American was responsible for two.[599]

Airport	Flight	Checkpoint	Airline/Screening Company
Logan (Boston)	AA 11	North (Main or B5) Checkpoint	American/Globe
Logan (Boston)	AA 11	Mid (B4) Checkpoint	American/Globe
Logan (Boston)	UA 175	Checkpoint C3	United/Huntleigh
Newark	UA 93	Terminal A, Checkpoint 1	United/Argenbright
Washington Dulles	AA 77	Checkpoint IADO2	United/Argenbright

At each of the checkpoints, the primary method for passenger screening was walk-through metal detectors calibrated to detect items with metal content no less than that of a .22-caliber gun. If a passenger triggered the walk-through alarm, he or she was to be screened with a hand-held metal detector to identify the object triggering the alarm. Carry-on bags were primarily screened by X-ray machines, backed up by physical search, explosive trace detectors, or both.[600]

The exception was the checkpoint at Dulles, which relied primarily on two walk-through metal detectors. If passengers set off the alarm of the first, they were sent through the second. If they triggered the second metal detector, they were screened with the hand-held device.[601]

Screening checkpoint for Flight 11 (Logan). Passenger screening for Flight 11 was conducted at the main checkpoint (B5).[602] Two lanes were operational. Each was outfitted with a walk-through metal detector to screen passengers and an X-ray machine to screen carry-on bags. A second screening checkpoint (B4 or middle) was opened at 7:15 A.M. This checkpoint was used primarily for "overflow" from B5.

The FAA conducted a comprehensive assessment of the B5 checkpoint on October 30, 2000, and found ▮ security weaknesses or violations. The previous assessment on October 20, 1999, found ▮ security weaknesses, all related to the ▮▮▮▮▮ system. Between September 11, 1999, and September 11, 2001, the FAA conducted ▮ screener evaluations at checkpoint B5. In the ▮ tests involving the metal detectors, the test object was detected in ▮ percent of the cases. In ▮ physical search tests, the detection rate was ▮ percent; in the ▮ X-ray tests, the detection rate was ▮ percent. With respect to 2001 national averages, B5 screeners met or exceeded the average for overall, physical search, and X-ray detection, while falling below the norm for metal detection.[603]

The combined detection rate for tests conducted at this checkpoint for the two years leading up to 9/11 was ██ percent; the national average was ██ percent.[604] In 2000, the checkpoint reported confiscating 13 guns, 8 grenades, and zero knives.[605]

Screening checkpoint for Flight 175 (Logan). Passenger screening for Flight 175 was conducted at checkpoint C3. It had two operational lanes, each was with a walk-through metal detector and an X-ray machine.[606]

The FAA conducted comprehensive assessments of this checkpoint on December 14, 1999, and November 15, 2000, uncovering ██ security weaknesses or violations. Between September 11, 1999, and September 11, 2001, the FAA conducted ██ screener evaluations at checkpoint C3. In the ██ tests involving the metal detectors, the test object was detected in ██ percent of the cases. In ██ physical search tests, the detection rate was ██ percent; in the ██ X-ray tests, the detection rate was ██ percent. With respect to 2001 national averages, C3 screeners met or exceeded the average for overall, physical search, and X-ray detection, while falling below the norm for metal detection.[607]

Screening checkpoint for Flight 93 (Newark). Passenger screening for Flight 93 was conducted at checkpoint A-1. On that day, the checkpoint featured two lanes. Each lane was outfitted with a walk-through magnetometer, an X-ray machine, and hand-wand magnetometers.

In October 2000, the FAA conducted a comprehensive assessment of this checkpoint. They found ██ security violations, both of which involved ████████████ In the 24 months prior to 9/11, the FAA conducted ██ screener evaluation tests at the checkpoint, including ██ metal detector tests, ██ physical search tests, and ██ X-ray tests. Metal test objects were detected 80 percent of the time. The detection rates for physical searches and X-rays were ██ percent and ██ percent, respectively. All of these detection rates met or exceeded the national averages for this time period.[610]

The combined detection rate for tests conducted at this checkpoint for the two years leading up to 9/11 was ██ percent; the national average was ██ percent.[611] The annual turnover rate of all checkpoint screeners at the airport was 100 to 199 percent.[612]

Screening checkpoint for Flight 77 (Dulles). Passenger screening for Flight 77 was conducted at both the east (IAD01) and west (IAD02) checkpoints in the Main Terminal. All five of the hijackers passed through the west checkpoint.[613]

The west checkpoint was assessed by the FAA on November 13, 2000, and no violations were detected. Over the two years preceding 9/11, the FAA conducted ██ screener evaluations. Of these, ██ involved metal detectors, ██ involved the physical searches, and ██ involved the X-ray machine. Detection rates were ██ percent, ██ percent, and ██

percent, respectively. While the physical search results exceeded the national average, both the metal detector and X-ray results were below average.

The combined detection rate for tests conducted at this checkpoint for the two years leading up to 9/11 was ▮percent; the national average was ▮percent.

A comprehensive airport security study prepared by a consulting firm in July 2001 found a number of problems and vulnerabilities at the Dulles checkpoints. These findings, based primarily on information provided by the air carriers' station managers, included "a considerably high turnover rate for screeners," the limited English-language skills of most of the screener workforce, a lack of a law enforcement presence during peak hours, and too few checkpoint supervisors.[616]

Red Team Testing. The FAA Red Team was an elite unit deployed to find vulnerabilities in the aviation security system. Red Team testing in 2000 and 2001 focused on the carriers' capabilities to detect explosives. The teams conducted tests at airports throughout the nation. In 1997, the Red Team found that test objects ▮ ▮were detected ▮percent of the time. In 1998, the X-ray detection rate was ▮percent. In addition, the Red Teams identified the following significant screening problems:

- •
- •
- •
- •
- •

- • lack of supervision over checkpoint procedures.[617]

Only two of the security checkpoints entered by the hijackers featured closed-circuit television surveillance—the checkpoint used by Mohamed Atta and Abdul Aziz al Omari at the Portland International Jetport and the one used by the Flight 77 hijackers at Dulles International Airport.

Commission staff reviewed the available videotapes to assess the security procedures applied to the hijackers. Because there was no video surveillance at Logan and Newark airports, the Commission was unable to assess the security procedures used to screen Flights 175, 11, and 93.

Supervisors and screening staff interviewed by law enforcement did not report any suspicions or problems associated with the screening of the hijackers. We have found no evidence to dispute these claims. However, at the request of the Commission staff, an expert in checkpoint security regulatory enforcement reviewed the videotapes from Portland and Dulles airports. With respect to Dulles International Airport, the expert told us that the quality of the screening of the hijackers was "marginal at best." He noted the following deficiencies: incomplete and sloppy hand-wanding procedures, the failure to resolve why two hijackers set off the walk-through magnetometers, the absence of "random and continuous" secondary screening of carry-on baggage, and the failure to properly rotate positions at the checkpoint.[619] With respect to Portland, he noted the absence of "random and continuous" secondary screening of carry-on baggage as required by the FAA, using either equipment to swipe the items for explosives or a physical search of the bag, which would have given screeners a better chance of finding the hijackers' weapons.[620]

Onboard Security

If the preflight layers of aviation security designed to keep dangerous people and weapons off the aircraft failed, onboard defenses represented the last chance to thwart an attack. FAA operated a Federal Air Marshal program to place specially trained law enforcement officials aboard high-risk flights.

In 2001, the program had 33 air marshals, a small fraction of its strength in the 1970s. The decline began after the implementation of checkpoint screening. A senior aviation security official told us that by the mid-1990s, air marshals were assigned exclusively to high-risk international flights on the basis of the prevailing threat assessment.[621] The highest-ranking FAA security official on 9/11 told us that the FAA did not discuss the need for a stronger domestic air marshal program, because the threat was considered to be overseas; in support of that view, he cited the fact that there had been no domestic hijackings in many years.[622]

FAA Administrator Garvey told us that the air marshal program had already been greatly diminished by the time she took office, and she and others—including members of Congress—thought other FAA needs had higher priority.[623] Another FAA official told us that air carriers did not want to give up the revenue they lost by providing free seats to air marshals.[624] Yet the air carriers' trade association had recommended to the Gore Commission in 1997: "Utilize Federal Air Marshals Effectively: Announce the immediate deployment of Federal Air Marshals at airport locations determined to warrant special security measures."[625] A high-ranking FAA official said that the Defense Department and the FBI did not like the air marshal program because the presence of armed personnel could cause tactical problems for emergency responders should hostage rescue operations by law enforcement or the military become necessary.[626] For a variety of reasons, therefore, the domestic air marshal program remained dormant.

Absent the presence of an armed and trained air marshal aboard, the crew was expected to respond to a hijacking in accordance with the FAA-approved tactics of the "Common Strategy."[627] This strategy, in which all flight crews were required to be trained, taught them to refrain from trying to overpower or negotiate with hijackers, to land the aircraft as soon as possible, to communicate with authorities, and to try delaying tactics.[628]

The strategy drew on previous experiences with domestic hijackings and aimed at getting passengers, crew, and hijackers safely landed. It offered no guidance for confronting a suicide hijacking.[629] One of the FAA officials most involved with the Common Strategy in the period leading up to 9/11 described it as an approach dating back to the early 1980s, developed in consultation with the industry and the FBI, and based on the historical record of hijackings. It was last updated in 1997.

The goal of the strategy was to "optimize actions taken by a flight crew to resolve hijackings peacefully" through systematic delay and, if necessary, accommodation of the hijackers. The FAA believed that the longer a hijacking persisted, the more likely it was to have a peaceful resolution. The strategy's fundamental assumptions were that hijackers issued negotiable demands, most often for asylum or the release of prisoners, and that "suicide wasn't in the game plan."[630] One aviation security commentator noted, "To the extent that the politically-motivated hijacking was even considered, it was lumped with all the others whose perpetrators had no suicidal intent, and thus could arguably be talked into a safe and non-lethal surrender, given enough time and aircrew patience."[631]

A frequently asked question about the 9/11 attacks is, How did the hijackers get into the cockpit? While FAA flight rules required the cockpit door to remain closed and locked at all times,[632] FAA regulations also required that the door be designed to facilitate the flight crew's entry and exit in the event of an emergency. Even if hardened cockpit doors had been installed, they would have been effective only with proper policy, management, and procedures to safeguard cockpit keys.[633] As of 9/11, one key opened the cockpits of all Boeing aircraft.

Moreover, a senior airline security executive pointed out that a hardened door would not have helped on 9/11, because the Common Strategy was to cooperate.[634] Indeed, the chairman of the Security Committee of the Air Line Pilots Association agreed. According to media accounts, when proposals were made in early 2001 to install reinforced cockpit doors, the chairman responded: "But even if you make a vault out of the door, if they have a noose around my flight attendant's neck, I'm going to open the door."[635]

The FAA acknowledged the possibility of suicide hijacking in its intelligence assessments. It understood that suicide was an increasingly common tactic among terrorists in the Middle East and that, historically, civil aviation was a favored target of terrorists. Nevertheless, the FAA-approved training for commercial flight crews contained no guidance on how to respond if hijackers were bent on suicide, resorted to violence on the aircraft, or attempted to unseat the flight crew from the cockpit. One air carrier's video presentation called on flight crew to "keep aggression out of the cockpit."[636] However, the Commission staff could find no instructional material addressing how that could be accomplished.[637]

The same training video, produced in 1984, showed actors playing hijackers holding a short-bladed knife to the throat of a flight crew member. The video said "knives are always a threat and have been used by hijackers in the past."[638] Another air carrier's training material included a CBS news report about a knife-wielding hijacker addicted to aviation video games who broke into the cockpit so that he might fly the plane. The hijacker killed the pilot and seized the controls before he was subdued by the co-pilot. The training material stated, "While this proved to be successful in this incident, remember, the Common Strategy tells us not to attempt to overtake a hijacker."

Thus, prior to 9/11, onboard security was a security layer only in the most modest sense of the term—a particularly ineffective barrier to those whose violent intentions reflected the growing terrorist trend to maximize casualties, rather than follow the traditional model of hijacking for transport or barter.

Former FAA administrator Jane Garvey summarized the Common Strategy and its relation to the 9/11 attacks as follows:

> The most powerful weapons that hijackers carried on 9/11 . . . was their knowledge that our aviation system's policy was to get the passengers on the ground safely and that meant negotiation, not confrontation. We can all share some blame in hindsight for not seeing the jeopardy of the policy. But it was developed and continued over decades as a policy that we knew from experience would save lives.[639]

A Layered System?

In addition to designating aviation security as a "national security issue," the Gore Commission in 1997 reiterated the importance of security layering. The panel stated that "aviation security should be a system of systems, layered, integrated and working together to produce the highest possible levels of protection."[640] The National Research Council, in a major study of aviation security, also strongly endorsed this principle.[641]

The concept of "layering" in the realm of aviation security is closely related to the principle of "redundancy" incorporated into aviation safety policy and regulation. The U.S. civil aviation system requires all critical flight systems to be backed up by redundant capabilities.[642] This policy aims at reducing the chances that failure at a single point could result in a catastrophic accident. Because the mathematical chances that two systems will fail simultaneously are far less than the probability that either of the systems will fail independently, redundancy is an effective risk management strategy. Indeed, civil aviation safety policies, designed to reduce the risk of catastrophic systems failure to one in a billion, are based partly on this principle.[643]

Achieving such a precise and ambitious mathematical goal is difficult in any discipline; it is even a greater challenge in the area of aviation security, where human factors, such as criminal imagination and screener performance, predominate.[644] Nevertheless, aviation experts have long agreed that effective layering in security, like redundancy in safety, can greatly reduce the likelihood of catastrophic failure. Realizing the potential benefits of a layered system, however, rests on two key factors.

First, the layers must be designed to guard against the right problems. For instance, a security checkpoint not designed to stop knives, and onboard security not designed to stop a suicide hijacker, may represent two layers of security, but they will not defeat a knife-wielding suicide hijacker.

Second, each layer must effectively address in its own right whatever it is designed to prevent. Two ineffectual layers operating in tandem may be little or no better than a single defense. Given the serious holes in aviation security demonstrated by the system's performance on 9/11 and discussed above, it is difficult to conceive of the defenses in place on that day as a "system of systems, layered, integrated and working together to produce the highest possible levels of protection."

As DOT Inspector General Kenneth Mead testified before the Commission:

> I think that the system we had in place before September 11 had in fact undergone incremental improvements over the years . . . and I believe in fact it provided a deterrent value for certain types of threat. Overall, though, the model on which the system was based did not work very well, and there were significant weaknesses in the protections it provided, even for the types of threats the system was designed to prevent.[645]

2.3 THE STAGE IS SET

Throughout 2001, the senior leadership of the FAA was focused on congestion and delays within the system and the ever-present issue of safety, but they were not as focused on security.[646] The Administrator recalled that "every day in 2001 was like the day before Thanksgiving."[647] The Deputy Administrator told the Commission that not a day went by in the spring of 2000 through the summer of 2001 that system delays were not priorities for him and the Administrator.[648]

Heeding calls for improved service and increased capacity, Congress focused its legislative and oversight attention on measures to improve the capacity, efficiency, and customer service of the aviation system. Its efforts included passage of a "passenger bill of rights," mainly to ensure greater convenience and comfort for passengers. The air carriers' trade association chief pointed out that all the while, the Department of Transportation was rating the air carriers by their on-time arrival records which added pressure to the effort to process people with great speed.[649] At the same time, the air carriers were struggling to keep up with demand, provide better customer service, and improve their economic health.

The American public—the customers of the aviation industry and the constituents of members of Congress—were generally sanguine about commercial aviation safety and security in the period leading up to 9/11. In an ABC poll taken just after the 1999 EgyptAir crash off the East Coast of the United States, 58 percent of the respondents indicated their belief that flying was safer than driving; and in a Fox News/Opinion Dynamics survey conducted during the same period, 78 percent cited poor maintenance as "a greater threat to airline safety" than terrorism.[650]

On September 11, 2001:

- The no-fly lists updated by FAA security directives offered an opportunity to prevent potential hijackers from boarding civilian aircraft in or traveling to the United States. As of September 11, 2001—only 12 individuals were listed—and not any of the 9/11 hijackers, even though two of them (Khalid al Mihdhar and Nawaf al Hazmi) were already on the State Department's TIPOFF terrorist watchlist (which contained more than 60,000 names).
- Checkpoint screener performance and the detection rate of prohibited items at airport checkpoints were spotty, and these weaknesses were widely known.
- Deadly knives were permitted aboard aircraft despite FAA's recognition that this policy was a vulnerability.
- A wide range of deadly weapons were undetectable by the screening equipment using the sensitivity levels then employed at security checkpoints.
- Selectees of the passenger prescreening risk profiling system (CAPPS) were subject to a search of their checked bags for explosives but underwent no additional scrutiny of their person or carry-on baggage.
- The official aircrew protocol for hijacking was cooperation and accommodation.

Thus, on 9/11 the challenge for would-be hijackers of domestic flights of U.S. air carriers boiled down to grasping three easily understood points: avoid prior notice by the U.S. intelligence and law enforcement communities, carry items that could be used as weapons that were either permissible or not detectable by the screening systems in place, and understand the in-flight hijacking protocol.

While intelligence authorities perceived the continuing terrorist threat to civil aviation, on September 10, 2001, the view of policymakers, air carriers, and the public contemplating civil aviation security was that there had not been a hijacking or bombing of a U.S. air carrier in many years and that aviation security measures were apparently gaining ground against the terrorists.[651]

In fact, the system was broken.

---

1 Colgan Air is a US Airways Express carrier providing regional service to east coast destinations. US Airways and American Airlines had an agreement that allowed passengers to make reservations for both airlines in the same booking.
2 FBI report,"The Final 24 Hours," Dec. 8, 2003.

3 Michael T. interview, (May 27, 2004); FBI report of investigation, interview of Diane G., Sept. 19, 2001.

4 Michael T. interview, (May 27, 2004).

5 CAPPS was an FAA-approved automated system run by the airlines that scored each passenger's profile to identify those who might pose a threat to civil aviation, and identified other passengers at random to be selectees. Also, ticket agents were to mark as "selectees" those passengers who failed to show proper identification, or met other criteria. See FAA report, "Air carrier Standard Security Program," May 20, 2001, pp. 75-76; FAA record of interview, Donna Thompson, Sept. 23, 2001. See Al Hickson briefing (June 8, 2004).

6 FAA report, "Air Carrier Standard Security Program," May 20, 2001, pp. 75-76.

7 Portland International Jetport briefing,(Aug. 18, 2003).

8 FBI report,"The Final 24 Hours," Dec. 8, 2003. See also FBI report, "Copy of surveillance video, ATTA/ALOMARI in Portland, Maine," Sept. 11, 2001.

9 Portland International Jetport briefing,(Aug. 18, 2003).

10 FBI report of investigation, "Copy of Surveillance Video ATTA/ALOMARI in Portland, Maine," Sept. 11, 2001.

11 FBI report of investigation, interview of Kenneth Anderson, Sept. 11, 2001.

12 US Airways record, passenger manifest for Colgan Air Flight No. 5930 on September 11, 2001.

13 FBI report of investigation, interview of Kenneth Anderson, Sept. 11, 2001.

14 FBI report of investigation, interview of Susan Yochelson, Oct. 12, 2001.

15 The FBI's Portland office pursued 600 leads related to the presence of Atta and Omari in Portland, with each lead resulting in between 3 and 10 interviews. The Portland police pursued more than 60 leads. regarding the presence of Atta and Omari; but none shed any light on the question of their travel to and from Portland, Maine. South Portland Police Chief and authorities with the Maine State Police also indicated that while their departments did investigate the hijackers' trip to Portland and shared the results of their work with the FBI, they turned up no information to indicate why this travel occurred. See Michael Chitwood briefing, undated; See also Edward Googins briefing, (June 21, 2004); and William Snedeker briefing, (June 21, 2004).

16 As the operational leader, Atta would have been particularly inclined to have such concerns and may have believed he was the one most likely to have been identified and placed under surveillance by U.S. authorities.

17 FBI response to Commission briefing request no. 6, undated (topic 11).

18 Tom Kinton interview, (Nov. 6, 2003).

19 See also, Matt Carroll, "Fighting Terror Sense of Alarm; Airlines Foiled Logan Police Probe," Boston Globe, Oct. 17, 2001, p. B1.

20 The FBI also reported that on Aug. 27, 2001, Atta possibly attempted to purchase box cutters in Florida. Among the possessions Atta left behind was a large folding knife. FBI report, "Summary of Penttbom Investigation," Jan. 31, 2003.

21 See FBI report of investigation, witness, Sept. 11, 2001.

22 FBI report, "The Final 24 Hours," December 8, 2004. A rental car associated with Al-Shehri was found later in the day in the Logan parking lot. An individual who had parked his car in the lot in order to catch an early morning flight from Boston reported that three Middle Eastern men were parked in a car next to him. One of the men opened their car door to exit, effectively preventing the traveler from getting out of his car. After a time, he grew tired of waiting for the individual who was "fiddling with his things" to collect his belongings and depart. At that point, the citizen pushed the others' car door away from his and up against the Middle Eastern man so that he could exit. The citizen reported that the three subjects said nothing to either him or each other and offered no response. When he heard about the attacks, he contacted the authorities to report the incident. See FBI report of investigation, interview with witness, Sept. 11, 2001. Logan parking records showed that rental cars associated with the hijackers had been in and out of the airport's parking facility over several days previous to 9/11. Massport report, response to Commission questions for the record, undated.

23 TSA report, "Selectee Status of September 11th Hijackers," (undated).

24 TSA report, "Selectee Status of September 11th Hijackers," (undated).

25 The two bags that Atta checked in Portland were not loaded aboard Flight 11 before the flight departed. A witness from American Airlines told the FBI that the bags came over from US Airways to American's baggage area too late to make it on to the flight. The bag tags were marked designating them to be put

aboard the airline's next flight to Los Angeles. After the attacks the bags were opened and law enforcement officers found a Koran, tape on flying a jetliner, a large folding knives and a distance measuring ruler. See FBI report of investigation, interview of witness, Sept. 19, 2001.

26 FAA report, "Air Carrier Standard Security Program," May 20, 2001.

27 FAA briefing materials, "Assessment and Testing Data for BOS, EWR, and IAD," Oct. 24, 2001.

28 Air Transport Association/Regional Airlines Association (ATA/RAA) report, "Air Carriers Checkpoint Operations Guide," Aug. 1999; FAA report, "Air Carrier Standard Security Program," May, 2001, appendix VI

29 FBI reports of investigation, interview of Nilda Cora, Oct. 4, 2001. See also, Mary Carol Turano interview (Mar. 11, 2004). See also, FBI reports of investigation, supervisor of B4 checkpoint, Sept. 15, 2001.

30 FBI response to Commission briefing request no. 6, undated (topic 11). [LES]

31 The times for check-in and boarding for the American flights are approximate because the airline's reservations and ticketing systems did "not provide exact times for such activities." See American Airlines report, "SABRE response for Flight 11, September 11, 2001,"; The records for Flight 11 indicated that some passengers had "boarded" after the aircraft had pushed back from the gate. AAL response to Commission questions for the record, Mar. 15, 2004.

32 AAL response to Commission questions for the record, Mar. 15, 2004.

33 AAL record, Dispatch Environmental Control/Weekly Flight Summary for Flight 11, Sept. 11, 2001.

34 AAL report, "Flight Attendant Jump Seat Locations During Takeoff and Flight Attendant Typical Cabin. Positions During Start of Cabin Service," undated.

35 AAL record, "Schematic of 767 aircraft," undated.

36 AAL record, "Passenger Name List Flight 11/September 11," undated.

37 AAL report,"Average Load Factor by Day-of Week," undated (for Flights 11 and 77 from June 11, 2001 b Sept. 9. 2001); AAL response to the Commission's supplemental document requests, Jan. 20, 2004.

38 FBI report, "Summary of Penttbom Investigation," Jan. 31, 2003; The FBI investigated individuals who were "no shows" for the flights and did not find terrorist links. See also, FBI response to Commission briefing request no. 6, undated (topic 11). [LES]

39 American Airlines response to Commission questions for the record, Mar. 15, 2004. See also, American Airlines record, Dispatch Environmental Control/Weekly Flight Summary for Flight 11, Sept. 11, 2001.

40 Craig Marquis and others interview (Nov. 19, 2003).

41 14 CFR § 121.587, "Closing and locking of flight crew compartment door."

42 Each American Airlines flight was assigned a "dispatcher" by the air carrier. The dispatcher located in the airline's operations center at its Texas headquarters was responsible for authorizing and monitoring the operation of the flight. See AAL system operations control personnel interview (Jan. 8, 2004).

43 JET A fuel was the type used on 9/11 and the normal fuel used by the airline. For amount loaded on Flight 11 see AAL record, Dispatch Environmental Control/Weekly Flight Summary for Flight 11, Sept. 11, 2001; American Airlines response to Commission questions for the record, Mar. 15, 2004.

44 AAL record, Dispatch Environmental Control/Weekly Flight Summary for Flight 11, Sept. 11, 2001.

45 NTSB report, "Flight Path Study—American Airlines Flight 11," Feb. 19, 2002; Commission analysis of NTSB and FAA air traffic control and radar data; System Operations Control interviews interview (Jan. 8, 2004).

46 United flight operations briefing (Nov. 20, 2003).

47 NTSB report, Air Traffic Control Recording—American Airlines Flight 11, Dec. 21, 2001; FAA report, Aircraft Accident File ZBW-ARTCC-148, Feb. 15, 2002.

48 American Airlines, "Flight Attendant Jump Seat Locations During Takeoff and Flight Attendant Typical Cabin Positions During Start of Cabin Service for Flights 11 and 77," undated.

49 Given that the Flight 11 cockpit crew had been acknowledging all previous instructions from ATC that morning within a matter of seconds, and that when the first reporting of the hijacking was received a short time later (Betty Ong's 8:18:47 call) a number of actions had already been taken by the hijackers, it is most likely that the hijacking of Flight 11 occurred at 8:14 A.M. or very shortly thereafter.

50 8:18:47 a.m. according to phone records. FBI report, "American Airlines Airphone Usage," Sept. 20, 2001.

51 Nydia Gonzalez interview (Nov. 19, 2003).

52 Nydia Gonzalez interview (Nov. 19, 2003).

53 AAL transcript, telephone call from Betty Ong to Nydia Gonzalez, Sept. 11, 2001.
54 "Daniel Lewin," Washington Post, Sept. 22, 2001, p. B7.
55 AAL transcript, telephone call from Betty Ong to Nydia Gonzalez, Sept. 11, 2001.
56 AAL System Operations Control interviews (Jan. 8, 2004).
57 Under FAA rules all aircraft traveling over 10,000 feet are required to emit a signal while in flight. This signal was received by FAA to create a radar image providing aircraft identification and some flight information. See DOD radar file, 84th Radar Evaluation Squadron, "9/11 autoplay." Also, see NTSB, "Flight Path Study—American Airlines Flight 11," Feb. 19, 2002.
58 AAL transcript, telephone call from Betty Ong to Nydia Gonzalez, Sept. 11, 2001; AAL transcript, telephone call from Nydia Gonzalez to Craig Marquis, Sept. 11, 2001.
59 Michael Woodward interview (Jan. 25, 2004).
60 FBI report, "American Airlines Airphone Usage," Sept. 20, 2001.
61 Most ACARS messages include ellipses in the original message. They do not signify deleted material; AAL record, Dispatch Environmental Control/Weekly Flight Summary for Flight 11, Sept. 11, 2001.
62 AAL transcript, telephone call from Betty Ong to Nydia Gonzalez, Sept. 11, 2001; AAL transcript, telephone call from Nydia Gonzalez to Craig Marquis, Sept. 11, 2001.
63 AAL transcript, telephone call from Nydia Gonzalez to Craig Marquis, Sept. 11, 2001.
64 FBI report, "American Airlines Airphone Usage," Sept. 20, 2001.
65 FAA report, ZBW-ARTCC-148,46R, at 8:24:38, and 8:24:56; see also, Peter Zalewski interview (Sept. 23, 2003).
66 FAA memo, "Full Transcript; Aircraft Accident; AAL 11; New York, NY; September 11, 2001," Feb. 15, 2002. p.11; Peter Zalewski interview (Sept. 23, 2003).
67 Peter Zalewski interview (Sept. 23, 2003); John Schippani interview (Sept. 22, 2003).
68 American Airlines record, Dispatch Environmental Control/Weekly Flight Summary for Flight 11, Sept. 11, 2001.
69 Michael Woodward interview (Jan. 25, 2004).
70 Terry Biggio interview (Sept. 22, 2003) and Dan Bueno interview (Sept. 22, 2003); and Daily Record of Facility Operation, Boston Center, OMIC Position, page 1, (September 11, 2001).
71 AAL transcript, telephone call from Nydia Gonzalez to Craig Marquis, Sept. 11, 2001.
72 FAA audio file, Herndon Command Center, position # 15, at 8:28; Daniel Bueno interview (Sept. 22, 2003).
73 AAL transcript, telephone call from AAL System Operations Control to Boston FAA Air Traffic Control center, Sept. 11, 2001; AAL transcript, telephone call from Nydia Gonzalez to Craig Marquis, Sept. 11, 2001.
74 FAA recording, ATCSCC, NOM Position, Line 4525, Sept. 11, 2001.
75 FBI report, "American Airlines Airphone Usage," Sept. 20, 2001. In trying to regain a connection after her 8:25 A.M. call had been cut off, Sweeney was also connected briefly at 8:29 A.M.
76 Michael Woodward interview (Jan. 25, 2004); AAL notes, Michael Woodward handwritten notes, Sept. 11, 2001; FBI report of investigation, interview of Michael Woodward, Sept. 13, 2001; AAL report, interview of Michael Woodward, Sept. 11, 2001; AAL transcript, telephone call from Nancy Wyatt to Ray Howland, Sept. 11, 2001.
77 Michael Woodward interview (Jan. 25, 2004).
78 Gerard Arpey interview (Jan. 8, 2004).
79 AAL transcript, telephone call from Nydia Gonzalez to Craig Marquis, Sept. 11, 2001.
80 American Airlines response to Commission questions for the record, April 26, 2004 and July, 2004.
81 AAL transcript, telephone call from Nydia Gonzalez to Craig Marquis, Sept. 11, 2001.
82 FAA memo, "Full Transcript; Aircraft Accident; AAL 11; New York, NY; September 11, 2001," Feb. 15, 2002. p.12.
83 Terry Biggio interviews (Sept. 22, 2003 and Jan. 8, 2004); Daniel Bueno interview (Sept. 22, 2003); FAA audio file, Herndon Command Center New York Center position, line 5114, September 11, 2001, from 8:30 to 8:46.
84 AAL transcript, telephone call from Nydia Gonzalez to Craig Marquis, Sept. 11, 2001.
85 AAL transcript, telephone call from Nydia Gonzalez to Craig Marquis, Sept. 11, 2001.
86 AAL transcript, telephone call from Nydia Gonzalez to Craig Marquis, Sept. 11, 2001; AAL report, SOCC Chronology, Jan, 15, 2002. At 8:38 A.M. and 8:48 A.M. additional ACARS messages were sent

from the airline to Flight 11 requesting that the pilot contact Air Traffic Control. See AAL record, American Airlines record, Dispatch Environmental Control/Weekly Flight Summary for Flight 11, Sept. 11, 2001.

[87] AAL transcript, telephone call from Nydia Gonzalez to Craig Marquis, Sept. 11, 2001. AAL also sent ACARS messages asking Flight 11 to contact FAA Air Traffic Control at: 8:38 A.M and 8:48 A.M.

88 Published timelines from the FAA and NORAD place the notification time at 8:40. NEADS recordings indicate, however, that the actual call came in at 8:37:15 to the Weapons Director Technician position, Channel 14.

89 Published timelines from the FAA and NORAD place the notification time at 8:40 A.M. NEADS recordings indicate, however, that the actual call came in at 8:37:15 A.M to the Weapons Director Technician position, Channel 14. Robert Marr interview (Jan. 23, 2004).

90 Larry Arnold testimony (May 23, 2003).

91 Larry Arnold, quoted in Air War Over America, by Leslie Filson, p. 56.

92 William A. Scott testimony (May 23, 2003).

93 Michael Woodward interview (Jan. 25, 2004).

94 For report on passengers see Michael Woodward interview (Jan. 25, 2004); AAL transcript, telephone call from Nancy Wyatt to Ray Howland, Sept. 11, 2001. The other flight attendants were assisting their fellow attendants who had been injured and passengers while Ms. Ong and Sweeney remained in communication with ground authorities.

95 AAL transcript, telephone call from Nydia Gonzalez to Craig Marquis, Sept. 11, 2001; FAA rules require air carriers to provide immediate notification of an "act or suspected act of airplane piracy." Sec, XI, May 20, 2001, p. 110.

96 AAL transcript, telephone call from Nydia Gonzalez to Craig Marquis, Sept. 11, 2001.

97 AAL transcript, telephone call from Nydia Gonzalez to Craig Marquis, Sept. 11, 2001.

98 Michael Woodward interview (Jan. 25, 2004).

99 AAL, transcript of call from Nancy Wyatt to Ray Howland, Sept. 11, 2001.

100 AAL security interview (Jan. 8, 2004).

101 NEADS audio file, Mission Crew Commander position, Channel 2, at 8:44:48.

102 NEADS audio file, Mission Crew Commander position, Channel 2, at 8:44:58.

103 Joseph McCain interview (Oct. 28, 2003); Dawne Deskins interview (Oct. 30, 2003).

104 NTSB report, "Flight Path Study—American Airlines Flight 11," Feb. 19, 2002.

105 American Airlines response to Commission questions for the record, April 26, 2004 and July 7, 2004; Gerard Arpey interview (Jan. 8, 2004).

106 Peter Zalewski interview (Sept. 23, 2003.)

107 AAL transcript, telephone call from AAL system operations control to FAA Air Traffic Control System Command Center, Sept. 11, 2001.

108 Boston Center was reporting information it had received from an FAA headquarters teleconference. NEADS audio file, Identification Technician position, Channel 7, at 9:21:10.

109 The report of Flight 11 heading south – the cause of the Langley scramble – is reflected not just in taped conversations at NEADS, but in taped conversations at various FAA centers, on NORAD's instant messaging system, and on taped conversations of the Pentagon-convened "significant event" (which transitioned to an "air threat") conference call. The report was also readily acknowledged in Commission interviews of operational personnel in FAA and NORAD. Nonetheless, it is not recounted in a single public timeline or statement issued by the FAA or the Department of Defense. Instead, the scramble at Langley was publicly attributed to the reported hijacking of Flight 77, Flight 93, or some combination of the two.

110 Kevin J. Nasypany interview (Jan. 22-23, 2004). (9:09 A.M. NEADS ordered alert fighters at Langley Air Force Base to battle stations (in response to receiving word that Flight 175 had crashed into the World Trade Center).

111 NEADS Mission crew commander technician log, Sept. 11, 2001.

112 Kevin J. Nasypany interview (Jan. 23, 2004).

113 NEADS audio file, Mission Crew Commander position, Channel 2, at 9:28:16.

114 DOD radar files, 84th Radar evaluation squadron, "9/11 Autoplay."

115 AAL report, "Systems Operation Command Center (SOCC) Chronology for September 11, 2001," Jan. 15, 2002.

116 FAA security personnel interview (Sept. 11, 2003).

117 AAL security personnel interview (Nov. 19, 2003).

118 AAL transcript, telephone call from Betty Ong to Nydia Gonzalez, Sept. 11, 2001; AAL transcript, telephone call from Nydia Gonzalez to Craig Marquis, Sept. 11, 2001; Nydia Gonzales interview (Nov. 19, 2003); Michael Woodward interview (Jan. 25, 2004); Michael Woodward notes, Sept. 11, 2001; AAL, email from Woodward to Schmidt, "Flight 11 Account of Events," Sept. 19, 2001.

119 AAL transcript, telephone call from Nydia Gonzalez to Craig Marquis, Sept. 11, 2001;

120 FBI report, "Summary of Penttbom Investigation," Jan. 31, 2003.

121 FBI report, "Summary of Penttbom Investigation," Jan. 31, 2003.

122 Jawahir recalled that her encounter with the Ghamdis occurred at "shortly before 7 A.M., and when shown photos of the hijackers she indicated that Mohand Al Shehri resembled one of the two she checked in. Thus, her experience may have actually been with Fayez Banihammad and Mohand al Shehri, who checked in at 6:53 A.M. However, Jawahir recalled that the two individuals she spoke with had the same last name and had assigned seats on Row 9, characteristics that both fit the Ghamdis; therefore, that account has been adopted here. In either case, it is almost certain that she was dealing with one set of the hijackers. UAL, "Flight 175—11Sep01 Passenger ACI Check-in History," July 11, 2002.

123 UAL, "Flight 175—11Sep01 Passenger ACI Check-in History," July 11, 2002.

124 FBI report of investigation, interview of Manuel Carreiro, Sept. 28, 2001.

125 FBI reports of investigation, interviews of Gail Jawahir, Sept. 21, 2001 and Sept. 28, 2001. Customer service representative Gail Jawahir recalled that her encounter with the Ghamdis occurred at "shortly before 7 A.M., " and when shown photos of the hijackers, she indicated that Mohand al Shehri resembled one of the two she checked in (suggesting they were Banihammad and Shehri). However, she also recalled that the men had the same last name and had assigned seats in row 9 (i.e. the Ghamdis), and that account has been adopted here. In either case, she almost certainly was dealing with one set of the Flight 175 hijackers.

126 UAL, "Flight 175—11Sep01 Passenger ACI Check-in History," July 11, 2002.

127 UAL, "Flight 175—11Sep01 Passenger ACI Check-in History," July 11, 2002.

128 Logan Site Visit and Briefing (Aug. 15, 2003).

129 FBI response to Commission briefing request no. 6, undated (topic 11).

130 UAL, "Flight 175—11Sep01 Passenger ACI Check-in History," July 11, 2002.

131 TSA report, "Selectee Status of September 11th Hijackers," (undated).

132 The time range for checkpoint screening of the hijackers is that between check-in and boarding: Marwan al Shehhi (*6:45 A.M.–7:27 A.M.*); Fayez Banihammad (*6:53 A.M.–7:23 A.M.*); Mohand al Shehri (*6:53 A.M.–7:23 A.M.*); Ahmed al Ghamdi (*6:20 A.M.–7:27 A.M.*);Hamza al Ghamdi (*6:20 A.M.–7:27 A.M.*).

133 FBI reports of investigation, interviews of William Thomas, Sept. 14, 2001; Jennifer Gore, Sept. 12, 2001; Claudia Richey, Sept. 15, 2001.

134 UAL, "Flight 175—11Sep01 Passenger ACI Check-in History," July 11, 2002; UAL, response to Commission questions for the record, May 13, 2004.

135 FAA report, "Executive Summary Chronology of a Multiple Hijacking Crisis, September 11, 2001," September 17, 2001.

136 UAL report, "United Flight 175: Flight Attendant Positions/Jumpseats," undated.

137 FAA report, "Executive Summary Chronology of a Multiple Hijacking Crisis, September 11, 2001," September 17, 2001; UAL report, Flight 175, Flight Data Recap; UAL response to Commission questions for the record, May 13, 2004.

138 Flight 175 was canceled on Monday, July 16, 2001, and contained a load factor of only 28.6 percent on Wednesday, August 29, 2001.

139 In addition, the September 11, 2001 passenger load was similar to the loads on comparable Tuesday dates in 1999 (37.2 percent on 9/14/99) and 2000 (36.6 percent on 9/12/00).UAL report, "Flight 175 BOS-LAX Load Factors," undated (from June 1, 2001 to Sept. 11, 2001; UAL report, "Explanation of Load Factors."

140 FBI report, response to Commission briefing request no. 6, undated (topic 8).

141 UAL record, "Weight and Balance Information—Flight number 175, Sept. 11, 2001."

142 UAL, "United Flight 175: Flight Attendant Positions/Jumpseats," undated; UAL flight operations briefing (Nov. 20, 2003)

143 UAL response to Commission questions for the record, April 5, 2004.

144 Ed Ballinger interview (Apr. 14, 2004).

145 FAA, "Executive Summary Chronology of a Multiple Hijacking Crisis, September 11, 2001," September 17, 2001; NTSB report, "Flight Path Study—United Flight 175," Feb. 19, 2002.

146 FAA Memo, "Full Transcript; Aircraft Accident; UAL 175; New York, NY; September 11, 2001," FAA Boston Center, position 47R. FAA transcripts of air traffic controllers' communications with Flight 175 include relevant communications with the FAA's Boston and New York Centers, but are titled "New York, NY" because the aircraft crash occurred in New York.

147 "Full Transcript; Aircraft Accident; UAL 175; New York, NY; September 11, 2001; FAA Boston Center, position 20R.

148 UAL, "United Flight 175: Flight Attendant Positions/Jumpseats," undated.

149 "FAA Memo, "Full Transcript; Aircraft Accident; UAL 175; New York, NY; September 11, 2001," FAA New York Center, position 42R. On September 11, 2001, passengers aboard United Airlines flights could monitor communications between FAA air traffic controllers and the pilots by selecting channel 9 on their headsets. United Airlines is the only U.S. airline to permit passengers to monitor air traffic control communications. Commission staff's interview of a United Airlines pilot revealed that United Airlines' passengers were permitted to monitor ATC communications after September 11, 2001 and at least as late as January 2004. See Timothy Duffy interview (Jan. 7, 2004).

150 NTSB report, Air traffic Control recording—United Airlines Flight 175, Dec. 21, 2001

151 FAA Memo, "Full Transcript; Aircraft Accident; UAL 175; New York, NY; September 11, 2001," FAA New York Center, position 42R.

152 NTSB report, Air traffic Control recording—United Airlines Flight 175, Dec. 21, 2001.

153 Interview of UAL System Operations Control Center personnel (Nov. 21, 2003).

154 UAL System Operations Control Center briefing (Nov. 20, 2003).

155 NTSB report, Air traffic Control recording—United Airlines Flight 175, Dec. 21, 2001.

156 Passenger Peter Hanson was assigned to seat 19E, but called from row 30 CDE. Another passenger was seated in 6F, but called from row 32 CDE, and passenger Brian David Sweeney was originally in 15A but called from row 31 AB. The flight attendant calls to UAL's maintenance facility in San Francisco (By dialing *fix) were made from row 31. FBI report of investigation, air phone records of for flights 93 and 175 on Sept. 11, 2001, Sept. 18, 2001; UAL report, "Flight 175—11Sep01 Passenger ACI Check-in History," July 11, 2002.

157 NTSB report, "Flight Path Study—United Flight 175," Feb. 19, 2002. Flight 175's transponder code changed nearly simultaneously with the impact of American 11 into the North Tower of the World Trade Center.

158 NTSB report, "Flight Path Study—United Flight 175," Feb. 19, 2002.

159 FAA Memo, "Full transcript; Aircraft Accident; UAL 175; New York, NY; September 11, 2001," FAA New York Center, position 42R.

160 FAA Memo, "Full transcript; Aircraft Accident; UAL 175; New York, NY; September 11, 2001," FAA New York Center, position 42R.

161 NTSB report, "Flight Path Study—United Flight 175," Feb. 19, 2002.

162 FAA memo, "Full Transcript; Aircraft Accident; UAL175; New York, NY; September 11, 2001." May 8, 2002, p. 9.

163 FAA Memo, "Full transcript; Aircraft Accident; UAL 175; New York, NY; September 11, 2001," FAA New York Center, position 42R. At 8:57, the following exchange between David Bottiglia and another New York controller occurred: "I got some handoffs over here. We got some incidents going over here. Is Delta 2433 going to be okay at thirty-three [thousand feet]? I had to climb him for traffic.

164 FBI report of investigation, air phone records for flights 93 and 175 on Sept, 11, 2001, Sept. 18, 2001.

165 FBI report of investigation, interview of Lee Hanson, Sept. 11, 2001.

166 The time of 8:52 A.M. is based on GTE Airfone records, which indicate two completed calls to the SAMC Star-fix location from Flight 175, the first of 75 seconds duration beginning at 8:52:01, and the second of 31 seconds beginning at 8:56:19. The recipient of the Star-fix call(s) from Flight 175, Marc Policastro, recalled only one such communication. United investigators determined that only one call was received. See UAL, letter from Jeff Plantz, United Senior Staff Investigator, to Assistant U.S. Attorney

David J. Novak, July 31, 2002. Whether or not there were two calls or only one, the longer first communication is more consistent with Policastro's recollection of the duration and information imparted during the call. See also, interview of Marc Policastro, (Nov. 21, 2003).

167 Flight crew onboard United aircraft could contact this office by simply dialing *349 on an air phone. FBI report of investigation, interview of David Price, Jan. 24, 2002.

168 Marc Policastro interview (Nov. 21, 2003); FBI report of investigation, interview of Marc Policastro, Sept. 11, 2001; Notes of Marc Policastro, Sept. 11, 2001. Rich Miles interview (Nov. 21, 2003).

169 FBI report of investigation, interview of David Price, Jan. 24, 2002.

170 FBI report of investigation, "Lead To Contact Final Phone Numbers Called From Airphones," undated[LES]; FBI report of investigation, interview of family member related to call, Sept. 12, 2001 [LES]; and FBI report of investigation, air phone records for flights 93 and 175 on Sept. 11, 2001, Sept. 18, 2001.

171 FAA recording, ATCSCC, Pos 14C, tape 1230-1330, operations line 1540, Sept. 11, 2001.

172 UAL System Operations Control Center briefing (Nov. 20, 2003); UAL report, [System Operations Control Center personnel] September 11, 2001 Timeline.

173 Evanna Dowis interview (Sept. 30, 2003); and FAA, "Executive Summary Chronology of a Multiple Hijacking Crisis, September 11, 2001," Sept. 17, 2001.

174 NTSB report, "Flight Path Study—United Flight 175," Feb. 19, 2002.

175 FAA Memo, "Full transcript; Aircraft Accident; UAL 175; New York, NY; September 11, 2001," FAA New York Center, position 42R.

176 FBI report of investigation, air phone records for flights 93 and 175 on Sept. 11, 2001, Sept. 18, 2001

177 FBI report of investigation, interview of Julie Sweeney, Oct. 10, 2001.

178 UAL report, Flight 175 ACARS; and FBI report of investigation, Interview of Edward D. Ballinger, January 29, 2002.

179 The Commission attempted to precisely identify the time that the SAMC notified United's headquarters about the call from the flight attendant aboard Flight 175. However, United reported that that on 9/11, none of the calls into or out of SAMC were recorded by United because the telephone system was not set up to record calls. Furthermore, "no usage billing was created for these calls. United did not keep any records of calls that left SAMC and no call-by-call detail reporting was created for calls made over this tie-line." See: UAL report, "Explanation of SAMC Phone Records for Calls to United WHQ." July 16, 2004.

180 UAL System Operations Control Center personnel interview (Nov. 21, 2003).

181 The operations center manager recalled that the operations center director's briefing on his 8:50 call to the FAA had triggered the manager's first communication with senior corporate leadership that day. UAL System Operations Control Center briefing (Nov. 20, 2003).

182 On call to airline's security chief see Marc Policastro interview (Nov. 21, 2003); UAL System Operations Control Center personnel interview (Nov. 21, 2003); UAL System Operations Control Center briefing, (Nov. 20, 2003).

183 UAL response to Commission questions for the record, July 13, 2004.

184 FBI report of investigation, air phone records for flights 93 and 175 on Sept. 11, 2001, Sept. 18, 2001.

185 FBI report of investigation, interview of Louise Sweeney, Sept. 28, 2001.

186 FBI report of investigation, air phone records for flights 93 and 175 on Sept. 11, 2001, Sept. 18, 2001.

187 Lee Hanson took two sheets of notes during the call, which served as the basis for his reconstruction of its contents. The only additional detail he recalled was that after his son had made the comment about the plane going to Chicago to fly into a building, a woman had screamed in the background. See FBI report of investigation, interview of Lee Hanson, Sept. 11, 2001.

188 FBI report of investigation, interview of Lee Hanson, Sept. 11, 2001.

189 Ed Ballinger interview (Apr. 14, 2004).

190 FAA Memo, "Full Transcript; Command Center; NOM Operational Position; September 11, 2001," Oct. 14, 2003, pp. 15-17.

191 FAA Memo, "Full transcript; Aircraft Accident; UAL 175; New York, NY; September 11, 2001," Jan. 17, 2002, p. 3.

192 FAA audio file, Herndon Command Center, New York Center position, line 5114, 9:02:34 a.m.

193 Joseph McCain interview (Oct. 28, 2003); Robert Marr interview (Jan. 23, 2004); James Fox interview (Oct. 29, 2003); Dawne Deskins interview (Oct. 30, 2003); NEADS audio files, Identification Technician positions, channels 4, 5 and 7, 9:02 to 9:15 a.m.

194 NTSB report, "Flight Path Study—United Flight 175," Feb. 19, 2002; and staff analysis of radar data.

195 NTSB report, "Flight Path Study—United Flight 175," Feb. 19, 2002.

196 FAA audio file, Herndon Command Center; New York Center position, line 5114, 9:03:22 a.m.

197 UAL report, Flight 175 ACARS on Sept. 11, 2001; Ed Ballinger interview (Apr. 14, 2004).

198 UAL report, Flight 175 ACARS on Sept. 11, 2001.

199 FAA audio file, Herndon Command Center, New York Center position, line 5114, 9:04 a.m.

200 NEADS audio files, Identification Technician positions, channels 4, 5 and 7, 9:04 to 9:07 a.m. Maureen Dooley interview (Oct. 27, 2003); Shelley Watson interview (Oct. 27, 2003); Stacia Roundtree interview (Oct. 27, 2003).

201 FAA audio file, Herndon Command Center, Boston Center position, line 5115, 9:05 a.m.

202 FAA audio file, Herndon Command Center, Boston Center position, line 5115, 9:05 a.m.; Michael McCormick interview (Oct. 1, 2003); David LaCates interview (Oct. 2, 2003).

203 FAA audio file, Herndon Command Center, New York Center position, line 5114, 9:07 a.m.; Terry Biggio interviews (Sept. 22, 2003; Jan. 8, 2004).

204 NEADS audio file, Mission Crew Commander position, channel 2, 9:07:32 a.m.

205 Robert Marr interview (Oct. 27, 2003); Larry Arnold interview (Feb. 3, 2004); Robert Marr, quoted in Air War Over America, by Leslie Filson, p. 60: "The plan was to protect New York City."

206 NEADS audio file, Mission Crew Commander position, channel 2, 9:08:36 a.m.; Robert Marr interviews (Oct. 27, 2003; Jan. 23, 2004); Larry Arnold interview (Feb. 3, 2004); Kevin Nasypany interview (Jan. 22-23, 2004).

207 FAA Memo, "Full transcript; Aircraft Accident; UAL 175; New York, NY; September 11, 2001," Boston Center Air Traffic Controller position 31R.

208 UAL report, Mike B. September 11, 2001 Timeline.

209 UAL System Operations Control Center briefing (Nov. 20, 2003).

210 UAL report, Mike Barber September 11, 2001 Timeline; UAL report "Timeline for Dispatch/SMFDO Activities—Terrorist Crisis," undated.

211 Daniel Nash interview (Oct. 14, 2003); Timothy Duffy interview (Jan. 7, 2004); NTSB report, "Flight Path Study—United Flight 175," Feb. 19, 2002; Commission analysis of FAA radar data.

212 FAA audio file, Herndon Command Center, Boston/Cleveland Center position, line 5115, 9:15:32 a.m.; Daniel Bueno interview (Sept. 22, 2003).

213 Ellen King interview (Apr. 5, 2004).

214 Ed Ballinger interview (Apr. 14, 2004).

215 UAL report, Mike Barber September 11, 2001 Timeline. An FAA executive summary of the 9/11 hijackings, prepared on September 17, 2001 by FAA, indicated that UAL 175 was "missing from radar" at 9:20 A.M. See FAA report, "Executive Summary Chronology of a Multiple Hijacking Crisis, September 11, 2001," Sept. 17, 2001.

216 UAL report, "UAL Timeline for Operational Messages ATC/UAL—Terrorist Crisis," September 11, 2001; and Rich "Doc" Miles interview (Nov. 21, 2003).

217 Rich "Doc" Miles interview (Nov. 21, 2003).

218 UAL report, Flight 175 ACARS on Sept. 11, 2001; and Ed Ballinger interview (Apr. 14, 2004).

219 Ed Ballinger interview (Apr. 14, 2004); and FBI report of investigation, interview of Edward D. Ballinger, Jan. 29, 2002.

220 Daniel Nash interview (Oct. 14, 2003); Timothy Duffy interview (Jan. 7, 2004); NTSB report, "Flight Path Study—United Flight 175," Feb. 19, 2002; Commission analysis of FAA radar data.

221 FBI report, "Summary of Penttbom Investigation," Jan. 31, 2003.

222 AAL record, SABRE information on Flight 77, Sept. 11, 2001. As is true of Flight 11, all of the times for check-in for Flight 77 are approximate because the airline's reservations and ticketing systems did "not provide exact times for such activities." See AAL response to Commission questions for the record, Mar. 15, 2004.

223 Metropolitan Washington Airports Authority videotape, Dulles Main Terminal checkpoints, September 11, 2001.

224 Metropolitan Washington Airports Authority videotape, Dulles Main Terminal checkpoints, September 11, 2001.

225 AAL report, "SABRE information on Flight 77," Sept. 11, 2001. In response to questions from the Commission, American Airlines has been unable to locate information about the check-in time for Hani Hanjour. However, it had to have taken place between 7:25 A.M., when he may have parked the rental car in the airport parking lot, and 7:35 A.M., when he appears on the checkpoint videotape.

226 The videotape evidence reviewed by the Commission indicates that all five Flight 77 hijackers passed through the west checkpoint, that three of the five set off at least one magnetometer alarm, and that two set off both magnetometers and were hand-wanded. See Metropolitan Washington Airports Authority videotape, Dulles Main Terminal checkpoints, September 11, 2001. Immediately after the attacks, the FAA's Washington Civil Aviation Security Field Office (WDC CASFO) began an investigation into the screening operations at Dulles on 9/11. After interviewing 43 of the 44 screeners (the other individual was in the hospital) identified by Argenbright as being on duty on September 11, 2001, the WDC CASFO made the following report: Overall, the responses provided by the screeners were consistent. They reported nothing out of ordinary nor suspicious activity on the morning of September 11, 2001. None of the screeners on duty at the East and West checkpoints recalled handling any passengers identified as selectees. See FAA report, Washington, DC Civil Aviation Security Field Office, "Executive Summary, American Airline Flight #77: Hijacking and Crash into the Pentagon, September 11, 2001."

227 TSA report, "Selectee Status of September 11th Hijackers," (undated). See FBI report of investigation, interview of Vaughn Allex, Sept. 12, 2001; Vaughn Allex interview (July 12, 2001).

228 TSA report, "Selectee Status of September 11th Hijackers," (undated);Vaughn Allex interview (July 12, 2001).

229 TSA report, "Selectee Status of September 11th Hijackers," (undated).

230 AAL record, "SABRE information for Flight 77," Sept. 11, 2001.

231 FAA report, "Executive Summary, American Airline Flight #77: Hijacking and Crash into the Pentagon, September 11, 2001."

232 AAL record, "Flight Attendant Jump Seat Locations During Takeoff And Flight Attendant Typical Cabin Positions During Start of Cabin Service for Flights 11 and 77," undated.

233 Wednesdays were the next lowest at 40.3 percent. AAL report,"Average Load Factor by Day-of Week," undated (for Flights 11 and 77 from June 11, 2001 to Sept. 9. 2001); and AAL report, email response from Christopher R. Christensen to Commission questions for the record, January 20, 2004.

234 FBI report, response to Commission briefing request no. 6, undated (topic 8).

235 AAL record, American Airlines record, Dispatch Environmental Control/Weekly Flight Summary for Flight 11, Sept. 11, 2001; AAL response toe Commission questions for the record," Mar. 15, 2004.

236 Craig Marquis, Craig Parfitt, Joe Bertapelle and Mike Mulcahy interview (Nov. 19, 2003).

237 AAL response to Commission questions for the record, March 15, 2004.

238 The departure gate was in the C/D Midfield Terminal

239 FAA report, "Chronology of the September 11, 2001 Attacks and Subsequent Events Through October 24, 2001."

240 "Partial Transcript; Aircraft Accident; AAL77; Washington, DC; September 11, 2001," Henderson radar position, Dec. 3, 2001, at 8:40:13.

241 NTSB report, "Flight Path Study—American Flight 77," Feb. 19, 2002

242 AAL report, "Flight Attendant Jump Seat Locations During Takeoff and Flight Attendant Typical Cabin Positions During Start of Cabin Service," undated.

243 NTSB report, "Flight Path Study—United Flight 77," Feb. 19, 2002;" FAA recording, Indianapolis Air Traffic Control, Position HNNR, Sept. 11, 2001.

244 NTSB report, "Flight Path Study—United Flight 77," Feb. 19, 2002."

245 Primary radar contact for Flight 77 was lost because the "preferred" radar covering this geographic area did not have a "primary" radar system, the "supplemental" radar had poor primary coverage in this geographic area, and the FAA ATC software did not allow the display of primary radar data from the "tertiary" and "quadrary" radars for this geographic area. See FAA, "Summary of Air Traffic Hijack Events: September 11, 2001," Sept. 17, 2001; Richard Byard interview (Sept. 24, 2003); Linda Povinelli interview (Sept. 24, 2003).

246 NTSB report, "Flight Path Study—United Flight 77," Feb. 19, 2002; and NTSB report, Air Traffic Control Recording—American Airlines Flight 77, Dec. 21, 2001.

247 "Partial Transcript; Aircraft Accident; AAL77; Washington, DC; September 11, 2001," Henderson radar position, at 8:57:39 (transcript dated December 3, 2001).

248 "Partial Transcript; Aircraft Accident; AAL77; Washington, DC; September 11, 2001," Henderson radar position, at 9:06:39 (transcript dated Oct. 4, 2001).

249 AAL response to Commission questions for the record, April 26, 2004; AAL report, reponse to Commission request for information, July 7, 2004; and AAL record, "Dispatch Environmental Control/Weekly Flight Summary: Flight 77, September 11, 2001."

250 Larry Wansley interview (Jan. 8, 2004); Gerard Arpey interview (Jan. 8, 2004)

251 NTSB report, "Flight Path Study—United Flight 77," Feb. 19, 2002.

252 FAA report, Criminal Acts Against Civil Aviation 2001, p. 40.

253 AAL report, "Systems Operation Command Center (SOCC) Chronology for September 11, 2001." Commission staff was told that shortly after 9:00 A.M., the American Airlines managing director of dispatch operations telephoned his brother who worked at United and that the director's brother told him that UAL had "some planes missing. However, the airline informed Commission staff that the brother did not recall the conversation. See Craig P. interview (Nov. 19, 2003).

254 FAA Indianapolis Center (ZID) after action report on AAL77 flight path and Commission staff analysis.

255 NTSB report, "Flight Path Study—United Flight 77," Feb. 19, 2002. One minute later, its autopilot was disconnected for about three minutes. This is based on information recovered from Flight 77's flight data recorder.

256 AAL report, "Systems Operation Command Center (SOCC) Chronology for September 11, 2001."

257 FAA report, "FAA Summary of Air Traffic Hijack Events September 11, 2001," Sept. 17, 2001: [9:09:00] ZID notified Great Lakes Regional Operations Center a possible aircraft accident of AAL 77 due to the simultaneous loss of radio communications and radar identification." John Thomas interview (Sept. 24, 2003).

258 FAA report, "Summary of Air Traffic Hijack Events September 11, 2001," Sept. 17, 2001.

259 In his interview with the Commission, Craig Marquis placed this time at approximately 9:00 A.M., while in his interview Gerard Arpey recalled the time as between 9:05 and 9:10. The most recent information from AAL now indicates the Halleck call to Herndon took place "some time after" 9:10 A.M. No evidence relating to this call has been found in the Commission's review of the Herndon tapes and transcripts. See Craig Marquis interview (Nov. 19, 2003); Gerard Arpey interview (Jan. 8, 2004); and AAL response to Commission questions for the record, April 26, 2004; AAL report, response to Commission questions for the record, July 7, 2004.

260 FBI report, "American Airlines Airphone Usage," Sept. 20, 2001.

261 FBI report of investigation, interview of Ronald and Nancy May, Sept. 12, 2001.

262 Patty Carson interview (Nov. 19, 2003); AAL report, email response from Christopher R. Christensen to Commission in response to questions for the record, January 20, 2004.

263 Gerard Arpey interview (Jan. 8, 2004)

264 AAL transcript, telephone call from Bill Halleck to FAA ATC system Command Center;" FAA recording, ATCSCC NOM Line 5149, position 34B, Sept. 11, 2001.

265 The records available for the phone calls from American Airlines Flight 77 do not allow for a determination of which of four "connected calls to unknown numbers" represent the two connections between Barbara and Ted Olson, although it is believed that all four of these calls represent communications between Barbara Olson and her husband's office (all family members of the Flight 77 passengers and crew were canvassed to see if they had received any phone calls from the hijacked flight, and only Renee May's parents and Ted Olson indicated that they had received such calls). The four calls were at 9:15:34 for one minute, 42 seconds; 9:20:15 for four minutes, 34 seconds; 9:25:48 for two minutes, 34 seconds; and 9:30:56 for four minutes, 20 seconds. FBI report, "American Airlines Airphone Usage," Sept. 20, 2001.

266 A witness in Theodore Olson's office recalled that at approximately 9:00 A.M., she received a series of six to eight collect calls from an unknown caller that did not go through. These were followed by a collect call from Barbara Olson, via an operator, which the witness accepted and transferred to Ted Olson. According to the witness, this call was followed a few (perhaps five) minutes later by a direct call from Barbara Olson, which the witness put through to Ted Olson. FBI report of investigation, interview of witness, September 14, 2001.

267 FBI report of investigation, interview of Theodore Olson, Sept. 11, 2001; FBI report of investigation, interview of witness, Sept. 4, 2001.

268 The Department of Justice's Command Center Watch Log contained an entry at 9:33 indicating that Ted Olson had contacted the center to apprise them of the call from his wife, and requested that someone for the command center come to his office. Department of Justice record, "Department of Justice Command Center Watch Officer Log, 0001-2400 HRS, September 11, 2001."

269 John Thomas interview (Sept. 14, 2003).

270 Command Center, Position # 25(B), Miller Transcript, Parts 2-4, pp. 5-6.

271 FBI report, "American Airlines Airphone Usage," Sept. 20, 2001.

272 FBI record of investigation, interview of Theodore Olson, Sept. 11, 2001.

273 FAA recording, Herndon Command Center Tape, NTMO Position #26, Line 4530 (FAA Transcript, p. 15).

274 Danielle O'Brien interview (Jan. 23, 2003).

275 FAA report, Summary of Air Traffic Hijack Events: September 11, 2001, AAT-20, 9/17/01.

276 FAA recording, ATCSCC, NTMO Position #26, Line 4530, Sept. 11, 2001. (FAA Transcript, p. 15).

277 John White interview (May 7, 2004); Ellen Riley interview (Apr. 5, 2004); Linda Schuessler interview (Apr. 6, 2004); Benedict Sliney interview (May 21, 2004); FAA memo, "Full Transcription; Air Traffic Control System Command Center, National Traffic Management Officer, East Position; September 11, 2001," Oct. 21, 2003, pp. 14, 27. By no later than 9:25, there were serious concerns within the FAA over the safety of other aircraft. A manager from Command Center specifically asked FAA Headquarters if they wanted to order a "nationwide ground stop."277 While executives at FAA headquarters discussed the issuance of a national ground stop, at 9:25, Command Center exercised initiative and ordered all aircraft in the United States not to depart from any airports until further notice.277 Command Center's National Operations Manager, Ben Sliney, told the Commission that he gave this order based on his belief the attacks would continue, concern that the FAA could not locate Flight 77 and reports that other commercial aircraft may have been hijacked. Sliney said he believed he possessed the authority to issue this order and ordered the ground stop in an attempt to mitigate any potential further damage. See Benedict Sliney interview (May 21, 2004).

278 NTSB report, "Flight Path Study—United Flight 77," Feb. 19, 2002; FAA report, "Report of Aircraft Accident," Nov. 13, 2001; John Hendershot interview (Dec. 22, 2003); FAA report, "Summary of Air Traffic Hijack Events: September 11, 2001," Sept. 17, 2001; Commission analysis of radar data.

279 FAA letterhead memorandum, "Report of Aircraft Accident Washington National (DCA) ATCT," Nov. 13, 2001; John Hendershot interview (Dec. 22, 2003); FAA report, "Summary of Air Traffic Hijack Events: September 11, 2001," Sept. 17, 2001; NTSB, "Flight Path Study—American Airlines Flight 77;" and staff analysis of radar data.

280 NTSB report, "Flight Path Study—American Airlines Flight 77;" and staff analysis of radar data.

281 NEADS audio file, Identification Technician position, Channel 2, between 9:32:10 and 9:33:58.

282 Noteworthy for its omission in this account is the claimed 9:24 A.M. FAA notification to the military that Flight 77 was hijacked. In the official NORAD timeline of 9/11 (released September 18, 2001), and as presented to the Commission in May 2003, NORAD claimed to have received notification that Flight 77 was a hijacked aircraft at 9:24 A.M. NORAD officials also indicated that the fighters at Langley Air Force Base were immediately scrambled to meet the threat to Washington posed by Flight 77. Retired General Larry Arnold (CONR Commander on 9/11) amplified, and confused, the issue in testimony before the Commission, stating: "9:24 was the first time that we had been advised of American 77 as a possible hijacked airplane. Our focus – you have got to remember that there's a lot of other things going on simultaneously here -- was on United 93, which was being pointed out to us very aggressively I might say by the FAA. ... We were advised [American 77] was possibly hijacked. And we had launched almost simultaneously with that, we launched the aircraft out of Langley to put them over top of Washington, DC, not in response to American Airlines 77, but really to put them in position in case United 93 were to head that way." Based on its review of the tapes, transcripts and other records obtained under subpoena, as corroborated by witness interviews at NEADS, the Commission can state unequivocally that the 9:24 A.M. notification time was not accurate. The 9:24 notification time was inaccurately derived from a handwritten log maintained by the staff working for the Mission Crew Commander (the operational commander on watch) at NEADS. Called the "MCC/T Log," it was the principal log of events kept at NEADS on 9/11.

At 9:24 A.M., the log records: "American Airlines #N334AA hijacked."[282] This tail number refers not to Flight 77 but to Flight 11, the first hijacked aircraft. The subpoenaed tapes confirm that this time corresponds to the receipt of the tail number information on Flight 11 and to reports that Flight 11 was still airborne and headed towards Washington DC.[282]

[283] AAL report, "Systems Operation Command Center (SOCC) Chronology for September 11, 2001."

[284] FAA audio file, Washington Tower, Tyson/Fluky Position, 9:36 A.M.; FAA letterhead memorandum, "Partial Transcript; Aircraft Accident; AAL 77; Washington, DC; September 11, 2001," Sept. 20, 2001.

[285] NEADS audio file, Identification Technician position, Ch. 7, at 9:35:50. The Commission staff was told by AAL's operations center leadership, during interviews, that the management did not request that dispatchers send warnings to the cockpits of its flights in the air on 9/11. The airline cited requirements of the Air Carrier Standard Security Program that information on hijacked flights be restricted to those with operational need to know. AAL reported that the management did, however, instruct dispatchers to contact aircraft with instructions to divert in order to implement the shut down of the airspace. On August 9, 2004 American Airlines sent the Commission a letter indicating that several dispatchers, improvising and acting on their own accord, sent messages to certain aircraft including one sent at 9:22 to the crew of an American flight requesting they "maintain extreme vigilance...USA today reporting acft being flown into the World Trade Center. Unconfirmed AA acft." A message sent to another flight by a different dispatcher at 9:36 a.m. was a more explicit hijack warning, "To all Captains and crew. Security must be at top of the list...AAL aircraft have be [been] hijacked this morning and may have been forced down...2 acft have been flow into the World Trade center   Please all of you be on hi alert keep us posted on your situation." See AAL letter to Commission, August 9, 2004.

[286] NEADS audio file, Mission Crew Commander "Op" position, at 9:36:34; Kevin J. Nasypany interview (January 22-23, 2004).

[287] NEADS audio file, Mission Crew Commander "Op" position, at 9:39:00, and 9:39:37; Kevin J. Nasypany interview (January 22-23, 2004).

A combination of three factors explains why the Langley fighters initially traveled so far to the east, when their initial scramble order directed them on a heading to the north. First, the Langley scramble order did not convey complete instructions. It instructed the fighters to "Scramble immediately time 1324... Scramble on a heading of 010 flight level 290." Though the order did include a direction to fly – "010" and a flight altitude – 29,000 feet – it did not include a distance to the target, nor the target's location, two key components that are normally included in a scramble order. Indeed, NEADS did not know the location of the mistakenly reported southbound American 11 – at the time, there was no discernable target. Second, a "generic" flight plan assigned to the Langley fighters incorrectly led them to believe that they were being ordered to fly due east (090) for 60 miles. In order to launch aircraft, the Langley AFB Tower was required to file an automated flight plan specifically designating the direction and distance of intended flight. Prior to 9/11, the standard – or generic – flight plan for aircraft departing Langley AFB to the east was "090 for 60" – meaning head 90 degrees (due east) for 60 miles. The generic "090 for 60" flight plan was utilized to expeditiously get aircraft airborne and out of the base's airspace. Langley Tower personnel assumed that once fighters got airborne they would be vectored to the target of interest by either NEADS or the FAA. Third, both the lead Langley pilot and the FAA's Norfolk TRACON facility – which was briefly controlling the aircraft once it departed the Langley AFB airspace – assumed the flight plan instruction to go "090 for 60" was newer guidance that superceded the original scramble order instructions. In fact, shortly after the fighters got airborne, the lead Langley pilot was asked by Norfolk TRACON in what direction he wanted to head. After brief discussion between the lead pilot (identified as "Quit 25") and Norfolk TRACON, it was mutually decided that the fighters would follow the flight plan guidance. Put simply, the Langley pilots received flight direction guidance from both the scramble order and the Langley AFB departure flight plan, and continued on the latter heading for several minutes until a direction and geographic destination was provided.

[288] NTSB report, "Flight Path Study—American Airlines Flight 77," Feb. 19, 2002.

[289] Federal Aviation Administration, Criminal Acts Against Civil Aviation 2001, p. 41.

[290] FAA audio file, Washington Tower, Tyson/Fluky Position, 9:38:52 A.M.; FAA letterhead memorandum, "Partial Transcript; Aircraft Accident; AAL 77; Washington, DC; September 11, 2001," Sept. 20, 2001, p. 7.

[291] Larry Wansley interview (Jan. 8, 2004).

292 AAL report, "Systems Operation Command Center (SOCC) Chronology for September 11, 2001."

293 FAA recording, NTMO East Position #26, Line 4530, Sept. 11, 2001. (FAA Transcript, p. 17).

294 Craig Marquis and others interview (Nov. 19, 2003); UAL response to Commission questions for the record, July 13, 2004.

295 Craig Marquis interview (Nov. 19, 2003).

296 UAL report, Flight 93 EWR Full Bag loading status, Sept. 11, 2001; and UAL report, Flight 93 11 Sep EWR ACI Passenger History, Sept. 11, 2001. Jarrah arrived at the Newark Airport parking lot and parked his rental car. See FBI report, The Final 24 Hours, December 8, 2003.

297 TSA report, "Selectee Status of September 11th Hijackers," (undated).

298 The checkpoint featured three walk-through metal detectors, two X-ray machines, and explosive trace detection equipment. On 9/11, after the attacks, the FAA's New York Civil Aviation Security Field Office (CASFO) conducted an investigation of the checkpoint used to screen passengers for Flight 93. The investigation found that all equipment was operating in compliance with FAA regulations. Each of the screeners on duty was interviewed. The report stated: "There were no significant findings disclosed from the interviews conducted." FAA report, New York Civil Aviation Security Field Office, "United Air Lines Flight 93 September 11, 2001," undated.

299 FBI report, "The Final 24 Hours," Dec. 8, 2003; and UAL record, Flight 93 EWR ACI passenger history, Sept. 11, 2001.

300 In the six months prior to 9/11, Flight 95 had operated six times a week, Monday through Saturday, from 6/11/01 through 7/7/01, then five times a week, Monday through Friday, from 7/9/01 through 8/31/01. Daily service had started only with the week of 9/3/01. UAL report, "Flight 93 BOS-SFO Load Factors" undated.

301 UAL response to Commission questions for the record, April 5, 2004.

302 UAL response to Commission questions for the record, April 5, 2004.

303 UAL response to Commission questions for the record, April 5, 2004

304 Except for five flights that were canceled, on 6/11/01, 6/19/01, 6/25/01, 7/3/01, and 8/22/01.

305 Except for Sundays, on which there was but a single flight in the six-month period, with a load of 42.19 percent. UAL records, "Flight 93 BOS-SFO Load Factors," undated.

306 FBI report, response to Commission briefing request no. 6, undated (topic 8).

307 UAL record, "Weight and Balance Information—Flight number 175, Sept. 11, 2001;" See also, UAL report, "Information Concerning Boeing Key and Who Sat in Jump Seats on the Hijacked Flights." [SSI]

308 UAL aircraft briefing (Nov. 20, 2003).

309 UAL response to Commission questions for the record, April 5, 2004; Ed Ballinger interview (Apr. 14, 2004).

310 UAL response to Commission questions for the record, Jan. 23, 2004.

311 UAL response to Commission questions for the record, April 5, 2004.

312 NTSB report, "Flight Path Study—United Flight 93," Feb. 19, 2002.

313 Bob Jordan briefing (Nov. 20, 2003).

314 UAL response to Commission questions for the record, April 5, 2004.

315 UAL record, Flight 93 ACARS message, Sept. 11, 2001; Ed Ballinger interview (Apr. 14, 2004).

316 UAL record, Flight 93 ACARS message, Sept. 11, 2001; Ed Ballinger interview (Apr. 14, 2004).

317 UAL record, Flight 93 ACARS message, Sept. 11, 2001; Ed Ballinger interview (April 14, 2004).

318 UAL record, communication to dispatchers on Sept. 11, 2001.

319 UAL record, Flight 93 ACARS message, Sept. 11, 2001.

320 UAL record, Flight 93 ACARS message, Sept. 11, 2001; Ed Ballinger interview (Apr. 14, 2004).

321 FAA memo, "Full Transcript; Aircraft Accident; N591UA (UAL93) Somerset, PA; September 11, 2001," position E 155, Sept. 13, 2001, p.t 6 (cleared to 10,000 feet, not to exceed 250 knots); p. 7 (resume normal speed); FAA memo, "Full Transcript; Aircraft Accident; N591UA (UAL93) Somerset, PA; September 11, 2001," position E 155, B43, Sept. 13, 2001, p. 1 (heading 330; left turn); p. 2 (cleared to fourteen thousand feet; then to seventeen thousand feet); FAA memo, "Full Transcript; Aircraft Accident; N591UA (UAL93) Somerset, PA; September 11, 2001," position R39, Sept. 13, 2001, p. 6 (cleared to twenty-eight thousand feet); 9 (cleared "direct dimmo"); FAA memo, "Full Transcript; Aircraft Accident; N591UA (UAL93) Somerset, PA; September 11, 2001," position R73, Sept. 27, 2001, p. 4 (climbing to 28,000 feet); p. 7 (cleared to thirty-five thousand feet); p. 13 (United reports light chop at 9:22:39, and is passed to Cleveland Center).

322 FAA memo, "Full Transcript; Aircraft Accident; N591UA (UAL93) Somerset, PA; September 11, 2001," position FKL-R, Sept. 17, 2001, p. 1; LOR-R, 5/10/02, Tr. at 8.
323 FAA memo, "Full Transcript; Aircraft Accident; N591UA (UAL93) Somerset, PA; September 11, 2001," Lorain Radar position, May 10 2002, p. 1-8.
324 FAA memo, "Full Transcript; Aircraft Accident; N591UA (UAL93) Somerset, PA; September 11, 2001," Lorain Radar position, May 10 2002, p. 8 (acknowledgment at 9:25:09).
325 FAA memo, "Full transcription; Air Traffic Control System Command Center, National Traffic Management Officer, East position; September 11, 2001," Line 4530, Line 4530, p. 13.
326 FAA memo, "Full Transcript; Aircraft Accident; N591UA (UAL93) Somerset, PA; September 11, 2001," Lorain Radar position, May 10 2002. Again, on September 11, 2001, passengers aboard United Airlines flights could monitor communications between FAA air traffic controllers and the pilots by selecting channel 9 on their headsets. It is possible that the hijackers on board Flight 93 could have heard the conversations between the Cleveland controller and the other aircraft in which the serious situation in New York City was mentioned.
327 UAL record, Ed Ballinger's ACARS log, Sept. 11, 2001; Ed Ballinger interview (April 14, 2004).
328 FAA recording, Cleveland ATC Center certified transcript, 9:27:25, Sept. 11, 2001.
329 The United 93 timeline in FAA report, 'Summary of Air Traffic Hijack Events September 11, 2001,' Sept. 17, 2001, states that at 9:28:54 a 'second radio transmission, mostly unintelligible, again with sounds of possible screaming or a struggle and a statement, 'get out of here, get out of here' from an unknown origin was heard over the ZOB [Cleveland Center] radio.
330 FAA memo, "Full Transcript; Aircraft Accident; N591UA (UAL93) Somerset, PA; September 11, 2001," Lorain Radar position, May 10 2002, p. 10; FAA report, "FAA Summary of Air Traffic Hijack Events September 11, 2001," Sept. 17, 2001. FAA memo, "Full Transcript; Aircraft Accident; N591UA (UAL93) Somerset, PA; September 11, 2001," Lorain Radar position, May 10, 2002, p. 10.
331 On FDR, see NTSB report, "Specialist's factual Report of Investigation—Digital Flight Data Recorder for United Airlines Flight 93, Feb. 15, 2002; on CVR, see FBI report, "CVR from UA Flight #93," Dec. 4, 2003; FAA report, "Summary of Air Traffic Hijack Events; September 11, 2001," Sept. 17, 2001; NTSB report, Air Traffic Control Recording—United Airlines Flight 93, Dec. 21, 2001.
332 FAA memo, "Full Transcript; Aircraft Accident; N591UA (UAL93) Somerset, PA; September 11, 2001," Lorain Radar position, May 10 2002, p. 10; FAA report, "FAA Summary of Air Traffic Hijack Events September 11, 2001," Sept. 17, 2001. FAA memo, "Full Transcript; Aircraft Accident; N591UA (UAL93) Somerset, PA; September 11, 2001," Lorain Radar position, May 10, 2002, p. 10.
333 UAL response to Commission questions for the record, July 13, 2004.
334 ZOB-ARTCC-287, LOR-R, 5/10/02, Tr. at 13. At 9:31:21, ExecuJet 56 also called in, reporting that "we're just answering your call. We did hear that, uh, yelling too." The FAA responded, at 9:31:51: "Okay, thanks. We're just trying to figure out what's going on."
335 UAL record, Flight 93 ACARS message, Sept. 11, 2001; Ed Ballinger interview (Apr. 14, 2004)
336 In accordance with FAA regulations, United 93 had a cockpit voice recorder that recorded in 30 minute loops via microphones in the pilots' headsets, as well as in the overhead panel of the flight deck. This is the only cockpit voice recorder from the four hijacked airplanes to survive the impact and ensuing fire. It recorded the last 31 minutes of the flight. The CVRs and flight data recorders (FDRs) from American 11 and United 175 were not found, and the CVR from American Flight 77 was badly burned and not recoverable. The Flight 93 recording started at 9:32 A.M. through the end of the flight. See FBI report, "Transcript of the Flight Voice Recorder for United Flight 93," Dec. 4, 2003; See also 14 §§ CFR 25.1457,91.609,91.1045, and 121.359. Evidence derived from audio readout of CVR from Flight 93.
337 Like Atta on Flight 11, Jarrah apparently did not know how to operate the communication radios; thus his attempts to communicate with the passengers were broadcast on the ATC channel. FBI report, "CVR from UA Flight #93," Dec. 4, 2003.
338 UAL record, Flight 93 ACARS message, Sept. 11, 2001; Ed Ballinger interview (Apr. 14, 2004). United reported that Ed Ballinger in handling his various duties, with the assistance of a fellow controller, sent out this and other "high security" alerts as a means of responding to various flights that had either asked for additional information or acknowledged receipt of his original "Beware cockpit intrusion" message. See UAL response to Commission questions for the record, July 16, 2004.
339 ZOB-ARTCC-287, LOR-R, 5/10/02, Tr. at 19.

340 FAA memo, "Full transcription; Air Traffic Control System Command Center, National Traffic Management Officer, East position; September 11, 2001," October 31, 2003, pp. 10, 13; FAA audio file, Herndon Command Center, New York Center position, line 5154.

341 GTE cell phone records indicate that an air phone call was made from Flight 93 to United's maintenance facility in San Francisco at 9:32 A.M. lasting 95 seconds. Another call of longer duration was indicated at 9:36. The SAMC personnel interviewed by the airline, the FBI, and the Commission report receiving only a single phone call from Flight 93, most likely the later one. According to United, the first call may have never been received, because it was in a queue among other calls being received by the facility. See FBI record, "United Air Lines Flight 93 Telephone Calls."

342 Rich B. interview (Nov. 21, 2003); Andrew L. interview (Nov. 21, 2003); Notes of Rich B.; notes of Rich B., Sept.11, 2001; notes of Andrew L., Sept. 11, 2001.

343 Details of information on the hijacking, shared during the communications on which the Commission based its analysis, are derived from tape recordings of several of the calls, as well as notes and official accounts by those receiving the communications.

344 FBI record, GTE phone records

345 NTSB report, "Flight Path Study—United Flight 93," Feb. 19, 2002.

346 UAL report, "Timeline for Dispatch/SMFDO Activities—Terrorist Crisis, September 11, 2001."

347 UAL response to Commission questions for the record, July 13, 2004.

348 UAL record, Flight 93 ACARS message, Sept. 11, 2001; Ed Ballinger interview (Apr. 14, 2004).

349 FBI report of investigation, interview of recipients of call from Mark Bingham, Sept. 13, 2001 [LES]

350 FBI report of investigation, interviews with recipients of calls from passengers Beamer, Bingham, Bradshaw, Glick, Lyles [LES]

351 14 CFR.§121.547

352 For jump seat information, see UAL records, Weight and Balance Information for Flight 93 and Flight 175, Sept. 11, 2001; AAL records, Dispatch Environmental Control/Weekly Flight Summaries for Flight 11 and Flight 77, Sept. 11, 2001.

353 FBI report of investigation, interview with Robert C., Sept. 11, 2001.

354 United Air Lines manifest records for Flight 93 show that passengers Thomas Burnett, Mark Bingham, Joseph DeLuca, Edward Felt, Linda Grondlund, and Mark Rothenberg were the six passengers holding first-class cabin seats, in addition to all four hijackers. Only Rothenberg is not known to have communicated with the ground during the flight.

355 UAL record, personnel records of pilot and first officer.

356 FBI report of investigation, interview of recipient of calls from Thomas Burnett, Sept. 11, 2001; Witness briefing (Apr. 26, 2004).

357 FBI report of investigation, interview of recipients of call from Jeremy Glick, Sept. 12, 2001; Lyzbeth Glick briefing (Apr. 22, 2004).

358 FBI report, "CVR from UA Flight #93," Dec. 4, 2003.

359 UAL dispatch sent several ACARS messages to the cockpit of Flight 93 after the cockpit had been taken over by the hijackers. UAL record, Ed Ballinger's ACARS log, Sept. 11, 2001.

360 FBI report of investigation, interview of recipients of call from Lauren Grandcolas, Sept. 11, 2001.

361 UAL response to Commission questions for the record, July 13, 2004.

362 UAL report, Flight 93 ACARS message, Sept. 11, 2001; Ed Ballinger interview (April 14, 2004).

363 NTSB report, "Flight Path Study—United Flight 93," Feb. 19, 2002.

364 FAA memo; "Full Transcript; Aircraft Accident; N591UA (UAL93) Somerset, PA; September 11, 2001," Lorain Radar position, May 10, 2002, p. 26-32.

365 Command Center tape recording, NTMO East Position # 26, Line 4530, pages 16-17 of FAA transcript.

366 FBI report of investigation, recipient of communication from Joseph DeLuca, Sept. 13, 2001.

367 Rich "Doc" Miles interview (Nov. 21, 2003); UAL report, "Timeline for Dispatch/SMFDO Activities—Terrorist Crisis, September 11, 2001."

368 FBI report of investigation, recipient of communication from Linda Gronlund, Sept. 11, 2001. FBI transcript, phone call of Linda Gronlund, Sept. 11, 2001.

369 Command Center tape recording, NTMO East Position # 26, Line 4530, page 19 of FAA transcript.

370 FBI report of investigation, recipient of communications from CeeCee Lyles, Sept. 15, 2001.

371 FBI report of investigation, recipient of call from Marion Britton, Sept. 14, 2001.

372 Command Center, NTMO East Position # 26, Line 4530, page 21 of FAA transcript.
373 UAL report, Flight 93 ACARS message, Sept. 11, 2001; UAL report, Timeline for Dispatch/SMFDO Activities—Terrorist Crisis, September 11, 2001.
374 FAA memo, "Full transcription; Air Traffic Control System Command Center, National Traffic Management Officer, East position; September 11, 2001," Line 4530, p. 23. Neither Monte Belger nor the deputy director for air traffic services could recall this discussion with their interviews with us. Monte Belger interview (April 20, 2004) ; Peter Challon interview (March 26, 2004). Subsequently, Belger told us that he does not believe the conversation occurred. Monte Belger e-mail to the Commission, July 12, 2004. However, tapes from the morning reveal that at 9:53 a.m., a staff person from headquarters told the command center "Peter's talking to Monte now about scrambling." FAA memo, "Full Transcription: Air Traffic Control System Command Center, National Traffic Management Officer, East Position; September 11, 2001," October 21, 2003, p. 23.
375 FBI report of investigation, recipient of call from Honor Wainio, Sept. 11, 2001.
376 NTSB report, Flight 93 flight data recorder.
377 FBI report of investigation, recipient of call from Todd Beamer, Sept. 11, 2001; Lisa Jefferson interview (May 11, 2004).
378 FAA memo, "Full transcription; Air Traffic Control System Command Center, National Traffic Management Officer, East position; September 11, 2001," Line 4530, p. 24.
379 FBI report of investigation, recipient of call from Sandy Bradshaw, Sept. 11, 2001; Philip B. interview (June 15, 2004).
380 FBI report, "CVR from UA Flight #93," Dec. 4, 2003.
381 FBI report of investigation, interview of recipient of call from Edward Felt, Sept. 11, 2001; FBI transcript, call from Edward Felt call, Sept. 11, 2001.
382 Given the timing of this call, we believe that Lyles was referring to the passengers, not the hijackers. See FBI report, interview of recipient from call from CeeCee Lyles, Sept. 15, 2001.
383 Flight 93 FDR and CVR data
384 FAA memo, "Full transcription; Air Traffic Control System Command Center, National Traffic Management Officer, East position; September 11, 2001," Line 4530, p. 26.
385 Ibid.
386 Command Center, NTMO East Position # 26, Line 4530, page 27 of FAA transcript.
387 Ibid.
388 Ibid.
389 The military did not receive notice at 9:16 A.M. that Flight 93 was hijacked, as was reported to the Commission in May 2003 by NORAD. At 9:16 A.M., the NEADS "MCC/T Log" records: "United tail #N612UA/75 SOB/." The tail number in the log belonged to Flight 175, not Flight 93. A corresponding conversation on recorded conversations on the NEADS floor confirms that at 9:16 A.M., NEADS was receiving (from an FAA facility) confirmation of the tail number of Flight 175 (see NEADS audio file, Identification Technician position , Channel 5, at 9:16:19).
390 Commission transcript of 9/11 NEADS recording DRM1, DAT2, Channel 4 ID op." Sept. 11, 2001.
391 NEADS audio file, Mission Crew Commander "Op" position, at 14:10:36. The timing of the Mission Crew Commander's instruction on ROE also belies various NORAD officials' public recounting of their awareness of, and response to Flight 93. "Air War Over America," for instance, offers the following accounts by two of the key NORAD participants: (Colonel Robert Marr, NEADS Commander): "With all available alert fighters in the air, Marr and his crew were still faced with United Flight 93. The plane was headed west, so controllers began looking for any other fighter jets that might be nearby. `We don't have fighters that way and we think he's headed toward Detroit or Chicago,' Marr says. `I'm thinking Chicago is the target and know that Selfridge Air National Guard Base (Mich.) has F-16s in the air. We contacted them so they could head 93 off at the pass. The idea is to get in there, close in on him and convince him to turn. ... As United Airlines Flight 93 was going out, we received the clearance to kill if need be. In fact, General Arnold's words almost verbatim were: `We will take lives in the air to save lives on the ground.'" (General Larry Arnold, CONR Commander): "...we watched the 93 track as it meandered around the Ohio-Pennsylvania area and started to turn south toward DC. By now the Pentagon has been hit and we have aircraft on orbit ... . They are now orbiting over Washington, DC, and have been for a while. As United 93 headed toward DC, the desire

is to move the fighters toward that aircraft." The record demonstrates, however, that no-one at any level in NORAD (or DOD) ever "watched the 93 track" start to turn south towards Washington DC. In fact, the military never saw Flight 93 at all. The Selfridge base was contacted by NEADS not regarding Flight 93, but in response to another commercial aircraft in the area that was reported hijacked (Delta Flight 1989, which ultimately was resolved as not hijacked). Most important, NORAD certainly never "received the clearance to kill if need be" on Flight 93.

392 NEADS audio file, Mission Crew Commander "Op" position, at 14:11:50

393 Command Center, NTMO East Position #26, Line 4530, page 34 of FAA transcript.

394 NORAD record, NEADS MCC/T log, September 11, 2001.

395 UAL response to Commission questions for the record, July 13, 2004.

396 UAL report, "Timeline for Operational Messages ATC/UAL—Terrorist Crisis, September 11, 2001."

397 AAL report, "Systems Operation Command Center (SOCC) Chronology for September 11, 2001."

398 NEADS audio file, Mission Crew Commander "Op" position, at 14:32:12; "MCCT Log," September 11, 2001; "CONR Chat Log," September 11, 2001.

399 Kevin J. Nasypany interview (Jan. 22- 23, 2004); Robert Marr interview (Jan. 23, 2004).

400 Robert Marr interview (Jan. 23, 2004).

401 Kevin Nasypany interview (Jan. 22-23, 2004); James Fox interview (Oct. 29, 2003).

402 Both Atta and Mihdhar established frequent flier accounts with American in late August, possibly in an effort to appear like normal travelers. In both cases the only reservations booked on the account were for travel on 9/11. See AAL response to Commission questions for the record, April 15, 2004

403 Flight standards rules at that time required the door facilitate access in and out of the cockpit in the event of an emergency. See Shirley Miller interview (Mar. 30, 2004).

404 Don Dillman briefing (Nov. 18, 2003); and Bob Jordan briefing (Nov. 20, 2003)

405 FAA report, Air Carrier Standard Security Program, Sec. XIII.J, May 20, 2001.

406 AAL response to Commission questions for the record, Mar. 15, 2004; AAL record, American Airlines record, Dispatch Environmental Control/Weekly Flight Summary for Flight 11, Sept. 11, 2001; AAL record, American Airlines record, Dispatch Environmental Control/Weekly Flight Summary for Flight 77, Sept. 11, 2001. UAL record, "United Air Lines Weight and Balance Information: Flight 93-2001-09-11; and Flight 175:2001-09-11."

407 The hijackers began their takeover about 15 minutes into Flight 11, about 28 minutes Flight 175, about 31 minutes into Flight 77, and about 47 minutes into Flight 93.

408 According to financial transaction data, at least seven knives were purchased by the 9/11 hijackers including two Victoronox Swiss Army knives, three Leatherman multi-tool knives, two pocket knives, and one Stanley two-piece snap knife set. The FBI collected 14 pieces of evidence of knives or portions of knives, including a box cutter, at the Flight 93 crash. None of the blades or knife housings recovered indicated a blade length longer than 3.5 inches. FBI report, "Summary of Penttbom Investigation," Jan. 31, 2003.

409 FAA Flight Standards Service briefing, Jan. 13, 2004; FBI report, "Summary of Penttbom Investigation," Jan. 31, 2003. Atta received flight training at facilities in Florida and Georgia; Shehhi received flight training in Florida and Georgia; Hanjour received flight training at facilities in Arizona, New Jersey and Maryland; and Jarrah received flight training at facilities in Florida and Pennsylvania. See FBI report, suspected suicide pilot training timeline, undated.

410 David Tew briefing

411 FAA Flight Standards Service briefing, Jan. 13, 2004; FBI report, "Summary of Penttbom Investigation," Jan. 31, 2003.

412 FAA Flight Standards Service briefing, Jan. 13, 2004; FBI report, "Summary of Penttbom Investigation," Jan. 31, 2003.

413 FAA Flight Standards Service briefing (Jan. 13, 2004); Ed Soliday interview (Nov. 21, 2003); and David Tew briefing (Jan. 25, 2004).

414 A number of computer-based software programs that provide cockpit simulation available on the open market to the general public. According to experts at the FAA, such computer-based ackages, including products that simulate cockpit controls of the Boeing 757 and 767, provided effective training. The terrorists were known to use computers, and there is no reason to believe they did not have the computer

literacy necessary to take advantage of computer-based training aids. FAA Flight Standards Service briefing (Jan. 13, 2004); Ed Soliday interview (Nov. 21, 2003); and David Tew briefing (Jan. 25, 2004).
415 FAA Flight Standards Service briefing (Jan. 13, 2004).
416 FAA Flight Standards Service briefing (Jan. 13, 2004).
417 FAA Flight Standards Service briefing (Jan. 13, 2004).
418 FAA Flight Standards Service briefing (Jan. 13, 2004); Ed Soliday interview (Nov. 21, 2003); and David Tew briefing (Jan. 25, 2004).
419 FBI report, "Summary of Penttbom Investigation," Jan. 31, 2003.
420 FAA Flight Standards Service briefing, Jan. 13, 2004; Ed Soliday interview (Nov. 21, 2003); and David Tew briefing (Jan. 25, 2004).
[421] Jane Garvey testimony, May 22, 2003.
[422] Based on the examination of FAA intelligence case files, daily intelligence summaries, interviews and other sources.
[423] Jane Garvey testimony, Jan. 27, 2004; Claudio Manno testimony, Jan. 27, 2004.
[424] FAA presentation, 2001 CD-ROM Terrorism Threat Presentation to Aviation Security Personnel at Airports and Air Carriers, Slide 24. [SSI]
[425] [SECRET] FAA memos, Office of Civil Aviation Security Intelligence, "Usama Bin Ladin/World Islamic Fronb Hijacking Threat," 1998 and 1999.
[426] The event in 1991 involving a Southwest Flight was not a case of terrorism: an American citizen who was angry that he was prohibited from smoking informed the flight crew he had a bomb and wanted to be flown to Cuba. He was arrested when the aircraft made its normally scheduled stop in San Diego. Mike Canavan testimony, May 23, 2003.
[427] Brian Jenkins, "Aviation Security in the United States," in Wilkinson and Jenkins, eds., *Aviation Terrorism and Security* (Frank Cass, 1999), p. 104.
[428] In 1998 UBL was reported to have stated "...All Islamic military have been mobilized to strike a significant U.S. or Israeli strategic target, to bring down their aircraft and hijack them." See: FAA response of 2/04/03 to Congressional Joint Inquiry staff letter dated 11/06/02
[429] FAA Alert Level III.
[430] The briefing was provided to FAA, air carrier and airport security officials for Newark Airport on March 14, 2001; Washington-Dulles Airport on March 22, 2001; and Logan Airport May 15, 2001. See FAA memo, Scott B. to Ross H. , May 17, 2002.
[431] Testimony of Jane Garvey, U.S. Senate Committee on Commerce, Science and Transportation. Sept. 20, 2001.
[432] Jane Garvey testimony, May 22, 2003.
[433] FAA Administrator Garvey testified before the Commission that she was aware that the summer of 2001 was a time of heightened terrorist threat. See Jane Garvey testimony, January 27, 2004.
[434] John H. interview (Oct. 8, 2003)
[435] [SECRET] ▮▮▮▮ summaries mentioned Usama Bin Ladin or al Qaeda threats overseas. Others indicated threats to U.S. interests, but only in the context of military and diplomatic facilities or of commercial interests overseas. ▮▮▮▮ FAA . reports, Daily Intelligence Summaries, 2001. FAA security analysts did perceive an increasing terrorist threat to U.S. civil aviation at home. Numerous FAA documents, including agency accounts published in the *Federal Register* in July 2001, clearly demonstrated the FAA's understanding that terrorist groups were active in the United States and maintained a historic interest in targeting aviation, including hijacking.
[436] [SECRET] FAA Daily Intelligence Summaries, May 1, 2001–Sept. 11, 2001.
[437] [SECRET] FAA Daily Intelligence Summaries, July 13, 2001.

SUBJECT TO CLASSIFICATION REVIEW

[438] At the Commission's May 23, 2003, hearing, Commissioner Gorelick observed that the FAA's invitation to the meeting suggested that "clearly the NSC thought that there would be or could be an aviation security piece to the emergency." The head of FAA civil aviation security, Gen. Mike Canavan, who attended the CSG meetings, agreed with her assessment.

[439] Mike Canavan testimony, May 23, 2003.

[440] Jane Garvey testimony, Jan. 27, 2004. See, for example, Carol H. interview (Oct. 27, 2003), Jane Garvey interview (Oct. 21, 2003); and Cathal Flynn interview (Sept. 9, 2003).

[441] Mike Canavan testimony, May 23, 2003.

[442] A security directive issued April 24, 2000, did issue an alert regarding Al Qaeda operatives, including Khalid Shaikh Mohammed (whom the FBI identifies as the main planner of the 9/11 attack) and five other individuals associated with Ramzi Ahmed Yousef and the 1995 Bojinka plot. (SSI)

[443] [SSI] The security directive issued on July 27, 2001, cautioned the aviation community about the use of fake credentials to penetrate secure areas at facilities overseas: "one can be certain that terrorists who might be contemplating an attack against civil aviation in the United States have taken note of the attractiveness of this modus operandi."

[444] Seven security directives were issued in 2001 prior to 9/11. (This number does not include five that followed up on several of the seven to make slight adjustments in their requirements.): SD 95-06J (Mar. 22, 2001), requiring ███████████████████████████████████████ SD 108-98-01D (Mar. 22, 2001), requiring that ██ , SD 108-98-02G (July 27, 2001), establishing ██████████████████████████████ ; SD 108-00-02D (July 27, 2001), warning the commercial aviation industry about the use of counterfeit law enforcement badges to gain access to airports. (A similar directive was sent to airports also on July 27, 2001—EA 107-00-1D); SD 108-00-03B (July 27, 2001), warning airlines to "no fly" and Egyptian, thought to be insane, who posed a threat to U.S. air carriers in Cairo: SD 108 108-01B (Aug. 28), issuing no-fly list and ████████████████████ SD 108-01-02A (Sept. 6), requiring extra security measures for flights carrying the author Salman Rushdie. Of the 16 security advisories known as "information circulars" sent by the FAA to the commercial aviation industry, 12 focused on security issues overseas, particularly the Middle East; two provided information on the threats of the Algerian-born terrorist Ahmed Ressam against Los Angeles Airport during the so-called millennium crisis; one discussed the threat to civil aviation of ground-to-air missiles (MANPADS); one alerted airports and air carriers to the tactic of disguising weapons as everyday items (a knife concealed in a cigarette lighter was found at the crash site of United Flight 93); and one discussed the possible terrorist threat to Americans posed by extremists but had expired on August 22, 2001. See FAA memos, Information circulars, 2001. [(SSI] Each of the 27 special security briefings that FAA provided to air carriers between May 1, 2001, and September 11, 2001, dealt with threats to civil aviation overseas, primarily in the Middle East. One of the briefings in May addressed hijacking threats overseas; another in August addressed the threat to commercial aviation worldwide, including potential ██ None of these briefings addressed the use of aircraft as weapons.

[SSI] Seven security directives were issued in 2001 prior to 9/11: SD 95-06J (March 22) requiring ██ ; SD 108-98-01D (March) requiring that passengers be CAPPS selectees if the travel was ██████████████████████████████████████ ██████████████████ ; SD 108-98-02G (July 27th) establishing explosives ██████████████ SD 108-00-02D (July 27th) warning the commercial aviation industry about the use of counterfeit law enforcement badges to gain access to airports; SD 108-00-03B (July 27th) warning airlines to "no fly" an Egyptian thought to be insane and a danger to U.S. air carriers in Cairo; SD 108 108-01B

(August 28th) issuing "No Fly" and ███████████████████████ SD 108-01-02A (September 6th) requiring extra security measures for flights carrying author Salman Rushdie; (SSI) Of the 16 security advisories known as Information Circulars sent by the FAA to the commercial aviation industry, 12 of them focused on security issues overseas, particularly the Middle East, two provided information on Algerian-Born terrorist Ahmed Ressam's threats against Los Angeles Airport during the millennium; one discussed the threat to civil aviation of ground to air missiles (MANPADS); one alerted airports and air carriers to the tactic of disguising weapons as every day items (a knife concealed in a cigarette lighter was found at the crash site of United Flight 93); and one discussed the possible terrorist threat to Americans posed by extremists but had expired on August 22, 2001.

[445] [SSI] FAA report, Information Circular 2001-4A , July 31, 2001. Another circular issued on August 16 also mentioned hijacking and warned about the potential use of disguised weapons. [SSI] See FAA report, Information Circular, August 16, 2001 (IC 2001-12)

[446] Monte Belger interview (Nov. 24, 2003); Shirley M. interview (Mar. 30, 2004). We interviewed a number of FAA security officials, including those on the front lines, who were unaware that the United States was on high alert regarding the terrorist threat during the summer of 2001. The security directors for American Airlines and United Air Lines told the Commission that they knew the summer of 2001 was a time of high threat, but neither of the senior operating executives for American and United Air Lines were aware. See Andy Studdert interview (Nov. 20, 2003); Gerard Arpey interview (Jan. 8, 2004). The Commission was contacted by commercial pilots who had been unaware of the heightened threat period and believed strongly that the threat information should have been more broadly shared with them.

[447] See Andy Studdert interview (Nov. 20, 2003); Gerard Arpey interview (Jan. 8, 2004).

[448] "The decade of the 1980s was a disastrous one for aviation. The period confirmed the existence of a dangerous trend toward greater violence against air transportation. Overall, 25 planes were sabotaged by explosives, causing 1,207 casualties as compared to 650 deaths caused by 44 explosions in the 1970s and 286 deaths in the 1960s." Alexander T. Wells, *Commercial Aviation Safety*, 3rd ed. (McGraw-Hill, 2001), p. 303.

[449] On the night of July 17, 1996, TWA Flight 800, which had departed from New York's JFK International Airport bound for Paris, France, crashed into the Atlantic Ocean near East Moriches, N.Y., killing all 230 individuals on board.

[450] These recommendations included immediate deployment of explosives detection technology to the airports for baggage screening; passenger and bag matching on domestic flights (a measure already applied overseas, which was explicitly linked to the need to determine the presence of explosives in checked baggage; it required each checked bag to be matched to a boarded passenger before being loaded onto an aircraft); additional deployment of canine explosives-sniffing teams.

[451] [SECRET] FAA report, "Civil Aviation Security Threat and Security Assessment Procedures and Matrix in effect on 9/11/01."

[452] James U. interview (Sept. 17, 2003); Timothy A. interview (Jan. 8, 2004).

[453] James U. interview (Sept. 17, 2003).

[454] Larry W. interview (Jan. 8, 2004).

[455] Rand–St. Andrews University Chronology of Terrorist Acts.

[456] FAA report, "Criminal Acts Against Civil Aviation," 2000.

[457] FAA report, "Civil Aviation Security Reference Handbook," May 1999, pp. D-9, D-11, D-22.

[458] The July 17, 2001, *Federal Register* stated: "Terrorism can occur anytime and anywhere in the United States. Members of foreign terrorist groups, representatives from state sponsors of terrorism, and radical fundamentalist elements from many nations are present in the United States. The activities of some of these individuals and groups . . . now include recruiting other persons for terrorist activities and training them to use weapons and make bombs." It continued: "Thus an increasing threat to civil aviation from both foreign sources and potential domestic ones exists and needs to be prevented and countered."

[459] James U. interview (Sept. 17, 2003).

[460] FAA Information Circular 2000-01 issued April 27, 2000. [SSI]

[461] FAA, *2001 CD-ROM Terrorism Threat Presentation to Aviation Security Personnel at Airports and Air Carriers,* slide 24. [SSI]

[462] FAA report, "Total Architecture for Aviation Security," June 2001, p. 10. However, the Commission also heard testimony from various FAA and aviation industry leaders, including two former FAA associate administrators of civil aviation security, that the civil aviation security system was designed to stop "crazies" and "criminals" but not necessarily committed terrorists who could always find a way to defeat the system.

[463] See Title 49 U.S.C. § 44903(b). The rules FAA imposed on certificated airports and air carriers to achieve security objectives were set forth primarily in 14 C.F.R. §§ 107, 108, 109, 129. The FAA's enforcement tools included imposing civil fines and withholding an air carrier's or airport's federal certificate to operate. Beginning in 1986, the FAA's responsibility "to protect passengers and property" was augmented to include the evaluation of intelligence on threats to the civil aviation system

[464] The rules FAA imposed on certificated commercial air carriers were required by Title 49 of the U.S. Code and set forth primarily in 14 C.F.R. §§ 108, 129; an FAA-approved Air Carrier Standard Security Program (ACSSP); an industry-generated Checkpoint Operations Guide (COG) that specified the ways and means by which air carriers would meet federal aviation security requirements.

[465] FAA Report, Administrator's Fact Book, October 2001, p. 16; FAA Report, Civil Aviation Security Handbook, May 1999, pp. 117–118. [SSI]

[466] See, *Report of the President's Commission on Aviation Security and Terrorism,* Washington, D.C., 1990, p. 40.

[467] Jane Garvey interview (Oct. 21, 2003); Mike Canavan interview (Nov. 4, 2003).

[468] To facilitate the flow of data and promote interagency cooperation on civil aviation security issues, the FAA assigned liaison personnel to key intelligence community agencies, including the FBI, CIA, and State Department. Although the NSA and the DIA maintained collection requirements on behalf of the FAA, liaisons were not assigned to either agency. Claudio Manno interview (Oct. 1, 2003).

[469] FAA intelligence officials stated that the division did not receive a daily stream of raw intelligence from the FBI. Claudio Manno interview (Oct. 1, 2003).

[470] Section 111(a) of the Aviation Security Improvement Act of 1990 (P.L. 101-604) required "the agencies of the intelligence community [to] . . . ensure that intelligence reports concerning international terrorism are made available . . . to the Department of Transportation and the Federal Aviation Administration." The U.S. intelligence community, including the FBI, CIA, National Security Agency (NSA), Defense Intelligence Agency (DIA); and the Department of State, among others, was responsible for collecting and analyzing intelligence data bearing on the security of the United States and for that data to the FAA's Office of Civil Aviation Security Intelligence (ACI). The

kinds of intelligence data that were supposed to flow to the FAA were determined by collection requirements set out in a "statement of intelligence interest" and other arrangements between the FAA and various intelligence community agencies. Claudio Manno testimony, Jan. 27, 2004); Claudio Manno interview (Oct. 1, 2003); Matt K. interview (Feb. 13, 2004).

[171] Pat M. interview (Sept. 24, 2003)

[172] Among the other products created by the Office of Civil Aviation Security Intelligence were "intelligence notes" and special assessments to provide detailed analysis on specific security issues, as well as "information circulars" that were sent to airports and air carriers to warn them of general security threats and concerns. Additionally, the Office of Secretary of Transportation had a director of security and intelligence to keep the secretary up to date on transportation security issues. To that end, the director was provided copies of intelligence products prepared by the FAA Office of Civil Aviation Intelligence.

The FAA's Intelligence Division produced four main products to help keep policymakers and the industry informed about threats to security so that they could make informed decisions about whether security policies, practices, and procedures were sufficient to counter the perceived threat. The first of these was the Daily Intelligence Summary (DIS). The intelligence data was rolled up each day into a summary and presented to key policymakers, including the FAA associate administrator of civil aviation security, the FAA administrator, and the FAA deputy administrator. The Department of Transportation's director of security and intelligence would also receive the information and use the material to produce a more comprehensive security briefing for the secretary of transportation. The second main product of the Intelligence Division was the information circular. It was designed to alert policymakers and the commercial aviation industry to more general threats and issues bearing on civil aviation security, but in the FAA's view did not necessitate the implementation of extraordinary security procedures. Whereas the security directive was a regulatory mechanism, the information circular was advisory. In addition, FAA intelligence published intelligence notes and assessment reports to expound on security issues such as terrorist methods of operation. These products were mainly intended to help justify and support regulatory and policy decisionmaking.

[473] James U. interview (Sept. 17, 2003); Claudio Manno interview (Oct. 1, 2003). If the assistant reviewed something in the DIS that she thought merited the attention of the Deputy Administrator, she would see that he was informed. The Deputy Administrator in turn would determine whether the information needed to be raised with the Administrator. Monte Belger interview (Nov. 24, 2003); Shirley M. interview (Mar. 30, 2004). Several interviewees indicated that the FAA Administrator maintained an open-door policy and was accessible if an intelligence or security matter needed to be raised, although one associate administrator said he rarely addressed security issues with her, going instead to the Deputy Administrator. The Administrator told us that she counted on her highly capable security staff to notify her of any pressing issues. Jane Garvey interview (Oct. 21, 2003); Cathal Flynn interview (Sept. 9, 2003); Monte Belger interview (Nov. 24, 2003); Shirley M. interview (Mar. 30, 2004).

[474] In addition, the analyst would determine whether to open an intelligence case file (ICF) to track and assess the particular security threat or issue. Between 1993 and 2001, the FAA had opened more than 1,200 ICFs; key intelligence inputs and taskings were recorded in a daily log sheet to make possible monitoring and supervision.

[475] Pat M. interview (Sept. 24, 2003); Bruce B. interview (Sept. 29, 2003). All airports certificated by the FAA to operate were required to implement a standard set of minimum security measures which were set forth in the Air Carrier Standard Security Program. Similarly, FAA-certificated airports were required to abide by an Airport Operator Standard Security Program. The FAA was authorized to require that air carriers and airports implement immediate, temporary measures to increase or alter security procedures. It did so by issuing security directives to air carriers (FAR 108) and emergency amendments to airports (FAR 107).

[476] Claudio Manno interview

[477] FAA report, Air Carrier Standard Security Program, appendix XV, May 2001. [SSI]

[478] Nick G. interview (May 26, 2004); Claudio Manno interview (Oct. 1, 2003); Mike Canavan interview (Nov. 4, 2003); Wells, *Commercial Aviation Safety*, p. 308.

[479] FAA Security Directive 95-11E, Aug. 25, 1995. (SSI)

[480] FAA Security Directive 97-01C, May 26, 1998 [SSI]; FAA Security Directive 96-03J, May 27, 1998. [SSI] Ironically, this language accompanied an FAA security directive that, in part, implemented the automated prescreening system (CAPPS I) that lowered the level of screening for carry-on items required of selectees.

The conviction of Ahmed Ressam for a plot to bomb the Los Angeles International Airport around January 1, 2000, was specific proof that terrorists sought to attack civil aviation in the United States.

[481] FAA report, Security Directive 96-03K, Dec. 1, 1998.

[482] Department of Transportation rulemaking, "14 CFR Parts 107 and 139 Airport Security; Final Rule," *Federal* Register vol. 66, No. 137 (July 17, 2001).

[483] Cathal Flynn interview (Sept. 9, 2003); Claudio Manno interview (Oct. 1, 2003).

[484] Cathal Flynn testimony, Jan. 27, 2004.

[485] ▮▮▮▮▮▮▮▮▮▮▮▮▮▮▮▮▮▮▮▮▮▮▮▮▮▮▮▮▮▮▮▮

[LES] ▮▮ See

FBI report, "Response to Commission Request 29-3 [Airport vulnerability assessments].

[486] Norman Mineta testimony, May 23, 2003; Lee L. interview (Oct. 28, 2003).

[487] However, according to an FBI official, their assessment of the terrorist threat to aviation was based on a matrix provided to them by the FAA. This matrix measured the threat ▮▮▮▮▮▮▮▮▮▮▮▮▮▮▮▮▮▮▮▮▮▮▮ Staff believes that this is another example of a troubling phenomenon observed in other areas of aviation security—that of plausible deniability. While the FAA could point to the FBI terrorist threat assessment as being "low" therefore imposing no obligation to increase security at home; the FBI could point to the assessment as one based on criteria established by the FAA—criteria that required ▮▮▮▮▮▮▮▮▮▮▮▮▮▮

[488] Matt K. interview (Sept. 24, 2003); Cathal Flynn interview (Sept. 9, 2003); James P. interview (Oct. 7, 2003); Claudio Manno interview (Oct. 1, 2003); The issues and

problems associated with the FBI culture in regard to intelligence versus criminal investigation is addressed extensively by the Commission's Team Five.

[489] Cathal Flynn interview (Sept. 9, 2003)

[490] Cathal Flynn testimony (Jan. 27, 2004)

[491] Matt K. interview (Feb. 13, 2004)

[492] The Phoenix EC was a 2001 FBI memo produced by a Special Agent in Phoenix, Arizona expressing his concern about flight training by individuals from Arab countries. FAA records indicate that no case file was established by the FAA specifically on the issue of pilot training by terrorists. One FAA Intelligence Official indicated that had this information been known to the FAA, perhaps the FAA's Intelligence division would have had the opportunity to focus on pilot training as a security issue in the period leading up to September 11, 2001. See Matt K. interview (Feb. 13, 2004).

[493] The FBI agent in charge of the tasking indicates that the liaison was consulted and, in fact, reviewed the tasking memo sent to the field office. See Bev W. interview (Feb. 17, 2004); Jack S. interview (Nov. 3, 2003); The FBI agent in charge of the tasking indicates that the liaison was consulted and, in fact, reviewed the tasking memo sent to the field office.

[494] Bev W. interview (Feb. 17, 2004)

[495] Carol H. interview (Oct. 27, 2003). In its recommendations to the Gore Commission, the ATA called for: "the dedication of specific FBI staff resources to the unique issues relating to aviation terrorism which, consistent with current intelligence assessments, require particular attention."[495] Letter from President and Chief Executive Officer of the Air Transport Association, to General John Michael Loh (Retired) of the Gore Commission, August 23, 1996.

[496] Agency leadership referred to FAA personnel assigned to Intelligence Community agencies as "liaisons." See reponse of TSA to Congressional Joint Inquiry questions for the record, Feb. 4, 2003.

[497][SECRET]See: CIA report: "Robert W's Responses to Commission Questions for the Record, 8 July 2004."

[498] [SECRET] FAA report, Intelligence Case File, 980096; FAA report, Intelligence Case File, 980199. See FAA, Daily Intelligence Summaries from May 1, 2001 to September 10, 2001

[499] [SECRET] FAA report, Information Circular 2000-01, April 27, 2000; FAA Intelligence Case File 950007; FAA Intelligence Case File 980199. In 1998 UBL was reported to have stated "...All Islamic military have been mobilized to strike a significant U.S. or Israeli strategic target, to bring down their aircraft and hijack them." See: FAA response of 2/04/03 to Congressional Joint Inquiry staff letter dated, Nov. 6, 2002. [SSI] The indictment of one of the co-conspirators with Bin Ladin in the Africa embassy bombings in 1998 stated that the defendant had "trained in a number of camps in Afghanistan, including a number of camps affiliated with al Qaeda. The [defendant] was trained in explosives, hijacking, kidnapping, assassination and intelligence techniques..." See United States District Court Southern District of New York v. Usam Bin Laden, S(10) 98 Cr. 1023 (LBS)

[500] [SECRET] FAA report, Intelligence Case File 980096; FAA report, Intelligence Case File 980199.

[501] [SECRET] FAA report, Intelligence Case File 980096.

[502][SECRET] FAA Intelligence Case File 950009.

[503] [SECRET] FAA report, Intelligence Case File 20010133; See FAA reports, Daily Intelligence Summaries, 2001. [Pre 9/11]

---

[504] [SECRET] See FAA report, Intelligence Case File 20010061.

[505] [SECRET] An earlier UBL hijacking threat in 1999 had resulted in a security directive to increase defenses at New York City airports, but the directive expired a few weeks later when the threat information on which the action was taken was deemed no longer credible.

[506] [SECRET] FAA report, Intelligence Case File 20010140; [SECRET] Claudio Manno interview (Oct. 1, 2003).

[508] [SECRET] FAA report, Intelligence Case File 95009.

[509] In the case of an Air India hijacking in December 1999 and the Alas Chiricanas Airlines hijacking in July 1994, even though the hijackers were not known to operate the aircraft, they clearly possessed advanced knowledge of aviation. Matt K. interview (Feb. 13, 2004)

[510] [SECRET] FAA report, Intelligence Case File 20010064.

[511] Jack S. interview (Nov. 3, 2003); Claudio Manno interview (Oct. 1, 2003). See also FAA report, Intelligence Case File 940305.

[513] Hijacking of an Air France jetliner. The hijackers' destination was Paris. While the plane was in Marseille the hijackers requested that the plane be filled with 27 tons of fuel, even though the trip to Paris would require a little more than one-third of that amount. The presence of explosives placed on the aircraft and other evidence indicated to authorities that the hijackers may have planned to blow the plane up over Paris. See Pat M. interview (Sept. 24, 2003); and Jack S. interview (Nov. 3, 2003); See also FAA report, Intelligence Case File 940305.

[514] [SECRET] FAA report, Intelligence Case File 940230. A reuters story in the case file said of the incident: "Police said, however, the third prospect of a Kamikaze-style attack on the White House is the worst case scenario, a dangerous how-to example for other would be assassins willing to give their lives for a greater goal.

[515] [SECRET] FAA report, Intelligence Case Files 940230 and 940237. Also, in 1974 a man attempted to commandeer a commercial jet at BWI with the intent of slamming the aircraft into the White House, but was shot before he could execute his plan. "Hijacker Targeted President in 1974--www.insightmag.com/news/2002/06/24.

[516] Pat M. interview.

[517] [SECRET]Claudio Manno interview (Oct. 1, 2003).

[518] [SECRET] Jack S. Interviews (Nov. 3, 2003 & June 13, 2004). See also, FAA report, Intelligence Case File 980162.

[519] [SECRET] FAA report, Daily Intelligence Summary, July 12, 2001.

[520] [SECRET] FAA report, Daily Intelligence Summary, July 12, 2001. FAA report, Intelligence Case File, 20010141, July 11, 2001.

[521] [SECRET] FAA report, Intelligence Case File 20010216.

---

[522] [SECRET] FAA report, Intelligence Case File 20010216.

[523] [SECRET] FAA Rebuttal, "Joint Staff Statement, Part I, Eleanor Hill, Staff Director, Joint Inquiry Staff, September 18, 2002--Rebuttals" (SSI); and Intelligence Note 99-06, "Usama Bin Ladin/World Islamic Front Hijacking Threat, Issued August 4, 1999.

[524] One FAA security official told the Commission that the theme of crashing airplanes into building was something that was "inevitable" because of the high profile of civil aviation. A number of interviewees expressed surprise that in the aftermath of 9/11 the FAA's leadership told Congress that they had never conceived of the use of aircraft as weapons, when in fact the agency had considered the threat, and as one official put it, "logic" dictated that such a possibility was a concern. See Jack S. interview (Nov. 3, 2003).

[525] [SECRET] FAA report, "Usama Bin Ladin/World Islamic Front (WIF) Threat to U.S. Civil Aviation," Sept. 15, 1998; FAA report, "Usama Bin Ladin/World Islamic Front Threat to U.S. Civli Aviation," July, 1999; See also FAA report, Intelligence Case File 20000024.

[526] Matt K. interview, (Feb. 13, 2004)

[527] Jack H. interview (Oct. 8, 2003)

[528] Federal Aviation Administration, *2001 CD-ROM Terrorism Threat Presentation to Aviation Security Personnel at Airports and Air Carriers,* Slide 24. [SSI]

[529] Mike Canavan testimony (May 23, 2004). We note that the final report of the Congressional Joint Inquiry on intelligence regarding 9/11 indicated that the FAA had not considered the use of aircraft as weapons. In response to the report, the FAA's intelligence unit sent a letter to the Joint Inquiry explaining that it had considered the use of aircraft as weapons and providing the facts to substantiate the rebuttal. Commission staff believes that the Intelligence division deserves substantial credit for its efforts to ensure that the public record was accurate regarding what the agency knew. See FAA Rebuttal, "Joint Staff Statement , Part I, Eleanor Hill testimony" (SSI); Security expert Brian Jenkins noted that: "…Security authorities almost invariably failed to foresee the terrorists' adoption of fresh methods of attacking aviation…." Even when potential tactics were perceived, the absence of an actual event or the intelligence regarding a "specific" plot to implement it meant little in terms of alterations to the security baseline.

[530] James P. interview (Oct. 7, 2003); Matt K. interview (Feb. 13, 2003); Ed. S. interview (Nov. 21, 2003)

[531] Rich S. interview (Mar. 1, 2004) (SSI)

[532] Claudio Manno interview (Oct. 1, 2003); and Lynne O. interview (Oct. 3, 2003)

[533] Lee L. interview (Oct. 28, 2003); James P. interview (Oct. 7, 2003); and Jane Garvey testimony, Jan. 27, 2004.

[534] [SSI] Commission interviewees stated that to be listed in a security directive an individual would have had to pose a "direct" threat to aviation—which meant that an individual, ▮▮ Lee L. interview (Oct. 28, ▮▮ James P. interview (Oct. 7, 2003); Jane Garvey testimony, Jan. 27, 2004; and Cathal Flynn testimony, Jan. 27, 2004.

[535] Cathal Flynn testimony, Jan. 27, 2004

[536] Matt K. interview (Feb. 13, 2004).

[537] Claudio Manno interview (Oct. 1, 2003). Claudio Manno testimony, Jan. 27, 2004.

SUBJECT TO CLASSIFICATION REVIEW

[538] Matt K. interview (Feb. 13, 2004).

[539] [SSI] FAA reports, SD95—issued April 24, 2000; SD 108-01—issued August 21, 24 & 28, 2001

[540] Final Report, White House Commission on Aviation Safety and Security, Feb. 12, 1997; One of the members of the Gore Commission told the 9/11 Commission that the intent of this recommendation was to assure maximum use of terrorist watch lists to prohibit known and suspected terrorists from getting on aircraft. The language of the recommendation appears to be somewhat ambiguous in regard to the "intelligence information" it calls on the FBI and CIA to use for the purpose of passenger profiling, if not the terrorists' names themselves. However, we stress that it would make exceedingly little sense to suggest that the FAA use information about known and suspected terrorists to create a profile capable of identifying them by their profile at airports in order to stop them from flying, but fail to use their known names for the same purpose..

[541] James P. interview (Oct. 7, 2003); See also: FAA report, Security Directive SD 97-01 (SSI)

[542] FAA report, Security Directive SD-96-05 (A-G) [SSI]

[543] FAA report, Security Directive 96-02 issued on July 25, 1996. "...carry-on items of selectees...shall be...emptied and the contents physically searched by a qualified screener." [SSI] FAA report, Security Directive SD-96-05 (A-G) (SSI); Janet R. interview (Feb. 26, 2004); and Rich S. interview (Mar. 1, 2004)

[544] FAA report, Security Directive SD-96-05 (A-G) (SSI); and FAA report, Security Directive SD 97-01 (SSI)

[545] Janet R. interview (Feb. 26, 2004)

[546] Ed S. interview (Nov. 21, 2003)

[547] FAA report, Air Carrier Standard Security Program, May, 2000. [SSI]

[548] FAA report, Air Carrier Standard Security Program, May 2001. [SSI]

[549] Nick G. interview (May 26, 2004).

[550] FAA Security Directive 97-01 issued October 27, 1997 stated that the directive "Requires profiling of ONLY those passengers checking baggage." [SSI]

[551] James P. interview (Oct. 7, 2003)

[552] Carol H. interview (Oct. 27, 2003)

[553] [SSI] Mr. R. interview (Feb. 26, 2004). We would note that such a decrease occurred at a time when the terrorist threat to the United States was on the increase, including the bombing of American Embassies in East Africa, Usama Bin Ladin's declaration of war against the United States; the bombing of the U.S.S Cole and the millennium threat posed by Ahmed Ressam.[SECRET]

SUBJECT TO CLASSIFICATION REVIEW

[554] FAA report, Baseline Working Group final report, 1996. FAA interviewees also stated that, as originally conceived, CAPPS was supposed to include extra screening of selectee's person, carry-on belongings and checked bags. See James P. interview (Oct. 7, 2003)

[555] FAA report, Air Carrier Standard Security Program, Appendix XV, May 2001, pp.1-9.

[556] Metropolitan Washington Airports Authority, videotape of Main Terminal checkpoints, September 11, 2001 [SSI]

[557] In the aftermath of the TWA 800 disaster in 1996, Congress, the Gore Commission and the FAA's Aviation Security Advisory Committee were pushing for large scale deployment of expensive explosive detection equipment at the nation's airports. At a cost of $1,000,000 million per machine, the initiative promised to be an expensive proposition for air carriers and the FAA. By linking the efforts to identify "risky" passengers through CAPPS to the use of Explosive Detection Technology – the system could ration the limited availability of the equipment at the time. It is quite possible that the industry also envisioned it as a means of avoiding the expense of having to apply EDT to all passenger bags when more machines could be made available.

[558] Passengers would perceive increased screening as an additional "hassle" factor of flying. The Department of Justice perceived the potential for complaints about discrimination by a system that singled out passengers for secondary screening. Finally, Congress did not like to hearing constituent complaints about either passenger inconvenience or charges of discrimination likely to arise from secondary screening.

[559] Air carriers, which were always concerned about operational efficiency, surely realized that requiring selectees to undergo additional screening of their person or hand searches of carry-on baggage could slow down checkpoint operations and thereby increase the difficulty of staying on schedule.

[560] Marcus A. interview (Oct. 24, 2003)

[561] While endorsing the "manual and automated profiling systems, such as the one under development by the FAA and Northwest Airlines," the latter of which was the progenitor of the CAPPS program, the Gore Commission adopted a lengthy "augmenting recommendation" with respect to the subject: "The Commission strongly believes the civil liberties that are so fundamentally American should not, and need not, be compromised by a profiling system. The Commission recommends the following safeguards: 1) no profile should contain or be based on material of a constitutionally suspect nature; 2) factors to be considered for elements of the profile should be based on measurable, verifiable data indicating that the factors chosen are reasonable predictors of risk; 3) passengers should be informed of airline security procedures and of their right to avoid any search of their person or luggage by electing not to board the aircraft; 4) searches arising from the use of an automated profiling system should be no more intrusive than search procedures that could be applied to all passengers; 5) neither the airlines nor the government should maintain permanent databases on selectees; 6) periodic independent reviews of profiling procedures should be made; 7) the Commission reiterates that profiling should last only until Explosive Detection Systems are reliable and fully deployed; and 8) the Commission urges that these elements be embodied in FAA standards that must be strictly observed." See *Final Report of the White Commission on Aviation Safety and Security*, Washington, DC, 1997.

[562] Marcus A. interview (Oct. 24, 2003)

[563] See FAA letter from Principal Security Inspector dated January 11, 1998. UAL response to Commission questions for the record, April 16, 2004.

[564] Ed S. interview (Nov. 21, 2003); Former FAA Administrator Garvey told the Commission that concerns were raised about security profiling at airports by the Arab American community that feared it might be the target of such security measures. She recalled receiving a similar complaint on behalf of the Arab-American community from a member of Congress. In response to the concerns, she and the Associate Administrator of Civil Aviation Security Chathal Flynn traveled to Detroit in 1998 to meet with members of the Arab American community who expressed deep concerns about passenger prescreening and the potential for discrimination. See Jane Garvey interview (Oct. 21, 2003); An article about the visit that appeared in the Arab American News on September 18, 1998 contained an account of an Arab American who told the member of Congress that he felt discriminated against and humiliated when he was told to open his luggage for hand-searching in front of other passengers at the local airport. It is worth noting that the issue of CAPPS was highly contentious at the time the developing program was considered by the Gore Commission, and it has continued to be so to the present day. Gore Commission member and terrorism expert Brian Jenkins highlighted the key concerns in a 1999 article: "Americans would prefer their security to be democratic and passive; that is, equally applied to everyone, and reactive only to behavior indicating criminal intent – such as attempting to smuggle a gun on board – rather than attempting to identify in advance the most likely smuggler. Criteria based on ethnic identity, national origin, gender, and religion are all out of bounds to civil libertarians. Nor should profiling provide airlines with access to personal information about travelers, including their criminal record if they have one. Arab-Americans, who have been subject to suspicion and in some cases mistreatment following terrorist incidents that were correctly or incorrectly blamed on Middle Eastern groups, have expressed particular concern." See Brian Jenkins, 'Aviation Security in the United States," in Wilkinson and Jenkins, eds., *Aviation Terrorism and Security* (London and Portland, OR: Frank Cass Publishers, 1999), p. 106.

[565] Al H. briefing (June 8, 2004)

[566] Information about the weapons used by the 9/11 hijackers is derived from reports provided by passengers who contacted the ground from the hijacked aircraft, from evidence found at the crime scenes, and from the hijackers' financial records. At least seven knives were purchased by the hijackers, including Victorinox Swiss Army knives, Leatherman multi-tool knives, pocket knives, and a Stanley two-piece snap knife set. The FBI collected evidence of 14 knives or portions of knives, including a boxcutter type implement, at the Flight 93 crash site. None of the blades that were found appeared to be 4 inches in length or longer. However, one of the pieces of evidence which the FBI referred to as a "green plastic handle for utility knife," did not have a blade, so it was not possible to ascertain how long it was. Short-bladed knives were not expressly prohibited by FAA regulations, so it is entirely possible that had they been found on the hijackers as they passed through checkpoint, they would have been returned to them (unless they were determined by the screener to be "menacing.") [LES]

[567] Federal Aviation Regulation Part 108 and the FAA's Air Carrier Standard Security Program specified the means by which air carriers, or their designees, were to screen passengers and their carry-on belongings. 14 CFR §108.9.

[568] Cathal Flynn testimony, Jan. 27, 2004.

[569] The airline retained the responsibility for overseeing the contractor's compliance with FAA regulations. See FAA report, Air Carrier Standard Security Program, May 2001. [SSI] Testimony of Robert W. Baker, Vice Chairman of American Airlines, to Senate Committee on Governmental Affairs Hearing on "Weak Links: How Should the Federal Government Manage Airline Passenger and Baggage Screening?" S. Hearing 107-208, September 25, 2001, pp. 107-108.

[570] FAA report, Air Carrier Standard Security Program, May 2001. [SSI]

[571] Appendix I of the ACSSP provided FAA's "Deadly or Dangerous Weapons Guidelines" for use in determining what objects should not be allowed to be carried into the cabin of an aircraft. They were to be used by screeners "in making a reasonable determination of what property in the possession of a person should be considered a deadly or dangerous weapon. They are only guidelines, however, and "common

sense should always prevail." Within the list were the following relevant entries: <u>Knives</u> – Including sabers, swords, hunting knives, souvenir knives, martial arts devices, and such other knives with blades 4 inches long or longer and/or knives considered illegal by local law; <u>Disabling or Incapacitating Items</u> – All tear gas, mace, and similar chemicals and gases whether in pistol, canister, or other container, and other disabling devices such as electronic stunning/shocking devices; <u>Other Articles</u> – Such items as ice picks, straight razors, and elongated scissors; though not commonly thought of as a deadly or dangerous weapon, but could be used as a weapon, including toy or "dummy" weapons or grenades. See FAA report, Air Carrier Standard Security Program, Appendix I, May 2001. [SSI]

[572] The book provided an example citing the "sewing scissors" in the hands of a woman who possessed other sewing equipment is permissible, while such scissors in the possession of a man who possessed no other sewing equipment should be prohibited. See ATA/RAA, *Checkpoint Operations Guide*, Revision 007, September 10, 2001, pp. 5-6 through 5-9 [SSI]

[573] The *Checkpoint Operations Guide* (COG) was developed, "in cooperation with the FAA," by the Air Transport Association (ATA) and the Regional Airline Association (RAA) to implement the security checkpoint related provisions of the ACSSP, and was subject to FAA review.*Checkpoint Operations Guide*, Revision 007, September 10, 2001, cover page [SSI] Courtney T. interview (June 3, 2004). Email response to Commission, Courtney T., June 14, 2004; The *Air Transport Association* (ATA) was founded in 1936 and remains the trade association for the major U.S. airlines. It represents their interests before Congress, federal agencies (including the FAA), and state and local governments. The ATA seeks to coordinate industry and government safety programs, to help standardize industry practices and to enhance the efficiency of the air transportation system. Of particular relevance to this report, the ATA took the lead role for the airlines in the FAA rulemaking process, and in developing – with FAA cooperation – the Checkpoint Operations Guide (COG) for passenger and carry-on baggage screening and the training materials for the "Common Strategy" for dealing in-flight with hijackings.

[574] *Checkpoint Operations Guide*, Revision 007, September 10, 2001, pp. 5-6 through 5-9 [SSI]

[575] Tim A. interview (Jan. 8, 2004)

[576] One entry in FAA's database on security incidents in 2001 regarding an incident at Logan Airport on 1/31/2001 in which a passenger entered a checkpoint "with a box cutter inside is jacket pocket." The report stated that "The item was discovered during x-ray screening. State police were notified and trooper cleared passenger for travel. Box cutter was placed in the TSA prohibited items bin." See FAA report, Security incident, Logan Airport, January 31, 2001

[577] One of the checkpoint supervisors working at Boston's Logan International Airport on September 11, 2001, recalled that, at that time, while box-cutters were not permitted to pass the checkpoint without the removal of the blade, any knife with a blade of less than four inches was permitted to pass through security. FBI report of investigation, interview of screener, (Sept. 30, 2001) [LES]

[578] May stated, "Under pre-9/11 FAA regulations only "knives with blades four inches long or longer and/or considered illegal under local law" were prohibited. Under a non-regulatory Checkpoint Operations Guide, developed by the FAA, the Regional Airline Association and the ATA, with FAA approval interpreting the FAA regulations, box cutting devices were considered a restricted item posing a potential danger. This meant that if such a device was identified, it could be kept off the aircraft. The FAA mandated metal-detection walk-through systems, however, were designed and tested to detect metallic items about the size of a small handgun or larger. The pre-9/11 screening system was not designed to detect or prohibit these types of small items." Testimony of James C. May, Chairman and CEO, Air Transport Association of America, to National Commission on Terrorist Attacks Upon the United States at Hearing on Civil Aviation Security, May 22, 2003

[579] FAA report, Air Carrier Standard Security Program, Appendix VI, May 200. FAA "Office of Civil Aviation Security National Assessment Manual" second edition, 6/30/1999; Bruce P. interview (Oct. 27, 2003). An FAA form titled "Screening Activities" that certificated airports were required to submit annually contained a field for the listing "weapons detected" at checkpoint screening operations. The field featured two categories, one titled "firearms" and the other titled "explosives and incendiaries." There was no field provided for knives. See Massport report, FAA Form 1650-7. Nevertheless, a U.S. government database which recorded suspicious security incidents at U.S. airports contained nine entries regarding "deadly and dangerous items" for 2001 prior to 9/11. Among them was an entry of an incident on March 15, 2001, at the Kansas City airport which stated" "passenger attempted to enter checkpoint with three and one-half inch knife in carry-on baggage. Passenger surrendered the item." Presumably this was an instance in which "common sense rather than a strict interpretation of the Air Carrier Standard Security Program and the Checkpoint Operations Guide of prohibited items. Another entry dated January 31, noted that a box cutter was confiscated from a passenger at Boston Logan and "placed into the prohibited items bin." And still another which occurred in June reported that a "pair of folding scissors" had been taken from a female passenger also in Boston. See TSA report, Security Incidents Reports 1/12001 to 9/11/2001.

[580] FAA report, "The Threat to U.S. Civil Aviation in the United States" September, 1994.[SSI]

[581] FAA security experts indicated to the Commission that the standard was based on a size of blade that could be considered "menacing" as well as a survey of local laws to determine what localities allowed citizens to carry in a concealed fashion in public. This canvas resulted in the establishment of the four-inch standard. See Lynne O. interview (Oct. 3, 2003); and Lee L. interview (Oct. 28, 2003); In regard to knives with blades shorter than 4 inches long, FAA's former civil aviation security chief testified before the Commission that "the menace conveyed by them is less than the innocent reasons for having them in people's possession." At the same hearing, former FAA Administrator Jane Garvey noted that prior to 9/11 knives were "commonplace" at airports and were used for meals services on aircraft. See Cathal Flynn testimony, Jan. 27, 2004; and Jane Garvey testimony, Jan. 27, 2004; In 1993, the FAA considered placing all knives on the prohibited items list, but the proposal was dropped because officials viewed such a mandate as unenforceable. See Leo B. interview (Sept. 17, 2003).

[582] The "Air Carriers Checkpoint Operations Guide" in effect on 9/11 stated: "knives with blades under 4 inches, such as Swiss Army Knives, scout knives, pocket utility knives, etc. may be allowed to enter the sterile areas. However knives with blades under 4 inches that could be considered by a reasonable person to be a "menacing" knife and/or may be illegal under local law and should not be allowed to enter the sterile area." See FAA, "Air Carriers Checkpoint Operations Guide,"Aug. 1999. See also, FAA report, Air Carrier Standard Security Program, May, 2000. [SSI]; Cathal Flynn interview (Sept. 9, 2003); Lee L. interview (Oct. 28, 2003); Leo B. interview (Sept. 17, 2003).

[583] Including among others: GAO reports, Aviation Security: FAA Preboard Passenger Screening Test results (GAO/RCED-87-125FS, Apr. 30, 1987); Aviation Security: Additional Actions Needed to Meet Domestic and International Challenges (GAO/RCED-94-38, January 27, 1994); Aviation Security: Urgent Issues Need to Be Addressed (GAO/T-RCED/NSIAD-96-251, September 11,1996); Aviation Security: Slow Progress in Addressing Long-Standing Screener Performance Poblems (GAO/T-

RCED-00-125, March 16, 2000); and Aviation Security: Long-standing Problems Impair Airport Screeners' performance (GAO/RCED-00-75, June 28, 2000.

[584] Including DoT-IG report, Audit Report on Deployment of Explosives Detection Systems, Oct. 5, 1998; Statement on Aviation Security by Alexis Stefani, Deputy Assistant Inspector General for Aviation, before House Subcommittee on Aviation, May 14, 1998; Statement on Aviation Security by Alexi Stefani, Deputy Assistant Inspector Generel for Aviation, before House Subcommitee on Aviation, March 10, 1999; and Statement on Aviation Security by Alexis Stefani, Deputy Assistant Inspector General for Aviation, before Senate Aviation Subcommittee, Arpil6, 2000.

[585] The high failure rate of screeners to detect weapons was discerned by the FAA using tests designed only to evaluate the system's ability to detect prescribed very obvious "test items" used by government inspectors. ██

████████████████ See Leo B. interview (Sept. 17, 2003). Many of the government reports cited low pay, insufficient training and high-turnover rates that reached nearly 400% among screeners at the nation's airports as the reason for consistently poor rates of detection. [SSI]

[586] Dr. John Jay Nestor, FAA Office of Civil Aviation Security Policy and Planning, "Evaluation of Checkpoint Screening Performance 10/1/1998 to 9/20/2000." [SSI]

[587] Testimony of Gerald L. Dillingham, General Accounting Office, to Senate Aviation Subcommittee of the Committee on Commerce, Science and Transportation at Hearing on Vulnerabilities in Aviation Security System, April 6, 2000. The author of the testimony also served on staff to the 9/11 Commission.

[588] Numerous interviewees noted that the air carriers awarded screening contracts to the lowest bidder who paid low wages and suffered high levels of employee turnover. They stated that air carriers considered fines imposed on them by the FAA for security violations as a "cost of doing business" that they simply factored into their annual budgets as part of the financial calculus Cathal Flynn interview (Sept. 9, 2003); Rich S. interview (Mar. 1, 2004); Jane Garvey interview (Oct. 21, 2003); Mike M. interview (Sept. 15, 2003).

[589] Mike M. interview (Sept. 15, 2003)

[590] *Federal Register*, July 17, 2001, p. 37331.

[591] Janet R. interview (Feb. 26, 2004).

[592] A veteran FAA Principal Security Inspector to a major airline told the Commission the FAA's standard of performance for checkpoints was "detection." The Principal Security Inspector told the Commission that while "detection" could be tested, measured, and enforced, "deterrence" was more subjective.

[593] James C. May testimony, May 22, 2003; One air carrier interviewee observed that the air carriers had done an excellent job of deterring for many years given the absence of a consequential security incident. See Timothy A. interview (Jan. 8, 2004)

[594] Cathal Flynn interview (Sept. 9, 2003)

[595] James C. May testimony, May 22, 2003.

[596] James Underwood interview (Sept. 17, 2003)

[597] Bogdan Dzakovic testimony, May 23, 2003

[598] Report of the President's Commission on Aviation Security and Terrorism, May 15, 1990, p. 47.

[599] The checkpoint at Portland was operated by Delta which had contracted with Globe; Aviation Operations Litigation Support, TSA, "Table of Screening Checkpoints, Contracted Screening Companies, and Responsible Air Carriers for September 11th Flights." [SSI]

[600] For Portland, ME checkpoint, see Site visit to Portland International Jetport, Portland, Me (Aug. 18, 2003). For Boston checkpoints, see Logan site visit and briefing (Aug. 15, 2003). For Newark checkpoint see FAA Office of Civil Aviation Security Operations, "Assessment and Testing Data for BOS, EWR, and IAD." [SSI]

[601] Metropolitan Washington Airports Authority, videotape of Main Terminal checkpoints, September 11, 2001 [SSI]

[602] Located in Terminal B.

[603] The results of FAA testing of x-ray and metal detection screening at the B4 checkpoint were similar to the result of B5 for all tests conducted since October 1, 2000, FAA report, "Assessment and Testing Data for BOS, EWR, and IAD." **See also, FAA report [SSI]** The FAA report produced by the Boston Civil Aviation Security Field Office (CASFO) stated: "Soon after hijacking, CASFO personnel tested the screening equipment at the screenign checkpoints at issue: At screening checkpoints B-4 and B-5, the X-rays units passed a ▓▓▓▓▓▓▓ However, walk-through metal detectors at both checkpoints failed tests using .22 cal encapsulated weapon." See FAA report of Boston CASFO, Sept. 12, 2001.

[604] No FAA "Red Teams" Special Assessments were done at Logan security checkpoints in the two years prior to 9/11.

[605] FAA Office of Civil Aviation Security Operations, "Assessment and Testing Data for BOS, EWR, and IAD." [SSI]

[606] Logan Briefing and Site Visit, August 15, 2003. [SSI]

[607] No FAA "Red Team" Special Assessments were done at Logan security checkpoints over the two years prior to 9/11/01.

[608] Federal Aviation Administration, Office of Civil Aviation Security Operations, "Assessment and Testing Data for BOS, EWR, and IAD: Boston-Logan International Airport (BOS)," September 21, 2001 [SSI]

[609] FBI/FAA Joint Vulnerability Assessment, "Airport Security Analysis: BOS," 1999 [SECRET]

[610] No FAA "Red Team" Special Assessments were done at Newark security checkpoints in the two years prior to 9/11.

[611] Federal Aviation Administration, Office of Civil Aviation Security Operations, "Assessment and Testing Data for BOS, EWR, and IAD: Newark International Airport (EWR)," September 21, **2001 [SSI]**

[612] FBI/FAA Joint Vulnerability Assessment, "Airport Security Analysis: EWR," 1999

[613] Metropolitan Washington Airports Authority, videotape of Main Terminal checkpoints, September 11, 2001 [SSI]

[614] No "Red Team" FAA Special Assessments were conducted at Dulles security checkpoints over the two years prior to 9/11. The "Red Team" did test the explosive detection systems for checked baggage, and the checkpoint passed ▓▓▓▓▓ such tests in the period Federal Aviation Administration, Office of Civil Aviation Security Operations, "Assessment and Testing Data for BOS, EWR, and IAD: Washington-Dulles International Airport (IAD)," September 21, 2001 [SSI]

---

[615] FBI/FAA Joint Vulnerability Assessment, "Airport Security Analysis: IAD," 1998-1999. [SECRET]

[616] A post-9/11 assessment performed by the Dulles Airport Security Office found that 269 checkpoint screeners employed by Argenbright at Dulles as of 9/11, 42 were from Pakistan, 35 from Sudan, 10 from Afghanistan, nine from Egypt, six from Bangladesh, three from Iran, and one from Morocco. Only India, with 56, was the home to more screeners than Pakistan or Sudan. Thirty-one of the 269 were American nationals.In December 2001, the FAA audited Argenbright's Dulles operations. One-fourth of the screeners were screening passengers even though their required criminal history check had not been completed. The FAA concluded that United Air Lines, through Argenbright Security, "never properly conducted criminal background checks on these screeners."CTI Consulting, "Comprehensive Airport Security Study, Washington Dulles International Airport: Survey and Assessment Report," July 23, 2001, pp. 49-50. Federal Aviation Administration, Office of Civil Aviation Security Operations, "Assessment and Testing Data for BOS, EWR, and IAD: Washington-Dulles International Airport (IAD)," September 21, 2001 [SSI]

[617] FAA "Special Activities Staff, ACS-50, Security Checkpoint Screening."(SSI)

[618][SECRET] Intelligence report interrogation of Ramzi Binalshibh, Oct. 1, 2002; FAA Intelligence Case File 2001-216

[619] Tim J. interview (Apr. 12, 2004)

[620] Tim J. interview (Apr. 12, 2004). For checkpoints that possessed explosive trace detection (ETD) equipment, the bags were to be swiped for explosives. In the absence of such equipment screeners were required to conduct physical searches of carry-on luggage.

[621] Lynne O. interview (Oct. 3, 2003)

[622] Mike Canavan interview (Nov. 4, 2003)

[623] Jane Garvey interview, (Oct. 21, 2003)

[624] Mr. T. interview, (June 3, 2004)

[625] Letter from Carol Hallett, President and Chief Executive Officer of the Air Transport Association, to General John Michael Loh (Retired) of the Gore Commission, August 23, 1996.

[626] Cathal Flynn testimony, Jan. 27, 2004. Admiral Flynn told the Commission: "Checkpoint screening was the primary measure to prevent hijackings of aircraft. The Federal Air Marshal program was a supplemental measure. Because the threat of hijackings was greater there, nearly all FAM missions were on international routes. The FAM program became controversial within the federal government in late 1993 and early 1994. The Department of Defense and the FBI sought to have it terminated because in their view there was unacceptable risk, in the event of a hijacking, of their hostage rescue efforts being dangerously complicated by the presence of armed FAM's in the aircraft. Blue on Blue friendly fire incidents were central to their concerns. The FAA did not agree there was appreciable risk, and insisted on continuing the program for deterrence. The National Security Council staff resolved the matter in the FAA's favor. Thereafter, the FAA's efforts to maintain a small, high-quality FAM corps continued, notably by relocating its base to the technical center in Atlantic City where it had ready access to greatly improved training facilities."

[627] [SSI] Section XIII.J of the ACSSP set forth air carrier responsibilities for security and anti-hijacking training for flight crews. The program included the following requirements███████████of initial security training for all crew members on aircraft██
████████████recurrent training██

██████████████████████An outline of "Inflight Hijacking Tactics" for both the cockpit and cabin crews, which, among other things advised "do not try to overpower hijacker(s), do not negotiate with hijackers, try to land the aircraft, relay specified information to ground about hijackers, and try delaying tactics." See FAA report, Air Carrier Standard Security Program, Change 56, 5/1/2000 [SSI]

[628] Air carrier responsibilities for security and anti-hijacking training in the Common Strategy for flight crews were set forth in the Air Carrier Standard Security Program. In addition to specifying the

requirements of security training, it provided an outline of in-flight hijacking tactics for both the cockpit and cabin crews. FAA report, Air Carrier Standard Security Program, Appendix XIII.4.b(2), May 2001, pp. 7-8. [SSI]

[629] Testimony of Jane Garvey, former FAA Administrator, to National Commission on Terrorist Attacks Upon the United States, at Hearing on Civil Aviation Security, May 22, 2003

[630] Mike M. interview (Sept. 15, 2003); In testimony before the Commission the former Inspector General at the Department of Transportation said that according to her research of the 823 hijacking that had occurred worldwide since 1970, crew and passengers fought back and were able to overcome the hijackers in 115 cases. See Mary Schiavo testimony, May 23, 2003.

[631] John Nance, "Denial of Access: Hardening our Defenses Against Terrorist Manipulation of Commercial Aircraft," CCH Inc. Issues in Aviation Law and Policy, September 28, 2001, p. 1.

[632] Prior to 9-11 cockpit doors on commercial aircraft were not reinforced, even though the FAA was increasingly concerned with the growing incidence of air rage that had included cases of cockpit intrusion, including two fatalities in 2000. See Bryon Okada, "Air Rage Prompts Call for Safety Measures," *Ft. Worth Star-Telegram*, January 10, 2001. Former FAA Administrator Garvey told the Commission that after Operation Desert Storm she discussed the issue of reinforcing cockpit doors with the Israelis who had installed such fortifications on their commercial aircraft because of the terrorist threat. Such an initiative was also considered as one way to combat "air rage" that had resulted in incident of cockpit intrusion and threats or attempt to use violence against aircrew. The Administrator said that while she struggled with this issue, FAA Flight Standards believed that hardened doors could create a safety hazard to the airframe and avionics in the event of decompression, and could also make egress from the cockpit in the event of an emergency more difficult. See Jane Garvey interview Oct. 21, 2003); and Monte Belger interview (Nov. 24, 2003). Another FAA witness testified that hardening the door would have increased weight to the aircraft, thereby increasing fuel costs to operate the flight, a consequence that the industry opposed. See Mike Canavan testimony, May 23, 2003; 14 CFR § 121.587, "Closing and locking of flight crew compartment door." .

[633] The Commission received testimony from an American Airlines employee that disciplined key security was not practiced by American personnel and that keys would be lost or mishandled by employees without any significant repercussions or concern by management. See Michael W. interview (Jan. 25, 2004)

[634] Timothy A. interview (Jan. 8, 2004)

[635] Ft. Worth Star-Telegram, January 10, 2001, p. 1.

[636] UAL instructional video, "Hijacking Cope and Survive," 1984.

[637] Mr. M. interview (Sept. 15, 2003). The Commission learned that FAA was seeking to update the Common Strategy in the summer of 2001. At an FAA Aviation Security Advisory Committee held on June 21, 2001 in Washington DC, Morse informed the panel that "our review of the principles involve suggest that for the most part the doctrine that's been used in the past is sound; we'll be continuing it." Morse told the Commission that he intended to raise the possibility of suicide hijacking in the new strategy, but the update had not yet been completed.

[638] UAL instructional video, "Hijacking Cope and Survive," 1984

[639] Jane Garvey testimony, May 22, 2003.

[640] Final Report of the White House Commission on Aviation Safety and Security, February 12, 1997, p. 20.

[641] National Research Council, *Making the Nation Safer: The Role of Science and Technology in Countering Terrorism* (Washington, DC: The National Academies Press, 2002).

[642] Ed S. interview (Nov. 21, 2003)

[643] FAA report, system design and analysis.

[644] Lynne O. interview (Oct. 3, 2003)

[645] Testimony of Kenneth Mead, DOT IG, to National Commission on Terrorist Attacks Upon the United States at Hearing on Civil Aviation Security, May 22, 2003.

[646] Monte Belger interview (Nov. 24, 2003); Mike Canavan interview (Nov. 4, 2003); and, Jane Garvey interview (Oct. 21, 2003).

[647] Jane Garvey interview (Oct. 21, 2003)

[648] Monte Belger interview (Nov. 24, 2003)

[649] Carol H. interview (Oct. 27, 2003)

[650] For poll on safety of flying vs. driving see, ABC News Poll by TNS Intersearch, November 1999; For poll on airline safety vs. security, Fox News/Opinion Dynamics Poll, Nov. 3-4, 1999.

[651] Brian Jenkins, "Aviation Security in the United States," in Wilkinson and Jenkins, eds., *Aviation Terrorism and Security* (London and Portland, OR: Frank Cass Publishers, 1999), p. 104.

9/11 PUBLIC DISCOURSE PROJECT PROGRESS REPORTS

FOLLOWING THE RELEASE of its official 567-page report, the 9/11 Commission, in accordance with its founding statute, disbanded as a government entity on August 21, 2004. Although the work of the Commission was officially completed, the Commissioners felt that more needed to be done to fulfill their mandate of guarding against future terrorist attacks.

Therefore, all ten original Commission members banded together to form the 9/11 Public Discourse Project. Its mission was to advocate for the recommendations made by the Commission and to educate the public about the issues of terrorism and what could be done to make our country safer. In the same bipartisan spirit that guided the 9/11 Commission in the previous 20 months, the Discourse Project examined the progress that had been made in making the necessary changes to our public policy.

Over the course of one year, from September 2004 to December 2005, the Discourse Project released three reports detailing the failings and occasional triumphs of the U.S. government in its progress towards implementing the recommendations made by the 9/11 Commission. These progress reports, which factor in post-9/11 events such as the London subway bombings and Hurricane Katrina, paint a picture even more startling than that of the original report. In short, the Commissioners have established what needs to be accomplished, but without more governmental support, the nation will again fail to prevent a terrorist attack, and fail to adequately respond when one does inevitably occur.

The following section includes the three progress reports released by the 9/11 Public Discourse Project in September, October, and November 2005 as well as the final report card, originally released on December 5, 2005, which summarizes the findings of the first three progress reports. All were revised and updated for this edition by members of the Commission in April 2006 to reflect the most current state of affairs. They are published here for the first time.

Final Report on 9/11 Commission Recommendations
A Summary of Parts I, II, and III

December 5, 2005
(updated April 2006)

EMERGENCY PREPAREDNESS AND RESPONSE

Provide adequate radio spectrum for first responders　　　**C**

The President signed legislation in January 2006 reallocating analog broadcast spectrum, including the provision of additional bandwidth for public safety purposes. However, the transfer of broadcast spectrum to first responders does not take place until February 2009. The date is too distant given the urgency of the threat. A 2007 handover date would make the American people safer sooner.

Establish a unified Incident Command System　　　**C**

Although there is awareness of and some training in the ICS, Hurricane Katrina demonstrated the absence of full compliance during a multi-jurisdictional/statewide catastrophe—and its resulting costs.

Allocate homeland security funds based on risk and vunerability　　　**F**

Congress still has not changed the underlying statutory authority for homeland security grants, or benchmarks to ensure that funds are used wisely. As a result, homeland security funds continue to be distributed without regard for risk, vulnerability, or the consequences of an attack, diluting the national security benefits of this important program.

Regularly assess national critical infrastructure risks and vulnerabilities　　　**D**

A draft National Infrastructure Protection Plan (November 2005) spells out a methodology and process for critical infrastructure assessments. However, no risk and vulnerability assessments are actually made; no national priorities are established; no recommendations on allocation of scarce resources are given. All key decisions are at least a year away. It is time that we stop talking about setting priorities, and actually set some.

Promote private sector preparedness　　　**C**

National preparedness standards are only beginning to find their way into private sector business practices. Private sector preparedness needs to be a higher priority for the Department of Homeland Security (DHS) and for American businesses.

TRANSPORTATION SECURITY

Develop a national strategy for transportation security   C–

DHS has transmitted its National Strategy for Transportation Security to the Congress. While the strategy reportedly outlines broad objectives, this first version lacks the necessary detail to make it an effective management tool.

Improve airline passenger pre-screening   F

Few improvements have been made to the existing passenger screening system since right after 9/11. The completion of the testing phase of the Transportation Security Administration's pre-screening program for airline passengers has been delayed. A new system, utilizing all names on the consolidated terrorist watchlist, is therefore not yet in operation.

Improve airline screening checkpoints to detect explosives   C

While more advanced screening technology is being developed, Congress needs to provide the funding for, and TSA needs to move as expeditiously as possible with, the appropriate installation of explosives detection trace portals at more of the nation's commercial airports.

Improve checked bag and cargo screening   D

Improvements here have not been made a priority by the Congress or the administration. Progress on implementation of the more advanced in-line screening equipment has been slow. The main impediment is inadequate funding.

BORDER SECURITY

Develop a better terrorist travel strategy   Incomplete

The first Terrorist Travel Strategy was due in December 2005 as required by PL 108-458. A classified strategy was sent to Congress in February 2006; no unclassified document has been released.

Develop a comprehensive screening system   C

We still do not have a comprehensive screening system. Although agencies are moving ahead on individual screening projects, there is lack of progress on coordination between agencies. DHS's new Screening Coordination Office still needs to establish and implement goals for resolving differences in biometric and traveler systems and standards for credentialing and identification.

Implement a biometric entry-exit screening system   B

US-VISIT biometric entry procedures are currently in place at 115 airports, 15 seaports, and in the secondary inspection areas of 154 land ports of entry. US-VISIT exit procedures are operating at 12 airports and two seaports; the exit component of the system has not been widely deployed. The numerous border screening systems operated by DHS, including US-VISIT, are not yet interoperable.

Collaborate internationally on border and document security   D

There has been some good collaboration between US-VISIT and Interpol, but little progress elsewhere. There has been no systematic diplomatic effort to share terrorist watchlists, nor has Congress taken a leadership role in passport security.

Standardize secure identification   B-

The REAL ID Act has established by statute standards for state-issued IDs acceptable for federal purposes, though states' compliance needs to be closely monitored. New standards for issuing birth certificates (required by law by December 17, 2005) are delayed. Without movement on the birth certificate issue, state-issued IDs are still not secure.

THE INTELLIGENCE COMMUNITY

Appoint a Director of National Intelligence   B

The framework for the Director of National Intelligence and his authority is in place. Now his challenge is to exercise his authority boldly to smash stovepipes, drive reform, and create a unity of effort—and act soon. He must avoid layering of the bureaucracy and focus on transformation of the Intelligence Community. The success of this office will require decisive leadership from the DNI and the President, and active oversight by the Congress.

Establish a National Counterterrorism Center   B

Shared analysis and evaluation of threat information is in progress; joint operational planning is beginning. But the NCTC does not yet have sufficient resources or personnel to fulfill its intelligence and planning role.

Create an FBI national security workforce   C

Progress is being made—but it is too slow. The FBI's shift to a counterterrorism posture is far from institutionalized, and significant deficiencies remain. Reforms are at risk from inertia and complacency; they must be accelerated, or they will fail. Unless there is improvement in a reasonable period of time, Congress will have to look at alternatives.

Assign new missions to the CIA Director   Incomplete

Reforms are underway at the CIA, especially of human intelligence operations. But their outcome is yet to be seen. If the CIA is to remain an effective arm of national power, Congress and CIA leadership need to be committed to accelerating the pace of reforms, and must address morale and personnel issues.

Provide incentives for information sharing   D

Changes in incentives for information sharing have been minimal. The office of the Program Manager for Information Sharing is still a start-up, and is not getting the support it needs from the highest levels of government. There remain many complaints about lack of information sharing between federal authorities and state and local-level officials.

Encourage government-wide information sharing D

Designating individuals to be in charge of information sharing is not enough. These individuals need resources, active presidential backing, policies, and procedures in place that compel sharing, and systems of performance evaluation that appraise personnel on how well they carry out information sharing.

Regularly assess homeland airspace defense B-

Situational awareness and sharing of information has improved. But it is not routine or comprehensive, no single agency currently leads the interagency response to airspace violations, and there is no overarching plan to secure airspace outside the National Capital region.

CIVIL LIBERTIES AND EXECUTIVE POWER

Balance security and civil liberties B

The debate surrounding the now-completed reauthorization of the Patriot Act has been strong, and concern for civil liberties has been at the heart of it. Robust and continuing oversight, both within the Executive and by the Congress, will be essential.

Establish a Privacy and Civil Liberties Oversight Board D

We saw long delays and little urgency in the creation of this board. The President did not send the nominations of a Chair and Vice Chair to the Senate until September 2005, and the Senate did not act to confirm them until February 2006. The Board held its first meeting in March 2006. Now constituted, the Board needs to establish a work plan and move forward expeditiously with its important mission.

Set privacy guidelines for government sharing of personal information D

The Privacy and Civil Liberties Oversight Board has just begun its work. The DNI named a Civil Liberties Protection Officer in November 2005.

CONGRESSIONAL AND ADMINISTRATIVE REFORM

Reform intelligence oversight D

The House and Senate have taken limited positive steps, including the creation of oversight subcommittees. However, the ability of the intelligence committees to perform oversight of the intelligence agencies and account for their performance is still undermined by the power of the Defense Appropriations subcommittees and Armed Services committees.

Consolidate homeland security committees   B

The House and Senate have taken positive steps, but Secretary Chertoff and his team still report to too many bosses. The House and Senate homeland security committees should have exclusive jurisdiction over all counterterrorism functions of the Department of Homeland Security.

Declassify overall intelligence budget   F

No action has been taken. The Congress cannot have robust intelligence oversight when funding for intelligence programs is buried within the defense budget. Declassifying the overall intelligence budget would allow for a separate annual intelligence appropriations bill, allowing Congress to better judge how intelligence funds are being spent.

Standardize security clearances   B

The President put the Office of Management and Budget (OMB) in charge of standardizing security clearances. OMB issued a plan to improve the personnel security clearance process in November 2005, and in December issued guidance to improve reciprocal recognition of security clearances, with most deadlines for action March 31, 2006. The Deputy Director of OMB is committed to the success of this initiative. Much hard work is ahead.

NONPROLIFERATION

Maximize effort by U.S. government to secure WMD   D

Countering the greatest threat to America's security is still not the top national security priority of the President and the Congress.

FOREIGN POLICY

Make a long-term commitment to secure and stabilize Afghanistan   B

Progress has been made, but attacks by Taliban and other extremists continue and the drug situation has worsened. The U.S. and its partners must commit to a long-term economic plan in order to ensure the country's stability.

Support Pakistan against extremists   C+

U.S. assistance to Pakistan has not moved sufficiently beyond security assistance to include significant funding for education efforts. President Musharraf has made efforts to take on the threat from extremism, but has not shut down extremist-linked madrassas or terrorist camps. Taliban forces still pass freely across the Pakistan-Afghanistan border and operate in Pakistani tribal areas.

Support reform in Saudi Arabia   D

Saudi authorities have taken initial steps but need to do much more to regulate charities and control the flow of funds to extremist groups, and to promote tolerance and moderation. A U.S.-Saudi strategic dialogue to address topics including reform and exchange programs only recently started.

Identify and prioritize terrorist sanctuaries   B

Strategies have been articulated to address and eliminate terrorist sanctuaries, but they do not include a useful metric to gauge progress. There is little sign of long-term efforts in place to reduce the conditions that allow the formation of terrorist sanctuaries.

Develop a comprehensive Coalition strategy against Islamist terrorism   C

Components of a common strategy are evident on a bilateral basis, and multi-lateral policies exist in some areas. But no permanent contact group of leading governments has yet been established to coordinate a coalition counterterrorism strategy.

Develop Coalition standards for terrorist detention   F

The U.S. has not engaged in a common coalition approach to developing standards for detention and prosecution of captured terrorists. Indeed, U.S. treatment of detainees has elicited broad criticism, and makes it harder to build the necessary alliances to cooperate effectively with partners in a global war on terror.

Pursue liberalized economic policies abroad   B+

There has been measurable progress in reaching agreements on economic reform in the Middle East, including a free trade agreement with Bahrain and the admission of Saudi Arabia to the World Trade Organization. However, it is too early to judge whether these agreements will lead to genuine economic reform.

Vigorously track terrorist financing   A-

The U.S. has won the support of key countries in tackling terrorism finance, though there is still much to do in the Gulf states and in South Asia. The government has made significant strides in using terrorism finance as an intelligence tool. However, the State Department and Treasury Department are engaged in unhelpful turf battles, and the overall effort lacks leadership.

PUBLIC DIPLOMACY

Define the U.S. message   C

Despite efforts to offer a vision for U.S. leadership in the world based on the expansion of democratic governance, public approval ratings for the U.S.

throughout the Middle East remain at or near historic lows. Public diplomacy initiatives need to communicate our values, way of life, and vision for the world without lecturing or being condescending.

Spread U.S. ideals through international broadcasting   B

Budgets for international broadcasting to the Arab and Muslim world and U.S.-sponsored broadcasting hours have increased dramatically, and audience shares are growing. But we need to move beyond audience size by exposing listeners to new ideas and accurate information about the U.S. and its policies, and then measuring the impact and influence of these ideas.

Rebuild scholarship, exchange, and library programs   D

Funding for educational and cultural exchange programs has increased. But more American libraries abroad (in Pakistan, for example) are closing rather than opening. The number of young people coming to study in the U.S. from the Middle East continues to decline (down 2 percent in 2005, following declines of 9 percent and 10 percent in the previous two years).

Support secular education in Muslim countries   D

An International Youth Opportunity Fund has been authorized, but has received no funding; secular education programs have been initiated across the Arab world, but are not integrated into a broader counterterrorism strategy. The U.S. has no overarching strategy for educational assistance, and the current level of education reform funding is inadequate.

PART I:
Homeland Security and
Emergency Preparedness and Response
September 14, 2005 (updated April 2006)

Emergency Preparedness and Response

PROVIDE ADEQUATE RADIO SPECTRUM FOR FIRST RESPONDERS

"Congress should support pending legislation which provides for the expedited and increased assignment of radio spectrum for public safety purposes. Furthermore, high-risk urban areas such as New York City and Washington, D.C., should establish signal corps units to ensure communications connectivity between and among civilian authorities, local first responders, and the National Guard. Federal funding of such units should be given high priority by Congress." (p. 397)

Grade: MINIMAL PROGRESS

What we found: On 9/11, inadequate radio spectrum hindered first responder communications. Firefighters at the World Trade Center had a difficult time communicating with one another and with their commanders. As the units in both towers climbed higher, their radio transmissions were disrupted by the many floors between them and their commanders.

What has happened: The President signed legislation in January 2006 reallocating analog broadcast spectrum, including the provision of additional bandwidth for public safety purposes. However, the transfer of broadcast spectrum to first responders does not take place until February 2009.

Why this is still important: New spectrum is needed to facilitate interoperable communications between responder agencies; to allow effective radio communications during large-scale responses to major disasters; and to allow emergency response agencies to deploy next-generation communications technologies.

What needs to be done: First responders should not have to wait three more years to accommodate politically powerful broadcasters. Congress should mandate the reallocation of broadcast spectrum for public safety purposes by January 1, 2007, or the earliest possible date.

ESTABLISH A UNIFIED INCIDENT COMMAND SYSTEM

"Emergency response agencies nationwide should adopt the Incident Command System (ICS). When multiple agencies or multiple jurisdictions are involved, they should adopt a unified command. . . . In the future, the Department of Homeland Security should consider making funding contingent on aggressive and realistic training in accordance with ICS and unified command procedures." (p. 397)

Grade: MINIMAL PROGRESS

What we found: Response operations on 9/11 lacked integrated communications and unified command. Problems existed both within and among individual agencies. The Incident Command System in the city of New York did not function to integrate awareness among agencies, inform decision-making, or facilitate interagency response.

What has happened: Many fire and police departments and state and local authorities are already well versed in using the ICS—others are being trained in it. Hurricane Katrina demonstrated a major failure: the absence of unified command.

Why this is still important: In the event of terrorist attack or natural disaster, clear lines of command and control for responding authorities are essential to minimize civilian and responder casualties.

What needs to be done: The Department of Homeland Security set the deadline for full Incident Command System compliance "to the maximum extent possible" as October 1, 2004. The hard deadline for full compliance as a condition for federal preparedness funds is October 1, 2006. This date must not slip. All jurisdictions must train and exercise the Incident Command System as it applies to them.

ALLOCATE HOMELAND SECURITY FUNDS BASED ON RISK AND VULNERABILITY

"Homeland security assistance should be based strictly on an assessment of risks and vulnerabilities. Washington, D.C., and New York City are certainly at the top of any such list. We understand the contention that every state and city needs to have some minimum infrastructure for emergency response. But federal homeland security assistance should not remain a program for general revenue sharing. It should supplement state and local resources based on the risks and vulnerabilities that merit additional support. Congress should not use this money as a pork barrel." (p. 396)

Grade: MINIMAL PROGRESS

What we found: Billions of federal homeland security dollars have been distributed with no consideration of risk factored in to the allocation process. No requirement has existed to ensure that funds are distributed within states according to risk.

What has happened: Congress has considered legislation to overhaul the homeland security grant program. The House three times passed a very good bipartisan bill that would allocate funds based on risks and vulnerabilities. The Senate has passed a reform amendment as well. The two chambers have been unable to agree on a bill to send to the President.

Why this is still important: Preventing terrorist attacks is a matter of national security. Federal resources are scarce in proportion to the number of potential targets. Congress and the Administration must set priorities based on the risk, vulnerability, and consequences of an attack on a given site.

What needs to be done: Congress should act to ensure that all federal homeland security assistance is allocated based on an assessment of risk and vulnerability—not as general revenue sharing. The House and Senate should agree and send a bill to the President that distributes dollars based on risks and vulnerabilities. This should happen before the end of the 109th Congress.

REGULARLY ASSESS NATIONAL CRITICAL INFRASTRUCTURE RISKS AND VULNERABILITIES

"The Department of Homeland Security and its oversight committees should regularly assess the types of threats the country faces to determine (a) the adequacy of the government's plans—and the progress against those plans—to protect America's critical infrastructure and (b) the readiness of the government to respond to the threats that the United States might face." (p. 428)

Grade: UNSATISFACTORY

What we found: Many officials complained to us about unfair allocations of homeland security funding. We found little analytic justification for the allocations of federal funding, based on assessments of risks and vulnerabilities. Therefore, we recommended a regular assessment of risks and vulnerabilities, so that scarce resources can be applied to protect us against the greatest threats.

What has happened: The Intelligence Reform and Terrorism Prevention Act of 2004 (PL 108-458) required DHS to issue a report by June 15, 2005, assessing the risks and vulnerabilities of the nation's critical infrastructure. This report has not yet been released. A draft National Infrastructure Protection Plan (November 2005) spells out a methodology and process for critical infrastructure assessments. However, no risk and vulnerability assessments are actually made; no national priorities are established; no recommendations as to how to allocate scarce resources are given.

Why this is still important: Regular national assessments of threat, vulnerability, and preparedness will ensure that government efforts are making measurable progress in reducing the overall terrorist threat.

What needs to be done: DHS should produce the report required by PL 108-458 as soon as possible, and demonstrate its capability to regularly review and modify the assessment to reflect the changing threat environment and state of readiness.

PROMOTE PRIVATE SECTOR PREPAREDNESS

"We endorse the American National Standards Institute's recommended standard for private preparedness... and urge the Department of Homeland Security to promote its adoption. We also encourage the insurance and credit-rating industries to look closely at a company's compliance with the ANSI standard in assessing its insurability and creditworthiness." (p. 398)

Grade: MINIMAL PROGRESS

What we found: Many building occupants in the World Trade Center did not take preparedness seriously. Neither full nor partial evacuation drills were held; participation in drills varied greatly from tenant to tenant. Because 85 percent of our nation's critical infrastructure is controlled by the private sector, firms and individual civilians are likely to be the first responders in future emergencies. Therefore, we made recommendations to improve private sector preparedness.

What has happened: In a May 2005 speech to private sector representatives, Secretary Chertoff correctly noted that preparedness is not solely a government responsibility. The insurance and credit-rating industries are beginning to incorporate national preparedness standards into their underwriting and risk-analysis criteria. Leaders in the legal profession are beginning to evaluate the National Preparedness Standard as a "legal standard of care." Still, awareness of the Standard throughout the corporate sector is low.

Why this is still important: The terrorists have repeatedly targeted private sector assets. In another attack and in any natural disaster, private-sector employees will likely again be on the front lines. As the 9/11 Commission Report showed, employees of enterprises that institutionalize a high level of emergency preparedness are far more likely to survive in a disaster.

What needs to be done: Corporate leaders should take the lead in encouraging all American businesses, especially those in high-risk areas, or who own critical national infrastructure, to incorporate National Preparedness Standards into their business practices. DHS should make private-sector preparedness a higher priority. The insurance and credit-rating industries should incorporate the National Preparedness Standard into their evaluations.

Transportation Security

DEVELOP A NATIONAL STRATEGY FOR
TRANSPORTATION SECURITY

"The U.S. government should identify and evaluate the transportation assets that need to be protected, set risk-based priorities for defending them, select the most practical and cost-effective ways of doing so, and then develop a plan, budget, and funding to implement the effort. The plan should assign roles and missions to the relevant authorities (federal, state, regional, and local) and to private stakeholders." (p. 391)

Grade: UNSATISFACTORY

What we found: As of 2004, over 90 percent of Transportation Security Administration funds went to aviation security—to fight the last war. The money was spent mainly to meet congressional mandates to federalize checkpoint screeners and to deploy existing security methods and technologies at airports. Efforts did not reflect a forward-looking strategic plan assessing assets, risks, costs, and benefits across all sectors of transportation.

What has happened: The Intelligence Reform and Terrorism Prevention Act of 2004 (PL 108-458) required DHS to prepare a National Strategy for Transportation Security, due April 1, 2005. DHS transmitted a classified National Strategy for Transportation Security to the Congress in September 2005, followed later with an unclassified four-page summary. While the strategy outlines broad objectives, this first version lacks the necessary detail to make it an effective management tool.

Why this is still important: With limited resources available for transportation security, resources must be allocated according to rational, risk-based priorities.

Without a comprehensive assessment of the security needs of the nation's transportation system, this will be impossible.

What needs to be done: DHS must produce this report as soon as possible, and maintain a capability to review and modify the assessment to reflect the changing threat environment and state of transportation security.

IMPROVE AIRLINE PASSENGER PRE-SCREENING

"Improved use of 'no-fly' and 'automatic selectee' lists should not be delayed while the argument about a successor to CAPPS continues. This screening function should be performed by the TSA, and it should utilize the larger set of watchlists maintained by the federal government. Air carriers should be required to supply the information needed to test and implement this new system." (p. 393)

Grade: UNSATISFACTORY

What we found: As of 9/11, the Federal Aviation Administration's "no-fly" list contained the names of just 12 terrorist suspects, even though government watchlists contained the names of thousands of known and suspected terrorists (including 2 of the 19 hijackers). On 9/11, the 19 hijackers were screened at the airport by a computer-assisted passenger pre-screening system called CAPPS. More than half were identified for further inspection, which applied at that time only to their checked luggage.

What has happened: Contrary to the Commission recommendation, the TSA test program is combining watchlist screening with the use of commercial databases to verify passenger identities, which has produced controversy over privacy issues. This has delayed completion of the testing phase. TSA now hopes to begin operation of the new system in 2006.

Why this is still important: With the airlines still responsible for implementing the "no fly" and "automatic selectee" lists, the names of many known or suspected terrorists are still not being included on these lists, making airline passengers less secure than they should be.

What needs to be done: As recommended by the Commission and mandated by the Intelligence Reform and Terrorism Prevention Act of 2004 (PL 108-458), TSA should focus its priority attention on taking over implementation of passenger pre-screening so that all names on the comprehensive terrorist watchlist are utilized.

IMPROVE AIRLINE SCREENING CHECKPOINTS
TO DETECT EXPLOSIVES

"The TSA and the Congress must give priority attention to improving the ability of screening checkpoints to detect explosives on passengers. As a start, each individual selected for special screening should be screened for explosives. Further, the TSA should conduct a human factors

study, a method often used in the private sector, to understand problems in screener perfor-
mance and set attainable objectives for individual screeners and for the checkpoints where
screening takes place." (p. 393)

Grade: MINIMAL PROGRESS

What we found: Since 9/11, CAPPS is still part of the screening process, and the consequences of selection now include personal searches of the individual and carry-on bags. While other measures (hardening of cockpit doors, banning of knives and other sharp items on the aircraft, the presence of Federal Air Marshals, armed pilots in the cockpit, etc.) have had a significant impact on reducing the likelihood of a repeat of the tactics of the 9/11 attack, the threat of explosives to aircraft has not been addressed adequately.

What has happened: The Intelligence Reform and Terrorism Prevention Act of 2004 (PL 108-458) required DHS to develop and deploy effective checkpoint explosives and WMD detection equipment, to screen all selectees and their carry-on property for explosives, and to report to Congress within 180 days on the results of any human factors study it has conducted. TSA has deployed explosives trace detection devices at all airports to examine selectees' carry-on items, and installed explosives detection trace portals ("puffers") at 17 airports (with seven more airports due for installation in the near future) to scrutinize the persons of selectees. After the suicide bombing of Russian commercial aircraft in August 2004, TSA stepped up the use of "pat-down" searches for explosives, but after privacy-related protests it took steps to reduce the intrusiveness of these searches. While TSA has indicated that human factors analysis is being carried out at a Research & Development facility in Atlantic City and elsewhere, it has not yet submitted to Congress the report required by statute.

Why this is still important: Following improvements in on-board defenses against suicide hijacking, explosives currently represent the major security threat to passenger aviation.

What needs to be done: Congress needs to provide the funding for, and TSA needs to move as expeditiously as possible with, the installation of explosives detection trace portals at more of the nation's 441 commercial airports, while both continue to support the development of more advanced screening technology. Furthermore, until such time as the trace portals, or more effective successors, are fully deployed, TSA must utilize other means (including the canine teams and "pat-down" searches) to ensure that selectees are searched for explosives, no matter what airport they fly from.

IMPROVE CHECKED BAG AND CARGO SCREENING

"More attention and resources should be directed to reducing or mitigating the threat posed
by explosives in vessels' cargo holds. The TSA should expedite the installation of advanced

(in-line) baggage-screening equipment. Because the aviation industry will derive substantial benefits from this deployment, it should pay a fair share of the costs. The TSA should require that every passenger aircraft carrying cargo must deploy at least one hardened container to carry any suspect cargo. TSA also needs to intensify its efforts to identify, track, and appropriately screen potentially dangerous cargo in both the aviation and maritime sectors." (p. 393)

Grade: MINIMAL PROGRESS

What we found: Prior to 9/11, selection by CAPPS meant that a passenger's checked baggage was screened for explosives or held off the airplane until the passenger boarded. This policy reflected the perception that nonsuicide sabotage was the primary threat to civil aviation. Since 9/11, extensive measures have been implemented to screen the carry-on baggage of all passengers. However, we still do not have comprehensive screening of cargo carried by passenger aircraft.

What has happened: The Intelligence Reform and Terrorism Prevention Act of 2004 (PL 108-458) incorporated the Commission's recommendations for deployment of "in-line" screening equipment, converted the hardened container requirement into a pilot program, and established a detailed program for air cargo security. In response, TSA does not appear to have expedited its plans for in-line installation, with just nine operational systems and eight more under construction as of mid-2005. There has been little progress on the hardened container pilot project. The agency's air cargo security efforts have centered on a slow-moving regulatory proceeding. Efforts by the Department of Homeland Security's Custom and Border Protection (CBP) division have improved upon the pre-9/11 state of maritime cargo security, yet these programs have received relatively little funding. The Government Accountability Office, among others, has documented continuing problems in each of them.

Why this is still important: Deployment of in-line explosives detection equipment has been shown to improve security and to significantly reduce operational costs. Air and maritime cargo continue to be very vulnerable to terrorist attack.

What needs to be done: The main impediment to improved checked bag and cargo security is inadequate funding. If the Congress and the administration believe these to be priorities, they must determine the costs and specify how they will pay for these improvements.

Border Security

DEVELOP A BETTER TERRORIST TRAVEL STRATEGY

"The United States should combine terrorist travel intelligence, operations, and law enforcement in a strategy to intercept terrorists, find terrorist travel facilitators, and constrain terrorist mobility." (p. 385)

Grade: SOME PROGRESS

What we found: Before 9/11, no agency of the U.S. government systematically analyzed terrorists' travel strategies and their exploitation of weaknesses in our border security. As many as 15 of the 19 hijackers were potentially vulnerable to interception by border authorities. Analyzing their characteristic travel documents and travel patterns could have allowed authorities to intercept 4 to 15 hijackers, and more effective use of the information available in U.S. government databases could have identified up to 3 hijackers.

What has happened: The National Counterterrorism Center, the Human Smuggling and Trafficking Center, and representatives of multiple government agencies are jointly developing the first terrorist travel strategy. They are taking steps to integrate terrorist travel intelligence into border operations.

Why this is still important: As terrorists move across international borders to meet, train, and carry out their operations, they make themselves vulnerable to detection and interdiction. Targeting terrorist travel can help detect terrorists and help prevent attacks.

What needs to be done: The U.S. government must develop and implement a long-term terrorist travel strategy, comparable to the multi-faceted strategies currently directed at terrorist finance and terrorist communications. Completing a terrorist travel strategy (and report) is a first major benchmark. A classified strategy, due December 2005, was sent to Congress in February 2006. An unclassified strategy has not been released. What to look for: Progress in implementing a program to screen travel documents for terrorist indicators.

DEVELOP A COMPREHENSIVE SCREENING SYSTEM

"The President should direct the Department of Homeland Security to lead the effort to design a comprehensive screening system, addressing common problems and setting common standards with systemwide goals in mind." (p. 387)

Grade: SOME PROGRESS

What we found: In our investigation, we found a series of ad hoc, fragmented measures relating to: (1) the compilation of information about individuals; (2) how that information was checked; (3) how individuals were screened, and (4) the consequences of finding suspicious indicators. "Feeder" documents used in identifying individuals did not contain standardized information. Checks of databases for potential terrorists were neither systematic nor comprehensive. Border, immigration, and law enforcement officials who screened visitors and immigrants were given little training in terrorist travel intelligence. Before 9/11, responses to suspicious indicators were often ineffective or produced no further information. For example, four of the 9/11 attackers were pulled into secondary border inspection, but then admitted.

What has happened: Presidential Homeland Security Directive 11 (August 27, 2004) announced a new U.S. policy to "implement a coordinated and comprehensive approach to terrorist-related screening—in immigration, law enforcement, intelligence, counterintelligence, and protection of the border, transportation systems, and critical infrastructure—that supports homeland security, at home and abroad." A working group developed an implementation plan, and Secretary Chertoff has announced the establishment of a new Screening Coordination Office at DHS.

Why this is still important: Having too many different biometric standards, travel facilitation systems, credentialing systems, and screening requirements hampers the development of information crucial for stopping terrorists from entering the country. It is also expensive and inefficient. A coordinating body should raise standards, facilitate information sharing, and survey systems for potential problems.

What needs to be done: The Screening Coordination Office should set standards and break down bureaucratic stovepipes that prevent the match-up of information. Goals need to be set and implemented for resolving differences in biometric systems, traveler systems, and credentialing and identification standards.

IMPLEMENT A BIOMETRIC ENTRY-EXIT SCREENING SYSTEM

"The Department of Homeland Security, properly supported by the Congress, should complete, as quickly as possible, a biometric entry-exit screening system, including a single system for speeding qualified travelers. It should be integrated with the system that provides benefits to foreigners seeking to stay in the United States." (p. 389)

Grade: SOME PROGRESS

What we found: The 9/11 conspirators attempted to enter the United States 34 times over 21 months, through nine airports. They succeeded all but once. No border inspectors or agents were trained in terrorist travel intelligence and document practices. The culture at the airports was one of travel facilitation and lax enforcement, with the exception of programs to interdict drug couriers and known criminals.

What has happened: Some biometric entry procedures (called US-VISIT) are currently in place at 115 airports, 15 seaports, and in the secondary inspection areas of 154 land ports of entry. US-VISIT exit procedures are operating at 12 airports and 2 seaports; the exit component of the system has not been widely deployed. The numerous border screening systems operated by DHS, including US-VISIT, are not yet interoperable.

Why this is still important: It is imperative for national security that the government can effectively verify identities and knows who is coming into our country, how long they have been here, and when they leave.

What needs to be done: Continuing to build this system, developing and deploying the exit component of US-VISIT, and making entry-exit and immigration benefits systems interoperable should remain top priorities for DHS.

COLLABORATE INTERNATIONALLY ON BORDERS AND DOCUMENT SECURITY

"We should do more to exchange terrorist information with trusted allies, and raise U.S. and global border security standards for travel and border crossing over the medium and long term through extensive international cooperation." (p. 390)

Grade: UNSATISFACTORY

What we found: Before 9/11, the U.S. shared terrorist watchlists for border security only with Canada and Australia. Global security standards for travel documents were inadequate.

What has happened: Terrorist watchlists—the most basic tool of border control—need to be shared. More information should be shared with a greater number of allies. The U.S. is not moving to include fingerprints in passports and therefore is not taking a leadership role in passport security.

Why this is still important: The U.S. government does not have complete information on terrorist identities; much information is held by foreign governments. U.S. security will be greatly strengthened by access to this information and the help of other governments in interdicting terrorist travel. If terrorists are to enter, prepare for, and carry out operations in the United States, they need travel documents. International collaboration on document standards and security is needed to ensure that foreign travelers' documents are legitimate and secure, and to keep out suspected terrorists.

What needs to be done: Watchlist sharing must be a higher priority, and it needs a systematic diplomatic effort. Congress should make fingerprints in passports a priority.

STANDARDIZE SECURE IDENTIFICATIONS

"The federal government should set standards for the issuance of birth certificates and sources of identification, such as drivers licenses." (p. 390)

Grade: SOME PROGRESS

What we found: The 9/11 hijackers obtained a total of 13 state-issued drivers licenses and 21 U.S.- or state-issued identification cards. The drivers licenses themselves were all legal (not forged), but were not all legally obtained. Seven hijackers used false statements of residency to acquire identifications in Virginia. We recommended strong federal standards for the issuance of birth certificates and other sources of identification, such as drivers licenses, to avoid the identity fraud that terrorists can exploit.

What has happened: The Intelligence Reform and Terrorism Prevention Act of 2004 (PL 108-458) started a regulatory process to establish standards for state-issued IDs acceptable for federal purposes. The REAL ID Act (PL 109-13) superseded this regulatory process and established these standards by statute. The fragmented and easily exploitable system of birth certificate issuance has not yet been addressed. New standards for issuing birth certificates (required by law by December 17, 2005) are delayed. Without movement on the birth certificate issue, state-issued IDs are still not secure.

Why this is still important: Birth certificate security is critical to preventing fraud in the acquisition of U.S. passports and other identification, such as drivers licenses. Drivers license issuance affects terrorist mobility and presents an opportunity to screen terrorists.

What needs to be done: Congress will need to monitor states' compliance with the REAL ID Act. Congress should insist on the issuance of new birth certificate standards, as required by PL 108-458, as soon as possible.

PART II:
Reforming the Institutions of Government
October 20, 2005 (updated April 2006)

The Intelligence Community

APPOINT A DIRECTOR OF NATIONAL INTELLIGENCE

"The current position of Director of Central Intelligence should be replaced by a National Intelligence Director with two main areas of responsibility: (1) to oversee national intelligence centers on specific subjects of interest across the U.S. government and (2) to manage the national intelligence program and oversee the agencies that contribute to it." (p. 411)

Grade: CONGRESS: FULFILLED/EXECUTIVE: SOME PROGRESS

What we found: Before 9/11, the Director of Central Intelligence had too many jobs—serving as the President's chief intelligence adviser, running the CIA, and managing the Intelligence Community. The third job did not get done. The DCI had little ability to set priorities or move resources across agency boundaries. He had little ability to set standards and practices across the intelligence community (for information sharing, analysis, personnel, and security clearances) to enhance unity of effort and overall performance. Therefore, we recommended a Director of National Intelligence assigned responsibility for managing the national intelligence program.

What has happened: The Intelligence Reform and Terrorism Prevention Act of 2004 (PL 108-458) established the position of DNI, placing 15 agencies under his leadership. The Act gives the DNI access to all national intelligence; authority to develop and execute the intelligence budget, transfer and reprogram funds, and appoint and transfer personnel; and responsibilities in tasking, setting standards, and ensuring information sharing across the intelligence community. John Negroponte was confirmed as DNI on April 22, 2005. The Office of the DNI is now in charge of preparing the President's Daily Briefings, and the DNI has replaced the DCI as the President's chief intelligence adviser. In order to improve intelligence, the DNI has set improving analysis, building a sense of community, and gaining control of the budget as his priorities. The Office of the DNI reports that it has implemented new procedures for ensuring that an Intelligence Community–wide range of analytical views on priority issues, including dissents, is reflected in the analytic product. The Office issued a National Intelligence Strategy in October 2005.

Why this is still important: The Commission recommended a DNI not to create a new "czar" or a new layer of bureaucracy, but to catalyze transformation and manage and forge unity of effort in a more efficient and effective Intelligence Community.

What needs to be done: The framework for the DNI and his authorities is now in place. But that is not enough. To ensure success, the DNI needs to exercise all his authorities, especially budget and personnel authorities, to drive reform. Information sharing must be a high priority reform. Success will require bold DNI leadership, direct presidential support, active congressional oversight, and public vigilance.

ESTABLISH A NATIONAL COUNTERTERRORISM CENTER

"We recommend the establishment of a National Counterterrorism Center (NCTC), built on the foundation of the existing Terrorist Threat Integration Center (TTIC). Breaking the older mold of national government organization, this NCTC should be a center for joint operational planning and joint intelligence, staffed by personnel from the various agencies. The head of the NCTC should have authority to evaluate the performance of the people assigned to the Center." (p. 403)

Grade: CONGRESS: FULFILLED, EXECUTIVE: SOME PROGRESS

What we found: Before 9/11, no single individual or agency was in charge of the counterterrorism efforts of the U.S. government. In our hearings we regularly asked: Who is the quarterback? Who is calling the plays and assigning counterterrorism responsibilities so that agencies execute as a team? The answers were never clear. Therefore, we recommended the creation of a National Counterterrorism Center to perform joint planning and unify counterterrorism efforts across the government.

What has happened: The Intelligence Reform and Terrorism Prevention Act of 2004 (PL 108-458) established the NCTC within the Office of the DNI, and required the NCTC to begin operations by June 17, 2005. Vice Admiral John Scott Redd was confirmed as Director of NCTC on July 28, 2005. The NCTC brings intelligence and policy agencies in the federal government together daily to share, analyze, and evaluate threat information and terrorist intelligence. Joint strategic operational planning for counterterrorism, as called for in the statute, is beginning. So far, NCTC has only about one-half of its necessary analytic capability and one-third of its necessary personnel.

Why this is still important: The NCTC's purpose is to bring all the participants to the table for information sharing and planning and direction to respond to the al Qaeda enemy. Its purpose is to unify the intelligence effort and operational response to terrorism.

What needs to be done: Strong and effective leadership from both the DNI and the Director of the NCTC are essential to ensure that the Center has sufficient resources and personnel to fulfill its intelligence and planning role.

CREATE AN FBI NATIONAL SECURITY WORKFORCE

"A specialized and integrated national security workforce should be established at the FBI consisting of agents, analysts, linguists, and surveillance specialists who are recruited, trained, rewarded, and retained to ensure the development of an institutional culture imbued with deep expertise in intelligence and national security." (p. 425–6)

Grade: INSUFFICIENT PROGRESS (Analytic capability: Minimal Progress, Information systems: Unsatisfactory)

What we found: Before 9/11, the FBI had critical shortfalls in its ability to carry out an effective, preventative counterterrorism strategy. Shortfalls included limited intelligence collection and analysis, poor information sharing within the FBI and with other agencies, and inadequate training and resources. After 9/11, Director Mueller began a series of reforms to make counterterrorism the number one priority of the FBI.

What has happened: The Intelligence Reform and Terrorist Prevention Act (PL 108-458) enacted the Commission's recommendations on the FBI. The trend line on FBI reform has been in the right direction, but far too slow. It is widely recognized that there are still numerous problems impeding the Bureau's ability to carry out its new counterterrorism function effectively. There are still significant deficiencies in the FBI's analytic capabilities; information sharing with other agencies and with local law enforcement is still inadequate; leadership of counterterrorism and intelligence has changed repeatedly; to date, initiatives to improve information technology capabilities have failed. Problems in management turnover and shortfalls in human capital development (recruitment, hiring, training, and career development) continue. The FBI's culture continues to resist Director Mueller's changes.

Why this is still important: The FBI's shift to a preventive counterterrorism posture must become institutionalized if it is to survive beyond Director Mueller's tenure. A strong and effective domestic intelligence function is not an option for the United States—it is an obligation. Our nation's security depends on it.

What needs to be done: A sense of urgency within the Bureau is essential. The FBI must complete reforms now underway: the creation of a robust and qualified national security workforce to carry out the domestic counterterrorism mission. The FBI's culture must change to meet its new challenges and counterterrorism role. Director Mueller's timeframe for effecting reform at the FBI is not indefinite. The terrorists will not wait. Reforms must be accelerated, or they will fail. Unless there is improvement in a reasonable period of time, Congress will have to look at alternatives.

ASSIGN NEW MISSIONS TO THE CIA DIRECTOR

"The CIA Director should emphasize (a) rebuilding the CIA's analytic capabilities; (b) transforming the clandestine service by building its human intelligence capabilities; (c) developing a stronger language program, with high standards and sufficient financial incentives; (d) renewing emphasis on recruiting diversity among operations officers so they can blend more easily in foreign cities; (e) ensuring a seamless relationship between human source collection and signals collection at the operational level; and (f) stressing a better balance between unilateral and liaison operations." (p. 415)

Grade: SOME PROGRESS

What we found: Before 9/11, the CIA had experienced serious problems with both analysis and human intelligence. No comprehensive National Intelligence Estimate on the foreign terrorist threat to the United States had been written since 1995; numerous panels pointed out weaknesses in all-source analysis and security rules that blocked the sharing of information with analysts. The CIA never developed human intelligence sources that had access to Bin Ladin and reliable information about his whereabouts; DCI George Tenet testified in 2004 that it would take "at least five years" to rebuild human intelligence.

What has happened: Many of the recommended reforms were already underway at the CIA even before the Intelligence Reform and Terrorism Prevention Act of 2004 (PL 108-458) wrote them into law as responsibilities of the CIA Director. These measures will take years to bear fruit. The DNI has established the National Clandestine Service and named the CIA Director as the National Human Intelligence (HUMINT) Manager to coordinate the human intelligence collection efforts of CIA, FBI, and the Pentagon. Low morale and high turnover in senior ranks at the CIA are areas of concern.

Why this is still important: Rebuilding the CIA's analytic and operational capabilities is a key factor in fighting the war on terror. It is essential that the CIA's human intelligence operations have strong and effective leadership.

What needs to be done: Strong, determined leadership committed to accelerating the pace of the reforms already underway is critical if the nation is to have the intelligence system it requires. Congress and CIA leadership should regularly evaluate the effectiveness of the National Clandestine Service structure, to determine if it improves coordination of human intelligence collection operations and produces better intelligence results. Congress and CIA leadership should also address morale and personnel issues at the CIA to ensure it remains an effective arm of national power.

PROVIDE INCENTIVES FOR INFORMATION SHARING

"Information procedures should provide incentives for sharing, to restore a better balance between security and shared knowledge." (p. 417)

Grade: MINIMAL PROGRESS

What we found: Government agencies missed several opportunities to share information in order to piece together and disrupt the 9/11 plot. For example, the CIA did not inform the FBI in early 2000 about suspected terrorists (and future hijackers) al Mihdhar and al Hazmi's visas and travel to the United States, or provide watchlist information to the State Department.

What has happened: According to the Intelligence Reform and Terrorism Prevention Act of 2004 (PL 108-458), the President shall require the heads of federal departments and agencies to promote a culture of information sharing by both reducing disincentives and providing affirmative incentives for sharing information. The DNI also has responsibility for establishing policies and procedures to ensure the maximum availability of, and access to, intelligence information within the intelligence community. A program manager has been designated by the President as responsible for information sharing across the federal government. This office is still a start-up. So far, changes in incentives in favor of information sharing are minimal.

Why this is still important: The 9/11 story included numerous examples of how a mentality of limiting information sharing to those with a "need to know" in fact kept information from getting to the right people at the right time. Cultures will not change without policies in place that actively encourage such change.

What needs to be done: The President and the DNI need to make change in the culture of information sharing a priority through clear and visible support. They need to develop positive incentives for information sharing to balance the many disincentives on the books. Information sharing must be improved not only across the federal government, but with state and local authorities.

ENCOURAGE GOVERNMENT-WIDE INFORMATION SHARING

"The President should lead the government-wide effort to bring the major national security institutions into the information revolution. He should coordinate the resolution of the legal, policy, and technical issues across agencies to create a 'trusted information network.'" (p. 418)

Grade: MINIMAL PROGRESS

What we found: Efforts since 9/11 to improve information sharing have been partial and uneven, especially by the intelligence community with other federal agencies, and by the federal government with state and local authorities. No single agency can solve the problem. Therefore, we recommended that the President lead a government-wide information sharing initiative.

What has happened: The Intelligence Reform and Terrorism Prevention Act of 2004 (PL 108-458) required that the President create an information sharing environment to provide and facilitate the means for sharing information through the use of policy guidelines and technologies. Within the intelligence community, the DNI has all necessary support and authority from the President to ensure maximum availability of and access to intelligence information. A program manager designated by the President as responsible for information sharing across the federal government has been replaced. Momentum has been lost. There are few signs of the actual implementation of a "trusted information network."

Why this is still important: Only with White House leadership can legal and policy obstacles be overcome to bring our national security institutions into the information revolution

What needs to be done: The President needs to make information sharing a priority. Designating officials to be in charge is not enough; they need resources and active presidential backing to change the information systems that enable information sharing, the policies and procedures that compel sharing, and the systems of performance evaluation so that personnel are appraised on how they carry out information sharing.

REGULARLY ASSESS HOMELAND AIRSPACE DEFENSE

"The Department of Defense and its oversight committees should regularly assess the adequacy of Northern Command's strategies and planning to defend the United States against military threats to the homeland." (p. 428)

Grade: SOME PROGRESS

What we found: On 9/11, the Federal Aviation Agency (FAA) and the North American Aerospace Defense Command (NORAD) were unprepared for a missile attack based on the use of domestic civilian aircraft. They struggled to improvise a homeland defense against a threat they had never encountered and had never trained to meet. Therefore, we recommended regular oversight of plans for homeland airspace defense.

What has happened: Situational awareness has improved. FAA and NORAD share the same radar feeds and have established strong liaison relationships through the exchange of personnel. FAA's Domestic Events Network provides a 24/7 open, unclassified line that facilitates immediate situational awareness for all agencies, in particular DOD, on any aircraft deviation. The National Capital Region Coordination Center, comprised of representatives of the military and civilian agencies, coordinates action in the event of a threat from unidentified aircraft to the Washington, D.C., region. Committees, including House Armed Services and Government Reform, have held oversight hearings of strategies and plans for national air defense.

Why this is still important: Clear delineations of responsibility and authority for national defense are essential, in the few minutes available when aircraft deviate from standard flight paths into restricted airspace.

What needs to be done: No single agency leads the interagency response to airspace violations. No overarching plan exists to secure airspace outside of the National Capital region. Agency database records documenting violations are not routinely shared; agencies do not have a common definition of airspace violation. More needs to be done to standardize definitions and procedures, and unify leadership and response to airspace violations.

Civil Liberties and Executive Power

BALANCE SECURITY AND CIVIL LIBERTIES

"Because of concerns regarding the shifting balance of power to the government, we think that a full and informed debate on the Patriot Act would be healthy....The burden of proof for retaining a particular government power should be on the executive, to explain (a) that the power actually materially enhances security and (b) that there is adequate supervision of the executive's use of the powers to ensure protection of civil liberties. If the power is granted, there must be adequate guidelines and oversight to properly confine its use." (p.394–5)

Grade: SOME PROGRESS

What we found: After 9/11, Congress quickly passed the USA PATRIOT Act, providing substantial new powers to the investigative agencies of the government. We heard many concerns about the shifting balance of power from the individual to the government. Therefore, we recommended a full and informed debate on the future of the Patriot Act, as several of its controversial provisions were set to expire at the end of 2005.

What has happened: Congress held numerous hearings, with at least 16 in the House and Senate Judiciary Committees devoted exclusively to review of provisions of the Patriot Act, and several more in other committees of jurisdiction. Numerous voices across the political spectrum were heard in the debate. The House and the Senate completed action on separate bills before the end of 2005, and the Congress twice provided temporary extensions of expiring Patriot Act authorities while a conference committee worked out the differences between the two bills. The President signed a renewal of the Patriot Act into law on March 9, 2006.

Why this is still important: Out of a full and informed debate, a better policy will emerge. Guidelines and oversight are essential for the protection of our freedoms.

What needs to be done: Following renewal of the Patriot Act, the Executive Branch and the Congress need to continue robust oversight over the use of its authorities.

ESTABLISH A PRIVACY AND CIVIL LIBERTIES OVERSIGHT BOARD

"At this time of increased and consolidated government authority, there should be a board within the executive branch to oversee adherence to the guidelines we recommend and the commitment the government makes to defend our civil liberties." (p. 395)

Grade: MINIMAL PROGRESS

What we found: During our inquiry, we were told that there is no office within the government whose job it is to look across the government at the actions we are taking to protect ourselves, to ensure that civil liberty concerns are appropriately considered. Because we recommended substantial changes in the way government collects and shares information, we also strongly recommended an institutional voice within the executive branch where civil liberty concerns could be expressed.

What has happened: Section 1061 of the Intelligence Reform and Terrorism Prevention Act (Public Law 108-458) created a Privacy and Civil Liberties Oversight Board. On June 10, 2005, the President appointed Lanny Davis, Ted Olson, and Francis X. Taylor members of the Board, and nominated Carol Dinkins and Alan Charles Raul as Chair and Vice Chair respectively. Their names were sent up to the Senate on September 28, 2005, and they were confirmed on February 17, 2006. The Administration requested $750,000 for the Board for Fiscal Year 2006; the Congress provided $1.5 million. Sixteen months after its creation by statute, the Board held its first meeting in March 2006.

Why this is still important: The Privacy and Civil Liberties Oversight Board is the only office within the executive branch to look across the government at the actions we are taking to protect ourselves, to ensure that privacy and civil liberties concerns are appropriately considered.

What needs to be done: Now constituted, the Board needs to establish a work plan and move forward expeditiously with its important mission.

SET PRIVACY GUIDELINES FOR GOVERNMENT SHARING OF PERSONAL INFORMATION

"As the President determines the guidelines for information sharing among government agencies and by those agencies with the private sector, he should safeguard the privacy of individuals about whom information is shared." (p. 394)

Grade: MINIMAL PROGRESS

What we found: At our first public hearing we noted the need for balance as our government responds to the real and ongoing threat of terrorist attacks. Even without the changes we recommend, the American public has vested enormous authority in the U.S. government. While protecting our homeland, Americans need to be mindful of the threats to vital personal and civil liberties.

What has happened: The Intelligence Reform and Terrorism Prevention Act (PL 108-458) created the Privacy and Civil Liberties Oversight Board, as well as a Civil Liberties Protection Officer in the Office of the Director of National Intelligence. The Privacy and Civil Liberties Oversight Board held its first meeting in March 2006. The Director of National Intelligence named a Civil Liberties Protection Officer in December 2005.

Why this is still important: The shift of power and authority to the government calls for an enhanced system of checks and balances to protect the liberties that are vital to our way of life.

What needs to be done: The Privacy and Civil Liberties Oversight Board must begin its important work. The Congress should continue to provide sufficient funding and pay close attention to the work of the Board and the DNI's Civil Liberties Protection Officer.

Congressional and Administrative Reform

REFORM INTELLIGENCE OVERSIGHT

"Congressional oversight for intelligence—and counterterrorism—is now dysfunctional. Congress should address this problem. We have considered various alternatives: A joint committee on the old model of the Joint Committee on Atomic Energy is one. A single committee in each house of Congress, combining authorizing and appropriating authorities, is another.

• The new committee or committees should conduct continuing studies of the activities of the intelligence agencies and report . . . to all members of the House and Senate.

- *[T]he total level of funding for intelligence [should] be made public. . . the national intelligence program [should] be appropriated to the National Intelligence Director, not to the Secretary of Defense.*
- *[T]he intelligence committee should have a subcommittee specifically dedicated to oversight. . . .*
- *[G]rant subpoena authority to the committee or committees. The majority party's representation on this committee should never exceed the minority's representation by more than one.*
- *Four of the members appointed to this committee or committees should be a member who also serves on each of the following additional committees: Armed Services, Judiciary, Foreign Affairs, and the Defense Appropriations subcommittee.*
- *Members should serve indefinitely on the intelligence committees, without set terms. . . .*
- *The committees should be smaller. . . so that each member feels a greater sense of responsibility, and accountability, for the quality of the committee's work." (p. 420–1)*

Grade: MINIMAL PROGRESS

What we found: We interviewed numerous members of Congress from both parties and found dissatisfaction with congressional oversight to be widespread. The word members most often used to describe Congressional oversight of intelligence was "dysfunctional." Therefore, we recommended a substantial strengthening of the oversight committees.

What has happened: The Senate Select Committee on Intelligence (SSCI) eliminated term limits, pared its membership roster, cut the majority/minority divide to one, and created an oversight subcommittee. The House Permanent Select Committee on Intelligence (HPSCI) created an oversight subcommittee.

The primary problem remains: the oversight committees have insufficient authority over the funding of the agencies in the intelligence community. First, the agencies' purse strings are controlled by the defense appropriations subcommittees, for whom intelligence is not a primary concern. Second, the power of the Armed Services committees constrains the legislative authority of the intelligence committees.

The SSCI and HPSCI are the premier repositories of intelligence expertise in the Congress. Both committees are conducting vigorous oversight, often well and certainly as best they can, within the limitations noted.

Why this is still important: By its very nature, much of the work of intelligence must be conducted in secret. The American people rely on committees of the Congress to ensure that the critical agencies responsible for their safety are getting the job done. This is especially important in the wake of major intelligence reform—only strong Congressional oversight can ensure that this historic legislation is properly implemented.

What needs to be done: If the Intelligence Committees are not vested with appropriating authority, each house should create a separate appropriations sub-committee on intelligence. This would give the intelligence community's designated overseers the carrots and sticks they need to hold those agencies accountable.

The SSCI and the HPSCI should be made permanent standing committees of the Congress. The HPSCI should eliminate term limits, so that committee members can build the expertise needed to conduct rigorous oversight over sensitive intelligence programs.

CONSOLIDATE HOMELAND SECURITY COMMITTEES

"Congress should create a single, principal point of oversight and review for homeland security. Congressional leaders are best able to judge what committee should have jurisdiction over this department and its duties. But we believe that Congress does have the obligation to choose one in the House and one in the Senate, and that this committee should be a permanent standing committee with a nonpartisan staff." (p. 421)

Grade: SOME PROGRESS

What we found: Prior to 9/11, terrorism came under the jurisdiction of at least 14 different committees in the House alone. Budget and oversight functions in both the House and Senate were splintered badly among committees, contributing to the problems of the executive branch in formulating an integrated counterterrorism policy. In 2003, the House created a Select Committee on Homeland Security, but its effectiveness was undermined by the presence on it of powerful chairs from other committees dedicated to protecting their turf. Because of the compelling need for Congressional oversight, we recommended strong Homeland Security committees in both the House and Senate.

What has happened: The House created a permanent Committee on Homeland Security (HSC). The Senate gave the Governmental Affairs Committee responsibility for the Department of Homeland Security (DHS), and renamed it the Homeland Security and Governmental Affairs Committee (HSGAC).

Both committees have conducted effective oversight over department-wide homeland security policy. Both have worked in a bipartisan fashion.

However, the HSGAC was not given authority over the Transportation Security Administration (TSA), the Coast Guard, the immigration functions of Customs and Border Protection (CBP) and Immigration and Customs Enforcement (ICE), the DHS Directorate of Border and Transportation Security, or several other major DHS agencies.

Why this is still important: Holes in the HSGAC's jurisdiction make it difficult for the committee to pass an annual DHS authorization bill—as the HSC did in

2005. An annual authorization would give Congress a regular legislative vehicle to influence the direction of, and increase accountability within, the Department.

What needs to be done: The homeland security committees should have exclusive jurisdiction over all counterterrorism elements of DHS, and should make it their goal to send a DHS authorization bill to the President.

DECLASSIFY THE OVERALL INTELLIGENCE BUDGET

"...[T]o combat the secrecy and complexity we have described, the overall amounts of money being appropriated for national intelligence and to its component agencies should no longer be kept secret. Congress should pass a separate appropriations act for intelligence, defending the broad allocation of how these tens of billions of dollars have been assigned among the varieties of intelligence work." (p. 416)

Grade: UNSATISFACTORY

What we found: Excessive secrecy hampers public understanding and congressional oversight of the intelligence community. Even the most basic information about how much money is allocated for what purposes within the intelligence community and its key components is shrouded from public view. As a result, the intelligence community suffers from a lack of public debate and review, losing the opportunity to build support for its programs and needed reforms.

What has happened: This recommendation was included in the Senate-passed bill, but was not adopted by the House. It was dropped in conference committee.

Why this is still important: It is certainly possible to protect America's intelligence capabilities and intelligence sources and methods while declassifying the top-line appropriations figures for the intelligence budget. Without some disclosure, the American public and most members of Congress cannot judge adequately how well funds are being allocated toward our nation's security. More public information would promote a greater sense of accountability as to how those funds are spent. Some secrecy is necessary for our security; unnecessary concealment of information from the American people is not.

What needs to be done: Congress should pass a separate appropriations act for intelligence, making public the overall amounts being appropriated from national intelligence and being assigned to the various components of the intelligence community.

STANDARDIZE SECURITY CLEARANCES

"A single federal agency should be responsible for providing and maintaining security clearances, ensuring uniform standards—including uniform security questionnaires and financial report requirements, and maintaining a single database." (p. 422)

Grade: MINIMAL PROGRESS

What we found: We found time and again that the lack of standard security clearances delayed the sharing of terrorism information across agency lines, slowed and undermined the process of bringing needed talent into government, and contributed to long vacancies and dangerous gaps in senior national security posts during the transition of administrations.

What has happened: The President issued an Executive Order on June 27, 2005, "taking appropriate account of Title III of Public Law 108-458 [the Intelligence Reform Act]" stating that "agency functions relating to determining eligibility for access to classified national security information shall be appropriately uniform, centralized, effective, timely, and reciprocal." The Executive Order's statement of policy is excellent. It also puts the Office of Management and Budget in charge, and OMB is expected to delegate its authorities to the Office of Personnel Management. OMB issued a plan to improve the personnel security clearance process in November 2005, and in December 2005 issued guidance spelling out actions to improve reciprocal recognition of security clearances, with most deadlines for action March 31, 2006.

Why this is still important: The balkanized process for investigating, adjudicating and administering security clearances results in (1) great delays in getting good people into government; and (2) significant blockages to the timely sharing of information within the government.

What needs to be done: Urgency is necessary. The Office of Management and Budget needs to make the issue of standardized security clearances a much higher priority. It needs to take charge and carry out the intent of the Executive Order. The Deputy Director of OMB is committed to the success of this initiative. Much hard work is ahead.

PART III:
Foreign Policy, Public Diplomacy, and Nonproliferation
November 14, 2005 (updated April 2006)

Nonproliferation

MAXIMIZE EFFORT BY U.S. GOVERNMENT TO SECURE WMD

"Our report shows that al Qaeda has tried to acquire or make weapons of mass destruction for at least ten years. There is no doubt the United States would be a prime target. Preventing the proliferation of these weapons warrants a maximum effort—by strengthening counterproliferation efforts, expanding the Proliferation Security Initiative, and supporting the Cooperative Threat Reduction program." (p. 381)

Grade: INSUFFICIENT PROGRESS

What we found: We documented the efforts of al Qaeda dating back at least a decade to acquire weapons of mass destruction. Testifying in a federal courtroom in early 2001, an al Qaeda member explained his mission: "It's easy to kill more people with uranium." Bin Ladin's intent is clear. He is patient. He plans carefully. He would use a nuclear device if he could acquire one.

What has happened: The agreement reached by Presidents Bush and Putin in February 2005 provided positive movement on programs to secure nuclear warheads and materials. Access has improved: Russia has made several dozen additional nuclear weapons storage sites available for inspection and security upgrades. The U.S. and Russia have mostly resolved liability issues that had long delayed efforts to eliminate plutonium from dismantled weapons. In the past 18 months, with U.S. assistance, four shipments of highly enriched uranium have been returned from Soviet-supplied research reactors in Eastern Europe and the former Soviet republics to secure storage in Russia. The Fiscal Year 2006 Defense Authorization Act includes an amendment by Senator Lugar that removes bureaucratic hurdles to the timely expenditure of Cooperative Threat Reduction funds (repealing annual certification requirements imposed by Congress and delegating from the President to the Secretary of Defense the authority to use such funds outside the former Soviet Union).

The Cooperative Threat Reduction program has made significant accomplishments over the past 14 years in dismantling former Soviet weaponry (40 percent of ICBMs [Intercontinental Ballistics Missiles], 51 percent of warheads, 64 percent of strategic bombers, and 58 percent of missile silos), but much remains to be done to secure weapons-grade nuclear materials. The size of the problem still dwarfs the policy response. Seventy-five percent of the buildings in the former Soviet Union that contain nuclear weapons material have completed "rapid upgrades" of security, and 54 percent have completed "comprehensive upgrades." The total amount of nuclear material being protected inched upward this past year, from 26 to 29 percent (counting comprehensive upgrades only) and from 46 to 49 percent (including rapid upgrades). However, this pace is less than half the rate the U.S. had intended, in large part because of access disputes. Approximately half of former Soviet nuclear materials still lack adequate security protection.

Most troubling is that over 100 research facilities worldwide—in some 40 countries—contain enough highly enriched uranium to fashion a nuclear device. Many of these sites lack even basic security features.

The Administration's Proliferation Security Initiative, an international effort to disrupt proliferation-related shipments and stop the proliferation trade, has now expanded to over 70 countries, and counts 11 successful interdictions in the past year.

Why this is still important: As the President has stated, "The gravest danger our nation faces lies at the crossroads of radicalism and technology. Our enemies have openly declared that they are seeking weapons of mass destruction, and evidence indicates they are doing so with determination." The consequences of a WMD attack in an American city would be catastrophic.

What needs to be done: Preventing terrorists from gaining access to weapons of mass destruction must be elevated above all other problems of national security because it represents the greatest threat to the American people. The President should develop a comprehensive plan to dramatically accelerate the timetable for securing all nuclear weapons-usable material around the world and request the necessary resources to complete this task. The President should publicly make this goal his top national security priority, and ride herd on the bureaucracy to maintain a sense of urgency.

The Congress should provide the resources needed to secure vulnerable materials at the fastest possible rate.

Finally, the U.S. and Russia must renew the Cooperative Threat Reduction umbrella agreement before it expires in 2006, to prevent suspension of the program's critical work.

Foreign Policy

MAKE A LONG-TERM COMMITMENT TO A SECURE AND STABLE AFGHANISTAN

"Now the United States and the international community should make a long-term commitment to a secure and stable Afghanistan, in order to give the government a reasonable opportunity to improve the life of the Afghan people. Afghanistan must not again become a sanctuary for international crime and terrorism. The United States and the international community should help the Afghan government extend its authority over the country, with a strategy and nation-by-nation commitments to achieve their objectives." (p. 370)

Grade: SOME PROGRESS

What we found: The United States and the international community lost interest in Afghanistan after the last Soviet troops left in 1989. The country slipped into civil war. Promising stability, the Taliban came to power in 1996 and provided a sanctuary from which al Qaeda planned and executed terrorist attacks. The lack of international interest or involvement in Afghanistan contributed to its growth as a terrorist sanctuary.

What has happened: Afghanistan elected President Hamid Karzai in late 2004 and a national assembly in mid-September 2005. Both elections took place with minimal civil disruption. With the installation of the national assembly, Afghanistan will have its first entirely democratically elected government. According to the Afghan constitution, each of the country's 34 provinces will have at least two women representatives. The international community provided $160 million to ensure that the elections proceeded smoothly.

As required by law, the administration has submitted to Congress a five-year strategy for Afghanistan, and a report on the implementation of the strategy. NATO forces are playing a bigger role in providing security. Allies have made progress in standing up the Afghan National Army, which now has over 20,000 operational troops and comprises 37 battalions. The Afghan National Army deployed in support of the national assembly elections. A total of 50,000 police and 12,000 border police will be initially trained and deployed throughout Afghanistan by the end of the year. Rehabilitation of hydroelectric power plants, dams, and gas turbine plants is underway. Substantial improvements of provincial highways have occurred and capacity building for the ministries of finance, telecommunications, and the central bank is ongoing. Millions of children are being educated, have been vaccinated, and have improved access to healthcare. Rural women are being trained as teachers, women's literacy is increasing, and more girls are going to school.

The challenges facing the country are still formidable: Taliban and other extremist forces stepped up attacks against the Karzai government in the spring and summer of 2005, and attacks continue; new fighters are being drawn from Pakistan. Eighty-nine U.S. military personnel were killed in action in Afghanistan in 2005 (52 were killed in 2004), and the insurgency is growing. Karzai has not extended his authority throughout the entire country. With U.S. and allied help—the U.S. currently has about 17,900 troops in Afghanistan—he is attempting to strengthen regional governments in the provinces.

The Taliban derives some of its financing from Afghanistan's drug trafficking. The U.S. and allies are combating opium cultivation and the labs that make Afghanistan the world's leading supplier of heroin. But last year's campaign against opium has been characterized by some U.S. officials as a failure. Although the amount of land used to grow opium poppies was reduced by 20 percent, a higher-than-average rainfall still produced a big crop. A Department of State/Department of Defense report on counter-drug efforts in Afghanistan states that the drug situation in Afghanistan has worsened.

The U.S. assistance request for Afghanistan for Fiscal Year 2007 ($802 million) is nearly double the level of funds appropriated in 2005. Some senior coalition military leaders have emphasized that the U.S. and its partners must commit to a long-term economic plan for Afghanistan in order to ensure the country's stability.

Why this is still important: Before 9/11 Afghanistan was a terrorist sanctuary, an al Qaeda training center, and a launching pad for al Qaeda attacks on U.S. interests.

It is imperative that the United States and allies remain focused on Afghanistan, support its democratic government, reinforce its security, and help build its economy to ensure that it never again becomes a haven for terrorists.

What needs to be done: The U.S. and allies need to press forward on training and standing up the Afghan National Army and Afghan security forces. These forces should be used in consolidating the central government's control over the country. The coalition should help Karzai and his government develop more effective means for eradicating Afghanistan's poppy cultivation, as opium production and criminal drug trafficking threaten to undermine the government and its democratic institutions. The U.S should exert every effort to implement the five-year Afghanistan strategy that the administration has submitted to Congress. In particular, priority should be given to helping the country build a solid economic infrastructure and develop a sound economy. Congress should continue to provide generous economic and development aid to Afghanistan, and provide robust funding to the Afghan National Army, police forces, and border police.

SUPPORT PAKISTAN AGAINST EXTREMISTS

"If Musharraf stands for enlightened moderation in a fight for his life and for the life of his country, the United States should be willing to make hard choices too, and make the difficult long-term commitment to the future of Pakistan. Sustaining the current scale of aid to Pakistan, the United States should support Pakistan's government in its struggle against extremists with a comprehensive effort that extends from military aid to support for a better education, so long as Pakistan's leaders remain willing to make difficult choices of their own." (p. 369)

Grade: SOME PROGRESS

What we found: Since 9/11, Pakistan has been a critical partner of the United States in combating al Qaeda. However, Pakistan's endemic poverty, widespread corruption, and often ineffective government creates ample opportunity for Islamist recruitment. Therefore, we recommended that a long-term U.S. commitment to support Pakistan against extremists must also be matched by Pakistan's own efforts in support of reform and moderation.

What has happened: Language in the Intelligence Reform and Terrorism Prevention Act of 2004 (PL 108-458) provided a sense of Congress in support of the Commission's recommendations. Increases in the Fiscal Year 2006 budget and a five-year, $3 billion package of assistance are encouraging signs of a long-term commitment to Pakistan. But there is still little movement beyond security assistance: Too much of our assistance is in the form of a cash transfer, and funding to improve education in Pakistan is still far from sufficient.

President Musharraf has made real efforts to take on the threat of extremism, yet Pakistan remains a sanctuary and training ground for terrorists. Musharraf does not appear to have lived up to his promises to properly regulate the madrassas or close down all those that have known links to extremist groups. Taliban forces still pass freely across the Pakistan-Afghanistan border and operate in Pakistani tribal areas. Terrorists from Pakistan carry out operations in Kashmir. The results of promised democratization efforts are yet to be seen.

Reports indicate that the rapid U.S. aid in response to the devastating October 8th earthquake has enhanced the standing of the U.S. in Pakistan. Many elements of Pakistani society see such aid as a sign of strong U.S. commitment.

Why this is still important: A politically and economically stable Pakistan that is a committed partner in the war on terror is critical to U.S. counterterrorism efforts. This cannot happen unless Pakistan is wholly committed to practical reform. The United States must be equally committed to helping Pakistan achieve practical economic and political reform.

What still needs to be done: U.S. assistance to Pakistan must move beyond security assistance. $35 million is not adequate to the task of helping to revive Pakistan's failing basic education system. Funding for education efforts must be increased. The U.S. government should pressure Pakistan to act forcefully to close Taliban-linked madrassas, shut down terrorist training camps, and prevent Taliban forces from operating across the Pakistan-Afghanistan border.

SUPPORT REFORM IN SAUDI ARABIA

"The problems in the U.S.-Saudi relationship must be confronted, openly. The United States and Saudi Arabia must determine if they can build a relationship that political leaders on both sides are prepared to publicly defend—a relationship about more than oil. It should include a shared commitment to political and economic reform, as Saudis make common cause with the outside world. It should include a shared interest in greater tolerance and cultural respect, translating into a commitment to fight the violent extremists who foment hatred." (p. 374)

Grade: INSUFFICIENT PROGRESS

What we found: Before 9/11, U.S.-Saudi ties consisted of a basic trade of security for access to oil. The participation of 15 Saudis in the 9/11 attacks radically altered perceptions, causing many Americans to see Saudi Arabia as an enemy, not an ally. In turn, educated Saudis sympathetic to our perspective now see the U.S. as hostile. Therefore, we recommended that the United States and Saudi Arabia build a broader relationship based on a shared commitment to practical reform, not just oil.

What has happened: Administration statements in support of democracy and political reform in the Middle East are more pointed and pronounced than those of previous Administrations. Saudi Arabia held elections in early 2005 for one-half of the seats in municipal councils (the other half to be appointed by the government); however, the councils have yet to meet and their authorities are unclear. On economic reform, Saudi Arabia completed talks with the U.S. and joined the World Trade Organization in 2005, accepting greater transparency and openness in its economy.

Saudi security forces have acted forcefully against al Qaeda following the May 2003 bombing in Riyadh. Bilateral counterterrorism cooperation with the U.S. has also greatly improved. Saudi official statements on encouraging tolerance and moderation are good, but it is unclear if there has been much positive change in their religious establishment, educational textbooks, or daily life. A U.S.-Saudi strategic dialogue to address topics beyond oil and security, including reform and expansion of citizen-to-citizen contacts, is just beginning.

Why this is still important: Cooperation with Saudi Arabia against violent Islamic extremism is very much in the U.S. national interest; such cooperation is difficult to sustain in the absence of public support and broader ties between the two countries.

What needs to be done: Both governments should accelerate efforts to give life and substance to U.S.-Saudi strategic dialogue, increase exchange programs, and promote pragmatic reform. The Saudi government needs to take additional steps to regulate charities and promote tolerance and moderation.

IDENTIFY AND PRIORITIZE TERRORIST SANCTUARIES

"The U.S. government must identify and prioritize actual or potential terrorist sanctuaries. For each, it should have a realistic strategy to keep possible terrorists insecure and on the run, using all elements of national power. We should reach out, listen to, and work with other countries that can help." (p. 367)

Grade: SOME PROGRESS

What we found: Many impoverished states with weak governments and empty rugged terrain, similar to Afghanistan, could offer sanctuary to terrorists. Therefore, we recommended that strategies be devised to work with these countries so they do not become failed states and terrorist sanctuaries.

What has happened: The Intelligence Reform and Terrorism Prevention Act of 2004 (PL 108-458) expressed the sense of Congress in support of this recommendation, but did not put in place specific programs to identify and prioritize sanctuaries. In its report to Congress, the State Department described a U.S. strategy to address and eliminate terrorist sanctuaries that includes: coordinating cooperative programs to build ties with foreign partners and boost counterterrorism capabilities, increasing impediments to terrorist funding and travel, and diminishing the underlying conditions that terrorists seek to exploit. But this strategy does not include a useful metric for overall progress against terrorist sanctuaries. There is little sign of long-term efforts in place to reduce the conditions that allow the formation of terrorist sanctuaries.

Why this is still important: Even as terrorist groups increasingly make use of technology to establish links with other groups, raise funds, spread propaganda, and plan attacks, the 9/11 story tells us that complex operations still require space and resources to recruit, train, and plan. We cannot afford to allow failing or failed states to become home bases for tomorrow's terrorists.

What needs to be done: The National Security Council Office for Combating Terrorism, the National Counterterrorism Center, the State Department, the Department of Defense, and the CIA should, as a priority matter, agree on which countries are currently terrorist sanctuaries, and which countries have the potential for becoming such sanctuaries. Together these organizations should develop and implement comprehensive strategies for responding to terrorist sanctuaries and potential sanctuaries. These strategies should include metrics for evaluating progress toward making these countries and regions less attractive to terrorists. The State Department should then take the lead in winning the endorsement of key international allies for implementing these strategies.

DEVELOP A COMPREHENSIVE COALITION STRATEGY AGAINST ISLAMIST TERRORISM

"The United States should engage other nations in developing a comprehensive Coalition strategy against Islamist terrorism. There are several multilateral institutions in which such issues should be addressed. But the most important policies should be discussed and coordinated in a flexible contact group of leading Coalition governments. This is a good place, for example, to develop joint strategies for targeting terrorist travel, or for hammering out a common strategy for the places where terrorists may be finding sanctuary." (p. 379)

Grade: MINIMAL PROGRESS

What we found: Counterterrorism success requires close cooperation with key allies and partners. Each tool of American policy—military power, intelligence, covert action, foreign assistance, diplomacy, border security, aviation security, etc.— is far more effective when used in cooperation with allies and partners.

What has happened: The Intelligence Reform and Terrorism Prevention Act of 2004 (PL 108-458) authorized the Secretary of State, in consultation with other U.S. government agencies, to negotiate international agreements on a bilateral or multilateral basis, under which parties work in partnership to address and interdict acts of international terrorists. The Act also authorized the president to establish an international contact group of leading nations to develop common policies and strategies against terrorists. Components of a common counterterrorism strategy have been generated and/or implemented on a bilateral basis. For example, the U.S. has strong cooperative relationships on intelligence sharing and law enforcement with a number of partners. There has also been progress establishing multilateral policies on preventing terrorist travel and combating terrorist financing, addressing the threat to transportation infrastructure, and promoting best practices for transportation security. No permanent international contact group of leading nations has yet been established.

Why this is still important: International cooperation on counterterrorism strategy is not just advantageous to U.S. efforts. As the recent attacks in Bali and London once again demonstrate, cooperation is essential to successfully conduct a global war on terror. The global community needs joint strategies to strengthen its ability to erode the roots of terrorism.

What needs to be done: Just as the U.S. needs to use all instruments of power against the terrorist threat, we need to forge a comprehensive Coalition strategy on all fronts in the war on terror. This must include a broader approach to targeting the roots of terrorism, including implementing joint strategies for encouraging reform efforts in Saudi Arabia and Pakistan, improving educational and economic opportunities in the Muslim world, identifying and eliminating terrorist sanctuaries, and making progress in the Arab-Israeli peace process.

DEVELOP COALITION STANDARDS FOR TERRORIST DETENTION

"The United States should engage its friends to develop a common Coalition approach toward the detention and humane treatment of captured terrorists. New principles might draw upon Article 3 of the Geneva Conventions on the law of armed conflict. That article was specifically designed for those cases in which the usual laws of war did not apply. Its minimum standards are generally accepted throughout the world as customary international law." (p. 380)

Grade: UNFULFILLED

What we found: Allegations that the United States abused prisoners in its custody make it harder to build the diplomatic, political, and military alliances necessary for success against terrorism. Therefore, the United States should work with friends to develop mutually agreed-upon principles for the detention and humane treatment of captured international terrorists.

What has happened: The U.S. government's detention and prosecution of suspected terrorists in military prisons and secret detention centers abroad, as well as reports on the abuse of detainees, have elicited criticism from around the globe. There have also been inquiries into the U.S. government's internment policies and the status of their prisoners under international law both at home and abroad. A new Department of Defense Directive and revised Army interrogation manual, both currently under review, will provide important guidance for the U.S. military on detention and interrogation standards for captured terrorists, reportedly drawing upon Article 3 of the Geneva Conventions. The Defense Appropriations Act for Fiscal Year 2006 prohibits cruel, inhumane, and degrading treatment of prisoners in the custody of the U.S. government. The President's signing statement construes this ban "in a manner consistent with the constitutional authority of the President . . . as Commander in Chief." No international standards have been agreed to.

Why this is still important: The closer our detention policies can be to international law, the fuller our cooperation can be with international partners on other aspects of counterterrorism strategy.

What needs to be done: Administration policies that provide standards for captured terrorists in accordance with international law should be adopted. These standards should cover the treatment of detainees held by all elements of the U.S. government. The U.S. should work with its allies to develop mutually acceptable standards for terrorist detention.

PURSUE LIBERALIZE ECONOMIC POLICIES ABROAD

"A comprehensive U.S. strategy to counter terrorism should include economic policies that encourage development, more open societies, and opportunities for people to improve the lives of their families and to enhance prospects for their children's future." (p. 379)

Grade: GOOD PROGRESS

What we found: Terrorism is not caused by poverty. Indeed, many terrorists come from relatively well-off families. Yet when people lose hope, when societies break down, when countries fragment, the breeding grounds for terrorism are created. Backward economic policies and repressive regimes leave people without hope, where ambition and passions have no constructive outlet.

What has happened: The Administration has continued to pursue trade liberalization and the integration of the Arab and Muslim world into the global trading system, in support of the goal of a Middle East Free Trade Area by 2013. The United States has entered into free trade agreements (FTAs) with Jordan, Morocco, and the Palestinian Authority (via the US-Israel FTA), concluded FTA negotiations with Bahrain (September 2004) and Oman (October 2005), and opened FTA talks with the United Arab Emirates (March 2005). The United States is also actively considering an FTA with Egypt, which has reduced tariffs, accelerated privatization, and increased exchange rate flexibility, significantly improving its investment climate. In addition, the Administration has entered into bilateral Trade and Investment Framework Agreements with 13 Arab states (Algeria, Bahrain, Egypt, Iraq, Jordan, Kuwait, Morocco, Oman, Qatar, Saudi Arabia, Tunisia, United Arab Emirates, and Yemen) as well as Afghanistan and Pakistan. Saudi Arabia became a member of the World Trade Organization in December 2005, joining nine Arab states—Bahrain, Egypt, Jordan, Kuwait, Morocco, Oman, Qatar, Tunisia, and UAE—that are already members of the WTO.

Why this is still important: Economic stagnation and social dislocation create a breeding ground for terrorism. Economic reforms foster growth, create jobs, and provide hope.

What needs to be done: Economic liberalization of the Arab and Muslim world needs to continue to be pursued, so that a virtuous cycle of growth can take hold. Growth expands the middle class, creating a constituency for further economic and political reform.

VIGOROUSLY TRACK TERRORIST FINANCING

"Vigorous efforts to track terrorist financing must remain front and center in U.S. counterterrorism efforts." (p. 382)

Grade: GOOD PROGRESS

What we found: Initially, the U.S. government saw attacks on terrorist finance as a way "to starve the terrorists of money." Aggressive actions to designate financiers and freeze assets have not been enforced worldwide, have been easily circumvented, and been confronted by legal challenges forcing some reversals of asset freezes. A better strategy has emerged: using intelligence about terrorist financing as a critical tool to understand terrorist networks, search them out, and disrupt their operations.

What has happened: There is widespread international recognition that terrorist financing cannot be ignored, and growing agreement on standards to combat it. With U.S. support, the 33-member Financial Action Task Force (FATF) agreed this past year to create regional groups in Eurasia (including Russia and China) and in the Middle East and North Africa (including 14 countries) to implement FATF recommendations to fight money laundering and terrorist financing. The U.S. is an observer in both regional groups. The U.S. is providing technical assistance and training to develop and strengthen counterterrorist financing capabilities of frontline states, including Saudi Arabia, the UAE, Kuwait, Qatar, Egypt, and Pakistan.

Why this is still important: Tracking terrorist funding provides critical intelligence, helping to understand terrorist networks, search them out, and disrupt their operations. While any individual terrorist operation is inexpensive, terrorist organizations need steady funding to train, recruit, and pay operatives.

What needs to be done: Priorities include the Gulf states and South Asia. The U.S. needs to persuade Saudi Arabia to establish a fully functioning Charities Commission, providing oversight of international Islamic and relief organizations headquartered there. Pakistan needs to enact terrorist finance legislation. U.S. assistance is critical in helping Saudi Arabia, Jordan, and Kuwait develop Financial Intelligence Units; no country in South Asia yet has one. FIUs are essential for information sharing and maintaining compliance with international standards to combat terrorist financing.

Public Diplomacy

DEFINE THE U.S. MESSAGE

"The U.S. government must define what the message is, what it stands for. We should offer an example of moral leadership in the world, committed to treat people humanely, abide by the rule of law, and be generous and caring to our neighbors. America and Muslim friends can agree on respect for human dignity and opportunity. To Muslim parents, terrorists like Bin Ladin have nothing to offer their children but visions of violence and death. America and its friends have a crucial advantage—we can offer these parents a vision that might give their children a better future. If we heed the views of thoughtful leaders in the Arab and Muslim world, a moderate consensus can be found. That vision of the future should stress life over death: individual educational and economic opportunity. This vision includes widespread political participation and contempt for indiscriminate violence. It includes respect for the rule of law, openness in discussing differences, and tolerance for opposing points of view." (p. 376)

Grade: MINIMAL PROGRESS

What we found: Support for the U.S. has plummeted. Polls taken in Islamic countries immediately after 9/11 suggested that many or most people thought the United States was doing the right thing in its fight against terrorism. By 2003, polls showed that "the bottom had fallen out of support for America in most of the Muslim world." The small percentage of Muslims who are committed Bin Ladin supporters are impervious to persuasion. It is among the large majority that we must encourage reform, freedom, democracy, and opportunity, even if the effectiveness of our message is limited because of mistrust of the United States.

What has happened: In his second inaugural address, the President offered a vision for American leadership in the world based on the expansion of democratic governance to all countries. The President and the Secretary of State have articulated this message widely, including in the Middle East. The United States has shown moral leadership in support of democratic elections and the rule of law in Muslim countries and in generous assistance to the victims of the Indian Ocean tsunami and the recent South Asia earthquake. However, mistrust and dislike of America remain high in many areas of the world, especially in Arab and Muslim countries. Detainee abuse at Abu Ghraib, Guantanamo Bay, and elsewhere undermines America's reputation as a moral leader, committed to humane treatment and the rule of law. Public opinion approval ratings for the United States throughout the Middle East remain at or near historic lows.

Why this is still important: The generational struggle that began on 9/11 will not be won by military or intelligence operations alone—it will require all elements of national power. During the Cold War, the appeal of Western ideals rallied the people of the world, including behind the Iron Curtain, against totalitarian

Communism. Similarly, to defeat Bin Ladin and his allies, we must defeat their ideology of hate and death.

What needs to be done: The global appeal of our core values and our culture of education, equal opportunity, and tolerance still have powerful appeal around the world. Public diplomacy initiatives should seek to explain the civic principles and system of government contained in our founding documents, and to portray the American way of life factually.

The challenge is to communicate our values, our way of life, and our vision for the world, without lecturing or condescension. That task will fall to President Bush, Secretary Rice, Undersecretary Hughes, and countless other U.S. government officials. The media, the private and nonprofit sectors, and individual citizens should also be encouraged to participate in this effort.

SPREAD U.S. IDEALS THROUGH INTERNATIONAL BROADCASTING
"Recognizing that Arab and Muslim audiences rely on satellite television and radio, the government has begun some promising initiatives in television and radio broadcasting to the Arab world, Iran and Afghanistan. These efforts are beginning to reach large audiences. The Broadcasting Board of Governors has asked for much larger resources. It should get them." (p. 377)

Grade: SOME PROGRESS

What we found: Bin Ladin has succeeded in reaching out to Muslim audiences, through the vehicle of tapes delivered to satellite television (such as al Jazeera) and radio. The United States needs to defend its own ideals and values vigorously. If the United States does not act to define itself in the Islamic world, the extremists will gladly do the job for us.

What has happened: The budgets for international broadcasting to the Arab and Muslim world have increased dramatically since 9/11, from $45 million in Fiscal Year 2002 to $152 million in the Fiscal Year 2006 request—an overall 237 percent increase. Arabic-language Radio Sawa began in 2002 and Alhurra TV in 2004. The number of U.S.-sponsored broadcasting hours to the broader Middle East has nearly quadrupled since 2001, from 13,000 hours to over 50,000 hours.

Audience shares are growing. According to an August 2005 ACNielsen survey, Radio Sawa and Alhurra TV are now reaching a total audience of 35 million adults per week. Radio Sawa is the top international broadcaster in the Middle East. Alhurra is making inroads, reaching on average 25 percent of adult audiences weekly in 11 Arab countries, compared to 65 percent for al Arabiya and 80 percent for al Jazeera. According to the survey, 77 percent of Alhurra's viewers and 73 percent of Radio Sawa's listeners consider their news reliable.

Why this is still important: In a region where 40 percent of adult Arabs are illiterate, radio and TV are the most important sources of news and information.

What needs to be done: Building audience share is a first step toward shaping public opinion. With audiences citing Radio Sawa and Alhurra TV as reliable sources of news, the challenge is to see whether these services can make a difference by exposing listeners to new ideas and accurate information about the United States and its policies. Metrics beyond audience size should be developed to measure impact and influence.

REBUILD SCHOLARSHIP, EXCHANGE, AND LIBRARY PROGRAMS
"The United States should rebuild the scholarship, exchange, and library programs that reach out to young people and offer them knowledge and hope. Where such assistance is provided, it should be identified as coming from the citizens of the United States." (p. 377)

Grade: UNFULFILLED

What we found: Since 9/11, young Muslims who want to visit or study in the United States have had difficulties and delays in getting visas. Upon arrival, they often experience additional searches and discrimination. Such stories undermine our efforts to shape perceptions and build ties with Muslim elites and the general population. Exchange programs are still heavily oriented toward Europe. Embassy libraries in the Middle East and South Asia have closed because of security concerns.

What has happened: Congress funded the administration's request for $430.4 million for Fiscal Year 2006 for Educational and Cultural Exchange Programs, up from $367.4 million in Fiscal Year 2005. The administration requested $474 million for Fiscal Year 2007.

Overseas American libraries are closing in the regions we want to reach most, largely due to safety concerns. The American Consulate and Library in Istanbul, Turkey, was targeted at least six times by terrorists until it was closed in 2003. The United States closed the American Center in Islamabad, Pakistan, in 2005. Even the American Center in New Delhi, India, frequently touted as a model public diplomacy facility, is being closed in 2007 due to security concerns. Over the past two years, the State Department has increased its investment in interactive websites and American reading sections in host country libraries. Neither initiative includes the presence of U.S. personnel for dialogue, reading guidance, and educational counseling, important factors in shaping the attitudes of foreign users.

A Partnerships for Learning youth initiative, funded at $10 million, is aimed at the Muslim world. While U.S.-funded efforts directed at the Muslim world are increasing, the overall level of young people coming to visit or study in the United States from Muslim countries is static or declining.

Why this is still important: Interaction with citizens of target countries is one of the most effective ways to expose them to American values and culture, which help build positive perceptions and ties.

What needs to be done: The U.S. needs to make library posts abroad viable, even in the face of security challenges. The U.S. should increase support for scholarship and exchange programs, our most powerful tool to shape attitudes over the course of a generation.

SUPPORT SECULAR EDUCATION IN MUSLIM COUNTRIES

"The U.S. government should offer to join with other nations in generously supporting a new International Youth Opportunity Fund. Funds will be spent directly for building and operating primary and secondary schools in those Muslim states that commit to sensibly investing their own money in public education." (p. 378)

Grade: MINIMAL PROGRESS

What we found: Across the Islamic world, millions of poor families send their children to religious schools, or madrassas, as they are often the only opportunity available for education. These schools leave graduates without marketable skills, creating a large pool of unemployable youth. Some of these schools indoctrinate students with a radical, militant interpretation of Islam. These young graduates form an attractive pool of potential targets for al Qaeda recruiters.

What has happened: The Intelligence Reform and Terrorist Prevention Act (PL 108-458) authorized the creation of the International Youth Opportunity Fund and instructed the Secretary of State to seek international cooperation in funding it. To date, Congress has appropriated no funding to establish the program.

The Middle East Partnership Initiative (MEPI) and USAID have initiated programs across the Arab world to support secular education improvements and the teaching of English. A number of these programs focus on female education. In Fiscal Year 2006, the administration requested $120 million for MEPI, of which $30 million is earmarked for education reform programs.

Why this is still important: As Secretary of Defense Rumsfeld wrote in October 2003, the challenge of counterterrorism is "capturing, killing, or deterring and dissuading more terrorists every day than the madrassas and radical clerics are recruiting, training, and deploying against us."

What needs to be done: The International Youth Opportunity Fund would reduce the share of costs borne by U.S. taxpayers for improving international education. Congress should make appropriations to initiate this program, which would allow the Secretary of State to begin seeking international contributions to the Fund.

Secular education programs through MEPI and USAID are a constructive start to answering the challenge of secular education in Muslim countries. These programs should not, however, operate in a vacuum. They should be components of an overarching strategy for educational assistance—itself one component of an overall U.S. strategy for counterterrorism—targeted where the need, and the benefit to U.S. national security, are greatest. Once such a strategy exists, this important long-term counterterrorism tool should receive significantly increased funding from the Congress. The current level of education reform funding is not sufficient given the scale of this challenge.

INDEX

Please note: This index contains references only to the complete Report, Interim Reports, the Third Monograph, and any notes. Page numbers in *italics* indicate illustrations. Those followed by *n* refer to endnotes.